1 Samuel

OLD TESTAMENT AND CPH EDITOR

Christopher W. Mitchell

NEW TESTAMENT EDITOR

Curtis P. Giese

CONCORDIA COMMENTARY VOLUMES

Leviticus, John W. Kleinig

Joshua, Adolph L. Harstad

Ruth, John R. Wilch

1 Samuel, Andrew E. Steinmann

*2 Samuel, Andrew E. Steinmann

Ezra and Nehemiah, Andrew E. Steinmann

Proverbs, Andrew E. Steinmann

Ecclesiastes, James Bollhagen

The Song of Songs, Christopher W. Mitchell

Isaiah 40–55, R. Reed Lessing

Isaiah 56–66, R. Reed Lessing

Ezekiel 1–20, Horace D. Hummel

Ezekiel 21–48, Horace D. Hummel

Daniel, Andrew E. Steinmann

Amos, R. Reed Lessing

Jonah, R. Reed Lessing

Matthew 1:1–11:1, Jeffrey A. Gibbs

Matthew 11:2–20:34, Jeffrey A. Gibbs

Mark 1:1–8:26, James W. Voelz

Luke 1:1–9:50, Arthur A. Just Jr.

Luke 9:51–24:53, Arthur A. Just Jr.

John 1:1–7:1, William C. Weinrich

Romans 1–8, Michael P. Middendorf

Romans 9–16, Michael P. Middendorf

1 Corinthians, Gregory J. Lockwood

Galatians, A. Andrew Das

Ephesians, Thomas M. Winger

Colossians, Paul E. Deterding

Philemon, John G. Nordling

*Hebrews, John W. Kleinig

2 Peter and Jude, Curtis P. Giese

1–3 John, Bruce G. Schuchard

Revelation, Louis A. Brighton

For a current list of available Concordia Commentary volumes, visit our website: cph.org/commentaries.

*In preparation

CONCORDIA COMMENTARY

A Theological Exposition of Sacred Scripture

1 SAMUEL

Andrew E. Steinmann

Concordia Publishing House
Saint Louis

Copyright © 2016 Concordia Publishing House
3558 S. Jefferson Avenue, St. Louis, MO 63118-3968
1-800-325-3040 • www.cph.org

Unless otherwise indicated, Scripture quotations are the author's translation.

Scripture quotations marked ESV are from the ESV® Bible (The Holy Bible, English Standard Version®), copyright © 2001 by Crossway, a publishing ministry of Good News Publishers. Used by permission. All rights reserved.

Quotations from Scripture and the Apocrypha marked NRSV are from the New Revised Standard Version of the Bible with the Apocrypha, copyright 1989, Division of Christian Education of the National Council of the Churches of Christ in the United States of America. Used by permission. All rights reserved.

Quotations designated NET are from the NET Bible® copyright ©1996–2006 by Biblical Studies Press, L.L.C. http://netbible.com. Scripture and notes quoted by permission. All rights reserved.

Scripture quotations marked GW are taken from GOD'S WORD®, © 1995 God's Word to the Nations. Used by permission of Baker Publishing Group.

Scripture quotations marked HCSB are taken from the Holman Christian Standard Bible®, copyright © 1999, 2000, 2002, 2003, 2009 by Holman Bible Publishers. Used by permission. Holman Christian Standard Bible®, Holman CSB®, and HCSB® are federally registered trademarks of Holman Bible Publishers.

Scripture quotations marked NASB are taken from the NEW AMERICAN STANDARD BIBLE®. Copyright © 1960, 1962, 1963, 1968, 1971, 1972, 1973, 1975, 1977, 1995 by The Lockman Foundation. Used by permission.

Quotations marked *NETS* are taken from *A New English Translation of the Septuagint*, © 2007 by the International Organization for Septuagint and Cognate Studies, Inc. Used by permission of Oxford University Press. All rights reserved.

Unless otherwise indicated, the quotations from the Lutheran Confessions in this publication are from THE BOOK OF CONCORD: THE CONFESSIONS OF THE EVANGELICAL LUTHERAN CHURCH, edited by Theodore G. Tappert, copyright © 1959 Fortress Press. Used by permission of Augsburg Fortress.

Quotations of the Small Catechism taken from *Lutheran Service Book* (*LSB*) originally come from *Luther's Small Catechism with Explanation*, copyright © 1986, 1991 by Concordia Publishing House.

The map "Kingdom and Battles of Saul" (figure 18) is adapted from *The Lutheran Study Bible* © 2009 by Concordia Publishing House. All rights reserved.

The SymbolGreekU, NewJerusalem, Jacobite, and TranslitLSU fonts used to print this work are available from Linguist's Software, Inc., PO Box 580, Edmonds, WA 98020-0580, USA; telephone (425) 775-1130; www.linguistsoftware.com.

Manufactured in the United States of America

Library of Congress Cataloging-in-Publication Data
Names: Steinmann, Andrew, author.
Title: 1 Samuel / Andrew E. Steinmann.
Other titles: First Samuel
Description: St. Louis : Concordia Publishing House, 2016. | Series:
    Concordia commentary: a theological exposition of sacred scripture |
    Includes bibliographical references and index.
Identifiers: LCCN 2015049877 | ISBN 9780758606945 (alk. paper)
Subjects: LCSH: Bible. Samuel, 1st—Commentaries.
Classification: LCC BS1325.53 .S74 2016 | DDC 222/.43077—dc23 LC record available at
http://lccn.loc.gov/2015049877

---

1 2 3 4 5 6 7 8 9 10   25 24 23 22 21 20 19 18 17 16

To Rebecca, who, like Abigail before her, provided wise advice

Contents

EDITORS' PREFACE   xii
AUTHOR'S PREFACE   xvi
PRINCIPAL ABBREVIATIONS   xviii
HEBREW VERBAL SYSTEM   xxii
ICONS   xxiii
BIBLIOGRAPHY   xxv
INTRODUCTION TO THE BOOK OF SAMUEL   1

Authorship, Composition, and Date   1
The Composition of Samuel   1
Critical Theories of Samuel's Composition   3
   Source-Critical Theories   3
   Tradition-Historical Theories   4
Redaction-Critical Theories   5
   The Deuteronomistic History Theory   5
   Editorial Layers in Samuel   7

Literary Features of Samuel   8
Biographical Studies of Saul and David   8
David in Samuel and Chronicles   9

Historical and Archaeological Issues   10
The Historicity of David   10
The Tel Dan Inscription   11
The Khirbet Qeiyafa Inscription   12

Chronological Issues in Samuel   13
Samuel and Eli as Judges   13
The Basic Chronology of the United Monarchy   14
The Reign of Saul (c. 1049–1009)   16
The Reign of David (Nisan 1009–969t)   18
   David's Reign in Hebron (Nisan 1009–1002t)   18
   David's Reign in Jerusalem (1002t–969t)   18

Christ in Samuel   23
The Promise to David (2 Samuel 7)   23
Other Messianic Passages in the Book of Samuel   24
David and the Messianic Promise   25

Law and Gospel in Samuel   26

Other Theological Themes in Samuel   29
Prosperity and Success Come Only from God   29
Prophecy   30
The Spirit of Yahweh   30

The Text of Samuel   31
The Masoretic Text   31
The Septuagint   33
    The Old Greek   33
    The Kaige Recension   34
    LXX 1–2 Kingdoms and Textual Criticism of the Book of Samuel   34
Samuel Manuscripts from Qumran   34

This Commentary's Translation Technique   37

COMMENTARY

1:1–8:22	**Israel without a King**	
1:1–2:11	**Samuel Is Dedicated to God's Service**	
1:1–20	The First Trip to Shiloh: Hannah Asks Yahweh for a Son	41
1:21–28	The Second Trip to Shiloh: Samuel Is Given to Yahweh	58
Excursus	*Polygamy in the Bible*	64
2:1–11	Hannah's Prayer	68
2:12–36	**The Unfaithful Sons of Eli Contrasted to Samuel**	
2:12–17	Eli's Sons and Their Sins	83
2:18–21	Samuel Ministers before Yahweh	89
2:22–26	Eli Rebukes His Sons	92
2:27–36	A Prophecy against Eli's House	97
3:1–21	**Yahweh Calls Samuel to Be a Prophet**	108
Excursus	*The Prophet Samuel in Scripture*	116
4:1–7:1	**Israel's Struggle with the Philistines**	
4:1–11	The Philistines Capture the Ark of the Covenant	118
4:12–22	The Death of Eli and the Birth of Ichabod	128
5:1–12	Yahweh Judges the Philistines and Their God Dagon	134
6:1–7:1	The Ark Is Returned to Israel	141
7:2–17	**Samuel's Ministry as Judge: God Delivers Israel from the Philistines**	154
8:1–22	**Israel Demands That Samuel Appoint a King**	162

9:1–31:13	**The Reign of Saul**	
9:1–12:25	**Transition to a Monarchy**	
9:1–25	Saul Meets the Prophet Samuel	175
9:26–10:16	Saul Is Anointed King	189
10:17–27a	Saul Is Publicly Made King	200
10:27b–11:15	Saul Saves Jabesh-gilead	205
12:1–25	Samuel's Warning about the Monarchy	216
13:1–15:35	**Saul's Military Accomplishments**	
13:1–23	Saul's First Philistine Campaign, Part 1: His Preparation	230
14:1–23	Saul's First Philistine Campaign, Part 2: Jonathan Routs the Philistines	246
14:24–46	Saul's First Philistine Campaign, Part 3: Saul's Impetuous Vow	258
Excursus	*The Urim and Thummim*	272
14:47–52	Saul's Military Successes	276
15:1–35	The Amalekite Campaign: Saul Is Rejected as King	281
16:1–31:13	**Saul's Decline and David's Rise**	
16:1–18:5	**David Becomes a Commander in Saul's Army**	
16:1–13	David Is Anointed King and Receives God's Spirit	301
16:14–23	David Ministers to Saul with Music	314
17:1–58	David as Israel's Champion: The Victory over Goliath	321
18:1–5	David in Saul's Service and Jonathan's Love for David	344
18:6–26:25	**David in Saul's Disfavor**	
18:6–16	Saul's Jealousy of David	350
18:17–30	David Becomes Saul's Son-in-Law	357
19:1–17	Saul Tries to Have David Killed	364
19:18–24	Saul Searches for David in the Pastures at Ramah	374
Excursus	*Luther on the Prophet Samuel*	380
20:1–21:1	Jonathan Warns David (ET 20:1–42)	386
21:2–10	David in Nob (ET 21:1–9)	406
21:11–16	David in Gath (ET 21:10–15)	414
22:1–5	David in Adullam and Moab	420
22:6–23	Saul Kills the Priests at Nob	424
23:1–13	David Rescues Keilah	434
23:14–24:1	David in Ziph and Maon (ET 23:14–29)	443
24:2–23	David Spares Saul's Life at En-gedi (ET 24:1–22)	452
25:1–44	David Marries Abigail	469
26:1–25	David Spares Saul's life at Ziph	490

27:1–31:13   **The Philistine Resurgence**

27:1–12   David in the Service of Achish of Gath   505

28:1–2   David Gains Achish's Trust   515

28:3–25   Saul's Second Philistine Campaign, Part 1: Saul and the Medium at Endor   518

29:1–11   Saul's Second Philistine Campaign, Part 2: The Philistines Dismiss David   541

30:1–31   David Rescues His Wives from the Amalekites   549

31:1–13   Saul Dies in Battle   564

INDEX OF SUBJECTS   573

INDEX OF PASSAGES   591

LIST OF FIGURES

Figure   1   "To This Day" Notices in the Book of Samuel   3

Figure   2   Old Testament Parallels to Passages in Samuel   11

Figure   3   Chronology of Eli's Life   13

Figure   4   Basic Chronology of the United Monarchy   16

Figure   5   Chronology of Saul's Reign   17

Figure   6   Chronology of David's Reign in Hebron   18

Figure   7   Chronology of David's Reign in Jerusalem   22

Figure   8   Chronology of 1 Samuel   22

Figure   9   English and Hebrew Versification Differences in Samuel   33

Figure 10   Contents of the Qumran Samuel Manuscripts   36

Figure 11   Movements of the Ark of the Covenant   124

Figure 12   Places Where the Tabernacle Rested in Israel   133

Figure 13   Places Where Samuel Judged Israel   161

Figure 14   Promonarchical and Antimonarchical Sections in 1 Samuel 8–12   167

Figure 15   Samuel's Instructions to Saul (1 Sam 10:1–8)   197

Figure 16   Saul's Faltering Accession   198

Figure 17   Comparison of 1 Samuel 12:8–13 with Other Historical Reviews in the Old Testament   225

Figure 18   Kingdom and Battles of Saul   245

Figure 19   Elide Priests from Samuel to David   257

Figure 20   Saul's Family Genealogy   280

Figure 21   Parallels between 1 Samuel 15 and 2 Samuel 24   291

Figure 22   Traits of Saul and David Given by the Narrator When They Are Introduced   305

Figure 23   David's Genealogy   312–13

Figure 24   David on the Run from Saul   372–73

Figure 25   David's Raids   514
Figure 26   Military Maneuvers in 1 Samuel 28–31   526–27
Figure 27   Chronology of Events in 1 Samuel 28–2 Samuel 1   548
Figure 28   Places That Received Gifts from David (1 Sam 30:27–31)   563

Editors' Preface

What may a reader expect from the Concordia Commentary: A Theological Exposition of Sacred Scripture?

The purpose of this series, simply put, is to assist pastors, missionaries, and teachers of the Scriptures to convey God's Word with greater clarity, understanding, and faithfulness to the divine intent of the original Hebrew, Aramaic, or Greek text.

Since every interpreter approaches the exegetical task from a certain perspective, honesty calls for an outline of the presuppositions held by those who have shaped this commentary series. This also serves, then, as a description of the characteristics of the commentaries.

First in importance is the conviction that the content of the scriptural testimony is Jesus Christ. The Lord himself enunciated this when he said, "The Scriptures ... testify to me" (Jn 5:39), words that have been incorporated into the logo of this series. The message of the Scriptures is the Good News of God's work to reconcile the world to himself through the life, death, resurrection, ascension, and everlasting session of Jesus Christ at the right hand of God the Father. Under the guidance of the same Spirit who inspired the writing of the Scriptures, these commentaries seek to find in every passage of every canonical book "that which promotes Christ" (as Luther's hermeneutic is often described). They are *Trinitarian* and *Christological* commentaries.

As they unfold the scriptural testimony to Jesus Christ, these commentaries expound Law and Gospel. This approach arises from a second conviction—that Law and Gospel are the overarching doctrines of the Bible itself and that to understand them in their proper distinction and relationship to each other is a key for understanding the self-revelation of God and his plan of salvation in Jesus Christ.

Now, Law and Gospel do not always appear in Scripture labeled as such. The palette of language in Scripture is multicolored, with many and rich hues. The dialectic of a pericope may be fallen creation and new creation, darkness and light, death and life, wandering and promised land, exile and return, ignorance and wisdom, demon possession and the kingdom of God, sickness and healing, being lost and found, guilt and righteousness, flesh and Spirit, fear and joy, hunger and feast, or Babylon and the new Jerusalem. But the common element is God's gracious work of restoring fallen humanity through the Gospel of his Son. Since the predominant characteristic of these commentaries is the proclamation of that Gospel, they are, in the proper sense of the term, *evangelical*.

A third, related conviction is that the Scriptures are God's vehicle for communicating the Gospel. The editors and authors accept without reservation that the canonical books of the Old and New Testaments are, in their entirety, the inspired, infallible, and inerrant Word of God. The triune God is the ultimate author of the Bible, and every word in the original Hebrew, Aramaic, and Greek is inspired by the Holy Spirit. Yet rather than mechanical dictation, in the mysterious process by which the Scriptures were divinely inspired (e.g., 2 Tim 3:16; 2 Pet 1:21), God made use of the human faculties, knowledge, interests, and styles of the biblical writers, whose individual books surely are marked by distinctive features. At the same time, the canon of Scripture has its own inner unity, and each passage must be understood in harmony with the larger context of the whole. This commentary series pays heed to the smallest of textual details because of its acceptance of *plenary and verbal inspiration* and interprets the text in light of the whole of Scripture, in accord with the analogy of faith, following the principle that *Scripture interprets Scripture.* The entirety of the Bible is God's Word, *sacred* Scripture, calling for *theological* exposition.

A fourth conviction is that, even as the God of the Gospel came into this world in Jesus Christ (the Word Incarnate), the scriptural Gospel has been given to and through the people of God, for the benefit of all humanity. God did not intend his Scriptures to have a life separated from the church. He gave them through servants of his choosing: prophets, sages, evangelists, and apostles. He gave them to the church and through the church, to be cherished in the church for admonition and comfort and to be used by the church for proclamation and catechesis. The living context of Scripture is ever the church, where the Lord's ministry of preaching, baptizing, forgiving sins, teaching, and celebrating the Lord's Supper continues. Aware of the way in which the incarnation of the Son of God has as a consequence the close union of Scripture and church, of Word and Sacraments, this commentary series features expositions that are *ecclesiological* and *sacramental.*

This Gospel Word of God, moreover, creates a unity among all those in whom it works the obedience of faith and who confess the truth of God revealed in it. This is the unity of the one holy Christian and apostolic church, which extends through world history. The church is to be found wherever the marks of the church are present: the Gospel in the Word and the Sacraments. These have been proclaimed, confessed, and celebrated in many different cultures and are in no way limited nor especially attached to any single culture or people. As this commentary series seeks to articulate the universal truth of the Gospel, it acknowledges and affirms the confession of the scriptural truth in all the many times and places where the one true church has been found. Aiming to promote *concord* in the confession of the one scriptural Gospel, these commentaries seek to be, in the best sense of the terms, *confessional, ecumenical,* and *catholic.*

All of those convictions and characteristics describe the theological heritage of Martin Luther and of the confessors who subscribe to the Book of Concord (1580)—those who have come to be known as Lutherans. The editors and authors forthrightly confess their subscription to the doctrinal exposition of Scripture in the Book of Concord. As the publishing arm of The Lutheran Church—Missouri Synod, Concordia Publishing House is bound to doctrinal agreement with the Scriptures and the Lutheran Confessions and seeks to herald the true Christian doctrine to the ends of the earth. To that end, the series has enlisted confessional Lutheran authors from other church bodies around the world who share the evangelical mission of promoting theological concord.

The authors and editors stand in the exegetical tradition of Martin Luther and the other Lutheran reformers, who in turn (as their writings took pains to demonstrate) stood in continuity with faithful exegesis by theologians of the early and medieval church, rooted in the hermeneutics of the Scriptures themselves (evident, for example, by how the New Testament interprets the Old). This hermeneutical method, practiced also by many non-Lutherans, includes (1) interpreting Scripture with Scripture according to the analogy of faith, that is, in harmony with the whole of Christian doctrine revealed in the Word; (2) giving utmost attention to the grammar (lexicography, phonetics, morphology, syntax, pragmatics) of the original language of the Hebrew, Aramaic, or Greek text; (3) seeking to discern the intended meaning of the text, the "plain" or "literal" sense, aware that the language of Scripture ranges from narrative to discourse, from formal prose to evocative poetry, from archaic to acrostic to apocalyptic, and it uses metaphor, type, parable, and other figures; (4) drawing on philology, linguistics, archaeology, literature, philosophy, history, and other fields in the quest for a better understanding of the text; (5) considering the history of the church's interpretation; (6) applying the text as authoritative also in the present milieu of the interpreter; and (7) above all, seeing the fulfillment and present application of the text in terms of Jesus Christ and his corporate church; upholding the Word, Baptism, and the Supper as the means through which Christ imparts salvation today; and affirming the inauguration, already now, of the eternal benefits of that salvation that is yet to come in the resurrection on the Last Day.

To be sure, the authors and editors do not feel bound to agree with every detail of the exegesis of our Lutheran forefathers. Nor do we imagine that the interpretations presented here are the final word about every crux and enigmatic passage. But the work has been done in harmony with the exegetical tradition that reaches back through the Lutheran confessors all the way to the biblical writers themselves, and in harmony with the confession of the church: grace alone, faith alone, Scripture alone, Christ alone.

The editors wish to acknowledge their debt of gratitude for all who have helped make possible this series. It was conceived at CPH in 1990, and a couple of years of planning and prayer to the Lord of the church preceded its formal launch on July 2, 1992. During that time, Dr. J. A. O. Preus II volunteered his enthusiasm for the project because, in his view, it would nurture and advance the faithful proclamation of the Christian faith as understood by the Lutheran church. The financial support that has underwritten the series was provided by a gracious donor who wished to remain anonymous. Those two faithful servants of God were called to heavenly rest not long after the series was inaugurated.

During the early years, former CPH presidents Dr. John W. Gerber and Dr. Stephen J. Carter had the foresight to recognize the potential benefit of such a landmark work for the church at large. CPH allowed Dr. Christopher W. Mitchell to devote his time and energy to the conception and initial development of the project. Dr. Mitchell has remained the CPH editor and is also the Old Testament editor and the author of the commentary on the Song of Songs. Dr. Dean O. Wenthe served on the project since its official start in 1992 and was the general editor from 1999 until 2016; he is also the author of the commentaries on Jeremiah and Lamentations. Julene Gernant Dumit (M.A.R.) has been the CPH production editor for the entire series. Dr. Jeffrey A. Gibbs served on the editorial board as the New Testament editor from 1999 until 2012 and is the author of the commentaries on Matthew. Dr. Curtis P. Giese, author of the commentary on 2 Peter and Jude and the commentary on James, joined the board in 2011 and now serves as the New Testament editor.

CPH thanks all of the institutions that have enabled their faculty to serve as authors and editors. A particular debt of gratitude is owed to Concordia Theological Seminary, Fort Wayne, Indiana, for kindly allowing Dr. Dean O. Wenthe to serve on the editorial board and to dedicate a substantial portion of his time to the series for many years. CPH also thanks Concordia Seminary, St. Louis, Missouri, for the dedication of Dr. Jeffrey A. Gibbs during his tenure as the New Testament editor. Moreover, Concordia University Texas is granting Dr. Curtis P. Giese a reduced load to enable him to carry on as the New Testament editor of the series. These institutions have thereby extended their ministries in selfless service for the benefit of the greater church.

The editors pray that the beneficence of their institutions may be reflected in this series by an evangelical orientation, a steadfast Christological perspective, an eschatological view toward the ultimate good of Christ's bride, and a concern that the wedding feast of the King's Son may be filled with all manner of guests (Mt 22:1–14).

> Now to him who is able to establish you by my Gospel and the preaching of Jesus Christ, by the revelation of the mystery kept secret for ages past but now revealed also through the prophetic Scriptures, made known to all the nations by order of the eternal God unto the obedience of faith—to the only wise God, through Jesus Christ, be the glory forever. Amen! (Rom 16:25–27)

Author's Preface

When Dr. Christopher Mitchell of Concordia Publishing House first approached me about writing commentaries on the book of Samuel, I was quite reluctant to undertake this project. I had already written and published three volumes in the Concordia Commentary series (*Ezra and Nehemiah*, *Proverbs*, and *Daniel*) and was not convinced I ought to write others. However, eventually I agreed, and I am glad that I did. The book of Samuel is a rich trove of narratives of the late premonarchial period and early monarchy of Israel. But it is more than that—it is a record of God's love and mercy toward Israel and ultimately toward all humankind. The author of Samuel does not often place overt theological analysis of the narrative into his work. The challenge for readers is to understand the theological thrusts of his writings, his often subtle messages of God's Law and God's gracious Gospel. I have attempted to draw these out in this commentary.

Since our present 1 Samuel and 2 Samuel in English Bibles were originally one book, this volume contains an introduction to the entire book of Samuel. A second volume will contain commentary on 2 Samuel without an extensive introduction.

When seeking to understand historical narrative, it is most helpful to know when and where events took place. Throughout this commentary readers will find dates for the individual narratives. These are based on my published chronological work *From Abraham to Paul*. The identification of ancient sites with modern places is based in large part on the very helpful *Student Map Manual: Historical Geography of the Bible Lands* (J. Monson, general consultant; Jerusalem: Pictorial Archive [Near Eastern History] Est., 1979). In addition, I have included several maps as visual helps in understanding the events in 1 Samuel.

I would like to express my thanks to those who have made this work possible: Concordia University Chicago provided a sabbatical and Concordia Publishing House a grant, which allowed me leave from teaching for a year to complete this work. The very helpful librarians at the Klinck Memorial Library at Concordia University Chicago helped me obtain many of the articles and essays listed in the bibliography and provided workers to scan articles to PDF files for my use. The able editorial work by Dr. Christopher Mitchell and Julene Dumit is also appreciated. The opportunity to work with them again was another incentive for me to accept this assignment. Dr. Christopher Begg graciously sent me copies of some of his articles on Josephus' treatment of the book of Samuel that I could not obtain elsewhere. And, of course, I am grateful for the support of my wife, Rebecca, who followed my progress and at times, when I was a little too obsessed with the project, urged me to take a break and go for a walk with my binoculars and ornithology field guide.

May our gracious God continue to bless all who study his Word and trust his promises.

May 16, 2016
Pentecost Monday

Principal Abbreviations

Books of the Bible

Gen	2 Ki	Is	Nah	Rom	Titus
Ex	1 Chr	Jer	Hab	1 Cor	Philemon
Lev	2 Chr	Lam	Zeph	2 Cor	Heb
Num	Ezra	Ezek	Hag	Gal	James
Deut	Neh	Dan	Zech	Eph	1 Pet
Josh	Esth	Hos	Mal	Phil	2 Pet
Judg	Job	Joel	Mt	Col	1 Jn
Ruth	Ps (pl. Pss)	Amos	Mk	1 Thess	2 Jn
1 Sam	Prov	Obad	Lk	2 Thess	3 Jn
2 Sam	Eccl	Jonah	Jn	1 Tim	Jude
1 Ki	Song	Micah	Acts	2 Tim	Rev

Books of the Apocrypha and Other Noncanonical Books of the Septuagint

1–2 Esdras	1–2 Esdras
Tobit	Tobit
Judith	Judith
Add Esth	Additions to Esther
Wisdom	Wisdom of Solomon
Sirach	Sirach/Ecclesiasticus
Baruch	Baruch
Ep Jer	Epistle of Jeremiah
Azariah	Prayer of Azariah
Song of the Three	Song of the Three Young Men
Susanna	Susanna
Bel	Bel and the Dragon
Manasseh	Prayer of Manasseh
1–2 Macc	1–2 Maccabees
3–4 Macc	3–4 Maccabees
Ps 151	Psalm 151
Odes	Odes
Ps(s) Sol	Psalm(s) of Solomon

Reference Works and Scripture Versions

ABD	*The Anchor Bible Dictionary.* Edited by D. N. Freedman. 6 vols. New York: Doubleday, 1992
AC	Augsburg Confession
AE	*Luther's Works.* St. Louis: Concordia, and Philadelphia: Fortress, 1955– [American Edition]
ANET	*Ancient Near Eastern Texts Relating to the Old Testament.* Edited by J. B. Pritchard. 3d ed. Princeton: Princeton University Press, 1969
ANF	*The Ante-Nicene Fathers.* Edited by A. Roberts and J. Donaldson. 10 vols. Repr., Peabody, Mass.: Hendrickson, 1994
Ap	Apology of the Augsburg Confession
BDB	Brown, F., S. R. Driver, and C. A. Briggs. *A Hebrew and English Lexicon of the Old Testament.* Oxford: Clarendon, 1979
BHS	*Biblia Hebraica Stuttgartensia.* Edited by K. Elliger and W. Rudolph. Stuttgart: Deutsche Bibelgesellschaft, 1967/1977
CAL	*The Comprehensive Aramaic Lexicon.* Cincinnati: Hebrew Union College—Jewish Institute of Religion; http://cal1.cn.huc.edu
CDCH	*The Concise Dictionary of Classical Hebrew.* Edited by D. J. A. Clines. Sheffield: Sheffield Phoenix, 2009
DOTHB	*Dictionary of the Old Testament: Historical Books.* Edited by Bill T. Arnold and H. G. M. Williamson. Downers Grove, Ill.: InterVarsity, 2005
ESV	English Standard Version of the Bible
ET	English translation
FC Ep	Formula of Concord, Epitome
FC SD	Formula of Concord, Solid Declaration
GCS	Die griechischen christlichen Schriftsteller der ersten drei Jahrhunderte
GKC	*Gesenius' Hebrew Grammar.* Edited by E. Kautzsch. Translated by A. E. Cowley. 2d ed. Oxford: Clarendon, 1910
GW	God's Word translation of the Bible
HALOT	Koehler, L., W. Baumgartner, and J. J. Stamm. *The Hebrew and Aramaic Lexicon of the Old Testament.* Translated and edited under the supervision of M. E. J. Richardson. 5 vols. Leiden: Brill, 1994–2000
HCSB	Holman Christian Standard Bible

HOTTP[2]	*Preliminary and Interim Report on the Hebrew Old Testament Text Project.* 2d ed. Volume 2: *Historical Books.* New York: United Bible Societies, 1979
IBH	Steinmann, A. E. *Intermediate Biblical Hebrew: A Reference Grammar with Charts and Exercises.* St. Louis: Concordia, 2007, 2009
Jastrow	Jastrow, M., comp. *A Dictionary of the Targumim, the Talmud Babli and Yerushalmi, and the Midrashic Literature.* 2 vols. Brooklyn: P. Shalom, 1967
Joüon	Joüon, P. *A Grammar of Biblical Hebrew.* Translated and revised by T. Muraoka. 2 vols. Subsidia biblica 14/1–2. Rome: Editrice Pontificio Istituto Biblico, 1991
KJV	King James Version of the Bible
KTU	*Die keilalphabetischen Texte aus Ugarit.* Vol. 1. Edited by M. Dietrich, O. Loretz, and J. Sanmartín. Alter Orient und Altes Testament 24/1. Neukirchen-Vluyn: Neukirchener Verlag, 1976
LC	Large Catechism of M. Luther
LSB	*Lutheran Service Book.* St. Louis: Concordia, 2006
LSB Agenda	*Lutheran Service Book: Agenda.* St. Louis: Concordia, 2006
LXX	*Septuaginta: Id est Vetus Testamentum graece iuxta LXX interpretes.* Edited by A. Rahlfs. 2 vols. Stuttgart: Deutsche Bibelgesellschaft, 1935, 1979
MT	Masoretic Text of the Hebrew Bible
Muraoka	Muraoka, T. *A Greek-English Lexicon of the Septuagint.* Louvain, Belgium: Peeters, 2009
n	Used after a year date to indicate that the year began in the spring month of Nisan (e.g., 969n began in the spring of 969 BC and ended after winter in early 968 BC)
NASB	New American Standard Bible
NET	NET Bible (New English Translation)
NETS	*A New English Translation of the Septuagint and the Other Greek Translations Traditionally Included under That Title.* Edited by A. Pietersma and B. G. Wright. Oxford: Oxford University Press, 2007. For 1 Reigns (1 Samuel), this is an English translation of Rahlfs, *Septuaginta* (LXX), except where noted in *NETS*
NIV	New International Version of the Bible
NPNF[1]	*The Nicene and Post-Nicene Fathers.* Series 1. Edited by P. Schaff. 14 vols. Repr., Peabody, Mass.: Hendrickson, 1994

NPNF[2]	*The Nicene and Post-Nicene Fathers.* Series 2. Edited by P. Schaff and H. Wace. 14 vols. Repr., Peabody, Mass.: Hendrickson, 1994
NRSV	New Revised Standard Version of the Bible
NT	New Testament
OT	Old Testament
PL	Patrologia latina. Edited by J.-P. Migne. 217 vols. Paris, 1844–1855
SA	Smalcald Articles
SC	Small Catechism of M. Luther
t	Used after a year date to indicate that the year began in the fall month of Tishri (e.g., 969t began in the fall of 969 BC and ended after summer in 968 BC)
TDOT	*Theological Dictionary of the Old Testament.* Edited by G. J. Botterweck, H. Ringgren, and H.-J. Fabry. Translated by J. T. Willis et al. 15 vols. Grand Rapids: Eerdmans, 1974–2006
Triglotta	*Concordia Triglotta: The Symbolical Books of the Ev. Lutheran Church.* St. Louis: Concordia, 1921
TWOT	*Theological Wordbook of the Old Testament.* Edited by R. L. Harris, G. L. Archer Jr., and B. K. Waltke. 2 vols. Chicago: Moody, 1980
WA	*D. Martin Luthers Werke: Kritische Gesamtausgabe.* 73 vols. in 85. Weimar: Böhlau, 1883– [Weimarer Ausgabe]
WA DB	*D. Martin Luthers Werke: Kritische Gesamtausgabe. Die Deutsche Bibel.* 12 vols. in 15. Weimar: Böhlau, 1906–1961 [Weimarer Ausgabe Deutsche Bibel]
Waltke-O'Connor	Waltke, B. K., and M. O'Connor. *An Introduction to Biblical Hebrew Syntax.* Winona Lake, Ind.: Eisenbrauns, 1990

Hebrew Verbal System

	G-Stem System[1] *Basic*	D-Stem System[2] *Doubling*	H-Stem System *H-Prefix*
Active	G (Qal)	D (Piel)	H (Hiphil)
Passive	Gp (Qal passive)	Dp (Pual)	Hp (Hophal)
Reflexive/Passive	N (Niphal)	HtD (Hithpael)	

---

[1] "G" is from the German *Grundstamm,* "basic stem."

[2] This also includes other doubling patterns such as Polel (D), Pilpel (D), Polal (Dp), Polpal (Dp), Hithpolel (HtD), and Hithpalpel (HtD).

Icons

These icons are used in the margins of this commentary to highlight the following themes:

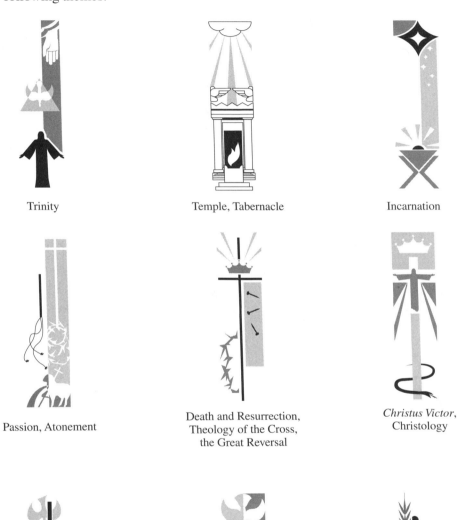

Trinity

Temple, Tabernacle

Incarnation

Passion, Atonement

Death and Resurrection,
Theology of the Cross,
the Great Reversal

Christus Victor,
Christology

Baptism

Catechesis,
Instruction, Revelation

Lord's Supper

Ministry of Word and Sacrament,
Office of the Keys

The Church,
Christian Marriage

Worship

Sin, Law Breaking,
Death

Hope of Heaven,
Eschatology

Justification

Bibliography

Aberbach, David. "מנה אחת אפים (1 Sam. i 5): A New Interpretation." *Vetus Testamentum* 24 (1974): 350–53.

Ackerman, James S. "Who Can Stand before YHWH, This Holy God? A Reading of 1 Samuel 1–15." *Prooftexts* 11 (1991): 1–24.

Ackroyd, Peter R. "The Verb Love—*ʾĀhēb* in the David-Jonathan Narratives—A Footnote." *Vetus Testamentum* 25 (1975): 213–14.

Adam, Klaus-Peter. "Nocturnal Intrusions and Divine Interventions on Behalf of Judah: David's Wisdom and Saul's Tragedy in 1 Samuel 26." *Vetus Testamentum* 59 (2009): 1–33.

———. "Saul as a Tragic Hero: Greek Drama and Its Influence on Hebrew Scripture in 1 Samuel 14,24–46 (10,8; 13,7–13a; 10,17–27)." Pages 123–83 in *For and against David: Story and History in the Books of Samuel*. Edited by A. Graeme Auld and Erik Eynikel. Leuven: Peeters, 2010.

Aejmelaeus, Anneli. "Hannah's Psalm: Text, Composition, and Redaction." Pages 354–76 in *Houses Full of All Good Things: Essays in Memory of Timo Veijola*. Edited by Juha Pakkala and Martti Nissinen. Helsinki: Finnish Exegetical Society, 2008.

———. "Hannah's Psalm in 4QSamᵃ." Pages 23–37 in *Archaeology of the Books of Samuel: The Entangling of the Textual and Literary History*. Edited by Philippe Hugo and Adrian Schenker. Leiden: Brill, 2010.

———. "What Rahlfs Could Not Know: 1 Sam 14,4–5 in the Old Greek." Pages 81–94 in *After Qumran: Old and Modern Editions of the Biblical Texts: The Historical Books*. Edited by Hans Ausloos, Bénédicte Lemmelijn, and Julio Trebolle Barrera. Leuven: Peeters, 2012.

Allegro, John M. *Qumran Cave 4.I (4Q158–4Q186)*. Discoveries in the Judaean Desert 5. Oxford: Clarendon, 1968.

Allis, Oswald T. "The Punishment of the Men of Bethshemesh." *Evangelical Quarterly* 15 (1943): 298–307.

Alter, Robert. *The David Story: A Translation with Commentary of 1 and 2 Samuel*. New York: Norton, 1999.

Althann, Robert. "Consonantal *ym*: Ending or Noun in Isa 3,13; Jer 17,16; 1 Sam 6,19." *Biblica* 63 (1982): 560–65.

———. "Northwest Semitic Notes on Some Texts in 1 Samuel." *Journal of Northwest Semitic Languages* 12 (1984): 27–34.

Amit, Yairah. "Progression as a Rhetorical Device in Biblical Literature." *Journal for the Study of the Old Testament* 28 (2003): 3–32.

Angert-Quilter, Theresa, and Lynne Wall. "The 'Spirit Wife' at Endor." *Journal for the Study of the Old Testament* (2001): 55–72.

Ansell, Nicholas John. "On (Not) Obeying the Sabbath: Reading Jesus Reading Scripture." *Horizons in Biblical Theology* 33 (2011): 97–120.

Arnold, Bill T. "The Amalekite's Report of Saul's Death: Political Intrigue or Incompatible Sources?" *Journal of the Evangelical Theological Society* 32 (1989): 289–98.

———. "Necromancy and Cleromancy in 1 and 2 Samuel." *Catholic Biblical Quarterly* 66 (2004): 199–213.

———. "A Pre-Deuteronomistic Bicolon in 1 Samuel 12:21?" *Journal of Biblical Literature* 123 (2004): 137–42.

———. "Soul-Searching Questions about 1 Samuel 28: Samuel's Appearance at Endor and Christian Anthropology." Pages 75–83 in *What about the Soul? Neuroscience and Christian Anthropology.* Edited by Joel B. Green. Nashville: Abingdon, 2004.

Aster, Shawn Zelig. "What Was Doeg the Edomite's Title? Textual Emendation versus a Comparative Approach to 1 Samuel 21:8." *Journal of Biblical Literature* 122 (2003): 353–61.

Athas, George. " 'A Man after God's Own Heart': David and the Rhetoric of Election to Kingship." *Journal for the Evangelical Study of the Old Testament* 2 (2013): 191–98.

Auld, A. Graeme. *I and II Samuel: A Commentary.* Old Testament Library. Louisville, Ky.: Westminster John Knox, 2011.

Auld, A. Graeme, and Craig Y. S. Ho. "The Making of David and Goliath." *Journal for the Study of the Old Testament* 56 (1992): 19–39.

Avioz, Michael. "Could Saul Rule Forever? A New Look at 1 Samuel 13:13–14." *Journal of Hebrew Scriptures* 5, article 16 (2005). http://www.jhsonline.org/Articles/article_46.pdf.

———. "Josephus' Rewriting of 1 Samuel 25." *Journal of Jewish Studies* 59 (2008): 73–85.

———. "The Incineration of Saul's and His Son's Corpses according to Josephus." *Journal for the Study of the Pseudepigrapha* 18 (2009): 285–92.

Bach, Alice. "The Pleasure of Her Text." *Union Seminary Quarterly Review* 43 (1989): 41–58.

Backon, Joshua. "Prooftext That Elkanah Rather Than Hannah Consecrated Samuel as a Nazirite." *Jewish Bible Quarterly* 42 (2014): 52–53.

Baden, Joel. *The Historical David: The Real Life of an Invented Hero.* New York: HarperCollins, 2013.

Bailey, Randall C. "Reading the Book of Samuel as a Message to the Exiles: A Hermeneutical Shift." *Journal of the Interdenominational Theological Center* 18 (1990–1991): 95–118.

———. "The Redemption of YHWH: A Literary Critical Function of the Songs of Hannah and David." *Biblical Interpretation* 3 (1995): 213–31.

Baird, James O. "Difficult Texts from Ruth, 1 and 2 Samuel." Pages 267–76 in *Difficult Texts of the Old Testament Explained*. Hurst, Tex.: Winkler, 1982.

Bakon, Shimon. "David's Sin: Counting the People." *Jewish Bible Quarterly* 41 (2013): 53–54.

Baldwin, Joyce G. *1 and 2 Samuel: An Introduction and Commentary*. Tyndale Old Testament Commentaries 8. Leicester, England: Inver-Varsity, 1988.

Bar, Shaul. *A Letter That Has Not Been Read: Dreams in the Hebrew Bible*. Translated by Lenn J. Schramm. Cincinnati: Hebrew Union College Press, 2001.

———. "Saul and the 'Witch of En-Dor.' " *Jewish Bible Quarterly* 39 (2011): 99–107.

Barr, James. "Seeing the Wood for the Trees: An Enigmatic Ancient Translation." *Journal of Semitic Studies* 13 (1968): 11–20.

Barthélemy, D., and J. T. Milik. *Qumran Cave 1*. Discoveries in the Judaean Desert 1. Oxford: Clarendon, 1955.

Barthélemy, Dominique, David W. Gooding, Johan Lust, and Emanuel Tov. *The Story of David and Goliath: Textual and Literary Criticism: Papers of a Joint Research Venture*. Göttingen: Vandenhoeck & Ruprecht, 1986.

Batten, Loring W. "The Sanctuary at Shiloh, and Samuel's Sleeping Therein." *Journal of Biblical Literature* 19 (1900): 29–33.

Bauck, Peter. "1 Samuel 19—David and the *Teraphim*: יהוה עם דוד and the Emplotted Narrative." *Scandinavian Journal of the Old Testament* 22 (2008): 212–36.

Bautch, Richard J. *Developments in Genre between Post-Exilic Penitential Prayers and the Psalms of Communal Lament*. Atlanta: Society of Biblical Literature, 2003.

Beck, John A. "The Narrative-Geographical Shaping of 1 Samuel 7:5–13." *Bibliotheca sacra* 162 (2005): 299–309.

———. "David and Goliath, a Story of Place: The Narrative-Geographical Shaping of 1 Samuel 17." *Westminster Theological Journal* 68 (2006): 321–30.

Beck, Martin. "Messiaserwartung in den Geschichtsbüchern? Bemerkungen zur Funktion des Hannaliedes (1 Sam 2,1–10) in seinen diversen literarischen Kontexten (vgl Ex 15; Dtn 32; II Sam 22)." Pages 231–51 in *Auf dem Weg zur Endgestalt von Genesis bis II Regum: Festschrift Hans-Christoph Schmitt zum 65. Geburtstag*. Berlin: De Gruyter, 2006.

Beckwith, Roger T. "The Day, Its Divisions and Its Limits, in Biblical Thought." *Evangelical Quarterly* 43 (1971): 218–27.

Begg, Christopher T. "The Abigail Story (1 Samuel 25) according to Josephus." *Estudios bíblicos* 54 (1996): 5–34.

———. "The Ark in Philistia according to Josephus: Ant 6,1–6." *Ephemerides theologicae lovanienses* 72 (1996): 384–97.

———. "The Loss of the Ark according to Josephus." *Liber annuus* 46 (1996): 167–86.

————. "The Rape of Tamar (2 Samuel 13) according to Josephus." *Estudios bíblicos* 54 (1996): 465–500.

————. "David's Philistine Service: According to Josephus." *Jian Dao* 7 (1997): 1–16.

————. "David's Second Sparing of Saul according to Josephus." *Tyndale Bulletin* 48 (1997): 93–117.

————. "The Massacre of the Priests of Nob in Josephus and Pseudo-Philo." *Estudios bíblicos* 55 (1997): 171–98.

————. "Samuel Leader of Israel according to Josephus." *Antonianum* 72 (1997): 199–216.

————. "Samuel's Farewell Discourse according to Josephus." *Scandinavian Journal of the Old Testament* 11 (1997): 56–77.

————. "Saul's Royal Start according to Josephus." *Sacris erudiri* 37 (1997): 5–32.

————. "David's Double Escape according to Josephus." *Journal of Progressive Judaism* 10 (1998): 28–45.

————. "The Return of the Ark according to Josephus." *Bulletin for Biblical Research* 8 (1998): 15–37.

————. "King Saul's First Sin according to Josephus." *Antonianum* 74 (1999): 685–96.

————. "David's Fourfold Escape according to Josephus." *Antonianum* 80 (2005): 433–52.

————. "The Anointing of Saul according to Josephus." *Bulletin for Biblical Research* 16 (2006): 1–24.

————. "The First Encounter between Saul and David: According to Josephus." *Andrews University Seminary Studies* 44 (2006): 3–11.

————. "The Youth of Samuel according to Josephus." *Sacris erudiri* 45 (2006): 15–45.

Ben-Barak, Zafrira. "The Mizpah Covenant (I Sam 10:25): The Source of the Israelite Monarchic Covenant." *Zeitschrift für die alttestamentliche Wissenschaft* 91 (1979): 30–43.

Ben-Meir. "Nabal, the Villain." *Jewish Bible Quarterly* 22 (1994): 249–51.

Bergen, Robert D. *1, 2 Samuel.* New American Commentary 7. Nashville: Broadman & Holman, 1996.

Berger, Yitzhak. "Ruth and Inner-Biblical Allusion: The Case of 1 Samuel 25." *Journal of Biblical Literature* 128 (2009): 253–72.

Berginer, Vladimir M., and Chaim Cohen. "The Nature of Goliath's Visual Disorder and the Actual Role of His Personal Bodyguard: נֹשֵׂא הַצִּנָּה (I Sam 17:7,41)." *Ancient Near Eastern Studies* 43 (2006): 27–44.

Berlin, Adele. "Hannah and Her Prayers." *Scriptura* 87 (2004): 227–32.

Bernat, David A. "Biblical *Waṣf*s beyond Song of Songs." *Journal for the Study of the Old Testament* 28 (2004): 327–49.

Beuken, W. A. M. "1 Samuel 28: The Prophet as 'Hammer of Witches.'" *Journal for the Study of the Old Testament* 6 (1978): 3–17.

Bewer, Julius A. "The Original Reading of I Sam 6:19a." *Journal of Biblical Literature* 57 (1938): 89–91.

———. "Notes on 1 Sam 13:21; 2 Sam 23:1; Psalm 48:8." *Journal of Biblical Literature* 61 (1942): 45–49.

Bič, Miloš. "Saul Sucht die Eselinnen (1 Sam 9)." *Vetus Testamentum* 7 (1957): 92–97.

Biddle, Mark E. "Ancestral Motifs in 1 Samuel 25: Intertextuality and Characterization." *Journal of Biblical Literature* 121 (2002): 617–38.

Billington, Clyde E. "Goliath and the Exodus Giants: How Tall Were They?" *Journal of the Evangelical Theological Society* 50 (2007): 489–508.

Biran, Avraham, and Joseph Naveh. "An Aramaic Stele Fragment from Tel Dan." *Israel Exploration Journal* 43 (1993): 81–98.

———. "The Tel Dan Inscription: A New Fragment." *Israel Exploration Journal* 45 (1995): 1–18.

Birch, Bruce C. "Development of the Tradition on the Anointing of Saul in 1 Sam 9:1–10:16." *Journal of Biblical Literature* 90 (1971): 55–68.

Blenkinsopp, Joseph. "Jonathan's Sacrilege: 1 Sm 14:1–46: A Study in Literary History." *Catholic Biblical Quarterly* 26 (1964): 423–49.

———. "Did Saul Make Gibeon His Capital?" *Vetus Testamentum* 24 (1974): 1–7.

———. "Saul and the Mistress of the Spirits (1 Samuel 28.3–25)." Pages 49–62 in *Sense and Sensitivity: Essays on Reading the Bible in Memory of Robert Carroll.* Edited by Alastair G. Hunter and Phillip R. Davies. London: Sheffield Academic, 2002.

Blumenthal, Fred. "The Ghost of Samuel: Real or Imaginary?" *Jewish Bible Quarterly* 41 (2013): 104–6.

Bodner, Keith. "Ark-Eology: Shifting Emphases in 'Ark Narrative' Scholarship." *Currents in Biblical Research* 4 (2006): 169–97.

———. *1 Samuel: A Narrative Commentary.* Hebrew Bible Monographs 19. Sheffield: Sheffield Phoenix, 2008.

———. "Mouse Trap: A Text-Critical Problem with Rodents in the Ark Narrative." *Journal of Theological Studies* 59 (2008): 634–49.

Boogaart, Thomas Arthur. "Narrative Theology in the Story of the Capture of the Ark." *Reformed Review* 41 (1988): 139–46.

Borgman, Paul. *David, Saul, and God: Rediscovering an Ancient Story.* Oxford: Oxford University Press, 2008.

Bosworth, David A. "David, Jether, and Child Soldiers." *Journal for the Study of the Old Testament* 36 (2011): 185–97.

Boyle, Marjorie O'Rourke. "The Law of the Heart: The Death of a Fool (1 Samuel 25)." *Journal of Biblical Literature* 120 (2001): 401–27.

Branch, Robin Gallaher. "Women Who Win with Words: Deliverance via Persuasive Communication." *In die Skriflig* 37 (2003): 289–318.

Bratcher, Robert Galveston. "How Did Agag Meet Samuel? (1 Sam. 15:32)." *Bible Translator* 22 (1971): 167–68.

Brauner, Ronald A. " 'To Grasp the Hem' and 1 Samuel 15:27." *Journal of the Ancient Near Eastern Society of Columbia University* 6 (1974): 35–38.

Brenner, Athalya. "Female Social Behaviour: Two Descriptive Patterns within the 'Birth of the Hero' Paradigm." *Vetus Testamentum* 36 (1986): 257–73.

———. "Michal and David: Love between Enemies?" Pages 260–70 in *The Fate of King David: The Past and Present of a Biblical Icon*. Edited by Tod Linafelt, Claudia V. Camp, and Timothy Beal. New York: T&T Clark, 2010.

Brettler, Marc Zvi. "The Composition of 1 Samuel 1–2." *Journal of Biblical Literature* 116 (1997): 601–12.

Bridge, Edward J. "Self-Abasement as an Expression of Thanks in the Hebrew Bible." *Biblica* 92 (2011): 255–73.

Brooke, Alan England, Norman McLean, and Henry St John Thackeray, eds. *The Old Testament in Greek*. Vol. 2: *The Later Historical Books*. Part 1: *1 and 2 Samuel*. Cambridge: Cambridge University Press, 1927.

Brooks, Simcha Shalom. "Was There a Concubine at Gibeah?" *Bulletin of the Anglo-Israel Archaeological Society* 15 (1996–1997): 31–40.

Brown, C. R. "I Sam ii. 10 as Illustrative of Gen. vi. 3." *Journal of the Society of Biblical Literature and Exegesis* 5 (1885): 91.

Brueggemann, Walter. "Narrative Intentionality in 1 Samuel 29." *Journal for the Study of the Old Testament* 43 (1989): 21–35.

———. *First and Second Samuel*. Interpretation: A Bible Commentary for Teaching and Preaching. Louisville, Ky.: Westminster/John Knox, 1990.

———. "I Samuel 1: A Sense of a Beginning." *Zeitschrift für die alttestamentliche Wissenschaft* 102 (1990): 33–48.

———. "Narrative Coherence and Theological Intentionality in 1 Samuel 18." *Catholic Biblical Quarterly* 55 (1993): 225–43.

———. "(I)chabod Departed." *Princeton Seminary Bulletin* 22 (2001): 115–33.

———. *David's Truth in Israel's Imagination and Memory*. 2d ed. Minneapolis: Fortress, 2002.

———. *Ichabod toward Home: The Journey of God's Glory*. Grand Rapids: Eerdmans, 2002.

Byington, Steven T. "Brief Communications: I Sam 13:21." *Journal of Biblical Literature* 39 (1920): 77–82.

Calabro, David. "The Lord of Hosts and His Guests: Hospitality on Sacred Space in Exodus 29 and 1 Samuel 1." *Proceedings of the Eastern Great Lakes and Midwest Biblical Societies* 27 (2007): 19–29.

Campbell, Antony F. "From Philistine to Throne (1 Samuel 16:14–18:16)." *Australian Biblical Review* 34 (1986): 35–41.

———. "The Reported Story: Midway between Oral Performance and Literary Art." *Semeia* 46 (1989): 77–85.

———. "Structure Analysis and the Art of Exegesis (1 Samuel 16:14–18:30)." Pages 76–103 in *Problems in Biblical Theology: Essays in Honor of Rolf Knierim.* Edited by Henry T. C. Sun and Keith L. Eades. Grand Rapids: Eerdmans, 1997.

———. *1 Samuel.* Forms of the Old Testament Literature 7. Grand Rapids: Eerdmans, 2003.

———. *Joshua to Chronicles: An Introduction.* Louisville, Ky.: Westminster John Knox, 2004.

Caquot, André, and Philippe de Robert, *Les livres de Samuel.* Commentaire de l'Ancien Testament. Geneva: Labor et Fides, 1994.

Carasik, Michael. "Why Did Hannah Ask for 'Seed of Men'?" *Journal of Biblical Literature* 129 (2010): 433–36.

Carmichael, Calum. "David at the Nob Sanctuary." Pages 201–12 in *For and against David: Story and History in the Books of Samuel.* Edited by A. Graeme Auld and Erik Eynikel. Leuven: Peeters, 2010.

Carmignac, J. "Précisions apportées au vocabulaire d'hébreu biblique par la guerre des fils de lumière contre les fils de ténèbres." *Vetus Testamentum* 5 (1955): 345–65.

Cartledge, Tony W. "Hannah Asked, and God Heard." *Review and Expositor* 99 (2002): 143–44.

Chalmers, Aaron. "RS 25.460 and Early Hebrew Poetry." *Ugarit-Forschungen* 36 (2004): 1–9.

Chapman, Cynthia R. "'Oh That You Were like a Brother to Me, One Who Had Nursed at My Mother's Breasts': Breast Milk as a Kinship-Forging Substance." *Journal of Hebrew Scriptures* 12, article 7 (2012). http://www.jhsonline.org/Articles/article_169.pdf.

Cheyne, T. K. "Some Supposed Archaisms in the Old Testament." *Journal of Biblical Literature* 18 (1899): 210–11.

Chisholm, Robert B., Jr. "Yahweh versus the Canaanite Gods: Polemic in Judges and 1 Samuel 1–7." *Bibliotheca sacra* 164 (2007): 165–80.

Clements, Ronald E. "Deuteronomistic Interpretation of the Founding of the Monarchy in 1 Sam 8." *Vetus Testamentum* 24 (1974): 398–410.

Coats, George W. "Self-Abasement and Insult Formulas." *Journal of Biblical Literature* 89 (1970): 14–26.

Cogan, Mordechai. "The Road to En-dor." Pages 319–26 in *Pomegranates and Golden Bells: Studies in Biblical, Jewish, and Near Eastern Ritual, Law, and Literature in Honor of Jacob Milgrom.* Edited by David P. Wright, David Noel Freedman, and Avi Hurvitz. Winona Lake, Ind.: Eisenbrauns, 1995.

Coggins, Richard J. "On Kings and Disguises." *Journal for the Study of the Old Testament* 50 (1991): 55–62.

Cohen, Naomi G. "'בי ... דבר': An 'Enthusiastic' Prophetic Formula." *Zeitschrift für die alttestamentliche Wissenschaft* 99 (1987): 219–32.

Collins, C. John. "The *Wayyiqtol* as 'Pluperfect': When and Why." *Tyndale Bulletin* 46 (1995): 117–40.

Collins, John J. *The Scepter and the Star: The Messiahs of the Dead Sea Scrolls and Other Ancient Literature.* New York: Doubleday, 1995.

Collins, Nina L. "The Start of the Pre-exilic Calendar Day of David and the Amalekites: A Note on 1 Samuel xxx 17." *Vetus Testamentum* 41 (1991): 203–10.

Conrad, Joachim. "Davids Königtum als Paradoxie: Versuch zu I Sam 21,2–10." Pages 413–23 in vol. 1 of *Gott und Mensch im Dialog: Festschrift für Otto Kaiser zum 80. Geburtstag.* Edited by Markus Witte. Berlin: De Gruyter, 2004.

Conrad, Lawrence I. "The Biblical Tradition for the Plague of the Philistines." *Journal of the American Oriental Society* 104 (1984): 281–87.

Cook, Edward M. "1 Samuel xx 26–xxi 5 according to 4QSam[b]." *Vetus Testamentum* 44 (1994): 442–54.

Cook, Joan E. "The Magnificat: Program for a New Era in the Spirit of the Song of Hannah." *Proceedings of the Eastern Great Lakes and Midwest Biblical Societies* 15 (1995): 35–43.

Cook, Stephen L. "The Text and Philology of 1 Samuel xiii 20–1." *Vetus Testamentum* 44 (1994): 250–54.

Cooley, Jeffrey L. "The Story of Saul's Election (1 Samuel 9–10) in the Light of Mantic Practice in Ancient Iraq." *Journal of Biblical Literature* 130 (2011): 247–61.

Cooley, Robert. "Gathered to His People: A Study of a Dothan Family Tomb." Pages 47–58 in *The Living and Active Word of God: Studies in Honor of Samuel J. Schultz.* Edited by Morris Inch and Ronald Youngblood. Winona Lake, Ind.: Eisenbrauns, 1983.

Couffignal, Robert. "David et Goliath: Un conte merveilleux: Étude littéraire de *1 Samuel* 17 et 18, 1–30." *Bulletin de littérature ecclésiastique* 99 (1998): 431–42.

Craig, Kenneth M., Jr. "Rhetorical Aspects of Questions Answered with Silence in 1 Samuel 14:37 and 28:6." *Catholic Biblical Quarterly* 56 (1994): 221–39.

Cross, Frank Moore. "The Oldest Manuscripts from Qumran." *Journal of Biblical Literature* 74 (1955): 147–72.

———. "The History of the Biblical Text in the Light of Discoveries in the Judaean Desert." *Harvard Theological Review* 57 (1964): 281–99.

———. *Canaanite Myth and Hebrew Epic: Essays in the History of the Religion of Israel.* Cambridge, Mass.: Harvard University Press, 1973.

————. "The Ammonite Oppression of the Tribes of Gad and Reuben: Missing Verses from 1 Samuel 11 Found in 4QSamuelᵃ." Pages 148–58 in *History, Historiography and Interpretation: Studies in Biblical and Cuneiform Literatures.* Edited by H. Tadmor and M. Weinfeld. Jerusalem: Magnes, 1983.

Cross, Frank Moore, and Donald W. Parry. "A Preliminary Edition of a Fragment of 4QSamᵇ (4Q52)." *Bulletin of the American Schools of Oriental Research* 306 (1997): 63–74.

Cross, Frank Moore, Donald W. Parry, Richard J. Saley, and Eugene Ulrich. *Qumran Cave 4.XII: 1–2 Samuel.* Discoveries in the Judaean Desert 17. Oxford: Clarendon, 2005.

Crowell, Bradley L. "Good Girl, Bad Girl: Foreign Women of the Deuteronomistic History in Postcolonial Perspective." *Biblical Interpretation* 21 (2013): 1–18.

Curtis, John B. "A Folk Etymology of *Nābîʾ*." *Vetus Testamentum* 29 (1979): 491–93.

Dahood, Mitchell. "The Divine Name *ʿĒlî* in the Psalms." *Theological Studies* 14 (1953): 452–57.

Darshan, Guy. "The Reinterment of Saul and Jonathan's Bones (II Sam 21,12–14) in Light of Ancient Greek Hero-Cult Stories." *Zeitschrift für die alttestamentliche Wissenschaft* 125 (2013): 640–45.

Davies, Philip R. "Ark or Ephod in I Sam. xiv. 18?" *Journal of Theological Studies* 26 (1975): 82–87.

Day, John. "Bedan, Abdon or Barak in 1 Samuel xii 11?" *Vetus Testamentum* 43 (1993): 261–64.

De Vries, Simon J. "David's Victory over the Philistine as Saga and as Legend." *Journal of Biblical Literature* 92 (1973): 23–36.

Debergé, Pierre. "Les fondements bibliques de la laïcite?" *Bulletin de littérature ecclésiastique* 106 (2005): 219–38.

Deboys, David G. "1 Samuel 29:6." *Vetus Testamentum* 39 (1989): 214–19.

Deenick, Karl. "Priest and King or Priest-King in 1 Samuel 2:35." *Westminster Theological Journal* 73 (2011): 325–39.

Derby, Josiah. "Expletives in the Bible." *Jewish Bible Quarterly* 26 (1998): 255–59.

Dhorme, Edouard. *Les livres de Samuel.* Paris: Victor Lecoffre, 1910.

Dick, Michael B. "The 'History of David's Rise to Power' and the Neo-Babylonian Succession Apologies." Pages 3–19 in *David and Zion: Biblical Studies in Honor of J. J. M. Roberts.* Edited by Bernard F. Batto and Kathryn L. Roberts. Winona Lake, Ind.: Eisenbrauns, 2004.

Dietrich, Walter. "Die Erzählungen von David und Goliat in I Sam 17." *Zeitschrift für die alttestamentliche Wissenschaft* 108 (1996): 172–91.

Diffey, Daniel S. "David and the Fulfilment of 1 Samuel 2:35: Faithful Priest, Sure House, and a Man after God's Own Heart." *Evangelical Quarterly* 85 (2013): 99–104.

Dragga, Sam. "In the Shadow of the Judges: The Failure of Saul." *Journal for the Study of the Old Testament* 38 (1987): 39–46.

Driver, G. R. "A Lost Colloquialism in the Old Testament (1 Sam 25:6)." *Journal of Theological Studies* 8 (1957): 272–73.

———. "Old Problems Re-examined." *Zeitschrift für die alttestamentliche Wissenschaft* 80 (1968): 174–83.

Eaton, M. R. "Some Instances of Flyting in the Hebrew Bible." *Journal for the Study of the Old Testament* 61 (1994): 3–14.

Edelman, Diana. "Saul's Rescue of Jabesh-Gilead (1 Sam 11:1–11): Sorting Story from History." *Zeitschrift für die alttestamentliche Wissenschaft* 96 (1984): 195–209.

———. "Saul's Battle against Amaleq (1 Sam 15)." *Journal for the Study of the Old Testament* 35 (1986): 71–84.

———. "Saul's Journey through Mt. Ephraim and Samuel's Ramah (1 Sam. 9:4–5, 10:2–5)." *Zeitschrift des deutschen Palästina-Vereins* 104 (1988): 44–58.

Edenburg, Cynthia. "How (Not) to Murder a King: Variations on a Theme in 1 Sam 24; 26." *Scandinavian Journal of the Old Testament* 12 (1998): 64–85.

———. "Notes on the Origin of the Biblical Tradition regarding Achish King of Gath." *Vetus Testamentum* 61 (2011): 34–38.

Edenburg, Cynthia, and Juha Pakkala, eds. *Is Samuel among the Deuteronomists? Current Views on the Place of Samuel in a Deuteronomistic History.* Atlanta: Society of Biblical Literature, 2013.

Eppstein, Victor. "Was Saul Also among the Prophets?" *Zeitschrift für die alttestamentliche Wissenschaft* 81 (1969): 287–304.

Esler, Philip Francis. "The Role of Hannah in 1 Samuel 1:1–2:21: Understanding a Biblical Narrative in Its Ancient Context." Pages 15–36 in *Kontexte der Schrift*, vol. 2: *Kultur, Politik, Religion, Sprache-Text.* Edited by Christian Strecker. Stuttgart: Kohlhammer, 2005.

Eslinger, Lyle M. "Viewpoints and Point of View in 1 Samuel 8–12." *Journal for the Study of the Old Testament* 26 (1983): 61–76.

———. *Kingship of God in Crisis: A Close Reading of 1 Samuel 1–12.* Decatur, Ga.: Almond, 1985.

———. "A Change of Heart: 1 Samuel 16." Pages 341–61 in *Ascribe to the Lord: Biblical and Other Studies in Memory of Peter C. Craigie.* Edited by Lyle Eslinger and Glen Taylor. Sheffield: JSOT, 1988.

Eves, Terry L. "One Ammonite Invasion or Two? 1 Sam 10:27–11:2 in the Light of 4QSam[a]." *Westminster Theological Journal* 44 (1982): 308–26.

Exum, J. Cheryl. *Tragedy and Biblical Narrative: Arrows of the Almighty.* Cambridge: Cambridge University Press, 1992.

Exum, J. Cheryl, and J. William Whedbee. "Isaac, Samson, and Saul: Reflections on the Comic and Tragic Visions." *Semeia* 32 (1984): 5–40.

Eynikel, Erik. "The Relation between the Eli Narratives (1 Sam. 1–4) and the Ark Narrative (1 Sam. 1–6; 2 Sam. 6:1–19)." Pages 88–106 in *Past, Present, Future: The Deuteronomistic History and the Prophets*. Edited by Johannes C. de Moor and Harry F. van Rooy. Leiden: Brill, 2000.

———. "Das Lied der Hanna (1 Sam 2,1–11) und das Lied Davids (2 Sam 22): Ein Vergleich." Pages 57–72 in *For and against David: Story and History in the Books of Samuel*. Edited by A. Graeme Auld and Erik Eynikel. Leuven: Peeters, 2010.

Falk, Marcia. "Reflections on Hannah's Prayer." *Tikkun* 9 (1994): 61–64.

Feldman, Louis H. "Prophets and Prophecy in Josephus." *Journal of Theological Studies* 41 (1990): 386–422.

Fenton, Terry L. "Deuteronomistic Advocacy of the *Nābî*ʾ: 1 Samuel ix 9 and Questions of Israelite Prophecy." *Vetus Testamentum* 47 (1997): 23–42.

Fernández Marcos, Natalio. "On Double Readings, Pseudo-Variants and Ghost-Names in the Historical Books." Pages 591–604 in *Emanuel: Studies in Hebrew Bible, Septuagint, and Dead Sea Scrolls in Honor of Emanuel Tov*. Edited by Shalom M. Paul et al. Leiden: Brill, 2003.

Fidler, Ruth. "A Wife's Vow—the Husband's Woe? The Case of Hannah and Elkanah (I Samuel 1,21.23)." *Zeitschrift für die alttestamentliche Wissenschaft* 118 (2006): 374–88.

Finkel, Joshua. "Filial Loyalty as a Testimony of Legitimacy: A Study in Folklore." *Journal of Biblical Literature* 55 (1936): 133–43.

Finkelstein, Emunah. "An Ignored Haplography in Samuel." *Journal of Semitic Studies* 4 (1959): 356–57.

Finkelstein, Israel. "Shiloh Yields Some, but Not All, of Its Secrets." *Biblical Archaeology Review* 12/1 (January/February 1986): 22–41.

———. "The Philistines in the Bible: A Late-Monarchic Perspective." *Journal for the Study of the Old Testament* 27 (2002): 131–67.

Firth, David G. " 'Play It Again, Sam': The Poetics of Narrative Repetition in 1 Samuel 1–7." *Tyndale Bulletin* 56 (2005): 1–17.

———. "The Accession Narrative (1 Samuel 27–2 Samuel 1)." *Tyndale Bulletin* 58 (2007): 61–81.

Flowers, H. J. "1 Samuel 1:1: אִישׁ אֶחָד." *Expository Times* 66 (1955): 273.

Fokkelman, J. P. *Narrative Art and Poetry in the Books of Samuel: A Full Interpretation Based on Stylistic and Structural Analysis*. 4 vols. Vol. 2: *The Crossing Fates (I Sam 13–23 and II Sam 1)*. Assen: Van Gorcum, 1986.

———. *Narrative Art and Poetry in the Books of Samuel: A Full Interpretation Based on Stylistic and Structural Analysis*. 4 vols. Vol. 4: *Vow and Desire (I Sam 1–12)*. Assen: Van Gorcum, 1993.

Fontaine, Carole R. "The Bearing of Wisdom on the Shape of 2 Samuel 11–12 and 1 Kings 3." *Journal for the Study of the Old Testament* 34 (1986): 61–77.

Foote, Theodore Clinton. "The Ephod." *Journal of Biblical Literature* 21 (1902): 1–47.

Fouts, David M. "Who Really Killed Goliath? 2 Samuel 21:19 versus 1 Chronicles 20:5." *Journal of Translation and Textlinguistics* 13 (2000): 14–24.

Freedman, David Noel. Review of Stanley Gevirtz, *Patterns in the Early Poetry of Israel*. *Journal of Biblical Literature* 83 (1964): 201–3.

———. "Psalm 113 and the Song of Hannah." Pages 243–61 in *Pottery, Poetry, and Prophecy: Studies in Early Hebrew Poetry*. Winona Lake, Ind.: Eisenbrauns, 1980.

Frisch, Amos. " 'For I Feared the People, and I Yielded to Them' (I Sam 15,24)—Is Saul's Guilt Attenuated or Intensified?" *Zeitschrift für die alttestamentliche Wissenschaft* 108 (1996): 98–104.

Fritz, Volkmar. "Where Is David's Ziklag?" *Biblical Archaeology Review* 19/3 (May/June 1993): 58–61.

Frolov, Serge. "Succession Narrative: A 'Document' or a Phantom?" *Journal of Biblical Literature* 121 (2002): 81–104.

———. "Man of God and the Deuteronomist: Anti-Deuteronomistic Polemics in 1 Sam 2,27–36." *Scandinavian Journal of the Old Testament* 20 (2006): 58–76.

———. "Bedan: A Riddle in Context." *Journal of Biblical Literature* 126 (2007): 164–67.

———. "The Semiotics of Covert Action in 1 Samuel 9–10." *Journal for the Study of the Old Testament* 31 (2007): 429–50.

———. " 'Certain Men' in Judges and Samuel: A Rejoinder to Mark Leuchter." *Catholic Biblical Quarterly* 73 (2011): 251–64.

Frolov, Serge, and Vladimir Orel. "A Nameless City." *Jewish Bible Quarterly* 23 (1995): 252–56.

———. "Was the Lad a Lad? On the Interpretation of I Sam 1:24." *Biblische Notizen* 81 (1996): 5–7.

Frolov, Serge, and Allen Wright. "Homeric and Ancient Near Eastern Intertextuality in 1 Samuel 17." *Journal of Biblical Literature* 130 (2011): 451–71.

Galpaz-Feller, Pnina. "David and the Messenger—Different Ends, Similar Means in 2 Samuel 1." *Vetus Testamentum* 59 (2009): 199–210.

Garfinkel, Yosef, and Saar Ganor. "Khirbet Qeiyafa: Shaʾarayim." *Journal of Hebrew Scriptures* 8, article 22 (2008). http://www.jhsonline.org/Articles/article_99.pdf.

Garfinkel, Yosef, Saar Ganor, and Michael G. Hasel. "The Contribution of Khirbet Qeiyafa to Our Understanding of the Iron Age Period." *Strata* 28 (2010): 39–54.

Garfinkel, Yosef, and Hoo-Goo Kang. "The Relative and Absolute Chronology of Khirbet Qeiyafa: Very Late Iron Age I or Very Early Iron Age IIA?" *Israel Exploration Journal* 61 (2011): 171–83.

Garr, W. Randall. "Necromancy and 1 Samuel 19:22." Pages 23–31 in *Sacred History, Sacred Literature: Essays on Ancient Israel, the Bible, and Religion in Honor of R. E. Friedman on His Sixtieth Birthday*. Edited by Shawna Dolansky. Winona Lake, Ind.: Eisenbrauns, 2008.

Garsiel, Moshe. "Wit, Words, and a Woman: 1 Samuel 25." Pages 161–68 in *On Humour and the Comic in the Hebrew Bible*. Edited by Yehuda T. Radday and Athalya Brenner. Sheffield: Almond, 1990.

Gehman, Henry Snyder. "A Note on I Samuel 21:13 (14)." *Journal of Biblical Literature* 67 (1948): 241–43.

Geoghegan, Jeffrey C. "Israelite Sheepshearing and David's Rise to Power." *Biblica* 87 (2006): 55–63.

George, Mark K. "Constructing Identity in 1 Samuel 17." *Biblical Interpretation* 7 (1999): 389–412.

———. "Yhwh's Own Heart." *Catholic Biblical Quarterly* 64 (2002): 442–59.

Gevirtz, Stanley. *Patterns in the Early Poetry of Israel*. Chicago: University of Chicago Press, 1963.

Gilmour, Rachelle. "Suspense and Anticipation in 1 Samuel 9:1–14." *Journal of Hebrew Scriptures* 9, article 10 (2009). http://www.jhsonline.org/Articles/article_112.pdf.

Gilmour, Rachelle, and Ian Young. "Saul's Two Year Reign in 1 Samuel 13:1." *Vetus Testamentum* 63 (2013): 150–54.

Gitay, Yehoshua. "Reflections on the Poetics of the Samuel Narrative: The Question of the Ark Narrative." *Catholic Biblical Quarterly* 54 (1992): 221–30.

Gitin, Seymour, Trude Dothan, and Joseph Naveh. "A Royal Dedicatory Inscription from Ekron." *Israel Exploration Journal* 47 (1997): 1–16.

Goldingay, John. *Israel's Gospel*. Old Testament Theology 1. Downers Grove, Ill.: InterVarsity, 2003.

Gooding, David W. "An Approach to the Literary and Textual Problems in the David-Goliath Story." Pages 55–86 in *The Story of David and Goliath: Textual and Literary Criticism*. Göttingen: Vandenhoeck & Ruprecht, 1986.

Gordis, Robert. "Notes on 1 Sam 13:21." *Journal of Biblical Literature* 61 (1942): 209–11.

Gordon, Robert P. "Saul's Meningitis according to Targum 1 Samuel 19:24." *Vetus Testamentum* 37 (1987): 39–49.

———. "Word-Play and Verse-Order in 1 Samuel 24:5–8." *Vetus Testamentum* 40 (1990): 139–44.

Gosse, Bernard. "Le salut et le Messie en 1 Sam 2,1–10, et Yahvé juge, à l'œuvre sur la terre et dans l'histoire, dans la tradition des cantiques et du Psautier." *Biblische Notizen* 111 (2002): 18–22.

Green, Adam. *King Saul: The True History of the First Messiah*. Cambridge: Lutterworth, 2007.

Green, Barbara. "Enacting Imaginatively the Unthinkable: 1 Samuel 25 and the Story of Saul." *Biblical Interpretation* 11 (2003): 1–23.

———. *How Are the Mighty Fallen? A Dialogical Study of King Saul in 1 Samuel.* Sheffield: Sheffield Academic, 2003.

———. "Experiential Learning: The Construction of Jonathan in the Narrative of Saul and David." Pages 43–58 in *Bakhtin and Genre Theory in Biblical Studies.* Edited by Roland Boer. Atlanta: Society of Biblical Literature, 2007.

Greenstein, Edward L. "Recovering 'the Women Who Served at the Entrance.'" Pages 165–73 in *Studies in Historical Geography and Biblical Historiography: presented to Zechariah Kallai.* Edited by Gershon Galil and Moshe Weinfeld. Leiden: Brill, 2000.

Grohmann, Marianne. "Psalm 113 and the Song of Hannah (1 Samuel 2:1–10): A Paradigm for Intertextual Reading?" Pages 119–35, 289–94 in *Reading the Bible Intertextually.* Edited by Richard B. Hays, Stefan Alkier, and Leroy A. Huizenga. Waco, Tex.: Baylor University Press, 2009.

Grossman, Yonatan. "The Design of the 'Dual Causality' Principle in the Narrative of Absalom's Rebellion." *Biblica* 88 (2007): 558–66.

Guillaume, A. "מְאֹד in I. Samuel xx, 19." *Palestine Exploration Quarterly* 86 (1954): 83–86.

Gunn, David M. "Traditional Composition in the 'Succession Narrative.'" *Vetus Testamentum* 26 (1976): 214–29.

———. *The Story of King David: Genre and Interpretation.* Sheffield: JSOT, 1978.

———. *The Fate of King Saul: An Interpretation of a Biblical Story.* Sheffield: JSOT, 1980.

Hallberg, Calinda Ellen. "Storyline and Theme in a Biblical Narrative: 1 Samuel 3." *Occasional Papers in Translation and Textlinguistics* 3 (1989): 1–35.

Halpern, Baruch. *The Constitution of the Monarchy in Israel.* Chico, Calif.: Scholars, 1981.

———. *David's Secret Demons: Messiah, Murderer, Traitor, King.* Grand Rapids: Eerdmans, 2001.

Hamilton, Mark W. "The Creation of Saul's Royal Body: Reflections on 1 Samuel 8–10." Pages 139–55 in *Saul in Story and Tradition.* Edited by Carl S. Ehrlich. Tübingen: Mohr Siebeck, 2006.

———. "At Whose Table? Stories of Elites and Social Climbers in 1–2 Samuel." *Vetus Testamentum* 59 (2009): 513–32.

Hamori, Esther J. "The Spirit of Falsehood." *Catholic Biblical Quarterly* 72 (2010): 15–30.

Harding, James E. *The Love of David and Jonathan: Ideology, Text, and Reception.* Sheffield: Equinox, 2013.

Harris, Scott L. "Hannah's Vow to Yahweh in I Samuel 1: An Issue of Faithfulness." *Lutheran Forum* 26 (1992): 28–33.

Harstad, Adolph L. *Joshua.* Concordia Commentary. St. Louis: Concordia, 2004.

Harvey, John E. "*Tendenz* and Textual Criticism in 1 Samuel 2–10." *Journal for the Study of the Old Testament* 96 (2001): 71–81.

―――. "Eli Failing Aaron." Pages 56–63 in *From Babel to Babylon: Essays on Biblical History and Literature in Honour of Brian Peckham.* Edited by Joyce Rilett Wood, John E. Harvey, and Mark Leuchter. New York: T&T Clark, 2006.

Hauer, Christian E. "Does 1 Samuel 9:1–11:15 Reflect the Extension of Saul's Dominions." *Journal of Biblical Literature* 86 (1967): 306–10.

―――. "Shape of Saulide Strategy." *Catholic Biblical Quarterly* 31 (1969): 153–67.

Haupt, Paul. "Heb. *Mardût,* Chastisement and Chastity." *Journal of Biblical Literature* 39 (1920): 156–58.

Hawk, L. Daniel. "Saul's Altar." *Catholic Biblical Quarterly* 72 (2010): 678–87.

Hawkins, Ralph K., and Shane Buchanan. "The Khirbet Qeiyafa Inscription and 11th–10th Century BCE Israel." *Stone-Campbell Journal* 14 (2011): 219–34.

Hays, J. Daniel. "Reconsidering the Height of Goliath." *Journal of the Evangelical Theological Society* 48 (2005): 701–14.

―――. "The Height of Goliath: A Response to Clyde Billington." *Journal of the Evangelical Theological Society* 50 (2007): 509–16.

Heacock, Anthony. "Wrongly Framed? The 'David and Jonathan Narrative' and the Writing of Biblical Homosexuality [sic]." *Bible & Critical Theory* 3 (2007).

―――. *Jonathan Loved David: Manly Love in the Bible and the Hermeneutics of Sex.* Sheffield: Sheffield Phoenix, 2011.

Heiser, Michael S. "Should אלהים (*'ĕlōhîm*) with Plural Predication Be Translated 'Gods'?" *Bible Translator* 61 (2010): 123–36.

Hendel, Ronald. "Plural Texts and Literary Criticism: For Instance, 1 Samuel 17." *Textus* 23 (2007): 97–114.

Hentschel, Georg. "Die Verantwortung für den Mord an den Priestern von Nob." Pages 185–99 in *For and against David: Story and History in the Books of Samuel.* Edited by A. Graeme Auld and Erik Eynikel. Leuven: Peeters, 2010.

Hertzberg, Hans Wilhelm. *I and II Samuel: A Commentary.* Translated by J. S. Bowden. Old Testament Library. Philadelphia: Westminster, 1964.

Hilbert, Benjamin D. H. "Joseph's Dreams, Part One: From Abimelech to Saul." *Journal for the Study of the Old Testament* 35 (2011): 259–83.

Hill, Andrew E. "A Jonadab Connection in the Absalom Conspiracy." *Journal of the Evangelical Theological Society* 30 (1987): 387–90.

Ho, Craig Y. S. "Conjectures and Refutations: Is 1 Samuel xxxi 1–13 Really the Source of 1 Chronicles x 1–12?" *Vetus Testamentum* 45 (1995): 82–106.

Hobbs, T. Raymond. "Hospitality in the First Testament and the 'Teleological Fallacy.'" *Journal for the Study of the Old Testament* 95 (2001): 3–30.

Hoffmeier, James K. "The Aftermath of David's Triumph over Goliath." *Archaeology in the Biblical World* 1 (1991): 18–19, 22–23.

Hoffner, Harry A., Jr. "Second Millennium Antecedents to the Hebrew *ʾôḇ*." *Journal of Biblical Literature* 86 (1967): 385–401.

———. "Hittite Analogue to the David and Goliath Contest of Champions." *Catholic Biblical Quarterly* 30 (1968): 220–25.

Holter, Knut. "Was Philistine Dagon a Fish-God? Some New Questions and an Old Answer." *Scandinavian Journal of the Old Testament* 3 (1989): 142–47.

Hoop, Raymond de. "Saul the Sodomite: Genesis 18–19 as the Opening Panel of a Polemic Triptych on King Saul." Pages 17–26 in *Sodom's Sin: Genesis 18–19 and Its Interpretations*. Edited by Ed Noort and Eibert Tigchelaar. Leiden: Brill, 2004.

Hornkohl, Aaron D. "Her Word versus His: Establishing the Underlying Text in 1 Samuel 1:23." *Journal of Biblical Literature* 133 (2014): 465–77.

House, Paul R. "Examining the Narratives of Old Testament Narrative: An Exploration in Biblical Theology." *Westminster Theological Journal* 67 (2005): 229–45.

Houtman, Cornelis. "The Urim and Thummim: A New Suggestion." *Vetus Testamentum* 40 (1990): 229–32.

Howard, David M., Jr. "The Transfer of Power from Saul to David in 1 Sam 16:13–14." *Journal of the Evangelical Theological Society* 32 (1989): 473–83.

Hubbard, Robert L. "The Hebrew Root *Pgʿ* as a Legal Term." *Journal of the Evangelical Theological Society* 27 (1984): 129–33.

Hummel, Horace D. "Enclitic *Mem* in Early Northwest Semitic, Especially Hebrew." *Journal of Biblical Literature* 76 (1957): 85–104.

Hurowitz, Victor. "Eli's Adjuration of Samuel (1 Samuel iii 17–18) in the Light of a 'Diviner's Protocol' from Mari (*AEM* I/1, 1)." *Vetus Testamentum* 44 (1994): 483–97.

Hwang, Jerry. "Yahweh's Poetic *Mishpat* in Israel's Kingship: A Reassessment of 1 Samuel 8–12." *Westminster Theological Journal* 73 (2011): 341–61.

Hyman, Ronald T. "Power of Persuasion: Judah, Abigail, and Hushai." *Jewish Bible Quarterly* 23 (1995): 9–16.

———. "Four Acts of Vowing in the Bible." *Jewish Bible Quarterly* 37 (2009): 231–38.

Isbell, Charles D. "A Biblical Midrash on David and Goliath." *Scandinavian Journal of the Old Testament* 20 (2006): 259–63.

Jacobs, Jonathan. "The Role of the Secondary Characters in the Story of the Anointing of Saul (I Samuel ix–x)." *Vetus Testamentum* 58 (2008): 495–509.

Jacobs, Rachel Miller. "Hannah: Her Story." *Vision* (Winnipeg, Manitoba) 4 (2003): 51–56.

Jacobson, Howard. "The Judge Bedan (1 Samuel xii 11)." *Vetus Testamentum* 42 (1992): 123–24.

———. "Nonnulla Onomastica." *Vigiliae christianae* 50 (1996): 210–11.

Jagt, Krijn A. van der. "What Did Saul Eat When He First Met Samuel? Light from Anthropology on Biblical Texts." *Bible Translator* 47 (1996): 226–30.

Janzen, David. "The Sacrifices of Saul Thoroughly Examined: An Essay in Honor of James Franklin Armstrong." *Princeton Seminary Bulletin* 26 (2005): 136–43.

Janzen, J. Gerald. " 'Samuel Opened the Doors of the House of Yahweh' (1 Samuel 3:15)." *Journal for the Study of the Old Testament* 26 (1983): 89–96.

———. "Prayer and/as Self-Address: The Case of Hannah." Pages 113–27 in *A God So Near: Essays on Old Testament Theology in Honor of Patrick D. Miller*. Edited by Brent A. Strawn and Nancy R. Bowen. Winona Lake, Ind.: Eisenbrauns, 2003.

Jassen, Alex. "Literary and Historical Studies in the Samuel Apocryphon (4Q160)." *Journal of Jewish Studies* 59 (2008): 21–38.

Jobes, Karen H., and Moisés Silva. *Invitation to the Septuagint*. Grand Rapids: Baker Academic, 2000.

Jobling, David. "Saul's Fall and Jonathan's Rise: Tradition and Redaction in 1 Sam 14:1–46." *Journal of Biblical Literature* 95 (1976): 367–76.

———. *1 Samuel*. Berit Olam: Studies in Hebrew Narrative and Poetry. Collegeville, Minn.: Liturgical, 1998.

Johnson, Benjamin J. M. "Reconsidering 4QSamª and the Textual Support for the Long and Short Versions of the David and Goliath Story." *Vetus Testamentum* 62 (2012): 534–49.

Johnson, Bo. "On the Masoretic Text at the Beginning of the First Book of Samuel." *Svensk exegetisk årsbok* 41 (1977): 130–37.

Jones, Barry A. "1 Samuel 20:1–17." *Interpretation* 58 (2004): 172–74.

Joosten, Jan. "1 Samuel 16:6, 7 in the Peshitta Version." *Vetus Testamentum* 41 (1991): 226–33.

———. "Workshop: Meaning and Use of the Tenses in 1 Samuel 1." Pages 72–83 in *Narrative Syntax and the Hebrew Bible: Papers of the Tilburg Conference 1996*. Edited by Ellen van Wolde. Leiden: Brill, 1997.

Joüon, Paul. "Notes philologiques sur le texte hebreu de Josué 6, 18; 10, 13; 23, 13; Juges 7, 8; 7, 14; 12, 5; 14, 17; 18, 31; 1 Samuel 6, 4–5; 12, 8–9; 12, 23; 12, 24; 13, 17; 13, 28." *Biblica* 9 (1928): 161–66.

Kaiser, Walter C., Jr. "The Blessing of David: The Charter for Humanity." Pages 298–318 in *The Law and the Prophets: Old Testament Studies Prepared in Honor of Oswald Thompson Allis*. Edited by John H. Skilton, Milton C. Fisher, and Leslie W. Sloat. Nutley, N.J.: Presbyterian and Reformed, 1974.

Kalmin, Richard. "Doeg the Edomite: From Biblical Villain to Rabbinic Sage." Pages 390–405 in *The Interpretation of Scripture in Early Judaism and Christianity: Studies in Language and Tradition*. Edited by Craig A. Evans. Sheffield: Sheffield Academic, 2000.

Kang, Hoo-Goo, and Yosef Garfinkel. "Finger-Impressed Jar Handles at Khirbet Qei-yafa: New Light on Administration in the Kingdom of Judah." *Levant* 47 (2015): 186–205.

Kapelrud, Arvid S. "The Covenant as Agreement." *Scandinavian Journal of the Old Testament* 2 (1988): 30–38.

Kauhanen, Tuukka. *The Proto-Lucianic Problem in 1 Samuel.* De Septuaginta investigationes 3. Göttingen: Vandenhoeck & Ruprecht, 2012.

Keil, C. F. *Biblical Commentary on the Books of Samuel.* Translated by James Martin. Edinburgh: T&T Clark, 1866. Repr., Grand Rapids: Eerdmans, 1976.

Kent, Grenville J. R. *Say It Again, Sam: A Literary and Filmic Study of Narrative Repetition in 1 Samuel 28.* Cambridge: Lutterworth, 2012.

Kessler, Martin. "Narrative Technique in 1 Sm 16:1–13." *Catholic Biblical Quarterly* 32 (1970): 543–54.

Kim, Eun Chul. "Cult of the Dead and the Old Testament Negation of Ancestor Worship." *Asia Journal of Theology* 17 (2003): 2–16.

Kim, Jeong Bong, and Dirk J. Human. "Nagid: A Re-examination in the Light of the Royal Ideology in the Ancient Near East." *Hervormde teologiese studies* 64 (2008): 1475–97.

Kio, Stephen Hre. "What Did Saul Ask For: Ark or Ephod? (1 Samuel 14.18)." *Bible Translator* 47 (1996): 240–46.

Kitz, Anne Marie. "The Plural Form of *ʾÛrîm* and *Tummîm*." *Journal of Biblical Literature* 116 (1997): 401–10.

Klein, Johannes. "Davids Flucht zu den Philistern (1 Sam xxi 11ff; xxvii–xxix)." *Vetus Testamentum* 55 (2005): 176–84.

Klein, Ralph W. *1 Samuel.* 2d ed. Word Biblical Commentary 10. Nashville: Thomas Nelson, 2008.

Kleinig, John W. *Leviticus.* Concordia Commentary. St. Louis: Concordia, 2003.

Knoppers, Gary N. "Ancient Near Eastern Royal Grants and the Davidic Covenant: A Parallel?" *Journal of the American Oriental Society* 116 (1996): 670–97.

Ko, Ming Him. "Fusion-Point Hermeneutics: A Theological Interpretation of Saul's Rejection in Light of the Shema as the Rule of Faith." *Journal of Theological Interpretation* 7 (2013): 57–78.

Koch, Klaus. *The Growth of the Biblical Tradition: The Form-Critical Method.* Translated by S. M. Cupitt. New York: Scribner, 1969.

Kooij, Arie van der. "The Story of David and Goliath: The Early History of Its Text." *Ephemerides theologicae lovanienses* 68 (1992): 118–31.

Kotzé, Robert J. "The Circumstantial Sentence—A Catch-Them-All Term: A Study in Sentence Relationships in 1 Samuel 1–12." *Journal of Northwest Semitic Languages* 15 (1989): 109–26.

———. "Reading between the Sentences: Notes on the Sentence Relations in 1 Samuel 1:1–8." *Journal of Northwest Semitic Languages* 16 (1990): 61–84.

Krašovec, Jože. "Two Types of Unconditional Covenant." *Horizons in Biblical Theology* 18 (1996): 55–77.

Kreuzer, Siegfried. " 'Saul war noch zwei Jahre König …': Textgeschichtliche, literarische und historische Beobachtungen zu 1 Sam 13,1." *Biblische Zeitschrift* 40 (1996): 263–70.

Krinetzki, Leo. "Ein Beitrag zur Stilanalyse der Goliathperikope (1 Sam 17,1–18,5)." *Biblica* 54 (1973): 187–236.

Kruger, Paul A. "The Symbolic Significance of the Hem (*kānāf*) in 1 Samuel 15.27." Pages 105–16 in *Text and Context: Old Testament and Semitic Studies for F. C. Fensham.* Edited by W. Claassen. Sheffield: JSOT, 1988.

———. " 'Liminality' in 2 Samuel 19:1–9: A Short Note." *Journal of Northwest Semitic Languages* 24 (1998): 195–99.

Labuschagne, C. J. "The Divine Title עֶלִי, 'The High One,' in the Song of Hannah." *Vetus Testamentum* 58 (2008): 644–49.

Landy, Francis. "Are We in the Place of Averroes? Response to the Articles of Exum and Whedbee, Buss, Gottwald, and Good." *Semeia* 32 (1984): 131–48.

Langlamet, François. "1 Samuel 13–2 Samuel 1: Fokkelman et le prêtre de Nob (1 Sam 21:2–7)." *Revue biblique* 99 (1992): 631–75.

Lasine, Stuart. "Guest and Host in Judges 19: Lot's Hospitality in an Inverted World." *Journal for the Study of the Old Testament* 29 (1984): 37–59.

———. *Knowing Kings: Knowledge, Power, and Narcissism in the Hebrew Bible.* Atlanta: Society of Biblical Literature, 2001.

Lawton, Robert B. "1 Samuel 18: David, Merob, and Michal." *Catholic Biblical Quarterly* 51 (1989): 423–25.

———. "Saul, Jonathan and the 'Son of Jesse.' " *Journal for the Study of the Old Testament* 58 (1993): 35–46.

Leithart, Peter J. "David's Threat to Nabal: How a Little Vulgarity Got the Point Across." *Bible Review* 18/5 (October 2002): 18–23, 59.

Lemaire, André. "La stèle de Mésha et l'histoire de l'ancien Israël." Pages 143–70 in *Storia e tradizioni di Israele: Scritti in onore di J. Alberto Soggin.* Edited by Daniele Garrone and Felice Israel. Brescia, Italy: Paideia Editrice, 1991.

———. "The Tel Dan Stela as a Piece of Royal Historiography." *Journal for the Study of the Old Testament* 81 (1998): 3–14.

Lemardelé, Christophe. "Saül le nazir ou la légende d'un roi." *Scandinavian Journal of the Old Testament* 22 (2008): 47–62.

Lemche, Niels Peter. "חפשׁי in 1 Sam. xvii 25." *Vetus Testamentum* 24 (1974): 373–74.

———. "The Hebrew and the Seven Year Cycle." *Biblische Notizen* 25 (1984): 65–75.

Lemos, T. M. "Shame and Mutilation of Enemies in the Hebrew Bible." *Journal of Biblical Literature* 125 (2006): 225–41.

Leneman, Helen. *Love, Lust, and Lunacy: The Stories of Saul and David in Music.* Sheffield: Sheffield Phoenix, 2010.

Lenzi, Alan C. "An Incantation-Prayer: Ghosts of My Family 1." Pages 133–44 in *Reading Akkadian Prayers and Hymns: An Introduction.* Edited by Alan C. Lenzi. Atlanta: Society of Biblical Literature, 2011.

Lerner, Berel Dov. "Saul and Genocide." *Jewish Bible Quarterly* 42 (2014): 39–44.

Lessing, R. Reed, and Andrew E. Steinmann. *Prepare the Way of the Lord: An Introduction to the Old Testament.* St. Louis: Concordia, 2014.

Leuchter, Mark. "Something Old, Something Older: Reconsidering 1 Sam 2:27–36." *Journal of Hebrew Scriptures* 4, article 6 (2003). http://www.jhsonline.org/Articles/article_28.pdf.

———. "A King Like All the Nations: The Composition of I Sam 8,11–18." *Zeitschrift für die alttestamentliche Wissenschaft* 117 (2005): 543–58.

———. "The Cult at Kiriath Yearim: Implications from the Biblical Record." *Vetus Testamentum* 58 (2008): 526–43.

———. *Samuel and the Shaping of Tradition.* Oxford: Oxford University Press, 2013.

Levenson, Jon D. "1 Samuel 25 as Literature and as History." *Catholic Biblical Quarterly* 40 (1978): 11–28.

Lewis, Peter E. "Is There a Parallel between 1 Samuel 3 and the Sixth Chapter of the Egyptian Book of the Dead?" *Journal for the Study of the Old Testament* 31 (2007): 365–76.

Lewis, Theodore J. "The Textual History of the Song of Hannah: 1 Samuel ii 1–10." *Vetus Testamentum* 44 (1994): 18–46.

Linafelt, Tod, Claudia V. Camp, and Timothy Beal, eds. *The Fate of King David: The Past and Present of a Biblical Icon.* New York: T&T Clark, 2010.

Lindblom, Johannes. "Lot-Casting in the Old Testament." *Vetus Testamentum* 12 (1962): 164–78.

Lipiński, Edward. "ʾŪrīm and Tummīm." *Vetus Testamentum* 20 (1970): 495–96.

Lockwood, Gregory J. *1 Corinthians.* Concordia Commentary. St. Louis: Concordia, 2000.

Long, Burke O. "Framing Repetitions in Biblical Historiography." *Journal of Biblical Literature* 106 (1987): 385–99.

Long, V. Philips. *The Reign and Rejection of King Saul: A Case for Literary and Theological Coherence.* Atlanta: Scholars, 1989.

———. "Interpolation or Characterization: How Are We to Understand Saul's Two Confessions?" *Presbyterion* 19 (1993): 49–53.

Longman, Tremper, III. "1 Sam 12:16–19: Divine Omnipotence or Covenant Curse?" *Westminster Theological Journal* 45 (1983): 168–71.

Luck, G. Coleman. "The First Meeting of Saul and Samuel." *Bibliotheca sacra* 124 (1967): 254–61.

Lunn, Nicholas P. "Patterns in the Old Testament Metanarrative: Human Attempts to Fulfill Divine Promises." *Westminster Theological Journal* 72 (2010): 237–49.

Lust, J. "The Story of David and Goliath in Hebrew and Greek." *Ephemerides theologicae lovanienses* 59 (1983): 5–25.

MacDonald, Duncan B. "Notes, Critical and Lexicographical." *Journal of Biblical Literature* 14 (1895): 57–62.

MacLeod, Ian. "Samuel's Little Robe." *Expository Times* 97 (1986): 144–45.

Maeir, Aren M. "A New Interpretation of the Term *ʿopalim* (עפלים) in the Light of Recent Archaeological Finds from Philistia." *Journal for the Study of the Old Testament* 32 (2007): 23–40.

———. "Did Captured Ark Afflict Philistines with E.D.?" *Biblical Archaeology Review* 34/3 (May/June 2008): 46–51.

Magennis, Feidhlimidh T. *First and Second Samuel.* New Collegeville Bible Commentary 8. Collegeville, Minn.: Liturgical, 2012.

Mangan, Edward A. "The Urim and Thummim." *Catholic Biblical Quarterly* 1 (1939): 133–38.

Mann, Thomas W. *The Book of the Former Prophets.* Eugene, Oreg.: Cascade, 2011.

Margalith, Othniel. "The Meaning of *ʿplym* in 1 Samuel 5–6." *Vetus Testamentum* 33 (1983): 339–41.

Marttila, Marko. "The Song of Hannah and Its Relationship to the Psalter." *Ugarit-Forschungen* 38 (2006): 499–524.

Mastin, B. A. "The *Miqneh* of 1 Samuel xxiii 5." *Vetus Testamentum* 53 (2003): 379–96.

McAleese, Killian. "Danger at the King's Table: Insult and Family Conflict at Saul's New Moon Feast." Pages 24–38 in *Text, Theology, and Trowel: New Investigations in the Biblical World.* Edited by Lidia D. Matassa and Jason M. Silverman. Eugene, Oreg.: Pickwick, 2011.

McCarter, P. Kyle, Jr. *I Samuel: A New Translation with Introduction, Notes and Commentary.* Anchor Bible 8. Garden City, N.Y.: Doubleday, 1980.

McCarthy, Dennis J. "The Inauguration of Monarchy in Israel: A Form-Critical Study of I Samuel 8–12." *Interpretation* 27 (1973): 401–12.

McFall, Leslie. "The Chronology of Saul and David." *Journal of the Evangelical Theological Society* 53 (2010): 475–533.

McKane, William. "Note on Esther 9 and 1 Samuel 15." *Journal of Theological Studies* 12 (1961): 260–61.

McKenzie, Cameron S. "Echoes of Time and Space: The Ark and the Exodus in 1 Samuel 4–6." *Didaskalia* (Otterburne, Manitoba) 12 (2001): 59–80.

McKenzie, Steven L. *King David: A Biography.* Oxford: Oxford University Press, 2000.

————. "The So-Called Succession Narrative in the Deuteronomistic History." Pages 123–35 in *Die Sogenannte Thronfolgegeschichte Davids: Neue Einsichten und Anfragen*. Edited by Albert de Pury and Thomas Römer. Fribourg, Switzerland: Universitätsverlag, 2000.

————. "Elaborated Evidence for the Priority of 1 Samuel 26." *Journal of Biblical Literature* 129 (2010): 437–44.

McKinlay, Judith E. "To Eat or Not to Eat: Where Is Wisdom in This Choice?" *Semeia* 86 (1999): 73–84.

McLean, Paul D. "The Kaige Text of Reigns: To the Reader." Pages 271–76 in *A New English Translation of the Septuagint and the Other Greek Translations Traditionally Included under That Title*. Edited by Albert Pietersma and Benjamin G. Wright. Oxford: Oxford University Press, 2007.

Mendenhall, George E. "From Witchcraft to Justice: Death and Afterlife in the Old Testament." Pages 67–81 in *Death and Afterlife: Perspectives of World Religions*. Edited by Hiroshi Obayashi. Westport, Conn: Greenwood, 1992.

Menn, Esther. "Child Characters in Biblical Narratives: The Young David (1 Samuel 16–17) and the Little Israelite Servant Girl (2 Kings 5:1–19)." Pages 324–52 in *The Child in the Bible*. Edited by Marcia J. Bunge. Grand Rapids: Eerdmans, 2008.

Meredith, Christopher. "A Case of Open and Shut: The Five Thresholds in 1 Samuel 1:1–7:2." *Biblical Interpretation* 18 (2010): 137–57.

Merwe, C. H. J. van der. "Workshop: Text Linguistics and the Structure of 1 Samuel 1." Pages 157–65 in *Narrative Syntax and the Hebrew Bible: Papers of the Tilburg Conference 1996*. Edited by Ellen van Wolde. Leiden: Brill, 1997.

Meyers, Carol L. "An Ethnoarchaeological Analysis of Hannah's Sacrifice." Pages 77–91 in *Pomegranates and Golden Bells: Studies in Biblical, Jewish, and Near Eastern Ritual, Law, and Literature in Honor of Jacob Milgrom*. Edited by David P. Wright, David Noel Freedman, and Avi Hurvitz. Winona Lake, Ind.: Eisenbrauns, 1995.

Michelson, Marty Alan. *Reconciling Violence and Kingship: A Study of Judges and 1 Samuel*. Eugene, Oreg.: Pickwick, 2011.

Middendorf, Michael P. *Romans 1–8*. Concordia Commentary. St. Louis: Concordia, 2013.

————. *Romans 9–16*. Concordia Commentary. St. Louis: Concordia, 2016.

Millard, A. R. "The Armor of Goliath." Pages 337–43 in *Exploring the Longue Durée: Essays in Honor of Lawrence E. Stager*. Edited by J. David Schloen. Winona Lake, Ind.: Eisenbrauns, 2009.

Miller, J. Maxwell. "Saul's Rise to Power: Some Observations concerning 1 Sam 9:1–10:16; 10:26–11:15 and 13:2–14:46." *Catholic Biblical Quarterly* 36 (1974): 157–74.

————. "Geba/Gibeah of Benjamin." *Vetus Testamentum* 25 (1975): 145–66.

Miller, Patrick D., Jr., and J. J. M. Roberts. *The Hand of the Lord: A Reassessment of the "Ark Narrative" of 1 Samuel*. Baltimore: Johns Hopkins University Press, 1977.

Miscall, Peter D. *1 Samuel: A Literary Reading*. Indiana Studies in Biblical Literature. Bloomington: Indiana University Press, 1986.

Mitchell, Christopher W. *The Song of Songs*. Concordia Commentary. St. Louis: Concordia, 2003.

Moberly, R. W. L. "To Hear the Master's Voice: Revelation and Spiritual Discernment in the Call of Samuel." *Scottish Journal of Theology* 48 (1995): 443–68.

———. "'God Is Not a Human That He Should Repent' (Numbers 23:19 and 1 Samuel 15:29)." Pages 112–23 in *God in the Fray: A Tribute to Walter Brueggemann*. Edited by Tod Linafelt and Timothy K. Beal. Minneapolis: Fortress, 1998.

Mommer, Peter. "Ist auch Saul unter den Propheten: Ein Beitrag zu 1 Sam 19:18–24." *Biblische Notizen* 38–39 (1987): 53–61.

Monson, J., general consultant. *Student Map Manual: Historical Geography of the Bible Lands*. Jerusalem: Pictorial Archive (Near Eastern History) Est., 1979.

Moran, William L. "The Ancient Near Eastern Background of the Love of God in Deuteronomy." *Catholic Biblical Quarterly* 25 (1963): 77–87.

Morgenstern, Julian. "David and Jonathan." *Journal of Biblical Literature* 78 (1959): 322–25.

Morse, Benjamin. "The Defence of Michal: Pre-Raphaelite Persuasion in 2 Samuel 6." *Biblical Interpretation* 21 (2013): 19–32.

Mulder, Martin Jan. "Un euphémisme dans 2 Sam 12:14." *Vetus Testamentum* 18 (1968): 108–14.

Müller, Reinhard. *Königtum und Gottesherrschaft: Untersuchungen zur alttestamentlichen Monarchiekritik*. Tübingen: Mohr Siebeck, 2004.

Mulzac, Kenneth D. "Hannah: The Receiver and Giver of a Great Gift." *Andrews University Seminary Studies* 40 (2002): 207–17.

———. "The Role of Abigail in 1 Samuel 25." *Andrews University Seminary Studies* 41 (2003): 45–53.

Muraoka, T. "1 Sam 1,15 Again." *Biblica* 77 (1996): 98–99.

Murray, Donald F. "Under Yhwh's Veto: David as Shedder of Blood in Chronicles." *Biblica* 82 (2001): 457–76.

Na'aman, Nadav. "The Pre-Deuteronomistic Story of King Saul and Its Historical Significance." *Catholic Biblical Quarterly* 54 (1992): 638–58.

———. "In Search of the Ancient Name of Khirbet Qeiyafa." *Journal of Hebrew Scriptures* 8, article 21 (2008). http://www.jhsonline.org/Articles/article_98.pdf.

———. "Shaaraim—The Gateway to the Kingdom of Judah." *Journal of Hebrew Scriptures* 8, article 24 (2008). http://www.jhsonline.org/Articles/article_101.pdf.

———. "David's Sojourn in Keilah in Light of the Amarna Letters." *Vetus Testamentum* 60 (2010): 87–97.

Nakarai, Toyozo W. "*Lmh* and *Mduʿ* in the Tanak." *Hebrew Studies* 23 (1982): 45–50.

Naveh, Joseph. "Achish-Ikausu in the Light of the Ekron Dedication." *Bulletin of the American Schools of Oriental Research* 310 (1998): 35–37.

Nicholson, Sarah. *Three Faces of Saul: An Intertextual Approach to Biblical Tragedy.* Sheffield: Sheffield Academic, 2002.

Nicol, George G. "David, Abigail and Bathsheba, Nabal and Uriah: Transformations within a Triangle." *Scandinavian Journal of the Old Testament* 12 (1998): 130–45.

Nihan, Christophe. "L'injustice des fils de Samuel, au tournant d'une époque (Quelques remarques sur la fonction de 1 Samuel 8,1–5 dans son contexte littéraire)." *Biblische Notizen* 94 (1998): 26–32.

———. "Du voyant au prophète: Royauté et divination en Israël selon 1 Samuel 9,1–10,16." *Foi et vie* 98/4 (September 1999): 7–25.

———. "Saul among the Prophets (1 Sam 10:10–12 and 19:18–24): The Reworking of Saul's Figure in the Context of the Debate on 'Charismatic Prophecy' in the Persian Era." Pages 88–118 in *Saul in Story and Tradition*. Edited by Carl S. Ehrlich. Tübingen: Mohr Siebeck, 2006.

Noort, Edward. "Eine weitere Kurzbemerkung zu 1 Samuel 14:41." *Vetus Testamentum* 21 (1971): 112–16.

Noth, Martin. *The Deuteronomistic History.* Sheffield: JSOT, 1981.

O'Connor, M. "War and Rebel Chants in the Former Prophets." Pages 322–37 in *Fortunate the Eyes That See: Essays in Honor of David Noel Freedman in Celebration of His Seventieth Birthday*. Edited by Astrid B. Beck et al. Grand Rapids: Eerdmans, 1995.

Olmo Lete, Gregorio del. "David's Farewell Oracle (2 Samuel 23:1–7): A Literary Analysis." *Vetus Testamentum* 34 (1984): 414–38.

Olyan, Saul M. " 'Surpassing the Love of Women': Another Look at 2 Samuel 1:26 and the Relationship of David and Jonathan." Pages 7–16, 165–70 in *Authorizing Marriage? Canon, Tradition, and Critique in the Blessing of Same-Sex Unions*. Edited by Mark D. Jordan. Princeton, N.J.: Princeton University Press, 2006.

Oosthuizen, Rudolph. "2 Sam 14:16: Stop the Wicked Man." *Scriptura* 68 (1999): 13–27.

Orel, Vladimir E. "The Great Fall of Dagon." *Zeitschrift für die alttestamentliche Wissenschaft* 110 (1998): 427–32.

Orton, David E. "We Felt like Grasshoppers: The Little Ones in Biblical Interpretation." *Biblical Interpretation* 11 (2003): 488–502.

Parry, Donald W. "4QSamᵃ (4Q51): A Preliminary Edition of 1 Samuel 25:3–31:4." Pages 58–71 in *The Provo International Conference on the Dead Sea Scrolls: Technological Innovations, New Texts, and Reformulated Issues*. Edited by Donald W. Parry and Eugene Ulrich. Leiden: Brill, 1999.

———. "More Fragments from 4QSamª (4Q51): A Preliminary Edition of 1 Samuel 14:24–24:22." Pages 19–29 in *The Dead Sea Scrolls: Fifty Years after Their Discovery*. Edited by Lawrence W. Schiffman, Emanuel Tov, and James C. VanderKam. Jerusalem: Israel Exploration Society, 2000.

———. " 'How Many Vessels'? An Examination of MT 1 Sam 2:14/4QSamª 1 Sam 2:16." Pages 84–95 in *Studies in the Hebrew Bible, Qumran, and the Septuagint Presented to Eugene Ulrich*. Edited by Peter W. Flint, Emanuel Tov, and James C. VanderKam. Boston: Brill, 2006.

———. "Hannah in the Presence of the Lord." Pages 53–73 in *Archaeology of the Books of Samuel: The Entangling of the Textual and Literary History*. Edited by Philippe Hugo and Adrian Schenker. Leiden: Brill, 2010.

Paul, Shalom M. "Gleanings from the Biblical and Talmudic Lexica in Light of Akkadian." Pages 242–56 in *Minḥah le-Naḥum: Biblical and Other Studies Presented to Nahum M. Sarna in Honour of His 70th Birthday*. Edited by Marc Brettler and Michael Fishbane. Sheffield: JSOT, 1993.

———. "A Rejoinder concerning 1 Samuel 1:11." *Journal of Biblical Literature* 130 (2011): 45.

Payne, J. Barton. "Saul and the Changing Will of God." *Bibliotheca sacra* 129 (1972): 321–25.

Penchansky, David. "Four Vignettes from the Life of David: Recollections of the Royal Court." Pages 55–65 in *The Fate of King David: The Past and Present of a Biblical Icon*. Edited by Tod Linafelt, Claudia V. Camp, and Timothy Beal. New York: T&T Clark, 2010.

Pick, Bernhard. "The Masoretic Piska in the Hebrew Bible." *Journal of the Society of Biblical Literature and Exegesis* 6 (1886): 135–39.

Pigott, Susan M. "1 Samuel 28—Saul and the Not So Wicked Witch of Endor." *Review and Expositor* 95 (1998): 435–44.

Pioske, Daniel D. "Memory and Its Materiality: The Case of Early Iron Age Khirbet Qeiyafa and Jerusalem." *Zeitschrift für die alttestamentliche Wissenschaft* 127 (2015): 78–95.

Pisano, Stephen. *Additions or Omissions in the Books of Samuel: The Significant Pluses and Minuses in the Masoretic, LXX and Qumran Texts*. Göttingen: Vandenhoeck & Ruprecht, 1984.

———. "The Prophecy against the House of Eli (1 Sam 2,27–36)." Pages 97–124 in *Biblical Exegesis in Progress: Old and New Testament Essays*. Edited by J. N. Aletti and J. L. Ska. Rome: Editrice Pontificio Istituto Biblico, 2009.

Pleins, J. David. "Son-Slayers and Their Sons." *Catholic Biblical Quarterly* 54 (1992): 29–38.

Polzin, Robert. "On Taking Renewal Seriously: 1 Sam 11:1–15." Pages 493–507 in *Ascribe to the Lord: Biblical and Other Studies in Memory of Peter C. Craigie*. Edited by Lyle Eslinger and Glen Taylor. Sheffield: JSOT, 1988.

———. *Samuel and the Deuteronomist: A Literary Study of the Deuteronomic History, Part Two: 1 Samuel.* San Francisco: Harper & Row, 1989.

———. *David and the Deuteronomist: A Literary Study of the Deuteronomic History, Part Three: 2 Samuel.* Bloomington: Indiana University Press, 1993.

Powell, Matthew. "Sound and Silence in Samuel's Call Narrative." *Lutheran Forum* 44 (2010): 13–15.

Provan, Iain, V. Philips Long, and Tremper Longman III. *A Biblical History of Israel.* Louisville, Ky.: Westminster John Knox, 2003.

Pury, Albert de, Thomas Römer, and Jean-Daniel Macchi, eds. *Israel Constructs Its History: Deuteronomistic Historiography and Recent Research.* Sheffield: Sheffield Academic, 2000.

Raffalovich, Samuel. "I Sam 13:21." *Journal of Biblical Literature* 40 (1921): 184.

Ratner, Robert. "Three Bulls or One? A Reappraisal of 1 Samuel 1:24." *Biblica* 68 (1987): 98–102.

Rebera, Basil A. " 'He Got Up'—or Did He? (1 Samuel 20.25)." *Bible Translator* 40 (1989): 212–18.

Reinhartz, Adele. "Anonymity and Character in the Books of Samuel." *Semeia* 63 (1993): 117–41.

Reis, Pamela Tamarkin. "Collusion at Nob: A New Reading of 1 Samuel 21–22." *Journal for the Study of the Old Testament* 61 (1994): 59–73.

———. "Eating the Blood: Saul and the Witch of Endor." *Journal for the Study of the Old Testament* 73 (1997): 3–23.

Reiss, Moshe. "Serah Bat Asher in Rabbinic Literature." *Jewish Bible Quarterly* 42 (2014): 45–51.

Rendsburg, Gary A. "Some False Leads in the Identification of Late Biblical Hebrew Texts: The Cases of Genesis 24 and 1 Samuel 2:27–36." *Journal of Biblical Literature* 121 (2002): 23–46.

Richards, Kent Harold. "Psalm 34." *Interpretation* 40 (1986): 175–80.

Robert, Philippe de. "1 Samuel 3: Une vocation prophétique?" *Foi et vie* 83/5 (September 1984): 4–10.

Roberts, Jim. "The Legal Basis for Saul's Slaughter of the Priests of Nob (1 Samuel 21–22)." *Journal of Northwest Semitic Languages* 25 (1999): 21–29.

Robertson, Edward. "The ʾŪrīm and Tummīm: What Were They?" *Vetus Testamentum* 14 (1964): 67–74.

Rofé, Alexander. "The Acts of Nahash according to 4QSamᵃ." *Israel Exploration Journal* 32 (1982): 129–33.

———. "The Battle of David and Goliath: Folklore, Theology, Eschatology." Pages 117–51 in *Judaic Perspectives on Ancient Israel.* Edited by Jacob Neusner, Baruch A. Levine, and Ernest S. Frerichs. Philadelphia: Fortress, 1987.

———. "4QSam^a in the Light of Historico-Literary Criticism: The Case of 2 Sam 24 and 1 Chr 21." Pages 109–19 in *Biblische und Judaistische Studien: Festschrift für Paolo Sacchi*. Edited by Angelo Vivian. Frankfurt am Main: Peter Lang, 1990.

———. "Midrashic Traits in 4Q51 (So-Called 4QSam^a)." Pages 75–88 in *Archaeology of the Books of Samuel: The Entangling of the Textual and Literary History*. Edited by Philippe Hugo and Adrian Schenker. Leiden: Brill, 2010.

Rogers, Cynthia M., and Danna Nolan Fewell. "No Greater Love: Jonathan and His Friendship with David in Text, Tradition, and Contemporary Children's Literature." Pages 123–51 in *Text, Image, and Otherness in Children's Bibles: What Is in the Picture?* Edited by Caroline Vander Stichele and Hugh S. Pyper. Atlanta: Society of Biblical Literature, 2012.

Rook, John. "When Is a Widow Not a Widow? Guardianship Provides an Answer." *Biblical Theology Bulletin* 28 (1998): 4–6.

Rost, Leonhard. *The Succession to the Throne of David.* Translated by Michael D. Rutter and David M. Gunn. Sheffield: Almond, 1982. Translation of *Die Überlieferung von der Thronnachfolge Davids*. Stuttgart: Kohlhammer, 1926.

Roth, Wolfgang M. W. "The Numerical Sequence x/x+1 in the Old Testament." *Vetus Testamentum* 12 (1962): 300–311.

Routledge, Robin L. " 'An Evil Spirit from the Lord'—Demonic Influence or Divine Instrument." *Evangelical Quarterly* 70 (1998): 3–22.

Rowe, Jonathan Y. *Michal's Moral Dilemma: A Literary, Anthropological and Ethical Interpretation.* New York: T&T Clark, 2011.

Rowley, H. H. "Note on the Septuagint Text of 1 Samuel 15:22a." *Vetus Testamentum* 1 (1951): 67–68.

Rudman, Dominic. "The Patriarchal Narratives in the Books of Samuel." *Vetus Testamentum* 54 (2004): 239–49.

Salibi, Kamal S. "The 'Goliath' Problem." *Theological Review* 12 (1991): 3–13.

Sasson, Jack M. "Doeg's Job." *Scriptura* 87 (2004): 317–22.

———. "The Eyes of Eli: An Essay in Motif Accretion." Pages 171–90 in *Inspired Speech: Prophecy in the Ancient Near East: Essays in Honor of Herbert B. Huffmon.* Edited by John Kaltner and Louis Stulman. London: T&T Clark, 2004.

Sasson, Victor. "The Inscription of Achish, Governor of Eqron, and Philistine Dialect, Cult and Culture." *Ugarit-Forschungen* 29 (1997): 627–39.

Schäfer-Lichtenberger, Christa. "ELLA, ARES und die Samuel-Überlieferung." Pages 73–90 in *For and against David: Story and History in the Books of Samuel.* Edited by A. Graeme Auld and Erik Eynikel. Leuven: Peeters, 2010.

Schmidt, Brian B. "The 'Witch' of En-Dor, 1 Samuel 28, and Ancient Near Eastern Necromancy." Pages 111–29 in *Ancient Magic and Ritual Power.* Edited by Marvin Meyer and Paul Mirecki. Leiden: Brill, 1995.

Schreiner, David B. "What Are They Saying about Khirbet Qeiyafa?" *Trinity Journal* 33 (2012): 33–48.

Schroer, Silvia, and Thomas Staubli. "'Jonathan aima beaucoup David': L'homoé-
rotisme dans les récits bibliques concernant Saül, David et Jonathan." *Foi et vie*
99/4 (September 2000): 53–64.

Schürer, Emil. *The History of the Jewish People in the Age of Jesus Christ (175 B.C.–
A.D. 135)*. Revised and edited by Geza Vermes and Fergus Millar. Rev. ed. 3 vols.
in 4. Edinburgh: T&T Clark, 1973–1987.

Schwartz, Joshua. "Dogs, 'Water' and Wall." *Scandinavian Journal of the Old Testament* 14 (2000): 101–116.

Scolnic, Benjamin E. "Did David Kill Goliath: Historical Criticism and Religious
Meaning." *Conservative Judaism* 42 (1989): 31–40.

Seebass, Horst. "Zum Text von 1 Sam 14:23b–25a und 2:29, 31–33." *Vetus Testamentum* 16 (1966): 74–82.

Seger, Joe D. "A Note on the Early Antiquity of the Song of Hannah." Pages 47–51 in
Biblical and Humane: A Festschrift for John F. Priest. Edited by Linda Bennett
Elder, David L. Barr, and Elizabeth Struthers Malbon. Atlanta: Scholars, 1996.

Segert, Stanislav. "Symmetric and Asymmetric Verses in Hebrew Biblical Poetry."
Pages 33–37 in *Proceedings of the Ninth World Congress of Jewish Studies,
Jerusalem, August 4–12, 1985*. Jerusalem: World Union of Jewish Studies, 1986.

Sellars, Dawn Maria. "An Obedient Servant? The Reign of King Saul (1 Samuel
13–15) Reassessed." *Journal for the Study of the Old Testament* 35 (2011):
317–38.

Shackleton, David M. *Wild Sheep and Goats and Their Relatives: Status Survey and
Conservation Action Plan for Caprinae*. Gland, Switzerland: IUCN, 1997.

Shaviv, Shemuel. "*Nābîʾ* and *Nāgîd* in 1 Samuel ix 1–x 16." *Vetus Testamentum* 34
(1984): 108–13.

Shedinger, Robert F. "Who Killed Goliath? History and Legend in Biblical Narrative." Pages 27–38 in *Who Killed Goliath? Reading the Bible with Heart and
Mind*. Valley Forge, Pa.: Judson, 2001.

Shemesh, Yael. "Lies by Prophets and Other Lies in the Hebrew Bible." *Journal of
the Ancient Near Eastern Society of Columbia University* 29 (2002): 81–95.

———. "David in the Service of King Achish of Gath: Renegade to His People or a
Fifth Column in the Philistine Army?" *Vetus Testamentum* 57 (2007): 73–90.

———. "Suicide in the Bible." *Jewish Bible Quarterly* 37 (2009): 157–68.

Shields, Mary E. "A Feast Fit for a King: Food and Drink in the Abigail Story." Pages
38–54 in *The Fate of King David: The Past and Present of a Biblical Icon*. Edited by Tod Linafelt, Claudia V. Camp, and Timothy Beal. New York: T&T Clark,
2010.

Simon, Uriel. "A Balanced Story: The Stern Prophet and the Kind Witch." *Prooftexts*
8 (1988): 159–71.

———. "1 Samuel 28:3–25: The Stern Prophet and the Kind Witch." Pages 281–87 in *"Wünschet Jerusalem Frieden": Collected Communications to XIIth Congress of the International Organization for the Study of the Old Testament, Jerusalem, 1986.* Edited by Matthias Augustin and Klaus-Dietrich Schunck. Frankfurt am Main: Peter Lang, 1988.

Skinner, Macy M. "הֲעָלֶיהָ, I Sam. ix. 24." *Journal of Biblical Literature* 15 (1896): 82–86.

Smelik, Klaas A. D. "The Ark Narrative Reconsidered." Pages 128–44 in *New Avenues in the Study of the Old Testament: A Collection of Old Testament Studies, Published on the Occasion of the Fiftieth Anniversary of the Oudtestamentisch Werkgezelschap and the Retirement of Prof. Dr. M. J. Mulder.* Edited by A. S. van der Woude. Leiden: Brill, 1989.

Smith, Brett W. "The Sin of Eli and Its Consequences." *Bibliotheca sacra* 170 (2013): 17–30.

Smith, Henry Preserved. *A Critical and Exegetical Commentary on the Books of Samuel.* International Critical Commentary. Edinburgh: T&T Clark, 1899.

———. "Old Testament Notes." *Journal of Biblical Literature* 24 (1905): 27–30.

Smith, J. Alfred. "Break the Silence: 'Justice Is Waiting for You to Speak.'" *Review and Expositor* 110 (2013): 15–23.

Sonnet, Jean-Pierre. "God's Repentance and 'False Starts' in Biblical History (Genesis 6–9; Exodus 32–34; 1 Samuel 15 and 2 Samuel 7)." Pages 469–94 in *Congress Volume Ljubljana 2007.* Edited by André Lemaire. Leiden: Brill, 2007.

Speiser, E. A. "Of Shoes and Shekels (I Samuel 12:3; 13:21)." *Bulletin of the American Schools of Oriental Research* 77 (1940): 15–20.

Spina, Frank A. "A Prophet's 'Pregnant Pause': Samuel's Silence in the Ark Narrative (1 Sam 4:1–7:2)." *Horizons in Biblical Theology* 13 (1991): 59–73.

———. "Eli's Seat: The Transition from Priest to Prophet in 1 Samuel 1–4." *Journal for the Study of the Old Testament* 62 (1994): 67–75.

Steinmann, Andrew E. *Intermediate Biblical Hebrew: A Reference Grammar with Charts and Exercises.* St. Louis: Concordia, 2007, 2009.

———. *Daniel.* Concordia Commentary. St. Louis: Concordia, 2008.

———. *Proverbs.* Concordia Commentary. St. Louis: Concordia, 2009.

———. *Ezra and Nehemiah.* Concordia Commentary. St. Louis: Concordia, 2010.

———. *From Abraham to Paul: A Biblical Chronology.* St. Louis: Concordia, 2011.

———. "What Did David Understand about the Promises in the Davidic Covenant?" *Bibliotheca sacra* 171 (2014): 19–29.

Stern, Philip D. "I Samuel 15: Towards an Ancient View of the War-Ḥerem." *Ugarit-Forschungen* 21 (1989): 413–20.

Sternberg, Meir. "The Bible's Art of Persuasion: Ideology, Rhetoric, and Poetics in Saul's Fall." *Hebrew Union College Annual* 54 (1983): 45–82.

Steussy, Marti J. *Samuel and His God.* Columbia: University of South Carolina Press, 2010.

Stirrup, A. " 'Why Has Yahweh Defeated Us Today before the Philistines?' The Question of the Ark Narrative." *Tyndale Bulletin* 51 (2000): 81–100.

Stoebe, Hans Joachim. "Die Goliathperikope 1 Sam. xvii 1–xviii 5 und die Textform der Septuaginta." *Vetus Testamentum* 6 (1956): 397–413.

———. "Noch Einmal die Eselinnen des *Kîš* (1 Sam ix)." *Vetus Testamentum* 7 (1957): 362–70.

Stokes, Ryan E. "The Devil Made David Do It … Or *Did* He? The Nature, Identity, and Literary Origins of the *Satan* in 1 Chronicles 21:1." *Journal of Biblical Literature* 128 (2009): 91–106.

Sturdy, John. "The Original Meaning of 'Is Saul Also among the Prophets?' " *Vetus Testamentum* 20 (1970): 206–13.

Taggar-Cohen, Ada. "Political Loyalty in the Biblical Account of 1 Samuel xx–xxii in the Light of Hittite Texts." *Vetus Testamentum* 55 (2005): 251–68.

Talmon, Shemaryahu. "1 Sam. xv 32b—A Case of Conflated Readings?" *Vetus Testamentum* 11 (1961): 456–57.

Talmon, Shemaryahu, and Weston W. Fields. "The Collocation משתין בקיר ועצור ועזוב and Its Meaning." *Zeitschrift für die alttestamentliche Wissenschaft* 101 (1989): 85–112.

Taylor, Bernard A. "The Old Greek Text of Reigns: To the Reader." Pages 244–48 in *A New English Translation of the Septuagint and the Other Greek Translations Traditionally Included under That Title.* Edited by Albert Pietersma and Benjamin G. Wright. Oxford: Oxford University Press, 2007.

Thiemann, Ronald F. "Radiance and Obscurity in Biblical Narrative." Pages 21–41 in *Scriptural Authority and Narrative Interpretation.* Edited by Garrett Green. Philadelphia: Fortress, 1987.

Thomas, D. Winton. "A Note on וְנוֹדַע לָכֶם in I Samuel vi. 3." *Journal of Theological Studies* 11 (1960): 52.

———. "A Note on נוֹדַע in I Samuel xxii. 6." *Journal of Theological Studies* 21 (1970): 401–2.

Thompson, J. A. "The Significance of the Verb *Love* in the David-Jonathan Narratives in 1 Samuel." *Vetus Testamentum* 24 (1974): 334–38.

Thornhill, Raymond. "A Note on אל־נכון, 1 Sam. xxvi 4." *Vetus Testamentum* 14 (1964): 462–66.

Tidwell, Neville. "Linen Ephod: 1 Sam 2:18 and 2 Sam 6:14." *Vetus Testamentum* 24 (1974): 505–7.

Tiemeyer, Lena-Sofia. "Prophecy as a Way of Cancelling Prophecy: The Strategic Uses of Foreknowledge." *Zeitschrift für die alttestamentliche Wissenschaft* 117 (2005): 329–50.

Toeg, A. "A Textual Note on 1 Samuel xiv 41." *Vetus Testamentum* 19 (1969): 493–98.

Toorn, Karel van der, and Cornelis Houtman. "David and the Ark." *Journal of Biblical Literature* 113 (1994): 209–31.

Tov, Emanuel. *The Text-Critical Use of the Septuagint in Biblical Research.* Jerusalem: Simor, 1981.

———. *Textual Criticism of the Hebrew Bible.* 2d rev. ed. Minneapolis: Fortress, 2001.

Trebolle Barrera, Julio C. "The Story of David and Goliath (1 Sam 17–18): Textual Variants and Literary Composition." *Bulletin of the International Organization for Septuagint and Cognate Studies* 23 (1990): 16–30.

Tsevat, Matitiahu. "Studies in the Book of Samuel." *Hebrew Union College Annual* 32 (1961): 191–216.

———. "The Biblical Account of the Foundation of the Monarchy in Israel." Pages 77–99 in *The Meaning of the Book of Job and Other Biblical Studies: Essays on the Literature and Religion of the Hebrew Bible.* New York: KTAV, 1980.

Tsumura, David Toshio. "*Hamôr Lehem* (1 Samuel xvi 20)." *Vetus Testamentum* 42 (1992): 412–14.

———. "The Poetic Nature of Hebrew Narrative Prose in 1 Sam. 2:12–17." Pages 293–304 in *Verse in Ancient Near Eastern Prose.* Edited by Johannes C. de Moor and Wilfred G. E. Watson. Neukirchen-Vluyn: Neukirchener Verlag, 1993.

———. "Bedan, a Copyist's Error? (1 Samuel xii 11)." *Vetus Testamentum* 45 (1995): 122–23.

———. "List and Narrative in I Samuel 6,17–18a in the Light of Ugaritic Economic Texts." *Zeitschrift für die alttestamentliche Wissenschaft* 113 (2001): 353–69.

———. *The First Book of Samuel.* New International Commentary on the Old Testament. Grand Rapids: Eerdmans, 2007.

Ulrich, Eugene Charles, Jr. *The Qumran Text of Samuel and Josephus.* Missoula, Mont.: Scholars, 1978.

———. "David, the Plague, and the Angel: 2 Samuel 24 Revisited." Pages 63–80 in *After Qumran: Old and Modern Editions of the Biblical Texts: The Historical Books.* Edited by Hans Ausloos, Bénédicte Lemmelijn, and Julio Trebolle Barrera. Leuven: Peeters, 2012.

Van Dam, Cornelis. *The Urim and Thummim: A Means of Revelation in Ancient Israel.* Winona Lake, Ind.: Eisenbrauns, 1997.

Van Seters, John. "Two Stories of David Sparing Saul's Life in 1 Samuel 24 and 26: A Question of Priority." *Scandinavian Journal of the Old Testament* 25 (2011): 93–104.

Van Wijk-Bos, Johanna W. H. *Reading Samuel: A Literary and Theological Commentary.* Macon, Ga.: Smyth & Helwys, 2011.

Van Zyl, A. H. "1 Sam 1:2–2:11—A Life-World Lament of Affliction." *Journal of Northwest Semitic Languages* 12 (1984): 151–61.

Vartejanu-Joubert, Madalina. "Les 'anciens du peuple' et Saül: *Temps, espace* et *rite de passage* dans Nombres xi et 1 Samuel x." *Vetus Testamentum* 55 (2005): 542–63.

Vehse, Charles Ted. "Long Live the King: Historical Fact and Narrative Fiction in 1 Samuel 9–10." Pages 435–44 in *The Pitcher Is Broken: Memorial Essays for Gösta W. Ahlström*. Edited by Steven W. Holloway and Lowell K. Handy. Sheffield: Sheffield Academic, 1995.

Veijola, Timo. "David in Keïla: Tradition und Interpretation in 1 Sam 23:1–13." *Revue biblique* 91 (1984): 51–87.

Vermeylen, Jacques. "'Comment sont tombés les héros?': Une lecture de 1 S 31 et 2 S 1,1–2,7." Pages 99–116 in *Analyse Narrative et Bible: Deuxième colloque international du RRENAB, Louvain-la-Neuve, Avril 2004*. Edited by Camille Focant and André Wénin. Leuven: Leuven, 2005.

Vette, Joachim. "Der letzte Richter? Methodische Überlegungen zur Charaktergestaltung in 1 Sam 11." *Communio viatorum* 51 (2009): 184–97.

———. "Samuel's 'Farewell Speech': Theme and Variation in 1 Samuel 12, Josephus, and Pseudo-Philo." Pages 325–39 in *Literary Construction of Identity in the Ancient World*. Edited by Hanna Liss and Manfred Oeming. Winona Lake, Ind.: Eisenbrauns, 2010.

Viberg, Åke. "Saul Exposed by Irony: A New Understanding of 1 Samuel 15:27 Based on Two Symbolic Acts." *Svensk exegetisk årsbok* 70 (2005): 301–8.

Wagner, Volker. "Plante Absalom eine Reform der Gerichtsordunung in Israel? (2 Sam 15:2–4)." *Vetus Testamentum* 63 (2013): 159–65.

Wahl, Otto. *Die Sacra-Parallela-Zitate aus den Büchern Josua, Richter, 1/2 Samuel, 3/4 Könige sowie 1/2 Chronik*. Göttingen: Vandenhoeck & Ruprecht, 2004.

Waldow, Hans Eberhard von. "The Concept of War in the Old Testament." *Horizons in Biblical Theology* 6 (1984): 27–48.

Walters, Stanley D. "Hannah and Anna: The Greek and Hebrew Texts of 1 Samuel 1." *Journal of Biblical Literature* 107 (1988): 385–412.

———. "The Light and the Dark." Pages 567–89 in *Ascribe to the Lord: Biblical and Other Studies in Memory of Peter C. Craigie*. Edited by Lyle Eslinger and Glen Taylor. Sheffield: JSOT, 1988.

———. "After Drinking (1 Sam 1:9)." Pages 527–46 in *Crossing Boundaries and Linking Horizons: Studies in Honor of Michael C. Astour on His 80th Birthday*. Edited by Gordon D. Young, Mark W. Chavalas, and Richard E. Averbeck. Bethesda, Md.: CDL, 1997.

Warren, A. L. "A Trisagion Inserted in the 4QSam^a Version of the Song of Hannah, 1 Sam 2:1–10." *Journal of Jewish Studies* 45 (1994): 278–85.

Weingreen, Jacob. "Rabbinic-Type Gloss in the LXX Version of 1 Samuel 1:18." *Vetus Testamentum* 14 (1964): 225–28.

Wellhausen, Julius. *Die Text der Bücher Samuelis untersucht*. Göttingen: Vandenhoeck & Ruprecht, 1871.

Wénin, André. "Marques linguistiques du point de vue dans le recit biblique: L'example du mariage de David (1 S 18,17–29)." *Ephemerides theologicae lovanienses* 83 (2007): 319–37.

Wesselius, Jan-Wim. "A New View on the Relation between Septuagint and Masoretic Text in the Story of David and Goliath." Pages 5–26 in *Early Christian Literature and Intertextuality*. Vol. 2: *Exegetical Studies*. London: T&T Clark, 2009.

Westbrook, Raymond. "1 Samuel 1:8." *Journal of Biblical Literature* 109 (1990): 114–15.

White, Ellen. "Michal the Misinterpreted." *Journal for the Study of the Old Testament* 31 (2007): 451–64.

White, Marsha. "Saul and Jonathan in 1 Samuel 1 and 14." Pages 119–38 in *Saul in Story and Tradition*. Edited by Carl S. Ehrlich. Tübingen: Mohr Siebeck, 2006.

Whitney, G. E. "Alternative Interpretations of *Lōʾ* in Exodus 6:3 and Jeremiah 7:22." *Westminster Theological Journal* 48 (1986): 151–59.

Wicke, Donald W. "The Structure of 1 Sam 3: Another View." *Biblische Zeitschrift* 30 (1986): 256–58.

Wiesmann, Hermann. "Die Einführung des Königtums in Israel (1 Sam 8–12)." *Zeitschrift für katholische Theologie* 34 (1910): 118–53.

Wilkinson, John. "Philistine Epidemic of I Samuel 5 and 6." *Expository Times* 88 (1977): 137–41.

Williams, Gillian Patricia, and Magdel Le Roux. "King Saul's Mysterious Malady." *HTS Teologiese Studies/Theological Studies* 68 (2012).

Willis, John T. "Cultic Elements in the Story of Samuel's Birth and Dedication." *Studia theologica* 26 (1972): 33–61.

———. "Function of Comprehensive Anticipatory Redactional Joints in 1 Samuel 16–18." *Zeitschrift für die alttestamentliche Wissenschaft* 85 (1973): 294–314.

———. "The Song of Hannah and Psalm 113." *Catholic Biblical Quarterly* 35 (1973): 139–54.

Winger, Thomas M. *Ephesians*. Concordia Commentary. St. Louis: Concordia, 2015.

Wolde, Ellen van. "A Leader Led by a Lady: David and Abigail in I Samuel 25." *Zeitschrift für die alttestamentliche Wissenschaft* 114 (2002): 355–75.

Wong, G. C. I. "Who Loved Whom? A Note on 1 Samuel xvi 21." *Vetus Testamentum* 47 (1997): 554–56.

Wong, Gregory. "Goliath's Death and the Testament of Judah." *Biblica* 91 (2010): 425–32.

———. "A Farewell to Arms: Goliath's Death as Rhetoric against Faith in Arms." *Bulletin for Biblical Research* 23 (2013): 43–55.

Wood, Bryant G. "From Ramesses to Shiloh: Archaeological Discoveries Bearing on the Exodus–Judges Period." Pages 256–82 in *Giving the Sense: Understanding and Using Old Testament Historical Texts*. Edited by David M. Howard Jr. and Michael A. Grisanti. Grand Rapids: Kregel, 2003.

―――. "Hittites and Hethites: A Proposed Solution to an Etymological Conundrum." *Journal of the Evangelical Theological Society* 54 (2011): 239–50.

Wood, Irving F. "Folk-Tales in Old Testament Narrative." *Journal of Biblical Literature* 28 (1909): 34–41.

Wright, G. E. "1 Samuel 13:19–21." *Biblical Archaeologist* 6 (1943): 33–36.

Yadin, Azzan. "Goliath's Armor and Israelite Collective Memory." *Vetus Testamentum* 54 (2004): 373–95.

Yadin, Yigael. "Goliath's Javelin and the מנור ארגים." *Palestine Exploration Quarterly* 87 (1955): 58–69.

Yaron, Reuven. "The Coptos Decree and 2 Sam xii 14." *Vetus Testamentum* 9 (1959): 89–91.

Yoo, Yoon Jong. "The Shema (Deut 6:4–5) in the Story of Samuel (1 Samuel 1–15)." *Expository Times* 123 (2011–2012): 119–21.

Young, Theron. "Psalm 18 and 2 Samuel 22: Two Versions of the Same Song." Pages 53–69 in *Seeking Out the Wisdom of the Ancients: Essays Offered to Honor Michael V. Fox on the Occasion of His Sixty-Fifth Birthday*. Edited by Ronald L. Troxel, Kelvin G. Friebel, and Dennis R. Magary. Winona Lake, Ind.: Eisenbrauns, 2005.

Zakovitch, Yair. "בדן = יפתח." *Vetus Testamentum* 22 (1972): 123–25.

Zehnder, Markus. "Observations on the Relationship between David and Jonathan and the Debate on Homosexuality." *Westminster Theological Journal* 69 (2007): 127–74.

Ziegler, Yael. " 'So Shall God Do …': Variations of an Oath Formula and Its Literary Meaning." *Journal of Biblical Literature* 126 (2007): 59–81.

―――. " 'As the Lord Lives and as Your Soul Lives': An Oath of Conscious Deference." *Vetus Testamentum* 58 (2008): 117–30.

Zimran, Yisca. " 'The Lord Has Rejected You as King over Israel': Saul's Deposal from the Throne." *Journal of Hebrew Scriptures* 14, article 5 (2014). http://www.jhsonline.org/Articles/article_199.pdf.

Zorn, Jeffrey R. "Reconsidering Goliath: An Iron Age I Philistine Chariot Warrior." *Bulletin of the American Schools of Oriental Research* 360 (2010): 1–22.

Zwickel, Wolfgang. "Dagons Abgeschlagener Kopf (1 Samuel v 3–4)." *Vetus Testamentum* 44 (1994): 239–49.

Introduction to the Book of Samuel

Some of the most memorable accounts from Israel's history are found in the book of Samuel: Hannah's prayer for a son, God calling to the boy Samuel at night in the tabernacle, the capture of the ark of the covenant and the death of Eli, the ark causing disease and panic in Philistia, Saul seeking to pin David to the wall of his palace with his spear, David and Goliath, and David and Bathsheba. These incidents are told with skill, allowing readers to feel the tension, pathos, triumphs, and failures of Israel and its kings.

The fifty-five chapters of this single Hebrew book (1 and 2 Samuel in English Bibles) trace Israel's transition from a tribal confederacy designed to live under God's rule to a monarchy established and supported by God. When the Israelites felt that they could no longer defend themselves against the Philistines, they asked for a king "like all the nations" (1 Sam 8:5). Their vulnerability was not a sign of God's failure but of Israel's failure. They had abandoned Yahweh for the worship of the gods of the nations who lived in Canaan, and God, in turn, had given them over to the nations. Would an earthly king solve their problems? Perhaps temporarily, but as Samuel himself suggests, it would not be a permanent solution but a new burden (1 Samuel 8; 12). Yet within this book is hope: Hannah expects the messianic king (1 Sam 2:10); David receives the messianic promise (2 Samuel 7); and David affirms God's eternal salvation (2 Sam 23:1–6).

One of the longest books in the OT, Samuel follows the stories of three major persons: Samuel, the Levite, prophet, and last judge; Saul, Israel's first king; and David, the second and greatest Israelite king. In English Bibles Samuel is divided into two books, a division that most likely first appeared when Samuel was translated into Greek sometime before Christ.[1] 1 Samuel covers the ministry of Samuel and the reign of Saul, while 2 Samuel depicts the reign of David.

Authorship, Composition, and Date[2]
The Composition of Samuel

Like many of the historical books of the OT, Samuel does not name its author. Clearly the writer composed his narrative based on historical sources. While some of them may have been oral, written records played a major part, as indicated, for instance, by the various lists of David's officials (2 Sam 8:15–18; 23:8–39). Perhaps books by the prophets Samuel, Gad, and Nathan were also employed (cf. 1 Chr 29:29).

---

[1] This is the common conclusion drawn by scholars, since the Hebrew text of Samuel was considered one book throughout antiquity, but manuscripts containing the oldest known translation of Samuel (LXX 1–2 Reigns) split it into two books.

[2] This material is adapted from Lessing and Steinmann, *Prepare the Way of the Lord*, 146–49, 189–93.

Though the book is named after Samuel, he could hardly be its author since all of the events related after 1 Sam 25:1 take place after his death. Moreover, the latest event narrated in the book is David uttering his "last words" (2 Sam 23:1). Since David died in about 969 BC,[3] Samuel could not have been written before that time. In addition, 2 Sam 5:9 states:

וַיֵּשֶׁב דָּוִד֙ בַּמְּצֻדָ֔ה וַיִּקְרָא־לָ֖הּ עִ֣יר דָּוִ֑ד
וַיִּ֤בֶן דָּוִד֙ סָבִ֔יב מִן־הַמִּלּ֖וֹא וָבָֽיְתָה׃

So David lived in the stronghold, and he named it the City of David.
David built all around from the Millo and toward the house.

The author mentions David's construction in Jerusalem as extending from the current location of the Millo. However, the Millo itself was built later by Solomon (1 Ki 9:15, 24; 11:27). Therefore, the author of Samuel must have been writing *after* Solomon's construction of it.

A further clue to the writer's own time may be his frequent noting of events that led to situations that were still present in Israel "to this day" (עַד הַיּוֹם הַזֶּה).[4] See figure 1.

The most telling of these is the note that the city of Ziklag belongs to "the *kings* of *Judah* to this day" (1 Sam 27:6). Tsumura argues that the final composition of Samuel took place during the reign of Rehoboam (932–915 BC),[5] but this is probably too early, especially since 1 Sam 27:6 refers to "*kings* of Judah," implying that as least two Judean monarchs (Rehoboam and Abijah) and possibly several more had occupied the throne before this verse was written.

On the other hand, it is common for critical scholars to date Samuel to the postexilic period as part of the so-called Deuteronomistic History.[6] This dating, however, is probably too late, and there is little evidence in the Hebrew text to support it. For instance, in Samuel the name "David" is always spelled *ḥaser*, or defectively (without the vowel letter), דָּוִד, and the *male*ʾ, or plene, form דָּוִיד, so common in books from the postexilic period (e.g., Chronicles, Ezra, Nehemiah, Zechariah), is never found in Samuel. Therefore, although books such as Joshua, Judges, Samuel, and Kings display clear affinities to the theological accents found in Deuteronomy and might for that reason be called part of a Deuteronomistic History, that does not thereby make them late compositions.

It is best, therefore, to view Samuel as a preexilic book written sometime after the death of Rehoboam (915t[7])—probably several generations removed

---

[3] See "The Basic Chronology of the United Monarchy" in "Chronological Issues in Samuel" below.

[4] 1 Sam 5:5; 6:18; 27:6; 30:25; 2 Sam 4:3; 6:8; 18:18 (cf. 1 Sam 8:8; 12:2; 29:3, 6, 8; 2 Sam 7:6).

[5] Tsumura, *The First Book of Samuel*, 11–32.

[6] See "The Deuteronomistic History Theory" in "Redaction-Critical Theories" below.

[7] A year with a trailing lowercase "t" indicates a year that began in the fall month of Tishri, rather than the spring month of Nisan (designated with "n"). See Steinmann, *From Abraham to Paul*, 20–21.

from Solomon's era (which ended in 932 BC)—but before the Babylonian exile (587 BC) by a Judean author. A more specific date cannot be determined for the composition of this OT book.

Figure 1

"To This Day" Notices in the Book of Samuel

Verse	Notice	Earliest Possible Date
1 Sam 5:5	The priests of Dagon do not step on the threshold of his temple	Reign of Saul (c. 1049–1009)
1 Sam 6:18	The rock on which the ark was placed is in the field of Joshua of Beth-shemesh	Reign of Saul (c. 1049–1009)
1 Sam 27:6	Ziklag belongs to the kings of Judah	Reign of Abijah (915–912)
1 Sam 30:25	The troops who remain with the supplies divide the spoils with the troops who fight the battle	Reign of Solomon (971–932)†
2 Sam 4:3	The Beerothites live in Gittaim	David's reign in Jerusalem (1002–969)
2 Sam 6:8	The place where Uzzah died is called Perez-uzzah	Some years after the ark was moved to Jerusalem (975)
2 Sam 18:18	The pillar set up by Absalom is called Absalom's Monument	Some years after Absalom's rebellion (974)

†Solomon enjoyed peace until the very end of his reign, making this statement not applicable until that time (cf. 1 Kings 11) and perhaps not even until the reign of his son Rehoboam (932–915).

Critical Theories of Samuel's Composition

Source-Critical Theories

Early critical theories of the composition of Samuel often sought to find conflicting sources behind the book, much akin to the search for source documents proposed for the Pentateuch. These scholars perceived numerous repetitions, doublets, and contradictions. Among these were issues such as the following: When was Saul was first introduced to David? When was David recruited to serve Saul? Was it as a court musician (1 Sam 16:14–23) or during

3

the challenge from Goliath (1 Sam 17:32–39)? Who killed Goliath—David (1 Sam 17:50) or Elhanan (2 Sam 21:19)?

Most important of these issues was the supposed tension between two hypothetical sources, one displaying a positive attitude toward the monarchy (e.g., 1 Sam 9:15–16) and one portraying a negative evaluation of kings and kingship (e.g., 1 Sam 12:16–19). Julius Wellhausen thought this tension represented two sources: a promonarchial source that was preexilic and an antimonarchial source that reflected disillusionment with the monarchy brought about by the experience of the Babylonian exile. Therefore, he dated the final form of Samuel to the postexilic period.[8] Later scholars thought the tension may have come from various premonarchical movements in Israel, dating back to the days of Gideon (Judg 8:22–9:29), that reflect a debate about the merits of having a monarchy.

Ultimately, these source-critical approaches indicate more about the expectations of the critics as they approach the text. Their theories shed little light on the composition of the text itself. Since they reflect the biases and perspectives of the individual critics, these proposed theories of Samuel's composition have largely fallen out of favor.

Tradition-Historical Theories

Instead of arguing for two intertwined sources that lay behind the present text of Samuel, scholars who used tradition-historical approaches sought to isolate original collections of narratives organized around various themes that were allegedly used by the final author or editor to construct the book's history. The most influential of these theories is that of Leonhard Rost, who identified three large blocks of material that were supposedly incorporated into Samuel: an ark narrative (1 Sam 4:1–7:1; 2 Samuel 6), a history of David's rise (1 Sam 16:14–2 Sam 5:10), and a succession narrative (2 Samuel 9–20 and 1 Kings 1–2).[9] Subsequently others proposed additional sources such as a prefixed account of Samuel's childhood (1 Samuel 1–3) or an appendix of material from David's reign (2 Samuel 21–24) that became an intrusion into the succession narrative.

Recent currents in scholarship have called into question the concept of such independent sources. Bodner examined the work of a dozen scholars to demonstrate that there is now widespread skepticism about whether an independent ark narrative ever existed.[10] He points out that Yehoshua Gitay argued that the ark narrative is inseparable from the rest of Samuel[11] and that Graeme Auld noted that it is tightly integrated with its antecedent material.[12] A similar analysis by

---

[8] Wellhausen, *Die Text der Bücher Samuelis untersucht*, 4–33.

[9] Rost, *Succession to the Throne of David.*

[10] Bodner, "Ark-Eology: Shifting Emphases in 'Ark Narrative' Scholarship."

[11] Bodner, "Ark-Eology: Shifting Emphases in 'Ark Narrative' Scholarship," 176–77, citing Gitay, "Reflections on the Poetics of the Samuel Narrative: The Question of the Ark Narrative."

[12] Bodner, "Ark-Eology: Shifting Emphases in 'Ark Narrative' Scholarship," 185–86, citing Graeme Auld, "1 and 2 Samuel" in *Eerdmans Commentary on the Bible* (ed. James D. G.

Firth of the account of David's rise argued that this block of material, too, was so linked by literary ties to the rest of Samuel that the text should be read as a coherent whole.[13] Frolov's analysis of the succession narrative's seamless integration into the book of Samuel led him to conclude that "a large, continuous, self-contained, and distinctive 'document' underlying 2 Sam 1–1 Kgs 2 is a figment of scholars' imagination."[14]

This, of course, leads one to question whether proposed independent sources such as the ark narrative or the account of David's rise actually existed. If the book of Samuel is a tightly integrated, inseparable whole, then the attempt to isolate underlying sources becomes more a matter of how a particular scholar reads, understands, and ultimately divides the text of Samuel. This scholarly endeavor is not a reliable method for identifying predecessors that were combined to form the received text.

This is not to assert that the author of Samuel had no literary resources for his work. Clearly, he must have had access to earlier documents to write a history, since history cannot be written without access to sources that relay information about past events and people. Most likely passages such as 2 Sam 21:15–22 (David's troops who defeated Philistine giants) and 2 Sam 23:8–39 (a list of David's prominent warriors) indicate that the author used records from David's court. However, there should be a healthy skepticism about the ability of scholars to confidently differentiate various sources behind the now skillfully integrated narrative of the book of Samuel. Except when the author indicates the origin of his material (see possible source references in 1 Sam 10:25 [Samuel's scroll about the privileges of a king]; 2 Sam 1:18 [the Book of Jashar]), it is best simply to read the narrative as a whole and not speculate on theories of composition that rely on reconstructed sources that are dubious.

Redaction-Critical Theories

The Deuteronomistic History Theory

It is common for scholars to speak of a Deuteronomistic History that includes Joshua, Judges, Samuel, and Kings and supposedly builds on the ideology found in the book of Deuteronomy, especially the dual concept that Israel would experience blessing in the land for its faith as demonstrated by keeping the Sinaitic covenant but would experience God's wrath when the nation abandoned it. This emphasis is the reason Samuel is considered part of this complex of books that allegedly originated from the same school that produced Deuteronomy toward the end of the seventh century BC. This view of the

---

Dunn; Grand Rapids: Eerdmans, 2003) 213–45. Auld considers the major source material used by the writer of Samuel to have been a Book of the Two Houses (Yahweh's house and David's house), which contained the ark material. See his comments in, for example, *I and II Samuel*, 12, 65.

[13]   Firth, "The Accession Narrative (1 Samuel 27–2 Samuel 1)."

[14]   Frolov, "Succession Narrative: A 'Document' or a Phantom?" 103.

Former Prophets as a Deuteronomistic History was first developed by Noth in the mid twentieth century[15] and has become an accepted interpretation among critical scholars.

Noth treated Deuteronomy, Joshua, Judges, Samuel, and Kings as a unified history of Israel, which he called the Deuteronomistic History. According to his theory, the corpus was written by the Deuteronomist, a term that applies not to a single author but to a school of authors active from the seventh century BC onward into the Babylonian exile. The Deuteronomistic History was composed to explain the exile as God's rejection of Israel and contained a negative message: there was no hope for Israel's future. The Deuteronomist used earlier sources, but according to Noth, the book of Samuel contained some material that was composed by the Deuteronomist himself as well as insertions made after the time of the Deuteronomist (e.g., the presumed appendix, 2 Samuel 21–24). Ultimately, however, Noth emphasized the unified character of the Deuteronomistic History. Other critics propose several redactions to this corpus.

Noth's concept of a Deuteronomistic History was widely adopted, and much of critical scholarship to this day still refers to Deuteronomy–Kings as the Deuteronomistic History. However, subsequent studies have pointed out that God's eternal promise to David is an important theme throughout this corpus, calling into question Noth's assertion that there is no hope offered to Israel in these books.[16]

Later critics sought to modify Noth's theory. Cross proposed that the Deuteronomistic History has two redactional layers.[17] The first came from the time of Josiah in support of his reforms (623t). This layer was optimistic about Israel's future. The second layer originated in the exile by a redactor who emphasized the conditions placed on the Davidic covenant. This layer was more pessimistic in outlook. Cross' theory has influenced further work by American scholars.

In Europe a group of scholars in Göttingen, Germany, proposed that the Deuteronomistic History had three redactional layers. The first layer (DtrG) provided the basic historical framework and was optimistic, as it assumed the conquest of the land of Canaan had been successfully accomplished. The next redaction (DtrP) added prophetic narratives. The final layer (DtrN) inserted legal ("nomistic") material. This redactor portrayed the conquest as incomplete and Israel's hold on the land of Canaan as precarious.

More recently even critical scholars have begun to question the existence of a Deuteronomistic History or have proposed even further modifications of

---

[15] Noth, *The Deuteronomistic History*.

[16] See, e.g., Kaiser, "The Blessing of David"; Collins, *The Scepter and the Star*, 22–23; Knoppers, "Ancient Near Eastern Royal Grants and the Davidic Covenant"; J. J. M. Roberts, "Davidic Covenant," *DOTHB*, 206–11.

[17] Cross, *Canaanite Myth and Hebrew Epic*.

this theory.[18] Clearly, there is much doubt about whether one can hold that the book of Samuel is part of a wider group of documents in the OT that were produced by one or more Deuteronomistic editors.

Without denying that theological currents found in Deuteronomy play a large part in the worldview of the authors of books like Joshua, Judges, Samuel, and Kings, the critical view that Samuel is simply a theological narrative of what Israel thought its history should have been is doubtful and driven more by the ideology of critical scholars than by evidence from the text or from extrabiblical sources. Such critical reconstructions assume any historical writing that has a theological viewpoint cannot be historically accurate—a common but unverifiable assumption among critical scholars. Moreover, by placing the composition of Joshua so late in Israel's history, these theories fail to explain many of the features of the Deuteronomistic History that point to a much earlier date for its writing. For instance, why did Joshua depict the Canaanites as living in Gezer (Josh 16:10) when other supposedly Deuteronomistic editors claimed that the Canaanites had been exterminated from the city (1 Ki 9:16–17)? How is it that Hurrian names such as Hoham, Piam, Sheshai, and Talmai (Josh 10:3; 15:14) are preserved in Joshua when Hurrian culture had disappeared by the tenth century BC? With regard to Samuel, why does 1 Sam 27:6 claim that Ziklag belongs to the kings of Judah "to this day" if the kingdom had fallen to the Babylonians? These issues are often overlooked or ignored by critical scholars because of their assumptions that lead them to conclude that Israel could not have accurately preserved its early history in the land.

Editorial Layers in Samuel

Some scholars, building on tradition-historical theories, identify distinct editorial layers within the text of Samuel as well as Joshua, Judges, and Kings. For instance, one hypothetical editorial layer attempted to justify Josiah's reforms (2 Ki 22:1–23:25). The final redaction was supposedly done in the exile and holds out hope for a return to the promised land (2 Ki 25:27–30). The book of Samuel allegedly was also part of this process of producing the history of Israel from after the death of Moses to the Babylonian captivity. Critics who posit several redactions to these books claim that telltale signs of this process remain embedded in the final text. Foremost among these are ostensibly competing and even contradictory theological outlooks.

While these approaches continue to have their adherents, they remain problematic. All of them rely on assertions that conflicting interests are evident in the extant texts of the books that comprise the Deuteronomistic History. Often, however, the presence of these supposedly incompatible ideologies stems from purposeful disharmonization of passages that do not prima facie require such readings. Moreover, each of them assumes that multiple theologies are intrinsic to books like Samuel. These hypothetical incongruent theologies are rather

---

[18] See especially the essays in Edenburg and Pakkala, *Is Samuel among the Deuteronomists?*

one-dimensional and pedestrian, devoid of nuance and subtlety. In contrast, a holistic reading of a book such as Samuel without preconceived notions of redactional layers could lead one to see a multidimensional theology full of nuanced views of God and humans often portrayed with wonderful subtleties in style and substance. Such a holistic approach can appreciate the skill of the author as he delves into the complicated events of God's history in dealing with Israel and the multifaceted motivations of kings and commoners alike. As a result, Samuel should be seen as giving a realistic picture of humans and a reliable picture of God's interaction with them. The inspired book is a divine revelation both of judgment against sin and of the gracious salvation to be fully accomplished in Christ.

Literary Features of Samuel[19]

Samuel is primarily narrative history. Although it contains poems (notably 1 Sam 2:1–10; 2 Sam 1:19–27; 22:2–51; 23:1–7) and other materials, even these were included by the author in the service of the narrative that runs from Samuel's birth to the end of David's reign. Samuel itself covers three main eras: the end of the period of the judges, when Israel had no king (c. 1109–1049 BC; 1 Samuel 1–8), the reign of Saul (c. 1049–1009 BC; 1 Samuel 9–2 Samuel 1), and the reign of David (1009–968 BC; 2 Samuel 2–24).

Biographical Studies of Saul and David

Given the narrative history in Samuel and its two long treatments of the reigns of Saul and David, it is not surprising that this has given rise to a number of studies that seek to produce biographical character studies of these kings. There are fewer of these on Saul, but most of them view him in some way as a failed king at the head of a failed experiment in monarchy.[20] Perhaps only Sellars attempts to view Saul in a somewhat positive light, and this only in that he is obedient to the people of Israel, though disobedient to God.[21]

A number of recent biographical studies of David have sought to cast David or God in a less than flattering light. Some, such as those by Gunn and Brueggemann, have concluded that Saul was a victim of God's favoring David and that David was the recipient of an inscrutable God's blessing.[22] Halpern and McKenzie, on the other hand, assume that the book of Samuel seeks to rehabilitate David from what he actually was—a scheming, petty, and violent

---

[19] Some of this material is adapted from Lessing and Steinmann, *Prepare the Way of the Lord*, 193–94.

[20] These include Adam Green, *King Saul: The True History of the First Messiah*; Barbara Green, *How Are the Mighty Fallen? A Dialogical Study of King Saul in 1 Samuel*; and Michelson, *Reconciling Violence and Kingship: A Study of Judges and 1 Samuel*. There are even fewer studies of Samuel; see Leuchter, *Samuel and the Shaping of Tradition*.

[21] Sellars, "An Obedient Servant? The Reign of King Saul (1 Samuel 13–15) Reassessed."

[22] Gunn, *The Story of King David: Genre and Interpretation*; Brueggemann, *David's Truth in Israel's Imagination and Memory*.

despot who pushed aside his predecessor to seize the throne and who eliminated some of his sons in order to cling to his crown.[23] The story of David in Samuel seems to them too good to be true, and getting behind the text's portrait of David reveals him as simply another minor Near Eastern potentate. Polzin goes even farther, claiming that the text of Samuel itself mainly portrays David in a negative light, consistently condemning him through explicit and implicit characterizations.[24]

On the other hand, Borgman argues that David is gradually revealed to the audience as a complex person whom God chooses over Saul because of David's grasp of the moral imperatives of the world that he inhabits and because of David's delight in God and his mercy, something that Saul consistently lacks.[25] According to this view, David's God is not the inscrutable and arbitrary deity that many scholars perceive in the book of Samuel, but a God who makes excellent sense in a more subtle and complex way than is often grasped by many contemporary biblical scholars.

What all of these treatments of Saul and David lack in some way is the recognition (to which Borgman comes closest) that the narrative of Samuel is knit together not by the human characters but by Yahweh. The book's literary goal is to portray a God who deals patiently and mercifully with sinners—Israel as a whole as well as its leaders: Eli, Samuel, Saul, David, and to a lesser extent Jonathan, Abner, Joab, and others. The skillful literary weaving together of the events of Israel's history is designed to show the readers that their God is gracious despite human failings, joyful when humans respond to his love in faith and obedience, and long-suffering with human failures and recalcitrance. These divine qualities will be definitively exemplified in David's Son and Lord (Mt 22:42–45).

David in Samuel and Chronicles

There are a number of parallel passages in Samuel and Chronicles. They begin with the death of Saul and extend through the reign of David. Scholars have debated whether the writer of Chronicles was using and adapting Samuel or whether there was a common source underlying both Samuel and Chronicles. No matter which is the case, it is clear that the writer of Chronicles had his own outlook on the history of God's dealing with Israel through David.

Chronicles emphasizes God's working with all Israel,[26] so the writer was not interested in the division of the kingdom after Saul's death when David

---

[23] Halpern, *David's Secret Demons: Messiah, Murderer, Traitor, King* (2001); McKenzie, *King David: A Biography* (2000). See also the more recent work by Baden, *The Historical David: The Real Life of an Invented Hero* (2014).

[24] Polzin, *David and the Deuteronomist*.

[25] Borgman, *David, Saul, and God: Rediscovering an Ancient Story*.

[26] This can be seen by the forty-six occurrences of the phrase "all Israel" (כָּל־יִשְׂרָאֵל) in Chronicles (1 Chr 9:1; 11:1, 4, 10; 12:39 [ET 12:38]; 13:5, 6, 8; 14:8; 15:3, 28; 17:6; 18:14; 19:17; 21:4, 5; 28:4, 8; 29:21, 23, 25, 26; 2 Chr 1:2 [twice]; 7:6, 8; 9:30; 10:1, 3, 16 [twice];

ruled only Judah from Hebron (2 Samuel 1–4). Chronicles emphasizes the line of David as the God-chosen royal line (2 Chr 13:5, 8; 21:7; 23:3). Thus, the Chronicler omits the account of David's dealings with Mephibosheth, Saul's grandson and Jonathan's son (2 Samuel 9), and David's interactions with Saul's family in response to the complaint of the Gibeonites (2 Sam 21:1–14). In addition, the Chronicler generally excludes references to David's failures and troubles: David's adultery and its aftermath (2 Sam 11:2–12:28), the series of tribulations that came upon David as a result of his adultery (2 Samuel 13–20), and the late Philistine war (2 Sam 21:15–17). However, Chronicles does include David's sin of taking a census of Israel (2 Sam 24:1–25; 1 Chr 21:1–22:1), since this incident leads to David acquiring the land upon which the temple would be built (2 Chr 3:1).

Although Samuel depicts David as a skilled musician and composer (1 Sam 16:16, 23; 18:10; 19:9), the Chronicler emphasizes David as the one who designated certain Levites to be in charge of music and song in worship.[27] In fact, in Chronicles David is never depicted as producing music except when he sings with the rest of Israel (1 Chr 13:8). Therefore Chronicles leaves out three songs by David: his lament over Saul and Jonathan (2 Sam 1:17–27), the version of Psalm 18 in 2 Samuel 22, and the last words of David (2 Sam 23:1–7). See figure 2.

Historical and Archaeological Issues[28]
The Historicity of David

In the late twentieth century a number of biblical scholars known as minimalists, or members of the Copenhagen School, held that the Israelite kingdom of David and Solomon was an invention by exilic or postexilic Judean writers. Other scholars maintain that David and his son Solomon were rulers of a kingdom, but that it was much more modest in size and in influence than depicted in the books of Samuel and Kings. Recent archaeological finds, however, cast doubt upon these theories.

11:3, 13; 12:1; 13:4, 15; 18:16; 24:5; 28:23; 29:24 [twice]; 30:1, 5, 6; 31:1; 35:3). This phrase is not unknown to the writer of Samuel. In Samuel it occurs thirty-six times (1 Sam 2:14, 22; 3:20; 4:1, 5; 7:5; 11:2; 12:1; 13:4, 20; 14:40; 17:11; 18:16; 19:5; 24:3 [ET 24:2]; 25:1; 28:3, 4; 2 Sam 3:12, 21, 37; 4:1; 5:5; 8:15; 10:17; 11:1; 12:12; 14:25; 15:6; 16:21, 22; 17:10, 11, 13; 18:17; 19:12 [ET 19:11]).

[27] 1 Chr 6:16–33 (ET 6:31–48); 15:16–24; 16:41–42; 25:1–31; 2 Chr 7:6; 23:18; 29:25–27, 30; 35:15.

[28] This section is adapted from Lessing and Steinmann, *Prepare the Way of the Lord*, 199–202.

Figure 2

Old Testament Parallels to Passages in Samuel

Saul dies in battle	1 Sam 31:1–13	1 Chr 10:1–12
David is made king over all Israel	2 Sam 5:1–3	1 Chr 11:1–3
A summary of David's reign over Israel:		
David conquers Jerusalem	2 Sam 5:6–10	1 Chr 11:4–9
David reigns in Jerusalem	2 Sam 5:11–16	1 Chr 14:1–7
David's sons are born in Jerusalem	2 Sam 5:14–16	1 Chr 3:5–8
David defeats the Philistines	2 Sam 5:17–25	1 Chr 14:8–16
David brings the ark to Jerusalem:		
David's first attempt to move the ark	2 Sam 6:1–11	1 Chr 13:1–14
The ark is brought to Jerusalem	2 Sam 6:12–16	1 Chr 15:25–29
David's worship before the ark	2 Sam 6:17–19	1 Chr 16:1–3
God's covenant with David:		
God's promise to David	2 Sam 7:1–17	1 Chr 17:1–15
David's prayer in response to God's promise	2 Sam 7:18–29	1 Chr 17:16–27
David's victories	2 Sam 8:1–14	1 Chr 18:1–13
David's officials	2 Sam 8:15–18	1 Chr 18:14–17
The Ammonite war:		
Joab attacks Rabbah	2 Sam 10:1–11:1	1 Chr 19:1–20:1a
David conquers Rabbah†	2 Sam 12:30–31	1 Chr 20:2–3
The defeat of four Philistine giants	2 Sam 21:18–22	1 Chr 20:4–8
David's song of deliverance	2 Sam 22:1–51	Psalm 18
David's mighty men	2 Sam 23:8–39	1 Chr 11:10–41a
David's census leads to repentance and a place to build the temple	2 Sam 24:1–25	1 Chr 21:1–22:1

†2 Sam 12:26–31 tells how Joab all but captured Rabbah (cf. 1 Chr 20:1b) but called on David to make the final assault and claim the victory.

The Tel Dan Inscription

In 1993 and 1994 excavators at Tel Dan, the site of the biblical city of Dan in northern Israel, discovered three fragments of a stele apparently erected by the Aramean king Hazael (or, less probably, by Hazael's son Bar-hadad). In the Aramaic inscription on this stele the Aramean king claims to have killed both Joram the king of Israel and Ahaziah of the house of David.[29] However, accord-

---

[29] See Biran and Naveh, "An Aramaic Stele Fragment from Tel Dan"; Biran and Naveh, "The Tel Dan Inscription: A New Fragment"; Lemaire, "The Tel Dan Stela as a Piece of Royal

11

ing to 2 Ki 8:29, Hazael merely wounded Joram. Both Joram and Ahaziah were killed by Jehu (2 Ki 9:14–28).

Most important though, Ahaziah is identified as a descendant of David in this inscription, thereby confirming the accounts in Samuel and Kings that David founded a dynasty. When the Tel Dan inscription was first published a number of minimalist scholars attempted to argue that the phrase ביתדוד, written without a word divider, should not be read as "the house of David." Instead, while conceding that the first element in the phrase was indeed "house" (בית), they argued that the second element (דוד) might be understood as "beloved" or a place-name (i.e., Dod) or something else because the phrase lacks a word divider. Such arguments were quickly dismissed by the majority of scholars who demonstrated the faulty logic used to support them. Moreover, André Lemaire reexamined the Mesha Stele, an inscription first discovered in 1868 at the site of ancient Dibon in Moab.[30] He found that it also contains the phrase "the house of David," though written as two words (בית דוד). As a result, there is now general agreement that these two inscriptions confirm the presence of a kingdom ruled by a dynasty established by David.

The Khirbet Qeiyafa Inscription

Khirbet Qeiyafa overlooks the Elah Valley in southwest Israel near the site that 1 Samuel 17 describes as the setting for the contest between David and Goliath.[31] This site, which probably housed no more than about five or six hundred people inside a fortified wall, gives evidence for a strong central government that could construct such a city during the late eleventh or early tenth century BC.

During excavations at Khirbet Qeiyafa in 2008, a pottery shard with a faint inscription was discovered. It seems to be in Hebrew, making it at the time of its discovery the oldest known Hebrew inscription, dating to about the early tenth century BC. In addition, four burned olive pits were found in the city's destruction layer. Subsequent cabon-14 dating of the pits indicated a date of 1051–969 BC, a date consistent with pottery found at the site.[32] It appears that the location was abandoned before the middle of the tenth century, probably sometime during the latter part of David's reign. Subsequent statements by the excavators and others have said that this site must have been an outpost built by the

---

Historiography." Line 7 of the reconstructed inscription mentions the killing of Joram, although the name is only partially preserved. Line 8 of the reconstructed inscription mentions the killing of Ahaziah, though here also the name is only partially preserved. Line 11 mentions Jehu as the new ruler of Israel, thereby confirming the reconstructions of the names of Joram and Ahaziah.

[30] Lemaire, "La stèle de Mésha et l'histoire de l'ancien Israël."

[31] For a good summary and analysis of the evidence from Khirbet Qeiyafa, see Schreiner, "What Are They Saying about Khirbet Qeiyafa?"

[32] Garfinkel and Kang, "The Relative and Absolute Chronology of Khirbet Qeiyafa," especially 178–81, who estimate that the site was occupied for about twenty years within that time frame.

kingdom ruled by David and Solomon.[33] However, the dates are too early for Solomon and actually appear to be confirmation of an outpost guarding Israel's border with Philistia during the reigns of Saul and David.

The presence of an inscription at Khirbet Qeiyafa most likely indicates royal scribal activity. Coupled with the proximity to Saul's confrontation with the Philistines that led to David's slaying of Goliath, the discoveries at Khirbet Qeiyafa provide support for the biblical depiction of a substantial kingdom ruled by Saul and later by David. This kingdom was powerful enough to organize, build, and support an outpost at this location. While some critical scholars have tended to minimize David's kingdom and claim that he was in reality only a local chieftain, the evidence from Khirbet Qeiyafa would suggest that Saul and David were rulers of a realm with enough logistical, political, and financial resources to have built such a site.

Chronological Issues in Samuel[34]

Samuel and Eli as Judges

Once dates have been established for the reign of Saul (c. 1049–1009),[35] it is possible to calculate dates for events surrounding the ministries of Eli and Samuel. 1 Sam 7:2–6 states that twenty years passed between the time that the ark was returned to Israel and Samuel interceded for the people at Mizpah shortly before Saul was anointed king. This would place the return of the ark in 1068 BC. The season was spring, since it was the time of harvesting wheat (1 Sam 6:13). The death of Eli, seven months earlier (1 Sam 6:1), would have been in 1069 BC. Given other information from 1 Samuel, we can reconstruct Eli's life as shown in figure 3.

Figure 3

Chronology of Eli's Life

1167	Eli is born (1 Sam 4:15)
1109–1069	Eli serves as priest and judge (1 Sam 1:9; 4:18)
1069	Eli dies (1 Sam 4:15)

This dating also aligns well with the archaeology of Shiloh, which indicates that Shiloh was destroyed about 1050 BC. This would have been at the time of

---

[33] Garfinkel, Ganor, and Hasel, "The Contribution of Khirbet Qeiyafa to Our Understanding of the Iron Age Period"; Kang and Garfinkel, "Finger-Impressed Jar Handles at Khirbet Qeiyafa"; Pioske, "Memory and Its Materiality"; Hawkins and Buchanan, "The Khirbet Qeiyafa Inscription and 11th–10th Century BCE Israel."

[34] This section is adapted from Steinmann, *From Abraham to Paul*, 108–23.

[35] See "The Basic Chronology of the United Monarchy" and "The Reign of Saul (c. 1049–1009)" below.

the ark's capture by the Philistines and the death of Eli (see Jer 7:12–14; 26:6, 9; Ps 78:60).[36]

If Josephus' information is correct that Samuel was a judge for twelve years,[37] Samuel's career as a judge lasted from 1060 BC to 1049 BC. Note that Samuel's judgeship closely follows the death of Abdon in 1061.[38] Therefore, the indication that Samuel was a judge (1 Sam 7:6, 15, 16, 17) seems to fit with the chronology of the judges and provides for nearly uninterrupted leadership from Othniel until the institution of the monarchy, or nearly uninterrupted leadership from Moses to Joshua and the elders through the judges ending in Samuel.

The Basic Chronology of the United Monarchy

The period between the anointing of Saul and the death of Solomon is often characterized as Israel's "united monarchy" in contrast to the division of Israel into the kingdoms of Israel (north) and Judah (south) after Solomon's death. This characterization is accurate except for the first years of David's reign when David reigned over Judah alone and Saul's son Eshbaal reigned over the rest of Israel (2 Sam 2:10).

The reign of Solomon can be securely dated as 971t–932t.[39] David reigned forty years (2 Sam 5:4; 1 Ki 2:11). This was calculated by accession-year reckoning, since in 1 Ki 2:11 he is credited with forty years: seven in Hebron and thirty-three in Jerusalem. However, David was actually king in Hebron for seven years and six months (2 Sam 2:11; 5:5). This means that his first six months in Hebron were reckoned as his accession year and not counted in the total. Thus, David began to reign during the month of Nisan, and his first regnal year was reckoned from Tishri of that same year.

As 1 Ki 1:5–2:12 and 1 Chronicles 23–29 make clear, Solomon shared the throne of Israel with David for some time. As related in 1 Chronicles 23–29, during this coregency David made extensive preparations for the construction of the temple and organized the duties of the priests and Levites. Those preparations seem to require a period of at least a year or two. But since David had been forbidden by God from building the temple (2 Sam 7:12–13; 1 Chr 17:11–12; 28:3), he had certainly died by the time Solomon began to build it in Ziv 967 BC (1 Ki 6:1).[40] Taking those things into consideration, it is reasonable to assume that David's last year was 969t.[41] David's first year as king over

---

[36] Wood, "From Ramesses to Shiloh," 280–81.

[37] Josephus, *Antiquities*, 6.294.

[38] Steinmann, *From Abraham to Paul*, 107.

[39] See Steinmann, *From Abraham to Paul*, 37–45.

A year with a trailing lowercase "t" indicates a year that began in the fall month of Tishri, rather than the spring month of Nisan (designated with "n"). See Steinmann, *From Abraham to Paul*, 20–21.

[40] Ziv is the month that follows Nisan.

[41] As indicated above, a year denoted with a lowercase "t" indicates a year that began in the fall month of Tishri. Thus, 969t = fall 969 BC through the end of summer 968 BC.

Israel in Jerusalem, therefore, was 1002t (969t + 33). His first year as king over Judah in Hebron was 1009t (969t + 40), with his reign actually commencing in Nisan of 1009 BC.

Sometime during the period when David was king in Hebron, Eshbaal's great-uncle Abner made Eshbaal king over the northern tribes of Israel.[42] The narrative of 2 Sam 5:1–8 implies that shortly after Eshbaal's death (2 Samuel 4), David was acknowledged to be king over all Israel and conquered Jerusalem. This means that Eshbaal's two-year reign as king over northern Israel (2 Sam 2:8–10) began no earlier than 1009t but no later than 1004t, two years before David was made king of all Israel and conquered Jerusalem (2 Sam 5:1–8).

As for Saul's reign, the text of MT 1 Sam 13:1 appears corrupt since it credits Saul with an impossibly short reign of two years.[43] However, Acts 13:21 and Josephus[44] indicate that Saul reigned forty years. This may be a round number, but it is most likely close to the actual total.

One confirmation of this can be seen in the birth of Saul's youngest son, Eshbaal, who was forty years old when he became king of most of the tribes of Israel (2 Sam 2:10). Only three sons of Saul are mentioned at any one place in texts dealing with his reign. 1 Sam 14:49 mentions Jonathan, Ishvi, and Malchishua. 1 Sam 31:2 mentions Jonathan, Abinadab, and Malchi-shua. Since Ishvi is mentioned only one time in the entire OT, whether or not he is to be equated with Abinadab is a topic of debate. He may have been a son who died early, and Abinadab may have been born after Saul began to reign. It is most likely that Eshbaal was Saul's youngest son and did not participate in battle with his father and brothers to ensure survival of the royal line. However, there is no mention in Samuel of the birth of Saul's fourth son, Eshbaal (it is mentioned in 1 Chr 8:33; 9:39). Thus, it would appear that Eshbaal was born after Saul began to reign about 1049 BC. Eshbaal was forty years old when he became king and reigned two years during David's seven years and six months in Hebron (2 Sam 2:10–11). This means that Eshbaal began to reign no earlier than Nisan 1009 and no later than 1004t.[45] Therefore, he was born no earlier than sometime in 1049 or late 1050 BC and no later than 1044 BC. Eshbaal's age at his accession to the throne confirms that Saul reigned about forty years and certainly no less than thirty-five years.

---

[42] Eshbaal is called Ish-bosheth in 2 Samuel (e.g., 2 Sam 2:8–10). It is likely that the name Ishbosheth ("man of shame") is a purposeful scribal bowdlerization of Eshbaal ("man of Baal" or "man of the master"). Although later readers probably assumed that the name Eshbaal was a reference to the pagan god Baal, Saul may have understood this name given to his son as a reference to Yahweh as Israel's Master or Lord.

[43] See Steinmann, *From Abraham to Paul*, 45, 105–6.

[44] Josephus, *Antiquities*, 6.378.

[45] See the discussion above in this section about when David's reign began.

Since Saul died in the spring of 1009 BC,[46] his reign must have commenced about 1049 BC. We cannot know whether, like David's dynasty, Saul reckoned his regnal years from Tishri. If so, his official reign would have been c. 1050t–1010t. If, however, he reckoned his regnal years from Nisan, then his reign would have been ca. 1049n–1009n. Since 1 Sam 13:1 credits Saul with two years on the throne, it may be argued that original text may have read "forty-two years," with only the number "two" surviving in the now-corrupt MT text. However, this is unlikely, since the number "two" in 1 Sam 13:1 appears to be secondary (see the textual note on it there).

Thus, the basic chronology of the united monarchy is shown in figure 4.

Figure 4

____

Basic Chronology of the United Monarchy

c. 1049–1009	The reign of Saul
Nisan 1009–1002t	David's reign in Hebron
1002t–969t	David's reign in Jerusalem
971t–969t	Solomon's coregency with David
969t–932t	Solomon's sole reign

The Reign of Saul (c. 1049–1009)

There are few explicit chronological markers in the narrative of Saul's reign in 1 Samuel 10–31. Therefore, any reconstruction of the events during Saul's reign will contain some degree of uncertainty.

Before David is introduced in the narrative in 1 Samuel 16, Saul led a campaign against the Philistines (1 Samuel 13–14) and a campaign against the Amalekites (1 Samuel 15). In both instances Saul failed in some way to obey God, prompting Samuel to inform Saul that God had already chosen someone else as king (1 Sam 13:13–14; 15:26–28). These statements imply that David was already living. Since David was thirty years old before he became king (2 Sam 5:4; making his birth between mid 1040 and early 1039 BC), these statements imply that, apart from the acts of Saul at the very beginning of his reign (1 Samuel 10–12), most of the first three decades of Saul's reign are passed over in silence. Most likely David was approaching the age of twenty—the normal age for military service (Num 1:3)—when Saul was informed that someone else had been chosen to be king. This would place the Philistine campaign around 1021 BC, no more than about two years before 1019 BC, when David turned twenty, and the Amalekite campaign about a year later than the Philistine campaign, c. 1020 BC.

---

[46] This is based on the calculation that David's reign in Hebron began in Nisan 1009. See the discussion above in this section.

David volunteered to confront Goliath (1 Sam 17:32), implying that he was at least twenty years old, but not much older, since he was a young man and despised by the older Goliath (1 Sam 17:33, 42).[47] Moreover, David had no experience wearing armor or with a sword (1 Sam 17:38–39), which also implies that he was just over the age for military service. Therefore, David most likely killed Goliath about 1019 BC and had been anointed by Samuel (1 Samuel 16) shortly before that.

Well into his reign David did not know of the existence of Jonathan's son Merib-baal (Mephibosheth; 2 Sam 9:3).[48] This implies that David most likely fled from Saul's court before Merib-baal's birth. Since Merib-baal was five years old when Saul died (2 Sam 4:4), he was born in 1014 BC. David, therefore, fled Saul's court about 1015 BC. This places the events of 1 Samuel 18 between c. 1019 BC and c. 1015 BC.

During the last sixteen months of Saul's reign (Tebeth late 1011 or early 1010 BC to Nisan 1009 BC), David served as a mercenary for the Philistine king Achish (1 Sam 27:7). If we allow a year or two for the events between the death of Samuel and David entering Achish's service, Samuel's death can be dated to c. 1012 BC (1 Sam 25:1). This, in turn, places the events of 1 Samuel 19–24 between c. 1015 BC and c. 1012 BC.

Major events during Saul's reign can be summarized as shown in figure 5.

Figure 5

___

Chronology of Saul's Reign

c. 1049	Saul is made king (1 Samuel 9–12)
c. 1045	Eshbaal (Ish-bosheth) is born
c. 1039	David is born
c. 1021	Saul's Philistine campaign (1 Samuel 13–14)
c. 1020	Saul's Amalekite campaign (1 Samuel 15)
c. 1019	David is anointed, and David kills Goliath (1 Samuel 16–17)
c. 1016	David marries Michal (1 Sam 18:27)
c. 1015	David flees Saul's court (1 Samuel 19–21)
1014	Merib-baal (Mephibosheth) is born
c. 1012	Samuel dies (1 Sam 25:1)
c. 1011	David marries Abigail and Ahinoam (1 Sam 25:42–43)
1010–1009	David is in Achish's service for sixteen months (1 Samuel 27; 29–30)

___

[47] Numbers 1 indicates that twenty years of age was the minimum for military service in Israel (see also Num 26:2, 4).

[48] Merib-baal is called Mephibosheth in 2 Samuel (e.g., 2 Sam 4:4; 9:6). It is likely that the name Mephibosheth ("from the mouth of shame") is most like a purposeful scribal bowdlerization of Merib-baal ("contending with Baal").

The Reign of David (Nisan 1009–969t)

The narratives of David's reign are found in 2 Samuel 2–24 and 1 Chronicles 11–29. In contrast to the narrative for Saul's reign, there are several notices in the narratives of David's reign that are useful in reconstructing a chronology of events during this period. However, even with this information, many of the dates for individual events will be approximate.

David's Reign in Hebron (Nisan 1009–1002t)

The majority of the account of David's time in Hebron when he reigned over Judah (2 Samuel 2–4) concerns the two years in which Eshbaal reigned over the rest of Israel (2 Sam 2:8–4:12). The narrative of 2 Samuel 5 implies that David was made king over all Israel shortly after Eshbaal was assassinated. This, in turn, implies that for about four years after Judah acknowledged David as king, the rest of Israel had no recognized king until Saul's uncle Abner, who had been commander of Israel's army (1 Sam 14:50), made Saul's son Eshbaal king (2 Sam 2:8–9).

Confirmation of this can be found in Abner's later comment to the elders of Israel that for some time they had been considering acknowledging David as king (2 Sam 3:17). By placing Eshbaal on the throne, it would appear that Abner was attempting to stanch the erosion of the power he and his family had held during the previous four decades. Therefore, we can date Eshbaal's reign to about 1005t–1003t.[49] This, in turn, allows us to construct the chronology for David's reign over Judah in Hebron as shown in figure 6.

Figure 6

Chronology of David's Reign in Hebron

Nisan 1009	David is made king of Judah in Hebron (2 Sam 2:1–7)
Mid 1005	Abner makes Eshbaal king (2 Sam 2:8–10)
Early 1004	Joab defeats Abner at Gibeon (2 Sam 2:11–32)
Late 1003	Joab murders Abner (2 Samuel 3)
Early 1002	Eshbaal is assassinated (2 Samuel 4)
Mid 1002	David is made king of all Israel and conquers Jerusalem (2 Sam 5:1–8)

David's Reign in Jerusalem (1002t–969t)

To the careful reader it quickly becomes obvious that the material about David's reign in 2 Samuel 5–24 (and its parallel, 1 Chronicles 11–21) is not arranged in strict chronological order. First, it is clear that 2 Sam 5:9–16 is a summary of David's activity in Jerusalem throughout his reign there. 2 Sam

---

[49] A year with a trailing lowercase "t" indicates a year that began in the fall month of Tishri, rather than the spring month of Nisan (designated with "n"). See Steinmann, *From Abraham to Paul*, 20–21.

5:11–12 (∥ 1 Chr 14:1–2) notes that David's building activity was aided by Hiram of Tyre, whose reign began in 980t, about twenty years after David conquered Jerusalem. Clearly, this notice, plus the summary of the sons born to David in 2 Sam 5:13–16 (∥ 1 Chr 14:3–7), marks this section as a summary of David's thirty-three years of reigning in Jerusalem.

Another indication that the events during David's reign in Jerusalem are not always narrated in chronological order is the Philistine war in 2 Sam 5:17–25 (∥ 1 Chr 14:8–17). This clearly was initiated before David conquered Jerusalem in mid 1002 BC. 2 Sam 5:17 notes that the Philistines threatened to attack shortly after David was anointed king over all Israel (1002t). In response, David went down to the "stronghold" (מְצֻדָה, 2 Sam 5:17), a term used earlier to describe Jerusalem (2 Sam 5:7, 9). Heretofore the Philistines probably considered David their ally, since they both opposed the house of Saul. However, as soon as David became king over a united Israel, the Philistines attacked him and he found a more secure capital in Jerusalem before retaliating and defeating the Philistines.

The very next event in the accounts of David's reign is David's bringing the ark to Jerusalem (2 Samuel 6; 1 Chronicles 13; 15–16). As 1 Chr 15:1 makes clear, the ark was brought to Jerusalem after David had built his palace—that is, after 980t, when Hiram became king of Tyre (2 Sam 5:11).

Later, the Ammonite war is related (2 Sam 10:1–11:1; 12:29–31; 1 Chr 19:1–20:3). There are two indications that this war took place before 980 BC. One is that the war was precipitated by the disrespect shown by the new Ammonite king Hanun to David's ambassadors (2 Sam 10:1–5; 1 Chr 19:1–5). This had to have taken place early in David's reign before he had become powerful. Later in David's reign Hanun would not have dared to insult him. In addition, Hanun was the son of Nahash (2 Sam 10:2; 1 Chr 19:2), who attacked Jabesh-gilead at the beginning of Saul's reign (1 Sam 11:1–11). If Hanun precipitated the Ammonite war sometime after 980t as required by a strict chronological arrangement of the material in 2 Samuel 5–24, then Nahash would have had to reign almost eighty years! If, however, the Ammonite war took place early in David's reign, Nahash would have had a very—but not impossibly—long reign of forty-five or fifty years.

A second indication that the Ammonite war happened early is the age of Solomon. Although we do not know exactly how old Solomon was when he became king, shortly after David's death he characterized himself as "a young child" (נַעַר קָטֹן, 1 Ki 3:7; cf. 1 Chr 22:5). While this is most certainly hyperbole on Solomon's part, it is probable that Solomon was in his early twenties when he took the throne. His eldest son, Rehoboam, was born in 973 BC,[50] two years before Solomon's first regnal year (971t). This, in turn requires Solomon to have been at least in his middle teens and more likely closer to twenty years old when his wife Naamah became pregnant (1 Ki 14:21). Since Solomon's birth

---

[50] Steinmann, *From Abraham to Paul*, 147.

followed David's adultery with Bathsheba during the Ammonite war (2 Sam 11:1–12:23), Solomon, Bathsheba's second child with David, was most likely born within two or three years after the siege of Rabbah. Thus, if we assume that Hanun ascended to the Ammonite throne in 998t, after a fifty-year reign by his father, the outbreak of the Ammonite war can also be placed that year. The siege of Rabbah would then have been in the spring of 997 BC (2 Sam 11:1; 1 Chr 20:1) and the birth of Solomon about 994 BC (2 Sam 12:24). Solomon would have been twenty-one years old when Rehoboam was born and about twenty-three years old at the beginning of his own first regnal year (971t).

All this demonstrates that the material for David's reign is not arranged in precise chronological order and that each incident in the narrative must be examined carefully to determine when it took place. Sufficient clues exist, however, to estimate the dates of most major incidents in David's reign.

Key to determining the chronology of the remaining major events of David's reign is the narrative concerning Absalom (2 Samuel 13–19). The sequence of the events is related as follows:

1. Amnon raped Absalom's sister Tamar (2 Sam 13:1–22). At this time Absalom was old enough to have his own household—at least twenty years of age (2 Sam 13:20).
2. Two years later Absalom murdered Amnon (2 Sam 13:23–33, especially 2 Sam 13:23) and fled to Geshur (2 Sam 13:34–39). Absalom remained in exile in Geshur for three years (2 Sam 13:38).
3. Absalom's return from exile is facilitated by Joab (2 Sam 14:1–27).
4. Absalom is received by David two years after returning from exile (2 Sam 14:28–33).
5. Absalom spends four years preparing to overthrow David (2 Sam 15:1–11, especially 2 Sam 15:7).
6. Absalom leads a rebellion, is defeated, and is killed by Joab (2 Sam 15:13–19:43).

There are two indications that Absalom's rebellion took place after David built his palace and moved the ark to Jerusalem. First, Absalom's defiling of David's concubines took place on the roof of David's palace (2 Sam 16:22). Second, when David fled Jerusalem, Zadok attempted to take the ark from the city, but David ordered him to return it (2 Sam 15:24–29). Thus, Absalom's rebellion took place several years after 980t, when Hiram became king of Tyre (2 Sam 5:11; 1 Chr 14:1). The most opportune time for Absalom to begin his political campaign to gain the support of the elders of Israel would have been while David was immersed in building his palace and moving the ark to Jerusalem. If we assume that Hiram made his first overture to David soon after assuming the throne of Tyre in 980t, then we can estimate that David began work on his palace in 979 BC.

About three years would have been a reasonable time to build a palace, placing the completion in 976 BC. The ark would have been brought to Jerusalem the next year, 975 BC. Thus, a reasonable period for Absalom's four years spent undermining David's authority would have been from about 978 BC, when David was in the midst of palace construction, to about 974 BC, when Absalom rebelled.

Working backward yields 980 BC as the year when Absalom returned from exile, 983 BC as the date when Absalom murdered Amnon and went into exile, and 985 BC as the time when Amnon raped Tamar. It should be noted that Amnon was David's eldest son, the first of David's six sons born during the seven and a half years he ruled in Hebron (2 Sam 3:2–5; 1 Chr 3:1–4). Since David had been married to Ahinoam, Amnon's mother, sometime before coming to Hebron (1 Sam 25:43; 27:3), it is possible that Amnon was born as early as 1009 BC. Absalom's birth probably came a year or two later in 1008 or 1007 BC. This would have made Amnon about twenty-four years old when he raped Tamar. Absalom would have been twenty-two or twenty-three years old at the time.

Following Absalom's rebellion, Sheba rebelled. This can be dated to about 973 BC. The census David ordered should probably be dated to most of 972 BC (2 Samuel 24; 1 Chronicles 21). It may have been a reaction to the two rebellions and a result of David's desire to know how large an army he could raise in case of another revolt. This would explain God's anger, since David was relying on human might instead of God's power to retain his kingdom.

The end of the narrative about the census tells of David buying the threshing floor of Araunah, which would become the site of the temple (2 Sam 24:16–25; 1 Chr 21:15–22:1). The remaining two or three years of David's reign were primarily spent with a renewed dedication to build the temple. David made preparations for the construction of the temple as he reigned with his coregent Solomon (1 Chr 22:2–29:25).

This leaves only two major events during David's reign undated: the avenging of the Gibeonites (2 Sam 21:1–14) and the later Philistine wars (2 Sam 21:15–22; 1 Chr 20:4–8). The avenging of the Gibeonites took place at the end of a three-year famine "during the days of David" (2 Sam 21:1). Since 2 Samuel 21 also relates the Philistine wars that took place after the capture of Rabbah (1 Chr 20:4), it is most likely that the famine and the avenging of the Gibeonites also should be placed after the conquest of Rabbah. The best that can be estimated chronologically is that both the famine and the Philistine wars are to be dated between the capture of Rabbah in about 997 BC and about 980 BC. A later date is not warranted, since by that time David had built his palace and God had granted him peace from his enemies (2 Sam 7:1, 9, 11; 1 Chr 17:8, 10).

Therefore, the approximate chronology of the events of David's reign in Jerusalem can be summarized as shown in figures 7 and 8.

21

Figure 7

Chronology of David's Reign in Jerusalem

1002	David conquers Jerusalem and defeats the Philistines (2 Sam 5:6–25; 1 Chr 11:4–9; 1 Chronicles 14)
998	The Ammonite war begins (2 Sam 10:1–11:1; 12:29–31; 1 Chr 19:1–20:3)
997	David commits adultery, and Rabbah is captured (2 Samuel 11–12)
994	Solomon is born (2 Sam 12:24–25)
985	Amnon rapes Tamar (2 Sam 13:1–22)
983	Absalom murders Amnon and goes into exile (2 Sam 13:23–39)
980	Absalom returns from exile (2 Sam 14:1–27)
979–976	David builds his palace (2 Sam 5:11; 1 Chr 14:1)
978	Absalom is received again by David (2 Sam 14:28–33)
975	The ark is moved to Jerusalem (2 Samuel 6; 1 Chronicles 13; 16); God's covenant with David (2 Samuel 7; 1 Chronicles 17)
974	Absalom rebels (2 Sam 15:13–19:43)
973	Sheba rebels (2 Samuel 20); Rehoboam is born (1 Ki 14:21; 2 Chr 12:13)
972	David orders a census taken (2 Samuel 24; 1 Chronicles 21)
972–969	David makes preparations for the construction of the temple (1 Chr 22:2–29:25)
971	Solomon is made coregent (1 Kings 1; 1 Chr 23:1)
969	David dies (1 Ki 2:10–12; 1 Chr 29:26–30)

Figure 8

Chronology of 1 Samuel

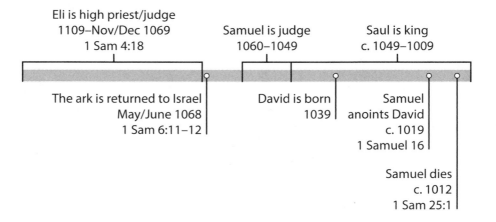

For a complete discussion of these dates, see Steinmann, *From Abraham to Paul*, 108–15.

Christ in Samuel[51]

The Promise to David (2 Samuel 7)

From the reign of David onward the most common association of the promised Messiah in the psalms and the prophets is with David.[52] This connection was prompted by the events related in 2 Samuel 7. The chapter opens with David relating to the prophet Nathan his desire to build a house for God, which Nathan initially approves. However, that night God revealed to Nathan that David was not to build a house for God, but that God would build a house (dynasty) for David (2 Sam 7:11, 15–16).[53] This oracle given to Nathan is the basis for the messianic hope connected with David and his house. Especially important are the last words of this oracle, "your house and your kingdom will be secured forever before me, and your throne will be established forever" (2 Sam 7:16; cf. Is 9:6 [ET 9:7]; Heb 1:8). This promise to David came as a partial fulfillment of God's promise to Abraham that kings would come from him (Gen 17:6). Moreover, God had provided regulations for kings in the laws given by Moses (Deut 17:14–20). Therefore, God's promise of a kingdom to David and his house was not a new plan, but was part of God's plan from the beginning. The raising up of David's "seed" (2 Sam 7:12) for this purpose recalls the original Gospel promise of the "Seed" who would crush the serpent's head (Gen 3:15).

In many ways this oracle is the high point of David's reign and, therefore, also of the book of Samuel. Although David would sin and bring misery to himself and his kingdom, nevertheless, God's promise remained with David and David remained confident of God's promise to him, even in his last words (2 Sam 23:5). In the Gospels the acclamation that Jesus is the "Son of David" makes the connection between this prophecy and Jesus as the Messiah.[54] Moreover, the Gospels affirm that the general opinion of the Pharisees and scribes in the first century was that the Messiah would be David's descendant (Mt 22:41–42; Mk 12:35).[55] Likewise, the relationship between God as "Father" and the royal "son" from David (2 Sam 7:14) fits with the Jewish equation of "the Son of God" with "the Christ" (Mt 26:63) and "the King of Israel" (Jn 1:49).[56]

---

[51] This section is adapted from Lessing and Steinmann, *Prepare the Way of the Lord*, 204–5.

[52] E.g., Pss 18:51 (ET 18:50); 89:4–5, 21, 36–37, 50 (ET 89:3–4, 20, 35–36, 49); 132:10–18; Is 11:1–16; 55:3; Jer 23:5–6; 30:9; 33:15–18; Ezek 34:23–24; 37:24–25; Hos 3:5; Amos 9:11–15; Micah 5:1 (ET 5:2).

[53] The Hebrew noun בַּיִת, "house," often refers to a "dynasty," as is applicable in 2 Sam 7:11, 15–16. In addition, "house" in 2 Sam 7:13 relates to the Solomonic temple and then suggests Jesus as the new temple (e.g., Jn 1:14; 2:19–21).

[54] See "Son of David" in Mt 1:1; 9:27; 12:23; 15:22; 20:30–31; 21:9, 15; Mk 10:47–48; Lk 18:38–39; cf. Rev. 3:7; 5:5; 22:16.

[55] In Mt 22:42–45 Jesus challenges the assumption that the Messiah would be only David's son by citing Ps 110:1 to demonstrate that he is also David's Lord.

[56] See the quote of 2 Sam 7:14a in Heb 1:5b. For Jesus as the Son of God the Father, see also, e.g., Mt 11:27; 28:19; Lk 1:35; Jn 1:14; 5:19–23.

Luther held that David understood this oracle (2 Samuel 7) as being about the Messiah, noting that in his response to Nathan's oracle he said, "And this is the manner of the man" (וְזֹאת תּוֹרַת הָאָדָם, 2 Sam 7:19).[57] Luther understood "the man" to be the promised Messiah. Perhaps there is support for Luther's interpretation in the parallel in 1 Chr 17:17, which could be read to say: "And you have viewed me according to the teaching about the ascending man" (וּרְאִיתַנִי כְּתוֹר הָאָדָם הַמַּעֲלָה), meaning that God saw in David the longing to see the Messiah, the "ascending man" (Prov 30:4; Jn 3:13; Eph 4:10). This is the position endorsed in this commentary (see the commentary on 2 Sam 7:19).

On the other hand, many scholars understand "the man" (הָאָדָם, 1 Chr 17:17) to be used in a generic sense to mean "mankind." David, then, comprehended this oracle as a "covenant/charter for mankind." This passage would then point forward to God's work through the house of David that would bring the kingdom to all people, something that is fulfilled in Jesus, who announced the arrival of the kingdom of God. Under this understanding David's words continue to be relevant through the mission of the church to bring the Gospel of Christ and his kingdom to all people. There are several problems with this position, however, including that fact that it requires an impossible understanding of the word הַמַּעֲלָה (1 Chr 17:17; see the commentary on 2 Sam 7:19).

Other Messianic Passages in the Book of Samuel

While 2 Samuel 7 is central in the messianic focus of the book of Samuel, we can also see several other passages as signaling Israel's messianic hope. At the very beginning of 1 Samuel, Hannah's Song proclaims confidence that God would strengthen the coming King, "his Anointed One" (מְשִׁיחוֹ, "his Messiah/Christ," 1 Sam 2:10). Then at the end of the book David's last words express confidence that God had made eternal provisions for an eternal covenant with him and for his salvation (2 Sam 23:5; cf. Heb 13:20). Thus, the book begins with a forward-looking confidence in God's work in the coming Messiah, reaches a climax in God's promise to David through Nathan, and then ends with David's assertion that God will do what he has promised.

In addition, God promised through Samuel that he would raise up a faithful priest (see the commentary on 1 Sam 2:35). This priest would act in accord with God's will. He would have a house that would endure and would walk before God forever. Moreover, this priest will not be from the house of Aaron (1 Sam 2:27–33). In the book of Hebrews, Jesus is portrayed as this priest in words that echo God's words to Samuel (Heb 2:17; 7:11–16).

Therefore, in Samuel we find the promise of the Messiah primarily in royal imagery but also in his portrayal as a priest. Because of Nathan's prophecy, David becomes the paradigm that molds messianic expectations throughout much of the prophetic books. In addition, the coming faithful priest who will

---

57 Luther, "The Last Words of David," AE 15:291: "This is the manner of a Man who is the Lord God."

not be from the line of Aaron shaped prophecy when the Anointed One to come is proclaimed in both kingly and priestly language (Psalm 110). In Samuel we find the historical foundation for these later messianic prophecies.

David and the Messianic Promise

In light of the passages noted above, it is not an exaggeration to say that the messianic promise in the book of Samuel is filtered through the lens of David's life. This should not be surprising, since from David's introduction to the reader in 1 Samuel 16 to his last sacrifice in 2 Samuel 24, almost every narrative involves David in some way.[58] David is the chosen king, Yahweh's anointed (1 Sam 16:12–13). This naturally raises the question for readers as to *why* God chose David. While God need not justify his choices, it is interesting to note that the book of Samuel does reveal something about God's choice of David—something it does not do for the previous choice of Saul.[59] When Samuel was sent to Jesse to anoint one of his sons, God told Samuel that he looks on the heart, not on outward appearance (1 Sam 16:7). What sets David's heart apart from others, especially from Saul's heart, is his trust in God, a trust God himself wrought in him by his Word and Spirit (see the commentary on 1 Sam 16:1–13). This trust is exhibited in David's defeat of Goliath (1 Samuel 17). It also led David to a high respect for God's Word (see the commentary on 1 Sam 23:6–13). David also honored God's decisions, even when it may have seemed more advantageous to him to have done otherwise. Thus, David twice refused to take Saul's life, since Saul was still "Yahweh's anointed,"[60] the one God originally anointed as king (1 Samuel 24; 1 Samuel 26). David trusted that God would remove Saul when the time was right (1 Sam 26:10).

God's work in David's heart is also shown in his willingness to repent of his sins. Without prompting by others David was sorry that he cut off a corner of Saul's robe (1 Sam 24:6–7 [ET 24:5–6]). After his decision to take a census (challenged by Joab, 2 Sam 24:3) he repented of this sin (2 Sam 24:10). When admonished by Nathan for his sin of adultery and murder, readers are shown how the prophetic Word worked in David's heart—he immediately repented and did not deny or make excuses for his sinful actions (2 Sam 12:13). When his own anger may have led him into sin, David's heart listened to Abigail (1 Samuel 25).

Therefore, the tracing of the arc of David's life from his anointing by Samuel to his last years on the throne reveals something about God's choice of David as king and as bearer of the messianic promise. As God enabled David to fulfill this messianic vocation, he was, in these ways, a prefiguration of Christ. Thus, reading about David in the book of Samuel is also instruction for us about

---

[58] Rare exceptions include Saul consulting the medium at Endor (1 Samuel 28) and Saul's death (1 Samuel 31).

[59] For a broad discussion of the biblical teachings of God's choosing or election, see FC SD XI, "Eternal Foreknowledge and Divine Election."

[60] מְשִׁיחַ יְהוָה, 1 Sam 24:7, 11 (ET 24:6, 10); 26:9, 11, 16, 23.

Christ. Even the ways in which David struggled and failed yet was brought to repentance and renewed faith teach us about the Christian life. Here we learn that Christ desires his people to trust him with their lives. We are instructed in repentance and in God's grace in Christ Jesus toward us sinners—God forgave David. We see God's favor toward all fallen humans in his choice of David as bearer of the messianic kingship culminating in Christ, who is not only King of Israel but also King of kings and Lord of all, who has opened the kingdom of grace to all people. We learn that Jesus earnestly desires that his people trust his Word and come to it for guidance in their lives as David did. We also are instructed by David's example to trust God's decisions as to what circumstances in this life will surround us and even beset us. By showing us how Yahweh interacted with David, the author of the book of Samuel is showing us Christ and his gracious heart. By telling us how David interacted with Yahweh, the author is telling us how we, like David, can rely on Christ to bless our lives and to patiently deal with us as sinners who daily need to repent of our sins.

Law and Gospel in Samuel[61]

The author of Samuel does not avoid depicting the aftereffects of transgressing God's Law. He points out the sins of every major character in the book (with the possible exception of the prophet Samuel). Most obvious of these are Eli's sin of not disciplining his sons (1 Sam 2:12–36; 3:11–14); Saul's repeated sin of lack of trust and confidence in God (1 Sam 13:1–15; 15:1–35); and David's sins, notably his adultery with Bathsheba (2 Sam 11:1–12:23) and his mistake in taking the census (2 Sam 24:1–25). All of these transgressions lead to consequences as God judges the sin and as the sinner sets into motion a chain of events triggered by his sins. Even David's repentance does not prevent an elaborate sequence of incidents that stem in some way from his adultery: the death of the child conceived with Bathsheba, the rape of Tamar, the murder of Amnon, and the rebellions of Absalom and Sheba. Clearly, the writer of Samuel wishes to demonstrate that sin often brings unintended and unanticipated consequences to the sinner and frequently to those around him. Even when the sinner repents and is forgiven and delivered from eternal death, the consequences of disobedience in this life are not ameliorated.

Another aspect of the Law that is highlighted is accountability, stressing the first use of the Law: God holds those whom he has placed in positions of authority especially accountable for their sins because their actions affect those whom they rule. Thus, Saul's decisions have dire consequences for all Israel. His failure of leadership, largely due to his lack of confidence in God, leads Israel astray and ultimately to defeat in battle against the Philistines. Because of Saul's sin, God punishes him with an evil spirit that vexes him (1 Sam 16:14–23; 18:10–11) and by giving the kingdom to young David (1 Sam 15:28; 16:1–13). Finally, Saul dies in battle as Israel is defeated by the Philistines (1 Sam 31:1–13).

---

[61] This section is adapted from Lessing and Steinmann, *Prepare the Way of the Lord*, 205–8.

It can be argued that Eli's poor supervision of his sons leads not only to their deaths but also to the capture of the ark by the Philistines (1 Sam 4:11) and a long, dark period in Israel's history (1 Sam 7:2) that ends only with Samuel's intervention (1 Sam 7:3–17). God held Eli accountable for his sin (1 Sam 3:11–14), and Eli's pitiable death (1 Sam 4:18) is an early step in God's holding him and his house liable.

Even David, the greatest of Israel's kings, is judged for his iniquitous actions. Because of his improprieties with Bathsheba, God humiliated him in the sight of all Israel (2 Sam 12:9–12; 16:20–22).

Despite the many sins of Israel and its leaders chronicled in Samuel, Yahweh continued to be merciful and gracious to his people—a frequent way in which the Gospel is proclaimed in Samuel. When Eli's leadership failed, Yahweh raised up Samuel to prophesy and to deliver Israel. When the people rejected God as their king and requested a human king to rule over them so that they could be like the other nations, God was patient and granted their request (1 Sam 8:7). Through David he blessed Israel with victory over all the surrounding nations and ushered in a period of extended peace.

Most important, God never forgot his ultimate gracious pledge to Israel—the messianic promise. Hope for this promise is evident in Hannah's prayer at the beginning of the book: "Yahweh will judge the ends of the earth. He will give strength to his King and lift up the horn of his Anointed One" (i.e., his Messiah or Christ; 1 Sam 2:10). The messianic promise given to David in 2 Samuel 7 is the focus of David's last words: "Because he has made an everlasting promise to me, with every detail arranged and secured" (2 Sam 23:5).

God's grace is especially evident because of his blessings on the lowly. Hannah is given a child, and God supports her through the loving words of her husband, Elkanah (1 Sam 1:23). The boy Samuel, a mere servant at the tabernacle, is called to be a prophet (1 Samuel 3). David, the youngest of Jesse's eight sons and a common shepherd boy, is chosen to be king (1 Sam 16:1–13).

This gracious blessing of the poor and humble is explicit in Hannah's prayer. By including her petition at the beginning of his work, the writer of Samuel is setting the tone for this theme in the rest of the book: "Yahweh kills and makes alive; he brings down to Sheol and brings up [again]" (1 Sam 2:6). In this way the book of Samuel points toward God's grace in Christ, who sacrificed himself for the sins of the world, but whom God made alive again for the saving of many that they might inherit a glorious throne in his eternal kingdom (2 Tim 2:11–12; cf. Rev 20:6).

From Hannah in 1 Samuel 2 to David's census in 2 Samuel 24, Yahweh frequently reverses what is expected and thereby shows the dynamic interplay of Law and Gospel. Consider these events: Hannah overcomes ridicule and barrenness (1 Samuel 1). The young man Samuel replaces Israel's supreme religious leaders, Eli and his wicked sons, Hophni and Phinehas (1 Samuel 3). Unbelieving Philistines gain a military victory over God's people because Israel is in such a woeful spiritual condition (1 Samuel 4). The idol of Dagon, the Philistines' God of grain who is credited with the triumph over the Israelites, falls flat on his face before Yahweh's ark (1 Samuel 5). Because of renewed trust in Yahweh, Israel defeats the Philistines who have a superior military (1 Samuel 7). Saul, a fearful man, becomes the first king in Israel (1 Samuel 9–11). Jonathan, Saul's son, is distinguished over his father in battle (1 Samuel 14). Israel's king Saul is embarrassed by Samuel, a mere prophet, who announces that Yahweh has taken the kingdom from Saul's hand (1 Samuel 15). David, the youngest son of Jesse, is anointed to serve as Israel's second king (1 Samuel 16). The shepherd boy David with just a sling and a stone is triumphant over the mighty armored Goliath (1 Samuel 17). Saul, the king of Israel and Yahweh's anointed one, dies and is mocked by the Philistines on Gilboa (1 Samuel 31). He is even beheaded (1 Sam 31:9).

This theme continues during David's reign: Michal, the powerful daughter of Saul, is sent away, never to have children (2 Samuel 6). Mephibosheth, the crippled son of Jonathan, is given a seat at King David's table (2 Samuel 9). Uriah, a Hittite soldier in the Israelite army, is more righteous than King David (2 Samuel 11). The prophet Nathan dares to condemn King David for his sin (2 Samuel 12). The wise woman from Tekoa knows more about the king's family troubles than he does (2 Samuel 14). Finally, David confesses that when God's people are in the dark, Yahweh will light their way (2 Sam 22:29). These reversals are all anticipated in Hannah's observation: "Yahweh makes poor and makes rich; he humbles, and he also elevates" (1 Sam 2:7).

This is not a new theme in the OT. Sarah (Gen 11:30), Rebekah (Gen 25:21), and Rachel (Gen 30:1) were all barren for a time after being married. They went on to become Israel's beloved matriarchs. Like Hannah (1 Sam 1:2), Leah was one of two wives, and though Leah initially was despised (Gen 29:23–31), she became an ancestress of the Messiah (Gen 29:35). The people of Israel, who had been slaves in Egypt, saw Pharaoh's army drowned while they escaped from his mud pits and straw bins (Ex 14:28). Moreover, in the NT Paul picks up this motif again: "God chose the foolish things of the world to shame the wise; God chose the weak things of the world to shame the strong. He chose the lowly things of this world and the despised things and the things that are not to nullify the things that are" (1 Cor 1:27–28). Christ crucified is a foolish stumbling block (1 Cor 1:23), but "God was pleased through the folly of preaching to save those who believe" (1 Cor 1:21).

This theme of reversal is most evident in Jesus and his ministry. He chose fishermen instead of Pharisees, sinners instead of Sadducees, and prostitutes instead of the princely line of Herod. Ultimately, Jesus wore thorns instead of silver and gold for a crown. His choices lead to torment and torture, darkness and death.

Jesus' work led to the greatest inversion of all. He rose and overturned death, replacing it with resurrection life. His ministry continued through his apostles, of whom some Jews in Thessalonica declared, "These men who have turned the world upside down have also come here" (Acts 17:6).[62]

Other Theological Themes in Samuel[63]

The book of Samuel is so large that it is difficult to speak of only a few other theological themes that characterize it. However, several stand out among the many that are found within this work.

Prosperity and Success Come Only from God

The book of Samuel repeatedly emphasizes that God provides prosperity and success by his grace alone and that when humans look to their own devices, they are turning their backs on God and will ultimately fail. This is seen first in the acts of Eli's sons, who corrupt the sacrifices and the priesthood (1 Sam 2:12–17), seeking to provide for themselves and satisfy their desires by their own efforts. Eli, who refused to discipline his sons (although he did rebuke them; 1 Sam 2:22–25), received a prophecy that he and his sons would die and the high priesthood would be taken away from his family (1 Sam 2:27–36).

Saul's initial success came from God's work in him (1 Sam 11:6). His ultimate failure also is ultimately tied to his rejection of God's Word. When God's displeasure over Saul's refusal to exterminate the Amalekites is announced by Samuel (1 Sam 15:1–31), the reader is being prepared for the fall of Saul's house that eventually leads to David's installation as king over Israel. It is because Yahweh was no longer with Saul that Saul would give way to David (1 Sam 16:14; 18:12). Saul's ultimate demise is prefixed by the condemnation of him for his unfaithfulness in consulting a medium rather than God (1 Samuel 28), again pointing out that without trust in God, Saul cannot succeed.

David was successful because "God was with him" (1 Sam 16:13, 18; 18:12, 14, 28; 2 Sam 5:10). Moreover, God remained with David, despite his sin with Bathsheba and against Uriah, as he confessed his sin and was forgiven (2 Sam 12:13). David specifically acknowledged his utter dependence on grace in his last words (2 Sam 23:1–7). Noting that when one rules with "the fear of God" (יִרְאַת אֱלֹהִים, 2 Sam 23:3)—that is, in a relationship characterized by divine favor and by one's repentance and trust in God—he brings prosperity to his people. This happened with David because God made it happen in his promise of an everlasting covenant (2 Sam 23:5; see the discussion of 2 Samuel 7 in "Christ in Samuel" above).

---

[62] The biblical theme of "reversal" or "inversion" is related to what Luther, in the German version of *The Freedom of a Christian*, called "the joyous exchange" (*der fröhlich Wechsel*, WA 7.25). See the translation of the Latin version of that work in AE 31:327–77 (see especially 31:351–52). See also, for example, AE 26:172–79, 276–91; 30:225; 31:297–99; 48:12–13; 51:316. Christ takes our sins on himself and in exchange gives us his own righteousness (2 Cor 5:21).

[63] This section is excerpted from Lessing and Steinmann, *Prepare the Way of the Lord*, 202–3.

Prophecy

The role of prophets and prophecy in Samuel is limited, but often noted at important junctures in the narrative. The culmination of Samuel's rise to prominence is marked by his acknowledgment as a "prophet" (נָבִיא, 1 Sam 3:20). God's choice of Saul as Israel's first king is confirmed by Saul's prophesying (the verb נָבָא, 1 Sam 10:10–13). God's covenant with David is announced by the prophet Nathan (2 Sam 7:1–17). The punishment on Israel for David's sin in connection with the census is announced by the prophet Gad (2 Sam 24:11–13). This eventually leads to God choosing Araunah's threshing floor as the site for an altar (2 Sam 24:18), which became the site of the temple in Jerusalem (2 Chr 3:1).

A prophet could also be called a "seer" (רֹאֶה, 1 Sam 9:9, 11, 18, 19; 2 Sam 15:27, or חֹזֶה, 2 Sam 24:11), presumably because prophets often received Yahweh's Word through a "vision" (חָזוֹן, 1 Sam 3:1; מַרְאָה, 1 Sam 3:15; חִזָּיוֹן, 2 Sam 7:17). In addition, prophesying could be manifested in ecstatic activities that involved music and dancing (1 Sam 10:5–13; 19:19–24). Because Saul engaged in such activities when God's Spirit came upon him, the question was raised whether Saul was among the prophets (1 Sam 10:11–12; 19:24).

Prophets mentioned by name in Samuel are Samuel (1 Sam 3:20), Nathan (2 Sam 7:2; 12:25), Gad (1 Sam 22:5; 2 Sam 24:11), and even the high priest Zadok (2 Sam 15:27). David also declares that his last words were a prophetic "oracle" (נְאֻם) and that God's Spirit spoke through him (2 Sam 23:1–2).

The Spirit of Yahweh

Closely associated in Samuel both with kings and their successes and prophets speaking God's Word is the divine "Spirit" (רוּחַ). The "Spirit of Yahweh" or the "Spirit of God" is mentioned thirteen times in Samuel.[64] Five of these are associated with prophesying (1 Sam 10:6, 10; 19:20, 23; 2 Sam 23:2) and three with the success or failure of kings (1 Sam 11:6; 16:13, 14). Clearly, God's work through both prophets and kings is carried out by his Spirit's presence in the lives of his people.

God also sent a harmful or tormenting spirit that served to hasten Saul's downfall and David's rise (1 Sam 16:14, 15, 16, 23; 18:10; 19:9). It is first described as "an evil spirit from Yahweh" (רוּחַ־רָעָה מֵאֵת יְהוָה, 1 Sam 16:14). Subsequently it is called "a spirit of/from God" (רוּחַ־אֱלֹהִים, 1 Sam 16:15, 16; 18:10) or "a spirit of/from Yahweh" (רוּחַ יְהוָה, 1 Sam 19:9) that is "evil" (רָעָה). In 1 Sam 16:23 it is introduced as "a spirit of/from God" (רוּחַ־אֱלֹהִים) and then designated "the spirit—the evil one" (רוּחַ הָרָעָה).

---

[64] 1 Sam 10:6, 10; 11:6; 16:13, 14, 15, 16, 23; 18:10; 19:9, 20, 23; 2 Sam 23:2.

The Text of Samuel

Samuel contains more text-critical problems than perhaps any other book of the OT. The LXX appears at times to have followed a different Hebrew text for the basis of its translation, and the writer of Chronicles, who incorporated large sections of Samuel into his work, also seems to have had a text that in some places had different readings than the current MT of Samuel.

The variations in the text of Samuel among the MT, the LXX, and other traditions have led to some extreme views of its textual history. Some critical scholars favor the LXX in nearly every place where it disagrees with the MT. At the other extreme, Tsumura seeks to defend the MT in almost every instance,[65] even when it appears to be hopelessly corrupt, that is, as the text was copied over the centuries some scribes inadvertently made mistakes such as omitting or misspelling words. Perhaps the best approach is to weigh each case of textual variation in its own context and make decisions according to which variant best explains the rise of the others. The textual decisions reflected in this commentary are explained in the textual notes. In cases where it is difficult to choose among the variant readings in the ancient witnesses, the translation will reflect the text-critical decisions of the present author, and the options will be explained in the textual notes. Not all variants among the MT, the LXX, and the various Qumran manuscripts are discussed in the textual notes, especially where the LXX differs from the MT but the LXX is judged to be semantically equivalent or clearly inferior. In such cases the translation will follow the MT. However, all of the major variants are discussed, and at times less important variants are noted (e.g., where the MT has one divine name and the LXX or a Qumran manuscript has an alternate divine name; see, e.g., the textual notes on 23:14, 16).

The Masoretic Text

The MT of Samuel for the most part presents a coherent and understandable narrative of the end of the period of the judges and the reigns of Saul and David. However, there are a number of places where the text appears to have suffered in transmission. The following are some examples.

1 Sam 14:41 is much longer (and more understandable) in the LXX than the same verse in the MT and may indicate that the MT became corrupted by some form of paralepsis (eye skip):

וַיֹּאמֶר שָׁאוּל אֶל־יְהוָה אֱלֹהֵי יִשְׂרָאֵל הָבָה תָמִים
וַיִּלָּכֵד יוֹנָתָן וְשָׁאוּל וְהָעָם יָצָאוּ׃

Saul said to Yahweh, "God of Israel, give complete." Jonathan and Saul were chosen, and Israel was exonerated. (MT 1 Sam 14:41)

καὶ εἶπεν Σαουλ κύριε ὁ θεὸς Ισραηλ, τί ὅτι οὐκ ἀπεκρίθης τῷ δούλῳ σου σήμερον; εἰ ἐν ἐμοὶ ἢ ἐν Ιωναθαν τῷ υἱῷ μου ἡ ἀδικία, κύριε ὁ θεὸς Ισραηλ,

---

δὸς δήλους· καὶ ἐὰν τάδε εἴπῃς ἐν τῷ λαῷ σου Ισραηλ, δὸς δὴ ὁσιότητα. καὶ κληροῦται Ιωναθαν καὶ Σαουλ, καὶ ὁ λαὸς ἐξῆλθεν.

And Saul said, "Lord God of Israel, why didn't you answer your servant today? If this sin is in me or in my son Jonathan, Lord God of Israel, give Urim. But if you say this, [that the sin is] in your people Israel, give Thummim." Jonathan and Saul were chosen, and the people were exonerated. (LXX 1 Sam 14:41)

1 Chr 21:16 reports that David saw Yahweh's messenger standing over Jerusalem, "and his sword was drawn in his hand" (וְחַרְבּוֹ שְׁלוּפָה בְּיָדוֹ). This notice is missing from 2 Sam 24:16, but is included in 4QSamᵃ, a manuscript that generally supports the MT readings, which may indicate that the MT is deficient in 2 Sam 24:16.

Several other important passages appear to have been damaged in the process of copying and transmitting the book of Samuel. For instance, 1 Sam 13:1 contains this information on Saul and his reign: "Saul was ... years old when he became king. He ruled ... and two years over Israel." Unfortunately, neither the MT nor the LXX, nor any of the other versions, preserves the numbers that apparently have been lost from this verse.

Other passages show signs that they may have been damaged due to scribal mistakes, especially when a scribe's eye may have skipped from a word in one line of text to an identical or similar word in a following line. In addition to 1 Sam 14:41, discussed above, another example is in 1 Sam 10:27, immediately before 1 Sam 11:1, which introduces the account of the Ammonite king Nahash's attack on Jabesh-gilead. The MT, though understandable, is somewhat laconic. However, both 4QSamᵃ and Josephus in book 6 of his *Antiquities of the Jews*[66] include a longer reading that explains Nahash's activity in Israelite territory east of the Jordan River. One possible explanation is that the longer reading was omitted when a scribe's eye skipped from a word in one line to the identical word in a subsequent line, thereby inadvertently shortening the text.[67] However, another explanation is that the additional text in 4QSamᵃ and Josephus is a later expansion of the shorter original text. Since expansions are known to have crept into the text of Samuel and since parablepsis (eye skip) appears to have occurred frequently in the MT of Samuel, cases such as this are difficult to adjudicate. (For a detailed discussion, see the first textual note on 1 Sam 10:27b.)

It ought to be noted that the versification of the MT of Samuel differs in several places from that found in English Bibles (whose versification is based on the LXX). These differences are shown in figure 9.

---

[66] Josephus, *Antiquities*, 6.66–72.

[67] Cross, "The Ammonite Oppression of the Tribes of Gad and Reuben: Missing Verses from 1 Samuel 11 Found in 4QSamuelᵃ," 153.

Figure 9

English and Hebrew Versification Differences in Samuel

English	Hebrew
1 Sam 20:4b (last clause)	1 Sam 21:1
1 Sam 21:1–15	1 Sam 21:2–16
1 Sam 23:29	1 Sam 24:1
1 Sam 24:1–22	1 Sam 24:2–23
2 Sam 18:33	2 Sam 19:1
2 Sam 19:1–43	2 Sam 19:2–44

The Septuagint

In the LXX the book of Samuel is divided into two books: 1 Kingdoms (= 1 Samuel in English Bibles) and 2 Kingdoms (= 2 Samuel in English Bibles).[68] Caution must be exercised in the use of the LXX when making text-critical decisions. It has long been recognized that the surviving LXX text of Samuel derives from two different translations, usually called the Old Greek and the Kaige versions.

The Old Greek[69]

In the LXX, 1 Kingdoms and 2 Kingdoms 1:1–11:1 are preserved in the Old Greek translation of Samuel. It tends to adhere closely to the word order of the Hebrew text that underlies it, but the grammar and syntax are clearly that of Koine Greek. This translation frequently transliterates Hebrew proper nouns and sometimes even common nouns. In addition, LXX 2 Kingdoms 1:1–11:1 shows some evidence of a reviser's work. One interesting translation feature of the Old Greek of Samuel is that it rather consistently translates the Hebrew פְּלִשְׁתִּי and פְּלִשְׁתִּים, "Philistine(s)," as ὁ ἀλλόφυλος and οἱ ἀλλόφυλοι, "foreigner(s)." The Old Greek also omits a number of verses found in the MT. For instance, the MT verses 1 Sam 13:1; 17:12–31; 18:1–5, 10–11, 17–19; 23:12 are not present in LXX 1 Kingdoms. The most significant of these omissions are the ones that present a considerably shorter version of the encounter between David and Goliath in 1 Samuel 17–18. Scholars have debated whether the longer MT or the shorter LXX version represents the original text of the David and Goliath account.[70] (For a detailed discussion of the text of 1 Samuel 17–18, see "The Text of 1 Samuel 17:1–18:30" at the beginning of the textual notes on 1 Sam 17:1–58.)

---

[68] 1 Kings in English Bibles = LXX 3 Kingdoms; 2 Kings in English Bibles = LXX 4 Kingdoms.

[69] For a more detailed discussion, see Taylor, "The Old Greek Text of Reigns."

[70] For a summary of the various scholars on each side of the debate, see Johnson, "Reconsidering 4QSam^a and the Textual Support for the Long and Short Versions of the David and Goliath Story," 534–35.

The Kaige Recension[71]

The name Kaige derives from this Greek translation's tendency to render the frequent Hebrew combination וְגַם, "and also," as καί γε, *kai ge*. Scholars usually hold that LXX 2 Kingdoms 11:2–24:25 is from the Kaige recension. The Old Greek tends to be a more dynamic, idiomatic translation, at least in its Greek syntax, whereas the Kaige recension is more of a formal correspondence (word-by-word) translation, which yielded much more awkward Greek.

While the Kaige portion of LXX 2 Kingdoms appears to be a revision that sought to bring an earlier Greek translation in line with a text very similar to the MT text of 2 Samuel, there are places where it differs from the MT, sometimes agreeing with the Hebrew text found in 4QSam[a].

LXX 1–2 Kingdoms and Textual Criticism of the Book of Samuel

Given that the current LXX text of Samuel is drawn from two different versions, one has to take into consideration two different sets of translation characteristics when considering the LXX of 1–2 Kingdoms for text-critical purposes. In addition, one cannot always assume that a variant reading in the LXX compared to the MT indicates a different Hebrew text underlying the Greek version, although—as Qumran manuscript 4QSam[a] demonstrates—this may often be the case.

Currently there is no critical edition of LXX 1–2 Kingdoms in the Göttingen series.[72] The older Cambridge Septuagint is the only critical edition available.[73] The most commonly used edition is the *Septauginta* of Rahlfs.[74] In this edition the versification of the LXX has been aligned with that of the MT.

Samuel Manuscripts from Qumran

The ancient manuscripts from Qumran appear to confirm that there were variant Hebrew manuscript traditions for Samuel. Fragments of four scrolls were found in Caves 1 and 4 at Qumran. At times 4QSam[a] (4Q51) supports readings found in the LXX and in Chronicles. At other times it agrees with the MT against the LXX. In addition, Johnson argues that 4QSam[a] supports the longer version of the David and Goliath account in 1 Samuel 17–18.[75] Overall, 4QSam[a] appears to be a conscious combination of the textual traditions behind both the MT and the LXX.[76]

---

[71] For a more detailed discussion, see McLean, "The Kaige Text of Reigns."

[72] *Septuaginta: Vetus Testamentum Graecum Auctoritate Academiae Scientiarum Gottingensis editum* (Göttingen: Vandenhoeck & Ruprecht, 1931–).

[73] Brooke et al., *The Old Testament in Greek*, vol. 2: *The Later Historical Books*, part 1: *1 and 2 Samuel*.

[74] Alfred Rahlfs, ed., *Septuaginta* (2 vols.; Stuttgart: Deutsche Bibelgesellschaft, 1935, 1979).

[75] Johnson, "Reconsidering 4QSam[a] and the Textual Support for the Long and Short Versions of the David and Goliath Story."

[76] See the discussion in Aejmelaeus, "Hannah's Psalm in 4QSam[a]," 36–37.

In contrast, 4QSam[b] (4Q52), 4QSam[c] (4Q53), and 1QSam (1Q7) generally follow the types of readings found in the MT.[77] In addition, there is another related work often called *The Vision of Samuel* or *The Samuel Apocryphon* (4Q160),[78] which apparently incorporates a quotation of 1 Sam 3:14–18 that sometimes agrees with the MT and sometimes with the LXX, but also contains variants not found in any other tradition.[79] It has been suggested that the non-aligned variants in 4Q160 may be purposeful modifications of 1 Samuel 3 for incorporation into *The Vision of Samuel*. For the contents of the Qumran Samuel manuscripts, see figure 10.

---

[77] For the text of 4QSam[a–c], see Cross et al., *Qumran Cave 4.XII*; for 1QSam, see Barthélemy and Milik, *Qumran Cave 1*, 64 and plate 11.

[78] For the text, see Allegro, *Qumran Cave 4.I*, 9–11 and plate 3.

[79] Jassen, "Literary and Historical Studies in the Samuel Apocryphon (4Q160)," 24–25. Jassen (35) notes that John Allegro, who first worked on 4Q160, called it *The Vision of Samuel*. However, Jassen believes that to be a misnomer and prefers the title first suggested by Geza Vermes: *The Samuel Apocryphon*. Jassen (35, n. 61) cites Geza Vermes in Schürer, *The History of the Jewish People in the Age of Jesus Christ*, 3/1:335, and Geza Vermes, trans. and ed., *The Complete Dead Sea Scrolls in English* (New York: Penguin, 2004), 587.

Figure 10

Contents of the Qumran Samuel Manuscripts

1QSam (1Q7)

1 Sam 18:17–18

2 Sam 20:6–10

2 Sam 21:16–18

2 Sam 23:9–12

4QSam^a (4Q51)

1 Sam 1:9, 11–13, 17–18, 22–28

1 Sam 2:1–10, 16–36

1 Sam 3:1–4, 18–21

1 Sam 4:3–4, 9–10, 12

1 Sam 5:8–12

1 Sam 6:1–13, 16–18, 20–21

1 Sam 7:1

1 Sam 8:7, 9–14, 16–20

1 Sam 9:6–8, 10–12, 16–24

1 Sam 10:3–12, 14, 16, 18, 24–27

1 Sam 11:1–2, 7–12

1 Sam 12:7–8, 10–19

1 Sam 14:24–25, 28–34, 47–51

1 Sam 15:20–21, 24–32

1 Sam 17:3–8, 40–41

1 Sam 18:4–5

1 Sam 20:37–40

1 Sam 22:10–11

1 Sam 24:3–5; 8–10; 14–23

1 Sam 25:3–12, 20–21, 25–27, 38–40

1 Sam 26:9–12, 21–24

1 Sam 27:1–2, 8–12

1 Sam 28:1–3, 22–25

1 Sam 29:1

1 Sam 30:22–31

1 Sam 31:1–4

2 Sam 1:4–5, 10–13

2 Sam 2:5–16, 25–32

2 Sam 3:1–15, 17, 21, 23–39

2 Sam 4:1–4, 9–12

2 Sam 5:1–3, 6–16, 18–19

2 Sam 6:2–18

2 Sam 7:6–7, 22–29

2 Sam 8:1–8

2 Sam 9:8–10

2 Sam 10:4–7, 18–19

2 Sam 11:2–12, 15–20

2 Sam 12:1, 3–5, 8–9, 13–20, 29–31

2 Sam 13:1–6, 13–34, 36–39

2 Sam 14:1–3, 14, 18–19, 33

2 Sam 15:1–7, 20–21, 23, 26–31, 37

2 Sam 16:1–2, 6–8, 10–13, 17–18, 20–22

2 Sam 17:2–3, 23–25, 29

2 Sam 18:1–11, 28–29

2 Sam 19:6–12, 14–16, 25, 27–29, 38

2 Sam 20:1–2, 4, 9–14, 19, 21–25

2 Sam 21:3–6, 8–9, 12, 15–17

2 Sam 22:17, 19, 21, 24, 26–28, 30–51

2 Sam 23:1–6, 14–16, 21–22, 38–39

2 Sam 24:16–22

4QSam^b (4Q52)

1 Sam 12:3, 5–6

1 Sam 14:41–42

1 Sam 15:17–18

1 Sam 16:1–11

1 Sam 19:10–13, 15–17

1 Sam 20:26–42

1 Sam 21:1–3, 5–10

1 Sam 22:8–9

1 Sam 23:8–23

4QSam^c (4Q53)

1 Sam 25:30–32

2 Sam 14:7–33

2 Sam 15:1–15

4Q160

1 Sam 3:14–18 (as a quotation)

This Commentary's Translation Technique

The Italians have a saying: *traduttore traditore*, "a translator is a traitor." This clever wordplay highlights the fact that a translation is always an approximation. Features of a text in the source language (e.g., the Hebrew OT) such as word order, idioms, wordplay, and sentence length often do not survive in the target language (English) of a good, readable translation. This often bothers biblical scholars, since in reading the source text they can see elements that are interesting and enlightening for understanding the message of the inspired ancient authors. For this reason, some translations in commentaries seek to preserve source language features and end up deforming the target language. This produces not so much a translation as a pidgin text that would have never flowed from the lips or out of the pen of a native user of the target language. Such pidgin texts expect readers to read in the target language but to understand the words as if they are in the argot of the source language. But this is self-defeating, since if one can read the source language, such a translation is not needed. On the other hand, if readers have little or no facility in the source language, to expect them to assign the source language function to the words in the target language is to expect what they are incapable of doing. In addition, a pidgin translation introduces other problems: It often makes the translation harder for its readers to understand than the original text was for its original intended audience. It can lead readers to wrong conclusions about the message of the text, since they are overlaying target-language meanings when the translator expects them to assign source-language connotations instead. A pidgin translation is a traitor to the target language out of an unnecessarily slavish affection for the modes of expression native to the source language.

In this commentary the translation attempts to bring the meaning of the Hebrew text of Samuel to readers in actual, living, contemporary English, while betraying the Hebrew as little as possible. This means that the translation not only presents English *words* that are the approximation of Hebrew words but also presents natural English *expressions and idioms* that convey the meaning accurately in natural English idiom. Thus, the translation presented here eschews a misguided, wooden, formal correspondence, a word-for-word mode of translation. Many times the transformations from Hebrew idiom to English expression are discussed in the textual notes. At other times they are not, and someone following with a Hebrew text is expected to understand the calculus of bringing the message into English. In short, this means that I have endeavored not only to translate the *words* but also to take Hebrew *constructions* and render them with corresponding English constructions as much as possible. Perhaps some readers will judge that I have been a traitor to the source language. However, I would argue that if I have rendered the *meaning* of the text correctly in contemporary English, I have minimized as much as possible the traitorous tendencies inherent in any attempt at translation.

For the sake of the Gospel, the Scriptures need to be heard (Rom 10:17). The best way for them to be heard in any language is for them to be rendered so as to speak that language in a way that—as much as possible—approximates what actual users of that language would say or write to convey the meaning intended by the inspired human authors God used to communicate his saving Word of Law and Gospel.

1 Samuel 1:1–8:22

Israel without a King

1:1–2:11   **Samuel Is Dedicated to God's Service**

1:1–20   The First Trip to Shiloh: Hannah Asks Yahweh
                for a Son

1:21–28   The Second Trip to Shiloh: Samuel Is Given to Yahweh

Excursus   *Polygamy in the Bible*

2:1–11   Hannah's Prayer

2:12–36   **The Unfaithful Sons of Eli Contrasted
                to Samuel**

2:12–17   Eli's Sons and Their Sins

2:18–21   Samuel Ministers before Yahweh

2:22–26   Eli Rebukes His Sons

2:27–36   A Prophecy against Eli's House

3:1–21   **Yahweh Calls Samuel to Be a Prophet**

Excursus   *The Prophet Samuel in Scripture*

4:1–7:1   **Israel's Struggle with the Philistines**

4:1–11   The Philistines Capture the Ark of the Covenant

4:12–22   The Death of Eli and the Birth of Ichabod

5:1–12   Yahweh Judges the Philistines and Their God Dagon

6:1–7:1   The Ark Is Returned to Israel

7:2–17   **Samuel's Ministry as Judge: God
                Delivers Israel from the Philistines**

8:1–22   **Israel Demands That Samuel Appoint
                a King**

The First Trip to Shiloh: Hannah Asks Yahweh for a Son

Translation

1 ¹There was a man from Ramathaim, a Zuphite, from the hill country of Ephraim. His name was Elkanah the son of Jeroham, the son of Elihu, the son of Tohu, the son of Zuph, a man from Ephraim. ²He had two wives. The name of one was Hannah, and the name of the second was Peninnah. Now Peninnah had children, but Hannah had no children. ³That man would go up from his city every year to worship and to sacrifice to Yahweh of armies at Shiloh. The two sons of Eli, Hophni and Phinehas, priests of Yahweh, were there.

⁴One day Elkanah sacrificed and gave portions to Peninnah his wife and to all her sons and her daughters. ⁵But he gave an expensive portion to Hannah because he loved Hannah even though Yahweh had closed her womb. ⁶Her rival would make her especially aggravated in order to make her depressed because Yahweh had closed her womb. ⁷This would happen every year whenever she went up to Yahweh's house: she would aggravate her this way, and she would weep and not eat. ⁸Elkanah, her husband, said to her, "Hannah, why are you crying, and why won't you eat? Why are you in a bad mood? Aren't I better for you than ten sons?"

⁹Hannah got up after [he had] eaten in Shiloh and after [he had] drunk, and the high priest Eli was sitting on the chair beside the doorpost of Yahweh's temple. ¹⁰She was distressed, and she prayed to Yahweh and began to weep bitterly. ¹¹She made a vow and said, "Yahweh of armies, if you will certainly see the affliction of your servant and remember and not forget your servant and give your servant a child, I will give him to Yahweh all the days of his life and a razor will never be used on his head." ¹²As Hannah prayed much before Yahweh, Eli was watching her mouth. ¹³And Hannah was praying silently. Only her lips were moving, but her voice was not heard, so Eli concluded that she was drunk.

¹⁴Eli said to her, "How long will you stay drunk? Get rid of your wine."

¹⁵Hannah answered, "No, sir. I am a discouraged woman. I have drunk no wine or beer, but I am pouring out my soul to Yahweh. ¹⁶Do not take your servant to be a good-for-nothing woman. Rather, I have been speaking out of my great anguish and aggravation."

¹⁷Eli replied, "Go in peace. May the God of Israel grant your request that you have asked from him."

¹⁸She said, "May your slave girl find favor in your eyes."

So the woman went on her way. She ate and no longer looked dejected.

¹⁹They got up in the morning and worshiped before Yahweh. Then they returned to their home in Ramah. Elkanah made love to Hannah his wife, and

**Yahweh remembered her. ²⁰After some time Hannah became pregnant and bore
a son. She called his name Samuel, because "I asked Yahweh for him."**

Textual Notes

1:1 וַיְהִי אִישׁ אֶחָד—Samuel is one of several books that begin with the verb וַיְהִי.[1]
The opening three words, literally "and there was one man" (the preterite[2] [imperfect
with *waw* consecutive] of הָיָה), appear elsewhere in the OT only in Judg 13:2, although
the first two words occur more often.[3] The masculine numeral אֶחָד, "one," serves as
an indefinite article, "*a* man" (Joüon, § 137 u; Waltke-O'Connor, § 13.8a, example 5).

מִן־הָרָמָתַיִם—The place-name "Ramathaim" is elsewhere simply called Ramah
(הָרָמָה), which means "the height." Hebrew always includes the article (הָ-) unless it
is compounded with another place-name, such as Ramath-mizpeh (רָמַת הַמִּצְפֶּה, Josh
13:26). Here, the dual form רָמָתַיִם with the article הָ-, literally "the two heights," is perhaps referring to two parts of the city, an upper and lower city, or two hills encompassed
by the city. There were several other cities in Israel with the name Ramah: a city in the
territory of Naphtali (Josh 19:36); a city on the border of Asher's territory (Josh 19:29);
a city in the territory of Benjamin near Rachel's tomb;[4] a city in Judah called Ramah
of the Negev (Josh 19:8), possibly the same place as Ramoth of the Negev (1 Sam
30:27). Ramah is also a shortened name for a city in Gilead usually called Ramoth-
gilead (compare 2 Ki 8:28 [∥ 2 Chr 22:5] with 2 Ki 8:29 [∥ 2 Chr 22:6]; see also, e.g.,
1 Ki 4:13; 22:3–4) or Ramoth in Gilead (Deut 4:43; Josh 20:8; 21:38; 1 Chr 6:65 [ET
6:80]). Elkanah's city may be the one later called Arimathea (Mt 27:57; Mk 15:43; Lk
23:50–51; Jn 19:38), called Rempthis by Eusebius,[5] and probably the modern village
of Rentis, about fifteen miles (twenty-four kilometers) east of Tel Aviv. This would
place it on the edge of the Ephraimite highlands.[6] If this is the case, then the Kohathites
descended from Zuph (see the next textual note) probably moved from one of the four
original Levitical cities in Ephraim—Shechem, Gezer, Kibzaim/Jokmeam, and Beth-
horon (Josh 21:20–22; 1 Chr 6:51–54 [ET 6:66–69]). 1 Chr 6:54 (ET 6:69) appears
to indicate that the Kohathites in Ephraim grew and spread out, since it includes two
Kohathite cities outside of Ephraim mentioned in Joshua's original allotment: Aijalon
and Gath-rimmon in the tribe of Dan (cf. Josh 21:23–24).

צוֹפִים מֵהַר אֶפְרָיִם—The translation "a Zuphite" assumes the reading צוּפִי, with
the final ם on צוֹפִים being a dittograph of the מ representing the preposition מִן, "from,"

---

[1] Joshua, Judges, 1 Samuel, 2 Samuel, Ruth, Esther, and Nehemiah are listed as beginning this
way in Joüon, § 118 c, note 2. For the sequence of imperfect and perfect verbs in 1 Sam 1:1–8,
see Waltke-O'Connor, § 33.2.1c, example 9; § 33.2.4b; § 33.3.4b, example 1.

[2] For "preterite," see *IBH*, § 52.

[3] See וַיְהִי אִישׁ in Gen 39:2; Judg 17:1; 19:1; 1 Sam 9:1; 2 Sam 21:20; 1 Chr 20:6. Num 9:6
has the plural אֲנָשִׁים. Job opens with a comparable construction, but with הָיָה in the perfect,
אִישׁ הָיָה, "there was a man" (Job 1:1).

[4] Josh 18:25; Judg 4:5; 19:13; 1 Ki 15:17; Is 10:29; Jer 31:15; Ezra 2:26; Neh 7:30; 2 Chr 16:5.

[5] Eusebius, *Onomasticon* (GCS 11/1.32.21–23, 144.27–29; cf. Jerome, *De situ et nominibus*
[PL 23:875]).

[6] Meyers, "An Ethnoarchaelogical Analysis of Hannah's Sacrifice," 86.

on מֵהַר, "from the hill country of" Ephraim. This reading is also indicated by the LXX (Σιφα; cf. NIV). The end of this verse states that Elkanah was a descendant of צוּף, "Zuph" (1 Sam 1:1; see also 1 Chr 6:10–12 [ET 6:25–27]; Zuph is called Zophai in 1 Chr 6:11 [ET 6:26]). Alternately, the MT could be read as it stands as "Ramathaim of the Zuphites," which still implies that Elkanah was a Zuphite.

אֱלִיהוּא—"Elihu" is called אֱלִיאָב, "Eliab," in 1 Chr 6:12 (ET 6:27) and אֱלִיאֵל, "Eliel," in 1 Chr 6:19 (ET 6:34). Both Elihu[7] and Eliab[8] are common names in the OT, and the name in either 1 Sam 1:1 or 1 Chr 6:12 (ET 6:27) may be a scribal mistake of substituting one of these common names for the other. The name אֱלִיאֵל, "Eliel," in 1 Chr 6:19 (ET 6:34) may have been a mistake for אֱלִיאָב, "Eliab," which differs only in the last consonant of the name.

תֹּחוּ—"Tohu" is נַחַת, "Nahath," in 1 Chr 6:11 (ET 6:26) and תּוֹחַ, "Toah," in 1 Chr 6:19 (ET 6:34). Toah and Tohu are unique in the OT, but seem to be related. There may have been an accidental scribal metathesis of the letters ח and ו. The name Nahath occurs also in Gen 36:13, 17; 1 Chr 1:37; 2 Chr 31:13. It is impossible to determine which of these three is original and which two may be scribal errors.

צוּף—"Zuph" (also in 1 Sam 9:5; 1 Chr 6:20 [ET 6:35]) is צוֹפַי, "Zophai," in 1 Chr 6:11 (ET 6:26).

אֶפְרָתִי:—This gentilic noun, "a man from Ephraim," indicates either an association with the tribe of Ephraim (אֶפְרַיִם, e.g., Num 1:32–33)[9] or with the Judahite clan of Ephrath that settled in and around Bethlehem and gave that city its alternate name "Ephrathah" (Micah 5:1 [ET 5:2]; Ps 132:6; Ruth 4:11; 1 Chr 2:50; 4:4).[10] Elkanah was not a member of either the tribe of Judah or the tribe of Ephraim, but was actually a Levite from the clan of Kohath (1 Chr 6:7–12 [ET 6:22–27]) and the family of Zuph, which had settled in the territory of Ephraim (cf. 1 Sam 9:5).

1:2 וְלוֹ שְׁתֵּי נָשִׁים—Literally "to him [were] two wives." The preposition לְ is used in the sense of possession: *he had two wives* (BDB, s.v. לְ, 5 b *a*). לְ recurs in this sense twice more in this verse, each time translated with the verb "had."

שֵׁם אַחַת חַנָּה וְשֵׁם הַשֵּׁנִית פְּנִנָּה—The first clause is literally "name of one, Hannah." The numeral "one" (feminine: אַחַת; anarthrous, GKC, § 134 l) is often used in place of the ordinal "first" (feminine: רִאשֹׁנָה) when there are a small number of countables (Waltke-O'Connor, § 15.2.1b). Since the next clause uses an ordinal to call Peninnah "second" (feminine: שֵׁנִית), the sense is that Hannah was Elkanah's "first" wife.

וַיְהִי לִפְנִנָּה יְלָדִים—The subject is masculine plural, יְלָדִים, "children," but the common singular form of the verb is used: וַיְהִי, "(he) was" (GKC, § 145 o (a)).

---

[7] Also Job 32:2, 5–6; 34:1; 36:1; 1 Chr 12:21 (ET 12:20).

[8] Also Num 1:9; 2:7; 7:24, 29; 10:16; 16:1, 12; 26:8–9; Deut 11:6; 1 Sam 16:6; 17:13, 28; 1 Chr 2:13; 12:10 (ET 12:9); 15:18, 20; 16:5; 2 Chr 11:18.

[9] אֶפְרָתִי means "a man from the tribe of Ephraim" in Judg 12:5; 1 Ki 11:26.

[10] That is the meaning of אֶפְרָתִי, "Ephrathite," in 1 Sam 17:12; Ruth 1:2. When the word is used in this sense, it denotes a descendant of Caleb's wife Ephrath (1 Chr 2:19). In 1 Chr 2:50; 4:4 "the firstborn of Ephrathah" probably denotes the first person in this clan to settle (or perhaps to be born) in Judahite Bethlehem.

1:3 וְעָלָה֩—A perfect with *waw* consecutive can denote repeated past action, "would go up" (see Joüon, § 119 v), as can an imperfect without *waw* (see the first and third textual notes on 1:7).

מִיָּמִים ׀ יָמִ֫ימָה—Literally this means "from days to days." The repetition of a noun can form a distributive idiom (GKC, § 123 c); the idiom here also has the preposition מִן on the first word and a directional *he* on the second (for the directional *he*, see *IBH*, § 18 D). This idiom means "yearly" or "every year." It occurs also in Ex 13:10; Judg 11:40; 21:19; 1 Sam 2:19. Cf. שָׁנָ֥ה בְשָׁנָֽה in the second textual note on 1:7.

לְהִשְׁתַּחֲוֺת—The preposition לְ with the infinitive construct expresses purpose (Joüon, § 124 l): he traveled to Shiloh "to worship." The verb חָוָה, "bow down (in worship)," occurs only in the Hishtaphel conjugation, a conjugation not used for any other verb but attested also in Ugaritic (see Joüon, §§ 59 g; 79 t; cf. Waltke-O'Connor, § 21.2.3d). It first prefixes -שׁ (as in the Shaphel conjugation) and then prefixes -הִתְ (as in the Hithpael conjugation), which would make -הִתְשׁ, but the consonants -תְשׁ- interchange by metathesis,[11] thus -הִשְׁתְּ. The ending -וֺת is regular for the infinitive construct of third-ה verbs (GKC, § 75 c; Joüon, § 79 f). In Samuel forms of this Hishtaphel verb appear in 1 Sam 1:3, 19, 28; 2:36; 15:25, 30, 31; 20:41; 24:9 (ET 24:8); 25:23, 41; 28:14; 2 Sam 1:2; 9:6, 8; 12:20; 14:4, 22, 33; 15:5, 32; 16:4; 18:21, 28; 24:20.

לַיהוָ֣ה צְבָא֗וֹת—"Yahweh of armies" is traditionally translated as "the LORD of hosts." The noun צָבָא denotes an "army." The English word "host" denoting an army derives from the Latin *hostis*, "stranger, enemy."[12] In military contexts "armies" in "Yahweh of armies" can refer to Israel's army (1 Sam 17:45). The noun צָבָא is often used for the army of Israel or for an enemy army (e.g., 1 Sam 12:9; 14:50; 17:55). In this phrase with יהוה, the noun צָבָא is always used in the plural, צְבָאוֹת. The plural is never clearly explained in the OT, but 1 Sam 17:45 indicates its military significance by using another plural in parallel to it: David refers to "Yahweh of armies, the God of the battle lines of Israel" (יְהוָה צְבָא֗וֹת אֱלֹהֵ֛י מַעַרְכ֥וֹת יִשְׂרָאֵֽל). The plural may denote that Yahweh commands a heavenly army (the angels; see BDB, s.v. צָבָא, 1 b; cf. 2 Ki 6:17) as well as an earthly one (Israel's army). The stars and other heavenly bodies can also be called an "army" (Gen 2:1; Is 40:26; 45:12; BDB, 1 c). In that case, it probably refers to the apparent regimented alignment of the stars like the alignment of soldiers in the army's ranks (i.e., the stars are grouped in constellations where each has its specific place and each appears in the sky in the proper season; see Gen 1:14).

1:4 וַיְהִ֣י הַיּ֔וֹם—This expression means "one day" (Waltke-O'Connor, § 13.5.1e, example 19). Some English versions translate it as "whenever" (HCSB, GW), probably in

---

[11] Similarly, when the first root letter of a verb is a sibilant, in the Hithpael conjugation that letter is transposed with the *taw* of the prefix.

[12] The English word "host" denoting someone who entertains guests derives from the Latin stem *hospit-*, "host, guest, stranger," while the English word "host" denoting the bread in the Lord's Supper derives from the late Latin *hostia*, "eucharistic wafer" (from Latin "victim, sacrifice").

anticipation of 1:7. However, this construction always refers to a specific day.[13] In this case it was the day when her rival began to taunt her (1:6).

1:5 מָנָה אַחַת אַפָּיִם—"Expensive portion" is literally "one portion, a pim's worth." The translation here follows the suggestion of Auerbach, who believes that אַפָּיִם is derived from the unit of weight פִּים, "pim," with a prosthetic *aleph*.[14] A pim was equal to two-thirds of a shekel (1 Sam 13:21). אַפָּיִם would then indicate a portion worth two-thirds of a shekel, an exceptionally large portion.[15] This expression is often understood to be an idiom ("a portion, one of face") meaning that Hannah received a double-size portion.[16] This interpretation takes אַפָּיִם to be the dual form of אַף, "nose," since the dual form אַפָּיִם is used some forty times in the OT to denote a "face."[17] However, the supposition that "face" can mean "double-size" is far from established, and it is not supported by the LXX here, which simply reads μερίδα μίαν, "one portion." Some have proposed emending the word אַפָּיִם to אֶפֶס, "however,"[18] but that emendation lacks textual support from Hebrew manuscripts or the versions.

וַיהוָה סָגַר רַחְמָהּ—Here the verb סָגַר, "to shut, close," takes a direct object with a feminine suffix, רַחְמָהּ, "her womb." Compare the fourth textual note on 1:6.

1:6 וְכִעֲסַתָּה ... גַּם־כַּעַס—The combination of the verb and its cognate noun is rendered as "(she) would make her especially aggravated." The form of the verb כָּעַס (Qal [G]: "be vexed, angry") is Piel (D) perfect third feminine singular with third feminine singular pronominal suffix (GKC, § 59 g). The *waw* consecutive form expresses repeated, habitual action, "would provoke her" or "was in the habit of provoking her," while the D stem signifies placing Hannah into a mood, not simply stirring up a passing emotion. (See Deut 32:21 for the only other occurrence of the D stem for this verb; its Hiphil [H] is common.) Hannah's mood is highlighted by the cognate noun כַּעַס, "aggravation," preceded by גַּם: "would aggravate her also with aggravation," that is, "would make her especially aggravated."

צָרָתָהּ—"Her rival" translates the feminine abstract noun צָרָה, "enmity" (*HALOT*, s.v. צָרָה II, B), with a feminine suffix. This noun is often associated with persecution by enemies (Pss 54:9 [ET 54:7]; 138:7; 143:11). However, here and in Sirach 37:11 it denotes a second wife who is a "rival" (cf. *HALOT*, s.v. צָרָה II, A) for a husband's attention.

בַּעֲבוּר הַרְעִמָהּ—When בַּעֲבוּר (בְּ + עֲבוּר) is used as a preposition with an infinitive, it indicates purpose, thus "in order to make her depressed." The verb is a Hiphil (H)

---

[13] 1 Sam 14:1; 2 Ki 4:8, 11, 18; Job 1:6, 13; 2:1. See GKC, § 126 s, and Joosten, "Workshop: Meaning and Uses of Tenses in 1 Samuel 1," 73.

[14] Aberbach, "מנה אחת אפים (1 Sam. i 5): A New Interpretation." Other nouns with prosthetic *aleph* include, e.g., אֶזְרוֹעַ, "arm" (from זְרוֹעַ); אֶזְרָח, "native" (from the root זרח, "be of pure lineage"); and אַרְגָּז, "chest, saddlebag" (presumably from the root רגז).

[15] Note that a quarter shekel was considered a large enough gift appropriate to present to a prophet (1 Sam 9:8). A portion of meat worth a pim—two-thirds of a shekel—would have been very generous.

[16] HCSB, ESV, NET, NIV, NRSV; cf. *HOTTP*[2], 146.

[17] E.g., 1 Sam 20:41; 24:9 (ET 24:8); 25:23, 41; 28:14; 2 Sam 14:4, 33; 18:28; 24:20.

[18] E.g., Auld, *I and II Samuel*, 25.

infinite construct with a third feminine singular object suffix. (The consonant ה rarely admits a *daghesh*; for -הָ- here, see *IBH*, § 4 C; GKC, §§ 20 h, 22 s; Joüon, § 18 k.) BDB believes that the verb is from the well-attested root רעם, "thunder" (cf. 1 Sam 2:10; 7:10; 2 Sam 22:14). *HALOT* and *DCH* include an additional root (citing Ezek 27:35 and this verse), a homograph רעם II, whose Qal (G; Ezek 27:35) means "be humbled, be humiliated" and whose Hiphil (H; here) means "to humiliate, make depressed." If BDB is correct, the sense is that Hannah was thunderstruck, paralyzed in her depression. If the alternate derivation in *HALOT* and *DCH* is correct, Hannah was humbled in spirit, placed in a state of depression.

סָגַר יְהוָה בְּעַד רַחְמָהּ:—This is almost identical to the last clause of 1:5 (see the last textual note on that verse), but here the verb סָגַר is used with the preposition בְּעַד (בְּ + עַד), which often means "away from" or "behind." בְּעַד can be used to form idioms with verbs denoting "shutting," especially סָגַר (as here) and also עָצַר (Gen 20:18), גָּדַר (Lam 3:7), and the by-forms שׂוּךְ, סוּךְ, or סָכַךְ (Job 1:10; 3:23).

1:7 וְכֵן יַעֲשֶׂה—The Qal (G) imperfect verb refers to past iterative action (Waltke-O'Connor, § 31.2b, example 3). The subject of the masculine verb could be Elkanah, "thus he would do," referring to his travel to Shiloh and/or his distribution of the portions (1:3–5). But the immediate context (1:6–7) pertains to the wives, so the subject probably is the rival wife's action in 1:6, hence "this would happen."

שָׁנָה בְשָׁנָה—This use of בְ on the repeated noun שָׁנָה, "year," is distributive: "year by year" or "every year" (*IBH*, § 27 G).

מִדֵּי—The compound preposition מִדֵּי (מִן + דֵּי) here means "as often as" (BDB, s.v. דַּי, 2 c α) or "whenever." In this verse it follows the temporal expression שָׁנָה בְשָׁנָה, "every year" (see the previous textual note), but in 1 Sam 7:16, as elsewhere, it precedes that phrase as part of an idiom that also means "every year." See the first textual note on 7:16.

תַּכְעִסֶנָּה—"She would aggravate her" is the Hiphil (H) imperfect third feminine singular of כָּעַס (see the first textual note on 1:6) with a third feminine singular object suffix. The subject must be Peninnah, and the object then is Hannah. The imperfect is iterative, referring to repeated past action.

וַתִּבְכֶּה וְלֹא תֹאכַל:—The subject of these two third singular feminine verbs (of בָּכָה and אָכַל) must switch to Hannah. She is the subject of these verbs again in 1:8, where they are second singular feminine (תִבְכִּי ... לֹא תֹאכְלִי). Like the preceding imperfect תַּכְעִסֶנָּה, the imperfect here, תֹאכַל, denotes iterative past action, as does also the preterite (imperfect with *waw* consecutive), וַתִּבְכֶּה (Joüon, § 79 m).

1:8 לָמֶה תִבְכִּי—The imperfect (here of בָּכָה) can be used for durative present action: "why are you crying?" (Joüon, § 113 d). The pointing לָמֶה, instead of לָמָּה, appears three times in this verse, and only here in the OT (GKC, § 102 l; Joüon, § 37 d).

וְלָמֶה יֵרַע לְבָבֵךְ—"Why are you in a bad mood?" is literally "why is your heart bad?" This idiom (the Qal [G] of רָעַע with לֵבָב as the subject) occurs also in Deut 15:10. For the imperfect form יֵרַע of the geminate verb רָעַע, see GKC, § 67 p.

1:9 אַחֲרֵי אָכְלָה בְשִׁלֹה—"After [he, i.e., Elkanah, had] eaten in Shiloh" takes the verb as a Qal (G) infinitive construct, although it could be parsed in other ways. The form

אָכְלָה could be a feminine singular Qal perfect, referring to Hannah, but "after she ate" would contradict 1:7, which ends by stating that she would "not eat" (וְלֹא תֹאכַל). It also could be the regular form of the infinitive construct, אֲכֹל, with a third feminine singular suffix (normally הָ-) but with the omission of the *mappiq* (hence הָ-) because of the following letter בְ (so GKC, § 91 e). However, the resulting meaning, "after her eating," would again contradict 1:7. Therefore it is best to take אָכְלָה as a so-called "feminine" form of the Qal infinitive construct, with no suffix (see GKC, § 45 d), literally "after eating in Shiloh." An infinitive is not marked for gender, person, or number, so the subject could be Elkanah, Hannah, Peninnah, or any combination of them. The translation takes Elkanah as the subject in light of 1:7 and because he was the speaker in the preceding verse, 1:8.

וְאַחֲרֵי שָׁתֹה—This is translated as "and after [he, Elkanah, had] drunk." As pointed, the verb שָׁתֹה is the usual form of a Qal (G) infinitive absolute, although it could be an infinitive construct (so GKC, §§ 75 n and y; Joüon, § 79 p), as was אָכְלָה in the preceding textual note. A translation for these two words (וְאַחֲרֵי שָׁתֹה) is missing from the LXX (except in the Lucianic recension; i.e., manuscripts boc₂e₂). However, they were probably present in 4QSamᵃ, whose fragments retain the final letter of "Shiloh" and the first two letters of this clause (…וא ה…). Their placement in the word order of the MT is unusual. One would expect the prepositional phrase about the location to be at the end, after both verbs: אַחֲרֵי אָכְלָה וְאַחֲרֵי שָׁתֹה בְשִׁלֹה, "after eating and after drinking in Shiloh." The MT word order is אַחֲרֵי אָכְלָה בְשִׁלֹה וְאַחֲרֵי שָׁתֹה, "after eating in Shiloh and after drinking." Thus, this commentary's author suspects that this clause ("and after drinking") may have been a scribal addition to the text. However, the Masoretic pointing could be a mistake, and the verb should be the Qal third masculine singular perfect, שָׁתָה, "he ate." A perfect aspect verb occasionally will directly follow a preposition in the MT (i.e., without an intervening pronominal suffix).[19] Examples with the preposition אַחַר/אַחֲרֵי are found in Lev 14:43; 25:48; 1 Sam 5:9; Job 42:7; Jer 41:16. Since Hannah refused to eat (1 Sam 1:7), the eating and drinking verbs most likely refer to Elkanah and, by extension, others worshiping with him.

The LXX also adds καὶ κατέστη ἐνώπιον κυρίου, and the Greek verb (unmarked for gender) would refer to Hannah, "and she stood before the Lord." It may reflect a Hebrew Vorlage such as ותתיצב לפני יהוה.[20] This insertion makes for a smoother transition by placing Hannah in the tabernacle before Yahweh and is most likely a scribal insertion in the text.

וְעֵלִי הַכֹּהֵן יֹשֵׁב עַל־הַכִּסֵּא—This construction with an initial *waw* and a predicate participle (יֹשֵׁב) indicates duration (GKC, § 141 e): Eli "was sitting" during the time of Hannah's actions in 1:9–10. The construction עֵלִי הַכֹּהֵן, a proper name (intrinsically

---

[19] Walters, "After Drinking (1 Sam 1:9)," 528–29, takes the verb שָׁתֹה as an infinitive absolute and considers it an anomaly, citing others who state that there are no other instances in the MT of an infinitive absolute following a preposition. However, Waltke-O'Connor, § 35.3.3a, examples 6 and 7, considers this construction in 1 Sam 1:9 and one in 2 Ki 13:17 to be cases where an infinitive absolute is the object of a preposition.

[20] *HOTTP*², 147.

definite) followed by the noun כֹּהֵן with the definite article (literally "Eli, the priest") is a way to designate the high priest, hence "the high priest Eli." Other examples of this construction in the book of Samuel are in 1 Sam 2:11; 21:2, 3 (ET 21:1, 2); 22:11; 23:9; 30:7; 2 Sam 15:27. The only exceptions are in Persian-period books, where the construction designates just a priest, not the high priest (Ezra in Ezra 7:11; 10:10, 16; Neh 8:2, 9; 12:26; Shelemiah in Neh 13:13).

1:10 וְהִיא מָרַת נֶפֶשׁ—This nominal clause, rendered as "she was distressed," is literally "and she, bitter of soul." A construct phrase is often used to name the body part or aspect of a person that is affected by a condition (GKC, § 128 y). The feminine form (in construct) of the adjective מַר describes her condition as "bitter," and the segholate noun נֶפֶשׁ (in pause נָפֶשׁ) denotes the aspect.

וַתִּתְפַּלֵּל עַל־יְהוָה—The Hithpael (HtD) of פָּלַל, "to pray, intercede," recurs in 1 Sam 1:12, 26, 27; 2:1, 25; 7:5; 8:6; 12:19, 23; 2 Sam 7:27. It can take various prepositional phrases. Here עַל־יְהוָה, "to Yahweh," is equivalent to אֶל־יְהוָה in 1 Sam 1:26.

וּבָכֹה תִבְכֶּה:—This is a textbook example of an infinitive absolute preceding an imperfect (with inceptive force) of the same verb (בָּכָה) to express intensity of action: "she wept bitterly" or "she began to weep bitterly" (*IBH*, § 47 C; Waltke-O'Connor, § 31.2c, example 10). See also רָאֹה תִרְאֶה, "you will certainly see," in the next verse (1:11).

1:11 וַתִּדֹּר נֶדֶר—This is another textbook example of a feature of Classical Hebrew. It is fond of using a verb (here נָדַר) with a cognate accusative noun (נֶדֶר): literally "and she vowed a vow." See *IBH*, § 17 B; GKC, § 117 p–r. See also 1 Sam 1:6, 17.

אִם־רָאֹה תִרְאֶה—In conditional sentences an infinitive absolute (רָאֹה) can be used with a finite verb (תִרְאֶה) to emphasize that the condition ("if you will certainly see …") must be fulfilled for the consequent action ("I will give him …") to take place (GKC, § 113 o (2)).

אֲמָתֶךָ—When addressing a superior, Hebrew speakers would often show deference by referring to themselves obliquely as "your servant." A woman speaking could use אֲמָתֶךְ (here in pause, אֲמָתֶךָ) or שִׁפְחָתֶךָ (1:18), while a man would use עַבְדְּךָ (3:9). This verse includes two more instances of אֲמָתֶךָ.

וּזְכַרְתַּנִי ... אֲמָתֶךָ—The verb with the first person pronominal suffix is "and remember me." Hannah refers to herself in the third person as "your servant" both before and after the verb. For the sake of clear English the pronoun "me" has been omitted in the translation. Otherwise, the reader might think that "your servant" and "me" are different persons when both refer to Hannah.

זֶרַע אֲנָשִׁים—Literally "a seed of men," this is translated as "a child." Carsik argues that this is a purposeful scribal change from זֶרַע אֱלֹהִים, "seed of God," meaning a child given by God.[21] However, Paul quite ably refutes this suggestion.[22] Cf. זֶרַע מִן־הָאִשָּׁה in 2:20.

---

[21] Carasik, "Why Did Hannah Ask for 'Seed of Men'?"

[22] Paul, "A Rejoinder concerning 1 Samuel 1:11."

וּמוֹרָה לֹא־יַעֲלֶה עַל־רֹאשׁוֹ׃—Literally "and a razor will not go up on his head." 4QSam^a has "go across" (יעבור) instead of "go up." While the noun מוֹרָה, "razor," appears feminine in form, it is actually masculine, and so is the subject of the masculine verb יַעֲלֶה (Qal [G] imperfect). This noun appears only here and in the two other instances of this expression (of Samson in Judg 13:5; 16:17).

1:12 וְהָיָה כִּי—The use of conjunctive *waw* with the perfect, וְהָיָה, at the start of a clause that continues the narrative is unusual (Joüon, § 119 z; cf. GKC, § 112 uu). Typically Classical Hebrew uses the preterite (imperfect with *waw* consecutive), וַיְהִי, as at the beginning of 1:1, 4, 20. The conjunction כִּי can have a temporal meaning in reference to time past, "as, when" (BDB, 2 a; GKC, § 164 d).

הִרְבְּתָה לְהִתְפַּלֵּל—Classical Hebrew employs various kinds of verbal coordination. The Hiphil (H) of certain verbs, including רָבָה, can take an infinitive construct (usually preceded by לְ) as an object. In such a construction the finite Hiphil serves adverbially, while the infinitive expresses the main verbal action (GKC, § 114 m, including note 2; Joüon, § 124 n). Here the Hiphil perfect, הִרְבְּתָה, takes as its object the Hithpael (HtD) infinitive (with לְ) לְהִתְפַּלֵּל (see the second textual note on 1:10), literally "she multiplied to pray," meaning "she prayed much" or "for a long time."

1:13 וְחַנָּה הִיא—Literally "and Hannah, she." The pronoun הִיא in apposition to the name is resumptive (see Joüon, § 146 c). 4QSam^a omits the name and simply reads "and she" (והיא), as does the LXX (καὶ αὐτή).

מְדַבֶּרֶת עַל־לִבָּהּ ... נָעוֹת ... יִשָּׁמֵעַ—The first participial clause is literally "speaking upon her heart," that is, "praying silently." The sequence of two participles (מְדַבֶּרֶת ... נָעוֹת) referring to action in the past is continued with an imperfect (יִשָּׁמֵעַ) with the same past temporal value (Joüon, § 121 f), "*was not heard.*"

וַיַּחְשְׁבֶהָ עֵלִי לְשִׁכֹּרָה—Literally "Eli deemed her to (be) a drunk woman." The verb is Qal (G) preterite (imperfect with *waw* consecutive) third masculine singular of חָשַׁב with third feminine singular pronominal suffix. In the G stem with a direct object and a prepositional phrase with the preposition לְ, this verb means "to consider" or "reckon" someone "to be" something.

1:14 תִּשְׁתַּכָּרִין—This second feminine singular Hithpael (HtD) imperfect of שָׁכַר, "be drunk," shows metathesis of -תְּתָשׁ to -תִּשְׁתַּ (Waltke-O'Connor, § 26.1.1b, including example 11), and its ending (ן-) is a paragogic *nun* (Waltke-O'Connor, § 31.7.1a, example 2a; cf. GKC, § 47 o). This is the sole instance of שָׁכַר in the Hithpael, which may have the nuance "make yourself drunken [a drunken spectacle]" (see BDB).

הָסִירִי אֶת־יֵינֵךְ מֵעָלָיִךְ׃—Literally "turn away your wine from upon you." The verb הָסִירִי is the Hiphil (H) imperative second feminine singular of סוּר.

1:15 וַתַּעַן חַנָּה וַתֹּאמֶר—Literally "Hannah answered and said." The two verbs, while eloquent in Hebrew, seem redundant in English and can be combined in one translation, e.g., "answered" (1:15) or "replied" (1:17). The combination of these two verbs, עָנָה, "to answer," and אָמַר, "to say," is common throughout the OT, including Samuel,[23]

---

23 Also, e.g., 1 Sam 1:17; 4:17; 9:21; 26:6, 14, 22; 29:9; 2 Sam 20:20.

and with the cognate verbs in Aramaic.[24] This Semitic idiom is also quite common in the Greek NT (e.g., Mt 3:15; 4:4; 11:4, 25).

קְשַׁת־רוּחַ—Literally "hard of spirit," this construct phrase is rendered as "discouraged." Muraoka takes this phrase to mean "determined."[25]

וְשֵׁכָר—Often translated as "strong drink," this word most likely denotes "beer"—a beverage made from fermented grain, often barley. (Distilled spirits were not produced in antiquity.) The Akkadian and Aramaic cognates denote beer. Oeming notes:

> Textual and iconographic evidence from Egypt and Mesopotamia documents the production of wine and beer since ca. 2800 B.C.E., but the practice is probably prehistoric. Alcohol enjoyed great popularity and was widely consumed among the Israelites and their neighbors, as a wealth of excavated production sites for alcoholic beverages attests. Many recipes for the manufacture of (strong) beer have been preserved. From Egypt we have clay models of breweries and pictures of brewers carved on tombs and temple walls.[26]

וָאֶשְׁפֹּךְ—This Qal (G) preterite (imperfect with *waw* consecutive), following a perfect (שָׁתִיתִי), is translated with a present force, "but I am pouring out," rather than as a punctiliar past ("but I poured out") because it is explanatory (cf. Joüon, § 118 j). Hannah is explaining that her prolonged praying stems from discouragement and not drunkenness.

1:16—אַל־תִּתֵּן אֶת־אֲמָתְךָ לִפְנֵי בַּת־בְּלִיָּעַל—Literally "do not place your servant before a daughter of a good-for-nothing," this idiom must mean something like "do not take your servant to be a good-for-nothing woman" (cf. *DCH*, s.v. נתן, Qal, 4 j; BDB, s.v. פָּנֶה, II 4 f). Like בֵּן, "son," בַּת, "daughter," can indicate a person's character or quality (BDB, s.v. בַּת, 5; GKC, § 128 v; Waltke-O'Connor, § 9.5.3b). בְּלִיָּעַל (in pause בְּלִיָּעַל) is a compound noun from בְּלִי, "not, without," and a nominal form of the verb יָעַל, which occurs only in the Hiphil and means "to avail, be beneficial" (see it in 12:21). בְּלִיָּעַל is often used to characterize people who are not simply useless but actively malicious and destructive. It recurs often in Samuel.[27] A Greek variant of this Hebrew word, Βελιάρ, is used by Paul as a term for Satan in 2 Cor 6:15. Tsumura argues that בְּלִיָּעַל is the name of an underworld goddess.[28] He defends this by noting the unusual phrasing of Hannah's words: "Do not give your maidservant before a daughter of Beliya'al." This supposedly means something like "bring your maidservant for judgment by Beliya'al's daughter," that is, "utterly destroy your maidservant." This seems far-fetched and without strong support in the text and has no extrabiblical support. Hannah is not asking not to be destroyed. She is asking Eli not to misconstrue her actions and appearance.

---

[24] E.g., Dan 2:7, 15, 20; 3:9, 14, 19, 24, 25, 26, 28; 4:16 (ET 4:19); 5:17; 6:14 (ET 6:13); 7:2.

[25] Muraoka, "1 Sam 1,15 Again."

[26] M. Oeming, "שָׁכַר *šākar*; שֵׁכָר *šēkār*," *TDOT* 15:2.

[27] Also 1 Sam 2:12; 10:27; 25:17, 25; 30:22; 2 Sam 16:7; 20:1; 22:5; 23:6. See also, e.g., Deut 13:14 (ET 13:13); Judg 19:22; 1 Ki 21:10, 13; Prov 6:12; 16:27; 19:28; 2 Chr 13:7.

[28] Tsumura, *The First Book of Samuel*, 123–24.

דִּבַּרְתִּי עַד־הֵנָּה:—Literally "I spoke until now," in English the force of this clause is best rendered with the English present perfect tense, "I have been speaking" (cf. HCSB, ESV, NIV, NRSV).

1:17 שֵׁלָתֵךְ אֲשֶׁר שָׁאַלְתְּ מֵעִמּוֹ—As in 1:11 (see the first textual note there), a verb takes a cognate accusative, literally "your request that you requested from him." The feminine noun שֵׁלָה, "a request, petition," is a form of שְׁאֵלָה (e.g., 1:27) with the elision of the quiescent א (GKC, §§ 23 f; 95 h) and is derived from the verb שָׁאַל, "to ask, request." The recurrence of the verb שָׁאַל at the end of 1:20 reinforces that Yahweh granted the son Hannah requested. See also הַשְּׁאֵלָה אֲשֶׁר שָׁאַל לַיהוָה in 1:27 and שְׁאֵלָתִי אֲשֶׁר שָׁאַלְתִּי in 2:20.

1:18 שִׁפְחָתְךָ—The noun שִׁפְחָה is used to describe a lowly household servant who was often assigned to serve the women of the household (*HALOT*, 1 a; see Gen 12:16; 16:1). Here Hannah uses "your slave girl" as a self-deprecating third person reference to herself. Cf. אֲמָתֶךָ in the third textual note on 1:11.

וּפָנֶיהָ לֹא־הָיוּ־לָהּ עוֹד:—Literally "her [distraught] face was not to her again," this means "she no longer looked dejected."

1:19 וַיִּשְׁתַּחֲווּ לִפְנֵי יְהוָה—For the verb, see the third textual note on 1:3.

וַיָּשֻׁבוּ וַיָּבֹאוּ—"They returned and they came" is a Hebrew hendiadys that recurs in 25:12 and in the singular in 27:9. Here it is rendered as "they returned."

וַיֵּדַע—When the verb יָדַע, "to know," is used as a circumlocution for sexual relations, it may denote a loving act between husband and wife (cf. Gen 4:1). Thus, the verb here is rendered as "made love."

וַיִּזְכְּרֶהָ יְהוָה:—"Yahweh remembered her" repeats the verb זָכַר from her vow in 1:11, וּזְכַרְתַּנִי, "and [if] you remember me," demonstrating literarily that Yahweh did so.

1:20 וַיְהִי לִתְקֻפוֹת הַיָּמִים—Literally "it came to be to/at the turning of the days." Idioms with the noun תְּקוּפָה refer to elapsed periods of time in Ex 34:22; 2 Chr 24:23 and to the completion of the sun's circuit in Ps 19:7 (ET 19:6). Cf. Gen 18:14.

שְׁמוּאֵל—"Samuel" most likely represents the combination שָׁמַע + אֵל, "God heard," and he is named this because God heard when Hannah asked for him.[29] The consonant ע likely was omitted for the sake of euphony, to avoid the clash of two consecutive guttural letters, ע followed by א. Other suggestions for the meaning of the name Samuel include "he who is from God" (שֶׁ + מִן + אֵל), "his name is God" (שְׁמָהוּ + אֵל) or perhaps (שְׁמוֹ + אֵל), and "asked of God" (שָׁאוּל + אֵל).

כִּי מֵיְהוָה שְׁאִלְתִּיו:—The conjunction כִּי has a causal force ("because") and also introduces direct discourse (BDB, 1 b). Her words are literally "because from Yahweh I asked him." However, pronominal suffixes on verbs do not always function as direct objects ("I asked him"). Instead, the suffix can have a datival force, hence "I asked *for* him" (see Joüon, § 125 ba). The pointing of the suffixed Qal (G) perfect with *hiriq* (-אִ-) instead of the usual *patach* (-אַ-) is a peculiarity of שָׁאַל and a few other verbs (GKC, § 44 d; Joüon, §§ 41 b; 42 d).

---

[29] Cartledge, "Hannah Asked, and God Heard."

Commentary

c. 1090 BC

Elkanah and His Family (1:1–3)

The first three verses of 1 Samuel acquaint us with Elkanah, his family, and the setting for Hannah's request for a son. Like Saul and David, the two other major figures in the book of Samuel and leaders of Israel, Samuel is introduced to us through his father (1 Sam 9:1–3; 16:1–12).

Elkanah is first introduced according to his hometown (Ramathaim in Ephraim) and patrimony (Zuphite), instead of being introduced by name. This emphasizes his identity as a Levite from the line of Kohath, specifically one of the Kohathite clans that were allotted cities within Ephraim's territory (Josh 21:20–22; see third textual note on 1 Sam 1:1). Elkanah's identity as a Levite is important for establishing Samuel's role as a Levite in service to God (1 Sam 2:18; 9:13; 10:8; 16:2). At the time of Moses God had selected the Levites to serve at the tabernacle (Ex 32:25–29; Num 1:47–54).

Elkanah's lineage is given when he is first identified by name. Here we have five generations back to Zuph, substantiating Elkanah's identity as a Zuphite. The Zuphites were descended from Kohath though Izhar, a brother of Amram, the father of Aaron and Moses (Ex 6:18; 1 Chr 5:27–29 [ET 6:1–3]; 6:3, 7–12 [ET 6:18, 22–27]).

Next we are introduced to Elkanah's wives. His first wife, Hannah, was barren, but his second wife, Peninnah, had children. Note that when the children are mentioned, the order of the wives changes.[30] Though Hannah was first (1 Sam 1:2) and loved (1:5), Peninnah is elevated to first place because of her children. This draws a subtle parallel with Rachel and Leah, and, earlier, Sarah and Hagar. God blessed the unloved Leah with children first (Gen 29:31), before Rachel (Gen 30:22), who was loved (Gen 29:18). Hagar bore Ishmael (Genesis 16) before Sarah bore Isaac (Genesis 21). Like Rachel and Sarah, Hannah remained childless for a time.

The final introduction is to Elkanah's piety. He would make a pilgrimage to the tabernacle at Shiloh every year[31] in order to worship "Yahweh of armies" (1:3). This title for God is used 259 times in the OT, but this is the first time.[32] It emphasizes God as a sovereign who presides over an army.[33] Its introduction

---

[30] In the first half of 1:2 the order is "Hannah ... Peninnah," but in the second half of 1:2 the order is "Peninnah ... Hannah."

[31] Israelites were to travel to the central sanctuary three times each year, for the Feast of Unleavened Bread and Passover, for the Feast of Weeks (Pentecost), and for the Feast of Booths (Succoth). See Ex 23:14–17; Deut 16:16. Elkanah's pilgrimage may have been on one of these occasions, but that is not stated in the text.

[32] 1 Sam 1:3; also 1:11 and often later.

[33] See the fourth textual note on 1:3.

here subtly prepares readers for God's later assertion that when Israel asked for a king, it was rejecting God as its king (8:7).

With the mention of Shiloh we also become aware for the first time of the high priest Eli and his sons Hophni and Phinehas. This begins the author's juxta-position of the pious Levitical family of Elkanah with the less-than-pious ways of the priestly family of Eli (2:12–17, 27–36). This contrast is maintained by interplay between Samuel and the Elides throughout 1 Samuel 1–7.

Elkanah and His Wives (1:4–8)

The narrative moves from Elkanah's regular yearly practice to a particular year, as signaled by the phrase "one day" (see the textual note on 1:4). The sac-rifice was apportioned by Elkanah to his family.[34] We first learn of the portions given to Peninnah and her children—both sons and daughters. We would expect that Elkanah would give a portion to Hannah too, since he is depicted as a pious leader of his household and he would want everyone to share in the joy of the sacrifice. The author points out a special portion given to Hannah (see the first textual note on 1:5). Elkanah singled out Hannah with this portion to empha-size that his love for her was not diminished by her inability to bear children.

No doubt Peninnah took note of the special portion given to Hannah, and she was able to nullify the attention that Elkanah gave to Hannah. By pointing out Hannah's barrenness, she was able to rob Hannah of the joy in the sacri-fice to the point where Hannah's sorrow made her unable to eat and appreciate Elkanah's loving gesture. The author goes on to point out that Peninnah would use this strategy every year.

Elkanah's words to Hannah ring of frustration at the dynamics of his fam-ily. He seems unable to grasp Hannah's sorrow—the grief of a woman who cannot bear children (Prov 30:15–16). While commentators are often quick to point out the importance of children—especially sons—as providing heirs for husbands in the world of the ancient Near East, the longing for a child is not simply an ancient cultural artifact. Childless couples who seek to start a fam-ily in contemporary society also experience the kind of pain that Hannah felt.

Elkanah's frustration blinds him in two ways, as revealed by his questions to Hannah. His first two questions depict him as unaware or unmindful of the tension between his two wives and especially of Peninnah's role in heighten-ing and perpetuating Hannah's anxiety. However, his third question, though not intended to be insensitive to Hannah's state, displays how he is unable to sympathize with Hannah. "Aren't I better for you than ten sons?" (1:8) is

---

[34] Elkanah's offering is called זֶבַח הַיָּמִים, "the annual sacrifice," in 1 Sam 1:21. The Torah pre-scribes various sacrifices to be offered at the tabernacle, some of which were not eaten or were eaten only by the priests. However, the peace offering (Lev 7:11–36) provided meat that could be eaten by the lay worshipers. See Kleinig, *Leviticus*, 38–39, 168–74. See also the sec-ond textual note on 10:8, which specifically refers to "peace offerings." A peace offering may be the sacrifice to which 1 Sam 1:24 refers; see the second textual note there and "Samuel Is Dedicated to Yahweh (1:24–28)" in the commentary on 1:21–28.

found on the lips of a man who has sons—and daughters too! Had Elkanah been monogamous, he would have felt the sting of childlessness much more sharply. However, polygamy has placed him in a position that creates an emotional distance from his first wife, and he seems to be oblivious to it. The very act of taking a second wife and producing children with her makes it impossible for him to fully realize his vocation as husband to Hannah, no matter how hard he tries to express his support for her.

Elkanah specifically refers to ten sons, an unusually large family. Westbrook believes that the number ten is drawn from standard adoption contracts dating to the Old Babylonian period.[35] These contracts use the standard trope that a first son, although adopted, will be heir even if the adopting father should subsequently have ten sons. This standard formula, Westbrook believes, is used by Elkanah to place himself in the position of being as valuable as an adopted son. If Westbrook is correct, it highlights all the more the troubled dynamic of a polygamous household, where Hannah can see the sons of the other wife and know that no matter how good a husband Elkanah might be, he cannot be as good for her as a son.

Hannah and Eli (1:9–18)

After the eating and drinking before Yahweh had ended, Hannah got up. The author again notes the location: Shiloh. This reminds readers that this was no ordinary meal, but part of worship.

Eli was sitting on his chair at the entrance to the tabernacle as Hannah approached God with her prayer. Eli's chair was a sign of his office as high priest, as most who served in the tabernacle and all of the worshipers at the tabernacle stood. When we first meet Eli and when we last read about him he is sitting on a chair (4:13, 18).

Interestingly, the tabernacle is called "temple" (הֵיכָל, 1:9), a term used for it again in 1 Sam 3:3 and 2 Sam 22:7. This is the first and earliest time the term appears in the OT. The Torah regularly employs the noun "tabernacle" (מִשְׁכָּן), but that term occurs only once in the book of Samuel (2 Sam 7:6), and there it is used to contrast the "tabernacle" as a tent with the permanent "house" (בַּיִת) that David desired to build for Yahweh. The author of Samuel is emphasizing that God, Israel's King, dwelt in a royal "temple" all along and that a new "temple" of wood and stone for God's dwelling would not change God's status.

Hannah's behavior before Yahweh is indicative of a person who is severely distressed but not without faith in God's power. She weeps, but she also trusts that Yahweh is able to provide her with relief from her torment. Her prayer is a promise that she will dedicate the child to God's service for his entire life. Smith incorrectly argued that this indicates that the author did not view Samuel as a Levite, since Levites were God's servants.[36] However, Levites were not lifelong

35   Westbrook, "1 Samuel 1:8."

36   Smith, *The Books of Samuel*, 9.

servants. The original generation of Levites served only twenty years, from age 30 to age 50 (Num 4:2–3, 22–23, 29–30, 34–35), although for later generations this was expanded to twenty-five years (ages 25 to 50; Num 8:24–25). Samuel, however, was a servant of God his entire life. As a boy he already served before God in an ephod (1 Sam 2:18), and he continued in service as God's prophet until his death.

The vow also included the promise that "a razor will never be used on his head" (1:11). Since ancient times this has been understood to be a promise that Samuel would be a Nazirite, since this phraseology occurs elsewhere in the OT only in connection with Samson, a Nazirite (Judg 13:5; 16:17). The LXX inserts "and he will not drink wine or beer" (καὶ οἶνον καὶ μέθυσμα οὐ πίεται) before mentioning the razor (cf. Judg 13:4–5). This reading apparently was also found in 4QSam[a].[37] Josephus seems to indicate this also when he describes how, in conformity with Hannah's vow, "his hair was allowed to grow long, and his drink was water."[38] All of these are secondary interpretive glosses, but cumulatively they depict an exegetical tradition that understood Samuel to have been a lifelong Nazirite.

From Hannah's silent prayer with moving lips, Eli misjudges her to be drunk and upbraids her for it. Hannah's words in reply are very carefully chosen. She had poured no alcohol into her mouth; instead, she was "pouring out" (שָׁפַךְ, 1:15) her soul to Yahweh. Her strange behavior came from what was inside her—but not because she had put something inside herself.

In his retelling of the story Josephus portrays Hannah as claiming to have drunk only water.[39] Moreover, she claims that her grief is because she has no children—a detail not in the biblical text, but something drawn by Josephus into Hannah's words from the context.[40] These additions make Hannah's somewhat cryptic response to Eli more understandable, but rob the biblical story of its heightened tension.

Eli's blessing on her begins with the clause "go in peace" (1:17), a clause used several times (with minor variations) in the book of Samuel to signal that the speaker holds no ill will toward the hearer.[41] He then blessed Hannah with the promise of the fulfillment of her request by God. The jussive verb יִתֵּן, "may he [God] grant" (1:17), in this case signals not simply a wish, but the actual promise given in a benediction, as in the well-known Aaronic benediction, which also uses jussive forms in this way (Num 6:24–26). With this benediction God states, "Thus will they put my name on the Israelites, *and I will bless them*" (Num 6:27).

---

[37] The text is not extant at this point, but there is room enough in the missing portion for the clause ויין ושכר לוא ישתה.

[38] κόμη τε οὖν αὐτῷ ἀνεῖτο καὶ ποτὸν ἦν ὕδωρ (Josephus, *Antiquities*, 5.347).

[39] Josephus, *Antiquities*, 5.345.

[40] Begg, "The Youth of Samuel according to Josephus," 28 (especially n. 58).

[41] 1 Sam 20:42; 29:7; 2 Sam 15:9; see also Gen 37:14; Ex 4:18; Judg 18:6; 2 Ki 5:19.

Hannah's reply contains a nice play on her name, which means "favored" (or "she who has been shown favor, grace"). "Hannah" (חַנָּה, *ḥannah*) asks that she find "favor, grace" (חֵן, *ḥen*, 1:18) from Eli.[42] Hannah appears to have understood Eli's blessing as a promise from God through his servant the high priest. Not only did she receive the blessing in faith, but she also lived in that faith as her entire outlook and behavior changed. Now she ate and no longer appeared dejected.

Hannah was trusting in the Word of God as delivered through the office of the high priest. Jesus would later give similar authority to his church when he said, "If you forgive anyone's sins, *they are forgiven. If you do not forgive them, they are not forgiven*" (Jn 20:23). Luther understood this well and teaches that "when the called ministers of Christ deal with us by His divine command, in particular when they exclude openly unrepentant sinners from the Christian congregation and absolve those who repent of their sins and want to do better, *this is just as valid and certain, even in heaven, as if Christ our dear Lord dealt with us Himself.*"[43]

Return to Ramah: The Birth of Samuel (1:19–20)

The piety of Elkanah's household is once again highlighted by the author: they worship before returning to Ramah. Then we see God working in concert with Elkanah. Yahweh remembered Hannah's prayer and Eli's promise.

Hannah's naming of her son is not unusual. Mothers are frequently the givers of names in the OT: Eve named Seth (Gen 4:25). Leah named her sons (Gen 29:32, 33, 34, 35; 30:17–18, 19–20) and her daughter (Gen 30:21). Leah also named the children of her slave girl Zilpah (Gen 30:10–11, 12–13). Rachel also named her children (Gen 30:22–24; 35:16–18) and the children of her slave girl Bilhah (Gen 30:4–6, 7–8). Judah's wife Shua named two of her sons (Gen 38:4, 5). Machir's wife Maacah named her son Peresh (1 Chr 7:16).[44]

The naming of the child "Samuel" (שְׁמוּאֵל, "God heard"; see the second textual note on 1 Sam 1:20) is explained by Hannah's thought that she "asked" (שָׁאַל, 1:20) Yahweh for him. She asked and God heard. Hannah's request for Samuel is highlighted by the use of the root שׁאל ("to ask, request" or "a request"; see the textual note on 1:17) throughout the narrative that features her (1:17, 20, 27, 28; 2:20).

Polzin, Miscall, and Bodner see in the account of Samuel's naming an anticipation of the reign of Saul, whose name means "asked" (שָׁאוּל, Qal passive

---

[42] Since Hannah had no children, she could not have merited favor in that way; her request is an appeal to grace alone.

[43] SC, "The Office of the Keys" (*LSB* 326; emphasis added).

[44] We might also include Bathsheba naming Solomon according to the Qere: וַתִּקְרָא אֶת־שְׁמוֹ שְׁלֹמֹה (2 Sam 12:24). The Kethib credits the naming to David: וַיִּקְרָא אֶת־שְׁמוֹ שְׁלֹמֹה.

[Gp] participle of שָׁאַל).[45] Indeed, the Israelites "asked" for a king (שָׁאַל, 8:10; 12:13, 17, 19). According to this view the lives and careers of the prophet and the king are intertwined from the beginning.

---

[45] Polzin, *Samuel and the Deuteronomist*, 2:25; Miscall, *1 Samuel*, 1, 14; Bodner, *1 Samuel*, 22–23.

The Second Trip to Shiloh: Samuel Is Given to Yahweh

Translation

1 **21**The man Elkanah and his entire household went up to sacrifice the annual sacrifice to Yahweh and [to repay] his vow. **22**But Hannah did not go up because she said to her husband, "[Wait] until the boy is weaned, then I will bring him and he will appear before Yahweh and stay there permanently."

23Elkanah said to his wife, "Do what you think is right. Stay until you have weaned him. Only may Yahweh fulfill his promise." So Hannah stayed and nursed her son until she had weaned him.

24So she brought him up with her when she had weaned him, along with a three-year-old bull, an ephah of flour, and a full container of wine. She brought him to the house of Yahweh in Shiloh, and the lad was [still] a boy. **25**They slaughtered the bull, and they brought the boy to Eli.

26She said, "Please, my lord, as you live, my lord, I am the woman who stood with you in this place to pray to Yahweh. **27**I prayed for this boy, and Yahweh gave me my request that I asked from him. **28**So I also am dedicating him to Yahweh. All the days which he lives he is dedicated to Yahweh."

And he worshiped Yahweh there.

Textual Notes

1:21 לִזְבֹּחַ לַיהוָה אֶת־זֶבַח הַיָּמִים—"To sacrifice a sacrifice" is another cognate accusative construction (*IBH*, § 17 B; GKC, § 117 p–r; previously in 1 Sam 1:6, 11, 17). What is literally "the sacrifice of the days" is rendered as "the annual sacrifice." This Hebrew phrase occurs only in the book of Samuel, here and again in 1 Sam 2:19; 20:6. The plural of יוֹם, "day," can signify a year (*HALOT*, 7). See 2:19; 20:6. The particular kind of sacrifice may be a peace offering; see the footnote on the peace offering at the beginning of "Elkanah and His Wives (1:4–8)" in the commentary on 1:1–20; the second textual note on 1:24; and the second textual note on 10:8.

וְאֶת־נִדְרוֹ:—"His vow" is a second direct object of the infinitive לִזְבֹּחַ, "to sacrifice." The fulfillment of vows is often closely connected to sacrifice (see, e.g., Lev 7:16; 22:21; Num 15:3, 8; Deut 12:6, 11; Prov 7:14).

1:22 עָלָתָה—This is the pausal form of עָלְתָה, the third feminine singular Qal (G) perfect of עָלָה, "go up."

יִגָּמֵל—The verb גָּמַל can be masculine in the Niphal (N) with a boy as subject, as here (also Gen 21:8), "be weaned." But naturally in the Qal (G) with the active meaning "to wean," it is feminine with a mother as subject (גְמָלַתּוּ, 1:24, shortened from גְמָלַתְהוּ

58

[see GKC, § 59 g]). The infinitive is a genderless form, but its two Qal infinitives in 1:23 have feminine pronominal suffixes as their subjects (גָּמְלָהּ, גָּמְלֵךְ).

וַהֲבִאֹתִיו—This is a classic example where an imperfect in a temporal clause (יִגָּמֵל in the preceding textual note) is followed by a perfect with *waw* consecutive (the Hiphil [H] of בּוֹא) to announce a future action (GKC, § 112 oo), "I will bring him."

וְנִרְאָה אֶת־פְּנֵי יְהוָה—It is unusual for a Niphal (N) verb to take a direct object, but the Niphal of רָאָה, "see," is used idiomatically with God's "face" as its object for "appearing before" Yahweh.[1] See GKC, § 121 a, b.

עַד־עוֹלָם:—The noun עוֹלָם, though often translated as "forever," actually denotes a long period of time. Here it denotes a long period of service ("permanently"), but not even Samuel's entire lifetime, since he would later serve God in other places (1 Sam 7:16–17). Only by context can one determine whether the word means "forever" or something like "a long period of time, but not forever." At times it refers to the past, to times beyond the experience of the audience (Deut 32:7; Jer 28:8; Prov 22:28; 23:10; cf. Ezra 4:15, 19). At other times when authors wish to ensure that the readers understand this word to mean "forever," they will compound it with itself or other words such as עוֹלָם וָעֶד (Jer 7:7; 25:5); לְמִן־עוֹלָם וְעַד־עוֹלָם (Ps 103:17; 1 Chr 29:10); מֵעוֹלָם וְעַד־עוֹלָם (Pss 10:16; 21:5 [ET 21:4]; 45:7 [ET 45:6]; 48:15 [ET 48:14]; 52:10 [ET 52:8]; 89:38 [ET 89:37]; 104:5); or לָעַד לְעוֹלָם (Pss 111:8; 148:6). This is also reflected in Jewish literature in Greek and in the NT by the phrase εἰς τοὺς αἰῶνας τῶν αἰώνων.[2]

4QSamᵃ adds [חיין] וּנְת[תיהו נזיר עד עולם כול ימי, "[and I] permanently dedicate him as a Nazirite all the days [of his life]."[3] McCarter believes that both the MT and the LXX have lost a clause such as this, which he translates as "for I shall dedicate him as a Nazirite forever."[4] However, it is most likely a secondary explanatory gloss.

1:23 הַטּוֹב בְּעֵינַיִךְ—Literally "the good in your eyes," this means "what you think is right." It is a common Hebrew idiom that expresses personal approval of an action.[5]

אַךְ יָקֵם יְהוָה אֶת־דְּבָרוֹ—The adverb אַךְ ("only") indicates a contrast to what precedes (BDB, 2 a). Elkanah allows Hannah to keep Samuel for now but wants her to fulfill her vow (1:11). "May Yahweh fulfill his promise" (1:23) is literally "may Yahweh establish his Word," a reference to the blessing of Eli (1:17). יָקֵם is a Hiphil (H) jussive masculine singular from the root קוּם. As Tsumura observes: "It should be noted that when God is the subject of the verb 'to establish,' its object is usually either *his* word or promise or the words of his prophets."[6]

---

[1] Ex 34:20, 23, 24; Deut 16:16; 31:11; Is 1:12; Ps 42:3 (ET 42:2).

[2] LXX Ps 83:5 (MT 84:5, ET 84:4); 4 Macc 18:24; Gal 1:5; Phil 4:20; 1 Tim 1:17; 2 Tim 4:18; Heb 13:21; 1 Pet 4:11; Rev 1:6, 18; 4:9–10; 5:13; 7:12; 10:6; 11:15; 15:7; 19:3; 20:10; 22:5.

[3] But see the commentary on 1 Sam 1:11 for the long-standing interpretation that Samuel was a Nazirite.

[4] McCarter, *I Samuel*, 56.

[5] Also, e.g., Gen 16:6; Judg 10:15; 19:24; 1 Sam 3:18; 11:10; 14:36, 40; 2 Sam 10:12; 19:19, 28, 39 (ET 19:18, 27, 38); 24:22; 2 Ki 10:5; 1 Chr 19:13; 21:23.

[6] Tsumura, *The First Book of Samuel*, 129, citing as examples Deut 9:5; 2 Sam 7:25.

Since it appears as if God has already kept his promise by the conception and birth of Samuel, this is a somewhat difficult reading. Thus, the LXX reading is likely a scribal change: ἀλλὰ στήσαι κύριος τὸ ἐξελθὸν ἐκ τοῦ στόματός σου, "but may the Lord establish what has come from your mouth." Similarly, 4QSamᵃ reads אך יקם יהו]ה היוצא מפיך[.[7]

1:24 וַתַּעֲלֵהוּ עִמָּהּ—The feminine pronoun on the preposition עִמָּהּ is reflexive because it refers back to the subject of the feminine verb (the Hiphil [H] of עָלָה), "she brought him up with *herself*" (see GKC, § 135 i; Joüon, § 146 k).

בְּפָרִים שְׁלֹשָׁה—Literally "with three bulls." The LXX reads ἐν μόσχῳ τριετίζοντι καὶ ἄρτοις, "with a three-year-old bull and loaves (of bread)." This probably reflects a Hebrew Vorlage as in 4QSamᵃ: בפר בן]בקר משלש ולחם[. Although most modern English translations follow the LXX and 4QSamᵃ by translating "a three-year-old bull," they also omit "and bread."[8] A single three-year-old bull makes the most sense in this context; three bulls would have been an excessive offering, and only one is mentioned in 1:25 (הַפָּר, "the bull"). Yet neither reading is without its problems, and the MT has its defenders.[9] Tsumura's argument in favor of the MT is that the offering of flour is an ephah, which is a little over three times what is required for a peace offering for a vow (see 0.3 ephah per bull in Num 15:9).[10] Therefore, he surmises that three bulls would be offered. Tsumura's argument would be more convincing had Elkanah brought 0.9 ephah. The wine required for a peace offering is half a hin (a half gallon or 1.9 liters; Num 15:10). Tsumura's conjecture would also imply that Elkanah brought a large vessel that could contain one and a half gallons of liquid, which would weigh about 12 pounds (5.4 kilograms) plus the weight of the container (see the next textual note). This would have been quite a load to bring from Ramah to Shiloh.

וְנֵבֶל יַיִן—This is translated as "and a full container of wine." The construct phrase here uses יַיִן as a genitive of material, indicating the substance with which the נֵבֶל is filled.[11] For a similar phrase, see נֹאד יַיִן, "a skin of wine," i.e., "a full wineskin," in 1 Sam 16:20. The noun here, נֵבֶל, though often translated as "skin," is most likely a jar or other hard container (cf. Lam 4:2; see *CDCH*, s.v. נֵבֶל I).

וְהַנַּעַר נָעַר:—The second word is the pausal form (without the article) of the first.[12] "And the lad was [still] a boy" is the most likely construal of the MT, as found in most modern English translations.[13] The LXX has a much longer text: καὶ τὸ παιδάριον μετ' αὐτῶν. καὶ προσήγαγον ἐνώπιον κυρίου, καὶ ἔσφαξεν ὁ πατὴρ αὐτοῦ τὴν θυσίαν ἣν ἐποίει ἐξ ἡμερῶν εἰς ἡμέρας τῷ κυρίῳ, "And the boy [was] with them, and they

---

[7] See also Hornkohl, "Her Word versus His."

[8] E.g., HCSB, ESV, NRSV. *HOTTP*² prefers the reading "a three-year-old bull," with a "B" rating, meaning that there is some doubt about its validity (*HOTTP*², 148; see also vii–viii).

[9] Ratner, "Thee Bulls or One?"

[10] Tsumura, *The First Book of Samuel*, 131.

[11] *IBH*, § 51 c; Waltke-O'Connor, § 9.5.3d; Joüon, § 129 f; GKC, § 128 o.

[12] נַעַר is a segholate noun and so is accented on the first syllable, but with *patach* in each syllable in place of *seghol* because of the guttural ע.

[13] That meaning is conveyed by the various translations in HCSB, ESV, NIV, NRSV.

brought [him] before the Lord. And his father slaughtered the sacrifice that he did yearly to the Lord" (1:24–25). This reading or something like it was also in 4QSamᵃ, which contains space for this longer text and also a few of the words, namely, הזבח [כ]אשר (= τὴν θυσίαν ἥν), "the sacrifice that." The suggestions that the second נַעַר be taken from the root נער, "growl" (Althann), or "shake, rouse up" (Frolov and Orel),[14] are far-fetched and difficult to justify contextually.

1:25 וַיִּשְׁחֲטוּ—This Qal (G) is plural: "and they slaughtered." The LXX (καὶ ἔσφαξεν) and 4QSamᵃ (שחט[וי]) read a singular: "and he [Elkanah] slaughtered."

וַיָּבִיאוּ—The MT has the plural "and they brought." The LXX reads καὶ προσήγαγεν Αννα ἡ μήτηρ τοῦ παιδαρίου, "and Anna, the mother of the boy, brought." This reading may have also been found in 4QSamᵃ, which contains room for the words "Hannah, the mother of the boy."

1:26 וַתֹּאמֶר בִּי אֲדֹנִי—Rather than the preposition בְּ with a suffix, this בִּי is a particle used to entreat a superior. It is always followed by אֲדֹנִי (or אֲדֹנָי), thus "please, my lord" (see Joüon, § 105 c).

חֵי נַפְשְׁךָ—This construct phrase has the unusual singular of the noun חַי, literally "[by] the life of your soul."[15] Hannah invokes Eli's life to put herself under oath to attest that she is telling the truth. Similarly, חַי־יְהוָה, "[by] the life of Yahweh," is used as an oath when appealing to Yahweh.[16] Both construct phrases are used together in 20:3; 25:26.

לְהִתְפַּלֵּל אֶל־יְהוָה:—For "pray," see the second textual note on 1:10; the same infinitive construct was in 1:12. The verb recurs in the perfect in 1:27: הִתְפַּלָּלְתִּי.

1:27 שְׁאֵלָתִי אֲשֶׁר שָׁאַלְתִּי מֵעִמּוֹ:—See the textual note on 1:17, which has the same wording but in the second person.

1:28 אָנֹכִי הִשְׁאִלְתִּהוּ ... הוּא שָׁאוּל—Usually שָׁאַל means "to ask, request" (1:17, 20, 27). The author will engage in wordplay with this verb since it is the derivation of the name שָׁאוּל, "Saul," meaning "requested"; he is the king whom Israel will request. See "Samuel Warns Israel about Kings (8:10–22)" in the commentary on 8:1–22; the first textual note on 10:22; the commentary on 12:13; the textual note on 14:37; and the second textual note on 20:6 (which also discusses שָׁאוּל נִשְׁאַל in 20:28). The meaning of the two forms of שָׁאַל here is difficult, but from the context they must mean something like "I am dedicating him" and "he is dedicated," not "I am granting him as a request" and "he is asked." הִשְׁאִלְתִּהוּ is the Hiphil (H) perfect first common singular with third masculine singular object suffix (-אִ- is attenuated from -אַ- [GKC, § 64 f]). The only other instance of the Hiphil is in Ex 12:36, where it has the similar meaning "to hand over." שָׁאוּל is a masculine singular Qal passive (Gp) participle.

---

[14] Althann, "Northwest Semitic Notes on Some Texts in 1 Samuel," 27–28; Frolov and Orel, "Was the Lad a Lad?"

[15] The same construct phrase is in 1 Sam 17:55; 20:3; 25:26; 2 Sam 11:11; 14:19.

[16] 1 Sam 14:39, 45; 19:6; 20:3, 21; 25:26, 34; 26:10, 16; 28:10; 29:6; 2 Sam 4:9; 12:5; 14:11; 15:21; 22:47; cf. 2 Sam 2:27.

וַיִּשְׁתַּחוּ—For this verb, see the third textual note on 1:3. The form here is the third masculine singular preterite (imperfect with *waw* consecutive).[17] For its subject, see the commentary.

Commentary

c. 1085 BC

Hannah Does Not Go to Shiloh (1:21–23)

Once again Elkanah took his family to the annual sacrifice at Shiloh (as in 1:3). The text also mentions "his vow" (1:21), though the only vow mentioned previously is Hannah's (1:11). According to Num 30:11–16 (ET 30:10–15), when a married woman took a vow, her husband could annul it when he first learned that she had made it. From the conversation between Hannah and Elkanah (1 Sam 1:22–23), it is apparent that Elkanah knew of his wife's vow and approved of it. Thus, Hannah's vow became Elkanah's vow, and he had taken responsibility for it. The mention of the vow and Hannah's delaying the dedication of Samuel meant that the fulfilling of the vow and its accompanying sacrifice would be postponed until the child was older.

Hannah waited until Samuel was weaned before bringing him to Shiloh. If 2 Macc 7:27 is any indication, Samuel might have been close to three years old when the vow was fulfilled. When Hannah asked to wait until the boy was weaned, Elkanah said, "Only may Yahweh fulfill his promise" (1:23). Yahweh already had given Hannah a son, so it might seem that he had already completed his half of the conditional sentence (1:11a) and that the rest is up to her (1:11b). However, Klein is certainly correct in noting that "Elkanah accepted her decision, but he expressed the wish that her vow—to give her son permanently to Yahweh … —would be brought to fruition by Yahweh."[18] God is the author of the believer's good works.[19]

Samuel Is Dedicated to Yahweh (1:24–28)

When the boy was weaned Hannah brought him with a sacrifice consisting of a three-year-old bull (see the second textual note on 1:24), an ephah of flour, and a full container of wine. An ephah was about 0.6 bushel or 22 liters. The items match well with those needed for a peace offering to fulfill a vow, although there is no mention of olive oil mixed with the flour (Num 15:8–10). That these items are associated with the fulfilling of Hannah's vow is implied by 1 Sam 1:25, which mentions both the slaughtering of the bull and the bringing of Samuel to Eli. The text also emphasizes that Samuel was still only a young boy when he was dedicated to Yahweh (see the fourth textual note on 1:24).

---

[17] The identical form recurs in 1 Sam 15:31; 20:41; 24:9 (ET 24:8); 28:14; 2 Sam 1:2; 9:6, 8; 12:20; 14:22, 33; 18:21, 28; 24:20.

[18] Klein, *1 Samuel*, 10.

[19] AC IV 122–39; FC SD II 36–39.

Hannah's speech not only reminds Eli of her prayer to Yahweh at Shiloh (1:10–11) but also states the reason she is dedicating Samuel to Yahweh. During her earlier conversation with Eli (1:9–18) she did not mention what her request from Yahweh was. Now she declares the contents of her prayer and vow. This is immediately followed by worship. The masculine verb "he worshiped" in 1:28 is ambiguous as to who worshiped Yahweh. Was it Elkanah, Samuel, or Eli? Since this statement about worship immediately follows Hannah's words about Samuel, he is the closest antecedent to the verb. So we ought to understand Samuel as beginning his worship of Yahweh in Shiloh at the time when Hannah presented him to Eli. This also continues the implied contrast between Elkanah's pious family and Eli's impious family (2:12–17), whose sins are catalogued immediately following the return of Elkanah to Ramah (2:11). The Hebrew of 1:28 maintains a theme already established in 1:1–20, that the lives of the prophet Samuel and the king Saul will be intertwined.[20]

---

[20] See the first textual note on 1:28, where Hannah designates Samuel as שָׁאוּל, which must mean "dedicated," although it is identical to the name "Saul." See also "Return to Ramah: The Birth of Samuel (1:19–20)" in the commentary on 1:1–20.

Excursus

Polygamy in the Bible

Any reader of the account of the birth of Samuel is immediately confronted by the problems in Elkanah's family caused by friction between his two wives. Moreover, Elkanah's polygamy makes him unable to be a true comfort to Hannah when she was discouraged because of her inability to have children (see the commentary on 1 Sam 1:8).

To most who are even casually acquainted with the OT it is clear that in addition to Elkanah several prominent men were polygamous: Abraham, Jacob, Gideon, David, and Solomon all had multiple wives. In addition, the following men had more than one wife:

- Lamech (Gen 4:19–24)
- Esau (Gen 28:9; 36:2, 6)
- Ahab (1 Ki 20:2–7)
- Jehoiachin (2 Ki 24:15)
- Jerahmeel (1 Chr 2:26)
- Ashhur (1 Chr 4:5)
- Shaharaim (1 Chr 8:8)
- Rehoboam (2 Chr 11:21)
- Rehoboam's sons (2 Chr 11:23)
- Abijah (2 Chr 13:21)
- Jehoram (2 Chr 21:14, 17)
- Joash (2 Chr 24:3)
- Zedekiah (Jer 38:23)

Thus, at least fifteen Israelite men, including two of Israel's patriarchs, are portrayed as polygamous. We probably ought to assume that most, if not all, of the kings of Israel and Judah practiced polygamy, since it was a common practice in the ancient Near East, and nine of the fifteen Israelite polygamists named above were kings. In addition, foreign kings such as Belshazzar (Dan 5:2, 3, 23) and Xerxes (the husband of Esther) were polygamous.

Polygamy in the ancient Near East was not only a marital practice, but it was also intertwined with economic and political expediencies. Unmarried women without a father or husband were likely to be poor, since they normally did not inherit, nor did they usually own land (although there were exceptions; see Num 27:1–11; 2 Ki 8:1–6; Job 42:15). In order to be provided food and shelter, they might remarry, and in some cases it would be marriage to a man who already had a wife. Poor men who could not support their entire household might sell their daughters as concubines to men who sought a wife (Ex 21:7–11). Often the purchaser was a rich man who could afford a second wife. Kings often married many wives to solidify relationships with powerful families within their kingdoms or for political alliances with other kingdoms.

Moreover, polygamy was not simply an OT practice. It was also extant in NT times, though no man in the NT is specifically portrayed as having more than one wife. Josephus, however, notes that Herod the Great had multiple wives.[1] He also notes that both King Monobazus of Adiabene and his son Izates had several wives.[2]

There is no indication anywhere in the text of the Bible that any of these polygamous marriages were illicit in the sense that they constituted adultery or fornication. They were marriages; there is no hint that the polygamous men were not in reality married to any wives other than their first wife. In fact, one can search in vain in the Scriptures for a general prohibition of polygamy.[3] Even concubines were considered wives (e.g., Gen 37:2), though of a lesser stature than wives for which one paid a bride-price.[4] Therefore, it would be wrong to state that polygamous marriages in the OT or that even such marriages today as found in some cultures were or are not marriages.

However, we ought not to conclude that polygamy has God's full approval or that it is not somehow contrary to his design for men and women. The Scriptures show by both negative and positive examples that God's design and ideal for marriage is monogamy. When God first created marriage, since it was "not good for the man to be alone" (Gen 2:18), he formed one woman to be his wife (Gen 2:22); his design is that "the two [one man and one woman] will become one flesh" (Gen 2:24).

The Pentateuch contains laws specifically for cases of polygamy. Ex 21:7–11 contains laws about a daughter who has been sold as a slave, in case she is married to her master or to her master's son. Ex 21:10 regulates what may become a polygamous relationship in such circumstances:

> If he takes another wife for himself, he shall not diminish her food, her clothing, or her marital rights.

Deut 17:14–20 contains laws limiting Israelite kings. Since it was common in the ancient Near East for kings to practice polygamy, Deut 17:17 states:

> And he shall not acquire many wives for himself, or his heart will turn away.
> Nor shall he acquire for himself excessive silver and gold.

This law apparently does not forbid polygamy—a king could have a few wives, but he was not to have many. Solomon was an example of a king who broke this law and whose heart did turn away from God (1 Ki 11:1–8).[5] Finally, Deut

---

[1] Josephus, *Jewish War*, 1.477, 480, 562–63; Josephus, *Antiquities*, 17.19.

[2] Josephus, *Antiquities*, 20.17–20, 85, 89.

[3] See the discussion below for 1 Tim 3:2, 12; Titus 1:6.

[4] Note that Josephus considers Jacob's concubines to be wives, stating that Jacob had four wives (*Antiquities*, 2.102).

[5] Cf. "Solomon's Polygamy (Song 6:8)" in Mitchell, *The Song of Songs*, 120–27.

21:15–17 regulates the granting of inheritances in polygamous circumstances; it assumes that in most cases a polygamous man will have only two wives:

> If a man has two wives, one loved and the other unloved, and both the loved and the unloved wives bear him sons, and if the unloved wife has the first-born son, when that man gives what he owns to his sons as an inheritance, he is not to designate the son of the loved wife as the firstborn over the first-born of the unloved wife. He must acknowledge the firstborn—the son of the unloved wife—by giving him two shares of all that is his, for he is the first-fruits of his virility. The custom for the firstborn is his.

Clearly, all of these laws anticipate problems precisely because of polygamy. None of the problems they address would exist in the family of a monogamous man. This in itself is a subtle indictment of the social, economic, and political systems that made polygamy acceptable or sometimes even preferable for the woman. We ought to remember that not all of the Pentateuchal laws were given by God to show his approval of practices that the laws tolerated. For instance, Jesus himself declared that the Pentateuchal law on divorce was not given because God approved of divorce, but because the Israelites in the hardness of their hearts did not live in marriage as God had originally intended (see Deut 24:1–4; Mt 5:31–32; 19:3–12; Mk 10:2–12).

Moreover, the OT often demonstrates the problems that can arise within polygamous families. There can be friction and jealousy among the several wives (Hannah and Peninnah; Sarah and Hagar [Gen 21:8–21]; Rachel and Leah [Gen 29:31–30:24]). There can also be friction and tension among the children of different wives. Joseph's half-brothers by the concubines Bilhah and Zilpah had to have resented the fact that he was placed over them by Jacob (Gen 37:2). In the book of Samuel we encounter problems among David's children from different mothers. Amnon's rape of his half-sister Tamar is the first of these incidents (2 Sam 13:1–22). This led to Absalom's hatred of Amnon and eventually to his murdering Amnon (2 Sam 13:23–33). This worked in Absalom's favor in two ways: he avenged the rape of his sister Tamar, and he killed the heir apparent to the throne, clearing the way for his own claim on the throne as the oldest surviving son of David. This rivalry among children from different mothers would continue into the book of Kings, where we learn of Adonijah's attempt to take the throne before David could place Solomon on it (1 Ki 1:5–27). By these negative examples Scripture demonstrates that polygamy is far from the ideal marital practice.

In addition, Scripture teaches that monogamy was God's original design for humankind. In the beginning God created Eve as the helper for Adam and blessed them in their marriage (Gen 1:27–28). And in what is probably the first narrational conclusion drawn for readers in the OT, we are told: "Therefore a man will leave his father and his mother and cling to his wife, and the two will become one flesh" (Gen 2:24). This statement presupposes that one man will have only one wife and suggests that the marriage union in some sense restores the unity of flesh that existed before the woman was taken from the man at the creation (Gen 2:21–23).

This ideal is also upheld in the NT when Paul instructs both Timothy and Titus that one of the qualifications of pastors and deacons is that they be "the husband of one wife" (1 Tim 3:2, 12; Titus 1:6).[6] As leaders in the church, they are to demonstrate God's ideal in marriage.

We ought also to note that one of the great pictures of God's relationship to his people is that of a husband to a wife, and this is always depicted as a monogamous relationship.[7] This metaphor is employed both in the OT, where Israel is Yahweh's wife, and in the NT, where the church is the bride of Christ.[8] In Eph 5:22–33 Paul sees Christian marriage as a reflection of the relationship between Christ and his church. Christ is the only Savior, and he has only one bride and body, the church comprised of all baptized believers.[9] Thus, the Christian ideal for marriage is monogamy, and faithful Christians who aspire to marriage and wish to please God ought to shun polygamy.

---

[6]   These statements have been interpreted in various ways. Some have understood them to deny the pastoral office and the deaconate to unmarried men. However, if that were the case, Paul himself would have been disqualified (1 Cor 7:8). Others have argued that it disqualifies men who remarry after being widowed, but this would contradict the principles about marriage Paul invokes in 1 Cor 7:39. The most likely meaning is that a pastor or deacon must have no more than one wife, which definitely rules out having more than one wife at a time and may also forbid pastors from divorcing faithful wives and then remarrying (which could be construed as serial polygamy).

[7]   Ezekiel 16 pictures Yahweh as marrying only one sister, personifying Jerusalem, but then later Ezekiel 23 speaks of Yahweh's marriage to two sisters, who represent Samaria and Jerusalem. The emergence of two sisters reflects the division of the kingdom into northern Israel and southern Judah, which was the result of the apostasy of the northern tribes. Originally Yahweh chose and redeemed Israel from Egypt to be his one people.

[8]   In the OT, see, e.g., Is 61:10; 62:5; Jer 2:2; 31:32; 33:11; Hosea 1–3. In the NT, see, e.g., Jn 3:29; 2 Cor 11:2; Rev 19:7; 21:2, 9; 22:17. See Mitchell, *The Song of Songs*, 40–66.

[9]   See Rom 12:4–5; 1 Cor 10:16–17; 12:12–13; Eph 4:4–6; 5:25–27.

Hannah's Prayer

Translation

2   ¹Hannah prayed. She said:

"My heart rejoices in Yahweh;
my horn is lifted in Yahweh.
My mouth is [opened] wide against my enemies,
    because I rejoice in your salvation.
²There is no one holy like Yahweh,
    because there is no one other than him,
    and there is no rock like our God.
³Do not speak a lot of very haughty words,
for arrogance will come out of your mouth,
    because Yahweh is a God of knowledge,
    and actions are weighed by him.

⁴The bow of mighty warriors is broken,
    but those who stumble are armed with strength.
⁵Those who are well-fed hire themselves out for bread,
and those who are hungry cease [being hungry].
Even a barren woman bears seven sons,
and one with many sons withers.
⁶Yahweh kills and makes alive;
he brings down to Sheol and brings up [again].
⁷Yahweh makes poor and makes rich;
he humbles, and he also elevates.

⁸He lifts a poor person from the dust;
he raises a needy person from the trash heap
    to seat [him] with nobles,
    and he makes him inherit an honored throne,
        because the foundations of the earth belong to Yahweh,
        and he set the world upon them.
⁹He guards the steps of his faithful ones,
and wicked people will be silenced in darkness,
    because a man does not prevail by [his own] strength.
¹⁰Yahweh—his adversaries will be shattered;
he will thunder in the heavens against them.
Yahweh will judge the ends of the earth

He will give strength to his King
and lift up the horn of his Anointed One."

[11]Then Elkanah went to his home in Ramah, and the boy was ministering to Yahweh in the presence of the high priest Eli.

Textual Notes

2:1 וַתִּתְפַּלֵּל—For this verb for "pray," see the second textual note on 1:10.

עָלַץ לִבִּי בַּיהוָה—The perfect verb עָלַץ, "rejoice, exult," and the three other perfects in the verse denote past action that remains in force during the present time (GKC, § 106 g), so they are translated with the English present tense.

רָמָה קַרְנִי בַּיהוָה—The Qal (G) perfect of רוּם, "be high, lifted," is feminine to match the gender of the noun קֶרֶן, "horn." See the third textual note on 2:10. In place of "in Yahweh" (בַּיהוָה), the LXX has ἐν θεῷ, "in God" (which would represent a Hebrew reading בֵּאלֹהִים; cf. כֵּאלֹהֵינוּ in 2:2), a reading preferred by McCarter and by Aejmelaeus.[1] However, 4QSam^a here agrees with the MT. Since 4QSam^a normally agrees with the LXX against the MT, the MT reading here is strongly reinforced by 4QSam^a. בַּיהוָה is to be preferred for this reason and because it is the more difficult reading.[2] The previous line ended with בַּיהוָה, and one would expect poetic variation here; see כַּיהוָה ... כֵּאלֹהֵינוּ in 2:2.

רָחַב פִּי עַל־אוֹיְבַי—This clause is translated as "my mouth is [opened] wide against my enemies." The verb (literally "be wide") has been understood in various ways by English translations: "boasts" (HCSB); "derides" (ESV) or "mocks" (GW). This precise idiom (פֶּה as the subject of רָחַב) is unique in the OT, but a similar idiom, the Hiphil (H) of רָחַב with פֶּה as its object ("make/open wide the mouth") appears three times. In two passages (Is 57:4; Ps 35:21) wicked persons are the subjects and it has a derisive or accusatory connotation, but here Hannah is rejoicing in God and his salvation. It refers to opening the mouth in hunger in Ps 81:11 (ET 81:10; cf. also Is 5:14), but that meaning would be inappropriate here with עַל־אוֹיְבַי, "against my enemies," and in light of the reversal in 1 Sam 2:5.[3]

2:2 This verse is different in each tradition. The LXX reads:

ὅτι οὐκ ἔστιν ἅγιος ὡς κύριος,
καὶ οὐκ ἔστιν δίκαιος ὡς ὁ θεὸς ἡμῶν·
οὐκ ἔστιν ἅγιος πλὴν σοῦ.

Because there is none holy like the Lord,
and there is none righteous like our God;
there is none holy besides you. (*NETS*)

---

[1] McCarter, *I Samuel*, 68; Aejmelaeus, "Hannah's Psalm," 358.

[2] Marttila, "The Song of Hannah and Its Relationship to the Psalter," 507, argues for the MT on the basis of it being the more difficult reading.

[3] In terms of the categories in 2:5, Hannah belongs metaphorically among those who were hungry but who now are filled by Yahweh; she would no longer be hungry.

4QSam^a reads:

[כ]יא אין קדוש כיה[וה]
[ואין צדיק כאלוהינו]
[ואין בלתך]
ואין צור כאלוהינו

[Bec]ause there is no one holy like Yah[weh],
[and there is no one righteous like our God,]
[and there is no one other than] you,
and there is no rock like our God.

In McCarter's judgment all of the witnesses contain a conflated text.[4] If the reconstruction of 4QSam^a is correct, then it appears either to be a conflation of the MT and the LXX or to retain the four original lines. If its four lines are original, then the second line dropped out from the MT and the fourth line is omitted in the LXX. On the theory that this verse ought to be a single bicolon, most commentators omit one line from the MT and emend the remaining two lines in some way.[5]

אֵין בִּלְתֶּךָ—In this verse the particle of negation, אַיִן, is used three times, each time in construct with what it negates. בִּלְתֶּךָ is another particle of negation, בִּלְתִּי, with a second masculine singular suffix. It is pausal for בִּלְתְּךָ. When בִּלְתִּי follows another negative (as here) it means "besides, except for, other than" (see BDB, s.v. בֵּלֶת, 2). Cf. Hos 13:4, וּמוֹשִׁיעַ אַיִן בִּלְתִּי, "and there is no Savior other than me."

2:3 אַל־תַּרְבּוּ תְדַבְּרוּ גְּבֹהָה גְבֹהָה—Literally, "do not multiply, (do not) speak high high," this means "do not speak a lot of very haughty words." A negative with an imperfect forms a negative imperative, "do not …" Here the negative אַל governs both of the imperfects, תַּרְבּוּ (Hiphil [H] of רָבָה) and תְדַבְּרוּ (Piel [D], דִּבֶּר). The second verb is attached without a *waw* and expresses the principal idea of the pair, that of speaking (GKC, § 120 g; Joüon, § 177 g). The repetition of the adjective (feminine of גָּבֹהַּ, "high, lofty") forms an absolute superlative, "very haughty."[6]

יֵצֵא עָתָק מִפִּיכֶם—The translation takes יֵצֵא as an imperfect (rather than a jussive) of יָצָא and interprets this clause as a result of ignoring the prior one: Hannah tells those who do speak haughty words (contrary to her prior admonition) that by doing so "arrogance will come out of your mouth." An alternate view is that the negative אַל that began the verse also extends over this clause, in which case יֵצֵא is jussive, "(do not) let arrogance come out from your mouth" (see GKC, § 152 z). The noun עָתָק occurs four times in the OT, always referring to "arrogance" displayed in speaking (also Pss 31:19 [ET 31:18]; 75:6 [ET 75:5]; 94:4).

דֵּעוֹת—This is the plural of the feminine noun דֵּעָה, "knowledge." The plural is an abstract (Joüon, § 136 g) or intensive (GKC, § 124 e). The only other occurrence of

---

4 McCarter, *I Samuel*, 68–69.

5 See Klein, *1 Samuel*, 12–13; Auld, *I and II Samuel*, 35, 37.

6 Joüon, § 141 k; see also Waltke-O'Connor, § 12.5a; GKC, § 133 k. Aejmelaeus, "Hannah's Psalm," 364, and Lewis, "The Textual History of the Song of Hannah," 29, consider this to be a case of dittography. However, for other instances of such repetition, see Deut 2:27; 16:20; Eccl 7:24.

this plural form is in Job 36:4. The feminine plural (genitive) noun in the LXX, θεὸς γνώσεων, supports the MT. 4QSamᵃ has the more common feminine singular noun דעת (to be pointed דֵּעַת), a secondary reading that substitutes the more common noun for the less common one.

וְלֹא נִתְכְּנוּ עֲלִלוֹת:—The Kethib לֹא would negate the Niphal (N) perfect of תָּכַן: "actions are not weighed/evaluated." Tsumura follows the Kethib and translates the clause as "and (his [God's]) deeds are immeasurable."[7] The weakness of Tsumura's argument is that he has to supply the pronoun that ought to be a suffix on the subject noun, i.e., עֲלִילוֹתָיו, "his deeds." The Qere is the homonym לוֹ, the suffixed preposition לְ with the sense of agency (BDB, 5 d): "by him [God]." In this context the Qere is obviously the correct reading and is also supported by the LXX (αὐτοῦ).[8]

2:4   קֶשֶׁת גִּבֹּרִים חַתִּים—This would literally mean "a bow of shattered warriors" if the masculine plural of the adjective חַת, "shattered, broken," modifies the masculine plural גִּבֹּרִים, "mighty warriors." The noun קֶשֶׁת, "bow," is feminine singular. In this context, however, it would make more sense for the "bow" to be broken. Therefore חַתִּים in the MT probably is the result of attraction to the preceding masculine plural noun (GKC, § 146 a).[9] In place of חַתִּים 4QSamᵃ reads חתה (singular), which could be the feminine singular of the adjective חַת or the feminine singular Qal (G) perfect of the verb חָתַת, "be shattered," a verbal form attested elsewhere in the OT. 4QSamᵃ is in agreement with the LXX, which has ἠσθένησεν, "was weak" (aorist indicative active, third person singular).

וְנִכְשָׁלִים אָזְרוּ חָיִל:—The Niphal (N) participle of כָּשַׁל is used as a substantive, "those who stumble." The verb אָזַר, "arm oneself, gird oneself," denotes binding something around the waist. In a military context it denotes girding one's equipment for battle. Here and in 2 Sam 22:40 it takes the object noun חַיִל (here pausal: חָיִל), "strength."[10] Instead of "those who stumble arm themselves with strength," the clause is translated as a passive, "those who stumble are armed with strength," because God is the one who supplies their strength.

2:5   שְׂבֵעִים בַּלֶּחֶם נִשְׂכָּרוּ—"Those who are well-fed" renders an adjective from the root שׂבע, which denotes being filled to satisfaction with food. "Hire themselves out" is a reflexive (cf. Greek middle) translation of the Niphal (N) perfect third common plural of שָׂכַר, "to hire." The N stem was originally a reflexive counterpart to the Qal (G) stem, and it retains this mode for many verbs.

---

7   Tsumura, *The First Book of Samuel*, 138.

8   Seger, "A Note on the Early Antiquity of the Song of Hannah," unconvincingly argues that neither the Qere nor the Kethib is correct and that the word ought to be read as לוֹא, "surely, certainly."

9   This suffices as a grammatical explanation for חַתִּים as the original reading; it need not imply that an original reading חַתָּה was changed to חַתִּים in the course of transmission (against Lewis, "The Textual History of the Song of Hannah," 32). For a contrary opinion, see Marttila, "The Song of Hannah and Its Relationship to the Psalter," 508, who argues that the MT contains the harder reading and ought to be retained on that basis.

10   Cf. Waltke-O'Connor, § 10.2.1h, example 51, which explains the verb אָזְרוּ as intransitive with חַיִל as a complement accusative.

עַד־עֲקָרָה—The preposition עַד here expresses degree: "even (more)" (see BDB, I 3). The reversal of a "barren woman" (עֲקָרָה) giving birth is an even greater and more astonishing reversal than those described in 2:4 and earlier in 2:5.

שִׁבְעָה—The feminine forms of numerals from three to ten are used with masculine nouns, so this feminine form of "seven" is translated as "seven sons."

אֻמְלָלָה:—"Withers" is a Pulal (Dp) perfect third feminine singular form of the root אמל. Here and in Jer 15:9, which also speaks of a woman who bore "seven sons," the contextual nuance of the verb is that a woman loses her fertility.

2:6 יְהוָה מֵמִית—"Yahweh" is the subject of the three participles that follow (see also the next two textual notes). Hebrew poetry often employs participles as titles for God.[11] In the Qal (G) מוּת means "die," and מֵמִית is Hiphil (H), which has the corresponding causative meaning, "put to death, kill." Elsewhere Yahweh is the subject of the Hiphil when he executes judgment (e.g., Gen 38:7; Deut 32:39; Is 14:30; 65:15; Hos 9:16).

The closest parallel to 1 Sam 2:6 employs this Hiphil as well as the following Piel (D; see the next textual note), but as imperfects rather than participles:

See now, for I, I am he,
and there is no [other] god with [besides] me [cf. 1 Sam 2:2].
  I, I kill and I make alive [אֲנִי אָמִית וַאֲחַיֶּה],
  I crush and I, I heal. (Deut 32:39)

וּמְחַיֶּה—This is the Piel (D) participle of חָיָה, "to live." The Piel can have the sense of preserving those who are already alive (see BDB, 1), but here it has the stronger meaning "to restore the dead to life" (see BDB, 3 a), as also in Deut 32:39; Hos 6:2; Ps 71:20. Hos 6:2, "after two days he will make us alive [יְחַיֵּנוּ]; on the third day he will raise us up [יְקִמֵנוּ], and we will live [וְנִחְיֶה] before him," is one of the chief OT passages that predict the resurrection of Christ on the third day (see Lk 24:46; 1 Cor 15:4). Ps 71:20 first uses the Piel, "you will again make me alive" (תְּחַיֵּינִי), and then, like 1 Sam 2:6 (see the last textual note on 2:6), the Hiphil (H) of עָלָה, "from the depths of the earth you will bring me up again."

מוֹרִיד—This is the Hiphil (H) participle of יָרַד with a causative meaning, "bring [someone] down." Its Qal (G), "go down," often refers to death as a descent into "Sheol" (Gen 37:35; Num 16:30, 33; Ezek 31:15, 17; 32:27; Ps 55:16 [ET 55:15]) or into the "pit," "corruption," "dust," "death," etc. (see BDB, 1 i). Likewise, the Hiphil can mean "to bring down" persons into "Sheol" (Gen 42:38; 44:29, 31; 1 Ki 2:6, 9; Ezek 31:16) or the "pit" or "corruption" (Ezek 28:8; Ps 55:24 [ET 55:23]).

שְׁאוֹל—"Sheol" is usually synonymous with death and the grave. For passages where it is used in parallel with מָוֶת, "death," see 2 Sam 22:6; Is 28:15, 18; 38:18; Hos 13:14; Hab 2:5; Pss 6:6 (ET 6:5); 18:6 (ET 18:5); 49:15 (ET 49:14); 89:49 (ET 89:48); Prov 5:5; 7:27; Song 8:6. The author of this commentary has concluded that the Hebrew "Sheol" in the OT and the Greek ᾅδης, "hades," in the NT are often designations for the

---

[11] Waltke-O'Connor, § 37.3d, note 28. A total of eight participles are used to characterize God in 1 Sam 2:6–8.

location or state of all the dead as they await the bodily resurrection.[12] In such cases the English word "hell" is not a good gloss for either the Hebrew term or the Greek term, since "hell" refers specifically to the place of the damned, those who die in unbelief and are condemned eternally. Note that in Rev 1:18; 6:8; 20:13–14, "death" (θάνατος) and "hades" (ᾅδης) are linked together, just as Sheol and death are linked in the OT. Also note that in Rev 20:13 the dead are pictured as being in "the sea" and in "death and hades" before they come forth for the bodily resurrection of all the dead and they are judged according to what they have done (as in our Lord's depiction of the judgment in Matthew 25).[13] note that both "death" and "hades" will be thrown into "the lake of fire," which is "the second death" (Rev 20:14; cf. Rev 20:6). This lake, which is the place of the eternal punishment and torment of unbelievers, corresponds more closely with the English word "hell" than does "hades." When the destruction of "death" itself will have happened (1 Cor 15:26), God will have delivered his people forever and they will inhabit the new earth, where they can eat from the tree of life in their reunited body and soul (Rev 2:7; 22:2, 14, 19).

וַיָּעַל:—This means "and he brings up [again]." It is unusual for this form (Hiphil [H] preterite [imperfect with *waw* consecutive] third masculine singular) to follow three participles (in 2:7 all four verbs are participles). The context requires it to have a habitual or frequentative meaning (something God does and will do on the Last Day) to match the force of the participles (GKC, § 111 u), rather than refer to a simple past action. Freedman suggests that it is an archaic form for the imperfect with conjunctive *waw*, וְיַעֲלֶה.[14] However, in poetry there are a number of instances of a preterite (imperfect with *waw* consecutive) following participles.[15] See GKC, § 116 x; Joüon, §§ 118 r; 121 h, including note 1; 121 j.

---

[12] "Sheol" in this sense is comparable to language in other passages, such as "sleeping in the dust of the earth" (Dan 12:2–3), that describes the location of all the dead, the righteous and the unrighteous, before they arise in the universal bodily resurrection and then are segregated into either eternal life or eternal condemnation. To be sure, some passages distinguish the present location of those who have died in the faith from that of dead unbelievers; believers who have died can be described as already now being in "the bosom of Abraham" (Lk 16:22), "in paradise" (Lk 23:43), or "under the altar" in heaven (Rev 6:9). Conversely, unbelievers who have died are already now "in torment" (Lk 16:23–24).

[13] In Rev 20:12–13, 15, all the dead are judged according to their works. However, the decisive criterion for eternal salvation or damnation is whether one's name is written in "the book of life" (Rev 20:12, 15; see also Phil 4:3; Rev 3:5; 13:8; 17:8; 21:27). All those whose names are written in the Lamb's book inherit eternal life, whereas all those whose names are not recorded in it are thrown into the lake of fire. Believers in Christ, therefore, are saved by grace alone; God elected them by writing their names in his book "before the foundation of the world" (Rev 13:8; see also Eph 1:4). Believers are not saved because of their works, even though their works are publicized in the judgment. Likewise in Mt 25:31–46, the King judges all the dead according to what they have done, but for the righteous (believers in Christ) he recalls only their good works (their sins are forgiven and forgotten), whereas the unbelievers are condemned for their evil works. See Ap IV 370–74.

[14] Freedman, "Psalm 113 and the Song of Hannah," 259, n. 25; cf. Lewis, "The Textual History of the Song of Hannah," 36.

[15] See, e.g., Pss 18:33, 48 (ET 18:32, 47); 29:5; 104:32; 107:40; Job 12:22, 23; 14:20; Prov 20:26.

2:8b וְכִסֵּא כָבוֹד יַנְחִלֵם—Literally, "and a throne of honor he makes them inherit." The suffix on the Hiphil (H) imperfect of נָחַל, "to inherit," is third masculine plural. However, if translated as "them," its natural antecedent in the English translation would be the prior plural noun "nobles," which would mean that God exalts the lofty. The intent of the verse is to express the reversal: God exalts the lowly. The intended antecedent is one or both of the earlier nouns דָּל, "poor," or אֶבְיוֹן, "needy" (2:8a). Each of those nouns is grammatically singular, but the plural pronoun here interprets one or both of them as collectives. To clarify the intended antecedent(s), the English translation renders the pronoun as singular: "makes him inherit."

2:8c–9 The LXX omits the last two lines found in MT 2:8 and has a completely different text for 2:9: διδοὺς εὐχὴν τῷ εὐχομένῳ καὶ εὐλόγησεν ἔτη δικαίου· ὅτι οὐκ ἐν ἰσχύι δυνατὸς ἀνήρ, "granting the prayer to the one who prays, he has even blessed the years of the righteous, because not by strength is a man mighty" (*NETS*). 4QSamᵃ, though fragmentary, seems to combine the MT and the LXX readings.

2:9 חֲסִידוֹ—This Kethib is singular, "his faithful one," but the translation follows the plural Qere, חֲסִידָיו, "his faithful ones," which is supported by many Masoretic manuscripts, the Targum, the Syriac, and the Vulgate. The plural agrees in number with the plural in the following antithetical clause, רְשָׁעִים, "wicked people." The singular may anticipate the singulars מַלְכּוֹ, "his King," and מְשִׁיחוֹ, "his Anointed One," in 2:10. Cf. the singular חֲסִידְךָ, "your faithful one," in the messianic promise of Christ's resurrection in Ps 16:10 (quoted in Acts 2:27; 13:35).

יִדָּמּוּ—This is the pausal form of יִדְּמוּ (Jer 49:26; 50:30), a Niphal (N) imperfect third masculine plural from the root דמם I, "be silent" or "be still, motionless" (so BDB). The Niphal then has the passive meaning "be made silent," although BDB adds "i.e. destroyed." *HALOT* (דמם III) and *DCH* (דמם IV) consider the Niphal forms of דמם in the OT[16] to be from a homographic root meaning something like "destroy," hence "be destroyed, cut off" or "perish," as in many English translations.

2:10 יְהוָה יֵחַתּוּ מְרִיבָיו—This is translated as "Yahweh—his adversaries will be shattered." This translation understands יְהוָה at the head of this clause to be an instance of *casus pendens*, a noun or pronoun "hanging" at the head of a clause to set it apart and emphasize it.[17] The verb is an imperfect third masculine plural from the root חתת, "be shattered" or "be terrified." The meaning is unaffected whether the form is parsed as Qal (G; so BDB) or Niphal (N; so *HALOT*, *DCH*). Some suggest following the reading in 4QSamᵃ, יחת, a Hiphil (H) imperfect third masculine singular form of the same verb, in which case יְהוָה would be the subject: "Yahweh will shatter."[18] This apparently is also the reading reflected in the LXX: κύριος ἀσθενῆ ποιήσει ἀντίδικον αὐτοῦ, "the Lord will make his adversary weak." However, in the MT the subject of the verb is the Qere מְרִיבָיו, "his adversaries," the plural Hiphil participle of רִיב with a pronominal suffix, a reading found in many Masoretic manuscripts and supported by the Syriac and

---

[16] Niphal (N) forms of דמם occur in 1 Sam 2:9; Jer 25:37; 49:26; 50:30; 51:6.

[17] Lewis, "The Textual History of the Song of Hannah," 40.

[18] E.g., Aejmelaeus, "Hannah's Psalm in 4QSamᵃ," 25.

the Vulgate. The Kethib is the singular participle מְרִיבוֹ, "his adversary," a reading also found in 4QSamª and supported by the LXX. See also the next textual note.

עָלָיו בַּשָּׁמַיִם יַרְעֵם—The first word (Qere: עָלָיו) is the normal form of the preposition עַל, "over; against," with a third masculine singular pronominal suffix, "him." This reading is found in many Masoretic manuscripts. The singular pronoun agrees with the singular Kethib reading מְרִיבוֹ at the end of the preceding clause (see the prior textual note). The Kethib here, עָלוֹ, would be an unusual form of the preposition with the same suffix and with the same meaning. The translation renders the pronominal suffix as plural, "against them," to agree with the preceding plural Qere מְרִיבָיו, "his adversaries." Dahood proposed the emendation to עֵלִי, which he claims is a divine name: "ʿĒlî thunders in the heavens."[19] This is a creative suggestion, but has little else to recommend it. In form יַרְעֵם ("to thunder") is a Hiphil (H) jussive of רָעַם, a denominative verb from the noun רַעַם, "thunder." The imperfect would be יַרְעִים, but that unshortened form is unattested in the OT (see, e.g., וַיַּרְעֵם in 1 Sam 7:10; Ps 18:14 [ET 18:13]; and יַרְעֵם in 2 Sam 22:14). This verb is a homograph of the רָעַם whose Hiphil occurred in 1:6 (see the third textual note there).

וְיָרֵם קֶרֶן מְשִׁיחוֹ:—The expression "to lift up [someone's] horn" with the Hiphil (H) of רום refers to God's action of saving or vindicating his faithful also in Pss 89:18 (ET 89:17); 92:11 (ET 92:10); 148:14; 1 Chr 25:5. The Hiphil is causative, whereas the result of God's action is expressed by Hannah with the Qal (G) of רום in 1 Sam 2:1, "my horn is lifted." See the Qal expression also in Pss 89:25 (ET 89:24); 112:9. The Hiphil יָרֵם is jussive in form (whereas the imperfect would be יָרִים), but Hebrew poetry often uses jussive forms with the force of imperfects (GKC, § 109 k), thus "he will lift up."

Insertion—LXX 1 Sam 2:10 has a long insertion, beginning with κύριος ἅγιος, "the Lord is holy," derived from Jer 9:22–23 (ET 9:23–24). 4QSamª, though very fragmentary, has a similar, albeit different insertion, beginning with [מי ק]דוש כיהוה, "who is h[oly like Yahweh]?" Klein notes: "Since the LXX here differs from the LXX of Jeremiah at a number of points, ... we must conclude that the Hebrew copy of Samuel used by the LXX translator had already been glossed. Both this gloss in [the] LXX and the gloss in 4Q[Samª] begin with references to the holiness of Yahweh."[20] The LXX reads:

κύριος ἀσθενῆ ποιήσει ἀντίδικον αὐτοῦ,
κύριος ἅγιος.
μὴ καυχάσθω ὁ φρόνιμος ἐν τῇ φρονήσει αὐτοῦ,
καὶ μὴ καυχάσθω ὁ δυνατὸς ἐν τῇ δυνάμει αὐτοῦ,

---

[19] Dahood, "The Divine Name ʿĒlî in the Psalms," 453–54, including n. 8, citing H. S. Nyberg, "Studien zum Religionskampf im Alten Testament," *Archiv für Religionswissenschaft* 35 (1938): 369 (cf. Lewis, "The Textual History of the Song of Hannah," 42, n. 31). This suggestion is also endorsed by Freedman, "Psalm 113 and the Song of Hannah," 261, including n. 27; Klein, *1 Samuel*, 13; McCarter, *I Samuel*, 70–71, 73. Labuschagne, "The Divine Title עֵלִי, 'The High One,' in the Song of Hannah," argues that this is a deliberate play on Eli's name.

[20] Klein, *1 Samuel*, 13; see also the discussion in Aejmelaeus, "Hannah's Psalm in 4QSamª," 33–35.

καὶ μὴ καυχάσθω ὁ πλούσιος ἐν τῷ πλούτῳ αὐτοῦ,
  ἀλλ᾽ ἢ ἐν τούτῳ καυχάσθω ὁ καυχώμενος,
  συνίειν καὶ γινώσκειν τὸν κύριον
  καὶ ποιεῖν κρίμα καὶ δικαιοσύνην ἐν μέσῳ τῆς γῆς.
κύριος ἀνέβη εἰς οὐρανοὺς καὶ ἐβρόντησεν,
αὐτὸς κρινεῖ ἄκρα γῆς
καὶ δίδωσιν ἰσχὺν τοῖς βασιλεῦσιν ἡμῶν
καὶ ὑψώσει κέρας χριστοῦ αὐτοῦ.

The Lord will make his adversary weak;
the Lord is holy.
Let not the clever boast in his cleverness,
and let not the mighty boast in his might,
and let not the wealthy boast in his wealth,
    but let him who boasts boast in this:
    to understand and know the Lord
    and to execute justice and righteousness in the midst of the land.
The Lord ascended to the heavens and thundered.
He will judge earth's ends
and gives strength to our kings
and will exalt the horn of his anointed.[21]

2:11 הָיָה מְשָׁרֵת—"Was ministering" translates הָיָה with a participle to indicate past action that is durative (Joüon, § 121 f). Alternatively, the action could be inchoative ("began to minister," Waltke-O'Connor, § 37.7.1b, example 15). The participle is Piel (D) masculine singular from the root שׁרת. This Piel verb takes a direct object (hence אֶת־ twice in the next textual note). The participle מְשָׁרֵת recurs as a verb in 2:18; 3:1. Elsewhere it can be used as a substantive (2 Sam 13:17, 18), often for Joshua as the ministerial assistant of Moses (e.g., Ex 24:13; Josh 1:1).

אֶת־יְהוָה אֶת־פְּנֵי עֵלִי הַכֹּהֵן:—In both instances אֵת (with maqqeph אֶת־) is the marker of a definite direct object. The first object is יְהוָה, literally "ministering *Yahweh*," but translated as "ministering *to Yahweh*" according to English idiom. The second direct object, literally "ministering … *the face of Eli the high priest*," is translated as "ministering … *in the presence of the high priest Eli*." For עֵלִי הַכֹּהֵן as a designation of Eli as "the high priest," see the third textual note on 1:9. The clause here is comparable to 2:18, where מְשָׁרֵת אֶת־פְּנֵי יְהוָה is translated as "ministering in the presence of Yahweh." See also מְשָׁרֵת אֶת־יְהוָה לִפְנֵי עֵלִי in 3:1, literally "ministering Yahweh to the face of Eli," translated as "ministering to Yahweh in the presence of Eli."

Commentary

c. 1085 BC

Hannah's prayer is one of four significant poems in the book of Samuel. The other three are David's Song of the Bow (2 Sam 1:17–27), his song of

---

[21] *NETS*; indents adapted.

deliverance (2 Samuel 22 ‖ Psalm 18), and his last words (2 Sam 23:1–7).[22] All four occur at important junctures in the narrative. Hannah's prayer prefaces the ministry of Samuel. The Song of the Bow closes the reign of Saul. David's song of deliverance summarizes his reign, and his last words look beyond his rule to the reign of the perfect King. All of these poems are united by one concept: anointing (1 Sam 2:10; 2 Sam 1:14, 16, 21; 22:51; 23:1). They signal that anointed kings ("christs") are important throughout the book. Samuel is the anointer of kings—both Saul (1 Sam 10:1) and David (1 Sam 16:13). Saul is the first person in Scripture to be called "anointed one" (מְשִׁיחוֹ, "his [Yahweh's] anointed one," 1 Sam 12:3), a title later assumed by David (2 Sam 23:1). The Hebrew מָשִׁיחַ becomes the title "Messiah," or in Greek, Χριστός, "Christ" (as explained in Jn 1:41; 4:25). Hannah's prayer prepares the reader for this as she is moved not only to pray in thanksgiving for the gift of a son, but also to prophesy of God's work that begins with the prophetic ministry of her son and culminates in Jesus, the great Anointed One.

Hannah's prayer has a number of thematic and verbal connections with 2 Samuel 22 ‖ Psalm 18 and 2 Sam 23:1–7. In addition, it shares connections with Psalms 24 and 30, also psalms of David. It is obvious that David was aware of Hannah's prayer and developed its themes.

However, David was not the only one to value Hannah's prayer. Most notably Psalm 113, whose author is unnamed; Mary's Magnificat (Lk 1:46–55); and Zechariah's Benedictus (Lk 1:67–79) contain echoes of Hannah's words. Like Hannah's Song, those of Mary and Zechariah are responses to God's miraculous provision of a child. The Magnificat celebrates the conception of Jesus Christ, and the Benedictus is prompted by the birth of his forerunner, John the Baptist. Thus, Hannah's prayer expressed sublime truths about Yahweh and his ways that later authors of Scripture incorporated into their praise of God.

Critical scholars have denied that the words of 1 Sam 2:1–10 are authentically Hannah's. Bailey notes that the only connection of the prayer to Hannah's life is the statement in 2:5 about the barren woman having children.[23] Also, the closing verse (2:10) connects the prayer to kingship, and Bailey argues that since there was no king yet in Israel in Hannah's time, these words were unlikely to be found on her lips.[24] One assumption behind these arguments is that Hannah could only have prayed a prayer of praise if it had direct relevance to her situation; she could not speak in general terms about Yahweh's power. Another assumption is that Hannah could not prophesy about a coming king. Of course, both assumptions are clearly false. Hannah, like believers before her and after her, could be moved by the Spirit to praise God with imagery that was

---

[22] The book of Samuel also includes a few short poetic utterances: 1 Sam 15:22–23; 18:7b = 21:12b (ET 21:11b) = 29:5b; 2 Sam 3:33b–34a; 20:1b.

[23] Bailey, "The Redemption of YHWH," 214; cf. Klein, *1 Samuel*, 14. See also the citations in Willis, "The Song of Hannah and Psalm 113," 139–40, nn. 8–9.

[24] Bailey, "The Redemption of YHWH," 214.

not directly drawn from her life. That accounts for the abundant use of biblical songs (as in Samuel and the Psalms) throughout church history and in Christian worship and proclamation today. As is common for critical scholarship, the presumption that there can be no true prophecy that anticipates future developments in Israel's life under God leads to the denial that 2:10 could be part of a prayer by Hannah. This critical bias against predictive prophecy leads to the denial of many of the OT messianic prophecies, including 2:10.

Rejoicing in Yahweh and His Work (2:1–3)

The first part of Hannah's prayer is her praise to God for who he is and for his work in her life (2:1) and in general (2:2–3). She starts with joy welling up in her heart for Yahweh, a thought similar to Mary's initial words in the Magnificat: "My soul magnifies the Lord" (Lk 1:46). Then Hannah immediately moves to a metaphor—her "horn is lifted" (1 Sam 2:1). This idiom occurs also in 1 Sam 2:10; Pss 75:5, 6, 11 (ET 75:4, 5, 10); 89:18, 25 (ET 89:17, 24); 92:11 (ET 92:10), 112:9; 148:4; Lam 2:17; 1 Chr 25:5. It denotes a change to a higher status.[25] Yahweh has elevated her position in her family and in the society of God's people through the gift of this son. And Hannah is given a role in salvation history, especially through her son's connection to David. Note that the prayer begins and ends with this metaphor—Yahweh lifts Hannah's horn, and he will lift the horn of his Anointed One (see the commentary on 1 Sam 2:10).

Next Hannah appears to say that she can now open her mouth to reply to her "enemies" (see the fourth textual note on 2:1), which would include her rival Peninnah (1:6–7), because she can rejoice in Yahweh's saving work. Similarly, Hannah will refer to the shattering of Yahweh's "adversaries" in 2:10, and salvation from enemies is a theme in Zechariah's Benedictus (Lk 1:71, 74). This "salvation" (1 Sam 2:1) leads Hannah to speak about the incomparability of God (1 Sam 2:2; cf. 1 Ki 8:23). No one is holy like him *because* there is no other God (see the same monotheism in 2 Sam 7:22; 22:32). In fact, all of 1 Sam 2:2 is drawn from God's own description of himself in Deuteronomy 32. The monotheism of the first two lines of 1 Sam 2:2 is drawn from Deut 32:39 (cf. also Deut 32:12), and the figure of God as a rock occurs throughout Moses' Song (Deut 32:4, 15, 18, 30, 31; cf. Deut 32:37). Hannah professes the faith of Moses and her Israelite ancestors of some 350 years earlier. The metaphor of God as the "rock (of salvation)" will be taken up again by David in his two poems at the end of the book of Samuel (2 Sam 22:3, 32, 47 ∥ Ps 18:3, 32, 47 [ET 18:2, 31, 46] and 2 Sam 23:3).

Next, Samuel's mother warns others about haughty words that reveal an arrogant heart (1 Sam 2:3)—perhaps with Peninnah in mind (1 Sam 1:6–7).

---

[25] Note the idiom especially in Ps 112:9, speaking of the righteous person who fears Yahweh: קַרְנוֹ תָּרוּם בְּכָבוֹד, "his horn will be lifted in honor." Conversely, it can at times be used to speak about someone lifting their own horn in an attempt at self-aggrandizement (Ps 75:5–6 [ET 75:4–5]).

The reason for everyone to avoid arrogance is that Yahweh is a God of knowledge who knows what is in the human heart (1 Sam 16:7); he weighs human thoughts and actions. Yahweh's omniscience leads to his acts of reversal that characterize the next section of the poem.

Yahweh Is a God of Reversals (2:4–7)

The next verses speak of God as reversing the state of affairs in order to redeem his contrite people and to humble the proud and arrogant. These include seven spheres of human experience: power (2:4), nourishment (2:5a), fertility (2:5b), life (2:6a), the grave (2:6b), wealth (2:7a), and honor (2:7b). In six of these seven reversals the first thought is that God deprives a prosperous person of something, and the second is that he blesses a deprived person. The only time the order is blessing first and then deprivation is in the one that was most relevant to Hannah—fertility (2:5b)—marking this prayer as truly Hannah's and not a poem from another context inserted by the author into Hannah's mouth.

In the first sphere, that of power (2:4), David would be elevated from humble shepherd to Israel's king, and in his praise of God for deliverance he also acknowledges that God armed him with strength (2 Sam 22:40).[26] Hannah's observation about nourishment (1 Sam 2:5a) is echoed in the Magnificat (Lk 1:53). However, Mary reverses the order, placing the feeding of the hungry before the deprivation of the well-fed.

When speaking of fertility (1 Sam 2:5b), Hannah mentions the barren woman bearing seven sons. In the Scriptures seven is the great number for completion and wholeness, probably based on the seven-day creation week in Gen 1:1–2:3. Hannah herself had six children, Samuel and five others (1 Sam 2:21). The blessing of a barren woman given a home where she bears children is also found in Ps 113:9.

Concerning life (1 Sam 2:6a), Hannah alludes to God's own words in Deut 32:39—he is the one who controls both death and life. This leads to the next sphere, that of the grave (1 Sam 2:6b). Hannah affirms that God brings people to Sheol and back again, a thought echoed by David in Ps 30:4 (ET 30:3). Through the declaration of the Law God kills, and in the Gospel he makes alive.[27] The words find literal fulfillment in the death and resurrection of Jesus Christ. It was the will of God the Father that Jesus suffer and die to atone for the sins of the world. His body was laid in a grave (Mt 27:57–66 and parallels). But on the third day God raised him from the dead bodily. After his resurrection Jesus affirmed that all this took place to fulfill what is written in the OT Scriptures (Lk 24:46; see also 1 Cor 15:4).[28]

---

26 Compare 1 Sam 2:4, וְנִכְשָׁלִים אָזְרוּ חָיִל, "but those who stumble are armed with strength," with 2 Sam 22:40, וַתַּזְרֵנִי חַיִל לַמִּלְחָמָה, "and you have armed me with strength for battle."

27 FC SD VI ("Third Use of the Law") 12.

28 See second and fourth textual notes on 1 Sam 2:6. See also, e.g., Hos 6:2; Ps 16:10, quoted in Acts 2:27–31; 13:34–37; Psalm 22, from which Jesus quotes while on the cross (Mt 27:46; Mk 15:34); and Ps 71:20.

The final two reversals involve wealth (1 Sam 2:7a; cf. Lk 1:53) and honor (1 Sam 2:7b). The loss of honor was especially feared in antiquity. Mary also refers to this reversal in the Magnificat (Lk 1:51–52).

Yahweh's Acts of Salvation (2:8–10)

God's ability to honor the humble serves as a transitional theme and becomes the first subject in the last portion of Hannah's prayer. The descriptions of Yahweh honoring the humble here (first column) and in Psalm 113 (second column) are nearly identical:

מֵקִים מֵעָפָר דָּל	מְקִימִי מֵעָפָר דָּל
מֵאַשְׁפֹּת יָרִים אֶבְיוֹן	מֵאַשְׁפֹּת יָרִים אֶבְיוֹן׃
לְהוֹשִׁיב עִם־נְדִיבִים	לְהוֹשִׁיבִי עִם־נְדִיבִים
וְכִסֵּא כָבוֹד יַנְחִלֵם	עִם נְדִיבֵי עַמּוֹ׃

He lifts a poor person from dust;	He lifts a poor person from the dust;
he raises a needy person from the trash heap	he raises a needy person from the trash heap
to seat [him] with nobles,	to seat him with nobles,
and he makes him inherit an honored throne. (1 Sam 2:8a–b)	with the nobles of his people. (Ps 113:7–8)

Hannah continues this thought by elaborating why God has the authority and power to do this—because he created the world and is its owner (1 Sam 2:8c). This same thought is expressed in Ps 24:1–2. "The foundations of the earth" are also mentioned again in the book of Samuel by David in his song of deliverance (מֹסְדוֹת תֵּבֵל, 2 Sam 22:16 ‖ Ps 18:16 [ET 18:15]).

Next, Hannah contrasts God's protection of his saints with his punishment of the wicked (1 Sam 2:9). His protection is also mentioned in almost identical words in Prov 2:8b. The third line of 1 Sam 2:9 explains why the faithful need God's protection and why the wicked will be silenced: because human strength cannot prevail either by providing unfailing protection or by preventing God's judgment.

The last verse of Hannah's prayer takes on an eschatological cast as she speaks of God's judgment of all the earth (1 Sam 2:10). First she notes Yahweh's role as he executes his Law, shattering his enemies and thundering against them (as in 2 Sam 22:14 ‖ Ps 18:14 [ET 18:13]). Then she notes God's role as a gracious and merciful Father, giving support to his people as he strengthens their King, who is called "his Anointed One" in the last line of the poem (see below).

In time God would give Israel kings who would fulfill this role as an anointed one imperfectly. Both Saul and David would bear the title "messiah."[29]

---

[29] Saul is called God's anointed one (מָשִׁיחַ) in 1 Sam 12:3, 5; 24:7, 11 (ET 24:6, 10); 26:9, 11, 16, 23; 2 Sam 1:14, 16; David in 2 Sam 19:22 (ET 19:21); 22:51; 23:1.

David would employ the imagery from Hannah's prayer to speak about God's defense of him as God's anointed king. Yahweh thundered in heaven against his enemies (2 Sam 22:14). Moreover, God saved him and was gracious to him (2 Sam 22:51).

However, neither Hannah's words nor David's words were completed by David or any other king of ancient Israel. While God gave David success and blessed Israel through him, he did not "judge the ends of the earth" (1 Sam 2:10) through him. Instead, Hannah's words prophesied of the great Messiah, God's Anointed, Jesus, the Son of David.[30] David, too, recognized this and prophesied that God would show favor "to his anointed, to David *and his offspring forever*" (2 Sam 22:51). That eternal favor of the Father rests on his Christ, and it was this hope that had moved Hannah to trust Yahweh both for a son and for his eternal blessing.

The closing line of Hannah's Song returns to the idiom of raising a horn, but instead of her own "horn" (1 Sam 2:1), she declares that Yahweh will "lift up the horn of his Anointed One" (1 Sam 2:10), that is, his Messiah, the Christ (Jn 1:41; 4:25), the one David will call "the horn of my salvation" (2 Sam 22:3). As Hannah's opening words (1 Sam 2:1) were echoed in Mary's Magnificat (Lk 1:46), her closing words also find their fulfillment in the first chapter of Luke's Gospel. Zechariah takes them up as he rejoices over the circumcision and naming of his son, John the Baptist, the forerunner of the Christ, who had been conceived by the power of the Holy Spirit three months earlier (Lk 1:26–38). Therefore Zechariah can use past-tense (aorist) verbs to speak of the event as having been accomplished:

> "Blessed be the Lord, the God of Israel,
>> for he visited and made redemption for his people
> and he raised up a horn of salvation for us,
>> in the house of David, his servant,
> just as he spoke by the mouth of his holy prophets of old."
>> (Lk 1:68–70)

This "horn of salvation" (Lk 1:69) is envisioned as the sacrificed Lamb with "seven horns" in Rev 5:6.

Samuel as Yahweh's Minister (2:11)

The fulfilling of Hannah's vow is noted in almost mundane terms as we learn that Elkanah went back to Ramah, but Samuel remained in Eli's presence as a minister to Yahweh. In fact, Samuel is the only person in the book of Samuel called Yahweh's minister, and this office is noted three times (מְשָׁרֵת אֶת־פְּנֵי יְהוָה, 1 Sam 2:11, 18; 3:1). This highlights him as the first of

---

[30] Mt 1:1; 9:27; 12:23; 15:22; 20:30–31; 21:9, 15; Mk 10:47–48; Lk 18:38–39.

the three great leaders of Israel in the book: Samuel (a Levite[31]), Saul, and David. The title "minister" is later applied to other Levites who served Yahweh in the temple (1 Chr 6:17 [ET 6:32]; 16:4; 2 Chr 13:10; 23:6; 29:11).

---

[31] See the last textual note on 1:1 and "Elkanah and His Family (1:1–3)" in the commentary on 1:1–20.

1 Samuel 2:12–17

Eli's Sons and Their Sins

Translation

2   ¹²**However, the sons of Eli were good-for-nothing men [because] they did not believe in Yahweh. (¹³Now the right of the priests with the people [was as follows]: Whenever a man was offering a sacrifice, the priest's servant would come with a three-pronged fork in his hand as the meat was boiling. ¹⁴He would thrust it into the pan, pot, cauldron, or kettle. Everything that the fork would bring out the priest would take with it. This is what they did to every Israelite who came there in Shiloh.) ¹⁵In addition, before the fat was burned away, the priest's servant would come and say to the man who was sacrificing, "Give the priest meat to roast, since he will not take boiled meat from you, only raw [meat]." ¹⁶When the man would say to him, "The fat certainly must be burned away first, then take what you wish for yourself," he would say, "No. Instead, give [it to me] now, and if you won't, I'll take it by force." ¹⁷The sin of the servants was very serious in the presence of Yahweh because the men disrespected the offerings to Yahweh.**

Textual Notes

2:12 בְּנֵי בְלִיָּעַל—"Sons of uselessness" means "good-for-nothing men"; see the first textual note on 1:16.

לֹא יָדְעוּ אֶת־יְהוָה:—Literally "they did not know Yahweh," this means "they did not believe in Yahweh." The expression "know Yahweh" denotes a relational knowledge of him. In most contexts it denotes a salvific relationship with him through faith (Is 19:21; Jer 31:34; Hos 2:22 [ET 2:20]; 6:3; Heb 8:11). Conversely, unbelievers (Pharaoh, Ex 5:2; Cyrus, Is 45:5), apostates (faithless Israelites, Is 1:3; 40:28; Jer 9:2 [ET 9:3]; Hos 5:4; apostate priests, Jer 2:8), and those who have not experienced his salvation (Judg 2:10) do not "know" (יָדַע) him. This expression here sets up a contrast between Eli's sons, who did not "know Yahweh" in the sense of not having faith in him, and Samuel, "before he knew Yahweh" in the sense of receiving a direct word of revelation and having a relationship with him as his prophet (1 Sam 3:7).

2:13 וּמִשְׁפַּט הַכֹּהֲנִים אֶת־הָעָם—"Now the right of the priests with the people [was as follows]: ..." The translation understands this as an introductory nominal clause and אֶת־ as the preposition "with." However, the LXX and some commentators interpret this to be a second thing that Eli's sons did not know: they didn't know "the custom of the priests with the people" concerning sacrifices.[1] But there are several problems with that interpretation. First, one would expect the direct object marker אֶת־ before the construct phrase מִשְׁפַּט הַכֹּהֲנִים, since it is definite and it would be the second direct object

---

1   Tsumura, *The First Book of Samuel*, 152; McCarter, *I Samuel*, 77–78; Auld, *I and II Samuel*, 40, 44.

for the verb יָדְעוּ in 2:12.[2] Second, the following narrative makes clear that the right of the priest to a portion of the sacrifices was known, but Eli's sons simply ignored the rules for it (2:15–16). Third, the rest of 2:13 through 2:14 is an explanation of the customary right of the priest to a portion of the sacrifice.[3] This initial clause is a necessary introduction. If it were a direct object attached to the preceding verse (2:12) instead of an introduction to what follows, the explanation would begin abruptly ("whenever …") without any transition for the reader from the mentioning of this otherwise unknown and undocumented priestly right to a description of it. The Torah stipulates that the priests receive portions of some offerings[4] but does not give any specific instructions (of the kind in 2:13–14) for how the priests were to take the meat.

כָּל־אִישׁ זֹבֵחַ זֶבַח וּבָא—The participial (זֹבֵחַ) clause ("whenever a man was offering a sacrifice") sets up a condition upon which the later action (וּבָא) is contingent: "the priest's servant *would come*" (GKC, §§ 116 w; 159 i; 164 a). In זֹבֵחַ זֶבַח, literally "sacrificing a sacrifice," the direct object (the noun זֶבַח) is a cognate accusative, that is, it is from the same root as the verb (זָבַח). Hebrew favors cognate accusatives, while English avoids them. See also the (first) textual notes on 1:6, 11, 17, 21 (1:21 also has זֶבַח with זָבַח).

כְּבַשֵּׁל הַבָּשָׂר—The preposition כְּ attached to an infinitive construct (the Piel [D] of בָּשַׁל) forms a temporal clause, literally "when boiling the meat." The noun בָּשָׂר, "flesh," denotes "meat" of a sacrificed animal here and twice in 2:15. בָּשַׁל, "to boil," recurs in the form of a Pual (Dp) participle, מְבֻשָּׁל, "boiled," toward the end of 2:15. The Torah prescribes boiling (Piel of בָּשַׁל) for only a few kinds of sacrifices (Ex 29:31; Lev 8:31; see also Num 6:19). The Passover lamb must be "roasted" (צָלִי) and *not* "boiled" (בָּשַׁל, Ex 12:9), so it is surprising that בָּשַׁל is used for "cooking" or "roasting" the Passover in Deut 16:7 and in 2 Chr 35:13, which adds "in fire" to clarify that roasting is meant. Boiling (בָּשַׁל) sacrificial meat is also pictured in eschatological visions in Ezek 46:20–24 and Zech 14:21, which refers to doing so in a "pot" (hence the meaning cannot be roasted there). For roasting, see also the second textual note on 1 Sam 2:15.

וְהַמַּזְלֵג שְׁלֹשׁ־הַשִּׁנַּיִם—The construct phrase שְׁלֹשׁ־הַשִּׁנַּיִם is in apposition to the definite noun הַמַּזְלֵג, literally "the fork, three of teeth" (*IBH*, § 21 A; Joüon, § 131 c). It means "a three-pronged fork." The definite article is used on הַמַּזְלֵג because this utensil is definite in the mind of the narrator, but it corresponds to an indefinite article in English.[5] Since the noun שֵׁן, "tooth," occurs only in the singular and the dual (for two rows of teeth, upper and lower), the dual form is used as a plural even though there are "three" (שָׁלֹשׁ).[6]

---

[2] This problem does not absolutely exclude the interpretation, since there are examples of a second definite direct object without a (repeated) direct object marker.

[3] Similarly, in Deut 18:3, which has the only other occurrence of the phrase מִשְׁפַּט הַכֹּהֲנִים, the explanation follows.

[4] E.g., Lev 5:13; 6:9, 19, 22 (ET 6:16, 26, 29); 7:6–9, 14, 31–34; 8:31; 10:13–14; Deut 18:3. See the overview and explanation in Kleinig, *Leviticus*, 38–39.

[5] See *IBH*, § 20 A; GKC, § 126 q; Joüon, § 137 m; Waltke-O'Connor § 13.5.1e.

[6] See Joüon, § 91 e; Waltke-O'Connor, § 7.3a; 12.3b, example 3.

2:14 יַעֲלֶה הַמַּזְלֵג—The form of this third masculine singular imperfect of עָלָה could be Qal (G), which would have the intransitive meaning "come up." But in context it must be Hiphil (H) with הַמַּזְלֵג as its subject and a transitive meaning: "… the fork would bring up/out."

יִקַּח הַכֹּהֵן בּוֹ—The referent of the third masculine singular suffix on בּוֹ is the masculine singular noun preceding this clause, הַמַּזְלֵג, thus "the priest would take with it [with the fork]."[7] Grammatically, the referent could be הַכֹּהֵן, "the priest." But to express "the priest would take with/for himself" the Hebrew idiom is for the verb לָקַח to be used with the preposition לְ (BDB, s.v. לָקַח, Qal, 4 a, b, d, e). This clause is often translated as if בּוֹ were לוֹ, "for himself," but there is no evidence for such a reading other than the LXX, which probably contains a translational variant, not a reflection of the translator's Vorlage.

לְכָל־יִשְׂרָאֵל הַבָּאִים—The singular "all Israel" serves to focus the narrative on each Israelite who came with a sacrifice, while the subsequent Qal (G) participle is masculine plural: הַבָּאִים, "who came." This plural participle lends a collective idea to the context, emphasizing that this action affected all Israel (GKC, § 132 g). However, English cannot efficiently express the simultaneous individual focus and the collective application as the Hebrew does. Here the translation chooses to emphasize the individual focus ("every Israelite") because the context is speaking about a specific action. However, it should be borne in mind that the Hebrew text also emphasizes that all Israel was afflicted by the priests' greedy demand.

2:15 יַקְטִרוּן אֶת־הַחֵלֶב—The verb form is the third masculine plural Hiphil (H) imperfect of קָטַר, with paragogic *nun* (Joüon, § 44 e). קָטַר is used thirty-three times in Leviticus (always Hiphil [H] except for one Hophal [Hp]) as a technical term for burning a sacrifice on the altar to produce an aroma pleasing to Yahweh.[8] Normally it is singular and its subject is a priest (priests in Lev 3:5). The action of burning the "fat" (חֵלֶב) was assigned to the priest.[9] However, in 1 Sam 2:15–16, the verb is plural with no specified subjects, and the priest himself appears to be absent. In both verses the translation renders this impersonal plural as a passive, "was/be burned away."

תְּנָה בָשָׂר לִצְלוֹת לַכֹּהֵן—Literally, "give meat to roast for the priest." The verb תְּנָה is the alternate form with paragogic ה (Joüon, § 48 d) of the imperative of נָתַן (the regular form is תֵּן). The infinitive construct לִצְלוֹת is of צָלָה, "to roast," with the preposition לְ indicating purpose. This rare verb occurs elsewhere only in Is 44:16, 19. The cognate noun צָלִי, "roasted," is used for the Passover lamb (Ex 12:8–9; its only other occurrence is in Is 44:16).

כִּי אִם־חָי:—"Only raw" is literally "only alive." The adjective חַי (pausal: חָי), "living," is a striking way to emphasize the rawness of the meat, since the sacrificed animal clearly would be dead. Ex 12:9 uses the adjective נָא to stipulate that the Passover lamb

---

7   Tsumura, "The Poetic Nature of Hebrew Narrative Prose in 1 Sam. 2:12–17," 296.

8   E.g., Lev 1:9, 13, 15, 17. Kleinig, *Leviticus*, 56–57, emphasizes that the verb denotes the production of smoke.

9   See קָטַר with חֵלֶב in, e.g., Ex 29:13; Lev 3:16; 4:19, 26, 31, 35; 6:5 (ET 6:12); 7:31.

is not to be eaten "raw." The combination כִּי אִם usually has a limiting or exceptive meaning: "except (for)," "unless," "only (if)."

2:16 קַטֵּר יַקְטִירוּן—Normally when an infinitive absolute is used to strengthen the force of a finite form of the same verb ("*certainly* must be burned away"), both forms of the verb are in the same conjugation. This is a rare exception since the infinitive absolute קַטֵּר is Piel (D) and the imperfect יַקְטִירוּן is Hiphil (H).[10] For this verb's meaning, see the first textual note on 2:15.

כַּיּוֹם—Literally "as the day," this is an idiom that occasionally means "first, beforehand" (Gen 25:31, 33; 1 Ki 1:51; 22:5; 2 Chr 18:4).

לֹא—The reading of the Kethib is לוֹ, "to him." The translation follows the Qere, the homonym לֹא, "no." This is also the reading found in 4QSamᵃ and the LXX.

וְאִם־לֹא לָקַחְתִּי בְחָזְקָה:—Literally "and if not, I'll take by force." לֹא negates an understood repetition of the preceding verb תִּתֵּן (Qal [G] imperfect of נָתַן), thus "if you won't [give]" (see Joüon, §§ 160 j, 167 o). The perfect aspect of לָקַחְתִּי denotes action that will take place immediately if the request is refused: "I'll take" (see Joüon, § 112 g). 4QSamᵃ has a *waw* consecutive with the perfect, [ולק]חתי, "then I'll t[ake]," while the LXX has a future indicative, λήμψομαι, "I'll take." 4QSamᵃ seems to be a secondary correction since it eliminates two words in the text, וְאִם־לֹא, whereas both the MT and the LXX begin the same way (וְאִם־לֹא = καὶ ἐὰν μή). The noun חָזְקָה, "strength, force" (five times in the OT), is always used with the inseparable preposition בְּ and functions adverbially (also Judg 4:3; 8:1; Ezek 34:4; Jonah 3:8): "forcefully" or even "violently."

2:17 אֶת־פְּנֵי יְהוָה—See the fourth textual note on 1:22.

Commentary

c. 1085–c. 1075 BC

The opening of this section immediately draws a comparison between Samuel, who was faithfully ministering to Yahweh, and the sons of Eli, who did not even believe in ("know," 2:12) Yahweh.[11] The author depicts Eli's sons as "good-for-nothing men" (בְּנֵי בְלִיַּעַל, 2:12). Ironically, Samuel's mother, Hannah, had felt that Eli falsely accused her of being a "good-for-nothing woman" (בַת־בְּלִיַּעַל, 1:16). It seems that Eli could not distinguish good from evil, even when they were right under his nose.

Eli's sons were "good-for-nothing" for two reasons according to the author. They were unbelieving (2:12), and "in addition" (2:15), "the men disrespected the offerings to Yahweh" (2:17).

Before the author can continue the narrative about Eli's sons, he must first explain to his readers how the priests customarily received their portion of the sacrifice at Shiloh (2:13–14). These verses are parenthetical material supplied so that the reader can appreciate the gravity of the offense when the priest requests "raw" meat (2:15). Readers might not understand the narrative without

---

[10] Joüon, § 123 p; Waltke-O'Connor, § 35.2.1e.

[11] See the second textual note on 2:12.

this explanation if what is described in 2:13–14 was no longer the practice for determining the priest's portion of the sacrifice after the tabernacle was moved from Shiloh. The custom was that the priest waited until the sacrificial meat was boiled,[12] and then the priest's servant could stick the fork into the well-cooked meat and take whatever meat the fork would bring out of the pot. Forks are mentioned in the OT only in connection with utensils used in the tabernacle and the temple.[13]

Hophni and Phinehas were not content to wait for whatever meat would fall off the bone when the fork was thrust into the pot. Instead, they instructed their servants to demand raw meat before the fat had been burned away. The regulations given through Moses called for all of the fat to be burned as a pleasing aroma for Yahweh (Lev 7:23–25, 31; 17:6). Thus, Eli's sons were demanding a portion of the sacrifice *before* it was sacrificed to Yahweh and before it was cooked. This way they ensured that they would receive a choice portion of the meat. In a culture where starvation was common, the eating of fat was highly prized.[14] In addition, in ancient cultures meat was not eaten frequently since there was no refrigeration to preserve it. Thus, there was always a danger that one could suffer ill health from having too little fat in one's diet. For this reason, fat was highly prized, as was olive oil, which is high in fat (cf. Is 39:2; Hos 2:10, 24 [ET 2:8, 22]; Prov 21:20; Rev 6:6).

Bible versions and commentators are split as to whether the noun נַעַר, "servant," in 2:13, 15, 17 refers to the priests' servants or to Eli's sons. Many treat the first two occurrences as a "servant" of Eli's sons (2:13, 15) and the last "servants" as Eli's sons themselves (2:17; cf. NRSV, NIV, ESV). However, there is no signal by the author that he is abruptly changing the referent from the servants to the priests themselves. Tsumura argues that all three instances refer to Eli's sons; he proposes that in 2:13, 15 the noun נַעַר functions adjectivally and means "young."[15] There is little evidence, however, for such a usage. Both McCarter and Klein offer a better solution: all three instances refer to the priests' assistants.[16] The sins of Eli's sons were doubly heinous because they disrespected Yahweh's sacrifices and also compelled their servants to participate in their sins. Thus, the author of Samuel concludes: "The sin of the *servants* was very serious … because *the men* [i.e., Eli's sons] disrespected the offerings to Yahweh" (2:17).

---

[12] See the third textual note on 2:13.

[13] The noun מַזְלֵג occurs only in Ex 27:3; 38:3; Num 4:14; 1 Sam 2:13–14; 1 Chr 28:17; 2 Chr 4:16.

[14] In some passages חֵלֶב, "fat," refers to the "richest" or "best" of foods, e.g., Gen 45:18; Num 18:12, 29; Deut 32:14; Ps 81:17 (ET 81:16).

[15] He argues that the construct phrase נַעַר הַכֹּהֵן means "young priest." Tsumura cites a number of instances where he claims that נַעַר is used adjectivally, but a close examination reveals that none of these are actual adjectival uses (*The First Book of Samuel*, 157, including n. 108).

[16] McCarter, *I Samuel*, 77; Klein, *1 Samuel*, 21. See also HCSB.

We are also told that "the sin of the servants was very serious *in the presence of Yahweh*" (אֶת־פְּנֵי יְהוָה, 2:17). This comment also draws a sharp contrast between Eli's sons and Samuel, who in the very next verse is said to have been "ministering in the presence of Yahweh" (2:18). Samuel's "ministering" (מְשָׁרֵת, 2:11, 18; also 3:1) brackets this account of Eli's sons, who were not faithful ministers of Yahweh. This contrast is heightened by the use of the same noun (נַעַר) regarding the sinful behavior of the priests' "servant(s)" (נַעַר, 2:13, 15, 17) and the faithful behavior of the "boy" Samuel (נַעַר, 2:11, 18).[17]

The text also contains an interesting connection to Numbers 16 through the verb נָאַץ, "to disrespect." In Numbers 16 the Levite Korah, along with Dathan and Abiram, disrespected Yahweh (Num 16:30) by desiring to usurp Aaron's priestly office for themselves. When they did this they disrespected Yahweh's choice of Aaron and his sons as priests. In the narrative of Samuel we are shown the opposite: the Levite Samuel is respecting God by serving under the direction of the priest Eli (1 Sam 2:11), while the priests Hophni and Phinehas were disrespecting Yahweh's sacrifices.

---

[17] The noun נַעַר, "boy," refers to Samuel also in 1:22, 24, 25, 27; 2:21, 26; 3:1, 8.

1 Samuel 2:18–21
Samuel Ministers before Yahweh

Translation

2 ¹⁸Now Samuel was ministering in the presence of Yahweh, a boy wearing a linen ephod. ¹⁹Now his mother would make a small robe for him and bring [it] up to him every year when she went up with her husband to offer the annual sacrifice. ²⁰And Eli would bless Elkanah and his wife. He would say, "May Yahweh restore to you children from this woman in place of the requested one that she dedicated to Yahweh." Then they would return to his place. ²¹Indeed, Yahweh paid attention to Hannah, and she conceived and bore three sons and two daughters. Meanwhile, the boy Samuel grew with Yahweh.

Textual Notes

2:18 מְשָׁרֵת אֶת־פְּנֵי יְהוָה—See the first and second textual notes on 2:11.

נַעַר—See the commentary on 2:11–17 for a discussion of the text's play on the different meanings of נַעַר, "servant" and "boy."

חָגוּר—This verb, "wearing," is a Qal passive (Gp) participle masculine singular. The root חגר specifically refers to wearing something around one's waist. What is worn is worded in the following accusative (GKC, § 116 k; Joüon, § 121 o).

אֵפוֹד בָּד:—This construct phrase, "an ephod of linen," is translated adjectivally, "a linen ephod." This same phrase refers to the vestments of the priests in 1 Sam 22:18 and to a garment worn by David when he danced before the Lord as the ark was brought to Jerusalem (2 Sam 6:14; 1 Chr 15:27). The Torah prescribed "linen" (בַּד; in pause: בָּד) as the material for the priests' undergarments that they were to wear whenever they went into the tabernacle or ministered at the altar (Ex 28:42–43). Linen was also stipulated as the material for the vestments that the high priest wore on the Day of Atonement (Lev 16:4, 23, 32) and for the garments worn by priests when taking the ashes of the burnt offering off the altar (Lev 6:3 [ET 6:10]). The "ephod" (אֵפוֹד) was a vestment worn on the chest (cf. the pastor's stole). The construction of the high priest's ephod and the breastpiece that was to be attached to it are described in Exodus.[1] An ephod is worn properly in, e.g., Lev 8:7; 1 Sam 2:18, 28. An ephod is use in heterodox worship in Judg 8:27; 17:5; 18:14–20.

2:19 וּמְעִיל קָטֹן—Like the ephod (see the previous textual note), Exodus details the construction of the high priest's "robe" (מְעִיל, Ex 28:4, 31, 34; 29:5; 39:22–26). This garment was donned before putting on the ephod (Lev 8:7). Robes were also worn by laypeople, including Saul (1 Sam 24:5 [ET 24:4]) and Jonathan (1 Sam 18:4).

תַּעֲשֶׂה ... וְהַעַלְתָה—Hannah is the subject of these two feminine singular verbs. The Qal (G) form of עָשָׂה is imperfect with the force of frequentative or habitual past

---

[1] Ex 28:4–30; 39:2–21; cf. Ex 25:7; 29:5; 35:9, 27.

action: every year she "would make" a robe. That imperfect is continued by a Hiphil (H) perfect of עָלָה with *waw* consecutive, which has a causative meaning with the same frequentative force: she "would bring up" the robe annually. See *IBH*, § 53 B 2; GKC, § 112 e; Joüon, § 119 u.

מִיָּמִים ׀ יָמִימָה—This means "yearly"; see the second textual note on 1:3.

בַּעֲלוֹתָהּ אֶת־אִישָׁהּ—Whereas the form of עָלָה earlier in the verse (וְהַעַלְתָה) was Hiphil (H), עֲלוֹת is the Qal (G) infinitive construct with the preposition בְּ and a third feminine singular suffix serving as its subject: "when she went up." Since the Qal is intransitive, אֶת־ must be the preposition, "*with* her husband," and not the direct object marker (not "she brought up her husband").[2]

לִזְבֹּחַ אֶת־זֶבַח הַיָּמִים:—See the first textual note on 1:21, which has these same words.

2:20 וּבֵרַךְ ... וְאָמַר ... וְהָלְכוּ—These three perfect verbs, each with *waw* consecutive, continue the sequence begun with the imperfect תַּעֲשֶׂה (2:19) and refer to past action with the same frequentative or habitual force: "would bless ... would say ... would return." The Piel (D) of בָּרַךְ with a human subject usually means "to utter a blessing," calling on God to display his grace. See further the third textual note on 9:13. In the context of the sanctuary and with a priest as the subject, it has formal liturgical force, "to pronounce a benediction."[3] Here Eli's benediction is the one quoted, rather than the Aaronic Benediction (Num 6:24–26), although יָשֵׂם appears in both (see the next textual note).

יָשֵׂם יְהוָה לְךָ—Benedictions are typically expressed with a verb in the jussive, which is an indirect imperative. יָשֵׂם is a jussive (the imperfect would be יָשִׂים) of שִׂים, "set, place." In context here with the preposition תַּחַת, "in place of," it means "replace" or "restore." Two other benedictions use this same jussive: Gen 48:20; Num 6:26. It is also used in the malediction of Jer 29:22. This benediction invokes "Yahweh" (יְהוָה) to carry out this action. The reading of 4QSam[a] is ישלם י[הוה] לך, and the verb would be pointed as יְשַׁלֵּם, the Piel (D) of שָׁלַם, "to repay, compensate, reward." It is probably supported by the LXX (ἀποτείσαι σοι κύριος). If original, the MT reading יָשֵׂם most likely resulted from the accident omission of a ל.

זֶרַע—Literally "seed," this singular noun was used for the child for whom Hannah asked in her vow (1 Sam 1:11). It can be used collectively to refer to children or later descendants (1 Sam 20:42; 24:22 [ET 24:21]; 2 Sam 4:8; 22:51). It is part of the messianic promise to David in 2 Sam 7:12.

הַשְּׁאֵלָה אֲשֶׁר שָׁאַל לַיהוָה—This cognate accusative construction meant "to request [שָׁאַל] a request [שְׁאֵלָה]" and referred to Hannah's prayer for Samuel in 1 Sam 1:17, 27 (cf. 1:20); see the textual notes there. Here, with the prepositional phrase לַיהוָה, "to Yahweh," the Qal (G) שָׁאַל would have to mean "to dedicate," as did the Hiphil (H) of שָׁאַל in 1:28 (see the textual note there). The difficulty of the MT is compounded

---

[2] If the verb were Hiphil, its expected form with the same preposition and suffix would be בְּהַעֲלוֹתָהּ, although occasionally the preformative ה of the Hiphil is elided, in which case the Hiphil could theoretically have the same form as the Qal here, בֵּעֲלוֹתָהּ.

[3] See also, e.g., Num 6:23–27; Lev 9:22, 23; Deut 10:8; 21:5; 1 Chr 23:13; 2 Chr 30:27.

because שָׁאַל is third masculine singular, and so Elkanah would have to be the subject. In the reading of 4QSam[a] the verb is Hiphil perfect. Its final letter could be supplied as [השאיל]ת, second feminine singular, "you dedicated," which is supported by the LXX, τοῦ χρέους οὗ ἔχρησας, "the loan that you made." The reading of 4QSam[a] could also be [השאיל]ה (so *BHS*), third feminine singular, which is adopted in the translation, "she dedicated to Yahweh." The definite feminine abstract noun הַשְּׁאֵלָה, "the request," is translated concretely as "the requested one," namely, Samuel.

2:21 כִּי־פָקַד—It is difficult to decide between this reading and the one found in 4QSam[a] (ויפקד) and the LXX (καὶ ἐπεσκέψατο). The conjunction כִּי can have an asseverative meaning, "indeed," and a strong affirmation fits the context here. The verb פָּקַד, traditionally translated as "visit," means to take a personal and special interest in someone, either for good or ill.[4] It can refer to Yahweh acting in a gracious way to fulfill his promises and accomplish his redemptive purposes; see, e.g., its use for Yahweh's action toward Sarah that resulted in her conception of Isaac (Gen 21:1; see also, e.g., Gen 50:24–25).

עִם־יְהוָה:—This means "with Yahweh." 4QSam[a] has [לפני י]הוה], "in Yahweh's presence." Cf. the LXX: ἐνώπιον κυρίου.

Commentary

c. 1085–c. 1075 BC

In contrast to Eli's sons, who were busy ministering to their own needs, Samuel was ministering before Yahweh. Two items of clothing are mentioned for Samuel: "a linen ephod" (אֵפוֹד בָּד, 2:18) and a "robe" (מְעִיל, 2:19). While linen was also used for priestly undergarments, the ephod was an outer garment worn on the priest's chest when conducting or assisting divine worship (see the fourth textual note on 2:18). The new "robe" (מְעִיל) Hannah brought Samuel each year may have been a vestment worn under the ephod (see the first textual note on 2:19). Thus, Samuel is depicted here as a Levite serving before Yahweh at an unusually early age.[5]

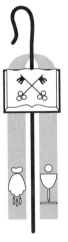

Once again we are given a glimpse into the life of Elkanah's family. Hannah and Elkanah supported Samuel when they made their annual pilgrimage to Shiloh. Hannah would bring him a robe, perhaps to wear with the ephod. The family was favored by Eli, who blessed Hannah. Yahweh worked through Eli's blessing to give Hannah five more children.

However, the focus returns to Samuel, the only child of Hannah named by the author. We are told that he grew with Yahweh (2:21; see further 2:26). Later this growing with God will be connected to Samuel's ministry as a prophet (3:19–4:1a).

---

4   See *TWOT*, § 1802, which says that this verb can denote "taking action to cause a considerable change in the circumstances … , either for the better or for the worse."

5   Levites normally did not begin service to Yahweh until age 25 (Num 8:24–25).

1 Samuel 2:22–26

Eli Rebukes His Sons

Translation

2 ²²Now Eli was very old. He kept hearing everything that his sons were doing to all Israel and that they were lying with the women who served at the entrance to the tent of meeting. ²³So he said to them, "Why are you doing these things—that I am hearing your evil deeds from all these people? ²⁴Do not [do this], my sons, because the report that I am hearing, which Yahweh's people are circulating, is not good. ²⁵If a person sins against [another] person, God can intercede for him. However, if a person sins against Yahweh, who will intercede for him?" But they would not listen to their father because Yahweh was determined to kill them. ²⁶But the boy Samuel continued growing and enjoyed favor both with Yahweh and with people.

Textual Notes

2:22–23 יַעֲשׂוּן ... יִשְׁכְּבוּן ... תַעֲשׂוּן—The imperfect aspect of these three Qal (G) verbs (each with paragogic *nun*; see Waltke-O'Connor, § 31.7.1a) denotes habitual action in the past ("were doing ... were lying," 2:22) and into the present ("are doing," 2:23).

2:22 וְעֵלִי זָקֵן מְאֹד וְשָׁמַע—The word זָקֵן could be a Qal (G) perfect third masculine singular (so BDB) or an adjective used in a nominal clause: "now Eli was very old." In either case, the following perfect with *waw* consecutive, וְשָׁמַע, signifies continuing action: "he kept hearing" (*IBH*, § 53 B 2; Joüon, § 119 v; cf. GKC, § 112 k).

אֵת כָּל־אֲשֶׁר—This is the first of two direct objects of the verb וְשָׁמַע, "he [Eli] kept hearing." Both begin with the direct object marker אֵת. The first object is כָּל־, which serves as a noun, "everything," and which is then elaborated by a relative clause beginning with אֲשֶׁר.

וְאֵת אֲשֶׁר־יִשְׁכְּבוּן אֶת־הַנָּשִׁים הַצֹּבְאוֹת פֶּתַח אֹהֶל מוֹעֵד:—This is the second direct object of וְשָׁמַע. The relative pronoun אֲשֶׁר has a nominalizing function: it enables the following verbal clause (... יִשְׁכְּבוּן) to serve as a noun object, "kept hearing ... *that* ..." (see the next textual note). However, this clause, "and that they were lying with the women who served at the entrance to the tent of meeting," is missing in 4QSam^a and in Codex Vaticanus. Harvey argues that the omission in Codex Vaticanus is due to a tendency in that manuscript to present priests in the most positive light.[1]

יִשְׁכְּבוּן אֶת־—Here the verb שָׁכַב, "to lie down," is used with the preposition אֵת, "with": "they were lying with." This idiom can have a variety of nuances, including death as "sleeping with one's fathers" (2 Sam 7:12). To denote sexual relations שָׁכַב is more commonly used with עִם, "with." This idiom can refer to marital relations (שָׁכַב עִם, 2 Sam 11:11; 12:24) but is often a euphemism for *illicit* sexual relations (שָׁכַב עִם,

---

[1] Harvey, "*Tendenz* and Textual Criticism in 1 Samuel 2–10," 72–73.

2 Sam 11:4; 12:11; rape is denoted by שָׁכַב עִם in 2 Sam 13:11 and by שָׁכַב אֶת in 2 Sam 13:14). The context indicates that שָׁכַב אֶת refers to illicit activity here. Elsewhere, for example, it refers to incestuous relations in Gen 19:33–34; 35:22; Lev 20:11–12, 20; to rape in Gen 34:2, 7; and to homosexuality in Lev 20:13 (to be punished by death).

הַצֹּבְאוֹת—This is the feminine plural Qal (G) participle of צָבָא with the definite article: "who served." The verb צָבָא is related to the noun in the title "Yahweh of armies" (צְבָאוֹת); see the fourth textual note on 1 Sam 1:3. The verb usually means "wage war, fight," but this is one of four passages where it means "be on duty" at a sanctuary (*HALOT*, s.v. צבא, 2 a and b). Elsewhere it refers to the Levites' service at the tabernacle in Num 4:23; 8:24 and to women serving at the entrance to the tent of meeting twice in Ex 38:8, similar to here.

2:23 אֲשֶׁר אָנֹכִי שֹׁמֵעַ אֶת־דִּבְרֵיכֶם רָעִים מֵאֵת כָּל־הָעָם אֵלֶּה—This relative clause, literally "which I am hearing your evil words, from with all these people," is in apposition to כַּדְּבָרִים הָאֵלֶּה, "(like) these things." For its syntax, see Joüon, § 154 fe. Since the singular noun (with the article) הָעָם, "the people," is a collective (see the fourth textual note on 2:24), it can be modified by a plural such as the demonstrative pronoun אֵלֶּה, "these." Although the demonstrative lacks a corresponding article, this feature is attested elsewhere (GKC, § 126 y; therefore Joüon, § 149 d, is unjustified in calling אֵלֶּה "incorrect").

2:24 אַל בָּנָי—"Do not [do this], my sons!" The negative particle אַל is used to negate volitive forms and in this case assumes an imperative such as "do this." Syntactically בָּנָי (pausal form of בְּנֵי) is a vocative.

לוֹא־טוֹבָה—Although earlier in the Hebrew word order, this is the predicate, so the English translation places "is not good" at the end of the sentence.

הַשְּׁמֻעָה אֲשֶׁר אָנֹכִי שֹׁמֵעַ—This is another cognate accusative construction.[2] The Qal (G) participle שֹׁמֵעַ, "hearing," takes as its object the definite feminine noun הַשְּׁמֻעָה, "the report," literally "the thing heard" since in form it is a feminine Qal passive (Gp) participle of שָׁמַע, "to hear."

מַעֲבִרִים עַם־יְהוָה:—The translation renders this as a relative clause modifying הַשְּׁמֻעָה, "the report": "which Yahweh's people are circulating." The verb עָבַר in the Hiphil (H) stem (literally "cause to pass through") can denote the circulation of a message (Ex 36:6; Ezra 1:1; 10:7; Neh 8:15; 2 Chr 30:5; 36:22). The subject is the construct phrase עַם־יְהוָה, "the people of Yahweh." עַם is grammatically singular but a collective. Therefore the Hiphil participle is plural, מַעֲבִרִים.

2:25 אִם־יֶחֱטָא ... וְאִם ... יֶחֱטָא—Each use of the hypothetical particle אִם with the Qal (G) imperfect of חָטָא, "to sin," sets up a conditional sentence: "if a person sins ..." The verb חָטָא recurs fairly often in Samuel,[3] mainly in confessions of sin, e.g., David's (2 Sam 12:13). Derived from it is the noun חַטָּאת, "a sin," in 1 Sam 2:17.

---

[2] *IBH*, § 17 B; GKC, § 117 p–r. See the (first) textual notes on 1:6, 11, 17, 21 and the second textual note on 2:13.

[3] Also 1 Sam 7:6; 12:10, 23; 14:33, 34; 15:24, 30; 19:4, 5; 24:12 (ET 24:11); 26:21; 2 Sam 12:13; 19:21 (ET 19:20); 24:10, 17.

אִישׁ—Here and in 2:26 this noun is used in the more generic sense of "person, human being" (see *HALOT*, s.v. אִישׁ I, 4) rather than "man, male."

לְאִישׁ ... לַיהוָה—In both of these prepositional phrases, לְ indicates acting "toward" another in a hostile sense, to sin "against" a person or Yahweh (see BDB, s.v. לְ, 1 d).

וּפִלְלוֹ ... מִי יִתְפַּלֶּל־לוֹ אֱלֹהִים—Both instances of the verb פָּלַל are translated as "intercede." The first (וּפִלְלוֹ) is in the Piel (D) stem (perfect with *waw* consecutive), which normally means "to pray." However, with God as the subject, it denotes intercession on someone's behalf. The pronominal suffix on וּפִלְלוֹ serves as an indirect object, "for him" (Joüon, § 125 ba), rather than a direct object. This is evident by the parallel prepositional phrase לוֹ, "for him," at the end of the second clause. The second form of פָּלַל is an imperfect in the Hithpael (HtD) stem, which often means "to pray" to God (as does Hannah in 1 Sam 1:10, 12, 26, 27; 2:1; David in 2 Sam 7:27), but frequently it denotes interceding with God on behalf of others (e.g., 1 Sam 7:5; 12:19, 23; cf. 8:6; see *HALOT*, B).

כִּי־חָפֵץ יְהוָה לַהֲמִיתָם:—"Because Yahweh was determined to kill them." The stative Qal (G) verb חָפֵץ involves someone's will. It is often translated as "be pleased" (as in Is 53:10, where Yahweh *was pleased* to crush" the Suffering Servant as a guilt offering), but here it is rendered as "Yahweh *was determined*." The Hiphil (H) stem of מוּת, "die" (לַהֲמִיתָם is the infinitive construct with לְ and a third masculine plural pronominal suffix), has the causative meaning "to put to death, kill" (see the first textual note on 2:6). This verse, then, is a fulfillment of a creedal affirmation in Hannah's Song, "Yahweh kills" (1 Sam 2:6, alluding to Deut 32:39). Neither that verse nor this one refers to predestination to damnation (as in double predestination). Rather, they refer to God's consequent will. Because of Eli's sons' habitual sinning and impenitence despite being warned (1 Sam 2:15–17, 22–24), the consequence was that God decided to kill them. God had given these priests the Torah to instruct them how to conduct the divine service and to warn them of the consequences of priestly malpractice (e.g., Lev 10:1–2), but they spurned the Torah as well as their father's rebuke (1 Sam 2:25). Nevertheless, if the conjunction כִּי has a causal sense here, "because" (as translated), it may indicate divine hardening. Because of their obduracy, God may have hardened them even more so that Eli's further appeals fell on deaf ears, further warranting God's determination to kill them. Cf. God giving over unrepentant sinners to more heinous sins in Rom 1:24, 26, 28 and the hardening of Pharaoh in Exodus and in Rom 9:17–18.[4]

2:26 הֹלֵךְ וְגָדֵל וָטוֹב—This is a rare but elegant syntactical construction (GKC, § 113 u; Joüon, § 123 s). Biblical Hebrew often employs the infinitive absolute (הָלוֹךְ) of הָלַךְ, "to walk, go," in combination with one other verb (usually another infinitive absolute) to express the idea of action that continues over time, grows, and/or intensifies. The construction here is rare because it employs three Qal (G) participles and no infinitive absolutes. The participle of הָלַךְ combines with the participles (or verbal adjectives) of גָּדֵל, "grow up, become great," and טוֹב, "be pleasing, good" (stative; Joüon, § 80 q).

---

4   For Rom 1:23–31, see Middendorf, *Romans 1–8*, 131–41. For Rom 9:17–18 and the biblical teaching of hardening, see "Is This Fair to the Pharaoh? (9:17–18)" in Middendorf, *Romans 9–16*, 883–92.

Thus, Samuel "continued growing and enjoyed favor." For similar constructions with participles of הָלַךְ but combined with only one other verb, see 1 Sam 17:41; 2 Sam 3:1 (twice); 15:12. For the more common kind of construction with the infinitive absolute of הָלַךְ, see 1 Sam 6:12; 14:19; 19:23; 2 Sam 3:16, 24; 5:10; 13:19; 16:13; 18:25.

וְגַם ... גַּם—This construction with the repeated adverb גַּם means "both ... and" (see BDB, 1).

Commentary

c. 1075 BC

We are told that Eli had heard what his sons were doing to Israel (see 2:12–17) and an additional report that they were fornicating with the women who served at the entrance to tent of meeting (2:22). This is the only place in the book of Samuel where the tabernacle is called "the tent of meeting" (אֹהֶל מוֹעֵד, 2:22).[5] The author probably intentionally employed this phrase in order to connect these women to the corps of women mentioned in Ex 38:8 "who served" (הַצֹּבְאוֹת, as in 1 Sam 2:22) at the entrance to the tent of meeting.

Eli rebuked his sons for their sins but did it in a general way without administering any punishment or warning of divine judgment (2:23–25a). He seemed more concerned about public opinion ("from all these people," 2:23; "people circulating," 2:24) than about Scripture and the divine will revealed therein.[6] He was an old man (probably close to ninety-eight years old; see 1 Sam 4:15), and it appears as if he had not disciplined his sons sufficiently for earlier transgressions. If parents correct minor behaviors when their children are young and impressionable, the children are less likely to stray into more serious offenses when they are older and are more likely to respond to adult admonitions to repent (Prov 13:24; 22:6).[7] Having failed to rein in his son's sinful tendencies when they were corrigible, his words now have no salutary effect and may even have hardened the sons' incorrigibility (see the fifth textual note on 1 Sam 2:25). As high priest, Eli ought to have used his authority to remove Hophni and Phinehas from office (cf. 3:13). However, he displays a weak oversight of his ministerial responsibilities, choosing only to scold his sons with a rhetorical question.

Eli states that if a person sins against another person, God can intervene on his behalf (2:25). God can call a person to repentance and absolve the penitent (2 Sam 12:1–13). God can even direct events to mitigate potential consequences

---

[5] The usual term for the "tabernacle" is מִשְׁכָּן, which appears 104 times in the Torah and which occurs in Samuel only in 2 Sam 7:6. The noun אֹהֶל, "tent," occurs 192 times in the Torah and often refers to the tabernacle. 2 Sam 7:6 is also the only other verse in Samuel (besides 1 Sam 2:22) to use אֹהֶל, "tent," for the tabernacle, although 2 Sam 6:17 refers to a "tent" David pitched for the ark of the covenant.

[6] In particular, his sons are violating the instructions for the priests in Leviticus, as well as the moral mandates in the Decalogue (Exodus 20; Deuteronomy 5). Doctrinally, the Law of God can be characterized as the immutable will of God.

[7] See Steinmann, *Proverbs*, 321, 441–43.

of one's sins (1 Sam 25:26, 31–34; but contrast 2 Sam 12:14). However, who can intervene when God is the one against whom the sin is committed (cf. Is 59:16; Jer 7:16)? The Scriptures never make an ironclad distinction between sins against humans and against God. All sins are against God in the sense that they violate his will and transgress his Law. Eli's point, however, is that if Yahweh is determined to exact punishment against someone for sin, no one can intercede to stop him. In fact, we are told that God was determined to punish Hophni and Phinehas by killing them (1 Sam 2:25), and he will do this by allowing the Philistines to defeat Israel, resulting in the deaths of Hophni and Phinehas, and capture the ark (4:1, 17).

Meanwhile, in contrast to the bad report about Eli's sons (2:22–24), Samuel continues to grow into manhood and by grace (2:26). He was favored by God, and moreover, the people also began to recognize him. God's favor was moving from the house of Eli to Samuel. The next two narrated events (2:27–36; 3:1–21) emphasize this shift. In 2:21 we were told that Samuel "grew with Yahweh" (וַיִּגְדַּל ... עִם־יְהוָה). Here his growth (וְגָדֵל) continues, not only "with Yahweh" (עִם־יְהוָה) but also "with people" (עִם־אֲנָשִׁים, 2:26). The NT appropriates this language for the growth of John the Baptist (τὸ δὲ παιδίον ηὔξανεν καὶ ἐκραταιοῦτο πνεύματι, "and the child grew and was strengthened in the Spirit," Lk 1:80), as well as for the true human development of God become man in the person of Jesus Christ (τὸ δὲ παιδίον ηὔξανεν καὶ ἐκραταιοῦτο πληρούμενον σοφίᾳ, καὶ χάρις θεοῦ ἦν ἐπ᾽ αὐτό, "and the child grew and was strengthened, filled with wisdom, and the grace of God was upon him," Lk 2:40). He is the high priestly Intercessor for our sins (Is 53:12; John 17; Rom 8:34; Heb 7:25).

A Prophecy against Eli's House

Translation

2 **²⁷**A man of God came to Eli and said to him, "Thus said Yahweh: Didn't I clearly reveal myself to your father's house when they were in Egypt [as slaves] belonging to the house of Pharaoh? **²⁸**I chose him from all the tribes of Israel for myself as a priest to offer [sacrifices] on my altar, to burn incense, to wear an ephod in my presence. I gave all the fire offerings of the Israelites to your father's house. **²⁹**Why do you [look at] my sacrifices and my offerings [with a selfish eye]? You have honored your sons more than me by fattening yourselves with the best of all the offerings of my people Israel. **³⁰**Therefore, a declaration of Yahweh, the God of Israel: I certainly said, 'Your house and your father's house—they will serve in my presence forever.' But now a declaration of Yahweh: I will certainly not allow this because those who honor me I will honor, and those who despise me will be disgraced.

³¹"Consider this: The days are coming when I will cut off your descendants and the descendants of your father's house, **³²**and there will never be an old man of yours in my house. **³³**A man of yours that I do not cut off from my altar, I will make his eyes fail and his soul grieve, and all your descendants will fall by the sword of men. **³⁴**And this will be the sign for you that will come to your two sons— to Hophni and Phinehas: on one day both of them will die. **³⁵**But I will raise for myself a faithful priest who will act in harmony with what is in my heart and my soul. I will build a secure house for him, and my Anointed One will serve in my presence forever. **³⁶**Then everyone left in your house will come to bow down to him for wages paid in silver or a round loaf of bread and say, 'Please appoint me to some priestly office so that I can eat a scrap of bread.'"

Textual Notes

2:27 אֵלָיו—"To him" is omitted in 4QSamᵃ and the LXX.

הֲנִגְלֹה נִגְלֵיתִי—"Didn't I clearly reveal myself?" translates a Niphal (N) infinitive absolute with interrogative *he* (הֲנִגְלֹה) and Niphal perfect first person singular of גָּלָה. In the N stem this verb is often reflexive, "reveal oneself," as here. The *he* interrogative, which reinforces that the answer should be obvious (GKC, § 150 e), is not reflected in the LXX. Perhaps it dropped out in the LXX's Vorlage by parablepsis or is a dittograph in the MT. An infinitive absolute can be used to strengthen an indignant question (GKC, § 113 q).

לְבֵית פַּרְעֹה:—This means "to the house of Pharaoh." The preposition לְ indicates possession, "belonging to" someone (BDB, 5 b (*a*)). Immediately before this phrase 4QSamᵃ includes עבדים (to be vocalized as עֲבָדִים), "slaves," and the LXX includes the corresponding Greek noun δούλων. The Hebrew word probably was lost in the MT due to homoioteleuton: each of the previous two words (בִּהְיוֹתָם בְּמִצְרַיִם) ends with ם, and so the scribe's eye skipped over this word (עֲבָדִים) that also ends in ם.

2:28 וּבָחֹר—When an infinitive absolute serves in place of a finite verb it is to be inflected based on the context, so this is translated as a first person singular, "I chose," to match נִגְלֵיתִי in 2:27 (see GKC, § 113 y, z; Waltke-O'Connor, § 35.5.2d, including example 12). The Qal (G) of בָּחַר often appears in passages that emphasize God's election or choice of Israel purely by grace and in his love, not because of any meritorious or advantageous traits in the people (e.g., Deut 4:37; 7:6–7; 14:2). Particularly relevant for Eli is Yahweh's choosing of the tribe of Levi and the priests (the descendants of Aaron) within that tribe (Deut 18:1–8, with בָּחַר in Deut 18:5). The verb also recurs in references to the place of worship God will choose (e.g., Deut 12:4–26; 14:23–25; 16:5–16), i.e., the Jerusalem temple. In 1 Sam 16:8–10 the verb is negated as God tells Samuel that he has not chosen the older sons of Jesse; instead, David is selected.

לַעֲלוֹת—Literally "to go up," this is translated as "to offer." This infinitive construct of עָלָה (with the preposition לְ) appears to be Qal (G), which usually has an intransitive meaning: "to go up." However, it could be the Hiphil (H), לְהַעֲלוֹת, but with elision of the Hiphil preformative ה (as with וְלַאֲדִיב in 2:33; see GKC, § 53 q, and the first textual note on 2:33). The Hiphil normally is transitive, "make [something] go up" or "offer up" a sacrifice (cf. the Hiphil in the next textual note). The usual explanation for the form here is that the Qal of עָלָה can have the same transitive meaning as the Hiphil, "to offer up" or "present" sacrifices (see *HALOT*, s.v. עלה, Qal, 4 a, and Hiphil, 4 c). Likewise, the forms of עָלָה in Lev 2:12; 1 Ki 18:29; Is 60:7; Ps 51:21 (ET 51:19) may be parsed as Qal with that transitive meaning.

לְהַקְטִיר קְטֹרֶת—This cognate accusative construction, literally "to cense incense," refers to a priestly duty; see, e.g., Ex 30:7–8; 40:27; Num 17:5 (ET 16:40); 2 Chr 13:11. The infinitive construct לְהַקְטִיר is Hiphil (H); for the verb, see the first textual note on 2:15. Its cognate noun קְטֹרֶת denotes "incense."

לָשֵׂאת אֵפוֹד—This means "to wear an ephod." The verb is a Qal (G) infinitive construct (with the preposition לְ) of the verb נָשָׂא, "bear, carry." For the priestly vestment אֵפוֹד, see the last textual note and the commentary on 2:18. This verse, however, likely refers to the unique vestments of the high priest (see the commentary). In 1 Samuel it appears as if "bear an ephod" is an idiom for "be vested in an ephod" (also 14:3; 22:18). Note especially 22:18, where there were eighty-five priests at Nob literally "bearing an ephod of linen," that is, wearing an ephod. It is unlikely that all of these men were carrying linen ephods in their arms.

לְפָנָי—"In my presence" (pausal for לְפָנַי) is absent in 4QSamᵃ and the LXX.

וָאֶתְּנָה—This lengthened form of נָתַן, "give," defies the general rule that a shortened form of the imperfect (when one exists) is used with *waw* consecutive. For this and other exceptions, see GKC, § 49 e. The more common and expected short form with *waw* consecutive is וָאֶתֵּן (seventeen times in the OT). The form here, which seems to be more emphatic, is used in Num 8:19, where Yahweh "gave" the Levites as ministerial gifts to the priests, and in 2 Sam 12:8 (twice), where God "gave" to David the house of Saul.[1] The cohortative (but with *waw* conjunctive) אֶתְּנָה is used when, e.g., God "gives" his covenant to Abraham (Gen 17:2) and the entire world to his Son, the messianic King (Ps 2:8).

אֶת־כָּל־אִשֵּׁי בְנֵי יִשְׂרָאֵל:—The noun אִשֶּׁה, "fire offering," appears to be related to the noun אֵשׁ, "fire." The Torah stipulates the rites for this kind of offering in, e.g., Ex 29:41; Lev 1:9, 13, 17; 2:2–3; 3:3–16. The prescriptions for the portions of such offerings that God provided as food for the priests are given in, e.g., Lev 2:10; 6:11 (ET 6:18); 7:35.[2]

2:29 לָמָּה תִבְעֲטוּ בְּזִבְחִי וּבְמִנְחָתִי אֲשֶׁר צִוִּיתִי מָעוֹן—A literal rendition of the MT could be "why do you [plural] kick at my sacrifice and at my offering which I commanded [to be offered at my] dwelling place?" The verb בָּעַט occurs elsewhere only in Deut 32:15, where it expresses contempt and rebellion against God, and the noun מָעוֹן often denotes God's "dwelling place" (in heaven or the temple). The LXX reads καὶ ἵνα τί ἐπέβλεψας ἐπὶ τὸ θυμίαμά μου καὶ εἰς τὴν θυσίαν μου ἀναιδεῖ ὀφθαλμῷ, "and why do you look at my incense and my sacrifice with a greedy eye?" The apparent reading of 4QSamᵃ (the lacunae is filled based on the LXX) is תביט ... [צרת עין], why do "you [singular] look ... [with a selfish eye]?" The verb in 4QSamᵃ would be pointed תַּבִּיט, a Hiphil (H) imperfect of נָבַט, with the construct phrase צָרַת עַיִן. Some of the vocabulary here recurs at the start of 2:32, where the MT reads וְהִבַּטְתָּ צַר מָעוֹן. The noun מָעוֹן in MT 2:32 is also here in MT 2:29. The verb תביט in 4QSamᵃ 2:29 is another form of the verb וְהִבַּטְתָּ in 2:29. The word צרת that is supplied in the lacuna of 4QSamᵃ 2:29 is another form of צַר in MT 2:32.[3]

לְהַבְרִיאֲכֶם—This is the Hiphil (H) infinitive construct of בָּרָא II, "be fat" (a verb that occurs only here in the OT), with a second masculine plural object suffix that functions reflexively: literally "to fatten yourselves."

מֵרֵאשִׁית כָּל־מִנְחַת יִשְׂרָאֵל לְעַמִּי:—In meaning, all five words go together. However, the rules of Hebrew syntax allow only the first four words to be expressed as a construct chain: literally "from the best of all of the offering(s) of Israel." The final genitive (*nomen rectum*) in that chain, יִשְׂרָאֵל, "Israel," is definite by virtue of being a proper name, so the entire construct chain is definite ("*the* best of ..."). Normally a definite noun cannot be in construct, so "Israel" cannot be in construct with עַמִּי, "my people" (which is definite because of the pronominal suffix). Therefore, instead of being appended to the construct chain, the fifth and final (definite) word is expressed in a separate prepositional phrase, לְעַמִּי, and the preposition לְ signifies possession, "*belonging to my people*."[4] The syntax of the English language allows all five Hebrew words to be combined in one phrase: "from the best of all of the offerings of my people Israel." In place of לְעַמִּי, the LXX reads ἔμπροσθέν μου, "in my presence."

---

[1] וָאֶתְּנָה appears also in Judg 6:9; Ezek 16:11; Ps 69:12 (ET 69:11); Eccl 1:17; Dan 9:3; Neh 2:1, 6, 9.

[2] See further Kleinig, *Leviticus*, 57, who translates אִשֶּׁה as "gift."

[3] See the discussion in McCarter, *I Samuel*, 87; cf. Klein, *1 Samuel*, 23.

[4] For this use of לְ as a periphrasis for the construct state when the word that would be the *nomen regens* (יִשְׂרָאֵל) is a proper name, see BDB, s.v. לְ, 5 c (*b*) (γ). For the לְ of possession, see also the third textual note on 2:27.

2:30 יִתְהַלְּכוּ לְפָנַי—Literally "they will walk back and forth before me," this is rendered as "they will serve in my presence." The verb is a Hithpael (HtD) imperfect third masculine plural of הָלַךְ, "walk." The verb recurs in the same sense in 2:35 (see the third textual note there). This verb is iterative in the HtD stem. When this root is used in the HtD stem and is followed by the preposition לְפָנַי, it usually forms an idiom meaning to serve, lead, or live one's life in the presence of someone.[5]

חָלִילָה לִּי—Literally "it is a profanity to me," this expression is used to introduce an oath that foreswears an action.[6] It is often translated as "far be it from me," but "I will certainly not allow this" conveys the sense more clearly in English. It corresponds to the negated Greek optative μὴ γένοιτο.[7]

מְכַבְּדַי אֲכַבֵּד וּבֹזַי יֵקַלּוּ—The first common singular pronominal suffix on מְכַבְּדַי, the Piel (D) participle of כָּבֵד, "to honor," is objective: "my honorers" means "those who honor me" (see GKC, § 116 g). This participle then serves as the direct object of the following Piel form of the same verb (first common singular imperfect), אֲכַבֵּד, "I will honor." The double use of this Piel verb here recalls its use in the previous verse (2:29).[8] Similarly, the suffix on וּבֹזַי, the Qal (G) participle of בָּזָה, "to despise," is also objective: "my despisers" means "those who despise me." That second participle then serves as the direct object of יֵקַלּוּ, the Qal[9] third masculine plural imperfect of קָלַל, "to be despised, disgraced."

2:31–32 The translation follows the reconstructed reading of 4QSamᵃ, based on the reading of the LXX:[10]

[הנה י]מ[י]ם באים וגדעתני את זרעך וזרע בית אביך ³¹

[ולוא] יהיה לך זקן בביתי כול [הימים] ³²

The MT appears to have a conflated reading that combines a variant of 2:32b to yield MT 2:31b with a variant of 2:29a to yield MT 2:32a:[11]

הִנֵּה יָמִים בָּאִים וְגָדַעְתִּי אֶת־זְרֹעֲךָ וְאֶת־זְרֹעַ בֵּית אָבִיךָ מִהְיוֹת זָקֵן בְּבֵיתֶךָ׃ ³¹

וְהִבַּטְתָּ צַר מָעוֹן בְּכֹל אֲשֶׁר־יֵיטִיב אֶת־יִשְׂרָאֵל וְלֹא־יִהְיֶה זָקֵן בְּבֵיתְךָ כָּל־הַיָּמִים׃ ³²

³¹Consider this: the days are coming when I will cut off your arm and the arm of your father's house *so there will not be an old man in your house.* ³²*And you will see distress in a dwelling in all that he does good for Israel,* and there will not be an old man in your house all the days [i.e., there will never be an old man in your house].

---

5 Gen 17:1; 24:40; 48:15; 1 Sam 2:30, 35; 12:2; 2 Ki 20:3; Is 38:3; Pss 56:14 (ET 56:13); 116:9.

6 *IBH*, § 64 A; Waltke-O'Connor, § 40.2.2c; Joüon, § 165 k.

7 E.g., Rom 3:4, 6; 6:2, 15; Gal 2:17; 3:21. See Middendorf, *Romans 1–8*, 220–21.

8 1 Sam 2:29: וַתְּכַבֵּד אֶת־בָּנֶיךָ מִמֶּנִּי. See Waltke-O'Connor, §§ 24.2h, example 10, and 33.3.3c, example 6.

9 The corresponding Niphal (N) form would be יֵקַלּוּ (as in Is 30:16).

10 LXX 1 Sam 2:31–32: ἰδοὺ ἡμέραι ἔρχονται καὶ ἐξολεθρεύσω τὸ σπέρμα σου καὶ τὸ σπέρμα οἴκου πατρός σου, καὶ οὐκ ἔσται σου πρεσβύτης ἐν οἴκῳ μου πάσας τὰς ἡμέρας.

11 See McCarter, *I Samuel*, 88–89; Klein, *1 Samuel*, 23.

2:31 הִנֵּה—This particle is used to draw attention to the conclusion of the prophecy, which contains the point of the previous declarations (see Waltke-O'Connor, § 40.2.1d, including example 17). It is translated as "consider this."

יָמִים בָּאִים—This participial clause (with בּוֹא), "(the) days are coming," can introduce an eschatological prophecy to be fulfilled at the first or second advent of Christ (e.g., Jer 16:14; 23:5; 31:31; Amos 9:13). But the prophecy here will be fulfilled soon (similarly, see 2 Ki 20:17 ‖ Is 39:6; Jer 51:47, 52).

2:32 כָּל־הַיָּמִים—Literally "all of the days," with the negative at the beginning of the clause (לֹא), this phrase is translated as "never": "and there will never be an old man …" 4QSamᵃ has the same wording but with כֹל (and probably לוֹא) spelled plene, or *maleʾ*: [הימים] כול ... [ולוא]. See the last textual note on 1 Sam 2:35.

2:33 לְכַלּוֹת אֶת־עֵינֶיךָ וְלַאֲדִיב אֶת־נַפְשֶׁךָ—The first infinitive construct is the Piel (D) of כָּלָה, "to exhaust (by weeping)" (see BDB, 2 b) or "to make fail." The second is the Hiphil (H) of אָדַב, "to grieve," a verb that appears only here in the OT; the preformative *he* is elided (GKC, § 53 q; Joüon, § 54 b; the expected form would be וְלִהַאֲדִיב). Both the first direct object, עֵינֶיךָ, "your eyes," and the second, נַפְשֶׁךָ (pausal for נַפְשְׁךָ), "your soul," have a second masculine singular suffix, which would refer to Eli alone. The translation "his eyes … his soul" follows the LXX (τοὺς ὀφθαλμοὺς αὐτοῦ … τὴν ψυχὴν αὐτοῦ), and in the case of the first word, also 4QSamᵃ (עיניו).[12] Since the prophecy is about וְאִישׁ, any surviving descendant of Eli, the third person singular makes much better sense contextually. Apparently under the influence of MT 2:32, the pronominal suffixes were changed in MT 2:33 to shift the referent to Eli instead of his descendants, especially Abiathar (1 Ki 2:26–27).[13]

וְכָל־מַרְבִּית בֵּיתְךָ—Literally "and all the increase of your house," this is rendered as "and all your descendants." The feminine singular noun מַרְבִּית is a collective denoting masculine persons, so the following verb יָמוּתוּ (in the next textual note) is masculine plural (GKC, § 145 e).

יָמוּתוּ אֲנָשִׁים—In context these two words probably indicate that Eli's descendants "will die [as] men," meaning "in the prime of life," before old age (GKC, § 118 q). (Cf. 1 Sam 4:9, where אֲנָשִׁים appears twice in exhortations for the Philistine soldiers to "be men," that is, be strong and brave.) However, the reading of 4QSamᵃ, יפולו בחרב אנשים (to be vocalized as יִפּוֹלוּ בְּחֶרֶב־אֲנָשִׁים), "they will fall by the sword of men," agrees with the LXX (πεσοῦνται ἐν ῥομφαίᾳ ἀνδρῶν) and fits the context well.[14]

2:35 וַהֲקִימֹתִי לִי—"I will raise up for myself" emphasizes divine monergism; salvation is entirely God's doing, and he accomplishes it not as a reward for good works, but for his own sake (for the sake of his name, his own glory, etc.). The shift of the accent from the second-to-last syllable (וַהֲקִימֹתִי) to the last one (וַהֲקִימֹתִי) indicates that the Hiphil (H) perfect of קוּם has *waw* consecutive. The suffixed preposition לְ has a

---

[12] See ESV.

[13] McCarter, *I Samuel*, 89; Klein, *1 Samuel*, 23.

[14] See HCSB; ESV; McCarter, *I Samuel*, 89; Klein, *1 Samuel*, 23.

reflexive sense, "for" the sake of the one who is the subject of the transitive verb (BDB, 5 h (a)), Yahweh himself.

כֹּהֵן נֶאֱמָן ... בַּיִת נֶאֱמָן—Note the play on words. Although translated differently, the same Niphal (N) masculine singular participle of אָמַן describes the "*faithful* priest" and the "*secure* house."

וְהִתְהַלֵּךְ לִפְנֵי־מְשִׁיחִי—This would literally seem to mean "he [the faithful priest] will walk back and forth before my Anointed One." For the Hithpael (HtD) of הָלַךְ (here singular and perfect with *waw* consecutive), translated as "to serve," see the first textual note on 2:30. However, instead of two different people, it is likely that the text is identifying the "faithful priest" (see the preceding textual note) *as* "my Anointed One." In 1:16 לִפְנֵי־ did not have its usual meaning "before, in the presence of," but rather signified identity: in Eli's estimation, Hannah *was* "a good-for-nothing woman."[15] Here לִפְנֵי־ may have the same sense: it identifies the "faithful priest" as "my Anointed One" who serves. This would result in the translation "and he will serve as my Anointed One." Alternatively, לִפְנֵי could be repointed to לְפָנַי, "before me," and again the "faithful priest" is "my Anointed One," and he is the subject of the verb וְהִתְהַלֵּךְ: "and my Anointed One will serve in my presence." There is a tendency in Biblical Hebrew for suffixed prepositions to follow the verb immediately (thus וְהִתְהַלֵּךְ לְפָנַי), although this is not absolutely necessary.[16]

כָּל־הַיָּמִים:—This construct phrase, literally "all of the days," occurs forty-six times in the MT, usually with the meaning of "always, continually, from now on" or, as here, "forever."[17] The exact nuance is determined by context. Here it clearly is a promise of a priest who will forever replace the Aaronic priesthood. Note that the phrase was used already in this prophecy in 2:32 to say that no one in Eli's line would ever (כָּל־הַיָּמִים) reach old age. In some OT passages this phrase has the more limited meaning of "continually for a specific period of time" (similar to the English "as long as"). In such cases it is usually modified by a trailing relative clause (... כָּל־הַיָּמִים אֲשֶׁר).[18]

2:36 לְהִשְׁתַּחֲוֹת—This is the infinitive construct (with the preposition לְ) of the Hishtaphel of חָוָה, "to bow down, worship." See the third textual note on 1:3.

לַאֲגוֹרַת כֶּסֶף וְכִכַּר־לָחֶם—This is translated as "for wages paid in silver or a round loaf of bread." The feminine noun אֲגוֹרָה (construct: אֲגוֹרַת) is a hapax legomenon that may be related to the Aramaic word אַגְרָא, "wages."[19] The feminine noun כִּכָּר (from the root כרר; so BDB) means "circle, disk," but elsewhere can refer to a geographical "plain" or to a "talent" as a measure of weight.

---

[15] BDB, s.v. פָּנֶה, II 4 f, defines לִפְנֵי־ in 1:16 as "*in the manner of, like,*" a rare meaning attested also in Job 3:24; 4:19, and suitable for 1 Sam 2:35.

[16] Joüon, § 155 t. See the discussion in Deenick, "Priest and King or Priest-King in 1 Samuel 2:35," 325–27.

[17] For other examples of the phrase meaning "forever," see Gen 43:9; Deut 5:29; Josh 4:24; 2 Ki 8:19 ‖ 2 Chr 21:7; Jer 32:39; cf. Ps 52:3 (ET 52:1). It has varying nuances in Gen 44:32; Deut 4:40; 6:24; 11:1; 14:23; 18:5; 19:9; 28:29, 33. Cf. BDB, s.v. יוֹם, 7 f.

[18] Deut 4:10; 12:1; 31:13; 1 Sam 1:28; 20:31; 27:11; 1 Ki 8:40; 2 Chr 6:31.

[19] *HALOT*; for the Aramaic word, see Jastrow, s.v. אֲגַר III, אַגְרָא I; *CAL*, s.v. 'gr, 'gr'.

אַחַת הַכְּהֻנּוֹת—Literally "one of the priestly offices," this is rendered as "some priestly office." The Hebrew number "one" can function as an indefinite article (see the first textual note on 1:1; Waltke-O'Connor, § 13.8a, example 10). The feminine noun כְּהֻנָּה, "priestly office" (e.g., Ex 29:9; 40:15; Num 3:10; 18:7), is clearly cognate to כֹּהֵן, "priest" (1 Sam 2:28, 35).

Commentary

c. 1075 BC

An Indictment of Eli (2:27–30)

The balance of 1 Samuel 2 is a message from a man of God to Eli. "Man of God" (2:27) is another term for a prophet that is used primarily in the books of Samuel and Kings (e.g., 1 Sam 9:6–10; 2 Ki 4:7–27; 5:8–20; 6:15). It connects the prophets to Israel's first prophet, Moses, the "man of God" (e.g., Deut 33:1; Josh 14:6; 1 Chr 23:14). Ultimately, it is "the man Christ Jesus" who is the one mediator between God and man (1 Tim 2:5). Paul calls Pastor Timothy a "man of God" (1 Tim 6:11). The inspired Scriptures equip every believer to be a "man of God" (2 Tim 3:16–17).

The indictment of Eli begins by noting that God revealed himself to the house of Eli, who as a priest was a descendant of Aaron, when they (Aaron and the rest of the tribe of Levi) were in Egypt (1 Sam 2:27). God chose Aaron as high priest (Exodus 28), and the man of God mentions three responsibilities for this priesthood: offering sacrifices, burning incense, and wearing an ephod (1 Sam 2:28). The ephod mentioned here is not simply the linen ephod worn by priests and Levitical ministers, including Samuel (1 Sam 2:18), but the high priest's ephod (Ex 28:2–12; 39:1–7). The Aaronic priesthood was given the honor of presenting all of the fire offerings to God and eating portions of them (see the last textual note on 1 Sam 2:28).

The prophet then transitions to Eli's abuse of the priestly office: he honored his sons more than he honored God because under Eli's supervision his sons grew fat on the best portions of the offerings (1 Sam 2:29; see also 2:12–17). The man of God next quotes Yahweh's promise that Aaron's house would serve God forever (1 Sam 2:30; see also Ex 29:9). But now God is abrogating that pledge because he will honor only those who honor him (1 Sam 2:30), a principle enunciated in formulaic language elsewhere.[20] Eli and his sons had despised God by showing disrespect for the holy offerings (2:17).

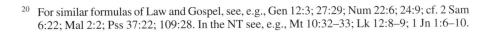

[20] For similar formulas of Law and Gospel, see, e.g., Gen 12:3; 27:29; Num 22:6; 24:9; cf. 2 Sam 6:22; Mal 2:2; Pss 37:22; 109:28. In the NT see, e.g., Mt 10:32–33; Lk 12:8–9; 1 Jn 1:6–10.

The Aaronic Priesthood Removed in Favor of the New Anointed Priest (2:31–36)

The second part of the prophecy pronounces Yahweh's judgment on Eli's house and on the Aaronic priesthood in general. Not only will Eli's descendants be cut off from the priesthood, so also will the descendants of his "father's house," that is, Aaron's descendants (2:31). Among Eli's descendants there would never be an old man in Yahweh's house (2:32). This is a direct reference to Eli's old age (2:22). Never again would a high priest from Eli's house die in office as an old man like Eli will (4:15–18). Any descendant of Eli that God would not cut off from his altar would face judgment, and the rest of Eli's descendants would be killed (1 Sam 2:33). Eli's descendant Abiathar would live to be an old man—he served as high priest for more than forty years, from before the reign of David (1 Sam 22:22) into the early years of Solomon's reign. However, he would be removed from office before his death (1 Ki 2:26–27, 35). The rest of Eli's descendants were killed by Saul (1 Sam 22:11–23). The "man of God" (2:27) also provided a sign for Eli to know that this prophecy was certain—Hophni and Phinehas would die on the same day (2:34). This will happen in 4:11 and be reported to Eli in 4:17.

Next the man of God states that Yahweh will replace the Aaronic priesthood in favor of a new, faithful priest (2:35). Many commentators take this to be fulfilled in Zadok (1 Ki 2:35), who, according to this understanding, served before David (e.g., 2 Sam 8:17), the Lord's anointed.[21] There is an insurmountable problem with this interpretation, however: the judgment here is not simply the removal of Eli's house, but includes the entire house of his father Aaron (1 Sam 2:31). Zadok was a descendant of Aaron (1 Chr 5:29–34 [ET 6:3–8]) and therefore cannot be the fulfillment of this prophecy. This was already noted in antiquity by Augustine[22] and reemphasized some 150 years ago by Keil, who identified the issue as not simply the replacement of the Elides as high priests, but the replacement of the entire Aaronic priesthood.[23]

The key to understanding this prophecy is found in the correct understanding of the end of 1 Sam 2:35. Instead of interpreting the MT to be a prophecy about two men, (1) the faithful priest who will serve in the presence of (2) Yahweh's Anointed One, the text ought to be understood (or repointed) to say that "my Anointed One" (= the "faithful priest") will serve (before Yahweh); see the third textual note on 2:35.[24] This, in fact, makes the most sense of this prediction, and for three reasons. First, although most of Samuel focuses its

---

[21] Bodner, *1 Samuel*, 35; Klein, *1 Samuel*, 27; McCarter, *I Samuel*, 92–93; Smith, *The Books of Samuel*, 23; Tsumura, *The First Book of Samuel*, 170.

[22] Augustine, *The City of God*, 17.5 (*NPNF*¹ 2:344).

[23] Keil, *The Books of Samuel*, 45–46.

[24] Deenick, "Priest and King or Priest-King in 1 Samuel 2:35," 325–27. Much of the following discussion follows the insights of Deenick. It ought to be noted that this interpretation is at least as old as Lactantius (c. AD 240–320), *The Divine Institutes*, 4.14 (*ANF* 7:113).

message on Israel's kings, 1 Samuel 1–7 concentrates on the failure of the priesthood, something that is already hinted at the very beginning (1:3; 2:12, 17, 22). The raising of a faithful priest is God's solution to this failure. Second, it should be noted that both the high priest and other priests were anointed when installed into office.[25] In addition, the high priest is called "the anointed priest" (הַכֹּהֵן הַמָּשִׁיחַ, Lev 4:3, 5, 16; 6:15 [ET 6:22]). Third, "his [Yahweh's] Anointed One" (מְשִׁיחוֹ) was introduced earlier in this chapter (see the commentary on 2:10), and this interpretation of 2:35 builds on the earlier passage. The prophecy recorded by the author now reveals more about this same figure. The "Anointed One" is equivalent to the "Messiah" and, in Greek, the "Christ."[26]

The first thought that might occur to readers is that Samuel himself is the solution to the priestly problem.[27] However, there are several hints that the author does not believe Samuel to be the "faithful priest" (כֹּהֵן נֶאֱמָן, 2:35). First of all, Samuel was confirmed (נֶאֱמָן) to be a prophet, not a priest (3:20). Second, his father's lineage (1:1) does not include Aaron, and only Aaronides were to be priests. Third, Samuel also failed in much the same way that Eli does: he made his sons judges, but they did not walk in his ways and instead perverted justice. This precipitated the leadership crisis that resulted in Saul's kingship (8:1–6).

Another connection that may occur to the reader is that in some sense David is the "faithful priest."[28] In 2 Sam 7:16 David is promised a "secure house" (as in 1 Sam 2:35) and kingdom (וְנֶאְמַן בֵּיתְךָ וּמַמְלַכְתְּךָ; cf. 1 Sam 25:28; 1 Chr 17:23). The description of the faithful priest as acting in harmony with God's heart and soul (1 Sam 2:35) is very similar to the description of David (1 Sam 13:14; cf. 1 Sam 16:7). Moreover, David appears as the leader of worship when the ark is brought to Jerusalem (2 Samuel 6). At that time David danced before the ark while wearing a linen ephod (2 Sam 6:14). He offered sacrifices (2 Sam 6:13, 17), although 1 Chr 16:1–2 clarifies that David offered them through the priests ("they" in 1 Chr 16:1). Moreover, David blessed the people (2 Sam 6:18), a common priestly privilege (although pronouncing a benediction was not an exclusively priestly prerogative). In addition, there are a number of linguistic connections to this prophecy in the conversation between Michal and David that followed the transporting of the ark to Jerusalem. The same interplay between the roots "bless" (ברך) and "curse, be disgraced" (קלל) that is found in 1 Sam 2:30 is also in David's words in 2 Sam 6:22. Just as those who despise (the verb בָּזָה) God will be disgraced (1 Sam 2:30), so Michal despised (וַתִּבֶז, 2 Sam 6:16) God's servant David and was disgraced in that she never bore children (2 Sam 6:23).

But while the reader here might initially suspect that David is the fulfillment of 1 Sam 2:35, later 2 Samuel 7–24 will clarify that he is not. God will build

---

[25] E.g., Ex 28:41; 29:7; 30:30; 40:13, 15; Lev 6:13 (ET 6:20); 7:36; 8:12; 16:32; Num 3:3.

[26] See further "Yahweh's Acts of Salvation (2:8–10)" in the commentary on 2:1–11.

[27] Deenick, "Priest and King or Priest-King in 1 Samuel 2:35," 327–28.

[28] Deenick, "Priest and King or Priest-King in 1 Samuel 2:35," 331–34.

David a house but not a priesthood (2 Sam 7:11). David will not serve in God's presence forever, for he will lie down with his fathers in death, and his son will build a temple (2 Sam 7:12–13). Even David's son cannot be the faithful priest, for he will sin and God will discipline him (2 Sam 7:14; cf. 1 Ki 11:1–10). Then 2 Samuel moves on to document David's sins: he commits adultery and murder (2 Samuel 11), and he fails to trust God when he takes a census (2 Samuel 24).

So who is the "faithful priest" (1 Sam 2:35)? He is the "Anointed One" with the "secure house" who "will serve in my [Yahweh's] presence forever" (2:35). Earlier the Anointed One was identified by Hannah as a king ("his King ... his Anointed One"; see the commentary on 2:10). Thus, this faithful priest who will replace the Aaronic priesthood is also a king like David—but greater. The rest of Samuel documents the fall of the Elides as the first step in the replacement of the Aaronic priesthood. It also records the establishment of kings. First is Saul, who is a poor substitute for the priesthood because of his sacrificial malpractice (15:7–23). Then comes David, who is a man in harmony with God's heart, but falls short of being either the ideal king or the replacement priest. Instead, the faithful priest is someone else.

We ought to note that the promise of the faithful priest is reminiscent of the declaration that Moses made concerning a prophet like himself (Deut 18:15–18):

- "Yahweh your God will raise up [the Hiphil (H) of קוּם] a prophet like me ..." (Deut 18:15).
- "I will raise up [the Hiphil of קוּם] a prophet like you for them ..." (Deut 18:18).
- "I will raise up [the Hiphil of קוּם] for myself a faithful priest ..." (1 Sam 2:35).

The parallel is even closer when we remember that Moses was "faithful [נֶאֱמָן] in all my [God's] house" (Num 12:7, quoted as a prophecy of Christ in Heb 3:2, 5). Thus, the prophecy in 1 Sam 2:35 joins with 1 Sam 2:10 and with Deut 18:15–18 to point the reader to a coming Anointed One who will be the utterly faithful Prophet, Priest, and King. As readers continue to read the book of Samuel they learn that this person is not Samuel or Saul or even great King David. Instead, readers will continue to look for a priest not in the old Aaronic order, but as David says in Psalm 110, a priest-king like Melchizedek. Thus, the prophecy here is of Jesus, the Christ, the "faithful High Priest in God's presence" (πιστὸς ἀρχιερεὺς τὰ πρὸς τὸν θεόν, Heb 2:17).[29] Moreover, his resurrection, exaltation, and session at God's right hand confirms his royal and priestly offices (Heb 5:5–6; cf. Ps 2:7).

Finally, the "man of God" (1 Sam 2:27) notes the disgraced state of the former Elides: they will beg for an appointment to a priestly office in order to earn subsistence wages. The message is bitingly ironic in that "appoint me" (סְפָחֵנִי, sephaheni, 2:36) is an anagram on the names "Hophni" (חָפְנִי, Hophni) and "Phinehas" (פִּינְחָס, Phinehas, 2:34), with "Hophni" using four of the five

---

[29] Note the similarity to LXX 1 Sam 2:35: ἱερέα πιστόν; "faithful priest."

consonants in the suffixed verb and "Phinehas" using all five.[30] The prophecy ends with the utter disgrace of Eli's house, no longer in contrast to the faithful boy Samuel (2:12–17 in contrast to 2:11, 18), but in stark contrast to the wholly faithful anointed High Priest who will serve forever (the theme of Hebrews 3–9).

---

[30] Fokkelman, *Vow and Desire*, 151.

1 Samuel 3:1–21

Yahweh Calls Samuel to Be a Prophet

Translation

3 ¹Meanwhile the boy Samuel was ministering to Yahweh in the presence of Eli. Now the Word of Yahweh was rare in those days—there was no frequent vision. ²At that time Eli was lying in his place, and his eyes had begun to grow dim. He could not see. ³Moreover, before God's lamp had gone out Samuel was lying in Yahweh's temple, where the ark of God was.

⁴Then Yahweh called, "Samuel!" And he said, "Here I am."

⁵Then he ran to Eli and said, "Here I am, because you called me."

He said, "I did not call. Return. Lie down." So he went and lay down.

⁶Yahweh called again, "Samuel!" So Samuel got up and went to Eli.

He said, "Here I am, because you called me."

He said, "I did not call, my son. Return. Lie down."

(⁷Now Samuel had not yet known Yahweh, that is, the Word of Yahweh had not yet been revealed to him.)

⁸Yahweh called again, "Samuel!" a third time. He got up and went to Eli.

He said, "Here I am, because you called me." Then Eli understood that Yahweh was calling to the boy.

⁹Eli said to Samuel, "Go lie down. If he calls to you, say, 'Speak, Yahweh, because your servant is listening.'" So Samuel went and lay down in his place.

¹⁰Yahweh came, stood, and called as previously, "Samuel! Samuel!"

Samuel said, "Speak, because your servant is listening."

¹¹Yahweh said to Samuel, "I am about to do something in Israel that whoever hears about it will have ringing ears. ¹²On that day I will carry out against Eli all that I spoke against his house, from beginning to end. ¹³I told him that I would be judging his house forever because of the iniquity that he knew, for his sons were cursing God, and he did not stop them. ¹⁴So therefore, I have sworn concerning the house of Eli, 'The iniquity of the house of Eli will never be atoned for by sacrifices or offerings.'"

¹⁵Then Samuel lay down until morning. He got up in the morning and opened the doors of Yahweh's house. Samuel was afraid to tell the vision to Eli. ¹⁶Eli called to Samuel and said, "Samuel, my son!"

He said, "Here I am."

¹⁷He said, "What is the message that he spoke to you? Don't hide [it] from me. Thus may God do to you, and thus may he add if you hide from me a [single] word from the entire message that he spoke to you." ¹⁸So Samuel told him all the words and did not hide [any] from him. So he said, "He is Yahweh. May he do what he considers good."

[19]Samuel grew, and Yahweh was with him and did not allow one of his [prophetic] messages to fail. [20]Then all Israel from Dan to Beersheba knew that Samuel was confirmed as a prophet of Yahweh. [21]Yahweh continued to appear in Shiloh, because Yahweh revealed himself to Samuel in Shiloh in the Word of Yahweh.

Textual Notes

3:1 וְהַנַּעַר—For the author's skillful play on this term, "boy" (3:1, 8), to refer to the faithful ministerial servant Samuel (2:11, 18, 21, 26; also 1:22–27) and also to the unfaithful "servant(s)" of the Elides (2:13, 15, 17), see the commentary on 2:12–17.

מְשָׁרֵת אֶת־יְהוָה לִפְנֵי עֵלִי—For the grammar of this predicate, "was ministering to Yahweh in the presence of Eli," see the first and second textual notes on 2:11.

וּדְבַר־יְהוָה—"The Word of Yahweh" reveals and imparts knowledge of Yahweh himself (3:7, 21). Yahweh is present at the speaking of his Word: "Yahweh came, stood, and called" (3:10). His Word can be heard (שָׁמַע, 3:9; 15:1). More concretely his Word can "come to" a prophet (הָיָה אֶל, 1 Sam 15:10; 2 Sam 7:4), be "revealed" (יִגָּלֶה, 3:7; cf. נִגְלָה in 3:21), or be visible in a "vision" (הַמַּרְאָה, 3:15; similarly, Gen 15:1; cf. 2 Sam 24:11). In the NT the Word is made flesh and is seen (Jn 1:14).

הָיָה יָקָר—Usually the adjective יָקָר means "valuable." It can describe scarce commodities such as precious jewels (2 Sam 12:30; 1 Ki 7:9–11; Ezek 28:13), hence the nuance "was rare" here.

אֵין חָזוֹן נִפְרָץ:—The noun חָזוֹן refers to a divine revelation by means of a prophetic "vision" (e.g., Is 1:1; Jer 14:14; Ezek 7:26; Hos 12:11 [ET 12:10]). It is derived from the verb חָזָה, "to see," which, like the noun, usually refers to the perception of divine revelation (e.g., Is 1:1; 2:1; Ezek 12:27), and so its participle, "seer," is a synonym of "prophet" (e.g., 2 Sam 24:11; 2 Ki 17:13). In the Qal (G) the verb פָּרַץ can have the geographical meaning "to spread out, be widely distributed, be abundant" (see BDB, Qal, 10; *HALOT*, Qal, 6). This is the sole instance of the Niphal (N), whose participle has the corresponding passive meaning, "be widespread," but the participle is negated by אֵין, hence "not common/frequent." Cf. Joüon, § 160 i.

3:2 וְעֵינָיו הֵחֵלּוּ כֵהוֹת—The subject precedes the predicate in this circumstantial clause (Joüon, § 155 nc). The Qere is plural, "his eyes," while the Kethib is singular, וְעֵינוֹ, "his eye." The Qere agrees with the plural verb הֵחֵלּוּ and the plural adjective כֵהוֹת. The Hiphil (H) of חָלַל commonly means "to begin" an action, as in 14:35; 22:15 (cf. the second textual note on 3:12). The adjective כֵּהֶה, "dim, dull, faint," serves as the verbal complement with הֵחֵלּוּ, thus "had begun to grow dim." It is quite rare for an adjective to serve as a verbal complement (see GKC, § 120 b). The common construction is for a verb to take an infinitive construct as its complement; see the next textual note.

לֹא יוּכַל לִרְאוֹת:—The verb יָכֹל, "be able," takes the infinitive construct לִרְאוֹת, "to see," as its verbal complement (GKC, § 114 c, m). The verb רָאָה commonly refers to physical sight, but "he was not able to see" may relate to the scarcity of the divine "Word" and the prophetic "vision" in 3:1 (see the third and fifth textual notes there); in 3:15 the "vision" is denoted by the noun מַרְאָה, which is derived from the verb רָאָה used here. Eli may have been dull to perceive divine revelation. Instead of communicating with Eli directly, God calls to Samuel (3:4–10). The divine "vision" (3:15) and words

109

(3:17–18) are communicated to Eli by Samuel, even as the divine warning in 2:27–36 was spoken to Eli by an anonymous "man of God" (2:27).

3:3 בְּהֵיכַל יְהוָה—This means "in Yahweh's temple." The LXX lacks a translation for "Yahweh." For הֵיכָל, "temple," as in 1:9, see "Hannah and Eli (1:9–18)" in the commentary on 1:1–20.

אֲרוֹן אֱלֹהִים:—This construct phrase, "ark of God," is the first appearance of the "ark" in Samuel. This phrase (with or without the article on אֱלֹהִים) recurs in chapters 4–6. It is called אֲרוֹן בְּרִית יְהוָה, "the ark of the covenant of Yahweh," in 4:3–5. In the Torah it is usually called אֲרוֹן הָעֵדֻת, "the ark of the testimony," or just "the ark." See also the second textual notes on 4:3 and 4:4 and the first textual note on 5:1.

3:4 וַיִּקְרָא יְהוָה אֶל־שְׁמוּאֵל—The MT reads "and/then Yahweh called to Samuel." 4QSamᵃ reads [ויקרא יהו]ה שמ[ואל], "and Yahw[eh called], 'Samuel!'" The LXX, probably under the influence of 3:10, reinforces God's call: καὶ ἐκάλεσεν κύριος Σαμουηλ Σαμουηλ, "and the Lord called, 'Samuel! Samuel!'"

הִנֵּנִי:—This demonstrative particle with suffix, "here I am," recurs in 3:5, 6, 8, 16 and indicates a readiness to serve as directed. See also, e.g., Is 6:8.

3:6 וַיֹּסֶף יְהוָה קְרֹא עוֹד שְׁמוּאֵל וַיָּקָם שְׁמוּאֵל וַיֵּלֶךְ אֶל־עֵלִי—"(And) Yahweh called again, 'Samuel!' So Samuel got up and went to Eli." The Hiphil (H) of יָסַף, "to add, increase; do again," functions adverbially and the Qal (G) infinitive construct קְרֹא, "to call," serves as the main verb, thus "called again" (see Joüon, §§ 102 g, 124 c, 177 b). The identical construction recurs in 3:8 with the same verbs and with different infinitives in 3:21; 9:8; 18:29; 19:8 (cf. 19:21); 20:17; 23:4; 2 Sam 2:22; 3:34; 5:22; 7:10, 20; 14:10; 24:1. This construction uses יָסַף in the Qal in 1 Sam 7:13; 15:35; 27:4; 2 Sam 2:28.

The LXX reads καὶ προσέθετο κύριος καὶ ἐκάλεσεν Σαμουηλ Σαμουηλ· καὶ ἐπορεύθη πρὸς Ηλι τὸ δεύτερον, "And the Lord called again, 'Samuel! Samuel!' So he went to Eli a second time." The words τὸ δεύτερον were probably added under the influence of 3:8, and the omission of a translation of the verb וַיָּקָם, which makes the adjoining names into a double call ("Samuel, Samuel"), may have been influenced by 3:10.

בְּנִי—In place of "my son," the LXX reads σε, "you."

3:9 וַיֹּאמֶר עֵלִי לִשְׁמוּאֵל—"(And) Eli said to Samuel." The LXX simply has καὶ εἶπεν, "and he said."

3:10 שְׁמַע עַבְדֶּךָ:—"Your servant (is) listening." To show abject humility and deference to a superior, a speaker can refer to himself (or herself) in the third person as a "servant." Hannah, too, did so; see the third textual note on 1:11.

3:11 הִנֵּה אָנֹכִי עֹשֶׂה—The particle הִנֵּה can be used with a participle (here עֹשֶׂה) to denote the imminent future: "I *am going to do*" (Waltke-O'Connor, § 37.6f, example 33).

כָּל־שֹׁמְעוֹ תְּצִלֶּינָה שְׁתֵּי אָזְנָיו:—Literally "everyone hearing it—the two of his ears will ring." Body parts that occur in pairs, including the אֹזֶן, "ear," generally are feminine in gender, hence the verb is feminine, the third plural Qal (G) imperfect of צָלַל, "to tingle, ring, quiver." This same idiom occurs also in 2 Ki 21:12; Jer 19:3. For the verb form here, see GKC, § 67 p. The pronominal suffix on אָזְנָיו is resumptive (GKC, § 155 c, d) since it refers back to כָּל־שֹׁמְעוֹ, which is a *casus pendens* (GKC, § 116 w).

3:12 בַּיּוֹם הַהוּא אָקִים—"On that day" often refers to the time of fulfillment for a prophecy, whether of weal (e.g., Is 4:2; 19:18–24; Ezek 29:21; Hos 2:18–23 [ET 2:16–21]; Amos 9:11) or, as here, woe (also, e.g., Deut 31:17–18; Is 2:11, 17; Micah 2:4; Zeph 1:9–10). In this prophetic context אָקִים (the Hiphil [H] of קוּם) is translated as "I will carry out."

הָחֵל וְכַלֵּה:—These two infinitive absolutes function adverbially in relation to אָקִים, "I will carry out."[1] The first is the Hiphil (H) of חָלַל, "to begin," as in 3:2. The second is the Piel (D) of כָּלָה, "to finish, fulfill, end." On that day Yahweh will both initiate the action and complete it.

3:13 כִּי־מְקַלְלִים לָהֶם בָּנָיו—Literally "because his sons were cursing themselves." This is one of the *tiqqûnê sôpherîm*, the "corrections of the scribes." The change was made to avoid any mention of God being cursed. See the LXX: ὅτι κακολογοῦντες θεὸν υἱοὶ αὐτοῦ, "because his sons were speaking evil against God." The *tiqqûnê sôpherîm* were intentional changes by Jewish scribes. Each is explained in the Masorah Magna, which was part of the textual tradition to be copied by subsequent scribes and passed down so that the original text was never lost.[2] The Qal (G) of קָלַל in 2:30 meant "be disgraced," but the Piel (D; as here) normally means "to curse" (1 Sam 17:43; 2 Sam 16:5–13; 19:22 [ET 19:21]).

כָהָה—This is the sole OT instance of the verb כָּהָה II, and it is Piel (D), "to rebuke" or "restrain." This verb is a homograph of the more frequent verb כָּהָה I, "be or grow dim/faint," whose cognate adjective כֵּהֶה is discussed in the first textual note on 3:2.

3:14 אִם־יִתְכַּפֵּר—Negative oaths often begin with the particle אִם,[3] hence the translation "will never." The verb is the only OT instance of the Hithpael (HtD) of the root כפר (which doesn't occur in the Qal). The meaning of the Hithpael is akin to that of the Pual (Dp; e.g., Is 6:7; 22:14) and is the passive of the Piel (D), "to atone" for sin (2 Sam 21:3; common in Leviticus, e.g., Lev 1:4; 5:6; 16:6, 10–11, 16–18).

בְּזֶבַח וּבְמִנְחָה—These two collective nouns, "sacrifice" and "offering," occurred together, each with the preposition בְּ, also in 2:29. Here בְּ is instrumental, "by means of."

3:15 עַד־הַבֹּקֶר—The MT has a single reference to "the morning." The LXX includes two references: ἕως πρωὶ καὶ ὤρθρισεν τὸ πρωί, "… until morning. And he got up in the morning." It is possible that the Hebrew originally included two words to be vocalized וַיַּשְׁכֵּם בַּבֹּקֶר but they were omitted by parablepsis as the scribe's eye jumped to the second בֹּקֶר. (The text of 4QSamᵃ is not extant for this passage.)

3:16 וַיִּקְרָא עֵלִי אֶת־שְׁמוּאֵל—Literally "and Eli called Samuel." Codex Leningradensis has the direct object marker אֶת. In its place many manuscripts have the preposition אֶל, "called *to* Samuel," as translated above.

3:17 כֹּה יַעֲשֶׂה־לְּךָ אֱלֹהִים וְכֹה יוֹסִיף—This jussive formula, "thus may God do … , and thus may he add if … ," puts a person under an oath without specifying what punishment God would mete out (and then increase) for not telling the truth or for not performing

---

[1] GKC, § 113 h; Joüon, § 123 r; Waltke-O'Connor, § 35.3.2a, including example 2.

[2] See Tov, *Textual Criticism of the Hebrew Bible*, 65–67, especially 66.

[3] Joüon, § 165 d; Waltke-O'Connor, § 40.2.2c.

an action (Joüon, § 165 a, including note 1). It recurs in 1 Sam 14:44; 20:13; 25:22; 2 Sam 3:9, 35; 19:14 (ET 19:13).

3:18 יְהוָה הוּא‎—The disjunctive *zaqeph* accent on הוּא‎ signifies that the Masoretes intended the words יְהוָה הוּא‎ to go together as a first sentence: "He is Yahweh," a confession of faith (cf. Deut 6:4 and יהוה הוא‎ in Deut 4:35, 39).

הַטּוֹב בְּעֵינָו יַעֲשֶׂה:‎—The Qere is the suffixed plural בְּעֵינָיו‎, "in his eyes," which is often used to express someone's opinion or estimation, thus "he considers." The Kethib is the singular בְּעֵינוֹ‎, "in his eye." The Qal (G) verb יַעֲשֶׂה‎ is probably jussive, literally "may he do the good in his eyes," that is, "may he do what he considers good." If so, Eli responds in faith (cf. "thy will be done," Mt 6:10; "let it be to me," Lk 1:38) and affirms the justice of Yahweh's impending judgment. The verb form could also be imperfect, in which case it could have a future meaning: "he will do." The imperfect could also have a timeless habitual meaning: "he (always) does." Either of these imperfect meanings would suggest that Eli expresses resignation to the inevitability that Yahweh will carry out the dire warning.

3:19 וַיִּגְדַּל שְׁמוּאֵל‎—The Qal (G) of גָּדַל‎, "grow, become big," was used of young Samuel earlier in 2:21, 26.

וַיהוָה הָיָה עִמּוֹ‎—For Yahweh to be "with" (the preposition עִם‎) a person indicates his showering of grace and blessing (e.g., Gen 21:22; 26:3, 28; 28:15; Judg 1:22; 6:12; אֵת‎, "with," in, e.g., Gen 39:2, 21). The author will use this expression for David (e.g., 1 Sam 16:18; 18:12, 14, 28; 2 Sam 7:3). Cf. also 1 Sam 20:13; 2 Sam 2:6. 1 Ki 1:37 uses the expression for both David and Solomon.

וְלֹא־הִפִּיל מִכָּל־דְּבָרָיו אָרְצָה:‎—Yahweh continues to be the subject, literally "and he did not make [any] of all his words fall to the ground," that is, he fulfilled all of his words. Here the idiom uses the causative Hiphil (H) of נָפַל‎, "to fall"; the same idiom but with Yahweh's "word" as the subject of the Qal (G) of נָפַל‎ occurs in Josh 21:45; 23:14; 1 Ki 8:56; similarly, 2 Ki 10:10. The same idea is expressed in different words in 1 Sam 9:6; see the fourth textual note there.

3:20 נֶאֱמָן‎—This Niphal (N) participle (here translated as "was confirmed") appeared twice in the messianic promise of 2:35 ("faithful … secure"); see the second textual note and the commentary there.

3:21 לְהֵרָאֹה‎—Literally "to be seen," translated as "to appear," this is an unusual form of the Niphal (N) infinitive construct of רָאָה‎, "see" (with לְ‎). The expected form would be לְהֵרָאֹת‎ (GKC, § 75 y).

The LXX has a long expansion in this verse: καὶ ἐπιστεύθη Σαμουηλ προφήτης γενέσθαι τῷ κυρίῳ εἰς πάντα Ισραηλ ἀπ᾽ ἄκρων τῆς γῆς καὶ ἕως ἄκρων. καὶ Ηλι πρεσβύτης σφόδρα, καὶ οἱ υἱοὶ αὐτοῦ πορευόμενοι ἐπορεύοντο καὶ πονηρὰ ἡ ὁδὸς αὐτῶν ἐνώπιον κυρίου, "And Samuel was believed to be a prophet of the Lord to all Israel from one end of the land to the other. And Eli was a very old man, and his sons kept advancing, and their way was evil before the Lord." McCarter believes that the first part of this expansion is a displaced variant of 2:20. He accepts the second part ("and Eli was …") as genuine and believes that it dropped out of the MT by a parablepsis that also affected 4:1 (see the textual note on 4:1).[4] However, this addition looks suspiciously like a summary of the problems of Eli and his sons as previously discussed in 1 Samuel 1–3. Thus, it is likely to be a secondary addition to the text added as a kind of recap preparing for 1 Samuel 4.

Commentary

c. 1073 BC

While the previous chapters have emphasized the contrast between the piety of Samuel and his family and the impious sons of Eli, this chapter depicts Samuel's rise and Eli's decline. We are once again introduced to Samuel as a minister of Yahweh under Eli (3:1). The author then gives us some background information that will set the stage for this account: the Word of Yahweh was rare, and since his Word could be revealed visually as well as aurally, this also meant that prophetic visions were infrequent (see the third and fifth textual notes on 3:1). There are two key words in this statement: "word/message" (דָּבָר) and "vision" (חָזוֹן, 3:1). The two are brought together when Samuel receives God's "message" and "words" (דָּבָר, 3:17) in a "vision" (מַרְאָה, 3:15).

At the beginning of the account we are told that Eli was lying in his place (3:2), though we are not told where that place was. Since Eli could not hear Yahweh's words to Samuel and Samuel had to run to Eli to speak to him, this place must have been out of earshot of the place where Samuel was lying. We are also told that Eli could no longer see. This will play an important role in this narrative, since Eli cannot see in order to tend to the lamp in the tabernacle (3:3), nor is he able to see in the sense of discerning a vision from God as Samuel did (3:15).

Samuel was lying in God's house, the tabernacle, which is called a "temple" (3:3) here, for one of only three times in the OT (also 1 Sam 1:9; 2 Sam 22:7). Samuel had seemingly replaced the high priest Eli, since he is in the presence of God's ark and is tending to God's lamp. The lamp was to burn continually, and it was the responsibility of the high priest and other priests to attend to it (Ex 27:20–21; Lev 24:2–3). However, the blind Eli cannot tend to the lamp, and apparently his derelict sons do not attend to it either. So it fell to the young Levite Samuel to keep watch over the lamp.

Three times we are presented with God calling (to) Samuel and Samuel reporting to Eli. After the second time Eli sent Samuel back to lie down, the author informs us that Samuel did not yet know Yahweh (3:7). At first one might think that he had this ignorance in common with Eli's faithless sons (2:12), but the author explains that in Samuel's case it means that Yahweh had not yet directly revealed his Word to Samuel. Samuel was not yet a prophet—a circumstance that would change quickly.

While Eli retained his hearing, his understanding of what was happening was slow to develop. The third time Yahweh called, Eli finally realized that

---

[4] McCarter, *I Samuel*, 97; similarly, Klein, *1 Samuel*, 30.

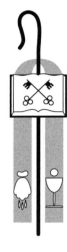

Samuel was being summoned by God. He instructed Samuel as to the proper way to respond, and the pious boy followed Eli's directions. The fourth time Yahweh came and stood before calling; presumably he stood beside the place where Samuel was lying. Since only the high priest could enter the tabernacle's Most Holy Place, we can only assume that Samuel was lying in the Holy Place where the lamp was. God, however, normally dwelt enthroned on the cherubim over the ark,[5] which was kept in the Most Holy Place (Ex 26:34). But in this case God moved toward Samuel in the Holy Place. This movement to communicate with humanity would culminate in the incarnation, the Word made flesh (Jn 1:14), as God now speaks to us through his Son (Heb 1:1–2; cf. Jn 9:37).

1 Samuel 3 is one of the more detailed accounts of the calling of a prophet,[6] punctuated with a dozen instances of the verb קָרָא, "call." The double "Samuel! Samuel!" (3:10[7]) evokes the call of the apostle Paul with "Saul, Saul."[8] Paul invoked his divine call to assert his apostolic authority, not for self-aggrandizement, but to verify the authenticity of the Gospel he preached: justification by grace alone and through faith alone.[9] Pastors today are called as servants of the Word.[10] They receive this call not directly from God but through the church,[11] and they preach the Word of the Scriptures, not any claimed private revelation. Ministers exercise the authority of the One whose Word they faithfully proclaim (e.g., Mt 28:19–20; Jn 20:21–23).

Yahweh's message to Samuel confirmed the previous prophetic message to Eli (1 Sam 2:27–36). God was now announcing that the time for the first stage of his judgment on Eli's house was near. God stated that when Israelites would hear the news about these events, their ears would ring. This expression (תְּצִלֶּינָה + אָזְנַיִם, 1 Sam 3:11) is always used to speak of shocking news about some calamity wrought by God (2 Ki 21:12; Jer 19:3).

God clarified that he will not relent of even a single element of the previous prophecy (1 Sam 2:27–36), since no amount of animal sacrifices or grain offerings could atone for the sins of Eli's house (3:12, 14). Eli will bear the brunt of this judgment, because as the high priest he was responsible for all of the priests and ought to have brought an end to his sons' evil practices (3:13).

The next morning Samuel continued to serve. He opened the doors to God's house (3:15). Attending to his work may have been a way of avoiding Eli, since

---

5   E.g., Ex 25:22; 30:6; Lev 16:2; Num 7:89; 1 Sam 4:4; 2 Sam 6:2; 2 Ki 19:15; 1 Chr 13:6.

6   For other prophetic call narratives, see, e.g., 2 Kings 2; Isaiah 6; Jeremiah 1; Ezekiel 1–2; Amos 7:14–15; Jonah 1; 3:1–3.

7   The first textual note on 1 Sam 3:4 observes that the LXX includes the double name also there.

8   Acts 9:4; 22:7; 26:14. The Gospels record Jesus personally "calling" his other apostles; see, e.g., καλέω in Mt 4:21 and προσκαλέω in Mt 10:1; cf. Jn 1:42.

9   See "call" (καλέω) in Gal 1:15, in the context of Galatians 1–2. He begins two of his epistles with the claim that he is a "called apostle" (κλητὸς ἀπόστολος, Rom 1:1; 1 Cor 1:1).

10 See the textual note on "the Word of Yahweh" in 3:1 (the phrase occurs also in 3:21).

11 No one is to exercise the public ministry of teaching, preaching, and administering the Sacraments without a divine call through the church to do so (AC XIV; see also AC V).

he was understandably afraid to bring such a stern prophecy to the high priest. Nevertheless, Eli not only prevailed upon the boy to tell him what Yahweh had said, but he also placed him under oath (3:17). Eli acquiesced to God's will (3:18). Throughout 1 Samuel 1–4 Eli is always a dedicated priest. He himself never displays contempt for God, dereliction of duty, or unbelief. His personal faith was not in doubt. Instead, he was held responsible as a leader who failed to execute the responsibilities of his office. In the same vein, James warned his readers that not many of them ought to seek positions of authority in the church as leaders, since God will judge such leaders more strictly than others (James 3:1). James was teaching only what Jesus had taught earlier: those who are put in charge of others have a greater responsibility to God (Lk 12:42–48).

The last verses of this chapter depict Samuel as Yahweh's prophet. All Samuel's prophecies were fulfilled (3:19; see also 9:6). Throughout Israel he was recognized as a true prophet of Yahweh (3:20). He continued to serve in Shiloh and to prophesy Yahweh's Word there (3:21).

The Prophet Samuel in Scripture

Samuel is the most important prophet in the book of Samuel.[1] He is the major figure in the narrative in 1 Samuel 1–4; 7–12 and also plays important roles in Saul's reign (1 Samuel 13; 15; 19; 28) and in anointing David (1 Samuel 16). All told, he is mentioned by name 129 times in 1 Samuel 1–28. But what is the depiction of this prophet elsewhere in Scripture?

Outside of the book of Samuel, he is mentioned most often in Chronicles. In the early chapters of that book we learn that Samuel was a Kohathite, the father of Joel and Abijah, who were among those in charge of music in worship (1 Chr 6:13, 18 [ET 16:28, 33]). His grandson Heman was a skilled musician who sang and played the cymbals and possibly other musical instruments (1 Chr 6:18 [ET 6:33]; 15:17, 19; 2 Chr 5:12; 35:15).

We also learn that Samuel was active in the administration of God's house, the tabernacle. He, like David after him, appointed gatekeepers (1 Chr 9:22). In addition, he dedicated gifts for God's house (1 Chr 26:28). His influence on worship must have been celebrated, since the Passover observed in Josiah's day is said to be greater than all the Passovers held since Samuel's time (2 Chr 35:18).

Finally, we learn that he wrote a chronicle of David's acts (1 Chr 29:29). This would have been limited to information about David during Saul's reign, since Samuel died before David became king (1 Sam 25:1; 28:3). Nevertheless, Samuel's influence outlived him, because the Chronicler tells us that Israel came to Hebron to make David king "according to the Word of Yahweh by the hand of Samuel" (1 Chr 11:3). Samuel's anointing of David (1 Sam 16:12–13) is probably in view in this comment.

Samuel is mentioned twice more in the OT. In Ps 99:6 we are told that Yahweh's priests included Moses and Aaron. Then the psalmist says that like them, Samuel called on Yahweh's name and he answered them. This is probably a reference to Samuel's intercession for Israel at Ebenezer (1 Sam 7:5–12, especially 7:9). The psalmist does not identify Samuel as a priest, but does compare him favorably to Moses and Aaron. Jeremiah also groups Samuel with Moses (Jer 15:1), as both intervened for Israel and God listened and acted. However, God prohibited Jeremiah himself from being such an intercessor (Jer 7:16; 11:14; 14:11), since God had already determined that Israel would be destroyed (Jer 15:1–9).

In the NT Samuel is mentioned in Acts and Hebrews. Acts 3:18–26 once again groups Samuel with Moses. Peter recalls the preaching of "all the prophets" (Acts 3:18). He quotes: "Moses said: 'The Lord God will raise up for you

---

[1] Others are Gad (1 Sam 22:5; 2 Sam 24:11), Nathan (e.g., 2 Sam 7:2; 12:25), and perhaps Zadok (2 Sam 15:27).

a prophet like me' " (Acts 3:22, citing Deut 18:15). The apostle then says that "all the prophets, *from Samuel and those afterward*, as many as spoke, also *proclaimed these days*" (Acts 3:24)—the days of God's Servant Jesus (Acts 3:26), who is the prophet like Moses. The only two prophets Peter singles out by name here are Moses and Samuel, attesting to Samuel's importance in the line of prophets in the OT. In a similar way, the writer to the Hebrews speaks of "Samuel and the prophets" at the end of his catalog of great OT men of faith (Heb 11:32).

In his review of Israel's history, Paul mentions Samuel as the last of the judges (Acts 13:20; cf. 1 Sam 7:6, 15). Thus, this apostle pictures Samuel as a transitional figure. He is the last of the judges and the prophet who anoints the first of Israel's kings. As a prophet he inaugurates a line of prophets stretching from the early monarchy (e.g., Elijah, Elisha, Hosea, Isaiah) to the Persian-period prophets (Haggai, Zechariah, Malachi).

Though not often considered by many today as a figure of the stature of Moses, David, or Elijah, in the Scriptures Samuel looms large as a seminal figure in both the monarchy and the line of prophets who pointed to Christ (cf. 1 Pet 1:10–12; 2 Pet 3:2).

The Philistines Capture
the Ark of the Covenant

Translation

4 **¹When the word of Samuel was for all Israel, Israel went out to meet the Philistines for battle. They camped at Ebenezer, and the Philistines camped in Aphek. ²The Philistines drew up battle lines to meet Israel, the battle became fierce, and Israel was defeated before the Philistines. They slew about four thousand men in the battle line in the field. ³When the troops came into the camp, the elders of Israel said, "Why has Yahweh defeated us before the Philistines today? Let's take the ark of the covenant of Yahweh for ourselves from Shiloh. It will come among us and save us from the grip of our enemies."**

⁴So the troops sent to Shiloh and took from there the ark of the covenant of Yahweh of armies, who is enthroned [over] the cherubim. Eli's two sons—Hophni and Phinehas—were there with the ark of the covenant of God. ⁵As the ark of the covenant of Yahweh came into the camp, all Israel gave a loud shout, and the earth shook.

⁶When the Philistines heard the sound of the shout, they said, "What is the sound of this loud shout in the Hebrews' camp?" They realized that the ark of Yahweh had come into the camp.

⁷The Philistines were afraid, because they thought that God had come into the camp. They said, "Woe to us, because nothing like this has ever happened before. ⁸Woe to us! Who will save us from the power of these majestic gods? These are the gods who struck Egypt with utter defeat in the wilderness. ⁹Be strong! Be men, Philistines! Otherwise you will serve the Hebrews as they have served you. So be men, and go to war!"

¹⁰The Philistines fought and Israel was defeated, and each man fled to his home. The slaughter was very great, and thirty thousand infantry troops fell from Israel. ¹¹Moreover, the ark of God was captured, and Eli's two sons—Hophni and Phinehas—died.

Textual Notes

4:1 וַיְהִי דְבַר־שְׁמוּאֵל לְכָל־יִשְׂרָאֵל—This is translated as "when the word of Samuel was for all Israel." Many commentaries take this first part of the verse to be a completion of the thought of the previous chapter, i.e., the Word of Yahweh came to Samuel, and the word of Samuel came to Israel.[1] It is best, however, to understand 4:1 as parataxis

---

[1] E.g., Brueggemann, *First and Second Samuel*, 28; Fokkelman, *Vow and Desire*, 158; Smith, *The Books of Samuel*, 30.

and this first clause as temporal.[2] (For other examples in this context of a verse beginning with a paratactic temporal clause, see 4:3, 6.) Thus, during the time when Samuel was prophesying to all Israel (rather than just to Eli, as in 1 Samuel 3), Israel went to war.

At this point the LXX has a different text: καὶ ἐγενήθη ἐν ταῖς ἡμέραις ἐκείναις καὶ συναθροίζονται ἀλλόφυλοι εἰς πόλεμον ἐπὶ Ισραηλ, "in those days the Philistines gathered themselves for war against Israel." Some commentators take this to be the original text, along with the extended ending of LXX 1 Sam 3:21.[3] However, this appears to be a secondary insertion that explicitly makes the Philistines the aggressors and also provides an explanation of why Israel went to war.

לִקְרַאת—This is the Qal (G) infinitive construct of קָרָא II, "to meet, encounter," with the preposition לְ. It recurs in 4:2 and is used over thirty times in Samuel, often for engaging in battle. Thus, it appears together with the noun מִלְחָמָה, "war," in 1 Sam 4:1, 2; 17:2; 2 Sam 10:9; 18:6; and elsewhere in the OT.

בָּאֲפֵק:—This means "at Aphek." Aphek was in the Plain of Sharon, just east of modern Tel Aviv.

4:2 וַיַּעַרְכוּ—This is translated as "drew up battle lines." The Qal (G) of עָרַךְ means "to arrange" and in this context refers to arraying troops in a line to meet the enemy in combat. This verb is the root of the noun מַעֲרָכָה, "battle line, array," used later in 4:2 (also, e.g., 4:12, 16; 17:8, 10, 20–22).

וַתִּטֹּשׁ הַמִּלְחָמָה—In form the verb is the third feminine singular Qal (G) preterite (imperfect with *waw* consecutive) of נָטַשׁ, which usually means "to leave, abandon, give up" something, but such a meaning does not fit this context with הַמִּלְחָמָה as its subject and no direct object. McCarter retains the consonantal text but proposes emending the vowels to וַתֻּטַּשׁ, a form that would be parsed the same way but from a Qal passive (Gp) stem, "and the battle was deployed."[4] A second proposed emendation is to וַתֵּט, the Qal of נָטָה, which often means "to spread out" (transitively, with a direct object) or "turn aside," which appears to have support from ἔκλινεν, "inclined, turned," in the LXX.[5] However, there is no other use of נָטָה in the OT meaning "to spread out" in the intransitive sense. Yet a third emendation is to וַתִּקֶשׁ, "became fierce," the third feminine singular Qal preterite (imperfect with *waw* consecutive) of קָשָׁה (cf. וַיִּקֶשׁ in 2 Sam 19:44 [ET 19:43]); those who advocate this emendation appeal to the cognate adjective קָשָׁה in 2 Sam 2:17, וַתְּהִי הַמִּלְחָמָה קָשָׁה, "and the battle became fierce."[6] The emendation to וַתִּקֶשׁ is adopted for this commentary's translation: "the battle became fierce."

וַיִּנָּגֶף—The identical form recurs in 4:10. The Niphal (N) of נָגַף has the passive meaning "be struck, defeated." The Qal (G) of נָגַף in 4:3 (נְגָפָנוּ) is the masculine singular

---

2 Spina, "A Prophet's 'Pregnant Pause,'" 66; Tsumura, *The First Book of Samuel*, 185; see Joüon, § 166 a.

3 See the textual note on 3:21. Advocates of this view include McCarter, *I Samuel*, 102–3; Klein, *1 Samuel*, 36–37.

4 McCarter, *I Samuel*, 102–3.

5 See already BDB, s.v. נָטָה, 3 a.

6 Smith, *The Books of Samuel*, 32; Klein, *1 Samuel*, 36–37.

perfect with first common plural suffix) has the corresponding active meaning "to strike" or "defeat."

וַיַּכּוּ—This Hiphil (H) preterite (imperfect with *waw* consecutive) of נָכָה, "to strike, smite," is translated as "they slew." The Hiphil participle and cognate noun מַכָּה occur in 4:8 (see the third textual note there).

4:3 הָעָם—While this often simply means "the people," in military contexts this word denotes "the troops," as here and also in 4:4, 17.

אֲרוֹן בְּרִית יְהוָה—This three-word construct chain, "the ark of the covenant of Yahweh," serves as a title for the ark thirty times in the OT (sometimes with additional wording appended). It recurs in 4:5 and in a unique expanded form in 4:4; see the second textual note on 4:4. See also the analogous אֲרוֹן בְּרִית הָאֱלֹהִים, "the ark of the covenant of God," in 1 Sam 4:4; 2 Sam 15:24. The "ark" was introduced in 1 Sam 3:3. Shorter phrases designate it elsewhere, e.g., אֲרוֹן יְהוָה, "the ark of Yahweh" (4:6), and more often אֲרוֹן (הָ)אֱלֹהִים, "the ark of God" (4:11, 13, 17–19, 21–22). The LXX omits "covenant" here and three more times in 4:4–5.

וְיָבֹא בְקִרְבֵּנוּ וְיֹשִׁעֵנוּ מִכַּף אֹיְבֵינוּ:—The verb יֹשִׁעֵנוּ, the suffixed Hiphil (H) imperfect (with conjunctive *waw*) of יָשַׁע, is a synonym of יַצִּילֵנוּ, the suffixed Hiphil imperfect of נָצַל, in 4:8. The subject of the two imperfect verbs here could be Yahweh, but the translation considers the "ark" to be the subject, "*it* will come … and save us," since the Israelites are treating it as a talisman that can give them victory. The Israelites' thinking is then inferior to that of the heathen Philistines, who conclude that "God" (4:7) or "gods" (4:8), not just his/their ark, had entered the Israelites' camp.

The prepositional phrase מִכַּף is literally "from [the palm side of] the hand of." It is a synonym of מִיַּד, "from the hand of," in 4:8.

4:4 וְשָׁם—The second instance in this verse of the adverb "there" is omitted in the LXX.

אֲרוֹן בְּרִית־יְהוָה צְבָאוֹת יֹשֵׁב הַכְּרֻבִים—"The ark of the covenant of Yahweh of armies, who is enthroned [over] the cherubim," is a four-word construct chain with an additional two-word appositional phrase modifying יְהוָה. This is the only instance of this full title in the entire OT. This long title emphasizes Yahweh as a warrior (cf. Ex 15:3) and a king at the head of his army (cf. 2 Sam 6:2). See the fourth textual note on 1 Sam 1:3. The LXX omits "of armies."

4:5 וַיָּרִעוּ … תְּרוּעָה גְדוֹלָה—Literally "they shouted a big shout," this is a cognate accusative construction. See the first textual note on 1:6 (see also, e.g., 1:11, 17, 21; 2:13, 24).

וַתֵּהֹם הָאָרֶץ:—The feminine noun אֶרֶץ, "earth," is the subject of the Niphal (N) third feminine singular preterite (imperfect with *waw* consecutive) of הוּם, "be in an uproar," hence "reverberate, shake."

4:6 קוֹל הַתְּרוּעָה—This construct phrase, "the sound of the shout," occurs twice in this verse, but the LXX omits "sound" both times.

הָעִבְרִים—"The Hebrews" is the way that Philistines referred to Israelites (1 Sam 13:19; 14:11; 29:3). It may have been a derogatory term (cf. 14:11). The designation is repeated in 4:9 (לָעִבְרִים).

4:7 וַיִּרְאוּ—If one ignores the accents, this form would be the third masculine plural Qal (G) preterite (imperfect with *waw* consecutive) of רָאָה "to see," which is common in the OT, e.g., 5:7; 6:13; 10:11. However, the *metheg* beside the *hireq* (-ִ-) indicates this is the defective, or *ḥaser*, spelling of וַיִּירְאוּ, the Qal imperfect of the stative verb יָרֵא, "be afraid."

אָמְרוּ—This is translated as "they thought." The verb אָמַר is used not only for "speak," but also for internal dialogue, "say to oneself," i.e., "think" (cf. *HALOT*, s.v. אמר, 4).

בָּא אֱלֹהִים—Literally "God came." The form בָּא could be the singular Qal (G) masculine participle, but the context indicates that it is the singular third masculine perfect. The LXX incorrectly emends the verb to a plural, οἱ θεοὶ ἥκασιν, "the gods had come," in anticipation of the plural forms that modify אֱלֹהִים in 4:8 and indicate that it means "gods" there (הָאֱלֹהִים הָאַדִּירִים הָאֵלֶּה אֵלֶּה הֵם הָאֱלֹהִים הַמַּכִּים). However, 4:7 is reporting on the internal thought of the Philistines *from a monotheistic Israelite viewpoint*. When the polytheistic Philistines' speech is reported in 4:8, their words reveal their conception of Israelite "gods" in a pantheon.

לֹא הָיְתָה כָּזֹאת—Literally "there has not been [anything] like this." Hebrew often expresses abstract ideas, such as events or circumstances, in the feminine singular, including the demonstrative זֹאת (GKC, § 122 q).

אֶתְמוֹל שִׁלְשֹׁם:—Literally this is "yesterday [and] a third day," i.e., the two previous days, since what we call "the day before yesterday" is the third day ago, counting inclusively (starting with today as the first day). This idiom means "before, previously." It also occurs in 1 Sam 10:11; 14:21; 19:7 (cf. 2 Sam 5:2).

4:8 יַצִּילֵנוּ—This is a synonym of יֹשִׁעֵנוּ in 4:3; see the third textual note there.

מִיַּד—Literally "from the hand of," this means "from the power of" and is a synonym of מִכַּף in 4:3; see the third textual note there.

הַמַּכִּים אֶת־מִצְרַיִם בְּכָל־מַכָּה—This is translated as "who struck Egypt with utter defeat." The masculine plural participle הַמַּכִּים (with the definite article functioning as a relative pronoun) is the Hiphil (H) of נָכָה, "to strike, smite." This verb is the root of the following noun מַכָּה, which, depending on context, can be translated as "plague" (4:8), "blow" (6:19), "slaughter" (4:10), "attack" (14:14), or "defeat" (14:30; מַכָּה גְדוֹלָה, "decisive defeat," 19:8; 23:5). Because of the allusions to the exodus by means of "Egypt" (מִצְרַיִם) and "in the wilderness" (בַּמִּדְבָּר), this singular could be treated as a collective and translated as "plagues." However, this Hebrew term is not used in the Torah for any of the ten plagues in Egypt. In the Torah מַכָּה occurs only in Num 11:33 regarding a plague that the Lord sent against the complaining Israelites in the wilderness; in Deut 25:3 regarding the punishment to be given to an individual Israelite found guilty of a crime; and in Lev 26:21; Deut 28:59, 61; 29:22 regarding future blows or plagues that the Israelites would experience if they were unfaithful to Yahweh. See further the next textual note.

בַּמִּדְבָּר:—This means "in the wilderness." If the word מַכָּה (see the preceding textual note) is interpreted as a reference to the ten plagues in Egypt, then this phrase might appear to be a contradiction, since those ten plagues took place in Egypt itself, not "in the wilderness." However, this commentary's translation takes מַכָּה to refer to the "defeat" of the Egyptians when they pursued Israel into the "wilderness" (מִדְבָּר in Ex 13:18, 20; 14:3, 11–12) and then drowned in the Red Sea. The LXX ameliorates the possible difficulty of translating מַכָּה as "plagues" by adding a conjunction, καὶ ἐν τῇ ἐρήμῳ, "*and* in the wilderness," so that there would be no contradiction if the plagues (LXX: ἐν πάσῃ πληγῇ) referred to the ones in Egypt. It is also possible that the reference could be to other foes of Israel who were defeated as the Israelites passed through the wilderness toward the promised land (e.g., Numbers 21; 32:33; Deut 2:18–3:11). On the other hand, the MT text may reflect that the Philistines were only generally familiar with Israel's history and were in error about the ten plagues having occurred "in the wilderness." Some propose emending בַּמִּדְבָּר to וּבַדֶּבֶר or וּבְמוֹ־דָבֶר, either of which would mean "and with pestilence."[7]

4:9 וִהְיִיתֶם לַאֲנָשִׁים וְנִלְחַמְתֶּם:—This Qal (G) perfect of הָיָה with *waw* consecutive and this Niphal (N) perfect of לָחַם with *waw* consecutive are parallel to the two preceding imperatives (הִתְחַזְּקוּ וִהְיוּ) and so function as imperatives: "so be men, and go to war!"

4:10 וַיִּלָּחֲמוּ פְלִשְׁתִּים—"The Philistines fought." The LXX reads καὶ ἐπολέμησαν αὐτούς, "they fought them."

אִישׁ לְאֹהָלָיו—"Each man … to his home" is the distributive use of the noun אִישׁ plus "to his tent." This is a stock idiom.[8]

רַגְלִי:—This is translated as "infantry troops." The singular adjective is formed from the noun רֶגֶל, "foot," with the gentilic suffix י. It denotes someone who travels by foot. In a military context it denotes an infantryman.

Commentary

Late fall/early winter 1069 BC

The Ark in the Plotline of the Book of Samuel

In 1926 Leonhard Rost proposed that the portions of Samuel in which the ark played a major role (1 Sam 4:1–7:1; 2 Samuel 6) were originally part of a separate ark narrative written by a priest for visitors to Jerusalem's temple who wanted to know how the ark had arrived there.[9] Rost's thesis went largely unchallenged among critical scholars for almost half a century. More recently, the idea of a separate independent ark narrative has met with skepticism, although it still has its defenders.[10]

There are a number of problems with the thesis of an independent ark narrative. For instance, the deaths of Hophni and Phinehas (4:11) and the account of Eli's death and Ichabod's birth (4:12–22) make no sense without the material

---

[7] See McCarter, *I Samuel*, 104; Klein, *1 Samuel*, 38.

[8] Judg 7:8; 20:8; 1 Sam 13:2; 2 Sam 18:17; 19:9 (ET 19:8); 20:1, 22; 2 Ki 14:12; 2 Chr 25:22; cf. 2 Chr 10:16.

[9] Rost, *The Succession to the Throne of David*.

[10] See Bodner, "Ark-Eology: Shifting Emphases in 'Ark Narrative' Scholarship." See also Smelik, "The Ark Narrative Reconsidered," and Gitay, "Reflections on the Poetics of the Samuel Narrative: The Question of the Ark Narrative."

in 1 Samuel 1–3. This suggests that one using this methodology ought to go farther than Rost and also excise 4:11–22 from the ark narrative. Yet without this poignant account of the ark's capture and its effects, the narrative in 4:1–10 becomes insipidly one-dimensional.

Another problem is that when David brings the ark to Jerusalem in 2 Samuel 6, there is no mention of Kiriath-jearim (1 Sam 6:21–7:2), the place from which he fetches the ark.[11] Instead, the alternate name of the place, Baalah in Judah, is used (2 Sam 6:2; cf. Josh 15:9). If 2 Samuel 6 was part of a coherent ark narrative, one would at least expect an explanation of the place-name Kiriath-jearim in 1 Sam 6:21–7:2 or of the place-name Baalah in 2 Sam 6:2.

Instead of looking for separate sources that contributed to the book of Samuel,[12] it is much more fruitful to ask why Samuel disappears from the narrative after 1 Sam 4:1 and does not reappear until 1 Sam 7:3. The reason for this ought to be obvious: The ark's story is the story of the failure of the leadership among the Elide priests, which leads to Israel's misuse of the ark (abetted by Eli's sons, 4:4, 11) as well as Israel's turning to idolatry and its continued twenty-year subjugation to the Philistines even after the return of the ark (7:2–3). During this time the Israelites were not listening to the prophecies of Samuel (3:19–4:1a) but were turning to the gods of the nations around them. In fact, 4:1 implies that the Israelites did not value Samuel's prophecy, since they went to war without first consulting the prophet or committing their hearts to Yahweh and serving only him (7:3). Thus, the accounts of the capture and return of the ark are presented by the author to illustrate the consequences of the crisis of leadership triggered by the failure of the high priest Eli and the corruption of his priestly sons.

Israel Attempts to Defeat the Philistines (4:1–5)

The author begins this section by noting that at the time Samuel was prophesying to Israel, Israel went to war (4:1). The implication of this is that the Israelites did not consult God through his prophet Samuel before seeking to free themselves from the Philistines (see Judg 10:7; 13:1; 1 Sam 4:9). Instead, Israel marched out to Ebenezer. Interestingly, the author uses the name of this place proleptically, since this place would not be called Ebenezer for another twenty years (7:12). The effect is subtle, but the implication is that Israel would have victory at Ebenezer only after it had repented and turned to Yahweh to hear his Word through his prophet (7:3–17).

---

[11] However, 1 Chr 13:5–6 and 2 Chr 1:4 mention David bringing the ark from Kiriath-jearim.

[12] See "Critical Theories of Samuel's Composition" in "Authorship, Composition, and Date" in the introduction.

Figure 11

Movements of the Ark of the Covenant

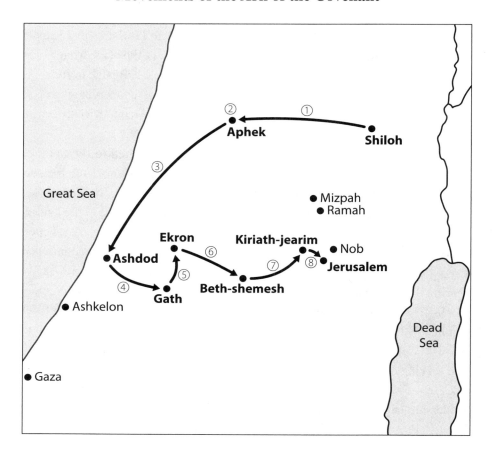

1. The ark, which was in Shiloh, is taken to war (1 Sam 4:1–4).
2. The ark is captured by the Philistines, who were camped at Aphek (1 Sam 4:1, 11).
3. The ark is taken to Ashdod (1 Sam 5:1).
4. The ark is moved to Gath (1 Sam 5:8).
5. The ark is moved to Ekron (1 Sam 5:10).
6. The ark is returned to Israel, coming first to Beth-shemesh (1 Sam 6:11–16).
7. The ark is taken to Abinadab's house in Kiriath-jearim (1 Sam 7:1).
8. The ark is brought by David to Jerusalem (2 Sam 6:1–23).

The exact location of Ebenezer is unknown, though it is often identified as modern ʿIzbet Sartah, about ten miles (sixteen kilometers) east of Tel Aviv. The Philistine camp was at Aphek, called Antipatris in Hellenistic and Roman times. It is modern Tell Ras el-ʿAin, about eight miles (thirteen kilometers) east of Tel Aviv.

The account of the first battle is told in brief, focused clauses without elaboration. The result is that four thousand Israelites were killed (4:2). In this way credit is withheld from the Philistines for any tactics or superior military might that may have played a role in the battle. In 4:2 the author most pointedly does not use an active construction to say that the Philistines defeated Israel (he does not use the active Qal [G] of נָגַף, "to defeat," which the Israelites will use in 4:3). Instead he uses a passive construction: "Israel was defeated before the Philistines" (4:2; the passive Niphal [N] of נָגַף, "to be defeated," as also in 4:10). Who was responsible for defeating Israel? Israel's elders knew the answer—it was not the Philistines but Yahweh ("Yahweh defeated us," נְגָפָנוּ יְהוָה, 4:3). Therefore, the elders' solution to this problem was an attempt at coercing Yahweh into giving them victory: they would take his ark of his covenant into battle. This is a form of idolatry—trusting in the ark instead of the one enthroned on it, who revealed his Word through his prophet Samuel. Their indifference to Yahweh's prophet is matched by their pagan use of the ark as a talisman.

Much of the message of the narrative concerning the ark is found in the questions of various persons. "Why has Yahweh defeated us before the Philistines today?" (4:3). The answer to the elders' question should have been obvious to them: "Because we have not listened to his Word through Moses and Samuel." Why did Israel not know this? The Formula of Concord tells us:

> If such a person [one who "will not hear preaching or read the Word of God"] despises the instruments of the Holy Spirit and will not hear, no injustice is done him if the Holy Spirit does not illuminate him but lets him remain in the darkness of his unbelief and be lost, as it is written, "How often would I have gathered your children together as a hen gathers her brood under her wings, and you would not!" (Matt. 23:37).[13]

The elders may not have been able to perceive the answer to their question, but the author of Samuel expects his readers to perceive it. By not listening to God's Word and by abusing the ark that bore his name (see 2 Sam 6:2), Israel was breaking the entire First Table of the Ten Commandments (Ex 20:1–11; Deut 5:1–15). Luther reminds us: "Since so much depends on God's Word that no holy day [and we might add no holy object such as the ark] is sanctified without it, we must realize that God insists upon a strict observance of this

---

[13] FC SD II 58. The wording "will not hear preaching or read the Word of God" comes from FC SD II 57.

commandment and will punish all who despise his Word and refuse to hear and learn it."[14]

The title for the ark when it was taken from Shiloh is unique and one of the most complete in the OT: "the ark of the covenant of Yahweh of armies, who is enthroned [over] the cherubim" (4:4).[15] This emphasizes that Israel was seeking to use the ark to make Yahweh into the king they would later request: a king to judge them, go out before them, and fight their battles (8:20). There is an ironic anticipation of that request here. In all their idolatrous actions they rejected Yahweh as their king, and so they would eventually seek to be ruled by a human monarch (8:7).

The text emphasizes that when the ark was retrieved from Shiloh, Eli's sons Hophni and Phinehas were with it (4:4). They must have accompanied the ark as it was transported into the camp and then into the battle because they were killed on the battlefield when the ark was captured (4:11). These two unfaithful priests were complicit in the idolatrous use of the ark, demonstrating their lack of faith in Yahweh (2:12). The presence of these priests and the ark gave the Israelite army a false confidence, as evidenced by their loud shout when the ark entered the camp (4:5).

Throughout these verses the ark is called "the ark ... of *Yahweh*" or "the ark of *God*."[16] Using the ark was using God's name. The elders of Israel and Hophni and Phinehas by their actions—and Eli by his inaction of not preventing the ark's misuse—were all guilty of breaking the Second Commandment (Ex 20:7; Deut 5:11). Luther reminds us: "If you are asked, 'How do you understand the Second Commandment? What does it mean to misuse or take the name of God in vain?' you should answer briefly: 'It is a misuse of God's name if we call upon the Lord God in any way whatsoever to support falsehood or wrong of any kind.' Therefore what this commandment forbids is appealing to God's name falsely ... when our heart knows or should know that the facts are otherwise."[17] And in a passage that applies to the priests Hophni and Phinehas and to pastors today, Luther reminds us: "The greatest abuse, however, occurs in spiritual matters, which pertain to the conscience, when false preachers arise and peddle their lying nonsense as the Word of God."[18] The Israelite misuse of the ark reminds us that in addition to deceiving others by using God's name in vain, we can also deceive ourselves (2 Tim 3:13; 1 Jn 1:8). His is the only

---

[14] LC I 95.

[15] See the second textual note on 4:4; cf. the second textual note on 4:3. A somewhat different but even longer designation appears in 2 Sam 6:2: "the ark of God that is called by [the] name, [the] name of Yahweh of armies, who is enthroned [over] the cherubim on it."

[16] See the second textual notes on 4:3 and 4:4.

[17] LC I 51.

[18] LC I 54.

saving name (Acts 4:12), and both the deceivers and the deceived will be cast into the lake of fire (Rev 19:20; 20:10).[19]

The Philistines Capture the Ark (4:6–11)

While 4:1–5 focuses on the Israelites and their words and actions, 4:6–11 shifts the emphasis to the Philistines and their words and actions. Their first reaction to the Israelite shout is fear. They have heard of Israel's God whom, in good pagan fashion, they take to be a consortium of gods in a pantheon (see the third textual note on 4:7). They may or may not have had an accurate historical knowledge of Yahweh's work in saving his people through the exodus from Egypt (see the third and fourth textual notes on 4:8; see also the second and third textual notes on 6:6), but they know of his overwhelming power. So they instead motivate themselves by their fear of being enslaved to Israel (4:9).

Once again the battle is related in summary fashion (4:10–11). Israel lost thirty thousand infantry, the ark, and two priests. The lack of detail as to *how* the battle was won once again minimizes any Philistine accomplishment in order to lead the reader to conclude that God himself controlled the outcome of the battle (as in 4:3).

---

[19] Deadly deception by the devil is a potent theme in Scripture; see 1 Kings 22; Mt 24:4–5, 11, 24; 1 Cor 6:9; 15:33; Gal 6:7; James 1:16; 1 Jn 2:26; 3:7; Rev 2:20; 12:9; 13:13–14; 20:2–3, 7–8.

1 Samuel 4:12–22

The Death of Eli
and the Birth of Ichabod

Translation

4 **12**Now a man from Benjamin ran from the battle line and came to Shiloh that day. His clothes were torn, and there was dirt on his head. **13**When he came, Eli was sitting on his chair beside the road watching, because he was anxious about the ark of God. The man came to report to the city, and the entire city cried out. **14**When Eli heard the sound of the cry, he said, "What is the sound of this commotion?" The man quickly came and told Eli. (**15**Now Eli was ninety-eight years old, and his eyes had failed—he could not see.) **16**The man said to Eli, "I am the one who came from the battle line. I fled from the battle line today." He [Eli] said, "What happened, my son?" **17**The messenger answered, "Israel fled from before the Philistines, and there was also a great slaughter among the troops. In addition, your two sons, Hophni and Phinehas, died, and the ark of God was captured." **18**As he mentioned the ark of God, he [Eli] fell backward from his seat away from the side of the gate. His neck was broken, and he died, for the man was old and heavy. He had judged Israel forty years.

19His daughter-in-law, Phinehas' wife, was pregnant and ready to give birth. When she heard the news that the ark of God had been captured and her father-in-law and husband had died, she went into labor and gave birth, because her labor pain came upon her. **20**As she was dying, the women who attended to her said, "Do not be afraid, because you have borne a son." But she did not answer, nor did she pay attention. **21**She named the boy "Ichabod," saying, "The Glory from Israel has gone into exile," referring to the capture of the ark of God and [the deaths of] her father-in-law and husband. **22**She said, "The Glory from Israel has gone into exile, because the ark of God has been captured."

Textual Notes

4:12 מֵהַמַּעֲרָכָה—For the noun מַעֲרָכָה, "battle line," which recurs twice in 4:16, see the second textual note on 4:2.

4:13 וְהִנֵּה עֵלִי יֹשֵׁב עַל־הַכִּסֵּא—Literally "behold, Eli sitting on the chair." הִנֵּה is often used to signal a change of some type in the narrative. Here it signals a change of focus from the runner to the following noun, "Eli" (see *HALOT*, s.v. הִנֵּה, 1).

יַד דֶּרֶךְ מְצַפֶּה—The Qere, יַד, is the noun יָד, "hand," in construct, meaning "*beside* the road." מְצַפֶּה is the Piel (D) participle of צָפָה, whose Qal (G) participle often refers to a "watchman" (e.g., 1 Sam 14:16; 2 Sam 13:34; 18:24–27), or, metaphorically, a prophet or evangelist (e.g., Is 52:8; Ezek 3:17; 33:7; Hos 9:8). The Piel participle is less common (also Is 21:6; Micah 7:4) and may indicate that Eli is watching with intensity or

128

foreboding (see the next textual note). The LXX reads παρὰ τὴν πύλην σκοπεύων τὴν ὁδόν, "beside the gate watching the road," and its reference to a "gate" may be a secondary adaptation to יַד הַשַּׁעַר in 4:18.

לִבּוֹ חָרֵד—Literally "his heart was trembling," this is translated as "he was anxious." BDB considers the form חָרֵד to be a verbal adjective (also, e.g., Is 66:2; Ezra 9:4).

כָּל־הָעִיר:—This means "the entire city." The LXX lacks "entire."

4:15 וְעֵינָיו קָמָה—"And his eyes had failed." The verb קוּם usually means "arise," but here it is used with "eyes" as its subject as an idiom for blindness (BDB, Qal, 7 j), as also in 1 Ki 14:4 (קָמוּ עֵינָיו). The verb קָמָה would appear to be the third feminine singular Qal (G) perfect of קוּם, which could be explained if the feminine dual subject ("eyes") were treated as one organ of sense. However, קָמָה likely is an archaic plural third feminine form (GKC, § 44 m). Earlier in 3:2 the author had noted that Eli's eyes had begun to fail (see the first textual note on 3:2).

וְלֹא יָכוֹל לִרְאוֹת:—This is nearly identical to the last clause of 3:2; the Qal (G) verb יָכוֹל is in the perfect here (plene, or *male*, for יְכֹל) versus the imperfect there.

The LXX adds καὶ εἶπεν Ηλι τοῖς ἀνδράσιν τοῖς περιεστηκόσιν αὐτῷ τίς ἡ φωνὴ τοῦ ἤχους τούτου; "And Eli said to the men standing around him, 'What is the sound of this noise?' " This is clearly a secondary reading, a repetition and expansion from 4:14.

4:17 מַגֵּפָה—This noun, "slaughter," is derived from the verb נָגַף, "to defeat," used in 4:2, 3, 10.

חָפְנִי וּפִינְחָס—The phrase "Hophni and Phinehas" is missing in the LXX.

וַאֲרוֹן הָאֱלֹהִים נִלְקָחָה:—The noun אֲרוֹן, "ark," usually is construed as masculine in gender, but here and in 2 Chr 8:11 it is regarded as feminine since it is the subject of feminine verbs. Here the verb is the third feminine singular Niphal (N) perfect of לָקַח, "to take; capture" (נִלְקָחָה is pausal for נִלְקְחָה). The same wording recurs in 4:22, but there the Niphal perfect is masculine: נִלְקַח אֲרוֹן הָאֱלֹהִים. The Niphal infinitive construct הִלָּקַח in 4:19, 21 likewise refers to the ark being captured.

4:18 אֲחֹרַנִּית—This feminine form of an adjective occurs seven times in the OT and always serves as an adverb: "backward."

מַפְרַקְתּוֹ—This feminine noun, מַפְרֶקֶת or מִפְרָקָה, "neck," appears only here in the OT, but the cognate ܡܦܪܩܬܐ is attested in Syriac.

וְכָבֵד—The adjective *kabed*, "heavy," in addition to being a historical fact, plays into the narrative because it is cognate to the "Glory" (כָּבוֹד, *kabod*) taken into exile (4:21–22). This helps explain why Phineas' wife names her son "Ichabod," *ʾi-kabod*, "where is Glory?" at the death of her (heavy) father-in-law (4:21). This Hebrew wordplay between "heavy" and "glory" may be supported by the LXX's translation of "Ichabod" in 4:21 with Οὐαὶ βαρχαβωθ, since βαρχαβωθ is a combination of the Greek root βαρ-, "heavy," and a transliteration of כָּבוֹד, *kabod*, "glory."

אַרְבָּעִים שָׁנָה:—For the sense of the verb שָׁפַט, "to judge," see the third textual note on 7:6. In place of "forty years," the LXX has εἴκοσι ἔτη, "twenty years."

4:19 לָלַת—This must represent a Qal (G) infinitive construct of יָלַד with the preposition לְ, "about to give birth." The expected form is לָלֶדֶת (Gen 4:2; 25:24; Is 26:17;

Eccl 3:2). Apparently the word here has been written phonetically with the assimilation of the leading dental consonant (דֿ) to the trailing one (תֿ). See GKC, §§ 19 d, 69 m.

וּמֵת חָמִיהָ וְאִישָׁהּ—The use of the singular verb מֵת instead of the plural (which would be מֵתוּ) with the compound subject gives greater emphasis to the nearer singular subject, חָמִיהָ. This could be rendered as "her father-in-law died, as well as her husband." Note the same order of these nouns in 4:21: חָמִיהָ וְאִישָׁהּ.

וַתִּכְרַע—Literally "and she bowed down," this is rendered as "she went into labor."

כִּי־נֶהֶפְכוּ עָלֶיהָ צִרֶיהָ:—Literally "because her labor pains were turned upon her." The noun צִיר, "pain," specifically denotes labor pains here and in Is 13:8; 21:3.

4:20 הַנִּצָּבוֹת עָלֶיהָ—"The women who attended to her" is literally "the ones standing over her." הַנִּצָּבוֹת is a Niphal (N) participle, feminine plural (with the article), of the verb נָצַב. Hannah used the singular form of this participle for herself in 1:26.

וְלֹא־שָׁתָה לִבָּהּ:—The idiom with the Qal (G) of שִׁית (third feminine singular perfect) and לֵב as an object, "and she did not set her heart," means "and she did not pay attention." The idiom occurs a total of a dozen times in the OT, including 2 Sam 13:20. More common is the idiom with the Qal of שִׂים and לֵב with the same meaning (e.g., 1 Sam 9:20; 25:25; 2 Sam 13:33; 18:3; 19:20 [ET 19:19]).

4:21 אִי־כָבוֹד—This compound name, "Ichabod," probably means "where is Glory?" and "Glory" refers to Yahweh himself (cf. כָּבוֹד in 2:8; 4:21–22; 6:5).[1] The Hebrew interrogative particle אִי, "where?" is a cognate of the Ugaritic ʾiy, "where?" as in the names ʾiy-balu, "where is Baal?" and ʾiy-tôru, "where is Bull?" (i.e., the god ʾEl).[2] In Hebrew see the names אִיזֶבֶל, "Jezebel," meaning "where is the prince?" (the "prince" being Baal),[3] and אִיתָמָר, "Ithamar," "where is the palm tree?"[4] As early as Josephus the name here has been explained as "no glory" (ἀδοξία).[5] The Phoenician particle אִי expresses negation.[6] However, the only OT passage where אִי may mean "no/not" is Job 22:30: אִי־נָקִי, "not innocent." The LXX gives the name here as Οὐαὶ βαρχαβωθ; see the third textual note on 1 Sam 4:18.

לֵאמֹר גָּלָה כָבוֹד מִיִּשְׂרָאֵל—These words, "saying, 'The Glory from Israel has gone into exile,'" are missing in the LXX. Either the MT has been expanded by adding the first part of 4:22 to 4:21 to further explain the boy's name or the quotation was purposely dropped in the LXX's textual tradition as superfluous. The Qal (G) of גָּלָה often means "go into exile" (BDB, 3) and is so used for the exiles of (northern) Israel and (southern) Judah (e.g., 2 Ki 17:23; 25:21; Is 5:13; Jer 1:3; Ezek 12:3). Its cognate noun גּוֹלָה, "exile," is commonly used in the same sense (e.g., 2 Ki 24:15–16; Ezek 1:1;

---

[1] See also כְּבוֹד־יהוה, "the glory of Yahweh," as a hypostasis of God, in, e.g., Ex 16:7; 40:34; 1 Ki 8:11; Is 40:5; 60:1; Ezek 1:28. The NT identifies this divine glory as Christ (e.g., Mt 25:31; Jn 1:14; 2:11; 17:24; 1 Cor 2:8; 2 Cor 4:4; Titus 2:13; Heb 1:3; cf. Rev 21:23).

[2] See McCarter, *I Samuel*, 116; Tsumura, *The First Book of Samuel*, 201.

[3] See *KTU* 1.6 IV 5 for this phrase used as a lament for Baal.

[4] Alternately, "Ithamar" may mean "island of the palm tree."

[5] Josephus, *Antiquities*, 5.360.

[6] Klein, *1 Samuel*, 45.

Esth 2:6). Cf. Hos 10:5, which refers to an idolatrous "glory" (כָּבוֹד, referring to a false god) going into exile (גָּלָה).

הִלָּקַח—For this Niphal (N) infinitive construct, here translated as "the capture of," see the third textual note on 4:17. A translation for it is missing in the LXX, which has some other significant differences from the MT (see the second textual note on 4:21).

Commentary

Late fall/early winter 1069 BC

The Death of Eli (4:12–18)

There are three reports bringing unwelcome news from a battlefield in the book of Samuel: this report of the defeat of Israel, the report of the defeat of Saul (2 Sam 1:1–16), and the report of the defeat of Absalom (2 Sam 18:19–32). In all three cases there is death to report: Hophni and Phinehas, Saul and Jonathan, Absalom. However, only the first two reports feature a messenger with torn clothes and dirt on his head (1 Sam 4:12; 2 Sam 1:2), a sign of grief and mourning. Moreover, the words of the messenger who reports to David in 2 Sam 1:3–4 are very similar to this messenger's report to Eli (1 Sam 4:16–17).

The messenger in this account is an unnamed Benjaminite (4:12). We are told that Eli was awaiting word of the battle because he was anxious about the ark (4:13). No mention is made of any concern for his sons, either because he had already accepted God's judgment on them (2:34) or because he did not suspect that they were in any danger. Ironically, Eli is said to be seated beside the road "watching" (מְצַפֶּה, 4:13). This may not strike the reader at first, since the reminder about Eli's failed eyesight has not yet been given (4:15; cf. 3:2). Once again, however, the writer of Samuel has used an ironic statement to emphasize the failure of Eli. He failed to prevent Israel from misusing the ark. Therefore, he was anxious about the ark and was watching for news about it using eyes that could not see.

However, the rest of Shiloh could see. As soon as the messenger entered the city to give his report of the battle, a cry went out. They could see his torn clothes and dirty head, and even before he could speak, they knew the news from the battlefield was not good. Eli reacted to the commotion in the city, not to the messenger's appearance—this is why the author reminds us of Eli's blindness (4:14–15).

Then the messenger delivered his news in three parts: Israel fled and many died, Hophni and Phinehas had died, and the ark was captured (4:17). It was not until the messenger mentioned the ark that Eli fell off his chair and broke his neck (4:18). The end of Eli's life is not mourned by the writer; he simply reports that Eli had judged Israel forty years (c. 1109–c. 1069).[7]

---

[7] Steinmann, *From Abraham to Paul*, 108–9. See "Samuel and Eli as Judges" in "Chronological Issues in Samuel" in the introduction. This would place Eli's birth c. 1167.

The Birth of Ichabod (4:19–22)

The birth of Ichabod completes the troubles for Eli's house (1 Samuel 1–3) to this point. The dying woman names her son "Ichabod," "where is Glory?" (see the first textual note on 4:21), a lament over the loss of "the ark of God."[8] Ironically, since the news was brought by a man from Benjamin, the author uses words similar to those that are part of the birth of Benjamin to the dying Rachel in Genesis: "The midwife said to her, 'Do not be afraid, because you have another son.' And with her last breath, since she was dying, she named him Benoni, but his father named him Benjamin" (Gen 35:17–18). Ichabod, however, is not the first child of Phinehas' wife. She was already the mother of Ahitub (1 Sam 14:3), who according to Josephus served as the first high priest under Saul.[9]

The "Glory" who had departed from Israel is a reference to Yahweh and his ark, which provided his throne, the place where he dwelt.[10] Now it appeared to Ichabod's mother that the God of glory (Ps 29:3; Acts 7:2; cf. "the Lord of glory" in 1 Cor 2:8; James 2:1) was taken captive into exile. This statement is pregnant with anticipation. What will happen to Yahweh and his ark in Philistia? Soon both Israel and the Philistines will discover that just as the ark of God cannot be treated as a talisman (4:3), so also God cannot be captured and treated like a prisoner of war.

The Destruction of Shiloh and the Location of the Tabernacle

Apparently in the wake of this battle the Philistines pressed on and destroyed Shiloh (Jer 7:12–14; 26:6, 9; Ps 78:60–66). Archaeological investigation seems to have confirmed this.[11] Shiloh was first settled in Middle Bronze Age IIB (1750–1650) and was destroyed already at the end of the Middle Bronze Age in the sixteenth century BC. There was a small settlement on the site from the fifteenth to the thirteenth centuries BC. Israelites appear to have made Shiloh an important center in the twelfth and eleventh centuries until it was destroyed sometime in the middle of the eleventh century BC, probably by the Philistines.

After the conquest of the promised land under Joshua, the tabernacle appears to have been originally placed at Shiloh (Josh 18:1), though for a time it was moved to Bethel (Judg 20:18, 26–28) before being returned to Shiloh (1 Sam 1:3). After the destruction of Shiloh (Jer 7:12–14; 26:6, 9; Ps 78:60–66), the tabernacle was at Nob, where David entered the house of God and ate the bread of God's presence (1 Sam 21:2–10 [ET 21:1–9]; 22:19; Mt 12:3–4). Whether this was the tabernacle from Shiloh that had been hurriedly relocated or whether it was a replacement structure after the earlier one was destroyed

---

[8] This is the consistent title of the ark in this passage (4:13, 17, 18, 19, 21, 22). For other titles, see the second textual notes on 4:3 and 4:4.

[9] Josephus, *Antiquities*, 6.122.

[10] 1 Sam 4:4; see also Ex 25:22; Num 7:89; 2 Ki 19:15; 1 Chr 13:6; Is 37:16; Heb 9:5.

[11] For a good summary, see Finkelstein, "Shiloh Yields Some, but Not All, of Its Secrets."

with the conquest of Shiloh cannot be determined. In any case, the ark was preserved and moved. Later the tabernacle was transported to Gibeon, and Solomon placed Zadok in charge of it (1 Chr 16:39; 2 Chr 1:3, 13). It would remain there until the temple was finished, after which the ark, along with the surviving tabernacle furnishings, was brought to Jerusalem (1 Ki 8:4; 2 Chr 5:5).

Figure 12

Places Where the Tabernacle Rested in Israel

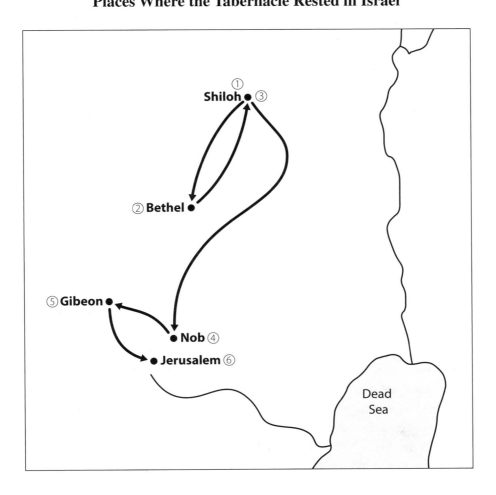

1 Samuel 5:1–12

Yahweh Judges the Philistines
and Their God Dagon

Translation

5 ¹The Philistines took the ark of God and brought it from Ebenezer to Ashdod. ²The Philistines took the ark of God and brought it to the house of Dagon and placed it beside Dagon. ³The Ashdodites got up the next morning, and there was Dagon, fallen on his face to the ground before the ark of Yahweh. So they took Dagon and returned him to his place. ⁴When they got up in the morning on the next day, there was Dagon, fallen on his face to the ground before the ark of Yahweh. His head and his two hands were cut off on the threshold. Only [the body of] Dagon was left. ⁵Therefore, to this day the priests of Dagon and everyone who enters the house of Dagon do not step on the threshold of Dagon in Ashdod.

⁶Yahweh's hand was heavy on the Ashdodites. He devastated them and struck them with swelling of the lymph nodes, both in Ashdod and its vicinity. ⁷The men of Ashdod saw this and said, "Do not let the ark of Israel's God dwell with us, because his hand is hard upon us and upon our god Dagon."

⁸So they sent and gathered to themselves all the Philistine governors. They said, "What should we do for the ark of Israel's God?"

They said, "Let the ark of Israel's God go around to Gath." So they brought the ark of Israel's God around [to Gath].

⁹After they brought it around [to Gath], Yahweh's hand was in the city, [causing] a very great panic. He struck the men of the city from the youngest to the oldest, and swelling of the lymph nodes broke out on them.

¹⁰So they sent the ark of God away to Ekron. As the ark of God came to Ekron, the Ekronites cried out, "They have brought the ark of Israel's God around to me to kill me and my people!" ¹¹So they sent and gathered all the Philistine governors. They said, "Send the ark of Israel's God away! Return it to its place! Don't let it kill me and my people!" for there was panic of death throughout the entire city. God's hand was very heavy there. ¹²The men who did not die were struck with swelling of the lymph nodes, and the cry of the city went up to heaven.

Textual Notes

5:1 אֲרוֹן הָאֱלֹהִים—The author of Samuel calls it "the ark of God" in his narrative in 5:1, 2, 10 (twice). Its title changes to "the ark of Yahweh" in the direct confrontation with the god Dagon in 5:3, 4. In the quoted speech of the Philistines, they refer to it in nationalistic terms as "the ark of the God of Israel" in 5:7, 8 (three times[1]), 10, 11. For titles of the ark, see the second textual notes on 4:3 and 4:4.

וַיָּבִאֻהוּ—This form of בּוֹא, "come," is the third masculine plural Hiphil (H) preterite (imperfect with *waw* consecutive), which has a causative meaning, "to bring." Its third masculine singular suffix (הוּ-) is its direct object and refers to the ark (as masculine; cf. the third textual note on 4:17), hence "brought it." The same verb form recurs in 5:2 but without the suffix: וַיָּבִיאוּ.

5:2 בֵּית דָּגוֹן—This construct phrase, "the house [temple] of Dagon," is an accusative of destination[2] (with no preposition such as אֶל), hence "to the house …" Similar accusatives recur throughout this chapter. For the meaning of "Dagon," see the commentary. This proper name of the false god occurs eleven times in this chapter and elsewhere in the OT only in Judg 16:23; 1 Chr 10:10 (aside from the place-name Beth-dagon in Josh 15:41; 19:27). See also the third textual note on 1 Sam 5:4.

וַיַּצִּיגוּ—The verb יָצַג occurs only in the Hiphil (H) and once in the Hophal (Hp; Ex 10:24). The Hiphil means "to set, place"; it recurs in 2 Sam 6:17. The י of the root is assimilated into the sibilant צ and marked by *daghesh* (-צִ-). See GKC, § 71.

5:3 מִמָּחֳרָת … וַיַּשְׁכִּמוּ—The noun מָחֳרָת usually has the prefixed preposition מִן and means "the next day." Here it is translated as "the next morning" because it follows the verb וַיַּשְׁכִּמוּ, the Hiphil (H) of שָׁכַם, "get up early." The same two Hebrew words recur in 5:4, but that verse also includes an explicit reference to the morning, בַּבֹּקֶר, "in the morning," so there מִמָּחֳרָת is translated as "on the next day." At the beginning of 5:3, the LXX has καὶ ὤρθρισαν οἱ Ἀζώτιοι καὶ εἰσῆλθον εἰς οἶκον Δαγων καὶ εἶδον, "and the Azotians rose early and entered into the house of Dagon and looked …" (*NETS*).

At the end of 5:3, the LXX adds the following, displaced from 5:6: καὶ ἐβαρύνθη χεὶρ κυρίου ἐπὶ τοὺς Ἀζωτίους καὶ ἐβασάνισεν αὐτοὺς καὶ ἐπάταξεν αὐτοὺς εἰς τὰς ἕδρας αὐτῶν, τὴν Ἄζωτον καὶ τὰ ὅρια αὐτῆς, "and the Lord's hand was heavy on the Azotians, and he tormented them and afflicted them on their seats, Azotus and its territory." Then the LXX expands the text of 5:6; see the second textual note on 5:6.

5:4 מִמָּחֳרָת—This is translated as "on the next day"; see the textual note on 5:3. It is missing in the LXX.

אֲרוֹן יְהוָה—For "the ark of Yahweh," the LXX has κιβωτοῦ διαθήκης κυρίου, "ark of the covenant of the Lord."

The LXX expands Dagon's disfigurement by adding καὶ ἀμφότεροι οἱ καρποὶ τῶν χειρῶν αὐτοῦ πεπτωκότες ἐπὶ τὸ πρόθυρον, "and both wrists of his hands had fallen in the doorway" (*NETS*).

רַק דָּגוֹן נִשְׁאַר עָלָיו—Literally "only Dagon was left upon himself," this must refer to the remaining portion of the idol (minus his head and hands), thus "only [the body of] Dagon was left."

---

[1] The third instance in 5:8 is part of the author's narrative, not Philistine speech, but it immediately follows the quotation of the Philistines.

[2] Joüon, § 125 n. GKC, § 118 d, e, f, places this in the category of an accusative of place; see also Waltke-O'Connor, § 10.2.2b.

5:5 At the end of the verse the LXX adds this detail about avoiding the threshold: ὅτι ὑπερβαίνοντες ὑπερβαίνουσιν, "for when they step over, they step over" (*NETS*).

5:6 וַיְשִׁמֵּם—The Hiphil (H) of שָׁמֵם means "to devastate, ravage." This is the third masculine singular preterite (imperfect with *waw* consecutive) with a third masculine plural object suffix: "he devastated them."

בָּעֳפָלִים—This Kethib (the plural of עֹפֶל with the preposition בְּ) is rendered as "with swelling of the lymph nodes," but is often translated as "with tumors." The Hebrew word עֹפֶל is sometimes defined as "hemorrhoid" (*DCH*, s.v. עֹפֶל II), which would fit with the anatomical location supplied in LXX 1 Sam 5:3, "on their seats" (εἰς τὰς ἕδρας αὐτῶν; see the textual note on 5:3), but hemorrhoids would not be fatal. From the description in this chapter and the infestation of rats (6:5), this word most likely denotes a symptom of bubonic plague (see the commentary). Plague causes swelling of the lymph nodes in the armpits and groin. The noun עֹפֶל, "swelling," is used to describe a portion of Jerusalem known as the Ophel (Is 32:14; Micah 4:8; Neh 3:26–27; 11:21; 2 Chr 27:3; 33:14). Apparently this "swelling" was a part of a hill. It is often identified as the hill that is between the City of David to the south and the Temple Mount to the north. This noun is also used to describe a hill of some sort in Samaria in 2 Ki 5:24. In addition, it is used in Deut 28:27 apparently as a reference to the boils with which God plagued the Egyptians (Ex 9:9–11). In Hab 2:4 the cognate verb עֻפְּלָה (Pual [Dp] perfect third feminine singular) is used to describe an inflated or swelled ego of an arrogant person (cf. Hab 2:5).

In Deut 28:27 and throughout 1 Samuel 5–6 the constant Qere is טְחֹרִים, "tumors." The Qere may be an attempt to explain the Kethib עֳפָלִים, or the Masoretes may have found the Kethib ("hemorrhoids") offensive and replaced it with a less offensive word.

LXX 1 Sam 5:6 reads καὶ ἐβαρύνθη χεὶρ κυρίου ἐπὶ Ἄζωτον, καὶ ἐπήγαγεν αὐτοῖς καὶ ἐξέζεσεν αὐτοῖς εἰς τὰς ναῦς, καὶ μέσον τῆς χώρας αὐτῆς ἀνεφύησαν μύες, καὶ ἐγένετο σύγχυσις θανάτου μεγάλη ἐν τῇ πόλει, "and the hand of the Lord was heavy upon Azotus and brought trouble on them, and it broke out upon them into the ships, and in the midst of its territory mice grew up, and there was great confusion of death in the city" (*NETS*).

5:8 סַרְנֵי פְלִשְׁתִּים—This means "the governors of the Philistines." The noun סֶרֶן appears to be a Philistine word for the leaders of each of their five cities.[3]

תִּסֹּב גַּת—The verb is the Qal (G) jussive of סָבַב, "to go around," and the city name גַּת is an accusative of destination: "to Gath."

וַיַּסֵּבּוּ—This verb is the Hiphil (H) preterite (imperfect with *waw* consecutive) of סָבַב; it has a causative meaning: "to bring around." The Hiphil perfect הֵסַבּוּ in 5:9 and 5:10 has the same meaning.

LXX 1 Sam 5:8b reads καὶ λέγουσιν οἱ Γεθθαῖοι μετελθέτω κιβωτὸς τοῦ θεοῦ πρὸς ἡμᾶς· καὶ μετῆλθεν κιβωτὸς τοῦ θεοῦ εἰς Γεθθα, "And the Gittites said, 'Let the ark of God come over to us.' And the ark of God came over to Gath."

---

[3] The word also occurs in Josh 13:3; Judg 3:3; 16:5, 8, 18, 23, 27, 30; 1 Sam 5:11; 6:4; 12, 16, 18; 7:7; 29:2, 6, 7; 1 Chr 12:20 (ET 12:19).

5:9 לָהֶם וַיִּשָּׂתְרוּ—The verb שָׂתַר appears only here in the OT. This Niphal (N) form apparently means the swellings "broke out for (on) them." Cf. the Syriac cognate ܣܬܪ, "destroy." The LXX reads καὶ ἐπάταξεν αὐτούς, "and he struck them."

At the end of the verse the LXX adds καὶ ἐποίησαν ἑαυτοῖς οἱ Γεθθαῖοι ἕδρας, "and the Gittites made seats for themselves."[4]

5:10 וַיְשַׁלְּחוּ—While the Qal (G) beginning 5:8 and 5:11 (וַיִּשְׁלְחוּ) simply means "to send" (something or someone), the Piel (D) here and in 5:11 (שַׁלְּחוּ, imperative) has the more forceful meaning "to send away" or "get rid of" something.

אֵלַי ... לַהֲמִיתֵנִי וְאֶת־עַמִּי—This means "to me ... to kill me and my people." 4QSamᵃ probably has the same reading. The LXX reads πρὸς ἡμᾶς ... θανατῶσαι ἡμᾶς καὶ τὸν λαὸν ἡμῶν, "to us ... to kill us and our people." The LXX is probably an interpretive reading that gives the sense of the more difficult wording of the Hebrew text. The LXX makes similar changes in 5:11.

5:11 וְיָשֹׁב לִמְקֹמוֹ וְלֹא־יָמִית—The Qal (G) jussive of שׁוּב is intransitive, "let/may it return," but since it follows an imperative (שַׁלְּחוּ), it is rendered more forcefully as transitive: "return it to its place!" Similarly, the following negated Hiphil (H) imperfect, יָמִית, is translated like a jussive: "don't let it kill!"

מְהוּמַת־מָוֶת—This construct phrase, "panic of death," is supported by the LXX: σύγχυσις θανάτου. 4QSamᵃ has מהמת יהוה, "panic from Yahweh."

כָּבְדָה מְאֹד יַד הָאֱלֹהִים שָׁם—"God's hand was very heavy there." The LXX reads ὡς εἰσῆλθεν κιβωτὸς θεοῦ Ισραηλ ἐκεῖ, "as the ark of God entered there," which may represent a Hebrew Vorlage of כבוא ארון האלהים שמה. The last two letters (מה) are extant in 4QSamᵃ, making it likely that it agreed with the LXX against the MT. The MT contains the harder reading, but it may be a corruption of the reading in the LXX and 4QSamᵃ.

5:12 וְהָאֲנָשִׁים אֲשֶׁר לֹא־מֵתוּ—This is translated as "the men who did not die." The LXX expands to καὶ οἱ ζῶντες καὶ οὐκ ἀποθανόντες, "and those who lived and did not die."

הַשָּׁמָיִם—The definite noun ("the heavens") is another accusative of destination (see the first textual note on 5:2), hence "to heaven," as reflected in the LXX (εἰς τὸν οὐρανόν).

Commentary

Late fall/early winter 1069–early spring 1068 BC

The Ark in the Temple of Dagon (5:1–5)

With this chapter the point of view of the narration shifts from observation of action within Israel to observation of action within the Philistine pentapolis.[5] It will remain that way until 6:17, when the point of view returns to Israel.

The Philistine triumph over Israel (1 Samuel 4) turns out *not* to be a triumph over Israel's God, as the Philistines will learn in two ways. The first is

---

4   The LXX translates עֳפָלִים as "seats" (ἕδρας) in 5:9, 12.

5   The Philistine pentapolis consisted of Gaza, Ashdod, Ashkelon, Gath, and Ekron. These five cities are listed in Josh 13:3 and 1 Sam 6:17.

the account of the ark in Dagon's temple (5:1–5). Here Yahweh progressively demonstrates his supremacy over Dagon. On the first morning the idol is found fallen in front of the ark with its face to the ground (5:3). It is as if Dagon has prostrated himself before Yahweh, acknowledging the superiority of the God of Israel. On the second morning Dagon has fallen and his hands and head have been severed from his body (5:4). Here Yahweh is the warrior who demonstrates his victory over the false god by slaying it. See the decapitations of the vanquished in 1 Sam 17:46, 51; 31:9 and the amputation of hands and feet in 2 Sam 4:12.

The narrator pauses his story to tell us that finding Dagon's hands and head on the temple threshold led to an enduring Philistine custom of not stepping on the threshold when entering Dagon's temple in Ashdod (5:5). He describes this custom as being practiced "to this day," the time when he wrote this narrative.

Dagon was a grain god.[6] The name derives from West Semitic words for grain: the Ugaritic *dgn*, the Phoenician *dgn*, and the Hebrew דָּגָן. Moreover, Philo of Byblos equated Dagon with the Greek σῖτος, "grain."[7] Attempts to identify Dagon as a fish god (from the Hebrew דָּג, "fish") date from as early as Jerome (c. AD 347–420) and the later Jewish commentators Rashi (AD 1040–1105) and Kimchi (c. AD 1127–c. 1190).[8] However, there is little evidence for this, and it is unconvincing. Rats thrive on grain, and the rats associated with the plagues on the Philistines[9] suggest that Yahweh sent these vermin as a pestilence that proved Dagon himself impotent (just as many of the ten plagues on Egypt targeted Egyptian deities).

Yahweh Sends a Plague on the Philistines (5:6–12)

The second way the Philistines learn that they have not defeated Israel's God is by the plague. It first broke out in Ashdod where the ark had been taken (5:6–7). The first attempt to stem the plague was to move the ark to another city of the pentapolis, Gath (5:8–9). Perhaps the Philistines thought that placing some distance between Dagon and the ark would mollify Israel's God. Clearly, the Philistines understood Yahweh to be similar to any other of the pagan gods— he could be manipulated into giving humans their desires. They may have reasoned that sending the ark closer to Israelite territory would appease Yahweh. When this did not work, they sent the ark to Ekron, the Philistine city closest to

---

[6] Orel, "The Great Fall of Dagon," 428.

[7] Lowell K. Handy, "Dagon," *ABD* 2:2, citing the quotation of Philo of Byblos in Eusebius, *Preparation for the Gospel*, 1.10.16. Philo is summarizing a Phoenician author named Sanchuniathon. Also note the ironic association between Dagon and grain in the Samson narrative: the blinded Samson was made subservient to the Philistines by being forced to grind grain (Judg 16:21) immediately before he was brought to Dagon's temple (Judg 16:23–25).

[8] Holter, "Was Philistine Dagon a Fish-God?" 142.

[9] The MT mentions the rats in 6:4, 5, 11, 18. The LXX includes them in the description of the plague already in 5:6 and again in 6:1 (see the second textual note on 5:6).

Israel's territory. However, the Ekronites panicked at the mere sight of the ark, and the plague also broke out there too (5:10–12).

There have been a number of attempts to identify the plague described in this account.[10] Some argue that it cannot be identified.[11] However, there is enough description in the text that we can make a probable diagnosis. The following characteristics of the plague are given:

- It could result in death (5:10–12).

- Those who did not die had conspicuous swellings (5:6, 9, 12).

- The Philistines associated the plague with an infestation of rats that destroyed the land (6:4, 5, 11, 18).

- The plague occasioned a panic among the Ekronites (5:11).

These phenomena align quite well with bubonic plague.[12] The earliest conclusion that this was bubonic plague was drawn by the Swiss physician J. J. Scheuchzer in his *Physica sacra*.[13] It was first adopted in a biblical commentary by Otto Thenius.[14] It has since become the consensus opinion among scholars.[15]

The plague bacterium *Yersinia pestis* is carried by the rat flea (*Xenopsylla cheopis*) that infests rats of the genus *Rattus*, most commonly the black rat (*Rattus rattus*). Those suffering from bubonic plague may exhibit swollen lymph nodes (buboes), especially in the armpits and groin. 1 Sam 5:12 notes that those who did not die had swellings. The major effect of bubonic plague is death, which occurs in two-thirds of victims within four days of infection. Those who die from plague often do so before the swelling of the lymph nodes becomes obvious. Panic among populations is a common reaction to outbreaks of the plague, as happened numerous times during the Black Death that swept Europe in the fourteenth century. No wonder Luther was moved to write his essay "Whether One May Flee from a Deadly Plague" in 1527.[16]

It would appear that bubonic plague matches the evidence from 1 Samuel 5. Other suggestions for the diagnosis of the plague, such as syphilis, bacillary dysentery,[17] or, most recently, erectile dysfunction,[18] do not account for all of these phenomena.

---

[10]   See the list in Wilkinson, "The Philistine Epidemic of I Samuel 5 and 6," 137–38.

[11]   Conrad, "The Biblical Tradition for the Plague of the Philistines."

[12]   Wilkinson, "The Philistine Epidemic of I Samuel 5 and 6," 138–40.

[13]   Johann Jakob Scheuchzer, *Physica sacra* (illustrated by Johann Andreas Pfeffel; n.p.: Augustae Vindelicorum & Ulmae, 1731).

[14]   Otto Thenius, *Die Bücher Samuels* (Leipzig: Weidmann'sche Buchhandlung, 1842), 20.

[15]   E.g., Klein, *1 Samuel*, 50; Miller and Roberts, *The Hand of the Lord*, 49.

[16]   AE 43:113–38.

[17]   Based on Josephus' description of the plague as δυσεντέριον (*Antiquities*, 6.3).

[18]   Maeir, "A New Interpretation of the Term ʿopalim (עפלים) in the Light of Recent Archaeological Finds from Philistia," and Maeir, "Did Captured Ark Afflict Philistines with E.D.?" See also the discussion in Wilkinson, "The Philistine Epidemic of I Samuel 5 and 6," 137–38.

The rats most likely multiplied and ate the Philistines' stores of grain (6:4)—a further judgment on the grain god Dagon. It is not surprising that the Philistines were desperate to rid themselves of the ark.

From a Christian standpoint, an astonishing feature of this narrative is what did *not* happen. Despite the deadly results of the Philistines' capture of Yahweh's ark and his humiliation, even decapitation, of their idol Dagon, they did not repent of their idolatry nor believe in the God who was so obviously superior to their own.[19] Although they discerned that the punishment came from Yahweh, the God of Israel (see also chapter 6, where they will attempt to placate him), and their lament "went up to heaven" (5:12), never did they call upon Yahweh by name to relent, let alone forgive.[20] They stubbornly clung to their false god despite the increasing severity of the consequences. God desires all people to be saved and promises that "everyone who calls on the name of Yahweh [LXX: 'the Lord'] will be saved" (Joel 3:5 [ET 2:32]; in Rom 10:9–13 Paul quotes that verse after explaining that everyone who confesses that "Jesus is Lord" and believes in his resurrection will be saved). To that end, he may send calamities to move people to contrition so that when they hear the Gospel, they may believe and be saved. Yet his grace is resistible. The total depravity of fallen human nature is on display when people refuse to repent and call on his saving name.[21]

---

[19] Contrast the Ninevites, who believed God's Word, repented of their evil, trusted in God's mercy, and were saved (Jonah 3).

[20] Their strategy in chapter 6 is to call on their own idolatrous priests and diviners; they do not call upon priests of Yahweh or the God of Israel himself.

[21] Similar scenarios play out in Revelation when God sends plagues for the purpose of moving unbelievers to repent, yet even after the death of swaths of humanity they refuse (Rev 9:20–21; 16:9–11).

1 Samuel 6:1–7:1

The Ark Is Returned to Israel

Translation

6 ¹Now the ark of Yahweh was in Philistine territory seven months. ²The Philistines summoned the priests and the diviners and said, "What should we do with the ark of Yahweh? Inform us as to how we should send it away to its place."

³They said, "If you are sending the ark of Israel's God away, do not send it away without anything [else], because you surely ought to return a guilt offering to him. Then you will be healed, and it will be forgiven you. Why shouldn't his hand turn away from you [then]?"

⁴They said, "What is the guilt offering that we ought to return to him?"

They said, "[Use] the number of the Philistine governors: five gold swellings and five gold rats, since there is a single plague for you and for your governors. ⁵Make images of your swellings and images of your rats that are destroying the land, and give glory to Israel's God. Perhaps he will lighten his hand from upon you and from upon your gods and from upon your land. ⁶Why should you be stubborn like the Egyptians and Pharaoh were stubborn? When he afflicted them didn't they send them away and they left? ⁷Now take and make a new cart and two nursing cows that have never been yoked. Hitch the cows to the cart and take their calves home. ⁸Then take the ark of Yahweh and set it on the cart. Set the gold items that you are returning to him as a guilt offering in a chest beside it. Then send it away and it will go. ⁹Watch—if it goes up on the way to its territory, to Beth-shemesh, then he brought this great calamity to us. But if not, we will know that his hand did not strike us—it happened to us by chance."

¹⁰So the men did that. They took two nursing cows and hitched them to the cart, but they confined the calves at home. ¹¹They set the ark of Yahweh, as well as the chest, the gold rats, and the images of swellings on the cart. ¹²The cows went straight on a route on the road to Beth-shemesh: they went on one thoroughfare, walking and lowing. They did not turn to the right or left. The governors of the Philistines were walking behind them until the border of Beth-shemesh.

¹³Now Beth-shemesh was harvesting the wheat harvest in the valley. They looked up and saw the ark and rejoiced to see [it]. ¹⁴The cart came to the field of Joshua the Beth-shemeshite and stood there. Now a large rock was there. So they split up the wood of the cart and offered the cows as a burnt offering to Yahweh. ¹⁵The Levites lowered the ark of Yahweh and the chest that was with it that had the gold items in it. They placed [them] on the large rock, and the men of Beth-shemesh offered burnt offerings and made sacrifices that day to Yahweh. ¹⁶The five governors of the Philistines saw [this], and they returned to Ekron that day.

¹⁷These are the gold swellings that the Philistines returned as a guilt offering to Yahweh: one for Ashdod, one for Gaza, one for Ashkelon, one for Gath, one for

Ekron. [18]And there were gold rats according to the number of all the Philistine cities belonging to the five governors—the fortified cities including the country villages. Even now the large stone upon which they set the ark of Yahweh is in the field of Joshua the Beth-shemeshite to this day.

[19]He struck some of the men of Beth-shemesh because they looked into the ark of Yahweh. He struck seventy men among the people. The people mourned because Yahweh struck a great blow among the people. [20]The men of Beth-shemesh said, "Who is able to stand in the presence of Yahweh, this holy God? And to whom will he go up from us?" [21]So they sent messengers to the inhabitants of Kiriath-jearim, saying, "The Philistines have returned the ark of Yahweh. Come down and bring it up to yourselves." [7:1]So the men of Kiriath-jearim came and brought the ark of Yahweh up. They brought it to the house of Abinadab on the hill, and they consecrated his son Eleazar to take care of the ark of Yahweh.

Textual Notes

6:1 אֲרוֹן־יְהוָה—This title, "the ark of Yahweh," recurs in 6:2, 8, 11, 15, 18, 19, 21; 7:1, but the Philistines use the fuller designation "the ark of the God of Israel" in 6:3. For these and other titles of the ark, see the second textual notes on 3:3; 4:3; 4:4; and the first textual note on 5:1. The LXX omits "Yahweh," and it probably was not present in 4QSam[a], since it appears there is not enough room for it in the missing portion of the verse. The same textual discrepancy, "the ark of Yahweh" in the MT versus simply "the ark" in the LXX, occurs in 6:8, 11.

בִּשְׂדֵה פְלִשְׁתִּים—"In Philistine territory" is literally "in the field of the Philistines" (cf. the LXX: ἐν ἀγρῷ τῶν ἀλλοφύλων, "in the field of the foreigners [i.e., the Philistines]").[1] The identical construct phrase with the preposition בְּ recurs in 27:7, 11.

6:2 וַיִּקְרְאוּ ... לְ—The root קרא followed by the preposition לְ prefixed to the direct object often means "to summon" or "invite" (see *HALOT*, s.v. קרא I, Qal, A 1 a).

לַכֹּהֲנִים—These are Philistine "priests," as in 5:5, not Israelite "priests," as earlier in the book (1:3, 9; 2:11–35).

וְלַקֹּסְמִים—In form קֹסְמִים, "diviners," is a Qal (G) participle masculine plural absolute of the verb קָסַם, "to consult an oracle, practice divination or necromancy." The verb and its cognate noun קֶסֶם can refer to a variety of occult practices.[2] The LXX adds τοὺς μάντεις καὶ τοὺς ἐπαοιδοὺς αὐτῶν, "their diviners and enchanters." 4QSam[a] apparently read וקוסמים ולחרטמים ולמעוננ[ין], "[the diviners, the enchanters,] and the magic[ian]s." The LXX and 4QSam[a] are probably expansive.

הוֹדִעֻנוּ בַּמֶּה נְשַׁלְּחֶנּוּ לִמְקוֹמוֹ:—Literally "make us know with what shall we send it away to its place." הוֹדִעֻנוּ is the Hiphil (H) imperative masculine plural of יָדַע, "to know," with a first common plural object suffix. בַּמֶּה is translated as "as to how" (see BDB, s.v. בְּ I, III 2 e), but the answer in 6:3–5 suggests that the preposition בְּ on the

---

[1] The plural noun ἀλλόφυλοι, "foreigners," is the default translation of פְּלִשְׁתִּים in LXX 1–2 Samuel.

[2] 1 Sam 15:23; 28:8; see also, e.g., Num 22:7; 23:23; Deut 18:10, 14; 2 Ki 17:17; Jer 14:14; 27:9; Ezek 13:6, 9; with arrows, teraphim, and a liver in Ezek 21:26 (ET 21:21).

interrogative מָה is one of accompaniment (BDB, III 1 a): the Philistines are asking what things should be sent along with the ark to accompany it when it is returned.

The verb וְנִשַׁלְּחֶנּוּ is a Piel (D) imperfect of שָׁלַח, "to send," first common plural, with a third masculine singular object suffix that refers to the ark. Here the imperfect has a modal sense, "we *should* send it." In the D stem this verb means "to send away" and is used several times in this context (5:10, 11; 6:3 [twice]; 6:8). In 6:6 it refers to the exodus from Egypt; see the third textual note there. 4QSamᵃ contains the synonymous reading [נ]שלחנו אל מקומו.

6:3 אִם־מְשַׁלְּחִים—The protasis of a conditional sentence (אִם, "if") usually has an imperfect instead of a participle (מְשַׁלְּחִים, "sending away"). 4QSamᵃ apparently included a subject pronoun, [אם משלחים אתם], "if you [masculine plural] are sending away," as does the LXX, εἰ ἐξαποστέλλετε ὑμεῖς. The MT reading without אַתֶּם is probably the result of homoioteleuton (ם … ם) or homoioarchton (א … א) with the following direct object marker, אֶת־.

אֶת־אֲרוֹן אֱלֹהֵי יִשְׂרָאֵל—Instead of the MT's "the ark of Israel's God," 4QSamᵃ reads [את ארון] ברית יהוה אלוהי ישראל, "the ark of the covenant of Yahweh, Israel's God." The LXX agrees: τὴν κιβωτὸν διαθήκης κυρίου θεοῦ Ισραηλ. The longer reading is probably expansive, given that elsewhere the Philistines never call it "the ark of the covenant"; only the Israelites do (1 Sam 4:3, 4 [twice], 5; 2 Sam 15:24).

רֵיקָם—This word is translated as "without anything [else]." It is from the root ריק, "to be empty," with the adverbial ending ָם-. It is one of only a few Hebrew words that are an adverb in form (see also יוֹמָם, literally "by day," in 1 Sam 25:16; 2 Sam 21:10). Here it is often translated by the adjective "empty" (even though the English adverb would be "emptily"). However, the Philistines are not placing objects into the ark, so the English phrase "without anything [else]" conveys the proper meaning. See 6:8, where the gold images are placed into a chest beside the ark on a cart.

הָשֵׁב תָּשִׁיבוּ לוֹ—The Hiphil (H) infinitive absolute of שׁוּב strengthens the force of the Hiphil imperfect of שׁוּב, which functions as an imperative (see Joüon, § 113 m). In context לוֹ here and in 6:4, 8 must mean "to him," that is, "to Yahweh" rather than "with it [the ark]," which would have been expressed with the preposition בְּ (see the third textual note on 6:2).

אָשָׁם—This noun, repeated in 6:4, 8, 17, is the term for a "guilt offering." In the theology of the Philistines it likely had deficient associations compared to those in the OT, where God provided a remedy for the total depravity of human nature and the guilt incurred by actual sins. It derives from the verb אָשַׁם, "to be guilty" (e.g., Lev 4:13, 22, 27; 5:2–5; Num 5:6–7; Is 24:6; Jer 2:3). Its rites are detailed in Lev 5:14–26 (ET 5:14–6:7); 7:1–7.[3]

וְנוֹדַע לָכֶם לָמָּה לֹא־תָסוּר יָדוֹ מִכֶּם:—The MT reads "and it will be known to you why his hand will not turn away from you." 4QSamᵃ apparently read [ו]נכפר ל[כם הלוא תסור ידו מכם], "[And] it will be forgiven y[ou. Why shouldn't

---

3 Some, however, argue that it refers to a "reparation offering." See Kleinig, *Leviticus*, 128–38, 166–68.

his hand turn away from you (then)?]" The LXX is similar to 4QSamᵃ.[4] [וְ]נִכְפֵּר] is a Nitpael (HtN) perfect with *waw* consecutive third masculine singular: "it will be atoned/forgiven."[5] It appears as if the MT tradition is a secondary reading that substituted a more familiar form (Niphal [N] stem of יָדַע, "to know") for a less familiar one and reduplicated two of the letters from לכם with the resulting sequence being וְנוֹדַע לָכֶם לֹם הֲלֹא. Then in order to make sense of the text, לֹם הֲלֹא had to be adjusted to לָמֶה לֹא by changing the word division.[6] לָמֶה, "why?" is an interrogative particle that normally stands at the head of a sentence (or following an opening vocative, as in the first occurrence in 1:8: חַנָּה לָמֶה, "Hannah, why … ?"). The use of לָמֶה in the middle of a sentence as a conjunction is rare, making the MT reading suspect, even though it is the harder reading.[7]

6:4 עָפְלֵי זָהָב—This means "swellings of gold." For the two plural nouns whose construct forms are here—the Qere, טְחֹרֵי, and the Kethib, עָפְלֵי—see the second textual note on 5:6. Suffixed forms of these words are Qere/Kethib readings in 6:5.

עַכְבְּרֵי זָהָב—This is translated as "gold rats." עַכְבָּר is often translated as "mouse" based on the LXX rendering μῦς (as in, e.g., 6:5). However, this word and its cognates in other Semitic languages are general terms for small rodents and can refer to rats as well.[8] For instance, the Akkadian cognate usually refers to jerboas, a genus of hopping rodents endemic to Asia and North Africa (*HALOT*). The Aramaic cognate is used to designate both rats and mice.[9] The LXX and 4QSamᵃ omit "five gold rats."

מַגֵּפָה—For this word, here translated as "plague," see the first textual note on 4:17.

לְכֻלָּם—This combination in the MT means "for all of them" but likely results from dittography of the ל. "For you" is the reading of the LXX (ὑμῖν) and apparently of 4QSamᵃ (ל[כם]).

6:5 צַלְמֵי עָפְלֵיכֶם וְצַלְמֵי עַכְבְּרֵיכֶם—Two of these nouns have pronominal suffixes: "images of *your* swellings and images of *your* rats." The reading in 4QSamᵃ is צלמי העפֹ[ל]ֹ[י]ם וצלמי העכברים, "[images of the swel]lings and images of the rats." It appears that 4QSamᵃ has a secondary reading that resulted from substituting the forms without suffixes since they are used more frequently in this account.

---

[4] καὶ ἐξιλασθήσεται ὑμῖν. μὴ οὐκ ἀποστῇ ἡ χεὶρ αὐτοῦ ἀφ᾽ ὑμῶν; "And it will be atoned for you. Why shouldn't his hand withdraw from you?"

[5] The Nitpael (HtN) stem is a mixed form combining the passive Niphal (N) stem and the passive/reflexive (Ht) formation. See וְנִכַּפֵּר in Deut 21:8.

[6] It ought to be borne in mind that in Paleo-Hebrew script and in early square script there was no difference between medial and final *mem*.

[7] For instance, לָמֶה (with occasional variations in spelling) occurs forty-nine other times in the book of Samuel, always as an interrogative (1 Sam 1:8 [three times]; 2:23, 29; 4:3; 6:6; 9:21; 15:19; 17:8, 28; 19:5, 17 [twice]; 20:8, 32; 21:15 [ET 21:14]; 22:13; 24:10 [ET 24:9]; 26:15, 18; 27:5; 28:9, 12, 15, 16; 2 Sam 2:22; 3:24; 7:7; 11:21; 12:23; 13:26; 14:13, 31, 32; 15:19; 16:9, 17; 18:22; 19:11, 12, 13, 26, 30, 36, 37, 43 [ET 19:10, 11, 12, 25, 29, 35, 36, 42]; 20:19; 24:3).

[8] *TWOT*, § 1618.

[9] *CAL*, s.v. ʿkbr, ʿkbrˀ.

לֵאלֹהֵי יִשְׂרָאֵל—Instead of "to Israel's God," the LXX reads τῷ κυρίῳ, "to the Lord."

אוּלַי יָקֵל אֶת־יָדוֹ מֵעֲלֵיכֶם—The hypothetical particle אוּלַי, "perhaps" (as also in 1 Sam 9:6; 14:6; 2 Sam 14:15; 16:12), and the Hiphil (H) imperfect of קָלַל signify the result anticipated by the pagan priests should the Philistines comply with their advice in 6:4–5a. The hope that God will "lighten" his hand is antonymous to the Qal (G) of כָּבֵד in 5:6, 11, where the hand of Yahweh was "heavy" on the Philistines. Cf. also the Piel (D) of כָּבֵד in the next textual note.

6:6   וְלָמָּה תְכַבְּדוּ אֶת־לְבַבְכֶם כַּאֲשֶׁר כִּבְּדוּ ... אֶת־לִבָּם—Literally this is "and why will you make your hearts heavy as they made their hearts heavy?" It is translated as "why should you be stubborn like they were stubborn?" Just as the author engaged in word-play in chapter 4 between כָּבֵד, "heavy," and כָּבוֹד, Yahweh's "glory" (see the third textual note on 4:18), so in chapter 6 there is a play in the contrast between giving God כָּבוֹד, "glory" (6:5), and כִּבֵּד, "making [one's heart] heavy," and refusing to glorify him.

הִתְעַלֵּל בָּהֶם—The verb עָלַל appears in the OT only in D conjugations, meaning "treat severely, violently; make sport of, abuse" (cf. *DCH*, s.v. עלל I). The Hithpael (HtD) always takes the preposition בְּ to introduce the object. The Hithpael refers to Yahweh's harsh treatment of Egypt here and in Ex 10:2. This verb, along with the two verbs that conclude the verse (see the next textual note), suggests that the Philistines had a precise knowledge of these events in the history of Israel's exodus. Cf. the third and fourth textual notes on 4:8. The Chronicler uses the Hithpael in his account of the demise of Saul (1 Chr 10:4).

וַיְשַׁלְּחוּם וַיֵּלֵכוּ׃—The implied subject of the first verb must be the Egyptians, while that of the second verb is the Israelites. This sequence describes what happened in the exodus. The Piel (D) of שָׁלַח, "to send away," occurs frequently in the exodus narrative. It occurs, for example, in Yahweh's repeated appeals through Moses to Pharaoh to "send away" or "let my people go" (e.g., Ex 4:23; 5:1; 6:11; 7:2, 16), and, as Pharaoh hardens his heart, it occurs in his refusals to "let them go" (e.g., Ex 7:14; 8:28 [ET 8:32]; 9:7, 17, 35). Finally, it is used for his expulsion of the people after he was compelled to do so by force: "when he lets you go, he will completely drive you out from this place" (Ex 11:1; see also Ex 12:33; 13:17).

6:7   עֲגָלָה חֲדָשָׁה אֶחָת—Occasionally the numeral "one" is used in Hebrew as an indefinite article (*HALOT*, s.v. אֶחָד, 3), as is more common in Aramaic, thus "a new cart." אֶחָת is pausal for אַחַת, which is the feminine form of אֶחָד. There is no need to emend the text by dropping the numeral based on the LXX's ἅμαξαν καινήν, "a new cart."[10]

פָּרוֹת עָלוֹת—This is translated as "nursing cows." The feminine plural participle of עוּל is used adjectivally, literally "cows that are suckling [their calves]." See also 6:10.

אֲשֶׁר לֹא־עָלָה עֲלֵיהֶם עֹל—"That have never been yoked" is literally "that a yoke has never gone up upon them."

וַהֲשֵׁיבֹתֶם בְּנֵיהֶם מֵאַחֲרֵיהֶם הַבָּיְתָה׃—"And take their calves home" is literally "and return their calves from after them to the house." The expected form of the Hiphil (H)

---

[10] As, e.g., McCarter, *I Samuel*, 129; Klein, *1 Samuel*, 53–54.

second masculine plural perfect with *waw* consecutive of שׁוּב would be הֲשִׁיבֹתֶם, with *hireq* in the second syllable, but with the accent shifted to the final syllable that vowel becomes *tsere*, וַהֲשִׁיבֹתֶם. See GKC, § 72 i. See also הֲשֵׁבֹתֶם in 6:8.

6:8 בָּאַרְגַּז—The noun אַרְגַּז, "chest," occurs only in this chapter (also 6:11, 15). The article is used because the noun is definite from the viewpoint of the speaker,[11] but it is not needed in English.

וְשִׁלַּחְתֶּם אֹתוֹ וְהָלָךְ:—The third person masculine singular forms (the pronominal suffix on אֹתוֹ and the verb וְהָלָךְ, pausal for וְהָלַךְ), both translated with "it," may refer to the ark (אָרוֹן), which usually is masculine (see the third textual note on 4:17), since it is by far the most important part of the assemblage. (Cf. וַיִּרְאוּ אֶת־הָאָרוֹן, "and they saw the ark," in 6:13, with no mention of the cart.) Or the referent could be the feminine "cart" (עֲגָלָה) since masculine forms are commonly used in place of feminine ones, especially when a number of words intervene (הָעֲגָלָה is the twelfth word prior to אֹתוֹ in 6:8). (In 6:14, the feminine verb בָּאָה immediately follows וְהָעֲגָלָה, with another feminine verb, וַתַּעֲמֹד, later.)

6:9 מִקְרֶה הוּא הָיָה לָנוּ—Literally "it [was] an accident [that] happened to us." The noun מִקְרֶה, derived from the verb קָרָה, "to meet; happen," corresponds to the English noun "an accident," or something that happened "by chance." This clause expresses a belief that purposeless events may occur by random chance.

6:10 כָּלוּ—"They confined" is a Qal (G) perfect third common plural of כָּלָא, "shut up, restrict." The expected form would be כָּלְאוּ, but third-*aleph* verbs often adopt the forms of third-*he* verbs (Joüon, § 78 g).

6:11 וְאֵת הָאַרְגַּז וְאֵת עַכְבְּרֵי הַזָּהָב וְאֵת צַלְמֵי טְחֹרֵיהֶם:—This is translated as "the chest, the gold rats, and the images of swellings." Codex Leningradensis has טְחֹרֵיהֶם, which could mean "their hemorrhoids," but many Masoretic manuscripts read עֲפֹלֵיהֶם, "their swellings" (for both terms, see the first textual note on 5:6). It appears as if the Qere has intruded into the text of Leningradensis here and in 6:17. The LXX omits "images of the swellings." McCarter claims that this entire list in both the MT and the LXX is a secondary expansion in the text. Given its awkward position in the Hebrew sentence and that there is no mention of the gold items being placed in the chest (as in 6:8), he may be correct.[12]

6:12 וַיִּשַּׁרְנָה הַפָּרוֹת—The Qal (G) of יָשַׁר means "to go straight." The subject is הַפָּרוֹת, "the cows," feminine plural. The verb form is an archaic third feminine plural imperfect (with *waw* consecutive) with the preformative -יְ instead of -תְּ (GKC, § 47 k). Introductory textbooks give the same form with preformative -תְּ (e.g., תִּשְׁמֹרְנָה) for the second and third feminine plural imperfects because the original third feminine plural form, which occurs here, is so rare. The form would then be וַיִּישַׁרְנָה, but the י of the root יָשַׁר is assimilated and marked by the *daghesh* in -שַּׁ-, hence וַיִּשַּׁרְנָה (GKC, § 71).

---

[11] *IBH*, § 20 A.

[12] McCarter, *I Samuel*, 130.

הָלֹךְ וְגָעוֹ—These two Qal (G) infinitive absolutes, "walking and lowing," could also be rendered as "lowing as they went" (see Joüon, § 123 m, s). The verb גָּעָה, "to low," occurs elsewhere in the OT only in Job 6:5 but is attested in Syriac (ܓܥܐ).

6:13 וַיִּשְׂאוּ אֶת־עֵינֵיהֶם—"They looked up" is literally "and they lifted up their eyes."

6:14 יְהוֹשֻׁעַ בֵּית־הַשִּׁמְשִׁי—Note the gentilic suffix ִי- on הַשִּׁמְשִׁי, thus "Joshua the Beth-shemishite." The word recurs in 6:18.

הֶעֱלוּ עֹלָה—This is a cognate accusative construction,[13] "to offer up [the Hiphil of עָלָה] a burnt offering [עֹלָה]." The noun עֹלָה denotes a "whole burnt offering," which was consumed in its entirety on the altar. Its derivation from the verb עָלָה, "go up," is probably because the entire offering was offered up to Yahweh (none of its meat was eaten by worshipers) and because the smoke ascended. Formal regulations for this offering are given in Lev 1:3–17.[14]

6:15 הוֹרִידוּ—The Hiphil (H) perfect of יָרַד, "they brought down," is translated as "(they) lowered," i.e., from the cart.

וַיִּזְבְּחוּ זְבָחִים—The cognate accusative construction "to sacrifice a sacrifice" appeared earlier in 1:21; 2:13, 19. See also 10:8; 11:15; 16:5; 2 Sam 15:12.

6:18 מֵעִיר מִבְצָר וְעַד כֹּפֶר הַפְּרָזִי—This merism, literally "from a fortified city and until a village of the hamlet-dweller," means "the fortified cities and unwalled villages." The noun כֹּפֶר IV, "village," occurs only here in the OT, and its cognate synonym כָּפָר appears twice.

וְעַד ׀ אָבֵל הַגְּדוֹלָה—The noun אָבֵל II, "meadow," occurs elsewhere only as or in a place-name (BDB), so this would mean something like "and until Great Meadow." However, since the phrase אֶבֶן גְּדוֹלָה, "a large stone," was used twice earlier (6:14, 15) and fits this context best, the reading אֶבֶן in a few Masoretic manuscripts with the support of the LXX (λίθου) is preferable. אָבֵל likely is a transcription error that substituted a *lamed* for a final *nun*.

הִנִּיחוּ—There are two different conjugations of Hiphil (H) forms of the verb נוּחַ. This form is from the conjugation that would appear to be from the root ננח, with gemination of the first radical, and it means "to put, place" (see Joüon, § 80 p).

6:19 וַיַּךְ בְּאַנְשֵׁי בֵית־שֶׁמֶשׁ כִּי רָאוּ בַּאֲרוֹן יְהוָה—"He struck some of the men of Beth-shemesh because they looked into the ark of Yahweh." "Some of the men" is literally "among the men" (similar to the prepositional phrase בָּעָם, "among the people," twice later in the verse). The LXX reads καὶ οὐκ ἠσμένισαν οἱ υἱοὶ Ιεχονιου ἐν τοῖς ἀνδράσιν Βαιθσαμυς ὅτι εἶδαν κιβωτὸν κυρίου, "and the sons of Jechonias were not pleased with the men of Beth-shemesh because they saw the ark of the Lord." Apparently, the LXX understands the disrespect for the ark by the sons of Jechoniah as the reason that God struck down some men of Beth-shemesh.

שִׁבְעִים אִישׁ חֲמִשִּׁים אֶלֶף אִישׁ—This is the reading of most Masoretic manuscripts: "seventy men, fifty thousand men." A few Masoretic manuscripts read שִׁבְעִים אִישׁ,

---

[13] See *IBH*, § 17 B; GKC, § 117 p–r.

[14] For an analysis, see Kleinig, *Leviticus*, 58–68.

"seventy men," which agrees with Josephus.[15] The second number in the MT, "fifty thousand men," must be an early intrusion into the text. Fifty thousand men is an incredibly large number for a small village like Beth-shemesh. Also, if the second number were original, one would expect שְׁבְעִים וַחֲמִשִּׁים אֶלֶף אִישׁ, "seventy *and* fifty thousand men," with a conjunction on the second number and the word אִישׁ, "men," used only once, at the end.[16] The solution proposed by Tsumura, "seventy men, that is, every five people out of a thousand," would still require an improbably large population of fourteen thousand in the small village of Beth-shemesh.[17] McCarter's solution is even more fanciful, as he emends the text based on a combination of the LXX and the mention of priests in Josephus' account of this incident.[18]

6:20 יְהוָה הָאֱלֹהִים הַקָּדוֹשׁ הַזֶּה—This means "Yahweh, this holy God." 4QSamᵃ reads יהוה הקדוש הזה, "this holy Yahweh," which is supported by the LXX (κυρίου τοῦ ἁγίου τούτου).

וְאֶל־מִי יַעֲלֶה מֵעָלֵינוּ׃—This rhetorical question, literally "and to whom will he go up from upon us?" probably asks whether there is anyone to whom Yahweh can go (after he would depart from being "upon us," that is, weighing heavily upon the men of Beth-shemesh) who will not suffer the same punishment of being struck down.

7:1 וַיַּעֲלוּ—This form of the third masculine plural preterite (imperfect with *waw* consecutive) of עָלָה could be either Qal (G) or Hiphil (H). Since it is transitive (see the next textual note for its direct object), it must be Hiphil: "they brought up" the ark. This agrees with the Hiphil imperative הַעֲלוּ in 6:21. The imperfect form יַעֲלֶה in 6:20 (also 6:9) could be either Qal or Hiphil, but since those contexts require the intransitive meaning "go up," it must be Qal.

אֶת־אֲרוֹן יְהוָה ... אֶת־אֲרוֹן יְהוָה׃—For both instances of "the ark of Yahweh" in the MT, the LXX reads τὴν κιβωτὸν διαθήκης κυρίου, "the ark of the covenant of the Lord." The LXX reading is supported by the reconstructed reading of the first instance of the phrase in 4QSamᵃ, but the latter part of the verse is not extant there.

אֲבִינָדָב—Instead of "Abinadab" in the MT, the LXX reads Αμιναδαβ, "Aminadab" (translating אֲמִינָדָב?), a name unattested in the MT. Αμιναδαβ is also used by Josephus to refer to the person in whose house the ark resided.[19] It appears as if the LXX is

---

[15] Josephus, *Antiquities*, 6.16.

[16] There are several examples of compounded numbers with the unit אִישׁ, which is never repeated, but always follows the final number (Num 16:35; 26:10; Judg 20:35; 1 Chr 21:5 [two examples]). Note LXX 1 Sam 6:19: ἑβδομήκοντα ἄνδρας καὶ πεντήκοντα χιλιάδας ἀνδρῶν, "seventy men and fifty thousand men." The καί was probably added in translation to make the text understandable.

[17] Tsumura, *The First Book of Samuel*, 226–27. Tsumura's reading requires a bit of linguistic gymnastics, including the positing of an enclitic *mem* on the number "five." It appears to be an attempt to justify the MT at all costs. Tsumura's solution is similar to the earlier solution of Allis, "The Punishment of the Men of Bethshemesh." Allis tries to read the text as "seventy men, fifty [from] one thousand men," which would imply a population of fourteen hundred in Beth-shemesh.

[18] McCarter, *I Samuel*, 131. Cf. Josephus, *Antiquities*, 6.16.

[19] Josephus, *Antiquities*, 6.18, 7.79.

substituting one labial consonant for another. Αμιναδαβ is also the LXX's equivalent for the name עַמִּינָדָב, "Amminadab" (e.g., Ex 6:23).

בַּגִּבְעָה—Instead of the MT's "on the hill," 4QSamᵃ probably read אשר בגבעה, "which is on the hill."[20] That reading appears to be supported by the LXX: τὸν ἐν τῷ βουνῷ.

קִדְּשׁוּ—The Piel (D) of קָדַשׁ has a factitive or declarative meaning (see Waltke-O'Connor, § 20.2m), "to sanctify, consecrate, pronounce or render holy." The person whom "they consecrated" was placed into a holy office; he was then able to serve in the presence of the "holy" God (הַקָּדוֹשׁ, 6:20). The Piel is common in the Torah for the consecration of the priests and the tabernacle appointments (e.g., Ex 28:3, 41; 29:1; 40:9–11, 13). It recurs in 1 Sam 16:5, while the Qal is in 1 Sam 21:6 (ET 21:5), the Hiphil (H) is in 2 Sam 8:11 (twice), and the Hithpael (HtD) is in 1 Sam 16:5; 2 Sam 11:4. Usually Yahweh uses the Piel in his declarations that he is the one who "sanctifies" his people (Lev 20:8; 21:8, 15, 23; 22:9, 16, 32).

Commentary

Spring 1068 BC

The Philistines Devise a Plan to Return the Ark to Israel (6:1–12)

The end of the ark's time in Philistine territory is marked by the author with a notice that the ark spent seven months there (6:1). Since it was returned to Beth-shemesh during the wheat harvest (6:13), which typically took place in May and June, the ark had been captured sometime in the previous November or December.

After the panic wrought by Yahweh, the Philistines were anxious to find a way to return it to Israel in hopes of ridding themselves of the plague. The conversation between the Philistines and their priests and diviners is interesting in several ways. The first is the acquisition of supernatural knowledge. The Philistines implicitly confess that they do not know how to deal with Yahweh; they are ignorant of how to rid themselves of the ark and the problems that came with it. They assume that their pagan clergy and occultists will be able to ascertain the answer. They say, "Inform us …" (6:2), as if these practitioners of the mantic arts can divine exactly what is to be done.

The second point of interest is the distance the text places between "the Philistines" (6:2) and their priests and diviners. The priests are not called "their priests," and the diviners are not "their diviners." And when these men speak, they keep the rest of the Philistine population at arm's length: "If *you* are sending the ark … *you* surely ought to return a guilt offering. … *You* will be healed, and it will be forgiven *you*. Why shouldn't his hand turn away from *you*?" (6:3). They do it again when they say, "Make images of *your* swellings and images of *your* rats. … Perhaps he will lighten his hand from upon *you* and from upon *your* gods and from upon *your* land" (6:5). It is as if the priests and diviners do

---

[20] The last extant word in the verse is אשׁ[ר], which was presumably followed by בגבעה.

not want to be associated with their fellow Philistines, their physical ailments, and any of their actions; they want to maintain as much distance as possible away from Yahweh. Finally, the words of the diviners "give glory to Israel's God" (6:5) are ironic in light of 4:21–22, where Phinehas' wife had said that the "Glory" had departed from Israel with the capture of the ark and the death of her priestly relatives. The return of the ark itself is a way of glorifying God. It is a tacit admission that Israel's God cannot be conquered and must be sent away from the defiled land of the pagan god Dagon, even as the Egyptians sent away the Israelites in the exodus (see the second and third textual notes on 6:6).

Immediately after counseling the Philistines to send guilt offerings to Israel's God (6:5), the priests and diviners also urge the Philistines not to be stubborn like Pharaoh and the Egyptians (6:6). It appears that they are familiar with the exodus and especially recall that Israel despoiled the Egyptians of their gold and other valuables before leaving the land of slavery (Ex 3:20–22). The priests and diviners counsel the making of a cart of which they say, "Send it away and it will go" (1 Sam 6:7–8), mirroring what they said of the Egyptians' release of the Israelites: "When he [Yahweh] afflicted them didn't they send them away and they left?" (6:6).

The very specific directions given for the returning of the ark meet the cultic requirements of the idolatrous clergy. The number of gold swellings and gold rats corresponds to the number of Philistine leaders, since there is one plague that accompanied the ark in its travels throughout Philistia (6:4). The cart is new (6:7). The two cows have never been yoked (6:7)—a requirement even in the laws given by Moses for some sacrificial cows (Num 19:2; Deut 21:3). The diviners leave nothing to chance, since the pagan attitude is that one must perform the correct actions and devote the proper offerings in order to make oneself presentable to the gods and then the gods may choose to look favorably upon the one who seeks their favor. It is a theology of works-righteousness, although the worshiper is always left in doubt whether his efforts have been sufficient.

This is the opposite of biblical worship, where God invites his people into his presence and provides the means by which they are admitted because of his grace.[21] In the OT this came through the sacrifices and other rites that Yahweh graciously gave through Moses to Israel so that the people could be assured of their forgiveness and worship in his presence.[22] In the NT God provides the sacrifice of Christ, through whom guilt is removed; sinners are forgiven and brought into God's church, his kingdom of grace. He provides his Word and the Sacraments of Baptism and the Lord's Supper as the means by which the saving benefits of Christ's sacrifice are received by each individual. Thus sanctified

---

[21] See Kleinig, *Leviticus*, 1–13.

[22] Forgiveness of sins is explicitly connected with several offerings: see Lev 4:20, 26, 31, 35; 5:10, 13, 16, 18; 5:26 (ET 6:7); 19:22; Num 15:25–26, 28. In sending the gold objects as a guilt offering (אָשָׁם), the Philistines were admitting their guilt and seeking forgiveness (see *TWOT*, § 180, for the root אשם). See also the fifth textual note on 1 Sam 6:3.

as saints, Christians are enabled to serve in the presence of the holy God (cf. 1 Sam 6:20; 7:1).[23]

The diviners provided a test that was rigged so that the ark probably would not go back to Beth-shemesh: the cows had never been yoked and had never pulled a cart, so they would not pull together in the same direction. As nursing mothers, they would have naturally tried to follow their calves back to their stalls. This test was the diviners' way of ensuring to their satisfaction that they were not mistaken. The ark probably would travel back to Philistia or go in circles or go nowhere. If the ark returned to Israelite territory, it must be because Yahweh willed it and was also responsible for the plague. The author emphasizes that the calves headed directly for Beth-shemesh (6:12). They were lowing—perhaps calling for their calves—yet they did not veer off course to either side. The Philistine governors followed to see this.

Why did the Philistines choose Beth-shemesh as the place to send the ark? The text does not say, but it may have been because it was a city of priests. According to Josh 21:8–16, Beth-shemesh within the territory of Judah was given to the descendants of Aaron (see also 1 Chr 6:39–45 [ET 6:54–60]). Thus, the ark was taken from the care of the negligent high priest Eli and his apostate sons in Shiloh and was returned to the priests who resided in Beth-shemesh.

The Ark in Beth-shemesh (6:13–18)

The account of the ark coming to Beth-shemesh shifts the point of view of the narration from action among the Philistines back to events in Israel. Since the ark came to a priestly city, the offering of a sacrifice (6:14) was not only most appropriate but was also aided by a ready reserve of Aaronic priests to preside over the sacrificial rites. The mentioning of Levites lowering the ark from the cart (6:15) may be a reference to other Aaronides who had not yet become priests (perhaps because they were under thirty years of age). The Philistine governors did not return to Ekron until they saw the sacrifices offered to Yahweh (6:16). They may have assumed that Israel's God had been appeased through their guilt offerings and the Israelites' sacrifices, and so the plague would be lifted from them.

The final verses of this section document both the gold items that accompanied the ark and the large rock upon which the ark was placed (6:17–18). Since the author claims that the rock is still in the field of Joshua the Beth-shemeshite "to this day," he is assuming that the whereabouts of Joshua's field was still known to his contemporaries when he wrote and that the rock could be located by anyone wishing to do so.

---

[23] See further the conclusion of "Beth-shemesh Sends the Ark to Kiriath-jearim (6:19–7:1)" below.

Beth-shemesh Sends the Ark to Kiriath-jearim (6:19–7:1)

Whether God struck down some seventy men from Beth-shemesh for looking into the ark (MT 1 Sam 6:19) or for disrespect of the ark by one clan (LXX 1 Sam 6:19; see the first textual note on 6:19), the reaction of the men of Beth-shemesh is similar to that of the Philistines—how can they rid themselves of the ark? It appears that their priestly status and familiarity with God led to casualness and laxity in the presence of Yahweh. This taking for granted the presence of the holy God is what caused the death of Eli's sons Hophni and Phinehas, as well as the earlier deaths of another pair of priests, Aaron's sons Nadab and Abihu (Lev 10:1–3). After the death of these men, the priests of Beth-shemesh were afraid to be in the presence of "Yahweh, this holy God" (1 Sam 6:20).

There is no reason given as to why the men of Beth-shemesh chose Kiriath-jearim as an appropriate place for the ark. Kiriath-jearim, whose name means "forest city," was earlier associated with the worship of Baal when it was a Gibeonite city (Josh 9:17) since its name had been Baalah or Kiriath-baal, "city of Baal" (Josh 15:9, 60; 18:14–15; 1 Chr 13:6). Kiriath-jearim was within the territory given to the clans of Judah and was eventually settled by the descendants of Shobal, a grandson of Caleb by his second wife, Ephrath (1 Chr 2:19, 50, 52). Caleb and Joshua were the only two in the wilderness generation who believed God's Word and so were granted entrance into the promised land (Num 13:30; 14:24; Deut 1:35–36; Josh 14:6, 13; 15:13). Thus, the ark was sent to the Ephrathites, who were related to David. David was an Ephrathite, descended from Ephrath through Salma, another grandson of Caleb (1 Sam 17:12; 1 Chr 2:50–51). Thus, for the first time the ark became associated with the tribe of Judah and David's clan Ephrath (cf. Ps 132:6).

There is an irony to the placing of the ark in the house of Abinadab (אֲבִינָדָב, 1 Sam 7:1), whose name combines the elements of the names of the unfaithful Aaronic priests Abihu (אֲבִיהוּא) and Nadab (נָדָב, Ex 6:32). Unlike the residents of Beth-shemesh, the men of Kiriath-jearim were not afraid of God's presence in their midst. Instead, they acknowledged God's holiness by placing the ark in charge of a man whom they consecrated for the care of it.[24] Thus, the ark would remain in Abinadab's house until David came to transport it to Jerusalem (2 Sam 6:2–3).

Abinadab's son Eleazar was consecrated "to take care of" or "guard" (לִשְׁמֹר, 1 Sam 7:1) the ark. He was not made a priest, nor does the root שׁמר imply any kind of priestly function.[25] Instead, it signifies guarding and protecting the ark as its custodian. Yet, even this simple function required consecrating Eleazar. The verb "consecrate" (the Piel [D] of the root קדשׁ; see the fifth textual note on 7:1) can be used of placing a person into the priesthood or Levitical

---

[24] Note the relation between the adjective "holy" (קָדוֹשׁ, 6:20) and verb "they consecrated" (קִדְּשׁוּ, 7:1). See the fifth textual note on 7:1.

[25] Contra some commentators, such as Klein, *1 Samuel*, 60.

service.[26] However, it can also be used for the consecrating of laypersons so that they may be in the presence of God.[27]

This entire account of the ark's time in Philistia and its eventual rest in Kiriath-jearim reminds readers of the great privilege given by God to those who believe in Christ. We can enter the presence of the holy God without fear because we, too, are sanctified—by our justification by grace alone, our baptismal incorporation into Christ, and our partaking of his body and blood in his Holy Supper.[28] Luther reminds us of this:

> I do not know how I can alter what I have heretofore constantly taught on this subject, namely, that by faith (as St. Peter says)[29] we get a new and clean heart and that God will and does account us as altogether righteous and holy for the sake of Christ, our mediator. Although the sin in our flesh has not been completely removed or become dead, he will not count or acknowledge it. (SA III XIII 1)

---

[26] Ex 28:3, 41; 29:1, 27, 33, 44; 30:30; 40:13; Lev 8:12, 30; 21:8, 15, 23; 22:9, 16; Num 6:11; 2 Chr 29:5.

[27] Ex 13:2; 19:10, 14, 23; Lev 20:8; 22:32; Josh 7:13; 1 Sam 16:5; Ezek 20:12; Joel 2:16; Job 1:5.

[28] For this sanctification by the forgiveness of sins through the means of grace, see, e.g., Mt 26:28; Jn 17:17–19; Acts 26:18; 1 Cor 1:2; 6:11; Eph 5:26; Heb 10:10, 29; 13:12.

[29] Luther probably has Acts 15:9 in mind.

Samuel's Ministry as Judge: God Delivers Israel from the Philistines

Translation

7 [2]From the day the ark dwelt in Kiriath-jearim there was a long time, twenty years. And the entire house of Israel lamented for Yahweh. [3]So Samuel said to the entire house of Israel, "If you are returning to Yahweh with all your heart, get rid of the foreign gods and the Astartes among you. Dedicate your heart to Yahweh, and serve only him. Then he will rescue you from Philistine domination." [4]So the Israelites got rid of the Baals and the Astartes and served only Yahweh. [5]Next Samuel said, "Gather all Israel at Mizpah, and I will pray to Yahweh on your behalf."

[6]Then they gathered at Mizpah, drew water, and poured it out in Yahweh's presence. They fasted that day and said there, "We have sinned against Yahweh." So Samuel judged the Israelites at Mizpah.

[7]Now the Philistines heard that the Israelites had gathered at Mizpah, so the governors of the Philistines went up to Israel. The Israelites heard [about it] and were afraid of the Philistines. [8]The Israelites said to Samuel, "Don't keep silent by not crying out to Yahweh our God for us, and he will save us from the power of the Philistines!" [9]Then Samuel took a nursing lamb and sacrificed it as a whole burnt offering to Yahweh. Samuel called to Yahweh on behalf of Israel, and Yahweh answered him.

[10]Samuel was sacrificing the burnt offering, and the Philistines came near to Israel for battle. Yahweh thundered loudly that day against the Philistines, and he threw them into a panic. They were defeated before Israel. [11]Then the men of Israel went out from Mizpah and pursued the Philistines and struck them as far as somewhere below Beth-car.

[12]Samuel took a stone and set it up between Mizpah and the Tooth. He called its name Ebenezer and said, "Thus far Yahweh has helped us." [13]So the Philistines were subdued and did not enter Israel's territory again. God's power was on the Philistines as long as Samuel was alive. [14]The cities that the Philistines had taken from Israel from Ekron to Gath returned to Israel. Israel liberated their territory from Philistine control. Moreover, there was peace between the Israelites and the Ammonites.

[15]Samuel judged Israel as long as he lived. [16]Every year he would go and make a circuit to Bethel, Gilgal, and Mizpah and judge Israel in all these places. [17]Then his return route was to Ramah, because his home was there. He would judge Israel there, and he built an altar to Yahweh there.

Textual Notes

7:2 וַיִּרְבּוּ הַיָּמִים וַיִּהְיוּ עֶשְׂרִים שָׁנֶה—Literally "the days increased, and there were twenty years."

וַיִּנָּהוּ ... אַחֲרֵי יְהוָה:—Literally "they lamented ... after Yahweh." This may be a pregnant clause, indicating both contrition and faith: "they lamented (their sin) and followed after Yahweh (in faith)." Cf. GKC, § 119 gg. The verb is a Niphal (N) preterite (imperfect with *waw* consecutive) third masculine plural of נָהָה. The plural is used with a singular subject that is a collective: כָּל־בֵּית יִשְׂרָאֵל, "the entire house of Israel." The Qal (G) of נָהָה occurs in Ezek 32:18; Micah 2:4 and means "to lament," and the Niphal occurs only here. The verb is probably related to the noun נְהִי, "wailing," with which it is used in Micah 2:4.

7:3 הָסִירוּ—"Get rid of" is a Hiphil (H) imperative masculine plural of the verb סוּר. In the H stem this verb signifies the removal of something (*HALOT*).

וְהָעַשְׁתָּרוֹת—Literally "and the Ashtaroth," this is translated as "and the Astartes." "Ashtoreth" (plural "Ashtaroth") is "the name by which the Canaanite goddess more commonly known as Astarte is referred to in the OT. ... Astarte was a consort of Baal."[1] "Astarte" is a Hellenized form of the name of the Mesopotamian goddess Ishtar, who was connected with love, fertility, and war. Her name also appears in 7:4 and 12:10. In these three verses (7:3, 4; 12:10), the LXX reads καὶ τὰ ἄλση, "and the groves." The plural of ἄλσος, "grove," is the LXX's usual translation of the name of a different goddess, "Asherah" (אֲשֵׁרָה; which often occurs in the plural).[2] Asherah was a Semitic mother goddess worshiped among trees or poles (probably phallic symbols). The only places where ἄλση in the LXX corresponds to עַשְׁתָּרוֹת in the MT are 7:3, 4; 12:10. This may indicate that a scribe systematically replaced אֲשֵׁרִים with עַשְׁתָּרוֹת throughout most of Samuel.[3]

וְיַצֵּל אֶתְכֶם—The Hiphil (H) jussive of נָצַל with conjunctive *waw* has a consecutive meaning: "then he will rescue you." A jussive form can have the same meaning as an imperfect (GKC, § 109 k).

מִיַּד פְּלִשְׁתִּים:—Literally "from the hand of the Philistines," this is rendered as "from Philistine domination."

7:6 וַיִּקָּבְצוּ—"Then they gathered" is a Niphal (N) preterite (imperfect with *waw* consecutive) third masculine plural of the verb קָבַץ. Here the Niphal has a reflexive nuance, "to gather themselves," as do the Niphal forms in 1 Sam 25:1; 28:4. This corresponds to the intransitive use of "gather" in English. Its Qal (G) imperative קִבְצוּ in 1 Sam 7:5 had the transitive meaning "to gather (people)," as do the Qal forms in 1 Sam 28:1, 4; 29:1; 2 Sam 2:30; 3:21. The Hithpael (HtD) perfect הִתְקַבְּצוּ in 1 Sam 7:7 has an intransitive

---

[1] John Day, "Ashtoreth," *ABD* 1:491.

[2] LXX Ex 34:13; Deut 7:5; 12:3; Judg 3:7; 1 Ki 14:23; 18:19; 2 Ki 17:10, 16; 18:4; 21:3; 23:14; Micah 5:13 (ET 5:14); 2 Chr 14:2 (ET 14:3); 17:6; 19:3; 31:1; 33:3, 19; 34:3, 4, 7.

[3] Except for 1 Sam 7:3, 4; 12:10, the LXX consistently transliterates עַשְׁתֹּרֶת, "Ashtoreth," as Ἀστάρτη, "Astarte" (Judg 2:13; 1 Ki 11:5 [LXX 11:6], 33; 2 Ki 23:13), or, for the plural עַשְׁתָּרוֹת, as Ασταρωθ (Judg 10:6) or Ἀσταρτεῖον (1 Sam 31:10).

155

meaning, "to gather (together)," as do the Hithpael forms in 1 Sam 8:4; 22:2; 2 Sam 2:25.

וַיִּשְׁפְּכוּ—"They poured it out." The LXX reads ἐξέχεαν … ἐπὶ τὴν γῆν, "they poured it out on the ground." Where they poured it is probably an interpretive translational gloss and not a reflection of the LXX's Vorlage.

וַיִּשְׁפֹּט—The verb "to judge" can refer to God's condemnation, as in 3:13. However, when it refers to Samuel's leadership of Israel (7:6, 15, 16, 17; cf. for Eli in 4:18), it refers to theological ministry and also what we would call military and political leadership of God's people, as church and state were combined in Israel. Thus, it involves both Law and Gospel. Yahweh was with Samuel, spoke his Word to him, and fulfilled all of those words (3:19–21). Samuel proclaims God's judgment to lead the people to repentance, as in 7:6 (see also 3:11–17). Yet he also intercedes on their behalf for God's mercy (7:5, 8–9) so that Yahweh will save them (וְיֹשִׁעֵנוּ, 7:8). He offers a sacrifice for atonement in 7:9 and will carry on the messianic promises (Gospel) by anointing David. In the book of Judges, the "judges" (שֹׁפְטִים, Qal [G] participle of שָׁפַט) often were God's agents to "save" his people,[4] and a judge can even be called a "savior" (the Hiphil participle of יָשַׁע, Judg 3:9, 15). In 1 Sam 8:5–6 Israel requests a "king" who would exercise his royal office "to judge us" (לְשָׁפְטֵנוּ).

7:7 וַיִּרְאוּ—See the first textual note on 4:7 for an explanation of this Qal (G) preterite (imperfect with *waw* consecutive) of יָרֵא, "be afraid."

7:8 אַל־תַּחֲרֵשׁ מִמֶּנּוּ מִזְּעֹק אֶל־יְהוָה אֱלֹהֵינוּ—Literally "don't keep silent from us from crying out to Yahweh our God." The negative אַל is used with the Hiphil (H) second person jussive (the imperfect would be תַּחֲרִישׁ) of חָרֵשׁ to form a negative command (Joüon, § 114 i). When the preposition מִן is prefixed to an infinitive construct (מִזְּעֹק) following a verb of restraint (תַּחֲרֵשׁ), it can have the force of negation (BDB, s.v. מִן, 7 b (*a*)): the people asked Samuel not to keep silent "by not crying out."

וְיֹשִׁעֵנוּ—See the third textual note on 4:3 for the identical suffixed Hiphil (H) imperfect of יָשַׁע with conjunctive *waw*, "and he will save us." It recurs without *waw* in 10:27.

7:9 טְלֵה חָלָב אֶחָד—Literally "a lamb of milk, one," this means "a nursing lamb." The Hebrew number "one" can function as an indefinite article (*HALOT*, s.v. אֶחָד, 3).

וַיַּעֲלֵהוּ—This is the Qere, "and he offered it up," which is the reading of a number of MT manuscripts and is supported by the LXX (ἀνήνεγκεν αὐτόν). The third masculine singular suffix (referring to טָלֶה, "lamb") serves as the direct object. The suffix (along with the second object in the double accusative construction, עוֹלָה, "as a whole burnt offering"; see Joüon, § 125 u) reveals that the verb is transitive and therefore must be Hiphil (H). Without the suffix, the form וַיַּעַל could be either Qal (G; as in, e.g., 1 Sam 1:21; 11:1) or Hiphil (as in 1 Sam 2:6 [where it is pausal, וַיָּעַל]; 13:9; 2 Sam 6:12, 17; 21:13; 24:25). The Kethib here, וַיַּעֲלֶה, which lacks the suffix, is Hiphil, as is יַעֲלֶה in 2:14 (but יַעֲלֶה is Qal in, e.g., 6:9, 20; 9:13). In each verse the context disambiguates which stem is intended.

---

[4] See the Hiphil (H) of יָשַׁע in Judg 2:16, 18; 3:9, 31; 6:14, 15, 36, 37; 7:7; 8:22; 10:1, 12; 13:5; and the Hiphil of נָצַל in Judg 9:17.

7:10 וַיַּרְעֵם יְהוָה ׀ בְּקוֹל־גָּדוֹל—Literally "and Yahweh thundered with a great voice/sound." The Hiphil (H) of רָעַם was also in 1 Sam 2:10 and recurs in 2 Sam 22:14.

וַיְהֻמֵּם—"And he threw them into a panic" is a Qal (G) preterite (imperfect with *waw* consecutive) third masculine singular of הָמַם, "to confuse, discomfit," with a third masculine plural pronominal suffix.

וַיִּנָּגְפוּ—"(And) they were defeated" is a Niphal (N) preterite (imperfect with *waw* consecutive) third masculine plural of נָגַף, "strike." The identical form recurs in 2 Sam 18:7. The singular of this Niphal form occurs in 1 Sam 4:2, 10; 2 Sam 2:17.

7:11 עַד־מִתַּחַת לְבֵית כָּר—Literally this is "as far as from below Beth-car." The location of Beth-car is unknown. It is mentioned only here in the OT. Since Philistine territory lay west of Mizpah, Beth-car is probably west of Mizpah.

7:12 הַשֵּׁן—"The Tooth" may be the name of a prominent outcropping of rock that resembled a tooth. McCarter would emend it to הַיְשָׁנָה, "the old [city]" or "Jeshanah" (see יְשָׁנָה in 2 Chr 13:19) based on the LXX's τῆς παλαιᾶς, "the old [city]."[5] Jeshanah, however, is northeast of Mizpah, an unlikely direction for the Philistines to have fled.[6]

אֶבֶן הָעֵזֶר—"Ebenezer" means "the rock of the helper." In 1 Sam 4:1; 5:1 this name was used proleptically.

7:13 וְלֹא־יָסְפוּ עוֹד לָבוֹא—The Qal (G) of יָסַף, "continue, do again," is coordinated with the Qal infinitive construct of בּוֹא, "to come," and strengthened by the adverb עוֹד, "again," literally "they did not continue again to enter." See Joüon, §§ 124 c, 177 b.

כָּל יְמֵי שְׁמוּאֵל׃—Literally "all the days of Samuel," this is translated as "as long as Samuel was alive." Similar is כָּל יְמֵי חַיָּיו, literally "all the days of his life," in 7:15.

7:16 מִדֵּי שָׁנָה בְּשָׁנָה—The compound preposition מִדֵּי (מִן + דֵּי) here forms an idiom with שָׁנָה בְּשָׁנָה, "year to year," that means "yearly" (BDB, s.v. דַּי, 2 c β) or "every year." This same idiom also occurs in Zech 14:16; 2 Chr 24:5. מִדֵּי is used in idioms for "month to month" and "Sabbath to Sabbath" in Is 66:23. The three words here are used in the order שָׁנָה בְּשָׁנָה מִדֵּי in 1 Sam 1:7; see the second and third textual notes there.

וְשָׁפַט אֶת־יִשְׂרָאֵל אֵת כָּל־הַמְּקוֹמוֹת הָאֵלֶּה׃—Here the verb וְשָׁפַט, literally "and he judged" (see the third textual note on 7:6), takes two definite direct objects, each marked by אֵת. The first is "Israel." The second is literally "all these places." Most often the object of "to judge" is people, although occasionally its object can be a place, e.g., a country (Ezek 7:3; 35:11) or the earth (Ps 82:8). Here one might expect בְּכֹל, "in all" these places; the LXX reads ἐν πᾶσι τοῖς ἡγιασμένοις τούτοις, "in all these holy places." It is tempting to posit an error in the MT, but the alternative would be to follow the LXX, which appears to be an interpretive rendering and not directly representative of its *Vorlage*. The English translation "in all these places" suitably conveys the thought of Samuel judging the people in these places even if "all these places" is the grammatical direct object in the Hebrew.

7:17 וּתְשֻׁבָתוֹ—This is the only place where the noun תְּשׁוּבָה, "a return" (derived from the verb שׁוּב), refers to "a return route" or "way home."

---

5   McCarter, *I Samuel*, 142.

6   Klein, *1 Samuel*, 64.

Commentary

1068–1049 BC

Israel Repents at Samuel's Urging: The Convocation at Mizpah (7:2–6)

When the author picks up his narrative after 7:1, twenty years have passed and Israel finally is moved to repentance. While it is not completely clear what Israel's lamenting for Yahweh involved, it clearly displayed a contrite attitude and was the precursor to the people's repentance (defined as contrition and faith; see the second textual note on 7:2). Samuel, in reaction to what he perceived as a return to Yahweh, counseled the extirpation of foreign gods (7:3). Twice Samuel mentioned Israel's "heart." The first uses the phrase "with all your heart" and immediately draws to mind Moses' words in Deuteronomy: after the great *Shema'* ("hear, O Israel, Yahweh our God, Yahweh is one," Deut 6:4), he exhorts the redeemed people to "love Yahweh your God with all your heart" (Deut 6:5). This monotheistic emphasis is also found here as Israel abandons all other gods (cf. the First Commandment, Ex 20:3; Deut 5:7).

When Samuel surmised that Israel had dedicated its heart to Yahweh alone, he summoned the Israelites to Mizpah (1 Sam 7:5). While there is some doubt about the location of Mizpah, the most likely place is modern Tel en-Nasbeh, about eight miles (thirteen kilometers) northwest of Jerusalem.[7] There are four reasons for this identification. First, Mizpah means "watchtower," and Tel en-Nasbeh is situated on the top of a prominent hill that provides a commanding view of the surrounding territory. Second, archaeological investigations have demonstrated that the site was occupied during Iron Age I, at the time of Samuel. Third, Judges 20–21 implies that Mizpah was situated on the road from Jerusalem to Shechem, as is Tel en-Nasbeh. Fourth, jug handles marked למלך, "belonging to the king," have been found there, marking this site as a prominent city during the later monarchy (see 1 Ki 15:22 ‖ 2 Chr 16:6). Mizpah is mentioned seven times in this narrative (1 Sam 7:5, 6 [twice], 7, 11, 12, 16) and only one more time in the entire book of Samuel (1 Sam 10:17). This is probably to highlight the importance of the events that took place in and around Mizpah, including the setting up of the monument at nearby Ebenezer (7:12).

The water ritual at the convocation (7:6) is not explained by the author and has no close parallels elsewhere in Scripture. However, given the immediate mention of fasting, it would appear that drawing water and then pouring it out undrunk demonstrated Israel's repentance (7:6). The combination of the verb שָׁאַב, "to draw," with the noun מַיִם, "water," recurs in 1 Sam 9:11, where women are going out to draw water (cf. John 4). In 2 Sam 23:16 (‖ 1 Chr 11:18) three of David's mighty men break through the Philistines, draw water from the well of Bethlehem, and bring it to David, but he refuses to drink it, probably as a sign

---

[7] See Beck, "The Narrative-Geographical Shaping of 1 Samuel 7:5–13," 303–4.

of humility—that he was unworthy of the risk taken by these men in their act of bravery—and so David pours out the water to Yahweh. The verb שָׁפַךְ, "to pour out," appears in messianic promises that Yahweh will pour out his Spirit, as with water (Ezek 39:29 [cf. Ezek 36:25–27]; Joel 3:1–2 [ET 2:28–29]; Zech 12:10), verses that are interpreted as baptismal allusions (e.g., the citation of Joel 3:1–2 [ET 2:28–29] on Pentecost in Acts 2:17–18; compare Ezek 36:25–27 to Eph 5:26).[8]

The admission of the Israelites that they had "sinned against Yahweh" (1 Sam 7:6) does not explain the exact nature of their sin. It certainly included idolatry (7:3–4), but was there more than that? The author's comment that "Samuel judged the Israelites at Mizpah" (7:6) may imply that they had sinned by not heeding Samuel's prophecies some twenty years earlier (see the commentary on 4:1).

God Defeats the Philistines (7:7–14)

The arrival of the Philistines at Mizpah is not explained other than by saying that they had heard of Israel's gathering there (7:7). Was this an opportunistic aggression? Or was it a preemptive strike in that the Philistines may have suspected that Israel was mustering for war? The author leaves us in the dark on this, perhaps on purpose. Without any stated rationale, the Philistine approach appears all the more menacing.

Israel was unprepared for battle, and in their fear the Israelites begged Samuel to pray for them (7:8). There is clearly a contrast between this battle at Ebenezer and the previous one (1 Samuel 4). Earlier the Philistines heard Israel, and they were afraid (4:6–7). Now Israel is fearful of the Philistines.[9] The contrast is also in Israel's attitude. Previously the Israelites ignored God's Word through Samuel and sought to manipulate God into fighting for them by carrying his ark into battle. Now they implore the prophet to pray for them and patiently watch as Samuel prepares a sacrifice and calls on Yahweh, who answers (7:8–9).

The sacrifice is a young lamb who was still nursing on its mother's milk (7:9). A very young animal could be sacrificed as long as it was at least eight days old (Ex 22:29 [ET 22:30]; Lev 22:27). The reason for Samuel's choice of such an immature animal is not given.[10]

Yahweh's answer to Samuel (1 Sam 7:9) appears to come in the form of thunder, which panics and routs the Philistines (7:10). In the book of Samuel

---

[8] See also the promise in Is 44:3 (with the verb יָצַק):

For I will pout out water on thirsty ground,
streams of water on the dry land;
  I will pout out my Spirit on your descendants
  and my blessing on your offspring.

[9] The Hebrew verb form in 7:7 is identical to that in 4:7. See the first textual note on 4:7.

[10] The noun טְלֵה, "lamb," in 7:9 appears elsewhere in the OT only in Is 40:11; 65:25 and so is not part of the sacrificial rites prescribed in the Torah.

thunder is most often associated with God's warfare against his enemies and the enemies of his people. Hannah mentioned God's thunder against those who oppose him (1 Sam 2:10), and David later said that God thundered against those who attacked him (2 Sam 22:14). Ironically, Israel will later find itself in the position of opposing God when the people insist on a king and God thunders against them (1 Sam 12:17–18).

The author does not credit Israel with the victory over the Philistines.[11] It was Yahweh who thundered and threw the Philistines into a panic, and so they were defeated (7:10). Only then did Israel pursue the fleeing Philistine army to a point below Beth-car (7:11). That place where the pursuit ended is probably Ebenezer, "the rock of the helper," where Samuel erected a monument to God's victory. What is not clear is what Samuel means by "*thus far* Yahweh has helped us" (7:12). Does he mean thus far in time? Or is he referring to this place far away from Mizpah? The context favors the latter, but the ambiguity of Samuel's words leaves open for the reader the possibility that God's help may or may not follow Israel any farther in time. It propels the reader forward to see whether and how God will continue to help Israel.

We are subsequently told of the subduing of Philistine power during Samuel's lifetime (7:13). The Philistines did not enter Israelite territory again as long as he was alive. Indeed, Saul and his son Jonathan would go on the offensive and attack the Philistines (13:1–14:48). The Philistines would advance on the border of Judah, but David would kill Goliath there, and the Philistines would be defeated (17:1–58). It would not be until after Samuel's death (25:1) that the Philistines would advance into Israel's territory and bring about the final defeat of Saul and his army (1 Samuel 28 and 31).

As a result of the victory at Mizpah, the Israelites were able to reclaim land between the Philistine cities of Ekron and Gath on Israel's western frontier (7:14). We are also told that there was peace on Israel's eastern border with the Ammonites. This comment recalls that Philistine aggression into Israel from the west began at the same time that the Ammonites advanced on Israel from the east (Judg 10:7–9).

Samuel as Judge (7:15–17)

Samuel's time as judge[12] is summarized quickly in only three verses. If Josephus' information is correct, these verses cover a dozen years.[13] Samuel's judging took place in the central part of Israel not very far from his home in Ramah. All three locations on his circuit were important places in Israel's history. The Israelites had made their first camp at Gilgal when they entered the

---

[11] Israel is not the subject of any verb in 7:10. Yahweh is the subject of the two active verbs in 7:10b, "thundered" and "threw into a panic." The victory over the Philistines is stated in the passive: "they were defeated."

[12] For his role in this capacity, see the third textual note on 7:6.

[13] Josephus, *Antiquities*, 6.294.

promised land (Josh 4:19–20). God had appeared to Jacob in his dream at Bethel (Genesis 28). And God gave Israel victory over the Philistines at Mizpah (1 Sam 7:10–11). We are also told that Samuel judged Israel at Ramah, where he erected an altar to Yahweh (1 Sam 7:17).

Figure 13

Places Where Samuel Judged Israel

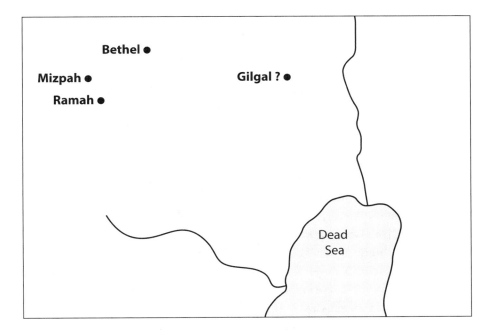

Israel Demands That
Samuel Appoint a King

Translation

8 ¹When Samuel became old, he appointed his sons as judges for Israel. ²The name of his firstborn son was Joel, and the name of his second was Abijah. They were judges in Beersheba. ³His sons did not walk in his ways. They sought dishonest income: they took bribes and perverted justice.

⁴All the elders of Israel gathered together and came to Samuel at Ramah. ⁵They said to him, "You are old, and your sons do not walk in your ways. So appoint a king for us to judge us like all the nations." ⁶Samuel was displeased when they said, "Give us a king to judge us." So Samuel prayed to Yahweh.

⁷Yahweh said to Samuel, "Listen to the people, to all that they are saying to you, because they have not rejected you. Rather, they have rejected me from reigning over them. ⁸[It is] like all the acts they have done from the day I brought them up from Egypt until today: they abandoned me and served other gods. So they are also doing [this] to you. ⁹Now listen to them. Yet be sure to warn them and tell them the rights of the king who will reign over them."

¹⁰Samuel said all Yahweh's words to the people who were requesting a king from him. ¹¹He said, "These are the rights of the king who will reign over you:

"He will take your sons and appoint them for his use in his chariots and among his horsemen, and they will run in front of his chariots. ¹²[It will be his right] to appoint [them] for his use as officers in charge of one thousand men and officers in charge of fifty men, and to [make them] plow his field, reap his harvest, and make his weapons and his chariot equipment.

¹³"He will take your daughters to serve as perfumers, cooks, and bakers.

¹⁴"He will take the best of your fields, your vineyards, and your olive orchards and give them to his officials.

¹⁵"He will take a tenth of your grain and your vineyards and give them to his eunuchs and officials.

¹⁶"He will take the best of your male slaves, your female slaves, your cattle, and your donkeys and make them do his work.

¹⁷"He will take a tenth of your flock.

Then you will become his slaves.

¹⁸"You will cry out at that time because of your king whom you chose for yourselves. But Yahweh will not answer you at that time."

¹⁹However, the people refused to listen to Samuel. They said, "No! Instead, a king will be over us! ²⁰Then we ourselves also will be like all the nations: our king

will judge us and go out in front of us and fight our battles." ²¹Samuel heard all the words of the people and told them to Yahweh.

²²Yahweh said to Samuel, "Listen to them. Appoint a king to reign over them." So Samuel said to the people of Israel, "Each one of you go to his city."

Textual Notes

8:1 כַּאֲשֶׁר—This combination, כְּ + אֲשֶׁר, has a temporal meaning: "when" (*IBH*, § 28 C). It recurs in 8:6.

וַיָּשֶׂם אֶת־בָּנָיו שֹׁפְטִים—In this double accusative construction, the verb שִׂים, "set, appoint," takes the persons appointed (בָּנָיו) as its first direct object, and the second direct object (שֹׁפְטִים) indicates the rank or office into which they are appointed (see *IBH*, § 18 C). The participle of שָׁפַט, "to judge," is often used as a substantive, "a judge." For the duties of this office in administering Law and Gospel, see the third textual note on 7:6. In 8:5–6 a "king" would use his royal office לְשָׁפְטֵנוּ, "to judge us" (the Qal [G] infinitive construct with the preposition לְ and a first common plural suffix).

8:3 וַיִּטּוּ אַחֲרֵי הַבָּצַע—In the Qal (G), נָטָה (here the preterite [imperfect with *waw* consecutive] third masculine plural) frequently is used with a noun for "arm" or "hand" to mean "stretch out the hand, reach out." That is the sense here, even without such a noun. The segholate noun בֶּצַע (in pause בָּצַע) refers to "gain made by violence, unjust gain" (BDB) or "dishonest income."

וַיַּטּוּ מִשְׁפָּט:—The *patach* under the preformative (-ֽיַ-) indicates that this is the Hiphil (H) of נָטָה (preterite [imperfect with *waw* consecutive] third masculine plural), versus the Qal (G) with *hireq*, וַיִּטּוּ, earlier in the verse (see the preceding textual note). The Hiphil has a causative meaning, "to turn [something] aside, lead astray," and is often used with מִשְׁפָּט to refer to the "*perverting* or *wresting* of justice" (BDB, Hiphil, 3 g).

8:4 וַיִּתְקַבְּצוּ—The Hithpael (HtD) of קָבַץ means "gather together" in an intransitive sense, as in 7:7. See the first textual note on 7:6.

כֹּל זִקְנֵי יִשְׂרָאֵל—Instead of the MT's "all the elders of Israel," the LXX reads ἄνδρες Ισραηλ, "(the) men of Israel" (cf. 8:22).

8:5 הִנֵּה ... עַתָּה—Literally this means "behold ... now." In Biblical Hebrew initial information is often prefaced with הִנֵּה, and the subsequent demand, request, advice, or conclusion based on that information is prefaced with עַתָּה.[1]

שִׂימָה—This is the alternate form with paragogic ה of the Qal (G) masculine singular imperative of שִׂים, "set, place, appoint" (Joüon, § 48 d). The regular form of the imperative would be שִׂים, as in 9:23, 24.

8:6 וַיֵּרַע הַדָּבָר בְּעֵינֵי שְׁמוּאֵל—Literally "the word/matter was evil in the eyes of Samuel" (see *HALOT*, s.v. רעע I, Qal, 2).

8:7 שְׁמַע בְּקוֹל הָעָם—The idiom "listen" (שָׁמַע) "to" (בְּ) a "voice" (קוֹל) means to accede to a request or to obey, as again in 8:9, 19, 22. It is common in Deuteronomy, meaning to obey God's Word in faith (e.g., Deut 4:30; 13:19 [ET 13:18]; 30:2, 8, 10, 20).

---

[1] E.g., Num 22:11, 38; Judg 16:10; 1 Sam 9:6, 12; 2 Sam 16:11; 2 Chr 25:19.

מִמְּלֹךְ—This is translated as "from reigning." It is the Qal (G) infinitive construct of מָלַךְ, "to rule, reign (as king)," with the preposition מִן, which has a negative force when prefixed to the infinitive (BDB, s.v. מִן, 7 b (*a*)), i.e., the Israelites oppose God's reign over them. Although not reflected in English translations, the verb מָלַךְ, "to rule, reign (as king)," is cognate to the noun מֶלֶךְ, "a king." The verb recurs in the Qal in 8:9, 11, and in the Hiphil (perfect with *waw* consecutive), וְהִמְלַכְתָּ, literally "and you shall make someone king," in 8:22. The noun appears in 8:5, 6, 9, 10, 11, 18, 19, 20, 22. Before this chapter, the only prior instance of מֶלֶךְ, "king," was in 2:10, in reference to Yahweh's Messiah or Christ, so the request for a "king" here is a repudiation of the "king" there. See Ps 2:2, 6.

8:8 הַמַּעֲשִׂים אֲשֶׁר־עָשׂוּ—This is a cognate accusative construction, literally "the deeds which they did." The LXX reads τὰ ποιήματα ἃ ἐποίησάν μοι, "the deeds which they did *to me*."

8:9 כִּי־הָעֵד תָּעִיד בָּהֶם—The Hiphil (H) of עוּד, "testify, bear witness" (here the infinitive absolute הָעֵד and the imperfect תָּעִיד), can have the nuance "to warn," particularly when the person(s) warned are introduced with the preposition בְּ in an adversative sense ("against," BDB, s.v. בְּ, II 4 a).

מִשְׁפַּט הַמֶּלֶךְ—This is translated as "the rights of the king." The noun מִשְׁפָּט can denote a legal claim to something (*HALOT*, s.v. מִשְׁפָּט, 3 a). This construct phrase recurs in 8:11.

8:11 וְרָצוּ—"And they will run." This is the Qal (G) perfect of רוּץ with *waw* consecutive. 4QSam[a] reads ורצי[ם], the Qal plural participle (וְרָצִים), "and runners."

8:12 שָׂרֵי אֲלָפִים וְשָׂרֵי חֲמִשִּׁים—Literally this means "officers of thousands and officers of fifties." Standard military organization consisted of smaller units of fifty or a hundred men collected into larger units of a thousand men.[2]

וְלַחֲרֹשׁ חֲרִישׁוֹ—Literally this means "to plow his plowing." This is the first of two adjacent cognate accusative constructions. Each construction has a Qal (G) infinitive construct prefixed with the conjunction *waw* and the preposition לְ, followed by a cognate noun with a third masculine singular suffix, and the nouns are of the same formation (קְטִיל). The Qal of חָרַשׁ can mean "to plow," and of the three instances of the noun חָרִישׁ in the OT, twice it refers to the act of "plowing."

וְלִקְצֹר קְצִירוֹ—This second cognate accusative construction literally means "to harvest his harvest." The LXX reads θερίζειν θερισμὸν αὐτοῦ καὶ τρυγᾶν τρυγητὸν αὐτοῦ, "to reap his harvest and to pick his grapes."

כְּלֵי־מִלְחַמְתּוֹ—This construct phrase, literally "the implements of his war," means "his weapons."

8:13 לְרַקָּחוֹת וּלְטַבָּחוֹת וּלְאֹפוֹת:—The feminine noun רַקָּחָה refers to a female maker of ointment or perfume and is derived from the verb רָקַח, "to mix (oil, perfume)." It appears in the OT only here. So, too, does the feminine noun טַבָּחָה, "a (female) cook," derived from the verb טָבַח, "to butcher." The masculine equivalent, טַבָּח, "a (male) butcher, cook," appears in 9:23, 24. אֹפוֹת is the feminine plural Qal (G) participle of

---

[2]   Ex 18:21, 25; Deut 1:15; 1 Sam 17:18; 18:13; 22:7; 2 Sam 18:1; 2 Ki 1:9, 11, 13.

אָפָה, "to bake." The verb's meaning is illustrated by its use in the description of a woman baking in 1 Sam 28:24. In Genesis 40 its masculine participle refers to Pharaoh's chief baker.

8:14 הַטּוֹבִים—An adjective (טוֹב, "good") with the definite article is one way to express a superlative (Joüon, § 141 j; cf. *IBH*, § 23), thus "best." In this verse the adjective modifies all of the preceding nouns. The identical form of the adjective recurs in 8:16 (see the first textual note on that verse).

לַעֲבָדָיו:—Literally this means "to his servants." In this context the king's servants are his officials. The identically inflected word recurs at the end of 8:15.

8:15 יַעְשֹׂר—This is the Qal (G) imperfect of עָשַׂר, a denominative verb based on the number עֶשֶׂר, "ten." Its Qal means "to take one-tenth," that is, to require a tithe, and recurs in 8:17 (the only other OT instance is in 1 Ki 22:49 [ET 22:48]). Its Piel (D) has the opposite meaning, "to give one-tenth, to tithe" (e.g., Deut 14:22; 26:12).

8:16 בַּחוּרֵיכֶם—The MT reads "your young men." The LXX reads τὰ βουκόλια ὑμῶν, "your cattle," which presupposes the Hebrew בְּקַרְכֶם (the singular בָּקָר is a collective) in place of בַּחוּרֵיכֶם. "Young men" would fit in 8:11–13, along with the discussion of "sons" and "daughters," but it seems contextually inappropriate here after "slaves." "Cattle" is congruent with the other animals 8:16b–17a. Therefore בַּחוּרֵיכֶם probably is due to an accidental homophonic substitution of ח for an original ק.

הַטּוֹבִים—In 8:14 this plural adjective functioned as a superlative, "best," modifying all three of the preceding suffixed nouns ("your fields, your vineyards, and your olive orchards"). Here in 8:16 it likewise functions as a superlative, "best," and three suffixed nouns precede it ("your male slaves, your female slaves, your cattle"), but a fourth suffixed noun then follows it ("your donkeys"). Some English translations consider הַטּוֹבִים to modify only the immediately preceding noun, which is בַּחוּרֵיכֶם in the MT, hence "your best young men" (HCSB, NASB; cf. ESV). That interpretation of the syntax makes sense if the suffixed noun "your young men" deserves particular emphasis as the most important of the four nouns (young men are more valuable than slaves and donkeys). Since, however, this commentary follows the LXX's "your cattle" (see the preceding textual note), it makes more sense to consider the superlative adjective "best" to modify all four of the suffixed nouns, as in the translation above.

וְעָשָׂה לִמְלַאכְתּוֹ:—Literally "and he will make [use them] for his work."

8:18 בַּיּוֹם הַהוּא ... בַּיּוֹם הַהוּא:—Literally "on that day," both times this is rendered as "at that time." For the second occurrence the LXX reads ἐν ταῖς ἡμέραις ἐκείναις, ὅτι ὑμεῖς ἐξελέξασθε ἑαυτοῖς βασιλέα, "in those days because you yourselves chose for yourselves a king." This is also the apparent reading of 4QSamᵃ, though it is fragmentary and the end of the verse contains only the word ההמ, to be vocalized הָהֵם, "those."

8:20 וְהָיִינוּ גַם־אֲנַחְנוּ—Since the first common plural verb is inflected ("we will be"), the appending of גַם, "also," and the redundant pronoun אֲנַחְנוּ, "we ourselves," is a strongly emphatic expression of the Israelites' defiance.

8:21 וַיְדַבְּרֵם בְּאָזְנֵי יְהוָה:—Literally "and he spoke them in the ears of Yahweh."

8:22 וְהִמְלַכְתָּ לָהֶם מֶלֶךְ—This cognate accusative construction is literally "and you shall make king for them a king." The Qal of מָלַךְ means "to reign, rule (as king)." The

Hiphil (here) has the corresponding causative meaning, "to make (someone reign as) king." This meaning is fortified by the use of the cognate noun מֶלֶךְ, "king," as its direct object. Essentially the same construction recurs in 12:1; 15:11. See the Hiphil of מָלַךְ also in 1 Sam 11:15; 15:35; 2 Sam 2:9.

אִישׁ—Literally "a man," this noun is used distributively: "each one of you."

Commentary

1049 BC

1 Samuel 8–12 and the Establishment of the Israelite Monarchy

Since the rise of historical-critical approaches to the OT, many scholars have hypothesized that the account of the choosing of Israel's first king is a compilation from various sources.[3] This approach seeks to isolate these sources based on two criteria: First, it is supposed that there are two opposing views of the monarchy in 1 Samuel 8–12. According this criterion 1 Samuel 8, 1 Samuel 12, and the last part of 1 Samuel 10 are supposedly antimonarchical, whereas 1 Samuel 9 and the first part of 1 Samuel 10 are in favor of the monarchy. Second, there are purportedly three different accounts of Saul's accession to the throne of Israel: 9:1–10:16; 10:17–27; and 11:1–15.

There are several problems with this analysis, starting with the fact that there is no external evidence for it (no hard manuscript evidence for separate sources). It also misconstrues the internal evidence in the text itself. For instance, in 1 Samuel 8, Samuel is definitely against the establishment of a monarchy (8:6), but Yahweh is portrayed with an ambivalent attitude, stating that Israel had rejected him as king (8:7–8), but twice telling Samuel to grant Israel's request for a king (8:9, 22). Moreover, it is not the request for a king per se that is problematic in 1 Samuel 8 (cf. Deut 17:14–20), but a request for a king *so that Israel can be like the nations* (8:5, 20). This smacks of a rejection of Yahweh's covenant with Israel, since God's people were and are set apart as different; among the nations, they are to be God's treasured possession (Ex 19:5–6). As Eslinger notes:

> Even this superficial review of the narrative reveals serious deficiencies in the segmentation of the text according to pro- and anti-monarchic viewpoints. Only one character, Samuel, voices absolute opposition to the idea of a human king over Israel, and that is only an initial reaction (8.6, 11–18, 22). Once Yahweh explains the concept of a designate to Samuel (9.15–16), Samuel is all for Saul and continues to be critical only of the request for a king "like all the nations" on account of the motivation for such a request. Yahweh is willing to appoint a royal designate from the beginning, and is critical only of the request that would replace him with a king "like all the nations" (8.9, 22; 9.15–17; 12.17). What the reader hears even in the voices of these *characters*

---

[3] See also "Critical Theories of Samuel's Composition" in "Authorship, Composition, and Date" in the introduction.

cannot be described as anti-monarchism. Rather, what Yahweh and Samuel are critical of is the anti-covenantal sentiment they hear in Israel's request.[4]

Tsevat and McCarthy have observed that the supposed antimonarchical statements come in the context of assemblies, whereas the narration of action appears to be more favorably disposed to the idea of a king.[5] This would argue that 1 Samuel 8–12 is a unified narration that records dissenting voices that existed among a populace that generally favored the establishment of the monarchy. Long offers the chart shown here as figure 14. Promonarchical sections are marked with a plus sign, and antimonarchical sections are marked with a minus sign.

Figure 14

Promonarchical and Antimonarchical Sections in 1 Samuel 8–12

– 8:4–22	Assembly	Elders demand a king
+ 9:1–10:16	Action	Secret anointing of Saul
– 10:17–27	Assembly	Lot casting and public presentation of Saul
+ 11:1–13	Action	Saul's first victory in battle
– 11:14–12:25	Assembly	Renewal of kingship and Samuel's warning

Provan, Long, and Longman, *A Biblical History of Israel*, 209.

Eslinger goes on to note that there are two promonarchic stances in the text: one that favors a king "like all the nations" (8:5, 20) in contrast to the leadership of Samuel and his sons and one that favors a monarchy that is subordinated to Yahweh's theocratic reign.[6] He notes:

> When we pay attention to the question of who says what, we can easily see the insensitivity of the division of the narrative into pro-monarchic and anti-monarchic scenes. In every scene both pro- and anti-monarchic attitudes are expressed or displayed by a variety of characters. Shifts in attitude occur, with Samuel moving from adamant anti-monarchism to one brand of pro-monarchism. Israel undergoes a transition from the pro-monarchism of the request, to a mixed reaction to the designate, Saul, to a final position in favour of the designated monarchy allowed by Yahweh. The historical-critical net was woven to catch big fish, the pro- and anti-monarchic authors (or sources, traditions, tradents and redactors). It allows the smaller fry, the characters and their separate voices to slip through, untouched. What, at first glance, looked like a few big fish, however, turned out to be schools of individual, smaller fish.[7]

---

[4] Eslinger, "Viewpoints and Point of View in 1 Samuel 8–12," 66.

[5] Tsevat, "The Biblical Account of the Foundation of the Monarchy in Israel," 83–84; McCarthy, "The Inauguration of Monarchy in Israel," 403.

[6] Eslinger, "Viewpoints and Point of View in 1 Samuel 8–12," 66–67.

[7] Eslinger, "Viewpoints and Point of View in 1 Samuel 8–12," 67.

Eslinger also notes that the narrator "appears to maintain a steadfast neutrality towards the subject of monarchy."[8]

With respect to the hypothesis of three accession accounts for Saul, Long has argued that, given the shape of the narrative, the reader ought to expect a three-stage procession: a designation of a candidate as king, a demonstration by the designee that he is fit for the office, and a confirmation of him in office by God and Israel.[9] According to Halpern, this pattern for king-making is common in the ancient Near East.[10] Long argues that Saul, by ignoring Samuel's intimation that he ought to attack the Philistines (10:7–8) and instead returning home in virtual silence about being designated king (10:16), necessitated another designation scene (10:17–27) and two more demonstrations (11:1–13; 13:1–3). Only then could his confirmation take place (13:4–15).[11] Whether or not one accepts Long's persuasive analysis, he succeeds in demonstrating that 1 Samuel 8–12 ought to be regarded as a coherent narrative and not clumsily aggregated sources that betray three separate and conflicting accounts of Saul's accession to the throne.

Some more recent treatments of the establishment of the monarchy seek to overcome the weaknesses of traditional source criticism by employing a "new literary criticism." While not necessarily denying that there may originally have been a number of sources upon which the author or editor drew to compose 1 Samuel 8–12, this approach seeks a single overarching authorial or editorial point of view that can be perceived when the narrative is treated as a coherent whole. Such an approach has the potential to be a major corrective for older source-critical analysis. Unfortunately, many of the practitioners of this method attempt to read the narratives concerning Saul and Israel without recognizing the overt theological emphases in the text. Instead, they attempt to get behind what they perceive to be the theological bias of the author of the book of Samuel. They presume that this bias is unhelpful for understanding Saul's reign, and so they search for a more authentic message under the narrative. Many of these treatments of Saul's reign, and especially of 1 Samuel 8–12, present Saul's reign as doomed to failure from the outset: Saul is a tragic figure, and Yahweh is an unpredictable God who unfairly condemns Saul for minor transgressions of vague divine instructions and irrational demands.[12] In essence such approaches maintain that Yahweh is no longer the righteous and

---

[8] Eslinger, "Viewpoints and Point of View in 1 Samuel 8–12," 68.

[9] Long, *The Reign and Rejection of King Saul: A Case for Literary and Theological Coherence*, 173–94. Long's work is based on the earlier work of Halpern, *The Constitution of the Monarchy in Israel*, and Edelman, "Saul's Rescue of Jabesh Gilead."

[10] Halpern, *The Constitution of the Monarchy in Israel*, 138–45.

[11] See Long's chart and the discussion in Provan, Long, and Longman, *A Biblical History of Israel*, 210–14. See also "Samuel Anoints Saul (9:26–10:8)" in the commentary on 9:26–10:16, where Long's chart is reproduced as figure 16.

[12] See, for example, Eslinger, *Kingship of God in Crisis*, 307; Exum, *Tragedy and Biblical Narrative*, 16–42; Gunn, *The Fate of King Saul*, 131; Nicholson, *Three Faces of Saul*, 36–76.

gracious God of Israel as portrayed throughout the book of Samuel (and the rest of Scripture); instead he is a God shaped by the interpreter's expectations and deformed by the reader's own befuddlement over difficult passages. Instead of acknowledging that a contributing factor is the scholar's own lack of understanding and theological deficiencies (due in part to the fallen, sinful nature of any human reader), the interpreter's solution is to project the perceived difficulties and ambiguities in the text onto God.

Rather than attempt to get behind the text to discern its proposed original sources (which relies on speculation as evidence) or to counter the author's theological perspective using methods that stem from the interpreter's own religious presuppositions, a more useful approach is to understand the text as a coherent whole. This commentary proceeds in this manner with the additional recognition that the inspired author's theological point of view is aligned with, and the result of, God's intention in the book of Samuel. It depicts not only his justice but even more his love and mercy as he acts to save his fallen creatures, working with sinful Israel and through its flawed leaders, especially Samuel, Saul, and David. In fact, this commentary also seeks to read the rest of the book this way, since the book itself intends readers to approach it from this perspective.[13]

Samuel's Dishonest Sons (8:1–3)

The chapter opens with an ominous note, an innovation for Israel from the now-elderly Samuel (cf. 1 Sam 12:2): he appointed his sons to be judges (8:1). Heretofore, judgeship was conferred by God (cf. Judg 2:16; 3:10). Samuel was the only judge who sought to make the office hereditary. Earlier Gideon refused such an arrangement when Israel offered it to him (Judg 8:22–23). In contrast, Samuel unilaterally made his sons judges.

While we are told the names of Samuel's two sons (1 Sam 8:2; 1 Chr 6:13 [ET 6:28]), Joel is the more prominent one. He is later mentioned as the father of the singer Heman (1 Chr 6:18 [ET 6:33]; 15:16–19). We are informed that they both judged Israel in Beersheba, the southernmost city.

The text does not say why Samuel appointed his sons. Was it because old age made it difficult for him to continue to serve in the office as he once had? Josephus, who claimed that one of Samuel's sons was a judge in Bethel and the other in Beersheba, thought this was the case.[14] But if this was so, why did he place his sons so far away from most of Israel's population? Was it an attempt at establishing a dynastic succession? Was it simply a father's attempt to favor his sons?

Whatever motivated Samuel to place his sons in charge of judging Israel, he was clearly blind to their corruption (8:3). The author tells us that they sought dishonest income, accepted bribes, and perverted justice. The first transgression

---

[13] See "Christ in Samuel," "Law and Gospel in Samuel," and "Other Theological Themes in Samuel" in the introduction.

[14] Josephus, *Antiquities*, 6.32.

would disqualify a person from leadership (Ex 18:21; Prov 28:16), for the righteous man refuses "dishonest income" (Is 33:15).[15] The combination of taking a bribe and perverting justice is repeatedly condemned in the OT.[16] The mention of "justice" introduces a key term for this chapter: justice/rights (מִשְׁפָּט, 8:3, 9, 11). Thus, while Samuel's leadership was clearly superior to that of Eli, he shared one weakness with the former high priest: he failed to properly supervise his sons (for Eli, see 2:12–17, 22–29).

Israel's Request for a King (8:4–9)

Apparently, the situation was so alarming that Israel's elders felt a special trip to Ramah to confront Samuel was necessary (8:4). Their words repeat what the narrator has already stated, reinforcing for the reader the reasons for their request: Samuel is old, and his sons are corrupt (8:5). When Samuel died, they did not want to be ruled by his crooked sons.

The presence of the elders demonstrated that all Israel recognized Samuel as their judge and looked to him for the authority to institute the monarchy they were proposing. Their request was significant: "appoint a king for us *to judge us* like all the nations" (8:5). Samuel was displeased that they said, "Give us a king *to judge us*" (8:6). Samuel was offended by the request because they sought to replace him—*he* judged Israel (7:6, 15).

Commentators often make this valid point about Israel's request for a king "like all the nations" (8:5, 20): a king "like all the nations" was intended to highlight that the request was for a monarchy to replace the system of judges.[17] Other passages disparage the idea of Israel being like all the nations.[18] However, this text never depicts Samuel or Yahweh as concerned about this portion of the request.[19] In fact, Israel had already made itself "like all the nations" in a much more serious way—the Israelites worshiped the gods of the nations (7:3; 8:8). God had already anticipated that the day would come for such a request, and through Moses he had given rules for a king in the event that Israel asked for a monarch "like all the nations" (Deut 17:14–20). These regulations were designed to keep Israel and its ruler under the reign of God.

---

[15] The noun in 1 Sam 8:3, בֶּצַע, "dishonest income," appears also in Ex 18:21; Is 33:15; Prov 28:16. It is condemned along with other serious crimes such as bloodshed. See, e.g., Is 57:17; Jer 8:10; 22:17; Ezek 22:13, 27; Hab 2:9; Prov 1:19; 15:27.

[16] Ex 23:2–8; Deut 16:19; Prov 17:23; Amos 5:7–12; on bribes alone, see Eccl 7:7; Is 1:23; 5:23; on perverted justice alone, see Deut 24:17.

[17] Brueggemann, *First and Second Samuel*, 62; Klein, *1 Samuel*, 75; McCarter, *I Samuel*, 160–61; Tsumura, *The First Book of Samuel*, 249.

[18] For example, in Deut 8:20 Israel is admonished not to be like the nations formerly in Canaan whom Yahweh extirpated so Israel could take possession of the land. In Ezek 20:32 Israel desires to be "like the nations" by worshiping gods of stone and wood (cf. 2 Ki 17:15).

[19] Although this commentary agrees with Eslinger's analysis quoted above, the point here is that the text itself never depicts either Samuel or Yahweh as objecting to the phrase "like all the nations."

Yahweh understood precisely why Samuel was displeased with the elder's demand: he felt and was rejected (1 Sam 8:7). But Samuel needed to be corrected—it was actually God whom the Israelites rejected as king. They had started doing this centuries earlier by serving other gods already at the time of the exodus (8:8), when God first redeemed them to be his covenant people (see, e.g., their worship of the golden calf in Exodus 32 and Baal of Peor in Numbers 25). It was no surprise, therefore, that they had also rejected Yahweh's servant Samuel. So God directed Samuel to warn the people and tell them the rights of a king (8:9).

Samuel Warns Israel about Kings (8:10–22)

The prophet-judge relayed the words of Yahweh to the people who had requested the king (8:10). There is a play on words here that anticipates the fulfilling of the people's demand. They were "requesting" (שָׁאַל, sha'al, 8:10) a king, and the king they are given is Saul (שָׁאוּל, sha'ul, e.g., 9:2), whose name means "requested."[20]

Samuel's warning covers seven categories: sons (8:11b–12), daughters (8:13), farmland (8:14), taxation of the products of the land (8:15), living property—slaves and livestock (8:16), taxation of the product of livestock (8:17a), and the people themselves (8:17b). In each of the first six categories the direct object of the verbs "he will take" (יִקַּח, 8:11, 13, 14, 16) or "he will take a tenth" (יַעְשֹׂר, 8:15, 17) are fronted in the Hebrew sentence to emphasize them. When the climactic seventh category arrives, the subject is fronted—"*you* will become his slaves" (8:17). The effect is stunning. The people may be willing to tolerate the king's use of their children and property, but will they be willing to have a king if they are enslaved?

Samuel efficiently ticks off what will happen to Israel. Sons will be pressed into service for the king's royal glory,[21] for his army, for supplying his food, and for manufacturing his weapons, both in peacetime and in war. Daughters, too, will be made to provide for the king's needs. The king will also confiscate what he needs both for his servants and in taxes.

Eunuchs are mentioned in 8:15 (לְסָרִיסָיו). The service of eunuchs to Israel's kings are occasionally mentioned in Scripture.[22] It is often argued that the term

---

[20] The form in 8:10 is הַשֹּׁאֲלִים, the Qal (G) active participle of שָׁאַל, "to ask," masculine plural, with the definite article. In form the name שָׁאוּל, "Saul," is the Qal passive (Gp) participle masculine singular of the same verb. Saul will be introduced in 1 Samuel 9. For wordplays between שָׁאַל, "to ask," and Saul's name, see also the first textual note on 1:28; the first textual note on 10:22; the commentary on 12:13; the textual note on 14:37; and the second textual note on 20:6 (which also discusses שָׁאוּל נִשְׁאַל נִשְׁאַל in 20:28).

[21] The chariots and horsemen here, though military, are primarily introduced to emphasize the way kings aggrandize themselves, as can be seen by the mention of runners in front of the chariots (cf. 2 Sam 15:1; 1 Ki 1:5).

[22] 1 Ki 22:9; 2 Ki 8:6; 9:32; 23:11; 24:12, 15; 25:19; Jer 29:2; 34:19; 38:7; 41:16; 52:25; 1 Chr 28:1; 2 Chr 18:8.

does not always denote a eunuch, but simply means "court official."[23] The rationale for this comes from the etymology of the word, which derives from the Akkadian *ša rēši*, "someone of the (king's) head." It is also argued that "such men would have been excluded from the congregation by Mosaic Law (Lev 22:24; Deut 23:2 [ET 23:1])."[24] However, there is no good reason to deny that these men were eunuchs. At times some are depicted as in charge of the queen or the king's harem, where eunuchs could be employed without fear of them being tempted to defile the king's wives (2 Ki 9:32; Esth 2:3). At least one of the eunuchs of Judah's kings was a foreigner (Jer 38:7). He should not have been eligible to own land within Israel permanently, since the land was to remain within the families to which it was originally allotted. It may be the case that this was the common practice—to employ foreign eunuchs. In fact, Is 56:3–4 implies that this was so: its Gospel promise is that foreigners and eunuchs would become equal servants of God in the church (see Acts 8:27–39). If this is the meaning of "eunuchs," Samuel is explaining the stark reality of living under a monarch: he will take your land—the land Yahweh pledged to the patriarchs Abraham, Isaac, and Jacob, which was to remain in Israelite possession as their divine inheritance—and give it to foreigners (1 Sam 8:15).

However, the most chilling action of kings would be that "you will become his slaves" (1 Sam 8:17). This is a reference to Israel's former slavery to another king—Egypt's pharaoh. When they were slaves in Egypt, the Israelites "cried out" to God (זָעַק, Ex 2:23), and he rescued them.[25] This time they will "cry out" (זָעַק) to Yahweh, but he will ignore their cry (1 Sam 8:18).

Despite the divine warning, the people stubbornly insist on a king (8:19–20). They emphasize the benefit of having someone to lead them into battle and do not react directly to the foreboding perils. The chapter ends with a brief report of the subsequent conversation between Samuel and God and Samuel's dismissal of the people (8:21–22). The dismissal was a tacit approval of Israel's request for a king, as depicted by God's permission that was repeated to Samuel (8:22; cf. 8:7–9).

---

[23] *TWOT*, § 1545.

[24] *TWOT*, § 1545.

[25] This same sequence appears in, e.g., Judg 3:9, 15; 6:6–14: the Israelites "cry out" (זָעַק) to Yahweh, and he saves them by means of his judges.

1 Samuel 9:1–31:13

The Reign of Saul

9:1–12:25	**Transition to a Monarchy**
9:1–25	Saul Meets the Prophet Samuel
9:26–10:16	Saul Is Anointed King
10:17–27a	Saul Is Publicly Made King
10:27b–11:15	Saul Saves Jabesh-gilead
12:1–25	Samuel's Warning about the Monarchy
13:1–15:35	**Saul's Military Accomplishments**
13:1–23	Saul's First Philistine Campaign, Part 1: His Preparation
14:1–23	Saul's First Philistine Campaign, Part 2: Jonathan Routs the Philistines
14:24–46	Saul's First Philistine Campaign, Part 3: Saul's Impetuous Vow
Excursus	*The Urim and Thummim*
14:47–52	Saul's Military Successes
15:1–35	The Amalekite Campaign: Saul Is Rejected as King
16:1–31:13	**Saul's Decline and David's Rise**
16:1–18:5	**David Becomes a Commander in Saul's Army**
16:1–13	David Is Anointed King and Receives God's Spirit
16:14–23	David Ministers to Saul with Music
17:1–58	David as Israel's Champion: The Victory over Goliath
18:1–5	David in Saul's Service and Jonathan's Love for David
18:6–26:25	**David in Saul's Disfavor**
18:6–16	Saul's Jealousy of David
18:17–30	David Becomes Saul's Son-in-Law
19:1–17	Saul Tries to Have David Killed
19:18–24	Saul Searches for David in the Pastures at Ramah
Excursus	*Luther on the Prophet Samuel*
20:1–21:1	Jonathan Warns David (ET 20:1–42)

21:2–10	David in Nob (ET 21:1–9)
21:11–16	David in Gath (ET 21:10–15)
22:1–5	David in Adullam and Moab
22:6–23	Saul Kills the Priests at Nob
23:1–13	David Rescues Keilah
23:14–24:1	David in Ziph and Maon (ET 23:14–29)
24:2–23	David Spares Saul's Life at En-gedi (ET 24:1–22)
25:1–44	David Marries Abigail
26:1–25	David Spares Saul's life at Ziph
27:1–31:13	**The Philistine Resurgence**
27:1–12	David in the Service of Achish of Gath
28:1–2	David Gains Achish's Trust
28:3–25	Saul's Second Philistine Campaign, Part 1: Saul and the Medium at Endor
29:1–11	Saul's Second Philistine Campaign, Part 2: The Philistines Dismiss David
30:1–31	David Rescues His Wives from the Amalekites
31:1–13	Saul Dies in Battle

Saul Meets the Prophet Samuel

Translation

9 ¹There was a man from Benjamin, and his name was Kish the son of Abiel, the son of Zeror, the son of Becorath, the son of Aphiah, a prominent Benjaminite man. ²He had a son, and his name was Saul, a handsome young man. None of the Israelites were more handsome than he. He was a head taller than everyone else. ³The female donkeys had wandered away for Kish, Saul's father. Kish said to Saul, his son, "Please take one of the servants and go search for the female donkeys."

⁴So they traveled through the hill country of Ephraim: They traveled through the region of Shalishah, but they did not find [them]. Then they traveled through the region of Shaalim, but they were not [there]. Next they traveled through the land of Benjamin, but they did not find [them]. ⁵When they came into the region of Zuph, Saul said to his servant who was with him, "Let's return [home]. Otherwise my father will quit [worrying about] the donkeys and will become worried about us."

⁶He said to him, "There is a man of God in this city. The man is highly respected: all that he says surely comes to pass. Now, let's go there. Perhaps he will tell us which way we should go."

⁷Saul said to his servant, "Suppose we go, what should we bring for the man, because the food from our sacks is gone, and there is no present to bring to the man of God? What do we have with us?"

⁸Again the servant answered Saul, "Look, I have a quarter shekel of silver with me. I'll give it to the man of God, and he'll tell us the way we should go."

(⁹Formerly in Israel this is what someone said when he went to seek God: "Let's go to the seer," because the [one called a] prophet today was formerly called a seer.)

¹⁰Saul said to his servant, "Your suggestion is good. Let's go." So they went to the city where the man of God was.

¹¹As they were going up the slope to the city, they found some young women going out to draw water. They said to them, "Is the seer in this [city]?"

¹²They answered them, "He is here, ahead of you. Hurry, now, because he came to the city today since there is a sacrifice today for the people at the high place. ¹³As you come into the city you might find him there before he goes up to the high place to eat. The people will not eat until he comes, because he will bless the sacrifice. After that those who have been invited will eat. So now, go up because—him—you can find him now!"

¹⁴They went up to the city. As they were coming into the city, there was Samuel going out to meet them in order to go up to the high place. (¹⁵Now Yahweh had revealed [this] to Samuel one day before Saul came: ¹⁶"At this time tomorrow I

will send you a man from the territory of Benjamin. Anoint him to be the designated ruler over the people of Israel. He will rescue my people from the domination of the Philistines, because I have seen my people, for their cry has come to me.") [17]When Samuel saw Saul, Yahweh answered him, "This is the man about whom I said to you, 'This man will restrain my people.'"

[18]Saul approached Samuel in the gate and said, "Please tell me, where is the house of the seer?"

[19]Samuel answered Saul, "I am the seer. Go up ahead of me to the high place. You will eat with me today. I will send you away in the morning, and I will tell you everything that is in your heart. [20]As for the female donkeys that wandered away from you three days ago, do not worry about them because they have been found. Whom does all Israel desire? Isn't it you and your father's entire house?"

[21]Saul answered, "Aren't I a Benjaminite, from the smallest of Israel's tribes, and isn't my clan the littlest of all the clans of the tribe of Benjamin? So why did you say something like this to me?"

[22]Samuel took Saul and his servant and brought them into the room and gave them a place at the head of those who had been invited. They were about thirty men. [23]Samuel said to the cook, "Bring the portion that I gave to you [and] of which I said to you, 'Keep it with you.'"

[24]The cook picked up the thigh and what was on it and set it in front of Saul. He said, "Here is what was left over; place it before you and eat, because it was kept for you for this event, as I said to the people I invited." So Saul ate with Samuel that day.

[25]They went down from the high place to the city. He spoke with Saul on the roof.

Textual Notes

9:1 בֶּן־אֲבִיאֵל—Literally this means "the son of Abiel." The Hebrew noun בֵּן, "son," can denote a male descendant in a later generation. Here it refers to Kish as Abiel's grandson (see the commentary on 14:50–51).

בֶּן־אִישׁ יְמִינִי—Literally "son of a man of a [Ben]jaminite," this must mean that Kish was a "Benjaminite man," as translated and as supported by the ancient versions. Apparently, in Hebrew the proper noun "Benjaminite" (בֶּן־יְמִינִי, as in 9:21) was sometimes shortened to "Jaminite" (יְמִינִי, also 1 Sam 9:4; 2 Sam 20:1; Esth 2:5).

גִּבּוֹר חָיִל:—This phrase often designates a skilled warrior,[1] but that does not seem to fit the context here. Occasionally it designates someone who is prominent in his community (1 Ki 11:28; Ruth 2:1). Thus, it is translated as "prominent" here.

9:2 בָּחוּר וָטוֹב—Literally "choice and good," this is translated as "a handsome young man." The adjective טוֹב is translated as "handsome" again in the next clause (see the next textual note). In form בָּחוּר is the Qal passive (Gp) participle of בָּחַר , "to choose,"

---

[1] Judg 11:1; 2 Ki 5:1; 1 Chr 12:29 (ET 12:28); 28:1; 2 Chr 13:3; 17:16–17; 25:6; 32:21.

thus "chosen," but it is frequently used as a noun to denote a young man of marriage-able age.[2]

טוֹב מִמֶּנּוּ—An adjective (טוֹב, "good") with the preposition מִן can form a compar-ative, thus "better than him" (see Joüon, § 141 g and also the next textual note). The construction can also express a superlative; see the second textual note on 9:21. Cf. the use of the article with this same adjective to form a superlative, הַטּוֹבִים, "the best," in the first textual note on 8:14 (also 8:16).

מִשִּׁכְמוֹ וָמַעְלָה גָּבֹהַּ מִכָּל־הָעָם:—Literally "from his shoulder and upward, he was higher than all of the people." The adjective גָּבֹהַּ, "high," with the preposition מִן forms the comparative "taller" (see Joüon, § 141 g).

9:3 וַתֹּאבַדְנָה הָאֲתֹנוֹת לְקִישׁ—Literally "the female donkeys went astray to Kish," this use of the preposition לְ is comparable to its use to denote possession, which could have been expressed with a construct phrase, i.e., אֲתֹנוֹת־קִישׁ, "Kish's female donkeys" (see Joüon, § 130 a). Here, however, לְ is in reference to the verb וַתֹּאבַדְנָה (Qal [G] preter-ite [imperfect with *waw* consecutive] third feminine plural of אָבַד, "perish; wander, stray"), thus "the female donkeys had wandered away for Kish," more like the English "had wandered away from Kish." See Joüon, § 130 g.

אַחַד מֵהַנְּעָרִים—This construct phrase is literally "one from the servants." The idea "one of the servants" could be expressed by the construct phrase אַחַד הַנְּעָרִים without the preposition מִן. The use of מִן might suggest that the reference is to one particular ser-vant among the others (GKC, § 117 d). Earlier in the book the author artfully employed נַעַר both for Samuel as a "boy" and for the "servant(s)" of Eli's wicked sons (see the commentary on 2:12–17 and the first textual note on 3:1). Rather than "boy" the noun נַעַר designates a "servant" here and again in 9:5, 7, 8, 10, 22, 27.[3]

וְקוּם לֵךְ בַּקֵּשׁ—These three imperatives (Qal [G] of קוּם, Qal [G] of הָלַךְ, and Piel [D] of בָּקַשׁ) are literally "arise, walk, search." The first two (קוּם לֵךְ) often appear together in the OT (e.g., Gen 28:2; Deut 10:11; Jonah 1:2; 3:2) and form a hendiadys, expressing one concept: "go." See also the feminine singular imperatives קוּמִי לְכִי in 2 Sam 13:15. Similarly, when imperatives of הָלַךְ recur in this chapter (the alternate form with paragogic ה of the masculine singular, לְכָה, in 9:5, 10, and the masculine plural לְכוּ in 9:9), they again are joined with another verb, forming a kind of hendi-adys. Cf. Joüon, § 177 f.

9:4 וַיַּעֲבֹר ... וַיַּעֲבֹר ... וַיַּעַבְרוּ ... וַיַּעֲבֹר—In Codex Leningradensis the first, sec-ond, and fourth instances of this Qal (G) preterite (imperfect with *waw* consecutive) of עָבַר, "cross, pass through," are singular, "he traveled through," while the third is plu-ral, "they traveled through," referring to both Saul and his servant. However, in all four instances the LXX has the plural verb διῆλθον. In addition, for the second, one other Masoretic manuscript has the plural וַיַּעַבְרוּ, and for the fourth, two other Masoretic

---

[2] E.g., Judg 14:10; 2 Ki 8:12; Is 9:16 (ET 9:17); 31:8; 40:30; Jer 9:20 (ET 9:21); 11:22; 18:21; 49:26; 50:30; 51:3; Ezek 30:17; Amos 2:11; 4:10; Ps 78:31; Ruth 3:10; Lam 1:15; 5:14; 2 Chr 36:17.

[3] See also, e.g., 2 Sam 19:18 (ET 19:17); Job 1:15; Esth 2:2; Neh 4:10 (ET 4:16); 6:5; cf. *HALOT*, 3.

manuscripts have the plural. The switching back and forth between singular and plural verbs in Leningradensis is awkward (but for that reason could be original). The translation above follows the consistently plural verbs in the LXX.

בְּאֶרֶץ־יְמִינִי—Literally "through the land of a [Ben]jaminite," this is translated as "through the land of Benjamin." For יְמִינִי, see the second textual note on 9:1.

9:5 הֵמָּה בָּאוּ בְּאֶרֶץ צוּף וְשָׁאוּל אָמַר—The first four words form a temporal clause, "when they came into the region of Zuph." (The LXX omits a translation of אֶרֶץ, "region.") The main clause in the verse is marked by a *waw* conjunctive prefixed to the first word in the clause, which is the subject: וְשָׁאוּל, "and Saul." In such clauses the subject is followed by a perfect aspect verb, here אָמַר, "said." For other examples, see 9:11, 27.

לְכָה וְנָשׁוּבָה—Literally "go, let's return." The two verbs form a hendiadys; see the third textual note on 9:3. נָשׁוּבָה is a cohortative. For its force, see Joüon, § 114 e.

פֶּן־יֶחְדַּל אָבִי מִן־הָאֲתֹנוֹת וְדָאַג לָנוּ:—Literally "lest my father cease from the female donkeys and be anxious for us." Often חָדַל is used in combination with another verb that expresses the main action, "to cease, quit" doing that action. This eloquent turn of phrase omits the main verb in the first clause but supplies it in the second clause: דָּאַג, "be anxious, worried."

9:6 הִנֵּה ... עַתָּה—See the first textual note on 8:5.

אִישׁ־אֱלֹהִים—For "a man of God" (also 9:7, 8, 10), see 2:27 and "An Indictment of Eli (2:27–30)" in the commentary on 2:27–36.

נִכְבָּד—"Highly respected" is a Niphal (N) participle masculine singular absolute from כָּבֵד, "to be honored."

בּוֹא יָבוֹא—The infinitive absolute conveys affirmation (Joüon, § 123 e), and it, together with the imperfect of בּוֹא, expresses certainty: "it surely comes to pass." See 3:19.

נֵלְכָה—For the force of this Qal (G) cohortative of הָלַךְ, "let us go," see Joüon, § 114 e. This form recurs in 9:9, 10, but each time it is pointed slightly differently. The textbook form, נֵלְכָה, is in 9:9, and its pausal form, נֵלֵכָה, is in 9:10.

אוּלַי יַגִּיד לָנוּ אֶת־דַּרְכֵּנוּ אֲשֶׁר־הָלַכְנוּ עָלֶיהָ:—Literally "perhaps he will tell us our way which we should go upon it." Cf. 9:8. This is a rare use of a perfect, הָלַכְנוּ, with a modal sense, "should go," referring to action in the near future (cf. GKC, § 106 g–l; Joüon, § 112 g–h).

9:7 וְהִנֵּה נֵלֵךְ וּמַה־נָּבִיא—Occasionally הִנֵּה may introduce a conditional clause (2 Sam 18:11; 2 Ki 7:2; *HALOT*, 10). The two first person plural imperfects (the Qal [G] of הָלַךְ and the Hiphil [H] of בּוֹא) then express the actions that would take place within the conditional: if "we go, what should we bring?" Normally the second verb would be pointed נָבִיא (identical to the noun נָבִיא, "prophet"), but it has *daghesh forte conjunctivum* (־נּ) because of the preceding interrogative מַה־ (GKC, §§ 20 d, 37 b, c). Yet even with this *daghesh* the identical pointing is also used for "prophet" in the context: לַנָּבִיא in 9:9.

וּתְשׁוּרָה—The noun תְּשׁוּרָה is a hapax legomenon in the OT but is attested in Rabbinic Hebrew, where it refers to a "traveler's gift," that is, a present that the traveler gives to a host (see Jastrow, s.v. תְּשׁוּרָה). That meaning can be inferred from its context here.

9:8 וַיֹּסֶף הַנַּעַר לַעֲנוֹת—For this construction, the Hiphil (H) imperfect of יָסַף, "to do again" (with *waw* consecutive), followed by an infinitive construct (לַעֲנוֹת, Qal [G] of עָנָה, "to answer"), see Joüon, §§ 102 g, 124 c, 177 b, and the first textual note on 3:6.

נִמְצָא בְיָדִי רֶבַע שֶׁקֶל כָּסֶף—The three-word construct chain "a quarter of a shekel of silver" is the subject of the Niphal (N) participle נִמְצָא with the prepositional phrase בְיָדִי, "is found in my hand."

וְנָתַתִּי—Instead of the MT's "and I'll give," the LXX has an imperative "and give" (καὶ δώσεις).

9:9 לְכוּ וְנֵלְכָה—"Let's go" is repeated in 9:10 (but with the pausal form נֵלֵכָה). See the third textual note on 9:3 and the second textual note on 9:5. The LXX translates this expression literally with δεῦρο πορευθῶμεν in 9:9 and with δεῦρο καὶ πορευθῶμεν in 9:10.

9:10 טוֹב דְּבָרְךָ—"Your suggestion is good." Often the noun דָּבָר, "word," must be translated as appropriate to context.

9:12 לְפָנֶיךָ—This means "ahead of you" (singular). The LXX has the pronoun "you" in the plural: κατὰ πρόσωπον ὑμῶν.

9:13 תִּמְצְאוּן … תִּמְצָאוּן—Both of these Qal (G) imperfects of מָצָא, "to find," have paragogic *nun* (Joüon, § 44 e). The imperfect can have a variety of modal nuances depending on context (Joüon, § 113 l–o). The first is "you *might* find," and the second is "you *can* find."

כִּי לֹא־יֹאכַל הָעָם—Literally this means "because the people will not eat." This is the first of two consecutive clauses beginning with the causal conjunction כִּי (see also the next textual note). Each is explanatory. They inform Saul (and the reader) of the liturgical customs that explain why Samuel could be found at that time and in that place. The כִּי in this first clause has been omitted in the English translation due to stylistic considerations.

כִּי־הוּא יְבָרֵךְ הַזֶּבַח—The action of "blessing" (the Piel [D] imperfect of בָּרַךְ) the sacrifice would include the pronunciation of an absolution of grace for the people, conferring the forgiveness of sins. The blessing declares that Yahweh has looked favorably upon their offering and is gracious toward them. See, e.g., the blessings in Lev 9:22–23; Num 6:23–27. See also the blessings given by Eli (1 Sam 2:20) and by David (2 Sam 6:18–20). The tribe of Levi, which would include Samuel,[4] was given the office of blessing the people (Deut 10:8; 21:5; 1 Chr 23:13). God may have intended the priests who offered the sacrifices to declare to the worshipers the statements of רָצוֹן, God's "favor," in, e.g., Lev 1:3; 19:5; 22:19–21; 23:11, and the assurances that the sacrifice is "pleasing" to God in, e.g., Lev 1:9, 13, 17; 2:2, 9, 12; 17:6.

הַקְּרֻאִים—Here and in 1 Sam 9:22, the Qal passive (Gp) participle (masculine plural with the article) of קָרָא, "to call, summon, invite," refers to guests at the meal as "those who have/had been invited."

---

4 Samuel's genealogy in 1 Sam 1:1 indicates that he was a Levite. See "Elkanah and His Family (1:1–3)" in the commentary on 1:1–20. See also the commentary on 2:18–21.

כִּי־אֹתוֹ כְהַיּוֹם תִּמְצְאוּן אֹתוֹ׃—This is translated as "because—him—you can find him now." The direct object marker with a pronominal suffix, אֹתוֹ, is repeated for emphasis. The first one (אֹתוֹ, "—him—") is fronted to suggest urgency. The LXX and many English translations omit the first occurrence, probably because of the resulting awkwardness in translation. Usually the definite article is elided between an inseparable preposition and a noun, so the expected form here would be כַּיּוֹם (sixty-nine times in the OT). However, sometimes the article is not elided, thus כְהַיּוֹם (eight times in the OT). See GKC, § 35 n.

9:14 לִקְרָאתָם—This is the Qal (G) infinitive construct of קָרָא II, "to meet, encounter," with the preposition לְ and a third masculine plural suffix: "to meet them."

9:15 גָּלָה אֶת־אֹזֶן שְׁמוּאֵל—Literally "he uncovered Samuel's ear." The idiom with the verb גָּלָה and the object noun אֹזֶן means "to reveal" something to someone (BDB, s.v. גָּלָה, Qal, 1). See also 1 Sam 20:2, 12, 13; 22:8, 17; 2 Sam 7:27.

9:16 וּמְשַׁחְתּוֹ לְנָגִיד—The Qal (G) perfect second masculine singular of מָשַׁח, "to anoint," with *waw* consecutive (and a third masculine singular object suffix), "you shall anoint him," functions as an imperative: "anoint him." The verb recurs often in Samuel.[5] Cf. also the discussion of the cognate noun מָשִׁיחַ, "Anointed One," in the commentary on 2:10, 35. The noun נָגִיד (often translated as "prince") is rendered as "designated ruler." There is a wordplay throughout this chapter with the verb נָגַד, whose Hiphil (H) occurs in 9:6, 8, 18, 19, "to declare, tell, designate," and נָגִיד in this verse.[6] Here Saul is the one God designated for Samuel to anoint to rule Israel.

רָאִיתִי אֶת־עַמִּי—"I have seen my people." The LXX reads ἐπέβλεψα ἐπὶ τὴν ταπείνωσιν τοῦ λαοῦ μου, "I have seen the humiliation of my people," perhaps reflecting a Hebrew Vorlage of ראיתי את עני עמי, with the noun עֳנִי (cf. Ex 3:7). If this was the original text, the MT may have suffered an omission by homoioarchton if the scribe's eye skipped from the first ע to the second ע and thus skipped over ני- in עני.

9:17 עָנָהוּ—The use of עָנָה, "to answer" (Qal [G] third masculine singular perfect with a third masculine singular suffix), instead of אָמַר or דִּבֶּר, implies that this is a continuation of the conversation Yahweh initiated with Samuel the previous day (9:16).

יַעְצֹר בְּעַמִּי׃—"He will restrain my people." The verb עָצַר in the Qal (G) with the preposition בְּ signifies keeping something in check (Job 4:2; 12:15; 29:9; *HALOT*, Qal, 1). See further the commentary.

9:18 וַיִּגַּשׁ שָׁאוּל אֶת־שְׁמוּאֵל—Usually the Niphal (N) of נָגַשׁ, "to draw near," takes the preposition אֶל, "to," but it takes an accusative (introduced with אֶת־) here and in Num 4:19; 1 Sam 30:21.

בְּתוֹךְ הַשָּׁעַר—This means "in the midst of the gate." The LXX (εἰς μέσον τῆς πόλεως) and 4QSamᵃ (בתוך הע[יר]) have "in the midst of the city," probably under the influence of 9:14.

אֵי־זֶה—Literally this is "where this?" The demonstrative pronoun זֶה can be used to emphasize an interrogative (GKC, § 136 c, d).

---

[5] 1 Sam 10:1; 15:1, 17; 16:3, 12, 13; 2 Sam 1:21; 2:4, 7; 3:39; 5:3, 17; 12:7; 19:11 (ET 19:10).

[6] In Samuel, the noun occurs also in 1 Sam 10:1; 13:14; 25:30; 2 Sam 5:2; 6:21; 7:8.

9:19 אָנֹכִי הָרֹאֶה—"I am the seer." The LXX (ἐγώ εἰμι αὐτός) and 4QSamᵃ (הו[א]) read "I am he."

וַאֲכַלְתֶּם—"And you [plural] will eat." The LXX has the singular imperative καὶ φάγε, "and eat."

לָךְ:—The preposition לְ appears to have a second feminine singular suffix (as if Samuel were speaking to a woman), but this form is pausal for לְךָ, with a masculine second singular suffix. The same is true of לֶךְ in 9:23.

9:20 הַיּוֹם שְׁלֹשֶׁת הַיָּמִים—Literally "today, three of the days," this means something like "for three days now" and is translated as "three days ago."

אַל־תָּשֶׂם אֶת־לִבְּךָ לָהֶם—Literally "do not set your heart to them," this means "do not think/worry about them." See the second textual note on 4:20.

וּלְמִי כָּל־חֶמְדַּת יִשְׂרָאֵל—Literally this means "for whom is all the desire of Israel?"

9:21 מִקַּטַנֵּי שִׁבְטֵי יִשְׂרָאֵל—The preposition מִן on the adjective קָטָן indicates origin, "from." A construct phrase can form a superlative, so this three-word construct chain, literally "from the small ones of the tribes of Israel," means "from the smallest/least of the tribes of Israel." The plural form of קָטָן (instead of the expected singular) may be due to attraction to the following plural form of שֵׁבֶט. The LXX translates this phrase as τοῦ μικροῦ σκήπτρου φυλῆς Ισραηλ, "of the least of the clan of the tribe of Israel," which would seem to represent a four-word construct chain with singular nouns, מִקְּטַן מִשְׁפַּחַת שֵׁבֶט יִשְׂרָאֵל. If so, then the noun מִשְׁפָּחָה, "clan," in the next clause of the MT apparently was included by dittography.

וּמִשְׁפַּחְתִּי הַצְּעִרָה מִכָּל־—Here the article with an adjective (the feminine form of צָעִיר, "little, insignificant"), along with the preposition מִן with a comparative sense, forms a superlative, "my clan is the littlest of all of . . ." See Joüon, § 141 g. Cf. the second textual note on 9:2, where the construction expressed a comparative. Cf. also the first textual note on 8:14.

מִשְׁפְּחוֹת שִׁבְטֵי בִנְיָמִן—This means "the clans of the tribes of Benjamin." One would expect "tribe" to be singular (שֵׁבֶט), as in the LXX (σκήπτρου Βενιαμιν = שבט בנימן). However, שֵׁבֶט here may refer to a subdivision of a tribe (BDB, 2 c) or be due to attraction to the preceding plural מִשְׁפְּחוֹת.

9:22 לִשְׁכָּתָה—The noun לִשְׁכָּה has a directional *he*. This noun can refer to a "room" adjacent to a sanctuary or temple, as in Jer 35:2, 4 and often in Ezekiel 40 and 42.

כִּשְׁלֹשִׁים—This means "about thirty." The LXX has ὡσεὶ ἑβδομήκοντα, "about seventy." Josephus also has "seventy."[7]

9:23 לַטַּבָּח—The noun טַבָּח is translated as "cook" (also in 9:24). The cognate verb טָבַח denotes butchering an animal (1 Sam 25:11). From the context it appears as if the butcher is also serving as the cook (*HALOT*, s.v. טבח, 1). This noun is the masculine counterpart to טַבָּחָה; see the textual note on 8:13.

9:24 וְהֶעָלֶיהָ—"And what was on it" is awkward and is not found in the LXX. The definite article is rarely attached to a preposition, but is here. The article functions as a

---

[7] Josephus, *Antiquities*, 6.52.

relative pronoun, "that which" or "what was," as it does also on the Niphal (N) participle הַנִּשְׁאָר ("what was left over") in the next textual note. See GKC, § 138 i.

הִנֵּה הַנִּשְׁאָר שִׂים־לְפָנֶיךָ אֱכֹל—Literally this means "behold, what was left over; place [it] before you and eat." The imperatives are the Qal (G) of שִׂים and אָכַל.

לַמּוֹעֵד שָׁמוּר־לְךָ—"It was kept for you for this event." מוֹעֵד signifies an appointed time or place and in this case is translated as "event." Instead of the Qal passive (Gp) participle שָׁמוּר, the LXX (τέθειται) and 4QSamᵃ (ש[ים]) read "it is placed."

לֵאמֹר הָעָם ׀ קָרָאתִי—Literally "... saying, 'I invited the people.'" The infinitive construct לֵאמֹר usually introduces direct speech. The translation takes it as a reference to the preceding clause, "it was kept for you for this event." The cook apparently tells Samuel that he had spoken these words to the people (or conveyed that the thigh portion would be reserved for Samuel) when he invited them. Alternatively, the cook could be quoting to Samuel his own words, which he had previously spoken to Samuel before the event: "I have invited the people." Perhaps at the time he invited the people he also set aside the thigh portion for Samuel.

9:25 וַיְדַבֵּר עִם־שָׁאוּל עַל־הַגָּג:—"He spoke with Saul on the roof." The LXX reads καὶ διέστρωσαν τῷ Σαουλ ἐπὶ τῷ δώματι, ²⁶καὶ ἐκοιμήθη, "and they spread [blankets?] for Saul on the roof, ²⁶and he slept." Josephus appears to follow the LXX: ἐπεὶ δὲ κοίτης ὥρα προσῆγεν, οἱ μὲν ἀναστάντες ἀνέλυον πρὸς αὐτοὺς ἕκαστοι, ὁ δὲ Σαοῦλος παρὰ τῷ προφήτῃ σὺν τῷ θεράποντι κατεκοιμήθη, "And when it was time for bed, the rest rose up, and all of them went home. But Saul slept beside the prophet with his servant."[8]

Commentary

1049 BC

Kish and His Son Saul (9:1–3)

Like Samuel earlier (1:1–3) and David later (16:1–12), Saul is introduced to the reader through his father. Kish's genealogy includes five generations (9:1), just as Elkanah's did (1:1).

The first- and last-mentioned attribute of Kish in 1:1 is that he was from the tribe of Benjamin. This is a baleful observation because of this tribe's earlier history, which almost caused it to be exterminated from Israel (Judges 19–21). This sense of foreboding will be magnified later, when we learn that Saul's hometown is Gibeah (1 Sam 10:10, 26), whose behavior mimicked the abominations of the men of Sodom (Judg 19:16–26; cf. Gen 19:1–11). The astute reader is led to suspect that Israel may get a king "like all the nations" (1 Sam 8:5, 20). Nevertheless, we are told that Kish was a prominent man (see the third textual note on 9:1). Perhaps the author is hinting that he had been among the delegation of elders that had gone to Ramah to request a king (8:4–5).

The narration quickly moves to Kish's son Saul. He is said to be exceptionally handsome and tall (9:2; cf. 10:23–24). These superficial features are

---

[8] Josephus, *Antiquities*, 6.52.

impressive to those who judge a person by his appearance (cf. 16:7); the reader is led to suspect that God is giving the people a king such as "all the nations" (8:5, 20) might choose. But what kind of qualifications are these for a monarch over Yahweh's chosen nation?

The only words of Kish recorded in Scripture are in 9:3. After this he will fade from the narrative and be mentioned only in passing (1 Sam 10:11, 21; 14:51; 2 Sam 21:14).

Saul Searches for His Father's Donkeys and for Samuel (9:4–13)

Saul's search is detailed for us (9:4). However, the route is not well understood, and there have been a number of attempts to identify the places mentioned.[9] Shalishah (שָׁלִשָׁה, 9:4) is usually identified with the area around Baal-shalishah (בַּעַל שָׁלִשָׁה, 2 Ki 4:42). Shaalim (שַׁעֲלִים, 1 Sam 9:4) is often identified with Shual (שׁוּעָל, 1 Sam 13:17). It would appear that both the regions of Shalishah and Shaalim were north of Benjamin in "the hill country of Ephraim," since we are told that Saul traveled through "the hill country of Ephraim" (9:4). The author does not say that Saul failed to find the donkeys anywhere in the hill country of Ephraim, as he does about Shalishah and Shaalim (and the land of Benjamin). Thus, "the hill country of Ephraim" must be a larger region which contained the two smaller regions of Shalishah and Shaalim. Then it seems that Saul doubled back through Benjamin (9:4 last places Saul in Benjamin), leading him toward the region of Zuph (9:5). "The region of Zuph" may have straddled the border of Benjamin and Ephraim, since Samuel's city of Ramah, which was in the hill country of Ephraim, appears to have been settled by the Zuphite clan of Levites (1 Sam 1:1; cf. 1 Chr 6:20 [ET 6:35]). At that point Saul was ready to call off the search.

Saul's servant suggests consulting "a man of God" in the nearby city (9:6). This title is another term for a prophet (see 2:27). In Scripture the title is first applied to Moses (Deut 33:1; also Josh 14:6; Ps 90:1 [ET superscription]; 1 Chr 23:14) and is primarily used in the book of Kings (e.g., 2 Ki 4:7–27; 5:8–20; 6:15). Elijah is the prophet most frequently designated by this phrase (about thirty-five times).

The reputation of this "man of God" is that all he prophesies comes to pass (1 Sam 9:6; see also 3:19). This is the mark of a true prophet of God (Deut 18:21–22).

Interestingly, the identity of both the city and the person under discussion is withheld from the reader, though it is obvious from earlier narration. The Zuphite city is Ramah (1:1, 19; 2:11; 7:17; 8:4), and the man of God is Samuel (8:4). Yet, by using the designation "man of God," which was previously used for an anonymous prophet (2:27), anonymity is maintained in the initial stage of Saul's introduction to Samuel.

---

9 See Edelman, "Saul's Journey through Mt. Ephraim and Samuel's Ramah," 44–48, as well as her own proposal on 50–58.

Why does the narrator not identify this person or his city? Partly it is to demonstrate the change in leadership from Samuel to Saul.[10] By not mentioning Samuel and his city, the narrator is able to focus more directly on Saul and his character. However, that is not the entire explanation, since Samuel will eventually be identified (9:14), though Ramah will not. Part of the narrator's strategy here is to keep the reader in suspense, as if he is on the quest with Saul. Since Saul does not yet know what is going to happen, keeping the identity of the man of God shrouded also submerges the previous chapter's identification of Samuel as Israel's requested kingmaker. The account of Saul's first evening encounter with Samuel moves slowly, and the information unfolds gradually and only partially. As one reads of the events of this evening, it becomes increasingly likely that Saul is the king whom Yahweh has chosen for Israel, but in this chapter this is only hinted at (9:20–21, 24).

Saul is reluctant to go to consult the man of God, giving as his excuse that he has nothing to bring as a present (see the second textual note on 9:7). Presents or gratuities given to a prophet are occasionally mentioned in the OT (1 Ki 14:3; 2 Ki 4:42; 5:5, 15–16; Amos 7:12; Micah 3:5). Saul's servant, however, offered a quarter shekel of silver (9:8), about one ounce. This exchange between Saul and his servant serves to introduce an interesting play on Saul's words "what shall we bring ... ?" (מַה־נָּבִיא, 9:7). The verb "we shall bring" is identical to the noun for "prophet" (see the first textual note on 9:7). Up to this point in the book, only Samuel has been identified as a prophet.[11] Thus, Saul's words give the author an opportunity once again to hint that the "man of God" (9:6) is Samuel, though that has not yet been explicitly revealed to the reader.[12]

Before disclosing that Saul has decided to seek the counsel of "the man of God" (9:10), the narrator includes a parenthetical comment that serves to heighten the tension that has been building concerning the identity of the prophet: he notes that the term "prophet" (נָבִיא) was current at his time of writing, but formerly the accepted term was "seer" (רֹאֶה), since God's revelations (even his "Word") often appeared to prophets in visual form (9:9).[13] This parenthetical aside is placed precisely at the turning point in the account when

---

[10] Gilmour, "Suspense and Anticipation in 1 Samuel 9:1–14," 5.

[11] Samuel is called a "prophet" in 1 Sam 3:20, as well as in 2 Chr 35:18; Acts 13:20. In 1 Sam 9:19 Samuel confirms that he is the "seer" Saul is seeking, and Samuel is called a seer in 1 Chr 9:22; 26:28; 29:29.

[12] Curtis, "A Folk Etymology of *Nābîʾ*," claims that Saul's words with the verb נָבִיא, "we shall bring," present the reader with a folk etymology for the noun נָבִיא, "prophet." However, there is no attempt in the text to claim that this verb and the noun "prophet" are somehow related. See also Shaviv, "*Nābîʾ* and *Nāgîd* in 1 Samuel ix 1–x 16," 108–10.

[13] See the third textual note on 3:1, which observes that some prophetic passages portray the divine "Word" as something not only heard but also seen. Cf. the Niphal (N) of רָאָה, "to see," for God "appearing" in 3:21 and the commentary on the double meaning of "he could not see" (רָאָה) in 4:15. In the prophets רָאָה, "to see," commonly refers to the prophets' perception of divine revelation. See, e.g., Jer 1:11–13; Ezek 1:1. The participle רֹאֶה, translated as "seer" in 1 Sam 9:9, serves as the verb for prophetic sight in, e.g., Amos 7:8; 8:2.

the search for the donkeys becomes a seeking for God (לִדְרוֹשׁ אֱלֹהִים, "to seek God," 9:9). The term "seer" will be used three more times (9:11, 18, 19) as Saul seeks God's disclosure through his prophet. But Yahweh himself has "seen" (רָאָה) and heard his people, and his gracious attentiveness to them is what has led him to choose Saul to be the one through whom he will save them (9:16).

The encounter with the women leaving the city to draw water (9:11) places Saul's first meeting with Samuel in the evening.[14] An ideal time to draw and carry water back up into the city was when the day began to cool. It was the normal time to do this (Gen 24:11).[15]

The women urged haste (1 Sam 9:12–13), since the seer was going up to the high place to eat the sacrificial meal. There would be no eating until he had blessed the sacrifice. This included a blessing of the worshipers as well as the portion of the sacrifice given to the invited guests after the priest had burned the rest of the sacrifice as an offering to God on an altar.[16] The evening sacrifice was normally offered around 3:00 p.m. If the priest had officiated over the offering of the sacrifice at the high place about that time and then Samuel was on his way up to utter the blessing and eat with the other guests, we may surmise that the time was about 4:00 p.m. when Saul and his servant found Samuel going up to the high place (9:14–18).

Samuel Finds Israel's King (9:14–25)

The identity of the man of God is finally revealed—it is Samuel (9:14). Samuel's timing was not by accident. The narrator is careful to tell the reader that Samuel was exiting the city *"to meet them"* (see the textual note on 9:14). Then he inserts another parenthetical comment explaining how Samuel knew to meet Saul and his servant at this time: God had revealed this to Samuel (9:15–16). Samuel knew that Saul would be in the city gate (9:18) through which everyone had to pass to enter Ramah. God told Samuel that Saul was specifically chosen to deliver Israel from Philistine domination. The dual language of Yahweh seeing his people and hearing their cry for salvation (9:16) is

---

[14] For other times when men met women drawing water, see Gen 24:15–20; 29:1–10; Ex 2:15–19; and Jesus meeting the Samaritan woman by the well in John 4.

[15] Note also Jn 4:6, which places the Samaritan woman at the well at "the sixth hour," i.e., 6:00 p.m., using Roman time, which reckoned the day to start at midnight and the second half of the day to start at noon. This is the same system commonly in use today. Some have sought to place this around noon using Jewish time, which reckoned the day to start at sundown and the daylight hours to begin at dawn (i.e., about 6:00 a.m.; cf. NIV). However, it is clear that John uses Roman time (e.g., compare "the sixth hour" in Jn 19:14, which in context must mean 6:00 a.m., counting from midnight, with "the sixth hour" in Mt 27:45; Mk 15:33; Lk 23:44, which in context must mean "noon" using Jewish time). See Steinmann, *From Abraham to Paul*, 293–97, especially nn. 463, 464, and 465.

[16] For "bless," see the third textual note on 9:13.

reminiscent of God seeing Israel and hearing the people's cry before he saved them from Egypt (Ex 2:23–25; 3:7).[17]

Yahweh identified Saul as the "designated ruler" of Israel (נָגִיד, see the first textual note on 9:16). Throughout the book of Samuel this word denotes God's *chosen and appointed* ruler (1 Sam 10:1; 13:14; 25:30; 2 Sam 5:2; 6:21; 7:8). More is involved than the general truth that all rulers receive their temporal authority, including the sword, from God (Jn 19:10–11; Rom 13:1; 1 Pet 2:13–14). The emphasis is on Yahweh's prerogative to select the man who administers Law and Gospel to govern his own redeemed people on his behalf, for the sake of their salvation. Israel's kings have this special appointment to their office, and Saul's comes through the prophet Samuel. In the church today God has established the pastoral office to administer Law and Gospel with the Word (but not the sword), to dispense Christ's grace through the Sacraments, and to exercise the office of the keys, all for the sake of his people's salvation. The pastor who is faithful shepherds God's flock with the divine authority conferred on him when he is called to this office of oversight.

When Samuel spotted Saul, God identified him as the man who would "restrain [יַעְצֹר] my people" (see the second textual note on 9:17). This accents his role in administering Law in the civic realm. From Judges 17–21 we learn that Israel was in dire need of restraint. The Israelites' tragic lawlessness is highlighted by the repeated refrain "there was no king in Israel" (Judg 17:6; 18:1; 19:1; 21:25). All governing requires curbing the innate sinful tendencies of humans, and Saul would be entrusted with punishing malefactors with the civil law of Israel in the Torah (cf. Rom 13:1–7). This is a blessing provided by God: good government restrains the sinful impulses of the populace, and equitable governors serve God in a noble calling with divine authority. Luther notes that God

> makes all creation help provide the comforts and necessities of life. … Moreover, he gives all physical and temporal blessings—*good government, peace, security.*[18]

Melanchthon identified these blessings:

> Temporal authority is concerned with matters altogether different from the Gospel. Temporal power does not protect the soul, *but with the sword and physical penalties it protects body and goods from the power of others.*[19]

---

[17] 1 Sam 9:16 uses the verb רָאָה for Yahweh "seeing" Israel and the noun צַעֲקָה for their "cry," which he has heard. The same verb was used for Yahweh "seeing" Israel's plight in slavery to Egypt in Ex 2:25; 3:7, and the identical noun (צְעָקָה) denoted their "cry" in Ex 3:7. A related verb (זָעַק) portrays their "crying" in Ex 2:23 (along with other synonyms in Ex 2:23–25). Cf. זָעַק for Samuel's intercessory "crying out" to God on behalf of oppressed Israel in 1 Sam 7:8, 9, and contrast the use of the same verb (זָעַק) when the people, after they are oppressed by the king they will choose for themselves, will "cry out" to God in 1 Sam 8:18.

[18] LC II 14–15; emphasis added.

[19] AC XXVIII 11; emphasis added.

God intended Saul as the "designated ruler" (1 Sam 9:16) to bring all of the blessings described above to Israel, both temporal benefits and eternal salvation.

When Saul asked Samuel for directions to the seer's house (9:18), Samuel not only identified himself but also gave Saul all the information he needed to know (9:19–20). He invited Saul to the sacrifice and told him that he would reveal what was in his heart when he sent him away in the morning (10:1–8).[20] He told him that the donkeys had been found. Finally, he identified Saul as the designated king when he stated that Saul was the one whom "all Israel desires" (9:20; cf. 8:4–5).

After Samuel identifies himself as the "seer" (9:19), the term will not be used again in 1 Samuel, signaling that the goal of the journey had been reached. Saul was looking for the "seer" in order to "seek God" (9:9). In finding Samuel, he found God through the divine Word imparted through the prophet. But it remained to be seen whether Saul would continue to seek God through his Word as revealed in the Torah and through his prophet.

Saul's first reaction to Samuel's words was not positive (9:21). He did not rejoice in God's choice or humbly accept God's will. Instead, he appeared to question and possibly even reject God's Word. Why should he be chosen from among the smallest clan of the smallest tribe of Israel? Like Israel (8:19–20; cf. 9:2), Saul was looking at kingship from a human perspective, not God's (cf. 16:7). Saul would continue to work at odds with God's Word to him (10:14–16, 21–22).

The scene quickly switches to the high place without any transition (9:22–24). There in a room Saul was given a thigh from the sacrifice. He supped at table with Samuel and about thirty other men. Sacral buildings at high places were not uncommon.[21] The specific portion given to Saul was a "thigh and what was on it" (9:24). It has been suggested that this was the right hind leg, a portion of the sacrifice for someone especially honored.[22] That Saul was the guest of honor is signaled by his place at the head of the guests (9:22), the portion of meat that was reserved for him (9:23–24), and the words "Saul ate with Samuel" (9:24).

Samuel and Saul therefore are fully in communion, sharing fellowship both at the altar and at the table. Their union in faith may be compared to that of the infant church, the baptized believers who devoted themselves to the apostles' teaching, the fellowship, the breaking of bread, and the prayers as they held everything in common (Acts 2:38–46). Such unity in doctrine and practice, expressed in communion together, is God's desire and the goal of the church. Tragically, Samuel will have to break his fellowship with Saul when

---

[20] Note also 1 Sam 10:9, which specifically states that God transformed Saul's heart: וַיַּהֲפָךְ־לוֹ אֱלֹהִים לֵב אַחֵר.

[21] 1 Ki 3:5; 12:31; 13:32; 2 Ki 17:29, 32; 23:19.

[22] Van der Jagt, "What Did Saul Eat When He First Met Samuel?"

Saul transgresses God's Word (1 Sam 15:24–28). Disregard for the Scriptures is the root cause of the schisms that rend asunder the fellowship of churches today.

When the feast was finished, Saul and Samuel went to Ramah. What happened that night in Ramah is not clear (see the textual note on 9:25). Either Samuel engaged Saul in a conversation (MT), or Saul was provided a place to sleep for the night (the LXX and Josephus).

Saul Is Anointed King

Translation

9 ²⁶They got up early, about dawn, and Samuel called to Saul on the roof, "Get up, and I will send you away." So Saul got up, and the two of them, he and Saul, went outside. ²⁷As they were descending at the edge of the city, Samuel said to Saul, "Tell your servant to go on ahead of us, but stay for a while, and I will inform you about God's message."

10 ¹Samuel took a flask of olive oil and poured it on his head and kissed him. He said, "Hasn't Yahweh anointed you to be designated ruler over his inheritance? ²When you leave me today, you will find two men near Rachel's tomb on the border of Benjamin at Zelzah. They will say to you, 'The female donkeys for which you went to search have been found. Moreover, your father has given up the matter of the female donkeys and is worried about you, thinking, "What will I do about my son?"' ³You will proceed from there and come to the terebinth at Tabor. Three men going up to God at Bethel will find you there. One will be carrying three kids, one will be carrying three loaves of bread, and one will be carrying a bottle containing wine. ⁴They will greet you and give you two [loaves] of bread. You will accept [the bread] from them. ⁵After this you will go to God's Gibeah, where there is a Philistine garrison. As you come to the city you will meet a group of prophets coming down from the high place preceded by harps, tambourines, flutes, and lyres. They will be prophesying. ⁶The Spirit of Yahweh will rush upon you. You will prophesy with them, and you will be transformed into another man. ⁷When these signs happen to you, do whatever you find to do, because God is with you. ⁸Then you will go down before me to Gilgal, and I will come down to you to offer whole burnt offerings and to make sacrifices of peace offerings. Wait seven days until I come to you. Then I will inform you about what you ought to do."

⁹As he turned to leave Samuel, God changed his heart. All these signs happened in that day. ¹⁰As he came from there to Gibeah, there was a group of prophets to meet him. The Spirit of God rushed upon him, and he prophesied among them. ¹¹When everyone who previously knew him saw that he was prophesying with prophets, the people said to each other, "What in the world has happened to the son of Kish? Is also Saul among the prophets?"

¹²A man from there replied, "And who is their leader?" Therefore it became a proverbial saying: "Is also Saul among the prophets?"

¹³When he finished prophesying, he went to the hill. ¹⁴Saul's uncle said to him and to his servant, "Where did you go?"

He said, "To look for the female donkeys. When we didn't find them, we went to Samuel."

¹⁵Saul's uncle said, "Please tell me what Samuel said to you."

16Saul said to his uncle, "He assured us that the female donkeys had been found." But on the subject of the monarchy he did not tell him what Samuel had said.

Textual Notes

9:26 וַיַּשְׁכִּמוּ—The verb שָׁכַם occurs only in the Hiphil (H), meaning "to rise early" or "make an early start" on a journey (BDB). It appears in Samuel eleven times, often with בַּבֹּקֶר, "in the morning" (1:19; 15:12; 17:20; 29:10 [twice], 11), or מִמָּחֳרָת, "on the next day" (5:3), or with both (5:4), but sometimes without any further elaboration as to the time (1 Sam 17:16; 2 Sam 15:2). This is its only instance with a temporal clause consisting of all three of the following words (see the next textual note), but Josh 6:15 is similar with two of those words, כַּעֲלוֹת הַשַּׁחַר.

וַיְהִי כַּעֲלוֹת הַשַּׁחַר—Literally "and it was about the coming up of the dawn." The preposition כְּ prefixed to the Qal (G) infinitive construct of עָלָה, "go/come up," has a temporal signification, "when." This is the only appearance of the noun שַׁחַר, "dawn," in Samuel.

9:27 אֱמֹר לַנַּעַר וְיַעֲבֹר לְפָנֵינוּ וַיַּעֲבֹר—The MT reads "tell your servant, and may he pass on [יַעֲבֹר is jussive] ahead of us; and he passed on." The last verb, וַיַּעֲבֹר (Qal [G] preterite [imperfect with *waw* consecutive]), is missing in the LXX and is omitted in the translation above. In the MT it is probably a secondary scribal addition to make explicit what was implicit in the text, that the "servant" did obey the instruction. For נַעַר, see the first textual note on 3:1.

10:1 The LXX contains a longer quotation from Samuel that gives Saul a more elaborate charge as king: οὐχὶ κέχρικέν σε κύριος εἰς ἄρχοντα ἐπὶ τὸν λαὸν αὐτοῦ, ἐπὶ Ισραηλ; καὶ σὺ ἄρξεις ἐν λαῷ κυρίου, καὶ σὺ σώσεις αὐτὸν ἐκ χειρὸς ἐχθρῶν αὐτοῦ κυκλόθεν. καὶ τοῦτό σοι τὸ σημεῖον ὅτι ἔχρισέν σε κύριος ἐπὶ κληρονομίαν αὐτοῦ εἰς ἄρχοντα; "Hasn't **the Lord anointed you ruler over** *his people, over Israel? You will reign among the people of the Lord, and you will save them from the hand of their enemies all around. This will be a sign to you that* **the Lord anointed you ruler over** *his inheritance.*" If the LXX is original, then the MT has suffered from haplography owing to a scribe's eye skipping from the first occurrence of מְשָׁחֲךָ יְהוָה (= κέχρικέν σε κύριος) to the second occurrence of that clause (= ἔχρισέν σε κύριος).[1] ESV and NRSV adopt the LXX reading. However, it is more likely that the LXX is a secondary addition for two reasons: It contains phrases drawn from elsewhere in 1 Samuel (e.g., "save from the hand," 7:8; 9:16; "enemies all around," 14:47; "sign to you," 2:34). In addition, the haplography would have had to have been an eye skip from one clause to another, and these would not have been completely identical clauses. The scribe's eye would have had to skip from מְשָׁחֲךָ יְהוָה עַל־עַמּוֹ לְנָגִיד to כִּי־מְשָׁחֲךָ יְהוָה עַל־נַחֲלָתוֹ לְנָגִיד. The preservation of the word כִּי argues against the loss by haplography, as does the presence of the differing words נַחֲלָתוֹ and עַמּוֹ in the two supposed trigger clauses. Admittedly, the MT's phrase הֲלוֹא כִי is unusual, but its

---

[1] McCarter, *I Samuel*, 171; Klein, *1 Samuel*, 83.

only other occurrence in the OT is found in a text from the author of the book of Samuel (2 Sam 13:28).

וַיִּצֹק פַּךְ הַשֶּׁמֶן—The noun פַּךְ, "flask," appears three times in the OT (also 2 Ki 9:1, 3) and always refers to a flask of "olive oil" (שֶׁמֶן) used for anointing. The verb וַיִּצֹק is the Qal (G) preterite (imperfect with *waw* consecutive) of יָצַק, "pour out," with assimilation of the י (GKC, § 71).

נַחֲלָתוֹ—The feminine noun נַחֲלָה means "heritage, inheritance" (cf. the denominative verb נָחַל, "to inherit"). In Samuel the noun almost always refers to the "inheritance" of Yahweh/God, as here (also 1 Sam 26:19; 2 Sam 14:16; 20:19; 21:3).[2] It does not refer to what God inherits (he already owns everything), but to the inheritance God bequeaths to his children according to his covenant or testament. It is a term of grace, denoting God's gift, and not something his people earn or deserve. The noun often refers to the promised land God gave his people after he redeemed them through the exodus (e.g., Deut 19:10, 14; 20:16; Josh 11:23; 13:6–8; Jer 2:7). But it can also refer to Yahweh himself; he is the "inheritance" of the priests, who receive no land (Num 18:20; the tithe is the Levites' inheritance [Num 18:21–26]). It can also refer to the redeemed people themselves (Deut 4:20; 9:26, 29; Joel 2:17; Micah 7:18), since they inherit all his blessings of grace (Is 54:17; Pss 28:9; 33:12; 74:2). This is its primary sense in Samuel: not so much the land as the people of God who have inherited his salvation, and Saul is given the office of reigning over them on God's behalf.

לְנָגִיד:—For the noun נָגִיד, "designated ruler," see the first textual note on 9:16.

10:2 וְהִנֵּה נָטַשׁ אָבִיךָ אֶת־דִּבְרֵי הָאֲתֹנוֹת וְדָאַג לָכֶם—"And look, your father abandoned the matters of the female donkeys and became anxious for you" fulfills the worry of Saul in 9:5b. See the third textual note on 9:5.

לֵאמֹר—For this word, here translated as "thinking," see the second textual note on 4:7.

10:3 וְחָלַפְתָּ מִשָּׁם וָהָלְאָה וּבָאתָ—Literally "and you shall pass on from there and farther, and you will come." Both שָׁם, "there" (מִשָּׁם, with the preposition מִן), and הָלְאָה, "farther," are adverbs.

אֵלוֹן—Traditionally translated as "oak," this tree is a *Pistacia palaestina*, a "terebinth," a member of the cashew family.

כִּכְּרוֹת לֶחֶם—The noun כִּכָּר derives from a root (כרר) that means "to be round" (*HALOT*, s.v. כרר II), hence "*loaf* of bread (from round shape)" (BDB, 2). The LXX has ἀγγεῖα, "baskets." 4QSamᵃ conflates both readings as כלובי כרות, "baskets of loaves."

נֵבֶל־יַיִן:—This construct phrase is rendered as "a bottle containing wine." The noun נֵבֶל denotes a container for foodstuff or liquid and is a hard-sided container, not a skin (*HALOT*, s.v. נֵבֶל I; *CDCH*, s.v. נֵבֶל I).

---

[2] The lone exception in Samuel is 2 Sam 20:1, where it refers to the "inheritance" of David, but its sense there is similar, since it refers to all that God has bequeathed to David, particularly the promise of the Messiah as the King of God's kingdom. See "Christ in Samuel" in the introduction.

10:4 וְשָׁאֲלוּ לְךָ לְשָׁלוֹם—Literally "and they will ask regarding you about [your] peace/ *shalom.*" To ask about someone's well-being is a common greeting[3] that persists in Modern Hebrew, מָה שְׁלוֹמֶךָ, "how is your peace?" Compare the English "how are you?"

שְׁתֵּי־לֶחֶם—"Two of bread" means "two loaves of bread" (cf. 1 Sam 21:4 [ET 21:3]: חֲמִשָּׁה־לֶחֶם, "five [loaves] of bread"; 2 Sam 16:1: מָאתַיִם לֶחֶם, "two hundred [loaves] of bread"; 2 Ki 4:42: עֶשְׂרִים־לֶחֶם שְׂעֹרִים, "twenty [loaves] of barley bread"). The LXX has δύο ἀπαρχὰς ἄρτων, "two firstfruits of bread," and 4QSamᵃ has]לחם [נו]פות[ת], "[w]ave offerings of bread." These are similar secondary readings that borrow from the firstfruits legislation in Lev 23:17: לֶחֶם תְּנוּפָה שְׁתַּיִם, "two wave offerings of bread."

10:5 גִּבְעַת הָאֱלֹהִים—There have been several suggestions for this place. Some take it as simply "the Hill of God"[4] (HCSB, GW; LXX: τὸν βουνὸν τοῦ θεοῦ[5]). Others take it to be another name for the Benjaminite town Geba.[6] However, it most certainly is Saul's hometown, Gibeah (NET, NIV).[7] There are three reasons for this identification. First, 10:10 identifies it as Gibeah, and second, 10:11 notes that there were people there who recognized Saul. Third, 13:3 connects Gibeah and a Philistine garrison (see the second textual note there).

נְצִבֵי פְלִשְׁתִּים—The noun נְצִיב can denote a "pillar," a "governor," or, most likely here, a military "garrison." The LXX (τὸ ἀνάστημα) and the reconstructed reading in 4QSamᵃ ([נציב[ים]]) have the singular, which is most likely the correct reading. The plural in construct in the MT (נְצִבֵי) is probably a result of accidental metathesis of the *yod* and *bet* in נְצִיב.

מִתְנַבְּאִים:—The participle (Hithpael [HtD]) denotes action continuing for a period of time: "they will be prophesying." The Hithpael of נָבָא occurs here and in 10:6, 10, 13 (also 18:10; 19:20, 21, 23, 24). There does not seem to be any distinction in meaning compared to the Niphal (N) forms in 10:11 and 19:20. All mean "to prophesy" and denote an activity of a נָבִיא, "a prophet" (e.g., 3:20; 9:9; 10:5, 10–12). The Hithpael form here and וַיִּתְנַבֵּא in 10:10, as well as the Niphal participle נִבָּא in 10:11, are as expected for נָבָא. However, the Hithpael forms וְהִתְנַבִּיתָ (perfect with *waw* consecutive) in 10:6 and מֵהִתְנַבּוֹת (infinitive construct with the preposition מִן) in 10:13 are formed as if from the root נָבָה. Forms of third-*aleph* verbs sometimes interchange with forms of third-*he* verbs (GKC, § 75 qq).

10:6 וְצָלְחָה עָלֶיךָ רוּחַ יְהוָה—While "the Spirit of Yahweh" denotes the third person of the Trinity, the noun רוּחַ is grammatically feminine, and so it is the subject of the feminine Qal (G) perfect of צָלַח I, "to rush upon." This noun is the subject of this verb again in 10:10; 11:6; 16:13; 18:10, and elsewhere in the OT only for the Spirit's empowering

---

3 E.g., Gen 43:27; Ex 18:7; Judg 18:15; 1 Sam 17:22; 25:5; 30:21; 2 Sam 8:10; 1 Chr 18:10.

4 Auld, *I and II Samuel*, 108.

5 ὁ βουνός, "the hill," is the LXX's most frequent translation for Gibeah; see also 10:10; 14:2; 22:6; 23:19; 26:1. In the MT the absolute form of גִּבְעָה is almost always preceded by the article (see BDB, s.v. גִּבְעָה II), which is reflected by the LXX's translation with the article.

6 Miller, "Geba/Gibeah of Benjamin."

7 Fokkelman, *Vow and Desire*, 419; Klein, *1 Samuel*, 91; McCarter, *I Samuel*, 181–82; Smith, *The Books of Samuel*, 68; Tsumura, *The First Book of Samuel*, 285.

action upon Samson in Judg 14:6, 19; 15:14. In 1 Sam 10:6 Samuel prophesies that "the Spirit of Yahweh" will rush upon Saul. That prophecy is fulfilled in 10:10, where the Spirit is called "the Spirit of God," as also in 11:6, where he again rushes upon Saul. Likewise, after Samuel anoints David to be king, "the Spirit of Yahweh" rushes upon him from that day forward (16:13). In a dramatic contrast, after the Holy Spirit had departed from Saul (16:14), "an evil spirit from God" rushes upon him (18:10).

וְנֶהְפַּכְתָּ לְאִישׁ אַחֵר:—Literally "and you will be turned/changed into another man." Saul did not become a different or separate person in a corporeal sense. He remained Saul, but a Saul transformed (Niphal [N] of הָפַךְ) by the Holy Spirit. See the similar clause but with the Qal (G) of הָפַךְ in the third textual note on 10:9.

10:7 תְּבָאנָה—This Qere (third feminine plural Qal [G] imperfect of בּוֹא, "come") is a form that appears three times in the OT with quiescent א (GKC, § 72 i, k). The Kethib, to be vocalized as תְּבֹאֶינָה, is the usual form with consonantal א.

לָךְ ... עִמָּךְ—These are pausal forms with a second *masculine* singular suffix, i.e., pausal for לְךָ and עִמְּךָ.

עֲשֵׂה לְךָ אֲשֶׁר תִּמְצָא יָדֶךָ—Literally "do for yourself that which your hand finds" means "make use of the opportunity at hand" or "carry out the action now made possible for you."

10:8 לְהַעֲלוֹת עֹלוֹת—This cognate accusative construction,[8] "to offer up [the Hiphil (H) of עָלָה] a burnt offering [עֹלָה]," appeared previously in 6:14, 15; 7:9, 10.

לִזְבֹּחַ זִבְחֵי שְׁלָמִים—For the cognate accusative construction "to sacrifice a sacrifice," see the second textual note on 6:15. The construct phrase זִבְחֵי שְׁלָמִים, "sacrifices of peace offerings," specifies that the particular kind of "sacrifices" being offered are "peace offerings." The "peace offerings" (Lev 3:1–17; 7:11–36) provided meat that could be eaten by the lay worshipers.[9] They are referenced again in 1 Sam 11:15; 13:9; 2 Sam 6:17, 18; 24:25.

שִׁבְעַת יָמִים תּוֹחֵל—"Seven days" is an accusative of extent of time. This same phrase, along with the Hiphil (H) of יָחַל, recurs in 13:8, where Saul *fails* to "wait seven days" for Samuel and instead offers the sacrifices himself.

10:9 וְהָיָה—This is probably a copyist error for וַיְהִי (cf. the LXX: καὶ ἐγενήθη).

כְּהַפְנֹתוֹ שִׁכְמוֹ לָלֶכֶת מֵעִם שְׁמוּאֵל—The Hiphil (H) infinitive construct of פָּנָה, "to turn toward/from," with the preposition כְּ forms a temporal clause: "when he turned his shoulder to go (away) from with Saul."

וַיַּהֲפָךְ־לוֹ אֱלֹהִים לֵב אַחֵר—Literally "and God changed regarding him another heart." The verb is the Qal (G) preterite (imperfect with *waw* consecutive) of הָפַךְ, "to turn, change," which depicts God's transformative action, as did the Niphal (N) in the second textual note on 10:6. As there in 10:6, אַחֵר does not mean a separate or corporeally "different" heart, but "another" heart, spiritually a new one. The preposition לְ (with a suffix לוֹ) is one of specification, "with respect to him," indicating that the action performed by God was done regarding Saul. However, the translation reflects it with a

---

[8]   See *IBH*, § 17 B; GKC, § 117 p–r.

[9]   See Kleinig, *Leviticus*, 38–39, 83–96, 168–74.

possessive pronoun, "his heart." The prophets speak of Yahweh's promise to transform the incorrigibly sinful human "heart" of fallen man (Gen 6:5; 8:21) into a new "heart" by the power of his sanctifying Spirit (Is 57:15; Jer 24:7; 32:39; Ezek 18:31; with baptismal water in Ezek 36:25–26). David speaks in similar terms of a God-given "clean heart" in Ps 51:12 (ET 51:10); cf. Ps 51:8, 19 (ET 51:6, 17).

10:10 וַיָּבֹאוּ שָׁם הַגִּבְעָתָה—The MT reads "and they came there to Gibeah." The LXX reads καὶ ἔρχεται ἐκεῖθεν εἰς τὸν βουνόν, "as *he* came *from* there to Gibeah," which would reflect the Hebrew text וַיָּבֹא מִשָּׁם הַגִּבְעָתָה. The MT appears to be a corrupt reading, since Saul's servant has not been mentioned for some time and will not be mentioned again until 10:14.

לִקְרָאתוֹ—See the second textual note on 4:1.

10:11 כָּל־יוֹדְעוֹ מֵאִתְּמוֹל שִׁלְשֹׁם—Literally "everyone knowing him from yesterday and three days ago." For the time signification, see the fifth textual note on 4:7.

מַה־זֶּה—"What [is] this?" The relative pronoun זֶה can be used with an interrogative such as מָה to form an emphatic question (*HALOT*, s.v. זֶה, 15), equivalent to the modern English "what in the world?"

10:12 אֲבִיהֶם—Literally this means "their father." A leader of prophets is called "father" (e.g., 2 Ki 2:12; 6:21; 13:14), while the prophets who are his disciples are "sons (of the prophets)."[10] Samuel served as the leader of a company of prophets (1 Sam 19:20).

הָיְתָה לְמָשָׁל—Hebrew can use feminine forms for abstract actions or ideas, as with this feminine singular verb with no express subject: "*it* became a proverb." The words spoken in this particular set of circumstances led to the formation of this proverb.

10:13 וַיְכַל מֵהִתְנַבּוֹת—This is translated as "when he finished prophesying." The Piel (D) of כָּלָה, "to complete, finish," takes an infinitive construct (the Hithpael [HtD] of נָבָא; see the third textual note on 10:5) as its direct object (see Joüon, § 124 c). When the preposition מִן is prefixed to an infinitive construct following a verb of cessation or restraint (here וַיְכַל), it denotes stopping an activity (BDB, s.v. מִן, 7 b (*a*)).

הַבָּמָה:—While the noun בָּמָה is often translated as "high place," implying the presence of a shrine of some type, sometimes it simply denotes an elevated place (Num 21:28; Deut 32:13; Is 58:14; Micah 3:12; Job 9:8), hence "the hill." The LXX reads τὸν βουνόν, "the hill"; however, this is also the LXX's standard translation for Gibeah (see the first textual note on 10:5). Some emend this to הַבַּיְתָה, "homeward," following a suggestion by Wellhausen.[11]

10:14 דּוֹד שָׁאוּל—"The uncle of Saul" is mentioned three times in three consecutive verses (10:14–16). Later an "uncle" (דּוֹד) of Saul is identified as Abner, who became the commander of his army (see the commentary on 14:50). Abner, therefore, is possibly the uncle to whom Saul was speaking. Throughout Samuel after 14:50 these consonants will always be vocalized דָּוִד, "David" (e.g., 16:13). Therefore the phrase דּוֹד שָׁאוּל in

---

[10] 1 Ki 20:35; 2 Ki 2:3, 5, 7, 15; 4:1, 38; 5:22; 6:1; 9:1.

[11] Klein, *1 Samuel*, 83; McCarter, *I Samuel*, 172. See Wellhausen, *Die Text der Bücher Samuelis untersucht*, 75.

10:14–16 may be a literary play that anticipates the drawn-out relationship between Saul and David that will be the central concern from 1 Samuel 16 through 2 Sam 22:1.

וַנִּרְאֶה כִּי־אַיִן—Literally "when we saw that there was not," this is translated as "when we didn't find them."

10:16 אֲשֶׁר אָמַר שְׁמוּאֵל:—This relative clause, "what Samuel had said," is present also in 4QSam[a] (אשר אמר [שמואל]). The LXX, however, lacks a translation for it.

Commentary

1049 BC

Samuel Anoints Saul (9:26–10:8)

In the morning when it was time to send Saul home (9:26), Samuel conducted a private anointing for Saul (9:27–10:1). The container of the oil is called a "flask" (פַּךְ, 10:1). The same term is used at the anointing of Jehu (2 Ki 9:1–3). In contrast, David and Solomon were anointed using a "horn" (קֶרֶן) of oil (1 Sam 16:1, 13; 1 Ki 1:39).

Samuel's rhetorical question (1 Sam 10:1) serves two purposes: It announces to Saul that he has been chosen by Yahweh as ruler over Israel, the treasured people who are God's inheritance, and it prepares for the signs that Samuel gives to Saul that will confirm that he is the designated ruler by God's authority. The signs are emphatic answers to the rhetorical question.

The first sign was to take place at Zelzah on the border of Benjamin, where Rachel's tomb was located (1 Sam 10:2; see figure 15 below). According to Gen 35:16–20 Rachel died on the road from Bethel to Ephrath (i.e., Bethlehem), while Jacob and his family were still some distance from Ephrath. Samuel's description places her burial place closer to Bethel (than Ephrath) and north of Gibeah. The first sign would confirm Samuel's words about the lost donkeys (1 Sam 9:20) and Saul's previous suspicion that his father was beginning to worry about him instead of the donkeys (9:5).

A second sign would take place at the terebinth at Tabor (10:3–4). This location is unknown, but it must have been within the territory of Benjamin, north of Gibeah and south of Zelzah. The three men would be heading to Bethel in the opposite direction of Saul's journey. They would have items intended to be offerings to God. That the men would give Saul two of the three loaves of bread originally intended as an offering to God indicates Saul's new status as God's anointed king. Samuel instructed Saul to accept the bread, apparently as a way of demonstrating his acceptance of God's designation of him as king.[12]

The final sign was to take place close to home (10:5–6). There Saul would meet prophets accompanied by music. Music and prophecy are associated with each other also when Elisha prophesied to Joram and Jehoshaphat (2 Ki 3:15–19). Saul was told that the Spirit of Yahweh would rush upon him (1 Sam 10:6), an expression that is used for the Spirit's endowment of Samson, Saul,

---

[12] This sharing of sacrificial bread may continue the theme of table fellowship for communion in the faith. See "Samuel Finds Israel's King (9:14–25)" in the commentary on 9:1–25.

and David (see the first textual note on 10:6). In the book of Samuel only Saul, Saul's messengers, and David are said to have a special gift of God's Spirit (1 Sam 10:10; 11:6; 16:13; 19:20, 23; 2 Sam 23:2). The outward manifestation of the Spirit served an evangelical purpose, signaling the arrival of the new ruler in the kingdom of God, as in the NT, when signs of the Spirit accompanied the preaching of the Gospel of Jesus Christ (Acts 2; 10:44–46; with prophesying in Acts 19:6; 1 Cor 12:10; 14:5–6, 22). For the connection between anointing, the gift of the Spirit, and Christian Baptism in the church age, see the commentary on 1 Sam 16:13.

Next Samuel gave Saul some instruction as to what he was to do (1 Sam 10:7–8). First, he was told, "Do whatever you find to do, because God is with you." Then he was told to go to Gilgal, where Samuel would offer sacrifices. Saul was to wait seven days for Samuel, who would give him further instructions. Since Gilgal was on Samuel's regular circuit (7:16), it is likely that the original plan was to publicly declare Saul as God's chosen king when Samuel came to Gilgal. However, since Saul did not go to Gilgal, Samuel continued on his circuit and summoned Israel to a summit when he arrived at Mizpah (10:17).

What was it that Samuel expected Saul to do before going to Gilgal? Samuel noted that there was a Philistine garrison at Gibeah (10:5). Surely Saul, who was from Gibeah, needed no lesson on Gibeah's situation. Yet Samuel went out of his way to point out that the Philistines had continued to maintain a garrison in the area despite no longer being able to invade Israel's territory (7:13). Samuel was implying that there was one specific task Saul was to do—attack the garrison and drive the Philistines out of Israel, thereby provoking the Philistines to further military action (note also God's words to Samuel in 9:16). By doing this, he would have successfully demonstrated that he was God's designated king whom Israel requested to "go out in front of us and fight our battles" (8:20). He was guaranteed success, since Samuel assured him that God was with him (10:7), and the signs confirmed Samuel's words (10:9–12). Then Saul was to go to Gilgal and wait for Samuel, where his public confirmation as king would be accompanied by the appropriate sacrifices to Yahweh, who had appointed him (10:8). At that time he would have received additional guidance on how to conduct a campaign against the Philistines. Long summarizes Samuel's instructions this way:

> Verses 7 and 8 … constitute the two parts of Saul's first charge: Saul's demonstration (v. 7) is to be followed by a meeting with Samuel in Gilgal for this confirmation and further instructions about how to deal with the Philistines, now that they have been provoked. Unfortunately, in the aftermath of his anointing and the fulfillment of all three signs, Saul simply fails to do what lies at hand. Indeed, it is not until 1 Samuel 13 that the Philistine garrison comes under attack, and it is not Saul but his son Jonathan who launches the attack (13:3). Jonathan's bold action has the desired effect (13:4a), and the Philistines come out in force (v. 5). Meanwhile Saul repairs to Gilgal (v. 4b)

to await Samuel's arrival, in keeping with the second part of his first charge (10:8).[13]

Samuel's Instructions to Saul (1 Sam 10:1–8)

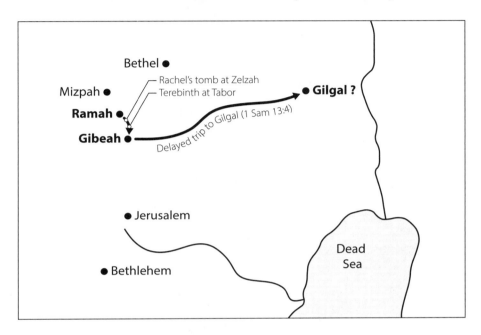

What Long and others miss is that Saul is consistently portrayed as hesitant to attack the Philistines. His inability to initiate a campaign against the Philistines would be underscored repeatedly in that Jonathan would have to attack the Philistine garrison at Gibeah (13:3; see the second textual note there) and again at Michmash (13:23–14:23); then Saul would send David to battle Goliath (17:37) and later send him out to defeat the Philistines (18:5–30). Before his final battle, Saul would cower in the face of the Philistine threat (28:5). Nowhere in the book of Samuel is Saul depicted as initiating war with the Philistines. He is constantly reactive to the success of Jonathan or David when they are victorious in their battles against the Philistines.[14] However, he is never proactive in his fight against Philistine forces.

---

[13] Provan, Long, and Longman, *A Biblical History of Israel*, 212.

[14] This is even subtly emphasized in the summary of Saul's military actions in 14:47, which comes *after* the defeat of the Philistines that was initiated by Jonathan's aggression against them.

Had Saul fulfilled this mission, there would have been the expected king-making pattern of designation (Saul's anointing in 10:1), demonstration of his divine office (driving the Philistines out of Israel), and confirmation (an inauguration at Gilgal).[15] Instead, Saul's inaction led to a second designation at Mizpah (10:17–27), a substitute demonstration by defeating the Ammonites at Jabesh-gilead (11:1–13), and a partial confirmation (11:14–15). Long outlines Saul's accession to Israel's throne as shown in figure 16.

Figure 16

Saul's Faltering Accession

Steps in the Process	**Text**	**Content**
Designation	9:1–10:13	Saul's anointing, first charge, and failure to do what lies at hand.
Interlude	10:14–16	Having faltered, Saul doesn't even mention the kingship to his uncle.
(Second Designation)	10:17–27	Saul is brought to public attention by lot casting and is found hiding behind the baggage; some "worthless fellows" ask, "How can this man save us?"
(Substitute Demonstration)	11:1–13	Saul demonstrates his military ability by rescuing Jabesh-gilead from the Ammonites, thus silencing his critics.
(Partial Confirmation)	11:14–15	Saul's kingship is "renewed"/confirmed(?) to the delight of Saul and the people (Samuel is not mentioned as joining the celebration).
Interlude	12:1–25	Samuel warns that a test remains: king and people must yet prove faithful to Yahweh.
Demonstration (originally intended)	13:1–3	Jonathan strikes the Philistine garrison (cf. 10:7).
Confirmation (withheld)	13:4–15	Saul goes to Gilgal (cf. 10:8), fails to wait for Samuel, and is not confirmed.

Provan, Long, and Longman, *A Biblical History of Israel*, 213 (table 8.3).

---

[15] See the discussion in Provan, Long, and Longman, *A Biblical History of Israel*, 201–14.

Saul Sees the Signs Fulfilled (10:9–12)

The narrator quickly tells us that Saul was changed and that all the signs Samuel had outlined came to pass (10:9). He concentrates on only one part of the last sign—Saul's prophesying—and the reaction of those who were acquainted with Saul (10:10–12). There was amazement that Saul would be a prophet, and as implied by one man's question, that he might even be the leader of a band of prophets (10:12). This is one of two incidents of Saul prophesying that led to a proverbial saying in Israel (for the other episode, see 19:19–24). The saying seems to be a way of noting something that is completely unexpected and out of character. "Is also Saul among the prophets?" (10:12) may have been equivalent to asking "who could have expected that?" The question may also have expressed a degree of doubt as to whether he was fit to hold the office—a skepticism that would quickly become justified.

Saul's Conversation with His Uncle (10:13–16)

After prophesying Saul went up a hill, apparently to his home (see the second textual note on 10:13). Saul's failure to follow Samuel's instructions to assault the Philistine garrison (10:5, 7) is highlighted by the conversation he had with his uncle, who may have been Abner (see the commentary on 14:50). Interestingly, it is Saul who first mentioned Samuel (10:14). That led to his uncle inquiring about Samuel's message, to which Saul gave only a partial answer (10:15–16). His avoiding the subject of the monarchy served to underscore his lack of action: Saul did not do whatever he found to do (10:7). Instead, he did nothing.

Saul Is Publicly Made King

Translation

10 ¹⁷Samuel summoned the people to Yahweh at Mizpah. ¹⁸He said to the Israelites, "This is what Yahweh, the God of Israel, says: 'I brought Israel up from Egypt, and I rescued you from the power of Egypt and from the power of all the kingdoms that were oppressing you.' ¹⁹Today you have rejected your God, who was your Savior from all your troubles and miseries, but you said, 'No! Appoint a king over us.' Now present yourselves before Yahweh by your tribes and your clans."

²⁰Samuel brought forward all the tribes of Israel, and the tribe of Benjamin was selected. ²¹So he brought forward the tribe of Benjamin by its families, and the family of Matri was selected. Then Saul the son of Kish was selected. They sought him, but he was not found.

²²So they inquired of Yahweh again, "Has the man come here yet?"

Yahweh said, "Look, he is hiding among the baggage."

²³They ran and they took him from there, and he stood among the people. He was a head taller than all the people. ²⁴Samuel said to all the people, "Do you see the one whom Yahweh has chosen, for there is no one like him among all the people?"

Then all the people shouted and said, "Long live the king!"

²⁵Samuel told the people the rights of the monarchy, and he wrote [them] in a scroll and placed it before Yahweh. Then Samuel sent all the people home. ²⁶Saul also went home to Gibeah, and the army whose heart God had touched went with him. ²⁷ᵃBut some good-for-nothing men said, "How can this guy save us?" So they despised him and would not bring him a present.

Textual Notes

10:17 וַיַּצְעֵק—The Qal (G) of צָעַק, "cry out," is common and is a by-form of the synonym זָעַק. The Hiphil (H) form of צָעַק here could have the causative meaning "to make messengers call out," i.e., to send messengers to proclaim a message or invitation or summons, but it is more naturally translated as "to call together" or "to summon." This is the only instance of the Hiphil of צָעַק in the OT, but the Hiphil of זָעַק has the same meaning in several passages (2 Sam 20:4, 5; also Judg 4:10, 13; Jonah 3:7).

10:18–19 הֶעֱלֵיתִי ... וָאַצִּיל ... הַלֹּחֲצִים ... מוֹשִׁיעַ—These verbs are classic terms associated with Yahweh's salvation of Israel through the exodus. For the Hiphil (H) of עָלָה, "to bring up" out of Egypt, see, e.g., Ex 3:8, 17; Deut 20:1. For the Hiphil of נָצַל, "to rescue, deliver," see Ex 3:8; 6:6; 18:4, 8–10; Deut 23:15 (ET 23:14). For לָחַץ, "to oppress," denoting the Egyptian oppression of Israel, see Ex 3:9 (cf. Ex 22:20 [ET 22:21]; 23:9; Deut 26:7). For the Hiphil of יָשַׁע, "to save," see Ex 14:30 (cf. Ex 2:17); Deut 20:4. Here the last two verbs are participles. The first, הַלֹּחֲצִים (with the definite article), is translated adjectivally: "all the kingdoms *that were oppressing* you." The second, מוֹשִׁיעַ, is rendered substantively: "Savior."

In the participial clause מוֹשִׁיעַ לָכֶם in 10:19, the preposition לְ is interpreted as denoting possession, hence "your Savior." It is also possible that the participle could function as a verb with לְ introducing the object, "he is the one (who has been) saving you." The Hiphil of יָשַׁע recurs in 10:27, but as a suffixed imperfect (יֹשִׁעֵנוּ) in a contemptuous question about Saul, "how can this guy save us?"

10:19 לֹא—"No!" is the reading in many MT manuscripts, which is also reflected in the LXX. Leningradensis has the homonym לוֹ, "to him."

תָּשִׂים—An imperfect (here the Qal [G]) can have the force of an imperative (Joüon, § 113 m), thus "appoint!"

הִתְיַצְּבוּ לִפְנֵי יְהוָה—The Hithpael (HtD) of יָצַב, "take one's stand," recurs in 10:23 and often later in Samuel. Here the people are to stand "before Yahweh" for adjudication. Ironically, in the first instance of this verb in the book, it was Yahweh who took his stand near Samuel to extend his gracious calling to the prophet (3:10).

וּלְאַלְפֵיכֶם:—"And by your clans" is literally "and to/by your thousands." At times אֶלֶף may denote a large family unit (Num 10:4; Judg 6:15). The LXX translates this as καὶ κατὰ τὰς φυλὰς ὑμῶν, "and according to your clans." In 1 Sam 10:21 the synonymous מִשְׁפָּחָה is used for "clan/family."

10:20 וַיַּקְרֵב—The Qal (G) of קָרַב often means "to come forward, approach" God (e.g., 1 Sam 14:36; also, e.g., Ex 40:32). The Hiphil (H) here and repeated at start of 10:21 has the causative meaning "to bring (people) forward" to God (also, e.g., Ex 29:4). It is frequent in Leviticus denoting the bringing forward of offerings to God (e.g., Lev 1:2, 3, 5, 10).

וַיִּלָּכֵד—Literally "and it was captured," this is the Niphal (N) preterite (imperfect with *waw* consecutive) third masculine singular from the verb לָכַד. This recurs in 10:21, along with the feminine equivalent. The meaning is "to be selected by lot" (*HALOT*, Niphal, 3; as in Josh 7:14–18). That the selection took place by lot is confirmed since Saul was selected but was not present (1 Sam 10:21).

10:21 וַיִּלָּכֵד שָׁאוּל בֶּן־קִישׁ—"Then Saul the son of Kish was selected." The LXX reads καὶ προσάγουσιν τὴν φυλὴν Ματταρι εἰς ἄνδρας, καὶ κατακληροῦται Σαουλ υἱὸς Κις, "and they brought forward the family of Matri man by man, and Saul the son of Kish was selected." If this reading, which is also found in the Old Latin text, is original, then the MT may have suffered its omission by haplography.

10:22 וַיִּשְׁאֲלוּ—The use of the verb שָׁאַל, "to ask, request," is likely a play on the name of שָׁאוּל, "Saul" (10:21, 26), which means "asked for, requested." See also the first textual note on 1:28; "Samuel Warns Israel about Kings (8:10–22)" in the commentary on 8:1–22; the commentary on 12:13; the textual note on 14:37; and the second textual note on 20:6 (which also discusses שָׁאוּל נִשְׁאַל נִשְׁאַל in 20:28).

הֲבָא עוֹד הֲלֹם אִישׁ—Literally "has a man come yet here?" The interrogative *he* is prefixed to the third masculine singular Qal (G) perfect of בּוֹא, "come," whose subject is the anarthrous אִישׁ, "a man," but it is translated as definite, "the man," because it refers to a certain one. הֲלֹם, "here," and עוֹד, "yet," are adverbs.

נֶחְבָּא—"He is hiding" is the Niphal (N) perfect third masculine singular or the masculine singular Niphal participle of חָבָא (BDB). In the Niphal, the sense of this word is passive, "be hidden," or reflexive, "hide oneself," as here. Oftentimes the intransitive use of the verb "hide" in English works best when translating the Niphal of חָבָא.

10:23 וַיִּגְבַּהּ מִכָּל־הָעָם מִשִּׁכְמוֹ וָמָעְלָה—This vocabulary is almost the same as that discussed in the third textual note on 9:2. Here a stative verb, גָּבַהּ, "be high, lofty," with the preposition מִן forms a comparative: "he was taller than all the people" (Joüon, § 141 h). Literally "from his shoulder and upward" (מִשִּׁכְמוֹ וָמָעְלָה, as in 9:2) states the extent to which he was "taller" in comparison to others.

10:24 הַרְּאִיתֶם—This is a rare instance of the gemination of the consonant *resh* (-רְּ-, with *daghesh*) following the interrogative *he* (Joüon, § 102 m; GKC, § 22 s) on the Qal (G) perfect of רָאָה: "do you see?"

בָּחַר־בּוֹ יְהוָה—The verb בָּחַר, "choose," often takes the preposition בְּ when it refers to a "divine choice" (BDB, s.v. בָּחַר, 1 a).

יְחִי הַמֶּלֶךְ:—Literally "may the king live." This expression with the Qal (G) jussive of חָיָה, "to live," serves as an acclamation, equivalent to the English "long live the king!"

10:25 מִשְׁפַּט הַמְּלֻכָה—This is translated as "the rights of the monarchy." For this nuance of מִשְׁפָּט denoting the legal rights or privileges to be asserted (or abused!) by the king, see 8:9–11.

וַיַּנַּח לִפְנֵי יְהוָה—This is another instance of the Hiphil (H) of נוּחַ formed as if it were from the root ננח and meaning "to put, place." See Joüon, § 80 p, and the third textual note on 6:18.

וַיְשַׁלַּח שְׁמוּאֵל אֶת־כָּל־הָעָם אִישׁ לְבֵיתוֹ:—Literally "and Samuel sent away all the people, each man to his own house." Similarly, 4QSam^a reads as follows: וישלח שמואל את כול העם איש למקומ[ו]. The LXX reads καὶ ἐξαπέστειλεν Σαμουηλ πάντα τὸν λαόν, καὶ ἀπῆλθεν ἕκαστος εἰς τὸν τόπον αὐτοῦ, "and Samuel sent away all the people, and each one went away to his own place."

10:26 הַחַיִל אֲשֶׁר־נָגַע אֱלֹהִים בְּלִבָּם:—Literally this reads "the force which God touched their heart." The noun חַיִל often means "strength," but it can also denote an "army" (e.g., Ex 14:4; Deut 11:4; Jer 32:2). Here "the army" probably denotes an armed band of men. The LXX (υἱοὶ δυνάμεων) and 4QSam^a (בני החיל) have "(the) sons of strength," that is, "(the) valiant men." The addition of "sons" may have been intended to draw a sharp contrast between the men whose heart God had touched (בְּנֵי־הַחַיִל, "the sons of strength") and the good-for-nothing men in 10:27 (בְּנֵי בְלִיַּעַל, literally "sons of uselessness") who refused to acknowledge Saul as king. The Qal (G) of נָגַע is used elsewhere with the preposition בְּ for God "touching" mountains or the earth with catastrophic consequences (BDB, s.v. נָגַע, Qal, 1 b, citing Amos 9:5; Pss 104:32; 144:5). This is the sole instance where it is used for God graciously touching a "heart" (לֵב) to volunteer in brave faith. Hebrew characteristically uses a retrospective object pronoun at the end of a relative clause (Joüon, § 158 h), thus בְּלִבָּם, "which God touched *their* heart," but the pronoun is redundant in English and so is omitted in translation.

10:27a בְּלִיַּעַל—For "good-for-nothing," see the first textual note on 1:16.

זֶה—At times this demonstrative pronoun is used derogatorily to express contempt (Joüon, § 143 d), thus "this guy." See also 1 Sam 21:16 (ET 21:15); 29:5; 1 Ki 22:27; and זֹאת in 2 Sam 13:17.

Commentary

1049 BC

The last time Samuel summoned the Israelites to Mizpah, God delivered them from Philistine aggression (7:5–11). Now he assembles the Israelites for a public declaration of God's choice of a king to lead them into battle against their enemies (10:17). This meeting was necessitated by Saul's inaction. Had Saul followed Samuel's instructions to conquer the Philistine garrison at Gibeah before proceeding to Gilgal, he could have been confirmed as king at Gilgal.[1]

Samuel begins by prophesying to the people (10:18–19). He quotes Yahweh, who notes that he delivered Israel from Egypt and later kingdoms that oppressed them, with the location of the convocation, Mizpah, being a reminder of God's latest deliverance (7:5–11). Samuel then repeats what Yahweh had told him—that in requesting a king (8:5, 19), the people had rejected God (8:7).

Samuel's order for the Israelites to present themselves before Yahweh by tribes and clans (10:19) begins the process of casting lots to determine whom God has chosen for Israel (10:20–21). Choosing by lot was not viewed as simply allowing random chance to determine one's fate. Instead, it was viewed as allowing God, who controls all things, including the fall of the lot, to pick (Prov 16:33). There are only a few instances of choosing persons by lot in the Scriptures. Two times it was used to determine someone who has done wrong (Achan in Josh 7:16–18 and Jonathan in 1 Sam 14:38–42). However, it was also used to choose an apostle of Christ to replace Judas Iscariot (Acts 1:23–26).[2]

The lots confirm God's choice of Saul. We learn that Saul was from "the family/clan of Matri" (מִשְׁפַּחַת הַמַּטְרִי, 1 Sam 10:21), a clan mentioned nowhere else in Scripture. It may be that Shimei, who later would curse David, was from this clan, since he was from "the family/clan of the house of Saul" (מִמִּשְׁפַּחַת בֵּית־שָׁאוּל, 2 Sam 16:5).

When Saul could not be found, Israel inquired of Yahweh—probably using the Urim and Thummim[3]—and Yahweh instructed them to look among the baggage (10:22). Why would Saul hide himself? Could it have been that he knew that this convocation was required because of his inaction? Was this a sign of his reluctance to confront the Philistines?

Despite Saul hiding among the baggage, when he was retrieved from there, he made a favorable impression on Israel because of his height. Samuel pointed this out to the people, who proclaimed him king (10:23–24). We ought

---

[1] See 10:7–8 and the explanation in "Samuel Anoints Saul (9:26–10:8)" in the commentary on 9:26–10:16.

[2] Contrast the Roman soldiers' casting of lots for Christ's tunic (Jn 19:23–24).

[3] See the excursus "The Urim and Thummim" following the commentary on 14:24–46.

to note that despite his impressive physical stature, Samuel emphasized Saul as *Yahweh's* choice.

The narration picks up its pace quickly with a summary statement of Samuel confirming the monarchy's rights both orally and in a written form placed before Yahweh (10:25). The people were dismissed, and Saul also went home.

The final verses depict a rift among the people (10:26–27a). Many, whose hearts were touched by God, accepted his choice of Saul despite the fact that he had no credentials to recommend him for the throne. They accompanied the new king to his home. However, some simply opposed God's choice. They asked, "How can this guy save us?" (10:27). Although "good-for-nothing" suggests that they were reprehensible apostates[4] and although they are disputing God's expressed will, theirs was not an unreasonable question from a worldly perspective, especially since Saul had ignored Samuel's instructions out of cowardice.[5] Had Saul attacked and driven off the Philistine garrison at Gibeah, these men would not have been able to raise such doubts. We are told that they despised Saul and displayed their contempt by refusing to bring him presents. Bringing presents to an honored person or tribute to a king was an acknowledgment of the recipient's elevated status.[6] Saul did not receive such acknowledgment from all Israel, since he had yet to demonstrate his ability to lead Israel into battle against its enemies.

---

[4] See the same term in, e.g., Deut 13:14 (ET 13:13); Judg 19:22; 1 Sam 2:12; 25:25; 2 Sam 16:7; 1 Ki 21:10, 13; Prov 6:12; 16:27; 19:28; 2 Chr 13:7.

[5] Again, see 10:7–8 and the explanation in "Samuel Anoints Saul (9:26–10:8)" in the commentary on 9:26–10:16.

[6] Gen 32:14–19 (ET 32:13–18); Judg 3:15; 6:18; 2 Sam 8:2, 6; 2 Ki 8:8.

1 Samuel 10:27b–11:15

Saul Saves Jabesh-gilead

Translation

10 ²⁷ᵇAbout a month later ¹¹:¹Nahash the Ammonite went up and besieged Jabesh-gilead. All the men of Jabesh said to Nahash, "Make a treaty with us, and we'll serve you."

²Nahash the Ammonite said to them, "Under this condition I will make [a treaty] with you: I'll gouge out each of your right eyes and bring disgrace upon all Israel."

³The elders of Jabesh said to him, "Let us alone for seven days. We will send messengers throughout the entire territory of Israel. If there is no one to save us, we will come out to you."

⁴When the messengers came to Saul's Gibeah, they announced the terms to the people, and the people wept aloud. ⁵Now Saul was coming behind the cattle from the countryside. Saul said, "Why are the people weeping?" So they repeated the words of the men of Jabesh to him.

⁶God's Spirit rushed upon Saul when he heard these words, and he became very angry. ⁷He took a pair of oxen, cut them in pieces, and sent them in the hands of messengers throughout the entire territory of Israel with the message "whoever does not come out behind Saul and Samuel will have this done to his cattle." The terror of Yahweh fell upon the people, and they came out united. ⁸He assembled them at Bezek. There were three hundred thousand Israelites and thirty thousand men of Judah. ⁹They said to the messengers who had come, "This is what you will say to the men of Jabesh-gilead: 'Tomorrow by the time the sun is hot, you will have victory.'" The messengers went and told [this] to the men of Jabesh-gilead, and they were overjoyed. ¹⁰The men of Jabesh said [to Nahash], "Tomorrow we will come out to you, and you may do to us whatever you think is right."

¹¹On the next day Saul put the troops in three commands. They entered the [Ammonite] camp during the morning watch and struck Ammon until the heat of the day. Those that were left were scattered, and no two of them were left together.

¹²The troops said to Samuel, "Who said, 'Should Saul rule us?' Give the men [to us], and we'll put them to death."

¹³Saul said, "No man will be put to death this day, because today Yahweh won a victory in Israel."

¹⁴Samuel said to the troops, "Let's go to Gilgal, and we'll renew the monarchy there." ¹⁵So all the troops went to Gilgal and made Saul king there before Yahweh in Gilgal. They sacrificed peace offerings there before Yahweh, and Saul and all the men of Israel celebrated.

Textual Notes

10:27b 4QSam[a], column 10, fragment a, lines 6–9, includes the following insertion between 10:27a and 10:27b. It is not found in the MT or the LXX.

[ונ]חש מלך בני עמון הוא לחץ את בני גד ואת בני ראובן בחזקה ונקר להם

כ[ול ע]ין ימין ונתן אין [מושי]ע ל[י]שראל ולוא נשאר איש בבני ישראל

אשר בעןבר הירדן אשןר לןוא נןקר לו נחןש מלך] בני עןמון כול עין ימין

ו[ה]ן שבעת אלפים איש [נצלו מיד] בני עמון ויבאו אל [י]בש גלעד

[Now N]ahash, king of the sons of Ammon, he oppressed the sons of Gad and the sons of Reuben severely. He gouged out [each] of their right [e]yes. He allowed no [savio]r for [I]srael. There was no man left in the sons of Israel who was ea[st of the Jordan who]se right eye Naha[sh, king] of the sons of [A]mmon, had not gouged out. H[ow]ever, seven thousand men [escaped from the power of] the sons of Ammon and came to [Ja]besh-gilead.

Josephus also includes most of this information in an expanded form that explains the reason for gouging out right eyes: it would make men incapable of taking up arms, since a right-handed man would hold his shield in his left hand, covering his left eye.[1] With no right eye, a man could not see his enemy to fight him. Also, a person needs two eyes for binocular depth perception to gauge the speed at which a soldier or weapon is coming toward him.

This text has been defended as original by a number of scholars and is included in the NRSV.[2] However, there are good reasons for rejecting this text. Auld offers the following:[3]

1. The time referent "about a month later" (ויהי כמו חדש, 10:27b; see the next textual note) *follows* the text in 4QSam[a], but the similar notice in Josephus (μηνὶ δ' ὕστερον) *precedes* the text.[4]

2. In this text Nahash is twice called "Nahash, king of the sons of Ammon" (נחש מלך בני עמון), but immediately after this text the MT calls him "Nahash the Ammonite" (נָחָשׁ הָעַמּוֹנִי, 11:1, 2).[5]

3. This text pairs Gad and Reuben, but they are never paired elsewhere in the book of Samuel. Gad is mentioned in 1 Sam 13:7 and 2 Sam 24:5. Reuben is never mentioned.

---

[1] Josephus, *Antiquities*, 6.68–70.

[2] Cross, "The Ammonite Oppression of the Tribes of Gad and Reuben: Missing Verses from 1 Samuel 11 Found in 4QSamuel[a]"; Eves, "One Ammonite Invasion or Two?"; Klein, *1 Samuel*, 102–3; McCarter, *I Samuel*, 198–99; Ulrich, *The Qumran Text of Samuel and Josephus*, 166–70.

[3] Auld, *I and II Samuel*, 118.

[4] Josephus, *Antiquities*, 6.68.

[5] Although Auld does not mention it, after the second occurrence of "Nahash" in 11:1, 4QSam[a] apparently supplies "king of the Ammonites" (מלך בני עמון), but only the initial *mem* is extant. This appears to be an adaptation to the expanded text of 10:27b. This strengthens the argument that the longer text is secondary. The LXX adds τὸν Αμμανίτην, "the Ammonite," under the influence of the previous mention of Nahash in 11:1 (cf. LXX 1 Sam 12:12: Ναας βασιλεὺς υἱῶν Αμμων, "King Nahash of the Ammonites").

In addition, the following ought to be noted:

4. Rofé notes that most of the elements in the expanded text could have been imported from elsewhere in the OT: the severe oppression of Israel by a foreign king (Judg 4:3); the gouging out of right eyes (1 Sam 11:2); the tribes of Gad and Reuben (in that order; Num 32:2–38); a remnant of seven thousand out of an entire population (1 Ki 19:18).[6]

5. Josephus makes no mention of the seven thousand men who escaped to Jabesh-gilead. Thus, Josephus does not agree completely with 4QSam[a] against the MT and the LXX.

6. If this longer text had been omitted by accident, there is no trigger for haplography. Usually such omission occurred when a scribe's eye skipped from a word or phrase (a trigger) to a similar word or phrase in the next line or lines.[7] Such is not the case here. Moreover, there is no good reason that this text would have been purposely omitted.

7. The position of the time referent "about a month later Nahash the Ammonite went up and besieged Jabesh-gilead" (10:27b–11:1a) is nonsensical in 4QSam[a]. About a month after what? After seven thousand men escaped to Jabesh-gilead? That would require a single mass escape from Nahash's custody. Surely that is not what is intended. Instead, the text is more reasonably understood as seven thousand men trickling into Jabesh-gilead as Nahash conducted a campaign of systematically gouging out right eyes among Gadites and Reubenites. 1 Sam 10:27b–11:1 makes much more sense as following Saul's investiture at Mizpah (1 Sam 10:17–27a): about a month later Nahash attacked Jabesh-gilead.[8]

This additional text in 4QSam[a] ought to be considered a secondary expansion of the MT. It was designed to make sense of Samuel's statement in 12:12, which is usually understood as "When you saw that King Nahash of the Ammonites came against you, you said to me, 'No! Rather, a king will reign over us,' although Yahweh was your King." This appears to say that Nahash's incursion into Israelite territory was the event that precipitated the request for a king. Thus, there was a perceived need to have Nahash actively campaigning *before* Saul was chosen as king. This led to the invention of the text in 4QSam[a] to explain Samuel's words in 12:12. Note that this text imports the epithet "Nahash, king of the sons of Ammon," from 12:12. However, this text arose from a misunderstanding of Samuel's words, which contain no explicit temporal clause (i.e., 12:12 does not explicitly say "*when* you saw …"). The text of 12:12 is composed of simple coordinated clauses that ought to be understood not as a temporal sequence but as a logical sequence that extends into 12:13 and that can be paraphrased as "You've

---

[6] Rofé, "The Acts of Nahash according to 4QSam[a]," 131. We could also add the epithet "Nahash, king of the sons of Ammon" (1 Sam 12:12).

[7] McCarter (*I Samuel*, 199) argues for the originality of the text that is unique to 4QSam[a], but he is forced to concede the weakness of his position:

> MT and LXX have lost everything from "Now Nahash …" to "… and entered into Jabesh-gilead" (*wnḥš … wybʾw ʾl ybš glʿd*), an extraordinary case of scribal oversight. The omission apparently was not haplographic—there seems to be nothing in the text to have triggered it. A scribe simply skipped an entire paragraph of his text.

[8] This is exactly how Josephus construes this passing month in *Antiquities*, 6.67–68.

seen Nahash attack you. You've [already] asked for a king [12:12]. Here is your king [who defeated Nahash; 12:13]." Samuel was not saying that Nahash's invasion was the *reason* for the request for a king. Instead, he is putting together Nahash's invasion with their previous request for a king to protect them in exactly such situations (8:20; cf. 9:16) and then pointing them to their king. The logic is as follows:

1. What happened (the siege of Jabesh-gilead in 10:27b–11:15) is what you feared.
2. A king was your proposed solution to alleviate such fears (8:20; cf. 9:16).
3. Here is your king (12:13), who will be the solution to your fears, but under one condition: "if you" fear Yahweh and obey his Word (12:14–15).

Thus, once 12:12 is correctly construed, there is no need for the expansion in 4QSamᵃ. See further the translation of 12:12 and the commentary on that verse.

וַיְהִי כְּמַחֲרִישׁ:—Literally the MT says "and he [Saul] was as one staying silent." He did not respond to the "good-for-nothing men" who despised him and refused to bring him tribute (10:27). The combination of the preterite (imperfect with *waw* consecutive), וַיְהִי, and the participle, מַחֲרִישׁ (the Hiphil [H] of חָרֵשׁ II, "be silent"), expresses action in the past that continued for some time. The preposition כְּ is the *kaph veritatis* (GKC, § 118 x; Joüon, § 133 g; akin to the *bet essentiae*), which can indicate equality, i.e., "he was a man keeping quiet."

The translation "about a month later" follows the reading found in the LXX (καὶ ἐγενήθη ὡς μετὰ μῆνα), 4QSamᵃ (ויהי כמו חדש), and Josephus (μηνὶ δ' ὕστερον).[9] The original reading most likely was (with pointing added) וַיְהִי כְּמֵחֹדֶשׁ, literally "and it was about from a month." The noun חֹדֶשׁ, "month," was prefixed by two prepositions, first מִן and then כְּ.[10] Twice elsewhere in the OT a word is prefixed with both of these prepositions.[11] The closest parallel is Gen 38:24: וַיְהִי ׀ כְּמִשְׁלֹשׁ חֳדָשִׁים, "and it was after about three months." If וַיְהִי כְּמֵחֹדֶשׁ was the original reading in 1 Sam 10:27, then the MT suffered from confusion of two similar letters: *daleth* and *resh*. When *resh* was accidentally written (כמחרש) instead of *daleth* (כמחדש), the only way to read the resulting text was to assume that the word כמחרש was the preposition כְּ prefixed to a Hiphil (H) participle (with preformative מ) from the root חרשׁ, and then a *yod* was added after the *resh* to signify the long vowel *hireq* (רִי-). 4QSamᵃ has the correct consonants כמחדש but took כמ as the form of the preposition כְּ with *mem*, כְּמוֹ (Joüon, § 103 g), and therefore added a *waw* with *holem* and a space between כְּמוֹ and the following *chet*, making כמחדש appear as if it were two words, כְּמוֹ חֹדֶשׁ.

11:1 נָחָשׁ—The name "Nahash" means "snake, serpent" in Hebrew (e.g., Gen 3:1, 14; Num 21:6; Is 27:1).

וַיִּחַן עַל־יָבֵשׁ גִּלְעָד—The verb is the Qal (G) preterite (imperfect with *waw* consecutive) of חָנָה, "encamp." In the book of Samuel it usually refers to establishing a military

---

[9] Josephus, *Antiquities*, 6.68.

[10] Cf. מֵחֹדֶשׁ, the noun חֹדֶשׁ, "month," with only the preposition מִן, in Esth 3:7.

[11] One example is in Lev 26:37: וְכָשְׁלוּ אִישׁ־בְּאָחִיו כְּמִפְּנֵי־חֶרֶב, "and they will stumble, each into his brother, *as from* the edge of a sword."

camp for warfare. Often it refers to an army laying siege to a town, in which sense it can take the preposition עַל in an adversative sense, "against" (BDB, s.v. חָנָה, Qal, 2 c).

כְּרָת־לָנוּ בְרִית—The verb כָּרַת with the noun בְּרִית, literally "to cut a covenant," is the standard Hebrew terminology for establishing a covenant or treaty.[12] A common explanation is that the verb "cut" refers to the cutting or severing of sacrificial animals, as in Gen 15:9–18, with the implication that a party who violates the covenant is punishable by a similar severing or dismemberment. Thus כָּרַת is also used in covenantal contexts for "cutting off" a person who transgresses the covenant.[13] The long "o" vowel, *holem*, in the Qal (G) imperative כְּרֹת is reduced to the short "o" vowel *qamets chatuph*, כְּרָת־, since the verb is joined to the suffixed preposition לְ in the sense of advantage, "for our benefit," but English idiom requires "with us." The verb כָּרַת recurs in the same sense, but without the noun בְּרִית, "covenant," in 11:2; see the first textual note there. Obviously the "covenant" or "treaty" in 11:1–2 is not a mutual agreement by equal parties; this request for a treaty is a capitulation to an overpowering enemy.

וְנַעַבְדֶךָ:—This Qal (G) preterite (imperfect with *waw* consecutive) of עָבַד, "to serve (as a slave)," serves as an apodosis of a conditional sentence, in effect "if you make a treaty with us, *then we will serve you*." The second masculine singular suffix has *daghesh forte affectuosum*, ךָ (see GKC, § 20 i), which strengthens the preceding vowel with *metheg* (-ֶ-ֶ-) in this pausal form.

11:2 אֶכְרֹת—"I will cut/make [a treaty]." The MT and 4QSamª lack the direct object (as also in 1 Sam 22:8; 1 Ki 8:9; 2 Chr 5:10), but it is implied since the idiom with the direct object preceded in 11:1 (see the third textual note there). The LXX supplies the implied object noun "covenant" (διαθήσομαι ὑμῖν διαθήκην).

בִּנְקוֹר לָכֶם כָּל־עֵין יָמִין—The preposition בְּ introduces the price (BDB, s.v. בְּ I, III 3): the granting of the treaty will cost the Israelites their right eyes. The infinitive construct נְקוֹר is one of only two instances of the Qal (G) of נָקַר, "gouge out," in the OT; the other is Prov 30:17, where ravens "peck out" an eye. The verb's Piel (D) has the same meaning in Num 16:14; Judg 16:21.

וְשַׂמְתִּיהָ חֶרְפָּה עַל־כָּל־יִשְׂרָאֵל:—"And I will place it [as a] disgrace upon all Israel." The feminine suffix on the verb ("it") refers to the abstract idea of the implementation of the requirement for the treaty.

11:3 הֶרֶף לָנוּ—The Hiphil (H) of רָפָה (this is the imperative) takes the preposition לְ with a person here and in 2 Ki 4:27 to mean "leave someone alone."

וְאִם־אֵין מוֹשִׁיעַ אֹתָנוּ—For the participle מוֹשִׁיעַ, see the textual note on 10:18–19, where it was translated as a substantive, "Savior." Here it functions verbally with אֹתָנוּ as its direct object: literally "and if there is no one saving us."

---

[12] The idiom recurs in 1 Sam 18:3; 23:18; 2 Sam 3:12, 13, 21; 5:3. Elsewhere in the OT see, e.g., Gen 9:11; 15:18; Ex 24:8; Deut 5:2–3; Is 55:3; 61:8.

[13] See, e.g., Gen 17:14; Ex 12:15; 31:14; Num 15:30–31; 1 Ki 9:7; cf. Ex 4:25; 1 Sam 2:33; 20:15.

11:4 וַיְדַבְּרוּ הַדְּבָרִים בְּאָזְנֵי הָעָם—Literally "and they said the words in the ears of the people." "Say in the ears" is often used as an idiom for making a public announcement.[14]

וַיִּשְׂאוּ כָל־הָעָם אֶת־קוֹלָם וַיִּבְכּוּ:—Literally "and all the people lifted up their voice and wept." "To lift up one's voice and weep" means "to weep aloud."[15]

11:5 הַשָּׂדֶה—The noun שָׂדֶה, translated as "countryside" (see *HALOT*, 1), is often used of the open country as opposed to the city, an urban area enclosed by a wall.

מַה־לָּעָם כִּי יִבְכּוּ—Literally "what [pertains] to the people that they continue weeping?"

11:7 כְּאִישׁ אֶחָד :—"As one man" is a common idiom for "united."[16]

11:8 וַיִּפְקְדֵם—The polysemous verb פָּקַד can have a variety of specific nuances, depending on context, including to "muster" troops for battle (BDB, Qal, A 4).

בְּבָזֶק—This means "at Bezek." 4QSam[a] expands to "at Bezek at the high place." The LXX is similar.

שְׁלֹשׁ מֵאוֹת אֶלֶף—The MT has "three hundred thousand." The LXX reads "six hundred thousand." Josephus has "seven hundred thousand."[17]

שְׁלֹשִׁים אֶלֶף:—The MT has "thirty thousand." The LXX, 4QSam[a], and Josephus[18] have "seventy thousand."

11:9 לְאִישׁ יָבֵישׁ גִּלְעָד—This reading in Leningradensis is literally "to the man of Jabesh-gilead." A few Masoretic manuscripts have the plural לְאַנְשֵׁי, "to the men of," in agreement with the LXX.

תִּהְיֶה־לָכֶם תְּשׁוּעָה—Literally "salvation will be to you [i.e., will be yours]." The noun תְּשׁוּעָה, derived from the verb יָשַׁע, "to save," is translated as "victory" here and in 11:13.

כְּחֹם הַשָּׁמֶשׁ— The Qere is חֹם, the Qal (G) infinitive construct of חָמַם, "to be hot," with the preposition כְּ in a temporal sense: "when the sun is hot." The Kethib בְּחֹם is the same infinitive but with the preposition בְּ, which can have the same temporal significance. In the phrase עַד־חֹם הַיּוֹם in 11:11, the homograph חֹם is the noun "heat": "until the heat of the day."

At the end of 11:9, 4QSam[a] contains an additional line of text, but only the first few words can be reconstructed: [ויאמרו] לכם פתחו השׁ[ער], "So they said to you, 'Open the gate. ...' " Since the rest of this extra line of text is missing, it is impossible to guess how these words came to be or what the full line might have meant.

11:11 הָעָם—In military contexts "the people" can refer to "the troops," as again in 11:12, 14, 15. See the textual note on 4:3.

שְׁלֹשָׁה רָאשִׁים—Literally "three heads," this means "three (division) commands."

---

[14] E.g., Gen 23:13, 16; Ex 11:2; 24:7; Num 14:28; Deut 5:1; 31:30; 32:44; 2 Ki 18:26; Is 36:11; Jer 26:15; 28:7.

[15] Also Gen 21:16; 27:38; 29:11; Num 14:1; Judg 2:4; 21:2; 1 Sam 24:17 (ET 24:16); 30:4; 2 Sam 3:32; 13:36; Job 2:12; Ruth 1:9, 14.

[16] Also Num 14:15; Judg 6:16; 20:1, 8, 11; 2 Sam 19:15 (ET 19:14); Ezra 3:1; Neh 8:1.

[17] Josephus, *Antiquities*, 6.78.

[18] Josephus, *Antiquities*, 6.78.

בְּאַשְׁמֹרֶת הַבֹּקֶר—Literally this means "in the watch of the morning." Nighttime guard duty was divided into "watches" (plural: אַשְׁמֻרוֹת) for military purposes.[19] Two of these are mentioned by name: "the middle watch" (הָאַשְׁמֹרֶת הַתִּיכוֹנָה, Judg 7:19) and the one here, "the morning watch" (הָאַשְׁמֹרֶת הַבֹּקֶר, Ex 14:24; 1 Sam 11:11). Since there is a "middle" watch, it appears that the night was normally divided into at least three watches. There must have been an earlier watch, and then "the morning watch" was the latest, extending until dawn. Beckwith has argued that the Hebrew phrase "between the evenings" (בֵּין הָעַרְבַּיִם, e.g., Ex 12:6; 16:12) refers to the first watch of the evening.[20]

עַמּוֹן—Here, as in Ps 83:8 (ET 83:7), "Ammon" stands alone. Everywhere else in the OT it occurs in the phrase בְּנֵי־עַמּוֹן, "the sons of Ammon," meaning "the Ammonites." A few Masoretic manuscripts and the LXX (τοὺς υἱοὺς Αμμων) have "the Ammonites" here, which is also the reconstructed reading of 4QSamᵃ (בני עמון).

11:12 מִי הָאֹמֵר שָׁאוּל יִמְלֹךְ עָלֵינוּ—The question with the interrogative pronoun מִי, "who?" and the participle with the definite article הָאֹמֵר asks, "Who is the one saying (who said)?" The next three words, שָׁאוּל יִמְלֹךְ עָלֵינוּ, "Saul should reign over us," are a quote within the quote. They could be taken as a statement: "Saul should/will reign over us." But the context (see the next textual note) requires these words to refer to what was said by the "good-for-nothing men" in 10:27a who opposed Saul becoming their king. Therefore they are taken as a question: "Should Saul reign over us?" While there is no formal indication that this is a question, Hebrew (like English) can indicate a question by intonation (Joüon, § 161 a), which is not readily apparent in the text.[21]

תְּנוּ הָאֲנָשִׁים וּנְמִיתֵם—The imperative (the Qal [G] of נָתַן) with the cohortative (the suffixed Hiphil [H] of מוּת) could be rendered as a purpose clause: "give [us] the men so that we can put them to death" (see Joüon, § 116 b). While the form of the suffixed verb נְמִיתֵם could be either imperfect or cohortative, its meaning clearly is cohortative since it is volitive, expressing the will and intent of the speakers (see Joüon, § 114 b). It is also true that an imperfect form can have a cohortative meaning.

11:13 יוּמַת—This is the Hophal (Hp) imperfect of מוּת, which has the passive meaning "be put to death," corresponding to the Hiphil (H) discussed in the preceding textual note.

11:14 לְכוּ וְנֵלְכָה—The imperative and cohortative forms of הָלַךְ are joined, forming a hendiadys: "let's go." See Joüon, § 177 f. The identical wording occurred in 9:9. See also the third textual note on 9:3.

וּנְחַדֵּשׁ—This is the Piel (D) imperfect of חָדַשׁ, which is related to the common adjective חָדָשׁ, "new." The verb חָדַשׁ occurs only in the Piel, meaning "renew" (as here and also in, e.g., Pss 51:12 [ET 51:10]; 104:30) or "repair," and once in the Hithpael

---

[19] Ex 14:24; Judg 7:19; 1 Sam 11:11; Pss 63:7 (ET 63:6); 90:4; 119:148; Lam 2:19; see also Judith 12:5; *Jubilees* 49:10–12.

[20] Beckwith, "The Day, Its Divisions and Its Limits, in Biblical Thought," 219.

[21] See, for example, Gen 27:24; Judg 14:16; 2 Sam 18:29; 1 Ki 1:24; 2 Ki 9:11; compare 1 Sam 16:4 with 1 Ki 2:13.

(HtD), "be renewed" (Ps 103:5). Some have proposed that the Piel here can also mean "inaugurate."[22] However, there is no firm evidence for this, and it is unconvincing.[23]

11:15 וַיַּמְלִכוּ—See the first textual note on 8:22.

וַיִּזְבְּחוּ־שָׁם זְבָחִים שְׁלָמִים—For the cognate accusative construction "to sacrifice a sacrifice," see the second textual note on 6:15. The noun שְׁלָמִים is in apposition to זְבָחִים to specify that the kind of "sacrifices" are "peace offerings." The appositional phrase here is equivalent to the construct phrase זִבְחֵי שְׁלָמִים in 10:8. For the "peace offerings," which provided meat for the worshipers to eat, see the second textual note on 10:8. See also "Elkanah and His Wives (1:4–8)" in the commentary on 1:1–20.

וַיִּשְׂמַח ... עַד־מְאֹד:—Literally "and he rejoiced ... greatly." The singular verb וַיִּשְׂמַח with the compound subject ("Saul and all the men of Israel") emphasizes the action of the (singular) party whose number agrees with the (singular) verb, namely, Saul's celebrating.

Commentary

1049 BC

Having previously disregarded Samuel's instructions to eradicate the Philistine garrison in Gibeah,[24] Saul would not be irrefutably recognized as king until he could demonstrate his ability to lead an army into battle. About a month later an opportunity presented itself in the person of Nahash the Ammonite. The city of Jabesh in Gilead, east of the Jordan River, conceded defeat by offering to become subject to Nahash when he besieged it (see the second textual note on 11:1). Nahash explains his condition for granting the treaty—that he gouge out the right eye of all the men—as a way to bring disgrace upon Israel (see the third textual note on 11:2). Although Josephus attempts to explain this as a way of making the men incapable of military service,[25] and although it would certainly inhibit their ability to fight, the text of Samuel depicts it as a matter of national shame. Not willing to concede their eyes immediately, the elders negotiate a week's period to ask for someone in Israel to come to their help before they surrender (11:3). Nahash apparently agreed, perhaps wishing to avoid a long siege and thinking that help was unlikely.

The scene immediately shifts to Gibeah, where the messengers from Jabesh have arrived (11:4). While the elders of Jabesh said they were sending messengers throughout Israel, only the messengers to Gibeah are mentioned by the author of Samuel. The people of Gibeah wept aloud—a sign of their distress over the potential shame and disability of fellow Israelites and the subjection of an Israelite city to a foreign power. A further cause of this lamentation was the

---

[22] Dhorme, *Les livres de Samuel*, 97; Wiesmann, "Die Einführung des Königtums in Israel," 137, n. 1.

[23] Polzin, "On Taking Renewal Seriously," 496, including n. 4.

[24] These instructions are implied in 10:7. See "Samuel Anoints Saul (9:26–10:8)" in the commentary on 9:26–10:16. See also the beginning of the commentary on 10:17–27a.

[25] Josephus, *Antiquities*, 6.68–70. See also the first textual note on 10:27b.

especially close connection between Gibeah and Jabesh. When Israel had gone to war against the tribe of Benjamin and had attacked Gibeah (Judges 19–21), Jabesh had sent no troops (Judg 21:8–9). Benjamin had been decimated and needed women for the remaining men to marry so as to not exterminate a tribe from Israel (Judg 21:1–3). Yet the other Israelites could not give their daughters as wives to the Benjaminites because of an oath not to do so (Judg 21:6–7). In fulfillment of a vow to put to death all who had not participated in the attack on Benjamin (Judg 21:5), Israel attacked Jabesh and nearly wiped it out (Judg 21:8–11). However, four hundred young women were taken from Jabesh and given to the men of Benjamin (Judg 21:12–14). So the people of Gibeah and elsewhere in Benjamin had kinship ties with the people of Jabesh.

Saul, we are told, was still not functioning as the anointed king Yahweh chose to save his people from foreign aggression (1 Sam 9:16; 10:1). Instead, he was driving his cattle when he received news of the message from Jabesh (11:5). Unlike the last time when God's Spirit rushed on him (10:10), Saul became angry at the indignity done to Israel (11:6) and took action (11:7). Saul's cutting up of the pair of oxen and sending a grisly message throughout Israel calls to mind the message sent by a Levite in reaction to the rape of his concubine by the residents of Gibeah (Judg 19:29), which had led to the war on Benjamin. Saul's message summoned Israel to war under his leadership *and* that of Samuel ("behind Saul and Samuel," 1 Sam 11:7). To this point Saul had been anointed by Samuel (10:1) and publicly proclaimed king (10:24), but had not begun his reign. Note that the summary of Saul's reign, which normally *precedes* the account of a king's acts, is not given until 13:1.[26] Thus, Saul as king designate (נָגִיד, "designated ruler," 9:16; 10:1) included the judge Samuel as his co-leader of Israel (11:7).

Saul's message incited "the terror of Yahweh" (פַּחַד־יְהוָה, 11:7) among Israel. This is the only time this terminology (with the noun פחד) is used in the book of Samuel.[27] In Chronicles "the fear of Yahweh" is associated with the fear of Judah's kings and their armies by foreigners (2 Chr 14:13 [ET 14:14]; 17:10) and is invoked by Jehoshaphat when he appoints judges and admonishes them to execute their office faithfully (2 Chr 19:7). Isaiah three times references the great "fear of Yahweh" that will come upon the earth at God's eschatological judgment (Is 2:10, 19, 21; cf. Is 33:14; 44:11). In each case such fear involves

---

[26] See similar summaries at the beginning of the concurrent reigns of Ish-bosheth and David (2 Sam 2:10–11) and at the beginning of David's reign over all Israel (2 Sam 5:4–16). This is also the general pattern in the book of Kings. See, for instance, Rehoboam (1 Ki 14:21–24), Abijam (1 Ki 15:1–3), Asa (1 Ki 15:9–11), Nadab (1 Ki 15:25–26), and Baasha (1 Ki 15:33–34).

[27] Elsewhere the book often uses terminology derived from the root ירא for "fearing" Yahweh/God, e.g., 1 Sam 4:7; 12:14, 18, 24; 2 Sam 23:3.

extreme effects of the Law whereby people are terrified into obedience out of fear of the impending consequences for defying God.[28]

When Saul mustered the army at Bezek, we are told of the large number of men who came, and the author specifically mentions the men of Judah separately (11:8). This separation of Judah from Israel is common in the book of Samuel.[29] It serves both to highlight the Judean perspective of the author and his presumed audience and also as a foreboding of the rift between Judah and the northern tribes of Israel that will lead to the division of the kingdom after the death of Solomon (2 Sam 19:11, 40–43 [ET 19:10, 39–42]; 20:2).

The army's message of deliverance was not tentative or speculative (see the second textual note on 11:9). Yahweh had promised to be with Saul (10:7, 24), and the Israelites, trusting in his promise, were confident of victory. The battle plan was clearly for a morning assault on the Ammonite camp, since Jabesh was promised deliverance before the day turned hot. In turn, the men of Jabesh sent a slyly worded ambiguous message to Nahash that they would come out to him the next day. The verb "come/go out" (נָצָא, 11:10) would have been understood by Nahash as a surrender, but it also could denote an attack (e.g., 1 Sam 28:1; 2 Sam 11:1; 21:17). It may imply that men from Jabesh came out to join the battle when Saul attacked the Ammonites.

The battle the next day is summarized quickly by the narrator, giving only Saul's tactics and his complete success (11:11). The attack came before dawn, during the morning watch—the last watch of night for ancient soldiers on guard duty (see the third textual note on 11:11). Note that this is "the next day" (11:11), because for ancient Israel the day had already begun at the previous sundown.[30] Although Saul's victory was impressive, there is no evidence that he killed Nahash, as Josephus claimed.[31] Later we learn that Nahash was on good terms with David (2 Sam 10:2).

Earlier some in Israel had doubted that Saul would be able to save Israel (1 Sam 10:27). Now the troops demanded their execution (11:12). Saul, however, put a stop to this, attributing the victory to Yahweh (11:13). Thus, we see

---

[28] The Law's three uses are these: "(1) to maintain external discipline against unruly and disobedient men, (2) to lead men to a knowledge of their sin, (3) after they are reborn, and although the flesh still inheres in them, to give them on that account a definite rule according to which they should pattern and regulate their entire life" (FC Ep VI ["The Third Use of the Law"] 1). Thus, the first two uses apply to unbelievers and believers alike; believers remain aware of their sinfulness and culpability even as they live by grace in faith. The third use of the Law applies only to believers as only they are able to live by faith in accord with God's righteous will (cf. Hab 2:4; Rom 1:17; Heb 11:6). In the passages that involve Israelites (e.g., here in 1 Sam 11:7 and in 2 Chr 19:7), many of the people may be believers who are also responding in faith according to the third use of the Law, even though the main emphasis of the text is on fearful obedience. The Israelites' confidence in 1 Sam 11:9 that God will grant them the victory is a display of their firm faith in God's salvation.

[29] 1 Sam 11:8; 17:52; 18:16; 2 Sam 2:10; 3:10; 5:5; 11:11; 12:8; 21:2; 24:1, 9.

[30] Steinmann, *From Abraham to Paul*, 8.

[31] Josephus, *Antiquities*, 6.79.

Saul as willing to acknowledge God's hand in granting victory. Despite his eventual rejection by Yahweh for ignoring God's Word (1 Sam 15:23, 26; 16:1), his reign was not a complete failure, and the author of Samuel also depicts his successes (1 Sam 14:47–48; 2 Sam 1:22–24). In this way the writer of Samuel reminds his readers that God can and does use rulers, even if they refuse to adhere to his Word, to accomplish his will (Rom 13:1–7; see also Mt 27:24–26; Jn 11:49–52).

Following the victory Samuel led the troops to Gilgal (1 Sam 11:14–15). Now at least a partial fulfillment of the plan to make Saul king publicly at Gilgal (10:8) took place.[32] Interestingly, Samuel says that this ceremony was to "renew" the monarchy (see the second textual note on 11:14). Given that Saul had previously aborted the establishment of the monarchy by not following Samuel's instructions,[33] it had to be renewed. In Gilgal Saul was made king (11:15). The people celebrated with "peace offerings," which provided them with a feast as they received some of the meat of the sacrifice.[34]

The victory at Jabesh had at least provisionally completed the expected pattern of designation (9:1–10:13), demonstration (11:1–13), and now confirmation (11:14–15).[35] However, the author also signals that the pattern is only provisional. Samuel's instructions had included the sacrifice of "burnt offerings" (עֹלוֹת) and further divine disclosures to direct the king (10:8), but neither takes place in 11:15. Most ominously, Saul still had done nothing about the Philistine garrison at Gibeah (10:5, 7).

---

[32] For this plan, see figure 16, "Saul's Faltering Accession," in the commentary on 9:26–10:16.

[33] See the interpretation of 10:7 in the commentary on 9:26–10:16.

[34] See the second textual note on 10:8.

[35] See figure 16, "Saul's Faltering Accession," in the commentary on 9:26–10:16.

Samuel's Warning about the Monarchy

Translation

12 ¹Samuel said to all Israel, "I have listened to you and to all that you have said to me, and I have made a king reign over you. ²Now there is a king leading you. I am old and gray-haired, and my sons are here with you. I have led you from my youth until this day. ³Now answer me in front of Yahweh and his anointed one: Whose bull have I taken? Whose donkey have I taken? Whom have I exploited? Whom have I oppressed? From whose hand have I taken a bribe to look the other way? I will return it to you!"

⁴They said, "You have not exploited us and have not oppressed us. You have not taken anything from anyone's hand."

⁵He said, "Yahweh is a witness against you, and his anointed one is a witness this day that you have not found anything in my hand."

They said, "[He is] a witness."

⁶Samuel said to the people, "Yahweh is the one who appointed Moses and Aaron and who brought your ancestors up from Egypt. ⁷Now stand, and I will put you on trial before Yahweh on the basis of all the righteous things he has done with you and your ancestors. ⁸After Jacob came to Egypt your ancestors cried out to Yahweh. So Yahweh sent Moses and Aaron. They brought your ancestors out of Egypt and settled them in this land. ⁹Yet they forgot Yahweh their God, so he sold them into the power of Sisera, commander of Hazor's army, into the power of the Philistines, and into the power of the king of Moab, and they waged war against them. ¹⁰They cried out to Yahweh and said, 'We have sinned because we have abandoned Yahweh and served the Baals and the Astartes. Now rescue us from the power of our enemies, and we will serve you.' ¹¹So Yahweh sent Jerubbaal, Barak, Jephthah, and Samuel and rescued you from the power of your surrounding enemies, and you lived securely. ¹²You have seen that King Nahash of the Ammonites came against you, and you had said to me, 'No! A king will reign over us,' although Yahweh was your King. ¹³Now here is the king whom you have chosen, whom you requested. Look—Yahweh has given you a king. ¹⁴If you will fear Yahweh, serve him, obey him, and do not rebel against Yahweh's Word, then you and the king who rules over you will follow Yahweh your God. ¹⁵If you will not obey Yahweh, but rebel against Yahweh's Word, Yahweh's hand will be against you and your king.

¹⁶"Now stand and see this great thing that Yahweh is doing in your sight. ¹⁷Isn't it the time of the wheat harvest? I will call to Yahweh, and he will send thunder and rain. Know and see that according to Yahweh's judgment you have done great evil by asking for a king for yourselves."

¹⁸Then Samuel called to Yahweh, and Yahweh sent thunder and rain that day. All the people were very afraid of Yahweh and Samuel. ¹⁹All the people said to

Samuel, "Pray to Yahweh your God on behalf of your servants and don't let us die, for we have added an evil to all our sins by asking for a king for ourselves."

²⁰Samuel said to the people, "Do not be afraid [although] you have done this entire evil thing. However, don't turn away from following Yahweh. Serve Yahweh with all your heart. ²¹Do not turn to follow useless idols that cannot benefit [you] or rescue [you] because they are useless. ²²For the sake of his great name Yahweh will not forsake his people, since he is determined to make you his people. ²³Also, as far as I'm concerned, I will certainly not sin against Yahweh by ceasing to pray on your behalf. Moreover, I will teach you the good and correct way. ²⁴Just fear Yahweh and serve him faithfully with all your heart. Consider the great things he has done for you. ²⁵But if you continue to act wickedly, both you and your king will be swept away.'"

Textual Notes

12:1–2 הִנֵּה֙ ... וְעַתָּ֗ה—See the first textual note on 8:5.

12:1 שָׁמַ֣עְתִּי בְקֹלְכֶ֔ם—Literally "I listened to your voice." The idiom "listen" (שָׁמַע) "to" (בְ) a "voice" (קוֹל) means to obey or accede to a request. See the first textual note on 8:7. This idiom recurs in 12:14 and 12:15, but in reference to obeying God.

וָאַמְלִ֥יךְ עֲלֵיכֶ֖ם מֶֽלֶךְ׃—For this cognate accusative construction, literally "and I made king over you a king," see the first textual note on 8:22.

12:2 מִתְהַלֵּ֥ךְ לִפְנֵיכֶ֖ם ... הִתְהַלַּ֧כְתִּי לִפְנֵיכֶ֛ם—These two instances of the Hithpael (HtD) of הָלַךְ with לִפְנֵי are translated as "leading you ... I have led you." On this idiom, see the first textual note on 2:30.

וְשַׂ֣בְתִּי—The Qal (G) verb שִׂיב, "to have gray hair," occurs only here and in Job 15:10. More common is the cognate noun שֵׂיבָה, "gray hair" (nineteen times in the OT).

12:3 הִנְנִ֣י עֲנ֣וּ בִ֡י—Literally "behold me; answer against me." The verb עָנָה with the preposition בְ can have the judicial meaning "to testify against" someone (BDB, s.v. עָנָה I, Qal, 3 a). Samuel establishes a courtroom setting with himself on the witness stand and Yahweh and his anointed king as judges, and he invites any accusers to come forward with their testimony. See also the judicial term עֵד, "a witness," three times in 12:5.

רַצּ֗וֹתִי—The Qal (G) of רָצַץ literally means "to crush," but when a person is the object, it can have the metaphorical meaning "to oppress" (BDB, 2).

וּמִיַּד־מִי֙ לָקַ֣חְתִּי כֹ֔פֶר וְאַעְלִ֥ים עֵינַ֖י בּֽוֹ—Literally "from the hand of whom have I taken a bribe so that I would hide my eyes in exchange for it?" The Hiphil (H) imperfect with conjunctive *waw* וְאַעְלִים forms a purpose clause. The nuance of the suffixed preposition בְ is that of exchange (see BDB, III 3 b), "in exchange for" the bribe. In place of וְאַעְלִים, the LXX reads καὶ ὑπόδημα, "and a sandal," a reading favored by some.[1]

12:5 וַיֹּ֨אמֶר֙—The prior verbs and forms in 12:1–5 referring to the people have been plural, but here the singular verb וַיֹּאמֶר must presuppose a singular collective subject,

---

[1] McCarter, *I Samuel*, 209–10; Speiser, "Of Shoes and Shekels," 15–18 (cf. Sirach 46:19).

either "Israel" (יִשְׂרָאֵל in 12:1) or "the people" (הָעָם in 12:6). The same situation recurs in 12:10; see the first textual note there.

עֵד:—In Biblical Hebrew the usual way to agree with a preceding statement is simply to repeat the words. The people say the noun עֵד, "a witness," to attest the truthfulness of Samuel's prior testimony in the verse, which included עֵד twice.

12:6 יְהוָה אֲשֶׁר עָשָׂה אֶת־מֹשֶׁה וְאֶת־אַהֲרֹן—Samuel's words are literally "Yahweh, who made Moses and Aaron." "Yahweh" is the subject, but there is no predicate, only the long relative clause beginning with אֲשֶׁר. Although one might have expected the pronoun הוּא to have been included (i.e., יְהוָה הוּא אֲשֶׁר), the sense must be "Yahweh is the one who …" The Qal (G) of עָשָׂה can mean "to appoint" a person (*DCH*, s.v. עָשָׂה I, 6 a). Cf. וַיִּשְׁלַח in 12:8.

הֶעֱלָה—The Hiphil (H) of עָלָה, "to bring up," in this exodus context reproduces the terminology of Exodus. See the textual note on 10:18–19. See also the second textual note on 12:8.

12:7 הִתְיַצְּבוּ—The Hithpael (HtD) of יָצַב has the nuance "to stand before" for adjudication; see also the third textual note on 10:19.

וְאִשָּׁפְטָה אִתְּכֶם—"And I will put you on trial." אִשָּׁפְטָה is a Niphal (N) cohortative singular of שָׁפַט. In the Niphal this verb has a reciprocal meaning (GKC, § 51 d), "take another person to court" or "enter into judgment with someone" (Is 59:4; Ps 109:7).

אֵת כָּל־צִדְקוֹת יְהוָה—The construct chain is not the direct object of any of the preceding verbs. The direct object marker אֵת must have the sense that Samuel is invoking "all the righteousnesses of Yahweh" as the legal basis of his adjuration, hence "on the basis of."

12:8 כַּאֲשֶׁר־בָּא יַעֲקֹב מִצְרָיִם—This means "after Jacob came to Egypt." In temporal uses כַּאֲשֶׁר usually means "when," but occasionally it means "after" (cf. Judg 16:22). The LXX has a longer reading: ὡς εἰσῆλθεν Ιακωβ καὶ οἱ υἱοὶ αὐτοῦ εἰς Αἴγυπτον, καὶ ἐταπείνωσεν αὐτοὺς Αἴγυπτος, "as Jacob and his sons entered Egypt, Egypt humbled them." Space considerations make it likely that this reading was also found in 4QSam[a].

וַיִּזְעֲקוּ—This Qal (G) form is repeated in 12:10. Like הֶעֱלָה in 12:6 (see the second textual note there), the verb זָעַק, "cry out," is another verb taken from the exodus narrative (Ex 2:23). See also the related noun צְעָקָה in Ex 3:7, 9.

וַיּוֹצִיאוּם ... וַיֹּשִׁבוּם—"They brought out … and settled them." These Hiphil (H) preterites (imperfects with *waw* consecutive) of יָצָא and יָשַׁב, respectively, are third person plural forms. The LXX has ἐξήγαγεν … κατῴκισεν, "he [Yahweh] brought out … settled." Since Moses and Aaron died before Israel entered and settled in the promised land, the LXX has adjusted the verbs to make Yahweh the subject.

12:9 סִיסְרָא שַׂר־צְבָא חָצוֹר—This is translated as "Sisera, commander of Hazor's army." The LXX, probably based on Judg 4:7, expands that to Σισαρα ἀρχιστρατήγου Ιαβιν βασιλέως Ασωρ, "Sisera, army commander for King Jabin of Hazor."

12:10 וַיֹּאמְרוּ—"And *they* said" is the reading of the Qere, which is supported by the LXX. The Kethib is the singular וַיֹּאמֶר, "and he said"; see the first textual note on 12:5.

הַצִּילֵנוּ—This is the Hiphil (H) imperative of נָצַל with a first common plural suffix: "rescue us." Other Hiphil forms of this verb recur in 12:11 (וַיַּצֵּל) and 12:21 (יַצִּילוּ).

הָעַשְׁתָּרוֹת—For "the Astartes," see the second textual note on 7:3.

12:11 בְּדָן—For the MT's "Bedan," the LXX reads Βαρακ, "Barak" (presupposing בָּרָק), which most English versions accept. For "Barak," see Judges 4–5. The MT's בְּדָן probably is the result of a double graphic confusion of *daleth* for *resh* and *nun* for *qoph*.[2] The reading "Barak" is supported by a wide range of interpreters.[3] Tsumura considers "Bedan" a phonetic variant of "Barak."[4] Other suggestions are less plausible. The Talmud equates "Bedan" with "Samson," apparently assuming that בְּדָן is a contracted form of בֶּן־דָּן, "the son of Dan" (cf. Judg 13:2).[5] Some argue that בְּדָן is a foreshortened form of עַבְדוֹן and that this judge is thus "Abdon" (Judg 12:13–15).[6] Zakovitch argued that "Bedan" was another name for "Jephthah" since in 1 Chr 7:17, "Bedan" is from the tribe of Manasseh and the family of Gilead, as was Jephthah (Judg 11:1).[7] In this view, the name "Jephthah" was added to 1 Sam 12:11 as a gloss on "Bedan."

שְׁמוּאֵל—It is striking that as Samuel recollects the rescuers sent by Yahweh, he also names himself in the third person (see the commentary). Perhaps because Samuel appears immodest the Syriac Peshitta and Lucianic LXX manuscripts have "Samson." Josephus omits the name altogether,[8] leading McCarter to conclude that this may be a later expansion of the text.[9] However, the Hebrew manuscripts are unanimous, and "Samuel" is supported by LXX A and B.

וַתֵּשְׁבוּ בֶטַח:—The noun בֶטַח, "security," is derived from the verb בָּטַח, "to trust" (often in God). It is commonly used together with the verb יָשַׁב, meaning "to live/dwell securely/in safety." In this combination the noun is an adverbial accusative here and in Deut 12:10. Elsewhere in the OT in this combination בֶטַח usually has the prefixed preposition לְ, as in, e.g., Lev 25:18–19; 26:5.

12:12 See the extended discussion of the import of this verse in its context in the first textual note on 10:27b in the commentary on 10:27b–11:15.

לֹא כִּי־מֶלֶךְ יִמְלֹךְ עָלֵינוּ—These words are only a slight paraphrase of what the people said in 8:19, לֹא [לוֹ] כִּי אִם־מֶלֶךְ יִהְיֶה עָלֵינוּ, and in 10:19, כִּי־מֶלֶךְ תָּשִׂים עָלֵינוּ.

12:13 אֲשֶׁר שְׁאֶלְתֶּם—This means "whom you requested." These words are missing in the LXX, and space considerations make it likely that they were also missing in 4QSamᵃ. Forms of the verb שָׁאַל, "ask, request," sometimes have the theme vowel *seghol* (-אֶ-), as here and in 25:5, or *hireq* (-אִ-) instead of the textbook *patach* (-אַ-). See GKC, §§ 44 d, 64 f.

---

2 Day, "Bedan, Abdon or Barak in 1 Samuel xii 11," 263.

3 E.g., Keil, *The Books of Samuel*, 118; Klein, *1 Samuel*, 111; Smith, *The Books of Samuel*, 86–87.

4 Tsumura, "Bedan, a Copyist's Error? (1 Samuel xii 11)."

5 Talmud, *Rosh Hashanah*, 25a.

6 See Jacobson, "The Judge Bedan (1 Samuel xii 11)."

7 Zakovitch, "בדן = יפתח."

8 Josephus, *Antiquities*, 6.90.

9 McCarter, *I Samuel*, 211.

For the play between this verb (also in 12:17, 19) and the name שָׁאוּל, "Saul," meaning "requested," see the first textual note on 1:28; "Samuel Warns Israel about Kings (8:10–22)" in the commentary on 8:1–22; the first textual note on 10:22; the commentary on 12:13; the textual note on 14:37; and the second textual note on 20:6 (which also discusses שָׁאוּל נִשְׁאַל in 20:28).

12:14 וְלֹא תַמְרוּ אֶת־פִּי יְהוָה—Literally "and you do not rebel [against] the mouth of Yahweh." The verb מָרָה means "to rebel" in both the Qal (G) and the Hiphil (H) and takes a direct object, hence אֶת־ here and in 12:15. The second masculine plural imperfect form here with *patach*, תַמְרוּ, is Hiphil; the equivalent Qal form would have *hireq*, תִּמְרוּ. (In 12:15 the Qal perfect with *waw* consecutive, וּמְרִיתֶם, has the identical meaning.) While the construct phrase פִּי יְהוָה (again in 12:15) is often translated as something like "the LORD's command,"[10] it is best rendered as "Yahweh's Word," as the Word will become incarnate (Jn 1:14; Rev 19:13). Samuel is warning not only about disobeying God's commandments (i.e., Law) but also about rejecting the Gospel message (as through Moses and the judges and prophets) and God's proffering of incarnate rescuers (12:8, 11; cf. 1 Cor 10:4). See also 1 Sam 12:15.

וִהְיִתֶם ... אַחַר יְהוָה אֱלֹהֵיכֶם:—Literally "and you will be ... after Yahweh your God," this idiom denotes "following God." The preposition אַחַר, "after," has the pregnant meaning "to follow after." See also מֵאַחֲרֵי יְהוָה in 12:20 and אַחֲרֵי הַתֹּהוּ in 12:21, both of which are translated with "follow."

1 Sam 12:14 appears incomplete. It begins with a conditional, "if you ... ," but lacks an apodosis or "then" clause; thus, it is an example of aposiopesis (GKC, §§ 159 dd, 167 a). One solution is to assume that the author intended the reader to supply an appropriate clause at the end of the verse such as וְטוֹב לָכֶם, "then it will go well for you," as in Deut 5:33. This solution is adopted by, e.g., ESV, NET. Another solution is to interpret the clause beginning with וִהְיִתֶם as the "then" clause, "then you ... will follow Yahweh," even though it seems tautological that fearing, serving, and obeying Yahweh will result in following him. Nevertheless, this is the expedient adopted in the translation above and also by, e.g., HCSB, GW, NASB.

12:15 וּבַאֲבֹתֵיכֶם:—"And against your ancestors" is the reading of the MT. However, it would not be in keeping with Scripture's depiction of God's justice for a divine judgment against a current generation of apostates to be applied retroactively against prior generations who have already died. The reading could be justified by translating it as "just as it [Yahweh's hand] was against your ancestors" (cf. GW), but this appears to be special pleading. Tsumura attempts to equate "you and ... your ancestors" with "your entire household,"[11] but that is another forced interpretation. The translation above follows the LXX, καὶ ἐπὶ τὸν βασιλέα ὑμῶν, "and against your king." The MT may have accidentally substituted the more familiar phrase "you and your ancestors."[12]

---

[10] HCSB; similar are ESV, NIV, NRSV.

[11] Tsumura, *The First Book of Samuel*, 324. "Household" is usually "father's house" (בֵּית אָב, e.g., Gen 12:1), not "you and your fathers."

[12] As in Ex 13:11; Jer 23:39; 25:5; 35:15; 44:21; cf. Deut 8:3; Joel 1:2. See also "we/us and our fathers" (Gen 46:34; 47:3; Josh 24:17; Jer 3:25; 44:17) and "they/them and their fathers" (Lev 26:40; Jer 19:4; 24:10; Ezek 2:3; 2 Chr 6:25).

12:17 הֲלוֹא קְצִיר־חִטִּים הַיּוֹם—Literally "is it not the harvest of wheat the/this day?"

וְיִתֵּן קֹלוֹת וּמָטָר—Literally "and he [Yahweh] will give voices and rain." The noun קוֹל can denote not only a "voice" (as in 12:1, 14, 15) but also any sound, including "thunder" (e.g., Ex 9:23, 29, 33; 19:16). Meteorological phenomena are often depicted as divine actions, particularly God's gift of "rain" (מָטָר, here and in 1 Sam 12:18). "The fire of God" (2 Ki 1:12; Job 1:16) and "the fire of Yahweh" (1 Ki 18:38; also Num 11:1, 3) may refer to lightning, and thunder is Yahweh's "voice" (קוֹל, Ps 29:3–9; cf. Deut 18:16).

וּדְעוּ וּרְאוּ—"Know and see." The verb יָדַע refers to apprehension by faith, while רָאָה denotes apprehension by sight. In this passage God provides visible and audible signs that confirm the veracity of his Word, spoken through his prophet. For the most part God's people are called to believe his Word even without visible attestation of its truth (Jn 20:29; 1 Pet 1:8).

בְּעֵינֵי יְהוָה—Literally "in Yahweh's eyes," this is translated as "according to Yahweh's judgment." See the first textual note on 1:23.

12:19 בְּעַד־עֲבָדֶיךָ—This means "on behalf of your servants." For self-deprecatory references to oneself as a "servant," see the third textual note on 1:11.

וְאַל־נָמוּת—"And don't let us die." The negative particle אַל normally precedes volitive forms. Here one would expect a cohortative form, but an imperfect form can be used with cohortative force, as is the Qal (G) imperfect נָמוּת here. For other examples, see 2 Sam 13:25; Ps 25:20; Job 32:21; 1 Chr 21:13.

12:21 וְלֹא תָּסוּרוּ כִּי—The first two words are translated as "do not turn." כִּי appears to be out of place, has no equivalent in the LXX, and is not in some MT manuscripts. Consequently, it is not usually translated in English translations. It may have been displaced from later in the verse.

אַחֲרֵי הַתֹּהוּ ... כִּי־תֹהוּ הֵמָּה׃—Literally "after nothingness ... because they are nothingness," this is translated as "to follow useless idols ... because they are useless." For the translation of the preposition אַחֲרֵי, "after," with the verb "follow," see the second textual note on 12:14. The noun תֹהוּ means "emptiness, nothingness" (Gen 1:2; Jer 4:23; Job 26:7). It can refer to an impotent, vacuous false god (Is 41:29) and also to those who make and venerate such worthless idols (Is 44:9). It is often used of a wilderness or desert that is nearly uninhabitable (Deut 32:10; Is 45:18; Ps 107:40; Job 6:18; 12:24; 26:7).

לֹא־יוֹעִילוּ—The Hiphil (H) of יָעַל means "to help, assist, benefit." Here and in Is 44:9; Jer 2:8, 11; Hab 2:18, it refers to false gods and idols who cannot save their worshipers; see also Is 47:12, which calls into question the benefit of occult practices, and Jer 23:32, where false prophets do not avail. This verb is the derivation for the second element in the compound noun בְּלִיַּעַל, a "worthless" or "good-for-nothing person" (see the first textual note on 1:16).

וְלֹא יַצִּילוּ—Literally "and they cannot rescue you." The inability of false gods to save (as in 2 Chr 25:15) contrasts with Yahweh's action of saving his people, denoted by the same verb, the Hiphil (H) of נָצַל, in, e.g., 1 Sam 7:3; 10:18; 12:10, 11; 17:37.

12:22 בַּעֲבוּר שְׁמוֹ הַגָּדוֹל—This prepositional phrase, "for the sake of his great name," expresses salvation by grace alone. God does not save his people based on their works or merit. Instead, he acts on the basis of his own gracious promises, reputation, and character, which are embodied in his name.[13]

12:23 גַּם אָנֹכִי—These words, translated as "also, as far as I'm concerned," make Samuel's statement especially emphatic. See the same words in 1 Sam 1:28; 2 Sam 2:6; and in Yahweh's words in, e.g., Gen 20:6; 2 Ki 22:19; Jer 7:11; Amos 4:7.

חָלִילָה לִּי—For this expression, translated as "I will certainly not," see the second textual note on 2:30.

וְהוֹרֵיתִי אֶתְכֶם בְּדֶרֶךְ הַטּוֹבָה וְהַיְשָׁרָה:—The Hiphil (H) of יָרָה can mean "shoot" arrows (1 Sam 20:20, 36; 31:3; 2 Sam 11:20, 24). But it often means "teach, instruct" and refers to the authoritative divine teaching from God and through his priests and prophets (BDB, 5). One would expect the noun דֶּרֶךְ, "way," to have the definite article (בַּדֶּרֶךְ) since the two adjectives modifying it are definite (הַטּוֹבָה וְהַיְשָׁרָה, "the good and the straight"), but see GKC, § 126 x.

12:24 הִגְדִּל עִמָּכֶם:—The Hiphil (H) of גָּדַל can be used intransitively with no direct object to mean "do great things" (BDB, 3), hence (literally) "he did great things with you."

12:25 הָרֵעַ תָּרֵעוּ—Like the Hiphil (H) in the preceding textual note, the Hiphil (H) of רָעַע can be used intransitively with no direct object, meaning "to do evil, act wickedly." The force of the Hiphil infinitive absolute used with the Hiphil imperfect may indicate continuing action, "if you continue to act wickedly," since the people have already confessed to having done רָעָה, "wickedness, evil" (12:19; cf. 20:17, 20).

תִּסָּפוּ:—The Niphal (N) of סָפָה means "be swept away, destroyed," or "perish," as again in 1 Sam 26:10; 27:1.

Commentary

1049 BC

1 Samuel 12 is often called "Samuel's Farewell," but that description is misleading, since Samuel continued to be a prophet for Israel and also pledged to continue to pray for and teach Israel (12:23). By context it would appear that this exchange between Israel and Samuel took place at Gilgal after the renewing of the monarchy under Saul (11:14–15).[14] Not only did Samuel address "all Israel" (12:1; cf. 11:7–8), but also Saul, God's anointed king, was present (12:5). There is no need to place this event at a later time.[15]

Samuel's words to Israel are in three sections. The first (12:1–5) confirms that Samuel did not abuse his office as judge. The second (12:6–19) is a historical review that charges Israel with sin, especially the sin of abandoning Yahweh. The third (12:20–25) is a call for Israel to be faithful to Yahweh and Samuel's pledge that he will support the people in remaining faithful.

---

[13] See, similarly, Ezek 20:9, 14, 22, 44; 36:22; Pss 23:3; 25:11; 31:4 (ET 31:3); 79:9; 106:8; 109:21; 143:11. In the NT, see the same soteriology in Acts 9:16; Rom 1:5.

[14] Bodner, *1 Samuel*, 110; McCarter, *I Samuel*, 212.

[15] Contra Tsumura, *The First Book of Samuel*, 317. See also Miscall, *1 Samuel*, 72, who says: "1 Sam. 12:1 stands in uncertain relation to 1 Sam. 11:14–15 in terms of time and setting."

Samuel Affirmed as an Honest Judge (12:1–5)

Samuel began his words with a reference to God's instructions that he ought to accede to Israel's request for a king (12:1; cf. 8:22). They now had a king who was leading them (12:2), as evidenced by Saul's liberation of Jabesh-gilead (11:1–15). Samuel also noted that he was old and that his sons, the judges whom he appointed in his old age (Joel and Abijah, 8:1–3), were also present. The mention of Samuel's sons might seem odd at this point, but they serve two purposes in this context. First of all, they were the apparent trigger for Israel's request for a king, since they did not walk in the ways of their father (8:3) and so were unfit to rule after him. Second, while they "took bribes and perverted justice" (8:3), Samuel would establish that he was not part of their corruption. Not only would his words lead to his personal vindication, but they would also be an oblique condemnation of his sons' actions. To that end, Samuel challenged Israel with a number of questions that served to establish that he had not sought financial gain at the expense of granting justice in any dispute that he had adjudicated (12:3). He had neither exploited (עָשַׁק) nor oppressed (רָצַץ) Israel. Moses had used these same two verbs to warn Israel that the people would be "exploited" and "oppressed" by foreign nations if they abandoned Yahweh (Deut 28:33). Oppression by fellow Israelites would have been even more bitter (cf. Hos 5:11; Amos 4:1).

After Israel confirmed that Samuel had not abused his position (1 Sam 12:4), Samuel invoked two witnesses to attest their affirmation of his innocence: Yahweh and his anointed king (12:5). This is the first time in the book of Samuel that a reigning king is called God's "anointed one" (מָשִׁיחַ). Samuel uses that term to reinforce that although Israel asked for a king, it was God who chose the king and commissioned Samuel to anoint him; indeed, it was Yahweh who anointed him (10:1). The people's concurrence that the Lord's anointed was a witness to their statement (12:5) had important implications: The king would be the chief magistrate in Israel. As a witness to the people's affirmation, he would be unable to rule against Samuel should charges of corruption be brought against him at a later time.

This affirmation of Samuel's tenure as judge was also important to the prophet himself. He had initially taken Israel's request for a king as a personal rejection (8:6–7). Now Israel had publicly declared that its request was not a criticism of his conduct in office (although it probably was a criticism of his decision to install his sons as judges).

The apostle Paul similarly ensured that his conduct in office was above reproach.[16] On one occasion he even offered to repay any money that may have previously been stolen by one of his converts (Philemon 18–19). His exemplary conduct was for the sake of the Gospel itself, that the saving name of Jesus Christ not be sullied. Likewise, in the rite of ordination, the pastor is asked

---

[16] See, e.g., 1 Cor 4:12; 9:1–27; 2 Cor 11:7–9; 1 Thess 2:5–9; 2 Thess 3:7–10; cf. Rom 13:8.

whether he will "honor and adorn the Office of the Holy Ministry with a holy life."[17] This the pastor does not to aggrandize himself, but to attest the holiness and genuineness of the Savior he proclaims.

Israel's History as Evidence for Its Repeated Unfaithfulness (12:6–19)

Once Samuel had established his fidelity in office, he moved on to indict Israel for its habitual sin of rejecting Yahweh and his authority. He began by noting that Yahweh had appointed Moses and Aaron and had brought Israel up from Egypt (12:6). This was a reminder that Yahweh was Israel's sovereign in that he had the sole prerogative to appoint leaders and that he was Israel's true Savior in that he alone could rescue his people. Saul, the anointed one, was appointed like Moses and Aaron.

However, Israel was never to think of Saul or any of their later kings as *the* savior of Israel, but only the one selected by Yahweh and through whom Yahweh led Israel against its enemies. Human leaders can become idols in which nations place their trust, but such leaders cannot save and are fallible and mortal. We are to trust God alone, who alone can provide permanent security (Jer 17:5–8; Psalm 146; cf. Ps 118:8–9).

This God, who was Israel's true King and had acted righteously with the Israelites in the past, was now to act as judge of Israel as Samuel brought charges against the people (12:7). The evidence Samuel presents consists of a historical review (12:8–13) from Jacob's entry into Egypt to the most recent deliverance under Saul (1 Samuel 11). This review is unique in that it contains few elements in common with most such reviews in the Bible: It has only a brief review of the patriarchal history, the exodus, and the conquest and occupation of the land. Instead, it concentrates on the period of the judges, including Samuel himself, since Israel sought to replace him, the last of the judges, with a new form of governance in the monarchy.[18] See figure 17.

The review begins with a brief overview of the sojourn in Egypt, the exodus, and the entry into the promised land (12:8). Here Samuel notes that God brought the Israelites out of Egypt in response to their cry to him (Deut 26:7). Now because of Israel's cry for a king, Yahweh has given them Saul (1 Sam 12:12–13).

The bulk of the historical recapitulation is concentrated on the period of the judges. It begins with Israel forgetting Yahweh (1 Sam 12:9).[19] This resulted in God *selling* Israel into the power of other nations (1 Sam 12:9; see also Judg 3:8; 4:2; 10:7; cf. Deut 32:30). Samuel names three of these oppressors, but not in strict chronological order: Sisera (Judges 4), the Philistines (Judg 3:31;

---

[17] *LSB Agenda*, 166.

[18] One might compare the way Samuel names himself in the third person in his summary of salvation history to the way Jesus refers to himself in Jn 17:3.

[19] See also Judg 3:7; cf. Deut 6:12; 8:11, 14, 19; Hos 2:15 (ET 2:13); 8:14; 13:6.

Figure 17

Comparison of 1 Samuel 12:8–13 with Other Historical Reviews in the Old Testament

Event	1 Samuel 12	Nehemiah 9	Psalm 78	Psalm 105	Psalm 106	Psalm 135	Psalm 136	Ezekiel 20
Creation		9:6				135:6–7	136:5–9, 25	
Patriarchs	12:8a	9:7–8		105:8–25				
Exodus	12:8b	9:9–12	78:12–14, 44–51	105:26–39	106:7–12	135:8–9	136:10–15	20:5–10
Wilderness		9:13–21	78:15–43, 52–53	105:40–41	106:13–33		136:16	20:11–26
Conquest of the land	12:8b	9:22–25	78:54–55	105:42–45	106:34–35	135:10–12	136:17–22	20:27–29
Occupation of the land					106:36–45			
A. *The judges*	*12:9–11*	*9:26–28*	*78:56–66*					
B. *The monarchy*	*12:12–13*	*9:29–30b, 34–35*	*78:67–72*					
Captivity and return from captivity		9:30c–32, 36–37			106:46–47		136:23–24	

This figure is adapted and expanded from Bautch, *Developments in Genre between Post-Exilic Penitential Prayers and the Psalms of Communal Lament*, 112. See also Steinmann, *Ezra and Nehemiah*, 534–35.

13:1–16:31; 1 Samuel 4–7), and the king of Moab (Judg 3:12–30). As the Israelites cried out to Yahweh when they were oppressed by the Egyptians, so they cried out to him again (1 Sam 12:10; see also Judg 10:10; cf. Deut 28:20; 31:16; Josh 24:16, 20). They confessed that they had abandoned Yahweh by worshiping the Baals and Astartes of the nations (1 Sam 12:10; see also Judg 2:11, 13; 1 Sam 7:3–4). God's response was to send judges as he had sent Moses and Aaron (1 Sam 12:11). Once again, Samuel does not list the judges in exact historical order: Jerubbaal (i.e., Gideon; Judges 6–9), Barak (Judges 4–5), Jephthah (Judges 11–12), and Samuel (1 Samuel 7). God's rescue was from the "surrounding enemies" (1 Sam 12:11), another link to Judges (Judg 2:14; 8:34). This allowed Israel to live securely (as in Lev 25:18–19; 26:5; Deut 12:10).

Next Samuel moved to the recent victory over Nahash (1 Samuel 11), which he used as confirmation of Saul's appointment as the king who would go out in front of Israel and fight its battles (8:20; 12:12). Saul's earlier investiture as king (10:17–27) had proven controversial (10:27), since he had not taken the initiative to do whatever he would "find to do" (10:7) and attack the Philistine garrison in Gibeah (10:5).[20] Now, however, Saul had rescued Jabesh-gilead (1 Samuel 11), and Samuel could point to him as a king with the ability to lead Israel into battle.

Oftentimes 12:12 is translated as if its first clause were a temporal clause, something like "when you saw that King Nahash …"[21] This has led to some discussion of a chronological difficulty with this text, since the request for a king (8:5) *preceded* Nahash's siege of Jabesh (11:1).[22] However, there is no formal marker of a temporal clause here.[23] Instead, the clauses are linked by simple consecution, which does not necessarily imply temporal sequence.[24] In this case Samuel is not employing temporal sequence. Instead, Samuel is making a logical argument (12:12–13): "You saw Nahash's attack, and you had [previously] requested a king despite having Yahweh as your King. So here is your king whom Yahweh gave you (i.e., to lead you in battle and defeat your enemies as he defeated Nahash)." By phrasing his argument in this manner, Samuel was able to accomplish two rhetorical goals. First, he was able to reinforce the people's sin of rejecting Yahweh's sovereignty by demanding a king. Second,

---

[20] See the discussion, including figure 16, "Saul's Faltering Accession," in "Samuel Anoints Saul (9:26–10:8)" in the commentary on 9:26–10:16.

[21] See, e.g., HCSB, ESV, GW, NET, NIV.

[22] Fokkelman, *Vow and Desire*, 514–15; McCarter, *I Samuel*, 215; Tsumura, *The First Book of Samuel*, 323.

[23] That is, the clause does not begin in a manner like this:

וַיְהִי בִּרְאוֹתְכֶם נָחָשׁ מֶלֶךְ בְּנֵי־עַמּוֹן בָּא

When you saw King Nahash of the Ammonites coming …

[24] This consecution is evident from the *waw* consecutive verbs: וַתֹּאמְרוּ … וַתִּרְאוּ, "you have seen … and you had said" (12:12).

he could point to Saul's defeat of Nahash as a public demonstration of Saul's ability to lead Israel to war.[25]

Samuel's rhetorical flourish also allowed him to move to his next statement that reinforced his emphasis on Israel's sinful attitude (12:13): Saul was the king whom the people had chosen in place of Yahweh (8:7), the one whom they had requested of Samuel (8:5). By placing the word "requested" after "chosen" (12:13), Samuel once again was able rhetorically to emphasize two points: First, he stressed that despite Israel's choice, the people were still dependent on Yahweh and had to request a king. Second, he highlighted the answer to their request by the implicit wordplay between "you requested" (שְׁאֶלְתֶּם) and the name "Saul" (שָׁאוּל), meaning "requested."[26] Yahweh answered their request despite their rejection of him as their king.

Next Samuel urged Israel and its king to "follow Yahweh your God" by instructing them on how to do that (12:14). Interestingly, Samuel omits a verb such as "follow" here, which is supplied in translation (see the last textual note on 12:14). Elsewhere in the OT such a verb can be a form of הָלַךְ, "to walk" (Deut 13:5 [ET 13:4]; 2 Ki 23:3; Hos 11:10; 2 Chr 34:31), or of the Piel (D) of מָלֵא, "be completely dedicated to" (Num 32:12; Deut 1:36; Josh 14:8–9, 14; 1 Ki 11:6). By omitting a verb, Samuel is able not only to imply that Israel ought to follow "after Yahweh," but also to imply that if the people follow Yahweh, they will never again have to lament "after Yahweh" (וַיִּנָּהוּ ... אַחֲרֵי יְהוָה, 7:2).

Samuel also defined what following Yahweh meant: fearing him, serving him, and believing his Word, both positively by listening to him in faith and negatively by not rebelling against him (12:14). Thus, fearing and serving Yahweh are not to be defined by a person's own wishes, but by God's revealed Word. For believers in every age, God's Word is their authoritative and inerrant source of faith and their infallible guide as to how to please him (Pss 105:1–45; 119:9). We are rendered pleasing to God by our baptismal incorporation into Christ as we trust in his work and promises and live by the power of his resurrection (Rom 4:16–6:13). Christ, who is our way and our life (Jn 14:6; Gal 2:20; Col 3:4), is revealed in the Scriptures, God's Word, as given through the prophets and apostles (Jn 5:39; Heb 1:1–2; 1 Pet 1:10–12). When the Israelites trusted in God's promises through the words of Moses and Samuel, they were following Yahweh, and that trust would lead them to keep the laws given to them by Moses. Thus, the fear of Yahweh here is not primarily fear of punishment, but instead a trust in our loving God as one might trust a father who graciously provides for his children.[27]

---

[25] See the discussion of the meaning of 12:12 in its context in the first textual note on 10:27b in the commentary on 10:27b–11:15.

[26] The name שָׁאוּל is a Qal passive (Gp) participle of the verb שָׁאַל. See also the first textual note on 1:28; "Samuel Warns Israel about Kings (8:10–22)" in the commentary on 8:1–22; the first textual note on 10:22; the textual note on 14:37; and the second textual note on 20:6 (which also discusses שָׁאוּל נִשְׁאַל נִשְׁאַל in 20:28).

[27] See Steinmann, *Proverbs*, 27–28.

Samuel followed his invitation to follow Yahweh with a warning of the consequences of not obeying but instead of rebelling against God: his hand would be against them (1 Sam 12:15). The consequences of God's hand being against the Philistines (7:13) were dire. Now the Israelites were told that they could face the same if they did not follow Yahweh.

To demonstrate God's ability to effect such judgments and to highlight Israel's sin, Samuel called on Yahweh to send a thunderstorm (12:16–17). It was late spring during the month of Sivan (May/June), the time of the wheat harvest.[28] This was well into the dry season in Palestine, when one would expect little, if any, rain and certainly not a thunderstorm (Prov 26:1). A storm could damage the crop before it could be harvested. The thunder and rain demonstrated not only God's power over creation but also what it would mean for the Israelites if they turned away from the God who had established his covenant with them; he would deal with them as his enemy.[29] The people's reaction to the thunderstorm was fear of both Yahweh and Samuel (1 Sam 12:18). By mentioning Samuel after Yahweh, the author is recognizing the divine office of Samuel as Yahweh's spokesman; he is in the same revered category as Moses and Joshua (Josh 4:14). In the same way, faithful pastors are rightly called "reverend" by virtue of their divine office. The people also begged Samuel to pray for them, specifically for forgiveness as they at last acknowledged that requesting a king was another sin they added to all of Israel's past rebellious acts against God (12:19).

Samuel Urges Israel to Be Faithful under a New King (12:20–25)

Samuel's final official pronouncement to Israel was aimed at reinforcing the people's relationship with Yahweh. Samuel first comforts them by telling them that they need not be afraid even though they had behaved evilly (12:20). Yahweh is a long-suffering, merciful God who is eager to forgive penitent sinners (Ex 34:6; Is 45:21–22). So Samuel urged the Israelites to never turn away from following Yahweh, but to serve him with "all [their] heart" (1 Sam 12:20). As in 7:3, serving God with one's entire heart necessitates the rejection of all other gods since they are "useless" (תֹהוּ, 12:21). This word, which is first used in Gen 1:2, brings to mind a vast wasteland that is unable to produce anything useful. Thus, trusting in anything more or other than the true God is futile.

Moreover, Samuel stressed that God was committed to making Israel his people and would not forsake them (12:22). God did this for the sake of his reputation, his "great name."[30] Later through David (2 Sam 7:23–24) and Ezekiel (Ezek 20:1–26, especially Ezek 20:9, 14, 22), God would make clear that his

---

28 See Steinmann, *From Abraham to Paul*, 16–17, especially the discussion of the Gezer Calendar, which places the wheat harvest nine months after the beginning of autumn.

29 Longman, "1 Sam 12:16–19: Divine Omnipotence or Covenant Curse?"

30 See Josh 7:9; 2 Sam 7:26; 1 Ki 8:42; Jer 10:6; 44:26; Ezek 36:23; Mal 1:11; Pss 76:2 (ET 76:1); 99:3; 138:2; 1 Chr 17:24; 2 Chr 6:32.

reputation was tied to the deliverance of his people from Egypt. He continued to be patient with Israel because of the reputation he established among the nations when he defeated Pharaoh's armies. Today he continues to be patient with those who bear the name of Christ, who redeemed us through his suffering, death, and resurrection, as he does not want any to perish (Rom 2:4; 2 Pet 3:9, 15).

Since the people of Israel had asked Samuel to pray for them (12:19; see also 7:5; 8:6),[31] Samuel explicitly committed himself to do that and added that he would continue to teach them "the good and correct way" (12:23). Thus, although Samuel would no longer have authority as a judge—since from this point on a king would judge Israel (8:5–6, 20)—he would continue to be Israel's teacher.

Samuel's teaching is summarized in 12:24–25: he repeated his invitation for the people to fear and serve Yahweh in faith with their whole heart (cf. 12:14, 20). The Law shows God's people how he expects them to live, but it is the Gospel, which proclaims the saving work of God on behalf of sinners, that has the power to justify and enable them so to live by faith (Hab 2:4; Rom 1:16–17). For this reason Samuel urged the people to consider the great things God had done for them (1 Sam 12:24). This alone could instill in them faith both to receive forgiveness and righteousness from God and to live according to his will. However, if they did not keep in mind the great things Yahweh had done for them, they would continue their evil actions (cf. 12:19–20), and they and their king would be swept away (1 Sam 12:25). This teaching is summarized well in the Formula of Concord:[32]

> The Apology states in Article XX:[33] "Peter teaches why we should do good works, namely, that we confirm our calling, that is, that we do not fall from our calling by lapsing again into sin [2 Pet 1:10]. He says: 'Do good works so that you remain in your heavenly calling, lest you fall away and lose the Spirit and his gifts, which you have not received because of your subsequent works but which have come to you by grace through Christ and which you retain through faith! Faith, however, does not remain in those who lead a wicked life, lose the Holy Spirit, and reject repentance.' "
>
> It does not, however, mean that faith accepts righteousness and salvation only at the beginning, and then delegates this function to works, as if works should henceforth preserve faith, the righteousness that has been received, and salvation. On the contrary, in order that the promise that we shall not only receive but also retain righteousness and salvation may be very certain to us, Paul ascribes to faith not only our entry into grace but also our present state of grace and our hope of sharing the glory of God (Rom 5:2). In other words, he attributes to faith alone the beginning, the middle, and the end of everything.

---

[31] Earlier Samuel's mother, Hannah, had prayed fervently for him: 1:10, 12, 26, 27; 2:1.

[32] FC SD IV ("Good Works") 33–34.

[33] Ap XX ("Good Works") 13.

1 Samuel 13:1–23

Saul's First Philistine Campaign, Part 1: His Preparation

Translation

13 ¹Saul was … years old when he became king, and he reigned … years over Israel. ²Saul chose for himself three thousand men from Israel, and two thousand were with Saul in Michmash and in the hill country of Bethel. One thousand were with Jonathan at Gibeah in Benjamin. He sent the rest of the people home. ³Jonathan attacked the Philistine garrison in Gibeah, and the Philistines heard about it. So Saul sounded the ram's horn throughout Israel with the message "Let the Hebrews listen." ⁴All Israel listened to the message, "Saul has attacked the Philistine garrison, and so Israel has become repulsive to the Philistines," and the troops were summoned to follow Saul at Gilgal.

⁵Now the Philistines gathered to fight against Israel, bringing up against Israel three thousand chariots, six thousand horsemen, and troops as numerous as the sand on the seashore. So they came up and camped at Michmash, east of Beth-aven. ⁶The men of Israel saw that they were in dire straits because the people were hard-pressed. So the people hid themselves in caves, thickets, cliffs, tombs, and cisterns. ⁷[Some] Hebrews crossed the Jordan River to the land of Gad and Gilead.

Saul was still at Gilgal, and all the troops following him were terrified. ⁸He waited seven days for the time appointed by Samuel. When Samuel did not arrive at Gilgal and the troops were deserting him, ⁹Saul said, "Bring the whole burnt offering and the peace offerings to me," and he sacrificed the whole burnt offering. ¹⁰As he finished sacrificing the whole burnt offering, Samuel was coming, and Saul went out to meet and greet him.

¹¹Samuel said, "What have you done?"

Saul said, "When I saw that the troops were scattering away from me, and you had not arrived within the appointed days, and the Philistines had gathered at Michmash, ¹²I thought, 'The Philistines will come down to me at Gilgal, and I have not sought Yahweh's favor.' So I forced myself to sacrifice the whole burnt offering."

¹³Samuel said to Saul, "You have acted foolishly. You did not keep the command of Yahweh your God, which he commanded you. For now Yahweh would have established your kingdom over Israel permanently. ¹⁴But now your kingdom will not endure. Yahweh has sought for himself a man according to his own heart, and he has commanded him to be designated ruler over his people because you have not obeyed what Yahweh commanded you."

¹⁵Then Samuel arose and went up from Gilgal on his way, but the remaining troops went up after Saul to meet the men of war. They came from Gilgal to Gibeah of Benjamin. Saul mustered the troops that were with him, about six hundred men.

¹⁶Now Saul, his son Jonathan, and the troops that were with them were staying in Geba in Benjamin. The Philistines were camped in Michmash. ¹⁷A raiding party went out from the Philistine camp in three commands. One command turned toward the Ophrah Road, toward the region of Shual. ¹⁸Another command turned toward the Beth-horon Road, and another command turned toward the Border Road that overlooks the Valley of the Hyenas toward the wilderness.

¹⁹Now no blacksmith was to be found in the entire land of Israel because the Philistines said, "Otherwise the Hebrews will make swords or spears." ²⁰So all Israel would go down to the Philistines to sharpen their plows, mattocks, axes, and sickles. ²¹The charge was a pim for plows and mattocks, and a third of a shekel for sharpening axes and repointing cattle prods. ²²So on the day of battle there was no sword or spear found in the possession of any of the troops that were with Saul and with Jonathan. However, Saul and his son Jonathan had them.

²³Now the Philistine encampment went out to Michmash Pass.

Textual Notes

13:1 The numbers in this verse have been lost or purposely deleted and altered (see the commentary). The verse is missing in the LXX.

בֶּן־שָׁנָה שָׁאוּל בְּמָלְכוֹ—Literally "a son of a year was Saul when he became king." The idiom "a son of [a number of] years" normally expresses someone's age (Joüon, § 129 j). The Qal (G) of מָלַךְ usually means "to be king, to reign" (as in the next textual note), but here its infinitive construct (with בְּ and a third masculine singular suffix) has the nuance "become king."

וּשְׁתֵּי שָׁנִים מָלַךְ עַל־יִשְׂרָאֵל:—Literally "and two years he reigned over Israel." However, "two years" is usually expressed by the dual form שְׁנָתַיִם or by שְׁתַּיִם שָׁנִים.[1] The dual feminine construct form here, שְׁתֵּי, is never used elsewhere to enumerate years. Moreover, Saul must have reigned more than two years, given all the events of his reign that are documented in 1 Samuel 13–31. Note that David's time in the service of Achish of Gath was sixteen months (1 Sam 27:7). This would mean that the events of 1 Samuel 13–26 would have had to have taken place in eight months! Nor can שְׁתֵּי be the remnant of a compound number such as twenty-two or forty-two with the first number accidentally omitted, since compound numbers are almost always expressed with an absolute form of the feminine dual, either שְׁתֵּים or שְׁתַּיִם.[2] A lone exception is the number forty-

---

[1] For שְׁנָתַיִם, the dual of שָׁנָה, "year," see Gen 11:10; 1 Ki 15:25; 16:8; 22:52 (ET 22:51); 2 Ki 15:23; Jer 28:3, 11; Amos 1:1. For שְׁתַּיִם שָׁנִים, see 2 Sam 2:10; 2 Ki 21:19; 2 Chr 33:21.

[2] The following are years attested in the OT with compound numbers that are theoretically possible for a king's reign:

- Twelve years: שְׁתֵּים עֶשְׂרֵה שָׁנָה (Gen 14:4; 1 Ki 16:23; 2 Ki 3:1; 21:1; 2 Chr 33:1) or שָׁנִים שְׁתֵּים עֶשְׂרֵה (Neh 5:14)
- Twenty-two years: עֶשְׂרִים וּשְׁתַּיִם שָׁנָה (Judg 10:3; 1 Ki 14:20; 16:29; 2 Ki 8:26; 21:19; 2 Chr 33:21)

two in 2 Ki 2:24, which in this one verse is used with the masculine singular construct numeral two, but it is employed with a partitive sense: אַרְבָּעִים וּשְׁנֵי יְלָדִים, "forty and *two of* the boys" (2 Ki 2:24). A partitive meaning is inappropriate for 1 Sam 13:1 in its context. See further the commentary.

13:2 אִישׁ לְאֹהָלָיו:—The stock idiom "each man to his own tent" is translated here as "[sent] home." See the second textual note on 4:10.

13:3 נְצִיב פְּלִשְׁתִּים—Samuel had referred to this "garrison of Philistines" in 10:5.

בְּגֶבַע—Instead of the MT's "in Geba," the LXX reads "in Gibeah" (ἐν τῷ βουνῷ; see the first textual note on 10:5). The reading גֶּבַע, "Geba," may be due to an accidental loss of the final *he* of גִּבְעָה; confusion caused by the similarity of the names of the two cities; and/or the assimilation of this verse to 14:4–5, where Jonathan is present at Geba. However, 13:2 located Jonathan at Gibeah, and in 10:5 we were told that a "garrison of Philistines" was there. Thus, this commentary follows the reading in the LXX.

וְשָׁאוּל תָּקַע בַּשּׁוֹפָר בְּכָל־הָאָרֶץ לֵאמֹר—Literally "and Saul blew on the ram's horn in all Israel, saying …" Here and in 13:4, לֵאמֹר, literally "saying," is translated more idiomatically in this context as "with/to the message."

הָעִבְרִים:—This gentilic noun, "the Hebrews," recurs in this chapter in 13:7, 19. It is rare for Israelites to call themselves "Hebrews." For this reason McCarter seeks to emend the word here.[3] However, the Philistines had called the Israelites "the Hebrews" in 4:6, 9, and will again in 13:19; 14:11; 29:3 (cf. 14:21). Here in 13:3 it appears that Saul is using a term that the Philistines used as a pejorative for Israel in order to stir Israel to action. In 13:7, the term is used in conjunction with the Israelites' cowardice in the face of the Philistine invasion. Later the Philistines use the same term to note this cowardly behavior of some of the Israelites (14:11). In 13:3 (and also in 14:21), the LXX has οἱ δοῦλοι, "the slaves," which may indicate that its Vorlage read העבדים. That reading probably arose from the common graphic confusion of *resh* and *daleth*. In 13:7 the LXX omits "the Hebrews."

13:4 וְכָל־יִשְׂרָאֵל שָׁמְעוּ לֵאמֹר—Literally "and all Israel listened [to the messengers] saying …" See the third textual note on 13:3.

וְגַם־נִבְאַשׁ יִשְׂרָאֵל בַּפְּלִשְׁתִּים—The Niphal (N) perfect of בָּאַשׁ literally means "Israel *became stinky* among the Philistines." The Qal (G) has the literal meaning "to emit a foul stench" when the Nile River became blood and its fish died in Ex 7:18, 21, and when there were heaps of rotting frogs throughout Egypt in Ex 8:10 (ET 8:14). Metaphorically, it means someone becomes offensive or reprehensible. The Niphal (N) of בָּאַשׁ recurs in the same sense in 2 Sam 10:6; 16:21, and the Hiphil (H), "to cause someone to stink," is used metaphorically in 1 Sam 27:12.

וַיִּצָּעֲקוּ הָעָם אַחֲרֵי שָׁאוּל—In the Qal (G) צָעַק means "to cry out." Its Hiphil (H) in 10:17 meant "to summon" (see the textual note there), and its Niphal (N) here has the corresponding passive meaning, "to be summoned." In military contexts הָעָם ("the

---

- Thirty-two years: שְׁלֹשִׁים וּשְׁתַּיִם שָׁנָה (2 Ki 8:17; 2 Chr 21:5)
- Fifty-two years: חֲמִשִּׁים וּשְׁתַּיִם שָׁנָה (2 Ki 15:2; 2 Chr 26:3)

[3] McCarter, *I Samuel*, 225.

people") often means "the troops," as again in 13:5 (without the article), 7, 8, 11, 15, 16, 22 (see the first textual note on 4:3). The preposition אַחֲרֵי, "after," has the pregnant meaning "to follow after," that is, the troops were summoned to follow Saul into battle. The preposition involves "following" also in 12:14, 20, 21, and in 13:7 (see the second textual note there).

13:5 לְהִלָּחֵם עִם־יִשְׂרָאֵל—After these words, "to fight against Israel," the LXX includes a clause that is absent from the MT: καὶ ἀναβαίνουσιν ἐπὶ Ισραηλ, "and they went up against Israel." If those words were originally in the Hebrew, then the MT lost the clause וַיַּעֲלוּ עַל יִשְׂרָאֵל by homoioteleuton (the scribe's eye skipped from the "Israel" in the MT to the "Israel" in this variant).

שְׁלֹשִׁים אֶלֶף—"Thirty thousand" is the reading of the MT and Codex Vaticanus (LXX). However, the Lucianic LXX manuscripts and the Syriac versions read "three thousand," as reflected in the translation above. Since there were six thousand horsemen to man the chariots, three thousand chariots are appropriate. Normally chariots were manned by a crew of two—a driver and an archer or other soldier.

כַּחוֹל אֲשֶׁר עַל־שְׂפַת־הַיָּם לָרֹב—Literally this means "like the sand which is on the shore of the sea with respect to abundance." The combination of the preposition לְ and the noun רֹב is translated adverbially, "as numerous as."

בֵּית אָוֶן:—"Beth-aven," which means "house of wickedness," was in the vicinity of Bethel (see 13:2). Hosea seems to use "Beth-aven" as an equivalent of Bethel (Hos 4:15; 5:8; 10:5), perhaps because of idolatry (Hos 10:5; cf. 1 Ki 12:26–29), though in Joshua "Beth-aven" appears to be a nearby village (Josh 7:2).

13:6 וְאִישׁ יִשְׂרָאֵל רָאוּ כִּי צַר־לוֹ—The first word is singular, as are the second verb and the suffix on the last word, but the verb in the middle is plural, literally "and the man of Israel, they saw that it was restricted to him [to Israel]." צַר is a Qal (G) perfect third masculine singular form of the verb צָרַר. When used intransitively this verb means "to be cramped, restricted, hampered" (see *HALOT*, s.v. צרר I, Qal, B). This is an impersonal construction (there is no grammatical subject of the verb, "*it* was restricted") employed as a passive, meaning "he [the man of Israel] was constricted," or more eloquently, "he was in dire straits."

וַיִּתְחַבְּאוּ—The Hithpael (HtD) of חָבָא, "to hide," has a reflexive meaning, "they hid themselves," as did its Niphal (N) in 10:22 (see the third textual note there).

13:7 וְעִבְרִים עָבְרוּ—Notice the alliteration: both the noun and the verb have the same root letters, עבר, and the clause both begins and ends with ו.

וְכָל־הָעָם חָרְדוּ אַחֲרָיו:—Literally "and all the people trembled after him," this means "and all the troops following him were terrified." For the pregnant sense of the preposition אַחֲרֵי (with suffix, אַחֲרָיו), see the third textual note on 13:4.

13:8 וַיּוֹחֶל | שִׁבְעַת יָמִים—"And he waited seven days." This is the same vocabulary (but with the verb in the third person) as a clause in 10:8, where Samuel instructed Saul to do this (with the second person verb; see the third textual note there). The Qere, וַיּוֹחֶל, is the expected Hiphil (H) form of a first-*yod* verb that originally was a first-*waw* verb, i.e., יָחַל. The Kethib is to be pointed וַיְיַחֶל, which is Niphal (N) (GKC, § 69 t) and has the same meaning; that Niphal form is attested in Gen 8:12 (which also refers to waiting seven days).

לַמּוֹעֵד֙ אֲשֶׁ֣ר [שָׁ֣ם] שְׁמוּאֵ֔ל—"For the time appointed by Samuel" is the reading of some Masoretic manuscripts; they include the verb שָׁם, the Qal (G) third masculine singular perfect of שִׂים, "to set, appoint." Most Masoretic manuscripts lack a verb, and in them שָׁם was probably lost due to parablepsis (שם שמו־). In place of שָׁם some Masoretic manuscripts supply אָמַר (cf. the LXX: ὡς εἶπεν Σαμουηλ).

וַיָּ֥פֶץ הָעָ֖ם מֵעָלָֽיו:—Literally "and the people scattered from beside him." The verb is the Hiphil (H) preterite (imperfect with *waw* consecutive) third masculine singular of פּוּץ. It has the same meaning, "to scatter" in the intransitive sense, as the Qal (G) by-form נָפַץ in 13:11.

13:9 הָעֹלָ֖ה וְהַשְּׁלָמִ֑ים—For עֹלָה, "whole burnt offering," see the second textual note on 6:14. For שְׁלָמִים, "peace offerings," see the second textual note on 10:8.

וַיַּ֖עַל הָעֹלָֽה:—The verb could be either Qal (G) or Hiphil (H). Since it is transitive (with הָעֹלָה as its direct object), it must be Hiphil. For this cognate accusative construction,[4] "to offer up [the Hiphil of עָלָה] a burnt offering [עֹלָה]," see also 6:14, 15; 7:9, 10; 10:8. In this chapter it recurs in 13:10 (see the next textual note) and 13:12.

13:10 כְּכַלֹּתוֹ֙ לְהַעֲל֣וֹת הָעֹלָ֔ה—The first infinitive construct is the Piel (D) of כָּלָה, "to finish, complete," with the preposition כְּ in a temporal sense, "when, as" and a third masculine singular suffix that serves as its subject: "as he finished." The second infinitive construct is the Hiphil (H) of עָלָה, "to offer up," with the preposition לְ. It serves as the object of the first infinitive (see Joüon, § 124 c) and supplies the action that Saul finished doing. When the preposition לְ is prefixed to such an object infinitive, the preposition has almost no semantic value or meaning (see Joüon, § 124 m).

וְהִנֵּ֥ה שְׁמוּאֵ֖ל בָּ֑א—Literally "and behold, Samuel (was) coming." In form בָּא could be the Qal (G) third masculine singular perfect, but in context it must be the masculine singular participle. Samuel was still coming and had not yet arrived, so Saul could go out "to meet him" (לִקְרָאתוֹ; see the second textual note on 4:1).

לְבָרֲכֽוֹ:—Literally this means "to bless him." This Piel (D) infinitive construct of בָּרַךְ with לְ forms a purpose clause. The Piel (D) of בָּרַךְ can refer to uttering a blessing as a form of greeting (e.g., 1 Sam 25:14 [cf. 1 Sam 15:13]; 2 Ki 4:29; 10:15; Ruth 2:4). Here Saul may intend his blessing to mask his disobedience to Yahweh and Samuel by impetuously sacrificing the burnt offering.

13:12 וּפְנֵ֤י יְהוָה֙ לֹ֣א חִלִּ֔יתִי—Literally "and the face of Yahweh I did not appease." Saul says that he had not yet sought Yahweh's favor. The verb is the Piel (D) perfect first common singular of חָלָה II, which occurs only in the Piel, meaning "to appease, entreat the favor" of someone. The verb idiomatically takes that person's "face" (פָּנִים) as its direct object.

וָאֶתְאַפַּ֗ק—The verb אָפַק, "to be strong," occurs only in the Hithpael (HtD). This form is the first common singular preterite (imperfect with *waw* consecutive). Elsewhere in the OT this Hithpael verb always means "to refrain" or "restrain oneself" from an

---

[4] See *IBH*, § 17 B; GKC, § 117 p–r.

action. This is the only verse where it means "to force/compel oneself" to perform an action.

13:13 נִסְכָּלְתָּ—This is the second masculine singular Niphal (N) perfect of סָכַל. Its Niphal has an active meaning, "to act foolishly." David will use its Niphal for himself after his foolish sin of numbering his troops in 2 Sam 24:10. The Hiphil (H) has the same meaning in 1 Sam 26:21. Its Piel (D) is causative in 2 Sam 15:31, "to make [something] foolish" or "to turn [something] into foolishness."

צִוְּךָ—The verb's suffix (ךָ-) appears to be second feminine singular, but this verb form is pausal for צִוְּךָ, which appears in the next verse (13:14). It is a Piel (D) third masculine singular perfect of צָוָה, "to command" (with Yahweh as subject), with a second masculine singular suffix, referring to Saul.

כִּי עַתָּה הֵכִין יְהוָה אֶת־מַמְלַכְתְּךָ—The syntax of this conditional sentence is abridged (GKC, § 159 dd). One must supply a prior thought to understand it: "[If you *had* kept the command of Yahweh,] then now he would have established your kingdom." However, this is an unreal or contrary-to-fact condition: Saul *had not* kept Yahweh's command, and so now Yahweh would not establish his kingdom, as Samuel declares in 13:14.

עַד־עוֹלָם:—Elsewhere in the OT this prepositional phrase often means "forever," and some translations render it so here. However, it does not necessarily mean forever, i.e., perpetually without end, as the English might imply. Here it is translated as "permanently" so as to accentuate this. The noun עוֹלָם can denote a distant time, either in the past or in the future—something beyond the experience of the persons who are using or hearing the term. *TWOT* notes:

> Though *ʿôlām* is used more than three hundred times to indicate indefinite continuance into the very distant future, the meaning of the word is not confined to the future. There are at least twenty instances where it clearly refers to the past. Such usages generally point to something that seems long ago, but rarely if ever refer to a limitless past. Thus in Deut 32:7 and Job 22:15 it may refer to the time of one's elders. In Prov 22:28; Prov 23:10; Jer 6:16; Jer 18:15; Jer 28:8 it points back somewhat farther. In Isa 58:12; Isa 61:4; Mic 7:14; Mal 3:4, and in the Aramaic of Ezr 4:15, 19 it clearly refers to the time just before the exile. In 1 Sam 27:8, in Isa 51:9 and Isa 63:9, 11 and perhaps Ezek 36:2, it refers to the events of the exodus from Egypt. In Gen 6:4 it points to the time shortly before the flood. None of these past references has in it the idea of endlessness or limitlessness, but each points to a time long before the immediate knowledge of those living. In Isa 64:3 [ET 64:4] the KJV translates the word "beginning of the world." …
>
> The LXX generally translates *ʿôlām* by *aiōn* which has essentially the same range of meaning. That neither the Hebrew nor the Greek word in itself contains the idea of endlessness is shown both by the fact that they sometimes refer to events or conditions that occurred at a definite point in the past, and also by the fact that sometimes it is thought desirable to repeat the word, not merely saying "forever," but "forever and ever."[5]

---

[5] *TWOT*, § 1631a.

13:14 אִישׁ כִּלְבָבוֹ—In this phrase, literally "a man like his heart," the preposition כְּ indicates likeness or conformity. The idea is idiomatically expressed in English as "a man after/according to his own heart." The combination of לֵב with כְּ has a similar meaning in Jer 3:15 (Yahweh promises to give his people faithful shepherds/pastors "after my own heart") but is somewhat different in 2 Sam 7:21; 17:10; 1 Chr 17:19.

לְנָגִיד—For נָגִיד as a "designated ruler," see the first textual note on 9:16.

13:15 וַיַּעַל מִן־הַגִּלְגָּל גִּבְעַת בִּנְיָמִן—The MT reads "and he went up from Gilgal [to] Gibeah of Benjamin." The LXX reads καὶ ἀπῆλθεν ἐκ Γαλγαλων εἰς ὁδὸν αὐτοῦ—καὶ τὸ κατάλειμμα τοῦ λαοῦ ἀνέβη ὀπίσω Σαουλ εἰς ἀπάντησιν ὀπίσω τοῦ λαοῦ τοῦ πολεμιστοῦ. αὐτῶν παραγενομένων ἐκ Γαλγαλων ... , "and he went up from Gilgal *on his way—but the remaining troops went up after Saul to meet the troops of war. When they had come from Gilgal* …" The italicized words are missing in the MT, which apparently suffered from homoioteleuton when a scribe's eye skipped from the first "from Gilgal" to the second.[6] The missing Hebrew text would have been this:[7]

וַיֵּלֶךְ לְדַרְכּוֹ וְיֶתֶר הָעָם עָלָה אַחֲרֵי שָׁאוּל לִקְרַאת עַם הַמִּלְחָמָה וַיָּבֹאוּ מִן הַגִּלְגָּל

Note that if the MT were correct, then Samuel would have gone to Gibeah, though there is no reason for him to go there.

וַיִּפְקֹד שָׁאוּל אֶת־הָעָם הַנִּמְצָאִים עִמּוֹ—For the Qal (G) of פָּקַד, "to muster" troops for battle, see the first textual note on 11:8. הַנִּמְצָאִים is a Niphal (N) masculine plural participle from the verb מָצָא, "to find," with the definite article. The participle is used adjectivally to describe the troops as *those who were found* with him." See also הַנִּמְצָא in 13:16.

13:17 הַמַּשְׁחִית—In form this is the masculine singular Hiphil (H) participle of שָׁחַת with the definite article, "the destroyer," the same term that denotes the angelic "destroyer" in Ex 12:23; 2 Sam 24:16. Since, however, it refers to human attackers, it is translated as "a raiding party" here and as "raiding parties" in 1 Sam 14:15. Some lexicons treat the word here as the Hiphil (H) participle (e.g., BDB, s.v. שָׁחַת, Hiphil, 1). Most lexicons also include a homographic noun מַשְׁחִית, "destruction," and some grammatical resources consider the word here to be that noun.

שְׁלֹשָׁה רָאשִׁים—For the translation of this phrase as "three commands," see the second textual note on 11:11.

הָרֹאשׁ אֶחָד—This phrase, literally "the head, one," recurs twice in 13:18. The number אֶחָד is used as an adverbial accusative to reinforce that the singular noun רֹאשׁ refers to just one "command." See GKC, § 118 q.

13:18 גֵּי הַצְּבֹעִים—This is translated as "the Valley of the Hyenas." In English the second element of the name is often simply transliterated: "the Valley of Zeboim." It is probably Shakh ed-Dubʿa, "ravine of the hyenas," in modern Israel.

הַמִּדְבָּרָה:—"Toward the wilderness" is missing in the LXX.

---

[6] McCarter, *I Samuel*, 227; Klein, *1 Samuel*, 123; ESV; GW.

[7] The consonants are from *HOTTP*², 174, but the pointing has been added. The text is rated "A" to indicate that the editors consider it highly probable that it represents the reading that is the earliest recoverable text (see *HOTTP*², vii–viii).

13:19 אָמְרוּ פְלִשְׁתִּים—"The Philistines said." The Qere, אָמְרוּ, is Qal (G) perfect third common plural, which is supported by the LXX. The Kethib is the singular אָמַר.

13:20 לִלְטוֹשׁ—The uncommon verb לָטַשׁ means "to sharpen" or, once, "to hammer." Here its Qal (G) infinitive construct with the preposition לְ forms a purpose clause.

אִישׁ אֶת־מַחֲרַשְׁתּוֹ—This literally means "[each] man his plow." The noun מַחֲרֵשָׁה, "plow," appears in the OT only in 13:20–21, a total of three times. Here and with the following phrases the use of the noun אִישׁ (with a third person pronominal suffix on the following noun) is distributive. The distributive idea is best represented in English by the plural pronoun "their" and plural nouns: "their plows, mattocks, axes, and sickles."

וְאֶת־אֵתוֹ—The noun אֵת, "mattock," appears five times in the OT.

קַרְדֻּמּוֹ—The noun קַרְדֹּם, "ax," is a quadriliteral that recurs in 13:21 and is found a total of five times in the OT.

מַחֲרַשְׁתּוֹ:—This is a pausal form of מַחֲרַשְׁתּוֹ, "his plow," repeated from earlier in the verse (see the second textual note on 13:20). The LXX has "his sickle," which probably reflects חרמשו, a suffixed form of the Hebrew noun חֶרְמֵשׁ, "sickle," a quadriliteral found only in Deut 16:9; 23:26 (ET 23:25). Since these two Hebrew words have the same consonants (but in different order), the LXX probably reflects the original and the MT is the result of transposition of some of the consonants. The translation follows the LXX.[8]

13:21 הַפְּצִירָה—This noun (with the definite article) is a hapax legomenon. Based on the context most interpreters assume פְּצִירָה means a "price, charge, fee" for the sharpening. Bewer proposed that it is derived from the root פרץ, "urge, coerce," and therefore has the connotation of money that is exacted for a service.[9]

פִּים—"Pim" is a unit of weight equal to two-thirds of a shekel (so *HALOT*), about a third of an ounce or 9.5 grams.

וְלִשְׁלֹשׁ קִלְּשׁוֹן וּלְהַקַּרְדֻּמִּים—The text as it stands says "and for three *qilleshon* and for the axes." For קַרְדֹּם, "ax," see the fourth textual note on 13:20. The noun קִלְּשׁוֹן is otherwise unattested. The translation above follows the suggestion of Bewer that the text suffered from disruption, including the loss of a *shin* due to haplography and misdivided words. He suggested that the original text was וּשְׁלֹשׁ שֶׁקֶל לָשׁוֹן הַקַּרְדֻּמִּים, "and a third of a shekel for sharpening the axes";[10] לָשׁוֹן would be the Qal (G) infinitive construct of שָׁנַן, "to sharpen."[11] The LXX also seems confused in this verse: καὶ ἦν ὁ τρυγητὸς ἕτοιμος τοῦ θερίζειν· τὰ δὲ σκεύη ἦν τρεῖς σίκλοι εἰς τὸν ὀδόντα, καὶ τῇ ἀξίνῃ καὶ τῷ δρεπάνῳ ὑπόστασις ἦν ἡ αὐτή, "and the harvest was ready to reap, but the implements were three shekels for the tooth, and for the axe and the pruning hook the arrangement was the same."

וּלְהַצִּיב הַדָּרְבָן:—Literally "and to set up the goad," this probably refers to putting a new point on a cattle prod. The noun דָּרְבָן, "goad, cattle prod," is another quadriliteral

---

[8] These commentators and versions also follow the LXX: McCarter, *I Samuel*, 234; Klein, *1 Samuel*, 123; HCSB, ESV, GW, NET, NIV.

[9] Bewer, "Notes on 1 Sam 13:21; 2 Sam 23:1; Psalm 48:8," 46.

[10] This reading is also followed by many English versions: HCSB, ESV, NET, NIV; see also McCarter, *I Samuel*, 235; Klein, *1 Samuel*, 123.

[11] Bewer, "Notes on 1 Sam 13:21; 2 Sam 23:1; Psalm 48:8," 45–46.

and another hapax legomenon (cf. דָּרְבֹנָה, "goad," in Eccl 12:11). The Hiphil (H) of נָצַב, "to set up, establish" (as in 1 Sam 15:12; 2 Sam 18:17, 18), here has the contextual meaning "restore (to original sharpness)" or "resharpen, repoint." (Its Niphal [N] means "to stand" in, e.g., 1 Sam 1:26; 19:20.)

13:22 מִלְחֶמֶת—The common form of this feminine noun for "war, battle," is מִלְחָמָה. The alternate form here is unique and may display the old feminine ending.

וַתִּמָּצֵא לְשָׁאוּל וּלְיוֹנָתָן בְּנוֹ׃—Literally "and it was found belonging to Saul and belonging to Jonathan his son." The repeated preposition לְ indicates possession ("belonging to"). The subject of the feminine singular verb וַתִּמָּצֵא could be either of the feminine nouns earlier in the verse, חֶרֶב, "sword," or חֲנִית, "spear"; both may be intended.

13:23 מַצַּב—This is the construct form of the noun מַצָּב, literally "a standing place" (as in Josh 4:3, 9), derived from the verb נָצַב, whose Niphal means "to stand" (see the last textual note on 13:21). In the book of Samuel this noun always denotes a "military base" or "encampment" (also 1 Sam 14:1, 4, 6, 11, 15; 2 Sam 23:14). It is often translated as "garrison." Here, however, it does not refer to the garrison at Gibeah, which is called a נְצִיב (1 Sam 10:5; 13:3, 4; see also 2 Sam 8:6, 14; 1 Chr 11:16; 18:13; 2 Chr 17:2).

Commentary

c. 1021 BC

Saul's Reign (13:1)

The information about Saul's age and reign is corrupt in all textual traditions available to us now. As 13:1 stands in the MT, no number is supplied for Saul's age, and the "two years" for the length of his reign is clearly a secondary reading (see the second and third textual notes on 13:1). A number of solutions have been offered for this problem. Saul's age cannot be determined from information in the book of Samuel, though Klein has suggested he was at least forty when he became king.[12] As for the length of his reign, a number of suggestions have been offered.[13] However, his reign must have lasted between thirty-five and forty years.[14] Acts 13:21 and Josephus[15] indicate that Saul reigned forty years.[16]

Gilmour and Young have proposed that the phrase "two years" (שְׁתֵּי שָׁנִים) in MT 13:1 was a later addition purposely chosen to minimize Saul's reputation as king, since later ineffective kings of Israel often reigned only two years. They state:

---

[12] Klein, *1 Samuel*, 122.

[13] See the discussion in Tsumura, *The First Book of Samuel*, 331–33.

[14] See "The Basic Chronology of the United Monarchy" in "Chronological Issues in Samuel" in the introduction.

[15] Josephus, *Antiquities*, 6.378.

[16] See Steinmann, *From Abraham to Paul*, 106. However, in *Antiquities*, 10.143, Josephus contradicts this, saying that Saul reigned twenty years.

The two year reign as symbolic of a failed kingship and dynasty is appropriate for Saul, the prototype of a failed northern king. The position of the regnal notice in 1 Sam 13:1 immediately before Saul's first rejection confirms the plausibility of this symbolic reading. By mentioning the duration of Saul's reign as "two years" the MT connects Saul with all the negative connotations associated with that length of reign.[17]

While this is an appealing argument, it does not explain why Saul's age at his accession to the throne is missing altogether or why 13:1 in its entirety is absent from the LXX. Perhaps we should take Gilmour and Young's suggestion two steps further:

1. Saul's reign of forty years would have been identical to the reigns of other mostly faithful kings of Judah: David (2 Sam 5:4; 1 Ki 2:11; 1 Chr 29:27), Solomon (1 Ki 11:42; 2 Chr 9:30), and Joash/Jehoash (2 Ki 12:2 [ET 12:1]; 2 Chr 24:1). Thus, a later scribe may have purposely substituted "two" for "forty," signaling a failed reign in place of a number perceived to signal a successful reign.

2. Saul appears to have had at least three sons when he assumed the throne (1 Sam 14:49). This would argue that he was close to thirty years old. If the text of 13:1 originally noted Saul's age as thirty and his reign as forty years, it would invite positive comparisons to David, who also was thirty when he became king and also ruled forty years (2 Sam 5:4). Thus, the same scribe who introduced the number two for Saul's reign may also have purposely omitted his age.

This would also explain the absence of 13:1 in the LXX. Its tradition apparently denied Saul a favorable comparison to David by deleting the entire verse.

Events Leading Up to Saul's First Philistine Campaign (13:2–23)

Having opened with a notice about Saul's reign, there is no indication as to when (during his reign) his campaign against the Philistines took place. However, there are a number of clues in the book of Samuel that allow an estimation of the date to about 1021 BC. See "The Reign of Saul (c. 1049–1009)" in "Chronological Issues in Samuel" in the introduction.

This chapter has ties to two other moments in Israel's history. The first and more recent is Samuel's instructions to Saul when he was anointed (10:5–8). There are six common elements between these two texts:

- Gibeah (10:5; 13:2–3)
- The Philistine garrison there (10:5; 13:3–4)
- Gilgal (10:8; 13:4, 7–8, 12, 15)
- Saul arrives at Gilgal before Samuel (10:8; 13:4, 7, 10)
- Burnt offerings and peace offerings (10:8; 13:9–10, 12)
- Waiting seven days (10:8; 13:8)

---

[17] Gilmour and Young, "Saul's Two Year Reign in 1 Samuel 13:1," 153.

Clearly, this chapter portrays the long-delayed attack on the Philistine garrison that Samuel had expected Saul to undertake immediately after being anointed.[18]

Second, this chapter has more distant ties to the account of Gideon's war with the Midianites. They include the following:

- Frightened Israelites hiding in caves (Judg 6:2; 1 Sam 13:6)
- Sounding a horn to summon volunteer troops (Judg 6:34–35; 1 Sam 13:3–4)
- Troops who were "terrified" (the adjective חָרֵד in Judg 7:6; the verb חָרַד in 1 Sam 13:7)
- A greatly reduced Israelite force (three hundred in Judg 7:2–8; six hundred in 1 Sam 13:8–15)

Like Gideon attacking the Midianites (Judg 7:2–14), Saul was to attack the Philistines with a reduced force and with instructions from God as to how to proceed. Saul's instructions were supposed to come from Yahweh through Samuel (1 Sam 10:8). However, because of the way events unfolded with Saul's impetuous action, Samuel would leave without giving Saul any instructions.

Apparently by this point in his reign Saul had an army of three thousand men, two thousand stationed with him in Michmash and a thousand stationed with his son Jonathan in Gibeah (13:2). While Saul had not taken the initiative to attack the Philistine garrison after he had been anointed many years earlier (cf. 10:7), Jonathan decided to carry out the mission and expel the Philistine presence from the heart of Israelite territory (13:3). The news would not take long to reach the Philistine pentapolis (see 6:17), and Saul immediately summoned volunteers from the general populace to assemble at Gilgal (13:4). In the message Saul is credited with the attack on the garrison (13:4), since he was the head of state. In addition, the message notes that "Israel has become repulsive [literally a stench] to the Philistines." Throughout the book of Samuel the concept of becoming repulsively odiferous (בָּאַשׁ; see the second textual note on 13:4) signals an alienation that leads to hostility or rejection (2 Sam 10:6; 16:21; cf. 1 Sam 27:12). When one nation becomes disgusting to another, a state of war is in the offing.

In choosing Gilgal as the place to muster these troops Saul showed that he had comprehended the instructions of Samuel that he had previously ignored: Samuel had implied that Saul was to attack the Philistines at Gibeah and then go to Gilgal (see the commentary on 10:7–8).

The narrative shifts to the Philistine force that marches to Michmash, the place where Saul had been bivouacking with his forces (13:5). The author notes the large number of chariots and uncountable troops. The idiom "numerous as the sand on the seashore" was famously in the Abrahamic blessing promise (Gen 22:17; 32:13 [ET 32:12]; cf. Gen 41:49), but it is used of the enemies of Israel also in Josh 11:4 and Judg 7:12. It is also used to depict Absalom's potential

---

[18] 1 Sam 10:7 strongly implies that Samuel expected Saul to eradicate the Philistine garrison in Gibeah. See the discussion in "Samuel Anoints Saul (9:26–10:8)" in the commentary on 9:26–10:16. See also the beginning of the commentary on 10:17–27a.

army in his rebellion against David (2 Sam 17:11). In these antagonistic verses it depicts what appears to be an overwhelming force that, nevertheless, will be routed on the battlefield by God's servants.

The invasion caused many Israelites to seek a place to hide from the attacking troops (1 Sam 13:6). Some sought to place the Jordan River between themselves and the Philistines, while Saul maintained his camp at Gilgal just west of the Jordan (13:7). The panic among the general population spilled over into Saul's troops.

Saul's actions at Gilgal appear at first to follow Samuel's instructions. Note the close parallel between what Samuel had told Saul and the description of what Saul did:

> Then you will go down before me to Gilgal, and I will come down to you to offer *whole burnt offerings and to make sacrifices of peace offerings.* **Wait seven days** until I come to you. Then I will inform you about what you ought to do. (10:8)

> He **waited seven days** for the time appointed by Samuel. When Samuel did not arrive at Gilgal and the troops were deserting him, Saul said, "Bring *the whole burnt offering and the peace offerings* to me," and he sacrificed the whole burnt offering. (13:8–9)

Saul waited for seven days at Gilgal just as Samuel had commanded, and he had animals for the offerings that Samuel had specified. These actions demonstrate that Saul had rightly perceived Samuel's directions given at his anointing and was adhering to them at this time. With the troops deserting and Saul feeling desperate, he ordered the sacrifices to begin (13:8–9). Nevertheless, when Saul went out to greet Samuel (13:10), the prophet asked an accusatory "what have you done?" (13:11).

Commentators are often hard-pressed to explain what Saul did wrong.[19] However, Auld helpfully points out that the most important part of Samuel's instructions was that *Samuel* would tell Saul what to do.[20] Instead, Saul took it upon himself to determine what he ought to do. Moreover, Saul did precisely what Samuel was supposed to do—offer the sacrifices. In addition, despite the fact that Saul waited seven days, it is clear that he did not wait until the end of the seventh day before concluding that Samuel would be late. As he finished offering the sacrifice on the seventh day, Samuel was arriving (see the second textual note on 13:10). Thus, although the narrator says that Saul waited for the appointed time (13:8; cf. 10:8), Saul clearly decided that he could carry out the action at any time on the seventh day, and he presumptuously did so prematurely when he felt pressured by troop desertions to entreat God through sacrifices.

In contrast to Samuel's terse accusation (two Hebrew words in 13:11), Saul's explanation is quite long (twenty-seven Hebrew words in 13:11–12). By

---

[19] Klein, *1 Samuel*, 126–27; Bodner, *1 Samuel*, 121–22; Miscall, *1 Samuel*, 86–87; Brueggemann, *First and Second Samuel*, 99–100.

[20] Auld, *I and II Samuel*, 141.

his verbosity he desperately sought to justify his actions by asserting the need to demonstrate his piety (in that he sought Yahweh's favor) and forcing himself into the role that was to have been Samuel's. He also sought to shift the blame to others: to the troops (they scattered), to Samuel (who did not arrive in time), and to the Philistines (whose menacing presence was at Michmash). Thus, he employed the same age-old strategy as Adam, who excused himself by indicting others, even blaming God for his predicament (Gen 3:8–12). This kind of situation is all too common in the church, as people disregard the Word of God and usurp the authority of those rightly called into divine offices.

Samuel's reply to Saul (13:13–14) does not seek to rebut Saul's self-justifications for his actions. He begins by telling Saul that he has behaved foolishly. His reply also states that Saul did not keep the command Yahweh had given him through his prophet Samuel. Had he obeyed, his kingdom would have been permanent—one that lasted beyond his lifetime (see the fourth textual note on 13:13).[21] God had intended that the monarchy be hereditary (Deut 17:20). Saul would eventually desire that his son Jonathan succeed him (1 Sam 20:30–31). But it was not to be. Thus, by not obeying the divine command when he first had opportunity (1 Sam 10:7–8), Saul first created a division over his fitness to be king (10:27). Then he raised a need for a new occasion to demonstrate his leadership (see the commentary on 11:1–13). This was followed by a renewal of the kingship at Gilgal, which solidified Saul's position as king, but did not confirm his permanent kingdom (see the commentary on 11:14–15).[22] Finally, almost three decades later, after Jonathan drove the Philistine garrison out of Gibeah, Saul found himself back in Gilgal with the potential to be confirmed not simply as king but as dynastic founder. His failure to obey God's Word cost him his dynasty. *At this time, however, Saul was not rejected as king—he was simply denied dynastic succession.* His rejection as king in favor of another (David) would not happen until he failed to carry out God's command to extirpate the Amalekites from the land (15:17–28).

Samuel tells Saul that his kingdom will not remain—he will have no dynasty to rule over Israel with Yahweh's approval (13:14). Instead, God has already chosen someone to succeed Saul—someone according to his own heart. This person is the new "designated ruler" (נָגִיד, 13:14), a term once applied to Saul (9:16; 10:1). Samuel concludes with his most devastating statement—Saul had not obeyed what Yahweh had commanded him.

It is unmistakable to readers familiar with the whole book that the person whom Yahweh has already sought, the man after Yahweh's own heart, is David.[23]

---

[21] Note Augustine's comments on this in *The City of God*, 17.6.2 (*NPNF*[1] 2:346).

[22] Note that this renewal at Gilgal was only a partial confirmation of Saul's monarchy—there were peace offerings (11:15), but no whole burnt offering (cf. 10:8).

[23] Brueggemann, *First and Second Samuel*, 102; McCarter, *I Samuel*, 229; Klein, *1 Samuel*, 127; Tsumura, *The First Book of Samuel*, 349.

The phrase "according to his own heart" highlights Yahweh's choice (see the first textual note on 13:14 and also 2 Sam 7:21; 1 Chr 17:19).[24]

The choice of Saul as king had also been Yahweh's, but he had granted Israel's request with its implied constraints—a king to judge Israel, a king to make Israel like all the nations, a king to lead Israel into battle (8:5, 20). When choosing Saul, Yahweh granted a king that was as much according to Israel's heart as it was according to his own heart. Now the choice is purely God's, and David will be all that Israel had requested and more.

Samuel's reply also begins to contrast Saul with David:

1. Saul's foolish behavior (the verb סָכַל) had to be pointed out to him (1 Sam 13:13), whereas David realized his own foolish behavior (the same verb, סָכַל, in 2 Sam 24:10).

2. Saul's "kingdom" (מַמְלָכָה) would not be "established" (the verb כּוּן) permanently (עַד־עוֹלָם, 1 Sam 13:13), whereas David's "kingdom" (מַמְלָכָה) would be "established" (the verb כּוּן, 2 Sam 7:12–13; see also 2 Sam 5:12; 7:16).

3. Saul's "kingdom" (מַמְלָכָה) would not "endure" (the verb קוּם, 1 Sam 13:14), whereas David's "kingdom" (מַמְלָכָה) would be "established" (the verb קוּם, 1 Ki 9:5; see also 1 Sam 24:21 [ET 24:20]; 2 Sam 3:10; 7:12).

While the phrase "according to his own heart" (1 Sam 13:14) emphasizes God's choice, it also implies something about David's character. David's God-given intellect and faith—especially his obedience in contrast to Saul's disobedience—distinguished him as the one God had chosen for Israel's benefit (2 Sam 7:10–11). That is, God himself molded a king according to how he envisioned royal divine service—not as Israel envisioned it. This conclusion about David was drawn at least as early as St. Paul, who said:

> καὶ μεταστήσας αὐτὸν ἤγειρεν τὸν Δαυὶδ αὐτοῖς εἰς βασιλέα ᾧ καὶ εἶπεν μαρτυρήσας· εὗρον Δαυὶδ τὸν τοῦ Ἰεσσαί, ἄνδρα κατὰ τὴν καρδίαν μου, ὃς ποιήσει πάντα τὰ θελήματά μου.

> And after removing him [Saul], God raised up David to be their king, of whom he also testified, "I have found David the son of Jesse a man **according to my own heart**, *who will do all the things I desire.*" (Acts 13:22)

Therefore, David was chosen as the man after God's own heart. People evaluate a man based on his outward appearance, but God looks on the heart (1 Sam 16:7). God chooses freely of his own accord out of his own love, not based on the worthiness or character of those he chooses, and his grace is also the reason his chosen ones obey him, succeed, and are blessed (Deut 4:34–40; 7:6–16; 10:11–15). St. Paul also expresses God's manner of freely choosing by grace alone and conforming his chosen ones to the likeness of Christ, who reveals the Father's heart of love: "the ones whom he foreknew he also predestined to be conformed to the image of his Son ... and the ones whom he predestined,

---

[24] Athas, " 'A Man after God's Own Heart': David and the Rhetoric of Election to Kingship."

these he also called; and the ones whom he called, these he also justified; and the ones whom he justified, these he also glorified" (Rom 8:29–30).[25]

Samuel did not give Saul instructions on how to handle the current crisis. He simply left Gilgal, while Saul and his troops went to meet "the men of war," perhaps a reference to Jonathan's forces in Gibeah (see the first textual note on 13:15; cf. 13:2). Upon arrival at Gibeah, Saul discovered that his forces had shrunk to only six hundred in the face of an uncountable Philistine army.

After Saul and his troops had joined with Jonathan and his soldiers, they both went to Geba to confront the Philistine forces in Michmash (13:16). However, the Philistines were not simply waiting for Israel to attack. They sent out three raiding parties (13:17–18). The word for "raiding party" (מַשְׁחִית; see the first textual note on 13:17) denotes troops sent to destroy crops and fruit trees, denuding the land and making it difficult for the populace and especially the opposing army to feed themselves (cf. Deut 20:19; Judg 6:4).

There was another pressing problem for Saul's troops however. The narrator notes that Israelites did not have the technical expertise to work with iron (1 Sam 13:19–22). This was nearing the end of what is commonly termed Iron Age I in Palestine (1200–1000 BC). Apparently the Philistines had acquired iron technology and had sought to keep knowledge of it from Israel in order to deny the Israelites the ability to make weapons. We are told that the Israelites had to go to the Philistines to have their iron farm implements sharpened, which also gave the Philistines a lucrative monopoly. As a consequence only the most well-to-do Israelites could afford to own iron weapons. In this case, only Saul and Jonathan had them. Pressing their advantage, the Philistines moved south into Michmash Pass toward Saul's camp in Geba (13:23). See figure 18.

---

[25] See similarly Eph 1:3–14; see also, e.g., 2 Cor 3:18; Col 3:10. Scripture reveals much but not all of the mystery of God's choosing (predestination or election). See the extended discussion in FC SD XI, "Eternal Foreknowledge and Divine Election."

Figure 18

Kingdom and Battles of Saul

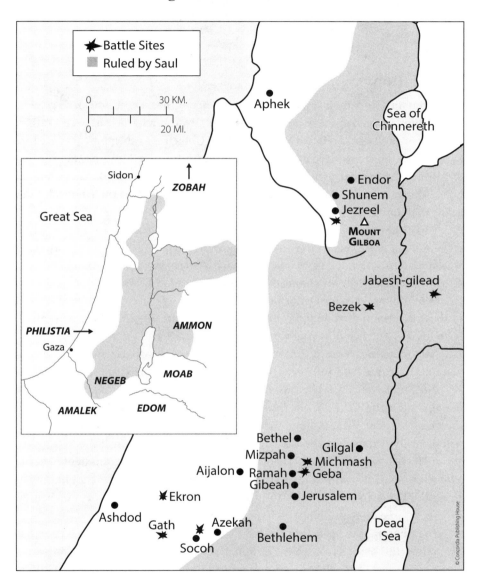

Saul defeated Nahash, leader of the Ammonites, at Jabesh-gilead (1 Sam 11:1–11). Jonathan routed the Philistines at Geba [or Gibeah], but they reassembled with a great force at Michmash (1 Sam 13:1–7). God gave Jonathan the victory at Michmash, and Saul pursued the Philistines beyond Aijalon (1 Sam 14:1–46). David slew Goliath near Azekah and Socoh, whereafter the Israelites pursued the Philistines to Gath and Ekron (1 Samuel 17). Israel's enemies included Philistia, Zobah, Ammon, Moab, Edom, and Amalek (1 Sam 14:47–48; 15:1–9). Saul fought against all of them. He and his sons, except Ish-bosheth, died on Mount Gilboa in battle against the Philistines (1 Samuel 31).

Saul's First Philistine Campaign, Part 2: Jonathan Routs the Philistines

Translation

14 ¹That day Saul's son Jonathan said to his armor bearer, "Come, let's go over to the Philistine encampment on the other side." However, he did not tell his father.

(²Now Saul was staying at the outskirts of Geba under the pomegranate tree in Migron, and there were about six hundred troops with him. ³Ahijah the son of Ahitub, the brother of Ichabod, the son of Phinehas, the son of Eli, [who had been] Yahweh's priest in Shiloh, was wearing an ephod. And the troops did not know that Jonathan had left.)

⁴On either side of the pass that Jonathan sought to cross to the Philistine encampment was a sharp crag on this side and a sharp crag on the other side. One was named Bozez, and one was named Seneh. ⁵One crag was to the north in front of Michmash, and the other was to the south in front of Geba.

⁶Jonathan said to his armor bearer, "Come, let's go over to the encampment of these uncircumcised men. Perhaps Yahweh will act on our behalf, since there is no limit to Yahweh in saving with many or with a few."

⁷His armor bearer said to him, "Do whatever you desire. Go ahead. I am with you, [and] I agree with you."

⁸So Jonathan said, "Then we're crossing over to the men, and we will show ourselves to them. ⁹If they say, 'Stop until we come to you,' we'll stand still and not go up to them. ¹⁰But if they say, 'Come up to us,' we'll go up, because Yahweh will have given them into our control, and this will be a sign for us."

¹¹The two of them showed themselves to the Philistine encampment, and the Philistines said, "Look! Hebrews are coming out of the holes where they hid themselves." ¹²The men of the outpost responded to Jonathan and his armor bearer, saying, "Come up to us, and we will teach you something!"

Jonathan said to his armor bearer, "Come up after me because Yahweh has given them into Israel's control." ¹³So Jonathan climbed up, and his armor bearer came after him. They fell before Jonathan, and his armor bearer finished killing them. ¹⁴In the first attack Jonathan and his armor bearer struck about twenty men in about half a furrow for a team [of oxen] in a field. ¹⁵There was panic in the camp, in the open field, and among all the troops, the encampment, and the raiding parties; they too panicked. The earth shook, and it became a panic caused by God. ¹⁶Saul's watchmen in Geba of Benjamin looked and [saw] the panicked crowd dispersing everywhere.

¹⁷Saul said to the troops who were with him, "Count now and see who left us." So they counted, and Jonathan and his armor bearer were not there.

18Saul said to Ahijah, "Bring the ephod," because at that time he wore the ephod in Israel's presence. **19**While Saul spoke to the priest, the panic in the Philistine camp grew worse and worse. So Saul said to the priest, "Withdraw your hand."

20So Saul and all the troops with him assembled and went into battle. There was very great confusion—each [Philistine] man using his sword against his neighbor. **21**Moreover, Hebrews who had previously been with the Philistines, who had gone up with them in the camp, turned. They also were with the Israelites who were with Saul and Jonathan. **22**Then all the men of Israel who had been hiding in the hill country of Ephraim heard that the Philistines had fled, and they also pursued them in battle. **23**So Yahweh saved Israel that day, and the battle moved past Beth-aven.

Textual Notes

14:1 הַיּוֹם—At times the article in Hebrew is weakly demonstrative, hence "that day."[1]

הַנַּעַר נֹשֵׂא כֵלָיו—This literally means "the servant carrying his equipment." A variation of this phrase, usually without הַנַּעַר, recurs in 14:6, 7, 12, 13, 14, 17; also 16:21; 31:4–6 (similarly with Joab in 2 Sam 18:15, 23:37). For consistency it is always translated as "his armor bearer."

לְכָה וְנַעְבְּרָה—"Come, let's go over." This pair of verbs is repeated in 14:6. The first is the Qal (G) masculine singular imperative of הָלַךְ with paragogic *he*. The second is the Qal cohortative of עָבַר, "to cross over." See the same imperative with another cohortative in the second textual note on 9:5; see also the textual note on 9:9.

מַצַּב פְּלִשְׁתִּים—This means "encampment of the Philistines." See the textual note on 13:23.

אֲשֶׁר מֵעֵבֶר הַלָּז—Literally this means "which is from across this (place)." הַלָּז is a shortened form of הַלָּזֶה, which is a rare strengthened form of the demonstrative pronoun זֶה, "this" (GKC, § 34 f).

14:2 הַגִּבְעָה—The MT and the LXX have "Gibeah." This Hebrew place-name recurs in the phrase בְּגִבְעַת בִּנְיָמִן in 14:16, where the LXX has "Geba." Saul was last with Jonathan at "Geba" (13:16). "Gibeah" appears to be impossible in this context, since it is too far from Michmash to observe any military movement (14:16; see figure 18 in the commentary on 13:1–23). The action appears to have taken place in "Geba" (14:5). This is another example of the confusion of these two places due to their similar names (see the second textual note on 13:3).

בְּמִגְרוֹן—This is translated as "in Migron." Migron is mentioned as being near Michmash in Is 10:28. Many commentators, however, take this to mean "on the threshing floor" (בְּמוֹ גֹרֶן), which requires positing an error in pointing and word division in the MT.[2] The LXX has ἐν Μαγδων (= במנדון), a confusion of the similar letters *resh* and *daleth*.

---

[1] Waltke-O'Connor, § 13.5.1d, including example 7.

[2] McCarter, *I Samuel*, 235; Klein, *1 Samuel*, 131; cf. Tsumura, *The First Book of Samuel*, 357.

14:3 נֹשֵׂא אֵפוֹד—Ahijah "was wearing an ephod." See the fourth textual note on 2:28.

14:4 וּבֵין—Normally the preposition בֵּין means "between." In context here it must mean "on either side," a meaning unique to this verse (cf. HCSB, GW, NET, NIV).

הַמַּעְבְּרוֹת—The feminine noun מַעְבָּרָה is always used in the plural for a "ford," and here for a "pass," probably a ravine or wadi.

שֵׁן־הַסֶּלַע—Literally "tooth of the cliff," this is rendered as "a sharp crag." When used alone in 14:5 the noun שֵׁן, "tooth," is rendered as "crag."

וְשֵׁם הָאֶחָד בּוֹצֵץ וְשֵׁם הָאֶחָד סֶנֶּה:—There is no certain way of knowing the meaning of these two names. It is often suggested that בּוֹצֵץ, "Bozez," means either "gleaming" (from the Arabic baṣṣa, "glitter, shine, gleam") or "miry" (from בֹּץ, "mire"; בִּצָּה, "swamp"). It is also suggested that סֶנֶּה, "Seneh," means "thorn" (from the Hebrew סְנֶה, "thorn bush," Ex 3:2–4; Deut 33:16).[3]

14:5 מָצוּק—The plural of מָצוּק referred to "pillars" or "foundations" of the earth in 2:8. However, the word here may be a corrupt dittograph of the following word, מִצָּפוֹן, "from north," meaning "to the north." It is omitted in the translation.[4]

14:6 מַעְצוֹר—This noun, a "limit" or "restriction," occurs only here in the OT, but it is derived from a common verb, עָצַר, "to restrain, prevent." The noun is also used in Sirach 39:18 in a similar context (see *DCH*).

14:7 כָּל־אֲשֶׁר בִּלְבָבֶךָ—Literally "all that is in your heart," this is translated as "whatever you desire." Here this is a God-given desire in accord with God's Word. See the textual note and the commentary on אִישׁ כִּלְבָבוֹ, "a man according to his own heart," in 13:14.

נְטֵה לְךָ—Literally "stretch out for yourself," this is translated as "go ahead." It is the Qal (G) imperative of נָטָה with a pausal form of לְךָ, the suffixed preposition לְ in a reflexive sense (BDB, s.v. לְ, 5 h).

הִנְנִי עִמְּךָ כִּלְבָבֶךָ:—Literally "behold, I [am] with you in accord with your heart," this is translated as "I am with you, [and] I agree with you." The LXX reading ὡς ἡ καρδία σοῦ καρδία μοῦ, "as your heart [so also is] my heart," suggests that the original Hebrew text may have been כִּלְבָבֶךָ כִּלְבָבִי. If so, the second word was lost from the MT by homoioarchton.

14:8 וְנִגְלִינוּ—The Niphal (N) of גָּלָה, "reveal," has a reflexive sense, "reveal/show oneself," here and in 14:11 (וַיִּגָּלוּ).

14:9 דֹּמּוּ—This is the Qal (G) imperative of דָּמַם, which can mean "be silent" or, as here, "be still, stop."

וְעָמַדְנוּ תַחְתֵּינוּ—Literally "we will stand [on the place] underneath us," this is an idiom for standing still and not moving (Judg 7:21) or not spreading (Lev 13:23, 28).

---

3   Smith, *The Books of Samuel*, 104; McCarter, *I Samuel*, 239; Klein, *1 Samuel*, 135; Tsumura, *The First Book of Samuel*, 359.

4   See McCarter, *I Samuel*, 235; Klein, *1 Samuel*, 131; *HALOT*. Tsumura's attempt to explain this word (*The First Book of Samuel*, 356, n. 9) appears to be special pleading in order to defend the MT at all costs.

14:11 מִן־הַחֹרִים אֲשֶׁר הִתְחַבְּאוּ־שָׁם׃—Literally this means "from the holes where they hid themselves there." For the Hithpael (HtD) of חָבָא, see the second textual note on 13:6. Hebrew often concludes a relative clause with a retrospective pronoun (Joüon, § 158 c, h–j), but here the demonstrative adverb שָׁם (Joüon, § 102 h) serves that function ("where … *there*"). Such retrospective words need not be translated in English.

14:12 הַמַּצָּבָה—The feminine noun מַצָּבָה is translated as "outpost." It is a hapax legomenon, but is likely a synonym of the masculine equivalent מַצָּב, "encampment," in 14:11 and elsewhere in the chapter (see the textual note on 13:23). The LXX reads μεσσαβ = מַצָּב.

14:13 וַיַּעַל יוֹנָתָן עַל־יָדָיו וְעַל־רַגְלָיו—Literally "and Jonathan went up on his hands and on his feet [i.e., using his hands and his feet]."

מְמוֹתֵת אַחֲרָיו׃—Literally this means "killing them off after him." The verb מְמוֹתֵת is a Polel (D) participle masculine singular absolute from the verb מוּת, "to die." The Hiphil (H) of מוּת has the causative meaning "to kill, put to death" (e.g., 2:6, 25; 5:10–11; 11:12). In the Polel, this verb usually denotes finishing off the wounded (also Judg 9:54; 1 Sam 17:51; 2 Sam 1:9, 10, 16).

14:14 וַתְּהִי הַמַּכָּה הָרִאשֹׁנָה אֲשֶׁר הִכָּה—The initial noun מַכָּה is a cognate of the verb הִכָּה (the Hiphil [H] of נָכָה) in the relative clause, literally "and the first attack which he attacked was …"

כְּבַחֲצִי מַעֲנָה צֶמֶד שָׂדֶה׃—This means "about in half a furrow for a team [of oxen] in a field." A furrow is a groove in the soil overturned by a plow. A typical furrow was about thirty to forty yards (twenty-seven to thirty-seven meters) long.[5] It is unusual for two prepositions to be prefixed to a noun (כְּבַחֲצִי = כְּ + בְּ + חֲצִי). The LXX reads ἐν βολίσι καὶ ἐν πετροβόλοις καὶ ἐν κόχλαξιν τοῦ πεδίου, "with darts and slings and pebbles of the field."[6]

14:15 חֲרָדָה … חָרְדוּ … וַתְּהִי לְחֶרְדַּת אֱלֹהִים—The two instances of the noun חֲרָדָה are translated as "panic," and the cognate verb חָרַד as "to panic" (but "to be terrified" in 13:7). The last clause is rendered as "and it became a panic caused by God"; the verb הָיָה with the preposition לְ can mean "to become" something. The implied subject of the feminine verb וַתְּהִי, "*it* became," is the abstract situation. In the construct phrase לְחֶרְדַּת אֱלֹהִים, the noun אֱלֹהִים is a genitive of agent: "a panic caused by God."[7]

וְהַמַּשְׁחִית—For "raiding parties," see the first textual note on 13:17.

וַתִּרְגַּז הָאָרֶץ—The feminine noun אֶרֶץ, "earth," is the subject of the Qal (G) of רָגַז, "shake, quake." Such language often appears in apocalyptic contexts that depict God's end-time judgment striking the entire world and devastating sinful humanity. See the same phraseology in Joel 2:10; Amos 8:8; Ps 77:19 (ET 77:18), and similar expressions in, e.g., 2 Sam 22:8 ‖ Ps 18:8 (ET 18:7); Is 13:13; Ps 99:1.

14:16 בְּגִבְעַת בִּנְיָמִן—The MT reads "in Gibeah of Benjamin," but the translation follows the LXX, "in Geba of Benjamin." See the first textual note on 14:2.

---

5   Klein, *1 Samuel*, 137.

6   Cf. the discussion in McCarter, *I Samuel*, 236; Auld, *I and II Samuel*, 149.

7   *IBH*, § 13 A; Waltke-O'Connor, § 9.5.1b.

וְהִנֵּה הֶהָמוֹן נָמוֹג—"And behold, the panicked crowd was dispersing." הָמוֹן often denotes a turmoil among a group of people (*HALOT*, 2), and "panicked" reflects the terminology discussed in the first textual note on 14:15. הֶהָמוֹן is the subject of נָמוֹג ("dispersing"), a Niphal (N) form of מוג, which usually means "to melt." While the Niphal form could be the third masculine singular perfect, most likely it is the masculine singular participle since the action is depicted as being in progress. Like the language discussed in the last textual note on 14:15, מוג often appears in contexts depicting eschatological and universal divine judgment: the earth itself melts away (Amos 9:5; Ps 46:7 [ET 46:6]; cf. Nah 1:5), or people melt in fear before armies that are carrying out God's judgment.[8]

וַיֵּלֶךְ וַהֲלֹם:—Literally "and it [the crowd] went and here/there." הֲלֹם is an adverb of place, "here" or "there." The LXX reads ἔνθεν καὶ ἔνθεν, "here and there," which may indicate that the original reading was הֲלֹם וַהֲלֹם, dispersing "both here and there." If so, the first הֲלֹם was misread and replaced with the more familiar word וַיֵּלֶךְ. However, no other OT passage has two instances of the adverb הֲלֹם.

14:17 פָּקְדוּ ... וַיִּפְקְדוּ—The Qal (G) of פָּקַד can mean "to muster" troops, but here it has the nuance of "pass in review" and is practically equivalent to "number" (see BDB, Qal, 4) or "count," "take a roll call."

14:18 הַגִּישָׁה אֲרוֹן הָאֱלֹהִים כִּי־הָיָה אֲרוֹן הָאֱלֹהִים בַּיּוֹם הַהוּא וּבְנֵי יִשְׂרָאֵל:—The MT literally reads "bring near God's ark, because God's ark was on that day, and the sons of Israel." The LXX reads προσάγαγε τὸ εφουδ ὅτι αὐτὸς ἦρεν τὸ εφουδ ἐν τῇ ἡμέρᾳ ἐκείνῃ ἐνώπιον Ισραηλ, " 'bring the ephod,' because at that time he wore the ephod in Israel's presence." This reading is also found in one Old Latin manuscript. The Hebrew text it presupposes would be this:

הַגִּישָׁה הָאֵפֹד כִּי־הוּא נֹשֵׂא הָאֵפֹד בַּיּוֹם הַהוּא לִפְנֵי יִשְׂרָאֵל

In addition to the incomplete ending of the verse in the MT, there are more good reasons for preferring the LXX to the MT here:[9]

---

8 Ex 15:15; Josh 2:9, 24; Is 14:31; Jer 49:23; Ezek 21:20 (ET 21:15); cf. Is 64:6 (ET 64:7).

9 Tsumura attempts to defend the MT (*The First Book of Samuel*, 364, n. 35, and 365–66), but his argument depends on special pleading and a questionable phonological analysis of the end of 14:18. Another attempt to defend the MT is made by Davies ("Ark or Ephod in I Sam. xiv. 18?"), who argues that there was a systematic replacement of "ark" with "ephod" in 1 Samuel, except for MT 1 Sam 14:18. (This is a revival of a theory first propounded by William R. Arnold, *Ephod and Ark: A Study in the Records and Religion of the Ancient Hebrews* [Cambridge, Mass.: Harvard University Press, 1917].) The most important argument of Davies is that priests are depicted as "carrying" (the verb נָשָׂא) the ephod instead of wearing it. However, in Samuel the verb נָשָׂא is used idiomatically with "ephod" to mean "wear" (see the fourth textual note on 2:28). Moreover, priests did not carry the ark; Levites did (see point 7 in the textual note on 14:18). Davies also argues on the basis of an assumed "Ark Narrative," which is a false construct; see "The Ark in the Plotline of the Book of Samuel" in the commentary on 4:1–11. His theory also relies on positing that the ark could be used in consulting God, though only the ephod is depicted in this way elsewhere (Ex 28:30; Num 27:21; Ezra 2:63; Neh 7:65). See also Toorn and Houtman, "David and the Ark," 210–15.

1. The ark remained at Kiriath-jearim until David brought it to Jerusalem (1 Sam 7:1–2; 2 Sam 6:1–3; 1 Chr 13:3).

2. Shortly Saul will consult the oracle of God (1 Sam 14:37). Oracular consultation is associated with the ephod (Ex 28:30; Lev 8:8; Num 27:21; 1 Sam 28:6; Ezra 2:63; Neh 7:65), not the ark. Here Saul commanded Ahijah to "withdraw" his hand (אֱסֹף, 1 Sam 14:19), apparently because Saul would not consult God through Urim and Thummim at this juncture, though he would later (14:37).

3. If "the priest" (14:3, 19) had put his hand on or in the ark (14:19), he would have died (Num 4:15; 2 Sam 6:6–8).

4. Earlier in this chapter the author explained that Ahijah was wearing the ephod (14:3), and this appears to prepare the reader for 14:18 and 14:36–41.

5. The verb נָגַשׁ, "to bring (near)" (14:18), is associated with the ephod when it is consulted for a decision from God (1 Sam 23:9; 30:7). Aside from MT 1 Sam 14:18 this verb is not associated with the ark.[10]

6. Bringing the ark into a military camp without explicit command or permission from Yahweh was clearly not countenanced by him (1 Sam 4:1–11). It is difficult to understand why the author would not have condemned Saul for bringing the ark with him when he was confronting the Philistines if God had not commanded such use of the ark. On the other hand, if God had commanded Saul or given him permission to take the ark into battle (e.g., as Joshua was commanded in Joshua 6), it is difficult to explain why the author does not note this.

7. Whenever the ark is transported, the movers (sometimes implicit in the verb) are mentioned in the plural (1 Sam 4:4; 5:1; 7:1; 2 Sam 6:3, 13). It would be strange (if not impossible) for one man—Ahijah—to bring the ark.[11] Moreover, Ahijah is a priest (1 Sam 14:3, 19), and the ark was carried by Levites.[12]

14:19 עַד דִּבֶּר שָׁאוּל—This means "while Saul spoke." It is the sole instance in the OT of the preposition עַד governing a form of דִּבֶּר, "to speak." The preposition and the perfect aspect verb form a temporal clause. Frequently a temporal clause is formed by prefixing the preposition בְּ or the preposition כְּ to the infinitive construct דַּבֵּר.[13]

וַיֵּלֶךְ הָלוֹךְ וָרָב—The idiomatic construction with the Qal (G) infinitive absolute הָלוֹךְ and the (pausal form of the) adjective רַב (from רָבַב), "much, great," as a verbal adjective means the panic "went continually greater" (see Jöuon, § 123 s), but since the panic is a negative entity for the Philistines, it is translated as "grew worse and worse." A similar construction with the Qal participle of הָלַךְ and the adjective רַב is וְהָעָם הוֹלֵךְ וָרָב, "and the people kept increasing," in 2 Sam 15:12.

14:20 וַיִּזָּעֵק—In the Qal (G) זָעַק means "to cry out" (e.g., 12:8, 10), as does its byform צָעַק. In the Niphal (N) both verbs mean "to be called together" or "assemble" for

---

[10] Keil, *The Books of Samuel*, 141.

[11] Kio, "What Did Saul Ask For: Ark or Ephod?" 243.

[12] Deut 31:25; 1 Sam 6:15; 2 Sam 15:24; 1 Ki 8:4; 1 Chr 15:2, 12, 14–15, 26–27; 16:4; 2 Chr 5:4; 35:3.

[13] With בְּ see, e.g., Gen 27:5; 50:17; Ex 19:9. With כְּ see, e.g., Gen 39:10; Ex 16:10; Judg 2:4; 2 Ki 7:18.

battle. See וַיִּצָּעֲקוּ in the third textual note on 13:4; see also *HALOT*, s.v. זעק, Niphal, 1 and 2.

וְהִנֵּה הָיְתָה חֶרֶב אִישׁ בְּרֵעֵהוּ מְהוּמָה גְדוֹלָה מְאֹד:—The Hebrew is laconic, literally "and behold, the sword of each man was against his neighbor, a very great confusion." The subject of the feminine verb הָיְתָה is the feminine noun חֶרֶב, "sword." The self-defeating situation is described by the feminine noun מְהוּמָה, "a confusion," which is related to the noun הָמוֹן, translated as "panicked crowd" in 14:16 and as "panic" in 14:19.[14]

14:21 כְּאֶתְמוֹל שִׁלְשׁוֹם—For the idiom "previously," see the last textual note on 4:7.

אֲשֶׁר עָלוּ עִמָּם בַּמַּחֲנֶה סָבִיב—This is a relative clause, literally the Hebrews "who went up with them into the camp all around." The adverb סָבִיב, "all around," indicates that these Hebrews went up and surrounded the camp. The LXX reads the adverb as a verb, ἐπεστράφησαν, "they turned," probably reflecting סָבְבוּ as its Hebrew Vorlage; the verb סָבַב can mean "turn" or "march around." The translation above follows the LXX.

14:22 הַמִּתְחַבְּאִים—This is a Hithpael (HtD) participle of חָבָא with the definite article, which functions as a relative pronoun: "who had been hiding." For the verb, see the second textual note on 13:6 and the textual note on 14:11.

וַיַּדְבְּקוּ ... אַחֲרֵיהֶם—In the Qal (G) דָּבַק means "to cling" to someone. Its Hiphil (H) can have the corresponding causative meaning. However, in a few passages the Hiphil (as here) is used in a military setting with the preposition אַחֲרֵי meaning "to pursue closely" (BDB, Hiphil, 2, citing also Judg 20:45; 1 Chr 10:2; and without אַחֲרֵי, 1 Sam 31:2; 2 Sam 1:6). The expected form of the third masculine plural Hiphil preterite (imperfect with *waw* consecutive) is וַיַּדְבִּיקוּ, as in Judg 18:22, but the Hiphil form here also appears in 1 Sam 31:2; 1 Chr 10:2 (see GKC, § 53 n).

14:23 בֵּית אָוֶן:—See the last textual note on 13:5.

Commentary

c. 1021 BC

Once again Jonathan took the initiative against the Philistines (14:1). He did not inform his father nor any other person in the camp (cf. 14:3) of his plan. The author of the book of Samuel has begun to draw a distinction between Jonathan, the heir apparent to the throne, and his father, King Saul. Jonathan boldly confronted the Philistines, whereas Saul was reluctant and even afraid to engage them in battle (cf. 28:5).[15] Later Jonathan would become David's close friend (18:1–5), even as Saul would become more and more estranged from him (18:6–16; cf. 19:1–7).

---

[14] According to BDB, the noun מְהוּמָה is derived from the verb הוּם, "to murmur, roar" in chaos or panic, and the noun הָמוֹן is derived from the verb הָמָה, which has the same meaning, "to murmur, roar." Both of those verbs are ultimately derived from the original biliteral root הם; hence the verbs and nouns are all closely related.

[15] Samuel had implied in 1 Sam 10:7 that Saul was to eradicate the Philistine garrison in Gibeah, but the one he had anointed failed to carry out the divine instructions. See the discussion in "Samuel Anoints Saul (9:26–10:8)" in the commentary on 9:26–10:16. See also the beginning of the commentary on 10:17–27a.

For the first time in the book of Samuel, an "armor bearer" is introduced into the narrative (see the second textual note on 14:1). Prominent soldiers such as kings and commanders had these battle assistants at their side. Among those who had armor bearers were Abimelech (Judg 9:54), Saul (in 1 Sam 16:21 David is his armor bearer; in 1 Sam 31:4–6 it is someone else), and Joab (2 Sam 23:37).

At the mention of Jonathan's father the narration is interrupted by a parenthetical description of Saul's position (1 Sam 14:2–3). We are reminded that he now commanded only six hundred men (14:2; cf. 13:15). We are also informed that the priest Ahijah was there wearing an ephod (14:3)—apparently identifying him as the high priest, since later this ephod will be used with its Urim and Thummim to inquire of God (14:37–41).

Ahijah's ancestry is given, tracing him back to Eli. This information helps us construct a line of Elide priests, including high priests, during the time of Samuel and in the reigns of Saul and David. Also helpful is Josephus, who names Eli, his grandson Ahitub, his great-grandson Ahijah, his great-grandson Ahimelech, and his great-great-grandson Abiathar as high priests.[16] Apparently, if Josephus is correct, Ahijah must have died without heir and the high priesthood passed to his brother Ahimelech and then to Ahimelech's son Abiathar. See figure 19 at the end of this pericope.

The author transitions back to the narrative concerning Jonathan by means of a description of the terrain Jonathan had to cross to reach the Philistine camp (14:4–5). The two sharp outcroppings must have been well-known to have been given names (see the last textual note on 14:4), perhaps because they were on either side of a prominent valley or pass between Michmash and Geba. (For the locations of Michmash and Geba, see figure 18 in the commentary on 13:1–23.)

When the narration resumes, we are given a fuller quotation from Jonathan that reveals his purpose for crossing over to the Philistine camp (14:6). He calls the Philistines "uncircumcised men," a pejorative that will also be used later by David (17:26, 36).[17] This characterization emphasizes that the Philistines are outside God's covenant of grace with Israel.[18] It was considered a disgrace for

---

[16] For Eli, see Josephus, *Antiquities*, 5.318, 338, 345, 358, 361–62; 6.294. For Ahitub, see *Antiquities*, 6.122–23 (Josephus has Ahitub as the unnamed high priest whom Saul consulted in 1 Sam 14:36–37). For Ahijah, see *Antiquities*, 6.107 (Ahijah is called Achias/Echias by Josephus, who uses Achias also for the prophet Ahijah in, e.g., *Antiquities*, 8.206; cf. 1 Ki 11:29–31). For Ahimelech, see *Antiquities*, 6.242, 254, 6.260–61 (in some manuscripts of Josephus Ahimelech is called Abimelech). For Abiathar, see *Antiquities*, 6.261; 7.200, 260, 293, 346, 359, 366.

[17] See also Judg 14:3; 2 Sam 1:20.

[18] See Gen 17:10–14; Ex 12:48; see also Is 52:1; Ezek 44:9. But God also called for a circumcision of faith; see Deut 10:16; 30:6; Jer 4:4; Rom 2:25–29; 4:11. The new covenant speaks of Baptism into Christ as the "circumcision of Christ" (Col 2:11–13; see also Gal 3:26–29). Physical circumcision no longer counts; rather, what matters is faith working through love and the new creation in Christ (Gal 5:2–6; 6:15; cf. 1 Cor 7:18–19; Col 3:11).

an Israelite to die at the hands of uncircumcised Philistines.[19] Jonathan's words again serve to contrast him with his father, Saul. Jonathan trusts that God can grant victory with even a few troops. On the other hand Saul, whose forces were reduced to a mere six hundred men, hesitated to attack. Jonathan's words are later expanded in a speech by Judas Maccabeus reported in 1 Macc 3:18–19:

> And Ioudas said, "It is easy for many to be ensnared by the hands of a few. And it makes no difference before heaven to save by many or by a few. For victory in war is not in the multitude of force, but rather, power is from heaven." (*NETS*)

Already the reader can begin to see qualities in Jonathan that will also be prominent in David, explaining Jonathan's affinity and love for David (18:1–5): like Jonathan, David is not afraid to confront uncircumcised Philistines, and he trusts Yahweh to save and give the victory (17:32–37).

God certainly can save by many or a few. This time God enabled his people to win the victory through the initiative of just two men, a leader and a follower, not the anointed king, Saul, but his son and his son's armor bearer. In time God would raise up David and then others. In the fullness of time (Gal 4:4) he would accomplish salvation for all humanity through one man alone: his own Son, named Jesus, "for he will save his people from their sins" (Mt 1:21). His weapon would not be the "sword" (1 Sam 14:20), but the very cross to which he was nailed—and his empty tomb. This royal "Anointed One" ("Messiah," "Christ," Jn 1:41) received his anointing not with oil, but the Holy Spirit without measure at his Baptism in the Jordan (Jn 1:32–33). He is the King, righteous and having salvation (Zech 9:9; cf. 2 Sam 22:51), who shall reign forever on the throne of David.[20] "Thanks be to God, who gives us the victory through our Lord Jesus Christ" (1 Cor 15:57).

Following his armor bearer's assent to his idea (1 Sam 14:7), Jonathan explains exactly what their plan will be (14:8–10). How Jonathan would know exactly by what sign Yahweh would favor their attack on the Philistines is not clear from the text. However, it may be that he simply assumed that if the Philistines invited them to engage in combat, God would grant him victory.

The Philistines derided Jonathan and his armor bearer when they saw them, not only mocking the Israelites for hiding but also referring to them as "Hebrews" (14:11). Most often in 1 Samuel this term is found on the lips of Philistines and was probably a depreciatory term (also 4:6, 9; 13:19; 29:3; see the fourth textual note on 13:3). The challenge they issue to Jonathan is that they will teach him and his armor bearer a lesson for daring to approach their camp, a challenge Jonathan takes as a sign that Yahweh has granted them victory (14:12).

---

[19] See Judg 15:18; 1 Sam 31:4; 1 Chr 10:4; also perhaps 1 Sam 18:25. To "die the death of the uncircumcised" was to perish eternally under God's judgment (Ezek 28:10; see also Ezek 31:18; 32:19–32).

[20] See 2 Sam 7:13, 16; Is 9:6 (ET 9:7); Ps 132:11; Lk 1:32; Heb 1:8.

Jonathan's attack was immediately successful, and he and his armor bearer slew twenty men in a short distance (14:13–14). The unusual way of referring to this distance—"about half a furrow for a team [of oxen] in a field" has led some commentators to propose other readings.[21] Jonathan's initial success led to panic in the Philistine camp and among the raiding parties (14:15). The cataclysmic, earth-quaking panic was due to God.[22] Israel's military victories against more powerful foes often came as a result of God sending a panic (Ex 14:24–25; 23:27; Deut 7:22–23; Josh 10:10; Judg 7:19–21; 1 Sam 7:10; Is 19:2). The confusion among the Philistines did not go unnoticed by Saul's pickets, who were watching the Philistine camp (1 Sam 14:16).

When word reached Saul, he must have suspected that someone from his command had begun an assault on the Philistines, since he took a roll call (14:17). Upon determining that it was Jonathan, Saul's first inclination was to consult God via the Urim and Thummim in the high priest's ephod (Ex 28:30; Lev 8:8; Num 27:21; see the textual note on 1 Sam 14:18). However, the Philistine panic kept growing worse, and this encouraged Saul to join the fray immediately, so he told Ahijah to take his hand out of the pouch where the Urim and Thummim were kept (14:19).

When Saul's troops engaged the enemy, they found that the Philistines were fighting one another (14:20). In addition, it appears as if some Israelites had joined the Philistine forces—perhaps as mercenaries—but turned on the Philistines in the heat of battle (14:21). These Israelites are called "Hebrews," which may indicate that this is the name given them by the Philistines. Later during Saul's second Philistine campaign, David, who was serving as a mercenary for the Philistine ruler Achish, was excluded from the Philistine forces precisely because the other Philistine commanders were afraid that he would turn against them when they attacked Saul (29:1–11).

Once the Philistines were routed, Israelites who had deserted Saul but were hiding just to the north in the Ephraimite hill country joined in the pursuit of the fleeing Philistines (14:22; cf. 13:6–7). The author clarifies that it was Yahweh who gave Israel victory that day (14:23)—reinforcing Jonathan's words (14:6). The Philistine forces fled to the west past Beth-aven (14:23), making them easy prey for anyone coming from the hills in Ephraim.

Jonathan's contention that Yahweh grants victory came from confidence that God had placed a king over Israel to deliver his people from Philistine domination (7:3; 9:16). Jonathan trusted God's promise and acted upon it, whereas his father was timid in the face of Philistine forces. While it is foolhardy to assume that God will act on our behalf simply because we desire it, it is equally foolhardy—if not more so—to fail to trust God and not to act boldly based on his clear promises when we have them. The most important of these promises is

---

[21] E.g., McCarter, *I Samuel*, 236.

[22] See the third textual note on 14:15 and the second textual note on 14:16.

the forgiveness of sins and eternal life in the Gospel of Jesus Christ; through this one man God has given us the victory (see the commentary on 14:6). With this promise we, like Jonathan, are to be bold in the face of our enemies—sin, death, and Satan with his assaults on our conscience. When we inwardly feel the accusations that we are defeated because of our sin, we are to cling to the promises of the Gospel in Word and Sacrament and put on the full armor of God (Eph 6:10–20). This also leads us to do good works as an external sign of the promise God has given us—a spiritual warfare against the sinister forces that threaten God's people (Eph 6:12). Melanchthon writes in the Apology:

> Nevertheless, Christ frequently connects the promise of forgiveness of sins with good works. He does not mean that good works are a propitiation—for they follow reconciliation—but he does so for two reasons. One is that good fruits ought to follow of necessity, and so he warns that penitence is hypocritical and false if they do not follow. *The other reason is that we need external signs of this exceedingly great promise, since a terrified conscience needs manifold consolations.* Baptism and the Lord's Supper, for example, are signs that constantly admonish, cheer, and confirm terrified minds to believe more firmly that their sins are forgiven. This same promise is written and pictured in good works, which thus urge us to believe more firmly. Those who fail to do good, do not arouse themselves to believe but despise these promises. But the faithful embrace them and are glad to have signs and testimonies of this great promise. Hence they exercise themselves in these signs and testimonies.[23]

Saul would soon show himself to be among those "who fail to do good" by not trusting the promise and by seeking instead to have victory through his own will (14:24). In this way he endangered the life of his son Jonathan and placed all God's people in jeopardy.

---

[23] Ap IV ("Justification") 275–76; emphasis added.

Figure 19

Elide Priests from Samuel to David

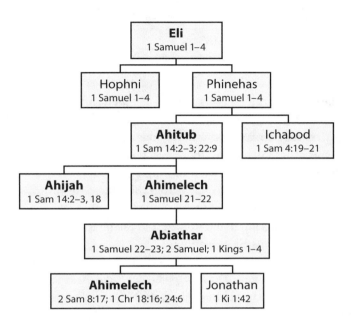

High priests are in bold. The text of Samuel gives no explanation for why there are two high priests (Ahijah and Ahimelech) from the same generation. These are possible explanations: (1) Ahijah ("my Brother is Yah[weh]") and Ahimelech ("my Brother is King") are alternate names for the same person. (2) Ahijah died young and without a male heir, so his brother became high priest in his place. (3) There is a mistake in textual transmission that accidentally substituted "Ahijah" for "Ahimelech" or vice versa. The author of this commentary believes that the second explanation is the most likely.

"Ahimelech the son of Abiathar" (2 Sam 8:17; 1 Chr 24:6; cf. 1 Chr 18:16) is a mystery. Elsewhere the Elide high priest during the end of Saul's reign and during David's reign was Abiathar, who was the son of Ahimelech (1 Sam 22:20–22; 23:6, 9; 30:7; 2 Sam 15:24, 27, 29, 35–36; 17:15; 19:12 [ET 19:11]; 20:25; 1 Ki 1:7, 19, 25, 42; 2:22, 26–27, 35; 4:4; 1 Chr 5:11). Since Abiathar served as high priest from the last years of Saul's reign (beginning c. 1014–1013) through the early years of Solomon's reign (c. 969–968), he had to be an old man (at least seventy-four) during the last part of this period. Since 1 Chr 24:6 apparently places Ahimelech the son of Abiathar as high priest at the very end of David's reign, it may be that he was functioning as high priest for his father although his father retained the title.

Saul's First Philistine Campaign, Part 3: Saul's Impetuous Vow

Translation

14 **24**Now the men of Israel were hard-pressed that day, and Saul had placed the troops under an oath, saying, "Cursed be the man who eats food until it is evening and I get revenge on my enemies." So none of the troops tasted food. **25**When all the troops went into the forest, there was honey on the ground. **26**The troops came into the forest, and they found it flowing with honey. Yet no one reached his hand to his mouth because the troops feared the oath. **27**However, Jonathan had not heard when his father put the troops under an oath. So he reached out with the end of the staff in his hand and dipped it in the honeycomb and returned his hand to his mouth, and his eyes brightened.

28One of the men from the troops responded, "Your father solemnly charged the troops, 'Cursed be the man who eats food today,' and the troops are exhausted."

29Jonathan said, "My father has ruined the land. See how my eyes brightened because I tasted a little of this honey. **30**If only the troops had freely eaten today from the spoils [captured] from their enemies that they found! So now the defeat of the Philistines has not been decisive."

31That day they struck the Philistines from Michmash to Aijalon, and the troops were terribly exhausted. **32**The troops pounced on the spoil and took sheep, cattle, and calves and slaughtered them on the ground. The troops ate meat with blood in it. **33**Saul was told, "Look! The troops are sinning against Yahweh by eating meat with blood in it."

So he said, "You have been unfaithful. Roll a large rock to me immediately." **34**Then Saul said, "Disperse among the troops, and say to them, 'Each man should bring to me his bull or his lamb, and slaughter [them] on this [rock] and eat [them]. Do not sin against Yahweh by eating meat with blood in it.'" So each of the troops brought his bull with him that night, and they slaughtered them there. **35**Saul built an altar to Yahweh. It was the first time he built an altar to Yahweh.

36Saul said, "Let's go down after the Philistines by night and plunder them until morning light, and we won't allow a single man to remain."

They said, "Do whatever you think is right."

The priest said, "Let's approach God here."

37So Saul asked God, "Should I go down after the Philistines? Will you hand them over to Israel?" But he did not answer him then.

38Saul said, "Come here, all leaders of the troops. Find out how this sin happened this day. **39**For as Yahweh, the Savior of Israel, lives, even if it is by my son Jonathan, he will certainly die!" But none of the troops answered him.

⁴⁰Then he said to all Israel, "You be on one side, and I and my son Jonathan will be on the other side."

The troops said to Saul, "Do whatever you think is right."

⁴¹Saul said to Yahweh, "God of Israel, why haven't you responded to your servant today? If the wrong is in me or my son Jonathan, give Urim, Lord God of Israel. And if it is said, 'In your people Israel,' give Thummim." Jonathan and Saul were selected, and the people were cleared.

⁴²Saul said, "Decide between me and my son Jonathan," and Jonathan was selected.

⁴³Saul said to Jonathan, "Tell me what you've done." Jonathan told him, "With the end of the staff that was in my hand I most certainly tasted a little bit of honey. Here I am; should I die?"

⁴⁴Saul said, "May God punish and even more, if you certainly don't die, Jonathan."

⁴⁵The troops said to Saul, "Should Jonathan who accomplished this great victory for Israel die? Certainly not! As Yahweh lives, no hair of his head will fall to the ground, because he accomplished [the victory] with God this day." So the troops ransomed Jonathan that day, and he did not die. ⁴⁶Then Saul stopped pursuing the Philistines, and the Philistines went to their territory.

Textual Notes

14:24 וְאִישׁ־יִשְׂרָאֵל נִגַּשׂ בַּיּוֹם הַהוּא—"Now the men of Israel were hard-pressed that day" is the reading of the MT. In the Qal (G) נָגַשׂ often means "to oppress." In form נִגַּשׂ could be the Piel (D) perfect of נָגַשׂ, but this verb occurs only in the Qal (G) and Niphal (N), so it is the Niphal third masculine singular perfect, meaning "be hard-pressed." The identical Niphal form had the same meaning in 13:6. The LXX reads καὶ Σαουλ ἠγνόησεν ἄγνοιαν μεγάλην ἐν τῇ ἡμέρᾳ ἐκείνῃ, "now Saul was ignorant [with] a great ignorance that day," which may represent a Hebrew Vorlage such as וְשָׁאוּל שָׁגַג שְׁגָגָה גְּדוֹלָה בַּיּוֹם הַהוּא, "now Saul erred a great error that day." This could be the reading of 4QSamᵃ, which contains two letters from the name "Saul" and room for the rest of this text. NRSV adopts this reading, as does McCarter, believing the MT to have been influenced by 13:6.[1]

וַיֹּאֶל—In the Qal (G) אָלָה can mean "to take an oath" or "to curse." This form is the Hiphil (H) preterite (imperfect with *waw* consecutive) third masculine singular. In the Hiphil the verb means "to put someone under an oath or a curse." This is accomplished by uttering an adjuration or curse formula (see the next textual note). This verb is a synonym of the Hiphil of שָׁבַע, "to put someone under an oath," in 14:27, 28. However, this verb also forms a double-entendre with the verb יָאַל I, "be foolish" (BDB).[2] That verb occurs in the OT only in the Niphal (N), but its Hiphil would have almost the same form as וַיֹּאֶל. (The verb וַיּוֹאֶל [Ex 2:21; Josh 17:12; Judg 1:27, 35; 17:11] is a Hiphil form of יָאַל II, "be willing, determined.") See further the commentary.

---

[1]   McCarter, *I Samuel*, 245.

[2]   Jobling, "Saul's Fall and Jonathan's Rise," 374.

אָרוּר—This Qal passive (Gp) participle of אָרַר is one of the strongest imprecatory curse words, as in the original curse after the fall into sin (Gen 3:14; with the feminine participle in Gen 3:17; also, e.g., Gen 9:25; Deut 27:15–26). Usually it refers to being cursed by God (not just by humans). It is the antonym of the Qal passive participle בָּרוּךְ, "blessed," in, e.g., Gen 27:29; Num 22:12; 24:9; Jer 20:14.

וְנִקַּמְתִּי מֵאֹיְבַי—Among other conjugations, the verb נָקַם, "avenge," occurs in the Qal (G), Niphal (N), and Piel (D), often with the preposition מִן in an adversative sense, "against" one's adversaries. The form וְנִקַּמְתִּי could be either the Niphal or the Piel perfect (with *waw* consecutive). In context it is most likely the Niphal with a reflexive meaning, "to avenge oneself," that is, to take revenge for one's own sake. Thus, it may reveal a self-centered motivation on the part of Saul.

14:25 The first part of the verse appears to have suffered from textual corruption. The MT reads as follows:

וְכָל־הָאָרֶץ בָּאוּ בַיָּעַר וַיְהִי דְבַשׁ עַל־פְּנֵי הַשָּׂדֶה:

And all the land went into the forest, and there was honey on the face of the field [i.e., on the ground].

The noun יַעַר usually means "forest," but rarely it (or a homograph) means "honey-comb," and that may be the meaning of the noun that occurs in 14:25, 26 (so BDB, s.v. יַעַר II; its only other OT occurrence is in Song 5:1). The feminine synonym יַעְרָה, "hon-eycomb," appears in 14:27. If יַעַר has that meaning here, then the first clause may mean "and they came to the honeycomb." The LXX is even more difficult: καὶ πᾶσα ἡ γῆ ἠρίστα καὶ ιααρ δρυμὸς ἦν μελισσῶνος κατὰ πρόσωπον τοῦ ἀγροῦ, "and all the land ate a meal, and Iaar [יַעַר, 'forest'] was a wood with a beehive on the ground." The best solution may be to understand "all the land" to mean "all the troops" of Israel. הָאָרֶץ may have a similar meaning when it recurs in 14:29 (although this commentary trans-lates it as "the land" in 14:29). One could also posit that הָאָרֶץ is a corruption of הָעָם. Either explanation results in the translation of 14:25 given above.

For הָעָם meaning "the troops" (as often later in this passage), see the first textual note on 4:3.

14:26 וְהִנֵּה הֵלֶךְ דְּבָשׁ—Literally this means "and behold, a flow of honey." The noun הֵלֶךְ is rare; its only other OT occurrence is in 2 Sam 12:4 in the sense of "a traveler." Some propose repointing to הֹלֵךְ, a Qal (G) masculine singular participle, "walking/flowing," for which הַיַּעַר in the preceding clause would be the implied subject: "… into the forest, and behold, it was flowing with honey," but for such a meaning one would expect the subject to be repeated in front of the participle, וְהִנֵּה הַיַּעַר הֹלֵךְ דְּבָשׁ. The revision of some critics to הָלַךְ דְּבֹרוֹ, "its bees had left," is unattested by any tradi-tion. However, some support for it might be discerned in the LXX; it reads ἐπορεύετο λαλῶν, "he went speaking," which could reflect הָלַךְ דֹּבֵר.[3] This would posit that the reason the honey was tempting was that the bees were gone, making the honey easily

---

[3]   Smith, *The Books of Samuel*, 118; McCarter, *I Samuel*, 246; Klein, *I Samuel*, 132.

accessible. However, Jonathan used the tip of his staff to obtain some honey and avoid being stung by bees (14:27).

וְאֵין־מַשִּׂיג יָדוֹ אֶל־פִּיו—Literally "and no one was reaching his hand to his mouth." The verb מַשִּׂיג is the Hiphil (H) masculine singular participle of נָשַׂג, which occurs only in the Hiphil, "to reach, overtake." Some prefer to follow the LXX's οὐκ ἦν ἐπιστρέφων, "*he did not return* his hand to his mouth."[4] This could mean that its Hebrew Vorlage read מֵשִׁיב, a Hiphil (H) masculine singular participle from שׁוּב, and would imply a graphic confusion of *gimel* for *bet* in the MT. Cf. וַיָּשֶׁב יָדוֹ אֶל־פִּיו, "and he returned his hand to his mouth," in 14:27.

14:27 וַיִּטְבֹּל אוֹתָהּ—"And he dipped it." The direct object marker has the third feminine singular object suffix (אוֹתָהּ). It refers to קְצֵה הַמַּטֶּה, "the end of his staff"; both קְצֵה and מַטֶּה are masculine in form and almost always construed as masculine. However, מַטֶּה appears to be treated as a feminine noun in Micah 6:9. Another explanation is that the feminine suffix is used here by attraction to the feminine noun יָד, "hand," since בְּיָדוֹ is the second word preceding אוֹתָהּ, whereas the construct phrase קְצֵה הַמַּטֶּה is farther away (the fourth and fifth preceding words).

בְּיַעְרַת הַדְּבָשׁ—Literally this says "in the honeycomb of the honey." The feminine noun יַעְרָה is a hapax legomenon.

וַתָּאֹרְנָה עֵינָיו:—"And his eyes shone/brightened." The Qere is the Qal (G) third feminine plural preterite (imperfect with *waw* consecutive) of אוֹר, "to shine," related to the noun אוֹר, "light." The Qal perfect of this verb is the sole reading in 14:29 (אֹרוּ עֵינַי, "my eyes brightened"). Here the Kethib is וַתִּרְאֶנָה, "and his eyes saw," the same form but of רָאָה. This apparently is the reading reflected by ἀνέβλεψαν in the LXX. However, וַתִּרְאֶנָה appears to be a corruption of וַתָּאֹרְנָה caused by the metathesis of *aleph* and *resh*, producing a more common word (וַתִּרְאֶנָה) for a less common one (וַתָּאֹרְנָה).

14:28 הַשְׁבֵּעַ הִשְׁבִּיעַ—"He solemnly charged" is a Hiphil (H) infinitive absolute followed by a Hiphil perfect from the root שׁבע. The Hiphil means "to place someone under an oath." The infinitive makes the action more serious. Cf. the Hiphil infinitive construction בְּהַשְׁבִּיעַ in 14:27 with בְּ in a temporal sense, "when [his father] put [the troops] under an oath." Cf. also the noun הַשְּׁבֻעָה, "the oath," in 14:26.

וַיָּעַף—This form recurs in 14:31. The verb עִיף II occurs only in the Qal (G) (five times in the OT) and means "to be faint, exhausted." It is a by-form of the slightly more common verb יָעֵף (cf. GKC, § 72 t).

14:29 וַיֹּאמֶר יוֹנָתָן—The MT has simply "(and) Jonathan said." The LXX reads καὶ ἔγνω Ιωναθαν καὶ εἶπεν, "and Jonathan knew and said." 4QSam[a] reads ויאמר יהונתן, but there is room at the end of the previous line for וידע, "and he knew."

עָכַר—This verb means "to trouble, disturb." See further the commentary.

דְּבַשׁ הַזֶּה:—This means "this honey." Normally if a noun is definite, the demonstrative pronoun that refers to it will have the definite article, but דְּבַשׁ is anarthrous. 4QSam[a] includes the article: הדבש הזה.

---

[4]   Smith, *The Books of Samuel*, 118; McCarter, *I Samuel*, 246; Klein, *1 Samuel*, 132.

14:30 אַף כִּי לוּא אָכֹל אָכַל הַיּוֹם הָעָם—"Freely eaten" translates the Qal (G) infinitive absolute followed by the Qal perfect of אָכַל, "eat." The particle לוּא (= לוּ) with a perfect verb forms a past unreal (contrary-to-fact) condition, "*if* the troops *had* freely eaten today," when in fact they have not eaten (see BDB, s.v. לוּ, 1 a). Since לוּ can also be an optative conjunction (BDB, s.v. לוּ, 2), this clause might instead be a wish, "would that the troops had freely eaten today"; if they had eaten, they may have been able to defeat the Philistines decisively.

כִּי עַתָּה לֹא־רָבְתָה מַכָּה בַּפְּלִשְׁתִּים:—This clause describes the present situation, literally "for now the striking against the Philistines is not great," meaning that the Philistines had not been defeated decisively. In 14:14 the feminine noun מַכָּה referred to the first "attack" against the Philistines. Here it is the subject of רָבְתָה, the Qal (G) third feminine singular perfect of רָבָה, "be much, great."

14:31 אַיָּלֹנָה—This is אַיָּלוֹן with a directive *he*: "to Aijalon." The LXX omits it. Aijalon was a few miles southwest of Beth-horon.

14:32 וַיַּעַט—This Qere, "and he pounced," is a Qal (G) preterite (imperfect with *waw* consecutive) of the verb עִיט, which recurs in 15:19 (its only other OT instance with this meaning; see also the third textual note on 25:14). See GKC, § 72 ff, for its form. It is a denominative verb formed from the noun עַיִט, "bird of prey; vulture" (Gen 15:11; Is 18:6; 46:11; Jer 12:9; Ezek 39:4; Job 28:7) and gives a vivid picture of the troops swooping down and devouring their prey. The Kethib is וַיַּעַשׂ, "and he did/made."

אֶל־הַדָּם:—This prepositional phrase, literally "upon the blood," is a technical expression for eating meat with blood in it, which is prohibited (Lev 19:26; Ezek 33:25). The identical expression recurs in 1 Sam 14:33, and the phrase אֶל־הַדָּם in 14:34 is equivalent, since it involves the common substitution of אֶל for עַל.

14:33 וַיַּגִּידוּ לְשָׁאוּל—Literally "and they declared to Saul," the impersonal plural verb (with no stated subject) is translated as a passive: "Saul was told."

בְּגַדְתֶּם—"You have been unfaithful." The Qal (G) verb בָּגַד denotes breaking faith and violating a relationship. When referring to one's relationship to God, it signifies apostasy or a transgression of the covenant (Jer 3:8, 11, 20; 5:11; Hos 6:7; Ps 78:57).

הַיּוֹם—This is translated as "immediately." Occasionally יוֹם, "day," with the definite article means "now, at once, immediately" (as in Prov 12:16), and that meaning probably is intended here. Some would emend to הֲלֹם, "here," based on the LXX's ἐνταῦθα.[5] Cf. the second textual note on 14:34.

14:34 פֻּצוּ—This is a Qal (G) masculine plural imperative of פּוּץ, "to scatter," thus "disperse." 4QSam^a reads נפצו, the same form but of the synonymous verb נָפַץ, "disperse, be scattered" (BDB, s.v. נָפַץ II).

אֵלָי—The MT reads "to me." The LXX reads ἐνταῦθα, "here."

14:35 אֹתוֹ הֵחֵל לִבְנוֹת מִזְבֵּחַ לַיהוָה:—Literally "it—he began to build an altar to Yahweh." The suffix on the direct object marker אֹתוֹ, "it," refers back to the preceding instance of the noun מִזְבֵּחַ, "altar," rather than the following instance. The Hiphil (H) of חָלַל can mean "to begin, start to do" something in the sense that this is the first time the

---

5   Smith, *The Books of Samuel*, 119; McCarter, *I Samuel*, 247; Klein, *1 Samuel*, 132.

person does it. The action undertaken for the first time is indicated by לִבְנוֹת, the Qal (G) infinitive construct of בָּנָה, "to build."

14:36 נֵרְדָה ... וְנָבֹזָה ... נִקְרְבָה—The first of the three Qal (G) cohortatives is of יָרַד, "descend." The second is of בָּזַז, "despoil, plunder," and the third of קָרַב, "draw near (to God)."

לַיְלָה—This is an adverbial accusative: "by night."

וְלֹא־נַשְׁאֵר—The expected form of the Hiphil (H) first common plural imperfect of שָׁאַר, meaning "cause to remain, make [something] be left over," would be נַשְׁאִיר. It is quite rare to find a shortened (jussive) form of the Hiphil (H) first common plural. This is a jussive form with a jussive meaning, literally "may we not let [anyone] remain." See GKC, § 48 g, including note 1, and 48 h.

כָּל־הַטּוֹב בְּעֵינֶיךָ—Literally "all the good in your eyes," this is translated as "whatever you think is right." See the textual note on 1:23. The expression (without "all") recurs in 14:40.

14:37 וַיִּשְׁאַל שָׁאוּל—Note the play on the verb שָׁאַל, "to ask, request," and the name שָׁאוּל, "Saul," meaning "requested." See the first textual note on 1:28; "Samuel Warns Israel about Kings (8:10–22)" in the commentary on 8:1–22; the first textual note on 10:22; the commentary on 12:13; and the second textual note on 20:6 (which also discusses שָׁאֹל נִשְׁאַל שָׁאוּל in 20:28).

14:38 כָּל־פִּנּוֹת הָעָם—This phrase is a vocative; Saul addresses "all leaders of the troops." פִּנּוֹת is literally "corners." This idiom also occurs in Judg 20:2; Is 19:13.

וּדְעוּ וּרְאוּ—The hendiadys "know and see" is translated as "find out."

בַּמָּה—Literally "by means of what [action]?" this is translated as "how."

14:39 כִּי אִם־יֶשְׁנוֹ בְּיוֹנָתָן—The word יֶשְׁנוֹ is the particle of existence, יֵשׁ, "there is," with נוֹ-, a rare form of third masculine singular suffix (GKC, §§ 67 o, note 1; 100 o). Although the suffix is masculine, it probably refers back to הַחַטָּאת, "the sin," in 14:38, thus "even if it was [the sin was committed] by Jonathan."

14:41 The MT reads as follows:

וַיֹּאמֶר שָׁאוּל אֶל־יְהוָה אֱלֹהֵי יִשְׂרָאֵל הָבָה תָמִים וַיִּלָּכֵד יוֹנָתָן וְשָׁאוּל וְהָעָם יָצָאוּ:

Saul said to Yahweh, "God of Israel, give complete." Jonathan and Saul were selected, and the people exited/were cleared.

The Niphal (N) stem of the verb לָכַד, "to capture, take," is used for being "chosen" or "selected" by lot, as in 1 Sam 10:20–21. See the second textual note on 10:20. Here the verb יָצָא, "to go out," is used as its antonym, "to be cleared," that is, not to be selected.

The LXX reads:

καὶ εἶπεν Σαουλ κύριε ὁ θεὸς Ισραηλ, **τί ὅτι οὐκ ἀπεκρίθης τῷ δούλῳ σου σήμερον; εἰ ἐν ἐμοὶ ἢ ἐν Ιωναθαν τῷ υἱῷ μου ἡ ἀδικία, κύριε ὁ θεὸς Ισραηλ, δὸς δήλους· καὶ ἐὰν τάδε εἴπῃς ἐν τῷ λαῷ σου Ισραηλ** δὸς δὴ ὁσιότητα. καὶ κληροῦται Ιωναθαν καὶ Σαουλ, καὶ ὁ λαὸς ἐξῆλθεν.

Saul said, "O Lord, God of Israel, **why have you not answered your servant today? If the wrong is in me or in my son Jonathan, O Lord, God of Israel, give clear ones [Urim], but if you should say these things, '[It**

is] in your people Israel,' give holiness [Thumim]." Jonathan and Saul were selected, and the people exited/were cleared.

Some defend the MT.[6] Others prefer the LXX and posit that the MT suffered a long homoioteleuton from the first occurrence of "Israel" in the LXX to the third occurrence. This commentary's translation follows the LXX.[7] The lost portion of the Hebrew can be reconstructed as follows:[8]

למה לא עניתי את עבדך היום אם יש בי או ביונתן נבי העון יהוה
אלהי ישראל הבה אורים ואם ישנו בעמך ישראל הבה תמים

With the loss, the Masoretes apparently read what ought to have been תֻּמִּים, "Thumim," as the singular adjective תָּמִים, "complete, whole," producing a difficult, if not impossible reading. תָּמִים is rarely used as a substantive. In the three instances where it is (Josh 24:14; Judg 9:16, 19), it denotes "integrity," a meaning not appropriate for this context. Because of this, some emend the pointing to תֻּמִּים. However, this would be the only place in the OT where Thummim is mentioned without Urim.[9] In addition, the MT requires a difficult decision as to whether "God of Israel" is a vocative (as translated at the beginning of the textual note), or should one read "Saul said to Yahweh, the God of Israel, 'Give ...'" with no vocative? The vocative יְהוָה אֱלֹהֵי יִשְׂרָאֵל is very common, but אֱלֹהֵי יִשְׂרָאֵל by itself as a vocative is quite rare.[10]

For Saul's self-deprecatory reference to himself (in the LXX) as "your servant," see the third textual note on 1:11.

14:42 הַפִּילוּ—The Hiphil (H) imperative of נָפַל is literally "make [something] fall," i.e., "cast (down)," but is translated as "decide." Many take this to mean "cast the lot";[11] a frequent idiom for casting lots is literally "to make a lot fall."[12] (The Niphal [N] of לָכַד in 14:41, "be selected," also implies the casting of lots; see the textual note on 14:41.) In most other verses where the Hiphil of נָפַל means "to cast lots," the noun גּוֹרָל, "lot,"

---

6 The MT is defended by Lindblom, "Lot-Casting in the Old Testament," 174–78, and Tsumura, *The First Book of Samuel*, 378–79. Both believe that a lot-casting ritual is in view and that Urim and Thummim were involved with this ritual. Tsumura claims that the procedure for casting lots was well-known to the intended readers of the book of Samuel, so a complete explanation was not needed. This, however, assumes knowledge on the part of readers that cannot be proven. It also assumes that the author would not have made the procedure explicit (whether or not his readers presumably knew what it was). More important, however, there is no evidence elsewhere in the OT that Urim and Thummim were associated with casting lots. See further in the excursus "The Urim and Thummim" following this pericope.

7 So too do NIV; ESV; McCarter, *I Samuel*, 247–48; Klein, *1 Samuel*, 132; Noort, "Eine weitere Kurzbemerkung zu 1 Samuel 14:41"; Toeg, "A Textual Note on 1 Samuel xiv 41."

8 *HOTTP*², 179. This text is rated "A" to indicate that the editors consider it highly probable that it represents the reading that is the earliest recoverable text (see *HOTTP*², vii–viii).

9 The reverse situation, where Urim is mentioned without Thummim, is in Num 27:21 and 1 Sam 28:6.

10 1 Ki 8:26 (where the LXX has κύριε ὁ θεὸς Ισραηλ!); Is 45:15; Ps 69:7 (ET 69:6).

11 Cf. HCSB, ESV, NET, NIV.

12 See BDB, s.v. נָפַל, Hiphil, 3, citing 1 Sam 14:42; Is 34:17; Jonah 1:7; Ps 22:19 (ET 22:18); Job 6:27; Prov 1:14; Esth 3:7; 9:24; Neh 10:35 (ET 10:34); 11:1; 1 Chr 24:31; 25:8; 26:13–14.

is its direct object, but that noun does not occur here. Apparently, Saul decided to use the Urim and Thummim as lots. The LXX has a long expansion here:

καὶ εἶπεν Σαουλ βάλετε ἀνὰ μέσον ἐμοῦ καὶ ἀνὰ μέσον Ιωναθαν τοῦ υἱοῦ μου· ὃν ἂν κατακληρώσηται κύριος, ἀποθανέτω. καὶ εἶπεν ὁ λαὸς πρὸς Σαουλ οὐκ ἔστιν τὸ ῥῆμα τοῦτο. καὶ κατεκράτησεν Σαουλ τοῦ λαοῦ, καὶ βάλλουσιν ἀνὰ μέσον αὐτοῦ καὶ ἀνὰ μέσον Ιωναθαν τοῦ υἱοῦ αὐτοῦ, καὶ κατακληροῦται Ιωναθαν.

And Saul said, "Cast [lots] between me and my son Jonathan. Whomever the Lord will cause to be selected by lot, let him die." The troops said to Saul, "This thing is not to be done." Saul prevailed against the troops, and they cast [lots] between him and his son Jonathan, and Jonathan was selected [by lot].

Some consider the LXX the better reading and believe that the MT lost text by homoioteleuton when a scribe's eye skipped from "my son Jonathan" to "his son Jonathan."[13] However, the additional text in the LXX appears to be an attempt to explain the anomalous use in this verse of הַפִּילוּ, "make fall, cast," without the noun גּוֹרָל, "lot," and also to be an expansion that anticipates the troops' opposition to Saul in 14:45.

14:43 הִנְנִי אָמוּת:—These two words are literally "behold I" and then either "I will die" or "should I die?" On the one hand, Jonathan's words could express his willingness to die for his action ("I will die"), even though he had not known that what he was doing was a sin. They could even be his admission that his sin, although inadvertent, deserved the punishment: "I should die." On the other hand, he could be asking a question; a Hebrew question need not have an interrogative (Joüon, § 161 a; see also the first textual note on 11:12). In context here it is best understood as a question: "should I die?"

14:44 כֹּה־יַעֲשֶׂה אֱלֹהִים וְכֹה יוֹסִף—Literally "thus may God do, and thus may he add," this is an oath formula stating that God should bring about punishment for some action not taken (*IBH*, § 64 C). At times the oath-taker states that the punishment for not fulfilling the oath should be inflicted upon himself: "thus may God do *to me*" (2 Sam 19:14 [ET 19:13]; 1 Ki 2:23; 2 Ki 6:31; cf. Ruth 1:17). However, in this case Saul includes no indirect object for the Qal (G) jussive יַעֲשֶׂה.

14:45 חָלִילָה—"Certainly not!" See the second textual note on 2:30. This is omitted from the LXX. Some believe it is a corrupt dittograph of the following words חַי־יְהוָה.[14]

חַי־יְהוָה אִם—Literally "the life of Yahweh if … ," this is translated as "as Yahweh lives, no …" This is an oath formula which often swears that something will not happen or that some statement is not true (cf. Gen 42:15; 1 Sam 19:6; see *IBH*, § 64 D).

וַיִּפְדּוּ—They "ransomed" is a Qal (G) preterite (imperfect with *waw* consecutive) third masculine plural of the verb פָּדָה. It usually involves paying a price to redeem someone or something (see *HALOT*, Qal, 1).

14:46 וַיַּעַל שָׁאוּל מֵאַחֲרֵי פְּלִשְׁתִּים—Literally "and Saul went up from after the Philistines," this means that he stopped pursuing them.

לִמְקוֹמָם:—"To their territory" is literally "to their place."

---

[13] Smith, *The Books of Samuel*, 124; McCarter, *I Samuel*, 248; Klein, *1 Samuel*, 132.

[14] McCarter, *I Samuel*, 248; Klein, *1 Samuel*, 132.

Commentary

c. 1021 BC

Jonathan Inadvertently Brings a Curse on Himself (14:24–30)

The battle had gone in Israel's favor. Nevertheless, after the Philistines had been routed and were fleeing westward (14:23), we find out that the troops were "hard-pressed" and operating at less than peak efficiency because of a curse that Saul had imposed upon them (14:24). Apparently Saul was unfamiliar with the adage that an army travels on its stomach. Curses uttered by people are fairly infrequent in OT narrative (Gen 9:25; 49:7; Josh 6:26; Judg 21:18). Saul's curse is the only one that is given with such impetuousness. Nevertheless, the narrator makes certain that readers know that the troops respected Saul's curse. The narrator also begins a series of wordplays that call into question the wisdom of Saul's action. The first one is in 14:24. We are told that Saul "had placed the troops under an oath" (14:24). The verb is וַיֹּאֶל. In an unpointed Hebrew text such as the book was originally written in, ויאל could be understood as deriving from the verb אָלָה, "to curse," which is contextually what is required. However, the verb could also be understood as a form of the verb יָאַל I, which would then mean that "Saul acted foolishly" (see the second textual note on 14:24). This verb signifies action that is not only foolish but also self-centered and stubborn.[15] It describes a person who cannot control his emotions and so makes rash decisions.[16]

Saul's sudden decision is shown to be foolish.[17] Perhaps his motivation for the curse was that he did not want the troops to take time to eat and lose the momentum toward complete victory. Yet they would not have needed to cease pursuing the Philistines because when the entered the forest, honey was readily available to them (14:25–26). The only one who ate the honey was Jonathan, who had not heard his father's oath (14:27). Jonathan's staff proved to be handy. He could obtain some honey without having to place his hands where the bees might sting him. Here the narrator engages in another wordplay. As he ate, Jonathan's eyes "brightened" (14:27). The verb is אוֹר, 'ur, "shine, be bright," but again in unpointed Hebrew ותארנה could also be from the root אָרַר, 'arar, "to curse." Thus, Jonathan's eyes brightened, but at the same time through a double entendre they are implied to be cursed. God's provision for the troops had become a curse for anyone who took advantage of it.

When one man informed Jonathan of his father's curse and its effect on the troops (14:28), Jonathan responded that his father had "ruined" (the verb עָכַר,

---

[15] Num 12:11; Is 19:13; Jer 5:4; 50:36; Sirach 37:19.

[16] The verb יָאַל I, "be foolish," is related to the root אול, and from that root are derived the nouns אֱוִיל, "stubborn fool," and אִוֶּלֶת, "stupidity." See the discussion of those nouns in Steinmann, *Proverbs*, 31.

[17] Cf. 13:13, where Samuel charged that Saul had "acted foolishly" (סָכַל), and 26:21, where Saul confessed that he had sinned by pursuing David and thus had "acted foolishly" (סָכַל).

'acar) the land (14:29). This verb denotes bringing trouble and devastation on someone. Simeon and Levi did this to Jacob when they slew the inhabitants of Shechem (Gen 34:30). Achan brought ruin on Israel when he disobeyed God's command at Jericho (Josh 7:25; cf. 1 Chr 2:7, where he is called 'Acar, "troubler"). Jephthah had uttered a reckless vow of what he would do if Yahweh would grant him victory over the Ammonites, and he refused to rescind it even though it required him to sacrifice his own daughter, whom he then accused of bringing ruin to him (Judg 11:30–35, with עָכַר in Judg 11:35). In each of these cases the cause of the problem was rash or reckless action that resulted in ruin and trouble. Saul's impetuous and ill-considered curse is in this same category, but is perhaps even worse. The Torah of Moses includes a provision for the forgiveness of a person who, in ignorance, spoke an ill-considered oath to do good or evil, then realized his guilt and confessed his sin (Lev 5:4–6). Saul, however, exacerbated his folly by refusing to confess his sin. As Prov 11:29 warns:

> Whoever troubles [עָכַר, 'acar] his family will inherit wind,
>> and a stubborn fool [אֱוִיל; from אול, related to the verb יָאַל] will be
>>> a slave to a person who is wise in heart.[18]

The wordplay introduced by the author in 1 Sam 14:27 climaxes in Jonathan's statement about his eyes brightening (14:29). The verbs "see" (רָאוּ, 14:29) and "brightened" (אֹרוּ, 14:29) contain identical consonants (although in different order). Indeed, Jonathan could see better than his father, who had not eaten. In addition, Jonathan "tasted" (the verb טָעַם) "a little" (the substantive מְעַט, 14:29), and those words too have the same consonants. It did not take much honey to brighten his eyes and give him insight into his father's foolishness. His insight is reminiscent of Prov 24:13–14:

> My son, eat honey, because it is good,
>> and flowing honey is sweet upon your palate.
> In the same way, know that wisdom is [like this] for your soul.
>> If you find [it], then there is a future,
>>> and your hope will never be cut off.[19]

The sugar in the honey was a quick source of energy that enabled Jonathan not only to continue the battle but also to see his father's folly: because the troops had not eaten, there would not be a decisive defeat of the Philistines (1 Sam 14:30).

The Troops Violate God's Law (14:31–35)

The battle extended from Michmash west to Aijalon (14:31), a distance of about twenty miles (thirty-two kilometers). With such a long pursuit and a daylong fast, it was no wonder that the troops were exhausted and immediately

---

18 Steinmann, *Proverbs*, 285.

19 Steinmann, *Proverbs*, 468.

began slaughtering the captured animals on the ground (14:32). Saul is told of their activity and halts it by having an altar built from a rock and instructing the troops to slaughter the animals there (14:33–34). When the animals were slaughtered on the ground, the blood was not able to drain from the meat. The altar allowed the blood to drain. The prohibition against eating meat without the blood drained is as old as God's permission to Noah about eating meat (Gen 9:3–4). The blood signified the life of the animal, and out of respect for God's gift of life, no blood was to be eaten. This prohibition is repeated several times in the laws given by Moses (Lev 17:10–14, 19:26; Deut 12:15–16). However, the only recorded instance of the violation of this command in the OT is in this account.

The rock became Saul's first altar to Yahweh (14:35). Thus, despite Saul's show of piety, he had not sought to build an altar until forced by an emergency that was largely his own creation. In fact, to this point in the battle account Saul had not once mentioned Yahweh (not even when he pronounced the curse in 14:24), even though Yahweh alone is the one who saves/grants victory (see the Hiphil [H] of יָשַׁע in 1 Sam 14:23, 39; also Deut 20:4; and the related noun in Prov 21:31). It was Jonathan who relied on Yahweh for success (14:6, 10, 12).

Saul Is Forced to Stop His Pursuit of the Philistines (14:36–46)

Following the troops' meal, Saul is keen to continue the pursuit of the fleeing Philistines, and the troops assent (14:36). However, God had not assented to Saul's plan, and the high priest Ahijah wisely suggested that they first consult God. The procedure was to use the Urim and Thummim to ask about God's will. The Urim and Thummim were given so that Israel could inquire of God (Ex 28:30; Lev 8:8; Deut 33:8). Judging from Num 27:21, where Joshua is to use Urim to know when Israel is to "go out [to battle]" (the verb יָצָא) and "come back [from battle]" (the verb בּוֹא), a primary use was to advise in military matters. Saul would seek to use Urim in preparing for his second battle with the Philistines, but God would not answer (1 Sam 28:6). Apparently David also used it in strategizing for war and received answers from God (1 Sam 23:9–13).

Saul inquired of God, asking two questions that really were one and the same: ought he to pursue the Philistines to a successful conclusion of the conflict (14:37)? No answer was forthcoming from God. This in itself was a sign that someone in Israel had caused a break in the people's relationship with God, since Yahweh had promised to speak to his covenant people Israel through the high priest as an oracle using Urim and Thummim (Ex 28:30). However, Israel had violated the covenant, so God did not answer.

Saul next decided that he must determine what sin had estranged Israel from God, and he summoned the troops for this purpose (1 Sam 14:38). Saul then took a second hasty oath that said more than he realized—that even if the sin was committed by his son Jonathan, the heir apparent to the throne, Jonathan would die (14:39). The troops' corresponding silence in the face of Saul's oath may have been caused by shock for two reasons: (1) they may have suspected that their eating of meat with blood in it was the offense and that their lives were now in danger, or (2) at least some of them knew what Jonathan had done, and they feared for his life.

Since God had not answered Saul, he resorted to using the Urim and Thummim as lots (14:40–41), although this was not their intended use. Urim and Thummim were to be used to determine a course of action—a decision (מִשְׁפָּט, Ex 28:30; Num 27:21), whereas lots were used to choose among alternatives where a course of action had already been generally determined.[20] There was no promise from God that using the Urim and Thummim would reveal God's will in the way Saul sought. Thus, the reader is left with uncertainty as to whether the Urim and Thummim actually revealed the offense that caused God to withhold his Word from Saul.

The first alternative was to choose between the commanders—Saul and Jonathan—and the troops. In what must have been a surprise to Saul, he and Jonathan were chosen by lot. The author clearly states that the troops were cleared; according to the lots, their sin of eating meat with blood in it was not the cause of the breach between Israel and God. When the lots were cast again between Saul and Jonathan, they showed Jonathan to be the guilty party (14:42).

A quick exchange between Saul and Jonathan highlighted the difference between father and son (14:43–44). Jonathan was quick to admit that he had eaten some honey, but he also did not believe that his transgression was worthy of death. After all, it was Saul who had "ruined the land" (14:29). However, Saul replied with his third vow—calling on God to mete out punishment if Jonathan was not executed for his transgression. That form of vow often included a punishment on the oath-taker if he were not to carry out the deed: "may God punish *me* if …" Interestingly, Saul does not use a pronoun in this vow (see the textual note on 14:44). Perhaps by this point he has become slightly more circumspect about his rash vows. The first (14:24) not only caught Jonathan in an inadvertent breach of an oath but also cost Saul complete victory over the Philistines. The second vow (14:39) unintentionally targeted Jonathan. Now for the third vow Saul called down God's punishment, but on no particular person. The ambiguity paved the way for Jonathan's discharge from the punishment.

The troops instantly came to Jonathan's defense (14:45). They credited the victory to Jonathan—not Saul. And the troops took an oath that Jonathan would not be harmed "because he accomplished [the victory] with God," implying that Saul had not been aligning his actions with God, despite his pious-sounding oaths. The vow that "no hair of his head will fall to the ground" was an expression of absolute protection from harm (2 Sam 14:11; 1 Ki 1:52; Lk 21:18; Acts 27:34). The author says that the troops "ransomed" Jonathan. It appears that their vow paid the ransom for Jonathan. They placed their lives in jeopardy if

---

[20] Lev 16:8; Josh 18:6, 8, 10; Joel 4:3 (ET 3:3); Obad 11; Jonah 1:7; Nah 3:10; Ps 22:19 (ET 22:18); Job 6:27; Esth 3:7; 9:24, 26; Neh 10:35 (ET 10:34); 11:1; 1 Chr 24:31; 25:8; 26:13–14; Add Esth 10:10–11; Mt 27:35; Mk 15:24; Lk 23:34; Jn 19:24; Acts 1:26.

Jonathan were to be harmed, thereby paying for his life with the offer of their own lives.

The author concludes the account of Saul's first Philistine campaign with a quick note that Saul stopped his pursuit and the Philistines returned to their territory. They would live to fight another day (1 Samuel 31). But the author does not answer the bigger question for the reader: Was Jonathan's consumption of honey (14:27) the real reason for Yahweh's displeasure and the lost opportunity to wipe out Israel's enemies? Or was it God's displeasure with Saul's impetuous oath (14:24), an oath that led to Jonathan's innocent transgression and to the troops' breaking Israel's covenant with Yahweh? In the end, Jonathan appears to be vindicated, since he worked "with God" (14:45). Saul, on the other hand, appears to have been censured, for his oath "ruined the land" (14:29).

In this account Saul's oaths play an important role, and they highlight the folly and uselessness of rash vows. Prov 26:2 reminds us:

> Like a migratory bird or a flying swallow,
>   so a gratuitous curse does not come [to rest].[21]

God alone can make a curse effective, and gratuitous curses like Saul's that call for God's punishment are a misuse of God's name and a transgression of the Second Commandment (Ex 20:7; Deut 5:11). There was no need for Saul to place a curse on any of the Israelite troops who ate that day (1 Sam 14:24), and his impulsive words created the unbearable conditions that led to them eating meat with blood in it (14:32). He further increased his sin by swearing that Jonathan would have to die (14:44), which was only averted when the troops put their own lives in danger (14:45). Authorities certainly have the right to require oaths of those under them when it is for the sake of justice, the good of society, and the benefit of others (Heb 6:16). Thus, Abraham asked his servant to swear an oath in order to find a godly wife for his son Isaac (Gen 24:2–4). Our Lord himself recognized this power of the authorities when he allowed himself to be placed under an oath to tell the truth (Mt 26:63–64; cf. Rom 13:1). However, when authorities misuse their power and require oaths to be taken simply for their own purposes or aggrandizement, they are guilty of misusing their authority and commit the further sin of compelling others to misuse God's name. For this reason the Augsburg Confession observes that "an ungodly vow, made contrary to God's command, is null and void."[22]

In addition, Saul personally took two oaths (1 Sam 14:39, 44), neither of which he was capable of keeping, thereby violating God's Law (Num 30:3 [ET 30:2]). Jesus, therefore, advised his disciples generally to avoid oaths and simply let their yes be yes and their no be no (Mt 5:33–37). None of Saul's oaths were necessary or helpful, and in each case he was unable to follow through on his vows.

Therefore, in the Large Catechism Luther reminds us:

---

[21] Steinmann, *Proverbs*, 516, 518, 525.

[22] AC XXVII 40.

We are not to swear in support of evil (that is, to a falsehood) or unnecessarily; but in support of the good and for the advantage of our neighbor we are to swear. This is a truly good work by which God is praised, truth and justice are established, falsehood is refuted, people are reconciled, obedience is rendered, and quarrels are settled. For here God himself intervenes and separates right from wrong, good from evil.[23]

Yet despite Saul's ill-considered oaths and acts, God gave Israel a victory over the Philistines, just as he promised when Saul was chosen as king (1 Sam 9:16). Jonathan was God's major instrument in achieving victory at Michmash, something that the author of the book of Samuel points out by his favorable comparison of the son to his father throughout 1 Samuel 13–14. Yet it was under Saul's authority that Jonathan acted, demonstrating that even when authorities act in ways that are not completely aligned with God's will, God nevertheless can use them for his purposes.

---

[23] LC I (Second Commandment) 66.

Excursus

The Urim and Thummim

Some of the least understood items mentioned in the OT are the Urim and Thummim that were kept in the high priest's ephod. The Urim and Thummim together are explicitly mentioned only six times (Ex 28:30; Lev 8:8; Deut 33:8; LXX 1 Sam 14:41;[1] Ezra 2:63; Neh 7:65). In addition, Urim alone is mentioned in Num 27:21 and 1 Sam 28:6. In these two passages the mention of Urim without Thummim is probably synecdoche, a literary device in which a part of something (Urim) is cited to refer to the whole (Urim and Thummim).

"Urim" (אוּרִים) mean "lights,"[2] and "Thummim" (תֻּמִּים) means "completeness," "innocence," or "perfection."[3] Both words are plural forms in Hebrew. There have been a number of suggestions as to what these names signify.[4] First, some propose that the two names could be a hendiadys meaning something like "perfect light" and that there was only one object, which was called "Urim and Thummim."[5] However, LXX 1 Sam 14:41 appears to treat Urim and Thummim as separate objects. Second, others believe that there were two singular objects.[6] If that is the case, the nouns may have retained an archaic *mem* suffix that later Hebrew scribes mistakenly took to signify a plural form. A third explanation is that these nouns are true plurals and refer to two *sets* of complementary objects.[7] Fourth, "Urim" could mean "cursed" if it is derived from the verb אָרַר, "to curse," and Thummim (תֻּמִּים) would have the antonymous meaning "innocent."[8] Earlier in this narrative Saul had used that verb in his rash oath: "cursed [אָרוּר] be the man who eats food until it is evening" (14:24; see also 14:28). In 14:41–42 Saul wanted the Urim and Thummim to tell him who had fallen under his curse. Fifth, yet another explanation is that

---

[1] See the textual note on 14:41. In the MT neither Urim nor Thummim is mentioned, though some believe the singular adjective תָּמִים, "complete," is mispointed and ought to be vocalized תֻּמִּים, "Thummim."

[2] In form אוּרִים could be the plural of the masculine noun אוּר, "flame, light," which appears five times in the OT (Is 31:9; 44:16; 47:14; 50:11; Ezek 5:2). Much more common is the related noun אוֹר, "light." Cf. also the verb אוֹר, "be light; shine."

[3] In form תֻּמִּים is the plural of the common masculine noun תֹּם, "completeness, innocence, integrity" (see BDB, s.v. תֹּם, under the root תמם). It probably is an abstract (or intensive) plural, and so it is translated as a singular above.

[4] A helpful summary of various suggestions is given in Kitz, "The Plural Form of ʾÛrîm and Tummîm," 401–2.

[5] See Van Dam, *The Urim and Thummim*, 137–39, 224; Houtman, "The Urim and Thummim: A New Suggestion," 230.

[6] See Robertson, "The ʾÛrîm and Tummîm: What Were They?" 68.

[7] See Van Dam, *The Urim and Thummim*, 137; Robertson, "The ʾÛrîm and Tummîm: What Were They?" 68.

[8] See Robertson, "The ʾÛrîm and Tummîm: What Were They?" 70, who cites Wellhausen and Moore as advocates of this interpretation.

272

the two names refer to the first and last letters of the Hebrew alphabet. "Urim," a plural of a noun derived from אוֹר, "light," denotes א, *aleph*, the first letter of the alphabet. This would be an appropriate name, since the first thing God created through his Word was "light" (אוֹר, Gen 1:3).[9] "Thummim," the plural of תֹּם, "completeness," denotes ת, *taw*, the last letter of the alphabet. This also is appropriate, since it is the completion or end[10] of the alphabet.[11]

No matter what the names signify, the first mention of the Urim and Thummim is in Ex 28:30, where Moses is instructed to place them in the breastpiece that was attached to the high priest's ephod, where they would always be when the high priest came into God's presence (see also Lev 8:8; Deut 33:8). They are said to be for the purpose of "decision" or "judgment" (מִשְׁפָּט, twice in Ex 28:30).[12] Interestingly, we are never told the origin or construction of these objects. Apparently they were not manufactured along with the breastpiece, the ephod, and the other priestly vestments and furnishings of the tabernacle. They most likely were gifts from God to his people Israel.

Key to identifying times when the Urim and Thummim were used is Num 27:21:

וְלִפְנֵי אֶלְעָזָר הַכֹּהֵן יַעֲמֹד וְשָׁאַל לוֹ בְּמִשְׁפַּט הָאוּרִים לִפְנֵי יְהוָה
עַל־פִּיו יֵצְאוּ וְעַל־פִּיו יָבֹאוּ הוּא וְכָל־בְּנֵי־יִשְׂרָאֵל אִתּוֹ וְכָל־הָעֵדָה׃

And he [Joshua] will stand before Eleazar the priest. He [the priest] will inquire for him [Joshua] by the decision of the Urim in Yahweh's presence. He [Joshua] and all the Israelites with him—the entire community—will go out [to battle] according to his [Yahweh's] authorization, and they will return [from battle] according to his authorization.

"According to his authorization" is עַל־פִּיו, literally "according to his mouth." Moses is stating that through the Urim, Yahweh would give the message authorizing Joshua's military actions (whether to attack or retreat), and it would come from the priest's mouth. The priest would act as God's spokesman.

Second, this verse speaks of "asking" or "inquiring" (the verb שָׁאַל) of Yahweh. This idiom of inquiring of Yahweh is used in relating fifteen instances of consulting God in the OT historical books, but never after the reign of David:

- Josh 9:14: Israel did not inquire of Yahweh before making a treaty with the Gibeonites.
- Judg 1:1: Israel inquired as to which tribe should first conquer its allotted territory.
- Judg 20:18, 23, 27: Israel inquired *three* times concerning its attack on the Benjaminites.

---

[9] Robertson, "The 'Ūrīm and Tummīm: What Were They?" 72.

[10] In some verses the verb תָּמַם, from which "Thummim" is derived, means "to finish, come to an end, be ended." See, e.g., Deut 2:14–16; 31:30; Jer 1:3; Job 31:40.

[11] Robertson, "The 'Ūrīm and Tummīm: What Were They?" 72.

[12] On the use of Urim and Thummim, see Van Dam, *The Urim and Thummim*, and Houtman, "The Urim and Thummim: A New Suggestion."

- 1 Sam 10:22: Israel inquired as to Saul's whereabouts.
- 1 Sam 22:10, 13: Ahimelech inquired of Yahweh for David.
- 1 Sam 23:2, 4: David *twice* inquired as to whether to attack the Philistines who were fighting against Keilah.
- 1 Sam 28:6: Saul inquired of Yahweh *by Urim*, but received no answer.
- 1 Sam 30:8: David inquired as to whether to pursue the Amalekites.
- 2 Sam 2:1: David inquired as to which city to make his base of operations.
- 2 Sam 5:19 ‖ 1 Chr 14:10: David inquired whether to wage war against the Philistines.
- 2 Sam 5:23 ‖ 1 Chr 14:14: David inquired about tactics for attacking the Philistines.

An additional incident of inquiring of Yahweh, but without the use of this idiom, is found in 1 Sam 23:9–12, when David summoned the priest to bring the ephod (where the Urim and Thummim were kept) and then asked God about the possible actions of Saul and the citizens of Keilah. Perhaps could be added the attempt to consult God that was aborted by Saul (see the commentary on 1 Sam 14:18–19). In these verses Urim is mentioned only in 1 Sam 28:6 and LXX 1 Sam 14:41, and Thummim only in LXX 1 Sam 14:41. However, all of these verses that speak of inquiring of Yahweh most likely involved the high priest consulting the Urim and Thummim. After the time of David neither the Urim and Thummim nor the idiom "inquire [שָׁאַל]" of Yahweh is mentioned, except in Ezra 2:63 ‖ Neh 7:65, which notes that in postexilic Judah there was no priest with Urim and Thummim who could give Yahweh's answer to a question (to ascertain whether certain men were members of the priesthood; if so, they could partake of the holy food).

Exactly how the Urim and Thummim were employed is never described in the OT, although 1 Sam 14:18 may imply that the priest held them in his hands as he inquired of God. Based on the meaning of "Urim" and "Thummim" as "light" and "perfection," respectively, Van Dam argues that the Urim and Thummim would glow when removed from the ephod to verify that the high priest's words had come from God.[13]

While some questions to God could be answered simply yes or no,[14] other questions required a longer answer. Thus, when Israel inquired about Saul's whereabouts—not a simple yes or no question—God answered: "Look, he is hiding among the baggage" (1 Sam 10:22). Again, when David asked to what city to go, Yahweh replied, "To Hebron" (2 Sam 2:1). The longest reply from God is his instructions on tactics to be used against the Philistines (2 Sam 5:23–24):

---

[13] Van Dam, *The Urim and Thummim*, 224.

[14] E.g., David's questions in 1 Sam 30:8 could be answered in this way, though Yahweh provides a much longer answer. David's first question in 2 Sam 2:1 could also have elicited a yes or no answer, and God's reply, "go up" (עֲלֵה), is essentially a yes.

וַיִּשְׁאַ֨ל דָּוִ֤ד בַּֽיהוָה֙ וַיֹּ֔אמֶר לֹ֖א תַעֲלֶ֑ה הָסֵב֙ אֶל־אַֽחֲרֵיהֶ֔ם וּבָ֥אתָ לָהֶ֖ם מִמּ֥וּל
בְּכָאִֽים׃ וִ֠יהִי כְּֽשָׁמְעֲךָ֞ אֶת־ק֤וֹל צְעָדָה֙ בְּרָאשֵׁ֣י הַבְּכָאִ֔ים אָ֖ז תֶּחֱרָ֑ץ
כִּ֣י אָ֗ז יָצָ֤א יְהוָה֙ לְפָנֶ֔יךָ לְהַכּ֖וֹת בְּמַחֲנֵ֥ה פְלִשְׁתִּֽים׃

So David inquired of Yahweh, and he [Yahweh] said, "Do not go up [i.e., do not attack directly]. Circle around behind them and attack them opposite the balsam trees. As you hear the sound of marching in the tops of the balsam trees, act decisively, for then Yahweh will have marched out ahead of you to attack the Philistine camp."

One widely held alternate theory as to how the Urim and Thummim were used is that they were a form of cleromancy or casting of lots.[15] Scholars often cite parallels with other lot-casting practices in the ancient Near East to reinforce this view. OT evidence for this theory is based largely on 1 Sam 14:41–42, where, according to the LXX, Saul used the Urim and Thummim, and both the LXX and the MT speak of "casting" (translated as "decide") and being "selected" by lot.[16] However, as noted in the commentary on 1 Sam 14:41–42, the text depicts Saul's use of the Urim and Thummim as lots *as a method not authorized or endorsed elsewhere in Scripture*. Thus, it is not appropriate to use 1 Sam 14:41–42 as a basis for comparing the regular use of the Urim and Thummim to lot-casting procedures in the ancient Near East.

Lots were used to choose between alternatives when a general course of action had already been determined. For instance, on the Day of Atonement two goats were brought to the high priest—one for a sacrifice and one to be the scapegoat. To determine which goat was which, the high priest was to cast lots (Lev 16:8). In another example, during the storm at sea in Jonah 1, the sailors had already determined that someone was to blame for their predicament. They used lots to determine that it was Jonah (Jonah 1:7). Thus, lots could only be employed to choose between alternatives, not to receive advice such as the specific tactics given to David (2 Sam 5:23–24).

Moreover, casting lots or selecting by lot *always* chooses one of the alternatives. There is no possibility of receiving absolutely no answer from lots, since one of the lots will be chosen. In at least two instances when Saul consulted the Urim and Thummim, he received no answer at all (1 Sam 14:37; 28:6). Therefore, we can conclude that the Urim and Thummim were not a lot oracle, but instead enabled an oral message from God to be spoken through the high priest.

---

[15] Kitz, "The Plural Form of *ʾÛrîm* and *Tummîm*," 402–10. Kitz (402–3, n. 8) lists a dozen scholars from Julius Wellhausen to Joseph Blenkinsopp who hold this view. See also Lindblom, "Lot-Casting in the Old Testament," 170–78.

[16] See the textual notes on 14:41 and 14:42.

1 Samuel 14:47–52
Saul's Military Successes

Translation

14 **47**Now Saul captured the kingship over Israel. He waged war all around against all his enemies: against Moab, against the Ammonites, against Edom, against the kings of Zobah, and against the Philistines. Against whomever he turned, he was victorious. **48**He acted forcefully and defeated Amalek and delivered Israel from the power of those who plundered it. **49**Saul's sons were Jonathan, Ishvi, and Malchishua. The names of his two daughters were [these]: the name of the firstborn was Merab, and the name of the younger was Michal. **50**The name of Saul's wife was Ahinoam the daughter of Ahimaaz. The name of the commander of his army was Abner the son of Ner, Saul's uncle. **51**Kish was Saul's father, and Ner, Abner's father, was the son of Abiel. **52**There was intense war against the Philistines all the days of Saul, and whenever Saul saw any man who was a warrior or any skilled soldier, he would conscript him.

Textual Notes

14:47 וְשָׁאוּל לָכַד לָכַד הַמְּלוּכָה—"Now Saul captured the kingship." In the Qal (G) לָכַד usually means "to capture, seize" a town or territory through warfare, along with the taking of captives and spoils (e.g., 2 Sam 5:7; 8:4; 12:26–29). The use of this verb implies that Saul acquired the kingship through his military actions in 1 Samuel 14 (initiated by Jonathan). See further the commentary.

יַרְשִׁיעַ—This Hiphil (H) of רָשַׁע, an imperfect with frequentative or habitual force, would mean that Saul "kept acting wickedly" or "would condemn [others], declare [them] guilty" (see BDB, Hiphil; *HALOT*, Hiphil). The LXX reads ἐσῴζετο (a durative imperfect of σῴζω), "he kept saving, being victorious," apparently reflecting a Hebrew text with יוֹשִׁיעַ (see the textual note on 10:18–19). The MT seems to have suffered from graphic confusion that replaced a *waw* (ו) with a *resh* (ר).

14:48 וַיַּעַשׂ חָיִל—"He acted forcefully" is literally "and he did strength." In military contexts this idiom (Qal [G] of עָשָׂה with the direct object noun חָיִל) refers to bravery and success in battle (Num 24:18; Pss 60:14 [ET 60:12]; 108:14 [ET 108:13]; 118:15–16).

וַיַּצֵּל—For the Hiphil (H) of נָצַל, meaning "to rescue, deliver," see the textual note on 10:18–19.

שֹׁסֵהוּ—This Qal (G) participle of שָׁסָה, "to plunder," is masculine singular and has a third masculine singular object suffix referring back to יִשְׂרָאֵל, "Israel," so "his plunderer" means "the one plundering Israel." "Amalek" in the context would be the implied subject. However, 4QSamᵃ has the plural participle [ש]סיו (to be vocalized שֹׁסָיו), "those who were plundering" Israel, as does the LXX (τῶν καταπατούντων αὐτόν). This would refer not only to Amalek but also to all other oppressors. The plural better fits the context of 14:47.

14:50 אֲבִינֵר—This spelling is "Abiner," meaning "my Father is a lamp" or "Father of [i.e., who is] a lamp," but elsewhere he is always called אַבְנֵר, "Abner," likely with the same meaning.

14:52 וְרָאָה—The Qal (G) perfect with *waw* consecutive signifies frequentative or habitual action: "whenever he would see …"

אִישׁ גִּבּוֹר—This means "a man [who was] a warrior." In military contexts the expanded phrase אִישׁ גִּבּוֹר חַיִל (for חַיִל, see the next textual note) denotes a man who is an accomplished soldier (plural in Josh 8:3; 1 Chr 5:24; 8:40; cf. the singular in Ruth 2:1).

בֶּן־חַיִל—Literally this is "a son of strength/valor." The phrase denotes a man who is strong, skilled, and brave. In military contexts it indicates someone who is proficient at the art of war (Deut 3:18; Judg 18:2; 1 Sam 18:17; 2 Sam 17:10; 1 Chr 5:18).

וַיַּאַסְפֵהוּ אֵלָיו:—Literally "and he [Saul] would gather him [the warrior or soldier] to himself," this is translated as "he would conscript him."

Commentary

1049–1009 BC

The author has waited until after the attack on the Philistine garrison at Gibeah and its aftermath (13:2–14:46) to present a summary of Saul's reign. This is an indication that he did not consider Saul's accession to the throne complete until Saul had carried out Samuel's initial instructions to attack the Philistine garrison (10:5–7).[1] Note that the author follows a similar procedure for David. Although David ruled in Hebron seven years and six months (2 Sam 2:11), it was not until after all Israel acknowledged him as king (2 Sam 5:1–3) that the author gives his summary of David's reign (2 Sam 5:4–16).

Saul's enemies listed in 1 Sam 14:47–48 are identical to those listed later among David's conquests, although the foes are listed in a different order:

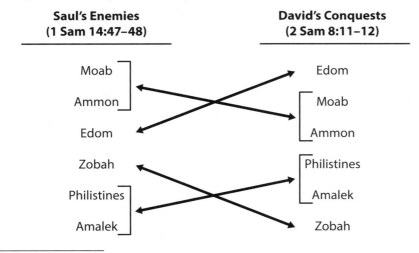

Saul's Enemies (1 Sam 14:47–48)	David's Conquests (2 Sam 8:11–12)
Moab	Edom
Ammon	Moab
Edom	Ammon
Zobah	Philistines
Philistines	Amalek
Amalek	Zobah

---

[1] 1 Sam 10:7 implies that Samuel expected Saul to eradicate the Philistine garrison in Gibeah as a necessary step in becoming the rightful king. See the discussion in "Samuel Anoints Saul (9:26–10:8)" in the commentary on 9:26–10:16. See also the beginning of the commentary on 10:17–27a.

In both cases the nations are listed in two groups of three. The first group of nations are those ethnically related to Israel—Moab (Gen 19:36–37) and Ammon (Gen 19:38) as well as Edom (Gen 25:30; 36:1). Edom is the last in the first group of three among Saul's enemies, but Edom is listed first among all of David's conquests. In both lists the second group of nations are those with no ethnic ties to Israel. Among Saul's enemies, the first nation in the second group—Zobah—is last of all in the list of David's conquests. One advantage (and possible reason) for the author's arrangement of the second group of Saul's enemies is that he has placed Amalek last here, which provides a convenient link to the next incident from Saul's reign (1 Samuel 15).

Saul's sons are listed next (14:49). There are several lists of Saul's sons in the OT:

1 Sam 14:49	1 Sam 31:2 ‖ 1 Chr 10:2	1 Chr 8:33; 9:39
Jonathan	Jonathan	Jonathan
Ishvi	Abinadab	Malchi-shua
Malchi-shua	Malchi-shua	Abinadab
		Eshbaal

There is much speculation among scholars as to the identity of Ishvi.[2] Compounding the problem is that the name in the LXX is Ιεσσιου, which would indicate the Hebrew name was יִשְׁוִי instead of the MT's יִשְׁוִי. Some scholars use this as evidence that the name may have actually been אִישְׁיוֹ, "man of Yahweh," and then attempt to identify him as Eshbaal ("man of the master").[3] However, there is no textual evidence to support this identification. Most likely Saul had either four or five sons by his wife. Perhaps 14:49 lists the sons at the beginning of his reign. That would imply that Ishvi may have died at a young age and that Abinadab and Eshbaal were born after Saul was made king.

Saul's two daughters (1 Sam 14:49) are mentioned again when Saul attempted to marry them to David. Merab was offered to David first (1 Sam 18:17–19), though she eventually married a certain Adriel from Meholah and bore five sons (2 Sam 21:8).[4] Michal became David's wife (1 Sam 18:27), but she bore no children (2 Sam 6:23).

Saul's wife was named Ahinoam (1 Sam 14:50). David also had a wife from Jezreel by this name (1 Sam 25:43; 27:3; 30:5; 2 Sam 2:2; 3:2; 1 Chr 3:1).

---

[2] See the discussions in McCarter, *I Samuel*, 254; Klein, *1 Samuel*, 141–42; Tsumura, *The First Book of Samuel*, 384.

[3] In the book of Samuel, Eshbaal is called Ish-bosheth (2 Sam 2:8, 10, 12, 15; 3:8, 14, 15; 4:5, 8, 12). It is likely that "Ish-bosheth," meaning "man of shame," is a purposeful scribal bowdlerization of "Eshbaal," meaning "man of Baal," although the element *ba'al*, "master, lord," may originally have been intended to refer to the God of Israel.

[4] Most MT and LXX manuscripts read "Michal." However, two MT manuscripts, some LXX manuscripts, and the Syriac versions read "Merab." This is undoubtedly the correct reading (followed by HCSB, ESV, GW, NET, NIV), since Michal had no children (2 Sam 6:23).

Though not mentioned here, Saul also had a concubine named Rizpah and two sons by her: Armoni and Mephibosheth (2 Sam 21:8–14).

Abner, the commander of Saul's army, was the son of Ner. His name is spelled "Abiner" (אֲבִינֵר) only in 14:50 (see the textual note), but elsewhere always "Abner" (אַבְנֵר). The text of 14:50–51 is somewhat ambiguous as to his relationship to Saul. Is Abner Saul's uncle? Or is Ner Saul's uncle, making Abner Saul's cousin? In 1 Sam 9:1 and 1 Chr 9:35–36 Kish and Ner both appear to be sons of Abiel/Jeiel, making Abner one of Saul's cousins. This is endorsed by Josephus.[5] However, in 1 Chr 8:33 and 1 Chr 9:39 Ner is Kish's father, making Abner Saul's uncle. The solution is a careful reading of the genealogical information in 1 Chr 9:35–39. There we see that there were two men named Kish. One was the son of Jeiel (1 Chr 9:36), whereas the other was the son of Ner (1 Chr 9:39), who was the son of Jeiel (1 Chr 9:36). Therefore, in 1 Sam 9:1 Saul's father Kish ought to be understood as the *grandson* of Abiel (see the first textual note on 9:1). This means that Abner was Saul's uncle. The genealogy of Saul and Abner is shown in figure 20.

The final note in this section (14:52) serves as a bridge to David, who will become Saul's designated replacement (15:26–29; 16:1, 11–13). While Saul fought many enemies, war with the Philistines was a constant throughout his time as king. As if to reinforce this, the Philistines will be mentioned eighty-eight more times in the rest of 1 Samuel, more often than any other ethnic group. David would be the most prominent recruit into Saul's army, and he would take the lead in fighting the Philistines.

---

[5]   Josephus, *Antiquities*, 6.130.

279

Figure 20

Saul's Family Genealogy

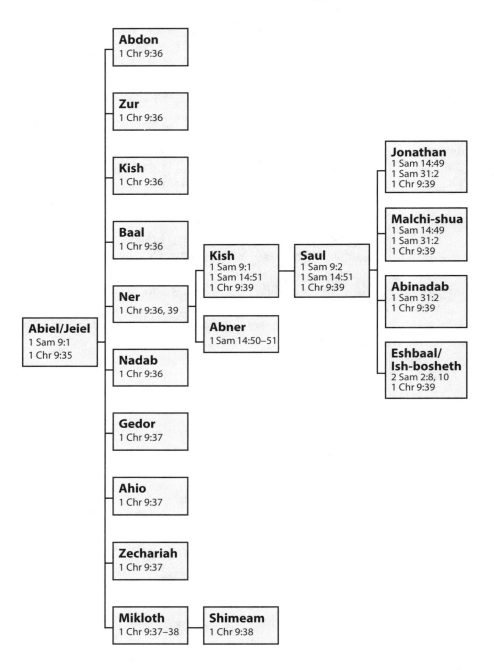

Saul had additional sons not listed in the chart above: Isvi by his wife, Ahinoam (1 Sam 14:49–50), and Armoni and Mephibosheth by his concubine, Rizpah (2 Sam 21:8). His daughters were Merab and Michal (1 Sam 14:49).

The Amalekite Campaign:
Saul Is Rejected as King

Translation

15 ¹Samuel said to Saul, "Yahweh sent me to anoint you king over his people, over Israel. Now listen to the voice of the words of Yahweh: ²Thus Yahweh of armies has said: 'I noted what Amalek did to Israel when he opposed him on the way when he came up from Egypt. ³Now go, attack Amalek and completely destroy all that is his. Do not spare him. Kill men and women, children and infants, herds and flocks, camels and donkeys.' "

⁴Saul summoned the troops and counted them at Telaim: two hundred thousand infantry and ten thousand men of Judah. ⁵Saul came to the city of Amalek and set up an ambush in the ravine. ⁶Saul said to the Kenites, "Go away! Get away from the Amalekites. Otherwise, I'll sweep you away with them. You showed kindness to all the Israelites when they came up from Egypt." So the Kenites got away from Amalek.

⁷Then Saul attacked Amalek from Havilah to Shur, which is next to Egypt. ⁸He captured King Agag of Amalek alive, but he completely destroyed all the people by the edge of the sword. ⁹Saul and the troops spared Agag and the best of the flocks, of the herds, and of the fattened calves, [and spared] the rams and the best of everything. They were not willing to completely destroy them. But all the despised and weak property—that they destroyed.

¹⁰Then the Word of Yahweh came to Samuel: ¹¹"I regret that I made Saul king, because he has turned from following me, and he has not carried out my words." Samuel was angry, and he called out to Yahweh all that night. ¹²Samuel rose early in the morning to meet Saul, and Samuel was told, "Saul went to Carmel where he is erecting a monument to himself. Then he turned, crossed over, and went down to Gilgal."

¹³Samuel came to Saul, and Saul said to him, "May you be blessed by Yahweh. I have carried out Yahweh's word."

¹⁴So Samuel said, "Then what is this sound of flocks in my ears and the sound of herds that I hear?"

¹⁵Saul said, "They brought them from Amalek, for the troops spared the best of the flocks and herds in order to sacrifice to Yahweh your God, and the rest we completely destroyed."

¹⁶Samuel said to Saul, "Stop! Let me tell you what Yahweh said to me last night."

So he said to him, "Speak."

¹⁷Samuel said, "Even if you consider yourself so insignificant, you are the head of the tribes of Israel, and Yahweh anointed you to be king over Israel. ¹⁸Yahweh

sent you on a mission and said, 'Go, completely destroy those sinners, Amalek. So wage war against him until you finish them off.' ¹⁹Why didn't you listen to Yahweh's voice? Why did you pounce on the plunder and do what Yahweh considers evil?"

²⁰Then Saul said to Samuel, "I obeyed Yahweh's voice. I went on the mission that Yahweh had sent me, and I brought back King Agag of Amalek, and I completely destroyed Amalek. ²¹The troops took from the spoils sheep and cattle, the best of what was to be destroyed, to sacrifice to Yahweh your God in Gilgal."

²²Samuel said, "Is Yahweh as pleased with whole burnt offerings and sacrifices as obeying Yahweh's voice?

"Look: To obey is better than sacrifice;
　　to listen [is better] than the fat from rams.
²³For rebellion is [like] the sin of divination,
　　and willfulness is [like] the wickedness of idolatry.
Because you have rejected Yahweh's word, he has rejected you as king."

²⁴Saul said to Samuel, "I have sinned because I transgressed Yahweh's command and your word, because I was afraid of the people, and I listened to them. ²⁵Now please forgive my sin, return with me, and let me worship Yahweh."

²⁶Samuel said to Saul, "I will not return with you, because you have rejected Yahweh's word, and Yahweh has rejected you from being king over Israel."

²⁷Then Samuel turned to go, and Saul grabbed the hem of his robe, and it tore. ²⁸So Samuel said to him, "Yahweh has torn the kingdom of Israel from you today, and he has given it to your neighbor, who is better than you. ²⁹In addition, the Glory of Israel does not lie, nor does he change his mind, because he is not a human who changes his mind."

³⁰He said, "I have sinned. Now please honor me before my people's elders and before Israel. Return with me, and I will worship Yahweh your God." ³¹So Samuel returned, following Saul, and Saul worshiped Yahweh.

³²Then Samuel said, "Bring King Agag of Amalek to me." Agag came to him trembling. Agag thought, "Surely death is bitter."

³³Samuel said, "As your sword has made women childless, so your mother will be childless among women." Then Samuel cut Agag to pieces in the presence of Yahweh in Gilgal.

³⁴Samuel went to Ramah, and Saul went up to his home in Gibeah of Saul. ³⁵Samuel did not see Saul again until the day he died, though Samuel grieved for Saul. Yahweh regretted that he had made Saul reign over Israel.

Textual Notes

15:1 לִמְשָׁחֲךָ—This means "to anoint you." The verb מָשַׁח was used for the anointing of Saul in 9:16; 10:1 and recurs often later in the book.[1] The form of the Qal (G) infinitive construct without a suffix would be מְשֹׁחַ. Normally in Hebrew an open syllable

---

[1] 1 Sam 15:17; 16:3, 12, 13; 2 Sam 1:21; 2:4, 7; 3:39; 5:3, 17; 12:7; 19:11 (ET 19:10). Cf. also the discussion of the cognate noun מָשִׁיחַ, "Anointed One," in the commentary on 2:10, 35.

has a long vowel, but the vowel (-שָׁ-) is *qamets chatuph*, a short "o" vowel, since it is reduced from the *holem* (-שֹׁ-) in the form without the suffix (מָשַׁח). This is confirmed by the *chateph qamets* under the following consonant (-חֳ-). See GKC, § 9 v.

עַל־עַמּוֹ עַל־יִשְׂרָאֵל—This means "over his people, over Israel." The LXX and one Masoretic manuscript omit "over his people."

שְׁמַע לְקוֹל דִּבְרֵי יְהוָה:—The MT reads "listen to the voice of *the words of* Yahweh." The shorter reading of the LXX is ἄκουε τῆς φωνῆς κυρίου, "listen to the voice of the Lord." On the one hand, the longer MT reading might appear to have added דִּבְרֵי, "words of," as an assimilation to the more common "listen to the Word of Yahweh."[2] On the other hand, in 15:13 Saul (falsely) claims, "I have carried out Yahweh's Word" (דְּבַר יְהוָה), which supports the inclusion of "words" here. In the book of Samuel the only other instance of the plural phrase is in the construct chain כָּל־דִּבְרֵי יְהוָה, "all the words of Yahweh," in 8:10.

15:2 יְהוָה צְבָאוֹת—For "Yahweh of armies," see the fourth textual note on 1:3.

פָּקַדְתִּי—"I noted." The verb פָּקַד often denotes taking an interest in something or closely observing a situation.[3] More commonly in Samuel, however, it refers to mustering troops for battle, as in 15:4, where וַיְפַקְדֵם essentially means Saul "counted/numbered them." For that meaning, see the textual note on 14:17.

שָׂם לוֹ בַּדֶּרֶךְ—This clause explains the preceding reference to "what Amalek did." Literally Amalek "placed against him [Israel] in the way," i.e., opposed Israel when the people were on the way to the promised land. The preposition לְ (with suffix: לוֹ) has the sense of disadvantage (BDB, s.v. לְ, 5 g (*b*) γ). For a similar use of שִׂים without a direct object to signify an attack, see 1 Ki 20:12.

בַּעֲלֹתוֹ מִמִּצְרָיִם:—This means "when he came up from Egypt." The clause recurs in 15:6 but with a plural suffix (בַּעֲלוֹתָם) on the Qal (G) infinitive construct of עָלָה, "to go up." In the exodus narrative עָלָה depicted Israel's deliverance from Egypt (e.g., Ex 12:38; 13:18). (For the Hiphil [H] of עָלָה, God "brought up" Israel, and other exodus vocabulary, see the textual note on 10:18–19.)

15:3 לֵךְ וְהִכִּיתָה—This is translated as "go, attack." These two verbs form a hendiadys in Hebrew. The Qal (G) imperative of הָלַךְ is often used asyndetically before another imperative (Joüon, § 177 e). In form וְהִכִּיתָה is a Hiphil (H) perfect (of נָכָה) with *waw* consecutive, but it functions as an imperative. It is one of a number of second masculine singular perfect verb forms in this chapter that have the longer ending תָה- instead of the usual shorter ending תָ-. See GKC, § 44 g. See also וְהֵמַתָּה in 15:3; עָשִׂיתָה in 15:6; וְהַחֲרַמְתָּה in 15:18; and מָאַסְתָּה in 15:26.

וְהַחֲרַמְתֶּם—"And completely destroy" is a second masculine plural Hiphil (H) perfect with *waw* consecutive of חָרַם. While often glossed as "place under the ban," it refers to total destruction in conquest, as, for example, Joshua was commanded to do to Jericho (Josh 6:17–18, 21). Hiphil (H) forms of this verb recur in 1 Sam 15:8, 9, 15, 18,

---

[2] 1 Ki 22:19; 2 Ki 7:1; 20:16; Is 1:10; 28:14; 39:5; 66:5; Jer 2:4; 7:2; 17:20; 19:3; 21:11; 22:2, 29; 29:20; 31:10; 34:4; 42:15; 44:24, 26; Ezek 13:2; 16:35; 21:3 (ET 20:47); 34:9; 36:1; 37:4; Hos 4:1; Amos 7:16; 2 Chr 18:18.

[3] See the discussion in *TWOT*, § 1802.

20. See also the cognate noun חֵרֶם in the textual note on 15:21. In the book of Samuel these terms appear only in 1 Samuel 15.

וְלֹא תַחְמֹל עָלָיו—The Qal (G) verb and the preposition in the prohibition here, literally "and you shall not have pity on him," are repeated in the record of Saul's direct disobedience, וַיַּחְמֹל ... עַל־, "and Saul ... had pity on" (15:9).

וְהֵמַתָּה מֵאִישׁ עַד־אִשָּׁה—The Hiphil (H) (second masculine singular perfect with *waw* consecutive) of מוּת, "die," has the causative meaning "to put to death." The combination of the prepositions מִן ... עַד, "from ... until," with the two opposites, "man" and "woman," encompasses the whole people. See the same wording in 1 Sam 22:19; 2 Sam 6:19; and also, e.g., in Josh 6:21, where Yahweh commands the destruction (Hiphil of חָרַם) of all the people in Jericho. The following phrase with the same combination of prepositions, "from child [עֹלֵל] to nursing infant [יוֹנֵק]," clarifies that even the youngest are to be included. Then the next two phrases with the same combination of prepositions indicate the inclusion of all domesticated animals in two classes. See further the first diagram in "Saul's Attack on the Amalekites (15:1–9)" in the commentary.

15:4 וַיְשַׁמַּע שָׁאוּל—The Piel (D) of שָׁמַע, "to hear," has a causative meaning, "to make (people) hear" a mandate or summons, thus "Saul summoned." The form is a preterite (imperfect with *waw* consecutive) third masculine singular. This verb occurs in the D stem only twice in the OT, both times in Samuel: here and in 1 Sam 23:8.

בַּטְּלָאִים—This means "at the lambs," but apparently טְלָאִים is a place-name not mentioned elsewhere in the OT, hence "at Telaim." However, a place called טֶלֶם, "Telem," in the southern reaches of Judah is mentioned in Josh 15:24. This would fit well with the account of pursuing the Amalekites to Shur on the border of Egypt (1 Sam 15:7). Perhaps the original reading was טלם but it was misvocalized as the plural noun טְלָאִים. The LXX reads ἐν Γαλγαλοις, "at Gilgal."

מָאתַיִם אֶלֶף רַגְלִי וַעֲשֶׂרֶת אֲלָפִים אֶת־אִישׁ יְהוּדָה:—This means "two hundred thousand infantry and ten thousand men of Judah." The noun רַגְלִי, "infantry," is the combination of רֶגֶל, "foot," and the gentilic suffix ־ִי, forming a noun meaning "one who travels by foot" or "a foot soldier." The LXX reads τετρακοσίας χιλιάδας ταγμάτων καὶ τὸν Ιουδαν τριάκοντα χιλιάδας ταγμάτων, "four hundred thousand units and Judah, thirty thousand units." The noun τάγμα denotes a military "unit" or "division, brigade." The LXX is a secondary reading that has suffered from the tendency to inflate numbers as texts are transmitted.

15:5 וַיֶּרֶב—"And (he) set up an ambush" is apparently a Hiphil (H) preterite (imperfect with *waw* consecutive) from אָרַב, "to lie in wait." It is contracted from וַיַּאְרֶב after the א quiesces (GKC, § 68 i). This meaning is supported by ἐνήδρευσεν in the LXX.

15:6 לְכוּ סֻּרוּ רְדוּ מִתּוֹךְ עֲמָלֵקִי—Three Qal (G) imperatives (of יָרַד, סוּר, הָלַךְ, and) are heaped up for emphasis: "Go! Turn aside! Go down from among (the) Amalekite(s)."

פֶּן־אֹסִפְךָ עִמּוֹ—Literally "lest I destroy you with him." The verb is the first common singular Qal (G) imperfect (with second masculine singular object suffix) of אָסַף (see Joüon, § 61 d, notes 3–4). In the Qal it usually means "to gather" (e.g., 14:52; 17:1), but occasionally it can mean "to destroy" (see BDB, Qal, 4).

15:7 שׁוּר בֹּאֲךָ מֵחֲוִילָה֙—Literally this means "from Havilah [until] *you* come to Shur." The Qal (G) infinitive construct of בּוֹא with the second masculine singular suffix is used with a place-name to signify an approximate region near a place.[4] Shur was in the Sinai Peninsula east of the Red Sea and the Bitter Lakes.[5]

15:9 וְעַל־מֵיטַב הַצֹּאן֙ וְהַבָּקָר וְהַמִּשְׁנִים—The construct phrase מֵיטַב הַצֹּאן֙ forms a superlative: "the best of the flocks." Normally in Hebrew one head noun (מֵיטַב) cannot be in construct with multiple nouns (Joüon, § 129 a) unless they are in construct with one another, forming a construct chain. But here מֵיטַב is in construct with each of the three following nouns: הַצֹּאן֙ וְהַבָּקָר וְהַמִּשְׁנִים. Similarly, in 15:15 מֵיטַב is in construct with the first two of the three nouns here (מֵיטַב הַצֹּאן֙ וְהַבָּקָר). English readily allows one head noun to be followed by multiple genitives, as in the translation: "the best of the flocks, of the herds, and of the fattened calves."

וְהַמִּשְׁנִים is literally "and the double portions." The LXX reads καὶ τῶν ἐδεσμάτων, "and the cooked foods." The translation "the fattened calves" for the noun is conjectural, but fits the context well. The original Hebrew may have been וְהַמִּשְׁמַנִים, "and the fatty foods" (the plural of מַשְׁמָן, as in Neh 8:10). If so, the MT suffered from the loss of a *mem*, whereas the LXX translators missed the nuance of the Hebrew.

וְעַל־כָּל־הַטּוֹב—The adjective טוֹב, "good," with the definite article forms a superlative, "the best." See the first textual note on 8:14.

וְכָל־הַמְּלָאכָה נְמִבְזָה וְנָמֵס—The definite feminine noun הַמְּלָאכָה here means "the property." The next two words appear to modify it adjectivally; in form נְמִבְזָה is feminine but נָמֵס is masculine. נְמִבְזָה might be a mixed form combining נִבְזָה, the feminine singular Niphal (N) participle of בָּזָה, "to despise," and the Hophal (Hp) participle of the same verb, מֻבְזָה (see GKC, § 75 y). The meaning "despised" is supported by the LXX's ἠτιμωμένον. The second word is a Niphal (N) masculine singular participle from מָסַס, "melt" or "be weak."

15:11 נִחַמְתִּי—This first common singular perfect form of נָחַם could be Piel (D), "to comfort" (as in 2 Sam 10:2–3; 12:24), but in this context it must be Niphal (N). The Niphal (N) has the nuance "regret" or "be sorry" (*HALOT*, 1 and 2, respectively) here and in 15:35. These verses refer to God's consequent will: Yahweh regrets making Saul king because of the disastrous consequences of Saul's sinful disobedience. In 15:29, however, the Niphal (twice) has the nuance "change one's mind." That verse refers to God's immutable will; God does not "lie" nor "change his mind" as fickle sinful people do (15:29). See also the second textual note on 15:29. In still other contexts, when God has threatened judgment or has even started to execute it, the Niphal of נָחַם can mean that God "relents" of the punishment as his disposition toward people changes from anger (caused by their transgression of his Law) to grace (according to his Gospel, which bestows forgiveness on the penitent). Thus, in 2 Sam 24:16 Yahweh "relented" of the plague that had already destroyed a large portion of the population. See also, famously, the Niphal of נָחַם in Jonah 3:9–10; 4:2.

---

[4] Gen 10:19, 30; 13:10; 25:18; Judg 6:4; 11:33; 1 Sam 17:52; 27:8; 1 Ki 18:46.

[5] See Gen 16:7; 20:1; 25:18; Ex 15:22; 1 Sam 27:8.

הִמְלַכְתִּי אֶת־שָׁאוּל לְמֶלֶךְ—For the Hiphil (H) of מָלַךְ in a cognate accusative construction, literally "to king a king," see the first textual note on 8:22.

שָׁב מֵאַחֲרַי—The preposition "after" has a pregnant sense, "he has turned from *following* me." See second textual note on 12:14. (Contrast the different nuance in וַיָּשָׁב שְׁמוּאֵל אַחֲרֵי שָׁאוּל in 15:31.)

וְאֶת־דְּבָרַי לֹא הֵקִים—The idiom with the Hiphil (H) of קוּם, literally "to raise up, cause to stand," and "word(s)" as the direct object, means "to carry out, fulfill," as again in 15:13 (see BDB, s.v. קוּם, Hiphil, 6 f). Here it is negated as a statement of fact; Saul makes his false claim with this idiom in the positive in 15:13.

15:12 וַיַּשְׁכֵּם—For "he rose up early," see the first textual note on 9:26.

לִקְרַאת—For "to meet," see the second textual note on 4:1.

יָד—Normally this noun means "hand." It is used twice in the book of Samuel (here and in 2 Sam 18:18) to mean "monument" (*HALOT*, 6 a).

At the end of the verse the LXX adds πρὸς Σαουλ, καὶ ἰδοὺ αὐτὸς ἀνέφερεν ὁλοκαύτωσιν τῷ κυρίῳ τὰ πρῶτα τῶν σκύλων, ὧν ἤνεγκεν ἐξ Αμαληκ, "to Saul, and he was offering to the Lord as a whole burnt offering the firsts of the spoils he had brought from Amalek." Some believe this text was lost by homoioteleuton from the presumed occurrence of אֶל־שָׁאוּל at the beginning of the missing section to אֶל־שָׁאוּל near the beginning of 15:13.[6] However, this does not explain the first two words in 15:13, וַיָּבֹא שְׁמוּאֵל, which ought to have been dropped from the text if this were a case of homoioteleuton. Instead, the LXX appears to be a deliberate expansion of the text in anticipation of 15:15.

15:13 בָּרוּךְ אַתָּה לַיהוָה—In context this is likely a prayer, "may you be blessed by Yahweh," rather than a simple statement of fact, "you are blessed by Yahweh." Such a blessing with the Qal passive (Gp) participle of בָּרַךְ is antonymous to a curse with אָרוּר, as in 14:24, 28.

15:15 מֵעֲמָלֵקִי—The MT reads "from an/the Amalekite(s)." The translation "from Amalek" is based on the LXX.

אֲשֶׁר חָמַל הָעָם עַל־ ... לְמַעַן זְבֹחַ—This is translated as "for the troops spared." אֲשֶׁר has a causal sense, "for, because" (see Joüon, § 170 e). In 15:9 the action of "taking pity on" or "sparing" was attributed first to Saul and then to the troops as well: וַיַּחְמֹל שָׁאוּל וְהָעָם עַל־, "Saul and the troops spared ..." Here Saul shirks his responsibility and shifts the blame by attributing the action to the troops alone. Then he offers a false pretense: "in order to sacrifice."

אֱלֹהֶיךָ—Saul repeats "your God" in 15:21, 30. Never in this chapter does Saul call Yahweh "my God," nor does Samuel ever call Yahweh "your [Saul's] God." Is Saul trying to appease Samuel by calling Yahweh "your God"? Or is Saul trying to seduce him into joining his apostasy (see the commentary)? Or does he unwittingly intimate that his disobedience has stemmed from a loss of faith so that he no longer calls upon Yahweh as "my God"?

---

[6] McCarter, *I Samuel*, 262–63; Klein, *1 Samuel*, 146.

הַיּוֹתֵר—This is the only instance in the OT of a Qal (G) form of the verb יָתַר, "to remain over." This (definite) masculine singular participle functions as an equivalent of the noun יֶתֶר, "remainder, remnant."

15:16 הֶרֶף—For this Hiphil (H) imperative of רָפָה, here translated as "stop!" see the first textual note on 11:3.

הַלַּיְלָה—This is translated as "last night." Like הַיּוֹם, which can mean "today," הַלַּיְלָה can mean "tonight," i.e., the night of the current solar day. Since Israel considered the solar day to begin at sundown, this refers to the night just past, which was part of the present day from Samuel's perspective. For English speakers who consider the day to begin at midnight (or more colloquially in the morning), it corresponds to "last night."

וַיֹּאמֶר—"And/so he said" is the Qere, which agrees with the LXX (καὶ εἶπεν); the Kethib is וַיֹּאמְרוּ, "and they said."

15:18 וְהַחֲרַמְתָּה אֶת־הַחַטָּאִים—The verb here is singular, which emphasizes Saul's responsibility to carry out the action; the verb in 15:3 was plural but otherwise identical (see the second textual note there). The article on הַחַטָּאִים has a demonstrative force, "*those* sinners."[7] Ironically, the root חטא appears in chapter 15 in this reference to "sinners" who should have been destroyed and in Saul's two confessions, "I have sinned" (חָטָאתִי, 15:24, 30), as if Saul belongs in the same category of "sinners" as the Amalekites. (The only other instance of the root in this chapter is the noun חַטָּאת, "sin," in 15:23, 25.) Each of his confessions is elicited only after Samuel declares that Yahweh has revoked his kingship (15:23, 28–29).

עַד כַּלּוֹתָם אֹתָם—Literally "until they finish off them," this is translated as "until *you* finish them off" since Samuel is speaking to Saul. The Piel (D) of כָּלָה has a transitive meaning, "to finish, complete" something, and in military contexts means to "destroy, exterminate" (see BDB, 2 c). The Piel (D) infinitive construct כַּלּוֹתָם has a third masculine plural suffix, which is its subject, "until they [Saul's troops] finish off." The third masculine plural suffix on the direct object marker, אֹתָם ("them"), refers to the Amalekites and their property.

15:19 וְלָמָּה—The translation considers the force of the interrogative, "why?" to extend through the end of the verse; the verse then consists of two questions.

וַתַּעַט—For עִיט, "pounce," see the first textual note on 14:32.

15:20 אֲשֶׁר—The relative pronoun introduces direct discourse here (Joüon, § 157 c; cf. 2 Sam 1:4).

15:21 רֵאשִׁית הַחֵרֶם—This construct phrase forms a superlative, "the first," i.e., "the best" of "what was to be destroyed." The noun חֵרֶם is cognate to the verb חָרַם; see the second textual note on 15:3.

15:22 הַחֵפֶץ לַיהוָה בְּעֹלוֹת וּזְבָחִים כִּשְׁמֹעַ בְּקוֹל יְהוָה—This is a comparison with the interrogative *he*, literally "does a desire belong to Yahweh in burnt offerings and sacrifices as (much as in) listening to the voice of Yahweh?"

---

[7] See Waltke-O'Connor, § 13.5.1d, including example 7.

הִנֵּה שְׁמֹעַ מִזֶּבַח טוֹב לְהַקְשִׁיב מֵחֵלֶב אֵילִים׃—The adjective טוֹב, "good," with the preposition מִן forms a comparative, "behold, to listen/obey is better than sacrifice; to pay attention [is better] than the fat of rams." Not counting הִנֵּה, each of the two clauses begins with an infinitive construct and consists of three Hebrew words.

15:23 חַטַּאת־קֶסֶם מֶרִי—The subject of this nominal clause is the noun מְרִי, "rebellion," which is derived from the verb מָרָה, "to rebel." In the book of Samuel the noun appears only here and the verb appears only in 1 Sam 12:14, 15, in Samuel's warning of divine judgment upon Israel and its king if they rebel.

וְאָוֶן וּתְרָפִים—The two nouns are juxtaposed, literally "wickedness and *teraphim*," but form a hendiadys, "the wickedness of idolatry" or "wicked idolatry." תְּרָפִים, *teraphim*, were idol images representing household gods.[8]

הַפְצַר—This is translated as "willfulness." It is the Hiphil (H) infinitive absolute of פָּצַר, which in the Qal (G) means "to urge, coerce." This is the only instance of the Hiphil, meaning "to be willful, arrogant, obstinate." The infinitive absolute serves as a verbal noun and so is the subject of the nominal-like clause וְאָוֶן וּתְרָפִים הַפְצַר.

יַעַן מָאַסְתָּ אֶת־דְּבַר יְהוָה וַיִּמְאָסְךָ מִמֶּלֶךְ׃—The Qal (G) of מָאַס I, "to reject, repudiate," appears twice here, twice more in 15:26, and again in 16:1, 7. To reject God's Word is to repudiate God and be rejected by him. The Word said, "Whoever rejects me rejects him who sent me" (Lk 10:16). See also Mt 10:33; Lk 12:9. The preposition מִן on מִמֶּלֶךְ has a privative sense, "from [being] king." See the longer synonymous expression מִהְיוֹת מֶלֶךְ in 15:26.

15:24 עָבַרְתִּי אֶת־פִּי־יְהוָה וְאֶת־דְּבָרֶיךָ—Literally "I have crossed over the mouth of Yahweh and your words." By metonymy "the mouth of Yahweh" (פִּי־יְהוָה, as in 12:14, 15) refers to what Yahweh's mouth has uttered, thus "Yahweh's command." By referring first to Yahweh and then to "*your* words" Saul acknowledges that Samuel served as Yahweh's mouthpiece.

15:25 שָׂא נָא אֶת־חַטָּאתִי—The verb שָׂא is the Qal (G) imperative of נָשָׂא, "bear, carry, take away," which can have the nuance "forgive" when used with sin (BDB, Qal, 3 c).

וְאֶשְׁתַּחֲוֶה לַיהוָה׃—For the Hishtaphel of חָוָה, "to worship," see the third textual note on 1:3. Different inflections of it recur in 15:30, 31.

15:27 וַיַּחֲזֵק בִּכְנַף־מְעִילוֹ—"And he grabbed the hem of his robe." The Hiphil (H) of חָזַק, "be strong," frequently means "take or keep hold of, seize" and often takes the preposition בְּ (see BDB, Hiphil, 6 and 6 a). The MT lacks an explicit subject for the verb; "Saul" is named in 4QSamᵃ (ויחזק שאול) and the LXX. The noun כָּנָף refers to something's edge or extremity, such as a bird's wing. Here it is the "hem" of Samuel's robe.

וַיִּקָּרַע׃—"And it tore" is a Niphal (N) preterite (imperfect with *waw* consecutive) of קָרַע. For this verb the Niphal is intransitive. 4QSamᵃ reads ויקרעהו, "and he tore it," a Qal (G) preterite with third masculine singular object suffix. Similar is the LXX: καὶ διέρρηξεν αὐτό. It is difficult to choose between these readings. The MT offers

---

8   Also Gen 31:19, 34, 35; Judg 17:5; 18:14, 17, 18, 20; 1 Sam 19:13, 16; 2 Ki 23:24; Ezek 21:26 (ET 21:21); Hos 3:4; Zech 10:2. See *TWOT*, § 2545, which states: "In all but one somewhat ambiguous context (I Sam 19:11–17), it is clear that the teraphim of ancient Israel were pagan household idols."

the harder reading, whereas 4QSamᵃ may preserve a lost suffix. In either alternative, the sense is the same.

15:28 וּנְתָנָהּ לְרֵעֲךָ הַטּוֹב מִמֶּךָּ—Here the adjective טוֹב with the definite article and the suffixed preposition מִן forms a comparative: "who is better than you." Cf. the second textual note on 15:9 and second textual note on 15:22.

15:29 נֵצַח יִשְׂרָאֵל—This is translated as "the Glory of Israel." Since נֵצַח can also mean "perpetual," some translate this title as "the Eternal One of Israel" (HCSB; cf. *HALOT*, 1 and 2).

וְלֹא יִנָּחֵם—"Nor does he change his mind." For the Niphal (N) of נָחַם, see the first textual note on 15:11. 4QSamᵃ reads ולו[א] ישוב [ולוא] ינחם, "nor does he turn or change his mind," as does the LXX: καὶ οὐκ ἀποστρέψει οὐδὲ μετανοήσει.

15:31 וַיִּשְׁתַּחוּ שָׁאוּל לַיהוָה:—"And Saul worshiped Yahweh." Despite appearing plural, the verb וַיִּשְׁתַּחוּ is singular (third masculine Hishtaphel preterite [imperfect with *waw* consecutive] of חָוָה; see the third textual note on 1:3). "Saul" is not named in 4QSamᵃ, which reads וישת[ח]ו ליהוה], "and he worshiped Yahweh," nor in the LXX, καὶ προσεκύνησεν τῷ κυρίῳ.

15:32 מַעֲדַנֹּת—This is understood to be an adverb meaning "trembling." Others take it as a feminine plural noun that is used as an adverbial accusative: "in fetters."[9] It is much debated. The NET note on 1 Sam 15:32 says:

> The word is found only here and in Job 38:31. Part of the problem lies in determining the root of the word. Some scholars have taken it to be from the root ענד (ʿnd, "to bind around"), but this assumes a metathesis of two of the letters of the root. Others take it from the root עדן (ʿdn) with the meaning "voluptuously," but this does not seem to fit the context. It seems better to understand the word to be from the root מעד (mʿd, "to totter" or "shake"). In that case it describes the fear that Agag experienced in realizing the mortal danger that he faced as he approached Samuel. This is the way that the LXX translators understood the word, rendering it by the Greek participle τρέμων (*tremon*, "trembling").

Tsumura believes that it means "cheerfully" since he follows the MT of the next clause[10] (see the next textual note).

אָכֵן סָר מַר־הַמָּוֶת:—The adverb אָכֵן can mean "surely, certainly" (see BDB, a). מַר (from the root מרר) could be an adjective, "bitter," or a substantive, "bitterness." Thus, the MT likely means "surely the bitterness of death has turned away," which suggests that Agag was confident that he would be spared yet again. However, the LXX reads εἰ οὕτως πικρὸς ὁ θάνατος; "is death thus bitter?" (*NETS*). Two Old Latin manuscripts and the Syriac Peshitta read "surely death is bitter," which fits the interpretation of the earlier word מַעֲדַנֹּת as "trembling" (see the preceding textual note). If that is the correct

---

[9] See BDB, s.v. מַעֲדַנּוֹת, under the root מעד; GKC, § 118 q; McCarter, *1 Samuel*, 264.

[10] Tsumura, *The First Book of Samuel*, 408, including n. 90.

meaning, it would presuppose a Hebrew reading אָכֵן סָר הַמָּוֶת. Then the MT might have resulted from a diplography of מר as סר, with a confusion of *samek* and *mem*.[11]

15:33 כַּאֲשֶׁר שִׁכְּלָה נָשִׁים חַרְבֶּךָ כֵּן־תִּשְׁכַּל מִנָּשִׁים אִמֶּךָ—As מָאַס, "reject," was repeated in both 15:23 and 15:26, the repetition of the same verb (שָׁכַל) in both clauses here reflects the *lex talionis*: the punishment fits the crime. In the first clause שָׁכַל is in the Piel (D) stem, which has a causative meaning, "to make someone childless, bereave." Its third singular perfect form is feminine, to match the gender of its subject noun חֶרֶב, "sword." In the second clause שָׁכַל is in the Qal (G) stem, "to be childless, bereaved." Most interpret the prepositional phrase מִנָּשִׁים as meaning "among women," but it could be a comparative or superlative, "most of all women," in the metaphorical sense that of all bereaved women Agag's mother might experience the greatest grief because the son she lost had been king.

וַיְשַׁסֵּף—The meaning of this Piel (D) preterite (imperfect with *waw* consecutive) of שָׁסַף is uncertain. This verb occurs only here in the OT. The context and versions support something like "cut to pieces."

15:35 וְלֹא־יָסַף שְׁמוּאֵל לִרְאוֹת אֶת־שָׁאוּל—For this construction, the Qal (G) of יָסַף, "to do again," followed by an infinitive construct, לִרְאוֹת (the Qal of רָאָה, "to see, look at"), see Joüon, §§ 102 g, 124 c, 177 b. See also the first textual note on 3:6. For the contextual meaning, see the commentary.

הִתְאַבֵּל שְׁמוּאֵל אֶל־שָׁאוּל—The Hithpael (HtD) of אָבַל, "to mourn," will recur in the same sense in 16:1. It referred to the mourning of the Israelites in 6:19 after they were defeated by the enemy.

Commentary

c. 1020 BC

In this chapter we learn that due to Saul's desire to strengthen his dominion over Israel by pleasing the people, he failed to carry out God's command completely (15:24). Thus, he only partly executed God's mandate given through Samuel (15:3). Later, David would seek to fortify his reign over Israel by conducting a census to determine how many men in Israel were of fighting age (2 Samuel 24).[12] In light of the rebellions of Absalom (2 Samuel 15–18) and Sheba (2 Samuel 20), David felt the need to know the total of men who might be drafted into his service. It is not surprising, then, that the author has narrated the historical events with a number of literary parallels to link these two chapters. See figure 21.

---

[11] Talmon, "1 Sam. xv 32b—A Case of Conflated Readings?" 457.

[12] Note that David commanded Joab, *the commander of the army*, to conduct the census (2 Sam 24:2). This indicates for what purpose David ordered the census taken.

Figure 21

Parallels between 1 Samuel 15 and 2 Samuel 24

Feature	1 Samuel 15	2 Samuel 24	Elsewhere in Samuel
פָּקַד (Qal), "to note, pay attention, muster, count"	15:2, 4	24:2, 4	1 Sam 2:21; 11:8; 13:15; 14:17; 17:18; 20:6; 25:15; 2 Sam 3:8; 18:1
Separate total for Judah	15:4	24:9	1 Sam 11:8
דְּבַר יהוה, "the Word of Yahweh"	15:1,† 10, 13, 23, 26	24:11	1 Sam 3:1, 7, 21; 8:10;† 2 Sam 7:4; 12:9
רָפָה (Hiphil), "stop, leave alone"	15:16	24:16	1 Sam 11:3
חָטָא (Qal), "to sin," or חַטָּאת, "a sin"—the king confesses his sin	15:24, 25, 30	24:10, 17	1 Sam 26:21; 2 Sam 12:13
נָשָׂא (Qal) or עָבַר (Hiphil), "to forgive (sin)"	15:25	24:10	2 Sam 12:13
נָחַם (Niphal) with God as subject: "regret" or "change one's mind"	15:11, 29, 35††	24:16	

†In 1 Sam 15:1 (as in 8:10) the MT has the plural, "the words of [דִּבְרֵי] Yahweh." LXX 1 Sam 15:1, however, omits "the words of." See the third textual note on 15:1.

††In 1 Sam 15:35, the subject of the verb is יהוה, "Yahweh." In 15:11 Yahweh speaks in the first person ("I regret"). In 15:29, the implied subject is נֵצַח יִשְׂרָאֵל, "the Glory of Israel," which refers to Yahweh. For the distinct nuances of the verb נָחַם, see the first textual note on 15:11.

This figure is adapted from Auld, *I & II Samuel*, 177.

Of these parallels between chapters 15 and 24, three stand out as particularly significant for the message of this chapter: First, the phrase "the Word/words of Yahweh" appears in both chapters as a characterization of the message from a prophet to the king: from Samuel to Saul in 1 Sam 15:1, 10, 13, 23,

26, and from Gad to David in 2 Sam 24:11.[13] However, there is a contrast in that the divine Word came to Saul *before* he sinned by transgressing it ("now listen to the voice of the words of Yahweh," 1 Sam 15:1), whereas it came to David (2 Sam 24:11) *after* he repented of his prior sin (2 Sam 24:10).

Second, in each chapter the king confessed his sin, but once again there is a contrast between David and Saul. Saul confessed his sin to Samuel twice (1 Sam 15:24–25, 30), but each confession came only *after* a harsh rebuke by Samuel and the revocation of Saul's kingship (1 Sam 15:22–23, 26–29). Saul never confessed his sin directly to Yahweh. But David repented and confessed his sin to Yahweh (2 Sam 24:10) *before* Gad spoke the Word of Yahweh to him (2 Sam 24:11–13).

Third, both chapters employ the verb נָחַם to say that Yahweh "regretted" or "relented" his action.[14] This also highlights the contrast between Saul and David. Yahweh "regretted" that he had made Saul king after he transgressed his Word (1 Sam 15:35; see also 1 Sam 15:11), whereas in the case of penitent David, God "relented" from the plague that was destroying Jerusalem (2 Sam 24:16), "the city of David" (2 Sam 5:7, 9; 6:10, 12, 16).

Although both Saul and David were chosen by God, these contrasts serve to demonstrate to readers why God rejected Saul and replaced him with David (1 Sam 15:26–29), who, despite his transgressions, remained in God's favor.[15] Saul spurned God's Word and did not allow it to give him a proper attitude toward it, nor did he learn a proper response to it—neither after receiving instructions from Samuel (1 Sam 15:2–3) nor after being confronted further by Samuel (1 Sam 15:14, 17–19). Instead, he made pious excuses in an attempt to justify his disobedient actions (1 Sam 15:15, 20–21). Although David initially overrode Joab's objections to his action (2 Sam 24:3–4), after further consideration of God's prior revelation his guilty conscience moved him to repent and confess (2 Sam 24:10) before being confronted by Gad. When Gad came with Yahweh's Word, David offered no excuse, but took refuge in God's "mercy" (2 Sam 24:14; cf. 2 Sam 12:13). Thus, Yahweh's favor remained on the adulterous, murderous, willfully self-centered David who repented and trusted in God—even the righteously angry God—rather than man (2 Sam 24:14).

---

[13] Note that "the Word of Yahweh" occurs five times in these two chapters (1 Sam 15:10, 13, 23, 26; 2 Sam 24:11) and only another five times elsewhere in the book of Samuel (1 Sam 3:1, 7, 21; 2 Sam 7:4; 12:9). The plural phrase "the words of Yahweh" appears once in these chapters (1 Sam 15:1) and only once elsewhere in the book (1 Sam 8:10).

[14] See the first textual note on 15:11.

[15] If one seeks to resolve the mystery of why some believe God's Word, continue in repentant faith, and ultimately are saved, whereas others who initially believe fall from the faith and ultimately are damned, a two-part answer must be given. First, God's choosing or election is by grace alone, not based on any superior quality or receptiveness on the part of those who are called to faith. He speaks his same Word of salvation to all humanity. Both God's initial calling to faith and his preservation of believers in the faith are actions he alone accomplishes. Second, those who fall from faith, refuse to repent, and are lost are solely to blame for their sinful rejection of God's Word. God does not predestine any to perish, but wills that all be saved. See FC SD II, "Free Will or Human Powers," and FC SD XI, "Eternal Foreknowledge and Divine Election."

Saul's Attack on the Amalekites (15:1–9)

This account opens rather abruptly with the simple statement that Samuel spoke to Saul (15:1). Samuel's words begin by emphasizing his relationship with Saul as the one whom Yahweh commissioned to consecrate Saul as king (10:1). In Hebrew the sentence places the pronoun *me* in the emphatic initial position: *"me* Yahweh sent to anoint you king …" (15:1). The pronoun calls attention to Samuel's role as God's spokesman to the monarchy (e.g., chapters 8–10). Samuel directly quotes God, calling him "Yahweh of armies" (15:2), a title that emphasizes that Israel's armies are ultimately God's.[16]

The preface to Saul's instruction recalls the incident of Amalek's attack on Israel in Ex 17:8–13. Moses prophesied that God would have victory over Amalek in every generation (Ex 17:14–16) and later instructed the Israelites that, after God gave them rest in the land, they were to blot out Amalek's memory (Deut 25:17–19). The Israelites had not done that, and so Amalek had continued to oppress them (Judg 3:13; 6:3, 33; 7:12; 10:12). Now Yahweh commands Saul to be his instrument to carry out his instructions through Moses.

Saul's orders were clear: he was to "completely destroy" the Amalekites (see the second textual note on 15:3). This type of warfare—the ban involving the total destruction of enemies and their property—had applied only to cities and people in the promised land (Deut 20:10–18), but God was now extending it into the south where the Amalekites lived. Even though the meaning of the verb "completely destroy" (the Hiphil [H] of חָרַם) left no doubt, Samuel elaborates it so that Saul cannot mistake what he is to do (15:3). Those to be destroyed are listed in four groups (each with two elements): adults, youth, animals used for agricultural production, and pack animals. Fokkelman notes God's multiple binary complements of those to be destroyed:[17]

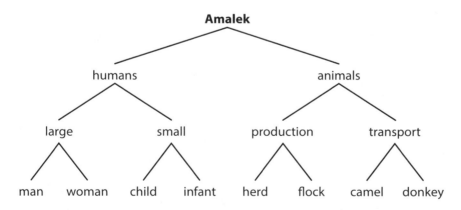

---

[16] See the fourth textual note and the commentary on 1:3.

[17] Fokkelman, *The Crossing Fates*, 89; the diagram is slightly adapted.

At first Saul appeared to have obeyed. He mustered his troops at Telaim on Judah's southern border (see the second textual note on 15:4) with a large army under his command. He then proceeded southward to "the city of Amalek" (15:5), an unknown location. However, judging from the geographical references, it appears to have been near Egypt. Perhaps the "ravine" (נַחַל) where Saul set up his ambush is the Brook of Egypt[18] on the southern border of Judah.

Saul gave the Kenites, who had been kind to Israel (Judg 1:16; 4:11–21; 5:24–27; cf. Num 24:20–21), opportunity to escape before he attacked (1 Sam 15:6). Had they stayed among the Amalekites, they would have been totally destroyed, so they took Saul's warning to heart and left. In showing this kindness, Saul demonstrated that he not only understood Yahweh's instructions but also the reason for them.

While at first it seemed that Saul was obedient, his execution of Yahweh's orders fell short. He appears to have been thorough enough in his geographic coverage—from Havilah to Shur (15:7; see the textual note on that verse)—but did not follow through by destroying everything. King Agag was captured—alive (15:8). To this point the reader might see Saul as completely obedient to Yahweh. However, the next verse brings disappointment as "Saul and the troops" selectively spared the best of the Amalekites (Agag) and the best of their animals (15:9). In doing this they subvert God's binary arrangement of the Amalekites into a set of new binary complements, as noted by Fokkelman:[19]

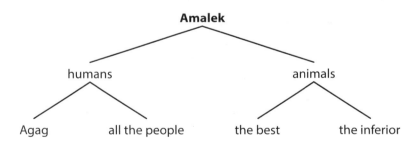

A partial obedience is no obedience. God calls his people to be holy and perfect, even as he is holy and perfect (Lev 19:2; 20:26; Deut 18:13; Mt 5:48). Whoever is guilty of breaking one of God's commands has broken all of them (James 2:10; cf. Num 15:39–40; Deut 28:15; Mt 5:19; Gal 5:3).

---

[18] נַחַל מִצְרַיִם, Num 34:5; Josh 15:4, 47; 1 Ki 8:65; 2 Ki 24:7; Is 27:12; 2 Chr 7:8; cf. Gen 15:18.

[19] Fokkelman, *The Crossing Fates*, 89; the diagram is slightly adapted.

Samuel Confronts Saul (15:10–35)

With the disobedience of Saul the scene shifts to Samuel as God informed him of the king's failure to carry out his instructions (15:10–11). God told Samuel that he regretted making Saul king. The verb "regret" (the Niphal [N] of נָחַם) expresses remorse or sorrow consequent to an action.[20] On many occasions God is its subject.[21] It is used twice this way in this chapter (15:11, 35). Many find these statements troubling, since Scripture clearly asserts that God does not change (Mal 3:6; Ps 102:27–28 [ET 102:26–27]; James 1:17).[22] Furthermore, Samuel told Saul that God does not lie or change his mind, for his will is perfect and immutable (1 Sam 15:29; a close parallel is Num 23:19; see also, e.g., Ps 110:4; Heb 7:21). How then are we to understand this seeming contradiction? When this verb (נָחַם) is used of God, the Scriptures are—or have been—revealing to us his compassion and long-suffering. In his forbearance he overlooks sin for a time in order to lead people to repentance (Rom 2:4; 2 Pet 3:9). The passages in which God "relents" or changes from judgment to grace—or even vice versa, after waiting patiently, as in the case of Saul—allow us to see the love and kindness of God.[23] This language in 1 Sam 15:11, 35 enables the reader to comprehend God's disappointment with one of his children. Yahweh himself had chosen, anointed, and endowed King Saul with his Spirit (10:1, 6, 10, 24; 11:6; 15:17), even though the omniscient God would have already known that the king would reject him (15:23, 26), even as the people had rejected God in asking for him (8:7; 10:19). Yet even then Yahweh did not strike Saul dead; instead, he sent Samuel to preach his Word and lead the fallen king to a recognition and confession of his sin. Although God had already chosen another (15:26–29), he would continue to appeal to Saul and even warn him in the depths of his apostasy[24] until his death (1 Samuel 31). Likewise, when Jesus chose his apostles, he already knew that Judas would betray him (Jn 6:64, 71), yet he still tried to dissuade his betrayer from the course of action that would lead to his perdition (Mt 26:21–25).

---

[20] See the first textual note on 15:11.

[21] See, e.g., Gen 6:6, 7; Ex 32:14; 2 Sam 24:16 ‖ 1 Chr 21:15; Jer 4:28; 15:6; 18:8, 10; 26:3, 13, 19; 42:10; Joel 2:13, 14; Amos 7:3, 6; Jonah 3:9, 10; 4:2; Ps 106:45.

[22] The understanding of God's relenting or change of disposition as a metaphor or anthropomorphism is long-standing. For instance, Gregory of Nyssa (c. AD 335–c. 395) explained it as an anthropomorphic metaphor (*Answer to Eumonius' Second Book*, 12.3 [*NPNF*[2] 5:292–93]). Barbara Green, *How Are the Mighty Fallen?* 250, expresses this view: "The notion is metaphorical and analogical, and some readers accept it more easily than others—which is to say that we tend to go along more easily with metaphors for God that do not trouble us than with those that do, which for many includes the notion of God changing the divine mind."

[23] In the book of Jonah, for example, God could have destroyed the Ninevites immediately, but instead he gave them forty days until judgment, then "relented" when they repented (Jonah 3:10; cf. Jonah 3:9; 4:2).

[24] 1 Sam 28:15–19. On that occasion (1 Sam 28:18) he is again reprimanded for his disobedience to the Word of Yahweh by not executing his wrath against Amalek here in 1 Samuel 15.

We are also told that Samuel was angry (1 Sam 15:11), but not against whom his anger was directed—although this will be made clear shortly (15:22–29). In the morning Samuel set out to meet Saul. We are not told who informed him of Saul's movements (perhaps Yahweh?), but they reveal Saul's lack of awareness of the seriousness of his disobedience to the divine command (15:12). He first glorified himself with a monument at the Judean city of Carmel (modern Khirbet al-Karmil), about eight miles (thirteen kilometers) southeast of Hebron (Josh 15:55; 1 Sam 25:2–42; 27:3; 30:5; 2 Sam 2:2; 3:3), and then proceeded eastward to Gilgal, the sacred location that has figured prominently in most of his interactions with Samuel (1 Sam 10:8; 11:14, 15; 13:4, 7, 8, 12, 15).

When Samuel caught up with Saul, the king exhibited no cognizance of his transgression of the very clear command he had been given (15:13; cf. 15:3). In fact, Saul expressly cloaked himself in outward piety, not only greeting Samuel with a blessing but also claiming to have fulfilled Yahweh's Word.

Samuel's reply directly points to Saul's sin—the best flocks and herds were spared (15:14). Instead of admitting his error, Saul made matters worse by attempting to justify his actions, disguising them under the mantle of even more false piety—the animals were for sacrifice to "Yahweh, *your* God" (15:15). By referring to Yahweh as Samuel's God, Saul added to his offense by seeking to recruit the prophet into an unholy alliance against God's expressed wishes. After such an outrageous attempt to corrupt the prophetic office, Samuel could only sharply rebuke Saul with a command to stop speaking and listen to what God had revealed to the prophet (15:16).

God's message was that even if Saul considered himself insignificant, he had a responsibility as the leader of Israel because of his God-given office as king (15:17). The characterizing of Saul as insignificant (קָטֹן, "little") is an indirect slight. As the tallest among Israel (9:2; 10:23), Saul was significantly more prominent than others. In addition, this is a veiled reference to Saul's initial reluctance to be king, since he came from the smallest of tribes (9:21).

As king, Saul was expected to obey God's command completely. He was told not only to completely destroy Amalek (חָרַם; see the second textual note on 15:3), but as Samuel further defined it, he was also to "finish them off" (see the second textual note on 15:18) specifically because that was God's punishment on them as "sinners" (חַטָּאִים, 15:18). Samuel's questions got to the heart of the matter: Why did Saul not obey? And why did he take plunder that was to be destroyed, thereby doing what Yahweh considered evil (15:19)? Each question places Yahweh's will at the center of the discussion. Samuel also accused Saul of "pouncing" (עִיט) on the spoil (15:19). Previously Saul had stopped the people from sinning when they had "pounced" (עִיט; see the first textual note on 14:32) on the spoil and ate meat with its blood (14:32–35). Now Saul was part of the pouncing on the spoil.

Saul countered that he had "obeyed Yahweh's voice" and accomplished his mission (15:20, rephrasing his assertion in 15:13). He maintained that sparing Agag while destroying the rest of the Amalekites was not a violation of

Yahweh's instructions. But his brazen defense started to crack as he diverted responsibility to the troops, a subtle indication that he knew he had sinned. In 15:21, as in 15:15, he blamed the troops for sparing the animals and construed their motive as wanting to offer a sacrifice. Moreover, he once again tried to recruit Samuel to participate in this fabricated rite by referring to "Yahweh *your* God" and to Gilgal.

The blame game is as old as humanity's fall into sin. Adam blamed Eve—and God by reminding him that he was the one who had given her to him (Gen 3:12); she then blamed the serpent for deceiving her (Gen 3:13). Moses' brother, Aaron, blamed the Israelites for the false god he created and set up for them to worship (Ex 32:2–6, 21–24). Likewise, Saul now blamed the people for the false worship over which he intended to preside.

For the third time Samuel replied to Saul with a question (15:22; previously 15:14, 19) before breaking into a short poetic discourse that spoke of the idolatry of the human will exalted over against God (15:22–23). The question and the first two lines of the poem state, restate, and restate again that a believer's faith is manifested in obedience and that the offering of sacrifices is no substitute for it. Subsequent prophets also make similar statements.[25] Offerings are not acceptable to God when they are presented with a prideful heart that insists that its way is better than God's. In the Torah God himself had made abundant provision for sacrifices that would meet with his favor and through which his people would be freely forgiven. The Israelites were to offer them in repentance and faith according to his Word; their trust in God and his gracious promises moved them to obey his commands.

In the last two lines of his poem Samuel characterized the opposite of obedience: rebellion and willfulness (15:23). The person who rebels against God or who simply places his will above God's will, as Saul had done, is guilty of idolatry, including "divination" (קֶסֶם, 15:23). Divination—an attempt to determine the hidden divine will—heretofore in Samuel was practiced by the polytheistic Philistines (1 Sam 6:2). Samuel was associating Saul with the very enemies whose attacks prompted Israel to ask for a king and whom Saul was to overcome (8:19–20; 10:1). Now he had become one of them. Samuel's words also provide the reader with deep insight into Saul and what his rebellion against Yahweh had made him—no better than the desperate Philistines who urgently sought to get rid of Yahweh's ark after he decapitated their god and struck them with the plague (chapter 6). Saul would eventually demonstrate the same religious desperation when he, too, resorted to divination (28:8).

Samuel's poem also recalls his warning to Israel about their king:

> Is Yahweh as pleased with whole burnt offerings and sacrifices as obeying [שָׁמַע, "hear, listen to"] Yahweh's voice?

---

[25] Is 1:10–11, 13; Jer 7:21–26; Hos 6:6; Amos 5:21–24; Micah 6:6–8; see also Pss 50:9; 51:18 (ET 51:16); Mk 12:28–34.

> Look: To *obey* [שָׁמַע] is better than sacrifice;
>> to listen [is better] than the fat from rams.
> For rebellion [the root מרה] is [like] the sin of divination,
>> and willfulness is [like] the wickedness of idolatry. (15:22–23)

> If you will fear Yahweh, serve him, obey [שָׁמַע] him, and do not rebel [the root מרה] against Yahweh's Word, then you and the king who rules over you will follow Yahweh your God. If you will not obey [שָׁמַע] Yahweh, but rebel [the root מרה] against Yahweh's Word, Yahweh's hand will be against you and your king. (12:14–15)

In fulfillment of Samuel's earlier words, God's hand turned against Saul, and Samuel pronounced God's rejection of Saul as king because of Saul's rejection of God's Word (15:23).

After his demotion Saul finally admitted his sin, but still clung to what he saw as extenuating circumstances: his fear of the people led to his incomplete execution of God's command (15:24). Instead of confessing his utter dependence on divine mercy, Saul was still trying to justify his works and hoping that his explanation would merit a measure of forgiveness and entice Samuel to bless his worship of Yahweh (15:25). It is no surprise then, that Samuel refused to go with Saul, since Saul was still rejecting the Word of Yahweh (15:26), the same Word who had condemned his actions (15:10).

The climax of Samuel's prophecy happened when Samuel turned to leave and Saul accidentally tore his robe as he grabbed the hem in an attempt to seek mercy (15:27). Like prophets who would follow him (see especially 1 Ki 11:29–31), Samuel used this as a prophetic illustration that God had torn the kingdom from Saul (1 Sam 15:26–29). Already God had chosen someone as Saul's replacement—someone Samuel characterized as "better than" Saul. The reference, of course, is to David. By grace David would show himself to be a more faithful believer than Saul in many ways, but especially in his confessing of his sins. When the prophet Nathan confronted David with his adultery and murder, he did not ignore the plain meaning of the prophet's words (versus Saul in 15:20), did not seek to lay the blame on others (versus Saul in 15:21), and did not attempt to justify his actions rather than merely confess them (versus Saul in 15:24). David simply admitted his sin and threw himself on God's mercy (2 Sam 12:13, 16, 22–23; similarly, 2 Sam 24:10–14, 17).

Moreover, Samuel emphasized that God's revocation of Saul's kingship and his choosing of another king was irrevocable (1 Sam 15:29). God does not lie or change his mind like humans. The verb "change his mind" (Niphal [N] of נָחַם, 15:29) immediately leaps out of the Hebrew text since earlier the same verb signified that God "regretted" making Saul king (15:11). The difference is subtle, but important. In both cases the verb helps the reader understand God's nature and work.[26] In regretting having made Saul king, God displayed

---

[26] See the first textual note on 15:11 and the commentary above at the beginning of "Samuel Confronts Saul (15:10–35)."

his continuing compassion toward Israel and his desire to bring all people to salvation. This remains his gracious will—but his grace is resistible, as Saul had shown. In not changing his mind, God displayed his unchangeable nature and his immutable will. He was determined to give his people the blessing of a righteous ruler, and nothing could thwart his plan, which would culminate in the Son of David, Christ the King. Thus, it is no accident that Samuel's words call to mind Balaam's prophecy:

> God is not a man that he could lie nor a son of man that he could change his mind [the Hithpael (HtD) of םחנ]. Does he talk and not act or speak and not fulfill it? Look, I received [Yahweh's command] to bless; since he has blessed, I cannot change it. (Num 23:19–20)

The polytheistic prophet Balaam had been hired to curse the Israelites as they traveled to the promised land. Yahweh, however, had spoken his blessing promises to Abraham (Gen 12:1–3; 18:17–18; 22:17–18; 26:3–4; 28:13–14), redeemed his people from Egypt, and would promise them every blessing in the land (e.g., Deut 28:1–12; 30:1, 16, 19; 33:1). Balaam, therefore, was unable to curse them and was instead compelled by Yahweh to bless them because the Word of God cannot be broken (Jn 10:35).

When the people asked for a king so they could be "like the nations" (1 Sam 8:5, 20), God granted their request. Saul was such a king—he embodied a king like the nations had in ways that were not only intended by the Israelites (i.e., to lead them out to war, 8:20) but also in ways beyond the intention of their words. He became the king who rejected God, just as the nations had, and who acted in his own self-interest (as Samuel had warned in 8:11–17), rather than for the good of the people. And he would become the king who desperately sought to determine the divine will through divination (28:8, as prophesied by Samuel about Saul in 15:23), as the nations did (Deut 18:9–14; Balaam, Josh 13:22; the Philistines, 1 Sam 6:2). God's regret demonstrated his compassion in that he was intervening to keep the Israelites from so quickly becoming apostate like the polytheistic nations around them, though they would eventually do just that (2 Ki 17:17; Jer 14:14; 27:9; 29:8; Ezek 13:9, 23).

However, the replacement for Saul would not be such a king. Instead, he would be someone whom God would enable to be "better" (15:28)—not the tall, impressive Saul, but the less-than-impressive young David, whose heart God saw and knew (16:7), the ancestor of Jesus Christ (Mt 1:1–18). God would not change his mind about David, and that also demonstrated his compassion for his people. God's irrevocable choice of David involved his promise of the eternal covenant in Christ: "Incline your ear; come to me! Listen, and your soul shall live. I will cut for you an eternal covenant, even the sure mercies of David" (Is 55:3).

Eventually, Saul quit his attempts to divert the blame elsewhere and simply admitted his sin, accepting God's verdict on his actions (1 Sam 15:30). Once again Saul asked Samuel to accompany him before the elders so that he could be honored and could worship "Yahweh *your* God." After Saul's confession, Samuel was now willing to accompany Saul, who worshiped in Gilgal (15:31).

However, there was some unfinished business—Agag could not be allowed to live, since God had commanded that all Amalek be punished (15:32). The meaning of the last part of the verse is unclear (see the textual notes on 15:32). However, I would argue that Agag had been relieved to have been initially spared by Saul but now was trembling and afraid; his words mean that his death was a final bitter blow.

Samuel's words to Agag highlight the sin for which the Amalekites were being judged—their actions against Israel had killed many mothers' sons, and now Agag's mother would experience the judgment of God as her son was killed (15:33). Saul and the troops had kept the best of the flocks and herds to slaughter as sacrifices to God at Gilgal. Ironically, the only slaughter there was of the Amalekite king.

The narrative quickly draws to a conclusion, with Saul and Samuel parting ways (15:34), each to his own home. The author tells us that Samuel never "saw" (רָאָה) Saul again (see the first textual note on 15:35). This statement has raised questions over the years because of the later account of Saul prophesying naked in front of Samuel (19:18–24). The most likely explanation is that in this context the verb does not simply mean "to lay eyes upon," but to "oversee" or supervise. This verb is used this way in Gen 39:23: "the warden did not *oversee* [רֹאֶה ... אֵין] anything for which Joseph was responsible because Yahweh was with him, and Yahweh made whatever he did successful." Thus, the author tells us that Saul no longer had the prophet Samuel to advise and correct him, for God had rejected and abandoned Saul in favor of David.[27]

The narrative ends with Samuel and Yahweh having quite different reactions to Saul's removal from the kingship: Samuel *"grieved"* (the Hithpael [HtD] of אָבַל) as if Saul had died, whereas Yahweh *"regretted"* (the Niphal [N] of נָחַם, 15:35; see the comments on 15:11, 29). The difference highlights Samuel's humanity—he mourned the loss of his relationship with the king he had installed—versus Yahweh's concern for Israel and the world as its Redeemer and loving Sovereign.

---

[27] Thus, the next narrative finds Samuel anointing David (1 Sam 16:1–13), and later Samuel provides protection for David (1 Sam 19:18–24). Also note that the same point is made in the next chapter as God's Spirit comes on David (16:13) but leaves Saul (16:14). Another popular explanation is that "see" here is used in the sense of "visit," similar to the English idiom "go to see" someone (HCSB translates with "visit"). However, all of the examples cited to support "visit" use a verb of motion (either בּוֹא, "go," or יָרַד, "go down") with the Qal (G) infinitive construct of רָאָה, "to see" (2 Sam 13:5; 2 Ki 8:29; 9:16; Ps 41:7 [ET 41:6]; 2 Chr 22:6), and the construction here has no verb of motion.

David Is Anointed King and Receives God's Spirit

Translation

16 ¹So Yahweh said to Samuel, "How long will you continue to grieve for Saul now that I have rejected him from being king over Israel? Fill your horn with olive oil. Go, for I am sending you to Jesse the Bethlehemite because I have seen a king for myself among his sons."

²Samuel said, "How can I go? When Saul hears about it, he will kill me."

Yahweh said, "Take a young cow with you, and say, 'I have come to sacrifice to Yahweh.' ³Invite Jesse to the sacrifice, and I will make known to you what you are to do. Anoint for me whomever I will say to you."

⁴Samuel did what Yahweh spoke. He came to Bethlehem, and the city elders shook with fear when they met him. They said, "Seer, do you come in peace?"

⁵He said, "In peace. I have come to sacrifice to Yahweh. Sanctify yourselves, and come with me to the sacrifice." He sanctified Jesse and his sons and invited them to the sacrifice. ⁶When they came, he saw Eliab and thought, "Surely before Yahweh is his anointed."

⁷But Yahweh said to Samuel, "Do not look at his appearance or how tall he is, because I have rejected him. For God does not see as man sees, since man looks at appearances, but God looks at the heart."

⁸Jesse called Abinadab and had him pass in front of Samuel, but he said, "This one also Yahweh has not chosen." ⁹So Jesse had Shammah pass [in front of Samuel], but he said, "This one also Yahweh has not chosen." ¹⁰Jesse had his seven sons pass in front of Samuel, and Samuel said to Jesse, "Yahweh has not chosen these." ¹¹Then Samuel said to Jesse, "Is this all of the young men?"

He said, "The youngest still remains. However, he is a shepherd with the flock."

So Samuel said to Jesse, "Send and fetch him, since we will not recline at table until he comes here." ¹²So he sent and brought him. He was ruddy with beautiful eyes and a handsome appearance.

Then Yahweh said, "Arise and anoint him, because this is he."

¹³So Samuel took the horn of olive oil and anointed him in the midst of his brothers. Then the Spirit of Yahweh rushed upon David from that day forward. Then Samuel got up and went to Ramah.

Textual Notes

16:1 אַתָּה֙ מִתְאַבֵּ֣ל אֶל־שָׁא֔וּל—For the verb, see the second textual note on 15:35. This is the Hithpael (HtD) participle, which has a durative meaning, "keep on grieving."

וַאֲנִ֣י מְאַסְתִּ֔יו—Literally this is "and I, I rejected him." The pronoun אֲנִי is emphatic. For the verb and Yahweh's action, see 15:23, 26.

מַלֵּא קַרְנְךָ שֶׁמֶן וָלֵךְ—The two imperatives, the Piel (D) of מָלֵא and the Qal (G) of הָלַךְ, "fill … go," establish the volitive mood that will continue through 16:3 even though other verb forms will be used. See the second and fourth textual notes on 16:2.

16:2 עֶגְלַת בָּקָר—Literally this phrase means "a heifer from the herd." Elsewhere it is used to denote a "young cow" (Deut 21:3; Is 7:21).

תִּקָּח—"Take" is a Qal (G) imperfect second masculine singular of לָקַח. The imperfect can be used with the volitional force of an imperative (Joüon, § 113 m), especially when it continues a sequence of events initiated with earlier imperatives (see the third textual note on 16:1).[1] The LXX (λαβέ) and 4QSam[b] (קן[ח]) have an imperative, which appears to be a secondary substitution of a more familiar volitional form for a less familiar one.

בְּיָדֶךָ—"With you" is literally "in your hand."

וְאָמַרְתָּ—This perfect with *waw* consecutive also (like תִּקָּח in 16:2) serves as a volitional equivalent to an imperative as it continues the imperatives in 16:1 (Joüon, § 119 i). So too do the perfects with *waw* consecutive in 16:3 (וְקָרָאתָ and וּמָשַׁחְתָּ).

לִזְבֹּחַ לַיהוָה בָּאתִי:—Literally this means "to sacrifice to Yahweh I have come." The purpose clause (with the infinitive) is placed first for emphasis. The word order is the same when Samuel speaks these words in 16:5.

16:3 בַּזֶּבַח—This is the pausal form of the segholate noun זֶבַח with the preposition בְּ and the definite article. The preposition בְּ has a pregnant meaning that implies motion: invite Jesse to come to be "at" the sacrifice, hence invite him "to the sacrifice." The identical form recurs at the midpoint of 16:5, but the more expected preposition לְ is used in the form לַזֶּבַח, "to the sacrifice," at the conclusion of 16:5.

וּמָשַׁחְתָּ—For "anoint," see 9:16; 10:1.

16:4 וַיֶּחֶרְדוּ זִקְנֵי הָעִיר—The verb חָרַד signifies trembling, often caused by fear or anxiety (see 13:7; 14:15; see also the verbal adjective in 4:13), thus "and the city elders shook with fear."[2]

לִקְרָאתוֹ—See the second textual note on 4:1.

וַיֹּאמֶר—Codex Leningradensis has the singular "and he said." The plural וַיֹּאמְרוּ, "and they said," is the reading of the Masoretic *sebir* (noted in the margin of *BHS*), many Masoretic manuscripts, the LXX, the Syriac, and the Vulgate.

שָׁלֹם בֹּאֶךָ:—The suffixed infinitive construct of בּוֹא serves as a verbal noun, "your coming," and the noun שָׁלוֹם is an adverbial accusative, "peaceful, in peace." These words are most naturally understood as a question, and one Masoretic manuscript has the interrogative *he*, הֲשָׁלֹם בֹּאֶךָ, making them explicitly a question: "do you come in peace?" Likewise the interrogative *he* is used with these words in 1 Ki 2:13: הֲשָׁלוֹם בֹּאֶךָ. The LXX reads εἰρήνη ἡ εἴσοδός σου, ὁ βλέπων; "do you come in peace, seer?" The addition of "seer" is supported by 4QSam[b], whose extant text contains only that last word of the Hebrew question: השלם בואך] הראה]. The word is to be vocalized הָרֹאֶה,

---

[1] See also *IBH*, § 47 E; Waltke-O'Connor, § 31.5b.

[2] See the verb also in, e.g., Gen 27:33; Ex 19:16, 18; 1 Ki 1:49; Is 10:29; 32:11; 41:5; Ezek 26:18; Amos 3:6; Ruth 3:8.

the Qal (G) participle of רָאָה with the definite article. This participle serves as a term for a prophet (9:9, 11, 18–19); see the discussion in "Saul Searches for His Father's Donkeys and for Samuel (9:4–13)" in the commentary on 9:1–25.

16:5 הִתְקַדִּשׁוּ—The Hithpael (HtD) of קָדַשׁ, "be holy," has a reflexive sense, "sanctify yourselves." This form could be perfect, but it is the imperative.

וּבָאתֶם אִתִּי בַּזֶּבַח—"And come with me to the sacrifice." The LXX reads καὶ εὐφράνθητε μετ' ἐμοῦ σήμερον, "and rejoice with me today." This is probably a secondary change in the words spoken to the elders of the city to accommodate the fact that, according to the rest of the verse, only Jesse and his sons were sanctified by Samuel.

16:6 מְשִׁיחוֹ:—This means "his anointed one." Hannah uses this title in her prophecy of the Messiah/Christ in 2:10; similarly see מְשִׁיחִי, "my Anointed One/Christ," in 2:35.

16:7 גְּבֹהַּ קוֹמָתוֹ—This construct phrase is literally "the height of his stature."

כִּי מְאַסְתִּיהוּ—This means "because I have rejected him." The Qal (G) of מָאַס is the same verb used in 15:23, 26; 16:1, where Yahweh "rejected" Saul as king for his disobedience to the divine Word. Here, however, Eliab is not being condemned for any disobedience, nor is he being expelled from the company of God's redeemed people. Here "reject" simply means that he is not the one chosen to be Saul's replacement. This clause has the same meaning as the clause discussed in the second textual note on 16:8.

כִּי ׀ לֹא אֲשֶׁר יִרְאֶה הָאָדָם—The laconic MT is "for not what a man sees," which implies that God sees differently. The LXX has the fuller reading ὅτι οὐχ ὡς ἐμβλέψεται ἄνθρωπος ὄψεται ὁ θεός, "for not as a man will see will God see." 4QSam^b is not extant at this point, but space considerations make it likely that it contained a reading such as the following (with vowels added): לֹא כַּאֲשֶׁר יִרְאֶה הָאָדָם יִרְאֶה הָאֱלֹהִים.[3] If so, then the MT may have suffered from parablepsis as a scribe's eye skipped from the first הָאָדָם to the next one in כִּי הָאָדָם and thereby omitted יִרְאֶה הָאֱלֹהִים.

הָאָדָם יִרְאֶה לַעֵינַיִם—Literally "man looks to the eyes," this is ironic in that David is described as having "beautiful eyes" (see the second textual note on 16:12). In five OT passages the noun עַיִן, "eye," means "appearance" (BDB, 4 b). The meaning "man looks at appearances" here is confirmed by the first half of the verse, which referred to observing מַרְאֵהוּ, "his appearance" (the suffixed noun מַרְאֶה is derived from the verb רָאָה, used here), and stature (see the first textual note on 16:7). Similar wording appears in Is 11:3. Yahweh foretells the Messiah as the shoot and branch from the stump of Jesse (Is 11:1), who was David's father. Anointed with the Spirit (Is 11:2), the Christ will not judge the way man typically judges: וְלֹא־לְמַרְאֵה עֵינָיו יִשְׁפּוֹט (Is 11:3), literally "and he will not judge by the appearance of his eyes," meaning the appearance of people whom he sees with his eyes.

16:8 וַיַּעֲבִרֵהוּ לִפְנֵי שְׁמוּאֵל—The Hiphil (H) of עָבַר has the causative meaning "to make someone pass across" also in 16:9, 10. The prepositional phrase לִפְנֵי שְׁמוּאֵל, literally "to the face of Samuel," recurs in 16:10 and is implied in 16:9 (supplied in brackets in the translation).

גַּם־בָּזֶה לֹא־בָחַר יְהוָה:—Literally "also in this one Yahweh has not chosen." This whole clause recurs in 16:9b and בָחַר plus בְּ is also in 16:10b. The verb בָחַר, "to choose," often takes the preposition בְּ on the person or thing chosen; this includes passages such as 16:8–10, where the construction refers to a "divine choice" (BDB, Qal, 1 a). However, in English idiom "choose" takes a direct object, and so בְּ is not reflected in the translation.

16:9 שַׁמָּה—Jesse's third-eldest son's name is spelled this way here and in 17:13: "Shammah." In 2 Sam 13:3, 32; 21:21 (Qere), his name is Shimeah (שִׁמְעָה). In 1 Chr 2:13; 20:7 his name is Shimea (שִׁמְעָא). In 2 Sam 21:21 (Kethib) his name is Shimei (שִׁמְעִי).

16:10 וַיֹּאמֶר שְׁמוּאֵל אֶל־יִשַׁי—"And Samuel said to Jesse." The LXX omits "to Jesse."

16:11 הֲתַמּוּ הַנְּעָרִים—Literally "are the young men completed/finished?" The verb is the Qal (G) of תָּמַם with an interrogative *he*. Earlier in the book the author frequently employed the noun נַעַר, "boy, servant," to contrast the faithful ministerial servant Samuel (1:22–27; 2:11, 18, 21, 26; 3:1, 8) to the unfaithful "servant(s)" of the Elides (2:13, 15, 17). See the commentary on 2:12–17.

הַקָּטָן—The adjective קָטָן, "little, young," with the definite article forms a superlative (Joüon, § 141 j), "the youngest."

וְהִנֵּה רֹעֶה בַּצֹּאן—Literally "and behold, (he is a) shepherd with the flock." In form רֹעֶה is a Qal (G) participle of רָעָה, "to tend, shepherd," but it is used as a noun. This idiom, רֹעֶה with צֹאן plus הַ plus בְּ, recurs in 17:34 and elsewhere in the OT only in Gen 37:2.

שִׁלְחָה וְקָחֶנּוּ—"Send and fetch him." These are two Qal (G) masculine singular imperatives. The first is the alternate imperatival form with paragogic *he* of שָׁלַח. The second is of לָקַח and has the form of the third masculine singular object suffix with energic nun.

כִּי לֹא־נָסֹב—"Since we will not recline at table." The Qal (G) of סָבַב (this is the first common plural imperfect) usually means "to surround." More specifically it can have the nuance "**gather around** a table to dine, **recline**" (*DCH*, 9, citing Sirach 9:9; 35:1) or "**close a circle**," i.e., sit down to meal" (*DCH*, 10, citing only 1 Sam 16:11). This meaning is confirmed by the LXX, ὅτι οὐ μὴ κατακλιθῶμεν, "because we will not recline."

16:12 אַדְמוֹנִי—This adjective, *ʾadmoni*, "ruddy, reddish," might refer to skin tone, or it might mean "red-haired." It appears here and in 17:42 describing David and elsewhere in the OT only in Gen 25:25, portraying Esau, who was subsequently given a name cognate to this adjective, אֱדוֹם, "Edom," because he sold his birthright for some אָדֹם, *ʾadom*, "red stew" (Gen 25:30–34).

עִם־יְפֵה עֵינַיִם—Literally this means "with beautiful of eyes." Hebrew can use an adjective in construct with a noun that specifies the thing that displays the quality expressed by the adjective (see Joüon, § 129 i). Thus, the adjective יָפֶה, "beautiful," is used in construct with the part or aspect of a person that is beautiful. Here David's "eyes" are what make him "beautiful." In this construction with the preposition עִם, "with," the adjective יָפֶה might serve as a substantive, "beauty" (so BDB at the end of its entry for יָפֶה), as in the LXX, μετὰ κάλλους ὀφθαλμῶν, "with beauty of eyes." Similar is the phrase עִם־יְפֵה מַרְאֶה, literally "with beautiful of appearance," describing David in 17:42. Elsewhere in the OT יָפֶה, "beautiful," often appears in construct with מַרְאֶה, "appearance" (Gen 12:11; 29:17; 39:6; 41:2, 4; 2 Sam 14:27) or with תֹּאַר, "(female) figure, (male) physique" (Gen 29:17; 39:6; 41:18; Deut 21:11; 1 Sam 25:3; Esth 2:7). Other passages that evaluate a person's appearance by devoting particular attention to the eyes (positively or negatively) include Gen 29:17; Is 3:16; Song 1:15; 4:1, 9; 5:12; 6:5; 7:5 (ET 7:4).

וְטוֹב רֹאִי—Literally "and good of appearance," this is another adjective in construct with a noun, the same kind of construct phrase described in the preceding textual note. See *HALOT*, s.v. טוֹב I, 5, for examples where this adjective, "good," is used to denote beauty or handsomeness. The noun רֳאִי (in pause: רֹאִי), "appearance," is an uncommon synonym of מַרְאֶה (discussed in the preceding textual note); both are derived from the verb רָאָה, "to see."

16:13 וַתִּצְלַח רוּחַ־יְהוָה אֶל־דָּוִד—"Then the Spirit of Yahweh rushed upon David." The wording is almost identical to the rushing of the Spirit upon Saul in 10:10; 11:6; see the first textual note on 10:6 and "Samuel Anoints Saul (9:26–10:8)" in the commentary on 9:26–10:16.

Commentary

c. 1019 BC

This pericope is the first of three introductions of David to the reader: he is anointed (16:1–13), he is a skilled musician (16:14–23), and he is a warrior (17:1–58). This is parallel to the tripartite introduction to Saul: he is anointed (9:1–10:16), he is publicly made king (10:17–27a), and he is a warrior (10:27b–11:15). By this rough parallel the writer of Samuel indicates that David is Yahweh's choice and the authentic replacement for Saul.

However, these parallels are made clearer by the parallel traits noted for both Saul and David when they are introduced. See figure 22.

Figure 22

Traits of Saul and David Given by the Narrator When They Are Introduced

Trait	Saul	David
Name	9:2; 10:21; 11:5	16:13, 19; 17:12
Genealogy	9:1; 10:21	16:1, 18, 19; 17:12, 58
Kinship	9:1, 21; 10:20	16:1, 18; 17:58
Hometown	10:26; 11:4	16:4, 18; 17:12, 15, 58
Physical attributes	9:2; 10:23	16:12, 18; 17:42
Military prowess	11:1–11	16:18; 17:34–37, 45–47, 48–51
Theological attributes	10:1, 9, 10–11; 11:6, 13	16:13, 18; 17:37, 45–46

This figure is adapted from George, "Yhwh's Own Heart," 448.

Moreover, we could also list the following thematic parallels connected with the anointing of Saul and that of David:[4]

1. Both were anointed at or after a sacrifice hosted by Samuel (9:19–10:1; 16:1–13).
2. Neither expected to be anointed.
3. Both were unlikely candidates: Saul was from the *smallest* tribe of Israel (מִקַּטַנֵּי שִׁבְטֵי יִשְׂרָאֵל, 9:21); David was the *smallest* (youngest) son (הַקָּטָן, 16:11).
4. Both were striking in appearance, though in different ways (9:2; 16:12).
5. Both events were private or semiprivate: Saul's anointing was strictly between him and Samuel (9:27–10:1), while only David's family is mentioned as present at his anointing (16:13).
6. Both men were designated by Yahweh's words to Samuel: Saul: "this is the man about whom …" (… הִנֵּה הָאִישׁ אֲשֶׁר, 9:17); David: "because this is he" (כִּי־זֶה הוּא, 16:12).
7. "The Spirit" of God/Yahweh "rushed upon" both men following their anointing (10:10; 16:13).

This careful recording of parallels between Saul's investiture as king and David's designation as Saul's successor underscores God's rejection of Saul and his abiding favor toward David throughout the rest of the book of Samuel. This is heightened by the juncture of the two pericopes in 1 Samuel 16; the first concludes when the Spirit of Yahweh rushes upon David (16:13), and the second begins with the Spirit leaving Saul (16:14). Moreover, both pericopes are framed by inclusios: the first begins and ends with a "horn" filled with "olive oil" for anointing (קֶרֶן הַשָּׁמֶן, 16:13; קַרְנְךָ שֶׁמֶן, 16:1), while the second begins and ends with the Spirit of Yahweh or a spirit from Yahweh departing from Saul (16:14, 23). In addition, the two are linked in a couple more ways:

1. God says, "I have seen" (רָאִיתִי) a king among Jesse's sons "for me/myself" (לִי, 16:1). Saul asks his servants to "see" (רְאוּ) a man "for me" (לִי, 16:17), and a servant replies, "I have seen" (רָאִיתִי) a son of Jesse (16:18).
2. David is described in both pericopes (16:12, 18).

With all of this careful structuring of the narrative, the author of the book of Samuel is able to signal the importance of the transition from Saul's reign to David's that will occupy the rest of the narrative in 1 Samuel.

The beginning of this section links to the end of 1 Samuel 15 with Yahweh referencing Samuel's "grieving" over Saul (16:1; see 15:35). God considers Samuel's continued grieving to be inappropriate, and his emphatic statement "*I* have rejected him" (see the second textual note on 16:1) stresses the impropriety of the prophet's reaction to Saul's rejection. God's initial instructions include a "horn" (קֶרֶן) as a container for the anointing oil (16:1; also 16:13). The only other time a horn for anointing oil is mentioned in the OT is when Zadok anointed Solomon as king (1 Ki 1:39). However, two other passages refer to a "horn" in connection with Yahweh's "Anointed One" (מָשִׁיחַ), that is, his

---

[4] Based on Walters, "The Light and the Dark," 576.

Messiah or Christ. The first was in Hannah's song of praise (see the commentary on 2:10). The second is in Psalm 132, which recounts the faithful ministry of David and Yahweh's promise to him of a son who would reign on his throne forever (2 Samuel 7): "I will make a horn sprout for David; I have prepared a lamp for my Anointed One" (Ps 132:17). Zechariah takes up this theme in his Benedictus: God "has raised up a horn of salvation for us in the house of David his servant" (Lk 1:69).

It is curious that God revealed to Samuel that one of Jesse's sons would be anointed but did not name which son, David (1 Sam 16:1). This is not unlike the choosing of Saul. Samuel also received only a general description of God's choice for Israel's first king before meeting him (9:15–16). Samuel's reply to God's initial instructions to anoint a son of Jesse expressed fear over Saul's reaction should he find out that Samuel was traveling to Bethlehem to anoint a king (16:2a). Samuel had already informed Saul that God had chosen someone to replace him (15:26–29), and Samuel may have thought that Saul was keeping close tabs on him in an attempt to prevent the anointing and forestall being deposed.

God's next instructions to bring a cow as a sacrifice and to invite Jesse to take part in it (16:2b–3) have been construed by some as divinely sanctioned deception.[5] However, there is an unstated—and perhaps unrecognized—assumption behind this construal: that Yahweh had completed his instructions to Samuel in 16:1 and that the provisions in 16:2b–3 were added specifically to hide the reason for Samuel's trip to Bethlehem. Yet we do not know that to be the case. In 16:2a Samuel may well have interrupted Yahweh's instructions because of his anxiety. Even at the end of 16:3 Yahweh indicates that he had not finished his revelations: his final statement, "anoint for me whomever I will say to you," is clearly not part of any subterfuge against Saul. How was Samuel to know which son was to be anointed? God would tell him when the time came. Therefore, the sacrifice may well have been part of Yahweh's plan all along and was not intended to deceive anyone. Indeed, it is hard to see how Samuel's traveling to Bethlehem with a sacrifice would not have raised Saul's suspicions of Samuel's intentions, since Bethlehem was not on Samuel's usual circuit (cf. 7:15–17). However, given the ensuing narrative, Saul appears at first to be completely unaware that Samuel had already anointed anyone to be his successor.

Samuel's arrival in Bethlehem was not met with joy, but with fear as the city elders trembled and inquired as to the seer's intentions (16:4). The reason for their trepidation is not clear, but given Samuel's most recent actions of announcing Saul's rejection (15:23, 26) and hacking the Amalekite king Agag into pieces (15:33), they may well have been justifiably anxious.

After reassuring the elders of his peaceful intentions to offer sacrifice, Samuel instructed them to sanctify themselves, and then Samuel sanctified Jesse's sons to take part in the sacrifice (16:5). Apart from washing one's clothes,

---

[5] E.g., Shemesh, "Lies by Prophets and Other Lies in the Hebrew Bible," 90; Smith, *The Books of Samuel*, 144; Brueggemann, *First and Second Samuel*, 121.

the procedure for sanctification for offering sacrifices or for otherwise being in God's presence is not spelled out in great detail in the OT, though it is mentioned on several occasions (Ex 19:10, 14; Josh 3:5; 7:13; Job 1:5). The sanctification of all God's people, particularly those in the ministry, is a major theme of the sacrificial legislation of the Torah that is fulfilled in Christ.[6]

When Jesse and his sons arrived at the sacrifice, Samuel immediately concluded that Eliab was the one he ought to anoint, referring to him as "his [Yahweh's] anointed" (16:6). When a king of Israel is called "anointed one" (מָשִׁיחַ), the context always makes clear that he is Yahweh's anointed one—not Israel's—and Samuel's thought shows that he conceived of the king in those terms.[7]

The narrator does not clarify why Samuel assumed Eliab was God's choice. God's rejection of Eliab—"do not look at his appearance or how tall he is" (16:7)—implies that his height may have been the reason, making him similar to Saul (9:2; 10:23–24). Then Yahweh emphasized that his way of choosing is different that the way humans choose, since he looks at the heart. When God chose Saul he gave the Israelites the king they had requested, and so Saul was a choice that accorded with the way humans would have chosen. This is why Samuel could refer to Saul as the king Israel had chosen (12:13), even though God had the ultimate choice. God had given the Israelites their type of king in Saul. However, in rejecting Saul (15:23, 26), God had also rejected Israel's way of choosing. The choice of a new king was not prompted by Israel's demand, as was the case for Saul. In this instance, God's rejection of Saul prompted him to choose a new king, and the choice would be made now solely by God's criteria—according to God's heart ("Yahweh has sought for himself a man according to his own heart," 13:14).

The declaration that "God looks at the heart" (16:7) is also, then, a statement about David's heart. When Saul was anointed, God saw fit to change his heart (10:9). In Hebrew idiom God "changed" his heart into "another heart" (וַיַּהֲפָךְ־לוֹ אֱלֹהִים לֵב אַחֵר), implying that Saul's heart was defective. He needed to "be transformed into another man" (10:6). If Saul had been an apostate Israelite, an unbeliever, this could explain why those who had known him were astonished when he began to prophesy among the prophets (10:11).

No such statement is ever made in Samuel about Yahweh transforming David or giving him another heart. This may imply that he was already a believer and an Israelite who lived by faith in accord with the Torah. This does not mean that David was without fault; he was born with a sinful nature just like every human (save Christ). But he had been incorporated into the covenant of Abraham, a covenant of righteousness through faith alone (Gen 15:6; see Romans 4). As a redeemed son of Abraham, David's inclination by faith

---

[6] See especially Ex 28:41; Lev 20:7–8, 26; 21:6–8; 22:31–33. In the NT, see Jn 10:36; 17:17–19; 1 Cor 1:30; Eph 5:26; Heb 2:11; 13:12; 1 Pet 1:2.

[7] Depending on which references to Yahweh's anointed are taken to refer to Israel's kings, there are at least twenty-five such uses of "anointed one" in the OT. Klein counts thirty-four uses (*1 Samuel*, 160).

was to trust in God and believe and obey his Word. When he fell into sin and was rebuked (2 Sam 11:1–12:12), he confessed his sin (2 Sam 12:13). In his extended prayer (Psalm 51), he implored God to forgive his iniquities, grant him "a clean heart," and renew a "right spirit" within him, that is, to sustain him in faith through the power of the "Holy Spirit" (Ps 51:11–13 [ET 51:9–11]), the Spirit who had rushed upon him at his anointing (1 Sam 16:13). His regeneration by grace restored him to be a man after Yahweh's own heart. For the believer, such repentance and renewal are not one-time events, nor are they only necessary after sins such as murder and adultery. Rather, they are a continual way of life as one daily begs God's forgiveness and seeks his guidance according to his Word (e.g., Rom 12:1–2; Eph 4:22–24; Titus 3:3–7).

This is demonstrated in the balance of 1 Samuel by David's reliance on God's counsel. As George has noted: "David continually inquires of Yhwh: David inquires before he attacks the Philistines (1 Sam 23:2, 4) and the Amalekites (1 Sam 30:7–8), when he flees Keilah (1 Sam 23:10–12), and he is reported by others to have asked Ahimelech to inquire of the deity for him (1 Sam 22:10, 13, 15)."[8] From this George concludes:

> David is different from Saul (and David's heart is different from Saul's heart) because David continually seeks Yhwh's counsel and guidance before he acts. David's need for divine counsel and guidance results in a relationship with Yhwh different for him from that for Saul. David and Yhwh have a dialogue, something Saul and Yhwh do not have. … To put this another way, David serves Yhwh with his heart, and therefore David has a heart after Yhwh's own heart. Thus David's relationship with Yhwh is different from Saul's relationship with Yhwh, not simply because Yhwh is predisposed toward David, but because of who David is and what his heart is like.[9]

David's trust is also shown in his actions. He even declares his trust in Yahweh *before* the action unfolds. Again, George aptly summarizes this aspect of David's heart:

> In the very first words David speaks in the narrative, he refers to the Israelite army as "the armies of the living God" (1 Sam 17:26). This statement is a reconceptualization in this chapter of the theological nature of the Israelite army as the army of God and reflects the orientation and nature of David's heart. Later, when standing before Saul, David explains that he is qualified to fight Goliath because "[t]he LORD, who saved me from the paw of the lion and from the paw of the bear, will save me from the hand of this Philistine" (1 Sam 17:37). David is confident that Yhwh will save him from Goliath. Finally, David declares his faith in Yhwh again when he meets Goliath on the battlefield (1 Sam 17:45–47), mentioning the name of Yhwh four times in his speech (v. 45 once, v. 46 once, and v. 47 twice), a repetition that stresses who will save him. Like Jonathan before him, David declares his faith that Yhwh will act on his behalf, both before going out to fight Goliath and when confronting Goliath. And David's declarations and fighting serve to inform "this

---

8   George, "Yhwh's Own Heart," 453.

9   George, "Yhwh's Own Heart," 454–55.

assembly" about Yhwh and that Yhwh acts on their behalf [1 Sam 17:47]. David serves and is faithful to Yhwh.[10]

After the rejection of Eliab, we are told that Jesse presented his second son, Abinadab, and his third son, Shammah, as well as the rest of his seven eldest sons, but none of them were God's choice (16:8–10). The number of Jesse's sons, therefore, was eight, including David (cf. 17:12). This has occasioned some comment, since 1 Chr 2:13–15 lists only seven sons of Jesse, with David as the seventh. Various solutions have been offered, from positing that one son died in early adulthood and so is not listed in 1 Chronicles 2 to claiming that 1 Sam 16:1–13 is dealing in epic writing so that David is actually the seventh, but climactically termed the eighth.[11] None of those solutions are convincing. It ought to be noted that in addition to the seven sons of Jesse listed in 1 Chronicles 2, an eighth son, Elihu, is mentioned in 1 Chr 27:18.[12]

It is likely that the genealogical information in 1 Chronicles 2 is selective and that Elihu was omitted to give David the prized seventh position. Selective genealogies are found elsewhere in the Scriptures. For instance, ten generations are listed from Perez to David in Ruth 4:18–22, though there had to have been more than ten generations in the eight centuries they span.[13] Moreover, Boaz is listed as the seventh generation and David as the tenth, both honored positions. Another example can be found in Mt 1:1–17, where Matthew lists three sets of fourteen generations, whereas a close reading of 1 Chronicles 2 and 1 Chronicles 4 demonstrates that he skipped several generations to make his threefold fourteen-generation scheme. Unlike modern genealogical procedure, in ancient Semitic cultures it was not seen as defective or deceptive to list genealogical information selectively and for effect or emphasis.

When none of Jesse's seven eldest sons were chosen, the brief conversation between Samuel and Jesse identified David as the youngest and as a shepherd for Jesse's flock (16:11). When David is called "the youngest" (הַקָּטָן; see the second textual note on 16:11), there is a direct contrast to the impressively tall Saul (9:2; 10:23) since the adjective can also mean "smallest" or "littlest."

Samuel's order to fetch David also emphasized the importance of Jesse's youngest son (16:11). Nothing further would happen until David arrived, and by now it must have been clear to Samuel whom God had chosen as the next king. Immediately after reporting David's arrival, the narrator interrupts the action to give us a description of David (16:12). While God may look into the

---

[10] George, "Yhwh's Own Heart," 456.

[11] See the discussion in Tsumura, *The First Book of Samuel*, 420–21.

[12] LXX 1 Chr 27:18 reads "Eliab," which is most likely a secondary reading caused by assimilation to 1 Sam 16:6; 17:13, 28; 1 Chr 2:13; 2 Chr 11:18.

[13] This assumes a 430-year Egyptian sojourn and the early date for the exodus (1446 BC). See Steinmann, *From Abraham to Paul*, 45–53, 68–70. However, even if one assumes a short 215-year Egyptian sojourn (critiqued in Steinmann, *From Abraham to Paul*, 68–70) and the late date of the exodus (c. 1250; critiqued in Steinmann, *From Abraham to Paul*, 54–64), there would still have been four centuries for the ten generations to span.

heart, David's countenance was striking. We are told that he was ruddy (אַדְמוֹנִי, 16:12). Besides David, the only other person described with this adjective was Esau at his birth (Gen 25:25). The exact nature of this description is unclear, though it has been proposed that it means that David had red hair, or less likely, reddish skin.[14] The other two descriptors are unique to David in the OT: beautiful eyes (יְפֵה עֵינַיִם) and handsome appearance (טוֹב רֹאִי; see the textual notes on 1 Sam 16:12). While Saul's height was impressive and recommended him as a warrior, David's attractiveness enhanced his personal appeal.

Only after learning about David's appearance are we told of Yahweh's order to Samuel to anoint David (16:12). David's anointing took place in a semiprivate setting (16:13). Only his brothers are mentioned as present, though presumably Jesse was also there. Then we are told that with the anointing came the Holy Spirit, who rushed upon David that day as he had previously rushed upon Saul (10:10; 11:6; cf. 10:6). However, there is also a contrast between Saul and David: the Spirit twice rushed upon Saul (10:10; 11:6), but only once upon David (16:13), and we are informed that Yahweh's Spirit continued to rush upon David from that day forward.

Apparently the coming of the Spirit upon David was manifested in a recognizable way. For Saul it resulted in prophesying (10:6–13). At the Baptism of Jesus the Father spoke and the Spirit descended in bodily form (Lk 3:21–22 and parallels). On Pentecost the outpouring of the Spirit on the followers of Jesus was manifested verbally by the speaking of the Gospel message in many different languages (Acts 2). Unbelievers who repented were invited to be baptized into Christ for the forgiveness of sins and to receive the gift of the Spirit (Acts 2:38–39). This sets the pattern for the church.[15] Christian Baptism is the divine anointing with the Spirit. In the OT era priests and kings were anointed, but now all are welcome to receive this anointing into the royal priesthood of all believers in Christ (1 Pet 2:5, 9).

The final, almost mundane, notice that Samuel returned to Ramah seems almost like a throwaway line at the end of this account (1 Sam 16:13). However, its significance ought not to be underestimated. Except for the time that David fled to Ramah for protection (1 Samuel 19), the prophet will not interact with David or Saul again during his lifetime. This also signals a difference between Saul and David. Saul constantly needed Samuel to inject himself into royal affairs in order to correct Saul's faulty course as king (10:17–27a; 13:8–15; 15:1–35). David, however, would reign successfully many years without prophetic correction and did not need such major prophetic intervention to correct his actions until he committed adultery and murder (2 Samuel 11–12).

See figure 23 for a genealogy of David.

---

[14] See, e.g., Klein, *1 Samuel*, 161.

[15] See, e.g., Acts 1:5; 8:12–16, 38; 9:18; 10:48; 11:16; 16:15, 33; 18:8; 19:3–5; 22:16. Furthermore, see the further expositions of the efficacy of Baptism in Rom 6:1–6; 1 Cor 12:13; Gal 3:26–29; Eph 4:4–6; 1 Pet 3:21.

Figure 23

David's Genealogy

(Men are in plain type; women are in *italics*; dotted lines indicate marriages.)

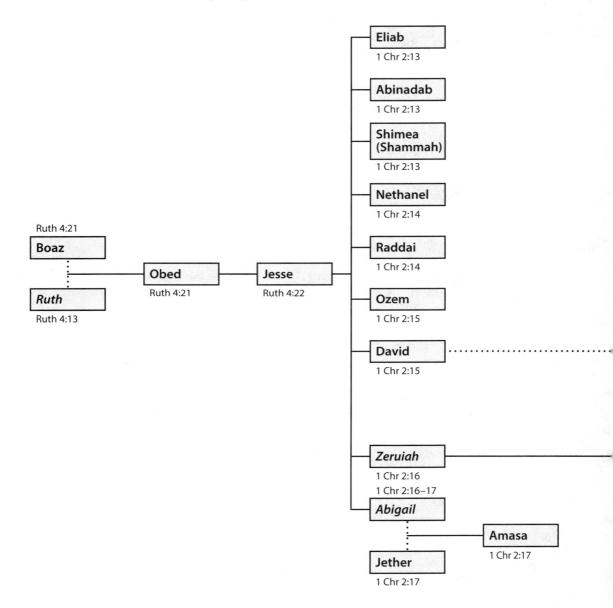

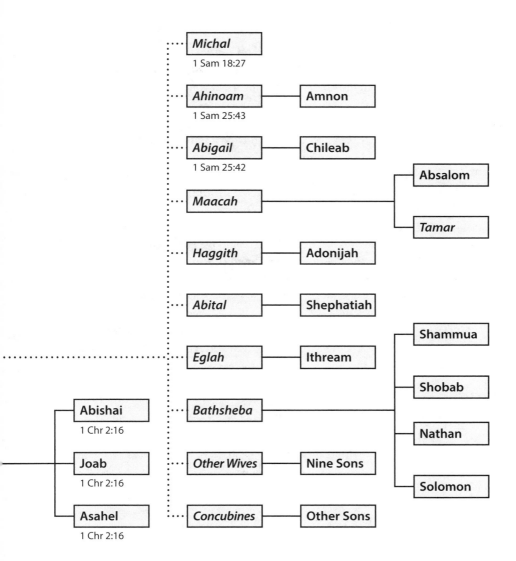

For David's seventh brother, see the commentary on 1 Sam 16:8–10.

For David's sons, see 2 Sam 3:2–5; 5:13–16; 1 Chr 3:1–9; 14:3–7.

The sons of David and Bathsheba are shown in the order given in 2 Sam 5:14; 1 Chr 3:5; 14:4, although Solomon was the oldest.

1 Samuel 16:14–23
David Ministers to Saul with Music

Translation

16 **¹⁴**Now Yahweh's Spirit had left Saul, and an evil spirit from Yahweh began to terrify him. **¹⁵**Saul's servants said to him, "Look, an evil spirit from God is terrifying you. **¹⁶**Let our lord tell your servants who are in your presence to seek a man who knows how to play the lyre. Then when an evil spirit from God is upon you, he will strum and you will be better."

¹⁷Saul said to his servants, "Please find for me a man who is good at playing stringed instruments and bring him to me."

¹⁸One of the servants replied, "Look, I have seen a son of Jesse the Bethlehemite who knows how to play stringed instruments, a prominent man, a warrior, eloquent, a handsome man, and Yahweh is with him."

¹⁹So Saul sent messengers to Jesse and said, "Send to me your son David, who is with the sheep." **²⁰**Jesse took a donkey loaded with bread, a skin full of wine, and one young goat and sent them with his son David to Saul.

²¹David came to Saul, and he stood before him, and he loved him very much, and he became his armor bearer. **²²**So Saul sent [a message] to Jesse: "Please allow David to serve me because he has found favor in my eyes."

²³Whenever a spirit from God came to Saul, David would take his lyre and strum it. Then Saul would be relieved and be better, and the spirit—the evil one—would turn from upon him.

Textual Notes

16:14 וְרוּחַ יְהוָה סָרָה מֵעִם שָׁאוּל—Literally "and the Spirit of Yahweh departed from with Saul," this Hebrew word order is unusual since the subject precedes a perfect verb. It can be a pluperfect or anterior construction, "the Spirit of Yahweh *had* left Saul." See Joüon, § 118 d; GKC, § 106 f; Waltke-O'Connor 33.2.3a. The feminine noun רוּחַ is the subject of the Qal (G) perfect third feminine singular of סוּר. The same verb form (but with *waw* consecutive) recurs in 16:23.

וּבִעֲתַתּוּ—"And it began to terrify him" is a Piel (D) third feminine singular perfect of the verb בָּעַת (with a conjunctive *waw* and a third masculine singular object suffix). The expected form would be וּבִעֲתָתְהוּ, but the ה is assimilated and marked by the *daghesh* in -תּ- (see GKC, § 59 g). In the D stem this verb most often denotes causing fright or terror,[1] as does its participle discussed in the second textual note on 16:15. The LXX reads καὶ ἔπνιγεν αὐτόν, "and it choked him." See also Josephus: πνιγμοὺς αὐτῷ καὶ στραγγάλας ἐπιφέροντα, "inflicting choking and strangulation on him."[2]

---

[1] Is 21:4; Job 7:14; 9:34; 13:11, 21; 15:24; 18:11; 33:7.
[2] Josephus, *Antiquities*, 6.166.

רוּחַ־רָעָה מֵאֵת יְהוָה:—Literally this means "an evil spirit from with Yahweh." The combination of prepositions מֵאֵת (מִן plus אֵת, "with") clarifies that the "evil spirit" is not the Spirit of Yahweh, the Holy Spirit.

16:15 רוּחַ־אֱלֹהִים רָעָה—Literally this means "a spirit *of* God, an evil (one)." Here and in 16:16 this phrase is translated as "an evil spirit *from* God" to match the wording of 16:14 and to clarify that this does not refer to the Spirit of God, the Holy Spirit. רָעָה lacks the definite article. Normally רוּחַ־אֱלֹהִים would be considered definite, "(the) Spirit of (the) God," since אֱלֹהִים denotes the one true God, but the indefinite feminine adjective רָעָה modifying רוּחַ shows that is "*a* spirit." See Joüon, § 139 c. See also the third textual note on 16:23. Here in 16:15 the LXX has "an evil spirit of the Lord"; in 16:16 it has only "an evil spirit."

מְבַעִתֶּךָ:—This is the feminine singular Piel (D) participle of בָּעַת, "to terrify" (as in 16:14), with a second masculine singular suffix. The older form of the feminine singular Piel (D) participle was מְבַעַת, and it was developed to מְבַעֶתָת, but with the suffix the second ת is assimilated and marked by the *daghesh* in -תֶ-. See GKC, § 80 d.

16:16 יֹאמַר־נָא אֲדֹנֵנוּ עֲבָדֶיךָ לְפָנֶיךָ—Literally "please let our lord say—your servants are before you." The verb יֹאמַר is the Qal (G) jussive of אָמַר. The "servants" address their king in the third person as "our lord." Normally with אָמַר, "say, speak," the Hebrew preposition לְ or אֶל introduces those to whom the speech is directed, but no preposition is used here with עֲבָדֶיךָ. No English preposition is required in the translation "tell your servants."

יֹדֵעַ מְנַגֵּן—These are participles, literally a man "knowing, playing," i.e., "knowing how to play." The second participle is the object complement of the first (GKC, § 120 b). The Piel (D) of נָגַן, "to play" a stringed instrument, often denotes playing the כִּנּוֹר, "lyre," as here. The verb occurs in 16:16 (twice), 17, 18, 23. Instead of two participles, the expected construction would be a participle with an infinitive construct, as in 16:17 (יֹדֵעַ לְנַגֵּן) and 16:18 (מֵיטִיב לְנַגֵּן).

וְנִגֵּן בְּיָדוֹ—Literally "and he will play with his hand." The expression is translated with "strum." It recurs in 16:23.

וְטוֹב לָךְ:—This is an impersonal construction (Joüon, § 152 d), literally "and it will be good for you." See also וְטוֹב לוֹ in 16:23. The verb is the Qal (G) perfect of טוֹב, translated in a comparative sense, "be better." לָךְ is the pausal form of לְךָ, with a (second singular) masculine suffix. The LXX adds καὶ ἀναπαύσει σε, "and he will refresh you."

16:17 רְאוּ־נָא—Literally "please see," this is translated as "please find."

מֵיטִיב לְנַגֵּן—This is translated as "good at playing stringed instruments." The first verb is the Hiphil (H) participle of יָטַב, which can mean "to do something well, skillfully" (see BDB, Hiphil, 3). The second verb is the Piel (D) infinitive construct of נָגַן, for which, see the second textual note on 16:16.

16:18 בֵּן לְיִשַׁי—This means "a son belonging to Jesse." The construction with a noun followed by a prepositional phrase is used in place of the construct phrase בֶּן־יִשַׁי, "Jesse's son," since Jesse had other sons besides David (16:1–13).

וְגִבּוֹר חַיִל—This construct phrase means "a prominent man" (see the third textual note on 9:1), but since David himself had not yet risen to prominence, it is most likely an affirmation of the high standing of Jesse's family. See further the commentary.

וְאִישׁ מִלְחָמָה—This construct phrase, "a man of war," is rendered as "a warrior."

וּנְבוֹן דָּבָר—"Eloquent" is literally "discerning of word." The verb נָבוֹן (in construct: נְבוֹן) is a Niphal (N) participle masculine singular of בִּין.

וְאִישׁ תֹּאַר—This construct phrase, "a man of [physical] form," means "a handsome man." For similar construct phrases signifying a handsome appearance, see the second and third textual notes on 16:12.

16:20 חֲמוֹר לֶחֶם—If the first noun in this construct phrase is חֲמוֹר II, then "a donkey of bread" must mean "a donkey loaded with bread." However, that noun might be a unit of measure.[3] A homograph חֲמוֹר I, "a heap," occurs only in Samson's saying in Judg 15:16. Alternatively, one might read with the LXX γομορ ἄρτων (= חומר לחם), "a homer of bread."

16:21 וַיֶּאֱהָבֵהוּ מְאֹד—"And he loved him very much." The subject of the verb (Qal [G] of אָהַב) and the referent of its object suffix are left ambiguous. See the discussion in the commentary.

נֹשֵׂא כֵלִים:—For "armor bearer," see the second textual note on 14:1.

16:22 יַעֲמָד־נָא דָוִד לְפָנַי—Literally "may David please stand before me." The verb is a Qal (G) jussive masculine singular of עָמַד. (In the closed unaccented syllable the vowel -ָ- is *qamets chatuph*, a short "o," reduced from *holem*, -ֹ-.) The idiom of עָמַד with לִפְנֵי in 16:21, 22 ("stand before") means "attend upon, be(come) servant of" (BDB, s.v. עָמַד, Qal, 1 e). A servant would stand before his master, who could be seated or (if a king) enthroned. Cf. the second textual note on 17:15.

16:23 רוּחַ־אֱלֹהִים—This is translated as "a spirit *from* God." See the first textual note on 16:15. The LXX reads πνεῦμα πονηρόν, "an evil spirit," which is an assimilation to the phrase τὸ πνεῦμα τὸ πονηρόν later in the verse (see the third textual note on 16:23).

וְרָוַח לְשָׁאוּל—Literally "and it will be wide for Saul," this is another impersonal construction; see the fourth textual note on 16:16. The verb is the third masculine singular Qal (G) perfect of רָוַח with *waw* consecutive, denoting frequent action (GKC, § 112 oo), hence "whenever … then Saul would be relieved." Generally in the OT the idea of narrowness or constriction implies distress, whereas the idea of spaciousness implies relief (see Joüon, § 152 d). This verb רָוַח occurs only twice elsewhere in the OT. The Qal (G) appears in a similar impersonal construction in Job 32:20. The Pual (Dp) participle in Jer 22:14 refers to "spacious" rooms.

וְסָרָה מֵעָלָיו רוּחַ הָרָעָה:—Literally "and a spirit—the evil (one)—would depart from upon him." The identical verb סָרָה (but without *waw* consecutive) referred to the departure of the Holy Spirit from Saul in 16:14a; see the first textual note on 16:14. But this verse refers to an evil spirit (cf. 16:14b, 15–16). The adjective רָעָה is marked as definite by the article, but the noun it modifies, רוּחַ, does not have an article. The lack of

---

[3] Tsumura, "*Hamôr Lehem* (1 Samuel xvi 20)," who adduces evidence from Akkadian to support this theory.

an article on רוּחַ calls special attention to Saul's being possessed by *an* evil spirit rather than *the* Spirit (of Yahweh/God).[4] This is the only example of רוּחַ in such a construction. The construction draws attention to two contrasts: (1) Saul was originally indwelt and under the influence of the Holy Spirit (10:10; 11:6; cf. 16:14) but now is vexed by an evil spirit. (2) David is now indwelt by the Holy Spirit (16:13), while Saul is possessed by an evil spirit.

Commentary

c. 1019 BC

This section begins with Yahweh's Spirit departing from Saul (16:14) in direct contrast with Yahweh's Spirit rushing upon David (16:13). Saul had repeatedly disobeyed the Word of God spoken directly to him.[5] God freely forgives all who repent and turn to him in faith, but persistent sinning is incompatible with faith. A life of willful violation of God's Word can eventually drive out the Holy Spirit,[6] and this is what happened to Saul. After the departure of the Spirit, a person becomes vulnerable to evil spirits (Mt 12:43–45). We are told that after the Spirit left Saul, God sent "an evil spirit" (רוּחַ־רָעָה, 16:14), which began to terrify him. This statement has led to much discussion, since God cannot be the author and originator of evil in the sense of his making or endorsing something opposed to his holy nature and will. God made everything "very good" (Gen 1:31). However, Satan rebelled against God, and many of the originally good angels fell when they joined in his rebellion (cf. Rev 12:3–4). Everything is under God's dominion. God allows the demonic forces some latitude to carry out their evil in this fallen world (cf. the "lying spirit" in 1 Ki 22:19–23; Satan himself in Job 1–2; the dragon chained and then set loose for a "little while" in Rev 20:1–10). Nevertheless, God's overarching purpose is always to lead people to repentance (e.g., Rev 9:20–21; 16:9–11) since he desires all people to be saved (1 Tim 2:4).

The Hebrew word translated as "evil" (רָעָה, 1 Sam 16:14–16, 23) has a wide range of meanings, and here it denotes a spirit that is opposed to God and his work (cf. Eph 6:12). Its visitation upon Saul was meant to punish him, and it did bring terrors upon him (16:14–15).[7] That it truly was an evil spirit and

---

[4] The LXX adds an article to the noun to match the article with the adjective, resulting in a normal Greek phrase τὸ πνεῦμα τὸ πονηρόν, "the evil spirit."

[5] 1 Sam 10:7 implies that God expected Saul to eradicate the Philistine garrison in Gibeah, which he failed to do. See the discussion in "Samuel Anoints Saul (9:26–10:8)" in the commentary on 9:26–10:16. See also the beginning of the commentary on 10:17–27a. Moreover, in 13:7–14 he disobeyed Samuel's instructions to wait at Gilgal for the prophet to come to offer the sacrifices. His rash oath in 14:24 inflicted hardship on the Israelite troops, prevented a complete victory over the Philistines, and brought a curse on his son Jonathan. In chapter 15 he did not carry out Samuel's instructions to completely destroy Amalek.

[6] See, e.g., Ap IV 142–44, 219; Ap XX 13; SA III III ("Penance") 43–45; FC Ep IV 19.

[7] For example, see Amos 3:6, where the noun רָעָה, "evil," denotes a disaster brought upon a city by God, and Lev 26:6; Jer 23:17; Ezek 34:25, where the noun or adjective רָעָה, "evil," is contrasted with שָׁלוֹם, "well-being, peace."

that God's will permitted it to afflict Saul ought not to be denied, since the passage is clear that even Saul's servants recognized that this spirit was evil and came from God (16:15–16). This is affirmed again in the author's summary statement (16:23).[8]

There are several passages that speak of God controlling evil spirits in order to punish those who reject him and bring the curse of his Law upon them (Judg 9:23–24; 1 Ki 22:19–23; 2 Ki 19:7; Is 19:13–14).[9] One might also include the incident related in Acts 19:13–16, where some Jews who were not believers in Jesus tried to cast out an evil spirit in Jesus' name and the demon-possessed man turned on them and beat them. Nevertheless, the evil spirits are subject to God, and in the NT Jesus' power over them demonstrates that he is the true God Incarnate.[10] In addition, as God the Son, Jesus gave authority to his disciples to drive out demons (Mk 3:15; Lk 9:1).

It is important to note that evil spirits cause torment and harm to those whom they possess.[11] The manifestation of possession by the evil spirit sent by God was a twofold torment for Saul: it brought him terror (1 Sam 16:14) and eventually a paranoid fear and loathing of David, who had Yahweh's Spirit (18:11–12; 19:9–10). The evil spirit even caused Saul to "prophesy," that is, to engage in some form of supernatural utterance (18:10), but because this action took place under the influence of the evil spirit, any words uttered by Saul would have been false prophecy (as in 1 Ki 22:19–23). Thus, Saul "prophesied" both under the control of the Holy Spirit (10:10–11; 19:23–24[12]) and under the control of an evil spirit sent by God (18:10).

The reaction of Saul's servants to his misery is noteworthy (16:15–16). Twice they stated that Saul was suffering because of an evil spirit and that the spirit was from God. Moreover, they prescribed music therapy for Saul, a treatment to which he readily assented (16:17).

As soon as Saul commissioned his courtiers to find a music therapist, one of them volunteered information about David, whom he described with seven characteristics (16:18):

---

[8] Note that Luther apparently also understood this to be an evil spirit (LC II 36). Alternate explanations include the proposals that the spirit was destructive—perhaps a holy angel meant to punish Saul, but not an angel who was evil in himself (e.g., Tsumura, *The First Book of Samuel*, 427–28; Bergen, *1, 2 Samuel*, 182), or that the spirit was actually a psychosis in Saul (e.g., Williams and Le Roux, "King Saul's Mysterious Malady").

[9] See the discussion of these passages in Hamori, "The Spirit of Falsehood," 18–24.

[10] Mt 9:32–34; 10:8; 12:22–28; 17:14–18; Mk 1:34, 39; 3:22; 7:26–30; 16:9; Lk 4:33–36, 41; 7:21; 8:1–3, 27–39; 9:38–42; 11:14–20; 13:32.

[11] Mt 12:43–45 ‖ Lk 11:24–26; see also Mt 9:32–34; Mt 17:14–18 ‖ Mk 9:14–27 ‖ Lk 9:37–42; Lk 8:27–39.

[12] It does not seem likely that in 19:23–24 Saul was regenerated to become a believer once again for a day and a night before relapsing into his apostasy. Rather than being indwelt by the Spirit to utter inspired prophecy, it appears more probable that the Spirit overcame Saul to thwart his intent to harm David and that Yahweh demonstrated his control over Saul by the ecstatic utterance. See further the commentary on 19:18–24.

1. He is "a son of Jesse the Bethlehemite" (cf. 16:1).

2. He knows how to play stringed instruments well.

3. He is a "prominent man" (גִּבּוֹר חַיִל), which is a statement about the high social standing of Jesse's family (see the third textual note on 9:1). Note that David's ancestor Boaz was also described this way, demonstrating the long-standing prominence of this Ephrathite family (Ruth 2:1).

4. He is "a warrior" (אִישׁ מִלְחָמָה), which may refer to David's training. Before he met Goliath in battle he already knew how to use a sling (17:40, 49–50) and had slain formidable animals (17:34–36).[13]

5. He is "eloquent" (נְבוֹן דָּבָר) and thus able to adorn his musical talent with words.

6. He is "a handsome man" (אִישׁ תֹּאַר). Note that the noun תֹּאַר is used to describe other good-looking persons in the OT: the physique of the men Joseph (Gen 39:6) and Adonijah (1 Ki 1:6) and the comely figures of Rachel (Gen 29:17), Abigail (1 Sam 25:3), and Esther (Esth 2:7).

7. "Yahweh is with him." This last quality is the most important feature of David and is repeated a number of times (1 Sam 18:12, 14, 28–29; 2 Sam 5:10; cf. 1 Sam 17:37; 20:13; 2 Sam 7:3 ‖ 1 Chr 17:2) to emphasize that he was indwelt by God's Holy Spirit (cf. Rom 8:9–11; 1 Cor 3:16; 2 Tim 1:14; James 4:5) and that God perpetually remained with him. The statement is ironic in that Yahweh's Spirit had left Saul (1 Sam 16:14), and the courtier's statement was the first hint to Saul that David was the designated ruler to replace him. However, at this point Saul did not negatively react to Yahweh's grace upon David as he would later.

Saul sent a message to Jesse asking for David to come to the royal court (16:19). Apparently, he or the courtier who composed the message had been informed of David's status as the one who tended Jesse's sheep, which provides a tie back to David's anointing (16:11) and forward to David's confrontation with Goliath (17:15, 34–37, 40).

The gifts Jesse sent with David are noted by the author (16:20). There might seem to be little reason in this context for the author's recording of the specific items that Jesse gave to Saul—bread, wine, and a goat. However, it ought to be noted that the same three items came to Saul immediately after his anointing by Samuel (10:3–4). Thus, the author is subtly signaling to the reader that David's anointing superseded Saul's.

The next verb begins with David as the subject: "David came to Saul" (16:21). The author then follows with three ambiguous statements: "*he* stood before *him*"; "*he* loved *him* very much"; and "*he* became *his* armor bearer." In the first and third statements the subject must be David and the antecedent of the other pronouns is Saul. Most English versions and many commentators reverse

---

[13]   Note that this was David's reply when Saul implied that David was no warrior like Goliath (17:33).

the persons in their interpretations of the middle statement: Saul loved David.[14] However, this reversal seems peculiar for two reasons:[15]

First, there is no good reason to think that the subject referenced by the third person verb of the middle statement is any different than the subject of the third person verbs in the first and third statements. Some interpreters appeal to Saul's following statement to Jesse that David "has found favor" with him (16:22). However, finding favor with the king is much different than being beloved by the king.

Second, Saul is never depicted as showing love for David. He displayed favor toward David (16:22), jealousy of David (18:8), suspicion of David (18:9), hostility toward David (18:11), and fear of David (18:15). On the contrary, it was David who demonstrated his love for Saul in his bafflement over why Saul tried to kill him (20:1), in twice sparing Saul's life (24:2–23 [ET 24:1–22], especially 24:22–23 [ET 24:21–22]; 26:1–25, especially 26:22–24), and in his lament over Saul (2 Sam 1:19–27, especially 2 Sam 1:23–24).

Therefore, it is best to understand David as the subject of all four Hebrew verbs in 1 Sam 16:21. David came to Saul. David stood before—that is, served—Saul. David loved Saul, a statement of his loyalty to the king throughout Saul's life, and even afterward (2 Sam 1:19–27). David became Saul's armor bearer. This last statement might seem premature, since David has not yet experienced war and his first taste of combat has yet to be presented to the reader (1 Sam 17:1–58). It may simply mean that David became one of Saul's menial servants—a squire or adjutant—and the notion of his assisting Saul in battle is not yet entailed at this point in the narrative.[16] If Joab later had ten armor bearers (2 Sam 18:15), it is likely that David was simply one of many such servants of King Saul.

Upon seeing David's service, loyalty, and utility (1 Sam 16:21), Saul requested Jesse to allow David to serve him permanently (16:22). Then the narrator emphasizes that this service was used to bring Saul relief from the evil spirit that afflicted him (16:23). This last statement involves a play on words: "be relieved" (רָוַח, *rawach*) from the "spirit" (רוּחַ, *ruach*), as both words have the identical consonants (רוח). This adds an ironic twist to the words since David is under the influence of "the Spirit of Yahweh" (רוּחַ־יְהוָה, 16:13) as Saul's successor. He provides relief from the "spirit from God" (רוּחַ־אֱלֹהִים), that is, "the spirit—the evil one" (רוּחַ הָרָעָה; see the third textual note on 16:23).

---

[14] HCSB; ESV; GW; NET; NIV; Keil, *The Books of Samuel*, 172; Smith, *The Books of Samuel*, 149; McCarter, *I Samuel*, 279–80; Klein, *1 Samuel*, 167; Bodner, *1 Samuel*, 174; Bergen, *1, 2 Samuel*, 183; Auld, *I and II Samuel*, 190.

[15] See Wong, "Who Loved Whom?"

[16] Note that the Hebrew term is נֹשֵׂא כֵלִים, "bearer of equipment" (also, e.g., 14:1), which does not necessarily refer to armor or weapons exclusively. For this interpretation, see Keil, *The Books of Samuel*, 172; Smith, *The Books of Samuel*, 149; McCarter, *I Samuel*, 282; Klein, *1 Samuel*, 167; Tsumura, *The First Book of Samuel*, 432.

1 Samuel 17:1–58

David as Israel's Champion: The Victory over Goliath

Translation

17 ¹The Philistines gathered their camps for war. They gathered at Socoh, which is in Judah, and they camped between Socoh and Azekah in Ephes-dammim. ²Then Saul and the men of Israel gathered and camped in the Valley of the Terebinth. They arranged their army for war to meet the Philistines. ³The Philistines were standing on the hill on one side, and Israel was standing on the hill on the other side, and the valley was between them.

⁴Then a certain soldier came out from the Philistine camps. His name was Goliath; [he was] from Gath. He was four cubits and a span tall. ⁵He wore a bronze helmet on his head and scale armor. The weight of his armor was five thousand shekels of bronze. ⁶[He wore] bronze greaves on his shins and a bronze javelin between his shoulders. ⁷The shaft of his spear was like a weaver's beam, and his spear's head weighed six hundred shekels of iron. His shield bearer walked in front of him.

⁸He stood and called to Israel's battle lines. He said to them, "Why did you come out in battle formation? Aren't I the Philistine and you are slaves to Saul? Choose a man for yourselves, and let him come down to me. ⁹If he is able to fight with me and strike me down, then we will become your slaves. But if I am able [to defeat] him and strike him down, you will become our slaves, and you will serve us." ¹⁰The Philistine also said, "I mock the battle lines of Israel today! Give me a man, and let's fight each other!" ¹¹When Saul and all Israel heard these words of the Philistine, they were demoralized and very afraid.

¹²Now David was a son of this Ephrathite from Bethlehem in Judah whose name was Jesse. He had eight sons, and in Saul's days the man was old and advanced in years. ¹³The three eldest sons of Jesse had followed Saul to war. Now the names of his three sons who followed to war were Eliab, the firstborn; his second, Abinadab; and the third, Shammah; ¹⁴and David was the youngest. The three eldest followed Saul. ¹⁵However, David would go back and forth from Saul to tend his father's flock in Bethlehem. ¹⁶Meanwhile, for forty days the Philistine came forward and took his stand every morning and evening.

¹⁷Jesse said to his son David, "Take this ephah of roasted grain and these ten loaves of bread for your brothers. Take [them] to your brothers' camp quickly. ¹⁸Also bring these ten portions of cheese to the company commander. Check on your brothers' welfare, and take their pledge. ¹⁹Saul and they and all Israel are in the Valley of the Terebinth fighting the Philistines."

²⁰So David got up early in the morning and left the flock with a keeper, loaded up, and went as Jesse had commanded. He came to the outskirts of the camp as the army was going out to the battle line and raising a battle cry. ²¹Israel and the Philistines arranged battle line to battle line. ²²David left the items he was carrying with the quartermaster and ran to the battle line. He came and asked his brothers about their welfare. ²³While he was speaking with them, the soldier—Goliath the Philistine was his name ([he was] from Gath)—was coming up from the battle lines of the Philistines. He spoke his usual words, and David listened. ²⁴When they saw the man, all the men of Israel fled from him and were very afraid.

²⁵The men of Israel said, "Do you see this man coming up? He most certainly is coming up to mock Israel. The man who will strike him down—the king will make him very rich and give him his daughter and make his family tax-exempt in Israel."

²⁶David said to the men who were standing with him, "What will be done for the man who strikes down this Philistine and removes the disgrace from Israel? After all, who is this uncircumcised Philistine that he mocks the battle lines of the living God?"

²⁷The troops answered him in the same way, "This will be done for the man who strikes him down."

²⁸His oldest brother, Eliab, heard when he was speaking to the men. Eliab became angry with David and said, "Why in the world have you come down? With whom have you left those few sheep in the wilderness? I know your insolence and your bad intentions—you came down to see the battle!"

²⁹David said, "What have I done now? Wasn't it just talk?" ³⁰He turned away from him to face another man and asked the same questions. The troops answered as they had the first time.

³¹The words that David spoke were overheard, and when they reported [his words] to Saul, he sent for him. ³²David said to Saul, "Don't let anyone despair because of him. Your servant will go and fight this Philistine."

³³Saul said to David, "You aren't able to go fight this Philistine, because you are an inexperienced young man, but he has been a man of war since his youth."

³⁴David said to Saul, "Your servant has been a shepherd for his father among the flock. Whenever a lion or a bear would come and take one of the sheep from the flock, ³⁵I would go out after it, strike it down, and rescue [the sheep] from its mouth. If it attacked me, I would grab it by the fur on its head, strike it down, and kill it. ³⁶Your servant has struck down both a lion and a bear, and this uncircumcised Philistine will be like one of them, because he has mocked the battle lines of the living God." ³⁷David added, "Yahweh, who rescued me from the power of a lion and a bear, will rescue me from the power of this Philistine."

Saul said to David, "Go, and may Yahweh be with you." ³⁸Then Saul dressed David in his clothes, put a bronze helmet on his head, and dressed him in armor. ³⁹David strapped his sword on his waist over his clothes. He attempted to walk, for he had not tried [this previously].

So David said to Saul, "I am not able to walk in these, because I have not tried [this previously]." So David took them off. ⁴⁰He took his staff in his hand and chose five smooth stones from the dry stream and put them in his shepherds' pouch—in his bag—and his sling was in his hand. Then he approached the Philistine.

[41]The Philistine came, continually approaching David, and the man carrying his shield was in front of him. [42]The Philistine looked down and observed David. He despised him because he was a young man, ruddy with a handsome appearance. [43]The Philistine said to David, "Am I a dog that you are coming to me with sticks?" Then the Philistine cursed David by his gods. [44]The Philistine said to David, "Come to me, and I'll give your flesh to the birds in the sky and to the wild beasts."

[45]David said to the Philistine, "You are coming to me with a sword, a spear, and a javelin, but I am coming to you in the name of Yahweh of armies, the God of the battle lines of Israel, whom you mocked. [46]Today Yahweh will hand you over to me, and I will strike you down, remove your head, and give the corpse of the camp of the Philistines today to the birds in the sky and to the wild animals. Then all the earth will know that Israel has a God, [47]and this entire assembly will know that Yahweh is able to save without a sword or a spear because war belongs to Yahweh. He will hand you over to us."

[48]When the Philistine arose and came near to confront David, David quickly ran from the battle line to confront the Philistine. [49]David put his hand in his pouch and took a stone from it. He slung [it] and struck the Philistine in his forehead. The stone sank into his forehead, and he fell face forward to the ground. [50]David with a sling and a stone was stronger than the Philistine. He struck the Philistine and killed him, even though he had no sword. [51]David ran and stood over the Philistine. He took his sword, drew it from its sheath, and finished killing him and cut off his head with it. The Philistines saw that their hero was dead, so they fled.

[52]The men of Israel and Judah rose up and shouted. They pursued the Philistines as far as Gath and the gates of Ekron. The slain Philistines fell on the Shaaraim road as far as Gath and Ekron. [53]When the Israelites returned from pursuing the Philistines, they plundered their camps. [54]David took the Philistine's head and brought it to Jerusalem and put his equipment in his tent.

[55]Now as Saul had watched David going out to confront the Philistine, he had said to Abner, the army's commander, "Whose son is this young man, Abner?"

Abner said, "I swear by your life, Your Majesty, I don't know."

[56]The king said, "Inquire whose son this young man is."

[57]As soon as David returned from striking down the Philistine, Abner took him and brought him before Saul. The head of the Philistine was in his hand. [58]Saul said to him, "Whose son are you, young man?"

David said, "The son of your servant Jesse the Bethlehemite."

Textual Notes

The Text of 1 Samuel 17:1–18:30

Among scholars one of the most discussed textual issues in 1 Samuel is the difference between the longer edition of 1 Samuel 17–18 as represented by the MT and many ancient versions and the shorter edition as represented by the LXX. The longer edition was probably also found in 4QSam[a]. This is significant, because most often 4QSam[a] agrees with the LXX against the MT, but here it supports the MT.[1] The shorter edition is missing 17:12–31, 41, 50, 55–58; 18:1–6a, 8a, 10–11, 17–19, 21b, 26b, 29b–30. The majority of critical scholars believe that the shorter edition is more original or at least that the MT is a parallel expanded edition.[2] However, there is no agreement among them as to exactly how the longer edition came into existence. Many assert that it is a blending of two sources. According to this theory, the shorter edition reveals one coherent source, whereas the longer one also contains expansions that were inserted into the shorter source from a second account (and these expansions by themselves present a more-or-less coherent parallel account of the David-Goliath encounter and its aftermath). A sizable minority of critical scholars[3] and most evangelical scholars[4] hold that the longer edition is original and that the shorter edition is an abbreviation of it. The position of this commentary is that the MT has a greater claim to authenticity and that the LXX appears to be a purposeful editing of it to omit material. Van der Kooij has noted:

> The motives behind the shortening of 1 Sam 17 may have been manifold. First of all, on the level of the text itself, it is likely that the aim was to create a version of our story which does fit in better with the preceding chapter (1 Sam 16). Omissions such as 17,12–31 and 17,55–58 do make sense in this respect.[5]

In fact, van der Kooij may be too conservative in his comments. The two longest omissions in the LXX, which are MT 17:12–31 and MT 17:55–18:6a, contain material that repeats information from 1 Samuel 16 (e.g., the introduction of Jesse's sons [16:6–12; 17:12–14]). Some portions of MT 1 Samuel 17 were probably excised by the LXX (or its Hebrew Vorlage) because of perceived conflicts with 1 Samuel 16. For instance, David is characterized as a warrior in 16:18 and as Saul's armor bearer in 16:21, but in 17:12–31 David's three eldest brothers are depicted as member of Saul's

---

[1]   See Johnson, "Reconsidering 4QSam[a] and the Textual Support for the Long and Short Versions of the David and Goliath Story."

[2]   E.g., Smith, *The Books of Samuel*, 151; Stoebe, "Die Goliathperikope"; McCarter, *I Samuel*, 284–309; Klein, *1 Samuel*, 173–75; Campbell, *1 Samuel*, 167–93; Auld, *I and II Samuel*, 198–99; Lust, "The Story of David and Goliath in Hebrew and in Greek," in Barthélemy et al., *The Story of David and Goliath*, 5–18; Tov, "The Nature of the Differences between MT and the LXX in 1 Sam. 17–18," in Barthélemy et al., *The Story of David and Goliath*, 19–46; Auld and Ho, "The Making of David and Goliath"; McKenzie, *King David: A Biography*, 70–73; Hendel, "Plural Texts and Literary Criticism."

[3]   E.g., Pisano, *Additions or Omissions in the Books of Samuel*, 78–86; de Vries, "David's Victory over the Philistine as Saga and as Legend"; Rofé, "The Battle of David and Goliath"; Polzin, *Samuel and the Deuteronomist*, 2:259–61, n. 21; van der Kooij, "The Story of David and Goliath"; Dietrich, "Die Erzählungen von David und Goliat"; Wesselius, "A New View on the Relation between Septuagint and Masoretic Text in the Story of David and Goliath"; Barthélemy, "Trois niveaux d'analyse (a propos de David et Goliath)," in Barthélemy et al., *The Story of David and Goliath*, 47–54; Gooding "An Approach to the Literary and Textual Problems in the David-Goliath Story: 1 Sam 16–18," in Barthélemy et al., *The Story of David and Goliath*, 55–86.

[4]   E.g., Bergen, *1, 2 Samuel*, 27, 187, n. 42; Tsumura, *The First Book of Samuel*, 434–36. Among earlier scholars Keil supported the MT as original and the LXX as a condensation of it. He also discussed the opinions of scholars on both sides of the issue in his day. See Keil, *The Books of Samuel* (1866), 176–78, n. 1.

[5]   Van der Kooij, "The Story of David and Goliath," 130.

army, and David is not. The presence of Goliath's shield bearer preceding him (17:41) may have been seen as an insuperable impediment to David killing Goliath with a sling stone (17:49). David's not using a sword to defeat Goliath in 17:50 could be seen as in conflict with 17:51. In yet another case, David is described to Saul as Jesse's son in 16:18, whereas in 17:55–58 Saul does not appear to know who David's father is. In some cases, verses may have been eliminated because they appeared duplicative of other accounts. 1 Sam 18:1–4 is thematically similar to 20:41–42, perhaps leading to the LXX's elimination of 18:1–4. 1 Sam 18:5 and 18:29b–30 may have been omitted because of their similarity to 18:14–16 (see also 18:6b–7).[6] 1 Sam 18:10–11 may have been eliminated since it appeared to duplicate the similar incident in 19:9–10 with Saul seeking to kill David with a spear. In still other cases, once earlier material was expunged from the text, later text need to be eliminated for consistency. Thus, the elimination of 17:25 (Saul's promise of his daughter as a bride) required also the elimination of 18:17–19 (the failure to give Merab to David), which in turn required excision of 18:21b and perhaps also 18:26b. Therefore, with the possible exception of 18:6a and 18:8a, all the texts missing from the LXX can be reasonably explained as attempts to eliminate perceived conflicts with other texts in 1 Samuel or to avoid duplication.

17:1 וַיַּאַסְפ֣וּ ... וַיֵּאָסְפ֣וּ—Both instances of אָסַף are third masculine plural preterite (imperfect with *waw* consecutive). The first is Qal (G) and transitive, "they gathered [their camps]." The second is Niphal (N) and intransitive, "they gathered (together)," as again in 17:2 (נֶאֶסְפ֔וּ, perfect) and previously in 13:5, 11.

וַיַּחֲנ֣וּ ... מַחֲנֵיהֶם֙—The noun מַחֲנֶה, denoting a military "camp" (17:1, 4, 17, 46, 53), is derived from the verb חָנָה, whose Qal (G) means "to camp" (17:1, 2).

שֹׂכֹה—There were two places in Judah named "Socoh." This one is the city in the Shephelah southeast of Azekah (also mentioned in Josh 15:35; 2 Chr 11:7; 28:18). It is probably modern Khirbet es-Shuweikeh. The other was in southern Judah about ten miles (sixteen kilometers) southwest of Hebron (Josh 15:48). It is probably modern Khirbet Shuweikeh.

עֲזֵקָה—"Azekah" is probably modern Tell Zaqareyeh, which is on the north side of the Valley of the Terebinth (Wadi es-Sant) and three miles (five kilometers) northwest of Socoh. It is also mentioned in Josh 10:10–11; 15:35; Jer 34:7; Neh 11:30; 2 Chr 11:9.

בְּאֶפֶס דַּמִּים׃—"Ephes-dammim" is somewhere between Socoh and Azekah. It is called Pas-dammim in 1 Chr 11:13. It may be modern Damun, west of Socoh and southeast of Azekah.

17:2 בְּעֵמֶק הָאֵלָה—The "Valley of the Terebinth," or the "Valley of Elah," is modern Wadi es-Sant, south of the Sorek Valley (Wadi es-Surar) and parallel to it. The Valley

---

6 Some scholars propose that the LXX omitted 18:1–5 and 18:29b–30 because they conflict with Saul's statement in 17:33, which they interpret to mean that David was not yet a seasoned warrior. However, Saul's statement in 17:33 was that David was still a youth; Saul did not claim that David had no prior battle experience. Moreover, David defended his abilities in 17:34–36, and his possession of a sling and his obvious skill in using it testified to his training as a warrior, even if he previously had no actual combat experience.

of the Terebinth is also mentioned in 17:19; 21:10 (ET 21:9). אֵלָה denotes a terebinth, *Pistacia palaestina*, a tree species native to the Levant.

וַיַּעַרְכוּ מִלְחָמָה—The Qal (G) of עָרַךְ, "to arrange" or "set in battle array," recurs in 17:8 and in both verses the noun מִלְחָמָה is an adverbial accusative (GKC, § 118 q), "for war." The verb also appears in 17:21 with its cognate noun מַעֲרָכָה, "battle line"; for the noun, see the first textual note on 17:8.

לִקְרַאת—The Qal (G) infinitive construct of קָרָא II, "to meet, encounter," with the preposition לְ often appears in a hostile sense for engaging in military action, as again in 17:21, 48 (twice), 55.

17:4 אִישׁ־הַבֵּנַיִם—Literally this may mean "a man of the in-betweens," but it is translated as "a certain soldier." The noun בֵּנַיִם (dual in form; with definite article: הַבֵּנַיִם) appears in the OT only here and in the same phrase in 17:23. However, it is used nineteen times in the Qumran *War Scroll* to mean "soldier, skirmisher, combatant" (cf. LXX 1 Sam 17:4: ἀνὴρ δυνατός).[7] בֵּנַיִם is often assumed to be derived from the preposition בְּ, "between." If so, this phrase may have a literal meaning something like "in-between man" or "man of the interval," i.e., a soldier who takes his stand in between armies (see *CDCH*).

גָּלְיָת שְׁמוֹ מִגַּת—Literally "Goliath was his name, from Gath." Goliath is named twice in this chapter (also 17:23), and each time the author associates his name with his city of origin, גַּת, "Gath," which is spelled with the first and last consonants of his name. "Goliath" may be a Philistine name, or it may be of Hittite or Lydian origin.[8] He is also named later in 1 Sam 21:10 (ET 21:9); 22:10; 2 Sam 21:19; and in 1 Chr 20:5.

שֵׁשׁ אַמּוֹת וָזָרֶת:—The MT reads "six cubits and a span" and is supported by Symmachus' Greek recension, the fifth column of the Origen's *Hexapla*, and the Vulgate.[9] 4QSamᵃ reads ארבע[ן א[מות וזרת, "four cubits and a span," as does the LXX (τεσσάρων πήχεων καὶ σπιθαμῆς), the Lucianic Greek recension, and Josephus.[10] An ancient cubit could range anywhere from sixteen to eighteen inches, and a span—the width of a flared hand, thumb to little finger—was commonly reckoned as half of a cubit. According to the MT, then, Goliath was between eight feet, eight inches (264 centimeters), and nine feet, nine inches (297 centimeters). According to the LXX, he was between six feet (183 centimeters) and six feet, nine inches (206 centimeters). It is difficult to decide between these two readings, but Hays has made a good case that the smaller LXX reading is more likely correct.[11] The elements in Hays' argument are these:

---

[7] Carmignac, "Précisions apportées au vocabulaire d'hébreu biblique par la guerre des fils de lumière contre les fils de ténèbres," 356–57; see also the discussion in McCarter, *I Samuel*, 290–91. The suggestion that the word means "champion" is based on conjecture. A rationalization such as Tsumura's (*The First Book of Samuel*, 439–40) that the word must have changed meaning between Biblical Hebrew and Qumranic Hebrew relies on supposition.

[8] See the discussion in McCarter, *I Samuel*, 291; Tsumura, *The First Book of Samuel*, 440.

[9] Hays, "Reconsidering the Height of Goliath," 705.

[10] Hays, "Reconsidering the Height of Goliath," 703–4. See Josephus, *Antiquities*, 6.171.

[11] Hays, "Reconsidering the Height of Goliath" and "The Height of Goliath: A Response to Clyde Billington." Billington's attempt ("Goliath and the Exodus Giants: How Tall Were They?") to refute Hays' arguments is unconvincing.

1. The Greek text of Codex Alexandrinus adds the missing verses from the MT to 1 Samuel 17–18, probably under the influence of the Vulgate, but it nevertheless reads "four cubits and a span."[12]

2. It is difficult to explain why a scribe would make Goliath shorter, thereby diminishing David's accomplishment. However, simple eye skip can explain how the reading שֵׁשׁ אַמּוֹת, "six cubits," was mistakenly placed into the text. A careless scribe's eye skipped momentarily from אַרְבַּע אַמּוֹת ("four cubits") in 17:4 to שֵׁשׁ מֵאוֹת ("six hundred") in 17:7. Since the second word in both instances is similar, the number שֵׁשׁ was accidently transferred from 17:7 to 17:4. While it may seem like there is a large amount of text between the two verses, it ought to be borne in mind that the MT of the book of Samuel is beset with a large number of such parablepsis errors, some spanning quite large quantities of text (see, e.g., the textual note on 14:41).[13]

3. While some have thought that the larger height for Goliath was required so that he would be powerful enough to carry the equipment he is described as having (17:5–7),[14] there is no reason that a muscular, well-trained man of six feet or taller could not have carried it.[15]

4. The real contrast in the account is not between David and Goliath, but between David and Saul. David's height is never mentioned, but Saul's height is clearly his outstanding physical feature (9:2; 10:23). Moreover, Saul was chosen to be king specifically to fight the Israelites' battles (8:20). The average Israelite is thought to have been between five feet (152 centimeters) and five feet, three inches tall (160 centimeters), and tall Israelites were most likely about five feet, eight inches (173 centimeters) tall. Yet Saul was taller than even these literally "from his shoulders upward" (9:2; 10:23). Thus, Saul was a good ten inches (25 centimeters) taller than the tallest Israelite—in the same height range as Goliath according to the LXX. Therefore Saul ought to have fought the Philistine. One should also note that Saul never mentions Goliath's height as a reason why David ought not to engage the Philistine in battle. To do so would have made Saul's own cowardice all the more evident.[16]

17:5 וְכוֹבַע נְחֹשֶׁת—This means "and a helmet of bronze." The noun for "helmet" is most likely a loanword, perhaps from the Hittite *kupaḫ(ḫ)i* (*HALOT*), which led to it being spelled two ways: כּוֹבַע here (also Is 59:17; Jer 46:4; Ezek 27:10; 38:5; 2 Chr 26:14), but קוֹבַע in 1 Sam 17:38 (also Ezek 23:24).

וְשִׁרְיוֹן קַשְׂקַשִּׂים הוּא לָבוּשׁ—Literally "and [with] body armor of scales he was clothed." The noun שִׁרְיוֹן denotes a coat of armor and recurs later in 17:5 and in 17:38 (also 1 Ki 22:34; Is 59:17; Neh 4:10 [ET 4:16]; 2 Chr 18:33; 26:14). The noun קַשְׂקֶשֶׂת (by reduplication of the biliteral root קשׂ; see GKC, § 84[b] o–p) means "fish scale" (also Lev 11:9, 10, 12; Deut 14:9, 10; Ezek 29:4) and is used here to depict the construction

---

12 Hays, "Reconsidering the Height of Goliath," 704.

13 Hays, "Reconsidering the Height of Goliath," 707.

14 This is Bergen's objection to the smaller LXX figure (*1, 2 Samuel*, 189, n. 49).

15 Hays, "Reconsidering the Height of Goliath," 708–9; Hays, "The Height of Goliath: A Response to Clyde Billington," 514–15.

16 Hays, "Reconsidering the Height of Goliath," 710–11.

of Goliath's armor. לָבוּשׁ, "clothed," is the Qal passive (Gp) participle of לָבֵשׁ, "to wear (clothing)."

חֲמֵשֶׁת־אֲלָפִים שְׁקָלִים נְחֹשֶׁת:—"Five thousand shekels of bronze" indicates a weight of approximately 121 pounds (55 kilograms). נְחֹשֶׁת is an accusative of material (cf. Waltke-O'Connor, § 10.2.3c) or an attributive accusative (cf. Joüon, § 127 b–d), since "bronze" designates the metal from which the armor was made. See also בַּרְזֶל in 17:7.

17:6 וּמִצְחַת נְחֹשֶׁת עַל־רַגְלָיו—The noun מִצְחָה refers to a "greave," a piece of armor for one's shin. The singular must refer to each of two, one for each leg. The noun רֶגֶל can refer to the leg, part of a leg, or a foot; here its suffixed dual denotes "his shins."

וְכִידוֹן—The noun כִּידוֹן recurs in 17:45. It is traditionally translated as "javelin," although it may mean "scimitar" (see *CDCH*). If "scimitar" is the correct meaning, then Goliath was armed with both a sword (חֶרֶב, 17:45, 51; 21:10 [ET 21:9]; 22:10) and what was probably a shorter knife-like weapon. Here and in 17:45, the LXX translates כִּידוֹן as ἀσπίς, "round shield."

17:7 וְעֵץ חֲנִיתוֹ כִּמְנוֹר אֹרְגִים—"And the shaft of his spear was like a beam of weavers." The identical description is in 2 Sam 21:19. The Qere of the first word, עֵץ, translated as "shaft," is literally "a tree" or "wood." The Kethib is חֵץ, "arrow." The noun מְנוֹר, "beam" (from the root ניר), appears four times in the OT (also 2 Sam 21:19; 1 Chr 11:23; 20:5), all with a form of אָרַג, "to weave," whose plural Qal (G) participle here is used as a substantive, "weavers." For the sake of English, the participle is translated as a singular: "a *weaver's* beam."

וְלַהֶבֶת חֲנִיתוֹ—Usually the noun לֶהָבָה (in construct: לַהֶבֶת) refers to a "flame" of fire (e.g., Is 4:5; 10:17), but here it refers to the (shiny) metal "head" or "point" of the spear.

שֵׁשׁ־מֵאוֹת שְׁקָלִים בַּרְזֶל—"Six hundred shekels of iron" weighed approximately 14.6 pounds (6.6 kilograms). Goliath's spear is his only "iron" (בַּרְזֶל) weapon mentioned, although his "sword" may also have been iron (חֶרֶב, 17:45, 51; cf. 21:10 [ET 21:9]; 22:10).

הַצִּנָּה—The noun צִנָּה refers to a large body "shield." Usually מָגֵן denotes a smaller shield that could be maneuvered more easily.

17:8 מַעַרְכֹת יִשְׂרָאֵל—The feminine noun מַעֲרָכָה is used as a technical term for the ranks of soldiers arranged for battle (*HALOT*, 2), thus this phrase means "the battle lines of Israel." The noun recurs in 17:10, 20, 21, 22, 23 (Qere), 26, 36, 45, 48. It is derived from the verb עָרַךְ, "to array for battle"; see the second textual note on 17:2.

לַעֲרֹךְ מִלְחָמָה—"In battle formation" is literally "to arrange for battle." See the second textual note on 17:2.

בְּרוּ־לָכֶם—"Choose for yourselves." The verb is a Qal (G) imperative masculine plural of בָּרָה II, "choose," a hapax legomenon (so *HALOT*, *DCH*). The verb might be a by-form of בָּרַר, "purify; choose."

17:9 לְהִלָּחֵם אִתִּי—In this chapter the Niphal (N) of לָחַם, "to fight," is used with the preposition אֵת, "with," here; with the adverb יַחַד, "together," in 17:10; and with the preposition עִם, "with," in 17:19, 32, 33.

17:10 חֵרַפְתִּי—"I mock" is a Piel (D) perfect first person singular of חָרַף. This verb denotes taunting and shaming (*HALOT*). Its Piel recurs in 17:25, 26, 36, 45; also 2 Sam 21:21; 23:9.

17:11 וַיֵּחַתּוּ—"They were demoralized" is a Niphal (N) preterite (imperfect with *waw* consecutive) third masculine plural of the verb חָתַת. The identical Niphal imperfect, but without *waw*, was used for the enemies of Yahweh in 2:10.

17:12 אֶפְרָתִי—For "Ephrathite," see the last textual note on 1:1, including the footnotes.

בָּא בַאֲנָשִׁים:—This unique expression literally means "he was advanced among men." The verb בּוֹא, "come," can be used in expressions meaning "to be advanced in age." The Qal (G) form בָּא here and in the similar expression elsewhere (בָּא בַיָּמִים, literally "advanced in the *days*," Gen 24:1; Josh 13:1a; 23:1; 1 Ki 1:1) could be either the third masculine singular perfect or the masculine singular participle. The expression בָּאִים בַּיָּמִים in Gen 18:11 has the participle (masculine plural), whereas perfect forms are so used in בָּאתָ בַיָּמִים in Josh 13:1b and in בָּאתִי בַּיָּמִים in Josh 23:2. The reading בָּא בַּשָּׁנִים, "advanced in the *years*," here is implied by the Greek Lucianic recension, the Peshitta, and the Vulgate. However, there is no other instance of that expression in the OT. The similar phrases in the previous verses cited all use the plural of יוֹם, "day," rather than שָׁנָה, "year."

17:13–14 וַיֵּלְכוּ ... הָלְכוּ ... הָלְכוּ—"They (had) followed." The verb is expressed twice in 17:13, first as a Qal (G) preterite (imperfect with *waw* consecutive) and second as a Qal perfect, which is repeated in 17:14.

הַגְּדֹלִים ... הַקָּטָן ... הַגְּדֹלִים—Each adjective with the definite article functions as a superlative: "the eldest ones ... the youngest one ... the eldest ones." David was designated הַקָּטָן also in 16:11. Here in 17:13 Eliab is named הַבְּכוֹר, "the firstborn," but he will be called הַגָּדוֹל, "the eldest/oldest one," in 17:28.

17:15 וְדָוִד הֹלֵךְ וָשָׁב—Literally "and David was going and returning." The two Qal (G) participles denote customary or ongoing acts.[17]

מֵעַל שָׁאוּל—Literally this means "from over Saul." The preposition עַל suggests that David would stand before and thus be "over" the seated or enthroned monarch in readiness to serve him. Cf. the idiom עָמַד לִפְנֵי, "stand before," in 16:21, 22.

17:16 הַשְׁכֵּם וְהַעֲרֵב—These are Hiphil (H) infinitive absolutes that serve as adverbs (GKC, § 113 k): "every morning and evening." The first is of שָׁכַם, whose Hiphil means "to rise early" (also in 17:20; see the first textual note on 9:26). The second is of עָרַב, a verb that is related to the common noun עֶרֶב, "evening." The verb occurs only three times in the OT: twice in the Qal (G), "to become evening" (Judg 19:9) or "to become dark" (Is 24:11), and once (here) in the Hiphil (H), "to do [something] in the evening."

17:17 וְהָרֵץ—"Take [them] quickly" translates the Hiphil (H) imperative of רוּץ, "to run." Its Hiphil (H) has the same meaning in Gen 41:14; 2 Chr 35:13.

---

[17] Waltke-O'Connor, § 37.6d.

17:18 חֲרִצֵי הֶחָלָב֒—This means "portions of cheese." It is the only instance of the noun חָרִיץ meaning "a cut, slice; portion" of food. Twice elsewhere it denotes a sharp iron "pick" (2 Sam 12:31; 1 Chr 20:3).

לְשַׂר־הָאֶלֶף—Literally "to the prince of the thousand," this means "the company commander." See the first textual note on 8:12.

וְאֶת־אַחֶיךָ תִּפְקֹד לְשָׁלוֹם—Literally "you shall visit/observe your brothers for peace," this means "check on your brothers' welfare." See, similarly, וַיִּשְׁאַל לְאֶחָיו לְשָׁלוֹם, literally "and he asked concerning his brothers regarding peace," in 17:22.

עֲרֻבָּתָם—This is translated as "their pledge." The noun עֲרֻבָּה is used only here and in Prov 17:18, where it denotes something given as a pledge of repayment, a kind of collateral. The meaning here is obscure.

17:20 וַיִּטֹּשׁ—This Qal (G) form of נָטַשׁ here and in 17:22 simply means that David "left" the sheep and the items without any negative connotation. But when Eliab uses this verb in 17:28 (נָטַשְׁתָּ), he may be insinuating that David "abandoned" the sheep to someone else and thereby shirked his responsibilities.

הַמַּעְגָּלָה—This means "to the outskirts of the camp." The masculine noun מַעְגָּל (here with the definite article and a directional *he*) is usually assumed to be related to the noun עֵגֶל, "calf," and is often understood to refer to a ring of wagons around a camp (*HALOT*). Its only other OT occurrences are in 26:5, 7.

וְהַחַיִל הַיֹּצֵא֙ אֶל־הַמַּעֲרָכָה וְהֵרֵעוּ בַּמִּלְחָמָה׃—Literally "and the force, the one going out to the battle line—and they shouted in the war," this is translated as a temporal clause: "as the army was going out to the battle line and raising a battle cry." The Hiphil (H) third common plural perfect (with conjunctive *waw*) of רוּעַ, "to shout," has the form הֵרֵעוּ only here; it is spelled הָרִיעוּ in Judg 15:14; Ezra 3:11.

17:21 וַתַּעֲרֹךְ—Since the form of the Qal (G) of עָרַךְ (see the second textual note on 17:2) is third feminine singular, grammatically מַעֲרָכָה must be its subject.

17:22 מֵעָלָיו—"From upon him" implies that he was carrying them, hence "the items *he was carrying.*"

שׁוֹמֵר הַכֵּלִים—"The quartermaster" is literally "the keeper of the items."

17:23 מִמַּעַרְכוֹת פְּלִשְׁתִּים—The first word is the Qere, "*from the battle lines of* the Philistines." The Kethib, מִמַּעֲרוֹת, "from the caves of," has suffered from haplography due to the juxtaposition of the similarly shaped letters *resh* and *kaph*.

כַּדְּבָרִים הָאֵלֶּה—Literally "according to these words," this is translated as "his usual words." The demonstrative pronoun אֵלֶּה must refer to the words in 17:8–10.

17:24–25 וְכֹל אִישׁ יִשְׂרָאֵל ... וַיֹּאמֶר ׀ אִישׁ יִשְׂרָאֵל—1 Sam 17:24 begins with a singular, "and every man of Israel," which has a collective sense, since the verse continues with plural forms referring to all the men. At the beginning of 17:25 the singular אִישׁ יִשְׂרָאֵל is the subject of the singular verb וַיֹּאמֶר, but it too has a collective sense.

17:25 הַרְּאִיתֶם֙—Literally "have you seen?" The consonant ר rarely accepts a *daghesh* but does so here (-רְּ-) after the interrogative *he*. See GKC, § 22 s.

כִּי—"Most certainly" is the asseverative or emphatic use of כִּי (*HALOT*, s.v. כִּי II, 1).

יְעַשְּׁרֶנּוּ הַמֶּלֶךְ ׀ עֹשֶׁר גָּדוֹל—Literally "the king will enrich him [with] great riches." יְעַשְּׁרֶנּוּ is the suffixed Hiphil (H) imperfect of עָשַׁר. It is rare for a Hiphil (H) imperfect to lose its theme vowel, *hireq* (GKC, § 60 g); the expected form would be יַעְשִׁירֶנּוּ. Here the Hiphil (H) of עָשַׁר has the causative meaning "to make someone rich" and is in a double accusative construction. The first accusative is its third masculine singular suffix, "him." The second accusative is the cognate noun עֹשֶׁר, "riches." A cognate of the verb is often used for an "accusative of the internal object" (Joüon, § 125 q). The accusative noun is then modified by the adjective גָּדוֹל, "great"; for this "qualified" construction, see Joüon, § 125 r.

חָפְשִׁי—This adjective normally means "free" (versus a slave), but in context it probably denotes freedom from taxation, thus "tax-exempt."

17:26 הַלָּז—For this rare demonstrative pronoun, "this," see the fifth textual note on 14:1.

17:27 כַּדָּבָר הַזֶּה—"In the same way" is literally "according to this word." For the plural equivalent, see the second textual note on 17:23. Here this phrase refers to the words in 17:25 that convey the king's promise.

17:28 לָמָּה־זֶּה—This is translated as "why in the world?" זֶה is used emphatically.[18]

זְדֹנְךָ—The noun זָדוֹן denotes "insolence" or "pride, arrogance."

רֹעַ לְבָבֶךָ—Literally "the evil of your heart," this is rendered as "your bad intentions." By context Eliab is not accusing David of continually having nothing but evil thoughts and intentions. He is simply accusing David of leaving his responsibilities at home in order to gawk at the battle scene. The only other instance of רֹעַ in construct with a word for "heart" also notes a temporary thought or mood (Neh 2:2).

17:29 הֲלוֹא דָבָר הוּא׃—Literally "isn't it (just) a word?" David is referring to his words in 17:26. He asks Eliab this rhetorical question here to make him think that he was merely asking questions in 17:26 without intending to take any action.

17:30 וַיִּסֹּב מֵאֶצְלוֹ אֶל־מוּל אַחֵר—Literally "and he turned from near him to in front of another (man)." The preposition אֵצֶל means "near, at the side of," and the preposition מוּל means "in front of."

וַיֹּאמֶר כַּדָּבָר הַזֶּה—Literally "and he said like this word," this means "and he asked the same questions." See the second textual note on 17:23 and the textual note on 17:27.

17:31 וַיִּקָּחֵהוּ׃—Literally "and he took him," this must mean that Saul sent for David or summoned him.

17:32 אַל־יִפֹּל לֵב־אָדָם עָלָיו—Literally "may the heart of a man not fall on account of him," this idiom means "do not let anyone despair because of him [Goliath]."

עַבְדְּךָ—For "your servant," see the third textual note on 1:11. The word recurs in 17:34, 36 (see also 17:58).

17:33 נַעַר ... מִנְּעֻרָיו׃—The noun נַעַר, "boy, lad; servant," in this context is emphasizing David's lack of proficiency relative to Goliath, hence "an inexperienced young

---

[18] *IBH*, § 25 B; GKC, § 136 c; Joüon, § 143 g; Waltke-O'Connor, § 17.4.3c.

man." Related to it is the abstract plural noun נְעוּרִים, "(time of) youthfulness," which heightens the contrast: Goliath was already a man of war when he was David's age.

17:34 וּבָא הָאֲרִי וְאֶת־הַדּוֹב—This is translated as "whenever a lion or a bear would come." In Hebrew the article is used on species to designate them as a class ("the lion," "the bear"). In such cases the corresponding English usage often requires an indefinite article or a plural (cf. 17:36, 37).[19] The use of the direct object marker אֶת in front of "bear" is unusual since the noun is a subject of the verb וּבָא. One would expect the conjunction אוֹ, "or." (Cf. 17:36, where גַּם אֶת־הָאֲרִי גַּם־הַדּוֹב are direct objects of the verb הִכָּה.)

מֵהָעֵדֶר:—This is translated as "from the flock." The noun עֵדֶר is a general word for a group of animals.

17:35 וַיָּקָם עָלַי—"If it attacked me" is literally "and it rose against me."

בִּזְקָנוֹ—In context this means "by the fur on its head." For men, זָקָן denotes a "beard," but for animals it refers to their cranial fur.

17:38 וַיַּלְבֵּשׁ שָׁאוּל אֶת־דָּוִד מַדָּיו—Twice in this verse the Hiphil (H) of לָבֵשׁ, "to clothe," takes a double accusative construction (see Joüon, § 125 u). The first accusative is the person who is clothed (here דָּוִד), and the second is the item of clothing put on him (here מַדָּיו, "his [Saul's] outer garments"). See also the third textual note on 17:38.

קוֹבַע נְחֹשֶׁת—For "a helmet of bronze," see the first textual note on 17:5.

וַיַּלְבֵּשׁ אֹתוֹ שִׁרְיוֹן:—"And he dressed him in armor" is missing in the LXX. For שִׁרְיוֹן, see the second textual note on 17:5.

17:39 וַיֹּאֶל—"He attempted." This is a Hiphil (H) preterite (imperfect with *waw* consecutive) of יָאַל. This verb occurs only in the Hiphil and means "to be willing; to undertake, try to do."

וַיְסִרֵם דָּוִד מֵעָלָיו:—This clause with the Hiphil (H) of סוּר is literally "and David removed them from upon himself."

17:40 מַקְלוֹ—The noun מַקֵּל denotes a "staff." Its plural is feminine in form; in 17:43 בַּמַּקְלוֹת is translated as "with sticks."

חַלֻּקֵי־אֲבָנִים—This construct phrase with the plural of the adjective חַלָּק (a hapax legomenon) is literally "smooth ones of stones." The construct adjective functions adjectivally: "smooth stones." See GKC, § 132 c, and Waltke-O'Connor, § 14.3.3b, including example 4, both of which allow for the possibility of a superlative, i.e., "smoothest stones."

בִּכְלִי הָרֹעִים אֲשֶׁר־לוֹ וּבַיַּלְקוּט—Literally this is "in a pouch of the shepherds, which belonged to him, and in a bag." וּבַיַּלְקוּט is epexegetical, explaining that the "pouch" is a "bag"; see Waltke-O'Connor, § 39.2.1b, including example 6. The noun יַלְקוּט is a hapax legomenon, and its meaning, "bag," is inferred from its context here.

וְקַלְעוֹ—The noun קֶלַע, "a sling," recurs in 17:50. For the cognate verb, see the first textual note on 17:49.

---

[19] *IBH*, § 20 F; GKC, § 126 g; Joüon, § 137 o; Waltke-O'Connor, § 13.5.1f.

17:41 וַיֵּלֶךְ הַפְּלִשְׁתִּי הֹלֵךְ וְקָרֵב אֶל־דָּוִד—The participle הֹלֵךְ, "walking," and the verbal adjective קָרֵב, "approaching," together depict an action in progress: "the Philistine came, *continually approaching* David," i.e., drawing closer and closer to him. See GKC, § 113 u (contra Joüon, § 123 s, who supposes that the participle הֹלֵךְ should be emended to the infinitive absolute הָלוֹךְ).

17:42 וַיַּבֵּט הַפְּלִשְׁתִּי—In some passages the Hiphil (H) of נָבַט refers to "looking down" from a higher elevation at something lower (see BDB, Hiphil, 1 b and 3). Such a nuance here would reinforce the height advantage of the Philistine over David.

וְאַדְמֹנִי—For "ruddy," see the first textual note and the commentary on 16:12.

עִם־יְפֵה מַרְאֶה:—"With a handsome appearance" is similar to עִם־יְפֵה עֵינַיִם, "with beautiful eyes" in 16:12 (see the second textual note there).

17:43 בֵּאלֹהָיו:—This is translated as "by his gods." The Philistines were polytheistic, as demonstrated in chapter 6, where they acknowledged Yahweh as a god.

17:44 וּלְבֶהֱמַת הַשָּׂדֶה:—Literally this means "and to the beast(s) of the field" (cf. Joel 1:20). See the similar prepositional phrase וּלְחַיַּת הָאָרֶץ, "and to the animal(s) of the earth," in 1 Sam 17:46.

17:45 וּבַחֲנִית וּבְכִידוֹן—Literally this is "and with a spear and with a javelin." For "spear," see the first textual note on 17:7, and for "javelin," see the second textual note on 17:6.

יְהוָה צְבָאוֹת—For "Yahweh of armies," see the fourth textual note on 1:3.

אֱלֹהֵי מַעַרְכוֹת יִשְׂרָאֵל אֲשֶׁר חֵרַפְתָּ:—See 17:10, 25, 26, 36.

17:46 יְסַגֶּרְךָ—In the Qal (G) סָגַר means "to shut, close." Its Piel (D) occurs here and three other times in the OT (1 Sam 24:19 [ET 24:18]; 26:8; 2 Sam 18:28), meaning "deliver up" or "hand over," as does its more common Hiphil (H).

17:47 יְהוֹשִׁיעַ—"He is able to save" is a modal use of this (Hiphil [H]) imperfect verb signaling capability.[20]

וְנָתַן אֶתְכֶם בְּיָדֵנוּ:—The Qal (G) perfect of נָתַן may have a conjunctive *waw*, "he (already) has given you into our hands," or a *waw* consecutive, "he will give you into our hands," as translated. In Codex Leningradensis, the consonants of בְּיָדֵנוּ are for the singular "our hand," but they are pointed with the vowels for the plural noun בְּיָדֵינוּ. Many Masoretic manuscripts have the plural, which is supported by the LXX (εἰς χεῖρας ἡμῶν).

17:48 וַיֵּלֶךְ וַיִּקְרַב לִקְרַאת—Literally "and he went, and he drew near to meet," the two verbs form a hendiadys: "and he came near." For לִקְרַאת, see the second textual note on 4:1.

17:49 וַיְקַלַּע—The verb קָלַע, "to sling," is cognate to the noun קֶלַע, "a sling" (see the fourth textual note on 17:40). The Piel (D), which occurs in the OT only here and in 1 Sam 25:29, has the same meaning as the Qal (G), found only in Judg 20:16; Jer 10:18.

---

[20] *IBH*, § 47 D.

וַתִּטְבַּע הָאֶבֶן בְּמִצְחוֹ—"The stone sank into his forehead." The noun אֶבֶן, "stone," is feminine, and so the form of the Qal (G) of טָבַע, "to sink down," is feminine (third singular preterite [imperfect with *waw* consecutive]).

17:51 וַיְמֹתְתֵהוּ—"And he finished killing him." The Polel of מוּת refers to finishing off the wounded. See the second textual note on 14:13.

17:52 עַד־בּוֹאֲךָ גַיְא—The MT has "until you come to a valley." For the suffixed infinitive construct בּוֹאֲךָ, see the textual note on 15:7. The LXX reads ἕως εἰσόδου Γεθ, "until arriving at Gath." There are two reasons to prefer "Gath" in the LXX here. The first reason is that the next destination is Ekron, another city of the Philistine pentapolis (6:17), and Gath and Ekron are the endpoints of the Israelite slaughter of Philistines later in this verse. Second, idioms that employ the suffixed infinitive construct בּוֹאֲךָ or בֹּאֲכָה and that designate goals always have a city as the goal.[21]

שַׁעֲרַיִם—"Shaaraim" is a place mentioned in the vicinity of Socoh and Azekah in Josh 15:35–36. Garfinkel and Ganor argue that Khirbet Qeiyafa, which overlooks the Valley of the Terebinth, ought to be identified as Shaaraim.[22] At that site archaeologists have found a small fortified city with two gates, and שַׁעֲרַיִם is a dual form of שַׁעַר, so it could mean "two gates." However, Na'aman notes that the ending *-ayim* (ַיִם-) in place-names does not necessarily form a dual and believes that Khirbet Qeiyafa does not meet the other geographic criteria to be identified as Shaaraim.[23] Instead, he believes Khirbet Qeiyafa is biblical Gob (2 Sam 21:18–19).[24]

17:53 מִדְּלֹק—This is the Qal (G) infinitive construct of דָּלַק with the preposition מִן. Usually דָּלַק means "to burn," but in military contexts it can mean "hotly pursue" (BDB, Qal, 2).

וַיָּשֹׁסּוּ—This is the Qal (G) of שָׁסַס, "to plunder." שָׁסַס is a rarer by-form (six times in the OT) of the slightly more common verb שָׁסָה (eleven times in the OT) in 14:48; 23:1.

17:54 יְרוּשָׁלָ͏ִם—According to Josh 15:63, in the early period following the conquest, Israelites lived together with Jebusites in Jerusalem, but its citadel was still in the hands of the Jebusites. For further discussion, see the commentary.

17:55 חֵי־נַפְשְׁךָ הַמֶּלֶךְ אִם־יָדַעְתִּי—Literally this means "[by] the life of your soul, O King, if I know." The article with הַמֶּלֶךְ marks it as a vocative.[25] The first clause is a common oath formula that begins with חֵי, the construct form of the adjective/substantive חַי, "alive; life" (see BDB, s.v. חַי, 1 b). If its contents are a denial, the second clause begins with אִם, as here. If the oath affirms something, the second clause begins with כִּי.[26]

17:56 שְׁאַל אַתָּה—Literally "ask—you!" means "you—ask!" The personal pronoun (second masculine singular) used with the imperative is emphatic. Since Saul is

---

[21] Gen 10:19, 30; 13:10; 25:18; Judg 6:4; 11:33; 1 Sam 15:7; 27:8; 1 Ki 18:46.

[22] Garfinkel and Ganor, "Khirbet Qeiyafa: Sha'arayim."

[23] Na'aman, "Shaaraim—The Gateway to the Kingdom of Judah."

[24] Na'aman, "In Search of the Ancient Name of Khirbet Qeiyafa."

[25] *IBH*, § 20 D.

[26] *IBH*, § 64 D.

speaking, the author may intend a play on the verb שָׁאַל, "to ask, request," and the name שָׁאוּל, "Saul," meaning "requested." The author engages in this wordplay elsewhere.[27]

הָעֶלֶם:—The masculine segholate noun עֶלֶם is a rare word that is a near synonym for נַעַר, "boy, young man." In the OT עֶלֶם occurs only here and in 20:22. The feminine equivalent, עַלְמָה, "a virgin," appears seven times in the OT.[28]

17:58 הַנַּעַר—"Young man" is a vocative marked with the article; see also הַמֶּלֶךְ in 17:55.

Commentary

c. 1019 BC

The account of David's defeat of Goliath is one of the best-known and most beloved stories in the Bible. In it David exhibits trust in Yahweh as well as military skill, while maintaining respect for Saul's authority. The story has become a classic paradigm for the triumph of an underdog, a byword, so that everyone knows what a "David versus Goliath" feat is, even if they have never read the Bible.

Despite the popularity of this narrative, there remain a number of problems noted by scholars:

1. Is the longer MT text original, or does the shorter LXX contain a better reporting of the encounter between David and Goliath? The longer MT text is most likely the original. (See "The Text of 1 Samuel 17:1–18:30" at the beginning of the textual notes.)

2. Who actually killed Goliath? According to 2 Sam 21:19, a certain Elhanan killed Goliath, although the parallel in 1 Chr 20:5 claims Elhanan killed Goliath's brother. The texts of both 2 Sam 21:19 and 1 Chr 20:5 seem to be problematic.[29] In 2 Sam 21:19, the name of Elhanan's father is given as יַעְרֵי אֹרְגִים בֵּית הַלַּחְמִי, "Jaare-oregim the Bethlehemite." Since "oregim" means "weavers," a word which occurs later in that verse, it appears to have been accidentally transferred after the name of Elhanan's father. Since the name of Elhanan's father in 1 Chr 20:5 is "Jair" (יָעִיר),[30] it appears as if the accidental transfer of "oregim" after "Jair" led to the adjustment of the absolute form "Jair" to the construct form "Jaare" to form a single-phrase name.[31] There is also a problem in 1 Chr 20:5, which says that Elhanan

---

27 See the first textual note on 1:28; "Samuel Warns Israel about Kings (8:10–22)" in the commentary on 8:1–22; the first textual note on 10:22; the commentary on 12:13; and the textual note on 14:37.

28 Gen 24:43; Ex 2:8; Is 7:14; Ps 68:26 (ET 68:25); Prov 30:19; Song 1:3; 6:8. (Its plural form serves as some kind of musical notation in Ps 46:1 [ET superscription]; 1 Chr 15:20.)

29 A helpful discussion of this passage in both 2 Samuel and 1 Chronicles and its text-critical problems is Fouts, "Who Really Killed Goliath?"

30 This is the Qere (see the LXX: Ιαϊρ). The Kethib is יָעוּר, "Jaur," and is most likely a result of graphic confusion of *yod* and *waw*.

31 One of the two homographic nouns יַעַר, "forest" or "honeycomb" (see the textual note on 14:25), is probably the origin of the word in both 2 Sam 21:19 and 1 Chr 20:5. Thus, the name of Elhanan's father would have the unlikely meaning of either "forest of weavers" or "honeycomb of weavers." In addition, the name "Jair" is unique to 1 Chr 20:5 and occurs nowhere else in ancient Hebrew literature. For this reason Fouts believes that the text originally listed

killed "Lachmi the brother of Goliath" (אֶת־לַחְמִי אֲחִי גָּלְיָת). However, אֶת־לַחְמִי appears to be a corruption of בֵּית הַלַּחְמִי, "the Bethlehemite," as in 2 Sam 21:19.[32] Thus, due to the textual disruptions that appear to have affected both 2 Sam 21:19 and 1 Chr 20:5, we cannot be certain of the name of Elhanan's father or of the name of Goliath's brother. However, it is likely that the original notice in both 2 Sam 21:19 and 1 Chr 20:5 said that Elhanan killed "the brother of Goliath the Gittite" (אֶת אֲחִי גָּלְיָת הַגִּתִּי). Thus, there is no conflict between 2 Sam 21:19 and 1 Samuel 17.[33]

3. Is the description of Goliath's armor (1 Sam 17:5–7) appropriate for the time period (early Iron Age Palestine)? Based on depictions of Philistine warriors in Egyptian reliefs, some argue that Goliath's armor is a late fabrication by hypothetical Deuteronomistic editors.[34] These scholars believe that the author is depicting Goliath in the sixth-century BC Greek armor of a hoplite. However, Zorn observes:

> It is important, then, to note that efforts to see the descriptions of Goliath's gear as reflecting some sort of mercenary Greek hoplite … or retrojection of a Hellenized "Philistine" culture of the sixth century and later into the past … are not without their own problems. The scale armor worn by the Philistine and the existence of the shield-bearer who accompanies him are not part of the seventh to fifth centuries' hoplite repertoire. … To be added to this list of incongruous elements is the giant's probable bronze sickle sword [see the textual note on "javelin"/"scimitar" in 17:6], a weapon of the second millennium. …
>
> First and foremost, it must be stated that there are no late 11th-century B.C. sources that document the appearance of Philistine warriors that would be contemporary with the biblical Goliath. This is a crucial point. Those who argue against an Iron Age I context for this gear note that the 1 Samuel 17 descriptions do not match the appearance of the Sea Peoples warriors depicted in the mortuary temple of Ramesses III at Medinet Habu ca. 1175 B.C. … This, however, is something of a red herring. It is well known that the material culture of the Philistines evolved in the period after their arrival in south coastal Canaan.[35]

Indeed, Zorn argues that Goliath's armor and weapons are all accurate depictions of a Levantine chariot warrior of the early Iron Age.[36] This would qualify Goliath

---

Elhanan's father as Dodo (cf. 2 Sam 23:24; 1 Chr 11:26). According to Fouts, the similarity of the names Dodo (דֹּדוֹ) and David (דָּוִד) led to a mistake where a scribe's eye skipped the name ("Who Really Killed Goliath?" 20).

[32] Note that the name "Lachmi" occurs nowhere else in ancient Hebrew literature and that it appears to have the gentilic ending יִ־, which would be highly unusual for a personal name.

[33] For a more complete discussion of 2 Sam 21:19, see Steinmann, *2 Samuel*.

[34] Finkelstein, "The Philistines in the Bible," and Yadin, "Goliath's Armor and Israelite Collective Memory."

[35] Zorn, "Reconsidering Goliath," 2.

[36] Zorn, "Reconsidering Goliath," 3–17.

as an elite warrior, exactly the type of soldier who would be sent out of the ranks to challenge the Israelites to a dual to the death.

4.   Saul's behavior toward David appears to conflict with information in 1 Samuel 16. When David was initially described to Saul, the king was told the name of David's father (16:18).[37] If David had been playing a lyre to calm Saul and had become Saul's armor bearer (16:21–23), why did Saul not know anything about David's family (17:55–58)? When David was initially described to Saul, he was characterized as a warrior (אִישׁ מִלְחָמָה, literally "a man of war," 16:18), so why did Saul state that David was unprepared to confront Goliath (17:33)? However, we ought to keep in mind that David was probably one of many squires or armor bearers who served Saul. Note that Joab, David's general, had ten armor bearers (2 Sam 18:15), and a king was likely to have more. Many of them may have functioned mainly as servants. If David was one of many such servants, Saul may have taken little note of him—servants are often taken for granted. Saul may have had no recollection of the exact description of the young man given by one of his courtiers (16:18). The requests sent to Jesse (16:19, 22) may have been composed by one of Saul's staff members on his behalf, since we cannot assume that the king attended to the details of such matters. Moreover, we ought not to presuppose that Saul was correct in assuming that David did not have adequate training or experience. David defended his qualifications to take up the Philistine's challenge (17:34–37). Moreover, David was proficient with a sling and apparently possessed one of his own, perhaps as a weapon for guarding his father's sheep (17:40). Therefore, we ought to see the dissonance concerning Saul's knowledge of David between 1 Samuel 16 and 1 Samuel 17 as Saul's problem, not as contradictions within the text of the book of Samuel. Only after Saul witnessed David going out to confront the Philistine did he become concerned enough to investigate David's family (17:55). Since he had promised to give one of his daughters to any man who could defeat Goliath (17:25; 18:17–29), he wanted to know whether a marriage into David's family would be worthy of a king's daughter.

Therefore, the questions that are often raised about the trustworthiness of the account in 1 Samuel 17 are not sufficient to raise doubts about the accuracy or historicity of the encounter between David and Goliath. Instead, the author of the book of Samuel has preserved for us a dramatic story from David's actual accomplishments that demonstrates that God saves his people by grace and through faith alone[38] as well as the wisdom of God's choice of David over Saul.

Goliath Challenges Israel (17:1–11)

Once again Saul was presented with a Philistine offensive. The location of the Philistine bivouac is described as being on the border between Philistine and Israelite territory at Ephes-dammim (17:1). Perhaps this was the Philistine

---

[37]   In fact, it ought to be noted that Saul's servant did not use David's name at all in his description of him.

[38]   See 17:45 and, in 17:47, "Yahweh is able to save without a sword or a spear." Of course, the theological truth of salvation by grace alone and through faith alone is based on the understanding that the grace is that of the God of Israel, the one true and triune God (Father, Son, and Holy Spirit), and that the faith is faith in him alone. Cf. 17:46: "then all the earth will know that Israel has a God." One cannot be saved by any other kind of grace or faith.

staging area, and the text may indicate this by referring to the Philistine "camps" (plural in 17:1, 4, 53), perhaps one for each of the five cities of the Philistine pentapolis (6:17). Saul immediately moved to check any Philistine advance, going out to the Valley of the Terebinth (17:2). Each army took up a position at the top of a hill, both seeking to have the advantage of the high ground in battle (17:3).

Into this stalemate came a soldier from the Philistine camp (17:4). We are told his name and that he was from Gath. Then we are given his most impressive feature—he was tall, probably about six and a half feet tall (see the third textual note on 17:4). In an age when the average Israelite probably was only a little over five feet tall, Goliath was a giant. The description of Goliath's armor and weapons makes him all the more impressive to the reader (17:5–7). Most of his equipment was bronze. The exception was his iron-tipped spear. The shaft of his spear is compared to a weaver's beam. The point of the comparison is not given to readers; the author assumes they will understand it. Some have taken the author's comparison to be a reference to the large circumference of the shaft.[39] However, a shaft the size of a weaver's beam would have been unwieldy even for a tall man with large hands. A better explanation is offered by Yadin, who notes that spears equipped with a thong and ring for throwing are known to have been used in Greece and Egypt, and these accessories make the shaft appear similar to the equipment used with a weaver's beam.[40] In addition, Goliath had a shield bearer to protect him from projectiles as he approached the Israelite ranks.

Goliath's challenge to the Israelite ranks contrasted his status as a Philistine to the Israelites' status as "slaves to Saul" (עֲבָדִים לְשָׁאוּל, 17:8). While many English versions understand this phrase as "servants of Saul," there are good reasons to understand it as an insult to the Israelites.[41] The usual phrasing for saying "Saul's servants" would be the construct phrase עַבְדֵי־שָׁאוּל. Moreover, Goliath next offered the Philistines as slaves to the Israelites if someone could defeat him (וְהָיִינוּ לָכֶם לַעֲבָדִים, literally "and we will be slaves to you," 17:9). This is typical bravado that sought to heap disrespect on the enemy. It was how he mocked the Israelite army (17:10). He was a large, intimidating warrior; to the Israelites he must have appeared to be nearly invincible. With his taunts, he sought to strike fear into the heart of every Israelite soldier. The reaction of Saul was typical (17:11)—he is never depicted as bold in the face of a Philistine threat. As the king reacted in cowardice, so did the troops.

Jesse's Sons and His Instructions to David (17:12–19)

Having described the scene in the Valley of the Terebinth, the author next turns to Jesse in Bethlehem (17:12–15). We are told of Jesse's eight sons (cf.

[39] Krinetzki, "Ein Beitrag zur Stilanalyse der Goliathperikope," 191; Tsumura, *The First Book of Samuel*, 443.
[40] Yadin, "Goliath's Javelin and the מְנוֹר אַרְגִים."
[41] Tsumura, *The First Book of Samuel*, 444, including n. 62.

16:10–11) and that the three eldest were serving in Saul's army, while David—despite being named one of Saul's armor bearers (16:21)—was traveling back and forth from Saul to tend the sheep in Bethlehem. This is a clue to Saul's later reaction to David's offer to fight the Philistine (17:33). David was not yet seen by Saul as a useful warrior as his brothers were. So while David—who would become the most important of Saul's soldiers (18:30)—was traveling back and forth, Saul cowered at the Philistine's challenge twice each day for forty days (17:16).

Ironically, Jesse also did not recognize David as a warrior, despite having seen Samuel anoint him to be king (16:6–13). Instead, David was a mere messenger and a supplier for his warrior brothers (17:17–19). In antiquity citizen-warriors were often responsible for their own daily rations, and Jesse was seeing to his older sons' needs because they had been stationed in the west for over a month. His gift of cheese for their company commander was no doubt intended to keep them in the good graces of the higher command.

David Arrives at the Battle Lines (17:20–30)

With a very quick description the author tells us of David's trip to the Valley of the Terebinth as he arrives at the camp in time for the army assembling its battle line (17:20–21). David quickly went to find his brothers and speak to them, and this put him in position to observe Goliath's taunts and the reaction of the Israelite troops (17:22–24). David also overheard that Saul was offering a bounty for defeating Goliath (17:25). David asked about this offer—seeking to confirm whether this was a legitimate bounty or simply army rumor—and also expressed his outrage over the indignity of the situation, especially Goliath's mocking of "the living God" (אֱלֹהִים חַיִּים, 17:26; also 17:36). This title for God was used by Moses to characterize Yahweh's presence on Mount Sinai (Deut 5:26).[42] Therefore, it also highlighted God's salvific covenant relationship with Israel. For David, Israel's fleeing in panic from someone who mocked the army of the living God was an unacceptable demonstration of lack of trust in Yahweh as Israel's Savior and Protector.[43]

Eliab, like Jesse, did not recognize David as a warrior (17:28) despite having seen Samuel anoint him to be king (16:6–13). He accused David of abandoning his vocation as shepherd and of simply wanting to be a spectator of the battle, a sort of military dilettante. David, in reply, dismissed his brother's accusation and continued to investigate the king's offer; he received additional confirmation of its validity (17:29–30).

---

[42] The wording אֱלֹהִים חַיִּים, "the living God," in Deut 5:26 is identical to that in 1 Sam 17:26, 36. The phrase with the adjective in the singular, אֱלֹהִים חַי, is synonymous, and it appears in 2 Ki 19:4, 16; Is 37:4, 17; Jer 10:10; 23:36.

[43] Cf. 2 Sam 22:3. Earlier passages in 1 Samuel connected the covenant name Yahweh, Israel's God, with his action of saving his people (1 Sam 4:3; 7:3, 8; 10:18; 12:11; 14:6, 23, 39; see also Yahweh's words in 1 Sam 9:16).

Saul Sends David to Battle Goliath (17:31–40)

Upon hearing what David had said, Saul had David brought to himself (17:31). Immediately David volunteered to confront the Philistine (17:32). Saul's reaction was to emphasize David's lack of experience in light of Goliath's proficiency as a soldier (17:33). Saul did not mention Goliath's stature, which would have drawn attention to Saul's own comparable height (9:2; 10:23) as well as to his own failure to take up the Philistine's challenge (see the third textual note on 17:4).

David replied with a lengthy defense of his ability as a warrior (17:34–37a). His experience with lions and bears—including close combat—implied that David was viewing Goliath as if he were simply a ferocious animal, a comparison David made explicit near the end of his defense (17:37). The Philistine was worthy of no respect because he—an uncircumcised man—had mocked the troops of the living God. Twice David characterized Goliath as "uncircumcised" (17:26, 36). For the reader this recalls Jonathan's words as he planned his attack on the Philistines (14:6a). David was behaving as the heir apparent to the throne. Moreover, as David's reference to "the living God" (1 Sam 17:26, 36) recalled Yahweh's covenant with Israel (Deut 5:26), so too his use of "uncircumcised" (1 Sam 17:26, 36), by way of contrast, highlighted Yahweh's gracious promise of blessing through Abraham and his seed.[44] The seal of this covenant promise was circumcision (Gen 17:7–14), although from the very start righteousness was imputed through faith (Gen 15:6).[45] Since the Philistine was "uncircumcised" he was excluded from that covenant (Gen 17:14), and his lack of faith in the God of Israel's patriarchs left him in his state of unrighteousness.

The narrator is careful to set off David's final statement with "David added/ said" (וַיֹּאמֶר דָּוִד, 17:37), the same words that introduced his reply to Saul (17:32; cf. 17:29). This serves to slow readers down so that they pay special attention to this statement. David asserts that it was Yahweh who rescued him from lions and bears—it was not David's own skill that saved him. Thus, David was confident that Yahweh would rescue him again. These words once more evoke readers' recollection of Jonathan's trust in Yahweh (14:6b, 12b), emphasizing David as the successor to Saul in place of Saul's eldest son.[46]

Saul's short reply to David wished him Yahweh's abiding presence (17:37b). It has an ironic ring to it, since the Spirit of Yahweh was already resting on David even as the Spirit had abandoned Saul (16:13–14). The irony is heighted by the almost comedic scene of Saul dressing David in his own royal armor and weapons and David having no experience walking in them (17:38–39). This

---

[44] Gen 12:1–3; 18:17–18; 22:17–18; 26:3–4; 28:13–14. See the original promise of salvation through the Seed of Eve in Gen 3:15. See also Paul's exposition in Galatians 3.

[45] See Paul's exposition in Romans 4.

[46] Cf. also Rom 4:11–16; Gal 3:7–14. Abraham, who was accounted righteous through faith alone, is the father of all who believe, who are likewise justified through faith alone. Thus, Jonathan and David are true sons of Abraham.

paradoxical incident magnifies the difference between Saul and David. Saul would not confront the Philistines without armor, but would confront them without Yahweh's presence (cf. 31:1–6). David, on the other hand, valued Yahweh's presence with him in battle more than he valued armor. Moreover, Saul, after his anointing, failed to confront the Philistines at the first opportunity, despite having Yahweh's Spirit (10:5–7, 10).[47] In contrast, David volunteered to fight the Philistine at his first opportunity.

The author is also careful to note David's weapons of choice—his shepherd's staff and sling, for which he carefully chose stones as projectiles (17:40). Slings, along with bows, were the artillery of Iron Age warfare (cf. 2 Ki 3:25; 2 Chr 26:14). Here another subtle contrast with Saul is brought into play. Saul, the king from Benjamin, ought to have confronted Goliath with a sling. Benjaminites were renown for their skill as slingers—they were even expert left-handed slingers (Judg 20:15–16; 1 Chr 12:2).[48]

David Defeats Goliath (17:41–51)

The Philistine, accompanied by his shield bearer, approached David (17:41). Upon seeing David's features, Goliath immediately despised him and expressed his scorn (17:42–44).[49] David had compared the Philistine to lions and bears (17:37), but the Philistine feigned much more insult, as if David was treating him like "a dog" (17:43a).[50] The insults continued to pour from Goliath's mouth—cursing David by the Philistine gods and threatening to feed his dead body to wild animals (17:43b–44).

---

[47] For Saul's failure to obey the Word of Yahweh spoken to him through Samuel, directing him to assault the Philistine garrison at Gibeah, see the discussion of 10:7 in "Samuel Anoints Saul (9:26–10:8)" in the commentary on 9:26–10:16. See also the beginning of the commentary on 10:17–27a.

[48] Note the added irony of left-handed slingers since the name "Benjamin" means "son of the right hand."

[49] Some, who have followed the MT's reading that Goliath was "six cubits and a span" (see the third textual note on 17:4), have suggested that because of his great height, the Philistine also suffered from a visual impairment often associated with giantism (e.g., Berginer and Cohen, "The Nature of Goliath's Visual Disorder and the Actual Role of His Personal Bodyguard"). Thus, when Goliath claims that David came out to attack him with "sticks" (17:43), it was because Goliath could not clearly see that David had only one stick (17:40). However, it ought to be noted that Goliath saw David clearly enough to discern his age and handsomeness (17:42), which strongly argues against any visual impairment in Goliath. The Philistine's reference to "sticks" was more likely rhetorical, belittling the effectiveness of David's "staff" (17:40), rather than an actual description of how many staffs he thought David had brought with him.

[50] In antiquity dogs were not kept as pets and were not highly esteemed. Instead, to compare someone (or oneself) to a dog or to throw a dead body to the dogs was a grave insult and a sign of disrespect (Ex 22:30 [ET 22:31]; Deut 23:19 [ET 23:18]; 1 Sam 24:15 [ET 24:14]; 2 Sam 3:8; 9:8; 16:9; 1 Ki 14:11; 16:4; 21:19, 23, 24; 22:38; 2 Ki 8:13; 9:10, 36; Pss 22:17, 21 [ET 22:16, 20]; 59:7, 15 [ET 59:6, 14]; 68:24 [ET 68:23]; Job 30:1; Prov 26:11; Eccl 9:4; Mt 7:6; 15:26–27; Mk 7:27–28; Lk 16:21; Phil 3:2; 2 Pet 2:22). In Deut 23:19 (ET 23:18) "dog" refers to a male cult prostitute, an "abomination." Similarly in Rev 22:15, "dogs" likely refers to homosexuals; they are excluded from the new Jerusalem.

David's reply to Goliath's verbal scorn and abuse raised the bar (17:45–47). He noted that unlike Goliath, he was armed with Yahweh. It was Yahweh whom Goliath had mocked. Note that previously Goliath had mocked "the battle lines of Israel" (17:10; cf. 17:26, 36), and the insult was to Israel (17:25). However, David now made Goliath out to be an impious polytheistic (see "his gods," 17:43) pagan who mocked the true Deity—and most gravely, Yahweh, the only living God (cf. 17:26, 36). He also surpassed Goliath's threat: the Philistine was as good as dead because Yahweh would hand him over to David, a statement made in 17:46 and expanded in 17:47; the verb וְנָתַן could mean that God would give the Philistine into David's hand or that God had already done so (see the second textual note on 17:47). Yahweh was the Victor even without a sword or a spear. David's threat, therefore, was that he would cut off the Philistine's head and feed not only Goliath's corpse to wild animals but also the "corpse of the camp of the Philistines" (17:46). This victory would be a message that "Israel has a God" (17:46), implying that the Philistines, like other heathen nations, had no gods, because their gods did not actually exist (2 Ki 19:18; Is 37:19; 44:9–17; Jer 2:11; 16:20) or were in fact demons (1 Cor 10:18–20; cf. Gal 4:8).

The pace of the action accelerates as the narrator describes the short conflict (1 Sam 17:48–51). With one stone sunk into the Philistine's forehead, David brought him down. In a short editorial comment, the author reinforces God's victory by noting that David was stronger with a sling (and by implication, with Yahweh's saving presence; see 17:37) than the tall, impressive Philistine warrior was with his panoply. While David used Goliath's own sword to decapitate him, the Philistines fled the scene. The apostle Paul may well have had this narrative in mind as he was inspired to take the divine message even further. For the believer in Jesus Christ, no physical weapon of any sort avails. Instead, God provides the full armor needed to withstand the schemes and flaming arrows of the devil (Eph 6:10–17). The believer's armaments are the belt of truth, the breastplate of righteousness, the shoes of the Gospel of peace, the shield of faith, the helmet of salvation, and, finally, the sword of the Spirit, which is the Word of God.[51]

The Aftermath (17:52–58)

The Israelites pursued the Philistine up to the gates of Gath and Ekron, the two easternmost of their five cities, with slain bodies littering the road (17:52). Upon returning to the Valley of the Terebinth, the looting of the Philistine camps took place, and David also shared in the plunder (17:53–54). We are told that he took Goliath's head to Jerusalem.[52] At this time Jerusalem was under Jebusite control, so it has been suggested that the text is anachronistic.[53] Others propose

---

[51] See Winger, *Ephesians*, 721–54.

[52] See the textual note on 17:54.

[53] McCarter, *I Samuel*, 294–95, who proposes that the text originally read "Nob" instead of "Jerusalem" (cf. 21:10 [ET 21:9]).

that the text may be speaking of David's eventual conquest of the city as the time that Goliath's head was brought there (cf. 2 Sam 5:6–8).[54] However, the narrative is a string of preterite (imperfect with *waw* consecutive) verb forms, which normally presents action in sequential steps.[55] Thus, it is unlikely that the head was taken to Jerusalem a number of years later. However, it ought to be noted that Israelites had access to Jerusalem, even under Jebusite rule (Judg 19:11). In addition, David appears to have been very familiar with the weak spot in the city's fortifications (2 Sam 5:8), which would have been unlikely had he never been in the city.

Another statement that frequently has been challenged is that David put Goliath's equipment in his tent (1 Sam 17:54).[56] However, as a shepherd, who spent many nights with his sheep, it would not have been unusual for David to own a tent. Considering that he had traveled from Bethlehem to the vicinity of Socoh and had planned to return to Jesse, it is likely that he brought his tent with him on a mission that would have been expected to take several days.

The author next uses a flashback to relate Saul's conversation with Abner about David's family connections (17:55–56). Neither Saul nor Abner were aware of David's pedigree, but it became important, since Saul had promised one of his daughters to the man who could defeat the Philistine (17:25). In addition, given David's bold confidence in Yahweh, Saul's question might be a sign that he may have had the very first inkling that David might be the one Yahweh had chosen as his replacement to take over the kingdom (15:26–29).

When Abner presented David to Saul, David was still carrying Goliath's head (17:57). When asked, David politely identified Jesse as his father (17:58). The scene was filled with irony as the future king stood before Saul with the head of Goliath, a sure sign that David had accomplished what Saul had failed to do in his responsibility as king (see 8:20). Yet David remained deferential to Saul, referring to his father, Jesse, as "your servant." Although he had been given the kingship, David persisted in not seizing it from Saul, but respected the Lord's anointed one as long as Saul lived.[57]

---

[54] Klein, *1 Samuel*, 181. Tsumura, *The First Book of Samuel*, 468–69, suggests that "Jerusalem" means the vicinity of the city.

[55] See Bergen, *1, 2 Samuel*, 198, n. 66.

[56] See the discussion in Klein, *1 Samuel*, 181.

[57] See 1 Sam 24:2–23 (ET 24:1–22); 26:1–25; and even after Saul's death, 2 Sam 1:14–16. Cf. the discussion of מָשִׁיחַ, "Anointed One" or "Messiah, Christ," in the commentary on 1 Sam 2:10, 35.

1 Samuel 18:1–5

David in Saul's Service
and Jonathan's Love for David

Translation

18 **¹As he stopped speaking to Saul, Jonathan was bound to David in close friendship, and he loved him as much as [he loved] his own life. ²Saul took him that day and did not allow him to return to his father's house. ³Jonathan and David made an agreement, because he loved him as much as his own life. ⁴Jonathan removed the robe he was wearing and gave it to David, as well as his armor, his sword, his bow, and his belt. ⁵David went out [to battle]. Wherever Saul sent him, he was successful. So Saul placed him over the warriors, and this was fitting in the eyes of all the troops and in the eyes of Saul's servants.**

Textual Notes

18:1–5 These verses are missing in the LXX. See "The Text of 1 Samuel 17:1–18:30" at the start of the textual notes in the commentary on 17:1–58.

18:1 וַיְהִי כְּכַלֹּתוֹ לְדַבֵּר—Literally this means "and it was when he [David; see 17:58] finished speaking." The Piel (D) of כָּלָה, "to finish" (infinitive construct with כְּ and a subjective pronominal suffix), takes another infinitive construct (Piel of דָּבַר, "speak") as its direct object. See Joüon, § 124 c. The same construction appears in 1 Sam 24:17 (ET 24:16); 2 Sam 13:36; cf. also 1 Sam 10:13; 2 Sam 6:18; 13:39.

וְנֶפֶשׁ יְהוֹנָתָן נִקְשְׁרָה בְּנֶפֶשׁ דָּוִד—Literally "and the soul of Jonathan was bound with the soul of David." The head noun (נֶפֶשׁ, "soul") of the first construct phrase (נֶפֶשׁ יְהוֹנָתָן) is feminine, and it is the subject of the feminine (Niphal [N] perfect) verb נִקְשְׁרָה. In the Qal (G) קָשַׁר means "to bind" or "conspire," and its Niphal has the passive meaning "be bound."

וַיֶּאֱהָבֵהוּ יְהוֹנָתָן כְּנַפְשׁוֹ:—Literally "and Jonathan loved him like his own soul/life." The idiom with the verb אָהַב and prepositional phrase כְּנַפְשׁוֹ recurs in 18:3; cf. 20:17. The difference here between the Qere וַיֶּאֱהָבֵהוּ and the Kethib וַיֶּאֱהָבוֹ is simply the form of the third masculine singular object suffix (see GKC, § 58 d). The Qal (G) of the verb אָהַב, "to love," will refer to Jonathan's love for David again in 18:3; 20:17. Elsewhere in the book of Samuel, it refers to marital love (1 Sam 1:5; cf. 1 Sam 18:20, 28); David's love for Saul (1 Sam 16:21; see the commentary there); Israel's love for David (1 Sam 18:16; similarly, the second instance in 2 Sam 19:7 [ET 19:6]; cf. 1 Sam 18:22); Yahweh's love for Solomon (2 Sam 12:24); Amnon's lust for Tamar (2 Sam 13:1, 4, 15); and David's love for Absalom (metaphorically, the first instance in 2 Sam 19:7 [ET 19:6]). See also the Niphal (N) in 2 Sam 1:23, where Saul and Jonathan were "loved." See further "Jonathan's Relationship with David" in the commentary.

18:3 וַיִּכְרֹת יְהוֹנָתָן וְדָוִד בְּרִית—Literally "and Jonathan and David cut a covenant." For this idiom, see the third textual note on 11:1. The phrase "Jonathan and David" is a compound subject, so both are acting to establish the agreement. However, the verb וַיִּכְרֹת is singular and "Jonathan" follows it immediately as the primary subject, so the emphasis is on Jonathan's initiative. Such language is usually used for God establishing a covenant of grace with his people or for treaties between nations. This בְּרִית between Jonathan and David is elaborated as "a covenant/agreement of Yahweh" in 20:8, and the same idiom, "cut a covenant," describes the establishment of their pact again in 23:18. See also 20:42, where Jonathan invokes Yahweh and extends the agreement to his and David's descendants. "Cut a covenant" is similarly used for a personal agreement between King David and Abner in 2 Sam 3:12–13.

בְּאַהֲבָתוֹ אֹתוֹ כְּנַפְשׁוֹ:—Literally this means "by his [Jonathan's] loving him [David] like his own soul/life." בְּאַהֲבָתוֹ is a so-called "feminine" form of the Qal (G) infinitive construct (אַהֲבָה; see GKC, § 45 d) of אָהֵב, "to love," with the preposition בְּ and a subjective pronominal suffix. In some verses it is difficult to tell whether אַהֲבָה is this infinitive construct or the homographic noun for "love." Here and in 20:17a it takes a direct object, אֹתוֹ, so it must be the infinitive of the verb. However, in 1 Sam 20:17b; 2 Sam 1:26; 13:15, אַהֲבָה may be the noun "love." For the prepositional phrase כְּנַפְשׁוֹ, see the third textual note and the commentary on 18:1.

18:4 וַיִּתְפַּשֵּׁט—"And he removed" is a Hithpael (HtD) preterite (imperfect with *waw* consecutive) of פָּשַׁט. It is reflexive and so denotes taking off one's own clothes. The Qal (G) of פָּשַׁט occurs in the same sense in 19:24, but it has the military meaning of troops "making a raid" or "plundering" in 23:27; 27:8, 10; 30:1, 14. The Piel (D) in 1 Sam 31:8; 2 Sam 23:10 and the Hiphil (H) in 1 Sam 31:9 refer to despoiling dead enemy soldiers, i.e., taking their weapons, clothing, and anything else of value.

וּמַדָּיו וְעַד־חַרְבּוֹ וְעַד־קַשְׁתּוֹ וְעַד־חֲגֹרוֹ:—The plural of מַד can refer to "clothing" in general (4:12), but it refers more specifically to military garb or "armor" here, as in 1 Sam 17:38, 39; 2 Sam 20:8. The preposition עַד, "until," repeated before each of the three items, signifies extent and could be rendered as "also" or "even."

18:5 וַיֵּצֵא דָוִד—"David went out [to battle]." In settings denoting military action the Qal (G) of יָצָא often signifies going out to battle. See also 1 Sam 18:13, 16, 30 (twice).

יַשְׂכִּיל—"He was successful." The verb in the MT is a Hiphil (H) imperfect of שָׂכַל, and the imperfect denotes frequentative or habitual action. 4QSamª has [וישכ]יל, the same form but with a *waw*, which may be a *waw* consecutive. The Hiphil of שָׂכַל recurs with the same meaning of military success in 18:14, 15, as does its Qal (G) in 18:30. Elsewhere in the OT the Hiphil of the verb often means "be wise." The cognate noun שֶׂכֶל in 25:3 indicates that Abigail was "discerning" or "astute." The verb and the noun are common terms for God-given wisdom in the Wisdom books of Proverbs, Job, and a number of psalms.

הָעָם—"The people" can refer specifically to "the troops"; see the first textual note on 4:3.

Commentary

c. 1019–c. 1016 BC

This short pericope alternates between Saul's relationship with David and Jonathan's relationship with David. In this way the author is able to contrast the difference between Jonathan's love for David and Saul's use of David. The first two verses are general statements that highlight this difference. Jonathan became bound to David and "loved him as much as [he loved] his own life" (וַיֶּאֱהָבֵהוּ ... כְּנַפְשׁוֹ, 18:1). Such fraternal affection is a fulfillment of the Torah's mandate "you shall love your neighbor as yourself" (Lev 19:18), and Christ affirmed that summary of the Second Table of the Decalogue as an ongoing way of life for his followers (Mt 19:19; 22:39; see also Rom 13:9; Gal 5:14; James 2:8). Jonathan valued David's life as much as his own, whereas Saul sought to employ David for his own purposes with little regard for David's life. Thus, Saul took David from his father's house and did not allow him to return (18:2). The rest of the chapter underscores Saul's lack of love for David as he manifests homicidal jealousy (18:6–11), fear (18:12–13, 28–29), and deceit (18:20–27). The contrast between father and son will manifest itself in Jonathan taking actions to protect David when Saul tries to have him killed (e.g., 19:1–6).

This contrast is further elaborated by Jonathan's actions in 18:3–4 and Saul's in 18:5. Jonathan's love for David is shown in two ways: First, he and David made an agreement. The covenantal language used here (see the first textual note on 18:3) emphasizes the deep mutual respect the two men have for each other. The agreement is not elaborated here, but is explained further in 20:8, 42; 23:18 as a mutual bond held together by Yahweh for both men and their offspring. David will display his fidelity to this covenant by his show of kindness for Jonathan's son Mephibosheth (2 Samuel 9).

Second, Jonathan gave David his robe and equipment. Throughout the book of Samuel the noun "robe" (מְעִיל, 18:4) is always associated with prophets or royalty.[1] Prophecy and kingship were associated when Saul tore Samuel's robe and the prophet interpreted the action to symbolize the tearing of the kingdom from Saul (15:27–28). Here Jonathan is acknowledging David's right to the kingdom, something Saul will do later (24:21 [ET 24:20]) after David cut off and took a corner of Saul's "robe" (מְעִיל, 24:5, 12 [ET 24:4, 11]).

Armed with Jonathan's equipment, David then went out to war, and the author summarizes David's time of service under Saul (18:5). Saul exploited David to gain his victories, and David became commander of the army, which pleased the troops and Saul's courtiers. That David "was successful" is repeated three more times in this chapter (the verb שָׂכַל in 1 Sam 18:5, 14, 15, 30), and nowhere else in the book of Samuel, in order to emphasize that God has turned

---

[1] A "robe" (מְעִיל) is worn by the prophet Samuel (or one thought to be Samuel) in 1 Sam 2:19; 15:27; 28:14; by King Saul in 24:5, 12 (ET 24:4, 11); and by the king's daughters in 2 Sam 13:18.

the kingdom over to David and taken it from Saul (see especially 18:14–15). Thus, what Jonathan freely acknowledged (18:4), Saul feared (18:12).[2]

Jonathan's Relationship with David

One topic first introduced in this chapter that has become much discussed in recent decades is the relationship between David and Jonathan. The love of these two men for each other is mentioned in 1 Sam 18:1, 3; 20:17; 2 Sam 1:26.[3] Some have argued that David and Jonathan's relationship had a sexual dimension and that they were homosexual lovers.[4] This proposal is conditioned by contemporary Western society's changing attitude toward same-sex unions. It is an anachronistic imposition of a modern antiscriptural perspective onto a biblical text. It also fails to deal adequately with the evidence from an ancient reader or writer's perspective.

First of all, it ought to be noted that the verb אָהֵב, "to love," occurs over two hundred times elsewhere in the OT and never once denotes homosexual activity or attraction. In fact, outside of the Song of Songs, it entails sexual attraction in only a minority of cases, and all of these are heterosexual.[5] Most often it has no sexual dimension (e.g., 2 Sam 19:7 [ET 19:6]; 1 Ki 5:15 [ET 5:1]). Moreover, a close parallel exists between the language of 1 Sam 18:1–5 and that of Gen 44:20, 30. Those verses employ the verbs אָהֵב, "to love," and קָשַׁר, "to bind," along with the noun נֶפֶשׁ, "soul, life." Genesis 44 portrays Jacob's love for Benjamin with the same two verbs and the same noun: Jacob "loved" (אָהֵב) his son Benjamin (Gen 44:20), and his "life" (נֶפֶשׁ) was "bound" (קָשַׁר) with Benjamin's "life" (Gen 44:30).[6] Thus, Jonathan's love and close relationship with David is akin to Jacob's love for his son. Zehnder also observes the context in which Jonathan's love for David is first described:

> It is noteworthy that the first encounter of David and Jonathan with the subsequent binding of Jonathan's נפשׁ ["soul, life"] is not combined with 1 Sam 16 where David's handsomeness is noted, but rather with 1 Sam 17 which focuses on his cleverness, prowess, and even cruelty. This creates an atmosphere probably less suggestive of homoeroticism than would be the case had the first encounter between Jonathan and David been linked to 1 Sam

---

2 For the theme of success in the book of Samuel, see "Prosperity and Success Come Only from God" in "Other Theological Themes in Samuel" in the introduction.

3 Other passages cited in scholarly discussion include 1 Sam 19:1; 20:1; 20:30, 41.

4 See the discussions in Heacock, "Wrongly Framed? The 'David and Jonathan Narrative' and the Writing of Biblical Homosexuality [sic]"; Olyan, " 'Surpassing the Love of Women': Another Look at 2 Samuel 1:26 and the Relationship of David and Jonathan"; Zehnder, "Observations on the Relationship between David and Jonathan and the Debate on Homosexuality."

5 See אָהֵב, "to love," in Gen 24:67; 29:18, 30, 32; 34:3; Deut 21:15 (twice), 16; Judg 14:16; 16:4, 15; 1 Sam 1:5; 18:20, 28; 2 Sam 13:1, 4, 15; 1 Ki 11:1; Hos 3:1 (twice); Eccl 9:9; Esth 2:17; 2 Chr 11:21. These verses are cited in Zehnder, "Observations," 144, n. 59.

6 Zehnder, "Observations," 140.

16; rather, it is the political and military sphere that is present in the description of their relationship from the very beginning.[7]

Zehnder's observation that the relationship had a political dimension has also been noted by others.[8]

Second, it ought to be noted that the relationship between Jonathan and David is depicted in covenantal terms ("made an agreement" in 18:3 is literally "cut a covenant").[9] That covenant involved Yahweh as the one who bound together David and Jonathan ("a covenant/agreement of Yahweh," 20:8; see also 23:18). Jonathan describes it in 20:42 as an oath invoking Yahweh, and he extends it to his and David's subsequent "seed" (זֶרַע). Given Pentateuchal prohibitions against homosexual activity such as Lev 18:22 and Lev 20:13, it is inconceivable that the author of the book of Samuel would portray Yahweh as a participant in a covenant that involved a homosexual relationship. Moreover, the agreement between Jonathan and David also bound *their offspring* (1 Sam 20:42), which assumes that both men were or would be active heterosexually. David's offspring would be born after Jonathan's death (2 Sam 3:2–5), and on the basis of this covenant David would graciously elevate Jonathan's son Mephibosheth in 2 Samuel 9. Thus, *their agreement assumes that the sexual attraction of both David and Jonathan was for women (not men) in accord with God's design for the natural procreation of children under his gracious blessing* (Gen 1:26–27; 9:1). There is no hint of any homosexual activity, which would be a cursed "abomination" (Lev 18:22; 20:13) eliciting the wrath of God (Rom 1:27; see also, e.g., 1 Cor 6:9; 1 Tim 1:9–10).

Finally, there is nothing in any of the texts concerning David and Jonathan's relationship that uses any of the Hebrew vocabulary for sexual relations elsewhere in the book of Samuel, such as בּוֹא אֶל, "to go into" (as in 2 Sam 3:7; 12:24; 20:3; see also Ps 51:2 [ET superscription]); the verb שָׁכַב, "to lie with" (1 Sam 2:22; 2 Sam 11:4, 11; 12:11, 24; 13:11, 14); the verb יָדַע, "to know" (1 Sam 1:19); the verb עָנָה in the Piel (D), "to oppress, rape" (2 Sam 13:12, 14, 22, 32). Neither does the account contain any of the explicit terminology for sexual relations found elsewhere in the OT. Thus, the alleged homosexual aspect of the relationship between these two men is *imagined* by contemporary readers with a libertine agenda, but is not stated or even intimated by the author.

Other passages that have been taken as indications of a homosexual relationship between David and Jonathan are found in 1 Samuel 20, where they kiss each other (the verb נָשַׁק, 20:41) and where Saul refers to Jonathan bringing shame on the nakedness of his mother (20:30). As far as two men kissing each other, it ought to be noted that in most cases in the OT kissing is not romantic

---

[7] Zehnder, "Observations," 157.

[8] Ackroyd, "The Verb Love—ʾĀhēb in the David-Jonathan Narratives—A Footnote," and Thompson, "The Significance of the Verb *Love* in the David-Jonathan Narratives in 1 Samuel."

[9] See the first textual note and the commentary on 18:3. The same idiom, "cut a covenant," describes their relationship again in 23:18.

or erotic. Of the thirty occurrences of נָשַׁק, "to kiss," only three (Prov 7:13; Song 1:2; 8:1) have an overtly romantic or erotic connotation, and all are heterosexual. In most instances in the OT, a person kisses a close relative as a sign of familial love.[10] Earlier in 1 Samuel a kiss had a political connotation when Samuel kissed Saul (10:1). In the case of David and Jonathan kissing each other, it likely indicated their friendship, their familial relationship as brothers-in-law, and even their political relationship, with David acknowledging Jonathan as a prince and Jonathan acknowledging David as the king-designate.

As for Saul's angry accusation against Jonathan because of his alliance with David (20:30), it appears in this context: Saul addressed him, "You son of a perverted, rebellious woman! Don't you know that you are choosing the son of Jesse to your shame and to the shame of your mother's nakedness?" Thus, "your mother's nakedness" refers to Jonathan's mother giving birth to him and, therefore, does not carry an erotic connotation.[11] Saul alleged that both Jonathan and his mother had been shamed by Jonathan's greater loyalty to Jesse's son than to Saul himself. Moreover, the "nakedness" was that of Jonathan's mother; there is no reference to "nakedness" on the part of Jonathan, which would be required if this were a reference to homosexual activity between David and Jonathan. Zehnder also notes the possibility of an alternate meaning for Saul's accusation: Saul may have been claiming that Jonathan was not his son and that Jonathan's mother was impregnated by another man.[12] That would explain why Saul called her "a perverted, rebellious woman." If that is the case, there is still no reference to homosexuality in Saul's words.

Therefore, nothing in the text of the book of Samuel is suggesting that Jonathan and David's relationship had a sexual aspect. In the text of the book of Samuel, it is clear that these two men had a close bond that can be characterized as *love* and that it had emotional, brotherly, and political components, all under the surpassing love of Yahweh and his administration of his kingdom (1 Sam 20:8, 42; 23:18).

---

[10] Zehnder, "Observations," 149, n. 79, lists these verses with נָשַׁק, "to kiss": Gen 27:26, 27 (Jacob kissed Isaac); Gen 29:13 (Laban kissed his nephew Jacob); Gen 31:28 and Gen 32:1 (ET 31:55; Laban wanted to and did kiss his grandchildren and his daughters); Gen 33:4 (Esau kissed Jacob); Gen 45:15 (Joseph kissed his brothers); Gen 48:10 (Jacob kissed the sons of Joseph); Gen 50:1 (Joseph kissed Jacob after he died); Ex 4:27 (Aaron kissed Moses); Ex 18:7 (Moses kissed Jethro); 2 Sam 14:33 (David kissed Absalom); 1 Ki 19:20 (Elisha wanted to kiss his parents good-bye); Ruth 1:9 (Naomi kissed her daughters-in-law); Ruth 1:14 (Orpah kissed Naomi). See also Gen 29:11, where Jacob kissed Rachel and wept at meeting her for the first time. Although Jacob would go on to marry Rachel, his actions at this point seem to indicate joy and relief at finding one of his mother's relatives (see also Gen 29:12).

[11] Zehnder, "Observations," 150.

[12] Zehnder, "Observations," 150.

1 Samuel 18:6–16
Saul's Jealousy of David

Translation

18 **⁶When they [the troops] came [from battle and] David returned from striking down the Philistine, the women came out from all the cities of Israel to sing and [rejoice with] dances, to greet King Saul with tambourines, with rejoicing, and with musical instruments. ⁷The women who were celebrating sang:**

> **"Saul has struck down his thousands**
>
> > **and David his tens of thousands."**

⁸Saul was very angry, and he took this song as an insult and said, "They gave ten thousands to David, but to me they gave the thousands. What more is there for him except the kingdom?" ⁹From that day onward Saul kept a jealous eye on David.

¹⁰The next day an evil spirit from God rushed upon Saul, and he prophesied in his house. Now David was strumming [a lyre] as usual, and Saul was holding a spear. ¹¹The Saul lifted the spear. He thought, "I'll nail David to the wall." But David got away from him twice. ¹²So Saul was afraid of David because Yahweh was with him but he had turned away from Saul. ¹³So Saul turned David away from himself and made him an officer in charge of a thousand men, and he [David] went out [to battle] and came back in front of the troops.

¹⁴Now David was successful wherever he went, since Yahweh was with him. ¹⁵Saul noticed that he was very successful, and he was afraid of him. ¹⁶However, all Israel and Judah loved David because he would lead them out and back [from battle].

Textual Notes

18:6a, 8a, 10–11 The LXX omits these verses. See "The Text of 1 Samuel 17:1–18:30" at the start of the textual notes in the commentary on 17:1–58.

18:6 וַיְהִ֣י בְּבוֹאָ֗ם בְּשׁ֤וּב דָּוִד֙ מֵהַכּ֣וֹת אֶת־הַפְּלִשְׁתִּ֔י—The initial וַיְהִי introduces two temporal clauses, each of which begins with a Qal (G) infinitive construct (of בּוֹא and שׁוּב, respectively) with the prefixed preposition בְּ, literally "and it was when they came, when David returned from striking the Philistine," i.e., Goliath. Often in this chapter the Qal of יָצָא, "go out" (18:5, 13, 16, 30; but not וַתֵּצֶאנָה in 18:6), and בּוֹא, "come" (18:6, 13, 16), refers to advancing for warfare and returning victorious from it, so the translation adds "to/from battle" in brackets in those verses. The pronominal suffix on בְּבוֹאָם is the subject; "they" could refer either to the troops or to Saul and David. In the book of Samuel the coordinated combination of יָצָא, "go out," and בּוֹא, "come in," always refers to military campaigns (1 Sam 18:13, 16; 29:6; 2 Sam 5:2; cf. 1 Sam 17:20; 18:6).

וַתֵּצֶאנָה—This is the third feminine plural Qal (G) preterite (imperfect with *waw* consecutive) of יָצָא, "go out."

לָשִׁיר—This Qere is the Qal (G) infinitive construct of שִׁיר, "to sing," with the preposition לְ. The Kethib is לָשׁוּר, which could mean "to travel" (שׁוּר I); "to look down" (שׁוּר II); or "to leap" (שׁוּר III). The Kethib probably resulted from graphic confusion of ו in place of י.

וְהַמְּחֹלוֹת—The feminine noun מְחֹלָה is derived from the verb חוּל I, "to whirl, dance, writhe." It is usually understood to denote a kind of circle dance (*HALOT*), although some dispute this, e.g., *CDCH*: "**dance, dancing**, not necessarily in a ring." The dancing denoted by this feminine noun, מְחֹלָה (also in 21:12 [ET 21:11]; 29:5), or its masculine equivalent, מָחוֹל, is often associated with musical instruments and the worship of Yahweh, as in Ex 15:20; Pss 149:3; 150:4, all of which also have תֹּף (see the next textual note).

בְּתֻפִּים—This is the plural of תֹּף, "tambourine" (with the preposition בְּ), whose singular was in 10:5. The plural recurs in 2 Sam 6:5; see also, e.g., Gen 31:27; Ex 15:20.

וּבְשָׁלִשִׁים:—This is translated as "and with musical instruments." The plural noun שָׁלִשִׁים is a hapax legomenon whose meaning is unknown. Since it comes from the same root as שָׁלוֹשׁ, "three," suggestions include a three-stringed lute (cf. Akkadian *šalaštu*), a triangle, and a three-stringed sistrum.[1]

18:7 וַתַּעֲנֶינָה ... וַתֹּאמַרְן—This could be the common combination of "to answer" and "to say" (as in, e.g., 1:15, 17; 16:18). More likely, however, the first verb is the Qal (G) preterite (imperfect with *waw* consecutive) third feminine plural of the verb עָנָה IV, "to sing" (so BDB and *HALOT*). It recurs in 21:12 (ET 21:11); 29:5.

הַמְשַׂחֲקוֹת—This is the feminine plural Piel (D) participle (with the article) of שָׂחַק (a by-form of צָחַק), whose Piel can mean "to make sport," as in 2 Sam 2:14, or "to play an instrument," as in 2 Sam 6:5. Here it could refer to the women as the players of the instruments, but it likely has the more general meaning "to celebrate," as also in 2 Sam 6:21.

הִכָּה שָׁאוּל בַּאֲלָפָיו—The Hiphil (H) of נָכָה, "strike (down)," often takes the preposition בְּ on the object signifying what is struck (*HALOT*, Hiphil, 1 b), as again in 18:11 (see the second textual note there); see also, e.g., 6:19; 14:31; 21:12 (ET 21:11); 29:5. The Qere here, בַּאֲלָפָיו, is plural, "his thousands," with the plene, or *male'*, spelling of the third masculine singular suffix. The Kethib is the defective, or *ḥaser*, spelling of the same word, בַּאֲלָפוּ. The identical clause recurs in 21:12 (ET 21:11), with the same Qere/Kethib, and in 29:5, where the sole reading has the plene, or *male'*, spelling.

וְדָוִד בְּרִבְבֹתָיו:—The subject switches to "David." The verb הִכָּה, "has struck down," in the preceding clause (see the previous textual note) is gapped, that is, here it is omitted but implied, as shown by the the preposition בְּ that the verb takes on its object (בְּרִבְבֹתָיו). The feminine noun רְבָבָה denotes a "myriad," that is, "ten thousand." This identical clause recurs in 21:12 (ET 21:11); 29:5.

18:8 וַיֵּרַע בְּעֵינָיו הַדָּבָר הַזֶּה—This clause with the Qal (G) of רָעַע is literally "and this word was evil in his eyes." Similar is the first clause of 1 Sam 8:6; see also 2 Sam 11:27.

---

[1] See McCarter, *I Samuel*, 311; *HALOT*, s.v. שָׁלִישׁ II.

18:9 עוֹיֵן—This Qere, "keeping a jealous eye on," is the Qal (G) participle of עִין, "to eye [someone]." This is a denominative verb from the noun עַיִן, "eye," and a hapax legomenon. The Kethib is עָוֶן, which is a different spelling of the same participle, but as if the root were עון instead of עין.

וָהָלְאָה:—This adverb with conjunctive *waw*, "and farther, onward, afterward," was in 10:3 and will recur in 20:22, 37.

18:10–11 Much of the vocabulary in these verses recurs in 19:9–10; 20:33.

18:10 רוּחַ אֱלֹהִים ׀ רָעָה—Literally "a spirit of God, an evil (one)," this same phrase was in 16:15, 16. See the first textual note on 16:15 and the commentary on 16:14–23.

וַיִּתְנַבֵּא—"And he prophesied." For the Hithpael (HtD) of נָבָא, see the third textual note on 10:5. Since this behavior (probably an ecstatic utterance) was under the influence of an evil spirit, it would have been a form of false prophesying, as in 1 Ki 22:19–23. See the fourth paragraph of the commentary on 16:14–23.

מְנַגֵּן בְּיָדוֹ—This is translated as "was strumming." See the third textual note on 16:16.

כְּיוֹם ׀ בְּיוֹם—Literally "as a day in a day," this is translated as "as usual."

וְהַחֲנִית בְּיַד־שָׁאוּל:—Literally "and the spear was in the hand of Saul." The noun חֲנִית recurs in 18:11; see also, e.g., 13:19; 17:7, 47.

18:11 וַיָּטֶל—This is the Hiphil (H) preterite (imperfect with *waw* consecutive) of the verb טוּל, "to throw, hurl." The identical form recurs in the same clause in 20:33. Its Hiphil appears seven times in other OT books, its Hophal (Hp) four times, and its Pilpel (D) once (Is 22:17). However, the translation "lifted" assumes that the verb should be pointed וַיִּטֹּל, a Qal (G) preterite (imperfect with *waw* consecutive) of נָטַל, "to lift (up)." Elsewhere in the OT נָטַל occurs in the Qal (G) three times; most similar is its sense in Is 40:15 (see also 2 Sam 24:12; Lam 3:28).[2] Also similar is the meaning of the Piel (D) of נָטַל, which occurs only in Is 63:9.

אַכֶּה בְדָוִד וּבַקִּיר—Literally "I will strike in David and in the wall," this means "I will strike through David and into the wall." See the second textual note on 26:8. The Hiphil (H) of נָכָה takes the preposition בְּ here; see the third textual note on 18:7.

וַיִּסֹּב דָּוִד מִפָּנָיו פַּעֲמָיִם:—Literally "but David turned around from his face twice." In the singular פַּעַם denotes one "occurrence" or "time," and dual form here, פַּעֲמָיִם (pausal for פַּעֲמַיִם), means "two times, twice."

18:12 וַיִּרָא שָׁאוּל מִלִּפְנֵי דָוִד—The verb is the Qal (G) preterite (imperfect with *waw* consecutive) of יָרֵא, "to fear" (not רָאָה, "to see"). This verb takes the combination מִלִּפְנֵי in a few other verses too (Eccl 3:14; 8:12, 13, all for fearing God).

18:13 וַיְסִרֵהוּ—This is the Hiphil (H) of סוּר, meaning "to remove." It is translated as "so Saul turned David away" to capture the author's play on words; a Qal (G) form of the same verb, סָר (Yahweh "had turned away" from Saul), was the preceding word, at the conclusion of the previous verse.

---

[2] "Lifted" is also the translation of Klein, *1 Samuel*, 185; similar is GW: "raised."

18:14 וַיְהִי דָוִד לְכָל־דְּרָכָו מַשְׂכִּיל—Literally "and David was, with respect to all his ways, succeeding." For the Hiphil (H) of שָׂכַל, see the second textual note on 18:5. Its participle here, מַשְׂכִּיל, recurs in 18:15. In place of the preposition לְ in לְכָל־, many manuscripts (and the Masoretic *sebir*) have בְּ, which is more common in this expression (six times in the OT[3]). This is the only OT verse where לְ is prefixed to כָּל־דְּרָכָיו. (The form דְּרָכָו is the defective, or *ḥaser*, spelling of דְּרָכָיו.)

18:15 וַיַּרְא שָׁאוּל אֲשֶׁר—This is translated as "Saul noticed that." Here the relative pronoun אֲשֶׁר has a nominalizing function: the relative clause (אֲשֶׁר־הוּא מַשְׂכִּיל מְאֹד) serves (like a noun) as the direct object of the verb וַיַּרְא, literally "and he saw."

וַיָּגָר מִפָּנָיו׃—"And he was afraid" is a Qal (G) preterite (imperfect with *waw* consecutive) of the verb גּוּר III, which often denotes fear accompanied by a sense of dread.[4] It takes the combination מִפְּנֵי also in Num 22:3; Deut 1:17; Job 19:29, but just מִן in Deut 18:22; Ps 22:24 (ET 22:23).

18:16 כִּי־הוּא יוֹצֵא וָבָא לִפְנֵיהֶם—This causal clause has two Qal (G) participles (יוֹצֵא וָבָא) denoting frequentative or habitual action, literally "because he kept going out and coming back before them." A battle setting is implied, hence "because he would lead them out and back [from battle]." See the first textual note on 18:6.

Commentary

c. 1019–c. 1016 BC

This section serves two functions. First, it is an explanation of 18:5 that relates how David became successful as a soldier and commander in Saul's army. Second, it prepares the readers for most of the rest of 1 Samuel and Saul's relentless efforts to eliminate David as his rival.

The Women's Victory Song (18:6–9)

The account begins by the author going back in time to the troops returning after David's victory over Goliath (18:6–8). Women came out from the cities rejoicing and singing. Such celebration by women in Israel was not new. We read of it with Miriam leading the women after God's victory over Pharaoh's army (Ex 15:20–21) and the celebration of Jephthah's daughter after his victory over the Ammonites (Judg 11:34).

The short song the women sang (five Hebrew words) is in the form of a graded numerical saying where one line introduces a number and the next line introduces a higher number, often either one unit higher (e.g., Job 5:19; Prov 6:16)[5] or ten times higher, as in this saying, "thousands … tens of thousands" (1 Sam 18:7). Other graded numerical sayings in the OT that have the

---

3   Deut 10:12; 11:22; Josh 22:5; 1 Ki 8:58; Ps 145:17; Prov 3:31 (cf. Ezek 16:47; Ps 91:11; Prov 3:6).

4   See *TWOT*, § 332.

5   See Roth, "The Numerical Sequence x/x+1 in the Old Testament."

progression "thousand(s) … ten thousand(s)" are found in Deut 32:30; 33:17; Micah 6:7; Pss 91:7; 144:13.[6] Since this is a stock device, Gevirtz argued that

> the implication that most would locate in the women's eulogy, therefore, that David's military prowess was being lauded over that of Saul's, appears poorly founded. And is it not furthermore incredible that the welcoming party of women—singing and dancing, obviously pleased and proud of the accomplishment of their men—should be thought to have seized just this opportunity, his return from victory, to insult their king? The song contains no insult. It is a lavish praise of both Saul and David, utilizing the largest (single) equivalent numerals available in Syro-Palestinian poetic diction: the fixed pair "thousands" // "ten-thousands."[7]

Thus, according to Gevirtz, the women were not elevating David over Saul and Saul's reported reaction is a misunderstanding of the women's song by the author of the book of Samuel.[8] However, Freedman has noted:

> On the basis of many examples of number-parallelism in Ugaritic and Hebrew poetry, Gevirtz is at pains to show that the women were praising both men equally (since "thousands" and "myriads" form a traditional pair); and contrary to the view of the biblical author and modern commentators, meant no slight to the king. This may readily be granted, but the biblical writer may still have been right in seeing in the episode and the offending couplet an occasion for Saul's outburst. The very fact that David was accorded equal treatment with the king in the song (which is the point of Gevirtz's argument) would be sufficient to arouse the suspicions of any monarch, and especially of one insecure in his position and jealous of his prerogatives. It is the other "pair" in the couplet (Saul // David) which provides the clue to the king's reaction. For this is the only example of standard number-parallelism, among all those cited by the author, in which there is a significant distinction of subjects: Saul and David. Once the king's suspicions had been triggered by this coupling of names, he might well have seen in the otherwise innocuous number-parallelism of the song further evidence of a plot to displace him.[9]

Thus, while the women may not have intended any insult to Saul, the very fact that he was paired with David, who at the time was not even a soldier in Saul's army, much less a top commander (he will be promoted later in 18:13; cf. 18:5), led to Saul's umbrage. It also heightened Saul's suspicion that David may have been the one chosen by Yahweh to replace him,[10] as indicated by his comment "what more is there for him except the kingdom?" (18:8). By killing one Philistine, albeit an exceptionally impressive one (1 Samuel 17), David was credited with ten times the accomplishments of Saul, who had been king for

---

[6] Note that Deut 33:17 is the only one of these where the progression is from a larger number to a smaller one.

[7] Gevirtz, *Patterns in the Early Poetry of Israel*, 24.

[8] Gevirtz, *Patterns in the Early Poetry of Israel*, 15, 23.

[9] Freedman, Review of Stanley Gevirtz, *Patterns in the Early Poetry of Israel*, 201–2.

[10] In 15:26–29 Samuel had informed Saul that Yahweh had chosen another to replace him as king and that God's decision was immutable.

many years. David already outranked his master as the most decorated in combat, and only the throne was currently beyond his reach. No wonder that from that day onward Saul "kept a jealous eye on David" (18:9).

Saul's First Attempts to Kill David (18:10–13)

The very next day the scene returns to Saul's court, where things appear to be back to the previous state (18:10). Saul was bedeviled by an evil spirit, and David was playing in order to soothe him.[11] Then the deathly jealousy in Saul's heart manifested itself as he tried to kill David (18:11). The scene, however, reveals a pathetic monarch, a seasoned warrior who cannot catch the young musician. So Saul's fear increased for good reason—Yahweh was with David, and not Saul (8:12). In an ironic use of the verb סור, we are told that just as Yahweh "had turned away" from Saul (18:12), so also Saul "turned away" David, the man with Yahweh's Spirit, and made him a top commander in his army (see the textual note on 18:13). David, who had been anointed king and indwelt by the Holy Spirit,[12] readily made the transition to acting like the king Israel requested by leading Israel's army out to battle (18:13; see 8:20). David, like Joshua before him, was God's chosen leader to take his elect people into battle and bring them back (Num 27:16–18). Ultimately, the Son of David will be the one to engage the devil in mortal combat (Mt 4:1–11), emerge victorious on Easter morning (Matthew 28), and institute the Great Commission of discipling, teaching, and baptizing in the triune name (Mt 28:19–20) that will enable all of God's chosen to withstand the lifelong spiritual battle,[13] confident of their victory in their risen Lord Jesus Christ.[14]

David's Success as a Commander in Saul's Army (18:14–16)

The author once again stresses Yahweh's presence with David as he became a successful soldier and Saul's fear escalated (18:14–15). In contrast to Saul's dread of David, we are told that "all Israel and Judah" loved David because of his successful leadership (18:16). Mentioning both "Israel" and "Judah" is not the most common way of referring to the united kingdom, but it is fairly frequent in the book of Samuel.[15] Here it serves to highlight David's tribe of Judah, but it is also a subtle reminder of the long-standing distance between Judah and the other tribes that would lead to a divided kingdom, first during David's early years as monarch (2 Sam 2:1–11), then later when David was restored to the throne after Absalom's rebellion (2 Sam 19:10–44 [ET 19:9–43]),

---

[11] See the commentary on 16:14–23.

[12] See the commentary on 16:12–13, which compares the sequence of anointing and the rushing of the Spirit to God's promise to pour out the Holy Spirit upon all who are baptized into Christ.

[13] See the discussion of Eph 6:10–17 in the commentary on 1 Sam 17:41–51.

[14] See, e.g., Rom 1:4; 7:22–25; 16:20; 1 Cor 15:54–57; 1 Jn 5:4.

[15] Also 1 Sam 11:8; 17:52; 2 Sam 2:10; 3:10; 5:5; 11:11; 12:8; 19:12, 41–44 (ET 19:11, 40–43); 20:2; 21:2; 24:1, 9.

and finally with the permanent division of the kingdom after Solomon's death (1 Ki 12:1–24).

That Israel and Judah loved David was an incipient recognition of David as king. The rhetoric of "love" for a leader signals that Saul in some sense had already been deposed as king in the hearts of the people. In the Amarna Letters as well as in Assyrian literature, one essential component in a healthy relationship between a monarch and his people was love. Moran notes:

> In view too of what we have seen one may perhaps appreciate more fully the significance of the statement in 1 Sm 18,16: "But all Israel and Judah loved (*'ōhēb*) David, for he went out and came in before them." It is clear that the writer sees this as another important step in David's way to the throne; the north as well as the south is attached to him. However, if we see in this attachment, as the Amarna and the Assyrian evidence encourages us to do, an essential requirement of the king-subject relationship, then the writer implies that the people at [that] point were already giving David a *de facto* recognition and allegiance, which his actual leadership and success in a sense justified.[16]

Much of the rest of 1 Samuel will portray the struggle of Saul to prevent the *de facto* allegiance that David had won from Israel from becoming a *de jure* recognition of David's right to the throne. However, God determines rulers (Rom 13:1). He sets them up and deposes them (Dan 2:21; 4:29 [ET 4:32]). He had already chosen Saul's successor (1 Sam 15:26–29; 16:12–13). The people's love for their ordained leader also has a religious dimension of abiding significance for the church. God's people are called to love and support their faithful pastors as those who minister on behalf of Christ. These shepherds and overseers (bishops) serve under the Great Shepherd and Overseer (Heb 13:20; 1 Pet 2:25), bestowing the love of Christ on his beloved through the authentic preaching of the Word and the faithful administration of the Sacraments (see, e.g., Eph 4:11–13; 1 Pet 5:1–5; 1 Tim 5:17–18).

---

[16] Moran, "The Ancient Near Eastern Background of the Love of God in Deuteronomy," 81.

David Becomes Saul's Son-in-Law

Translation

18 **17**Saul said to David, "Look, my elder daughter—I'll give her to you as a wife. Simply become a skilled soldier for me and wage Yahweh's wars," since Saul thought, "I won't lay a hand on him. Let the Philistines do that."

18David said to Saul, "Who am I, and who are my relatives [and] my father's clan in Israel that I should become the king's son-in-law?"

19When the time came to give Saul's daughter Merab to David, she was given to Adriel the Meholathite as a wife. **20**But Saul's daughter Michal loved David. This was told to Saul, and it was agreeable to him. **21**Saul thought, "I'll give her to him, and she'll become a trap to him, and the Philistines will overpower him." So Saul said to David a second time, "You will become my son-in-law today."

22Saul commanded his officials, "Tell David in private, 'Look, the king favors you, and all his officials love you. So now become the king's son-in-law.'"

23When Saul's officials repeated these words to David, David said, "Do you consider it an insignificant thing to become the king's son-in-law? I'm a poor, insignificant man!"

24Saul's officials told him, "David said these words."

25So Saul said, "Say this to David, 'The king has no desire for a bride-price except a hundred Philistine foreskins in order to take revenge against the king's enemies.'" (Saul intended to make David fall at the hands of the Philistines.)

26Saul's officials told David these words, and it was agreeable to David to become the king's son-in-law. So before the time expired, **27**David took action, and he and his men went and struck down two hundred Philistine men. David brought their foreskins and presented them to the king in order to become the king's son-in-law. So Saul gave him his daughter Michal as a wife.

28Saul realized that Yahweh was with David and that his daughter Michal loved him. **29**Saul became even more afraid of David. As a result, Saul was David's enemy from then on. **30**The Philistine commanders would go out to battle, and as often as they came out, David was more successful than all of Saul's officers, and he gained an excellent reputation.

Textual Notes

18:17–19, 21b, 26b, 29b–30   The LXX omits these verses. See "The Text of 1 Samuel 17:1–18:30" at the start of the textual notes in the commentary on 17:1–58.

18:17   בִּתִּי הַגְּדוֹלָה מֵרַב—Literally this means "my daughter, the big one, Merab." According to 14:49 Saul had two daughters. Merab was the firstborn, and Michal was the younger. Therefore the feminine adjective with the article, הַגְּדוֹלָה, is translated as a comparative, "elder" (see Joüon, § 141 g). If Saul had three or more daughters, it would be rendered as a superlative, "eldest"; see, e.g., הַטּוֹבִים in the first textual note on 8:14.

הֱיֵה־לִּי לְבֶן־חַיִל—The verb הָיָה with the preposition לְ often means "to become" something. For בֶּן־חַיִל as "a skilled soldier," see the third textual note on 14:52.

אַל־תְּהִי יָדִי בּוֹ וּתְהִי־בוֹ יַד־פְּלִשְׁתִּים:—Literally "let my hand not be against him, but let the hand of the Philistines be against him." The latter clause recurs in 18:21. The noun יָד is feminine, and so the repeated jussive תְּהִי is also feminine.

18:18 חַיַּי—This is the suffixed plural of the rare noun חַי, "relatives, kinfolk" (see BDB, s.v. חַי II; *HALOT*, s.v. חַי III). It ought not be confused with the homographic adjective/substantive חַי, "alive; life," or the plural noun חַיִּים, "life."

חָתָן—This noun can mean either "bridegroom" or, as here, "son-in-law." See the cognate verb in the third textual note on 18:21.

18:19 תֵּת ... נִתְּנָה—The first form of נָתַן is the Qal (G) infinitive construct, and the second is the Niphal (N) third feminine singular perfect.

לְעַדְרִיאֵל—This means "to Adriel." The name is the Aramaic equivalent of עַזְרִיאֵל, "Azriel" (Jer 36:26; 1 Chr 5:24; 27:19), meaning "God is my help."

הַמְּחֹלָתִי—A "Meholathite" was a person from Abel-meholah (Judg 7:22; 1 Ki 4:12; 19:16). This site may be either modern Tell Abû Sûs on the west side of the Jordan River, about twenty-three miles (thirty-seven kilometers) south of the Sea of Galilee, or Tell el-Maqlub, about eighteen miles (twenty-nine kilometers) south of the Sea of Galilee on the east side of the Jordan River in Gilead. Later it was the home of Elisha (1 Ki 19:16).

18:20 וַיַּגִּדוּ לְשָׁאוּל—Literally "and they declared to Saul." An impersonal plural verb (with no stated subject) can be rendered as a passive: "this was told to Saul." But in 18:24, 26, the same verb, וַיַּגִּדוּ (the Hiphil [H] of נָגַד), has an expressed subject: "Saul's officials told …"

וַיִּשַׁר הַדָּבָר בְּעֵינָיו:—Literally "and the matter was straight in his eyes." The Qal (G) of יָשַׁר almost always has the metaphorical meaning "be right, correct, pleasing" and usually is used with בְּעֵינֵי, "in the eyes of." The same construction recurs in 18:26.

18:21 וּתְהִי־בוֹ יַד־פְּלִשְׁתִּים—Literally "and the hand of the Philistines will be against him." See the third textual note on 18:17.

בִּשְׁתַּיִם—This is the feminine form of the dual noun שְׁנַיִם, "two," with the preposition בְּ. In light of Saul's broken promise in 18:17, it must mean "a second time." See also the identical prepositional phrase in Job 33:14.

תִּתְחַתֵּן בִּי—The verb חָתַן occurs only in the Hithpael (HtD) and means "marry; intermarry, become related by marriage" and often takes the preposition בְּ, "with." Here the specific relationship by marriage is that David will "become son-in-law" to Saul. The verb recurs in 18:22, 23, 26, 27, and is cognate to the noun חָתָן in 18:18 (see the second textual note there).

18:22 עֲבָדָיו—This plene, or *male'*, spelling is the Qere, which means "his servants." The Kethib עבדו might appear to be עַבְדּוֹ, "his servant," but in fact it is the same plural as the Qere, although spelled defectively, or *ḥaser*: עֲבָדוֹ. The marginal Masoretic note (חד מן ב כת חס בליש) indicates that this is one of two instances in which this plural Kethib has that defective, or *ḥaser*, spelling.

בַּלָּט—The noun לָט or לָאט (from the root לוט) means "secrecy" or "privacy." It is used with the preposition בְּ in an adverbial sense, "in private/secret," as again in 24:5 (ET 24:4; also Judg 4:21; Ruth 3:7).

חָפֵץ בְּךָ הַמֶּלֶךְ—Literally "the king delighted in you," this is translated as "the king favors you." The verb is a Qal (G) third masculine singular perfect of חָפֵץ, which, alone or with the preposition בְּ, can take on a variety of nuances, including "take pleasure in, desire or delight in [something]" and "be inclined toward/favor something" (see *HALOT*). It is used again with this same meaning in 19:1. The cognate noun חֵפֶץ in 18:25 denotes "a desire."

18:23 וַיְדַבְּרוּ עַבְדֵי שָׁאוּל בְּאָזְנֵי דָוִד אֶת־הַדְּבָרִים הָאֵלֶּה—Literally "and the servants of Saul spoke in David's ears these words."

הַנְקַלָּה בְעֵינֵיכֶם—Literally "is it lightweight in your eyes?" The verb הַנְקַלָּה is a Niphal (N) feminine singular participle of קָלַל, "be/become light," with interrogative *he*.

רָשׁ וְנִקְלֶה:—These two adjectival participles are translated as "poor, insignificant." The first masculine singular participle is the Qal (G) of רוּשׁ, "to be poor." The second is the Niphal (N) of קָלָה, "to be unesteemed, contemptible." It forms a wordplay with the participle הַנְקַלָּה earlier in the verse (see the preceding textual note); both Niphal participles have the identical consonants (נקלה).

18:25 בְּמֹהַר—The noun מֹהַר denotes a "bride-price," a payment by the bridegroom to the family of the bride. It occurs elsewhere in the OT only in Gen 34:12; Ex 22:16 (ET 22:17), and its cognate verb is used similarly in Ex 22:15 (ET 22:16). See further the commentary.

לְהִנָּקֵם—This infinitive construct with לְ forms a purpose clause, "in order to …" (see Joüon, § 124 l). The Niphal (N) of נָקַם means "avenge oneself" or "take (one's) vengeance" and often takes the preposition בְּ (here on בְּאֹיְבֵי) in the sense of disadvantage, "against."

18:26 וְלֹא מָלְאוּ הַיָּמִים:—Literally "and the days were not full/fulfilled," this serves as a temporal clause introducing the next verse, 18:27.

18:27 וַיָּקָם דָּוִד וַיֵּלֶךְ—Literally "and David arose and he went." Qal (G) forms of the verb קוּם are frequently used to signal the initiation of some further act. Here and also in, e.g., 3:6, 8; 16:13; 17:48, the further action is signified by וַיֵּלֶךְ.

מָאתַיִם—The dual suffix shows that this means "two hundred." The LXX reads ἑκατόν, "one hundred," and is probably an adaptation to 18:25.

וַיְמַלְאוּם—This is translated as "and presented them." This is a Piel (D) preterite (imperfect with *waw* consecutive) of מָלֵא, "be full." The Piel can mean "give/pay in full" (see BDB, Piel, 2); the foreskins fulfilled the required bride-price. The verb is masculine plural, so perhaps David's men helped him present the foreskins to the king. וַיְמַלְאוּם has a third masculine plural suffix referring to עָרְלֹתֵיהֶם, "their foreskins." The noun עָרְלָה, "foreskin," is grammatically feminine, but the verb's masculine plural suffix may be explained by attraction to the masculine plural suffix on עָרְלֹתֵיהֶם.

18:28 וַיַּרְא שָׁאוּל וַיֵּדַע—This is a verbal hendiadys: "and Saul saw and knew" means "Saul realized."

18:29 וַיֹּאסֶף—This is a third masculine singular Hiphil (H) form of יָסַף, "to do again; to do more, increase," thus "(he) became even more" (not a form of אָסַף, "to gather"). Here and in Ex 5:7 (cf. Job 27:19) a Hiphil (H) imperfect of יָסַף is written with א in place of ו (GKC, § 68 h, is unjustified in calling these forms a "mistake").

לֵרֹא—This is a Qal (G) infinitive construct of יָרֵא, "be afraid," with the preposition לְ. The expected form of the infinitive construct would be יְרֹא (cf. Josh 22:25), and the prefixed preposition would then have *hireq*, -לִ. However, the consonant י has been syncopated, and the vowel under the preposition has been lengthened to *tsere*, -לֵ, to compensate. Cf. GKC, § 69 n.

שָׁאוּל אֹיֵב אֶת־דָּוִד—More literally "Saul was being an enemy to David." The word אֹיֵב is the participle of the verb אָיַב, "be an enemy, be hostile." Usually the participle serves as a noun, "enemy," as in 18:25 and often elsewhere. Here, however, the participle functions as a verb with שָׁאוּל as its subject and אֶת־דָּוִד as its definite direct object.

כָּל־הַיָּמִים:—Literally this means "all the days."

18:30 מִדֵּי צֵאתָם—The noun דַּי, "sufficiency; enough," is frequently used with the prefixed preposition מִן and in construct (מִדֵּי) with an infinitive construct to mean "as often as" (BDB, s.v. דַּי, 2 c α). צֵאתָם is the infinitive construct of יָצָא in a military sense (see the first textual note on 18:6), "go out (to battle)," with a subjective pronominal suffix.

שָׂכַל—For this verb, "be successful," see the second textual note on 18:5 and the commentary on 18:5, 14–15.

וַיִּיקַר שְׁמוֹ מְאֹד:—Literally "and his name was esteemed, exceedingly." The verb יָקַר means "be precious, esteemed" (see *HALOT*, Qal, 3 and 4).

Commentary

c. 1018–c. 1016 BC

Saul had promised three things to the man who could defeat Goliath—to make him rich, to give him his daughter in marriage, and to free his family from taxation (17:25). This section of 1 Samuel deals directly with the second promise and indirectly with the first one (18:23).

Saul decided to use his promise of giving his daughter to be David's wife as a trap by demanding a bride-price for Merab (18:17). In this case for his older daughter, the price was simply to "wage Yahweh's wars" (18:17). Later, Abigail would recognize David as doing that, even after David had fled Saul's court (25:28). The portrait of Saul here is triply unflattering: he was using his daughter as bait to try to kill David; he was using David as the military leader to do the work that he ought to have been doing himself as king; and he was requiring an additional bride-price despite the fact that his original promise was contingent only on the defeat of Goliath (17:25).[1]

David's reply is a form of self-abasement (18:18) that was commonly used to reply to a superior (cf. Judg 6:15; 1 Sam 9:21; 2 Sam 7:18). It has the form of a question introduced by an interrogative particle (מַה, "what?" or מִי, "who?" as

---

[1] Similarly, Caleb offered his daughter to whoever conquered Kiriath-sepher; the conquest was the implied bride-price (Josh 15:16; Judg 1:12).

here) followed by an assertion introduced by כִּי, "that" (as here), or אֲשֶׁר, "who, which."[2] But despite David's protestation, Saul seems to have been obligated to give Merab to David, who paid the bride-price by his service. We are told that when the time came to give her "to David" (18:19), she was given to a certain Adriel the Meholathite. In giving Merab to another man, Saul may have been acting out of petulance when he saw that his scheme for David to be killed in battle had not panned out as he had planned. Later, David would give this couple's sons to the Gibeonites to execute in revenge for Saul's actions against them (2 Sam 21:5–9).

However, Saul perceived a second opportunity to use the Philistines to rid him of David (1 Sam 18:20–21). When Saul was informed of his younger daughter Michal's love for David, he decided to exploit her as he had exploited Merab. While his reported thought is not stated in the same words as when he proffered Merab (compare 18:17 and 18:21), his motivation was the same—he was hoping to lead David to his death.

It would seem that everyone mentioned in 1 Samuel 18 loved David except Saul. Jonathan loved David as a close friend and covenant partner (18:1, 3). All Israel and Judah loved David as the successful commander (18:16). Michal loved David romantically and as a spouse (18:20, 28). Saul's court officials loved David—or perhaps better, Saul had them claim such love in order to entice David into further battle with the Philistines (18:22).

David's protest to Saul's officials (18:23) was not as self-deprecating as his earlier reply to Saul had been (18:18). This time he noted that Saul's courtiers were asking him to do something that was beyond his station in life. He was a poor man, and an insignificant one (18:23). David may have been somewhat self-deprecating here, since we have been told repeatedly of David's renown and success (cf. 18:5, 7, 14). He was by no means "insignificant" as a commander in Saul's army. However, socially he may well have been insignificant—not from one of the leading families in Israel that might expect to marry into the royal family (cf. 18:18). However, David was also a "poor" man (רָשׁ, 18:23) who would not expect to have the resources to pay the kind of bride-price a king might demand for one of his daughters.[3] Moreover, David was insinuating that Saul had not kept his promise to "make very rich" the man who would strike down Goliath (17:25).

When Saul's servants reported David's words, Saul set a different bride-price that tacitly acknowledged David's lack of riches—he asked only for a hundred Philistine foreskins (18:24–25). The noun מֹהַר, "bride-price," is

---

[2] See Coats, "Self-Abasement and Insult Formulas," 14–17. See also, e.g., Ex 16:7; Num 16:11; 1 Sam 17:26; 2 Sam 9:8; Ps 8:5 (ET 8:4).

[3] Note also the play on words with the only other passage where רָשׁ, "poor," appears in the book of Samuel: 2 Sam 12:1, 3, 4, in the case of adjudication Nathan brought to David to illustrate David's sin against Uriah. In 1 Samuel 18, as a poor man, David could not afford a wife from the royal family. Later in 2 Samuel 12, as royalty himself, he would take the wife of another man, one who was poor, just as David had been.

mentioned only two other times in the OT: in Gen 34:12, where Shechem asks Jacob and his sons to set any bride-price they wish for Dinah, and in Ex 22:16 (ET 22:17), which required a man to pay the bride-price for violating a virgin. However, the concept is used elsewhere in the OT (implicitly in 1 Sam 17:25; 18:17), most notably in the account of Jacob's work to pay the bride-price set for Rachel by Laban (Gen 29:15–30). In fact, Genesis 29 has several parallels with this account:

1. In both accounts the father agreed to a bride-price in other than monetary terms (Gen 29:18, 27; Ex 22:15–16 [ET 22:16–17] implies that there was a standard bride-price for virgins).

2. In both accounts the father is depicted as cynically misusing his daughters (e.g., Laban first gave Leah instead of Rachel to Jacob [Gen 29:23]).

3. In both accounts the groom paid double in order to claim his wife: Jacob worked a total of fourteen years for Rachel (Gen 29:18, 27; 31:41), and David brought Saul twice as many Philistine foreskins as required (two hundred in 1 Sam 18:27 versus one hundred in 18:25).

It is intriguing that David learned of the bride-price from Saul's officials and not from Saul himself. Saul sent his officials to David with the terms (18:25), and David accepted the terms (18:26) and took action to fulfill the demand (18:27). David's doubling of the bride-price may have been a way of ensuring that this time Saul would not go back on his promise. For readers, it also emphasizes David's developing military expertise and contrasts his success against the Philistines against the background of Saul's failure ever to directly confront them, despite divine instructions to do so.[4]

Once again we are told that Saul reacted in fear because Yahweh was with David (18:28–29, as in 18:12).[5] This time the evidence was Michal's continued love for David, which she would later show by siding with David against her father (19:11–17). Saul's realization of God's abiding presence with David and his own daughter's allegiance to David, perhaps combined with a developing suspicion that David was the one Yahweh had picked to succeed him (15:26–29), led Saul to become David's constant enemy from then on (18:29). This provides readers with a transition to Saul's open enmity against David that will characterize much of 1 Samuel 19–26. Yet, despite this threat, David became the most successful of Saul's military men, especially when confronting Israel's most persistent enemy (18:30). We are also told that David gained an excellent reputation by his successes, a reputation that would enable him eventually to become king of all Israel.

---

[4] The prophet Samuel implied that Saul was to eradicate the Philistine garrison in Gibeah as a condition for becoming king (10:7). See the discussion in "Samuel Anoints Saul (9:26–10:8)" in the commentary on 9:26–10:16. See also the beginning of the commentary on 10:17–27a.

[5] Earlier David had been commended to Saul because Yahweh was with David (16:18), and Saul himself had prayed that Yahweh would be with David (17:37).

Once again, the life of David prefigures that of David's greater Son and Lord (Mt 22:42–45), whom King Herod sought to kill in infancy (Mt 2:16). On trial during Holy Week, he was condemned to death by those in authority (Pilate with the complicity of Herod the Tetrarch [Luke 23]). Yet not only was God with Jesus but he himself is "Immanuel," "God with us" (Mt 1:23), God Incarnate, the one anointed to be King of kings. The rage of rulers could not thwart him from ascending the throne of David (Is 9:6 [ET 9:7]; Lk 1:32) and receiving the most precious name.[6]

---

[6] See the third textual note on 18:30. See also, e.g., Acts 3:6; 4:12; Phil 2:9–10; 1 Pet 2:4–7.

Saul Tries to Have David Killed

Translation

19 ¹Saul told his son Jonathan and all his officials to kill David. But Saul's son Jonathan favored David very much. ²Jonathan reported to David, "Saul, my father, is seeking to kill you. Be on your guard in the morning. Stay somewhere out of sight and hide. ³I will go out and stand beside my father in the countryside where you are. I will talk about you to my father and see what [he says]. Then I'll report to you."

⁴So Jonathan spoke good things about David to Saul, his father. He said to him, "May the king not sin against his servant David, because he has not sinned against you and because his actions have been very good for you. ⁵He took his life in his hands and struck down the Philistine. Yahweh has worked great salvation for all Israel. You saw [it] and rejoiced. So why would you sin against innocent blood by killing David for no good reason?"

⁶Saul listened to Jonathan's advice, and Saul swore an oath, "As surely as Yahweh lives, he will not be put to death."

⁷So Jonathan summoned David, and Jonathan reported to him all these words. Then Jonathan brought David to Saul, and he served in his presence as previously.

⁸War broke out again, and David went out and fought against the Philistines. He decisively defeated them, and they fled from him. ⁹Now an evil spirit from Yahweh was with Saul. He was sitting in his house and had his spear in his hand. David was strumming [a lyre]. ¹⁰Saul sought to nail David to the wall with the spear, but he slipped away from Saul. He struck the spear into the wall, and David fled and escaped that night.

¹¹Saul sent messengers to David's house to watch him and kill him in the morning. His wife, Michal, told David, "If you don't escape with your life tonight, tomorrow you will be killed." ¹²Michal lowered David from the window, and he left, fled, and escaped. ¹³Then Michal took the household idols and put [them] on the bed. She put a goat-hair quilt at its head and covered [it] with a garment. ¹⁴Saul sent messengers to arrest David, and she said, "He's sick."

¹⁵So Saul sent messengers to see David with the instructions "bring him in the bed to me so that I can kill him." ¹⁶The messengers came and discovered the household idols in the bed and a goat-hair quilt at its head.

¹⁷Saul said to Michal, "Why did you deceive me like this and send my enemy away so that he could escape?"

Michal said to Saul, "He said to me, 'Send me away. Why should I kill you?'"

Textual Notes

19:1 לְהָמִית—This is the Hiphil (H) infinitive construct of מוּת, "to die," with the preposition לְ, indicating purpose or goal. The Hiphil has the causative meaning "put to death, kill." This same infinitive with prefixed preposition (sometimes also with a pronominal suffix) recurs in 19:2, 5, 11, 15; 20:33, all in reference to Saul's determination to have David killed. Yet in 19:6 Saul uses the Hophal (Hp) יוּמָת (with the corresponding passive meaning) to swear that David "will not be put to death." Cf. also the Hophal (Hp) participle מוּמָת in 19:11.

חָפֵץ בְּדָוִד—For the verb חָפֵץ plus the preposition בְּ, "*he favored* David," see the third textual note on 18:22.

19:2 וְיָשַׁבְתָּ בַסֵּתֶר—Literally "and you shall stay in the hiding place." The noun סֵתֶר, "hiding place; secrecy" is from the verb סָתַר, "to cover, conceal, hide."

וְנַחְבֵּאתָ:—This verb is a Niphal (N) perfect with *waw* consecutive of חָבָא, "hide," which does not occur in the Qal (G). In the Hiphil (H) it is transitive, "to hide [something]," while in the Niphal it is reflexive, "hide oneself." The English intransitive use of "hide" corresponds to the Hebrew Niphal.

19:3 בַּשָּׂדֶה וֹ—For "in the countryside," see the second textual note on 20:5.

19:4 אַל־יֶחֱטָא הַמֶּלֶךְ בְּעַבְדּוֹ בְדָוִד—Literally "may the king not sin against his servant, against David." When addressing a superior it is customary to show deference by referring to him in the third person (at least initially), rather than addressing him directly in the second person. In the rest of the verse, however, Jonathan switches to the second person; see the next textual note.

לְךָ ... לָךְ—These suffixed prepositions mean "against you ... for you." The first one, לָךְ, is a pausal form of the second, לְךָ; both prepositions have the second masculine singular suffix. The LXX omits the second one, לְךָ, probably in order to make David's actions seem even better—they are intrinsically good regardless of the beneficiary: τὰ ποιήματα αὐτοῦ ἀγαθὰ σφόδρα, "his deeds are exceedingly good."

19:5 חִנָּם:—This is translated as "for no good reason." It is one of the few Hebrew words that is an adverb in form. It is derived from the root חָנַן, which pertains to grace alone, apart from works or merit, with the adverbial ending ◌ָם. Thus, it can mean "*gratuitously, without cause, undeservedly*, esp[ecially] of groundless hostility or attack" (BDB, s.v. חָנַם, c), as also in 1 Sam 25:31. In 2 Sam 24:24 it means "gratis": King David refuses to offer donated sacrifices without first paying for them.

19:6 וַיִּשָּׁבַע—The Niphal (N) of שָׁבַע means "to swear an oath."

חַי־יְהוָה אִם־יוּמָת:—"As surely as Yahweh lives, he will not be put to death." The first three words are a standard oath formula; see the second textual note on 1:26 and the second textual note on 14:45. Regarding the Hophal (Hp) imperfect יוּמָת, see the first textual note on 19:1.

19:7 וַיְהִי לְפָנָיו—"And he served in his presence" is literally "and he was before him."

כְּאֶתְמוֹל שִׁלְשׁוֹם:—For "as previously," see the last textual note on 4:7.

19:8 וַתּוֹסֶף הַמִּלְחָמָה לִהְיוֹת—Literally "and the war continued to be." The feminine noun מִלְחָמָה is the subject of the feminine Hiphil (H) of יָסַף, "do again, do further," and the action that recurred is denoted by the Qal (G) infinitive construct of הָיָה, "to be." See Joüon, §§ 102 g, 124c, 177 b; see also the first textual note on 3:6.

וַיַּ֤ךְ בָּהֶם֙ מַכָּ֣ה גְדוֹלָ֔ה—Literally "and he struck them a great strike." Almost the same wording is in 6:19 (הִכָּ֤ה יְהוָה֙ בָּעָ֔ם מַכָּ֣ה גְדוֹלָ֑ה). The Hiphil (H) verb וַיַּ֤ךְ and the direct object noun מַכָּ֣ה are from the same root, נכה, forming a cognate accusative construction,[1] a very common construction in Hebrew, but one that is avoided in English.

19:9 ר֤וּחַ יְהוָ֣ה ׀ רָעָה֙—For "an evil spirit from Yahweh," see the first textual note on 16:15 and the commentary on 16:14–23. The same phrase, but with אֱלֹהִים, "God," in place of "Yahweh," was in 16:15, 16 (cf. 16:14, 23); 18:10.

מְנַגֵּ֖ן בְּיָֽד׃—For "was strumming," see the third textual note on 16:16.

19:10 לְהַכּ֛וֹת ... בְּדָוִ֥ד וּבַקִּ֖יר—For "to nail David to the wall," see the second textual note on 18:11.

וַיִּפְטַר֙—The rare verb פָּטַר (eight or nine times in the OT) is usually Qal (G), and only here has the intransitive meaning "to escape, slip away." Its Qal is transitive in Prov 17:14; 2 Chr 23:8.

וַיִּמָּלֵֽט—In the Niphal (N) מָלַט is intransitive, "to escape." This is the first instance of מָלַט in the book of Samuel, and it appears a total of thirteen times in the narrative of David's flight from Saul.[2] The identical form as here, a Niphal third masculine singular preterite (imperfect with waw consecutive), recurs in 19:12, 17, 18; also 22:1, 20. For its Piel (D), which is transitive, see the first textual note on 19:11.

בַּלַּ֥יְלָה הֽוּא׃—This means "(in/during) that night." The feminine-looking noun לַ֥יְלָה is actually masculine, with a penultimate accent (were it feminine the accent would be on the final syllable). Therefore it is modified by the masculine form of the demonstrative pronoun, הוּא. Usually the definiteness of a demonstrative agrees with that of the noun, but here הוּא lacks the article. This is fairly common; see GKC, § 126 y.

19:11 אִם־אֵֽינְךָ֞ מְמַלֵּ֤ט אֶת־נַפְשְׁךָ֙—The Piel (D) of מָלַט is transitive, "to save, deliver," so this participial clause is literally "if you are not saving your life."

מָחָ֖ר אַתָּ֥ה מוּמָֽת׃—Literally "tomorrow you are being put to death." The verb is a Hophal (Hp) participle from the verb מות (see the first textual note on 19:1). The use of a participle instead of an imperfect depicts the action (being killed) as so imminent that it is already happening.

19:12 וַתֹּ֧רֶד—This is the Hiphil (H) preterite (imperfect with waw consecutive) of יָרַד, "go down, descend." (The Qal [G] form would be וַתֵּ֖רֶד.) The Hiphil is causative: "Michal lowered David."

וַיִּבְרַ֖ח—This is the first instance of בָּרַח, "to flee," in the book of Samuel. This verb (always Qal [G]) refers to David fleeing from Saul here and in 1 Sam 19:18; 20:1; 21:11 (ET 21:10); 22:17; 27:4; to Abiathar fleeing to David in 1 Sam 22:20; 23:6; to David fleeing from Absalom in 2 Sam 15:14; 19:10 (ET 19:9); to Absalom's flight from David in 2 Sam 13:34, 37, 38; and to the flight of the Beerothites in 2 Sam 4:3.

19:13 הַתְּרָפִ֗ים—For "the household idols," see the second textual note on 15:23. See also the commentary on 19:13.

---

[1] *IBH*, § 17 B; GKC, § 117 p–r. See the first textual note on 1:6 (see also, e.g., 1:11, 17, 21; 2:13, 24; 4:5).

[2] 1 Sam 19:10, 11, 12, 17, 18; 20:29; 22:1, 20; 23:13; 27:1 (three times); 30:17.

כְּבִיר—This noun occurs only here and probably denotes a braided quilt or a cushion (*CDCH*). Perhaps it "serves as a wig."[3] The noun is probably related to the nouns כְּבָרָה, "sieve" (Amos 9:9); מִכְבָּר, "cover" (2 Ki 8:15); and מִכְבָּר, "grating" (Ex 27:4; 35:16; 38:4, 5, 30; 39:39). The noun recurs in 1 Sam 19:16.

מְרַאֲשֹׁתָיו—The feminine noun מְרַאֲשֹׁות occurs only in the plural and is used as an adverb. It is from רֹאשׁ, "head," and usually means "place at the head, head-place" (BDB). Here its third masculine singular suffix might refer back to הַמִּטָּה, "the bed," although that noun is feminine.[4] Or it might refer to David: "at his head," the place where he would lay his head. But most likely it refers to the whole arrangement of the covered idols as one fake man or dummy: "at its head." The same options are possible for מְרַאֲשֹׁתָיו in 19:16. See further the commentary on 19:13.

19:14 לָקַחַת—This is קַחַת, the Qal (G) infinitive construct of לָקַח, "to take," with the prefixed preposition לְ. The preposition usually has the vowel *qamets* (-לָ) in place of *shewa* (-לְ) when it immediately precedes the accented syllable (-קַ-) of an infinitive construct. See GKC, § 102 f.

19:15 לֵאמֹר—"With the instructions" is the Qal (G) infinitive construct of the verb אָמַר, "to say," which most often precedes direct discourse (quoted speech). Here it precedes the instructions given to the messengers.

לַהֲמִתוֹ:—The infinitive construct with לְ and an object suffix forms a purpose clause, literally "in order to kill him" (see the first textual note on 19:1). Since in context Saul is the agent of the action, it is translated as "so that I can kill him."

19:16 וְהִנֵּה—The particle הִנֵּה, "behold, look," often marks something as unexpected, as here, thus "and (they) discovered." The messengers made the unexpected discovery of a decoy.

19:17 לָמָּה כָּכָה רִמִּיתִנִי—The adverb כָּכָה, "thus, like this," is more emphatic that כֹּה. "[Why] did you deceive me?" translates a Piel (D) second feminine singular perfect of רָמָה with a first common singular pronominal suffix. It might also have the nuance "betray" (see *HALOT*, s.v. רמה II).

וַתְּשַׁלְּחִי ... שַׁלְּחִנִי—The verb שָׁלַח means "to send" in the Qal (G). Its Piel (D) means "to send [someone] away." Both forms here are feminine; the second is the feminine singular imperative (שַׁלְּחִי) with a first common singular suffix.

Commentary

c. 1015 BC

These verses contain three incidents from David's time in Saul's court that led to David's separation from Saul's army and from service to the king. In each incident a different member of the royal family plays a major role. First, Saul's son Jonathan defends David, resulting in Saul temporarily abandoning his threats against David's life (19:1–7). Next Saul himself proves unable

---

[3] McCarter, *I Samuel*, 326. He also discusses a possible etymology of the other Hebrew words cited above from the root כבר*.

[4] Hebrew prefers masculine forms and sometimes uses them when the referent is feminine. Thus, masculine is called the "prior gender" in GKC, §§ 122 g; 132 d; 146 d. In modern terminology it might be called the "default" gender.

to kill David (19:8–10). Finally, Saul's daughter Michal helps David escape (19:11–17). These three incidents combined illustrate that despite Saul's efforts, he is unable to do anything that will prevent Samuel's prophecy concerning the kingdom from being fulfilled (15:28; cf. 3:19). Subsequent kings will also attempt to prevent the words of Yahweh's prophets from coming to fruition, but, like Saul, they, too, will fail (1 Ki 11:26–40; 22:1–40).

While not as overt as some passages in the OT, this section of 1 Samuel emphasizes two important theological points:

1. *Yahweh's will—especially his salvific will expressed by the prophets—cannot be obviated by human effort.* God is the ultimate sovereign, and his decrees and judgments cannot be averted by human opposition to them. Moreover, when the prophets reveal God's grace and mercy, no one can keep his blessing from being bestowed on those who have received his favor. Saul cannot undo God's judgment that he be removed from the throne, nor can he prevent God's mercy and grace from being poured out upon David (2 Sam 7:8–9), and through David upon Israel (2 Sam 7:10–11), and ultimately through the Son of David upon the world (2 Sam 7:16; Is 11:1–16; Mt 1:1).

2. *The kingdoms of the world belong to God, and he places whomever he wishes over them* (Dan 2:21; 4:29 [ET 4:32]; Rom 13:1). God had told Saul that he was tearing the kingdom from him and giving it to someone else (15:28). Saul, though growing jealous of David, and by now suspecting that Yahweh had given the kingdom of Israel to this young man from Bethlehem, refuses to accept God's will.

Jonathan Defends David (19:1–7)

This account has been subjected to separation into sources by higher critics because of supposed contradictions it contains:[5] David was to hide, while Jonathan spoke to Saul (19:2), while on the other hand Jonathan would plan to have his conversation with Saul where David was in the countryside (19:3). Moreover, if David was to overhear the conversation, why did Jonathan have to report it to David (19:7)? However, these features of the text are not as contradictory as is claimed. First, nothing is said about David overhearing the conversation. Perhaps Jonathan simply wanted David to see that the conversation with Saul had taken place. However, even if David was within earshot of the conversation, there was no guarantee that he could hear all of it well enough to be certain about what was said. Often in the outdoors one can hear human voices without making out the words. Yet one can often judge the general demeanor of the participants from the tone of the conversation. Perhaps this is all that David might have detected, and it was necessary for Jonathan to report the details to David later.

The account opens with Saul seeking to enlist Jonathan and his own officials to kill David (19:1). However, these very people love David (אָהֵב, 18:1, 3, 22; 20:17). The author especially highlights that Jonathan "favored" David (חָפֵץ בְּ-,

---

[5] E.g., McCarter, *I Samuel*, 321–22.

19:1). This same phraseology was used by Saul in his devious instructions to his officials when he was trying to lure David into combat with the Philistines (18:22). Saul's message, "the king favors you" (חָפֵץ בְּךָ הַמֶּלֶךְ, 18:22), was a lie, but Jonathan truly did favor David.

Jonathan had an agreement with David (18:3–4), and he honored that agreement by warning David (19:2) and by devising a plan to deter Saul (19:3–5). Jonathan reported that Saul was "seeking" (the Piel [D] verb בִּקֵּשׁ, 19:2) to kill David. This "seeking" of David's life will be a repeated theme in Saul's future actions.[6] Three times Jonathan called Saul "my father" (אָבִי, 19:2, 3 [twice]), even though it was unnecessary in the context of 19:2 and it may have been more natural for him to have used a pronoun ("him") in 19:3. Clearly Jonathan had been placed in a position of conflicting loyalties. The Fourth Commandment requires honoring one's father and mother (Ex 20:12; Deut 5:16). Yet Jonathan favored David and thereby kept the Fifth Commandment (Ex 20:13; Deut 5:17) rather than choosing loyalty to his homicidal, demon-afflicted father.

In his conversation with Saul, Jonathan addressed him formally as "the king" (see the first textual note on 19:4), signaling not only respect for his father's office but also that he was speaking about official business of the kingdom. He used several arguments to persuade the king that his order to kill David was wrong:

1. He labeled Saul's order as a sin against David (19:4). He noted that David's behavior was just the opposite: "he has not sinned against you," and "his actions have been very good for you" (19:4).

2. He noted that David "took his life in his hands" (19:5; cf. Judg 12:3; 1 Sam 28:21; Job 13:14) when he killed "the Philistine," that is, Goliath.[7] David was willing to risk his life where Saul was not.

3. He noted that Yahweh worked a great salvation for Israel through David (19:5)— something that Yahweh had also done through Jonathan (14:45). To kill David would also by implication demonstrate ungratefulness for Yahweh's victory through Saul's own son.

4. Saul had rejoiced in David's triumph over Goliath (19:5). This was an appeal to Saul's own emotional connection to David's accomplishments.

5. Killing David would be a sin "against innocent blood" (בְּדָם נָקִי, 19:5). This phrase characterizes a sin against the Fifth Commandment, a murder that is abhorrent to Yahweh (cf. Prov 6:17).[8] Jonathan was appealing to Saul not to subject the kingdom to such lawlessness, which would harm the throne and bring God's judgment on all Israel (cf. 2 Ki 21:16; 24:4).

6. Killing David would be "for no good reason" (חִנָּם, 19:5), an unjustified, gratuitous murder that would accomplish no purpose other than to assuage Saul's fear of David.

---

[6] בִּקֵּשׁ, 19:10; 20:1; 22:23; 23:10, 14, 15, 25; 24:3 (ET 24:2); 25:26, 29; 26:2, 20; 27:1, 4.

[7] Twice in 1 Samuel 17 (17:4, 23), the author makes a point of the Philistine's name, "Goliath." Thereafter, he is always called "the Philistine" when referring to David's conflict with him.

[8] Cf. also Deut 19:10; 21:8; 27:25; Is 59:7; Jer 7:6; 22:3; 26:15; Pss 94:21; 106:38.

Saul was persuaded by Jonathan's words. He swore an oath by Yahweh that rescinded his order concerning David (19:6). Saul's solemn pledge, however, would be short-lived.

Jonathan's intervention accomplished a temporary reconciliation between Saul and David (19:7). David returned to serving Saul "as previously," which implies that he once again became one of Saul's attendants, especially in his duty to play music to soothe Saul when tormented by an evil spirit (16:14–23).

Saul Tries a Second Time to Kill David with a Spear (19:8–10)

David did not stay at Saul's court, however. Once again war with the Philistines meant that David went out to fight them, and he gained an impressive victory (19:8). This notice is placed in the narrative as a transition to Saul's second attempt to kill David with a spear (19:9–10; the first was in 18:10–11). Saul's jealousy of David flared up once more as David had success against an enemy that King Saul ought to have taken the lead in defeating (8:20). As previously, David slipped away from Saul. He fled and escaped (the verb מָלַט, 19:10). Just as Saul's seeking David's life will become a theme repeated throughout the rest of 1 Samuel (see the commentary on 19:2), so also David's escape will be repeated.[9]

Michal Helps David Escape (19:11–17)

David's escape from Saul was to "David's house" (19:11), probably a house in Gibeah given to him as part of his marriage to Michal. Saul's house was also in Gibeah (15:34). Since David escaped from Saul "that night" (19:10) and Saul sent men to wait and and kill him the next morning (19:11) but David escaped a second time during the same night (19:11–12), David's house must not have been too far from Saul's.

Saul now made no pretense of his intent. He ordered his messengers to watch the house the rest of the night and put David to death as soon as it was morning (19:11). How Michal learned of Saul's plan is not explained, but she emphasized the urgency of his leaving. Lowering David through a window to escape (19:12) most likely indicates that the house was in the city wall (cf. Josh 2:15; Acts 9:23–25; 2 Cor 11:32–33), since Saul's men who were watching the house presumably were stationed inside the city wall and perhaps also on top of it.

Michal's next actions (19:13) have caused some questions for readers. First, what were "household idols" (תְּרָפִים) doing in David's house? Since this house was most likely one given to him, the idols may well have been in the house before it became David's, not placed there by him. Note that Samuel had warned Saul about idolatry with the same kind of idols (תְּרָפִים; see the second textual note on 15:23), which may imply that Saul's family engaged in a type of syncretistic worship involving them.

---

[9] מָלַט, 19:11, 12, 17, 18; 20:29; 22:1; 23:13; 27:1.

Second, how many idols did Michal place in the bed—just one or several? Some commentators suggest that even though the Hebrew word תְּרָפִים ("household idols") has a plural form, it may be singular.[10] This argument primarily relies on the assumption that the resulting decoy is referenced with the masculine singular pronoun on מְרַאֲשֹׁתָיו, "at its head" (19:13, 16), but other interpretations of that pronoun are possible (see the third textual note on 19:13). Moreover, the noun תְּרָפִים is clearly plural in some passages (Gen 31:19, 34, 35; 2 Ki 23:24; Zech 10:2).[11] Moreover, if we are to imagine Michal moving a single wooden, metal, or stone idol similar in size to a man, she must have been muscular or large. It is more likely that she put several idols into the bed and covered them to form the body of the decoy.[12]

Michal was willing to defy her father not only by fabricating the dummy but also by telling lies. Her first lie was claiming that David was sick (19:14). Then she claimed that David had threatened to kill her if she did not help him escape (19:17). Her actions partially resemble Rachel's deception of her father, Laban, in the matter of "household idols" (תְּרָפִים, Gen 31:34–35). This passage does not overtly condone Michal's deceptions, but in the context of the narrative of David, she is implicitly commended as an intrepid ally of the man Yahweh had anointed as king to lead his people to salvation. Other passages narrate the telling of lies in order to protect God's people or enable them to escape, and occasionally Scripture lauds such actions as displays of saving faith by people who were justified, that is, righteous, e.g., Rahab the prostitute (Josh 2:1–24; 6:17–25; Heb 11:31; James 2:25), who was an ancestress of Christ (Mt 1:5). Within the book of Samuel, see further the commentary on 1 Sam 20:28–29 on telling lies to protect innocent lives. The deceptions by David in 21:3–4, 13–14 (ET 21:2–3, 12–13) and 27:10–11 are also portrayed in a favorable light.

Michal was not the first nor the last to rescue a believer who played a key role in the salvation of God's people by lowering him through a window in the city wall (1 Sam 19:12). Rahab had done the same thing for the Israelite spies sent to scope out the promised land (Josh 2:15, 18). The apostle Paul was lowered in a basket through an opening in the city wall of Damascus, enabling him to escape a plot to put him to death (Acts 9:23–25; 2 Cor 11:32–33).[13]

---

[10] Presumably, this would be an intensive plural or one suggesting (to the pagan worshiper) divine majesty (*pluralis majestatis*). See Waltke-O'Connor, § 7.4.3a, including n. 14; GKC, § 124 h; Joüon, § 136 d. Commentators who believe the noun refers to a single idol include McCarter, *1 Samuel*, 324, 326; Klein, *1 Samuel*, 197; Bergen, *1, 2 Samuel*, 208; and Tsumura, *The First Book of Samuel*, 494.

[11] Note especially Zech 10:2, where תְּרָפִים is the subject of a plural verb form.

[12] Commentators who believe Michal used several idols include Brueggemann, *First and Second Samuel*, 143; Auld, *I and II Samuel*, 225; and Bodner, *1 Samuel*, 206.

[13] The similarity of the incident includes watchers lying in wait for Saul (Acts 9:24); compare the messengers who watched to kill David in 1 Sam 19:11. Perhaps with some irony the apostle under the death threat is called Saul in Acts 9, with the same name as the king who sought to put David to death in 1 Samuel 19.

Saul, being determined to kill David, ordered his men to bring David to him even if it meant bringing him in his sickbed (1 Sam 19:15). However, Michal's ruse was discovered (19:16), and Saul could only ask his daughter why she would deceive him (19:17).

Like Jonathan's, Michal's love for David strained her relationship with her father. Such situations are always emotionally charged and sensitive. However, at times God calls his people to deny their family relationships in order to follow him in faith or to honor his commands. The first and greatest commandment is to "love the Lord your God" (Deut 6:5; Mt 22:37; Mk 12:30). Jesus declares, "Whoever loves father or mother more than me is not worthy of me" (Mt 10:37; see also Lk 12:51–53; 14:26–27).

Figure 24

David on the Run from Saul

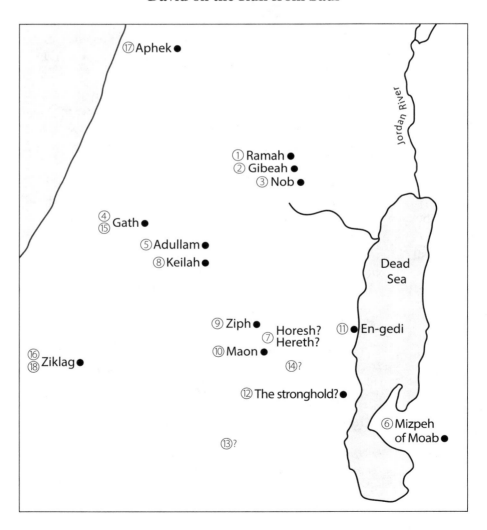

Key for Figure 24

1. David flees to Samuel at Ramah (19:18–24).
2. David meets Jonathan at Gibeah (20:1–21:1 [ET 20:1–42]; cf. 10:26).
3. David goes to Ahimelech at Nob (21:2–10 [ET 21:1–9]).
4. David goes to Achish at Gath (21:11–16 [ET 21:10–15]).
5. David is at Adullam (22:1–2).
6. David takes his parents to Mizpeh in Moab and stays in a stronghold (22:3–4).
7. David returns to Judah, to the forest of Hereth (22:5).
8. David rescues Keilah (23:1–13).
9. David is in the wilderness of Ziph at Horesh (23:14–18).
10. David escapes Saul in the wilderness of Maon (23:19–28).
11. David spares Saul's life in the cave near En-gedi (24:1–22 [ET 23:29–24:21]).
12. David is in the stronghold (24:23 [ET 24:22]).
13. David is in the wilderness of Paran, meets and marries Abigail, and also marries Ahinoam of Jezreel (25:1–43).
14. David spares Saul's life at the hill of Hachilah (26:1–25).
15. David goes to Achish at Gath (27:1–4).
16. David is given Ziklag as a base of operations (27:5–12).
17. David accompanies Achish to Aphek (29:1–11).
18. David returns to Ziklag and rescues his wives from the Amalekites (30:1–31).

Saul Searches for David
in the Pastures at Ramah

Translation

19 ¹⁸**David fled and escaped and came to Samuel in Ramah. He reported to him everything that Saul did to him. Then he and Samuel went and stayed in the pasture settlements.** ¹⁹**Saul was told, "David is in the pasture settlements at Ramah."** ²⁰**So Saul sent messengers to capture David. When they saw the company of the prophets prophesying and Samuel standing as their leader, the Spirit of God came upon Saul's messengers, and they, too, prophesied.** ²¹**They reported [this] to Saul, so he sent other messengers, and they, too, prophesied. Saul again sent messengers, a third group, and they, too, prophesied.** ²²**So he himself also went to Ramah, and when he came to the cistern of the threshing floor that is on the bare hill, he asked, "Where are Samuel and David?"**

[Someone] answered, "In the pasture settlements at Ramah."

²³**When he went there to the pasture settlements at Ramah, the Spirit of God came upon him too. He went, prophesying as he walked, until he came to the pasture settlements at Ramah.** ²⁴**He took off his clothes, and he, too, prophesied in front of Samuel. He lay there naked all that day and all night. Therefore, they say, "Is also Saul among the prophets?"**

Textual Notes

19:18 בָּרַח—For the Qal (G) verb "to flee," see the second textual note on 19:12.

וַיִּמָּלֵט—For the Niphal (N) verb "to escape," see the third textual note on 19:10.

וַיֵּלֶךְ הוּא וּשְׁמוּאֵל—This construction with a singular verb and a pronoun, literally "and he went—he and Samuel," keeps the focus on David. If, instead, a plural verb had been used, וַיֵּלְכוּ, "and they went," the focus would have been on both equally.

בְּנָיוֹת—This is the Qere; the pointing of the Kethib is uncertain but could be בְּנָיֹת. Both forms have the preposition בְּ. The word to which it is prefixed could be a place-name, "in Naioth," as in most English versions. This is unlikely, however, given that a named place—Ramah—follows it in 19:19, 22, 23.[1] Therefore the meaning "in the pasture settlements" is preferable here and for the same Qere and Kethib readings in 19:19, 22, 23b, similarly, for the same Qere and Kethib but without the preposition בְּ in 19:23a. The nouns נָיוֹת and נָיֹת (both are feminine plural in form) are most likely related to the masculine noun נָוֶה, "pasturage, grazing place, meadow, settlement," and/

---

[1] LXX 1 Sam 19:18 reads ἐν Ναυαθ ἐν Ραμα, "in Naioth in Ramah."

or its feminine equivalent נָוָה (see *HALOT; CDCH*).[2] Most III-ה roots in Hebrew were originally III-י (and the original final letter י is often preserved in forms with a suffix). Thus, נְוָיֹת may be the plural form of the noun נָוֶה. Its plural is unattested elsewhere in the OT. The plural of the feminine noun נָוָה is attested in the OT in the construct state and is spelled either נְוֹת (Zeph 2:6) or, more often, נְאוֹת (e.g., Ps 23:2).

19:19 הִנֵּה—Sometimes this word, "look, behold," simply signals that new or different information follows and is best left untranslated. The word recurs in 19:22.

19:20 וַיִּשְׁלַח שָׁאוּל מַלְאָכִים לָקַחַת אֶת־דָּוִד—These same words, "Saul sent messengers to capture/arrest David," were in 19:14. For לָקַחַת, see the textual note on 19:14.

וַיַּרְא—The verb is singular, "and he saw," possibly due to attraction to the preceding singular proper name, דָּוִד, "David," but it is translated as plural, "when they saw," since the implied subject is the plural מַלְאָכִים, "messengers."

אֶת־לַהֲקַת הַנְּבִיאִים—The noun לַהֲקָה, "company," occurs only here, and its derivation is unknown; no cognates of it occur in the OT. The LXX reads τὴν ἐκκλησίαν, which suggests a form of the Hebrew noun קָהָל (or the rare feminine equivalent, קְהִלָּה), "congregation, company, gathering," and implies that the MT has suffered from metathesis of ק and ל. Tsumura translates it as "elders" and references the Ethiopic *leḥiq*, "old man, elder," and the Akkadian *lēqû*, "foster father."[3] Similarly, for לַהֲקָה, *DCH* gives "seniority," "company (of elders)." However, since one cannot compare the semantic features of cognates across related languages without additional evidence to buttress a proposed meaning, this is simply speculation.[4]

נִבְּאִים—This is the masculine plural Niphal (N) participle of נָבָא, "to prophesy"; see the third textual note on 10:5. The subject is the noun with definite article, הַנְּבִיאִים, "the prophets," and the participle lacks an article, so instead of serving adjectivally ("prophesying prophets"), the participle serves as a verb, "the prophets" were "prophesying."

עֹמֵד נִצָּב עֲלֵיהֶם—This is translated as "standing as their leader." The first participle is the Qal (G) of עָמַד, "to stand." The second is the Niphal (N) masculine singular participle of נָצַב. In the Niphal נָצַב can mean "*stand = be stationed*" or "*be stationed = appointed* over (עַל)" (BDB, s.v. נָצַב, Niphal, 1 b and 2). BDB translates the clause here as "with Samuel *presiding over* (עַל) them" (BDB, Niphal, 2).

רוּחַ אֱלֹהִים—This construct phrase, "the Spirit of God," repeated in 19:23, refers to the Holy Spirit, the third person of the Trinity, since this Spirit is also implied as the one who was enabling the company of the prophets, with Samuel presiding, to prophesy earlier in the verse. Contrast the phrases with the adjective רָעָה that referred to an "evil spirit" from God/Yahweh in 16:14–16, 23; 18:10; 19:9 (see the first textual note on 16:15 and the commentary on 16:14–23).

---

[2] See McCarter, *I Samuel*, 328; Klein, *1 Samuel*, 198; Tsumura, *The First Book of Samuel*, 495–96; Bergen, *1, 2 Samuel*, 209–10.

[3] Tsumura, *The First Book of Samuel*, 496.

[4] If such methodology were to be applied to modern European languages, it might lead to false cognates such as these: (1) "robe" in English—a long loose garment worn over other clothes by men or women; "robe" in French—a woman's dress; (2) "become" in English—"come, change, grow"; "bekommen" in German—"get, receive, obtain."

וַיִּֽתְנַבְּאוּ—The Hithpael (HtD) of נָבָא, "to prophesy," is synonymous with the Niphal (N) of נָבָא. See נִבְּאִים earlier in 19:20. See also the third textual note on 10:5. This plural Hithpael (HtD) form recurs in 19:21 (twice), and its singular equivalent וַיִּתְנַבֵּא appears in 19:23, 24.

19:21 וַיֹּ֣סֶף שָׁאוּל֮ וַיִּשְׁלַח֒—The two verbs are coordinated, and the first serves adverbially: literally "and Saul did again/more and he sent" means "Saul again sent." For the Hiphil (H) of יָסַף in this type of construction, see Joüon, § 177 b, c.

מַלְאָכִים שְׁלִשִׁים—Literally this means "messengers, third ones." שְׁלִשִׁים is the masculine plural of the ordinal adjective שְׁלִישִׁי, "third," and it modifies the preceding noun, מַלְאָכִים. However, English does not have a plural form of the adjective "third," so the translation uses the appositional phrase "messengers, a third group."

19:22 בּוֹר הַגָּדוֹל אֲשֶׁר בַּשֶּׂכוּ—The MT reads "a cistern, the large one, which is in Secu." That reading has been challenged as corrupt for two reasons. First, there is no other mention of a place named Secu in the OT. Second, the noun בּוֹר, "cistern," has no definite article, but an article is attached to the adjective הַגָּדוֹל, "the large one," which modifies the noun (see GKC, § 126 x). The LXX reads τοῦ φρέατος τοῦ ἅλω τοῦ ἐν τῷ Σεφι, "the cistern of the threshing floor that is in Sephi." That would represent a Hebrew text such as בּוֹר הַגֹּרֶן אֲשֶׁר בַּשְׁפִי.[5] The last Hebrew word, בַּשְׁפִי, was partly translated and partly transliterated into Greek as ἐν τῷ Σεφι, but the noun שְׁפִי means "bare hill," as attested in other passages.[6] Thus, בּוֹר הַגֹּרֶן אֲשֶׁר בַּשְׁפִי can be translated as "the cistern of the threshing floor that is on the bare hill."[7] This commentary's translation follows that reading, which pictures the forlorn king standing on a windswept hill overlooking Ramah and inquiring about David.

19:23 וַתְּהִ֨י עָלָ֤יו גַּם־הוּא—The force of the preposition עַל with a suffix (עָלָיו, "upon him") extends over the following pronoun הוּא in apposition to the suffix, literally the Spirit "was upon him, also [upon] him" (see Joüon, § 146 d).

וַיֵּלֶךְ הָלוֹךְ וַיִּתְנַבֵּא—Literally "and he went, going, and he prophesied," this construction likely means "he went, prophesying as he walked." To express such a meaning usually וַיֵּלֶךְ, "and he went," would be followed by two infinitive absolutes, as is הָלְכוּ in 1 Sam 6:12 (GKC, § 113 s). Here הָלוֹךְ is the infinitive absolute of הָלַךְ, "walk," but the next verb, וַיִּתְנַבֵּא, is a Hithpael (HtD) preterite (imperfect with *waw* consecutive), rather than an infinitive absolute. The same kind of construction is attested in some other verses, including 2 Sam 16:13 (cf. 2 Sam 13:19). See GKC, § 113 t; Joüon, § 123 n (but Joüon's assertion that וַיִּתְנַבֵּא should be emended to an infinitive absolute is unwarranted).

19:24 וַיִּפְשַׁט גַּם־הוּא בְּגָדָיו ... עָרֹם—The first clause is literally "and he, also he, took off his garments." The clause itself may refer simply to taking off outer garments, as

---

[5] The corruption of this phrase into the MT's phrase would involve four instances of graphic confusion. Two instances resulted in הַגָּדוֹל in place of הַגֹּרֶן: the letter ד for ר and the letter ל for נ, with ו added later for full orthography. Two other instances resulted in בַּשֶּׂכוּ in place of בַּשְׁפִי: the letter כ for פ and the letter ו for י.

[6] Num 23:3; Is 41:18; 49:9; Jer 3:2, 21; 4:11; 7:29; 12:12; 14:6.

[7] Cf. Klein, *1 Samuel*, 193; Auld, *I and II Samuel*, 227.

in other verses with the same phraseology,[8] especially clauses with the Hiphil (H) of פָּשַׁט and the same direct object in Num 20:26, 28. The removal of an outer garment is conveyed by the Qal (G) or Hiphil (H) of פָּשַׁט with other direct objects in Gen 37:23; Micah 2:8; Song 5:3. See the first textual note on 1 Sam 18:4, which has the Hithpael (HtD) of פָּשַׁט. Thus, גַּם־הוּא, "also he," suggests that the other prophets had discarded their outer garments, probably due to the physical exertion involved in their activity as they prophesied.

Here, however, a second clause follows with the adjective עָרֹם, "naked." Similar phraseology with פָּשַׁט and then עָרֹם or the related verb עָרַר, "to strip (naked)," appears in Is 32:11; Hos 2:5 (ET 2:3); Job 22:6 (cf. Ezek 16:39). This phraseology refers to the removal of all garments. See further the commentary.

Commentary

c. 1015 BC

When David fled from Saul he headed north a couple of miles to Samuel's hometown of Ramah (19:18). The author is careful to note David's report to Samuel on Saul's behavior before the two of them went out to the settlements in the surrounding pastures. David's report to the seer serves as a way of validating for the reader Samuel's prophecy of God's rejection of Saul (15:26–29). David, however, would not find sanctuary with Samuel, since in short order Saul was told of his whereabouts (19:19).

Saul's three attempts to capture David are all thwarted by God's Spirit, who overtakes the messengers so that they prophesy (19:20–21). Many scholars opine that such prophesying took on an ecstatic character and cite this passage for support.[9] Nevertheless, the text does not offer sufficient details to confirm this opinion. However this prophetic activity manifested itself, in this passage the Spirit of God thwarted Saul's agents. Here God dealt gently with the king's messengers. In a similar situation later, when Ahaziah sent three different contingents to capture Elijah, God destroyed the first two with fire from heaven (2 Ki 1:2–17).

Saul, however, was not deterred in his pursuit of David and went to Ramah himself, inquiring about David's location as he approached. (For David's whereabouts, see the textual note on 19:22.) Saul, however, could not escape God's Spirit any more than his agents could (19:23). We are told that he prophesied as he walked.[10] Then, as he came to Samuel, he stripped off his clothes and lay naked before Samuel for an entire day and night. This is the second time in the book of Samuel that someone in the royal family "took off" (the verb פָּשַׁט) his clothes. The first was when Jonathan removed his robe and gave it to David, acknowledging David's leadership of Israel (18:4). Now Saul removed all his clothes and displayed his nakedness (see the textual note on 19:24). Assuming

---

[8] Lev 6:4 (ET 6:11); 16:23; Ezek 44:19; Neh 4:17 (ET 4:23).

[9] Also, e.g., 1 Sam 10:5, 6, 10, 11, 13; 18:10.

[10] See the second textual note on 19:23.

that this resulted from the influence of "the Spirit of God" (19:23; also 19:20), God was symbolically stripping the king of his royal garments in anticipation of Saul's loss of the kingdom.

Saul's sordid nakedness, however, revealed that he had lost even more: his faith and salvation.[11] His repeated rejection of the express Word of God had caused the Holy Spirit to depart from him and, in the Spirit's place, an evil spirit tormented him (see the commentary on 16:14–23). Here the Spirit exerted enough control over Saul to prevent him from carrying out his plans to kill David for a day and a night,[12] but Saul resumed his quest to execute David in the ensuing chapters. It does not appear, then, that Saul was briefly regenerated by the Spirit to saving faith for a day and night, only to relapse into apostasy the next day. Rather, he continued in his state of unbelief, impenitence, and hatred of the one chosen according to the prophetic Word (15:26–29). Saul remained bent on evil. Saul's nakedness highlighted his shame and sinfulness.[13] Before the fall into sin, the man and the woman were naked but had no shame (Gen 2:25). Since the fall, however, public nudity is always associated with shame.[14] Here Saul's shame was in full view before Samuel and the company of prophets with him.

Some commentators see a contradiction with 15:35, which states that Samuel did not see Saul again after he left him for the last time at Gilgal.[15] However, in that verse "see" probably denotes oversight, not simply looking upon Saul physically (see the commentary on 15:35).

The author notes that Saul's prophesying led to the saying "is also Saul among the prophets?" (19:24). The author had noted the same aphorism at the beginning of Saul's reign, when Saul prophesied after his anointing as he was going home (10:11–12). These two incidents form bookends on Saul's reign. He prophesied at the beginning of his reign as God's chosen king. Now he prophesied in shame as God stripped him of his dignity, along with stripping him of the kingdom. In the beginning God changed Saul's heart (10:9) as he assumed the throne. Now Saul had changed his own heart into one with murderous intent that would cause him to pursue David doggedly despite the divine warnings of how his life of willful disobedience would end (compare 15:23 to 28:7–19).

---

[11] Thus, God's judgment upon his people for their idolatry and apostasy is for them to be stripped naked in Is 32:11; Ezek 16:39; Hos 2:4–5 (ET 2:2–3), passages that use Hebrew terminology similar to that in 1 Sam 19:24. See the textual note on 19:24.

[12] The context of Saul in 1 Samuel is diametrically opposed to that in Acts 16, where the apostle Paul is preaching the Gospel of Jesus Christ. Nevertheless, compare Acts 16:6–7, where Paul and Timothy were forbidden by "the Holy Spirit" to speak the Word in Asia and "the Spirit of Jesus" did not allow them to go into Bithynia despite their attempt to travel there.

[13] See, e.g., Gen 3:7–12; Ezek 16:7, 22, 39; 23:29; Micah 1:11.

[14] See 2 Sam 10:4–5; also, e.g., Gen 9:20–27; Is 20:3–4. Passages such as Rev 3:18; 16:15 suggest that the damned remain naked for eternity. The greatest example of the shame of public exposure is the crucifixion of Christ after the soldiers had taken even his inner garment (Jn 19:23–24). He bore the shame of humanity's sin while on the cross: "he endured the cross, despising the shame" (Heb 12:2).

[15] E.g., McCarter, *I Samuel*, 330.

Because the adage "is also Saul among the prophets?" is attached to two different incidents in 1 Samuel, critical scholars often assume that the book preserves two traditions of separate origin, each offering a different explanation of the genesis of this saying.[16] A tacit assumption is that they cannot both be true. However, making this into an either-or situation misses the point being made in the book of Samuel. The maxim arose because of each—and both—of Saul's prophetic experiences under the influence of God's Spirit. Therefore, the saying has an irony to it. It can be spoken in admiration of the new king whom God has chosen (10:12). Or it can be uttered in abject pity of the aged king who has lost the entire dignity of his office (19:24) and who has been reduced to chasing his successor throughout the kingdom without hope of ever changing God's immutable decree against his failed reign (15:26–29).[17]

---

[16] E.g., McCarter, *I Samuel*, 330; Klein, *1 Samuel*, 195.

[17] Brueggemann, *First and Second Samuel*, 146.

Excursus

Luther on the Prophet Samuel

Narratives involving Samuel occupy just fourteen out of the fifty-five chapters in the book of Samuel.[1] In many ways he is a transitional figure—the last of the judges and the anointer of Israel's first two kings. He is mentioned nine more times in the OT and three times in the NT.[2] While his ministry prefigures that of Christ,[3] his prophetic utterances are less overtly messianic than some others in the book.[4] He is prominent enough to lend his name to be the book's title, but in the book of Samuel, he appears to be overshadowed by David and would seem to be surpassed by other prophets in the canon of the OT.

However, for Luther, Samuel was a pivotal figure among the prophets. Luther called him "the first great prophet."[5] Moreover, in commenting on Hab 3:13 ("You came out to save your people, to save your anointed one. You crushed the head of the house of the wicked and stripped him bare from head to toe"), Luther claimed: "This happened in the days of Samuel, Saul, [and] David. When they went forth to war, God helped them everywhere."[6] Interestingly, Habakkuk mentions "your anointed one," which could apply to either Saul or David (prefiguring the Anointed One, the Messiah or Christ), but not Samuel. Yet Luther includes the prophet in his comment, suggesting that Samuel was as important as either king in the salvation of God's people.[7]

---

[1] 1 Samuel 1–4; 7–13; 15–16; 19. His death is mentioned in 1 Sam 25:1, and he is mentioned by name seven times when Saul seeks to consult him through a medium (1 Sam 28:3, 11, 12, 14, 15, 16, 20).

[2] Jer 15:1; Ps 99:6; 1 Chr 6:13, 18 (ET 6:28, 33); 9:22; 11:3; 26:28; 29:29; 2 Chr 35:18; Acts 3:24; 13:20; Heb 11:32.

[3] See further "Christ in Samuel" in the introduction. Samuel serves as a lesser type of the greater Christ in a variety of ways, e.g., Samuel is consecrated to God even before he is conceived (1:11), while Jesus is the Son of God from eternity past. God reveals his Word through the prophet Samuel; Jesus is the Word of God. Samuel officiated over sacrifices for Israel and interceded for the people (e.g., 7:8–10; 10:8); Christ offered the once-for-all atoning sacrifice and is the high priestly Intercessor between mankind and God.

[4] Overtly messianic prophecies in the book of Samuel include those by Hannah (1 Sam 2:10); an anonymous "man of God" (1 Sam 2:35; see also 1 Sam 2:27); and the prophet Nathan (2 Samuel 7).

[5] AE 11:277. Apparently Luther considered Moses to be in a category by himself.

[6] AE 19:234.

[7] Defense, deliverance, and salvation can be depicted by a variety of terminology, so a word study gives only a partial picture. Nevertheless, one can find support for the statement above by noticing that the Hebrew vocabulary for "to save" (the Hiphil of יָשַׁע or נָצַל) appears in connection with the ministry of Samuel in 1 Sam 7:3, 8, 14; 12:10–11; with Saul in 1 Sam 9:16 (the noun תְּשׁוּעָה, "salvation, victory," in 1 Sam 11:9, 13); with Jonathan in 1 Sam 14:6, 23, 39, 48; although most often with David, e.g., in 1 Sam 17:37, 47 (the noun תְּשׁוּעָה in 1 Sam 19:5); 23:2, 5; 30:8; 2 Sam 3:18; 8:6, 14.

Samuel as a Prophet

When writing to Philip Melanchthon concerning the Zwickau prophets,[8] Luther questions their call as prophets of God, making his point by reference to Samuel. He notes: "God has never sent anyone, not even the Son himself, unless he was called through men or attested by signs." He then adds: "God did not even wish to speak to Samuel except through the authority and knowledge of Eli."[9] Luther appears to understand the account of Samuel's call in 1 Samuel 3 as purposely arranged by God for Samuel to consult Eli until Eli instructed Samuel to listen to God's call (1 Sam 3:9). Luther saw Samuel as an example of the uniform teaching of Scripture on the call to public ministry—whether that of the prophets, the apostles, pastors, or Christ himself.[10] All must have a proper call of God to be legitimate public ministers of the Gospel.[11]

Samuel on Vocation

One passage from Samuel's ministry that is frequently referenced by Luther is from Samuel's instructions to Saul at his anointing:

> The Spirit of Yahweh will rush upon you. You will prophesy with them, and you will be transformed into another man. When these signs happen to you, do whatever you find to do, because God is with you. (1 Sam 10:6–7)

Luther uses these verses to illustrate two points. First, when speaking of Saul's transformation by the Spirit, he notes that inward, spiritual transformation precedes any transformation in a person's actions. "Sin is taken away by a spiritual means," says Luther, not by changing one's outward deeds.[12] He bolsters this statement by additional references to Eph 2:10 and James 1:18. Thus, a Christian's good works are not what leads to overcoming sin. Instead, a Christian's sins have been overcome by Christ, who bestows the forgiveness of sins and the Holy Spirit on his people in their anointing in Baptism, through his Word, and with the sustenance of the Lord's Supper. Through these means

---

[8] The Zwickau prophets were a group of radical reformers who arose in the 1520s. They claimed to receive divine revelations directly from God without recourse to his written Word. On that basis they put themselves forward as prophets who had the authority to impose radical reforms on the church even though they had not been properly called to such an office through the church's order. They also opposed the Baptism of infants. Luther demanded that they demonstrate their claim to immediate divine authority by performing a miracle, which they refused to do. See Mark U. Edwards, *Luther and the False Brethren* (Stanford: Stanford University Press, 1975), especially 22–25.

[9] AE 48:366.

[10] Luther's inference that even Jesus Christ was "called through men" would apply to the ministry of John the Baptist, who publicly baptized the Christ and testified to the Father's voice from heaven and the descent of the Spirit onto him. Cf. also the words of Mary, Elizabeth, Simeon, and Anna (Luke 1–2), along with the consent of Joseph (Matthew 1).

[11] AC XIV states that no one is to preach in the church or administer the Sacraments unless he has received a "proper call" (author's translation; German: *ordentlichen Beruf*; Latin: *rite vocatus* [*Triglotta*, 48]).

[12] AE 25:323.

of grace Christians are transformed and willingly serve God and their neighbors by the power of the Spirit (see, e.g., Acts 2:38; Rom 6:1–4; 12:1–2).

Second, Luther notes several times that Samuel instructed Saul to "do whatever you find to do" (1 Sam 10:7). Christians transformed by God's Holy Spirit are set free to do acts of love that present themselves in whatever circumstances they find themselves.[13] Christians guided by the Spirit act out of love in accord with the Word to carry out their responsibilities and take advantage of their opportunities in the vocations in which God has placed them. Thus, "faith has no need of a teacher of good works, but he does whatever the occasion calls for."[14] Moreover, such works are valued by God:

> Therefore when your heart and spirit are upright, and your faith is pure, whatever you do afterwards, no matter how lowly and despised it is, will be precious before God, because these works are done by the will and at the direction of faith and the Holy Spirit.[15]

Thus, Samuel's words to Saul teach Christians this lesson:

> Accordingly, let those who want to live in a godly manner fear God and trust in Him, and then let them attend to their calling. Then they will have more than enough to do. Let them commend their way to the Lord, in the morning and in the evening. Let them sleep in the name of the Lord, rise from their beds, and do what comes to hand in whatever kind of life.[16]

It ought to be noted that Samuel's words—not Saul's actions—are the focus of Luther's comments. Samuel's words taught Saul how Christian vocation ought to be conducted. However, Saul did not heed Samuel's words.[17] Yet Samuel followed his own admonition. According to Luther:

> Also we read in the Old Testament how Samuel travelled around, now to Ramah, ... now to Gilgal and other places, not out of delight for taking a walk but out of love and a sense of duty in his ministry and because of the want and need of the people.[18]

Samuel as a Faithful Minister of God

Another passage from the life of Samuel that Luther frequently cites is Samuel's challenge to Israel concerning his faithful conduct as their minister:[19]

---

[13] AE 7:356, 367; 27:203; 44:26.

[14] AE 44:26.

[15] AE 7:356.

[16] AE 7:367.

[17] 1 Sam 10:7 implies that Samuel expected Saul to eradicate the Philistine garrison in Gibeah, but Saul failed to carry out Samuel's instructions (1 Sam 10:9–16). See "Samuel Anoints Saul (9:26–10:8)" in the commentary on 9:26–10:16. See also the beginning of the commentary on 10:17–27a.

[18] AE 40:269. See 1 Sam 7:17; 10:8; 11:14; 13:8–10.

[19] AE 17:195; 28:284; 30:136; 51:273.

Now there is a king leading you. I am old and gray-haired, and my sons are here with you. I have led you from my youth until this day. Now answer me in front of Yahweh and his anointed one: Whose bull have I taken? Whose donkey have I taken? Whom have I exploited? Whom have I oppressed? From whose hand have I taken a bribe to look the other way? I will return it to you! (1 Sam 12:2–3)

Luther notes that these words teach that for Christians, "love should issue from a heart which has a joyful, quiet conscience both toward men and toward God."[20] Every Christian ought to be blameless in their dealings with other people. Not only was Samuel an example of this, but as Luther comments, he was following Moses' example (Num 16:15).[21]

However, in commenting on 1 Tim 3:2, Luther notes that living a life that is irreproachable is especially important for a pastor and teacher in the church: "This is the first quality he must have. The man who wants to investigate, correct, and teach others should be above reproach." To be sure, "there is no one who is above reproach before God," and so the pastor and teacher must ever pray the Our Father, "Forgive us" (Mt 6:12; Lk 11:4).

> Before God no one is above reproach, but before men the bishop is to be so, that he may not be a fornicator, an adulterer, a greedy man, a foul-mouthed person, a drunkard, a gambler, a slanderer. If he is falsely accused, no harm; he is still above reproach; no law can accuse him before men. Samuel and Moses are good examples.[22]

Moreover, Samuel was faithful in his office as a minister of God by praying for his people:

> Consequently, the duty of a priest[23] is twofold: in the first place, to turn to God and pray for himself and for his people; in the second place, to turn from God to men by means of doctrine and the Word. Thus Samuel states in I Sam. 12:23: "Far be it from me not to pray for you and not to lead you to the good and the right way." He acknowledges that this is essential to his office.[24]

In addition, as a prophet Samuel was taught by God. Thus, when Samuel went to Bethlehem to anoint a replacement for Saul, God had to tell him which of Jesse's sons he had selected. God also reproved Samuel's perspective on choosing men for the ministry: humans judge by outward appearances, but Yahweh looks at the heart (1 Sam 16:7). God's teaching about the ministry

---

[20] AE 51:273.

[21] AE 30:136; 51:273.

[22] AE 28:284.

[23] Luther is not using "priest" in the sense of a person from the line of Aaron. (In fact, here he is commenting on Gen 6:3, a narrative set long before Aaron's day.) Instead, Luther is using the term "priest" as was common in his day to denote the office of the holy ministry. Thus, Luther is not calling Samuel an Aaronic priest—something he was not. Although he was from the tribe of Levi, he was not a descendant of Aaron (1 Chr 6:1–15 [ET 6:16–30]; cf. 1 Sam 1:1).

[24] AE 2:19.

exemplifies that salvation is by grace and through faith, not based on works. In commenting on Heb 11:4, Luther says: "Here the apostle determines clearly that the importance of the sacrifices and the entire value of the merit did not lie in the worthiness or the greatness of the work, but that faith is the cause; for God weighs the spirits and looks at the hearts."[25] In support, he goes on to cite, among other verses, 1 Sam 16:7.

Samuel's Reaction to Saul's Failures

A third incident from Samuel's ministry frequently mentioned by Luther is his condemnation of Saul's actions during the Amalekite war (1 Sam 15:1–35).[26] Especially prominent is Luther's use of 1 Sam 15:23, where Samuel speaks of Saul's sin as idolatry. In one instance Luther says that Samuel labeled as idolatry Saul's denial of his disobedience to God's instructions through Samuel and Saul's attempt to defend his actions.[27] Another time Luther says that Samuel called the disobedience itself idolatry.[28] This is not a contradiction in Luther, since Saul's denial and defense of his actions (1 Sam 15:20–21) are of themselves part of his defiance of the prophetic Word of God.

Luther also notes that Samuel took up the sword to execute King Agag of the Amalekites after Saul had failed to comply with the divine mandate to do so (1 Sam 15:33). In *Temporal Authority: To What Extent It Should Be Obeyed*, Luther argues that Samuel, like saints before and after him, used the sword to execute God's judgment in the world.[29]

On more than one occasion Luther comments on Samuel's mourning over Saul being rejected as king and God's reaction to Samuel's grief (1 Sam 15:35–16:1).[30] The reformer sees this mourning as a common action by saints when they see disaster coming as a result of sin.[31] Yet he notes that Samuel shed tears over Saul in vain and warns us: "We must be on our guard against those who [like Saul] are thus given over to a wicked disposition, lest we share in their sin and perish together with them."[32] In fact, Luther understands Samuel's grief to be extreme: "He cries and wails so long that God is compelled to restrain him (1 Sam 16:1)."[33]

---

[25] AE 29:232.

[26] AE 3:283, 285; 5:152–53; 22:397; 34:77; 45:96; 47:269.

[27] AE 34:77.

[28] AE 47:269.

[29] AE 45:96.

[30] AE 2:50, 91; 3:285.

[31] AE 2:91.

[32] AE 3:285.

[33] AE 2:50.

Did Samuel Appear to Saul from the Dead?

One account in 1 Samuel involves Samuel after his death: Saul asked the witch at Endor to bring Samuel back from the dead (1 Sam 28:3–25). Was the specter that appeared to Saul actually Samuel? Luther twice answers this in the negative:

> That Samuel was brought up by a medium or wizard was surely a spectre of the devil, not only because the Scriptures in that place declare that it was done by a woman who was filled with devils ... but also because Saul and the woman when they inquired of the dead were clearly acting contrary to this divine commandment [Deut 18:9–12]. ...

> The Scriptures do not expressly state whether it was really Samuel or not; they only call him Samuel. This proves that the Scriptures put the matter as it was in the heart of Saul, who did not know but that it was Samuel; and the [evil] spirit skilfully spoke all the words of Samuel and added more to them.[34]

In another place Luther said:

> Therefore we may easily see that the bringing up of Samuel from the dead, 1 Samuel 28, was trickery and deceit; the whole event is against this commandment of God [Deut 18:9–11]. Accordingly we may not assume that the real prophet Samuel was brought from the dead by the medium. But when the Scriptures are silent and do not tell us whether this was the real Samuel or not, it demands from all of us that we should well know that through Moses God has forbidden necromancy.[35]

---

[34] AE 36:196.

[35] AE 52:180.

1 Samuel 20:1–21:1 (ET 20:1–42)

Jonathan Warns David

Translation

20 ¹David fled from the pasture settlements at Ramah. He came to Jonathan and said, "What have I done? What is my offense? What is my sin in relation to your father that he is seeking my life?"

²He said to him, "Certainly not! You will not die. My father does not do any major deed or minor deed and not tell me personally. Why would my father hide this matter from me? This isn't so."

³David took an oath and said, "Your father certainly knows that I have found favor in your eyes and he thought, 'Don't let Jonathan know this, or he will be distressed.' Nevertheless, as Yahweh lives and as you live, there is about a step between me and death."

⁴Jonathan said to David, "What do you desire? I will do it for you."

⁵David said to Jonathan, "Tomorrow is the new moon, and I am certainly expected to sit with the king to eat. However, you should send me away, and I will hide in the country until the evening after tomorrow. ⁶If your father actually takes notice of my absence, say, 'David requested permission to run to his city Bethlehem because there is a yearly sacrifice there for his entire clan.' ⁷If he says, 'Good,' then your servant is safe. If he becomes very angry, know that he is determined to harm me. ⁸Deal mercifully with your servant, because you have brought your servant into an agreement with you sealed by Yahweh. If there is iniquity in me, kill me yourself. Why would you bother to bring me to your father?"

⁹Jonathan said, "Certainly not you! But rather if I really know that my father is determined to do this evil thing to you, wouldn't I tell you about it?"

¹⁰David said to Jonathan, "Who will tell me if your father answers you harshly?"

¹¹Jonathan said to David, "Come, let's go out into the country." So the two of them went out into the country. ¹²Then Jonathan said to David, "Yahweh, the God of Israel, is a witness: I will sound out my father about this time tomorrow or the next day. If he is favorable toward David, won't I then send for you and inform you? ¹³Thus may Yahweh do to Jonathan, and thus may he add if my father intends to harm you and I don't inform you and send you away and you go safely. May Yahweh be with you as he was with my father. ¹⁴If I am still alive, certainly deal with me [according to] the kindness of Yahweh, but if I die, ¹⁵do not ever cut your kindness off from my house, not even when Yahweh cuts off each of David's enemies from the land." ¹⁶Then Jonathan made [an agreement] with David's house, [saying,] "May Yahweh hold David's enemies accountable." ¹⁷Then Jonathan again put David under oath out of his love for him, because he loved him [as much as] his love of his own life.

[18]Jonathan said to him, "Tomorrow is the new moon. You will be noticed, because your seat will be observed. [19]On the day after tomorrow, go down quickly, and go to the place where you hid on the day of the deed, and stay beside this mound. [20]I will shoot three arrows beside it as if I were shooting at a target. [21]Then I will send the boy, 'Go, and find the arrows.' If I deliberately say to the boy, 'Look, the arrows are on this side of you. Fetch them,' then come because it is safe for you, and there is no problem, as surely as Yahweh lives. [22]But if this is what I say to the young man: 'Look, the arrows are farther away from you,' go, because Yahweh has sent you away. [23]And [concerning] the matter about which you and I spoke: may Yahweh be a witness between you and me forever." [24]So David hid in the country.

When it was the new moon, the king sat down to eat the meal. [25]The king sat at his usual place at the seat on the wall. Jonathan sat opposite [him], and Abner sat beside Saul, and he took note of David's spot. [26]Saul did not say anything that day, because he thought, "It is an accident since he is not clean; he must not be clean." [27]On the next day, the second day of the month, David's spot was noticed. So Saul said to his son Jonathan, "Why didn't Jesse's son come to the meal both yesterday and today?"

[28]Jonathan answered Saul, "David urgently asked me [to go] to Bethlehem. [29]He said, 'Please allow me to go, because there is a family sacrifice for us in the city. My brother—he commanded me. Now if you favor me, please allow me to go and see my brother.' That is the reason he did not come to the king's table."

[30]Saul became angry with Jonathan and said to him, "You son of a perverted, rebellious woman! Don't you know that you are choosing the son of Jesse to your shame and to the shame of your mother's nakedness? [31]For as long as Jesse's son is alive on the land, you and your kingdom will not be established. Now send and take him to me, for he is a dead man."

[32]Jonathan answered Saul, his father, and said to him, "Why must he be put to death? What has he done?" [33]Saul lifted up his spear against him to strike him, and Jonathan knew that his father was determined to kill David. [34]Jonathan got up from the table angrily and did not eat food during the second day of the month because he was distressed about David, since his father had humiliated him.

[35]In the morning Jonathan went out into the country for the meeting with David, and a young boy was with him. [36]He said to his boy, "Run and find the arrows that I am shooting." The boy ran, and he shot an arrow beyond him. [37]The boy came to the place of the arrow Jonathan had shot. Jonathan called after the boy, "Isn't the arrow farther away from you?" [38]Then Jonathan called after the boy, "Hurry up! Don't stand around!" Jonathan's boy gathered the arrows and came to his master. [39]The boy did not know anything. Only Jonathan and David knew the situation. [40]Jonathan gave his equipment to his boy and said to him, "Go. Bring [them] to the city."

[41]When the boy went, David got up from beside the mound and fell face down on the ground and bowed three times. They kissed each other and wept together, but David wept more. [42]Then Jonathan said to David, "Go in peace, since the two of us have taken an oath in the name of Yahweh, [saying,] 'May Yahweh be between

you and me and between my descendants and your descendants forever.'"²¹:¹Then he rose and left, and Jonathan went to the city.

Textual Notes

20:1 וַיִּבְרַח—For "and he fled," see the second textual note on 19:12.

מִנָּוֹית—For this Qere, "from the pasture settlements" (Kethib: מִנָּוֹת), see the fourth textual note on 19:18.

וַיָּבֹא ׀ וַיֹּאמֶר לִפְנֵי יְהוֹנָתָן—Literally "and he came and he said before Jonathan," the word order has been adjusted to "he came to Jonathan and said" to match normal English usage. The adjusted English is supported by the LXX: καὶ ἔρχεται ἐνώπιον Ιωναθαν καὶ εἶπεν.

מְבַקֵּשׁ—The Piel (D) of בָּקַשׁ, "to seek," is a thematic verb in the narrative of Saul's pursuit of David. See 19:2, 10, and "Jonathan Defends David (19:1–7)" in the commentary on 19:1–17.

20:2 חָלִילָה—For "certainly not!" see the second textual note on 2:30. This exclamation recurs in 20:9.

לֹא־יַעֲשֶׂה—"He does not do" is the Qere, in agreement with the LXX, οὐ μὴ ποιήσῃ. The Kethib is לוֹ עָשָׂה, "he did for himself." The marginal Masorah indicates that this is one of six instances where the Qere is לֹא and the Kethib is לוֹ.

דָּבָר גָּדוֹל אוֹ דָּבָר קָטֹן—Literally this means "a large word/matter or a small word/matter."

וְלֹא יִגְלֶה אֶת־אָזְנִי—Literally "and he does not uncover my ear," this means "and not tell me personally." The idiom with the Qal (G) of גָּלָה, "reveal, uncover," and the direct object אֹזֶן, "ear," appears thirteen times in the OT, with eight of them in the book of Samuel.[1]

אֵין זֹאת:—Literally "this [feminine] does not exist." Hebrew often uses the feminine gender for abstracts, including ideas. Here the abstract is the idea that Saul is seeking to kill David.

20:3 וַיִּשָּׁבַע עוֹד דָּוִד—Literally "David swore again." There is no previous instance of David taking an oath (the Niphal [N] of שָׁבַע) in the book of Samuel. The adverb עוֹד, "again, more," implies that his words in 20:1 had already begun his sworn declaration that Saul was trying to kill him.

פֶּן־יֵעָצֵב—Literally "lest he be grieved." The Qal (G) of עָצַב means "to cause pain, grief," and the Niphal (N), as here, has the corresponding passive meaning. The Niphal perfect נֶעְצַב occurs in 20:34.

וְאוּלָם—The particle אוּלָם is a strong adversative: "nevertheless."[2]

חַי־יְהוָה וְחֵי נַפְשֶׁךָ—For "as Yahweh lives and as you live," see the second textual notes on 1:26 and 14:45. The invocation חַי־יְהוָה recurs in an oath in 20:21.

---

[1] 1 Sam 9:15; 20:2, 12, 13; 22:8 (twice), 17; 2 Sam 7:27.
[2] *TWOT*, § 47.

כְּפֶשַׂע—This is translated as "about a step." The noun פֶּשַׂע, "a step, stride," representing a very short distance, is a hapax legomenon and is related to the verb פָּשַׂע, "to march," which occurs only in Is 27:4.

20:4 מַה־תֹּאמַר נַפְשְׁךָ—The MT literally reads "what does your soul say?" Many English versions translate the MT as "whatever you say."[3] However, the only use of מָה as a relative particle in the OT (i.e., "whatever") is in Eccl 1:9, and there it is followed by the relative prefix -שֶּׁ.[4] Here there is no relative particle (אֲשֶׁר or -שֶׁ), which rules out a relative use of מָה. The verb אָמַר can refer to an inner thought process, "to think," and perhaps the intended nuance of תֹּאמַר in the MT is along those lines. The LXX reads τί ἐπιθυμεῖ ἡ ψυχή, "what does your soul desire?" which would reflect a Hebrew text such as מָה תְּאַוֶּה נַפְשְׁךָ. That same combination of the suffixed subject noun נַפְשְׁךָ and verb תְּאַוֶּה (third feminine singular Piel [D] imperfect of אָוָה, "to desire"), meaning "your soul desires/you desire," occurs in Deut 12:20; 14:26; 1 Sam 2:16; 2 Sam 3:21; 1 Ki 11:37. If this is the correct reading, then the MT may have resulted from a scribe accidentally substituting a more common verb (אָמַר) for a less common one (אָוָה).

20:5 חֹדֶשׁ—This noun can mean either "month" or "new moon," since, according to a lunar calendar, a month began at the new moon. In this chapter this noun refers to the "new moon" here and in 20:18, 24, but it designates the "month" in 20:27, 34.

בַּשָּׂדֶה—This is translated as "in the country." Though often translated as "field," the noun שָׂדֶה denotes land outside of a walled city, such as open fields (*HALOT*, 1). Note the contrast set up between the country and the city by 20:35 and 21:1 (ET 20:42b). See 20:11, 35.

עַד הָעֶרֶב הַשְּׁלִשִׁית:—Literally this means "until the third evening." The noun עֶרֶב, "evening," is apparently construed as feminine here because it is modified by the feminine form of the adjective שְׁלִישִׁי, "third." Ancient Israelites counted days inclusively, starting with the present day. Thus, "the third evening" would be the evening of the day after the new moon, thus "the evening after tomorrow."[5] Cf. הַשְּׁלִשִׁית in the third textual note on 20:12.

20:6 פָּקֹד יִפְקְדֵנִי—Literally "he actually notices me." The Qal (G) of פָּקַד can mean to "miss, lack" (BDB, A 1 d), that is, to notice that someone is missing. The Qal infinitive absolute with the suffixed Qal imperfect is therefore rendered as "(he) actually takes notice of my absence." The Qal of פָּקַד often denotes looking carefully at something (*HALOT*, 1, 2, 3). Its Niphal (N) in 20:18, 25, 27 means that David's place at the table was "noticed," that is, Saul noticed David's absence.

---

[3] See also Tsumura, *The First Book of Samuel*, 503.

[4] See also 1QMysteries (1Q27), fragment 1, column 1, lines 3–4 (and 4QMysteries[b] [4Q300], fragment 3, lines 3–4): ולוא ידעו מה אשר יבוא עליהמה, "and they do not know whatever will come upon them," combining מָה with the relative pronoun אֲשֶׁר. (The combination מה אשר occurs also in 4Q481[b], fragment 1, line 3, but without enough text to determine its usage.) This later use of מה אשר may be in imitation of the Greek ὃ ἐάν.

[5] See Lk 13:32: "today and tomorrow and the *third day*." This explains why the NT declares that Jesus rose "on the third day," that is, on Easter Sunday morning, after being crucified on Good Friday (Mt 16:21; 17:23; 20:19; Lk 9:22; 18:33; 24:7, 46; Acts 10:40; 1 Cor 15:4).

נִשְׁאַל נִשְׁאַל—"He requested permission." The same wording (the Niphal [N] infinitive absolute and the Niphal third masculine singular perfect) recurs in 20:28. In the Qal (G), שָׁאַל means "to ask, request," but in the Niphal, it means "to ask for a leave of absence." Its Niphal occurs in only three OT passages (1 Sam 20:6, 28; Neh 13:6), all in this sense and always followed by the preposition מִן, "from," attached to the person from whom one takes leave (here מֵעִמָּדִי). Often in the book of Samuel the author engages in wordplay with the verb שָׁאַל and the name of Saul, שָׁאוּל, which means "requested."[6] This is evident when this clause recurs in 20:28 in the sequence שָׁאוֹל נִשְׁאַל נִשְׁאַל, *sha'ul nish'ol nish'al.*

זֶבַח הַיָּמִים—For "a yearly sacrifice," see the first textual note on 1:21.

20:7 שָׁלוֹם לְעַבְדֶּךָ—Literally "peace to your servant," this means "your servant is safe." For the self-effacing "your servant" (also twice in 20:8), see the third textual note on 1:11. עַבְדֶּךָ (here and in 20:8a) is the pausal form of עַבְדְּךָ (20:8b).

חָרָה יֶחֱרֶה לוֹ—Literally "it becomes very hot for him," this means "he becomes very angry." See the Qal (G) of חָרָה with the preposition לְ also in 1 Sam 15:11; 18:8; 2 Sam 3:8; 6:8; 13:21; 19:43 (ET 19:42); 22:8; 24:1.

דַּע כִּי־כָלְתָה הָרָעָה מֵעִמּוֹ—Literally "know that the evil is determined from with him." דַּע is the masculine singular Qal (G) imperative of יָדַע, "to know." The Qal of כָּלָה, "be finished, complete," can mean "be determined" (BDB, 1 d), and here its subject is the definite feminine noun הָרָעָה. The same wording recurs in 20:9. See also the similar wording in 20:33.

20:8 בִּבְרִית יְהוָה—This is translated as "into an agreement sealed by Yahweh." A noun in construct with another noun or (as here) a proper name may involve various relationships between the two words. Here the genitive, יְהוָה, is an adjectival genitive indicating what kind of an agreement—a "Yahweh agreement," that is an agreement made in Yahweh's name and with his participation as the one who seals and guarantees its terms.[7] See 23:18 and the first textual note and the commentary on 18:3.

הֲמִיתֵנִי—This is the Hiphil (H) masculine singular imperative of מוּת with a first common singular suffix (see GKC, § 67 v): "kill me."

לָמָּה־זֶּה—This is translated as "why would you bother?" The interrogative לָמָּה is combined with the relative pronoun זֶה used as an enclitic particle to add emphasis to the question.[8] In the translation the emphasis is brought out by the word "bother."

20:9 חָלִילָה לָּךְ—This is translated as "certainly not you!" Somewhat more literally it means "it would be unthinkable for you." Jonathan is saying that there certainly is no iniquity in David or fault on his part that would warrant capital punishment.

כִּי־כָלְתָה הָרָעָה מֵעִם אָבִי לָבוֹא עָלֶיךָ—Literally "that the evil is determined from with my father to come upon you." See the third textual note on 20:7.

---

[6] See the first textual note on 1:28; "Samuel Warns Israel about Kings (8:10–22)" in the commentary on 8:1–22; the first textual note on 10:22; the commentary on 12:13; and the textual note on 14:37.

[7] *IBH*, § 15 F; Waltke-O'Connor, § 9.5.3g.

[8] *IBH*, § 25 B; Waltke-O'Connor, § 17.4.3c.

וְלֹא אֹתָהּ אַגִּיד לָךְ:—Literally "and wouldn't I report it to you?" Here and again in 20:12 וְלֹא, "and not," forms a question expecting a positive answer, "wouldn't/won't I?" Here the LXX has the inexplicable καὶ ἐὰν μή εἰς τὰς πόλεις σου ἐγὼ ἀπαγγελῶ σοι, "if it were not against your cities I will tell you."

20:10 אוֹ מַה־יַּעַנְךָ אָבִיךָ קָשָׁה:—The MT literally reads "or what your father will answer you harshly." The feminine form of the adjective קָשֶׁה, "severe, harsh," functions as an adverbial accusative. The conjunction אוֹ, "or," can mean "if" (BDB, 3, citing this verse and Lev 26:41). For אוֹ מַה־, the LXX reads ἐάν, "if," which is followed by most commentaries and versions.[9]

20:11 לְכָה וְנֵצֵא—"Come, let us go out." For the use of the imperative of הָלַךְ as an interjection, see Joüon, § 177 f. Here it is used syndetically with וְ on the cohortative נֵצֵא.

20:12 יְהוָה אֱלֹהֵי יִשְׂרָאֵל—The invocation of "Yahweh, the God of Israel," apparently marks the rest of the utterance as a formal oath. In 12:5 Samuel had called upon "Yahweh" as "a witness" (עֵד יְהוָה). The Syriac begins with *nshd*, "a witness," which would suggest a Hebrew reading with עֵד, as reflected in the translation above, unless the Syriac added the word to try to make better sense of the MT. If עֵד is to be included as the first word, then the MT may have suffered from haplography due to homoioteleuton, since both עֵד and the previous דָּוִד end in *daleth*. See also the textual note on 20:23. The LXX reads κύριος ὁ θεὸς Ισραηλ οἶδεν, "the Lord God of Israel knows," which suggests that its Vorlage read יָדַע יהוה אֱלֹהֵי־יִשְׂרָאֵל (unless it added the verb to clarify what it assumed to be the meaning). This would indicate a different textual corruption, substituting the more common verb יָדַע for the similar but less common noun עֵד. Josephus' rather long paraphrase of Jonathan's words appears to suggest that the text he used had a conflation of the readings in the Syriac and the LXX: τὸν γὰρ θεόν εἶπε τοῦτον ὂν πολὺν ὁρᾷς καὶ πανταχοῦ κεχυμένον καὶ πρὶν ἑρμηνεῦσαί με τοῖς λόγοις τὴν διάνοιαν ἤδη μου ταύτην *εἰδότα μάρτυρα* ποιοῦμαι τῶν πρὸς σὲ συνθηκῶν, "he said, 'I appeal to that God, who, as you see, is spread forth everywhere and *knows* this intention of mine, before I explain it in words, as the *witness* of this my covenant with you.'"[10]

אֶחְקֹר—"I will sound out" is literally "I will examine."

מָחָר הַשְּׁלִשִׁית—Literally "tomorrow, the third [feminine]," this must mean "either tomorrow or on the third day," although the implied noun יוֹם is masculine. Cf. הַשְּׁלִשִׁית in the third textual note on 20:5.

וְלֹא־אָז—"Won't I then?" וְלֹא frames a question expecting a positive answer, as also in 20:9 (see the third textual note there).

וְגָלִיתִי אֶת־אָזְנֶךָ:—Literally "and I will uncover your ear." The expression recurs in 20:13. See the fourth textual note on 20:2.

[9] McCarter, *I Samuel*, 336; Klein, *1 Samuel*, 203; Bergen, *1, 2 Samuel*, 211; Auld, *I and II Samuel*, 238; HCSB; ESV; NET; NIV. However, see Tsumura, *The First Book of Samuel*, 505, who attempts to make sense of the MT without defending his translation.

[10] Josephus, *Antiquities*, 6.230.

20:13 כֹּה־יַעֲשֶׂה יְהוָה לִיהוֹנָתָן וְכֹה יֹסִיף—See the textual note on 3:17; see also 14:44 and GKC, § 149 d; Joüon, § 165 a.

כִּי־יֵיטַב אֶל־אָבִי אֶת־הָרָעָה עָלֶיךָ—Literally "if harm upon you is pleasing to my father." יֵיטַב is the Hiphil (H) third masculine singular imperfect of יָטַב. Elsewhere its Hiphil (H) is always transitive, "to do good," but here it is intransitive, "to be good." Many scholars propose emending it to the intransitive Qal, יִיטַב. The noun הָרָעָה is feminine, and it is preceded by the direct object marker אֶת־, so a verb of doing is probably implied, and the action of "doing harm" is the subject of the masculine verb יֵיטַב.

וִיהִי יְהוָה עִמָּךְ—The verb is the jussive יְהִי with conjunctive *waw*. עִמָּךְ is pausal for עִמְּךָ.

20:14 וְלֹא ... וְלֹא ... וְלֹא—The MT's threefold "and not" is difficult. The sense of the first two clauses must be positive, "while I am still alive you shall deal with me [according to] the kindness of Yahweh." The negative fits the third clause if the meaning is "so I will not die." The same fitting negative begins 20:15. Most commentaries repoint some or all of the three in 20:14 to וְלֻא (= וְלוּ), "and if only, and indeed," as rendered in most versions.[11] Whitney attempts to preserve the MT pointing by translating with "not only," though this appears to be special pleading.[12]

20:15 אֶת־אֹיְבֵי דָוִד אִישׁ—This means "each of David's enemies." אִישׁ, "man," is used distributively here: "each" (*HALOT*, 10).

20:16 The entire verse is difficult. The LXX is different: ἐξαρθῆναι τὸ ὄνομα τοῦ Ιωναθαν ἀπὸ τοῦ οἴκου Δαυιδ, καὶ ἐκζητήσαι κύριος ἐχθροὺς τοῦ Δαυιδ, "… to drive away the name of Jonathan from David's house, and may the Lord seek the enemies of David."

וַיִּכְרֹת יְהוֹנָתָן—As in 22:8 the verb כָּרַת, "cut," is used alone but the noun בְּרִית, "covenant, agreement," is implied. For the idiom with כָּרַת בְּרִית, see the third textual note on 11:1. This idiom is used for the covenant between Jonathan and David in 18:3; 23:18.

וּבִקֵּשׁ יְהוָה מִיַּד אֹיְבֵי דָוִד׃—The Piel (D) perfect with *waw* consecutive וּבִקֵּשׁ is apparently used with the force of a jussive. Literally the clause is "and may Yahweh seek from the hand of David's enemies."

20:17 לְהַשְׁבִּיעַ אֶת־דָּוִד—For the Hiphil (H) of שָׁבַע, "to put someone under oath," see 14:27–28.

בְּאַהֲבָתוֹ אֹתוֹ—For the identical phrase with the infinitive construct of אָהַב, "to love," see the second textual note on 18:3. See further "Jonathan's Relationship with David" in the commentary on 18:1–5.

20:18 וְנִפְקַדְתָּ כִּי יִפָּקֵד מוֹשָׁבֶךָ׃—"You will be noticed, because your seat will be observed." This means that Saul will notice that David's place is empty. Similar in meaning is the clause in the third textual note on 20:25. See the first textual note on 20:6.

---

[11] McCarter, *I Samuel*, 336; Klein, *1 Samuel*, 203; HCSB; ESV; GW; NET; NIV.

[12] Whitney, "Alternative Interpretations of *Lōʾ* in Exodus 6:3 and Jeremiah 7:22," 155.

20:19 וְשִׁלַּשְׁתָּ תֵּרֵד מְאֹד—"On the day after tomorrow, go down quickly" is difficult. וְשִׁלַּשְׁתָּ is a Piel (D) perfect with *waw* consecutive form of a denominative verb from the noun שָׁלוֹשׁ, "three." The LXX translates וְשִׁלַּשְׁתָּ literally as καὶ τρισσεύσεις, meaning "you will do on the third day [i.e., the day after tomorrow]" (cf. the last textual note on 4:7). The translation takes וְשִׁלַּשְׁתָּ תֵּרֵד as a hendiadys, "on the day after tomorrow, go down quickly." The adverb מְאֹד, "very, much," is taken in the sense of "quickly," although that is speculative.

הַמָּקוֹם אֲשֶׁר־נִסְתַּרְתָּ שָּׁם בְּיוֹם הַמַּעֲשֶׂה—Literally "the place where you hid there on the day of the deed," this refers to the place where David hid in 19:2. See the commentary.

אֵצֶל הָאֶבֶן הָאָזֶל:—The MT reads "beside the Ezel stone" or perhaps "beside this stone." אָזֶל (in pause with article, הָאָזֶל) is a hapax legomenon and of uncertain meaning. It could be a proper name or a noun derived from the verb אָזַל, "go away, disappear," thus "the stone of departure/escape." The LXX reads παρὰ τὸ εργαβ ἐκεῖνο, "beside this mound," with εργαβ being a transliteration of a presumed Hebrew noun אַרְגָּב, meaning "mound" (see *HALOT*, s.v. אַרְגָּב). This would suggest a Hebrew text of אֵצֶל הָאַרְגָּב הַלָּאז (for the rare demonstrative הַלָּאז, see the last textual note on 14:1, where it is spelled without an *aleph*). If such a reading is original, the MT would appear to have suffered from a double corruption, with הָאֶבֶן resulting from a graphic confusion of the letters רגב in הָאַרְגָּב and then הָאָזֶל showing a metathesis of the letters לאז-. Similarly, the LXX reads ἀπὸ τοῦ εργαβ, presupposing מֵאֵצֶל הָאַרְגָּב, "from the mound," in 20:41, where the MT has מֵאֵצֶל הַנֶּגֶב, "from beside the Negev/south." In 20:41 the MT seems to have suffered from graphic confusion of the letters *nun* and *resh*, resulting in the difficult reading הַנֶּגֶב.

20:20 צִדָּה—This is translated as "beside it." It is the noun צַד, "side," with a third feminine singular suffix (lacking a *mappiq*) that refers back to the feminine noun הָאֶבֶן, "the stone," in MT 20:19. Cf. מִצַּד (מִן plus צַד), "beside," in 20:25.

לְשַׁלַּח־לִי לְמַטָּרָה:—"As if I were shooting at a target" is literally "to send out [arrows] for myself to a target." The noun מַטָּרָה, "target," is derived from the verb נָטַר.

20:21 מִמְּךָ וָהֵנָּה—Literally this means "from you and hither." הֵנָּה is an adverb of place, "to this place; on this side."

קָחֶנּוּ ׀ וָבָאָה—The first Qal (G) imperative is of לָקַח, "take," with a third masculine singular suffix, even though the noun to which it refers, הַחִצִּים, "the arrows" (earlier in the verse), is plural. The second is the alternate form (with paragogic *he*) of the Qal imperative of בּוֹא, "come."

20:22 לָעֶלֶם—The only other OT instance of the noun עֶלֶם, "young man," is in 17:56; see the second textual note there.

מִמְּךָ וָהָלְאָה—Literally this means "from you and farther." The same phrase recurs in 20:37. The adverb הָלְאָה, "further, farther," previously appeared in 10:3; 18:9.

20:23 הִנֵּה יְהוָה בֵּינִי וּבֵינְךָ עַד־עוֹלָם:—The MT literally reads "behold, Yahweh is between me and between you through eternity." The LXX (ἰδοὺ κύριος μάρτυς ἀνὰ

393

μέσον ἐμοῦ καὶ σοῦ ἕως αἰῶνος) includes the noun "a witness" (see עֵד יְהוָה in 12:5 and the first textual note on 20:12). If "witness" is original, then the MT omitted עֵד.[13]

20:25 עַל־מוֹשָׁבוֹ כְּפַעַם ׀ בְּפַעַם—More literally "on his seat as once and again," this refers to Saul's usual seat as monarch. כְּפַעַם ׀ בְּפַעַם means "as usual" or "as previously." See 3:10 and *HALOT*, s.v. פַּעַם, 5 c.

וַיָּקָם יְהוֹנָתָן—The MT reads "and Jonathan arose." Though some follow the MT text as understandable,[14] the point of the verse seems to be the seating arrangement, not Jonathan's standing (which could have been to show respect for Saul). "Jonathan sat opposite" is based on the LXX: καὶ προέφθασεν τὸν Ιωναθαν, "and he went in front of Jonathan," which could reflect a Hebrew reading of ויקדם in place of וַיָּקָם.[15] In this setting ויקדם presumably would be the verbal root that gives us the preposition קֶדֶם, "before." Thus, ויקדם would mean "and he went before." It is left unpointed because (if the presumption is correct) we do not know in what stem it would carry that meaning. In Aramaic the cognate verb occurs in both the G and D stems with approximately the same meaning, "go before" (see *CAL*).

וַיִּפָּקֵד מְקוֹם דָּוִד:—"And David's spot was noticed." This clause recurs in 20:27. See the first textual note on 20:6.

20:26 בִּלְתִּי טָהוֹר הוּא כִּי־לֹא טָהוֹר:—Literally "not clean is he; for [he is] not clean." The adverb בִּלְתִּי here serves as a negative, "not."

20:27 וַיְהִי מִמָּחֳרַת הַחֹדֶשׁ הַשֵּׁנִי—This literally says "and it was on the next day, the second month." The phrase הַחֹדֶשׁ הַשֵּׁנִי must mean "on the second day of the month," since the new moon was the first day of the month. Similarly in 20:34, בְּיוֹם־הַחֹדֶשׁ הַשֵּׁנִי must mean "on/during the second day of the month."

אֶל־הַלָּחֶם:—Literally this means "to the food" (cf. אֶל־הַלֶּחֶם לֶאֱכוֹל, "to the food to eat," in 20:24). 4QSam[b] reads על השלחן, and the LXX reads ἐπὶ τὴν τράπεζαν, both meaning "to the table." Cf. אֶל־שֻׁלְחַן הַמֶּלֶךְ, "to the table of the king," in 20:29.

20:28 שָׁאוֹל נִשְׁאַל—Note the threefold repetition of the consonants שאל when the last word of the first clause, שָׁאוּל, is combined with the first two words of the second clause. See further the second textual note on 20:6.

נִשְׁאַל דָּוִד מֵעִמָּדִי—This is translated as "David urgently asked me." For the idiom, see the second textual note on 20:6.

20:29 זֶבַח מִשְׁפָּחָה—This means "a family sacrifice." מִשְׁפָּחָה denotes an extended family, a clan. 4QSam[b] reads למשפחה [זבח], "[the sacrifice] for the family."

וְהוּא צִוָּה־לִי אָחִי—Literally "and he/it—my brother commanded me." The pronoun הוּא might refer to the family sacrifice ("it"); if so, this would mean "it [is the thing about which] my brother commanded me," i.e., "my brother commanded me to come for it." Or הוּא could be emphatic and refer to אָחִי, "my brother," as in the translation: "my brother—he commanded me." 4QSam[b] reads ואני צוו לי אחי, "and me, my

---

[13] Finkelstein, "An Ignored Haplography in Samuel."

[14] GW; Tsumura, *The First Book of Samuel*, 515.

[15] Cf. HCSB; ESV; NET; NIV; McCarter, *I Samuel*, 338; Klein, *1 Samuel*, 204; Auld, *I and II Samuel*, 239; Bergen, *1, 2 Samuel*, 212.

brothers commanded me." See the LXX: καὶ ἐνετείλαντο πρός με οἱ ἀδελφοί μου, "my brothers commanded me."

אִם־מָצָאתִי חֵן בְּעֵינֶיךָ—Literally this means "if I have found favor in your eyes." In place of אִם 4QSam^b reads אם נא (to be vocalized אִם נָא), "if, please …" The same expression begins with אִם־נָא in 27:5.

אִמָּלְטָה—This singular Niphal (N) cohortative of מָלַט would most naturally mean "let me escape" (see the third textual note on 19:10), which is appropriate from David's perspective: he sought to escape from Saul. Jonathan, however, probably intended Saul to interpret it in the milder sense "let me go," since the entire pretense was devised to prevent Saul from realizing that David was indeed escaping and fleeing for his life. However, Saul's angry response (20:30) may indicate that he discerned the true meaning of the verb.

20:30 וַיִּחַר־אַף שָׁאוּל בִּיהוֹנָתָן—Literally "and the anger of Saul became hot against Jonathan." See, similarly, 11:6; 17:28. The adverb "very" is added by 4QSam^b (מאד) and the LXX (σφόδρα).

בֶּן־נַעֲוַת הַמַּרְדּוּת—This is translated as "you son of a perverted, rebellious woman." It is actually a construct chain, literally "son of a twisted woman of the rebelliousness." נַעֲוַת is the feminine singular Niphal (N) participle of עָוָה. Other Niphal forms of עָוָה appear three times in the OT (Is 21:3; Ps 38:7 [ET 38:6]; Prov 12:8) and mean "be bent, twisted, perverted." The noun מַרְדּוּת is a hapax legomenon with the feminine abstract ending וּת-. It denotes the (abstract) idea of "rebelliousness" and is derived from the verb מָרַד, "to rebel." 4QSam^b reads בן נערות המרדת, and the LXX reads υἱὲ κορασίων αὐτομολούντων, both meaning "son of young women of rebelliousness." This is clearly a secondary reading that substitutes a plural form of the common noun נַעֲרָה, "young woman," for the unique form נַעֲוַת.

בֹּחֵר אַתָּה—"You are choosing." בֹּחֵר is a Qal (G) participle that here probably denotes continuing action in progress. The LXX has μέτοχος εἶ σύ, "you are an accomplice."

עֶרְוַת אִמֶּךָ:—Literally "the nakedness of your mother," this refers to the (naked) state of Jonathan's mother when she gave birth to him. See the brief discussion in "Jonathan's Relationship with David" in the commentary on 18:1–5 as well as the commentary on 20:30.

20:31 כִּי כָל־הַיָּמִים אֲשֶׁר—"For as long as" is literally "for all the days that."

לֹא תִכּוֹן אַתָּה וּמַלְכוּתֶךָ—"You and your kingdom will not be established." The verb תִכּוֹן is a Niphal (N) imperfect of כּוּן. Its form could be second masculine singular, which fits with the masculine singular pronoun אַתָּה, "you," as its subject; it could also be third feminine singular, which fits with וּמַלְכוּתֶךָ, the suffixed feminine noun מַלְכוּת, "kingdom," as its subject. Most likely its form agrees with its first and nearer subject, אַתָּה. 4QSam^b reads לא תכן את ממלכתך, "you will not establish your kingdom" (with תָכֵן, the Hiphil of כּוּן). The LXX reads οὐχ ἑτοιμασθήσεται ἡ βασιλεία σου, "your kingdom will not be prepared."

בֶּן־מָוֶת—Literally "a son of death," this denotes someone who deserves capital punishment, thus "a dead man." It recurs in the same sense in 1 Sam 26:16 (where בֵּן is plural) and 2 Sam 12:5.

20:32 וַיַּעַן יְהוֹנָתָן אֶת־שָׁאוּל אָבִיו וַיֹּאמֶר אֵלָיו—"Jonathan answered Saul, his father, and said to him …" English style would not normally include the redundant "and said to him." The LXX simply reads καὶ ἀπεκρίθη Ιωναθαν τῷ Σαουλ, "and Jonathan answered Saul." 4QSam^b probably reads [ויען יונתן את] אביו ויאמר, "[and Jonathan answered] his father and said …"[16]

יוּמָת—This imperfect of מוּת is Hophal (Hp), "be put to death."

20:33 וַיָּטֶל שָׁאוּל אֶת־הַחֲנִית עָלָיו—1 Sam 18:11 has the same verb and phraseology (see the first textual note there).

כָלָה הִיא מֵעִם אָבִיו—Literally "it was determined from with his father." The feminine personal pronoun הִיא, "she/it," refers to the idea that Saul was monomaniacally fixated on killing David. Although feminine, it stands as the subject of the third masculine singular Qal (G) perfect of כָּלָה, which means "be determined." For the verb, see the third textual note on 20:7.

20:34 וַיָּקָם יְהוֹנָתָן מֵעִם הַשֻּׁלְחָן—"Jonathan got up from the table." 4QSam^b reads ויפחז יונתן מעל השלחן, which may mean "and Jonathan jumped up from the table," since that is the meaning of the LXX, καὶ ἀνεπήδησεν Ιωναθαν ἀπὸ τῆς τραπέζης. Some favor that as the more original reading, since the verb פָּחַז is rare.[17] In fact, פָּחַז appears only twice in the OT, and in those passages it means "be ruthless" (Judg 9:4; Zeph 3:4).

בָּחֳרִי־אָף—Literally this means "in heat of anger."

נֶעְצַב—For the Niphal (N) of עָצַב, "be grieved, distressed," see the second textual note on 20:3.

הִכְלִמוֹ—The Hiphil (H) of כָּלַם can mean "insult, humiliate, put to shame" (see BDB, 1).

20:35 לְמוֹעֵד—The noun מוֹעֵד can refer to an "appointed time" or an "appointed place." To cover both possibilities it is translated as "meeting."

20:36 מוֹרֶה … יָרָה—The first verb is the masculine singular Hiphil (H) participle of יָרָה, and the second is the third masculine singular Qal (G) perfect of יָרָה. In both stems the verb can mean "to shoot."

הַחֵצִי לְהַעֲבִרוֹ:—Literally he shot "the arrow to cause it to pass over [him]" (see BDB, s.v. עָבַר, Hiphil, 3 c). The third masculine singular suffix on the Hiphil (H) infinitive construct לְהַעֲבִרוֹ refers back to הַחֵצִי. The LXX agrees with the MT. After these words 4QSam^b adds העירה (to be pointed הָעִירָה), over him "toward the city." It is possible that the last word in 4QSam^b was lost in the MT and the LXX's exemplar.

20:37 הֲלוֹא הַחֵצִי—"Isn't the arrow?" is the reading of the MT. The reconstructed reading in 4QSam^b is [הנה החץ], "look, the arrow," which is supported by the LXX, ἐκεῖ ἡ σχίζα. That reading may be a result of assimilation to 20:21.

---

[16] There is not enough room on the line for the missing words to have included שאול, "Saul."

[17] McCarter, *I Samuel*, 339–40; Klein, *1 Samuel*, 204.

20:38 הַנַּעַר—"The boy" is the reading of the MT and 4QSamᵃ; the LXX reads τοῦ παιδαρίου αὐτοῦ, "his boy," perhaps as an assimilation to 20:36. 4QSamᵇ reads עלמה, "his youth."

מְהֵרָה חֽוּשָׁה—"Hurry up" is literally "quickly hurry." The feminine noun מְהֵרָה, "haste," usually serves as an adverbial accusative, as here. The verb חֽוּשָׁה is a Qal (G) imperative masculine singular (with paragogic *he*) of חוּשׁ, "to hurry."

וַיְלַקֵּט—The Piel (D) of לָקַט means "to gather (up), collect; glean."

הַחִצִּים—"The arrows" is the reading of the Qere and the LXX (τὰς σχίζας), which agrees with the same plural in 20:36a. The Kethib, הַחֵצִי, reads "the arrow," which agrees with the same singular in 20:36b and 20:37 (twice). 4QSamᵃ (החץ) also reads "the arrow."

וַיָּבֹא אֶל־אֲדֹנָֽיו׃—"And he came to his master" is the reading of the MT, 4QSamᵃ, and probably 4QSamᵇ. Some LXX manuscripts read the Qal (G) verb וַיָּבֹא as the corresponding Hiphil (H) form וַיָּבֵא: καὶ ἤνεγκεν, "and he brought" the arrows to his master.

20:40 אֶל־הַנַּעַר אֲשֶׁר־לֹו—Literally this means "to the boy who was his." The preposition לְ is used to denote possession or "belonging to." The LXX reads ἐπὶ τὸ παιδάριον αὐτοῦ, "to his boy." Some versions translate with something like "to the boy who was with him" (see HCSB, NET), although there is no justification for such a rendering.

20:41 מֵאֵצֶל הַנֶּגֶב—This is translated as "from beside the mound." See the last textual note on 20:19.

וַיִּֽשְׁתַּחוּ—For the Hishtaphel of חָוָה, "to bow down, worship," see the third textual note on 1:3. The form here is a third masculine singular preterite (imperfect with *waw* consecutive).

וַיִּשְּׁקוּ—"They kissed." The Qal (G) of נָשַׁק was also used in 10:1, where Samuel kissed Saul after anointing him. See further "Jonathan Sends David Away (20:35–21:1 [ET 20:35–42])" in the commentary.

עַד־דָּוִד הִגְדִּיל׃—Literally this means "until David did greatly." The Hiphil (H) of גָּדַל can mean "to do [something] greatly, to a great extent" (see BDB, 3 c), and here a repetition of the verb בָּכָה, "to weep" (e.g., לִבְכּוֹת, the infinitive construct with לְ), is implied. The sense could be comparative: David wept more than Jonathan.

21:1 וַיָּקָם—"And he arose" is the reading of the MT. 4QSamᵇ reads ויקם דוד, "and David arose," supported by the LXX: καὶ ἀνέστη Δαυιδ. Perhaps the subject was supplied for clarity.

וַיֵּלַךְ—This is pausal for וַיֵּלֶךְ.

Commentary

c. 1015–c. 1014 BC

This chapter presents Jonathan investigating Saul's intentions toward David. In doing so, he was forced to choose between his obligation to his father and his love and duty to his neighbor, friend, and brother-in-law David. Obligations toward parents do not end when one becomes an adult, and ancient Near Eastern societies—including ancient Israel—placed a high value on respect and duty to parents by their adult children. At the same time, Jonathan and David had entered into a solemn agreement, with the invocation of Yahweh, at Jonathan's initiation (18:3; 20:8; see also 20:42; 23:18). This also obligated Jonathan both because he was a member of Yahweh's covenant people and because of societal expectations within the people of God. When David gave Jonathan reason to suspect that his father had murderous intentions toward David, Jonathan chose his obligation to his neighbor and fellow believer in Yahweh over his loyalty to his apostate father, whom Yahweh had rejected (15:23; 16:1) and from whom Yahweh's Spirit had departed (16:14). In this way Jonathan remained faithful to Yahweh, kept the Fifth Commandment against murder (Ex 20:13; Deut 5:17), and honored the covenant agreement he had made with David under God.

Ambrose wrote about this choice as honorable and commendable, especially since Jonathan placed his own life at risk; in fact, his father threatened to kill him in exactly the same way he had twice attempted to kill David (compare 18:11 and 19:10 to 20:33):

> For that commendable friendship which maintains virtue is to be preferred most certainly to wealth, or honours, or power. It is not wont to be preferred to virtue indeed, but to follow after it. So it was with Jonathan, who for his affection's sake avoided not his father's displeasure nor the danger to his own safety. So, too, it was with Ahimelech, who, to preserve the duties of hospitality, thought he must endure death rather than betray his friend when fleeing.[18]

Ambrose also wrote:

> Wherefore Saul was very angry and strove to strike Jonathan his son with a spear [20:33] because he thought that David's friendship held a higher place in his esteem than either filial piety or a father's authority.[19]

Jonathan and David's Conversation in the City (20:1–10)

When David fled from Ramah, he apparently went to wherever Jonathan was (20:1). Since David seems to have had no fear of going to Jonathan, it is likely that Saul had not yet returned to Gibeah and that Jonathan and David met there. Note that the next day would be the new moon feast at Saul's table (20:5), so the narrative implies that 1 Samuel 20 took place in the vicinity of Gibeah, where Saul lived (10:26). David's questions about Saul's deadly intentions elicited denials from Jonathan (20:2). Jonathan's denials may have been predicated upon the reconciliation he thought he had brought about between Saul and David (19:1–7). However, it would have been difficult for Jonathan not to have known about Saul's repeated attempts to kill David with a spear (18:11; 19:9–10) and the incident involving his sister Michal (19:11–17) as well as Saul's pursuit of David to Ramah (19:18–24). Unless Jonathan had somehow been absent during all of those events, had recently returned, and had not been informed of David's flight—an extremely improbable scenario—it appears as if his relationships with David and his father placed him at a conflicted intersection. This

---

[18] Ambrose of Milan, *On the Duties of the Clergy*, 3.21 (*NPNF*² 10:87).

[19] Ambrose of Milan, *On the Duties of the Clergy*, 2.7 (*NPNF*² 10:49).

may have brought about his denial despite the evidence that Saul was actively seeking David's demise. His denial may have been more of a coping mechanism for himself than an attempt to persuade David that he was mistaken.

David, on the other hand, insisted that he was in danger and offered Jonathan a rationale for why Saul has not told Jonathan of his plans—because he knew that Jonathan favored David (20:3). This logic persuaded Jonathan to offer David help (20:4).

David suggested a way to demonstrate Saul's intention to Jonathan—a test involving the new moon festival (20:5–7). The Law of Moses required that there be sacrifices at the beginning of each month at the new moon.[20] Apparently Saul also held a feast in conjunction with this monthly event that his important officers, including David, were expected to attend.[21] David would stay in hiding in the countryside, while Jonathan would present David's excuse to Saul if Saul noticed David's absence. If Saul became angry at the excuse—the need to attend to his familial responsibilities at an annual sacrifice in conjunction with this new moon—it would be obvious that Saul wanted to harm David, since respect for David's religious observance would normally have been expected.

David understood that he was asking Jonathan to deceive his father. For this reason he asked for Jonathan's mercy on the basis of the agreement between them, and under Yahweh, that Jonathan had initiated (20:8; cf. 18:3; 20:42; 23:18). If Jonathan thought David to be wrong, David suggested that Jonathan simply execute him immediately without bothering to bring him to Saul. That suggestion was likely hyperbolic, but it was successful in its design to prompt Jonathan's denial of any wrong in David and a denial of any complicity in Saul's schemes (20:9). With Jonathan's denial, David could assume Jonathan's cooperation, and so he followed with a question as to how Saul's reaction would be communicated to him (20:10).

Jonathan and David's Conversation in the Country (20:11–24a)

To continue their conversation, Jonathan suggested that they go outside the city into the country, probably so that they could speak in private (20:11). He not only promised to investigate his father's attitude, but he also called on Yahweh, Israel's covenant God, as a witness (20:12). Invoking "Yahweh, the God of Israel," is common in the book of Samuel.[22] First—on a hopeful note— Jonathan promised to tell David if Saul was favorable toward him.

Jonathan followed this with an oath, using a formula for self-imprecation (20:13). This formula (כֹּה יֹסִף ... כֹּה עָשָׂה) is also common in the book

---

[20] Num 28:11–15; see also 2 Ki 4:23; Is 1:13–14; Ezek 45:17; 46:6–7; Amos 8:4–5; Ezra 3:4–5; Neh 10:33–34 (ET 10:32–33).

[21] It is interesting to note that the only persons other than Saul mentioned in connection with the feast have military connections: Jonathan, Abner, and David.

[22] 1 Sam 2:30; 10:18; 14:41; 20:12; 23:10, 11; 25:32, 34; 2 Sam 12:7.

of Samuel[23] but is found only occasionally elsewhere.[24] By using this formal oath, Jonathan was binding himself to warn David, even though this act might be seen as treasonous by Saul. Moreover, Jonathan once again acknowledged God's selection of David as king to replace Saul (as he had in 18:4).

Jonathan recognized that his promise to David could lead to his own execution, since he took seriously the possibility that he might die for aiding the future king. Therefore, Jonathan now called on David to honor the agreement that they had made by showing kindness not only to him but also to his house, even after Yahweh had established David in power by overcoming his enemies (20:14–17). Later in 20:42 Jonathan would elaborate that the agreement extended to "my descendants and your descendants forever." David would keep this agreement when he provided for Jonathan's son (2 Sam 9:1–13).

The next verses relate Jonathan's instructions to David so that he could deliver news about Saul's attitude toward David (1 Sam 20:18–23). The arrow signal was an elaborate procedure designed to hide the message from Jonathan's attendant. David was to be in hiding in the place where he originally hid "on the day of the deed" (20:19). The deed must be a reference to Saul's order to kill David (19:1), since this is what originally led David to hide in the countryside (19:2–3). Before leaving David, Jonathan once again invoked Yahweh, this time as a witness to their agreement and pledge (20:23). And David hid in the country (20:24a).

Jonathan Discovers Saul's Intentions (20:24b–34)

The scene then moves to the next day and the feast with Saul, Abner, and Jonathan in attendance (20:24b–25). The first day Saul rationalized David's absence: David must have accidentally become unclean and, therefore, ineligible to eat the meat from the sacrifice (20:26). Saul assumed that David, like any observant Israelite, would not have intentionally done anything to make himself unclean and thereby become disqualified for the monthly observance of sacrifices to Yahweh. Any Israelite who became unclean (knowingly or not) and nevertheless ate a holy sacrifice was to be cut off from his people (Lev 7:20–21). The book of Leviticus deals with a wide variety ways in which a person could inadvertently become unclean.[25]

---

[23] 1 Sam 3:17; 14:44; 20:13; 25:22; 2 Sam 3:9, 35; 19:14 (ET 19:13); cf. 1 Sam 11:7; 17:27.

[24] 1 Ki 2:23; 19:2; 20:10; 2 Ki 6:31; Ruth 1:17.

[25] Uncleanness was a kind of contagion. A person became unclean by contact with any person or thing that was unclean and even as a result of some common bodily functions, regardless of whether or not the person was aware of the uncleanness. A person would become unclean by accidentally touching a carcass of an unclean animal or by touching any object (e.g., a garment, a sack, a piece of wood, or an earthenware vessel or any food or drink from such a vessel) that had been in contact with an unclean carcass or by touching anything that had been contaminated with uncleanness from another person (Lev 5:2–3; 7:21; 11:24–38). A woman became unclean for a time because of her monthly period and by childbirth (Lev 12:1–5; 15:18–26), and a man became unclean from having an unexpected discharge (Lev 15:2–17); in addition, everything on which they would sit or lie became unclean. Skin diseases rendered

However, Saul's rationalization was irrational. Since David had already fled the court after Saul had sought to kill him, Saul appears to have been in self-denial about the consequences of his murderous pursuit of David. Surely he could not have reasonably expected David to appear at the feast after having sent messengers to drag him out of his house in order to kill him (19:11–17) and then having chased him to Ramah (19:18–24)! David was fully cognizant of those attempts on his life (19:18).

When David did not come to Saul's table the next day, Saul inquired about his absence (20:27). This time, however, he displayed his animus toward David by calling him "Jesse's son" (20:27, 30, 31), a way of avoiding his personal name in order to show contempt and to depersonalize his own relationship to him (he had given his daughter Michal to be David's wife [18:20, 27; 19:11–17]). Saul would use this derisive reference to David again when accusing the priests at Nob of conspiring with David (22:7, 8, 13).[26]

Jonathan's answer to Saul followed the outlines of the excuse David had suggested that he use (20:28–29).[27] This involved telling a lie in order to protect an innocent life. Michal had done the same thing to save David from Saul in 19:11–17.[28] David would also lie in 21:3–4 (ET 21:2–3; cf. 21:13–14 [ET 21:12–13]) and 27:10–11. The Scriptures are quite harsh in their depiction of lies that would bring harm to innocent persons, lies that would deceive a neighbor in order to defraud him or lead him into sin, or lies that give false testimony in judicial proceedings.[29] However, some lies, like Jonathan's lie to Saul, and especially lies to protect the innocent or to obtain justice, are portrayed in a more favorable light in the OT. This is, in fact, in keeping with the spirit of admonitions such as Prov 31:8–9.[30] Shemesh notes:

> The Hebrew Bible recognizes that under certain circumstances lying is unavoidable, particularly when it serves the weak as their only weapon against some force seeking to harm them or other persons. Included in this category are various instances of lies intended to save the liar's life or altruistic lies (mainly on the part of women).
>
> Thus, for example, David lies to Ahimelech (1 Sam. 21:3 [ET 21:2]) and misleads King Achish of Gath (1 Sam. 21:13 [ET 21:2]) in order to save his own life. Saul's daughter Michal lies to her father's messengers in order to save her

---

a person unclean (Lev 13:1–46). A garment and even a whole house with all its contents could become unclean (Lev 13:59; 14:33–47).

[26] "Jesse's son" was also used derisively by Nabal (1 Sam 25:10) and Sheba (2 Sam 20:1).

[27] Jonathan apparently added the reference to David's brother.

[28] See further discussion of this topic in the last paragraphs of the exposition in "Michal Helps David Escape (19:11–17)" in the commentary on 19:1–17.

[29] E.g., Gen 37:31–32; 39:14–15, 17–18; Ex 20:16; Lev 19:11–12; Deut 5:20; 19:18–19; 1 Ki 21:13; 2 Ki 5:22–27; Is 59:3–4; Jer 9:4 (ET 9:5); 23:14; Pss 5:7 (ET 5:6); 7:15–16 (ET 7:14–15); 144:7–8, 11; Prov 6:16–19; 14:5, 25; 19:5, 9; Mt 26:59–61; Acts 6:11–14.

[30] "Speak out for those who cannot speak, for the rights of all those who are defenseless. Speak out, judge fairly, and defend the oppressed and needy" (Steinmann, *Proverbs*, 618).

husband David's life (1 Sam. 19:11–16), and then lies to her father in order to escape his rage (1 Sam. 19:17). Jonathan, too, lies to his father to save his friend David's life (1 Sam. 20:28–29), and the woman from Bahurim lies to Absalom's servants to save David's spies Ahimaaz and Jonathan, hidden in the well in her courtyard (2 Sam. 17:18–20). Proof that God may actually approve of such lies may be derived from His rewarding of the midwives in Egypt, who lied to Pharaoh out of compassion for the lives of the male children born to the Hebrew women (Ex. 1:15–21). A further indication to that effect is the narrator's comment concerning Hushai's deception of Absalom by pretending to support him: "The Lord had decreed that Ahithophel's sound advice be nullified, in order that the Lord might bring ruin upon Absalom" (2 Sam. 17:14).

A forgiving view of deception may also be discerned in cases where persons lie to secure what belongs to them by right but has been unjustly withheld. Thus, the initiative taken by Judah's daughter-in-law Tamar, who disguises herself as a prostitute in order to become pregnant by him after his failure to marry her to his son Shelah, is described in a favorable light, and indeed justified by Judah himself in the narrative (Gen. 38:26). Tamar is rewarded for her subterfuge by the birth of the twins Perez and Zerah, through whom the tribe of Judah is established (Gen. 38:27–30).

The biblical narrator also takes a favorable view of fraud when the object is some religious goal in keeping with the general outlook of the Bible. An example is Jehu's lying to the worshippers of Baal, which is aimed at killing all the prophets of Baal and eradicating his worship from the country (2 Kgs. 10:18–28).

In one case we even find God twisting the truth in order to preserve amicable relations between Abraham and Sarah and to prevent Abraham's feelings from being hurt. Upon overhearing the prediction that she was about to become pregnant, Sarah laughs, "Now that I am withered, am I to have enjoyment—*with my husband so old*?" (Gen. 18:12); God, however, quotes her in Abraham's hearing as having said, "Shall I in truth bear a child, *old as I am*?" (Gen. 18:13), making no reference to Abraham's inadequacy. This episode was used by the Sages of the Talmud as a proof-text showing that it is permitted to deviate from the strict line of truth in order to establish peace (BT [Babylonian Talmud] Yeb. [*Yebamoth*] 65b; BT B.M. [*Baba Meẓiʻa*] 87a).[31]

Thus, Christians may at times find themselves in positions where they may have to lie or deceive to protect themselves or innocent people from injustice. In such cases one may have to choose to honor God by disobeying men (Acts 5:29) and keep the Fifth Commandment's prohibition against murder (Ex 20:13; Deut 5:17) even if it involves a violation of the Eighth Commandment (Ex 20:16; Deut 5:20), since God places a high value on the sanctity of all human life and is especially concerned about protecting the innocent, the weak, and the

---

[31] Shemesh, "Lies by Prophets and Other Lies in the Hebrew Bible," 84–85.

helpless.[32] The NT even cites with approval one such OT instance. The prostitute Rahab lied to protect the Israelite spies (Josh 2:1–6; 6:17–25), and two NT writers praise her as an exemplar of righteousness. She was justified by her courageous saving faith (Heb 11:31). James adds that saving faith results in righteous actions, and so he commends Rahab as one who was "justified by works" (James 2:24–25).[33]

Jonathan's words brought out Saul's anger against David, which he now transferred to Jonathan (1 Sam 20:30). He insulted him, calling him the "son of a perverted, rebellious woman"—in effect disowning him as his own son and accusing him of treason. He called Jonathan's protection of David shameful and an act that brought shame upon his mother, who bore him. The "nakedness" to which Saul referred was a reference to Jonathan's mother's birth canal, through which Jonathan was delivered.[34] Saul thus implied that Jonathan's mother should have been ashamed that she gave birth to him. Moreover, he told Jonathan that he would not be able to succeed to the throne as long as David was alive (20:31). Thus, Saul was acknowledging that David was the successor to the throne about whom Samuel had told him (15:26–29). Then Saul ordered Jonathan to surrender David for execution.

When Jonathan protested, asking what David had done that was deserving of death (20:32), Saul sought to kill Jonathan with his spear, just as he had twice tried to kill David (20:33; cf. 18:10–11; 19:9–10). The similarity convinced Jonathan that his father was intent on killing David. Because of the humiliation he received from his father and because of his anxiety over David, Jonathan rose from the table and did not eat (20:34; cf. David's rationale for Saul hiding his intent from Jonathan in 20:3).

Jonathan Sends David Away (20:35–21:1 [ET 20:35–42])

On the appointed day, we are told that Jonathan went out to signal David (20:35–40). The author emphasizes that Jonathan's young assistant did not know the real intent of the trip to the countryside.

While David was free to flee, at this point he initiated a farewell with Jonathan (20:41). David's bowing to Jonathan three times was unusual. No one else in the OT is recorded as bowing three times at once. Thus, David displayed respect to Jonathan as well as to Saul, indicating by his act that he had no traitorous motives. The kiss exchanged by two persons of the same sex was often a sign of their close relationship. Thus, Moses kissed his father-in-law, Jethro (Ex 18:7), and Naomi kissed her daughters-in-law (Ruth 1:9). Here

---

[32] Deut 10:17–19; 24:17; 27:19; Is 1:16–17; Jer 7:6–7; 22:3; Zech 7:10; Pss 10:14, 17–18; 68:6 (ET 68:5); 82:3; 146:9.

[33] Rahab also became an ancestress of Christ (Mt 1:5). See also the exposition, including comments from Luther and Origen, in Harstad, *Joshua*, 114–20, 125, 131–36.

[34] Zehnder, "Observations," 150; McCarter, *I Samuel*, 343; Klein, *1 Samuel*, 209. Some take it as a reference to Jonathan's parentage, implying that Jonathan was not the son of Saul (Zehnder, "Observations," 150, mentions this view).

brothers-in-law exchanged a kiss. At other times kisses may have had political implications, as when David kissed Barzillai (2 Sam 19:40 [ET 19:39]) or when Absalom in his campaign to supplant David kissed those coming to see the king (2 Sam 15:5–6). Those who have rebelled against God's Son are urged to reconcile with their ultimate Sovereign by kissing him in worship lest they perish (Ps 2:12; contrast the kissing of Baal as an act of idolatry in 1 Ki 19:18). Here the exchange of a kiss may also have signaled David's honoring of Jonathan as prince and Jonathan's honoring of David as king designate.

When Jonathan sent David away, he once again reminded him of the oath, sworn by invoking Yahweh, that they had taken that bound them and their descendants together under God (20:42 [ET 20:42a]).[35] This is the third time in this chapter that the agreement between the two men is mentioned. David first appealed to it when he felt vulnerable and needed Jonathan to understand his father's murderous intent (20:8). Next, Jonathan appealed to the covenant when he knew that he might have to face his father's wrath and perhaps be accused of sedition (20:14–17). Now Jonathan appealed to their agreement as enduring and binding even though they were departing from each other (20:42). This signals that Jonathan once again was sensing his vulnerability, this time acknowledging that David would someday be in a position of power over him. Thus, Jonathan was reminding David to treat him and his descendants with mercy, as he had treated David with mercy.

The account ends with David leaving and Jonathan returning to the city, presumably Gibeah. The short sentence is numbered as 21:1 in the MT but is included in 20:42 in most modern English versions. It is labeled as 20:43 by the Vulgate, Luther's translation of 1524 and 1545,[36] and the Douay-Rheims Bible of 1609. These different chapter divisions are due to the complex history of dividing the OT books into chapters and verses.[37] While verse divisions (without numbers) were introduced by the Masoretes during the sixth through ninth centuries AD, chapter divisions were first introduced into the Vulgate in the Middle Ages. (This is traditionally credited to Stephen Langton, archbishop of Canterbury, AD 1207–1228.) These chapter divisions were subsequently transferred to the Hebrew text.[38] Later, during the Reformation era, Luther and Calvin sought to correct what they perceived to be a few infelicitous chapter divisions. These newer chapter divisions often appear in printed Bibles in English, German, French, and many other languages (while not necessarily retaining the same verse divisions, e.g., Luther's 20:42–43 = English 20:42). However, the older chapter divisions are retained in printed Hebrew editions.

---

[35] For their "covenant, agreement" (בְּרִית), see, previously, 18:3; 20:8; and later, 23:18. For "swearing" (the Niphal [N] of שָׁבַע), see 20:3, 42 (cf. 20:17); see also "as Yahweh lives" in 20:3, 21.

[36] WA DB 9/1.258–59.

[37] See the discussion in Steinmann, *Daniel*, 208–9.

[38] See Tov, *Textual Criticism of the Hebrew Bible*, 52–53.

Printed editions of the Septuagint in many places have the same verse divisions as the Hebrew text, but sometimes agree instead with the English versification or have a unique system corresponding to neither.[39] Verse divisions in the Vulgate at times agree with the Hebrew text and at other times with the English text.

---

[39] For a list of differences between English, Hebrew, and Greek versification, see *The SBL Handbook of Style* (2d ed.; Atlanta: SBL Press, 2014), 265–68.

David in Nob

Translation

21 ²David went to Nob to the high priest Ahimelech. Ahimelech was shaking with fear when he met David. He said to him, "Why are you by yourself? No one is with you!"

³David said to the high priest Ahimelech, "The king gave me an assignment and said to me, 'Do not let anyone know anything about the assignment on which I am sending you and that I have commanded you.' I have made an appointment with the young men to be at a certain place. ⁴Now what do you have on hand? Hand five loaves of bread to me or whatever you can find."

⁵The high priest answered David, "I do not have any ordinary bread on hand. There is only holy bread—only if the young men have kept themselves from women."

⁶David answered the high priest, "Of course women have been kept from us as previously when I went out [to battle]. All the young men are consecrated. This is the usual practice. How much more [is it] today when they are consecrated along with their equipment?"

⁷The high priest gave him holy [bread], since there was no bread there except the bread of the Presence that had been removed from before Yahweh in order to place warm bread [there] on the day when it was taken away.

(⁸Now one of Saul's servants was detained there before Yahweh that day. His name was Doeg the Edomite, Saul's chief shepherd.)

⁹David said to Ahimelech, "Don't you have a spear or sword on hand? I didn't take even my sword or equipment with me because the king's assignment was urgent."

¹⁰The high priest said, "The sword of the Philistine Goliath, whom you struck down in the Valley of the Terebinth—it is here wrapped in a garment behind the ephod. If you wish to take it for yourself, take [it], because there is no other one here except it."

David said, "There is none like it. Give it to me."

Textual Notes

21:2 נֹבֶה—This is a place-name, נֹב, "Nob," with a locative *he* ending, "to Nob." The locative ending has this form, הָ֫-, only on this name (again in 22:9) and a few other times (GKC, § 90 i).

אֲחִימֶלֶךְ הַכֹּהֵן—"Ahimelech the priest" means "the high priest Ahimelech." See the third textual note on 1:9. Likewise in 21:3, 5, 6, 7, 10 (ET 21:2, 4, 5, 6, 9), הַכֹּהֵן is rendered as "the high priest."

וַיֶּחֱרַד—For "he was shaking with fear," see the first textual note on 16:4.

לִקְרַאת—Literally this means "to meet." See the second textual note on 4:1.

אִתָּךְ:—This is the preposition אֵת, "with," with a second masculine singular suffix: "with you." This form is pausal for אִתְּךָ. 4QSamᵇ substitutes the more common and synonymous preposition עִם, likewise suffixed: עמך.

21:3 לַאֲחִימֶלֶךְ הַכֹּהֵן—Instead of "to the high priest Ahimelech," 4QSamᵇ (לכהן) and the LXX (τῷ ἱερεῖ) read only "to the (high) priest."

צִוַּנִי דָבָר—"He gave me an assignment" is literally "he commanded me a matter."

מְאוּמָה—"Anything" is missing in the LXX.

וְאֶת־הַנְּעָרִים יוֹדַעְתִּי אֶל־—The MT literally reads "and I made the young men know to …" This is the only OT instance of the Poel (D) stem of יָדַע, "to know," and it has a causative sense, "to inform," or in context here, "to make an appointment." David informed his men about a certain place, i.e., he made an appointment with them to meet there. Although יָדַע is normally used in the Hiphil (H) stem to express a causative meaning, it appears once in the Piel (D) stem with the same meaning (Job 38:12). 4QSamᵇ reads ידעתי, which could be a defective, or *ḥaser*, form (יֹדַעְתִּי) of the verb in the MT. The LXX reads the perfect verb διαμεμαρτύρημαι, which could mean "I have stated firmly" or "I have given firm guidelines" (see Muraoka, s.v. διαμαρτύρομαι, 4 and 6).

מְקוֹם פְּלֹנִי אַלְמוֹנִי:—The identical phrase occurs also in 2 Ki 6:8. The noun מָקוֹם, "a place," is in construct with the phrase פְּלֹנִי אַלְמוֹנִי, which occurs only three times in the OT and means "a certain place" (here and in 2 Ki 6:8) or "a certain person" (Ruth 4:1). This is a purposely vague phrase used when the speaker does not want to state the name.

21:4 מַה־יֵּשׁ תַּחַת־יָדְךָ—Literally "what exists under your hand?" is equivalent to the English idiom "what do you have on hand?" The idiom תַּחַת־יָד recurs in 21:5, 9 (ET 21:4, 8). The LXX translates literally with εἰ εἰσὶν ὑπὸ τὴν χεῖρά σου, "if there are under your hand …"

חֲמִשָּׁה־לֶחֶם תְּנָה בְיָדִי—This command with תְּנָה, the alternate form (with paragogic *he*) of the Qal (G) imperative of נָתַן, is literally "five loaves of bread give in my hand." It is translated with "hand" as an English verb: "hand … to me."

אוֹ הַנִּמְצָא:—Literally "or the found (thing)," this introduces a second, alternate direct object of the imperative תְּנָה. The Niphal (N) participle of מָצָא, "to find," is used with the article as a substantive.

21:5 חֹל—This noun, which recurs in 21:6 (ET 21:5), denotes the theological/liturgical category of "common" or "ordinary." This is a largely neutral category for things in God's creation. What is "common" is not "holy" by direct association with God; the "holy" may be suitable for priests, but too sacred for ordinary use by laypeople. However, what is "common" can become "unclean" and thus unsuitable for any of God's chosen people. See Lev 10:10.[1]

נִשְׁמְרוּ—The Niphal (N) of שָׁמַר, "guard, keep," has a reflexive meaning, "keep oneself."

---

[1] See the explanation in Kleinig, *Leviticus*, 6, 226, 228–39. Aside from Lev 10:10; 1 Sam 21:5–6 (ET 21:4–5), the only other OT uses of חֹל are by the prophet and priest Ezekiel (Ezek 22:26; 42:20; 44:23; 48:15).

At the end of the verse 4QSam^b adds וַאֲכַלְתֶּם מִמֶּנּוּ, "and you [masculine plural] will eat of it." This is probably a secondary addition to smooth out the laconic text. Cf. the LXX, which adds καὶ φάγεται, "and he will eat."

21:6 וַיֹּאמֶר לוֹ—"And he said to him." This redundant clause is omitted from the translation for the sake of English style.

כִּי אִם—The combination כִּי אִם can mean "truly, surely," especially in connection with oaths or solemn statements (BDB, s.v. כִּי אִם [under כִּי], 2 c).

אִשָּׁה עֲצֻרָה־לָנוּ—Literally "a woman is restrained regarding us." The verb עֲצֻרָה is a Qal passive (Gp) feminine singular participle of עָצַר, "restrain, be kept away (from)."

כִּתְמוֹל שִׁלְשֹׁם—For "as previously," see the last textual note on 4:7.

בְּצֵאתִי—This is the Qal (G) infinitive construct of יָצָא with בְּ in a temporal sense and a subjective suffix. In the book of Samuel יָצָא often refers to "going out" for battle; see the first textual note on 18:6.

וַיִּהְיוּ כְלֵי־הַנְּעָרִים קֹדֶשׁ—The MT reads "and the vessels/equipment of the young men are/have been holy/consecrated." If retained, the young men's "vessels" may be a reference to their genitals, though this meaning is not attested elsewhere. However, one would expect the noun קֹדֶשׁ to be plural (קֳדָשִׁים) to match כְּלֵי, the plural of the noun כְּלִי. Moreover, in place of כְּלֵי, "vessels/equipment of," 4QSam^b reads כל (כֹּל), "all," which is supported by the LXX: πάντα τὰ παιδάρια ἡγνισμένα, "all the young men are sanctified." If כֹּל is correct, כְּלֵי in the MT may have resulted from attraction to בַּכֵּלִי at the end of the verse. The singular collective כֹּל accords better with the singular noun קֹדֶשׁ (although הַנְּעָרִים is plural). The collective singular כֹּל then may also be the subject of the later singular verb יִקְדַּשׁ, "he is consecrated," as reflected in the translation of יִקְדַּשׁ בַּכֵּלִי as "they are consecrated along with their equipment."

וְהוּא דֶּרֶךְ חֹל—"This is the usual practice" is literally "and it is the way of the common/ordinary."

21:7 לֶחֶם הַפָּנִים—Literally "the bread of the face [of Yahweh]," this construct phrase refers to the bread of the Presence (Ex 25:30; 35:13; 39:36; also 1 Ki 7:48; 2 Chr 4:19). See further the commentary.

הַמּוּסָרִים—"That had been removed" is a masculine plural Hophal (Hp) participle of סוּר, "turn, turn aside," with the definite article. The Hiphil (H) of סוּר often means "to remove," and the Hophal's meaning is the corresponding passive. The LXX has the plural participle οἱ ἀφηρημένοι. Grammatically, one might expect the Hebrew participle to be singular to agree with לֶחֶם, "bread." However, the bread of the Presence consisted of twelve loaves (Lev 24:5–6), so the plural is probably *ad sensum*. Also, לֶחֶם may serve as a collective, and the participle could be plural by attraction to the plural הַפָּנִים, "face, presence." 4QSam^b has the singular המוסר, which is probably a secondary correction.

בְּיוֹם הִלָּקְחוֹ—This is translated as "on the day when it was taken away." The verb is a Niphal (N) infinitive construct (with a subjective pronominal suffix) of לָקַח. The bread of the Presence was to be replaced every Sabbath (Lev 24:8; see the commentary).

21:8 נֶעְצָר—"Detained" is a Niphal (N) masculine singular participle of עָצַר, "restrain." Compare the Qal passive (Gp) feminine singular participle of the same verb in the third textual note on 21:6 (ET 21:5).

אַבִּיר הָרֹעִים—The construct phrase "the mighty one of the shepherds" forms a superlative, "the strongest of the shepherds" or "the chief shepherd." Aster notes that parallel terms in Assyrian and Hittite texts often place the "chief shepherd" among other military offices.[2] Thus, it is not surprising that Doeg would also serve as an executioner for Saul (22:18–19). The LXX reads νέμων τὰς ἡμιόνους Σαουλ, "grazer of Saul's mules."

21:9 וְאִין יֶשׁ־פֹּה—"Don't you have … ?" The first word as pointed, אִין, is a hapax legomenon. Most likely it is an irregular form of the particle of negation, אַיִן, in construct (normally pointed אֵין), thus literally "and not does there exist here," which, in context, must be a question. See אֵין־יֵשׁ in Ps 135:17. Less likely, it could be the Aramaic אִין (equivalent to the Syriac ܐܢ), "whether?" or "if?"

נָחוּץ:—This is a Qal passive (Gp) participle of נָחַץ. This is the only occurrence of this root in ancient Hebrew (see *CDCH*). The translation "urgent" is based on the LXX's rendering of this word as κατὰ σπουδήν, literally "according to haste/speed."

21:10 בְּעֵמֶק הָאֵלָה—For "in the Valley of the Terebinth," see the first textual note on 17:2.

הִיא לוּטָה—The noun חֶרֶב, "sword" (earlier in the verse), is feminine, hence the feminine pronoun and feminine singular Qal passive (Gp) participle of לוּט, "to wrap." The rest of this verse has other feminine singular forms referring back to the "sword." The verb לוּט appears only three times in the OT: as a Qal passive participle here; in the Hiphil (H) in 1 Ki 19:13; and as a Qal participle in Is 25:7.

אַחֲרֵי הָאֵפוֹד—"Behind the ephod" (MT, 4QSam[b]) is missing in the LXX.

Commentary

c. 1014–c. 1013 BC

As David fled from Saul, he headed south toward Judah, the territory of his tribe. Nob (21:2 [ET 21:1]) was in the territory of Benjamin, apparently a short distance from Jerusalem (Is 10:32; Neh 11:32). It may be el-ʾIsawiyeh, just north of the old city of Jerusalem. Apparently, David had been to Nob previously and was acquainted with Ahimelech (22:14–15). Ahimelech was the brother of Ahijah, who had inquired of God for Saul (14:3, 18–19).

Ahimelech met David with trepidation, just as the elders of Bethlehem had met Samuel with trepidation (16:4). Ahimelech's fear apparently stemmed from David's arriving alone. Considering that for some time there had been tension in the royal court caused by Saul's jealousy and repeated attempts on David's life, Ahimelech may have sensed that David was in mortal danger when he came to Nob by himself.

David's reply to Ahimelech was a lie used to save his life (21:3 [ET 21:2]), similar to the lies Michal and Jonathan had previously told to help him (19:14; 20:28–29).[3] David would lie again in 27:10–11 (cf. his deception in 21:13–14

---

[2] Aster, "What Was Doeg the Edomite's Title?"; see also Sasson, "Doeg's Job."

[3] See the further discussion of such lies in "Michal Helps David Escape (19:11–17)" in the commentary on 19:1–17 and "Jonathan Discovers Saul's Intentions (20:24b–34)" in the commentary on 20:1–21:1 (ET 20:1–42). Bergen (*1, 2 Samuel*, 221) contends that because David

[ET 21:12–13]). Here David's lie was exceptionally vague: he called Saul "the king" and said that he could not disclose the king's assignment and that the young men who would normally have accompanied him were at "a certain place." Yet there may have been elements of truth in David's words. For instance, he may have had some men who were loyal to him and whom he had arranged to meet.[4]

David followed this with an immediate request for five loaves of bread or any other food that could be spared (21:4 [ET 21:3]). By requesting five loaves, David gave the impression that he was not alone on his mission, but also that he was not accompanied by many men.

Apparently, Ahimelech accepted David's pretext or at least chose not to challenge it (21:5 [ET 21:4]). Instead, he stated that he had only "holy bread" (21:5, 7 [ET 21:4, 6]), "the bread of the Presence" (see the first textual note on 21:7 [ET 21:6]). This bread consisted of twelve loaves—one for each tribe of Israel—placed on a table in the Holy Place each Sabbath Day (Lev 24:5–9). These loaves were very large, as each was made from about 12 cups (2.8 liters) of flour (Lev 24:5). When new bread was set before Yahweh on the Sabbath, the old bread was to be eaten by priests in a holy place (Lev 24:9). Since the bread was holy, only men ordained into the office of the holy ministry were qualified to ingest it (cf. also, e.g., Lev 21:6, 8, 22). Ahimelech lowered the biblical requirement for the bread's consumption when he responded to David: he was willing to give it to laymen (David and his men) as long as they had abstained from women. OT priests married and had normal relations with their wives.[5] However, conjugal relations rendered any Israelite man unclean until evening, when he would become clean again after washing (Lev 15:18). This prerequisite also applied to the priests: after intercourse they could not eat holy food until sundown after they had bathed (Lev 22:4–7). At Mount Sinai God called the entire congregation of Israel to be "a kingdom of priests and a holy nation" (Ex 19:6). On that occasion Moses consecrated the people (Ex 19:10), directed them to wash their garments (Ex 19:10), and demanded that all the men "not go near a woman" (Ex 19:15), that is, all the people were to abstain from conjugal relations (temporarily) because Yahweh would descend upon Sinai on the third

---

called Yahweh "king" in a number of psalms (Pss 5:3 [ET 5:2]; 24:7–10; 29:10; 68:25 [ET 68:24]; 145:1), he may not have told a lie, but this explanation is unconvincing. Even if David meant "I'm on a mission from Yahweh," his words were still deceptive. Moreover, there is nothing in the context to lead Ahimelech or the reader to conclude that by "king" David was referring to anyone other than Saul.

4 Jesus appears to indicate that David ate the bread *along with his men* (Mt 12:3–4; Mk 2:25–26; Lk 6:3–4).

5 Since the descendants of Aaron were the only men eligible to be priests (and all Aaron's descendants were priests by virtue of their lineage), priests had to marry and have children in order for the priesthood to continue through subsequent generations. God did add some restrictions on the kind of woman a priest could marry. A priest could not marry a prostitute or a woman who was defiled or divorced (but could marry a widow), and the high priest was to marry a virgin (Lev 21:7–15).

day (Ex 19:11). A similar temporary abstinence may have been entailed in the call for the people to consecrate themselves before their entry into the promised land (Josh 3:5). A faithful soldier might voluntarily abstain during his tour of duty out of dedication to Yahweh's warfare (as did Uriah in 2 Sam 11:8–11).

The high priest Ahimelech therefore had solid grounds, rooted in the Torah, for not allowing David and his men to eat from the Lord's table unless they had met the biblical requirement not only for being clean but also for being holy.[6] On the other hand, God prioritizes the showing of mercy over external conformity to regulations, so if this was simply a matter of using the holy bread to feed those in desperate need, the preservation of life should have been given precedence (cf. 1 Sam 15:22; Prov 25:21).[7] By only offering holy bread with the required stipulation, Ahimelech may have attempted to avoid helping David. He had been afraid when David arrived alone (21:2 [ET 21:1]) and so may have hoped that this restriction would serve as an excuse for not abetting the fugitive and thus becoming another target of the king's rage.[8] Surely, the bread of the Presence was not the only bread in Nob (though it was the only bread in the tabernacle, 21:7 [ET 21:6]). There must have been ordinary bread baked in homes that Ahimelech could have procured for David. Instead, by diverting the conversation to the need to maintain holiness before God, the high priest seems to have tried to avoid helping David without appearing to be inhospitable.

David's reply was a clever rejoinder to the priest's hesitancy to help. He stated that all the men were consecrated and had not been with women, and he further contended that this was his normal practice for military service (21:6 [ET 21:5]). The men's abstinence and holiness were in keeping with God's command for military units (Deut 23:10–15 [ET 23:9–14]). David declared that even the equipment had been consecrated for this particular mission (1 Sam 21:6 [ET 21:5]). Gear and equipment could be rendered unclean in various ways,[9] but everything in a military camp was to be holy in order for Yahweh to be in the

---

[6] The high priest's examination of David and his men may be compared to the duty of a pastor not to admit people to receive the body and blood of Christ in the Sacrament of the Altar without consideration of their readiness to receive this holy food. See 1 Cor 11:17–34 and especially 1 Cor 11:27–34, discussed under the title "Unworthy Reception of the Sacrament," in Lockwood, *1 Corinthians*, 396–410.

[7] That God is a God of love and mercy is reiterated throughout the OT and NT. See, e.g., 2 Sam 24:14, and in the psalms of David, Pss 23:6; 25:6; 28:6; 51:3 (ET 51:1); 55:2 (ET 55:1). See further the discussion below of Mt 12:1–8; Mk 2:25–26; Lk 6:3–4; 13:15; 14:5; Jn 7:22–23.

[8] Reis, "Collusion at Nob," argues that Ahimelech was actually conspiring to help David: he spoke carefully and used veiled language to aid David but in such a way to hide the true meaning from Doeg (21:8 [ET 21:7]). See also Bodner, *1 Samuel*, 226. However, this does not explain Ahimelech's consternation over David's arrival at Nob (21:2 [ET 21:1]), nor does it explain Ahimelech's condition that the men must have abstained from women (21:5 [ET 21:4]). Moreover, the author of the book of Samuel is not reluctant to inform his readers about the thoughts of characters in the accounts he is relating (e.g., 1 Sam 4:7; 15:32; 16:6; 18:11, 17, 21; 20:26). If this was guarded, coded language on the part of Ahimelech, it is hard to believe that the author would not tell the readers what Ahimelech was thinking.

[9] See some of the Leviticus passages cited in the commentary on 1 Sam 20:26.

411

midst of the camp, save his people, and defeat their enemies (Deut 23:15 [ET 23:14]). With no other reason to deny assistance other than that they were laymen, the priest gave David the holy bread.

Jesus used this incident to teach that God's Law was not designed to prevent actions that serve human needs and preserve life (Mt 12:3–4; Mk 2:25–26; Lk 6:3–4). This general principle is articulated by Jesus in other ways also. The priests were allowed to violate the Sabbath regulation against work in order to bring forgiveness and eternal life to Israel through the sacrifices (Mt 12:5; cf. Num 28:9–10). Circumcision was permitted on the Sabbath in order to bring a child into the blessings of God's covenant with Abraham (Jn 7:22–23; cf. Gen 17:10–13). Jesus taught that this principle even applies to animal welfare: one could do work on the Sabbath by providing water for animals (Lk 13:15) or rescue an animal that had fallen into a pit or well (Mt 12:11; Lk 14:5). Moreover, if the requirement of priesthood was set aside for the sake of feeding David and his men, how much more should the Son of David, "the Lord of the Sabbath" (Mt 12:8), be able to feed his disciples on the Sabbath (Mt 12:1)! All baptized believers in him comprise "a chosen people, a royal priesthood, a holy nation" (1 Pet 2:9; cf. 1 Pet 2:5).[10] He himself serves as their great High Priest.[11] For the sustenance of their faith and life, he provides them with the holy food of his own body and blood, given and shed for the forgiveness of sins, in his Holy Supper.[12]

Next, the author includes a parenthetical comment that Doeg the Edomite, one of Saul's officials, was present to observe Ahimelech and David (1 Sam 21:8 [ET 21:7]). This will be important later (22:9–10). We are told that Doeg was "detained" before Yahweh (נֶעְצָר, 21:8 [ET 21:7]). The meaning of this is not altogether clear. One might be detained if one were seeking to be declared clean by a priest after having a skin malady or secretion from one's body (Lev 13:2–5, 24–28, 29–32, 38, 39; 15:15). However, Doeg was an Edomite, not an Israelite. Later, when Israelites were hesitant to execute Nob's priests, Doeg felt no constraint preventing him from carrying out Saul's order (1 Sam 22:17–19). This implies that Doeg was not at the sanctuary at Nob due to religious obligations. Instead, Doeg may have been "detained" before Yahweh by Saul as an informant should David come to the priests there for assistance. This would lend a double irony to Doeg's presence. Saul was supposed to "restrain" (the verb עָצַר, 9:17) the sinful tendencies of Israel, but instead he had "detained" (another form of the same verb, עָצַר, 21:8 [ET 21:7]) an Edomite. In addition, women had been "kept" (yet another form of the same verb, עָצֻר, 21:6 [ET 21:5]) from

---

[10] In the new covenant, abstinence from conjugal relations is not a requirement for holiness or reception of the holy things of God—neither for clergy nor for laity. See AC XXIII, "The Marriage of Priests."

[11] This truth is the main theme of the book of Hebrews; see, e.g., Heb 2:17; 3:1; 4:14–15; 5:5–6; 7:17; 9:11, 25–26. See also John 17.

[12] See Mt 26:20–30 and its Synoptic parallels; 1 Cor 11:17–34.

David's young men so that his troops would keep God's Law,[13] whereas Doeg was "detained" before Yahweh to aid in Saul's defiance of God.

After mentioning Doeg, the author continues the conversation between David and Ahimelech. David once again sought to deceive the high priest by claiming that due to the urgency of Saul's command (which Saul had not actually issued), he had no weapon and had not had a chance to bring one (21:9 [ET 21:8]). At his request for one, the high priest mentioned Goliath's sword, which was wrapped in a garment behind the ephod (21:10 [ET 21:9]). The mention of the ephod, like the mention of Doeg, prepares the reader for subsequent events at Nob. When Doeg massacred the priests, Abiathar, Ahimelech's son, fled with the ephod (23:6). We are not told how Goliath's sword came to be at the sanctuary at Nob. The last mention of it was when David wielded it to cut off Goliath's head (17:51).[14] Since it is likely that this was not David's first visit to the sanctuary at Nob (cf. 22:14–15), David may have dedicated the sword to Yahweh in thanks for granting him victory over the Philistine. That may be the reason that Ahimelech offered it to David—since it was considered David's spoil, captured in battle. David was quick to accept the offer, noting that the sword was unique—probably an indication that it was a weapon of fine quality.

---

[13] See Deut 23:10–15 (ET 23:9–14) and the discussion above.

[14] It is often assumed that David placed this sword in his tent after the battle (Klein, *1 Samuel*, 214; Tsumura, *The First Book of Samuel*, 534). However, while 17:54 indicates that David put Goliath's "equipment" (כֵּלָיו) in his tent, the sword is not explicitly mentioned.

1 Samuel 21:11–16 (ET 21:10–15)

David in Gath

Translation

21 **11David rose and fled that day from Saul's territory and came to King Achish of Gath. 12Achish's servants said to him, "Isn't this guy David, the king of the land? For this man they sing in the dances, saying, 'Saul has struck down his thousands and David his tens of thousands.'"**

13David took this to heart and was very afraid of King Achish of Gath. 14So he changed his demeanor whenever they saw him. He pretended to be insane when he was under their authority. He scribbled on the doors of the city gate and made spittle run down his beard.

15Achish said to his servants, "Look! You can see that the man is crazy! Why have you brought him to me? 16Have I so few crazy men that you brought this one to me to act crazy in my presence? Should this man come into my house?"

Textual Notes

21:11 וַיִּבְרַח—For "and he fled," see the second textual note on 19:12.

מִפְּנֵי שָׁאוּל—Literally "from the face/presence of Saul," this is translated as "from Saul's territory."[1] This phrase explains why David went to Gath: it was not under Saul's control, and, therefore, David was out of Saul's presence. Gath was one of the five cities of the Philistine pentapolis (6:17).

21:12 הֲלוֹא־זֶה—"Isn't this guy … ?" For the derogatory use of the demonstrative pronoun זֶה, see the second textual note on 10:27a.

יַעֲנוּ—This is the third masculine plural Qal (G) imperfect of עָנָה IV, "to sing" (so BDB and *HALOT*). See the first textual note on 18:7.

בַּמְּחֹלוֹת—For "in the dances," see the fourth textual note on 18:6.

הִכָּה שָׁאוּל בַּאֲלָפָיו—For "Saul has struck down his thousands," see the third textual note on 18:7.

וְדָוִד בְּרִבְבֹתָיו׃—For "and David his tens of thousands," see the fourth textual note on 18:7. The Qere here, בְּרִבְבֹתָיו, is the same plene, or *maleʾ*, spelling of the plural of רְבָבָה with a third masculine singular suffix that was the sole reading in the last clause of 18:7. Here the Kethib is בְּרִבְבֹתָו, the defective, or *ḥaser*, spelling of the same word. The same Qere/Kethib is given when this clause recurs in 29:5.

21:13 וַיָּשֶׂם דָּוִד אֶת־הַדְּבָרִים הָאֵלֶּה בִּלְבָבוֹ—Literally "and David set these words in his heart."

---

[1] Tsumura, *The First Book of Samuel*, 535.

וַיִּרָא—This is the defective, or *ḥaser*, spelling of the third masculine singular Qal (G) preterite (imperfect with *waw* consecutive) of יָרֵא, "be afraid." The plene, or *male*ʾ, spelling is וַיִּירָא, as in 12:18.

21:14 וַיְשַׁנּוֹ אֶת־טַעְמוֹ בְּעֵינֵיהֶם—Literally "and he changed it—his demeanor—in their eyes." וַיְשַׁנּוֹ is the third masculine singular Piel (D) preterite (imperfect with *waw* consecutive) of שָׁנָה, meaning "to change, alter" (transitive in the Piel), with a third masculine singular object suffix that refers to the following noun, טַעְמוֹ. The proleptic object suffix need not be translated in English. Most commentators advocate reading the verb as וַיְשַׁן, the same form but without the object suffix. No object suffix is reflected in the LXX (ἠλλοίωσεν). The segholate noun טַעַם usually means "taste" or "discretion, judgment," but here it must refer to David's "demeanor" or "behavior."

וַיִּתְהֹלֵל—"He pretended to be insane" is a third masculine singular Hithpolel (HtD) preterite (imperfect with *waw* consecutive) of הָלַל. Since its root was originally biliteral, הל, its D form יְהוֹלֵל (Is 44:25; Job 12:17; Eccl 7:7) can be called either Polel or Poel, and hence the HtD form here can be either Hithpolel or Hithpoel. הָלַל occurs commonly (over a hundred times) in the Piel (D) meaning "to praise." It appears in the Hithpolel six times in the OT (also Jer 25:16; 46:9; 50:38; 51:7; Nah 2:5 [ET 2:4]), meaning "be crazy, insane; act madly." This is the only time the Hithpolel refers to a feigned state, "*pretend* to be insane."

בְּיָדָם—Literally "in their hand," this is translated as "when he was under their authority." The LXX reads ἐν τῇ ἡμέρᾳ ἐκείνῃ, "on that day" (equivalent to a Hebrew reading בַּיּוֹם הַהוּא, as in 21:11 [ET 21:10]), which may be an intentional change in the LXX or its Vorlage to remove the concept that David would have been under Philistine authority.

וַיְתָיו—"He scribbled." This Qere is a third masculine singular Piel (D) preterite (imperfect with *waw* consecutive) of תָּוָה, a denominative verb from the noun תָּו (the name of the Hebrew letter *taw*), "a *taw*, mark, sign, cross"; hence the Piel (D) verb means "to make marks, scribble." The only other OT instance of this verb is the Hiphil (H) in Ezek 9:4, "to make a mark on; write a cross; make the sign of a cross."[2] Since the original form of the last Hebrew letter, תָּו or *taw*, was an X or cross, it was a mark that even those who were unable to write could make as a substitute for signing their name (Job 31:35). Here the Kethib is the same verb but spelled וַיְתַו, and the loss of the second *yod* probably resulted from the close proximity of two *waw*s and two *yod*s in ויתיו. The LXX reads ἐτυμπάνιζεν, "he beat upon" or "tormented," which might reflect a Hebrew text of ויתף, with a verb from the root תפף.[3]

וַיּוֹרֶד רִירוֹ אֶל־זְקָנוֹ:—Literally "and he caused his spittle to go down to his beard." The verb וַיּוֹרֶד is the Hiphil (H) of יָרַד. The noun רִיר here means "spittle." Its only

---

[2] See Christopher W. Mitchell, "(How) Should Lutherans Read the Old Testament? A Test Case: The Saving Cross in Ezekiel 9," in *The Restoration of Creation in Christ: Essays in Honor of Dean O. Wenthe* (St. Louis: Concordia, 2014), 37–52.

[3] McCarter, *I Samuel*, 355, understands the verb to be from the Aramaic root תפף, "spit." The only thing to recommend this is the reference to spittle in the next sentence; see the next textual note.

other OT occurrence is in Job 6:6, where it apparently refers to egg white. The noun זָקָן can mean either "chin" or "beard"; the latter is chosen for the translation here. It is clearly related to זָקֵן, which can be either the verb "be old" or the adjective "old (man)."

21:15 תִּרְאוּ אִישׁ מִשְׁתַּגֵּעַ—Literally "you see a man who is crazy." מִשְׁתַּגֵּעַ is a Hithpael (HtD) participle of שָׁגַע, "to be mad, crazy." The sibilant שׁ undergoes metathesis with the prefixed תּ of the Hithpael stem (see Waltke-O'Connor, § 26.1.1b, including example 8). This verb appears in the OT in the form of a Pual (Dp) participle five times, including the next verse (1 Sam 21:16 [ET 21:15]; also Deut 28:34; 2 Ki 9:11; Jer 29:26; Hos 9:7), and twice in the Hithpael, here and in the next verse.

21:16 חֲסַר מְשֻׁגָּעִים אָנִי—Literally "am I lacking of crazy men?" The pronoun אָנִי, "I," is the subject, and the predicate is the adjective חֲסַר, "needy, lacking," in construct with the plural Pual (Dp) participle of שָׁגַע, "be crazy" (see the textual note on 21:15 [ET 21:14]). In context the adjective חֲסַר can be translated as an elliptical comparison (see Joüon, § 141 i): "am I so lacking in crazy men that you have brought this man?" or "have I so few crazy men … ?" This initial question in 21:16 (ET 21:15) is not marked by an interrogative, but Hebrew questions need not be marked (GKC, § 150 a), and the second question (the last clause) of the verse is marked with an interrogative (on הֲזֶה). See Waltke-O'Connor, § 40.3b, including example 1.

לְהִשְׁתַּגֵּעַ עָלָי—Literally this means "to act crazy on/to me." The verb is the Hithpael (HtD) infinitive construct of שָׁגַע, for which, see the textual note on 21:15 (ET 21:14).

Commentary

c. 1014–c. 1013 BC

Upon leaving Nob, David went to King Achish of Gath, where Saul could not be a threat to him (21:11 [ET 21:10]). The name "Achish" may be Aegean/West Anatolian in origin. It is found in a list of Cretan names in an Egyptian text.[4] A seventh-century BC inscription from Ekron names "Akhayus [ʾkyš] son of Padi" as ruler of Ekron.[5] This same ruler is also mentioned as one of twelve kings of the seacoast who brought building materials to Nineveh for the palace of Esarhaddon (680–669 BC).[6] He is also named in a list of kings who took part in Ashurbanipal's first campaign to Egypt in 667 BC.[7] Naveh believes that the name "Akhayus" became Ἀχαιός in Greek, "Achaean," meaning "Greek."[8] This name may also be a cognate of the name Anchises, the father of Aeneas in the *Iliad*.[9] Such evidence may support the theory that the Philistines were originally from Crete (cf. Gen 10:14).

---

[4] Sasson, "The Inscription of Achish, Governor of Eqron, and Philistine Dialect, Cult and Culture," 632.

[5] Gitin, Dothan, and Naveh, "A Royal Dedicatory Inscription from Ekron," 8–11.

[6] *ANET*, 291. In *ANET* his name is spelled Ikausu.

[7] *ANET*, 294.

[8] Naveh, "Achish-Ikausu in the Light of the Ekron Dedication."

[9] See, for example, Homer, *Iliad*, 2.819; 20.160.

Achish is called "Abimelech" in Ps 34:1 (ET superscription). Evidence suggests that "Achish" may have been a traditional throne name for Gath's regents and that many of Gath's rulers assumed that name when they came to power. It ought to be noted that in 1 Samuel 21 the name of Achish's father is not given. However, in 1 Sam 27:2 Gath's ruler is called "Achish the son of Maoch, the king of Gath" (אָכִישׁ בֶּן־מָעוֹךְ מֶלֶךְ גַּת). This may indicate a change in rulers since David's first visit to Gath. Later, in 1 Ki 2:39 Gath's regent is "Achish the son of Maacah, the king of Gath" (אָכִישׁ בֶּן־מַעֲכָה מֶלֶךְ גַּת). While it is tempting to equate the very similar names "Maoch" and "Maacah," thereby equating the rulers mentioned in 1 Sam 27:2 and 1 Ki 2:39, we ought to note that the events in 1 Ki 2:39–46 took place at least three years after David's death (1 Ki 2:1–11), whereas the events in 1 Samuel 27 took place in the sixteen months before David became king (1 Sam 27:7). If the Achish in 1 Sam 27:2 were the same Achish in 1 Ki 2:39, then he would have reigned at least forty-five years (since David reigned forty years and six months [2 Sam 5:4–5]). That is an extremely long reign, making it likely that the Achish in 1 Sam 27:2 was a different person from the Achish in 1 Ki 2:39.[10] Thus, we probably know of three kings of Gath, all of whom took the throne name Achish: (1) Abimelech, who was king when David first went to Gath (1 Sam 21:11–16 [ET 21:10–15]; Ps 34:1 [ET superscription]); (2) the son of Maoch, under whom David served as a mercenary (1 Sam 27:1–12); and (3) the son of Maacah, to whom the servants of Shimei fled (1 Ki 2:39–46).

Achish is called "king" (1 Sam 21:11 [ET 21:10]). Collectively the rulers of the Philistine cities are called סְרָנִים, which this commentary translates as "governors," but this Hebrew noun always is used in the plural.[11] Since there apparently is no singular form for this title, the near-equivalent מֶלֶךְ, "king," is used here.

Interestingly, David is said to have come to Achish, not simply to the city of Gath. This may indicate that David offered his services to Achish, as he did to the later Achish (1 Sam 27:1–12). However, at this point in time, the rift between David and Saul may not have been apparent to the Philistines, leading Achish's courtiers to be suspicious of David (21:12 [ET 21:11]; cf. 29:1–11). They called David "the king of the land." The phrase "kings of the land" (מַלְכֵי הָאָרֶץ, Josh 12:1, 7) is used to describe rulers of various city-states in Palestine. Perhaps the Philistine courtiers were calling David some type of

---

[10] Of the forty-two kings of Israel and Judah (beginning with David since we have no definitive attestation in the OT to the length of Saul's reign), only three reigned more than forty years. Asa reigned forty-one years (1 Ki 15:9–10; 2 Chr 16:13), Azariah/Uzziah reigned fifty-two years (2 Ki 15:1–2; 2 Chr 26:3; fifty-one actual years), and Manasseh reigned fifty-five years (2 Ki 21:1; 2 Chr 33:1; fifty-four actual years). See Steinmann, *From Abraham to Paul*, 127–51, especially tables 31 and 32 on pages 141–42.

[11] Josh 13:3; Judg 3:3; 16:5, 8, 18, 23, 27, 30; 1 Sam 5:8, 11; 6:4, 12, 16, 18; 7:7; 29:2, 6, 7; 1 Chr 12:20 (ET 12:19).

local chieftain, but their words contain irony, since David had been anointed king of Israel (1 Sam 16:1–13).

The Philistines were also well-acquainted with David's reputation (21:12 [ET 21:11]). They quoted the song about him word-for-word as it appears in 18:7. While the Philistines may have originated in the Aegean Islands, by this time they had probably adopted some Semitic language akin to Hebrew, since David was able to understand their words and became afraid of Achish (21:13 [ET 21:12]).[12]

David exhibited his innate shrewdness by devising a plan to demonstrate that he was not a threat to Achish (21:14 [ET 21:13]). His feigned insanity took place in the city gate, the most public arena where it was common for the more important people of any city to congregate. David's lunacy did not go unnoticed by Achish (21:15–16 [ET 21:14–15]). His words are comical: "Have I so few crazy men that you brought this one to me?" He sardonically implies that he has other subjects—perhaps including some of his high officials—whom he might at times consider to be equally insane.

The verb שָׁגַע, "be crazy" (21:15 [twice], 16 [ET 21:14, 15]), elsewhere can designate prophets: they spoke for Yahweh and performed the actions he sent them to do, but the apostate people considered the prophets' words and behavior to be crazy (2 Ki 9:11; Jer 29:26).[13] This introduces another irony: David was perceived to behave like a prophet, just as Saul had on several occasions (1 Sam 10:9–13; 19:23–24). This serves to highlight the contrast between David and Saul. On the one hand, Saul had prophesied when the Spirit rushed upon him (10:6, 10; cf. 11:6).[14] However, Saul then rejected the Word of Yahweh (15:23, 26), and so the Spirit departed from him (16:14) and instead an evil spirit frequented him (16:14–23; 18:10; 19:9). On the other hand, the Spirit had rushed upon David (16:13) and remained with him as he was faithful to the Word. We may surmise that the Spirit gave him the insight into what kind of behavior would free him from danger in the court of Achish. We are not told how David was able to depart from Gath, although Ps 34:1 (ET superscription) says that Achish "expelled him" (וַיְגָרְשֵׁהוּ).

In the NT too God's spokesmen are sometimes alleged to be insane. During Jesus' earthly ministry some of his fellow kinsmen accused him of being possessed by an unclean spirit, and even his closest relatives considered him to be out of his mind (Mk 3:21–35). When the apostle Paul preached the Gospel of Jesus Christ in the presence of King Agrippa, Festus concluded that Paul's

---

[12] Note also that the Philistine Goliath had challenged Israel in a language that the Israelites could understand (17:10–11), and David could converse with him (17:43–47).

[13] The same verb for "be crazy" is in Hos 9:7, where, however, it appears to describe false prophets. The next verse, Hos 9:8, refers to true prophets.

[14] In 1 Sam 19:23–24 "the Spirit of God came upon" Saul and prevented him from harming David, but by that time Saul had become apostate (15:23, 26; 16:1). On that occasion (19:23–24) the Spirit overpowered Saul, but he remained in his state of unbelief.

erudition had driven him crazy (Acts 26:24–25). Pastors today may face the same allegation by those who disbelieve the Gospel they proclaim.

This short account serves to underscore the difference between David and Saul. Saul was reluctant to confront the Philistines and disobeyed Yahweh's instructions to do so.[15] David, however, was bold in engaging the Philistines, and even despite his fear of Achish (1 Sam 21:13 [ET 21:12]), he managed to outfox the Philistine king (21:14–16 [ET 21:13–15]). While Saul never managed to gain the upper hand against the Philistine foes of Israel, this is the second time that David had proven himself to be superior to the Philistines. In the first instance he overcame Goliath's skill as a warrior (1 Samuel 17). Now he outsmarted Achish, something he would do again when serving as a mercenary for another Achish (27:8–12).

---

[15] Samuel's instructions in 1 Sam 10:7 implied that Saul was to eradicate the Philistine garrison in Gibeah, but he failed to do so (later his son Jonathan did so in 14:1–16). See the discussion in "Samuel Anoints Saul (9:26–10:8)" in the commentary on 9:26–10:16, including figure 16, "Saul's Faltering Accession." See also the beginning of the commentary on 10:17–27a.

1 Samuel 22:1–5

David in Adullam and Moab

Translation

22 ¹David went from there and escaped to the cave at Adullam. His brothers and his father's entire house heard [about it] and came down to him there. ²Every man who was in trouble, every man who was in debt, and every man who was discontented gathered to him, and he became their leader. About four hundred men were with him. ³David went from there to Mizpeh in Moab. He said to the king of Moab, "Let my father and my mother live with you until I know what God will do to me." ⁴So he left them in the presence of the king of Moab, and they lived with him the entire time David was in the stronghold.

⁵The prophet Gad said to David, "Do not stay in the stronghold. Leave and go to the land of Judah." So David left and went to the forest of Hereth.

Textual Notes

22:1 וַיִּמָּלֵט—For "and he escaped," see the third textual note on 19:10.

מְעָרַת עֲדֻלָּם—A construct phrase can express a variety of relationships between the two nouns. Here מְעָרָה, "cave," is in construct with the place-name עֲדֻלָּם, which designates its location, hence "the cave *at* Adullam." See also מִצְפֵּה מוֹאָב, "Mizpeh in Moab," in 22:3.

22:2 וַיִּתְקַבְּצוּ—This Hithpael (HtD) of קָבַץ, "and they gathered," is discussed in the first textual note on 7:6.

כָּל־אִישׁ מָצוֹק—This construct chain is literally "every man of trouble." Here the relationship between the nouns is equivalent to the English "every man *in* trouble." The noun מָצוֹק signifies extreme duress or misery (Deut 28:53, 55, 57; Jer 19:9; Ps 119:143) and is derived from the verb צוּק, whose Hiphil (H) means "to constrain, press upon." This is the sole instance of this noun in the book of Samuel.

וְכָל־אִישׁ אֲשֶׁר־לוֹ נֹשֶׁא—Literally this means "and every man who had a creditor." The preposition לְ is used in the sense of possession (לוֹ means "he had"). נֹשֶׁא is a Qal (G) masculine singular participle of נָשָׁא, "to lend." Normally the stem vowel in a Qal participle of a third-*aleph* verb would be *tsere* (נֹשֵׁא), but this is an example of the vowels of a third-*he* verb being used for a third-*aleph* verb (נֹשֶׁא, as if it were נֹשֶׂה); see GKC, § 75 oo. Sometimes נָשָׁא is used for making a loan with interest charged (see Neh 5:7–11) even though charging interest was prohibited among Israelites (Ex 22:24 [ET 22:25]). In the Qal this verb usually appears as a participle used as a substantive, "a lender," and in relation to the person who owes a debt to him, hence "a creditor."

וְכָל־אִישׁ מַר־נֶפֶשׁ—Literally "and every man bitter of soul," this can be rendered as "and every discontented man" or "and every malcontent." The construct phrase מַר־נֶפֶשׁ is in apposition to the noun אִישׁ.

420

22:3 יֵצֵא־נָ֨א אָבִ֤י וְאִמִּי֙ אִתְּכֶ֔ם—The MT with the jussive יֵצֵא literally reads "please let my father and my mother go out with you [plural]." This might refer to David's parents exiting the cave (22:1) to be with (live among) the residents of Mizpeh.[1] The translation follows the proposal to emend יֵצֵא to יֵשֶׁב, the jussive of יָשַׁב, meaning "let my father and mother live/stay with you," based on the Vulgate (*maneat*) and the Syriac (ܢܬܒ). יָשַׁב is used in the clause וַיֵּשְׁב֥וּ עִמּ֖וֹ, "and they lived with him," in 22:4.

22:4 וַיַּנְחֵ֕ם אֶת־פְּנֵ֖י מֶ֥לֶךְ מוֹאָ֑ב—The MT reads "and he led them (to) the face/presence of the king of Moab." The verb וַיַּנְחֵם is the Hiphil (H) third masculine singular preterite (imperfect with *waw* consecutive) of נָחָה, "to lead, guide," with a third masculine plural object suffix. The syntax may be compared to וְלִפְנֵ֖י גְדֹלִ֣ים יַנְחֶֽנּוּ in Prov 18:16. Many emend the verb to וַיַּנִּחֵם, a Hiphil third masculine singular preterite (imperfect with *waw* consecutive) of נוּחַ with a third masculine plural object suffix, meaning "and he left them" (ESV; similarly, HCSB). The two Hiphil conjugations of נוח have different meanings; וַיַּנִּחֵם would be in the conjugation formed as if from the root ננח and with the meaning "place, put, leave." That form, but spelled plene, or *maleʾ*, וַיַּנִּיחֵם, appears in 2 Chr 1:14; 9:25.

בַּמְּצוּדָֽה:—The noun מְצוּדָה II, "stronghold, fortress" (derived from צוּד I), recurs in the next verse (22:5) and in 1 Sam 24:23 (ET 24:22); 2 Sam 5:7, 9, 17; 22:2; 23:14.

22:5 גָּ֨ד הַנָּבִ֜יא—The noun with the article, הַנָּבִיא, "the prophet," is in apposition to the proper name גָּד, "Gad," and denotes his vocation (Joüon, § 131 k).

לֵ֤ךְ וּבָֽאתָ־לְּךָ֙—After the imperative לֵךְ ("leave"), the perfect with *waw* consecutive, וּבָאתָ, functions as another imperative, "and go." The preposition לְ is used here reflexively (BDB, 5 h (*b*); GKC, § 119 s). It has a *daghesh forte conjunctivum* (־לְּ) since the two words וּבָֽאתָ־לְּךָ֙ are joined by a *maqqeph* and the first word, וּבָאתָ, has no full accent and only the secondary accent *metheg* (־בָ֑־). See GKC, § 20 f.

יַ֣עַר חָֽרֶת:—The noun חָרֶת is the pausal form of the segholate חֶרֶת. For its meaning and the relationship between these two words, see the commentary.

Commentary

c. 1014–c. 1013 BC

David's escape from Gath led him ten miles (sixteen kilometers) to the southeast, to the caves in the vicinity of Adullam (22:1). Adullam was a city in central Judah and is mentioned several times in the OT.[2] It may have been at what is now modern Tell esh-Sheikh Madhkur. Immediately David's whereabouts

---

[1] Tsumura (*The First Book of Samuel*, 539, including n. 7) seeks to defend the MT by claiming that "go out" is short for "go out and in," meaning "live [in a place]." In some passages the combination of the verbs יָצָא and בּוֹא may have such a meaning (2 Ki 19:27 ‖ Is 37:28; Ps 121:8). However, there are no other examples of יָצָא alone with this meaning. Often in the book of Samuel the verb יָצָא refers to "going out" to wage war (see the first textual note on 18:6), but such a meaning does not fit this context. In Samuel the coordinated combination of יָצָא and בּוֹא, "go out" and "come in," always refers to military campaigns (1 Sam 18:13, 16; 29:6; 2 Sam 5:2).

[2] Also Josh 12:15; 15:35; 2 Sam 23:13; Micah 1:15; Neh 11:30; 1 Chr 11:15; 2 Chr 11:7. In addition, a certain Adullamite is mentioned in Gen 38:1, 12, 20.

became known. He first attracted his family (22:1) and then men who were somehow disaffected under Saul's reign (22:2). At this point David led four hundred men, a number that eventually would grow to six hundred (23:13; 25:13; 27:2; 30:9–10).

David next went to Moab to find a safe haven for his parents (22:3). The location of Mizpeh is unknown, but it appears to be Moab's capital at this time. David's request to the king of Moab was for temporary domicile for his parents—"until I know what God will do to me." Although he knew God (through Samuel) had anointed him to be king (16:1–13), he did not know what events would transpire along the route to the throne. In keeping the Fourth Commandment (Ex 20:12; Deut 5:16), he sought to provide for his parents as Joseph had provided for his father (Gen 47:11–12) and Jesus would later provide for his mother (Jn 19:26–27).

David's choice of Moab most likely came from family connections through his ancestor Ruth (Ruth 4:13, 18–22). In addition, the king of Moab might have been willing to supply sanctuary for adversaries of his enemy Saul (1 Sam 14:47). There are several other instances of such sanctuary in the OT (1 Sam 27:4–5; 1 Ki 11:17–18, 40; 12:2; 2 Ki 25:26).

David left his parents in Mizpeh, where they stayed while he was "in the stronghold" (1 Sam 22:4). Opinions vary as to where this stronghold was located. Some claim that it was in Moab, while others suggest that it was at modern Masada, just west of the Dead Sea, and still others propose that it was at Adullam.[3] However, Gad's prophecy commanding David to go to Judah suggests that this particular stronghold could not have been located at Adullam or Masada, both of which were in the territory of Judah. Another factor is that Gad's directive (22:5) may have been an application of Deut 23:4–7 (ET 23:3–6), which prohibited alliances with Moab.[4] Thus, a stronghold somewhere in Moab is the most logical candidate, and David had to leave Moab to keep Yahweh's command. It does not appear as if David was in Moabite territory for very long.

David took his parents (since they stayed with the king of Moab only as long as David was in the stronghold [22:4]) and went to the forest of Hereth in Judah (22:5). The location of Hereth is unknown, though it has been suggested that "Hereth" is the Old Aramaic equivalent of "Horesh" (23:15).[5] The Hebrew חֹרֶשׁ, *ḥoresh*, means "woods" (Is 17:9; Ezek 31:3; 2 Chr 24:7), and the Aramaic חורשׁ means "forest" (*CAL*). If correct, this would probably locate Hereth at modern Khirbet Khoreisa, about six miles (ten kilometers) southeast of Hebron. This also would allow for the possibility that instead of יַעַר חָרֶת

---

[3] See the options listed in Bergen, *1, 2 Samuel*, 225–26; Tsumura, *The First Book of Samuel*, 540; Auld, *I and II Samuel*, 265. McCarter, *I Samuel*, 357, favors Adullam.

[4] This factor is set forth by Bergen, *1, 2 Samuel*, 226.

[5] This was first suggested by Wellhausen, *Die Text der Bücher Samuelis untersucht*, 124; see also Klein, *1 Samuel*, 223.

(22:5) being a construct phrase ("the forest of Hereth"), the second noun could be in apposition to the first, "the forest, that is, the woods." This location has much to commend it. It would place the Hereth/Horesh forest on the southern reaches of the wilderness of Ziph (1 Sam 23:15, 16, 18, 19). Thus, when David returned to Judah, he went farther away from Saul. Moreover, it would mean that David left Hereth/Horesh to go north to rescue Keilah (23:1–6), and then when Saul was advancing on Keilah, he returned to the wilderness of Ziph and eventually to Hereth/Horesh (23:7–18).

The prophet Gad appears in the narrative without introduction. He will appear again at the end of the book of Samuel with a prophecy of judgment on David for taking a census (2 Sam 24:11–19; 1 Chr 21:9–19). He must have been a regular member of David's inner circle, since he later wrote an account of David's reign (1 Chr 29:29) and, along with David and Nathan, organized the musicians who would serve in the temple (2 Chr 29:25).

Saul Kills the Priests at Nob

Translation

22 **⁶**Saul heard that David and the men who were with him were known. Saul was sitting in Gibeah under the tamarisk tree at the high place with a spear in his hand, and all of his servants were standing around him. **⁷**Saul said to his servants who were standing around him, "Listen, Benjaminites! Will Jesse's son give all of you fields and vineyards? Will he make all of you commanders in charge of a thousand men or commanders in charge of a hundred men? **⁸**Yet all of you have conspired against me. None of you informs me when my son makes an agreement with Jesse's son. No one is sorry for me and informs me that my son has raised up my servant as an ambush against me, as is the case today."

⁹Doeg the Edomite answered (he was in charge of Saul's servants). He said, "I saw Jesse's son come to Nob to Ahimelech the son of Ahitub. **¹⁰**He inquired of Yahweh for him, gave him provisions, and gave him the sword of Goliath the Philistine."

¹¹The king sent to summon the high priest Ahimelech the son of Ahitub and his entire family, the priests who were in Nob. All of them came to the king. **¹²**Saul said, "Listen, son of Ahitub!"

He replied, "Yes, my lord."

¹³Saul said to him, "Why have you and Jesse's son conspired against me by giving him bread and a sword and by inquiring of God for him? [You did this] to set up an ambush against me, as is the case today."

¹⁴Ahimelech answered the king, "Who among all your servants is as trustworthy as David, the king's son-in-law, the commander of your bodyguard, and an honored man in your house? **¹⁵**Is today the beginning of my inquiring of God for him? Certainly not! Your Majesty shouldn't blame your servant and my entire family for in all this your servant did not know anything whatsoever."

¹⁶The king said, "You will surely die, Ahimelech—you and your whole family."

¹⁷Then the king said to the runners standing around him, "Turn and kill the priests of Yahweh, since they also support David and since they knew that he was fleeing and they did not inform me." But the king's servants were not willing to lift a hand to strike the priests of Yahweh.

¹⁸So the king said to Doeg, "You turn and strike the priests." So Doeg the Edomite turned, and he himself struck the priests. That day he killed eighty-five men who wore linen ephods. **¹⁹**And Nob, the city of the priests, he struck with a sword—men and women, children and infants, herds and donkeys and flocks.

²⁰But one son of Ahimelech the son of Ahitub escaped. His name was Abiathar. He fled to David, **²¹**and Abiathar reported to David that Saul had killed the priests of Yahweh. **²²**So David said to Abiathar, "I knew on that day when Doeg the

Edomite was there that he would certainly tell Saul. I turned against every life in your family. ²³Stay with me. Don't be afraid, because the one who is seeking your life is [also] seeking my life. However, you will be safe with me."

Textual Notes

22:6 כִּי נוֹדַע דָּוִד וַאֲנָשִׁים אֲשֶׁר אִתּוֹ—The phrase "David and the men who were with him" is the compound subject of the third masculine singular Niphal (N) perfect נוֹדַע, of יָדַע, "to know." It is translated as "were known." It is often understood to mean "had been found" or "were discovered" (see *HALOT*, Niphal, 3). However, such a meaning would be unique to this passage. Instead, Saul may have received reports about David now having a band of men with him, not necessarily a report of David's whereabouts. This would explain why Saul twice mentions David setting up an ambush for him (22:8, 13). Saul may have assumed that David was gathering forces to overthrow him.

הָאֶשֶׁל—Eight species of "the tamarisk tree" are native to Palestine. Tamarisks have slender branches and grey-green foliage. They are flowing trees whose blossoms range from pink to white and are grouped in dense masses. Abraham planted a tamarisk tree at Beersheba where he called on Yahweh, the everlasting God (יהוה אֵל עוֹלָם, Gen 21:33). Ironically, Saul will be buried under a tamarisk tree (1 Sam 31:13).

בָּרָמָה—This is translated as "at the high place." Four times in Ezekiel 16 (Ezek 16:24, 25, 31, 39), the noun רָמָה I, "high place," denotes a shrine. If רָמָה does so here, it would reinforce Saul's apostasy (cf. 1 Sam 15:23, 26). רָמָה II is the place-name (thus "in Ramah," KJV), but elsewhere it never refers to a location in Gibeah.

נִצָּבִים עָלָיו—Literally this means "standing over him." The Niphal (N) participle of נָצַב, "to stand," can be used for attendants (see the first textual note on 4:20), as again in 22:7, 17. Its singular can also signify a position of leadership over others, as in 19:20; 22:9.

22:7 בְּנֵי יְמִינִי—This means "Benjaminites." The singular "Benjaminite" is the construct phrase בֶּן־יְמִינִי (e.g., 9:21). The plural here is formed by making only the first word of the construct phrase plural, בְּנֵי, "sons of …" See Joüon, § 136 m.

לְכֻלְּכֶם יָשִׂים שָׂרֵי אֲלָפִים וְשָׂרֵי מֵאוֹת—"Will he make all of you commanders in charge of a thousand men or commanders in charge of a hundred men?" For these military offices, see the first textual note on 8:12. Usually when שׂוּם or שִׂים (here יָשִׂים is Qal [G]) means "to make someone (be) something," it takes a double accusative construction.[1] Here, however, the people (normally the first accusative) are in a prepositional phrase, לְכֻלְּכֶם, literally "to all of you," probably in imitation of the preceding clause, which also has לְכֻלְּכֶם, but there it was an indirect object ("give to all of you").

22:8 קְשַׁרְתֶּם כֻּלְּכֶם עָלַי—In the Qal (G) קָשַׁר can mean "to bind (together)" (cf. the Niphal [N] in 18:1), but it can also mean "to conspire," with עַל in the adversative sense, "against" someone. The same idiom recurs in 22:13 (קְשַׁרְתֶּם עָלָי). See also the verb's

---

[1] See Joüon, § 125 w, which, however, cites 1 Sam 22:7 as if שִׂים took a double accusative construction (as in 1 Sam 11:11; 18:13).

425

participle, meaning "conspirators," in 2 Sam 15:31, and the cognate noun קֶשֶׁר, "conspiracy," in 2 Sam 15:12.

וְאֵין־גֹּלֶה אֶת־אָזְנִי ... וְגֹלֶה אֶת־אָזְנִי—"None of you informs me … and informs me." For this idiom, literally "uncovers my ear," see the textual note on 9:15 and the fourth textual note on 20:2. It recurs in 22:17.

בִּכְרָת־בְּנִי עִם־בֶּן־יִשַׁי—Literally this means "when my son cuts with the son of Jesse." בִּכְרָת is the Qal (G) infinitive construct of כָּרַת with the preposition בְּ in a temporal sense. Normally the Hebrew idiom is כָּרַת with the noun בְּרִית, "covenant, agreement," but occasionally the verb is used alone, with the noun implied, as here (also 1 Sam 11:2; 20:16; 1 Ki 8:9; 2 Chr 5:10). For the full idiom, see the third textual note on 11:1. It is used for the covenant between Jonathan and David in 18:3; 23:18.

וְאֵין־חֹלֶה מִכֶּם עָלַי—Literally "and there is no one from you being sick over me," this means "and none of you feels sorry over me." The verb חָלָה, "be weak, sick," is apparently metaphorical here. Some propose emending חֹלֶה to חֹמֵל, "having compassion."

הֵקִים בְּנִי אֶת־עַבְדִּי עָלַי לְאֹרֵב כַּיּוֹם הַזֶּה:—Literally "my son raised up my servant against me to (be an) ambusher, as this day." אֹרֵב is the Qal (G) participle of אָרַב, "to lie in wait." This verb usually occurs as a participle used as a substantive, meaning "ambush" (BDB, Qal). A similar clause concludes 22:13.

22:9 נִצָּב עַל—Literally "standing over," this signifies a position of leadership, "in charge of." See the end of the fourth textual note on 22:6.

22:10 וַיִּשְׁאַל־לוֹ בַּיהוָה—Literally "he inquired for him of Yahweh." The prepositional phrase לוֹ, "for him," has the sense of advantage ("for his sake/benefit") and refers to David. In place of בַּיהוָה, "of Yahweh," 4QSamᵃ (באלו]הים) and the LXX (διὰ τοῦ θεοῦ) read "of God," perhaps by attraction to 22:13.

וְצֵידָה—The singular collective צֵידָה, translated as "provisions," refers to the loaves of holy bread (21:5–7 [ET 21:4–6]).

22:11 הַכֹּהֵן—For the translation of this as "the high priest," see the third textual note on 1:9. The LXX omits this term here.

כָּל־בֵּית אָבִיו—Literally "the whole house of his father," this is common phraseology for close relatives, including cousins, uncles, aunts, nephews, and nieces. Variations of the phrase recur in 22:15, 16, 22 (cf. 22:1).

22:12 הִנְנִי אֲדֹנִי:—Literally "behold I, my lord," this indicates readiness to serve. See הִנֵּנִי (pausal: הִנֵּנִי) in 3:4, 5, 6, 8, 16; also Is 6:8.

22:13 קְשַׁרְתֶּם ... בְּתִתְּךָ לוֹ לֶחֶם וְחֶרֶב—An infinitive construct (בְּתִתְּךָ) can follow a finite verb (קְשַׁרְתֶּם) and describe in more detail how the action was accomplished (see Joüon, § 124 o), thus "you conspired … *by your giving* to him bread and a sword." בְּתִתְּךָ is the Qal (G) infinitive construct of נָתַן, "give," with the preposition בְּ and a subjective pronominal suffix.

וְשָׁאוֹל לוֹ בֵּאלֹהִים—This is a rare case where a finite verb followed by an infinitive construct with a preposition (see the preceding textual note) is then continued by an infinitive absolute without a preposition (שָׁאוֹל). The infinitive absolute then has the

426

same force as an infinitive construct, thus "you conspired … by giving … *and by inquiring* of God for him." See Joüon, § 124 r.

לָקוּם—Saul phrases his accusation as a purpose clause (Qal [G] infinitive construct with לְ), as if Ahimelech had carried out these actions deliberately "to set up" an ambush (see the last textual note on 22:8).

22:14 וְסָר אֶל־מִשְׁמַעְתֶּךָ—The noun מִשְׁמַעַת appears three times in the OT with the meaning "bodyguard" (also 2 Sam 23:23; 1 Chr 11:25; it denotes a "subjugated people" in Is 11:14; see *HALOT*). In form סָר appears to be the Qal (G) participle of סוּר, which could mean that David "turns aside (from his other duties) to (be part of) your bodyguard." More likely, however, סָר is an orthographic variant (or homophonic substitution) for שַׂר, "commander," as suggested by the LXX (καὶ ἄρχων) and the Targum (see also HCSB, ESV, GW, NET, NIV). Samuel is one of the OT books in which the preposition אֶל is often used in place of עַל (BDB, s.v. אֶל, note 2). Here אֶל means "over," which is more frequently a meaning of עַל.

22:15 הַחִלֹּתִי לִשְׁאָל־לוֹ בֵאלֹהִים—The OT contains more than one homographic verb חָלַל. This one, in the Hiphil (H), can mean "to begin" or "to do for the first time" (see BDB, s.v. חָלַל III, Hiphil, 2; *HALOT*, s.v. חלל I, Hiphil, 2). For the form הַחִלֹּתִי, see Joüon, § 82 n. This verb regularly takes an infinitive construct as its object (Joüon, § 124 c) to specify the action begun. Here the infinitive construct is the Qal (G) of שָׁאַל, "to ask, inquire, request." Its Qere form is לִשְׁאָל (the vowel under the *aleph*, ־ָא-, is *qamets chatuph*, shortened from וֹ), while its Kethib would be pointed with the usual *holem*, לִשְׁאוֹל. As elsewhere in the book the author may intend a play between the verb שָׁאַל and the name שָׁאוּל, "Saul," meaning "requested," especially since the unpointed Kethib here could be vocalized לְשָׁאוּל, "for Saul."[2]

חָלִילָה לִי—For "certainly not," see the second textual note on 2:30.

אַל־יָשֵׂם הַמֶּלֶךְ בְּעַבְדּוֹ דָבָר—Literally "the king should not set a word against his servant." The verb יָשֵׂם is the Qal (G) jussive of שִׂים. Here the preposition בְּ has the adversative sense "against." For the deferential third-person reference to oneself as someone's "servant," see the third textual note on 1:11.

בְּכָל־בֵּית אָבִי—This means "against my entire family." The MT lacks a conjunction, i.e., וּבְכָל, but one is supplied in the LXX, καὶ ἐφ᾽ ὅλον τὸν οἶκον τοῦ πατρός μου.

לֹא־יָדַע … דָּבָר קָטֹן אוֹ גָדוֹל:—"He did not know anything whatsoever" is literally "he did not know a word, small or large." See the similar expression in 25:36.

22:17 סֹבּוּ—This is the Qal (G) masculine plural imperative of סָבַב. In the Qal its meaning can be intransitive, "to turn," often as "preliminary to" carrying out another action (BDB, 1 a), which here would be to kill the priests (see וְהָמִיתוּ in the next textual note). That is its sense twice in 22:18, where Doeg is commanded to turn and kill the priests and does so. The Qal could also be transitive, with כֹּהֲנֵי יְהוָה as its direct object,

---

[2] For this wordplay elsewhere, see the first textual note on 1:28; "Samuel Warns Israel about Kings (8:10–22)" in the commentary on 8:1–22; the first textual note on 10:22; the commentary on 12:13; the textual note on 14:37; and the second textual note on 20:6 (which also discusses שָׁאוּל נִשְׁאַל in 20:28).

meaning "to surround," since the verb is used with this meaning for hostile purposes, such as laying siege to a town (BDB, 2 d; for marching around Jericho in Josh 6:3–15).

וְהָמִיתוּ כֹּהֲנֵי יְהוָה—This means "and kill the priests of Yahweh." The verb is the masculine plural Hiphil (H) imperative of מוּת, "to die." Its Hiphil has the causative meaning "to kill, put to death." Its Hiphil preterite (imperfect with *waw* consecutive) וַיָּמֶת is used in 22:18.

גַּם־יָדָם עִם־דָּוִד—Literally "also their hand is with David," this means that the other priests too (along with Ahimelech) support David.

וְלֹא גָלוּ אֶת־אָזְנִי—For "and they did not inform me," see the second textual note on 22:8. The Qere is אָזְנִי, "my ear," which is supported by the LXX, τὸ ὠτίον μου. The Kethib is אָזְנוֹ, "his ear," probably by confusion of the original *yod* with *waw*.

לִשְׁלֹחַ אֶת־יָדָם—"To lift a hand" is literally "to send a hand." This idiom means to extend one's hand to perform an action.

לִפְגֹעַ—This means "to strike." In 10:5 the Qal (G) of פָּגַע simply meant "to meet, encounter," but it is used with the meaning "strike down" or "execute" here, twice in the next verse (22:18), and in 2 Sam 1:15.

22:18 לְדוֹאֵג ... דּוֹאֵג—Twice in this verse and again in 22:22 the Qere is דּוֹאֵג, "Doeg," while the Kethib is דּוֹיֵג, "Doyeg."

וַיִּפְגַּע־הוּא—The LXX omits "and he himself struck."

שְׁמֹנִים וַחֲמִשָּׁה—"Eighty-five" is the reading of the MT. The LXX reads three hundred and five (τριακοσίους καὶ πέντε). Josephus reads "three hundred and eighty-five" (with "eighty-five" as a variant reading).[3] It appears as if the text probably used by Josephus was expanded by three hundred. The LXX appears to have had a similar text from which the word "eighty" had dropped out. It is unlikely that "three hundred" was original but accidentally dropped out of the MT, since this would require the omission of two words: שְׁלֹשׁ מֵאוֹת. However, there is a slight possibility that these two words were lost due to homoioarchton (if a scribe's eye skipped from the first שׁ of שְׁלֹשׁ to the שׁ of שְׁמֹנִים).

נֹשֵׂא אֵפוֹד בָּד:—For this idiom for wearing an ephod, see the fourth textual note on 2:28. A translation for the noun בָּד, "linen," is lacking in the LXX.

22:19 לְפִי־חֶרֶב—Literally "by mouth of a sword" (as in 15:8), this prepositional phrase is translated literally by the LXX as ἐν στόματι ῥομφαίας. It is repeated at the end of the verse in the MT but omitted there in the LXX and in the translation above.

מֵאִישׁ וְעַד־אִשָּׁה מֵעוֹלֵל וְעַד־יוֹנֵק וְשׁוֹר וַחֲמוֹר וָשֶׂה—This same phraseology and vocabulary was in 15:3. See the fourth textual note on 15:3 and the first diagram in "Saul's Attack on the Amalekites (15:1–9)" in the commentary on 15:1–35.

22:20 וַיִּמָּלֵט—"But he escaped." See the third textual note on 19:10.

וַיִּבְרַח אַחֲרֵי דָוִד:—Literally "and he fled after David." For the verb, see the second textual note on 19:12. The preposition אַחֲרֵי has a pregnant sense, meaning that he went to David and became one of his followers; see the second textual note on 12:14.

---

[3] Josephus, *Antiquities*, 6.260.

22:22 אָנֹכִי סַבֹּתִי בְּכָל־נֶפֶשׁ בֵּית אָבִיךָ‎:—Literally "I myself turned against every life of the house of your father." The verb סַבֹּתִי (the Qal [G] of סָבַב) likely has the same sense, "to turn," as in 22:17–18 (see the first textual note on 22:17). The sense of the preposition בְּ is adversative, "against," as in the third textual note on 22:15. David claims responsibility for the deaths of Abiathar's family members (cf. כָּל־בֵּית אָבִיו in the second textual note on 22:11), and the emphatic pronoun אָנֹכִי, "I myself," helps convey his personal feeling of guilt. The LXX translates with ἐγώ εἰμι αἴτιος, "I myself am responsible."[4] Based on the LXX some have proposed a Hebrew reading with the verb חוּב, "be guilty," either the Qal (G) perfect חַבְתִּי (so *DCH*, s.v. חוב, Qal), which would mean "I am guilty," or the Piel (D) perfect חִיַּבְתִּי, which could mean "I endangered" (see *DCH*, s.v. חוב, Piel). In the OT this verb occurs only in Dan 1:10, where its Piel perfect appears in the context "you made my head guilty to the king," i.e., "you endangered my life." Forms of this verb also appear in Sirach 11:18 and 4QTohBᵃ (4Q275) 1.2.

22:23 שְׁבָה—This is the alternate form (with paragogic *he*) of the masculine singular Qal (G) imperative of יָשַׁב, "live, stay."

אֲשֶׁר־יְבַקֵּשׁ אֶת־נַפְשִׁי יְבַקֵּשׁ אֶת־נַפְשֶׁךָ—Literally "(he) who is seeking my life (is he who) is seeking your life." However, that word order in English could imply that Abiathar is at greater risk if he joins David, so the translation reverses the order of the clauses. The imperfect Piel (D) verb יְבַקֵּשׁ denotes ongoing action in the present time.[5] The Piel (D) of בָּקַשׁ is thematic in the narrative of Saul's pursuit of David. See 19:2, 10; 20:1; and "Jonathan Defends David (19:1–7)" in the commentary on 19:1–17.

מִשְׁמֶרֶת אַתָּה עִמָּדִי‎:—Literally "you are something guarded with me." The feminine noun מִשְׁמֶרֶת usually has an active sense, referring to the act of watching or guarding, but here it has a passive sense, denoting something that is guarded or entrusted to someone for protection (*HALOT*, 1; *CDCH*, 4). David is stating that he is taking responsibility for Abiathar's safety against the threats from Saul.

Commentary

c. 1014–c. 1013 BC

The execution of the priests of Nob not only demonstrates Saul's apostasy (15:23, 26) and growing paranoia, but it also continues the theme of the judgment on the house of the high priest Eli that was first introduced in 2:27–36. Eli's sons perished in 4:11, and he himself expired in 4:18. Now most of Eli's other descendants would be killed, and only Abiathar would escape. Abiathar would serve as high priest, sharing that office with Zadok during David's reign (2 Sam 20:25). After David's death Solomon would banish Abiathar for supporting his half-brother Adonijah as David's successor, thereby completing the judgment on Eli's house (1 Ki 2:26–27).

---

[4] This reading is followed by HCSB, ESV, GW, NET, NIV.

[5] *IBH*, § 47 B; Waltke-O'Connor, § 31.3b; Joüon, § 113 d.

In Gibeah Saul Hears about David and His Men (22:6–10)

The scene opens with Saul receiving a report that David now had a band of men gathered around him (see the first textual note on 22:6). Saul was under a tamarisk tree holding court at the high place in Gibeah. Previously, on the day that Jonathan attacked the Philistine garrison at Gibeah, Saul was holding court under a pomegranate tree in Migron (14:2). Saul, as usual, was holding his spear (18:10; 19:9).

Saul began to challenge his servants, whom he addressed as Benjaminites and asked whether David, a Judahite, would grant them boons (22:7). Note that he once again referred to David disparagingly as "the son of Jesse" to avoid using his name (as in 20:27, 30–31). The favors Saul listed—fields, vineyards, positions as officers in the army—were kingly prerogatives about which Samuel had warned Israel (8:12, 14). Saul's words assumed that the right to grant these privileges was afforded a king and that David would avail himself of that right, but not for the benefit of Benjaminites. Saul clearly expected David to attempt to seize the throne.

Saul then accused his servants of conspiring against him by not reporting what he considered Jonathan's conspiracy to raise up David against him (22:8). We are not told how Saul came to know about the pact between David and Jonathan (cf. 19:1–7). This is the third time that Saul in some way has threatened Jonathan (previously in 14:43–45; 20:30–33). We are not told whether Jonathan was present to hear that he was accused of treason, but he is not recorded as defending himself, nor is anyone else recorded as defending him. Ironically, Saul's words make Saul appear to readers to be monomaniacal and out of control.

The only person to speak up was Doeg, an Edomite foreigner in Saul's service (22:9). He aligned himself with Saul by also calling David "the son of Jesse" and by reporting on David's time in Nob with Ahimelech. Doeg claimed that Ahimelech performed three services for David (22:10). He accused Ahimelech of inquiring of Yahweh for David, although that is not mentioned in 21:2–10 (ET 21:1–9). In fact, the only recorded instances when David inquired (שָׁאַל) of Yahweh are later in the book.[6] Doeg also asserted that Ahimelech gave David "provisions" (צֵידָה, 22:10). It is striking that Doeg did not mention that these provisions were loaves of the holy bread from the tabernacle (see 21:5–7 [ET 21:4–6]). Perhaps Doeg, an Edomite, did not know the significance of this bread or, if he did know it, did not think that to be the major transgression of the priest in light of the accusation of inquiring of Yahweh. Finally, he noted that Ahimelech gave Goliath's sword to David (see 21:10 [ET 21:9]).

---

[6] 1 Sam 23:2, 4; 30:8; 2 Sam 2:1; 5:19, 23. In all these verses David inquires of "Yahweh" (rather than "God").

Saul Accuses the Priests at Nob of Treason and Has Them Executed (22:11–19)

Because of Doeg's allegation Saul summoned Ahimelech and his family—presumably the males only—to Gibeah (22:11). All of them came. Saul addressed Ahimelech with the same type of reference he had used for David: "son of Ahitub" (22:12). Saul did not conduct a trial. He had already concluded that Ahimelech was guilty, so he simply accused the high priest of conspiring with David, attributing to him the same motive he had attributed to Jonathan (22:8): to set an ambush against him (22:13). Interestingly, Saul said that Ahimelech gave David "bread" (לֶחֶם, 22:13) instead of Doeg's term "provisions" (צֵידָה, 22:10). Perhaps Saul was using לֶחֶם in the more generic sense of "food." He placed the charge of inquiring of God last (in 22:13) to give it the most emphasis.

Ahimelech sought to defend himself, even though Saul had already condemned him. His defense had two parts. First, he pointed out David's status as a legitimate reason for him to have aided him—why would the high priest not assume that his cooperation was expected (22:14)? David not only had a reputation for being trustworthy, but he was also part of the royal family by marriage (18:27), an officer in Saul's court (18:13), and an honored member of Saul's household (18:30; cf. 18:7). Ahimelech had no reason not to help David, because Saul himself had treated David as trustworthy (cf. 17:31–39), made him his son-in-law, given him responsibility in his court, and honored him. Interestingly, Ahimelech called David "the commander of your [i.e., Saul's] bodyguard," although David is not given that title elsewhere. Later, Benaiah the son of Jehoiada would serve in that capacity for David (2 Sam 23:22–23; 1 Chr 11:24–25). Second, Ahimelech's rhetorical question in 22:15 implied that he had been inquiring of God for David for some time and that he had done so with Saul's knowledge (22:15). However, Ahimelech did not admit to inquiring of Yahweh for David during his most recent visit to Nob (21:2–10 [ET 21:1–9]). Perhaps Doeg had falsely accused the priest, but Ahimelech sensed that he could gain nothing by denying that allegation.

The high priest concluded that Saul ought not to blame Ahimelech and his family for anything related to David's time at Nob. Ahimelech's defense was credible and well-constructed. In essence he placed the problems with David back on Saul without directly indicting the king for his treacherous treatment of David. Saul should not blame Ahimelech, since by implication the fault lay with the king himself.

Saul, however, had already concluded that Ahimelech had acted seditiously and did not listen to the high priest's defense. He simply condemned him (22:16). The king ordered his runners to "kill the priests of Yahweh," which would include Ahimelech (22:17). Runners were not only the king's couriers,[7]

---

[7] Esth 3:13, 15; 8:10, 14; 2 Chr 30:6, 10.

but they also provided security as a corps of personal bodyguards.[8] Probably sensing his servants' reluctance to raise a hand against Yahweh's representatives, which was tantamount to violence against Yahweh himself,[9] Saul felt the need to justify his order—the priests had supported David against him and knowingly aided his flight from Saul. The runners, however, were still not willing to risk God's wrath by executing his ministers.

Doeg did not have such scruples. As an Edomite, he was probably not a worshiper of Yahweh and did not show the same respect for Yahweh's intermediaries (22:18). After killing the priests he went to Nob and completely devastated the city. The description of who and what Doeg destroyed—"men and women, children and infants, herds and donkeys and flocks" (22:19)—is nearly identical to Yahweh's instructions to Saul for the retribution against the Amalekites (15:3).[10] This introduces another subtle irony that only alert readers may see: Saul did not carry out God's instructions to completely destroy the Amalekites (15:1–35), who were "sinners" (15:18). However, through Doeg, Saul executed a similar plan against Yahweh's own priests. Saul had shown by negative example, a sin of omission (the Amalekite war in chapter 15), and by positive example, a grievous sin of commission (the destruction of Yahweh's priests and of Nob), that he was opposed to God, thereby providing further justification for Yahweh's rejection of him (15:23, 26–29; 16:1) and Yahweh's replacement of him with David (15:28; 16:12–13).

Abiathar Escapes and Flees to David (22:20–23)

One priest managed to escape. Abiathar fled and brought David news of the slaughter at Gibeah (22:20–21). David took responsibility for having initiated a chain of events that led to the priests' death. He was familiar with Doeg and had intuited that Doeg would report to Saul (22:22). David offered Abiathar protection (22:23). With the death of high priest Ahimelech, Abiathar was now the presumptive heir to the office his father had held. During David's reign Abiathar would share the high priesthood with Zadok. David would not remove Abiathar from the office, although he would force him to share it with a non-Elide. Perhaps this patient tolerance of an Elide high priest was in gratitude for Ahimelech's help and Abiathar's later assistance (23:6–14; 30:7–8).

David's treatment of Abiathar also serves as an example of respect for the office of the holy ministry that God had placed among the Israelites in the form of the OT priesthood. In contrast, Saul failed to show respect to either God's

---

[8] 1 Ki 14:27, 28; 2 Ki 10:25; 11:4, 6, 11, 13, 19; 2 Chr 12:10, 11; 23:12.

[9] David declares in a psalm: "The reproaches of those who reproach you [God] have fallen on me" (Ps 69:10 [ET 69:9]). The apostle Paul quotes this statement and applies it to Jesus Christ in Rom 15:3.

[10] Only "camels" (15:3) are omitted in 22:19. It appears as if camels were not commonly found among the Israelites. The only camels mentioned in possession of Israelites in the OT are from David's reign (1 Chr 12:41 [ET 12:40]; 27:30).

prophet Samuel[11] or Yahweh's priests at Nob. He repeatedly fell short of obeying Samuel's instructions (notably in chapter 15) and ordered the execution of faithful priests. They had not been guilty of abusing their office—not even when Ahimelech gave aid to David, who had already been anointed as king designate (16:12–13).

David's example of respect for the offices of prophet, priest, and Levite are a constant in his life. He repeatedly obeyed the instructions of God's prophets (Samuel;[12] Gad in 1 Sam 22:5; Nathan in 2 Samuel 12). He protected Abiathar (1 Sam 22:23). Later he made provisions for the priests and Levites who served in the temple (1 Chronicles 23–26). In this way David serves as an example for Christians today. They also are to honor those whom God has placed into the holy ministry and into auxiliary offices in the church and who serve faithfully:

> We request you, brothers, to recognize those who labor among you and stand over you in the Lord and who admonish you, and to esteem them most highly in love because of their work. Be at peace among yourselves. (1 Thess 5:12–13)

> Let the elders who rule well be considered worthy of double honor, especially those who labor in Word and doctrine. For the Scripture says, "A threshing ox you shall not muzzle," and, "The laborer is worthy of his wages." (1 Tim 5:17–18)

> Obey your leaders and submit, for they keep watch for the sake of your souls, as those who will have to give an account, so they may do this with joy and not be groaning, for that would be unprofitable for you. (Heb 13:17)

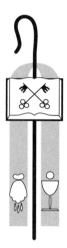

Luther also reminds us of this in his Large Catechism:

> Yet there is need to impress upon the common people that they who would bear the name of Christians owe it to God to show "double honor" [1 Tim 5:17] to those who watch over their souls and to treat them well and make provision for them. God will adequately recompense those who do so and will not let them suffer want.[13]

On the Last Day Jesus will say, "Whatever you did to one of the least of these my brothers you did to me" (Mt 25:40), and this most certainly pertains to those who preach the Gospel of Jesus (see "my brothers" in Mt 28:10), who make disciples by baptizing in the triune name and teaching all that Jesus has commanded (Mt 28:19–20), who feed his children with his Holy Supper, and attend to all their needs.

---

[11] Saul's disobedience began as soon as he had been anointed king. Samuel implied that he was to eradicate the Philistine garrison in Gibeah (10:7), but he failed to do so. (Later his son Jonathan did so in 14:1–16.) See the discussion in "Samuel Anoints Saul (9:26–10:8)" in the commentary on 9:26–10:16, including figure 16, "Saul's Faltering Accession." See also the beginning of the commentary on 10:17–27a.

[12] Samuel was a Levite as well as a prophet. See the last textual note and the commentary on 1:1.

[13] LC I (Fourth Commandment) 161.

David Rescues Keilah

Translation

23 ¹David was told, "The Philistines are attacking Keilah, and they're plundering the threshing floors."

²So David inquired of Yahweh, "Should I go to strike down these Philistines?"

Yahweh said to David, "Go for you will strike down the Philistines and save Keilah."

³David's men said to him, "We're afraid here in Judah! How much more [will we be in danger] if we go to Keilah to the battle lines of the Philistines?"

⁴So David again inquired of Yahweh. Yahweh answered, "Rise [and] go down to Keilah, because I am handing the Philistines over to you." ⁵Then David and his men went to Keilah. They fought the Philistines, led away their cattle, and decisively defeated them. So David saved the inhabitants of Keilah.

(⁶Now when Abiathar the son of Ahimelech had fled to David, he went down with David to Keilah, bringing an ephod with him.)

⁷When Saul was informed that David had gone to Keilah, Saul thought, "God has handed him over to me because he has trapped himself by entering a city with a barred double door." ⁸So Saul summoned all the troops to war to go down to Keilah to besiege David and his men.

⁹When David knew that Saul was plotting to do him harm, he said to the high priest Abiathar, "Bring near the ephod." ¹⁰David said, "Yahweh, the God of Israel, your servant has actually heard that Saul is planning to come to Keilah to destroy the city because of me. ¹¹Will the citizens of Keilah surrender me to him? Will Saul come down as your servant has heard? O Yahweh, the God of Israel, please inform your servant."

Yahweh said, "He will come down."

¹²Then David said, "Will the citizens of Keilah surrender me and my men to Saul?"

Yahweh said, "They will surrender."

¹³So David and his men (about six hundred men) rose and went out of Keilah and went wherever they could go. Saul was informed that David had fled from Keilah, so he ceased military operations.

Textual Notes

23:1 וַיַּגִּדוּ—Literally "and they informed David." The Hiphil (H) preterite (imperfect with *waw* consecutive) of נָגַד is the third masculine plural, but no subject is identified. An impersonal plural construction such as that can be translated as a passive: "David was told." Later in this chapter Hophal (Hp) forms of this verb are used, וַיֻּגַּד in 23:7 and

הֻגַּד in 23:13, each time with לְשָׁאוּל, literally "it was reported to Saul," but translated as "(when) Saul was informed."

שֹׂסִים אֶת־הַגְּרָנוֹת:—The verb שָׁסָה, "to plunder," appears once elsewhere in the book of Samuel, as another Qal (G) participle; see the third textual note on 14:48. This is the first instance of the noun גֹּרֶן, "threshing floor," which is masculine even though its plural, גְּרָנוֹת, is feminine in form. The "threshing floor" (גֹּרֶן) of Araunah figures prominently in the narrative of 2 Sam 24:16–24.

23:2 וַיִּשְׁאַל דָּוִד בַּיהוָה—"So David inquired of Yahweh." This is the first record in the book of Samuel of David doing so; he will again in 1 Sam 23:4; 30:8; 2 Sam 2:1; 5:19, 23. In all these verses David inquires of "Yahweh," the gracious covenant God of Israel. In 22:10 Doeg accused Ahimelech of inquiring of Yahweh for David, but that action was not mentioned in 21:2–10 (ET 21:1–9). When the clause is repeated in 22:13, 15, the speakers substitute "God" for "Yahweh." Presumably David inquires through the mediation of Abiathar, the successor of the high priest Ahimelech, whom Saul had put to death (22:16–23). Likewise, when Yahweh replies to David (e.g., 23:2b), he speaks through his high priest.

הַאֵלֵךְ וְהִכֵּיתִי ... לֵךְ וְהִכִּיתָ—Both pairs of verbs are the Qal (G) of הָלַךְ, "go," followed by the Hiphil (H) of נָכָה, "strike down." Both pairs are simply joined with *waw*, namely, a *waw* consecutive on a perfect form of נָכָה. The first pair, beginning with the interrogative *he* on an imperfect (הַאֵלֵךְ), expresses purpose: "should I go in order to strike down?" The second pair, beginning with the imperative לֵךְ, expresses causation: "go because you will strike down" (see Joüon, § 170 c).

וְהוֹשַׁעְתָּ—"And you will save." The Hiphil (H) of יָשַׁע was used in 10:19 for Yahweh saving his people from Egypt (see the textual note on 10:18–19) and from the Philistines in 7:8; 9:16; 14:6, 23, 39. It refers to new acts of salvation through David here in 23:2, again in 23:5 (וַיֹּשַׁע), as also in 1 Sam 17:47; 2 Sam 3:18; 8:6, 14. David recounts how Yahweh has saved him in 2 Sam 22:3–4; cf. also the nouns יֶשַׁע in 2 Sam 22:36, 47; 23:5; יְשׁוּעָה in 2 Sam 22:51; and תְּשׁוּעָה in 1 Sam 19:5; 2 Sam 23:10, 12.

23:3 מַעַרְכוֹת—For "battle lines," see the first textual note on 17:8.

23:4 וַיּוֹסֶף עוֹד דָּוִד לִשְׁאָל—"So David again inquired." For this construction, the Hiphil (H) preterite (imperfect with *waw* consecutive) of יָסַף, "to do again," followed by an infinitive construct (here with לְ), לִשְׁאָל, "to ask," see Joüon, §§ 102 g, 124 c, 177 b. See also the first textual note on 3:6.

קוּם רֵד—These are two Qal (G) masculine singular imperatives. The first is of קוּם, "arise," and the second is of יָרַד, "go down."

אֲנִי נֹתֵן אֶת־פְּלִשְׁתִּים בְּיָדֶךָ:—Literally "I am giving the Philistines into your hand." In a promise about the future, the use of a participle (נֹתֵן) depicts the action as already in progress. God will certainly fulfill his Word (*futurum instans*, GKC, § 116 p; see also Joüon, § 121 e).

23:5 וַאֲנָשָׁיו—"And his men" is the Qere. It is supported by the LXX, καὶ οἱ ἄνδρες οἱ μετ' αὐτοῦ, "and the men who were with him," but the added phrase in the LXX is a secondary expansion. The Kethib is a defective, or *ḥaser*, spelling of the same word, וַאֲנָשׁוֹ.

וַיִּנְהַג אֶת־מִקְנֵיהֶם—The Qal (G) of נָהַג, "to lead, drive," can refer to leading away herds and flocks after capturing them as booty in war (see BDB, s.v. נָהַג, 1). The noun מִקְנֶה is a general term for domesticated animals that could refer to large ones, "herds" or "cattle" (see BDB, 1 and 2), or small ones, "flocks," "sheep," and "goats" (see BDB, 2). See further the commentary. This same verb (נָהַג) and object noun (מִקְנֶה) recur in 30:20.

וַיַּךְ בָּהֶם מַכָּה גְדוֹלָה—This cognate accusative construction, "and he struck against them a great striking," is translated as "and (he) decisively defeated them"; see the second textual note on 19:8.

23:6 וַיְהִי בִּבְרֹחַ אֶבְיָתָר בֶּן־אֲחִימֶלֶךְ אֶל־דָּוִד קְעִילָה אֵפוֹד יָרַד בְּיָדוֹ—The MT literally reads "and it was when Abiathar the son of Ahimelech fled to David [to/in] Keilah, an ephod went down in his hand." This is an awkward reading at best for two reasons. First, the nearest noun that could be the subject of the Qal (G) perfect יָרַד is the preceding word אֵפוֹד, the "ephod."[1] Second, the MT wording implies that Abiathar fled to David when David was in Keilah. The LXX reads καὶ ἐγένετο ἐν τῷ φυγεῖν Αβιαθαρ υἱὸν Αβιμελεχ πρὸς Δαυιδ καὶ αὐτὸς μετὰ Δαυιδ εἰς Κεῖλα κατέβη ἔχων εφουδ ἐν τῇ χειρὶ αὐτοῦ, literally "and it was when Abiathar the son of Abimelech fled to David, he went down with David to Keilah, having an ephod in his hand." The LXX reading makes good sense and suggests a Hebrew text such as the following:

וַיְהִי בִּבְרֹחַ אֶבְיָתָר בֶּן־אֲחִימֶלֶךְ אֶל־דָּוִד וַיֵּרֶד עִם דָּוִד קְעִילָה וְאֵפוֹד בְּיָדוֹ

If correct, then it appears as if the MT has suffered haplography due to parablepsis; the words עִם דָּוִד could have been omitted as the scribe's eye skipped from the first דָּוִד to the second דָּוִד. Then the MT's word order could have been adjusted if the verb וַיֵּרֶד was moved from before the words קְעִילָה וְאֵפוֹד to be after those two words (and was changed to the perfect יָרַד) to try to make sense out of the end of the verse. There are three reasons why it is hardly likely that Abiathar fled from Gibeah directly to David at Keilah (as implied by the MT):

1. Abiathar's arrival at David's camp as related in 22:20–23 is implied to have occurred while David was still in the Hereth Forest (22:5b).

2. It is extremely unlikely that the events of 22:1–23:6 could have transpired as quickly as implied by the MT's text of 23:6. This would have required that four hundred men gathered to David at Adullam, then David and his men went to Moab, then to the Hereth Forest in only a short time (two months?). During this time Saul found out about David and his men (and the number of David's men had swelled to six hundred in 23:13) and had the priests from Nob executed and had Nob devastated while Abiathar made his way to David at Keilah. A more likely scenario is this: David returned from Moab to Judah (22:5) and attracted two hundred more men to join the four hundred he had in 22:2. Then Saul found out about David and his men and executed Nob's priests as Abiathar fled to David in the Hereth Forest.

---

[1] In the Qal (G) the verb יָרַד is intransitive, "go down, descend." One would expect the subject of the Qal verb to be אֶבְיָתָר, but the name "Abiathar" is rather distant, seven Hebrew words in front of the verb יָרַד. Another construction that might be expected would be for the verb יָרַד to be in the Hiphil (H), e.g., וַיּוֹרֶד (as in 21:14 [ET 21:13]) with אֶבְיָתָר as its subject and אֵפוֹד as its direct object, meaning "Abiathar brought down an ephod." (Whether the verb is Qal or Hiphil, the usual word order would be for the object noun, אֵפוֹד, to be after the verb.)

3. David inquired of Yahweh (23:2–4) *before* going to Keilah (23:5). The fact that he inquired of Yahweh and received an answer (23:2–4) implies that he already had access to the ephod and its Urim and Thummim brought by Abiathar. 1 Sam 23:9 explains that Abiathar had brought the ephod with him when he and David went to battle. This implies that Abiathar was treating David as the rightful king, since the Urim and Thummim were designated primarily to reveal God's advice in military matters to Israel's leader (Num 27:18–23).

23:7 וַיֹּאמֶר—The Qal (G) of אָמַר, "to say," can refer to an internal process, "to say (in one's heart)," i.e., "to think" (see BDB, 2).

נִכַּר אֹתוֹ אֱלֹהִים בְּיָדִי—The verb in the MT is a Piel (D) third masculine singular perfect of נָכַר, of which there are two homographs in the OT. נָכַר I is usually used in the Hiphil (H), meaning "to recognize, observe." Its Piel occurs in two OT passages, Job 21:29; 34:19, meaning "to recognize." If it is the verb here, the MT would mean "God has recognized him into my hand." The rare homograph נָכַר II is a denominative from נְכְרִי, "foreign(er)." Its Piel is attested in Jer 19:4, meaning "to treat as foreign; to profane," and in Deut 32:27, meaning "to misconstrue." If it is the verb here, the MT might mean "God has estranged him into my hand" (see BDB, s.v. נכר vb. denom.). However, neither of these two verbs appears elsewhere with the preposition and noun בְּיַד־, "in the hand of," nor with the meaning "hand over" or something similar as required by the context of this verse.

Many scholars advocate emending the verb to סִכַּר on the basis of Symmachus, the Syriac, the Targum, and the Vulgate.[2] סִכַּר is a Piel perfect of סָכַר I, meaning "to shut up; hand over." This rare verb occurs twice in the OT, the Niphal (N) in Ps 63:12 (ET 63:11) and the Piel in Is 19:4, where it is used together with בְּיַד־, meaning "hand over," in a context similar to 1 Sam 23:7.[3] סָכַר I is a by-form of the common verb סָגַר I, "shut" (Qal [G]) or "hand over" (Piel [D]); see the next textual note and the first textual note on 23:11.

Another proposal is to read the verb as the Qal perfect of מָכַר, "God *sold* him into my hand." The LXX reads πέπρακεν, "sold." The verb מָכַר is used with בְּיַד־, "to sell into the hand of," in Judg 2:14; 3:8; 4:2, 9; 10:7; 1 Sam 12:9; Ezek 30:12; Joel 4:8 (ET 3:8).

נִסְגַּר לָבוֹא—The Niphal (N) perfect of סָגַר, "to shut, close," could have a passive meaning, "he is shut in," or a reflexive meaning, as translated, "he has trapped himself." The Qal (G) infinitive construct לָבוֹא explains how the action of the preceding verb took place, "by entering" (see Joüon, § 124 o).

בְּעִיר דְּלָתַיִם וּבְרִיחַ:—Literally "in a city of two doors [דְּלָתַיִם is dual] and a bar." The bar was placed across the double door of the city gate to hold it shut.

23:8 וַיְשַׁמַּע—"So he summoned." See the first textual note on 15:4.

הָעָם—For the use of "the people" in a military sense meaning "the troops," see the first textual note on 4:3.

---

[2] See note a on 23:7 in *BHS*.

[3] The suggestion to read סָכַר based on Is 19:4 is offered in, e.g., BDB, s.v. נכר vb. denom.

לָרֶדֶת ... לְצוּר אֶל־דָּוִד—The first Qal (G) infinitive construct with לְ is of יָרַד, "go down." The second is of צוּר II, "to confine; besiege." Usually it takes the preposition עַל in an adversative/hostile sense; here אֶל is used with that sense of עַל. See צוּר אֶל־ also in Deut 20:19.

23:9 עָלָיו שָׁאוּל מַחֲרִישׁ הָרָעָה—Literally "against him [David] Saul was plotting the evil." The verb מַחֲרִישׁ is a Hiphil (H) participle of חָרַשׁ I (one of several homographs). This verb often occurs in the Qal (G) and can mean "plot, devise" (see BDB, 3). This is the only instance of its Hiphil in the OT.

23:10 עַבְדְּךָ—David, speaking to Yahweh, deferentially calls himself "your servant" here and again in 23:11. See the third textual note on 1:11.

מְבַקֵּשׁ—"Planning" is literally "seeking," a Piel (D) participle of בָּקַשׁ. This is a thematic verb in the narrative of Saul's pursuit of David. See "Jonathan Defends David (19:1–7)" in the commentary on 19:1–17.

בַּעֲבוּרִי:—This means "because of me" or "on my account" or "for my sake." The combination of בְּ + עֲבוּר is used as a preposition (see BDB, s.v. עָבַר II, under עָבַר). This is its only instance in the book of Samuel with a pronominal suffix. Cf. the third textual note on 1:6.

23:11 הֲיַסְגִּרֻנִי בַעֲלֵי קְעִילָה בְיָדוֹ—"Will the citizens of Keilah surrender me to him?" The verb סָגַר in the Hiphil (H) with the preposition and noun בְּיַד־ is an idiom for "hand over, deliver (someone) into someone's hand" (Josh 20:5; Ps 31:9 [ET 31:8]; Lam 2:7). It recurs in 1 Sam 23:12, 20; 30:15. The phrase בַעֲלֵי קְעִילָה, "the masters of Keilah," denotes the influential citizens of the city (see *HALOT*, s.v. בַּעַל I, A 2). The LXX has a different question at the beginning of this verse: εἰ ἀποκλεισθήσεται; "will it be shut up?" (*NETS*). And the space requirements in 4QSam^b indicate that the question was not present in that manuscript. Some, therefore, would omit it here, since is appears to be a near duplicate of the question in the next verse, 23:12.[4] However, the question in the next verse could not have been accidentally transferred into this verse, since it is significantly different in wording. Rather, this question is original to this verse. When God did not answer this first question by David in 23:11, David reworded and reiterated this inquiry in 23:12. The translators and scribes responsible for the text reflected in the LXX and 4QSam^b apparently did not recognize the reason for the repetitious question in 23:12 and purposely adjusted the text by rewording or eliminating the first question in 23:11.

יֵרֵד:—"He will come down." The repetition of a single word (the Qal [G] imperfect of יָרַד), which was the key word in David's second question (...הֲיֵרֵד), is sufficient to serve as an affirmative answer (Joüon, § 161 l (1)). Similarly, Yahweh will give the one-word answer יַסְגִּרוּ in 23:12.

23:13 וַיָּקָם דָּוִד וַאֲנָשָׁיו—The verb is singular, "so David rose," and the plural "and his men" then follows. This makes sense grammatically since David is the nearer part of the compound subject. It also makes sense in the drama of the narrative since David

---

4 Cross, "The Oldest Manuscripts from Qumran," 171; McCarter, *I Samuel*, 370; Klein, *1 Samuel*, 228.

438

is the leader and his men copy his actions. The next three verbs in the verse are plural, starting with וַיֵּצְאוּ.

וַיִּתְהַלְּכוּ בַּאֲשֶׁר יִתְהַלָּכוּ—"And (they) went wherever they could go" is literally "and they walked about where they could walk about." The verbs are Hithpael (HtD) forms of הָלַךְ. In the Hithpael this verb is iterative or frequentative, signifying walking back and forth at various times (see Waltke-O'Connor, § 26.1.2b–d, including n. 18; see also BDB, Hithpael, 1; *HALOT*, Hithpael, 1).

לָצֵאת:—This Qal (G) infinitive construct, literally "to go out," is translated as "[he ceased] military operations." In the context of war, the verb יָצָא frequently denotes the initiation of military and battle maneuvers. See the first textual note on 18:6; see also, e.g., 1 Sam 8:20; 18:30; 28:1; 2 Sam 11:1; 21:17.

Commentary

c. 1013–c. 1012 BC

This section relates the first in a series of attempts by Saul to capture David. More importantly, it draws two important contrasts between them. The first is that David led his men into battle against the Philistines. Saul, by contrast, joined the battle against them only after his men—Jonathan and his armor bearer (14:1–23) or David (17:40–54)—initiated the attack.[5] The second contrast is in their consultation of God. Saul inquired of Yahweh only *after* he had joined Jonathan's battle against the Philistines and only after being prompted by the high priest, and God did not answer him by Urim and Thummim (14:36–38). David, however, consulted Yahweh *before* attacking the Philistines (23:2–4) and again before Saul came to capture him (23:9–12), and Yahweh definitively answered his questions (23:2, 4, 11–12). The account of David and Keilah emphasizes David's trust in God and his reliance on the guidance of God's Word, revealed through his prophets[6] and priests.[7] Over half of the narrative in 23:1–13 is dedicated to David's receiving information and his consultations of God concerning that information (23:1–4, 9–12). David's actions are presented only in summary form (23:5, 13). Again, he stands in contrast to Saul, who received information, but erroneously assumed that he knew what God was doing (23:7).

These contrasts serve to highlight the salutary relationship between Yahweh and David. Because of God's promise to and grace toward David, he is led to trust God with his life in battle and to rely on God's counsel as to what he ought to do. In contrast, although God showed favor to Saul in choosing him to be king (1 Samuel 10), Saul did not respond with trust in God, nor did he follow God's

---

[5] Saul had failed to carry out the divine instructions given him by Samuel on the occasion of his anointing to be king: he was to eradicate the Philistine garrison in Gibeah (10:7). See the discussion in "Samuel Anoints Saul (9:26–10:8)" in the commentary on 9:26–10:16, including figure 16, "Saul's Faltering Accession." See also the beginning of the commentary on 10:17–27a.

[6] E.g., Samuel in 16:1–13; Gad in 22:5.

[7] E.g., Ahimelech in 21:2–10 (ET 21:1–9); Abiathar in 23:1–13.

specific directives given through Samuel[8] or those given in the Torah or those evident to human reason.[9] David is an example of a man with faith created and sustained by Yahweh's Word and favor toward him. God would reveal that his grace toward David and indeed toward all humanity would ultimately be rooted in the Son and everlasting King to be born from his line (2 Samuel 7).[10] David demonstrated that faith is not simply a matter of an intellectual comprehension of what God has said, but primarily a matter of trust and confidence in Yahweh and his promises, which center in Jesus Christ, the Son of David (Mt 1:1; cf. Lk 20:41–44). David's faith led him to act on the basis of God's Word instead of his own reasoning, whereas Saul acted of the basis of his presumptions about God (e.g., 23:7). Luther comments on David's days of persecution by Saul in light of this:

> Saul was a great king, chosen by God, and an upright man [see 1 Sam 9:15–10:13, 24]; but once he was secure on his throne and he let his heart depart from God, placing his confidence in his crown and power, he inevitably perished with all that he had; not one of his children remained. David, on the other hand, was a poor, despised man, hunted down and persecuted, his life nowhere secure, yet inevitably he remained safe from Saul and became king. … God will tolerate no presumption and no trust in any other object; he makes no greater demand of us than a hearty trust in him for all blessings.[11]

Throughout his time in the wilderness of Judah fleeing from Saul's pursuit, David demonstrated this trust in God and was given victory over his enemies. In a far greater way, the Son of David resolutely carried out his divine mission to achieve the victory of salvation for the entire world, despite the temptations of the devil (Mt 4:1–11); the increasing hostility of authorities, who sought to destroy him;[12] and finally his condemnation to the cross—all to fulfill the Scriptures with the promise of his resurrection from the dead, as written in the psalms of David.[13]

David Defeats the Philistines at Keilah (23:1–5)

This incident opens with some unnamed persons informing David of a Philistine raid on Keilah (23:1). Keilah was probably located at modern Tell Qila, about three miles (five kilometers) south of Adullam and eight miles

---

[8] In addition to Saul's disobedience in 10:7 (see several footnotes above), he also disobeyed the divine directives in 1 Samuel 15.

[9] Saul's attempts to kill David violate the Fifth Commandment (Ex 20:13; Deut 5:17) as well as the broad standards of justice in the Torah. His obsession with murdering his son-in-law, loyal military commander, and divinely anointed successor even defies human logic and the natural law written in the human heart and conscience.

[10] See further "Christ in Samuel" in the introduction.

[11] LC I (First Commandment) 45–47.

[12] Mt 2:13; 12:14; Mk 3:6; 11:18; Lk 22:2; Jn 5:18; 7:1.

[13] In the psalms of David, see particularly Pss 16:9–10; 22:17–32 (ET 22:16–31); 23:6; 110:1–7. See also, e.g., Lk 18:31; 24:19–27, 46; Jn 20:9.

(thirteen kilometers) northwest of Hebron. As part of the Judean Shephelah (Josh 15:44), it was near Philistine territory, due east of Gath. Since David had originally gathered men around him at Adullam (22:1–2), some of his men may have been from this area and had relatives who had sent them messages about Keilah. The opportunistic Philistines raids took place in late spring (barley harvest) or early summer (wheat harvest) when grain was being threshed on the threshing floors.

Upon hearing of the Philistine incursion, David inquired of Yahweh whether he ought to attack them (23:2). David was beginning to act like the king he had been anointed to be (1 Sam 16:12–13). Apparently, Saul had not come to rescue Keilah. The text does not state how David inquired of God. Josephus states that David consulted a prophet.[14] However, Josephus tends to introduce prophets or prophecy whenever the Bible lacks a clear statement of how God's Word was revealed to someone.[15]

The narration of this incident is preceded and followed by references to the high priest Abiathar (22:20–23; 23:7). This suggests that God communicated through Abiathar's use of the Urim and Thummim, a suggestion made more certain by the mention of the ephod in 23:6, 9, as the Urim and Thummim were kept in the high priest's breastpiece, worn over the ephod (Ex 28:28; Lev 8:7–8). In addition, the expression "inquire [the verb שָׁאַל] of Yahweh/God" appears to be a technical term for consulting God through the Urim and Thummim.[16] Moreover, it ought to be noted that after Abiathar's arrival (22:20–23), there is no mention of any prophet or prophecy to David during his days on the run from Saul. However, David did inquire of God through the ephod at least twice (23:9–12; 30:7–8), presumably using the Urim and Thummim.[17]

Upon hearing God's answer, David's men were reluctant to go to Keilah, which is on the border between Judah and Philistia and much closer to Saul's land of Benjamin (23:3). Unlike Saul, who simply listened to his people instead of God (15:24), David turned again to Yahweh, who ensured a victory over the Philistines (23:4–5). One statement that has puzzled readers is the note that David's men seized the Philistine's cattle (see the second textual note on 23:5). Why did the Philistines have cattle with them when they were raiding Judah? Mastin concluded that the cattle were animals the Philistines had captured as spoils during their raids.[18] The problem with this suggestion is that the text refers to the cattle as the Philistines' without any hint that the animals were

---

[14] Josephus, *Antiquities*, 6.271.

[15] Begg, "David's Double Escape according to Josephus," 30; Feldman, "Prophets and Prophecy in Josephus," 389–91.

[16] See the excursus "The Urim and Thummim" following the commentary on 14:24–46.

[17] In addition, David appears to have made use of the Urim and Thummim to inquire of God when he was king of Judah (2 Sam 2:1; 5:19, 23–24). After 1 Sam 22:5, the book of Samuel does not refer to David receiving further messages from prophets until he became king of all Israel (Nathan in 2 Samuel 7 and 2 Samuel 12; Gad in 2 Samuel 24).

[18] Mastin, "The *Miqneh* of 1 Samuel xxiii 5."

previously captured as spoil. McCarter suggested that the Philistines brought cattle with them to forage the threshing floors.[19] However, this seems improbable, since it would have been more economical and less risky to capture the grain and take it back to Philistia to their animals. Hertzberg suggested that the beasts were pack animals brought by the Philistines to carry equipment and the captured spoils.[20] This is the most appealing explanation, but must remain unproven for lack of solid evidence.

David Avoids Capture by Saul (23:6–13)

In 23:6 the narrator inserts information for the reader. We are told again that Abiathar had fled to David (23:6a, as previously recounted in 22:20–23), but new information is added: when Abiathar went with David to Keilah, he brought an ephod with him (see the textual note on 23:6). This apprises the reader how David had previously inquired of Yahweh (23:2–4) and also anticipates David's next questions for God (23:9–12).

The scene then briefly shifts to Saul (23:7–8), whose sources had informed him of events transpiring in Israel. In this case Saul learned that David had gone to Keilah. Since Keilah was a fortified city (with "a barred double door," 23:7), Saul believed that he could trap David inside by besieging the city to capture him (23:8).

However, David, too, had informants, and when he found out that Saul was on the move and would destroy the city in order to capture him, he consulted God (23:9–10). David asked God two questions. First, would the citizens of Keilah surrender him to Saul to save themselves and their city? Second, would Saul actually march against the city as David had heard (23:11)? Yahweh answered the second question by confirming that Saul would indeed advance (23:11), implying that Saul would attack Keilah in order to capture David. However, in that answer Yahweh did not specifically address the first query about the inhabitants giving David up, although his affirmative answer to the second question may have been an implicit assent to the first one too. David then reworded his first question, perhaps to clarify his understanding of God's answer (23:12). Yahweh confirmed that the people of Keilah would turn him over to Saul. Since Keilah would not defend David despite his rescue of the city from the Philistines, David and his men left and went wherever they could go (23:13). As a consequence, Saul called off his attack. By this time David's force of four hundred malcontents (22:2) had grown to six hundred men (23:13), the size it would remain until Saul's death (25:13; 27:2; 30:9).[21]

---

[19] McCarter, *I Samuel*, 371.

[20] Hertzberg, *I and II Samuel*, 191.

[21] According to LXX 1 Sam 23:13 and Josephus, *Antiquities*, 6.274, at this point David had "four hundred," probably by attraction to that number in 22:2.

1 Samuel 23:14–24:1 (ET 23:14–29)
David in Ziph and Maon

Translation

23 ¹⁴David dwelt in the wilderness in the fortresses, and he dwelt in the hill country in the wilderness of Ziph. Saul constantly sought him, but God did not deliver him to him.

¹⁵Now David saw that Saul had come out to seek his life when David was in the wilderness of Ziph at Horesh. ¹⁶So Saul's son Jonathan arose and went to David at Horesh, and he encouraged him in God. ¹⁷He said to him, "Don't be afraid because the hand of my father Saul will not find you. You will reign over Israel, and I will be second to you. My father Saul also knows this."

¹⁸So the two of them made an agreement before Yahweh. Then David stayed in Horesh, and Jonathan went to his home.

¹⁹Ziphites came up to Saul at Gibeah with this report: "Isn't David hiding with us in the strongholds in Horesh, on the hill of Hachilah, which is south of Jeshimon? ²⁰Now, whenever Your Majesty desires to come down, come down, and it will be our duty to hand him over to Your Majesty."

²¹Saul said, "May you be blessed by Yahweh because you have had compassion on me. ²²Go and check again. Investigate his place, where his swift foot is, because [someone] told me he can be very clever. ²³Investigate all the places where he might hide, and come back to me with accurate information. Then I will go with you. If he is in the land, I will search for him among all the clans of Judah." ²⁴So they left and went to Ziph ahead of Saul.

David and his men were in the wilderness of Maon in the Arabah to the south of Jeshimon. ²⁵Saul and his men went to seek him. David was informed, so he went down to the Rock and stayed in the wilderness of Maon. Saul heard [about this], and he pursued David into the wilderness of Maon. ²⁶Saul went on this side of the mountain, and David and his men went on the other side of the mountain. David was hurrying to get away from Saul, and Saul and his men were circling [the mountain] toward David and his men to capture them. ²⁷Then a messenger came to Saul with this report: "Come quickly, because the Philistines are plundering the land." ²⁸So Saul turned from pursuing David and went to confront the Philistines. Therefore that place is called Slippery Rock. ^{24:1}David went up from there and stayed in the strongholds of En-gedi.

Textual Notes

23:14 בַּמְּצָדוֹת—This means "in the fortresses/strongholds." It is the plural (feminine in form) of the noun מְצָד, which is cognate to the noun מְצוּדָה in 22:4–5; 24:23 (ET 24:22), with the preposition בְּ. The plural of מְצָד recurs in 23:19; 24:1 (ET 23:29).

וַיְבַקְשֵׁהוּ—"And he sought him." For this thematic Piel (D) verb in the narrative of Saul's pursuit of David, see "Jonathan Defends David (19:1–7)" in the commentary on 19:1–17. See also the infinitive construct (with לְ) לְבַקֵּשׁ in 23:15, 25.

כָּל־הַיָּמִים—Literally "all the days," this is rendered as "constantly."

וְלֹא־נְתָנוֹ אֱלֹהִים בְּיָדוֹ:—Literally "but God did not give him into his hand." This idiom (the verb נָתַן with בְּיַד־) appears often in the book of Samuel.[1] 4QSam^b reads [יהו]ה, "Yahweh," instead of "God," a reading supported by the LXX (κύριος).

23:15 וַיַּרְא—The MT's reading, "and he saw," is supported by the LXX, καὶ εἶδεν. Some would emend the pointing to וַיִּרָא, "and he was afraid," on the basis of אַל־תִּירָא in 23:17.[2] The form וַיִּרָא, the Qal (G) preterite (imperfect with *waw* consecutive) of יָרֵא, is used in 1 Sam 12:18; 18:12; 21:13 (ET 21:12); 28:5, 20; 2 Sam 6:9.

בַּחֹרְשָׁה:—The noun חֹרֶשׁ (a segholate, with the accent on the first syllable, חֹרֶשׁ) means "wooded height" or "woods" (see BDB). This noun with the unaccented locative *he* ending (הָ-) is used as the place-name "Horesh" in 23:15, 16, 18, 19. It also has the prefixed preposition בְּ in 23:15, 18, 19. Cf. the discussion of חֶרֶת, "Hereth," in the commentary on 22:5.

23:16 וַיְחַזֵּק אֶת־יָדוֹ בֵּאלֹהִים:—Literally "and he [Jonathan] strengthened his [David's] hand in God." For the idiom "strengthen [someone's] hand," meaning "to support" or "encourage," see Judg 9:24; Jer 23:14; Ezek 13:22; Job 4:3; Ezra 1:6; 6:22; Neh 2:18; 6:9. 4QSam^b reads ה[יהו], "Yahweh," instead of "God," a reading supported by the LXX (κύριος).

23:17 לְמִשְׁנֶה—For "second," see the commentary.

23:18 וַיִּכְרְתוּ שְׁנֵיהֶם בְּרִית לִפְנֵי יְהוָה—For the idiom כָּרַת בְּרִית, literally "cut a covenant," see the third textual note on 11:1. This idiom was used for the covenant between Jonathan and David in 18:3. See also the verb alone in the same sense in 20:16; 22:8.

23:19 זִפִים—"Ziphites" is the anarthrous reading of the MT. The LXX includes the definite article, οἱ Ζιφαῖοι, "the Ziphites." Ziph is modern Tell Ziph, about four miles (six kilometers) southeast of Hebron and thirteen miles (twenty-one kilometers) southeast of Keilah.

לֵאמֹר—The Qal (G) infinitive construct of אָמַר with לְ is often used to introduce direct discourse and ought to be translated as appropriate to context, thus here "with this report." It is translated the same way again in 23:27; 26:1.

מִסְתַּתֵּר—This Hithpael (HtD) participle of סָתַר, literally "keeping himself secret," is translated as "hiding." The identical participle recurs in 26:1. Cf. the Niphal (N) forms of סָתַר in 20:5, 19, 24 and the Hiphil (H) in 20:2.

הַחֲכִילָה—The name חֲכִילָה, "Hachilah," means "dark place." The location of the place is unknown, but it may be the ridge known as Dhahret el-Kolah.

---

[1] Also 1 Sam 14:10, 12, 37; 17:47; 23:4; 24:5, 11 (ET 24:4, 10); 26:23; 28:19; 30:23; 2 Sam 5:19 (twice); 16:8; 21:9.

[2] McCarter, *I Samuel*, 374; Klein, *1 Samuel*, 228.

מִיָּמִין—"South of" is literally "from the right of" (יָמִין with the prefixed preposition מִן). Directions in Hebrew may be given by assuming that a person is facing east. "To the right of" would be south. The same is true of אֶל יְמִין in 23:24.

הַיְשִׁימוֹן:—The name יְשִׁימוֹן, "Jeshimon," means "desert." It recurs in 23:24; 26:1, 3. The location of the place is unknown.

23:20 לְכָל־אַוַּת נַפְשְׁךָ הַמֶּלֶךְ לָרֶדֶת רֵד—Literally "to all the desire of your soul, O king, to come down, come down!" The noun אַוָּה denotes a "longing" or "desire." The article with הַמֶּלֶךְ marks it as a vocative,[3] and it is translated as "Your Majesty," as in 17:55; 22:15. לָרֶדֶת is the Qal (G) infinitive construct of יָרַד (with the preposition לְ), and רֵד is its Qal imperative.

וְלָנוּ—Literally "and to us," this use of the suffixed preposition לְ means "and it will be our duty." The Ziphites are taking upon themselves the responsibility to carry out the following action.

הַסְגִּירוֹ בְּיַד הַמֶּלֶךְ:—Literally "to shut him up in the hand of the king," this idiom with the Hiphil (H) of סָגַר (here the infinitive construct with an object suffix) and בְּיַד־ is also in 23:11, 12; 30:15. It means "to hand [someone] over" also when the idiom uses סָגַר in the Piel (D) stem (17:46; 24:19 [ET 24:18]; 26:8).

23:21 בְּרוּכִים אַתֶּם לַיהוָה—Literally "blessed are you [masculine plural] by Yahweh." בְּרוּכִים is the Qal passive (Gp) participle of בָּרַךְ, "to bless." Saul spoke the equivalent singular formula to Samuel in 15:13 as a pious disguise for his disobedience to God. Here too his display of piety is a sham. But David will use the same formula as here in a genuine way in 2 Sam 2:5.

23:22 לְכוּ־נָא הָכִינוּ עוֹד—Literally "go, please; make ready again." The verb הָכִינוּ is a masculine plural Hiphil (H) imperative of כּוּן, meaning "to prepare, make [things] ready," and can be used for setting up ambushes (see BDB, Hiphil, 2 a). The same imperative was in 7:3.

וּדְעוּ וּרְאוּ אֶת־מְקֹמוֹ אֲשֶׁר תִּהְיֶה רַגְלוֹ—Literally "and know and see his place, where his foot will be." The pair of Qal (G) imperatives, וּדְעוּ וּרְאוּ, can be translated as a hendiadys, "investigate," as again at the start of 23:23.

מִי רָאָהוּ שָׁם—The MT continues Saul's command to the Ziphites: they are also to investigate "who saw him there." According to this reading, Saul's concern is to identify who observed David's location, but elsewhere in this context Saul is only concerned about locating David. The conjectured reading of 4QSam[b] concludes with the same adverb of place, שם (to be vocalized שָׁם), "there," but instead of the previous two words in the MT, מִי רָאָהוּ, it has an adjective describing David's foot (רַגְלוֹ, a feminine noun) as המהרה (the definite feminine adjective הַמְּהֵרָה), "swift." The full sentence in 4QSam[b] would then literally be "and know and see his place, where his swift foot will be there," which can be translated as "investigate his place, where his swift foot is." This meaning makes better sense in the context, since Saul is asking the Ziphites to confirm David's whereabouts, and Saul knows that David is constantly on the run. The conjectured Hebrew reading of 4QSam[b] also makes good grammatical sense because

---

a relative clause that describes a location and that begins with the pronoun אֲשֶׁר, meaning "where," often concludes with the adverb שָׁם, "there."[4] This adverb is redundant in English ("his place where … *there*") and so need not be translated. It appears as if the MT's מִי רָאָהוּ, "who saw him," could be a corruption of הַמְהֵרָה.[5] The LXX reads ἐν τάχει, "in quickness" (= quickly?), for what may have been בִּמְהֵרָה.

עָרוֹם יַעְרִם הוּא:—"He can be very clever." The Qal (G) infinitive absolute of עָרַם, "be crafty, clever," precedes its Hiphil (H) imperfect, and the emphatic subject pronoun הוּא then follows the imperfect. The infinitive here is the only OT instance of a Qal form of עָרַם (so BDB). Aside from that form, this rare verb occurs only in the Hiphil and in the imperfect, here and in Ps 83:4 (ET 83:3); Prov 15:5; 19:25 (so BDB). It is related to the adjective עָרוּם, which can mean "wise, prudent" (e.g., Prov 12:23; 14:8, 15), but which was also used for the serpent (Gen 3:1) and can have a sinister connotation (Job 5:12; 15:5). Saul may intend such a connotation here. 4QSam[b] apparently omitted the infinitive absolute; after אֵלַי (אֵלַי) the only part of this clause that is extant is the initial consonant י (presumably the first consonant of יַעְרִם).

23:23 וּרְאוּ וּדְעוּ—For "investigate," see the second textual note on 23:22.

מִכֹּל הַמַּחֲבֹאִים אֲשֶׁר יִתְחַבֵּא שָׁם וְשַׁבְתֶּם אֵלַי אֶל־נָכוֹן—Literally "[investigate] from all the hideouts where he might hide there, and you will return to me for what is certain." The noun מַחֲבֹא, "hiding place," is a hapax legomenon. It is derived from the following verb חָבָא, whose Hithpael (HtD) stem (here, as in 13:6; 14:11, 22) means "to hide (oneself)," as does its Niphal (N) stem (1 Sam 10:22; 19:2; 2 Sam 17:9). נָכוֹן is the Niphal participle of כּוּן, meaning "to be sure, certain, reliable." The prepositional phrase אֶל־נָכוֹן must mean that the Ziphites will return to Saul to provide him with reliable military intelligence, that is, "with accurate information."

The LXX lacks a Greek translation of these nine Hebrew words, and some would omit them as an alternate version of 23:22 displaced into 23:23.[6] However, there is no good reason for omitting this text. It appears to have been present in 4QSam[b], which normally agrees with the LXX.[7] It may have been purposely omitted in the LXX because it appeared to be redundant after what was said in 23:22.

וְחִפַּשְׂתֶּי—In the Piel (D) חָפַשׂ can mean "search through" or, as here, "search for." The only other instance of חָפַשׂ in the book of Samuel is the Hithpael (HtD) in 28:8, which means "disguise oneself."

23:24 וַיָּקוּמוּ וַיֵּלְכוּ—This is the common Hebrew idiom "and they arose and went."[8]

---

4   See Joüon, § 158 j. For examples of relative clauses with אֲשֶׁר and שָׁם, see, e.g., Gen 2:11; 13:3, 4, 14; 19:27; 31:13; 33:19; 35:15, 27; 40:3; 50:10.

5   McCarter, *I Samuel*, 377; Klein, *1 Samuel*, 228; Hertzberg, *I and II Samuel*, 192; Auld, *I and II Samuel*, 259–60.

6   McCarter, *I Samuel*, 378; Klein, *1 Samuel*, 228.

7   Only three letters from this text are extant in 4QSam[b]: [ה]מחב[אים]. These letters represent the second word, הַמַּחֲבֹאִים.

8   Also 1 Sam 3:6, 8; 16:13; 18:27; 21:1 (ET 20:42b); 23:16; 28:25; 31:12; 2 Sam 6:2; 14:23; 15:9; 17:23.

אֶל יְמִין הַיְשִׁימֹן:—For "to the south of Jeshimon," see the fifth and sixth textual notes on 23:19.

23:25 לְבַקֵּשׁ—The MT simply has "to seek" without an object; the context clearly implies the object is David. The LXX includes an object pronoun, ζητεῖν αὐτόν, "to seek him," which may have been added to smooth out the syntax, or it may suggest a Hebrew reading of לְבַקְשׁוֹ. If that Hebrew reading was original, the loss of the final *waw* in the MT would be due to haplography since the next word, וַיַּגִּדוּ, begins with a *waw*.

וַיַּגִּדוּ לְדָוִד—Literally "and they reported to David," the impersonal plural is translated as a passive: "David was informed." See the first textual note on 23:1.

וַיִּרְדֹּף אַחֲרֵי־דָוִד—Literally "and he pursued after David." The Qal (G) of רָדַף, "to pursue," can be used with the preposition אַחֲרֵי, as here and again in 23:28 (also 24:15 [ET 24:14]; 26:18; 30:8a). Alternatively, it can take a direct object (e.g., 7:11; 17:52; 26:20; cf. 25:29; 30:8b, 10).

23:26 מִצַּד הָהָר מִזֶּה ... מִצַּד הָהָר מִזֶּה—Literally "from the side of the mountain from this ... from the side of the mountain from this," this is equivalent to the English "on this side of the mountain ... on the other side of the mountain." מִצַּד, "from the side of," is the noun צַד, "side," with the prefixed preposition מִן, as previously in 20:25 (where it was translated as "beside"); see also מִצַּד הָהָר in 2 Sam 13:34. Hebrew idiom repeats the demonstrative pronoun זֶה ... זֶה (e.g., Gen 29:27; Is 6:3; Ps 75:8 [ET 75:7]; Job 1:16), whereas English idiom requires the second word to be different: "this ... that" or "this ... the other."

נֶחְפָּז לָלֶכֶת—The Niphal (N) of חָפַז occurs four times in the OT, meaning "be in a hurry" or "be anxious" (also 2 Ki 7:15; Pss 48:6 [ET 48:5]; 104:7). Here the Niphal participle is followed by an infinitive construct (of הָלַךְ) that provides further detail about the action: "was hurrying to get away."

עֹטְרִים—"Were circling" is a Qal (G) participle of עָטַר. Note the cognate noun עֲטָרָה, a (circular) "crown, diadem, wreath." The only other OT instance of the Qal of עָטַר is in Ps 5:13 (ET 5:12), where it means "to surround, cover." Its Piel (D) in Pss 8:6 (ET 8:5); 65:12 (ET 65:11); 103:4; Song 3:11 means "to crown," as does its Hiphil (H) in Is 23:8.

23:27 מַהֲרָה וְלֵכָה—Literally "quickly come," the first of these two imperatives functions adverbially. Each is the alternate form of the imperative with paragogic *he*. The first is the Piel (D) of מָהַר, "do quickly," and the second is the Qal (G) of הָלַךְ.

פָּשְׁטוּ—For "they are plundering," see the first textual note on 18:4.

23:28 לִקְרַאת—The wartime context supports the rendition "to confront." The word is the Qal (G) infinitive construct of קָרָא II, "to meet, encounter," with לְ.

סֶלַע הַמַּחְלְקוֹת:—The genitive in this construct phrase is translated adjectivally, "*Slippery* Rock," suggesting that David slipped through (evaded) Saul's maneuver to capture him. The literal meaning of the phrase is probably "rock of the slippery places" (if הַמַּחְלְקוֹת is a concrete noun) or "rock of slipperiness" (if הַמַּחְלְקוֹת is an abstract plural). The feminine plural noun מַחְלְקוֹת is most likely a hapax legomenon derived from the verb חָלַק that means "be smooth, slippery" (BDB, s.v. חָלַק II; *CDCH*, s.v. חלק II; *HALOT*, s.v. חלק I). On the other hand, it could be the plural of the well-attested

447

feminine noun מַחֲלֹקֶת, denoting a "division, part" of land allotted to Israel, or a "division, rank" of priests and Levites, a noun derived from the homographic common verb חָלַק, "to divide, allot, apportion" (BDB, s.v. חָלַק I; *CDCH*, s.v. חלק I). This understanding is reflected in the LXX by Πέτρα ἡ μερισθεῖσα and in the Vulgate by *petram Dividentem*. If so, this construct phrase could mean "rock of divisions" or "rock of factions."[9] However, the latter verb חָלַק most often has to do with dividing spoils or apportioning land, and the context here does not refer to any such actions resulting from this particular conflict between Saul and the Philistines.

Commentary

c. 1013–c. 1012 BC

While the earlier part of 1 Samuel 23 emphasized David's reliance on God and his Word, this latter part of the chapter focuses on God's gifts to David. First is a brief notice that God did not allow Saul to capture David despite Saul's constant preoccupation with tracking him down. Then Jonathan's last interaction with David demonstrated God's blessing of strength to David through the encouragement of a believing friend. Finally, Saul proved to have allies even among David's own tribe when some Ziphites betrayed David's location to Saul. Despite good strategic intelligence about David's movements, Saul was prevented by circumstances beyond his control from capturing his former military commander (18:5), demonstrating God's ability to protect David. This illustrates God's foreknowledge and power to control events among humans, as noted in the Formula of Concord:

> God's foreknowledge sees and knows in advance the evil as well [as the good], but not in such a way as though it were God's gracious will that it should happen. To be sure, he sees and knows beforehand whatever the perverse and wicked will of the devil and of men will attempt and do. But even in wicked acts and works God's foreknowledge operates in such a way that God sets a limit and measure for the evil which he does not will—how far it is to go, how long it is to endure, and when and how he will interfere with it and punish it. For the Lord God governs everything in such a way that it must redound to the glory of his divine name and the salvation of his elect, and thereby the ungodly are confounded.[10]

Protecting David was indeed God governing affairs to his glory and the salvation of his elect in Christ Jesus, since David would become the bearer of the messianic promise from the tribe of Judah (Gen 49:8–10). This plan of salvation would unfold in greater detail in 2 Samuel 7, when God promised the Son of David, who would build God's house and reign on David's throne forever.[11]

---

9 See the discussion in McCarter, *I Samuel*, 379. McCarter does not believe the word derives from חָלַק I, "to divide."

10 FC SD XI ("Eternal Foreknowledge and Divine Election") 6.

11 See further "Christ in Samuel" in the introduction.

God Does Not Deliver David to Saul (23:14)

After David dwelt in unspecified "fortresses," presumably in Judah, he then moved to the wilderness of Ziph (23:14). During this time Saul was constantly seeking David, but we are not told how actively Saul was doing this. Was he simply gathering intelligence on David's movements and only occasionally making forays into central and southern Judah? Or was Saul constantly on the offensive, chasing David and his men around the countryside? Whatever the case, Saul was unsuccessful in finding David because "God did not deliver him to him" (23:14). This short statement colors the rest of the chapter, since it prompts us to read these events as governed by God even if some of the participants (Saul and the Ziphites) are ignorant of, or even hostile to, God's constant blessing on David for the sake of his plan to provide salvation for the whole world.

Jonathan's Last Visit with David (23:15–18)

While Saul was frustrated in finding David, Jonathan was able to locate David at Horesh and come to him (23:15–16). Horesh was probably located at modern Khirbet Khoreisa, about two miles (three kilometers) southeast of Ziph. This is the last encounter of these two friends, bound together under Yahweh (18:1–4; 20:1–21:1 [ET 20:1–42]; cf. 22:8), recorded in the book of Samuel. Jonathan came to encourage David in God. The Hebrew expression translated as "encourage" is literally "to strengthen [someone's] hand" (see the textual note on 23:16). Although it is a frequent idiom in the OT, this is the only place where someone encourages someone "in God," highlighting Jonathan's role as a fellow believer in Yahweh who brought the comfort and power of the Gospel to David. Jonathan's encouragement included the assurance that Saul's hand would not find David (23:17)—a way of stating that God was watching over David and would not deliver him into Saul's clutches. Jonathan also pointed to God's promise, given at David's anointing, that David would be king of Israel (16:1–13). This was to encourage him that Saul would not succeed in eliminating David as a rival for the throne. Moreover, Jonathan pledged his continued support for David after he became king, stating that he would serve as David's "second" (מִשְׁנֶה). Judging from Esth 10:2–3 and 2 Chr 28:7, this position appears to have been the king's chief of staff or prime minister. Finally, Jonathan stated that Saul was aware of all this—not only David's divinely appointed succession to the throne (cf. 1 Sam 24:21 [ET 24:20]; 26:25) but also Jonathan's unwavering support for David.

Finally, we are told that David and Jonathan entered into a bilateral agreement before Yahweh (23:18). Previously their agreements were initiated by Jonathan (18:3; 20:8, 42), but it now appears that the two men acted as equals in making their solemn pledges to each other. Earlier, at Jonathan's initiative, the two of them had sworn in the name of Yahweh that their covenant of peace would extend to their descendants forever (20:42).

The Ziphites Report David's Whereabouts to Saul (23:19–24a)

While Saul could not find David on his own, he eventually gained help from some Ziphites (23:19; cf. Ps 54:2 [ET superscription]). The clan of Ziph was descended from Caleb (1 Chr 2:42), who had trusted the promises of Yahweh and joined Joshua as the only two members of the wilderness generation who, by faith, were enabled to enter the promised land.[12] Despite the heroic faith of their progenitor, it appears that for some reason (which the author of Samuel does not reveal) some of the Calebites were hostile to David, as evidenced later by Nabal, who also was a Calebite (25:3).

These Ziphites came to Saul with information on David's location—in the strongholds of Horesh, on the hill of Hachilah, south of Jeshimon. The locations of Hachilah and Jeshimon are unknown. Hachilah is mentioned again in 26:1, 3. In the book of Samuel, Jeshimon appears to be used as the proper name of a place in Judah (see also 26:1, 3). Elsewhere it is a general term for a desert or wasteland.[13]

The Ziphites not only gave Saul information about David's location but also invited Saul to come and capture him, pledging their assistance (23:20). In reply Saul wished them Yahweh's blessing for having compassion on him (23:21). However, no prayer for God's blessing is fulfilled if it is contrary to God's will (cf. Prov 19:21), and Saul seems to have been assuming that he could capture David even though God had willed the opposite.

Saul went on to instruct the Ziphites to gather more detailed intelligence on David's various safe havens (23:22–23). He assured them that when they supplied this tactical data to him, he would then come and search for David, not only among the territory of their clan but also through the territory of every clan in Judah. The Ziphites then preceded Saul to Ziph (23:24a).

Saul Seeks to Capture David in the Wilderness of Maon (23:24b–24:1 [ET 23:24–29])

David, in the meantime, had moved to the far southeast of Judah (23:24b). He was in "the wilderness of Maon." Maon is probably modern Tell Ma'in, about nine miles (fourteen kilometers) southeast of Hebron and five miles (eight kilometers) south of Ziph. David, however, was not at Maon, but in the wilderness associated with it in the Arabah south of Jeshimon. The Arabah is the rift valley through which the Jordan River flows and in which is the Dead Sea. This geographic information places David somewhere east of Maon near the Dead Sea, but probably southwest of En-gedi. When David learned of Saul's movement toward him, he went to a place simply called "the Rock" (23:25). However, Saul continued to have his informants, and he followed David and caught up with him at this mountain, making a circling maneuver around it to

---

[12] See Num 13:30; 14:6–9, 24–38; 26:65; 32:11–12; Deut 1:35–36; Josh 14:13–14; 21:12.

[13] Num 21:20; 23:28; Deut 32:10; Is 43:19, 20; Pss 68:8 (ET 68:7); 78:40; 106:14; 107:4.

capture David (23:26). The writer implies that David was almost within Saul's grasp when Saul received news of Philistine incursions into Israel (23:27).

The verb used to denote the Philistine raids is a Qal (G) form of פָּשַׁט, which often means to strip clothes off someone (see the first textual note on 18:4). However, it can also be used of attacking or raiding and often in the context of stripping the land by capturing spoils (e.g., Job 1:17; 2 Chr 25:13). This connotation of stripping the land is especially prevalent in the book of Samuel (e.g., 1 Sam 27:8, 10; 30:1). Thus, the message was urgent, because the Philistines were plundering and pillaging. Saul was forced to break off his pursuit of David to check the Philistine incursions (23:28). The account implies not only that God, ironically, used the Philistines to save David but also that Saul's pursuit of David led him to neglect his duty as monarch to protect his citizens from foreign invaders. Saul was sinning by defying God's choice of David to be king, and he was sinning further by neglecting his own vocation as king and defender of Israel. We are not told whether Saul attacked the Philistines or simply stationed his army to block Philistine incursions into Israel. However, given Saul's previous reluctance to engage the Philistines in battle,[14] it is likely that he simply intended to stop their hostile activities by a show of force. The rock in the Desert of Maon where David had gone and where Saul had almost captured him became known as "Slippery Rock" (see the second textual note on 23:28), probably commemorating David's slipping through Saul's grasp.

David left the wilderness of Maon and went to En-gedi ("spring of the young goat," 24:1 [ET 23:29]) on the western shore of the Dead Sea about twenty miles (thirty-two kilometers) southeast of Hebron. This town, also called Hazazon-tamar ("gravel with a palm tree," Gen 14:7; 2 Chr 20:2) is mentioned several times in the OT. It had impressive fountains of warm water that poured out from beneath limestone cliffs. The spring there provided water for irrigation; the Song of Songs notes En-gedi's vineyards and blossoming henna (Song 1:14).[15] Josephus also mentions palm and balsam trees there.[16] It would have been a hospitable place for David and his six hundred men (see 1 Sam 23:13).

---

[14] Saul's cowardice in the face of the Philistines began as soon as he was anointed king. He was to eradicate the Philistine garrison in Gibeah (10:7), but it was only after his son led the attack that he followed afterward (14:1–16). See "Samuel Anoints Saul (9:26–10:8)" in the commentary on 9:26–10:16, including figure 16, "Saul's Faltering Accession." See also the beginning of the commentary on 10:17–27a.

[15] The topography of En-gedi, where the vineyards and blossoms are nestled in a ravine between slopes, lends itself to the metaphor in Song 1:13, and Solomon, the son of David and the author of the Song, may well have recalled his father's refuge there when he composed Song 1:13–14 (according to Mitchell, *The Song of Songs*, 635; see also 649–53).

[16] Josephus, *Antiquities*, 9.7.

David Spares Saul's Life at En-gedi

Translation

24 ²As Saul returned from going after the Philistines, they reported to him, "Look, David is in the wilderness of En-gedi."

³So Saul took three thousand men selected from all of Israel and went to seek David and his men in front of the Rocks of the Wild Goats. ⁴He came to the sheep pens beside the road, and a cave was there. Saul went [into the cave] to relieve himself while David and his men were sitting in the innermost part of the cave.

⁵Then David's men said to him, "Look! Today is the day about which Yahweh said to you, 'I am handing your enemy over to you.' You should do to him whatever you please." So David rose and secretly cut off the hem of Saul's robe.

⁶After this David's conscience bothered him because he had cut off the hem of Saul's [robe]. ⁷So David said to his men, "This certainly is not from Yahweh that I should do this thing to my lord, to Yahweh's anointed one, to stretch out my hand against him, because he is Yahweh's anointed one." ⁸Moreover, David castigated his men in this matter and did not allow them to attack Saul.

Saul got up from the cave and went in the road. ⁹David rose afterward and went out of the cave and called after Saul, "My lord, Your Majesty!" When Saul looked behind himself, David knelt with his face to the ground and bowed.

¹⁰David said to Saul, "Why have you listened to words of people who say, 'David is seeking to harm you'? ¹¹Note that today your eyes have seen that today Yahweh handed you over to me in the cave, but I refused to kill you and had pity on you. I thought, 'I will not stretch out my hand against my lord because he is Yahweh's anointed one.' ¹²My father, see! See also the hem of your robe in my hand, because when I cut off the hem of your robe, I did not kill you. Realize that I have done no wrong and no crime. I have not sinned against you, but you are setting an ambush for my life in order to take it. ¹³May Yahweh judge between you and me, and may Yahweh exact vengeance from you on my behalf, but my hand will never be against you. ¹⁴As the proverb of the ancients says, 'Wickedness comes from wicked people,' but my hand will never be against you. ¹⁵After whom has the king of Israel come out? Whom are you chasing? A dead dog? One flea? ¹⁶May Yahweh be a judge and decide between you and me. May he see [what you're doing], defend my cause, and vindicate me against you."

¹⁷As David finished speaking these words to Saul, Saul said, "Is that your voice, my son David?" Then Saul wept loudly. ¹⁸He said to David, "You are more righteous than I, because you treated me well although I treated you badly. ¹⁹Today you told me what good thing you did for me: when Yahweh handed me over to you, you did not kill me. ²⁰When a man finds his enemy, does he send him on his way unharmed? May Yahweh repay you well for what you have done for me this

day. ²¹Now I know that you will certainly rule, and the kingdom of Israel will be established under your control. ²²Now swear to me by Yahweh that you will neither cut off my descendants after me nor destroy my name from my father's house."

²³Then David swore an oath for Saul. Saul went to his home, and David and his men went up to the stronghold.

Textual Notes

24:2 שָׁב שָׁאוּל מֵאַחֲרֵי פְלִשְׁתִּים—Literally "Saul returned from after Philistines." The preposition אַחֲרֵי, "after," is used in a pregnant sense, that is, "from [pursuing] after …" Cf. the second textual note on 12:14.

24:3 אִישׁ בָּחוּר מִכָּל־יִשְׂרָאֵל—"Men selected from all Israel" specifies that Saul took the best, most able men to serve in his armed forces. The singular אִישׁ, "man," is used as a collective. Modifying it is בָּחוּר, the masculine singular Qal passive (Gp) participle of בָּחַר, "to choose, select." This passive participle is used a dozen times in the OT for chosen warriors (see BDB, s.v. בָּחַר, Qal, 7). Equivalent phrases occur in 1 Sam 26:2; 2 Sam 6:1; 10:9; 1 Chr 19:10. The same form, בָּחוּר, is often used in the OT as a noun, "young man"; see the first textual notes on 8:16 and 9:2.

לְבַקֵּשׁ—The Piel (D) verb בָּקֵשׁ, "to seek," is thematic in the narrative of Saul's pursuit of David. See 19:2, 10, and "Jonathan Defends David (19:1–7)" in the commentary on 19:1–17. Its participle occurs in 24:10 (ET 24:9), but in the opposite sense of who is seeking whom; see the textual note there.

עַל־פְּנֵי צוּרֵי הַיְּעֵלִים—This preposition and construct chain are literally "to the face of the rocks of the wild goats." These animals are Nubian ibexes (*Capra nubiana*), often considered a subspecies of the Alpine ibex (*Capra ibex*). Nubian ibexes live in jagged, dry, mountainous landscapes. Their diet consists largely of grass and leaves. Major predators of ibexes are leopards, eagles, and bearded vultures.[1]

24:4 גִּדְרוֹת הַצֹּאן—Literally "the walls of the flock," this construct phrase with the plural of גְּדֵרָה means "sheep pens" (see Num 32:16, 24, 36; Zeph 2:6).

לְהָסֵךְ אֶת־רַגְלָיו—Literally this means "to cover his feet." The verb is the Hiphil (H) infinitive construct of סָכַךְ I, which means "to cover" in the Qal (G) and the Hiphil (H). This Hebrew euphemism appears also in Judg 3:24 and means "to relieve oneself."

24:5 הִנֵּה הַיּוֹם אֲשֶׁר־אָמַר יְהוָה אֵלֶיךָ—The likely meaning is "behold, this is the day *about* which Yahweh said to you," and not "this is the day *on* which Yahweh said to you" (cf. GKC, § 138 b).

אָנֹכִי נֹתֵן אֶת־אֹיִבְךָ בְּיָדֶךָ—Literally "I am giving your enemy into your hand." The singular אֹיִבְךָ is the Qere, which is supported by the LXX, τὸν ἐχθρόν σου. The Kethib is the plural אֹיְבֶיךָ, "your enemies."

וְעָשִׂיתָ לּוֹ כַּאֲשֶׁר יִטַב בְּעֵינֶיךָ—Literally "and you will do to him as is good in your eyes," this could be part of the preceding quote of Yahweh's words (as most English translations assume). It seems more likely, however, that these are words of David's men urging him to take action because he now has the opportunity to fulfill (what they cite

---

[1] Shackleton, *Wild Sheep and Goats and Their Relatives*, 26.

as) Yahweh's prior promise. The verb יִטַב is the Qal (G) third masculine singular imperfect of יָטַב, "be good, pleasing." The usual form of this Qal imperfect is יִיטַב (nineteen times in the OT), but the form here, יִטַב, also appears in Judg 19:6; 1 Ki 21:7; 2 Ki 25:24.

וַיִּכְרֹת אֶת־כְּנַף־הַמְּעִיל—"And he cut off the hem of the robe." For the noun כָּנָף, "wing," meaning "hem," see the first textual note on 15:27. כָּנָף recurs in construct with מְעִיל twice in 24:12 (ET 24:11; as also in 15:27) and in the absolute state in 24:6 (ET 24:5). The noun מְעִיל denotes an outer "robe" of formal attire, probably a royal garment here, and so Saul would naturally take it off before relieving himself. Elsewhere מְעִיל may denote a liturgical vestment (see the first textual note on 2:19). One was worn by the prophet Samuel (15:27; cf. 28:14) and Jonathan the prince (18:4); see also 2 Sam 13:18.

בַּלָּט:—Literally "in the secret," this prepositional phrase functions as an adverb, "secretly." See the second textual note on 18:22.

24:6 וַיַּךְ לֵב־דָּוִד אֹתוֹ—Literally "the heart of David struck him," this identical idiom will refer to David's stricken conscience again in 2 Sam 24:10.

24:7 חָלִילָה לִּי מֵיהוָה—Literally "(it is) a profane thing to me from Yahweh," this means that David realizes his action "certainly is not from Yahweh." See the second textual note on 2:30.

לִמְשִׁיחַ יְהוָה ... מְשִׁיחַ יְהוָה—This means "to Yahweh's anointed one." The noun מָשִׁיחַ refers to Saul again in 24:11 (ET 24:10); also 1 Sam 26:9, 11, 16, 23; 2 Sam 1:14, 16. It refers to the Messiah or Christ in 1 Sam 2:10, 35. See also the verb מָשַׁח, "to anoint," for the anointing of Saul in 1 Sam 9:16; 10:1; 15:1, 17 (and for David in 1 Sam 16:3, 12, 13; 2 Sam 2:4, 7; 5:3, 17; 12:7; cf. 2 Sam 3:39).

24:8 וַיְשַׁסַּע דָּוִד אֶת־אֲנָשָׁיו בַּדְּבָרִים—Literally "and David tore apart his men with words." The Piel (D) of שָׁסַע occurs twice elsewhere in the OT, meaning "tear in pieces" (Lev 1:17; Judg 14:6), and the prepositional phrase בַּדְּבָרִים clarifies that the meaning here is metaphorical for a verbal upbraiding. The LXX reads καὶ ἔπεισεν Δαυιδ τοὺς ἄνδρας αὐτοῦ ἐν λόγοις, "and David persuaded his men with words," which is plausible but too mild in light of David's guilty conscience (24:6 [ET 24:5]) and forceful words in 24:7 (ET 24:6).

וְלֹא נְתָנָם לָקוּם אֶל־שָׁאוּל—Among the many nuances of נָתַן, "to give," is the sense "to permit, allow," usually with an accusative direct object (here the object suffix on נְתָנָם) and an infinitive construct with לְ (לָקוּם). See *HALOT*, s.v. נָתַן, Qal, 8. Thus the clause here literally means "and he did not allow them to arise against Saul." קוּם is often used with the preposition עַל or אֶל in the hostile sense of arising "against" someone, i.e., attacking that person (see BDB, s.v. קוּם, Qal, 2).

24:9 וַיִּקֹּד דָּוִד אַפַּיִם אַרְצָה וַיִּשְׁתָּחוּ:—The first of the two third masculine singular preterites (imperfects with *waw* consecutive) is of קָדַד, which occurs only in the Qal, meaning "bow down." The second verb, a synonym, is the Hishtaphel of חָוָה, "to bow, worship." See the third textual note on 1:3 and, for this form, וַיִּשְׁתָּחוּ, the second textual note on 1:28. These two verbs appear together in fifteen OT verses, as when the identical forms recur in 28:14. They often refer to the worship of Yahweh[2] or to the veneration of his king, as here and in 1 Ki 1:16, 31.

24:10 הִנֵּה דָוִד מְבַקֵּשׁ רָעָתֶךָ:—Literally "behold, David is seeking your harm." Usually in the narrative of David and Saul, the Piel (D) verb בַּקֵּשׁ refers to Saul "seeking" David (see the second textual note on 24:3 [ET 24:2]), but in this statement that misconstrues David's intentions, the reverse is purported to be true. רָעָתֶךָ, "your harm," is the feminine noun רָעָה, "evil, harm," with a suffix that can be rendered in English as a verbal object, "to harm you."

24:11 וְאָמַר לַהֲרָגְךָ—The MT literally reads "and he said to kill you." The nearest possible masculine singular subject of the masculine singular verb וְאָמַר, "and he said," is יְהוָה, "Yahweh," earlier in the verse. If Yahweh is the subject, "Yahweh said to kill you" could refer to the quotation of Yahweh by David's men in 24:5 (ET 24:4), where they urged David to dispatch Saul and claimed that Yahweh intended him to do so. Alternatively, the subject of the verb could be David's men, understood as a collective singular (as is אִישׁ in 24:3 [ET 24:2]); if that is the subject, "(they) said to kill you" refers to what David's men recommended to him in 24:5 (ET 24:4). Some English translations take the words in that sense, e.g., "and some told me to kill you" (ESV). Others translate similarly with a singular, e.g., "someone advised me to kill you" (HCSB). Ancient versions offer differing solutions. The LXX reads καὶ οὐκ ἠβουλήθην, "and I did not consent," meaning "I refused," which could reflect a Hebrew reading of וָאֵמָאֵן (the Piel [D] of מָאֵן). The Vulgate reads *et cogitavi*, "and I thought," which reflects the Hebrew consonants of the MT but pointed וָאֹמַר (that form is the third word following this clause). The Syriac and the Targum read "and men said," which may suggest the Hebrew וְאָמְרוּ.[3] Regardless of the subject here, David was urged to kill Saul in 24:5 (ET 24:4) but did not do so, and his self-restraint is conveyed by the translation "but I refused to kill you."

וַתָּחָס עָלֶיךָ—In Hebrew idiom the subject of the Qal (G) of חוס, "take pity (on someone)," frequently is the feminine singular noun עַיִן, "eye."[4] The suffixed dual עֵינֶיךָ, "your eyes," appeared earlier in this verse. Therefore here וַתָּחָס is to be parsed as a third feminine singular (not a second masculine singular) Qal (G) preterite (imperfect with *waw* consecutive) with עֵינִי, "my eye," implied as its subject.

24:12 דַּע וּרְאֵה כִּי אֵין בְּיָדִי רָעָה וָפֶשַׁע—Literally "know and see that there is not in my hand (any) evil and transgression."

וְלֹא־חָטָאתִי לָךְ—"I have not sinned against you." לָךְ is the pausal form of לְךָ. See the similar wording in 19:4b (also the analogous pausal form בָּךְ concluding 24:13 [ET 24:12] and 24:14 [ET 24:13]). Saul will use this identical verb form, חָטָאתִי, to confess to David his sin against him in 26:21.

---

2   E.g., Gen 24:26, 48; Ex 4:31; 12:27; Neh 8:6.

3   See note a on 1 Sam 24:11 (ET 24:10) in *BHS*.

4   This idiom occurs fifteen times in the OT, e.g., Gen 45:20; Deut 7:16; 19:13, 21; Ezek 9:5, 10.

צֹדֶה—"Are setting an ambush" is a Qal (G) participle of צָדָה I, "to lie in wait, set a trap" (see *CDCH*, s.v. צדה I). The only other OT instance of this verb is in Ex 21:13.

24:13   בֵּינִי וּבֵינֶךָ—The order of the Hebrew pronouns is "between *me* and between *you*," but they have been reversed in the translation to match English style, as also in 24:16 (ET 24:15).

וּנְקָמַנִי יְהוָה מִמֶּךָ—Literally "and Yahweh will avenge me from you," this means that Yahweh will avenge the injustice done to David by exacting revenge from Saul.

24:14   כַּאֲשֶׁר יֹאמַר מְשַׁל הַקַּדְמֹנִי—This means "as the proverb of the ancients says." The adjective קַדְמֹנִי, "former, ancient" (as in Ezek 38:17; Mal 3:4), is used here as a collective noun. Cf. Is 43:18, where its plural is used as a noun, "former things." Elsewhere in the OT it can mean "eastern."[5] 4QSamᵃ has the plural reading הקד[מֹניים]. If original, then the MT apparently suffered from the loss of the first *mem* in two consecutive occurrences, הַקַּדְמֹנִים* מְרָשָׁעִים.

24:15   אַחֲרֵי ... אַחֲרֵי ... אַחֲרֵי ... אַחֲרֵי—The repetition of this preposition, "after," is required in Hebrew, but for the sake of English idiom only the first one is translated.

יָצָא מֶלֶךְ יִשְׂרָאֵל—In the book of Samuel יָצָא often means to "come/go out" for battle; see the first textual note on 18:6.

רֹדֵף—The Qal (G) of רָדַף, "chase, pursue," often takes the preposition אַחֲרֵי (see the third textual note on 23:25).

כֶּלֶב מֵת—"A dead dog" (with the Qal [G] participle of מוּת) is one of the most abject self-deprecations, far stronger than referring to oneself as a "servant."[6] Both of the other two instances of this phrase in the OT are later in the book of Samuel. Mephibosheth humbles himself with it in 2 Sam 9:8. Abishai applies it to Shimei in 2 Sam 16:9 when he asks King David for permission to behead Shimei.

פַּרְעֹשׁ אֶחָד:—The noun פַּרְעֹשׁ, "flea," is a quadriliteral cognate of terms in Ugaritic and Akkadian (*HALOT*, s.v. פַּרְעֹשׁ I). Its only other OT occurrence is in 26:20. 4QSamᵃ reads או before the final אַחֲרֵי, "*or* after one flea." The LXX reads καὶ ὀπίσω ψύλλου ἑνός, "and after one flea."

24:16   לְדַיָּן—The noun דַּיָּן, a "judge," is derived from the verb דִּין, "to judge," and appears elsewhere only in Ps 68:6 (ET 68:5).

וְיֵרֶא—This is the Qal (G) jussive of רָאָה, hence "may he see."

וְיָרֵב אֶת־רִיבִי—Literally "and may he sue my lawsuit," this is a prayer that God would prosecute Saul for the injustice he has done to David. The verb יָרֵב is the Qal (G) jussive of רִיב, which can mean "conduct a legal case" or "file a lawsuit" (see BDB, Qal, 3). It takes the cognate accusative noun רִיב, a legal matter or "lawsuit."

וְיִשְׁפְּטֵנִי מִיָּדֶךָ:—The verb is another Qal (G) jussive, literally "and may he judge me from your hand." David is asking Yahweh to acquit him of any charge of wrongdoing in his dealing with Saul and thereby deliver him from Saul's power.

---

[5]   Ezek 10:19; 11:1; 47:18; Joel 2:20; Zech 14:8.

[6]   For the self-abasing term "servant," see the third textual note on 1:11 and the textual note on 3:10.

24:17 וַיִּשָּׂ֥א שָׁא֖וּל קֹל֥וֹ וַיֵּֽבְךְּ׃—Literally "and Saul lifted up his voice and wept." See the second textual note on 11:4.

24:18 צַדִּ֥יק אַתָּ֖ה מִמֶּ֑נִּי—The adjective צַדִּיק, "righteous," with the suffixed preposition מִן מִן forms a comparative phrase, "more righteous than." In the context of 24:16, 18 (ET 24:15, 17), the terminology for righteousness clearly is forensic. Cf. forensic justification in, e.g., Paul's epistles to the Romans and Galatians.

כִּ֤י אַתָּה֙ גְּמַלְתַּ֣נִי הַטּוֹבָ֔ה וַאֲנִ֖י גְּמַלְתִּ֥יךָ הָרָעָֽה׃—Literally this means "because you, you repaid me [with] the good, but I, I repaid you [with] the evil."

24:19 וְאַתָּה—"And you" (masculine singular) is the Qere. The Kethib is וְאַתְּ, the same form but without the final *he*. See GKC, § 32 g.

אֵ֣ת אֲשֶׁר־ ... אֵ֤ת אֲשֶׁר—Both relative clauses serve as direct objects of הִגַּ֣דְתָּ, "you told." Cf. GKC, § 117 c. 4QSamᵃ omits the second אֵת.

סִגְּרַ֧נִי יְהוָ֛ה בְּיָדְךָ֖—Literally "Yahweh closed me up in your hand." The Piel (D) of סָגַר is used with ‑בְּיָד, as in 17:46; 26:8. Cf. its Hiphil (H) with ‑בְּיָד in 23:11, 12, 20; 30:15.

24:20 וְשִׁלְּח֖וֹ בְּדֶ֣רֶךְ טוֹבָ֑ה—Literally "and he sends him in a good path." Here the noun דֶּרֶךְ is feminine and is modified by the feminine adjective טוֹבָה. Hebrew does not require an interrogative to mark a question, and in context this must be one.

תַּ֚חַת הַיּ֣וֹם הַזֶּ֔ה אֲשֶׁ֥ר עָשִׂ֖יתָה לִֽי׃—Literally this says "in return for this day which you did for me," but smooth English requires "for what you have done for me this day." When used as a preposition תַּחַת can have the nuance "*in exchange* or *return for*" (BDB, II 2 b (*b*)). The LXX reads καθὼς πεποίηκας σήμερον, "just as you have done today." 4QSamᵃ apparently reads הז]חן[היום אן]תה עשיתה כאשר], in agreement with the LXX. Thus both 4QSamᵃ and the LXX place "this day/today" at the end of the verse. Most English translations do the same.[7]

24:21 וְקָ֣מָה בְּיָדְךָ֔ מַמְלֶ֖כֶת יִשְׂרָאֵֽל׃—Literally "and the kingdom of Israel will be established in your hand." The feminine noun מַמְלָכָה (in construct: מַמְלֶכֶת), "kingdom," is the subject of the third feminine singular Qal (G) perfect of קוּם with *waw* consecutive. The Qal of קוּם can mean "be established, confirmed" (BDB, 7 b).

24:22 אִם־תַּכְרִית ... וְאִ֥ם תַּשְׁמִ֖יד—In this context these occurrences of אִם are translated as "neither ... nor." Oaths that foreswear actions often begin with אִם followed by an imperfect aspect verb.[8] The use of the verb כָּרַת, "cut" (in the Hiphil [H], meaning "cut off"), recalls its use (in the Qal [G]) for David "cutting off" the hem of Saul's garment (24:5 [ET 24:4]). Moreover, the covenant that Jonathan and David "cut" (כָּרַת, Qal, 18:3; 20:16; 23:18) would remain in force for their "seed/descendants" (זֶרַע, 20:42), even after Yahweh "cuts off" David's enemies (the Hiphil of כָּרַת, 20:15). Here Saul implores David not to "cut off" his "seed/descendants" (זֶרַע, 24:22 [ET 24:21]).

---

[7] HCSB, ESV, GW, NIV.

[8] *IBH*, § 64 A; Waltke-O'Connor, § 40.2.2b; Joüon, § 165 d.

Commentary

c. 1013–c. 1012 BC

The account of David sparing Saul's life near En-gedi brings forth two important themes. The first is David's reverence for the office held by Saul. David refused to kill "Yahweh's anointed one," and his conscience tormented him for cutting off the hem of Saul's robe (24:6–7 [ET 24:5–6]). While Saul had forfeited his right to claim any privileges as the anointed king of Israel[9] and David had been anointed as the new king to replace him (16:1–13), David showed great respect for God's original choice. Later, David expressed his trust that God would remove Saul when appropriate, and so he himself would not raise his hand to strike him (26:10–11; see also 2 Sam 1:14, 16). Although Saul was deeply flawed and at times opposed God's will, as the anointed one of Israel, he prefigured the greater Anointed One, Christ Jesus. When Saul defended Israel from its enemies, he foreshadowed Jesus' deliverance of his people from the powers of sin, death, and the devil. Therefore, in showing honor to Saul and refusing to attack him, David was honoring Christ. St. Augustine discerned this long ago:

> In this way, too, the kingdom of Saul himself, who certainly was reprobated and rejected, was the shadow of a kingdom yet to come which should remain to eternity. For, indeed, the oil with which he was anointed, and from that chrism he is called Christ, is to be taken in a mystical sense, and is to be understood as a great mystery; which David himself venerated so much in him, that he trembled with smitten heart when, being hid in a dark cave, which Saul also entered when pressed by the necessity of nature, he had come secretly behind him and cut off a small piece of his robe, that he might be able to prove how he had spared him when he could have killed him, and might thus remove from his mind the suspicion through which he had vehemently persecuted the holy David, thinking him his enemy. Therefore he was much afraid lest he should be accused of violating so great a mystery in Saul, because he had thus meddled even his clothes. For thus it is written: "And David's heart smote him because he had taken away the skirt of his cloak" [1 Sam 24:6 (ET 24:5)]. But to the men with him, who advised him to destroy Saul thus delivered up into his hands, he saith, "The Lord forbid that I should do this thing to my lord, the Lord's christ, to lay my hand upon him, because he is the Lord's christ" [1 Sam 24:7 (ET 24:6)]. Therefore he showed so great reverence to this shadow of what was to come, not for its own sake, but for the sake of what it prefigured.[10]

David's respect for Saul as Yahweh's anointed was motivated by his faith in Yahweh. However, it also would prove to be politically beneficial. David would one day reign on the throne as Yahweh's anointed king. He set an example of how God's anointed precursor of Christ ought to be respected by every Israelite (cf. 2 Sam 19:22). David would also demonstrate that he, like Saul,

---

[9] See especially 1 Samuel 15.

[10] Augustine, *The City of God*, 17.6 (*NPNF*[1] 2:346).

was an imperfect anointed one (2 Sam 12:7–9). Yet as God's anointed one he would rightfully claim God's blessing to him and through him to Israel and the world (2 Sam 22:51; 23:1).[11]

A second important theme that dovetails with the first one is respect for authority as instituted by God and as decreed in the Fourth Commandment.[12] Gregory the Great (c. AD 540–March 12, 604) recognized this theme in 1 Samuel 24:

> Subjects are to be admonished that they judge not rashly the lives of their superiors, if perchance they see them act blamably in anything, lest whence they rightly find fault with evil they thence be sunk by the impulse of elation to lower depths. They are to be admonished that, when they consider the faults of their superiors, they grow not too bold against them, but, if any of their deeds are exceedingly bad, so judge of them within themselves that, constrained by the fear of God, they still refuse not to bear the yoke of reverence under them. Which thing we shall shew the better if we bring forward what David did (I Sam. xxiv. 4 *seq.*). For when Saul the persecutor had entered into a cave to ease himself, David, who had so long suffered under his persecution, was within it with his men. And, when his men incited him to smite Saul, he cut them short with the reply that he ought not to put forth his hand against the Lord's anointed. And yet he rose unperceived, and cut off the border of his robe. For what is signified by Saul but bad rulers, and what by David but good subjects?[13]

David's deference to Saul and his preventing his men from taking the king's life (24:8 [ET 24:7]) demonstrated a faith that made every effort to keep God's commandment to honor authorities. David's conscience, enlightened by the Holy Spirit, would not allow him to raise a hand against Saul (24:6 [ET 24:5]; cf. Rom 13:5).

David Twice Spares Saul's Life—Comparing 1 Samuel 24 and 1 Samuel 26

Even the most casual reader of the book of Samuel cannot fail to notice the similarities between David sparing Saul's life at En-gedi (1 Samuel 24) and sparing it again at the hill of Hachilah (1 Samuel 26). Critical scholars often claim that these two chapters are alternate versions of the same event. However, even the relationship between the chapters is a matter of dispute among critical scholars. Some believe 1 Samuel 24 is older, while others propose that 1 Samuel 26 is older.[14]

---

[11] See further "Christ in Samuel" in the introduction.

[12] Ex 20:12; Deut 5:16. See also, e.g., Mt 15:4–6; 19:19; Rom 13:1–10; Eph 6:2; 1 Tim 6:1; 1 Pet 2:17.

[13] Gregory the Great, *The Book of Pastoral Rule*, 3.4 (NPNF[2] 12:27).

[14] See the discussion in Klein, *1 Samuel*, 237.

The most comprehensive presentation of this critical theory came from Klaus Koch.[15] The primary basis for this hypothesis is that both chapters share a similar outline:[16]

A. David was in the wilderness fleeing from Saul.
B. David had an opportunity to kill Saul.
C. Someone suggested that the opportunity was from Yahweh.
D. David refused to kill Yahweh's anointed.
E. David took a piece of evidence to prove what he could have done.
F. Saul recognized David's innocence and superiority.

Klein supplemented Koch's outline by noting a large number of specific parallels between the two accounts. However, some of these features are not exact equivalents, and they exhibit significant differences (noted below by added *italics*):[17]

1 Samuel 24	**1 Samuel 26**
Unidentified informers disclose David's location to Saul (24:2 [ET 24:1])	*Ziphites* disclose David's location to Saul (26:1; cf. 23:14, 15, 19)
Gibeah, Hachilah, Jeshimon (*23:19*)†	Gibeah, Hachilah, Jeshimon (26:1)
Three thousand select men from Israel seek David (24:3 [ET 24:2])	Three thousand select men from Israel seek David (26:2)
On the road (24:4, 8 [ET 24:3, 7])	On the road (26:3)
David and his men are sitting in the *cave* (24:4 [ET 24:3])	David and his men are sitting in the *wilderness* (26:3)
David's men: Yahweh is providing an opportunity to kill Saul (24:5 [ET 24:4])	Abishai: God is providing an opportunity to kill Saul (26:8)
David cuts off the hem of Saul's *robe* (24:5 [ET 24:4])	David takes Saul's *spear and water jug* (26:12)
David: May death be my lot if I harm Saul (24:7 [ET 24:6])	David: May death be my lot if I harm Saul (26:11)

†Note that, strictly speaking, this is not a parallel because it occurs in the previous account, not in the narrative about David sparing Saul's life.

---

[15] Koch, *The Growth of the Biblical Tradition*, 132–48.
[16] Cf. Koch, *The Growth of the Biblical Tradition*, 142.
[17] Klein, *1 Samuel*, 236–37 (adapted).

1 Samuel 24

David refers to Saul as "my lord" (24:7, 9, 11 [ET 24:6, 8, 10) and as the anointed of Yahweh (24:7 [twice], 11 [ET 24:6, 10])

David warns about stretching out one's hand against Saul (24:7, 11 [ET 24:6, 10])

David calls to *Saul* (24:9 [ET 24:8])

David asks Saul *why he listens to men* (24:10 [ET 24:9])

David: Yahweh gave you into my hand (24:11 [ET 24:10]; cf. 24:5 [ET 24:4])

"Today" as the time of David's innocence (24:11, 19, 20 [ET 24:10, 18, 19])

David protests his innocence by showing Saul *the piece of his robe* (24:12 [ET 24:11])

David: There is no evil in my hand (24:12 [ET 24:11])

David: I did not sin (24:12 [ET 24:11])

David: You hunt my life (24:12 [ET 24:11]); David calls Saul the king of Israel (24:15 [ET 24:14])

David: *Whom* are you pursuing? (24:15 [ET 24:14])

David: May Yahweh deliver (judge) me from *your hand* (24:16 [ET 24:15])

Saul: Is this your voice, my son? (24:17 [ET 24:16])

1 Samuel 26

David refers to Saul as "my lord" (26:17, 18, 19; cf. 26:15) and as the anointed of Yahweh (26:9, 11, 16, 23)

David warns about stretching out one's hand against Saul (26:9, 11, 23)

David calls to *the soldiers and Abner* (26:14)

David suggests that *human beings may have stirred Saul up* (26:19)

David: Yahweh gave you into my hand (26:23)

"Today" as the time of David's innocence (26:8, 19, 21, 23, 24)

David protests his innocence by showing Saul *the spear and water jug* (26:16)

David: What evil is in my hand? (26:18)

Saul: I sinned (26:21)

David: The king of Israel came to seek my life (26:20)

David: *Why* does my lord pursue? (26:18; cf. 26:20)

David: May he deliver me from *every trouble* (26:24)

Saul: Is this your voice, my son? (26:17; cf. 26:21, 25)

1 Samuel 24	1 Samuel 26
"Hand over" translates the Piel (D) of סגר (24:19 [ET 24:18]; cf. 23:12, 20)	"Hand over" translates the Piel (D) of סגר (26:8)
Saul: May Yahweh repay your goodness (24:20 [ET 24:19]); you are more righteous than I (24:18 [ET 24:17])	*David:* Yahweh will repay each man's righteousness (26:23)
Saul: You will surely *be king* (24:21 [ET 24:20])	Saul: You will surely *accomplish your work and have the upper hand* (26:25)
David and Saul go their respective ways (24:23 [ET 24:22])	David and Saul go their respective ways (26:25)

Klein also avers that in 1 Samuel 26 neither David nor Saul indicates that a similar incident had happened before.[18] However, this proves little. It is unreasonable to require both (1) that those involved in the history must have immediately recognized a resemblance to past history and (2) that such an explicit recognition must also be recorded in the narrative.[19] The author of the book of Samuel may have purposely guided his readers to see parallels that may not have been obvious to the actual participants at the time (but may have become clearer to them later). The selective inclusion of details common to both historical incidents may be part of the author's literary shaping as he recounted the events. In fact, the one overarching parallel between the two episodes is that in both David spared Saul's life because Saul was Yahweh's anointed one.

While Klein's analysis demonstrates correspondences between the two accounts, a close examination reveals that they are not two versions of the same incident. For instance, it is difficult, if not impossible, to explain how a single event was later interpreted as David cutting off the hem of Saul's robe and also as David taking Saul's spear and water jug. Moreover, there is a clear difference between David claiming that he *had not* sinned against Saul (24:12 [ET 24:11]) and Saul confessing that he *had* sinned against David (26:21). Additionally, while the parallel elements in the two scenes generally transpire in the same order, some appear in different places in the two narratives.

---

[18] Klein, *1 Samuel*, 236.

[19] That said, the responses of Saul and David in the conclusion of 1 Samuel 26 may indicate that this was the second time David had spared him. See the two concluding paragraphs of this section, "David Twice Spares Saul's Life—Comparing 1 Samuel 24 and 1 Samuel 26."

Tsumura points out some additional basic differences between the two texts:[20]

1 Samuel 24	1 Samuel 26
Setting: the wilderness of En-gedi	Setting: the wilderness of Ziph
Saul appeared before David	David sent spies to locate Saul
Saul was alone	Saul was with Abner and his soldiers
David called to Saul outside the cave	David called to Abner and the soldiers from a distance
Saul acknowledged David as the divinely appointed king	Saul simply prayed for blessing on David

Klein also adduces evidence that the two accounts derive from two different historical events:

> In chap. 24, after David took only the piece of Saul's robe instead of the king's life, the account consists of a speech by David to Saul (vv 10–16 [ET 24:9–15]) and a response by Saul to David (vv 17–22 [ET 24:16–21]). In chap. 26, by way of contrast, after David escaped from Saul's camp he spoke to Abner (v 14a), Abner responded (v 14b) and David replied again to Abner (vv 15–16). Then Saul (vv 17a, 21, 25a) and David (vv 17b–20, 22–24) engage in a two-way conversation.[21]

In addition, McCarter observes that in contrast to 1 Samuel 24, 1 Samuel 26 contains no "explicit statements about David's future and overt or extreme demonstrations of his innocence and piety and of Saul's abjection."[22]

Rather than proposing that a single author wrote two divergent accounts of the same episode, most scholars hypothesize that two different depictions of one historical event were transmitted to the author (or editor or final redactor) of the book of Samuel through separate channels of tradition. However, regardless of the supposed redactional process, this hypothesis would require that in the retelling of the story the detail that became the hem of Saul's robe in chapter 24 also became his spear and water jug in chapter 26.[23] It would also require that Saul's defecation in a cave became slumber in a camp (or vice versa) and that Saul's coming to David and his men alone became David and Abishai coming to Saul and his army (or vice versa), and so forth. Such a scenario is highly unlikely and does not cohere well when the evidence is considered in its entirety.

---

[20] Tsumura, *The First Book of Samuel*, 595 (adapted).

[21] Klein, *1 Samuel*, 238. This is also noted by Tsumura, *The First Book of Samuel*, 595.

[22] McCarter, *I Samuel*, 409. This is also noted by Tsumura, *The First Book of Samuel*, 595.

[23] The idiom "cover his feet" (see the second textual note on 24:4 [ET 24:3]) might suggest that Saul laid his robe somewhere near his feet. If so, this detail contrasts with the placement of his spear and water jug "at his head" in 26:7, 11, 12, 16.

A simpler and more probable explanation is that these two texts depict two discrete historical events that both contribute to one larger thematic message. The author of the book of Samuel related them in such a way as to reinforce their conjoint theology. However, he accurately recorded the individual accounts as separate sequences in the lives of David and Saul. Each takes place in its own setting with distinctive characteristics and unique experiences of the participants.

Finally, we ought to note that the difference in Saul's conclusion about David in 1 Samuel 26 exhibits a tacit recognition of this being the second time David had spared his life and what that implied about the future king. The contrast between the two conclusions demonstrates a progression in Saul's appreciation for Yahweh's choice of David from the earlier event (1 Samuel 24) to the later event (1 Samuel 26). When David first spared Saul's life, Saul affirmed that David would be king and asked David—who would occupy that future position of power—not to cut off his posterity from Israel (24:21–22 [ET 24:20–21]). When David spared Saul's life a second time, Saul invoked a blessing for David and conceded that he would accomplish much and be successful (26:25). At this later point in time Saul did not need to affirm David's right to the throne granted to him by God (a right he now took for granted—hence the blessing). Instead, he now predicted that faithful David, blessed by grace, would have a storied and prosperous reign.

David's disparate reactions to the two events also signals a recognition that the second one (1 Samuel 26) recapitulated some of the circumstances that had taken place during the first (1 Samuel 24). After the first time David spared Saul, Saul admitted his guilt (24:17–19 [ET 24:16–18]), possibly allowing David to be more at ease in Judah, hoping that Saul had suspended his pursuit of him. After spending some time in a stronghold (24:23 [ET 24:22]), he moved further out of Israel into the wilderness of Paran (25:1b). He eventually felt secure enough to return to the south-central cities of Maon and Carmel, where he married Abigail and even took a wife (Ahinoam) from Jezreel in the north (25:2–43). However, after the second time David spared Saul's life, David no longer trusted Saul's display of repentance (26:21–25). He had learned that Saul's contrition was short-lived and mercurial. Therefore, he concluded that he had to leave Israel for Philistia (27:1; cf. 26:19–20). David's more prudent second reaction also shows that his attitude developed from one incident to the other, thereby indicating that these are two separate historical events.

David Spares Saul's Life in the Cave (24:2–8a [ET 24:1–7a])

Apparently Saul immediately resumed his hunt for David once he had confronted the Philistines (24:2 [ET 24:1]). David had been in En-gedi since narrowly escaping capture (24:1 [ET 23:29]). Saul raised a force of three thousand of the best men in Israel, as he had previously (24:3 [ET 24:2]; cf. 13:2). He made his way to En-gedi and was at a specific area known as the Rocks of the Wild Goats. Because of the abundant water at En-gedi's oasis, it is a gathering spot for animals, including domestic sheep. "Sheep pens" were there, probably constructed with low stone walls (literally "the walls of the flock"; see the first textual note on 24:4 [ET 24:3]). Saul happened to choose the cave where David was hiding when he needed to relieve himself.

David's men immediately saw this as an opportunity to kill Saul, and they urged David to do just that (24:5 (ET 24:4)). They quoted Yahweh as having spoken a promise that he would hand over David's enemy to him. While this exact quotation of Yahweh is not recorded elsewhere, these words are reminiscent of 20:15–16 and in keeping with David's anointing as king to replace Saul (16:1–13), whom Yahweh had rejected (15:23, 26–29).[24] The additional words by David's men may be part of their quotation of Yahweh, "and you may do to him whatever you please," but such permission from Yahweh is not recorded elsewhere. Yahweh's instructions for the disposal of enemies are usually more specific (e.g., 15:2–3, 18; 23:2–4), but 10:7 may be comparable to the words here.[25] On the other hand, the men's additional words may be their own inference based on the circumstances: "you should do to him whatever you please."[26] They reason that since David now had the opportunity to do whatever he liked to Saul, Yahweh must have provided this opportunity and must approve of David taking full advantage of it.

David, however, did not kill Saul, but simply took the bottom part of his robe. Apparently the king had taken off this outer robe and laid it aside to relieve himself, so David was able to cut off its hem "secretly" (see the last two textual notes on 24:5 [ET 24:4]). Nevertheless, David's respect for Yahweh and his choice of Saul as anointed king left him conscience stricken even at this less aggressive act (24:6 [ET 24:5]). David would continue to show respect for Saul as Yahweh's anointed (1 Sam 26:9, 11, 16, 23), even after Saul's death (2 Sam 1:14, 16). This lesson would not be lost on David's nephew Abishai, who later would ask for Shimei's life for the crime of cursing David, Yahweh's anointed (2 Sam 19:22 [ET 19:21]; see also 1 Sam 26:6–11).

While David's men attributed his chance to kill Saul to Yahweh, David contradicted them by stating that even taking the hem of Saul's robe was not Yahweh's will (24:7 [ET 24:6]). David reprimanded them and prevented them from slaying Saul (24:8a [ET 24:7a]).

David Confronts Saul (24:8b–16 [ET 24:7b–15])

When Saul left the cave, David went after him, called to Saul as "my lord," and acknowledged him as king both in words and in bowing down to the ground

---

[24] For the theme of Yahweh delivering his faithful people from their enemies, see, e.g., 1 Sam 2:1; 4:3; 12:11; 14:47; 25:22, 26; 26:8; 30:26; 2 Sam 3:18; 4:8; 7:11.

[25] In 1 Sam 10:7 Samuel encouraged Saul to "do whatever you find to do." These words are rather vague, but the larger context implies that Saul was to eradicate the Philistine garrison in Gibeah. See "Samuel Anoints Saul (9:26–10:8)" in the commentary on 9:26–10:16, including figure 16, "Saul's Faltering Accession." See also the beginning of the commentary on 10:17–27a.

[26] See the second textual note on 24:5 (ET 24:4).

(24:8b–9 [ET 24:7b–8]). David's acts emphasized his respect for God's choice of Saul and the authority vested in the king by divine prerogative. What follows is the longest quotation of David in 1 Samuel (24:10–16 [ET 24:9–15]). His words are a long indictment of Saul for unjustly seeking his life. His argumentation divides into several parts:

1. Saul had listened to people who had slandered David, claiming that David was trying to harm the king (24:10 [ET 24:9]). We have no other record of anyone claiming that David was determined to harm Saul. Perhaps David was thinking of Doeg (22:9–10, 22) or the Ziphites (23:19). Since David had amassed a sizable contingent of troops (22:2; 23:13) and entered into a covenant with Saul's son Jonathan (18:3; 20:16; 22:8; 23:18), Saul's advisers may well have portrayed David as plotting to overthrow him.

2. David had had an opportunity to harm Saul and had not acted upon it, even though Yahweh had handed Saul over to David (24:11 [ET 24:10]). David, instead, showed pity on Saul *because Saul was Yahweh's anointed one*. David's pity was not for Saul as a person, but simply for Saul as one anointed by Yahweh. Therefore, David was implying that Yahweh stayed his hand.[27]

3. David invoked his relationship as Saul's son-in-law (18:21–27) by addressing him as "my father" (24:12 [ET 24:11]). David was implying that Saul did not act as a father to his daughter Michal or to her husband as he ought to have (cf. Eph 6:4).

4. David showed Saul the hem of the robe he had cut off, which proved that he had had an opportunity to kill the monarch (24:12 [ET 24:11]). Yet David claimed that he had committed no wrong or crime. Ordinarily showing disrespect for a ruler, such as taking a piece of his clothing, would have been treated as a crime. The hem of Saul's robe, however, was a subtle reminder that God had torn the kingdom from Saul and given it to David (15:27–28). David was willing to wait patiently in faith for the day when God would allow him to ascend the throne; he was not attempting to seize power by killing Saul. In contrast, Saul, who had no legitimate reason for seeking David's life, had set an ambush for him.

5. Yahweh would be the judge who would adjudicate the case between Saul and David—David would not take matters into his own hands (24:13–16 [ET 24:12–15]). This part of David's argumentation has two subparts that are prefaced and concluded by statements of Yahweh acting as judge (24:13, 16 [ET 24:12, 15]):

    a. Saul, David implied, was a textbook case of this proverb of the ancients: "wickedness comes from wicked people" (24:14 [ET 24:13]). Wickedness came from Saul, so his actions showed him to be wicked. However, David's actions would never display wickedness toward Saul.

    b. Saul was spending the kingdom's resources foolishly (24:15 [ET 24:14]). He was chasing "a dead dog"—a term of extreme contempt for someone who had committed an offense against the king or who was not worthy of the king's attention (cf. 2 Sam 9:8; 16:9). Pursing David was not worth the effort and expense to the kingdom. This was also emphasized by David comparing himself to a single flea. Flea infestations on humans can be quite annoying, since

---

27 Later Yahweh, working through Abigail, would prevent David from incurring bloodguilt by slaying Nabal; see 25:26, 31.

their bites cause itching. However, infestations involve large numbers of the parasites. A single flea is nearly impossible to find and hardly worth the effort.

David's censure of Saul was a masterful preaching of God's Law to a sinner who had been intent on defying God. David's self-restraint and pity on the vulnerable also modeled the Gospel. It was no crime for David to claim the kingdom that God had given him through his anointing (16:1–13), but he did not seize it. He had the mind of Jesus Christ, who, being God Incarnate, did not grab at equality with God, but emptied himself and became a servant and was obedient unto death, even death on the cross; therefore God highly exalted him (Phil 2:5–11).

Saul Admits That David Is More Righteous Than He (24:17–23 [ET 24:16–22])

Saul's reply to David's words (24:17–22 [ET 24:16–21]) is the longest quotation of Israel's first king anywhere in the Scriptures. Saul began by asking whether he had heard David's voice, clearly a rhetorical question, since there was no doubt about who had been speaking (24:17 [ET 24:16]). More importantly, Saul called David, "my son" and wept, showing that he understood that he had failed to act as a father ought to have acted toward his son-in-law and daughters.[28] Saul's next words acknowledged two truths: David was more righteous than Saul (24:18–20 [ET 24:17–19]), and David would someday be king of Israel (24:21–22 [ET 24:20–21]).

First there was Saul's admission that David was more righteous than he, as displayed by the behavior of each man (24:18 [ET 24:17]). Saul recognized that this was the only logical conclusion to be drawn from David's actions that day—Yahweh had handed Saul to David, but David did not kill him (24:19 [ET 24:18]). Saul then admitted that this was unexpected behavior; after the fall into sin, humanity is vengeful and selfish, and a sinful man does not naturally treat his enemy that way (24:20a [ET 24:19a]). This in itself demonstrates David's righteous behavior in that he repaid good for the evil he had received (cf. Gen 50:15–21; Is 63:7; Prov 3:30; 31:12). Such righteous mercy toward one's enemies has divine approval and elicits Yahweh's reward (Prov 25:21–22; see also Deut 32:35; Mt 5:43–48; Lk 6:27–28; Rom 12:14, 19–20). Therefore, Saul wished such a gracious reward for David (1 Sam 24:20b [ET 24:19b]).

Second, flowing out of Saul's admission was his recognition that David would someday be king of Israel (24:21 [ET 24:20]). This admission led Saul to beg for further leniency from David toward Saul's descendants so that Saul's own name would not be destroyed from his father's house (24:22 [ET 24:21]). Saul knew that David as king could exact vengeance on Saul's house.

---

[28] Saul had manipulated David in the arrangement for him to marry his daughter Michal, in the hope that the Philistines would kill David (18:21–27). Even worse was Saul's treatment of David regarding his older daughter, Merab. After promising her to David (18:17; cf. 17:25), he gave her to another man (18:19).

He implored him not to do it, perhaps showing that although he had accused Jonathan of being in league with David (22:8), he was ignorant of the details of the agreement between David and Jonathan, which established peace between their progeny (20:14–15, 42).

David swore the oath Saul requested and the men parted, Saul to Gibeah and David to a wilderness stronghold (24:23 [ET 24:22]). David would keep his oath to Saul by honoring his covenant with Jonathan (2 Sam 9:1–13; 21:7). Later, however, David would allow most of Saul's descendants to be killed (2 Sam 21:1–9). Even so, he continued to show respect for Saul and Jonathan by having their remains interred in Zela (2 Sam 21:12–14).

David Marries Abigail

Translation

25 ¹Samuel died, and all Israel gathered and mourned for him. They buried him in his hometown, in Ramah. Then David left and went down to the wilderness of Paran.

²There was a man in Maon, but his business was in Carmel. He was a very important man. He owned three thousand sheep and a thousand goats. At that time he was shearing his sheep in Carmel. ³The man's name was Nabal, and the name of his wife was Abigail. The woman was astute and beautiful. The man was harsh and evil in his dealings—he was a Calebite.

⁴In the wilderness David heard that Nabal was shearing his sheep. ⁵David sent ten young men. David said to the young men, "Go up to Carmel. When you come to Nabal, give him my greetings, ⁶and say this: 'May you live [long]! May you have peace! May your house have peace! May all that is yours have peace! ⁷Now I have heard that you are shearing. Now your shepherds were with us. We did not harass them, and nothing of theirs was missing the entire time they were in Carmel. ⁸Ask the young men, and they'll tell you. May the young men find favor in your eyes, because we have come on a special occasion. Please give whatever you have on hand to the young men and to your son David.'"

⁹David's young men came and spoke all these words to Nabal in David's name. Then they waited. ¹⁰Nabal replied to David's servants, "Who is David? Who is Jesse's son? Today many servants are deserting their masters. ¹¹Should I take my food and my water and my meat that I have slaughtered for my shearers and give it to men who came from I don't know where?"

¹²David's young men turned back to the way they had come. They returned, came, and reported to him all of these words. ¹³Then David said to his men, "Each man should put on his sword." So each man put on his sword, and David too put on his sword. About four hundred men went up following David, but two hundred stayed with the supplies.

¹⁴One of the young men told Abigail, Nabal's wife, "You should know that David sent messengers from the wilderness to bless our master, but he yelled at them. ¹⁵The men had been very good to us. We were not harassed, and we did not lose anything the entire time we went about with them when we were in the countryside. ¹⁶They were a wall around us both by night and by day the entire time we were with them tending the flock. ¹⁷Now ponder what you ought to do, because there is certain to be trouble for our master and his entire household. He is such a good-for-nothing man that no one can talk to him."

¹⁸Abigail quickly took two hundred loaves of bread, two bottles containing wine, five butchered sheep, five seahs of roasted grain, a hundred bunches of

raisins, and two hundred lumps of pressed figs and loaded them on donkeys. [19]She said to her young men, "Go in front of me—I will be following after you." (But she did not tell her husband, Nabal.) [20]She was riding on a donkey and going down under a covered mountain path, and David and his men were going up toward her, and she came upon them.

[21]David had thought, "I guarded all this guy's stuff in the wilderness for nothing. Nothing of all of his possessions went missing. He's repaid my good with evil. [22]Thus may God do to David and thus may he add, if I leave until morning any of his men who piss against a wall."

[23]When Abigail saw David, she quickly got down from the donkey and bowed facedown before David. [24]She fell at his feet and said, "The blame is mine, my lord. Please let your servant speak directly to you, and listen to the words of your servant. [25]My lord should not be concerned about this good-for-nothing man, Nabal, because as is his name, so is he. Nabal is his name, and foolishness accompanies him. However, I, your servant, did not see my lord's young men whom you sent. [26]Now, my lord, as Yahweh lives and as you live, since Yahweh has kept you from bloodshed and from saving yourself by your own power, now may your enemies and those who are seeking my lord's harm be like Nabal. [27]Now this blessing, which your slave girl has brought to my lord, let it be given to the young men who are traveling around under my lord's leadership. [28]Please forgive your servant's offense, since Yahweh will certainly give my lord a lasting dynasty because my lord is fighting Yahweh's wars, and evil will not be found in you as long as you live. [29]When a man rises up to pursue you and seek your life, then my lord's life will be bound in the bundle of life with Yahweh your God. He will sling away the life of your enemies in the pouch of a sling. [30]When Yahweh does for my lord every good thing that he said about you and appoints you to be designated ruler over Israel, [31]then this will not become for you, my lord, [a cause of] stumbling or a guilty conscience by having shed blood needlessly or by my lord saving himself. May Yahweh treat my lord well, and may you remember your servant."

[32]David said to Abigail, "Blessed be Yahweh, the God of Israel, who sent you to meet me today. [33]Blessed is your discretion, and blessed are you because you kept me from committing bloodshed and from saving myself by my own hand. [34]However, as Yahweh, the God of Israel, who prevented me from harming you, lives, if you had not come quickly to meet me, there would not have been left for Nabal by morning's light one of his men who piss against a wall."

[35]So David took from her what she had brought him and said to her, "Go up to your home in peace. See, I have listened to you and have shown you favor."

[36]So Abigail went home to Nabal. He was having a feast in his home like a king's feast. Nabal was in a good mood, and he was very drunk, so she did not tell him anything until morning's light.

[37]In the morning when Nabal had sobered up, his wife told him these things. His heart died within him, and he became like a rock. [38]About ten days later Yahweh struck Nabal, and he died.

³⁹When David heard that Nabal was dead, he said, "May Yahweh be blessed: he defended me against Nabal's insult, restrained his servant from doing evil, and brought Nabal's evil back upon his own head."

Then David sent [messengers] and spoke with Abigail to propose marriage. ⁴⁰David's servants came to Abigail at Carmel and spoke to her: "David sent us to you to propose marriage."

⁴¹She rose, bowed facedown on the ground, and said, "Your servant is a slave girl to wash the feet of my master's servants." ⁴²Then Abigail quickly arose and mounted a donkey, with five of her young women walking beside her, and she traveled behind David's messengers. She became his wife.

⁴³And David took Ahinoam from Jezreel. The two of them became his wives. ⁴⁴However, Saul gave his daughter Michal, David's wife, to Palti the son of Laish, who was from Gallim.

Textual Notes

25:1 וַיִּקָּבְצוּ—For "and they gathered," see the first textual note on 7:6.

וַיִּסְפְּדוּ־לֹו—"And they mourned for him." The identical third masculine plural Qal (G) preterite (imperfect with *waw* consecutive) of סָפַד, "to mourn," recurs in the similar notice of Samuel's death in 1 Sam 28:3, as well as in the notice of Saul's death in 2 Sam 1:12. Other forms of the verb appear in 2 Sam 3:31; 11:26.

וַיִּקְבְּרֻהוּ—"(And) they buried him." The same third masculine plural Qal (G) preterite (imperfect with *waw* consecutive) of קָבַר, "to bury," with a third masculine singular suffix, appears in the parallel notice of Samuel's death in 1 Sam 28:3, as well as in 2 Sam 2:32. Forms of the verb signify the burial of Saul (and his sons) in 1 Sam 31:13; 2 Sam 2:4–5; 21:14; and the burial of others in 2 Sam 2:32; 3:32; 4:12; 17:23.

בְּבֵיתֹו בָרָמָה—Literally this means "in his house in Ramah." This commentary understands "house/home" in this context to mean "hometown."

מִדְבַּר פָּארָן:—This means "the wilderness of Paran." This wilderness is mentioned also in Gen 21:21; Num 10:12; 12:16; 13:3, 26 (see also Gen 14:6; Deut 1:1; 1 Ki 11:18).[1] It apparently was a large swath of land bounded roughly on the north by Palestine, on the west by the wilderness of Etham, on the south by the desert of Sinai, and on the east by the Arabah.[2] Kadesh-barnea, in extreme southern Judah (Josh 15:3), was located in the wilderness of Paran (Num 13:26). Thus, David simply went south, just beyond the southern reaches of the more densely populated villages of Judah, perhaps in the Negev directly south of Maon.[3]

---

[1] "Mount Paran" occurs in Deut 33:2 and Hab 3:3.

[2] See also J. M. Hamilton, "Paran," *ABD* 5:162.

[3] See Tsumura, *The First Book of Samuel*, 575; cf. Fokkelman, *The Crossing Fates*, 474–75. McCarter, *I Samuel*, 388 (who notes that the wilderness of Paran did not extend farther north than the southern extreme of Canaan), and Klein, *1 Samuel*, 245 (who locates the wilderness of Paran in the southern Sinai Peninsula), argue that the wilderness of Paran was too far south for David to have gone there. They follow the reading "Maon" in LXX B.

471

25:2 וְלוֹ—The preposition לְ denotes possession, "(belonging) to him," hence "he owned."

וַיְהִי בִגְזֹז אֶת־צֹאנוֹ בַּכַּרְמֶל:—Literally "and it was in the shearing of his sheep in Carmel." The Qal (G) infinitive construct of גָּזַז, "to shear," with the preposition בְּ forms a temporal clause of a sentence that is completed in 25:4. The intervening verse, 25:3, supplies parenthetical information that interrupts the sentence. The thoughts to be connected are "when he was shearing his sheep, David heard …"

25:3 נָבָל—The man's name was "Nabal." In the OT a Hebrew adjective with this identical spelling, נָבָל, is attested meaning "foolish, stupid." It is cognate to the noun נְבָלָה, "folly, stupidity." See further the second textual note on 25:25. However, these are not the only possible derivations for Nabal's name; see "Introduction to Nabal and Abigail (25:2–3)" in the commentary.

אֲבִגַיִל—The name "Abigail" is a combination of אָבִי, "my father," possibly theophoric, referring to God as "my Father," and a form derived from the common verb גִּיל, "to rejoice," thus "my father rejoices." Cf. Prov 23:24: גִּיל יָגִיל אֲבִי צַדִּיק, "the father of a righteous man rejoices." The spelling here, אֲבִגַיִל, is defective, or *ḥaser*, without the first *yod*. Another short form, אֲבִיגַל, appears in 25:32. The full spelling אֲבִיגַיִל is given in 25:14, 23, 36, 39, 40, 42 and the Qere in 25:18. The Kethib in 25:18, אֲבוֹגַיִל, substitutes *waw* for the first *yod*.

טוֹבַת־שֶׂכֶל—This construct phrase, translated as "astute," is literally "good of sensibility." The noun שֶׂכֶל denotes the ability to follow God's ways even when circumstances seem to indicate some other course of action may be desirable or prudent (cf. Prov 19:11).

וִיפַת תֹּאַר—This construct phrase with *waw* is literally "and beautiful of form." The form of the adjective יָפֶה is feminine here (יָפָה in construct, יְפַת־), so this construct phrase refers to a woman, as also in Gen 29:17; Deut 21:11; Esth 2:7. When the masculine form is used, the construct phrase applies to a man (Gen 39:6; cf. 1 Sam 16:12; 17:42). The construct phrase with a feminine plural adjective is used for cows (Gen 41:18).

קָשֶׁה—This adjective can mean "severe, rough, rude" or "stubborn" (see BDB, 2 a and 3, respectively).

וְרַע מַעֲלָלִים—Literally "and evil of deeds," the man is characterized by his wicked works. The noun מַעֲלָל usually refers to bad practices or misdeeds. Thus, Nabal epitomizes the proverb of the ancients in 24:14 (ET 24:13).

וְהוּא כָלִבִּי:—"And he was a Calebite" is the reading of the Qere and a number of MT manuscripts; that reading is supported by the Targum and the Vulgate. The Kethib reads וְהוּא כְלִבּוֹ, "and he was like his heart." In place of וְהוּא 4QSam[a] reads והאיש, "and the man."[4] The LXX reads καὶ ὁ ἄνθρωπος κυνικός, "and the man was doglike," which implies a reading of והאיש כלבי, with the assumption that כלבי is related to כֶּלֶב, "dog" (17:43; 24:15 [ET 24:14]).

---

4   The word that follows in 4QSam[a] cannot be determined, since only three letters appear (כלב), and then the papyrus has a gap.

25:5 וּשְׁאֶלְתֶּם־לוֹ בִשְׁמִי לְשָׁלוֹם:—Literally "and you shall ask him in my name for peace." This is a formula for greeting. See the first textual note on 10:4; see also 17:22; *HALOT*, s.v. שָׁלוֹם, D 3; 2 Sam 8:10; 1 Chr 18:10.

25:6 לֶחָי—Literally "to alive," this is rendered as "may you live [long]." It is the pausal form of לְחַי, the adjective חַי with the preposition לְ. This use of the adjective חַי is somewhat unusual, but it is reflected in most of the ancient versions, although the LXX omits it. Josephus interpreted it as meaning ἐπ' ἔτη πολλά, "for many years."[5] Even so, it has puzzled commentators, and some have sought to emend it based on the Vulgate's *fratribus meis* to לְאָחִי, "to my brother."[6]

וְאַתָּה שָׁלוֹם—Literally "and you, peace," this is intended as a salutation and so a subjunctive verb must be supplied in English, "may you have peace!" The syntax of the next two salutations is similar.

25:7 שָׁמַעְתִּי כִּי גֹזְזִים לָךְ—Literally "I heard that shearers (are) yours," that is, "shearers" (גֹזְזִים, masculine plural Qal [G] participle) are working for Nabal. לָךְ is pausal for לָךְ.

לֹא הֶכְלַמְנוּם—In the Hiphil (H) stem (this is the first common plural perfect with a third masculine plural object suffix), כָּלַם can mean "to insult" or "humiliate" (see BDB, Hiphil, 1), thus "we did not harass them." The Hophal (Hp) perfect וְלֹא הָכְלַמְנוּ in 25:15 has the corresponding passive meaning, "we were not harassed."

וְלֹא־נִפְקַד לָהֶם מְאוּמָה—Literally "and nothing (belonging) to them was missed." The verb is a Niphal (N) perfect of פָּקַד. In 20:18, 25, 27, the Niphal of פָּקַד referred to David as "missing" or absent from Saul's table. See *HALOT*, Niphal, 1. A similar clause with the Niphal occurs in 25:21. A comparable clause with the active Qal (G) appears in 25:15, וְלֹא־פָּקַדְנוּ מְאוּמָה, "and we did not miss/lose anything."

25:8 עַל־יוֹם טוֹב בָּנוּ—Literally "on a good day we came." בָּנוּ is the Qal (G) first common plural perfect of בּוֹא, which normally would be spelled בָּאנוּ. See GKC, §§ 72 o, 74 k, 76 g.

25:9 וַיָּנוּחוּ:—"Then they rested/waited" is the reading of the MT, which is followed by most English versions. In this context the verb could mean "cease speaking" (BDB, s.v. נוּחַ, Qal, 1). The LXX reads καὶ ἀνεπήδησεν, "and he [Nabal] jumped up." On this basis and considering the reading of 20:34 in 4QSam[b] and the LXX (see the first textual note on 20:34), McCarter proposes that the verb here ought to be emended to וַיִּפֶז,[7] "but he [Nabal] was insolent/arrogant." This would involve a double graphic confusion of *nun* for *pe* and *waw* for *zayin*, two commonly confused pairs of letters in the Hasmonean script. This is supported by 25:9 in 4QSam[a], which reads נָ]בָל זַ[חַ]פֶן[וַיּ], "[and Na]bal was [in]sol[en]t/arrogant." McCarter's proposal is tempting, especially in light of 4QSam[a]. However, if that were the correct reading, the proper name "Nabal" as the subject of the verb ought to follow in 25:9, as in 4QSam[a], not after the initial verb in the next verse as in the MT and the LXX. It appears as if a scribe, sensing this, added

---

[5]   Josephus, *Antiquities*, 6.297.

[6]   See the discussion in McCarter, *I Samuel*, 392.

[7]   McCarter, *I Samuel*, 393.

נבל after the verb in 4QSamᵃ, thus supplying evidence that the MT's וַיְנֻחֵהוּ, though a difficult reading, is probably the correct text.

25:10 רַבּוּ עֲבָדִים הַמִּתְפָּרְצִים אִישׁ מִפְּנֵי אֲדֹנָיו—The plural noun עֲבָדִים, "servants," is the subject of רַבּוּ, "are many." The participle הַמִּתְפָּרְצִים then modifies עֲבָדִים. This plural participle is the Hithpael (HtD) of פָּרַץ, whose Qal (G) means "to break out/through/over." This is the sole instance of a Hithpael form, and the context suggests that it means "breaking away" or "deserting." It is followed by the singular distribute phrase "(each) man from before his master."

25:11 לָאֲנָשִׁים אֲשֶׁר לֹא יָדַעְתִּי אֵי מִזֶּה הֵמָּה—Literally "to men whom I don't know where from this they are."

25:14 נַעַר־אֶחָד מֵהַנְּעָרִים—Literally "one young man from the young men." This use of מִן is partitive.

הִנֵּה—The particle הִנֵּה can be used to call attention to something that is important, thus "you should know that."

וַיָּעַט בָּהֶם:—The verb here is the Qal (G) of עִיט, probably the same denominative verb as in 14:32; 15:19. In those verses it means "to swoop, pounce" as a vulture (see the first textual note on 14:32). Here, however, it means "scream at, shout at" (*DCH*, s.v. עִיט, Qal, 1). BDB (s.v. עִיט) considers it to be the sole OT instance of a separate verb, meaning "scream, shriek."

25:15 בַּשָּׂדֶה:—For "in the countryside," see the first textual note on 11:5.

25:17 דְּעִי וּרְאִי מַה־תַּעֲשִׂי—Literally "know and see what you should do." Imperatives of יָדַע and רָאָה were paired previously in 12:17; 14:38; 23:22, 23; 24:12 (ET 24:11); see also 2 Sam 24:13. As a hendiadys, here they could be rendered as "think carefully," "ponder," or "discern."

כָּלְתָה הָרָעָה—Literally "trouble is determined" (see *HALOT*, s.v. כלה I, Qal, 5). See the third textual note on 20:7.

בֶּן־בְּלִיַּעַל—Literally this means "a son of worthlessness." See the first textual note on 1:16.

מִדַּבֵּר אֵלָיו:—The preposition מִן prefixed to the Piel (D) infinitive construct דַּבֵּר forms an elliptical comparative (see Joüon, § 141 i). Thus, the clause could be rendered as "he is too much of a good-for-nothing to be able to talk to him."

25:18 אֲבִיַיִל—This Qere is the usual spelling of "Abigail." The Kethib אֲבוֹנַיִל results from a graphic confusion of *waw* in place of *yod*. Compare the third textual note on 25:18.

נִבְלֵי־יַיִן—This means "bottles containing wine." See the fourth textual note on 10:3. The noun נֵבֶל might already be a wordplay on Nabal's name; see 25:25.

עֲשׂוּוֹת—This Qere is the feminine plural Qal passive (Gp) participle of עָשָׂה, literally "things having been made." It modifies the "five sheep"; צֹאן is feminine singular, but a collective. The participle is translated as "butchered" in this context. The Kethib עֲשׂוּוֹת is the result of a graphic confusion of *waw* in place of *yod*.

וְחָמֵשׁ סְאִים—"Five seahs" is about nine and a half gallons (thirty-six liters).

צִמֻּקִים—The noun צִמּוּק denotes a raisin cluster.

דְּבֵלִים—The noun דְּבֵלָה refers to a cake, or pressed lump, of figs.

25:19 הִנְנִי אַחֲרֵיכֶם בָּאָה—The subject is the pronominal suffix ("I") on הִנְנִי. בָּאָה is the feminine singular Qal (G) participle of בּוֹא, thus literally "I am coming after you." (The third feminine singular Qal perfect would be accented on the first syllable, בָּאָה.)

25:20 בְּסֵתֶר הָהָר—If the noun סֵתֶר here means "hiding place" (as in 19:2) or "covering" (see *DCH*, s.v. סֵתֶר I), then this phrase means "in the cover of the mountain" or "under a covered mountain path," as translated. If the noun here means "cleft" (see *DCH*, s.v. סֵתֶר II), then the phrase probably refers to a ravine in the mountain.

וַתִּפְגֹּשׁ אֹתָם:—The Qal (G) preterite (imperfect with *waw* consecutive) of פָּגַשׁ, "to meet, encounter," is third feminine singular, thus "and she came upon them."

25:21 לַשֶּׁקֶר—This combination of the noun שֶׁקֶר, "lie, falsehood," with the article and the preposition לְ serves as an adverb and usually refers to swearing or prophesying "falsely" (e.g., Lev 5:24 [ET 6:5]; 19:12; Jer 3:23; 5:2; 27:15), so its negative force is stronger than its English translation here: "for nothing."

לָזֶה—The preposition לְ indicates possession, thus "this guy's stuff." The pronoun זֶה is sometimes used with a pejorative connotation, represented in the translation as "this guy" (see also 1 Sam 21:16 [ET 21:15]; 1 Ki 22:27 ‖ 2 Chr 18:26).

25:22 כֹּה־יַעֲשֶׂה אֱלֹהִים לְאֹיְבֵי דָוִד וְכֹה יֹסִיף—The MT reads "thus may God do to the enemies of David and thus may he add." For this oath formula, see the textual note on 3:17. Usually the speaker of this oath calls for God to punish *himself* if the speaker does not perform an action (1 Sam 14:44; 20:13; 2 Sam 3:9, 35; 19:14 [ET 19:13]), but that is not always the case (1 Sam 3:17). Here, according to the MT, the punishment would be done לְאֹיְבֵי דָוִד, "to the enemies of David." In place of that phrase, the LXX reads τῷ Δαυιδ, "to David," who is the speaker. The translation follows the LXX and assumes that the MT is a scribal emendation designed to prevent David from invoking a curse on himself.[8] In 2 Sam 12:14 both the MT (אֹיְבֵי יְהוָה) and the LXX (τοὺς ἐχθροὺς κυρίου) read "the enemies of Yahweh," but many translations assume that "the enemies of" was added to the text to avoid accusing David of scorning Yahweh.[9] It is noteworthy that in 2 Sam 12:14, 4QSam^a reads דבר יהוה, "the Word of Yahweh." Tsumura, following Yaron, argues that here, as in 2 Sam 12:14, the inclusion of "enemies" is not a scribal emendation, but was a euphemism in the original text, purposely employed by the author of the book of Samuel.[10] Yaron cites as evidence the Coptos Decree, an inscription from Egypt's thirteenth dynasty during the eighteenth century BC. This inscription uses the same euphemism and is older than the book of Samuel. Therefore, the author of Samuel could have also employed this euphemism. However, this argumentation for the authenticity of "enemies" is inconclusive on several counts. First, the fact that the euphemism existed in Egypt before the composition of the book of Samuel supports the *possibility* that the author of Samuel might have employed it, but it does not prove that

---

8 Most English versions agree: HCSB, GW, NET, NIV. However, ESV retains "the enemies of."

9 English translations that eliminate "the enemies of" in 2 Sam 12:14 include HCSB, ESV, GW, NET, NIV.

10 Tsumura, *The First Book of Samuel*, 585–86, following Yaron, "The Coptos Decree and 2 Sam xii 14."

he did. Second, there are other examples where scribes apparently made ideologically motivated changes to the text of Samuel to denigrate Saul and enhance David's reputation. An example is the elimination of Saul's age and length of reign in the MT 13:1 and the elimination of that verse completely in the LXX; this avoided any favorable comparison with David (see the commentary on 13:1). Third and finally, some names of members of Saul's family were most likely bowdlerized to avoid any royal association with the pagan god Baal: "Mephibosheth" ("from the mouth of shame," 2 Sam 4:4; 9:6, 10–13; 16:1, 4; 19:25, 26, 31 [ET 19:24, 25, 30]; 21:7, 8) in place of "Merib-baal" ("he contends with Baal," 1 Chr 8:34; 9:40) and "Ish-bosheth" ("man of shame," 2 Sam 2:8, 10, 12, 15; 3:8, 14, 15; 4:5, 8, 12) instead of "Eshbaal" ("man of Baal," 1 Chr 8:33; 9:39). Since the author of Chronicles most likely used Samuel as one of his sources, it is unlikely that the bowdlerized names were part of the original text of Samuel. But since these name changes are found in both the MT and the LXX of Samuel, the changes must have been made to the Hebrew text of Samuel prior to the translation of it in the LXX.

עַד־הַבֹּקֶר ... אִם־אַשְׁאִיר—After the oath formula (see the previous textual note), this אִם, "if," clause states what the speaker is determined not to let happen, literally "if I let [any man] remain ... until the morning." When the Hiphil (H) of שָׁאַר, "to cause to remain," is negated in context (as here), it means "leave no survivor" (BDB, Hiphil, 1).

מַשְׁתִּין בְּקִיר ... מִכָּל־אֲשֶׁר־לוֹ—Literally "from all who belong to him ... pissing against a wall." מַשְׁתִּין is a Hiphil (H) participle of שָׁתַן, whose Hiphil means "urinate." In the OT this verb occurs only as a participle and only in the phrase מַשְׁתִּין בְּקִיר, which recurs in 25:34 (also 1 Ki 14:10; 16:11; 21:21; 2 Ki 9:8). The singular participle מַשְׁתִּין is in apposition to the singular מִכָּל־, "all," with the preposition מִן in a partitive sense. The participial clause מַשְׁתִּין בְּקִיר is a strongly pejorative term for men and is translated with a comparably offensive English idiom (see also 25:34).[11]

25:23 וַתִּפֹּל לְאַפֵּי דָוִד עַל־פָּנֶיהָ—Literally the MT reads "and she fell to the nostrils of David on her face." The LXX reads καὶ ἔπεσεν ἐνώπιον Δαυιδ ἐπὶ πρόσωπον αὐτῆς, "and she fell before David on her face," which suggests a Hebrew reading of לִפְנֵי דָוִד in place of לְאַפֵּי דָוִד in the MT.

וַתִּשְׁתָּחוּ—This verb, which recurs in 25:41, is the Hishtaphel of חָוָה, "to bow down"; see the third textual note on 1:3. The feminine form here corresponds to the masculine וַיִּשְׁתַּחוּ, for which, see the second textual note on 1:28.

25:24 בִּי־אֲנִי אֲדֹנִי הֶעָוֹן—The majority of Masoretic manuscripts include the emphatic pronoun אֲנִי, literally "on me—me—my lord is the iniquity." The pronoun is omitted in a few Masoretic manuscripts, which read בִּי אֲדֹנִי הֶעָוֹן, "on me, my lord, is the iniquity," which agrees with the LXX, ἐν ἐμοί, κύριέ μου, ἡ ἀδικία. The pronoun אֲנִי may be a dittograph and corruption of the following אֲדֹנִי.

וּתְדַבֶּר־נָא אֲמָתְךָ בְּאָזְנֶיךָ—"And please let your female servant speak in your ears" is translated as "please let your servant speak directly to you." Abigail self-effacingly refers to herself in the third person with the feminine noun אָמָה, "female servant," twice in this verse and again in 25:25, 28, 31, 41. (She will employ שִׁפְחָה, "slave girl,"

---

[11] Leithart, "David's Threat to Nabal: How a Little Vulgarity Got the Point Across."

in 25:27, 41.) See the third textual note on 1:11. This is analogous to the use of עֶבֶד by male speakers, e.g., in 3:9.

25:25 אַל־נָא יָשִׂים אֲדֹנִי ׀ אֶת־לִבּוֹ—Literally "now my lord should not set his heart."

נָבָל שְׁמוֹ וּנְבָלָה עִמּוֹ—"Nabal/fool is his name, and foolishness is with him." Abigail's etymology implies that Nabal's name is derived from the Hebrew root נבל that pertains to stupidity (see the first textual note on 25:3), although other derivations are possible.[12] The noun נְבָלָה, "foolishness," and the adjective and substantive נָבָל, "foolish/fool," denote the most extreme kind of foolishness.[13] They connote not just unbelief in God, but apostasy, idolatry, and open hostility toward God (Deut 32:6, 21; Is 32:5–6; Ezek 13:3; Job 2:10). A "fool" (נָבָל) rejects the very existence of God and mocks him as if he were powerless (Pss 14:1; 53:2 [ET 53:1]; 74:22). Consequently, dying the death of a fool (2 Sam 3:33) is tragic because it leads to eternal punishment. In 2 Sam 13:12–13 נְבָלָה refers to the rape of a half-sister, and the rapist is categorized as being "like one of the fools" (כְּאַחַד הַנְּבָלִים). Similarly, נְבָלָה refers to the rape of Dinah in Gen 34:7. Elsewhere נְבָלָה can denote a vile sexual sin, an abomination, or lewdness deserving death (Deut 22:21; Josh 7:15; Judg 19:23–24; 20:6; Jer 29:23); see also נַבְלוּת in Hos 2:12 (ET 2:10).

25:26 חַי־יְהוָה וְחֵי־נַפְשְׁךָ—For "as Yahweh lives and as you live," see the second textual notes on 1:26 and 14:45. The first phrase recurs in 25:34.

מְנָעֲךָ יְהוָה מִבּוֹא בְדָמִים—Literally "Yahweh withheld you from entering into bloodshed." The Qal (G) of מָנַע, "withhold, hold back," governs the infinitive construct of בּוֹא (with a prefixed מִן in a privative sense) and also the infinitive construct הוֹשֵׁעַ (see the next textual note). מָנַע recurs in the same sense with a different infinitive in 25:34, and it is a synonym of כָּלָא in 25:33 and of חָשַׂךְ in 25:39. In Hebrew the plural of דָּם, "blood," is used to denote shed human blood (see also 2 Sam 1:16; 3:28; 16:7, 8; 21:1), and it is a plural of result.[14] David will repeat Abigail's words מִבּוֹא בְדָמִים in 1 Sam 25:33.

וְהוֹשֵׁעַ יָדְךָ לָךְ—This is the second action that Yahweh, working through Abigail, prevented David from doing, literally "and your hand accomplishing salvation for yourself." In form the Hiphil (H) infinitive הוֹשֵׁעַ (of יָשַׁע, "to save") appears to be the infinitive absolute (cf. GKC, § 53 k), but here and in 25:33 it is used as an infinitive construct (GKC, § 65 f). (The usual form of its Hiphil infinitive construct, הוֹשִׁיעַ, appears in 25:31.) It is the second infinitive construct governed by the verb מְנָעֲךָ (see the preceding textual note). יָדְךָ functions as the infinitive's subject. לָךְ is pausal for לְךָ, and the preposition לְ has the sense of advantage.

Yahweh's hand, not David's, should be the one to achieve salvation (see 1 Sam 5:6, 9; 7:13; see also Josh 4:24; Is 53:1; 66:14). The point Abigail is making is that such a victory would not be part of Yahweh's wars (cf. 1 Sam 25:28) but simply David's

---

[12] See "Introduction to Nabal and Abigail (25:2–3)" in the commentary.

[13] See "Fools in Proverbs" in Steinmann, *Proverbs*, 30–32, which distinguishes נָבָל as a "complete fool."

[14] *IBH*, § 11 C; Waltke-O'Connor, § 7.4.1b.

selfish vengeance. Abigail will use similar language in 25:31, and David will rephrase Abigail's words in 25:33.

25:27 הַבְּרָכָה—The feminine noun בְּרָכָה, "blessing," can denote a gift or benefaction bestowed on someone (see *CDCH*, 2, citing Gen 33:11). This sets up a play on words when David, in accepting the gifts, returns a triple blessing in thanks, praising Yahweh and Abigail (25:32–33).

אֲשֶׁר־הֵבִיא שִׁפְחָתֶךָ—This means "which your slave girl has brought." For Abigail's self-effacing use of שִׁפְחָה (again in 25:41), see the third textual note on 1:11 and the second textual note on 25:24. This feminine noun is the subject of the verb, although the verb in Codex Leningradensis and many Masoretic manuscripts is הֵבִיא, the masculine third singular Hiphil (H) perfect of בּוֹא. Many other Masoretic manuscripts have הֵבִיאָה, the expected feminine Hiphil (H) form.

וְנִתְּנָה—This is the Niphal (N) third feminine singular perfect of נָתַן with *waw* consecutive. Its subject is the definite feminine noun הַבְּרָכָה, and in context it has the force of a jussive, expressing polite advice, "let the blessing be given."

לַנְּעָרִים הַמִּתְהַלְּכִים בְּרַגְלֵי אֲדֹנִי:—Literally this means "to the servants/young men walking about at the feet of my lord." The verb is a Hithpael (HtD) participle of הָלַךְ, and the Hithpael denotes iterative action. The idiom "[move about or be] at someone's feet" denotes being under his or her command or leadership.[15] For a feminine equivalent, see the textual note on 25:42.

25:28 שָׂא נָא לְפֶשַׁע אֲמָתֶךָ—The idiom with the verb נָשָׂא, "lift up" (שָׂא is the Qal [G] masculine singular imperative), and the object noun פֶּשַׁע, "transgression, offense," refers to forgiving sins.

בַּיִת נֶאֱמָן—Literally "a confirmed house," this refers to a "lasting dynasty," which Abigail foresees as Yahweh's gift to David. The identical phrase was in the messianic promise of 2:35; see the second textual note and the commentary there. Cf. also the application of the same Niphal (N) participle נֶאֱמָן to the prophet Samuel in 3:20 and to David in 22:14. The prophet Nathan will employ similar wording, וְנֶאֱמַן בֵּיתְךָ, in 2 Sam 7:16 to elaborate the divine promise of an eternal dynasty for David's Son (see 2 Sam 7:11–17, 29).

מִלְחֲמוֹת יְהוָה—This is translated as "Yahweh's wars." Saul had used this same construct phrase when he had promised to give his daughter Merab to David as a wife and had commissioned him to fight "Yahweh's wars" (18:17; cf. 8:20). Here Abigail acknowledges that David has been carrying out his office faithfully.

מִיָּמֶיךָ:—Literally "from all your days," this means "as long as you live."

25:29 וְהָיְתָה נֶפֶשׁ אֲדֹנִי צְרוּרָה ׀ בִּצְרוֹר הַחַיִּים—Literally "and the life of my lord will be bundled in the bundle of life." The feminine noun נֶפֶשׁ, "soul, life," is the subject of the feminine verb וְהָיְתָה. The predicate adjective is the feminine singular Qal passive (Gp) participle צְרוּרָה (of צָרַר I, "to bind, tie up"), which is followed by the cognate noun צְרוֹר, "a bundle, pouch, bag," used for holding something precious (e.g., Gen 42:35; Song 1:13). This is a unique biblical expression for the gift of eternal life. In context

---

[15] See also Judg 4:10; 8:5; 2 Sam 15:16, 17, 18; 1 Ki 20:10; 2 Ki 3:9.

it implies God's protection from evil and preservation in the faith until the person is called from this life into the next (cf. Gen 5:24; Ps 73:24). That this "life" is eternal is confirmed by the next phrase: it is life אֶת יְהוָה אֱלֹהֶיךָ, "with Yahweh your God." See Lk 20:37–38 and parallels.

וְקִלְּעֶנָּה—Literally "he will sling it." The implied subject is "Yahweh" in the preceding clause, and the third feminine singular object suffix refers to נֶפֶשׁ, the "life/soul" of David's enemies. The Piel (D) of קָלַע also referred to David slinging his stone into Goliath in 17:49. The cognate noun קֶלַע denoted David's "sling" in 17:40, 50, and Abigail uses the same noun here. Her use of vocabulary from 1 Samuel 17 suggests that she was familiar with David's defeat of Goliath and foresaw David's future victories in similar terms.

25:30 לְנָגִיד—This means "to be designated ruler." See the first textual note on 9:16.

25:31 לְפוּקָה וּלְמִכְשׁוֹל לֵב—Literally this means "for a toppling and for a stumbling of heart." The noun פוּקָה, "a toppling, stumbling," is a hapax legomenon derived from the verb פּוּק I, "stumble" (*CDCH*, s.v. פּוּק I). In its place 4QSamᶜ reads למנקם, "for vengeance," with an erasure of the *mem*,[16] but that is most certainly a secondary reading, substituting a more common noun for a less common one. The second noun is a common synonym, מִכְשׁוֹל, "stumbling," from the verb כָּשַׁל, "stumble" (*CDCH*, s.v. כשל). The phrase לְמִכְשׁוֹל לֵב is translated metaphorically as "a guilty conscience." מִכְשׁוֹל can denote a physical "stumbling block" that causes a person to trip and fall (e.g., Lev 19:14) or a spiritual offense that causes a person to fall from faith into divine judgment, such as idolatry (e.g., Ezek 7:19; 14:3–4; 44:12). Similar vocabulary appears in the NT, e.g., σκάνδαλον, "scandal" (Mt 13:41; 18:7; 1 Jn 2:10), and πρόσκομμα, "stumbling block" (Rom 14:13, 20).

וּלְהוֹשִׁיעַ אֲדֹנִי לוֹ—Literally this means "and by my lord achieving salvation for himself." See the third textual note on 25:26.

25:32–33 בָּרוּךְ יְהוָה ... וּבָרוּךְ טַעְמֵךְ וּבְרוּכָה אַתְּ—"Blessed be Yahweh. ... Blessed is your discretion, and blessed are you." The verb is the singular Qal passive (Gp) participle of בָּרַךְ (twice masculine, then once feminine). This verb is commonly used in the Piel (D), "to bless," as in, e.g., 1 Sam 2:20; 9:13; 13:10; 25:14; 2 Sam 6:11–12. Earlier Saul had used similar blessing formulae with the Qal passive participle to pronounce a benediction on Samuel (1 Sam 15:13) and the Ziphites (23:21), but on both occasions his words were a pietistic sham, designed to mask his disobedience to Yahweh's Word (15:13) and his sinister intent to kill David (23:21).

Here, however, David rightly pronounces these three benedictions in faith and gratitude for Yahweh carrying out his own plan of salvation through the agency of Abigail. Through her discretion God saved David from the sin of attempting to save himself. This is not the first time a woman has been "blessed" for being God's instrument of salvation; see, e.g., the blessing of Jael in Judg 5:24. Nor is it the last; see the double blessing of Mary, "blessed are you among women ... blessed is she who believed" (Lk 1:42, 45), along with the blessing of her Child, "blessed is the fruit of your womb" (Lk 1:42).

---

[16] See Josephus, *Antiquities*, 6.303, who has ἐκδικήσει, "he [God] will avenge."

The second benediction is spoken over טַעְמֵךְ, "your [Abigail's] discretion." While the noun טַעַם appears thirteen times in the OT, in only five cases is it a term for divine wisdom (1 Sam 25:33; Ps 119:66; Job 12:20; Prov 11:22; 26:16). In Ps 119:66 it is parallel to "knowledge" (דַּעַת) taught by God in accord with his Word. Its only other appearance in the book of Samuel is in 1 Sam 21:14 (ET 21:13; see also Ps 34:1 [ET superscription]), where it refers to David's affected "demeanor." In most of its other OT occurrences it refers to the sense of "taste" (e.g., Ex 16:31; Num 11:8).

25:33 כְּלִתִנִי—This is the suffixed Qal (G) second feminine singular perfect of כָּלָא, "to restrain, hinder" (see BDB, 2). Thus, it is a synonym of מָנַע in 25:26, 34 and of חָשַׂךְ in 25:39. Its form here is pointed as if it were (shortened from כְּלִיתִנִי) a form of כָּלָה, "to finish," but forms of third-*aleph* verbs (כָּלָא) often interchange with forms of third-*he* verbs (כָּלָה). See GKC, § 75 oo.

מִבּוֹא בְדָמִים—See the second textual note on 25:26.

וְהוֹשֵׁעַ יָדִי לִי:—Literally this means "and by my hand accomplishing salvation for myself." David rephrases Abigail's words from 25:26 (see the third textual note there).

25:34 לוּלֵי ... כִּי אִם־—This sequence of particles forms an unreal or contrary-to-fact condition: "if you had not hurried … there would not have been …" See Joüon, § 167 f.

25:35 וָאֶשָּׂא פָנָיִךְ:—Literally "and I lifted up your face," this idiom with the verb נָשָׂא and the object noun פָּנֶה, "face," means to show favor to someone.[17]

25:36 וְלֵב נָבָל טוֹב עָלָיו—Literally "and the heart of Nabal was good upon him" (cf. 2 Sam 13:28). This idiom denotes merriment and being in a good mood (Prov 15:15; Eccl 9:7; Esth 5:9).

וְלֹא־הִגִּידָה לּוֹ דָּבָר קָטֹן וְגָדוֹל—"And she did not report to him a word, small or large," means "so she did not tell him anything." See the similar expression with the adjectives קָטֹן and גָדוֹל in 22:15 (see the fifth textual note there).

25:37 בְּצֵאת הַיַּיִן מִנָּבָל—Literally this means "when the wine had gone out of Nabal."

25:39 בָּרוּךְ יְהֹוָה—David's blessing begins with the first two words of Abigail's (see the textual note on 25:32–33).

רָב אֶת־רִיב חֶרְפָּתִי מִיַּד נָבָל—Literally "he contended the contention of my insult from the hand of Nabal." The verb רָב is the Qal (G) perfect third masculine singular of רִיב, "to strive, contend, sue." Its direct object is the cognate noun רִיב "lawsuit, dispute, contention," thus forming a cognate accusative construction.

חָשַׂךְ מֵרָעָה—This verb, "to withhold, keep back," is a synonym of מָנַע (25:26, 34) and כָּלָא (25:33). The noun רָעָה, "evil" (with מִן in a privative sense), is translated verbally, "from doing evil," since it refers to an action (that was precluded).

לְקַחְתָּהּ לּוֹ לְאִשָּׁה:—Literally this means "to take her for himself for a wife." The verb is קַחַת, the Qal (G) infinitive construct of לָקַח, "take," with a prefixed לְ and a third feminine singular object suffix. The same wording recurs in 25:40, but there the infinitive's suffix is second feminine singular.

---

[17] Gen 19:21; 32:21 (ET 32:20); Lev 19:15; Deut 10:17; 28:50; Mal 1:8, 9; 2:9; Job 32:21; 34:19; Prov 6:35; 18:5.

25:41 וַתִּשְׁתָּחוּ—See the second textual note on 25:23.

25:42 וְחָמֵשׁ נַעֲרֹתֶיהָ הַהֹלְכוֹת לְרַגְלָהּ—Literally "and five of her young women, the ones walking at her foot," this idiom signifies that the women were Abigail's servile attendants. It is comparable to the masculine idiom discussed in the fourth textual note on 25:27.

Commentary

c. 1012 BC (Samuel dies)

c. 1011 BC (David marries Abigail and Ahinoam)

The ultimate source of all good counsel is "the wisdom from above," which "first of all is pure, then peaceable, forbearing, open to reason, full of mercy and good fruits" (James 3:17).[18] This account of David's time on the run from Saul illustrates the wisdom of accepting good advice. Like preceding narratives, this one serves to illustrate the nature of faith, which God had created in David's heart (see 1 Sam 16:7), and which enables a person to be open to receiving godly counsel (Prov 12:15; 13:10; 19:20; 20:18). We are not privy to the details of Abigail's spiritual life, but apparently this daughter of Abraham[19] was familiar with God's Word and trusted that the Savior of Israel would guide David, Yahweh's anointed with the Spirit (1 Sam 16:1–13), to rescue her from the crisis created by her husband's foolishness. How much more does Jesus Christ, the Son of David and the sinless Son of God, the anointed Christ with the Spirit, save all who call upon him for help in every time of trouble.[20] In offering advice, Abigail commends herself to David as a woman who would be an excellent wife, not simply because of her beauty (1 Sam 25:3), but especially because of her godly wisdom, which preserves her household (cf. Prov 31:26–27). She exemplifies the biblical portrait of a woman of faith (e.g., 1 Pet 3:1–6). Although married to a coarse and ungodly man, she did not rebel against him but remained submissive; at the same time she acted wisely and was saved. Her patient faith was rewarded when, after her husband's death (cf. 1 Cor 7:39), she was privileged to marry the new king of Israel. Even so, the bride of Christ, the body of believers, lives in sacrificial, submissive love while awaiting the return of her Bridegroom from heaven.[21]

---

[18] See also James 1:17. Contrast the ultimately demonic origin of jealousy, bitterness, and selfish ambition (James 3:14–15).

[19] In Romans 4 the apostle Paul argues that justification is through faith alone and that Abraham is the father of all who believe, all who share "the faith of Abraham" (Rom 4:16).

[20] See "Christ in Samuel" in the introduction and the commentary on 1 Sam 2:10, 35. Jesus is the Davidide who is anointed with the Holy Spirit to bring salvation: Is 11:1–5; 61:1–3; Mt 3:13–17; Lk 4:18–19.

[21] Cf. Mt 25:1–13; Eph 5:21–33; 1 Thess 1:10; Rev 22:17.

Samuel's Death (25:1)

The chapter begins with a notice of Samuel's death, which must have taken place after the first time David spared Saul's life, at En-gedi (1 Samuel 24),[22] but before David's time in the wilderness of Paran (25:1). This notice appears almost superfluous in this context, since the reader does not need to know about Samuel's death until Saul's attempt to bring him back from the dead for advice on his final battle against the Philistines (28:1–25; see especially 28:3). However, it is important to note that the author includes this death notice immediately after Saul acknowledged David as king (24:21 [ET 24:20]).[23] Saul would not stop in his attempts to eliminate David after Samuel's death, but he had finally admitted the validity of Samuel's anointing of David as king (1 Sam 16:1–13).

Samuel was accorded an honor in his death that is said of no other person in the Bible and was befitting of his role as the most important prophet since Moses: "all Israel gathered and mourned for him" (25:1).[24] Samuel was interred in Ramah, his ancestral town where he had spent most of his adult life.

After Samuel's funeral, David, who had been in a stronghold somewhere in Judah (24:23 [ET 24:22]), moved to the wilderness of Paran in Judah's southernmost reaches (see the last textual note on 25:1). Apparently, after two close encounters with Saul,[25] David decided at first to go to the extreme southern portion of the land of Israel to see whether he could avoid Saul altogether. But circumstances would bring him north into south-central Judah once again.

Introduction to Nabal and Abigail (25:2–3)

In order to explain the next story from David's life, the author first introduces us to Nabal and Abigail. The description begins in 25:2 without mentioning his name until 25:3. He lived in Maon and had business just north of there in Carmel.[26] Since Abigail was from Carmel (27:3), Nabal's business there may have been the result of family ties. Carmel was where Saul had erected a monument to his victory over the Amalekites (15:12).

We learn from the author that the man was very prominent and owned a large flock of sheep and goats (25:2). It was springtime, and his sheep were being shorn in Carmel. To this point we know of the man, but he has not been named.

---

[22] David would spare Saul's life a second time in 1 Samuel 26. See "David Twice Spares Saul's Life—Comparing 1 Samuel 24 and 1 Samuel 26" in the commentary on 24:2–23 (ET 24:1–22).

[23] Bodner, *1 Samuel*, 259.

[24] All Israel (perhaps meaning only the northern tribes) is said to have mourned for Jeroboam's son Abijah (1 Ki 14:13, 18), but they did not gather to do it.

[25] Chapters 23 and 24 each narrate a major encounter between David and Saul. Briefer perilous encounters are narrated earlier.

[26] For the locations of these cities in south-central Judah, see the commentary on 23:24 and 15:12, respectively. See also figure 24 in the commentary on 19:1–17.

After this information, the couple is introduced formally: we are given Nabal's name and the name of his wife (25:3). The name "Nabal," which would be the subject of Abigail's pun later (25:25), as well as the author's pun (25:37), is not easily explained. It is hard to understand why parents would give their son such a name if its primary meaning were "fool, stupid." To be sure, that is a well-attested meaning of נָבָל (see the second textual note on 25:25), but his name probably was intended to represent a different Hebrew word with the same spelling.[27] It is not likely that it was derived from נֵבֶל, "harp," or נֵבֶל, "bottle,"[28] despite the author's quip in 25:37.[29] A more likely meaning is "noble," from the adjective נָבָל, as in Sirach 50:26 (*CDCH*, s.v. נָבָל III).[30] On the other hand, "Abigail" clearly means "my father rejoices" (see the second textual note on 25:3).

There is a chiastic arrangement to 25:3:

A   Nabal's name
   B   Abigail's name
   B'   A description of Abigail
A'   A description of Nabal

This allows Abigail to be at the center of the introduction and to highlight her as the more important of the two. Since she was "astute" and "beautiful," she was the perfect match for David. The description of her as "astute" (טוֹבַת־שֶׂכֶל, 25:3) uses a noun (שֶׂכֶל) that is cognate to the verb employed four times to depict David as "being successful" (שָׂכַל, 18:5, 14, 15, 30). The phrase portraying her as "beautiful" (וִיפַת תֹּאַר, 25:3) has the same noun (תֹּאַר) used in the designation of David as "handsome" (וְאִישׁ תֹּאַר, 16:18). On the other hand, Nabal was a poor mate for her, since he was harsh and evil (25:3). For the same reason he was also not a good benefactor for David, something that is signaled by the author's final remark, "he was a Calebite." Like the Ziphites, who also were Calebites, but who betrayed David (23:19–20), Nabal did not favor David.

David Sends Messengers with a Request to Nabal (25:4–8)

From somewhere in the wilderness David got word that Nabal was shearing his sheep (25:4). Therefore, it was spring, and with a flock of three thousand sheep Nabal would have had a number of men doing the work. He would have

---

[27] A very unlikely theory is that of Levenson ("1 Samuel 25 as Literature and History," 14), who believed that the man's actual name was suppressed and never supplied by the author so that the name "Nabal" could serve his purposes of characterization of this foolish man.

[28] For נֵבֶל, "bottle," see the third textual note on 1:24. A different Hebrew noun for "flask" or "bottle," בַּקְבֻּק (e.g., 1 Ki 14:3), is related to the names Bakbuk, "bottle" (Ezra 2:51; Neh 7:53), and Bakbukiah, "bottle of Yah(weh)," among postexilic Judeans (Neh 11:17; 12:9, 25), as well as "Bukki" (Ezra 7:4), which may be a shortened form of בָּקְיָהוּ, "my vessel is Yahweh."

[29] The author's statement that "the wine had gone out of Nabal" (נָבָל, 25:37) might wryly compare him to a drained "bottle of wine" (נֵבֶל, 25:18). See the commentary on 25:37.

[30] However, LXX Sirach 50:26 translates the adjective נָבָל as μωρός, "foolish."

had, therefore, a large quantity of food on hand for the workers (cf. 25:11). It was the opportune moment for David to ask for supplies for his men. David's rather long message to Nabal contained four parts:

1. The first part was a greeting, for which the words are not given, since David probably assumed that the messengers would use a common salutation (25:5).

2. Next followed four blessings—perhaps more than normal, but likely an indication that David may have had a suspicion that Nabal would not have been well-disposed toward him and his men (25:6).

3. The third part noted the shearing of the sheep and how David had safeguarded Nabal's shepherds—an implication that David's protection was one reason the sheep were kept safe and were now able to be sheared (25:7–8a). David and his men were not marauding bandits, and his message even suggested that Nabal might check with his shepherds to confirm this. Moreover, this part of David's message anticipated Nabal's rejection of David's request: Nabal might claim not to know anything about David (cf. 25:11).

4. Finally, David broached his request asking for favor toward his young men and a gift of food for them and himself (25:8b). David's self-referential "your son" places him in a deferential posture toward Nabal while simultaneously invoking a relationship that implies Nabal's obligation to David.

Nabal's Reply and David's and Abigail's Reaction to It (25:9–22)

The author is careful to note that David's messengers followed their instructions (25:9). Nabal's reply began with two revealing questions (25:10). The second one refers to David as "Jesse's son," a derogatory characterization found elsewhere in 1 Samuel as Saul's pejorative name for David (20:27, 30, 31; 22:7, 8, 13; cf. 22:9). Thus, Nabal, like the Ziphites, aligned himself with Saul—and he clarified this by noting that "many servants are deserting their masters" (25:10). Nabal implied that David was a disloyal servant of Saul who had deserted the king; he had not fled for his life from a murderous tyrant. Then Nabal insulted David's messengers, claiming that he did not know from where they came—implying that they might not have been sent by David (25:11). Overall, Nabal's reply was arrogant and imperious. He did not bother to check with his shepherds to see whether the young men were telling the truth and whether he ought to have been grateful to David. Instead, he brusquely dismissed David's men.

The author first completes the account of David's messengers by relating their return (25:12) and David's reaction of ordering his men to arm themselves for action (25:13). The author is careful to tell us that David took only four hundred of the six hundred men, leaving two hundred to guard their supplies. This indicates that David did not intend to stay in Carmel in south-central Judah, but would return to the wilderness of Paran after dealing with Nabal.

Next the narrative turns to Abigail, relating that "one of the young men," one of Nabal's shepherds, informed her of her husband's dismissal of David's request (25:14). To everyone except Nabal it must have seemed urgent to appease David (cf. 25:17), so the servant took the unusual step of appealing to his master's wife. He also went on to confirm the protection that David's men had afforded them—something that David had suggested Nabal should do (25:15–16; cf. 25:7–8a). The shepherd characterized the security provided by David's men as a "wall" (חוֹמָה, 25:16), the word used to refer to a city's fortifications that defend it from intruders. The servant also advised Abigail to take action, but he refrained from taking the bolder step of suggesting a specific plan (25:17). He was certain that Nabal had stirred up David's wrath and that the result would be nothing but trouble for anyone connected with Nabal. In addition, Nabal's rude behavior must have been so typical of him and so obviously irritating to Abigail that the servant was not hesitant to speak ill of his master to Abigail. The intrepid servant even said that Nabal was "such a good-for-nothing man that no one can talk to him" (25:17), thus explaining why the servant had not appealed to his master. Abigail acquiesced by her response; she too thought it futile to speak to Nabal (25:19).

Abigail had no trouble knowing what to do. She took a large amount of provisions (25:18). The bread and sheep were perishable and were clearly meant to provide an immediate banquet for David and his men. The other items would keep for some time if properly stored. Raisins and dried figs made into lumps (sometimes called "fig cakes") were common ways of keeping fruit for year-round consumption as a quick source of energy, especially for someone whose blood sugar had been seriously depleted (cf. 30:11–12). Abigail recruited some of the household servants to go with her but did not tell Nabal of her actions, as the author pointedly notes (25:19). She must have had some idea where David had been staying and which road he was likely to take to Carmel, since she came upon him as he was traveling toward Carmel (25:20).

Before relating the encounter between Abigail and David, the author turns to give further information about David's reaction to Nabal's rebuff. David was thinking about how he had provided protection for Nabal's possessions, and for the third time in the account mention is made of Nabal having lost nothing (25:21; see previously 25:7, 15). David was particularly incensed because Nabal had repaid David's good with evil, which once again connected Nabal with Saul (24:18 [ET 24:17]). Such behavior brings evil on one's household (Prov 17:13), so it is not surprising that David was thinking of taking an oath to destroy every man in Nabal's household by morning (1 Sam 25:22). The crude way in which David referred to men in Nabal's house—those "who piss against a wall" (מַשְׁתִּין בְּקִיר, 25:22)—when used elsewhere in the OT is always in a context of meting out violent death on a family unit for crimes and sins that are offensive to God (1 Ki 14:10; 21:21; 2 Ki 9:8) or, in one case, a brutal coup d'état (1 Ki 16:11).

Abigail's Appeal to David (25:23–31)

Abigail's appeal to David for the lives of her family began with her bowing to David as if he were her master or king (the last verb in 25:23 typically refers to worshiping God). The author quotes a long speech by Abigail—the longest individual discourse by a woman in the OT.[31] In order to seek David's forgiveness, Abigail assumed the blame for the insult David suffered from her husband and begged David to hear her out (25:24). She argued in essence that Nabal was so worthless that he was beneath David's contempt and that she was ignorant of David's initial request (25:25). Her wordplay on Nabal's name takes him from being noble (see the commentary on 25:3) to possessing godless foolishness (see the second textual note on 25:25). This kind of foolishness would later be aptly described by Isaiah as the behavior of a scoundrel who was no longer viewed as noble and who denied the hungry person food and the thirsty person drink (Is 32:5–8).

Next Abigail's words deftly assumed that David would favorably receive her plea—stating in an oath that Yahweh had kept David from bloodshed and, more importantly, from "from saving yourself by your own power" (25:26). Any victory over Nabal that was a product of David's indignation would have been a selfish act accomplished by David's own effort, not by Yahweh's gracious blessing (see "blessed," 25:32–33). Saving oneself by one's own hand is a form of works-righteousness that is actually a sign of unbelief (Judg 7:2), since true salvation is by God's own power (Deut 20:4), that is, by his grace in Jesus Christ and through faith alone (e.g., Eph 2:8–9), as it has always been (Gen 3:15; 12:1–3; see Romans 4; Galatians 3). By highlighting that Yahweh had prevented such sin on David's part, she revealed her own comprehension of Yahweh's gracious manner of saving. At the same time, she was appealing to David, her kinsman in the faith, in order to save her family.

After asking David to accept the provisions she had brought as a "blessing" (25:27), Abigail directly asked for forgiveness (27:28) by appealing to Yahweh's anointing of David and promise that he would be king (16:1–13). She forecast that God would give him a "lasting dynasty," since he was fighting divine wars (25:28; cf. 8:20; 18:17). Abigail's foretelling of a "lasting dynasty" anticipated God's great promise to David in 2 Samuel 7, and her statement that evil would never be found in him anticipated the innocence that David could claim in Yahweh's sight as he himself would state in his last words (2 Sam 23:3–5). To be sure, David was a sinner and did sin (most egregiously in 2 Samuel 11). David's innocence was credited to him not because he was sinless, but through faith in God's promises, especially his promise of the Savior to be born through David's own line (2 Sam 7:16, 19), the "Son of David" (Mt 1:1), whom David himself addressed as "my Lord" (Ps 110:1; see also Mk 12:35–37; Acts 2:34–35).[32] The book of Samuel, then, clearly teaches justification by grace alone through faith alone.

---

[31] The quotation is 153 Hebrew words in the MT. Only the Song of Deborah (Judg 5:2–31) is longer (352 Hebrew words). However, that song is attributed to Deborah *and* Barak (Judg 5:1; Bergen, *1, 2 Samuel*, 249).

[32] See Steinmann, "What Did David Understand about the Promises in the Davidic Covenant?"

Abigail then stated that David had no reason to kill Nabal, since it would not enhance his life—God had already bundled David "in the bundle of life" to be with himself forever, whereas Yahweh would banish enemies like Nabal away from his presence forever as if hurling them away with a sling (1 Sam 25:29; cf. Mt 8:12; 22:13; 25:30). Her words were adroitly designed to assure David that Nabal was no threat because God would keep his promises. She displayed wisdom in appealing to David's relationship with Yahweh, who had sustained him thus far in his flight from Saul. Then Abigail closed her remarks by confidently appealing to the outcome of Samuel's anointing of David at God's command (16:1–13). Yahweh would most certainly fulfill every good thing he had promised. David would become Israel's ruler, and by accepting her gift, David would avoid needless bloodshed, personal vengeance, and a future guilty conscience over sinful actions he might otherwise have taken on his path to the throne (25:30–31).

David's Reply to Abigail (25:32–35)

David's reaction to Abigail's words demonstrated that he saw in her a wisdom that could have come only from God. He praised God for sending Abigail (25:32) and then invoked Yahweh's blessings for Abigail's discretion and for Abigail herself, since she was Yahweh's instrument to keep him from bloodshed and self-serving conquest (25:33). Yet he also acknowledged in an oath that she and her quick reaction were all that stood between David and certain death for all of Nabal's men, vocalizing the previous oath he had considered only in his thoughts (25:34; cf. 25:22). In acknowledging Abigail's "discretion" (טַעַם, 25:33), he was in essence noting that it enhanced her outer beauty ("astute and beautiful," 25:3). Without it she would not have been useful to Nabal or a worthy future bride for David (Prov 11:22).[33] David sent her home with assurance of the safety of her household (1 Sam 25:35).

The Results of Abigail's Actions (25:36–42)

The narrative shifts to the scene in Nabal's home when Abigail arrived. Ironically, Nabal was feasting like a king (25:36)[34] after having refused to provide food or drink for Israel's anointed king David (25:11). Seeing that her foolish husband was drunk, she declined to speak with him. Nabal's drunken state was not fitting for someone playing the part of a king, and it was a corollary of his refusal to feed those who had less than he (Prov 31:4–5).

The events of the last days of Nabal are related quickly. The next day "the wine had gone out of Nabal" (25:37). The author's words seem to play on comparing "Nabal" (נָבָל, nabal) to an empty "bottle" (נֵבֶל, nebel) of wine that now

---

[33] Prov 11:22 has the same noun, טַעַם, "discretion," as 1 Sam 25:33. See Steinmann, *Proverbs*, 295. See further the discussion of טַעַם in the textual note on 25:32–33.

[34] Note also the conjunction of feasting and shearing in Absalom's attempt to make himself king (2 Sam 13:23–28).

had been drunk (see "two bottles containing wine," 25:18). Abigail's news caused Nabal's heart to die within him, "and he became like a rock" (25:37). This description is often identified in medical terms as a stroke or seizure.[35] However, we ought to be cautious in offering medical diagnoses through these metaphorical descriptions. They might just as easily be describing psychological and behavioral changes in Nabal—perhaps he was dispirited and offended and became petulantly nonresponsive to Abigail and others around him.

The ultimate blow came from Yahweh, who, about ten days later, took Nabal's life (25:38), justifying Abigail's advice to David that God would throw away the lives of David's enemies like a stone cast out of a sling (25:29). David, upon hearing the news of Nabal's death, acknowledged God's governance of all these events (25:39a).

David's proposal of marriage demonstrated his wisdom and good judgment (25:39b–40). His desire for her was a further acknowledgment of the inestimable value of her "discretion" (25:33). He found a way to graciously provide for the widow of his enemy, and he obtained a wise and beautiful wife. Abigail's wisdom is confirmed by her reply to David's marriage proposal: she assumed no special privilege but offered her service as the lowliest member of David's household, who would perform the menial task of showing hospitality by washing the feet of guests (25:41; cf. Gen 18:4; 19:2; 24:32; 43:24; Judg 19:21), a task Jesus Christ would perform for his disciples to exemplify his own mission as the Servant sent by God to serve and save even the lowliest (Jn 13:5–17). But as Hannah sang, Yahweh is a God who exalts the lowly:

> "Yahweh makes poor and makes rich;
> he humbles, and he also elevates.
> He lifts a poor person from the dust;
> he raises a needy person from the trash heap
>   to seat [him] with nobles,
>   and he makes him inherit an honored throne." (1 Sam 2:7–8)

Fittingly, then, Abigail arrived at David's camp not as a lowly servant girl, but as a rich widow with a donkey and five servant girls of her own (25:42).

David's Wives (25:43–44)

The chapter is concluded with a note about the wives David took while he was in Judah's wilderness. "Ahinoam" was probably his second wife (after Michal [18:27]) since her son Amnon was David's eldest son (2 Sam 3:2; 1 Chr 3:1). Her hometown was the Jezreel that was in the vicinity of Maon, Ziph, and Carmel in south-central Judah (Josh 15:55–56). David's second son, known as both "Chileab" and "Daniel," would be born to Abigail (2 Sam 3:3; 1 Chr 3:1). (See figure 23, "David's Genealogy," at the end of the commentary on 1 Sam 16:1–13.) Both Ahinoam and Abigail would accompany David

---

[35] HCSB; Bergen, *1, 2 Samuel*, 252; Tsumura, *The First Book of Samuel*, 593.

wherever he lived—going first to Gath (1 Sam 27:3) and then to Ziklag, where the Amalekites would capture them (1 Sam 30:5). Eventually they would be with him when he began his reign in Hebron (2 Sam 2:2–4).

In the meantime, Saul, who had given his daughter Michal to be David's first wife (18:20–27), betrayed his son-in-law by passing her off to Palti the son of Laish from Gallim (25:44). Saul had broken an earlier promise in a similar way when he had offered his older daughter, Merab, to David (18:17; cf. 17:25), but then gave her to another man instead (18:19). Although Michal was Saul's daughter, his action violated the holy marriage covenant between her and David and was an offense against God (cf. Gen 2:24; Mal 2:14–16; Mt 19:4–6). Saul may have taken back his daughter Michal to weaken David's claim to the throne, though it would have little effect, and eventually David would demand the return of Michal (2 Sam 3:14–16). The longer form of Palti's name is "Paltiel" (2 Sam 3:15), and his father's name is also vocalized as Lush (the Kethib in 2 Sam 3:15). Gallim was just north of Jerusalem in the same area as Laishah and Anathoth (Is 10:30).

David Spares Saul's Life at Ziph

Translation

26 ¹The Ziphites came to Saul at Gibeah with this report: "Isn't David hiding at the hill of Hachilah across from Jeshimon?" ²So Saul arose and went down to the wilderness of Ziph. With him were three thousand men selected from Israel to seek David in the wilderness of Ziph. ³Saul camped at the hill of Hachilah, which is opposite Jeshimon on the road, while David was dwelling in the wilderness. He saw that Saul had come after him in the wilderness.

⁴David sent spies and knew that Saul had definitely come. ⁵So David arose and came to the place where Saul was encamped. David saw the place where Saul and Ner's son Abner, the commander of his army, were lying. Saul was lying within the camp, and the troops were encamped around him. ⁶David then spoke to Ahimelech the Hittite and to Zeruiah's son Abishai, Joab's brother, "Who will go down with me to Saul, to the camp?"

Abishai said, "I will go down with you."

⁷So David and Abishai went to the troops at night. Saul was lying asleep within the camp, and his spear was stuck in the ground near his head. Abner and the troops were lying around him. ⁸Abishai said to David, "Today God has handed your enemy over to you. Now let me strike him with the spear into the ground one time. I will not need to do it to him a second time."

⁹But David said to Abishai, "Do not destroy him, for who can stretch out his hand against Yahweh's anointed one and remain guiltless?" ¹⁰David also said, "As Yahweh lives, certainly Yahweh will strike him down, or his day will come and he will die, or he will go down to battle and be swept away. ¹¹Because of Yahweh I will certainly not stretch out my hand against Yahweh's anointed one. Now take the spear that is at his head and the jug of water, and let's go."

¹²So David took the spear and the jug of water at Saul's head, and they went on their way. No one observed them, no one knew, and no one awakened, since all of them were sleeping because a deep slumber from Yahweh had fallen upon them.

¹³David crossed to the other side and stood atop the hill far away. The space between them was great. ¹⁴David called out to the troops and to Ner's son Abner, "Won't you answer, Abner?"

Abner replied, "Who are you that you call to the king?"

¹⁵David said to Abner, "Aren't you a man? Who is like you in Israel? Why haven't you guarded your master, the king? For a soldier came to destroy the king, your master. ¹⁶This thing you have done is not good. As Yahweh lives, you are dead men who have not guarded your master, Yahweh's anointed one. Now look! Where are the king's spear and the jug of water that was at his head?"

¹⁷Then Saul recognized David's voice and said, "Is this your voice, my son David?"

David said, "It is my voice, my master, Your Majesty." ¹⁸He also said, "Why would my master bother pursuing his servant? For what have I done, and what crime have I committed? ¹⁹Now let my master the king listen to the words of his servant: If Yahweh has incited you against me, let him accept an offering. If, however, humans [have incited you], may they be cursed in Yahweh's presence because today they have driven me away from sharing in Yahweh's inheritance, saying, 'Go serve other gods.' ²⁰May my blood not fall to the ground away from Yahweh's presence, because the king of Israel has come out to seek a single flea like someone pursing a partridge in the hills."

²¹Saul said, "I have sinned. Return, my son David, because I will not harm you again since you considered my life precious this day. I have acted foolishly, and I have made a terrible mistake."

²²David replied, "Here is the king's spear! Let one of the young men cross over and get it. ²³Yahweh will repay each man for his righteousness and faithfulness. When Yahweh handed you over to me today, I was not willing to stretch out my hand against Yahweh's anointed one. ²⁴Just as I considered your life important today, so may Yahweh consider my life important and deliver me from every trouble."

²⁵Saul said to David, "May you be blessed, my son David. Not only will you accomplish much, but you will also certainly succeed."

Then David went on his way, and Saul returned to his place.

Textual Notes

26:1 לֵאמֹר—This is translated as "with this report." See the second textual note on 23:19.

מִסְתַּתֵּר—This is the Hithpael (HtD) participle of סָתַר, literally "keeping himself secret." The identical form was discussed in the third textual note on 23:19.

עַל פְּנֵי הַיְשִׁימֹן:—Literally "upon the face of Jeshimon," this is rendered as "across from Jeshimon." In 23:19, 24 the hill of Hachilah is described as south of Jeshimon (מִימִין הַיְשִׁימֹון, 23:19; similar is 23:24). See the last two textual notes on 23:19.

26:2 אִישׁ בְּחוּרֵי יִשְׂרָאֵל—This is translated as "men selected from Israel." See the first textual note on 24:3 (ET 24:2). Here, however, the Qal passive (Gp) participle of בָּחַר, "choose, select," is plural *ad sensum* (whereas it is singular in 24:3 [ET 24:2]). אִישׁ is singular but a collective, "men," so the plural participle here matches its sense.

לְבַקֵּשׁ אֶת־דָּוִד—This means "to seek David." The infinitive construct לְבַקֵּשׁ, which recurs in 26:20, is the Piel (D) of בָּקַשׁ with the preposition לְ. This is a thematic verb in the narrative of Saul's pursuit of David. See 19:2, 10, and "Jonathan Defends David (19:1–7)" in the commentary on 19:1–17.

26:3 וַיִּחַן—This is the Qal (G) preterite (imperfect with *waw* consecutive) of חָנָה, "encamp." In the book of Samuel it usually refers to establishing a military camp for warfare. Its Qal perfect חָנָה refers to Saul's encampment in 26:5, and its Qal participle חֹנִים in 26:5 refers to Saul's soldiers "being encamped" around him.

26:4 מְרַגְּלִים— This is translated as "spies." It is the Piel (D) masculine plural participle of רָגַל, to "foot it" (BDB), a denominative verb derived from the noun רֶגֶל, "foot, leg." This verb usually appears in the Piel and with the meaning to "spy" (BDB, 2). The identical participle recurs in 2 Sam 15:10; see other forms of its Piel in 2 Sam 10:3; 19:28 (ET 19:27).

אֶל־נָכוֹן:—This prepositional phrase functions adverbially: "definitely, certainly, surely." It had a similar meaning in 23:23; see the second textual note on 23:23. נָכוֹן is the Niphal (N) participle of כּוּן, meaning "to be sure, certain, reliable." The LXX reads ἕτοιμος ἐκ Κεïλα, "prepared from Keilah," and ἕτοιμος probably represents אֶל־נָכוֹן. Some believe that the MT is a corruption of אל הכילה, "to Hacilah."[1]

26:5 הַמָּקוֹם אֲשֶׁר חָנָה־שָׁם שָׁאוּל ... הַמָּקוֹם אֲשֶׁר שָׁכַב־שָׁם שָׁאוּל—In relative clauses describing a place Hebrew typically includes the retrospective adverb שָׁם, literally "the place where Saul camped *there* ... the place where Saul lay *there*." See Joüon, § 158 j. The verb שָׁכַב, "lay," is singular, in agreement with its following (first) subject, שָׁאוּל, "Saul," but then a second man, וְאַבְנֵר, "and Abner," is appended to form a compound subject of the singular verb; see Joüon, § 150 q. English requires the verb שָׁכַב to be translated in the plural, "were lying."

בַּמַּעְגָּל—This prepositional phrase, "within the camp," recurs in 26:7. See the second textual note on 17:20.

וְהָעָם—For "and the troops," see the first textual note on 4:3.

סְבִיבֹתָיו:—This Qere has the usual spelling of the third masculine singular suffix appended to a plural. The feminine plural form of סָבִיב is usually used with the force of a preposition (BDB, s.v. סָבִיב, 2 b (*b*)), thus "around him." The same form, סְבִיבֹתָיו, is the Qere in 26:7.[2] In both verses the Kethib is סְבִיבֹתָו, which exhibits an accidental loss of the *yod* before the similarly shaped *waw*.

26:6 וַיַּעַן דָּוִד וַיֹּאמֶר—Literally "and David answered and said," this is translated as "David then spoke." The verb עָנָה often refers to responding to previous dialogue (as twice in 26:14), but it can also refer to responding to a situation. Here it refers to David articulating his plan after assessing the military situation.

אֲחִימֶלֶךְ הַחִתִּי— This means "Ahimelech the Hittite." "Hittite" is most likely a reference to his ancestry rather than his national origin. There is no archaeological evidence that ancient Hittites from Anatolia and northern Syria settled in Palestine. Regarding that nation, Wood summarizes:

> The origin of the Anatolian Indo-Europeans we call "Hittites" is unknown. They appeared in central Anatolia early in the second millennium BC and established a kingdom that lasted from the early seventeenth century to the early twelfth century BC. Their capital was at Ḫattusha, modern Boğazkale, in N-central Turkey. Hittite history can be divided into two major periods, the Old Kingdom, ca. 1670–1400 BC, and the Empire, or New Kingdom, ca. 1400–1177 BC. When the empire disintegrated, its second most important city

---

[1]   McCarter, *I Samuel*, 405; Thornhill, "A Note on אל נכון, 1 Sam. xxvi 4."

[2]   This form also appears in 2 Sam 22:12; Jer 50:32; Ezek 12:14; Eccl 1:6. See also the plene, or *male'*, form סְבִיבוֹתָיו, in Ezek 32:22, 25, 26; Ps 18:12 (ET 18:11).

Carchemish, along with other city-states in southern Anatolia and northern Syria, survived to become the Neo-Hittite states, which continued until the late eighth century BC when they were absorbed by the Assyrian empire.[3]

Wood goes on to note that the Indo-European Hittites or Neo-Hittites from Anatolia or northern Syria are always referenced in the OT with the *plural* gentilic הַחִתִּים, "the Hittites,"[4] or חִתִּית (1 Ki 11:1).[5] Wood's analysis also reveals that in Genesis the *singular* הַחִתִּי, "the Hittite,"[6] is juxtaposed several times with the phrase בְּנֵי־חֵת, "the sons of Heth."[7] These individuals called a "Hittite" (or "Hethite") were not the Indo-European Hittites, but rather the Semitic descendants of Heth, the son of Canaan (Gen 10:15; 1 Chr 1:13). The gentilic word used to refer to them as a group is the singular הַחִתִּי, "the Hittite."[8] They were Canaanite residents of Palestine. Two of them are mentioned in the book of Samuel: "Ahimelech the Hittite," who is mentioned only here, and the better-known "Uriah the Hittite."[9]

אֲבִישַׁי בֶּן־צְרוּיָה אֲחִי יוֹאָב—Literally "Abishai the son of Zeruiah, the brother of Joab," is translated as "Zeruiah's son Abishai, Joab's brother," to clarify the family relationships. The feminine Hebrew name "Zeruiah" was that of David's sister (1 Chr 2:16). Her sons were Joab, Abishai, and Asahel (1 Chr 2:16). Therefore, Abishai was David's nephew. Abishai and Joab were brothers.

אֶל־שָׁאוּל אֶל־הַמַּחֲנֶה—This means "to Saul, to the camp." The second prepositional phrase is in apposition to the first one. To go down "to Saul" involves going down "to the camp."

26:7 שֹׁכֵב יָשֵׁן— This means "lying asleep." The first word is a Qal (G) participle: "lying." In form the second word could be the Qal participle of יָשֵׁן, "to sleep," but grammatical resources regard it as an adjective, "sleeping" (BDB, s.v. יָשֵׁן I). This adjective recurs in 26:12.

וַחֲנִיתוֹ מְעוּכָה־בָאָרֶץ—The noun חֲנִית, "spear," is feminine. It is the subject of מְעוּכָה, the feminine singular Qal passive (Gp) participle of מָעַךְ, "to press," so the spear had been "thrust/stuck into the ground." The rare verb מָעַךְ appears elsewhere only in Lev 22:24, where its Qal passive participle means "crushed," and in Ezek 23:3, where its Pual (Dp) participle means "squeezed" or "caressed."

מְרַאֲשֹׁתָיו— This means "at/near his head." This Qere has the expected spelling of the third masculine singular suffix on a plural noun. This noun (derived from רֹאשׁ, "head") appears only in the feminine plural form מְרַאֲשׁוֹת, meaning "place where the head is." The identical suffixed form is attested in Gen 28:11, 18; 1 Sam 19:13, 16; 1 Ki 19:6. The Kethib is מְרַאֲשֹׁתָו, which exhibits an accidental loss of the *yod* before

3 Wood, "Hittites and Hethites," 240–41.

4 Josh 1:4; Judg 1:26; 1 Ki 10:29; 2 Ki 7:6; 2 Chr 1:17.

5 Wood, "Hittites and Hethites," 244, 248–49.

6 Gen 23:10; 25:9; 26:34; 36:2; 49:29–30; 50:13.

7 Gen 23:3, 5, 7, 10, 16, 18, 20; 25:10; 49:32. See Wood, "Hittites and Hethites," 242, 244.

8 Gen 15:20; Ex 3:8, 17; 13:5; 23:23, 28; 33:2; 34:11; Num 13:29; Deut 7:1; 20:17; Josh 3:10; 9:1; 11:3; 12:8; 24:11; Judg 3:5; 1 Ki 9:20; Ezra 9:1; Neh 9:8; 2 Chr 8:7.

9 2 Sam 11:3, 6, 17, 21, 24; 12:9, 10; 23:39; see also 1 Ki 15:5; 1 Chr 11:41.

the similarly shaped *waw*. The same Qere/Kethib spellings of this word recur in 1 Sam 26:11, 16, and the construct form of the noun occurs in 26:12.

26:8 סָגַּר ... בְּיָדְךָ—Literally this means "enclosed ... in your hand." The Piel (D) of סָגַר, "to shut, close," is used with בְּיָד־ in the sense of "deliver [someone] into the hand of," as in 17:46; 24:19 (ET 24:18). Cf. the Hiphil (H) of סָגַר with בְּיָד־ in 23:11, 12, 20; 30:15.

אַכֶּנּוּ נָא בַּחֲנִית וּבָאָרֶץ—Literally "let me smite him, please, with a spear and into the ground." The verb אַכֶּנּוּ is the Hiphil (H) first common singular imperfect of נָכָה in a cohortative sense, "let me strike," with a third masculine singular suffix, followed by נָא, a particle of entreaty ("please"). An imperfect form can have a cohortative meaning; see Joüon, § 114 b (1). The preposition בְּ is repeated on the next two words, but with different nuances; the first is instrumental ("with," BDB, s.v. בְּ I, III 1) and the second is local ("into," BDB, s.v. בְּ I, I 4). Abishai's plan is to thrust "with" the spear all the way through Saul and then "into" the ground underneath. A partially similar double use of the preposition בְּ, along with the same verb (the Hiphil imperfect of נָכָה), expressed Saul's intent to impale David in 18:11: אַכֶּה בְדָוִד וּבַקִּיר, literally "I will strike into [i.e., 'through,' BDB, s.v. בְּ I, I 1] David and into the wall." But most similar is the threefold use of the preposition בְּ in 19:10 for Saul's stratagem to pierce David: Saul sought לְהַכּוֹת בַּחֲנִית בְּדָוִד וּבַקִּיר, literally "to strike with the spear into [through] David and into the wall." (Cf. Num 25:7–8, where a spear impales two people.) These syntactical parallels (1 Sam 18:11; 19:10) weaken the proposal that the words here in 26:8, בַּחֲנִית וּבָאָרֶץ, were incorrectly divided and that the conjunctive *waw* on the second word should instead be a pronominal suffix appended to the first word: בַּחֲנִיתוֹ בָאָרֶץ, "with his spear into the ground."

אֶשְׁנֶה—This is the Qal (G) first common singular imperfect of שָׁנָה III, "to do [something] a second time; to repeat [an action]." It is related to the numeral שְׁנַיִם, "two."

26:9 אַל־תַּשְׁחִיתֵהוּ—This negative command is formed with the second masculine singular Hiphil (H) imperfect of שָׁחַת, "to destroy," with a third masculine singular object suffix. The Hiphil infinitive construct (with the preposition לְ) לְהַשְׁחִית will be used in 26:15 in the same sense for killing King Saul, as will the Piel (D) infinitive construct (with לְ) לְשַׁחֵת in 2 Sam 1:14.

מִי שָׁלַח יָדוֹ—"Who can stretch out his hand?" The verb שָׁלַח with the direct object יָד is a common idiom for reaching out to strike someone. It recurs in 26:11, 23; see also 1 Sam 22:17; 24:7, 11 (ET 24:6, 10); 2 Sam 1:14; 18:12; 24:16. A perfect verb (here שָׁלַח) can be used in reference to the future.[10] The LXX has the future tense verb ἐποίσει, which could reflect a Hebrew text with the imperfect יִשְׁלַח, unless the LXX simply interpreted the perfect in the sense required by the context. If the original text

---

[10] Joüon, § 112 i, observes that the use of a Hebrew perfect verb in reference to the future is especially common in conditional sentences. The thought of 26:9 could be expressed as a conditional, i.e., "if someone stretches out his hand against Yahweh's anointed, then he will not remain guiltless." Joüon, § 112 j, includes 26:9 in its discussion of perfect verbs in a "surprised question."

were מִי יִשְׁלַח then the MT suffered from haplography due to two consecutive *yod*s (i.e.,
(מי שלח → מי ישלח).

בִּמְשִׁיחַ יְהוָה—The phrase "Yahweh's anointed one," with the noun מָשִׁיחַ, referred
to Saul previously in 24:7, 11 (ET 24:6, 10). It will again in 26:11, 16, 23, as well as in
2 Sam 1:14, 16. מָשִׁיחַ refers to the Messiah or Christ in 2:10, 35; see the commentary
on those verses. See also the verb מָשַׁח, "to anoint" (from which the noun is derived),
for the anointing of Saul in 1 Sam 9:16; 10:1; 15:1, 17 (and for David in 1 Sam 16:3,
12, 13; 2 Sam 2:4, 7; 5:3, 17; 12:7; cf. 2 Sam 3:39).

וְנִקָּה:—This is the Niphal (N) third masculine singular perfect of נָקָה with *waw*
consecutive. In the Niphal this verb can mean to be "free from guilt, innocent" (BDB,
2) or to be "exempt from punishment" (BDB, 3). Both meanings apply here: anyone
who strikes the anointed one will be guilty and will receive divine punishment. See
2 Sam 1:14–16.

26:10 חַי־יְהוָה—For "as Yahweh lives," see the second textual notes on 1:26 and 14:45.
This invocation recurs in 26:16.

יִגָּפֶנּוּ—This is the third masculine singular Qal (G) imperfect of נָגַף, "strike down,"
with a third masculine singular suffix. Cf. 25:38, where the Qal of נָגַף referred to Yahweh
striking down Nabal, and 4:3, where Yahweh struck down Israel's troops.

וְנִסְפָּה:—This is the Niphal (N) perfect of סָפָה, meaning "be swept away." See
imperfect Niphal forms in 12:25; 27:1.

26:11 חָלִילָה לִּי מֵיהוָה—For "because of Yahweh I will certainly not," see the second
textual note on 2:30.

צַפַּחַת—This feminine noun, denoting a "jar" or "jug," recurs in 26:12, 16. Its only
other OT appearances are in 1 Ki 17:12, 14, 16; 19:6.

וְנֵלְכָה לָּנוּ:—The verb is the Qal (G) cohortative of הָלַךְ. The suffixed preposition
לְ has a conjunctive *daghesh*, -לָּ (GKC, § 20 c), and a reflexive sense (BDB, 5 h (*b*)).

26:12 מֵקִים—This is the Hiphil (H) participle of קִים I, which has the intransitive
meaning "wake up." This verb occurs only in the Hiphil and often refers to waking from
sleep (BDB, 1 a).

תַּרְדֵּמַת יְהוָה נָפְלָה עֲלֵיהֶם:—The feminine noun תַּרְדֵּמָה, "deep sleep," is used with
the verb נָפַל, "to fall," to refer to a divinely induced state of slumber also in Gen 2:21;
15:12. Cf. Is 29:10; Job 4:13; 33:15.

26:14 מִי אַתָּה קָרָאתָ אֶל־הַמֶּלֶךְ:—This clause with קָרָאתָ, the perfect form of the Qal
(G) of קָרָא, "call," could be rendered literally as "who are you (that) you have called to
the king?" David called to Abner by name (26:14a), but Abner responded as if David
had called to the king, perhaps to elevate his own office as a defender of the king. The
LXX translates the verb by a participle, ὁ καλῶν, "the one who calls," which may reflect
a participial form, הַקֹּרֵא. If that were the original reading, then the MT would have suffered from haplography due to two consecutive uses of *he*, which then required adjusting
the verb to second person singular, i.e., אתה קראת → אתה קרא → אתה הקרא.

26:15 אַחַד הָעָם—This construct phrase is literally "one of the people," meaning "one
of the troops" (see the first textual note on 4:3), "a soldier."

26:16   בְּנֵי־מָוֶת֙ אַתֶּ֔ם—David switches from his address to Abner in the singular to the second person plural, literally "men of death (are) you." For the corresponding singular construct phrase בֶּן־מָ֫וֶת, see the third textual note on 20:31. The next verb is plural, לֹא־שְׁמַרְתֶּ֗ם, "you have not guarded," but then David reverts to the singular with the imperative רְאֵ֣ה, "look!"

26:17   וַיַּכֵּ֣ר—The Hiphil (H) of נָכַר can mean "to observe, pay close attention" (as in 2 Sam 3:36) or, as here, to "recognize" (BDB, 2).

קוֹלִ֑י—"(It is) my voice." A question can be answered in the affirmative simply by repeating a word (as here) or words from the question (Joüon, § 161 l).

הַמֶּ֑לֶךְ:—This noun with the article is a vocative, "O King," equivalent to the English "Your Majesty."

26:18   לָ֥מָּה זֶּ֖ה—"Why would you bother?" See the last textual note on 20:8.

רֹדֵ֖ף אַחֲרֵ֣י עַבְדּ֑וֹ—The Qal (G) of רָדַף, "pursue," often takes the preposition אַחֲרֵי, "after," with its object, as here. It takes a direct object in 26:20. For more examples of both constructions, see the third textual note on 23:25.

וּמַה־בְּיָדִ֖י רָעָֽה:—Literally "and what evil is in my hand?" This is rendered as "and what crime have I committed?"

26:19   אִם־יְהוָ֞ה הֱסִֽיתְךָ֣ בִ֗י—The verb סוּת occurs only in the Hiphil (H). It seldom has a positive connotation, "to urge, allure" (see BDB, 1 b). Most often it has a negative connotation, "to incite" someone to take an action, and with that meaning it usually takes the preposition בְּ in an adversative sense: the action is done "against" someone (BDB, 2). See the parallel in 2 Sam 24:1.

יָרַ֣ח מִנְחָ֔ה—Literally "let him smell an offering." The verb is a Hiphil (H) jussive of רִיחַ, "to smell." This verb appears only in the Hiphil and is a denominative from the noun רֵיחַ, "odor." The noun usually refers to the God-pleasing fragrance of an atoning sacrifice (e.g., Ex 29:18, 25, 41; Lev 1:9; 2:2; 3:5; 4:31). The verb refers to God smelling with delight and being appeased by a fragrant sacrifice here and also in Gen 8:21. Cf. Is 11:3, where the verb means that the messianic Root and Branch of Jesse delights in the fear of Yahweh.

בְּנֵ֣י הָֽאָדָ֔ם—The construct phrase "the sons of (the) man" signifies humans as contrasted with God. This phrase generally refers to humankind, rather than to males exclusively.[11]

אֲרוּרִ֣ים הֵם֮ לִפְנֵ֣י יְהוָה֒—Literally "cursed (are/be) they before Yahweh." The verb is the Qal passive (Gp) participle of אָרַר, "to curse." The singular Qal passive (Gp) participle was used in a curse formula in 14:24, 28 (see the third textual note on 14:24). The plural expression here is the opposite of the plural blessing formula in 23:21. See also the singular benediction in 26:25.

גֵּרְשׁ֣וּנִי הַיּ֗וֹם מֵֽהִסְתַּפֵּ֜חַ בְּנַחֲלַ֣ת יְהוָ֗ה—The Piel (D) of גֵּרַשׁ, "drive away," can refer to expulsion from a desirable place, such as Adam and Eve from Eden (Gen 3:24) or the Canaanites from the promised land (Ex 23:28; 33:2; Josh 24:12). מֵֽהִסְתַּפֵּ֜חַ is the Hithpael (HtD) infinitive construct of סָפַח, "to join, attach," with the prefixed preposition מִן in a privative sense. This is the sole instance of the verb in the Hithpael, which

---

[11]   See Gen 11:5; 1 Ki 8:39; Ps 33:13; Eccl 2:8; 3:18–19, 21; 8:11; 9:3, 12; 2 Chr 6:30.

has a reflexive meaning, "join oneself to" something, and the preposition בְּ, "to," introduces its object here, "the inheritance of Yahweh." Thus, David is being deprived of joining or sharing in Yahweh's inheritance.

לֵאמֹר לֵךְ עֲבֹד אֱלֹהִים אֲחֵרִים׃—This is translated as "saying, 'Go, serve other gods.'" David is not necessarily claiming that people spoke these exact words to Saul to give as an order to David. The words spoken to Saul by the Ziphites were phrased quite differently (23:19–20; 24:2 [ET 24:1]; 26:1). Nevertheless, the construction here conveys result. The *effect* of those words to Saul has been to expel David from Yahweh's inheritance and thereby pressure him to turn to other gods for help, that is, to engage in idolatry.

26:20 פַּרְעֹשׁ אֶחָד—For this phrase, "a single flea," see the fifth textual note on 24:15 (ET 24:14).

כַּאֲשֶׁר יִרְדֹּף הַקֹּרֵא בֶּהָרִים׃—Literally this means "just as (someone) pursues a partridge in the hills." The noun קֹרֵא I, a "partridge," occurs elsewhere in the OT only in Jer 17:11.

After "the king of Israel has come out to seek," in place of the Hebrew discussed in these two textual notes, LXX 26:20 reads τὴν ψυχήν μου, καθὼς καταδιώκει ὁ νυκτικόραξ ἐν τοῖς ὄρεσιν, "my soul like the owl pursues [its prey] in the hills." On the basis of this reading some would emend פַּרְעֹשׁ אֶחָד, "a single flea," to נַפְשִׁי, "my life," on the theory that the text has been changed to harmonize it with 24:15 (ET 24:14).[12] Perhaps an unstated reason for this is also that in the MT David appears to mix animal metaphors since he uses both "flea" and "partridge" in the same sentence.

26:21 חָטָאתִי—"I have sinned." Saul spoke this same confession to Samuel in both 15:24 and 15:30, but his repentance did not endure.

יָקְרָה נַפְשִׁי בְּעֵינֶיךָ—Literally "my soul/life was precious in your eyes." The suffixed feminine noun נֶפֶשׁ is the subject of the Qal (G) third feminine singular perfect of יָקַר, "be precious, valuable." This verb also appeared in 18:30. Cf. the idiom in the first textual note on 26:24.

הִסְכַּלְתִּי—"I acted foolishly." This is the Hiphil (H) first common singular perfect of סָכַל. It is synonymous with the Niphal (N) form Samuel employed to tell Saul that his sin against Yahweh's command was foolish; see the first textual note on 13:13.

וָאֶשְׁגֶּה—Saul claims, "and I have made a mistake." The Qal (G) of שָׁגָה generally refers to committing an unintentional sin (Lev 4:13; Num 15:22; Ezek 45:20) or going astray from God's commandments (Ps 119:21, 118). In English "made a mistake" (or "accidentally sinned") conveys that the transgression was not deliberate, although Saul's claim may be hollow.

26:22 חֲנִית הַמֶּלֶךְ—This construct phrase, "the spear of the king," is the reading of the Qere and 4QSam[a] (חנית המלך), supported by the LXX (τὸ δόρυ τοῦ βασιλέως). The two words are in apposition in the Kethib, הַחֲנִית הַמֶּלֶךְ, "the spear, Your Majesty."

26:23 וַיהוָה יָשִׁיב לָאִישׁ אֶת־צִדְקָתוֹ וְאֶת־אֱמֻנָתוֹ—Literally "and Yahweh will bring back to a man his righteousness and his faithfulness." The Hiphil (H) of שׁוּב can refer

---

to divine retribution, either for evil (25:39) or for good, as here (BDB, 4 a). Previously צְדָקָה, "righteousness," referred to acts by Yahweh himself (12:7). It refers to deeds of David in 2 Sam 8:15; 22:21, 25. This is the sole instance of the noun אֱמוּנָה, "faithfulness," in the book of Samuel. Elsewhere it commonly refers to the faithfulness of God (Deut 32:4; Is 25:1; Pss 36:6 [ET 36:5]; 89:2–3 [ET 89:1–2]; 100:5) and his Davidic Messiah (Is 11:5).

נְתָנְךָ יְהוָה ׀ הַיּוֹם בְּיָד—Codex Leningradensis literally reads "Yahweh gave you today into a hand," i.e., "Yahweh handed you over today." Many Masoretic manuscripts include a pronominal suffix on יָד, בְּיָדִי, "into my hand," which is supported by the LXX (παρέδωκέν σε κύριος … εἰς χεῖράς μου).

26:24 גָּדְלָה נַפְשְׁךָ הַיּוֹם הַזֶּה בְּעֵינָי—Literally "your life was big/important this day in my eyes," this idiom is similar to the one discussed in the second textual note on 26:21. The nuance of גָּדֵל here may be equivalent, "become great in value" (see BDB, Qal, 2 b).

וְיַצִּלֵנִי—Earlier the Hiphil (H) of נָצַל, "to rescue, deliver," was used of God delivering his people from the Philistines (7:3; see also 7:14) and from Egypt (10:18). See also, e.g., 1 Sam 12:10, 11; 17:35, 37; 2 Sam 12:7.

26:25 בָּרוּךְ אַתָּה—This benediction could be a statement, "blessed are you," or a prayer, "may you be blessed." See the similar benedictions in 15:13; 23:21; 25:33. For the verb "to bless," see the first textual note on 2:20 and the third textual note on 9:13.

גַּם … וְגַם—This means "not only … but also."

Commentary

c. 1011 BC

For a discussion of the relationship between the two accounts of David sparing Saul's life, see "David Twice Spares Saul's Life—Comparing 1 Samuel 24 and 1 Samuel 26" in the commentary on 24:2–23 (ET 24:1–22).

This second narrative of David sparing Saul's life not only repeats the theme of respect for the life of God's anointed king (26:9, 11, 23; cf. 24:7, 11 [ET 24:6, 10]) but also emphasizes God's prerogative of taking human life (26:10, 24) and the respect for life that is required of all people (Gen 9:6; the Fifth Commandment, Ex 20:13; Deut 5:17). David was the one who spoke of God as the master of life. His words drew a contrast between himself and Saul in their opposite attitudes toward taking the life of an innocent person.[13] Moreover, they also contrasted David the fugitive, when he was the ultimate respecter of Saul's life, with David later at the height of his power, when he so callously ordered the death of Uriah (2 Sam 11:15).

This theme of life connects physical life to spiritual life through David's words in 1 Sam 26:19–20.[14] Saul's pursuit of David threatened to drive him

---

[13] Similarly, in the preceding chapter David was intent on killing Nabal, but Yahweh used Abigail to prevent him from carrying out that murder, and David praised Yahweh for restraining him from that crime (25:26–33, 39).

[14] See also Abigail's words about "the bundle of life with Yahweh your God" in 25:29.

away from sharing Yahweh's inheritance with the rest of God's redeemed people (26:19). The humans who incited Saul (the Ziphites, 23:19–20; 24:2 [ET 24:1]; 26:1) had committed an even more grave sin in that their actions endangered David's faith in Yahweh by implying that he ought to worship the pagan gods in another land (26:19). To drive someone away from the living God, who saves, to venerate false gods, who can offer no help in this world and no eternal life, is a most serious sin, since it is the primal sin (Gen 3:1–5) and it violates the First Commandment (Ex 20:2–6; Deut 5:6–10), the greatest commandment (Deut 6:5; Mt 22:37–38). This command is the most important, as Luther notes in his comments on Ex 20:5–6:

> Although these words apply to all the commandments … , yet they are attached precisely to this one [the First Commandment] which stands at the head of the list because it is of the utmost importance for a man to have the right head. For where the head is right, the whole life must be right, and vice versa.[15]

Saul and the Ziphites were driving David away from God, risking his whole life—body and soul, now and for eternity.

The Ziphites Inform Saul of David's Whereabouts (26:1–3)

Once again the Ziphites reported David's location to Saul (26:1; as previously in 23:19–20; 24:2 [ET 24:1]).[16] Apparently, after the death of Nabal (25:37–39), David had felt less danger from Saul and returned to south-central Judah, especially now that he had in-laws in the vicinity through his marriages to Abigail and Ahinoam (25:42–43).[17] But the Ziphite report would change his situation as Saul once again came from Gibeah to Judah with a force of three thousand men (26:2; cf. 24:3 [ET 24:2]). Saul went to the place mentioned by the Ziphites, the hill of Hachilah near Jeshimon, but David had retreated to the wilderness when he learned of Saul's incursion into Judah (26:3).

David Investigates Saul's Presence (26:4–6)

While Saul had the Ziphites to supply intelligence, David had his own spies that confirmed Saul's whereabouts (26:4). Though Saul was on the hill of Hachilah, David apparently was on higher ground and could observe the position of Saul, Abner, and the rest of the troops in the camp (26:5).[18] David then asked two of his men which of them wished to accompany him by going down into Saul's camp (26:6). We know nothing more of this Ahimelech,[19] but

---

[15] LC I (Explanation of the Appendix to the First Commandment) 31.

[16] For the identity of the Ziphites, see the first textual note on 23:19 and "The Ziphites Report David's Whereabouts to Saul (23:19–24a)" in the commentary on 23:14–24:1 (ET 23:14–29).

[17] Carmel (25:2), the hometown of Abigail (27:3), and the Jezreel (25:43) from which Ahinoam came, were in south-central Judah. See "David's Wives (25:43–44)" in the commentary on 25:1–44.

[18] Note that David speaks of going *down* to Saul's camp (26:6).

[19] He was not the Ahimelech who had been high priest at Nob, to whom David had appealed for food in 21:2–7 (ET 21:1–6). Saul had killed that Ahimelech and all but one of the other priests from Nob (22:16–20).

apparently he was one of David's more trusted men, since David offered him this opportunity.

Abishai, David's nephew, is mentioned here for the first time, as are Abishai's mother, Zeruiah (David's sister), and his brother Joab (another nephew of David).[20] The author felt no need to introduce any of these relatives of David to his readers, indicating that he assumed they were familiar with them. In fact, although Zeruiah is mentioned fifteen times in the book of Samuel,[21] the author never identifies her as David's sister.

David and Abishai in Saul's Camp (26:7–12)

After David's nephew Abishai volunteered, the two went to the camp, and the author makes a point of telling his readers that Saul was surrounded by Abner and his troops and that Saul's spear had been thrust into the ground near his head (26:7). Abishai concluded that God had given David an opportunity to kill Saul, and he asked for permission to do so (26:8). He included his tactic: with one blow of Saul's spear he could dispatch Saul and pin him to the ground. Abishai's offer had an ironic touch to it, since Saul had on two occasions tried to impale David to a wall with this same spear (18:10–11; 19:9–10), and the Hebrew wording of these three passages is similar (see the second textual note on 26:8). Abishai's instinct to rid David of his enemies would show itself again when later he would request permission to decapitate Shimei for cursing David (2 Sam 16:9; cf. 2 Sam 19:22 [ET 19:21]).

David's reason for denying Abishai's request here was that *no one* could attack Yahweh's anointed king and be guiltless (26:9). In the earlier incident when David's men urged him to kill Saul (24:5 [ET 24:4]), as he easily could have done, he simply stated that he himself would not attack God's anointed one (24:7 [ET 24:6]; cf. 24:11 [ET 24:10]). The more general principle here asserts that everyone ought to respect God's anointing and his choice of king.[22] David then expanded on why there was no need to kill Saul: Yahweh himself would end Saul's life in whatever manner he pleased (26:10; cf. Yahweh's way of terminating Nabal's life in 25:38–39). Perhaps Yahweh would allow Saul to live out his allotted days or he would sweep him away in battle (26:10). All of these point to God's power to remove Saul in any way he saw fit. Therefore, David concluded that he would not attack Saul *because of Yahweh* (26:11a).

---

[20] For their relationships to David, see the third textual note on 26:6.

[21] 1 Sam 26:6; 2 Sam 2:13, 18; 3:39; 8:16; 14:1; 16:9, 10; 17:25; 18:2; 19:22, 23 (ET 19:21, 22); 21:17; 23:18, 37.

[22] In broader biblical perspective, God's choosing and anointing of the king with the gift of the Holy Spirit (1 Sam 10:1–10; 16:13) relates to the anointing of Christ himself (Mt 3:16; Lk 4:18; Acts 10:38; "Christ" means "Anointed One") and to the Sacrament of Baptism (Acts 2:38–41; 22:16; Rom 6:1–4; 1 Cor 12:13). All baptized believers in Christ are his chosen ones and have received his anointing (2 Cor 1:21; 1 Jn 2:20, 27). They are royalty (Is 62:3; 2 Tim 2:12; 1 Pet 2:9; Rev 5:10; 22:5), and their redeemed lives are precious to God.

"The living God" (17:26, 36) is the Lord over life and death.[23] Hannah had expressed this in her song:

"Yahweh kills and makes alive;
he brings down to Sheol and brings up [again]." (2:6)

Since these are God's prerogatives, no person can take an innocent life (by whatever means, e.g., abortion, euthanasia, acts of violence) and "remain guiltless" (26:9). Every human life is endowed with sanctity by the Lord and Giver of life. Moreover, since Jesus Christ was crucified and raised again, he is "Lord both of the dead and of the living" (Rom 14:9). He possesses the keys of death and hell (Rev 1:18). "Children of the living God" (Hos 2:1 [ET 1:10]; Rom 9:26) are born again into the living hope of everlasting life in Christ (1 Pet 1:3). However God may permit them to die, they shall be delivered from their enemies and raised again to walk in the land of the living with their God.[24]

David's reasoning demonstrates his faith in God, who grants authority and life to some but removes the authority and life of others (Dan 2:21; Rom 13:1–2). As is often true in the life of David, his wisdom in trusting God also corresponded to benefits that would accrue to David himself. In this case, David's attitude toward Saul as God's anointed king also signaled to Abishai how David ought to be respected when he would take the throne.

David then ordered Abishai to take the spear and a jug of water (26:11b). Interestingly, the author writes that David took the spear and jug (26:12). Perhaps he simply means that David is credited with taking these items, since Abishai was under David's authority. We are also told that no one in the camp witnessed their actions because "a deep slumber from Yahweh" (תַּרְדֵּמַת יְהוָה, 26:12) had fallen on them. The word תַּרְדֵּמָה, "deep sleep," is associated with God's action elsewhere. God caused Adam to fall into a deep sleep when he created Eve (Gen 2:21), and Abram fell into a deep sleep before God affirmed his gracious covenant with him (Gen 15:12). Conversely, when the nation would later fall into apostasy, Isaiah would prophesy that God sent a deep slumber on the inhabitants of Jerusalem that blinded them to the message of his Word (Is 29:10; cf. Is 56:10; Jer 51:39, 57). In Gethsemane Jesus' disciples fell into a sleep that apparently prevented them from interfering in God's plan of salvation (Mt 26:40–46; Mk 14:37–42; Lk 22:44–47; cf. Lk 9:32).

David Challenges Abner (26:13–16)

Upon going some distance to another hill (26:13), David challenged the army and Abner, calling out to them (26:14). Evidently, no answer came after his initial challenge, and so David provoked Abner to respond. When Abner

---

[23] See also, e.g., Deut 5:26; Josh 3:10; Is 37:4, 17; Jer 10:10; 23:36; Hos 2:1 (ET 1:10); Pss 42:3 (ET 42:2); 84:3 (ET 84:2); Ruth 2:20; Dan 6:21, 27 (ET 6:20, 26); and in the NT, Acts 14:15; 2 Cor 3:3; 6:16; 1 Tim 3:15; 4:10; Heb 3:12; 9:14; 10:31; 12:22; Rev 7:2.

[24] Pss 27:13; 116:9; 142:6 (ET 142:5); cf. 1 Sam 25:29; Dan 12:2–3; Rev 21:1–4.

inquired as to who was calling, David did not answer directly. Instead, he pointed out that Abner had neglected his duty to guard the king (26:15). Abner and all the troops were deserving of death for their failure to protect God's anointed king ("dead men"; see the textual note on 26:16). As evidence of this David asked them to look for Saul's spear and water jug.

David and Saul Have Their Final Conversation (26:17–25)

Aroused from his sleep, Saul finally recognized David's voice, asking the same question (26:17) he had asked previously when David spared his life (24:17 [ET 24:16]). Saul once again called David "my son," though he had hardly treated David as a son. David was his son-in-law (18:21–27), and he addressed Saul as "my father" (24:12 [ET 24:11]), but recently Saul had severed his family relationship to David by giving his daughter Michal, David's wife, to another man (25:44). Nevertheless, David, for his part, politely answered Saul, showing him respect as master and king (26:17).

David followed his reply with a challenge to Saul for his actions: what reason would Saul have for seeking David's life (26:18)? David did not wait for an answer or defense from Saul, but instead exhorted Saul to listen to what he had to say about the matter (26:19). If, as a sign of divine wrath against the king because of his sins against God and David, God had "incited" (see 2 Sam 24:1) Saul to pursue an innocent man (thereby demonstrating to Saul's subjects the king's utter contempt for God's will), Saul ought to repent of those sins and offer a sacrifice that God would accept (1 Sam 26:19). The Hebrew text literally says that God should "smell" the sacrifice (see the second textual note on 26:19). The phrasing is similar to Gen 8:21, where God smelled Noah's sacrifice and declared that he would not again curse the ground because of humans. David may have been implying that should Saul offer a sincere sacrifice for his sin against David, God would lift the curse of Saul's jealousy. In any case, as Samuel had told Saul after his disobedience, what God truly desires even more than an offering is the response of faith in obedience to his Word (15:22–23; "the obedience of faith," Rom 1:5; 16:26).

On the other hand, humans may have incited Saul to action against David. In fact, this was the case, and the reference may well be an oblique indictment of the Ziphites (23:19–20; 24:2 [ET 24:1]; and most recently, 26:1). David called for them to be cursed in Yahweh's presence, even as their actions served to drive David from Yahweh's presence (26:19). The effect of their persecution was to drive David away from "Yahweh's inheritance" and toward the worship of other gods. To advocate the veneration of "other gods" was an act of apostasy and idolatry, a serious offense that merited the death penalty.[25] The avoidance of syncretism and idolatry is no less vital for God's people under the new covenant in Christ, who alone is Lord: "stay away from idols."[26]

---

[25] See especially Deut 13:2–12 [ET 13:1–11]; 18:20; see also, e.g., Ex 20:3, 13; Deut 5:7; 6:14; 7:3–4; 11:16, 28.

[26] 1 Jn 5:21; see also, e.g., Acts 15:29; Rom 2:22; 1 Cor 8:7; 2 Cor 6:16; Rev 2:14, 20; 9:20.

God's inheritance is the people of Israel (2 Sam 20:19; 21:3). David wanted to share in the true faith by worshiping with all of God's people, worship centered on the Word of God in the context of the liturgical and sacrificial rites he had prescribed for his sanctuary (e.g., Exodus 25–40; Leviticus). True faith in the one living God is moved to express itself in worship with others who hold that same faith.[27] Driving David from the land was cutting him off from the fellowship of believers in Yahweh, risking his spiritual well-being, and cutting him off from "the mutual conversation and consolation of brethren."[28] In the same manner, Christians gather to benefit from God's Word and Sacraments, the liturgical worship by which they devote themselves to the apostles' teaching and the fellowship, the breaking of bread, and the prayers.[29]

Finally, David pleaded that his blood not be shed away from the presence of Israel's covenant God (26:20). As he had previously (24:15 [ET 24:14]), David metaphorically depicted Saul's pursuit of him as seeking a single flea, which is nearly impossible to find and hardly worth the effort (26:20). Yet Saul was chasing David like a hunter chases a "partridge." These birds prefer to walk or run along the ground, since they fly only short distances. A common way of hunting the rock partridge (also known as the Greek partridge, *Alectoris graeca*) or the chukar (*Alectoris chukar*) was to chase it from place to place until it was fatigued and could be stunned with a stick. While such partridges were commonly hunted, much effort had to be expended to capture them. David's reference to the "partridge" also involved a play on words, since the Hebrew name of this bird, קֹרֵא (26:20), means "caller," in reference to the males that can often be heard calling in the hills in the early morning. Even so, David now "called out" (וַיִּקְרָא, 26:14) to Saul from a hill (26:13), and Abner asked, "Who are you that you call [קָרָאתָ] to the king?" (26:14).

In reply Saul not only admitted his sin but also asked David to "return," pledging not to harm him since David had not harmed the king (26:21). Saul then added two more descriptions of his sin—acting foolishly and making a terrible mistake (see the third and fourth textual notes on 26:21). However, David refused to trust Saul's promise. David's words had already revealed that he was contemplating leaving the territory of Israel (cf. 26:19–20), which he would do shortly as he traveled to the Philistine city of Gath (1 Samuel 27). He did not even deign to dignify Saul's plea with a direct reply. Instead, he offered to return the royal spear (26:22) and then launched into an indirect indictment of Saul: Yahweh should repay each man for "his righteousness [צְדָקָה] and faithfulness" (26:23)—an implicit reference to David's attitude toward Saul and the sparing of his life that Saul had not reciprocated. Earlier Saul had confessed to David, "You are more righteous [צַדִּיק] than I" (24:18 [ET 24:17]), but that had

---

[27] Pss 22:23, 26 (ET 22:22, 25); 35:18; 40:10–11 (ET 40:9–10); 68:27 (ET 68:26); 107:32; 111:1; Mt 18:20; Heb 10:24–25.

[28] SA III IV.

[29] Acts 2:41–44; "when you come together," 1 Cor 11:17–34; 14:26; see also Heb 10:23–25; 13:9–10.

not stopped Saul from embarking on another mission to destroy David (chapter 26). So as David spared Saul's life again, David would now trust Yahweh—not Saul—to watch over his own life (26:24).

Saul had the final word, praying for David to be blessed and asserting that David would succeed (26:25). However, this benediction, like his previous ones, may have been a pietism intended to mask his evil designs.[30] It had become obvious even to Saul that Yahweh was with David and that David would succeed him on the throne (24:21 [ET 24:20]). The two men then parted, never to meet again.

---

[30] Both of Saul's prior benedictions (15:13; 23:21) were hypocritical. The first (15:13), spoken over Samuel, was an attempt to conceal Saul's disobedience to God's Word through Samuel regarding the Amalekites (15:2–3). The second (23:21), uttered over the Ziphites, was gleeful praise for their betrayal of David.

David in the Service of Achish of Gath

Translation

27 **¹David thought, "Now I will be swept away one day by Saul's hand. There is nothing better for me other than that I should certainly escape to Philistine territory. Then Saul will give up seeking me again within all the territory of Israel, and I will escape from his grasp." ²So David rose, and he and six hundred men with him crossed over to Achish the son of Maoch, the king of Gath. ³David lived with Achish in Gath—he and his men, each man and his household, David and his two wives, Ahinoam the Jezreelitess, and Abigail the Carmelitess, the wife of Nabal. ⁴When Saul was told that David had fled to Gath, he no longer sought him.**

⁵David said to Achish, "If I have found favor in your eyes, please give me a place among the outlying cities, and let me stay there. Why should your servant live in the royal city with you?" ⁶So on that day Achish gave him Ziklag. Therefore, Ziklag has belonged to the kings of Judah to this day.

⁷The total time David lived in Philistine territory was a year and four months. ⁸David and his men went up and raided the Geshurites and the Amalekites, since they were ancient inhabitants in the land as far as Shur and the land of Egypt. ⁹David would strike the land and would not allow a man or woman to remain alive. He would capture sheep, cattle, donkeys, camels, and clothing. Then he would return and come to Achish. ¹⁰Achish would say to David, "Against whom did you conduct a raid today?"

David would say, "Against the Negev of Judah" or "Against the Negev of the Jerahmeelites" or "Against the Negev of the Kenites." ¹¹David would not allow a man or woman to remain alive to be brought to Gath, thinking, "Otherwise they will inform on us: 'This is what David did.'" This was David's customary practice during the entire time he lived in Philistine territory. ¹²Achish trusted David, thinking, "He is definitely making himself repugnant among his people, among Israel. He will be my servant permanently."

Textual Notes

27:1 וַיֹּאמֶר דָּוִד אֶל־לִבּוֹ—Literally "and David said to his heart," this indicates serious thought on the implication of Saul's relentless pursuit (chapters 24 and 26).

אֶסָּפֶה—This is the first common singular Niphal (N) imperfect of סָפָה, meaning "be swept away." David had used another Niphal form of this verb in 26:10 to speak of the possibility of Saul's death as allowed by God. See yet another Niphal form in 12:25.

אֵין־לִי טוֹב—Literally "there does not exist for me (anything) good." In the context of the rest of the verse, this forms a comparative: "there is nothing better (than for me …)."

כִּי הִמָּלֵט אִמָּלֵט—This is translated as "other than that I should certainly escape." The use of כִּי is exceptive here (*HALOT*, s.v. כִּי II, A 4). The Niphal (N) infinitive absolute of מָלַט, meaning "to escape," is followed by an imperfect form of it (see Joüon, § 123 d, e). Note also the Niphal perfect with *waw* consecutive וְנִמְלַטְתִּי at the end of the verse. This is a frequent verb in the narrative of David's flight from Saul (see the third textual note on 19:10). The LXX reads ἐὰν μὴ σωθῶ, "unless I be saved." On this basis some would emend the text to כִּי אִם אִמָּלֵט, "except that I escape."[1]

וְנוֹאַשׁ ... לְבַקְשֵׁנִי—"And he will give up ... seeking me." The first verb is a third masculine singular Niphal (N) perfect with *waw* consecutive of יָאַשׁ, "despair, give up hope" (see *CDCH*). The second verb, an infinitive construct with לְ, explains the action that Saul would give up doing (see Joüon, § 124 o). The Piel (D) of בָּקַשׁ is another thematic verb in the narrative of Saul's pursuit of David.[2] Note also לְבַקְשׁוֹ in 27:4. See "Jonathan Defends David (19:1–7)" in the commentary on 19:1–17.

מִיָּדוֹ:—Literally this means "from his hand."

27:2–3 ... וַיֵּשֶׁב דָּוִד ... וַיַּעֲבֹר הוּא—The Qal (G) form of עָבַר, "cross over," is singular, in agreement with the singular personal pronoun הוּא, "he," referring to David, even though the pronoun is only the first part of the verb's compound subject in 27:2, which continues "and six hundred men with him." The singular verb and corresponding pronoun emphasize David as the initiator of the action and the main concern of the narrative. Similarly, 27:3 begins with a singular verb and subject, וַיֵּשֶׁב דָּוִד, "and David lived," even though the rest of the verse explains that the subject (those who "lived" in Gath) includes הוּא וַאֲנָשָׁיו, "he [David] and his men," and also his wives. This too keeps the focus on David.

27:3 אֲחִינֹעַם הַיִּזְרְעֵאלִית וַאֲבִיגַיִל אֵשֶׁת־נָבָל הַכַּרְמְלִית:—This means "Ahinoam the Jezreelitess, and Abigail, the wife of Nabal, the Carmelitess." Both gentilic adjectives are translated with "-ess" because they are feminine in gender. The LXX reads Ἀβιγαια ἡ γυνὴ Ναβαλ τοῦ Καρμηλίου, "Abigaia, the wife of Nabal the Carmelite," translating the second gentilic with a masculine form to agree in gender with "Nabal" instead of his wife. This is an impossible reading for two reasons: (1) The Hebrew gentilic is clearly feminine, referring to Abigail, not Nabal. (2) Nabal was not from Carmel, but from Maon (25:2).

Abigail is identified by the name of her former husband. Abigail *had* been Nabal's wife (25:3), but he had died (25:38–39), and afterward she had consented to David's marriage proposal and became his wife (25:39–42). This much is in accord with the NT teaching that "a woman/wife is bound for as much time as her husband should live; but if the husband should fall asleep, she is free to be married to whomever she wishes, but only in the Lord" (1 Cor 7:39; see also Rom 7:2–3). Abigail, however, was probably David's third wife. Previously David had married Saul's daughter Michal, with Saul's approval (18:20–27). David was also married to Ahinoam (25:43), who was probably

---

[1] McCarter, *I Samuel*, 412; Klein, *1 Samuel*, 261.

[2] See the Piel (D) of בָּקַשׁ, "seek," previously in 19:2, 10; 20:1; 22:23; 23:10, 14, 15, 25; 24:3, 10 (ET 24:2, 9); 25:29; 26:2, 20.

his second wife (see the commentary on 25:43–44). Saul, however, had rescinded his consent to the marriage of David and Michal by giving his daughter to another man (25:44). Consequently, at this time David had only the two wives mentioned in 27:3, Ahinoam and Abigail.

27:4 וַיֻּגַּד לְשָׁאוּל—The verb is the Hophal (Hp) of נָגַד with no explicit subject, literally "and it was told to Saul." See Joüon, §§ 128 b; 155 i (3). Such an impersonal construction is often best translated in English with the object as the subject and the verb in the passive, thus "Saul was told."

גַּת—This is an accusative of destination: "to Gath." This is one of the five cities that comprised the Philistine pentapolis; see 6:17.

וְלֹא־יָסַף עוֹד לְבַקְשׁוֹ:—The Qere of the first verb is the Qal (G) perfect of יָסַף, "to do further, do again," which is often combined with an infinitive construct of another verb (here לְבַקְשׁוֹ, "to seek him") to explain the action done further/again (Joüon, §§ 102 g, 124 c, 177 b). The Qal of יָסַף is used in such a construction also in, e.g., 7:13; 15:35. Often the Hiphil (H) of יָסַף is used, as in, e.g., 3:6, 8, 21; 9:8; 19:8; 20:17. The Kethib here, יוסף, likely is intended to be vocalized as יֹסֶף, a defective, or *ḥaser*, spelling of the Hiphil יוֹסִיף.

27:5 יִתְּנוּ־לִי—The verb is the third masculine plural Qal (G) jussive of נָתַן, literally "may they give me," with no stated subject. Such an impersonal construction is a request that functions as a polite imperative, as translated: "please give me."

עָרֵי הַשָּׂדֶה—Literally "the cities of the field," this means "the outlying cities." See the second textual note on 20:5.

וְאֵשְׁבָה—"And let me stay." This cohortative, a Qal (G) first common singular form of יָשַׁב, continues the diplomatically worded request.

עִמָּךְ:—This is pausal for עִמְּךָ, "with you." The pronominal suffix is second masculine singular.

27:6 הָיְתָה צִקְלָג—The names of towns are feminine in gender, regardless of their form, hence צִקְלָג is the subject of the third feminine singular Qal (G) perfect of הָיָה, translated with a durative force, "has (belonged)."

27:7 מִסְפַּר הַיָּמִים—This construct phrase is literally "the number of the days."

בִּשְׂדֵה פְלִשְׁתִּים—"In Philistine territory" is literally "in the field of the Philistines." See the second textual note on 6:1.

יָמִים—The plural of יוֹם, "day," can signify a year (*HALOT*, 7). The LXX lacks a translation of this word and simply reads "four months."

27:8 וַיִּפְשְׁטוּ—Here and in 27:10 the Qal (G) of פָּשַׁט has the military meaning "make a raid." See the first textual note on 18:4. Both here and in 27:10 the verb is plural, emphasizing the active participation of David's men.

הַגְּשׁוּרִי—This singular gentilic noun serves as a collective and so is translated in the plural: "the Geshurites." Gentilic nouns usually are used with the definite article (Joüon, § 137 c). These people were associated with the Philistines and the Avvim as inhabitants of the land on the coast not conquered by Joshua (Josh 13:2–3). According to that information, they dwelt from the Shihor stream east of Egypt up to Ekron. There was also a kingdom of Geshur south of Maacah and east of the Sea of Galilee in western Bashan.

507

However, it is unlikely that David crossed Israelite territory controlled by Saul to attack that kingdom. Later David married Maacah, daughter of Talmai, king of Geshur, and she was the mother of Absalom and Tamar (2 Sam 3:3). Absalom fled to Talmai for safety after murdering Amnon (2 Sam 13:37–38).

וְהַגִּזְרִי—"And the Gizrites" is the reading of the Qere. For this gentilic noun the Kethib has a metathesis of *zayin* and *resh*, וְהַגִּרְזִי, "and the Girzites," but there is no known place called Girzah or Gerzah in the OT. "Gizrites" were inhabitants of Gezer, a Canaanite city on the southern border of Ephraim (Josh 16:10; Judg 1:29). Its location is modern Tell Jezer. Since a translation of this word is omitted in the LXX,[3] some omit it.[4] וְהַגִּרְזִי could be a corrupt dittograph of the previous word, הַגְּשׁוּרִי, "the Geshurites," with a conjunctive *waw* added for sense. David appears to have raided settlements to the south of Gaza out of the direct sight of Achish in Gath (see his claim to Achish in 27:10 that he was raiding in the Arabah). David and his men would have had to march past Gath and the neighboring city of Ekron to attack Gezer (see figure 25 at the end of this pericope). It would have been unlikely that Achish would have been unaware of such a raid. For those reasons the translation above omits this word.

הֵנָּה יֹשְׁבוֹת הָאָרֶץ—The plural personal pronoun הֵנָּה, "they," is feminine and is the subject of יֹשְׁבוֹת, the feminine plural participle of יָשַׁב, even though the preceding gentilic nouns are masculine. The feminine singular participle of יָשַׁב can be used in poetic texts as a collective to refer to "inhabitants" (BDB, Qal, 3). The phrase here is apparently the only time the feminine plural participle is so used; the meaning of the clause here is then literally "they were the populations of the land" (see BDB, Qal, 3).

אֲשֶׁר מֵעוֹלָם—Literally "who (were) from antiquity," this relative clause modifies the preceding clause, hence "ancient inhabitants." Although the noun עוֹלָם is often translated as "forever," it does not always mean that. It signifies a long time into the future or back into the past.[5] See also עוֹלָם in the third textual note on 27:12.

בּוֹאֲךָ שׁוּרָה—For these two words, "as far as Shur," see the textual note on 15:7. Here שׁוּר has the directional *he* ending.

27:9–11 The verbs narrating the actions of David and Achish in these verses (excluding the quotes in 27:10–11) refer to customary (frequentative, habitual) action and so are translated with "would." See further the next two textual notes.

27:9 וְהִכָּה ... וְלֹא יְחַיֶּה—"And he would strike ... and he would not allow to remain alive." The first verb, וְהִכָּה, is a Hiphil (H) perfect of נָכָה, "strike," with *waw* consecutive. A perfect with *waw* consecutive may follow a preterite (imperfect with *waw* consecutive), וַיִּפְשְׁטוּ, "and they raided" (27:8), to indicate customary action ("and he would strike"), as here.[6] The second verb, יְחַיֶּה, is a Piel (D) imperfect of חָיָה, whose Qal (G) means "to live." In the Piel its meaning is causative and it takes a direct object that participates passively, thus "and he would not allow or permit [someone] to remain

3   Josephus, *Antiquities*, 6.323 also omits it: Σερρίταις καὶ Ἀμαληκίταις.

4   McCarter, *I Samuel*, 413; Klein, *1 Samuel*, 262.

5   See, e.g., Gen 9:16; 17:8; Ex 29:28; 30:21; 40:15; Num 18:19; 25:13; Deut 15:17; Is 35:10; 54:8; 56:5; Jer 20:17; Ps 112:6; Job 40:28 (ET 41:4).

6   *IBH*, § 53 B 2; Waltke-O'Connor, § 32.2.1.

alive," a resultative force.[7] The same is true of לֹא־יְחַיֶּה in 27:11. This imperfect also indicates customary action ("and he would not allow to remain alive"). An imperfect is used here rather than a perfect with *waw* consecutive because a negative could not be inserted between the *waw* and a consecuted perfect.

וְלָקַח—"And he would take." Like the first verb in this verse (וְהִכָּה), this is another perfect with *waw* consecutive denoting customary action.

27:10 אַל־פְּשַׁטְתֶּם הַיּוֹם—The MT is awkward and reads "you should not have raided today." The grammatical difficulty is that the negative adverb אַל normally is used with an imperfect verb to form a negative command, but the verb here, פְּשַׁטְתֶּם, "you [plural] raided," is a perfect. In the OT there is no other instance of אַל being used with a perfect verb. The semantic difficulty is equally problematic: Achish was pleased with David's raids (27:12), and so he would not have scolded David here. In place of אַל־ the reading in 4QSam[a] is עַל מִ[י] (to be vocalized עַל־מִי), "against whom?" which is supported by the LXX, ἐπὶ τίνα, and the Vulgate (*in quem*). This reading is followed by most English translations.[8] Another proposal is to read אָן, "where?" with the Syriac and the Targum.

הַיְּרַחְמְאֵלִי—This means "Jerahmeelites." Jerahmeel was a great-grandson of Judah and his daughter-in-law Tamar (Genesis 38). Jerahmeel's grandfather was Perez, and his father was Hezron (1 Chr 2:3–5, 9). Apparently the clan descended from Jerahmeel settled in the Negev in southern Judah.

וְאֶל־נֶגֶב הַקֵּינִי—This is translated as "or 'Against the Negev of the Kenites.'" For the "Kenites," see the commentary on 15:6. The LXX reads κατὰ νότον τοῦ Κενεζι, "against the south [Negev] of the Kenizites/Kenizzites." The Kenizzites were an ethnic group native to Palestine that apparently was absorbed into the tribe of Judah (Gen 15:18–19; Num 32:12; Josh 14:6, 14). However, "the Kenites" is most likely the correct reading here; see the commentary.

27:11 לְהָבִיא—The Hiphil (H) infinitive construct of בּוֹא (with לְ) has the active meaning, "to bring," and its implied object would be any living "man or woman" (וְאִישׁ וְאִשָּׁה is the stated object of the preceding negated verb לֹא־יְחַיֶּה). To clarify the sense in English and to avoid supplying the implied object (a repetition of "a man or woman"), the infinitive is rendered in the passive, "be brought," with the previously stated "man or woman" as its subject.

כֹּה־עָשָׂה דָוִד וְכֹה מִשְׁפָּטוֹ—Literally "thus David would do, and thus was his custom." These two clauses can be translated as a hendiadys: "this was David's customary practice." The noun מִשְׁפָּט, "justice," can denote one's "custom, manner," or practice (BDB, 6 b).

27:12 וַיַּאֲמֵן אָכִישׁ בְּדָוִד—The Hiphil (H) of אָמַן, "to trust, believe," usually takes the preposition בְּ when it refers to "believing in" God (e.g., Gen 15:6; Jonah 3:5), but this construction can also be used with a human object, as with בְּדָוִד here (see BDB, s.v. אָמַן, Hiphil, 2 (*c*)).

---

[7]   See the discussion of the Piel (D) in *IBH*, §§ 37; 41 B; Waltke-O'Connor, §§ 21.2; 24.3.

[8]   HCSB, ESV, GW, NET, NIV.

הַבְאֵשׁ הִבְאִישׁ—The Hiphil (H) of בָּאַשׁ can have the intransitive meaning "emit a stinking odour" (BDB, Hiphil, 1), as well as the transitive meaning "cause [something] to stink" (BDB, Hiphil, 2). Here the Hiphil (H) infinitive absolute and perfect combine to express an emphatic intransitive meaning, "be utterly repugnant, abhorrent." See the discussion of the verb's Niphal (N) in the second textual note on 13:4.

לְעֶבֶד עוֹלָם:—In this construct phrase, "to (be) a servant of a long time," the noun עוֹלָם (see the fifth textual note on 27:8) is translated adverbially, "permanently."

Commentary

Tebeth (December/January) late 1011 or early 1010 BC–Nisan (March/April) 1009 BC

This account of David fleeing to Gath for the second time[9] is part of a much longer section concerning the final Philistine confrontation with Saul that brought David to the beginning of his reign. It places David in the service of the Philistines as preparation for their incursion into Israel. The interplay between David's role and Saul's role coordinated David's rise to the throne of Judah with Saul's final collapse. The narrative is organized by the author in the following sequence:

Part 1: David as Undaunted by the Philistines; Saul as Afraid of Them
David in the service of Achish (27:1–12)
David tells Achish that he will show him what he can do (28:1–2)
Saul, afraid of the Philistines, is told at Endor that he will die in battle against them (28:3–25)

Part 2: David Assumes Royal Responsibilities; Saul Loses His Life and His Throne
David is dismissed from Achish's service (29:1–11)
David behaves like a king: he rescues his and his men's wives and distributes spoils to his subjects (30:1–31)
Saul, afraid of the Philistines, commits suicide in battle against them (31:1–13)

Each of the two major parts has three scenes, and the scenes in part 1 are parallel to the scenes in part 2. The first scenes in each part relate to David's service to Achish: first his entry into service (27:1–12) and then his dismissal (29:1–11). The second scenes focus on David's action: in part 1 his enigmatic words to Achish about what he *could do* (28:1–2) and in part 2 what he *actually does* (30:1–31) that demonstrates his royal aptitude. The final scenes in each part highlight Saul's fear of the Philistines (28:3–25) and his death while in battle against them (31:1–13).

David Flees to Gath (27:1–4)

The narrative begins with David's internal conversation about his situation (27:1). He concluded that he would be "swept away" (the Niphal [N] of סָפָה,

---

[9]   The first time David fled to Gath is narrated in 21:11–16 (ET 21:10–15).

27:1) if he remained in Judah, so he once again decided to flee to Gath (as previously in 21:11–16 [ET 21:10–15]). David's fear of being swept away contains overtones of Yahweh's judgment. In 12:25 Samuel reminded the Israelites that if they did not remain faithful to Yahweh, they and their king would be "swept away" (the Niphal of סָפָה, as in 27:1). In 26:10 David refrained from killing Saul himself and stated that should God choose, Saul could enter battle and be "swept away" (the Niphal of סָפָה, as in 12:25; 27:1). Now David concluded that it may well be God's will that he himself leave Judah or be "swept away" (27:1). David certainly had been considering this for some time (cf. 26:19).

We are told that all six hundred of David's men[10] went to Gath, where Achish the son of Maoch reigned (27:2). After David's previous peril in Gath and his escape (21:11–16 [ET 21:10–15]), this may strike the reader as quite risky. However, there are several reasons why the situation was different enough to make Gath a more hospitable place this time. First of all, the king is identified as "Achish the son of Maoch" rather than simply as "Achish," as previously (21:11 [ET 21:10]). This may well signal that a change in rulers has occurred, with the previous Achish no longer in power.[11] Second, David now arrived as an established warlord with a sizable body of men instead of as a lone fugitive with a reputation as the heir to the throne of Israel (21:12 [ET 21:11]). Finally, Saul's pursuit of David may have been known to the Philistines,[12] moving Achish to decide to make common cause with David against their mutual enemy Saul.

At first David and his men and their households lived in Gath (27:3). The author makes a special point of telling us that David's household included the two wives he had previously married while in Judah (see the textual note on 27:3). Already David has taken on the appearance of a king with the beginnings of a harem. Saul, we are told, no longer "sought"[13] David when he learned of his residence in Gath (27:4).

Achish Gives Ziklag to David (27:5–6)

David eventually approached Achish with a request to be given an outlying city instead of living in Gath (27:5). This may have appealed to Achish on several levels: The influx of over a thousand people (including the families of the six hundred men) may have strained the resources of his city. The presence of so many Judeans may have been disruptive and caused ethnic tensions. Moreover, there may have been lingering doubts on his part as to where David's

---

[10] In 22:2 David had four hundred men, but their ranks had swelled to six hundred in 23:13.

[11] Achish may well have been a common Gittite throne name; see the commentary on 21:11 (ET 21:10).

[12] The Philistines may have even taken advantage of it for an incursion into Israelite territory (23:27–28).

[13] For the thematic verb "seek," see the fifth textual note on 27:1.

loyalty lay (cf. 29:3–5)—something that would not be resolved for some time (cf. 27:12–28:2).

Achish gave David the city of Ziklag (27:6). Ziklag was within the territory allotted to the tribe of Simeon (Josh 19:5; 1 Chr 4:30), though it was nominally reckoned with Judah (Josh 15:31), probably as Simeon lost its identity and was absorbed into the larger southern tribe. Ziklag was probably located at modern Tell esh-Shariah,[14] fifteen miles (twenty-four kilometers) southeast of Gaza and twenty-five miles (forty kilometers) southwest of Gath (see figure 25 at the end of this pericope). This location suited David well and may have served his purposes by removing him from everyday scrutiny by Achish. The author includes a note that subsequently Ziklag belonged to "the kings of Judah" and remained so in the author's own day. This notice anticipates David's initial seven-and-a-half-year reign over Judah (2 Sam 2:4; 5:5).

David's Raids (27:7–12)

We are next told that David was in Philistine territory for sixteen months (27:7; cf. 29:3). This anticipates the following verses that explain what David did during this time. David used his remote location to raid the Geshurites and Amalekites in the south and southwest (27:8). In raiding Geshur, David was continuing to fight "Yahweh's wars" (18:17; 25:28), since Joshua had left the Geshurites for Israel to conquer as part of receiving the promised land (Josh 13:2–3). In conquering the Amalekites, David was finishing what Saul had left undone (15:1–33). We are also told that David left no survivors, but captured domesticated animals, including camels, and clothing (27:9). Camels were not usual beasts of burden in Israel, and only during David's reign are they mentioned as Israelite domesticated animals (1 Chr 12:41 [ET 12:40]; 27:30). Clothing, though not frequently mentioned as part of the spoils of war, was taken on several other occasions (Judg 8:26; 2 Ki 7:8).

After these raids David would return to Achish in Gath, apparently to share some of the spoils with his patron. We are told that Achish would question David about whom he was raiding (27:10). David lied about his activity by telling Achish that he was pillaging various locations in Judah.[15] The Negev of Judah was probably in the vicinity of Beersheba (2 Sam 24:7). The Negev of Jerahmeel may have been south of Beersheba, perhaps near Hormah (Josh 15:21–30). The Kenite Negev most likely was near Arad to the east of Beersheba (Judg 1:16). The mention of the "Kenites" (27:10) is pivotal to the relating of this narrative, because the author is telling us that David led Achish to believe that he was denying mercy to the Kenites in direct opposition to what Saul had done (15:6). This would also have been a breach of historic ties between Israel and the Kenites, who had been kind to Israel (Judg 1:16; 4:11–21; 5:24–27; cf. Num 24:20–21).

---

[14] For other suggestions on the location of Ziklag, see Fritz, "Where Is David's Ziklag?"

[15] For his lying, see further the commentary below.

The author now reveals why David allowed no person to live when he raided—because he was deceiving Achish, he wanted no living informants who could contradict his reports to the Gittite ruler (1 Sam 27:11; cf. 27:9). This apparently worked, since we are told that Achish thought David was alienating himself from his people, possibly ruining his chances to become their ruler (27:12). David, he thought, would have no choice but to remain in his service permanently.

David had once again gotten the upper hand on the Philistines. He defeated Goliath (17:48–54), outwitted a previous Achish of Gath (21:11–16 [ET 21:10–15]), and now had misled Achish the son of Maoch. Throughout 1 Samuel, Saul is seen as reluctant to engage the Philistines and lacking faith in God to enable him to overcome them.[16] By contrast, David is seen as boldly confident in Yahweh's salvation (e.g., 17:34–37, 45–47), more than willing to seek encounters with the Philistines, and always able to outmaneuver them to his advantage and to the advantage of Israel (see also 2 Sam 5:17–25; 8:1; 21:15–22).

The author of Samuel has once again portrayed lying by an Israelite believer in a favorable light.[17] However, in this case the lies might appear to modern readers to be less justifiable. In the previous cases a lie was used to protect innocent lives. Here it could appear that David was simply dissembling in order to preserve his political ambitions. However, we ought to keep in mind that David was lying in order to further activity sanctioned by God—the continued conquest of the promised land as ordered by God and the ongoing victory over the Amalekites prophesied by Moses (Ex 17:14–16). Moreover, by deceiving the Philistine monarch Achish, David was favoring God's people instead of raiding and plundering throughout Judah. David as king-designate (1 Sam 16:1–13) was fighting "Yahweh's wars" (18:17; 25:28), fulfilling the leadership role the Israelites originally desired when they asked for a king (8:20), so the author does not portray David's lies in a negative light. Subterfuge may not have been the ideal way for David to carry out God's mandate. However, given that David had little choice but to find a place outside of Israel to survive and there was no way to avoid attacking God's chosen people without resorting to deception, the author reports David's words without portraying them as inappropriate. David's statements were not honest and did not live up to the ideal that David himself

---

[16] Saul failed to carry out the divine mandate given him by Samuel at his anointing (10:7) to eradicate the Philistine garrison in Gibeah. See "Samuel Anoints Saul (9:26–10:8)" in the commentary on 9:26–10:16, including figure 16, "Saul's Faltering Accession." See also the beginning of the commentary on 10:17–27a. Saul and his troops were terrified of the Philistines (13:7, 12). Later Saul's son Jonathan assaulted the Philistine garrison in Gibeah (14:1–16), and Saul joined the battle only after Jonathan was routing the Philistines (14:20).

[17] See the commentary on the lies by Michal in 19:11–17 and especially on those by Jonathan in 20:28–29. David apparently lied in 21:3–4 (ET 21:2–3) and deceived in 21:13–14 (ET 21:12–13). As noted in the commentary on 19:11–17, the NT even praises the lying of Rahab the prostitute (Josh 2:1–24; 6:17–25) as an act of justifying faith and a demonstration of righteousness through actions (Heb 11:31; James 2:25).

would later acknowledge (Ps 15:1–5), but they were at least partly the result of circumstances brought about by the sins of others against David (cf. 26:18–20). It would not be long before God would arrange circumstances in order to liberate David from potential warfare against Israel (29:1–11).

Figure 25

David's Raids

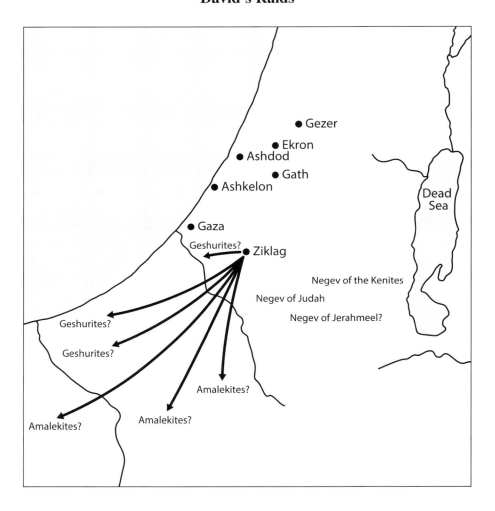

1 Samuel 28:1–2
David Gains Achish's Trust

Translation

28 **¹In those days the Philistines gathered their camps into an army for battle with Israel. Achish said to David, "You most certainly ought to know that you and your men will march out with me in the camp."**

²David said to Achish, "Surely you will find out what your servant can do."

Achish said to David, "In that case I will appoint you as my chief bodyguard permanently."

Textual Notes

28:1 וַיִּקְבְּצוּ פְלִשְׁתִּים אֶת־מַחֲנֵיהֶם לַצָּבָא—In the Qal (G) קָבַץ has the transitive meaning "to gather [people] together," often for military purposes, as also in 1 Sam 7:5; 28:4; 29:1; 2 Sam 2:30; 3:21. Here it takes the direct object אֶת־מַחֲנֵיהֶם, "their camps." The noun מַחֲנֶה is derived from the verb חָנָה (for which, see the second textual note on 11:1), and it recurs later in the verse (see the last textual note on 28:1). This is the only time in the book of Samuel that the noun צָבָא denotes the action of "warfare"; elsewhere it refers to an "army" (e.g., 17:55; 26:5), including Yahweh's "armies" (צְבָאוֹת; see the fourth textual note on 1:3).

לְהִלָּחֵם—This is the Niphal (N) infinitive construct of לָחַם, with the preposition לְ, forming a purpose clause. This verb appears in the Niphal, meaning "to wage war," thirty times in the book of Samuel.

יָדֹעַ תֵּדַע—The force of the Qal (G) infinitive absolute together with the Qal imperfect of יָדַע is that David "most certainly should/ought to know" that in return for the hospitality the Philistine king Achish has shown him, he is expected to demonstrate his loyalty by waging war against his fellow Israelites. The same second masculine singular Qal imperfect form, תֵּדַע, recurs in 28:2 but in a different sense; see the first textual note on 28:2.

אִתִּי תֵּצֵא בַמַּחֲנֶה אַתָּה וַאֲנָשֶׁיךָ:—The prepositional phrase is placed first for emphasis, literally "*with me* you will go out in the camp, you and your men." In the book of Samuel, the Qal (G) of יָצָא often refers to "going out" for battle; see the first textual note on 18:6. אַתָּה וַאֲנָשֶׁיךָ is a compound subject, but the agreement of the singular verb תֵּצֵא with the singular pronoun אַתָּה focuses the attention on the personal involvement of David as the key figure.

At the end of the verse 4QSam^a adds [למ]לחמה יזרעאל, "[for w]ar at Jezreel," and it apparently omits בְּמַּחֲנֶה, "in the camp."[1] The LXX omits "in the camp" and adds εἰς

---

[1] In 4QSam^a there is a lacuna between אכיש אל דויד ידוע ת[דע], "... Achish to David, 'You most certainly k[now],'" and [למ]לחמה יזרעאל, "[for w]ar at Jezreel." Space considerations leave no room for במחנה in this lacuna.

πόλεμον, "to war." Josephus reads εἰς τὸν πόλεμον εἰς Ῥεγάν, "for war to Rega."[2] On the basis of these other textual witnesses some scholars have argued that the text originally included לַמִּלְחָמָה, "to war."[3] However, it appears more likely that these witnesses preserve a secondary reading that substituted the easier לַמִּלְחָמָה, "for war," for the more difficult בַּמַּחֲנֶה, "in the camp," and added יִזְרְעֶאל, "Jezreel," in anticipation of 29:1, 11.[4]

28:2 לָכֵן אַתָּה תֵדַע—The adverb כֵּן with the preposition לְ introduces a consequence of the previously described conditions: "in that case, consequently, therefore" (see BDB, s.v. כֵּן II, 3 d (a)). The second masculine singular pronoun אַתָּה preceding the second masculine singular verb תֵדַע is emphatic: "you yourself will know." Since this knowledge will be gained, the verb has the nuance of "learn, find out." The LXX reads νῦν γνώσει, "now you will find out," which reflects a Hebrew text with *ayin* in place of *aleph*, עתה (עַתָּה) instead of אַתָּה.

שֹׁמֵר לְרֹאשִׁי אֲשִׂימְךָ—The Qal (G) participle שֹׁמֵר with לְרֹאשִׁי, literally "the one keeping/guarding for my head," a unique phrase in the OT, denotes an office that is rendered as "my chief bodyguard." The Qal (G) of שִׂים, " to set, appoint," takes a double accusative. The first accusative is its object suffix (ךָ-), "you." The second object is the participial phrase, which denotes the office into which the person (denoted by the first object) is installed. See the second textual note on 8:1 for the same construction; see also Joüon, § 125 w; *IBH*, § 18 C.

כָּל־הַיָּמִים:—Literally "all the days," this phrase functions adverbially and is rendered as "permanently."

Commentary

Nisan (March/April) 1009 BC

This short section is set off from the preceding narrative by the introduction "(and it happened) in those days" (וַיְהִי בַּיָּמִים הָהֵם, 28:1).[5] This rare clause creates a disjunction from the previous text.[6] The following verse (28:3) also signals the beginning of a new narrative by starting with a subject-initial clause, "after Samuel had died" (וּשְׁמוּאֵל מֵת), instead of a verb-initial clause that would have signaled continuation with the previous narrative, i.e., וַיָּמָת שְׁמוּאֵל, "(and) Samuel died" (25:1). Most commentators recognize 28:1–2 as a distinct, short

---

2 Josephus, *Antiquities*, 6.325. On Ῥεγάν as a corruption of יִזְרְעֶאל, see the discussion in Ulrich, *The Qumran Text of Samuel and Josephus*, 172.

3 E.g., McCarter, *I Samuel*, 414.

4 Klein, *1 Samuel*, 262.

5 For the place of this section (28:1–2) in the larger section of 27:1–31:13, see the beginning of the commentary on 27:1–12.

6 This clause occurs only three other times in the OT: Ex 2:11; Judg 19:1; and, with the inclusion of an adjective, Ex 2:23 (וַיְהִי בַיָּמִים הָרַבִּים הָהֵם). Similar clauses, but with the verb in the imperfect, looking toward a future situation, occur in Deut 17:9; 19:17; 26:3; Josh 20:6.

narrative created by the author of the book of Samuel and either consider it to be a separate account or a subsection of 27:1–28:2.[7]

The account begins with the Philistines gathering "their camps" (מַחֲנֵיהֶם) for battle with Israel (28:1). This plural may imply that each of the five Philistine overlords (see 6:17) marshaled his own camp. This narrative does not tell us where they gathered, though 28:4 will reveal that it was at Shunem.

In gathering his forces, Achish, the king of Gath, told David that he and his men were to accompany the Gittite army into the camp. David gave an enigmatic reply, "Surely you will find out what your servant can do" (28:2). The reader is left with the question as to what David can and would do *to whom*. Heretofore, David had deceived Achish by raiding Israel's enemies while claiming to have raided Israel (27:9–12). David had never sided with the Philistines against Israel, and David's words left open the possibility that he would show Achish his true colors by turning on the Philistines in battle, as the other Philistine commanders suspected (29:4–5).

Achish appears once again gullibly to have accepted David's words as full support for him. He promised that once David showed his capability in battle, he would make him his chief bodyguard, the "guardian/keeper" of his "head" (רֹאשׁ; see the second textual note on 28:2). Ashish's words were unconsciously ironic, since David had already shown himself to be the keeper of another Philistine's head—the severed "head" of Goliath (רֹאשׁ, 17:46, 51, 54)! In fact, it is precisely concern for what David might to with their "heads" (the plural of רֹאשׁ) that would cause the other Philistine commanders to insist that David be dismissed from the camp and sent back to Ziklag (29:4).

The casual reader of 28:1–2 might think that David was in danger of having to fight against Israel. However, a closer reading of the text implies that David was quite coy in his statement to Achish, holding out the possibility that he never intended to support the Philistine cause.[8]

---

[7] The follow commentaries treat 28:1–2 as a separate section: Auld, *I and II Samuel*, 319–20; Bergen, *1, 2 Samuel*, 262–63; Bodner, *1 Samuel*, 291–92; Campbell, *1 Samuel*, 278–79. These commentaries treat 28:1–2 as a subsection of 27:1–28:2: Brueggemann, *First and Second Samuel*, 191; Fokkelman, *The Crossing Fates*, 558–69; Miscall, *1 Samuel*, 166–67; Smith, *The Books of Samuel*, 234–37. A few commentaries treat 28:1–2 as part of 27:1–28:2 without discussing it as a subsection: Klein, *1 Samuel*, 261–66; McCarter, *I Samuel*, 411–16. The main reason for grouping 28:1–2 with 27:1–12 is that both sections feature Achish, the king of Gath (who is not mentioned again until 29:2). However, the strong disjunction at the beginning of 28:1 ("in those days"; see the commentary above) indicates that the author is signaling the start of a separate section.

[8] Thus, one might include 28:2 among the passages in the book in which the deception of an unbeliever by a believer is portrayed in a positive light. See especially the commentary on 20:28–29. See also the commentary on 19:13–17; 21:3–4, 13–14 (ET 21:2–3, 12–13); and 27:10–11.

Saul's Second Philistine Campaign, Part 1: Saul and the Medium at Endor

Translation

28 ³After Samuel had died, all Israel mourned for him and buried him in Ramah, that is, in his city. Saul had removed the necromancers and mediums from the land. ⁴The Philistines gathered, came, and camped in Shunem. So Saul gathered all Israel and camped at Gilboa. ⁵Saul saw the Philistine camp and was afraid and exceedingly terrified. ⁶Saul inquired of Yahweh, but Yahweh would not answer him, either by dreams or by the Urim or by the prophets.

⁷Saul said to his servants, "Find me a woman who is an expert necromancer. I will go to her and inquire of her."

Saul's servants said to him, "There is a woman who is an expert necromancer at Endor."

⁸Saul disguised himself by putting on different clothes. He and two of his men went and came to the woman at night. He said, "Please practice divination for me with a spirit of a dead person. Bring up for me whomever I say to you."

⁹The woman said to him, "Look, you know what Saul did when he cut off the necromancers and mediums from the land. Why are you setting a trap for my life in order to kill me?"

¹⁰Saul swore an oath to her by Yahweh, "As Yahweh lives, you will not be punished in this matter."

¹¹The woman said, "Whom should I bring up for you?"

He said, "Bring up Samuel for me."

¹²When the woman saw Samuel she cried out loudly. The woman said to Saul, "Why did you deceive me? You are Saul!"

¹³The king said to her, "Do not be afraid. But what did you see?"

The woman said to Saul, "I saw gods coming up from the earth."

¹⁴He said to her, "What is his appearance?"

She said, "An old man is coming up, and he is wrapped in a robe."

Saul knew that it was Samuel, so he knelt with his face to the ground and bowed.

¹⁵Samuel said to Saul, "Why did you disturb me by bringing me up?"

Saul said, "I'm in a very tight spot. The Philistines are attacking me. God has turned away from me and has not answered me either by the hand of the prophets or by dreams. So I called to you to let me know what I ought to do."

¹⁶Samuel said, "So why are you asking me when Yahweh has turned away from you and become your enemy? ¹⁷Yahweh has done to you as he spoke through me.

Yahweh has torn the kingdom from your hand and given it to your neighbor, to David. [18]Since you did not listen to Yahweh's voice and did not execute his anger on Amalek, Yahweh has done this thing to you today. [19]Yahweh will also hand Israel with you over to the Philistines, and tomorrow you and your sons will be with me. Yahweh will also hand the camp of Israel over to the Philistines."

[20]Then Saul quickly fell flat on the ground. He was very afraid because of Samuel's words. He also had no strength because he had not eaten any food all day and all night. [21]The woman came to Saul and saw that he was terrified. She said to him, "Your servant has listened to your voice. I have placed my life in my hand, and I listened to your words that you spoke to me. [22]Now please listen—you also—to the voice of your servant. Let me place before you a bit of food; eat! May you regain your strength, because you will be going on your way."

[23]He refused and said, "I won't eat." His servants and also the woman urged him, so he listened to their voice. He rose from the ground and sat down on the couch. [24]The woman had a fattened calf in her house. She quickly slaughtered it. She took flour, kneaded [it], and baked it [into] unleavened loaves. [25]She brought [it] to Saul and his servants, and they ate. They rose and went [away] during that night.

Textual Notes

28:3 וּשְׁמוּאֵל מֵת—This is translated as "after Samuel had died." This subject-initial clause signals the beginning of a new narrative. (The commentary on 28:1–2 argued that those two verses are a separate section of narrative.) Contrast the verb-initial clause beginning chapter 25 that signaled its continuation of the previous narrative, וַיָּמָת שְׁמוּאֵל, "(and) Samuel died" (25:1).

וַיִּסְפְּדוּ־לוֹ כָּל־יִשְׂרָאֵל וַיִּקְבְּרֻהוּ—See the second and third textual notes on 25:1.

בָרָמָה וּבְעִירוֹ—This is translated as "in Ramah, that is, in his city." The second prepositional phrase is in apposition to the first, and the conjunction is an explanatory or epexegetical *waw*.[1]

הָאֹבוֹת—The masculine noun אוֹב (whose plural is feminine in form, אֹבוֹת) usually denotes a "necromancer," a person who consults the spirits of the dead (BDB, 2). This meaning is confirmed by Deut 18:11, where a person "who asks a necromancer or medium" (וְשֹׁאֵל אוֹב וְיִדְּעֹנִי) is parallel to one "who seeks/inquires into the dead" (וְדֹרֵשׁ אֶל־הַמֵּתִים) or perhaps "who calls up the dead" (NASB); cf. וְהַעֲלִי, "bring up," in 1 Sam 28:8b. See also the first textual note on 28:7. In the Torah אוֹב appears only in God's commandments that his people not consult such people under penalty of death, for they are an abomination (Lev 19:31; 20:6, 27; Deut 18:11). Resorting to them is implicitly condemned in 2 Ki 21:6 ‖ 2 Chr 33:6; Is 19:3. Like Saul (1 Sam 28:3), Josiah banished them from the land (2 Ki 23:24). The chronicler attributes Saul's death to his unfaithfulness to Yahweh's Word and to his consultation of the necromancer (אוֹב, 1 Chr

---

[1] GKC, § 154 a, note 1 b; Waltke-O'Connor, § 39.2.4.

10:13). The noun אוֹב has cognates in Hittite, Ugaritic, Akkadian, and Sumerian and is connected with calling up the spirits of the dead from a pit in the ground (cf. "gods coming up from the earth," 28:13).[2] In eleven of the sixteen occurrences of אוֹב in the OT, it is paired with the noun יִדְּעֹנִי (see the next textual note).[3]

הַיִּדְּעֹנִים—The noun יִדְּעֹנִי, "medium," is derived from the verb יָדַע, "to know," possibly signifying that such a person knows (is familiar with or an expert in) occult phenomena, "one who consults a familiar spirit" (*DCH*). In every passage with this noun, it is the second word paired with אוֹב as the first word.[4]

28:4 וַיִּקָּבְצוּ—For the Niphal (N) of קָבַץ with an intransitive meaning, "(and) they gathered," see the first textual note on 7:6.

וַיַּחֲנוּ ... וַיַּחֲנוּ—"And they camped. ... And they camped." For the Qal (G) of חָנָה, see the second textual note on 11:1.

בְשׁוּנֵם—Shunem was in the territory of Issachar (Josh 19:18). It is identified with modern Solem, about four miles (six kilometers) north of Jezreel. See figure 26 in "The Chronological Displacement of 1 Samuel 28:3–25" in the commentary.

וַיִּקְבֹּץ—For the Qal (G) of קָבַץ with a transitive meaning, see the first textual note on 28:1.

בַּגִּלְבֹּעַ׃—Mount Gilboa is modern Jebel Fuquʿah on the eastern edge of the Plain of Esdraelon.

28:5 וַיַּרְא—This form, which recurs in 28:20, is the defective, or *ḥaser*, spelling of the third masculine singular Qal (G) preterite (imperfect with *waw* consecutive) of יָרֵא, "be afraid." The plene, or *male'*, spelling is וַיִּירָא, as in 12:18. Cf. תִּירְאִי, its second feminine singular imperfect, in 28:13.

וַיֶּחֱרַד לִבּוֹ מְאֹד׃—Literally "and his heart trembled exceedingly" (cf. Job 37:1).

28:6 וַיִּשְׁאַל שָׁאוּל בַּיהוָה—"(And) Saul inquired of Yahweh." Cf. וַיִּשְׁאַל שָׁאוּל בֵּאלֹהִים, "so Saul asked God," in 14:37. Elsewhere in the book of Samuel the author engages in wordplay with the verb שָׁאַל, "ask, request, inquire," and Saul's name, שָׁאוּל, meaning "requested," since Israel "requested" that "Yahweh" give them a king (8:10; 10:22; 12:13–19). Such wordplay is evident in the three words here.[5]

28:7 אֵשֶׁת בַּעֲלַת־אוֹב—Literally this means "a woman of a mistress of a spirit." This might mean "a woman possessing a spirit," that is, a woman possessed by a spirit. This phrase is a suspended-genitive formation where the first two nouns are in the construct state and are completed by the genitive in the form of the final noun in the absolute

---

[2]   Hoffner, "Second Millennium Antecedents to the Hebrew *ʾōb*.

[3]   These two nouns are paired in Lev 19:31; 20:6, 27; Deut 18:11; 1 Sam 28:3, 9; 2 Ki 21:6; 23:24; Is 8:19; 19:3; 2 Chr 33:6.

[4]   Lev 19:31; 20:6, 27; Deut 18:11; 1 Sam 28:3, 9; 2 Ki 21:6; 23:24; Is 8:19; 19:3; 2 Chr 33:6.

[5]   See also the first textual note on 1:28; "Samuel Warns Israel about Kings (8:10–22)" in the commentary on 8:1–22; the first textual note on 10:22; the commentary on 12:13–19; the textual note on 14:37; and the second textual note on 20:6, which refers to the Hebrew wording of 20:28.

state.[6] In 28:7 (twice) and 28:8 the noun אוֹב does not denote a "necromancer" (as it does in 28:3). Instead, it may refer to the practice of "necromancy" (so BDB, אוֹב 4), but more likely it refers to a "spirit" of the dead—or a demon masquerading as one. Is 29:4, a judgment oracle against Jerusalem, compares the voice of the destroyed city to the voice of a spirit of the dead (אוֹב). Compare the construct phrase בַּעֲלַת כְּשָׁפִים, "a mistress of sorcery," i.e., a sorceress or witch, in Nah 3:4. Here the LXX reads simply γυναῖκα ἐγγαστρίμυθον, "a woman ventriloquist."

וְאֵלְכָה אֵלֶיהָ וְאֶדְרְשָׁה־בָּהּ—"(And) I will go to her, and I will inquire of her." The Qal (G) cohortatives וְאֵלְכָה and וְאֶדְרְשָׁה express volition, namely, Saul's earnest desire, or even desperation, to receive some form of supernatural guidance (cf. 28:6).

בְּעֵין דּוֹר:—Endor is modern Khirbet Safsafeh, about six miles (ten kilometers) north of Gilboa (cf. Josh 17:11; Ps 83:11 [ET 83:10]).

28:8 וַיִּתְחַפֵּשׂ—"And he disguised himself." In the Piel (D) חָפַשׂ commonly means "to search for" (23:23). However, in the Hithpael (HtD), as here, it has the reflexive meaning "disguise oneself" (as also in 1 Ki 20:38; 22:30; 2 Chr 18:29; 35:22; cf. Job 30:18).

קָסֳמִי—This Qere is the Qal (G) feminine singular imperative of קָסַם, "to practice divination," as in 6:2. Cf. the cognate noun קֶסֶם, "divination," in 15:23. The masculine singular imperative would be קְסֹם or קְסׄום, with *holem* (a long "o" vowel). In the feminine singular form, the long vowel has been reduced to a *shewa* with a short "o" vowel, *chateph qamets* (-ֳ-), with a *qamets chatuph* (-ָק) preceding it. Cf. GKC, §§ 10 h, 46 d. The Kethib, קְסׄומִי, retains the *holem* of the masculine singular form.

וְהַעֲלִי לִי—"(And) bring up for me." This clause (without *waw*) recurs in 28:11. The verb is the Hiphil (H) feminine singular imperative of עָלָה. Since the dead were buried in the ground (וַיִּקְבְּרֻהוּ, 28:3), to conjure a spirit was to bring it up from from the realm of the dead. Cf. 2:6: Yahweh is the God who "brings down to Sheol [מוֹרִיד שְׁאוֹל] and brings up [וַיָּעַל]," that is, raises from the dead.

28:9 הַיִּדְּעֹנִי מִן־הָאָרֶץ—The MT has the singular noun, "the medium from the land." The LXX reads the plural, τοὺς γνώστας, "the mediums," and is followed by most English versions.[7] The MT probably suffered from haplography; the loss of the final *mem* on an original הַיִּדְּעֹנִים is due to the initial *mem* on the next word (מִן).

מִתְנַקֵּשׁ—Elsewhere in the OT the verb נָקַשׁ appears in the Qal (G), Niphal (N), and Piel (D), meaning "be ensnared" (Deut 12:30) or "ensnare" (Pss 9:17 [ET 9:16]; 38:13 [ET 38:12]; 109:11). This is the sole instance of a Hithpael (HtD) form, and this participle means "setting a trap."

לַהֲמִיתֵנִי:—The Hiphil (H) infinitive construct of מוּת with לְ and a first common singular suffix forms a purpose clause, "in order to kill me," as does the identical form in 5:10.

---

6 See GKC, § 130 d–e. For other examples, see שְׂפֻנֵי טְמוּנֵי חוֹל, "hidden things that are secreted in the sand" (Deut 33:19); נַהֲרֵי נַחֲלֵי דְּבַשׁ וְחֶמְאָה, "rivers that are rivers of honey and cream" (Job 20:17); and בְּתוּלַת בַּת־צִיּוֹן, "the virgin who is the daughter of Zion" (Is 37:22; cf. Is 23:12).

7 HCSB, ESV, GW, NET, NIV.

28:10 חַי־יְהֹוָה אִם—For "as Yahweh lives, if/not," see the second textual notes on 1:26 and 14:45.

יִקְרֵךְ עָוֹן—Literally "iniquity/punishment will not encounter you." The verb is the Qal (G) third masculine singular imperfect of קָרָה, "to meet, encounter, befall," with a second feminine singular suffix.

28:11 אַעֲלֶה־לָּךְ—The verb form could be either the Qal (G) or the Hiphil (H) first common singular imperfect of עָלָה. The context requires the Hiphil (H) with the caus-ative meaning, "I will bring up" (see the third textual note on 28:8). לָּךְ (with conjunctive *daghesh*, GKC, § 20 f), is pausal for לְךְ.

28:12 רִמִּיתָנִי—The Piel (D) of רָמָה II, "deceive, mislead," also appears in 1 Sam 19:17; 2 Sam 19:27 (ET 19:26).

28:13 אַל־תִּירְאִי כִּי—After a negative (אַל), the conjunction כִּי can have the adversa-tive meaning "but" (BDB, s.v. כִּי, 3 e).

אֱלֹהִים ... עֹלִים—Here the noun אֱלֹהִים, which is masculine plural in form, prob-ably has the plural meaning, "gods," since it is modified by the masculine plural Qal (G) participle of עָלָה, "come up." Contrast the third textual note on 28:15. However, in light of the singular forms in 28:14 that refer back to אֱלֹהִים here (note עֹלֶה), the plural here might refer to one spiritual or supernatural being.

28:14 מַה־תָּאֳרוֹ—"What is his appearance?" Saul responds to the woman's (plural) אֱלֹהִים with the question about *his* form." The noun תֹּאַר, "form, appearance" (16:18; 25:3), has a third masculine *singular* suffix.

אִישׁ זָקֵן עֹלֶה—"An old man is coming up." Contrast the singular Qal (G) partici-ple עֹלֶה here to the plural participle of the same verb, עֹלִים, in 28:13. In place of זָקֵן, "old," the LXX reads ὄρθιον, "upright," which might reflect a Hebrew text with זקף, and if so, זָקֵן in the MT could have resulted from a confusion of *nun* and *pe*. However, זקף appears only twice in the OT; its participle in Pss 145:14; 146:8 describes Yahweh as "raising up" the prostrate. While some prefer the LXX because it is the more diffi-cult reading,[8] it makes little sense in this context. There was no reason why Saul would necessarily recognize the description of an "upright man" in a robe as Samuel. In light of Samuel's death and burial in 28:3, the description of an "old man" in a robe is much more in keeping with what Saul might have expected.

וְהוּא עֹטֶה מְעִיל—For the noun מְעִיל, which often denotes a royal or priestly "robe," see the first textual note on 2:19 and the fourth textual note on 24:5 (ET 24:4). In the Qal (G), the verb עָטָה means "wrap/cover oneself," and with clothing it is equivalent to "wear."

וַיִּקֹּד אַפַּיִם אַרְצָה וַיִּשְׁתָּחוּ—For the identical wording (but with "David" as the explicit subject), see the textual note on 24:9 (ET 24:8).

28:15 הִרְגַּזְתַּנִי לְהַעֲלוֹת אֹתִי—In the Hiphil (H) רָגַז has the causative meaning "to dis-turb, bother" or even "to provoke, enrage." The Hiphil infinitive construct הַעֲלוֹת with לְ

---

8   McCarter, *I Samuel*, 419; Klein, *1 Samuel*, 268.

(and the direct object אֹתִי) explains how that action was accomplished (Joüon, § 124 o), "by bringing me up."

צַר־לִי מְאֹד—Literally "it is narrow to me, very." The verb צַר is a Qal (G) perfect of צָרַר, "be narrow, constricted." The verb lacks a subject, and in such an impersonal construction, the object (לִי) can be translated as the subject and the active verb rendered as a passive, thus "I am in a very tight spot."

וֵאלֹהִים סָר מֵעָלַי וְלֹא־עָנָנִי—Here אֱלֹהִים refers to the one true "God" and is the subject of the two Qal (G) perfect third masculine singular verbs (of סוּר and עָנָה, respectively). Contrast the second textual note on 28:13. In the OT there are some instances where אֱלֹהִים refers to the one true "God" and is modified by plural forms (Joüon, § 148 a) or is the subject of a plural verb (Joüon, § 150 f). The verb סוּר, "turn away, depart," is used with the combination of prepositions מֵעָל־, literally "from upon," again in 28:16. The verb סוּר was used in 16:14, where "the Spirit of Yahweh departed" from Saul, and again in 18:12, where Saul recognized that "Yahweh was with" David but that Yahweh "had turned away from Saul."

וָאֶקְרָאֶה—This unique form is the singular cohortative of קָרָא, "to call." The usual form of the first common singular imperfect is אֶקְרָא, and the expected form of the cohortative would be אֶקְרָאָה. See GKC, § 48 d; Joüon, § 78 h, including note 1.

28:16 וַיְהִי עָרֶךָ—"And he has become your enemy." The noun עָר, "enemy," is rare, occurring elsewhere only in Ps 139:20; Sirach 37:5; 47:7. It appears to be an Aramaic form of the common Hebrew noun צַר, "adversary." The LXX reads καὶ γέγονεν μετὰ τοῦ πλησίον σου, "and he [Yahweh] has become [is now] with your neighbor." (The "neighbor" would be David, as stated in 28:17, since Yahweh is "with" David; see 16:18; 17:37; 18:12, 14, 28; 20:13; cf. 16:13.) This may reflect a Hebrew text that may have read ויהי עם רעך, to be vocalized וַיְהִי עִם רֵעֶךָ.[9] If that Hebrew were original, עָרֶךָ in the MT might be explained by positing a corruption by an accidental metathesis of the *resh* and the *ayin* in רֵעֶךָ, but that would not explain the loss of the preposition עִם. Instead, it would appear that the LXX tradition has substituted an easier reading adapted to 28:17 (לְרֵעֶךָ) for the harder one in the MT here.

28:17 וַיַּעַשׂ יְהוָה לוֹ— Codex Leningradensis and the majority of Masoretic manuscripts read "and Yahweh did for himself," if the suffixed preposition לוֹ is to be understood in a reflexive sense, rather than a third-person reference to Saul, "to him." The LXX reads καὶ πεποίηκεν κύριός σοι, "and the Lord has done to you," and a few MT manuscripts have לְךָ, "to you." The second-person reading is followed by some English versions.[10] The reading לוֹ is probably the result of a damaged final *kaph* read as a *waw*.

בְּיָדִי—"Through me" is literally "by my hand."

---

[9] As favored by McCarter, *1 Samuel*, 419; Klein, *1 Samuel*, 268.

[10] ESV, GW. Others simply omit "to you" or "to him" (HCSB, NET, NIV).

וַיִּקְרַ֨ע יְהוָ֤ה אֶת־הַמַּמְלָכָה֙ מִיָּדֶ֔ךָ וַֽיִּתְּנָ֖הּ לְרֵעֲךָ֥ לְדָוִֽד׃—This repeats the vocabulary and thought of 15:28, where Samuel informed Saul that "Yahweh" had "torn the kingdom" from him and had "given" it to his "neighbor," i.e., to David.

28:18 וְלֹא־עָשִׂ֧יתָ חֲרוֹן־אַפּ֛וֹ בַּעֲמָלֵ֑ק—Literally "and you did not do the anger of his nose against Amalek." For Saul's failure to exterminate the Amalekites, see 1 Samuel 15.

28:20 וַיְמַהֵ֣ר שָׁא֔וּל וַיִּפֹּ֤ל—Literally "and/then Saul hurried, and he fell." The first verb functions adverbially: "and/then Saul quickly fell." See also the second textual note on 28:24.

מְלֹא־קֽוֹמָתוֹ֙—Literally this means "the fullness of his height." Saul was unusually tall (9:2; 10:23). The noun קוֹמָה also appeared in 16:7 when Yahweh told Samuel to pay no attention to the "height" of Jesse's son Eliab, for he was not the son chosen to replace Saul as Israel's anointed king; David was (16:12).

וַיִּרָ֖א—"And he was afraid." See the first textual note on 28:5.

גַּם־כֹּ֙חַ֙ לֹא־הָ֣יָה ב֔וֹ—Literally "also strength was not in him."

28:21 נִבְהַ֣ל מְאֹ֑ד—Literally "he was very terrified." The verb is a Niphal (N) perfect of בָּהַל. Its Niphal means "be terrified, dismayed."

28:22 וְאָשִׂ֧מָה—"(And) let me place." This is the first common singular Qal (G) cohortative of שִׂים with a conjunctive *waw*.

וִיהִ֥י בְךָ֖ כֹּ֑חַ—Literally "and let strength be in you." The verb וִיהִי is a Qal (G) third masculine singular jussive of הָיָה with a conjunctive *waw*.

28:23 וַיִּפְרְצוּ־ב֣וֹ—Normally the Qal (G) of פָּרַץ means "to break through/down." However, for פָּרַץ here and in 2 Sam 13:25, 27; 2 Ki 5:23, the context requires a meaning such as "urge," "insist," or "press upon," which are usual meanings of פָּצַר. Such a meaning here is supported by the LXX (παρεβιάζοντο) and found in most English translations.[11] One explanation is that the MT reading וַיִּפְרְצוּ is the result of accidental metathesis of the *tsade* and the *resh*. Another possibility is that the verb פָּרַץ that appears in 1 Sam 28:23; 2 Sam 13:25, 27; 2 Ki 5:23 is a by-form of פָּצַר, caused by metathesis, and so no emendation is needed in these verses.

28:24 עֵֽגֶל־מַרְבֵּ֣ק—Literally "a calf of a stall," this denotes "a fattened calf." Calves were kept in stalls to feed and fatten them before slaughter. All three other instances of the noun מַרְבֵּק, "stall," in the OT involve the plural of עֵגֶל (Jer 46:21; Amos 6:4; Mal 3:20 [ET 4:2]), and at least two refer to "fattened calves" (Jer 46:21; Amos 6:4).

וַתְּמַהֵ֖ר וַתִּזְבָּחֵ֑הוּ—Literally "and she hurried, and she slaughtered it." The first verb functions adverbially: "and she quickly slaughtered it." See also the first textual note on 28:20.

וַתָּ֖לָשׁ—"And she kneaded" is a Qal (G) third feminine singular preterite (imperfect with *waw* consecutive) of לוּשׁ, "to knead."

וַתֹּפֵ֖הוּ מַצּֽוֹת׃—Literally "and she baked it [into] unleavened loaves." The verb is the Qal (G) third feminine singular preterite (imperfect with *waw* consecutive) of אָפָה,

---

[11] HCSB, ESV, NET; cf. GW.

"to bake," with a third masculine singular suffix. This is one of the Hebrew verbs that often takes a double accusative construction (Joüon, § 125 w). The first accusative is the pronominal suffix ("it"), referring to the kneaded flour she baked, and the second accusative, מַצּוֹת, denotes the baked product, "unleavened loaves." The noun מַצָּה, *matsah*, "unleavened bread," usually appears in the plural. חַג הַמַּצּוֹת) is the term designating the Feast of Unleavened Bread.[12] מַצָּה can also denote bread baked in a hurry (Gen 19:3; Ex 12:39), as it does here.

28:25 בַּלַּיְלָה הַהוּא:—This phrase with the preposition בְּ means "in/on that night."[13] 4QSam³ (הלילה הן הוא[]) and the LXX (τὴν νύκτα ἐκείνην) lack the preposition and simply read "that night" (as in 2 Sam 2:29; Job 3:6, 7).

Commentary

Nisan (March/April) 1009 BC

The Chronological Displacement of 1 Samuel 28:3–25

It has long been noted that the account of Saul's nighttime trip to Endor is out of chronological sequence. It takes place the night before the battle in which Saul died (31:1–6), whereas 29:1–11 takes place in Aphek before the Philistines reach the vicinity of Jezreel to engage Saul's army (see figure 27 at the end of the commentary on 29:1–11). While older critical scholars held that this was due to accident or clumsiness on the part of a redactor who mishandled his sources, more recent scholars have admitted that the author or redactor of the book of Samuel has skillfully arranged this chronological displacement for literary purposes that draw distinctions between Saul and David.[14] (See the discussion of the structure of the final chapters of 1 Samuel in the commentary on 27:1–12.) In particular, the author has juxtaposed David's predicament—Achish expected him to go into battle against Israel (28:1–2)—with Saul's predicament—he inquired of Yahweh before going into battle, but Yahweh refused to answer him (28:6). Furthermore, when David next inquired of Yahweh before engaging in battle, Yahweh answered David with a message of victory (30:8), as Yahweh did on other occasions.[15]

See figure 26.

---

[12] E.g., Ex 12:17; 23:15; 34:18; Lev 23:6; Deut 16:16; cf. Ex 12:8–20; 13:6–7.

[13] The same prepositional phrase, sometimes without the article on the pronoun, occurs also in Gen 19:33, 35; 26:24; 30:16; 32:14, 22, 23 (ET 32:13, 21, 22); Num 14:1; Josh 8:9, 13; Judg 6:25, 40; 7:9; 1 Sam 19:10; 2 Sam 7:4; 2 Ki 19:35; Esth 6:1; 1 Chr 17:3; 2 Chr 1:7.

[14] See Campbell, *1 Samuel*, 276, 278. Campbell offers a brief summary of the observations of various commentators who perceive great literary skill on the part of the author of Samuel as evidenced by the chronological displacement of 28:3–25.

[15] 1 Sam 23:2, 4; 2 Sam 2:1; 5:19, 23–24. See the first textual note on 1 Sam 23:2.

Figure 26

Military Maneuvers in 1 Samuel 28–31

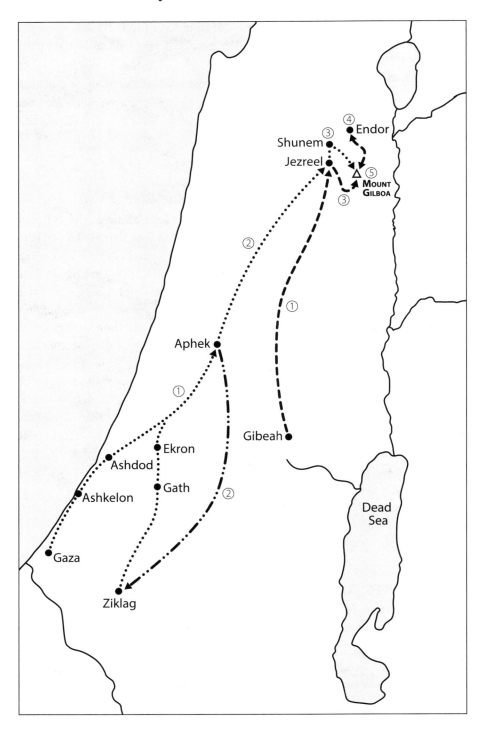

Key for Figure 26

1. The Philistines gather their forces at Aphek, while Saul moves his forces to Jezreel (29:1).
2. The Philistines order David to return to Ziklag, while they march on Jezreel (29:11–30:1).
3. Saul moves his forces to Mount Gilboa, and the Philistines move to Shunem (28:4).
4. Saul makes a night visit to Endor (28:8–25).
5. The Philistines attack and defeat Saul and Israel on Mount Gilboa (31:1–6).

Did Samuel Actually Appear to Saul at Endor?

Reasons for Saying Yes

One question that has been repeatedly asked about this narrative throughout the centuries is whether Samuel actually appeared from the dead to Saul. In antiquity many affirmed that Samuel was actually called up from the dead, starting with Ben Sira (Sirach 46:20) and Josephus.[16] Among the church fathers Justin Martyr,[17] Augustine,[18] John Chrysostom,[19] and Methodius[20] also argued that Samuel actually appeared to Saul. This is also the position of most modern scholars,[21] and many commentaries simply assume that the author of the book of Samuel was presenting Samuel as actually speaking to Saul from the realm of the dead.[22] Bergen offers reasons for such an interpretation:

> First, the plain statement of the Hebrew text is that she [the woman at Endor] did in fact see Samuel [28:12]. Second, the medium reacted to Samuel's appearance as though it was a genuine—and terrifying—experience: she "cried out at the top of her voice" [28:12]. Her strong reaction also suggests that Samuel's appearance was unexpected; perhaps this was the first time she had ever actually succeeded in contacting the dead. Third, the speeches attributed to Samuel contained allusions to a prior interchange between the two [Samuel and Saul], allusions that would have been appropriate only for the real Samuel to have made. Fourth, Samuel's role and message as a prophet, so much a part of his ministry in life, was unchanged in his encounter with Saul here.

> Indeed, a straightforward reading of the biblical account suggests the possibility that mediums may possess the capacity to contact dead persons and establish lines of communication between the living and the dead. This view is

---

[16] Josephus, *Antiquities*, 6.332–36.

[17] Justin Martyr, *Dialogue with Trypho*, 105 (*ANF* 1:252).

[18] Augustine, Letter 158.6 (*NPNF*[1] 1:511); *On Christian Doctrine*, 2.23 (*NPNF*[1] 2:547); *On Care for the Dead*, 18 (*NPNF*[1] 3:548); *On the Soul and Its Origin*, 4.29 (*NPNF*[1] 5:367).

[19] John Chrysostom, *Homilies on the Gospel of Matthew*, 6.4 (*NPNF*[1] 10:39).

[20] Methodius, *Discourse on the Resurrection*, 3.2.19 (*ANF* 6:377).

[21] E.g., Arnold, "Soul-Searching Questions about 1 Samuel 28." Baird, "Difficult Texts from Ruth, 1 and 2 Samuel," 272–74; Beuken, "1 Samuel 28: The Prophet as 'Hammer of Witches.'"

[22] E.g., McCarter, *I Samuel*, 422; Klein, *1 Samuel*, 269; Tsumura, *The First Book of Samuel*, 627.

not explicitly rejected elsewhere in Scripture; the Torah prohibits necromancy not because it is a hoax but because it promotes reliance on supernatural guidance from some source other than the Lord.[23]

An alternative reading of this passage suggests that it was not the skill of the medium but rather a unique act of God that brought Saul into contact with Samuel. The medium did not possess the capacity to disturb a dead saint; but God, as "a sign of [his] grace,"[24] permitted Saul to have one last encounter with the prophet who had played such a determinative role in the king's career.[25]

Reasons for Saying No

At the outset, one should note that on multiple occasions Saul had been tormented by an evil spirit sent by Yahweh (16:14–16, 23; 18:10; 19:9), and so it is possible that the appearance of the entity to Saul here could be another manifestation of that evil spirit or of another one. An additional potential parallel is the episode in 1 Kings 22, when Yahweh sent a lying spirit to speak through the court prophets of apostate King Ahab to entice him into battle so that he would die at Ramoth-gilead.[26] This is analogous to the spirit in 1 Sam 28:12–19 who, as we shall see, uttered inaccurate prophecies that ultimately caused Saul to commit suicide during battle.

Bergen appears to present a number of good reasons for defending the proposition that Samuel actually appeared from the dead to Saul. However, when each of them is examined carefully, they are less impressive.

First—before dealing with Bergen's points—it ought to be noted that there are the plain statements that Samuel spoke to Saul (28:15, 16–19). However, these may rely upon Saul's assumption that the apparition that the woman saw was Samuel (28:11, 14). Therefore the narration may simply be presenting the events as Saul perceived them, based on his premise, rather than as objective statements of fact.

Second, the medium's reaction (28:12) confirms that what she saw was frightening and unexpected. She assumed that the apparition she saw was Samuel (28:12) because Saul had asked her to bring up Samuel (28:11). However, this does not prove that she actually saw Samuel. It indicates that she saw something she had not previously experienced. She may have presumed that it must be the person for whom Saul had asked, or the apparition itself may have claimed to be Samuel. It may well have been true that such mediums primarily relied on

---

[23] Bergen may have in mind passages such as Lev 19:26, 31; 20:27; Deut 18:9–14.

[24] Bergen is quoting David F. Payne, *I and II Samuel* (Philadelphia: Westminster, 1982), 145 ("his" is in Payne).

[25] Bergen, *1, 2 Samuel*, 267.

[26] The true prophet Micaiah revealed what had happened in the heavenly council regarding this lying spirit (1 Ki 22:19–23). An additional correspondence is that Ahab disguised himself (1 Ki 22:30), as did Saul here (1 Sam 28:8).

fraudulent deceptions to convince their clients that they were communicating with the dead (as may also be true today). On the other hand, many mediums may have been possessed by demons who spoke through them and who represented themselves as being spirits of dead people (as may also happen today).

In this case, something supernatural happened—but it does not necessarily follow that what she saw was Samuel. In fact, she did not characterize the specter as "Samuel," but rather in the plural as "gods coming up from the earth" (see the second textual note on 28:13). Saul asked about the form of what the woman saw under the insistent implication that there was only one apparition (*"his* appearance," 28:14). In response the woman gave a description of one man (28:14), but we do not know whether she actually saw only one figure or whether she changed her description from plural to singular to match what she thought her patron expected. Thus, the woman herself *never* identified the apparition as "Samuel." Saul concluded from her description that it was "Samuel" (28:14), and the author shaped the narrative accordingly to give us Saul's perspective.

Third, while the speeches attributed to Samuel contained allusions to prior interchanges between Samuel and Saul, it ought to be obvious that knowledge of Samuel's interchanges with Saul were not confined to the two of them. Many of their exchanges took place in public or at least with others present, and the few that were private (e.g., 9:27–10:8) were recounted to the author of the book of Samuel.[27] Therefore their conversations were known to others, and that may well have included whatever spirit spoke to Saul. If this was a deceiving spirit, he would have sought to use some of Samuel's prior words in attempting to lend verisimilitude to his message.

Fourth, Bergen argues that the specter took on the role of a prophet, proving that it was Samuel. However, if this was some spirit impersonating Samuel, one would expect it to speak in prophet-like discourse. So the form of the spirit's communication does not prove that Samuel appeared to Saul. Note again the lying spirit who spoke through the mouths of wicked King Ahab's court prophets; their utterances and prophetic actions mimicked the style of true prophets (1 Ki 22:6, 10–12).

Fifth, as for the "straightforward" reading of the account and the Torah prohibitions against necromancy, it is true that divination is condemned because it promotes reliance on a source other than Yahweh. However, it does not necessarily follow that necromantic practices can actually bring up the spirits of the dead in order to communicate with the living. In fact, Scripture is clear that those who do not believe in the true God (including the apostate Saul) are under the power and deception of Satan and his angels (Acts 26:18; 1 Cor 10:19–20; 2 Thess 2:9; 1 Tim 5:15) and that Satan and his angels can appear to be messengers of the truth (2 Cor 11:14; 1 Tim 4:1). Thus, the practice of consulting

---

[27] Samuel himself likely recounted these incidents and may have committed them to writing.

the dead through mediums is condemned precisely because it is reliance on demons instead of on God.

Sixth and finally, Bergan's "alternative reading" relies on an assumption that cannot be proven and is not found in the text of 1 Sam 28:3–25 or anywhere else in Scripture—the assumption that God "permitted" Saul one last encounter with Samuel.

On the other hand, since antiquity there have also been those who have asserted that Samuel did not appear to Saul. Among the church fathers Hippolytus[28] and Tertullian[29] held this view. Luther also held that Samuel did not appear to Saul.[30] Luther offers several arguments:

- The activity was led by a woman who "was filled with devils,"[31] that is, she was known as an expert in necromancy, an occult practice (28:7).
- Saul and the woman were acting contrary to God's command, so they could not have brought Samuel back from Sheol.
- While the text calls the apparition "Samuel" (28:11, 12, 14, 15, 16, 20), it does not state that the vision was actually of Samuel. Instead the author was simply portraying the matter as perceived from Saul's viewpoint (28:11, 14).

While few modern scholars have sought to deny that the narrator is portraying the dead Samuel as appearing to Saul, there are additional observations that call into question whether the author intended for his readers to understand the specter to be the actual person of Samuel.[32] Three of these involve the accuracy of the predictions given to Saul, and one involves the nature of the supposed prophetic speech of Samuel in 28:16–19.

First of all, the "Samuel" apparition predicted that "tomorrow" Saul and his sons would "be with me" (28:19). Yet a close reading of the book of Samuel reveals sons of Saul who did not die the next day. Ish-bosheth/Eshbaal would survive to be assassinated later (2 Sam 2:8–10; 4:1–12). Armoni and Mephibosheth, the two sons of Saul's concubine Rizpah, would be executed during David's reign (2 Sam 21:8–9). This appears to be an indication by the author that the prophecy given to Saul was inaccurate—something Samuel's prophecies never were (3:19; 9:6). Kent comments on this:

> This puzzle encourages a re-reading of the Saulide death scenes to determine whether all Saul's sons died at Gilboa. There one notes in the narrator's choices a pattern of varied repetition. Reading of the killing of Jonathan, Abinadab, and Malchishua, "Saul's sons" (31:2), one can assume that this means all Saul's sons, but the narrator has not actually stated that, and has carefully qualified by name exactly which sons are mentioned. We are told

---

[28] Hippolytus, *On the Sorceress*, fragment (*ANF* 5:169–70, including n. 9).

[29] Tertullian, *Treatise on the Soul*, 57 (*ANF* 3:234).

[30] AE 36:196; 52:180. For these quotations, see "Did Samuel Appear to Saul from the Dead?" in the excursus "Luther on the Prophet Samuel" following the commentary on 19:18–24.

[31] AE 36:196.

[32] See especially Kent, *Say It Again, Sam*, 159–204.

"Saul died, and his three sons" (31:6), which is also a numerically qualified and careful statement, even if the reader who thinks Saul has *only* three sons will read it as comprehensive [emphasis original]. Then we are told "Saul and his sons were dead," but importantly this is focalized from the point of view of the trans-Jordan Israelites who "saw" this (31:7), without the narrator necessarily endorsing the view; it is an imperfect repeat showing up the imperfect intelligence of the stress of battle; it is also now in a context where the expression "Saul's sons" has been carefully defined. The narrator's statement that the Philistines stripped the bodies of "Saul and his three sons" (31:8) is also numerically qualified. Then the narrator says the men of Jabesh-Gilead reclaimed the bodies of "Saul and his sons" (31:12), which in context also has a numerically restricted range. Thus in chapter 31 the narrator alternates between two major expressions, producing the pattern:

"[Names], Saul's sons" (31:2)
"his three sons" (31:6)
"Saul and his sons" (31:7)
"his three sons" (31:8)
"Saul and his sons" (31:12)

None of this qualifies as outright deception, yet the reader can very easily assume that all of Saul's sons are dead. Pre-biased by the woman's prediction, we accept the observations of various characters, but this interpretation is shown to be false. *Alternating between the various characters' perceptions and the narrator's numerically accurate description alerts the observant reader that perception and reality differ.*[33]

Therefore, the text seduces unwary readers into adopting the viewpoint of Saul about the identity and reliability of the apparition, only to be contradicted by later accounts about other sons of Saul. This is a more powerful warning to readers about relying on occult practices—including words from specters that may appear to them or words reported to them through astrologers, mediums, or fortunetellers—than if the author had openly condemned Saul's actions.

Second, the ostensible "Samuel" predicted that Yahweh would "hand Israel … over to the Philistines" and "hand the camp of Israel [מַחֲנֵה יִשְׂרָאֵל] over to the Philistines" (28:19). At first blush this appears to be an accurate prediction. During the battle the men of Israel fled and were slain on Mount Gilboa (31:1). However, it is not long before the reader discovers that somehow Abner—the commander of Saul's troops—was not killed on Mount Gilboa (2 Sam 2:8). It is difficult, if not impossible, to construe Abner as not being included in "the camp of Israel." In fact, if the commander was not part of the camp, it is unlikely that any other soldier would have been considered a member of the camp. Once again, the apparition gave an unreliable prophecy and also misled Saul—and perhaps some of the readers of the book of Samuel as well. Concerning this prediction Kent notes:

---

[33] Kent, *Say It Again, Sam*, 162; final emphasis added.

It is worth a detailed reading of the narrative to determine to what extent it was fulfilled. The Philistines took aggressive initiative, causing Israelites to flee and/or to fall dead or dying (31:1). The Philistines focused their attacks on the royal family, killing three sons (31:2), and then Saul was the special focus of archery attack [31:3]. The reported death of Saul and "all his men" (31:6) cannot mean the entire army, because the narrator reports initial escapes (√נוס, 31:1), and two other groups of "men of Israel" see the army escaping (√נוס, a partial repeat of 31:1, leaving out the deaths, which they do not see), and they also escape (√נוס, 31:7). This is substantially confirmed by the report of the Amalekite:

אֲשֶׁר־נָס הָעָם מִן־הַמִּלְחָמָה וְגַם־הַרְבֵּה נָפַל מִן־הָעָם וַיָּמֻתוּ

["The people fled from the battle, and also many from the people fell and died."] (2 Sam 1:4)

Notice the Amalekite uses the same keyword for escapes but also reports deaths, the same two classes the narrator uses (31:1). Certain cities and towns are occupied (31:7), which forms part of a continuation of the swapping back and forward of border towns (cf. 7:14), yet there is still a clear line of "the land of the Philistines" (31:9), and no Philistine domination of Jabesh-Gilead (31:11–13).[34]

Third, the "Samuel" apparition predicted that Yahweh would "also hand Israel *with you* over to the Philistines" (28:19). Once again Kent notes:

This prediction is rather ambiguous. It is the fear of its fulfillment, a fear of being given alive into the hands of the Philistines, which prompts Saul's request for his weapon bearer to kill him "lest these uncircumcised come and stab me and abuse/make a fool of me" (31:4), and his subsequent suicide. Yet battles have been lost without necessarily losing the leader. And can it be said that Yahweh gives him over to the Philistines? There is no fulfillment in those words, and Saul is not actually given to the Philistines—he kills himself before they can get him. ... *Whether Saul was mortally wounded by archers or not, it would be difficult to see him as given into the hand of the Philistines after his death, because they only discover the body the next day* (31:8). ...

And even though Saul's body was taken, the men of Jabesh Gilead quickly recovered it and put it beyond Philistine reach (31:11–13). In what sense was he given into the hands of the Philistines? At Saul's death "there are not even Philistines present."[35] Yet his belief in this prophecy led to his suicide, which could be regarded as self-fulfilling prophecy.[36]

Most importantly, we ought to note that Saul was *not* given into the hands of the Philistines "tomorrow," as the apparition's words predicted,[37] and even when

---

34 Kent, *Say It Again, Sam*, 201.

35 Kent is quoting Brueggemann, *First and Second Samuel*, 207.

36 Kent, *Say It Again, Sam*, 202–3 (emphasis added).

37 The "Samuel" specter said, "Yahweh will also hand Israel with you over to the Philistines, and tomorrow you and your sons will be with me" (28:19). While he did not specify when Saul and Israel were to be handed over to the Philistines, if Saul was to be with him the next day, that must also be the day on which Saul was to fall into Philistine hands.

the Philistines obtained his body on the day after "tomorrow," they were unable to retain it. In addition, though they stripped Saul's body of his armor (31:9), there is no mention of the Philistines taking the symbols of his office—his crown and armlet. The reason for this is that they had probably already been taken by the Amalekite who reported Saul's death to David (2 Sam 1:10).[38] Therefore, Saul did not fall into the hands of the Philistines "tomorrow." He took his own life, and his dead body was looted by an Amalekite. Saul (that is, his corpse) fell into the hands of the Philistines a day later than the "Samuel" spirit predicted. Ironically, if Saul fell into the hands of a foreign people on the day of the battle, it was into the hands of the Amalekites! The careful reader will be forced to conclude that the "Samuel" specter's words were more than a false prophecy; they were a satanic deception that lured Saul into committing suicide because he feared its fulfillment.

Fourth, the "Samuel" apparition was quick to refer to the prophet's words to Saul in 15:1–3, 17–19, 26, 28–29: Yahweh had torn the kingdom from Saul and given it to David (28:17; cf. 15:28); Saul had not obeyed Yahweh and had not executed his anger on Amalek (15:19; see 15:2–3). However, it is striking that this ghostly "Samuel" figure did not mention Samuel's condemnation of Saul in 15:22–23, where rebellion against Yahweh was equated with "divination" (קֶסֶם; cf. 28:8). Were this the true prophet, it is nearly inconceivable that he would not have directly condemned Saul's occult activity through the medium at Endor since it was occurring at the same time he was speaking. Moses and other prophets did not hesitate to offer such condemnation.[39] Yet the specter, though expressing consternation at having been conjured up from the earth (28:15), failed to mention displeasure over Saul's occult idolatry. This points to a demon, one who would exploit occult rituals, but certainly not one who would condemn necromancy and thereby divide Satan against himself (Lk 11:18; cf. Mt 12:26; Mk 3:26).

Therefore, the discerning reader must come to the conclusion that the words of this "Samuel" were false prophecy and thus not attributable to Yahweh's prophet. Instead, the woman was shocked and alarmed at the sight of this ghost precisely because it was a new experience—the visual presence of a demon—though she may not have recognized it for what it was (28:12). She may have been accustomed to deceiving her clients into believing that she was communicating with the dead, or perhaps she was accustomed to being possessed by demons who spoke through her in the guise of the spirits of dead people. She was not familiar with *seeing* the dead. When this substitute "Samuel" appeared, she knew that her client had to be someone special—King Saul himself—to merit such attention from a spirit, which she assumed was of a person from beyond the grave.

---

[38] Arnold, "The Amalekite's Report of Saul's Death," 296.

[39] Deut 18:10, 14; Is 3:2; 44:25; Jer 14:14; 27:9; 29:8; Ezek 13:6, 9, 23; 21:26–28, 34; 22:28; Micah 3:6–7, 11; Zech 10:2.

Through indirect means the author is demonstrating the tragic consequences of trusting in necromancy and dabbling in satanic and occultic rites. He expects his readers to pay attention to the repeated failure of the predictions of the apparition and to conclude that it was not an actual appearance of the prophet with a reliable Word from God. He also wants them to conclude that the Mosaic prohibitions against occult practices are to be heeded not only because they are incompatible with trust solely in the one true God but also because they can have dire consequences. An apostate unbeliever who commits suicide condemns himself to hell for eternity.

Saul at Endor (28:3–25)

In order to set the scene the narration begins with information about previous events that are important for understanding Saul's nighttime journey to Endor (28:3). The death of Samuel was related earlier (25:1), since it probably happened shortly before David married Abigail (25:42). His death is noted here a second time, since the figure of Samuel is prominent in this narrative. In the same way, Saul's elimination of necromancers and mediums from Israel (28:3) is an important backdrop for this narrative.

Saul's final battle was about to commence.[40] The Philistines had massed their forces at Shunem, while Saul had encamped on the high ground of Mount Gilboa (28:4). Saul's fear of the Philistines (28:5) was nothing new. He had been too cowardly to take the initiative to attack them,[41] having reaped victory only when one of his men, such as Jonathan (14:1–23) or David (17:40–53), first took charge. However, after the death of Samuel, Saul may have been especially fearful, since he no longer could rely on the prophet to reveal God's advice when going into battle. Nevertheless, 28:6 states that Saul sought to inquire of Yahweh but Yahweh was not willing to answer Saul. The author tells us of Yahweh's unwillingness to use the three major ways in which he communicated to kings: dreams, Urim,[42] and prophets. This statement does not say that Saul attempted to use all of these, but that God was not willing to use them, even if Saul would have had access to them. In point of fact, Saul could not have consulted the Urim, since Abiathar had taken the Urim and Thummim with the high priest's ephod when he fled the slaughter of the priests at Nob (22:20–23; 23:6). David would consult God using the Urim and Thummim while Saul was on Gilboa (30:7–8). However, Saul would admit to the "Samuel" specter that he had hoped Yahweh would provide him guidance through one of the two other means, "prophets" or "dreams" (28:15).

---

[40] See "The Chronological Displacement of 1 Samuel 28:3–25" above.

[41] After Saul was anointed king, he failed to carry out Samuel's instructions to eradicate the Philistine garrison in Gibeah (10:7). See "Samuel Anoints Saul (9:26–10:8)" in the commentary on 9:26–10:16, including figure 16, "Saul's Faltering Accession." See also the beginning of the commentary on 10:17–27a. Saul was terrified of the Philistines (17:11; 28:5; cf. 13:7, 12).

[42] See further the excursus "The Urim and Thummim" following the commentary on 14:24–46.

Saul's order to find a female "expert necromancer" (28:7) demonstrated how desperate he had become in the face of the Philistine incursion into northern Israel. Curiously, Saul's servants know exactly where to find such a person. This may imply that some in Saul's court continued to syncretize their worship of Yahweh with pagan Canaanite beliefs. That they were familiar with this woman may also imply that she had patrons at the court or among the nobility who had protected her from Saul's purge of occultists in Israel (28:3). At least one Jewish tradition identifies her as the wife of Zephaniah and the mother of Abner, Saul's uncle and the commander of the army.[43]

Endor was a Canaanite city that Joshua did not conquer but that was to have been a city of Manasseh within the territory of Issachar (Josh 17:11–13). It had been the site of the defeat of Sisera and Jabin by Deborah and Barak (Ps 83:10–11 [ET 83:9–10]). Perhaps it remained in Canaanite hands due to the failure of the northern tribes to conquer all of their allotted territory (Judg 1:27–36). If so, this would explain the presence of the necromancer in this town.

Saul, we are told, disguised himself by changing his attire, probably into clothes that were not royal robes. In ancient times, it would not have been unusual for most people to have never seen the king. There was no coinage on which to portray his likeness, and obviously no photography or electronic media to show his image to his subjects. Many commoners would never have interacted with him or seen him in person. Thus, to most of his subjects he would have been identifiable only by his royal garments. Thus, Saul did not need a wig or makeup to disguise his office.

We are told that Saul took two of his men with him and came to the woman at night (28:8). Jewish tradition identifies these men as Amasa (David's nephew [1 Chr 2:17]) and Abner,[44] though the text of 1 Samuel does not specify who they were.[45] Many commentators believe that this visit to Endor would have required Saul to slip behind the enemy lines of the Philistines, since Endor was situated to the north of Shunem. However, Endor is also farther east than Shunem, and we do not know how far east Philistine pickets would have been stationed. It is entirely possible that Saul did not have to cross through Philistine-controlled territory to reach Endor.

Saul asked the woman to "practice divination" (see the textual note on קָסֳמִי, 28:8). Earlier the polytheistic Philistines had consulted their own practitioners of divination (קֹסְמִים, 6:2), and now Saul had become just like Israel's heathen enemies, whom he feared. This was another sign of Saul's continued rebellion

---

[43] *Pirqe de Rabbi Eliezer*, 33. Zephaniah here is simply the name given by the Jewish tradition to the medium's husband, perhaps assuming that Ner, Abner's father (14:50), had died and she had remarried. This Zephaniah, however, is not mentioned in the Bible.

[44] *Midrash Rabbah Shmuel* according to Blenkinsopp, "Saul and the Mistress of the Spirits," 53, n. 7.

[45] Nor does Josephus identify them (*Antiquities*, 6.330).

against God, and Samuel had warned the monarch that "divination" (קֶסֶם) was rebellion against Yahweh (15:23).

The woman was wary and cautious of Saul's request, thinking that it was a ruse to entrap her and have her executed (28:9). However, Saul sought to reassure her with an oath that promised that she would not be punished if she complied with the request (28:10). Saul's oath was taken in Yahweh's name, in keeping with the letter of the Law given by Moses (Deut 6:13–15), but contradicting that Law because he invoked Yahweh to sanction the kind of occultic idolatry practiced by the Canaanites whom Israel was to have extirpated. Moreover, the oath's form is highly ironic. It began with the standard formula "as Yahweh lives" (חַי־יְהוָה, 1 Sam 28:10).[46] Since Yahweh is the ever-living God (1 Sam 17:26, 36; see also Deut 5:26; Jer 10:10; 23:36), why would one consult dead humans? Saul had hypocritically invoked "Yahweh" by name on other occasions to conceal his evil intentions under the cloak of piety (e.g., 15:13; 23:21; 26:25).

Once convinced that Saul was not intending to entrap her, the woman asked whom her visitor wished to consult from the dead, and Saul requested Samuel (28:11). It is intriguing that the woman did not discern that this request revealed her visitor as the anti-occult king himself; perhaps her thought process was already clouded by demonic influence. The author passes over any description of incantations or other rituals that may have been used by the woman and immediately notes that she saw "Samuel" and was able to identify her visitor as "Saul" (28:12). The author's reasons for omitting the action between Saul's request and the appearance of the specter is not stated. However, the omission entails two important messages for readers. First, the lack of ritual serves to delegitimize occult rites. It was not the ritual or the incantation that brought about the apparition's presence—no humanly invented words or ceremony can command God or Satan. Second, the close juxtaposition of the request for "Samuel" (28:11) *and* the appearance of the specter (28:12) were the clues assembled by the woman that brought her to the realization that Saul was her nocturnal client. The appearance of something like the "Samuel" figure must have been new and wholly unanticipated even to this experienced necromancer since "she cried out loudly" in shock (28:12).

Saul assured the woman that she had nothing to fear from his trickery; he only wanted to know what she was observing (28:13). She described her vision from the viewpoint of her pagan assumptions, "I see gods coming up from the earth." The last time the author portrayed someone as unambiguously speaking of (plural) "gods" (אֱלֹהִים plus plural pronouns/modifiers or plural predication) was when the Philistines were characterizing the Israelite deity according to

---

[46] See the second textual notes on 1:26 and 14:45. In the book of Samuel, see the formula also in 1 Sam 14:39, 45; 19:6; 20:3, 21; 25:26, 34; 26:10, 16; 29:6; 2 Sam 4:9; 12:5; 14:11; 15:21; 22:47. On swearing an oath by the life of Yahweh or by a prominent person's life, see *IBH*, § 64 D.

their pagan viewpoint (4:8).[47] Some would argue that, grammar aside, Saul's following question, "what is *his* appearance?" means that the woman's words ought to be understood as singular: "I see a god coming up."[48] Kent rightly rejects this assertion:

> Some commentators are influenced to translate her [the woman's] plural with singular sense because of Saul's reply using the singular. ... He [Alter] sees here the "complication" of the plural participle but sees a "grammatical crossover" and "fluidity of usage in which the plural might sometimes be employed with a singular sense, even when the referent was not the one God."[49] ... Yet it would be more customary to use a singular when describing a group in which one member is very prominent. Thus it seems more logical to take her plural on face value, then note that Saul is speaking within his monotheistic paradigm, to which she soon adapts her speech because of his perceived power. She moves from plural participle [עֹלִים, "coming up," in 28:13] to singular participle [עֹלֶה, "is coming up," in 28:14], either changing her story to suit her audience or perhaps focusing on just one of the apparitions she sees arising (28:14).[50]

Thus, when her monarch Saul insisted that there should be only one person in her vision (28:14), she adapted her language to his worldview, since he was both king and client. Moreover, she described seeing an old man in a "robe" (מְעִיל, 28:14). The combination—Samuel was old when he died (8:1), and his customary outer garment from youth was a "robe" (מְעִיל, 2:19; 15:27)—led Saul to conclude that the woman had succeeded in summoning Samuel. However, we do not know whether the woman actually saw the figure in the form she described to Saul. She may have, or she may have simply catered to her royal patron's expectations and deceived him—after all, he could not see the specter, since he had to interrogate the woman as to what she saw. The careful reader will accept only her first characterization—"gods coming up from the earth" (28:13)—as likely to be a forthright reply to Saul's questioning. Her second reply ought to be read with at least enough skepticism to refrain from confidently concluding (as Saul did) that the apparition took on the appearance of Samuel, and with even more doubt about the actual prophet coming back from the dead.

Saul immediately knelt and honored the specter he could not see. This action introduces another irony into the narrative: the woman saw "gods," and Saul treated the "Samuel" phantom like his god! He was hoping that Samuel would communicate to him when the true God had not (28:15)!

---

[47] Goliath also cursed David "by his gods" (17:43), but in that case there are no plural pronouns referring to אֱלֹהִים and no plural words modifying it, and it is not the subject of a plural verb.

[48] E.g., Alter, *The David Story*, 174–75; McCarter, *I Samuel*, 421; Bergen, *1, 2 Samuel*, 267–68; similarly, Heiser, "Should אלהים (*ʾĕlōhîm*) with Plural Predication Be Translated 'Gods'?" 136.

[49] Kent is quoting Alter, *The David Story*, 174.

[50] Kent, *Say It Again, Sam*, 181–82.

When the apparition complained and asked why Saul had disturbed him, Saul in turn complained of being in a very tight spot (see the second textual note on 28:15). This constriction pressured him to resort to the occult, and his words contrast him with David, who at nearly the same point in time found himself in an equally tight spot, but found strength in Yahweh his God (30:6; see figure 27 at the end of the commentary on 29:1–11).

The reply Saul received (28:16) struck right at the problem with Saul's inquiry. Why did Saul seek advice from Samuel when Yahweh had "turned away"[51] from Saul and become his enemy? Did Saul believe that Samuel had some power to compel Yahweh to return to him or to manipulate God into revealing what he otherwise would not? Did Saul, lacking a current prophetic message from Yahweh, have more faith in Samuel than he did in Yahweh's prior prophetic messages through the prophet? In a pun on Saul's name (שָׁאוּל, sha'ul), the "Samuel" apparition used the verb שָׁאַל, sha'al, in his challenge, "so why are you asking me?" (וְלָמָּה תִּשְׁאָלֵנִי, 28:16).[52]

The faux "Samuel" then reviewed what Yahweh had done in reaction to Saul's unfaithfulness, sprinkling it with phraseology from Samuel's rebuke of Saul after his disobedience in the attack on the Amalekites (28:16–18; cf. 15:1–35), which was the last time the live Samuel spoke to the king. Three times Samuel's previous words are referenced:

Yahweh has torn the kingdom from your hand and given it to your neighbor, to David. (28:17)	Yahweh has torn the kingdom of Israel from you today, and he has given it to your neighbor, who is better than you. (15:28)
Since you did not listen to Yahweh's voice … (28:18)	Now listen to the voice of the words of Yahweh … (15:1)
	Why didn't you listen to Yahweh's voice? (15:19)
… and did not execute his anger on Amalek … (28:18)	[A general allusion to the instructions given in 15:2–3.]

The ghoul's references to Samuel's words were intended to reinforce the illusion that the speaker was Samuel come back from the dead. They were calculated to lend credibility to his rebuke of Saul. The apostate Saul hypocritically invoked "Yahweh" in 28:10 (cf. 28:6) but avoided the sacred name in 28:15,

---

[51] The same verb, סוּר, referred to the Spirit of Yahweh "turning away" from Saul in 16:14 and to Yahweh "turning away" from Saul in 18:12. See the third textual note on 28:15.

[52] For this wordplay, which occurs throughout the book of Samuel, see the textual note on 28:6.

using the more general term "God" instead, but the specter named "Yahweh" seven times in 28:16–19,[53] once again seeking to convince Saul that Yahweh's prophet Samuel was actually speaking.[54]

The discourse of the "Samuel" specter now included inaccurate predictions of what would happen on the following day (28:19).[55] The predicted death of Saul and his sons is sandwiched between two statements of Yahweh's handing Saul and Israel over to the Philistines. The structure serves to highlight the death of Saul and his sons:

A–B Yahweh will hand **Israel** with *you* over to the Philistines.

A' *You* and *your sons* will be with me.

B' Yahweh will also hand the camp of **Israel** over to the Philistines.

Like Eli and his sons, who died in one day (4:11, 18), so Saul and (three of) his sons would die in one day. Yahweh had put in motion the acts that would eventually remove the Elides from the high priesthood;[56] likewise, he also put in motion the act that would eventually remove the Saulides from the throne of Israel. Yahweh's judgment announced by the "Samuel" ghost was real—the kingdom would be given to David (28:17). But that was not a new prophecy; it had been stated in 15:28. The new information the apparition gave—that it would happen on the next day—was false. Not all of Saul's sons would die that day, and the threatened end of his dynasty did not occur that day. A Saulide throne would be briefly revived, and Ish-bosheth would rule for two years (2 Sam 2:8–11).

Saul was knocked to the ground with fright over "Samuel's words" (28:20). He believed and reacted more immediately with heart and mind to the words of this supposed "Samuel" than he had to any of the messages Samuel delivered to him during his lifetime.

He was weak and exhausted. The author does not tell us why Saul had not eaten. Had he lost his appetite from worry? Had he fasted in preparation for the evening's activity? The author leaves us without a clear reason, but with another hint of Saul's foolishness, as the reader can connect this to Saul's previous fasting because of a foolish vow (14:24–46).

---

[53] Once in 28:16 and twice in each of the following three verses (28:17–19).

[54] In the NT, demons name "Jesus" and recognize him as the holy one of God (Mk 1:24; Lk 4:34; Acts 19:15) even as they fear and oppose him. An evil spirit also acknowledges the name of the apostle "Paul" (Acts 19:15).

[55] See the analysis of the inaccuracies in "Did Samuel Actually Appear to Saul at Endor?" above.

[56] See "The Aaronic Priesthood Removed in Favor of the New Anointed Priest (2:31–36)" in the commentary on 2:27–36.

The woman acted with compassion and kindness to the king (28:21–22). As Fokkelman observes, her concern and pleading with Saul is highlighted with the chiastic arrangement of 28:20b–22 by the author of the book of Samuel:[57]

```
strength -
    eat -
        food -
            your servant
                voice
                    listen
                    listen
                voice
            your servant
        food +
    eat +
strength +
```

Saul initially refused, and he arose from the ground to eat only when the woman and Saul's men insisted (28:23). It would appear that Saul's men, who knew about necromancers and the necromancer herself (28:7), were wiser than Saul: the king's speech was constantly formulated in terms of a monotheistic faith in Yahweh, but his actions consistently rebelled against Yahweh, the only true God.

The meal included unleavened bread (28:24). In this case the use of unleavened bread was not because of religious observance, but because of the shortage of time. There was no time to wait for a loaf to rise before baking it, since Saul and his men would soon be on their way back to Mount Gilboa (28:25).

---

[57] Adapted from Fokkelman, *The Crossing Fates*, 620, who explains: "The minus and plus signs indicate what is absent and what is advised, respectively."

Saul's Second Philistine Campaign, Part 2: The Philistines Dismiss David

Translation

29 ¹The Philistines gathered all their camps at Aphek, while Israel was encamped at the spring that is in Jezreel. ²The governors of the Philistines were passing in review by hundreds and by thousands, and David and his men were passing in review in the rear with Achish. ³The Philistine commanders said, "What about these Hebrews?"

Achish said to the Philistine commanders, "Isn't this David, the servant of Saul, the king of Israel, who has been with me for some time now? I have not found any fault in him from the day he defected to this day."

⁴The Philistine commanders became incensed at him, and the Philistine commanders said to him, "Send back the man, and let him return to his place where you have assigned him. He must not go down with us into battle so that he will not become our adversary during the battle. With what could this guy make himself favorable to his lord? Would it not be with the heads of our men? ⁵Isn't this guy David whom they sing about in their dances: 'Saul has struck down his thousands, and David his tens of thousands'?"

⁶So Achish called David and said to him, "As Yahweh lives, you are an honorable man. Your going out [to battle] and your coming in with me in the camp [have been] good in my eyes since I have not found any wrong in you from the day you came to me until this day. But in the eyes of the governors, you are no good. ⁷So now return and go peaceably and don't do anything wrong in the eyes of the Philistine governors."

⁸David said to Achish, "What have I done? What [fault] have you found in your servant from the day I [first] was in your presence until this day that I shouldn't go and fight against the enemies of my lord, the king?"

⁹Achish answered David, "I know that you are as good in my eyes as an angel of God. However, the Philistine commanders said, 'He will not go up with us into battle.' ¹⁰Now rise early in the morning, [you] and your lord's servants who came with you. So when you rise early in the morning, [as soon as] you have light, go."

¹¹So David rose early—he and his men—to go during the morning to return to Philistine territory, and the Philistines went up to Jezreel.

Textual Notes

29:1 וַיִּקְבְּצוּ פְלִשְׁתִּים אֶת־כָּל־מַחֲנֵיהֶם—See the first textual note on 28:1.

אֲפֵקָה—See the third textual note on 4:1.

חֹנִים—This is the Qal (G) masculine plural participle of חָנָה, "to camp, establish a military base of operations." The same participle was in 26:5b.

בַּעַיִן אֲשֶׁר בְּיִזְרְעֶאל׃—This means "at the spring that is in Jezreel." The feminine noun עַיִן II denotes a "spring" of water. The relative clause refers to the northern city of Jezreel (not the Jezreel in Judah mentioned in 25:43; cf. 27:3). This Jezreel is usually identified with a modern archaeological site that is located on a low hill on the southern edge of the Jezreel Valley's eastern edge in northern Israel. The spring is probably the Harod Spring (Judg 7:1), now known as ʿAin Jalud, which flows from the north side of the base of Mount Gilboa.

29:2 וְסַרְנֵי פְלִשְׁתִּים—For "the governors of the Philistines," see the first textual note on 5:8.

עֹבְרִים ... עֹבְרִים—In this context the Qal (G) of עָבַר has the military nuance "pass by in review."

לְמֵאוֹת וְלַאֲלָפִים—This means "by hundreds and by thousands." See the first textual note on 8:12.

29:3 מָה הָעִבְרִים הָאֵלֶּה—The question is literally "what [about] these Hebrews?" (Waltke-O'Connor, § 18.2d, including example 23; cf. Joüon, § 144 c). For "Hebrews," see the second textual note on 4:6.

זֶה יָמִים אוֹ־זֶה שָׁנִים—Literally "this, days, or this, years," this is rendered as "for some time now." Some consider this to be a conflation of two variant readings joined by the conjunction אוֹ.[1] However, the LXX is similar: ἡμέρας τοῦτο δεύτερον ἔτος, "days this second year." This may be an interpretive rendering of the same text as in the MT; it may also be based on 27:7, where we are told that David was in Philistine territory for one year and four months, making this the second (partial) year of his service to Achish.

וְלֹא־מָצֵאתִי בוֹ מְאוּמָה—Literally "and I have not found in him anything," that is, "any fault." See the parallel in 29:6, לֹא־מָצָאתִי בְךָ רָעָה, "I have not found in you (any) wrong/evil." See also the second textual note on 29:8.

מִיּוֹם נָפְלוֹ—Literally "from the day of his falling," this means "from the day he defected." In military contexts the verb נָפַל can signal deserting to the enemy's side (BDB, Qal, 4 b; *HALOT*, Qal, 8). This form is the Qal (G) infinitive construct with a subjective third masculine singular suffix, and the vowel under the *nun* (-ָ) is *qamets chatuph* (see Joüon, § 65 b).

29:4 וַיִּקְצְפוּ עָלָיו—The Qal (G) of קָצַף means "become angry, incensed" and usually takes the preposition עַל, "at" someone. This is the verb's only appearance in the book of Samuel.

הָשֵׁב אֶת־הָאִישׁ וְיָשֹׁב—"Send back the man, and let him return." Both verbs are forms of שׁוּב. The first is the masculine singular Hiphil (H) imperative, which has a causative meaning, "make [him] return." The second is the third masculine singular Qal (G) jussive, which is intransitive in meaning.

מְקוֹמוֹ אֲשֶׁר הִפְקַדְתּוֹ שָׁם—Literally this means "his place where you have stationed him there." In the Hiphil (H), פָּקַד means to "set" or "station" someone (see BDB,

---

[1] McCarter, *I Samuel*, 425; Klein, *1 Samuel*, 275.

Hiphil, 1). הִפְקַדְתּוֹ is the Hiphil second masculine singular perfect with a third masculine singular object suffix. This is the only instance of a Hiphil form of פָּקַד in the book of Samuel. The retrospective adverb שָׁם, "there," is redundant in English and so need not be translated, but this use is common Hebrew style (Joüon, § 158 j).

לְשָׂטָן—The noun שָׂטָן can denote an "adversary, enemy" (BDB, 1), which is probably the meaning intended by the Philistines, or it can be the proper noun "Satan" (BDB, 2), as in the narrative of David in 1 Chr 21:1 (also, e.g., Zech 3:1–2; Job 1:6–9). The identical prepositional phrase appears in 2 Sam 19:23 (ET 19:22).

וּבַמֶּה יִתְרַצֶּה זֶה אֶל־אֲדֹנָיו—The preposition בְּ here has the nuance of price or exchange (BDB, s.v. בְּ I, III 3), thus וּבַמֶּה, "and with what?" more precisely means "and at what cost?" or "and in exchange for what?" (see also the next textual note). The subject is the demonstrative pronoun זֶה with the derogatory meaning "this guy," as also in 29:5; see the second textual note on 10:27a. In the Qal (G), רָצָה means "be pleased with, be favorable toward, graciously accept." This is the sole OT appearance of a Hithpael (HtD) form (third masculine singular imperfect), which has a reflexive meaning, "make oneself pleasing" to someone. The Philistines probably intended the prepositional phrase אֶל־אֲדֹנָיו to mean "to his lord," an intensive plural with a singular meaning, referring to a human master,[2] that is, "to Saul" (see "David, the servant of Saul," in 29:3). But אֶל־אֲדֹנָיו could also mean "to his Lord," with the plural form referring to God.[3] The author may intend for believing readers to perceive the double sense and understand the chapter within the larger narrative context of David being restored to his rightful place as the king under the Lord, that is, Yahweh, Israel's God. The same is true of אֲדֹנֶיךָ in 29:10.

בְּרָאשֵׁי הָאֲנָשִׁים הָהֵם:—Here again the preposition בְּ has the nuance of price or exchange (BDB, s.v. בְּ I, III 3). "With the heads of our men" means "in exchange for, at the cost of" their heads, i.e., by killing them. The third masculine plural personal pronoun הֵם, literally "they," with the definite article, functions here as a demonstrative pronoun, "*these* men." A demonstrative pronoun can function as a kind of possessive, thus "these men" is translated as "our men." See Joüon, § 143 e.

29:5 This couplet, introduced in 18:7 and recalled in 21:12 (ET 21:11), appears here for the final time in the book.

יַעֲנוּ—This verb is the third masculine plural Qal (G) imperfect of עָנָה IV, "to sing." The identical form was in 21:12 (ET 21:11). See the first textual note on 18:7.

בַּמְּחֹלוֹת—For "in the(ir) dances," see the fourth textual note on 18:6.

הִכָּה שָׁאוּל בַּאֲלָפָיו—See the third textual note on 18:7.

וְדָוִד בְּרִבְבֹתָיו:—See the fourth textual note on 18:7. For the alternate readings here, the Qere בְּרִבְבֹתָיו and the Kethib בְּרִבְבֹתָו, see the fifth textual note on 21:12 (ET 21:11).

29:6 חַי־יְהוָה—For "as Yahweh lives," see the second textual notes on 1:26 and 14:45. The Philistines were polytheists who acknowledged that Yahweh was the God of the

---

[2] See BDB, s.v. אָדוֹן, 2 (1) (f). The plural form refers to a human master or masters in, e.g., 20:38; 25:10, 14, 17; 26:15, 16.

[3] See BDB, s.v. אָדוֹן, 2 (2). The plural form refers to Yahweh/God in, e.g., 2 Sam 7:18–20, 22, 28, 29.

Israelites (e.g., 4:6–8; 5:7–8; 6:2), but was not their own god. Achish invokes Yahweh when speaking to David not out of personal faith in Yahweh, but because he knows David will honor an oath sworn in the name of David's God.

יָשָׁר—This adjective can mean physically "straight" or metaphorically "right, upright, just, righteous." In this context it is rendered as "honorable."

וְטוֹב בְּעֵינַי צֵאתְךָ וּבֹאֲךָ אִתִּי בַּמַּחֲנֶה—"And your going out [to battle] and your coming in with me in the camp [have been] good in my eyes." An infinitive construct, as a verbal noun, can be the subject of a nominal sentence (Joüon, § 124 b). Here the two suffixed Qal (G) infinitive constructs, צֵאתְךָ וּבֹאֲךָ, "your going out and your coming in," form a compound subject, to which the prepositional phrase "with me in the camp" is attached. In this nominal sentence the predicate adjective is טוֹב, "good," to which is attached the prepositional phrase "in my eyes." For the verbs יָצָא, "go out," and בּוֹא, "come in," referring to military campaigns, see the first textual note on 18:6.

29:8 כִּי ... כִּי—The first כִּי is recitative (BDB, 1 b), introducing direct discourse, and the second כִּי is resultative, "(with the result) that" (BDB, 1 f).

וּמַה־מָּצָאתָ בְעַבְדְּךָ—Literally "and what have you found in your servant?" The translation supplies "[fault]." See the third textual note on 29:3.

29:9 כְּמַלְאַךְ אֱלֹהִים—This phrase means "as an angel of God." A translation of it is missing in the LXX. Some scholars would omit it. They claim that in the other two cases where this phrase is applied to David (2 Sam 14:17; 19:28 [ET 19:27]), it refers to his judicial ability, and such a meaning is inappropriate here.[4] However, in those passages the phrase is used to make the point that David has the insight to make the right and just decision. That is precisely what Achish is stating here—David would make the right and just decision in battle (i.e., to support the Philistines), since Achish believes David has no other choice than to be beholden to him (27:12).

Achish, a Philistine, is polytheistic, but here, when speaking to David, he probably intends אֱלֹהִים to refer to David's "God," the God of Israel (as do the Philistines in, e.g., 5:7–8; cf. 4:7–8), rather than to "gods" (as in 28:13). See the first textual note on 29:6.

29:10 This verse is very difficult, and the translation attempts to make it intelligible. The MT reads as follows, with a literal translation following:

וְעַתָּה הַשְׁכֵּם בַּבֹּקֶר וְעַבְדֵי אֲדֹנֶיךָ אֲשֶׁר־בָּאוּ אִתָּךְ
וְהִשְׁכַּמְתֶּם בַּבֹּקֶר וְאוֹר לָכֶם וָלֵכוּ:

And now rise early in the morning, [you] and the servants of your lord/Lord who came with you, and [when] you [plural] rise early in the morning, and when it is light for you [plural], go [plural].

For the Hiphil (H) of שָׁכַם, "to get up early" (twice in 29:10 and once in 29:11), see the first textual note on 9:26. וְאוֹר is the third masculine singular Qal (G) perfect of אוֹר, "to be light," used impersonally with a conjunctive *waw* and forming a temporal clause: "when it is light."

The LXX is somewhat longer:

---

[4]   McCarter, *I Samuel*, 426; Klein, *1 Samuel*, 276.

καὶ νῦν ὄρθρισον τὸ πρωί, σὺ καὶ οἱ παῖδες τοῦ κυρίου σου οἱ ἥκοντες μετὰ σοῦ, καὶ πορεύεσθε εἰς τὸν τόπον οὗ κατέστησα ὑμᾶς ἐκεῖ, καὶ λόγον λοιμὸν μὴ θῇς ἐν καρδίᾳ σου, ὅτι ἀγαθὸς σὺ ἐνώπιόν μου· καὶ ὀρθρίσατε ἐν τῇ ὁδῷ, καὶ φωτισάτω ὑμῖν, καὶ πορεύθητε.

Now then rise up early in the morning, you and the servants of your lord who have come with you, and go to the place that I assigned you [plural], and entertain no evil thought in your heart, because you are good before me, and rise early in the way, and when it is light for you [plural], then go [plural].

Some scholars believe the LXX contains a better text and that the MT has suffered a loss by parablepsis.[5] See *HOTTP*[2], which, based on the LXX, offers the following conjectural reconstruction of the beginning of the verse:

השכם בבקר אתה ועבדי אדניך אשר באו אתך והלכתם אל המקום
אשר הפקדתי אתכם שם ודבר בליעל אל תשם בלבבך כי טוב אתה לפני

Rise early in the morning, you and your master's servants who came with you, and go to the place that I have assigned you, and do not set a worthless word in your heart because you are good before me.

HOTTP[2] assigns this reconstruction a "D," which signifies that this form of the text is highly doubtful and has a low probability of accurately representing the author's original text.[6] Therefore, although both the MT and the LXX exhibit difficulties that could indicate some corruption, it is impossible to reconstruct a better reading with any degree of confidence.

Commentary

Nisan (March/April) 1009 BC

This account continues the narrative from 28:2 within the structure of 27:1–31:13.[7] The Philistines were on their march north to engage Saul in battle and used Aphek as a staging area along the way (29:1; see figure 26 in the commentary on 28:3–25). The armies were marching into the camp under each of the five Philistine governors (see 6:4, 16–18) in organized units, and David and his men were in the rear with Achish, which allowed the rest of the Philistine forces to observe their arrival (29:2). The presence of David and his men did not escape the notice of the Philistine commanders, who immediately inquired about their presence (29:3). The author uses a play on words to highlight the irony of David and his men marching with the Philistines. The troops were "passing in review" (עֹבְרִים, ʿobrim, twice in 29:2), and among them were the "Hebrews" (עִבְרִים, ʿibrim, 29:3).

It would appear that the "Philistine commanders" (שָׂרֵי פְלִשְׁתִּים, 29:3, 4, 9) were identical to the "Philistine governors" (הַסְּרָנִים, 29:2, 7; סַרְנֵי פְלִשְׁתִּים,

---

5 McCarter, *I Samuel*, 426; Klein, *1 Samuel*, 276.

6 *HOTTP*[2], 203 (see also vii–viii).

7 For the place of this section (29:1–11) within the larger section of 27:1–31:13, see the beginning of the commentary on 27:1–12.

29:6). Earlier in the book the author preferred "Philistine governors" (5:8, 11; 6:4, 12, 16; 7:7; הַסְּרָנִים, 6:4, 18) but also used "Philistine commanders" (18:30). In this chapter the author seems to be alternating between these two titles for variety. Note that the "Philistine commanders" voiced their objection to David's presence to Achish (29:4–5), but when speaking to David of their opposition, Achish first called them "governors" (29:6, 7) and then "commanders" (29:9).

Achish's defense of David is curiously worded (29:3). While he defended him as blameless, he also called him "David, the servant of Saul, the king of Israel" (דָּוִד עֶבֶד ׀ שָׁאוּל מֶלֶךְ־יִשְׂרָאֵל). While readers would most naturally assume that the title "the king of Israel" applied to the nearer antecedent, "Saul," the Hebrew phrasing is ambiguous, and the author may have chosen this wording to recall that David had been anointed king as Saul's replacement (16:1–13; cf. 15:23–29). Note that when David first went to Gath, the Gittites called him "the king of the land" (21:12 [ET 21:11]).

Achish's infelicitous characterization of David as Saul's servant brought out the wrath of his fellow Philistine commanders, who demanded that David be sent back to the place Achish had assigned him (29:4), i.e., Ziklag (27:6). They immediately pounced on the description of David as Saul's servant by noting the following (29:4–5):

- He would turn on the Philistine forces in battle—something that Hebrew allies had done previously (14:21).
- He could reingratiate himself with Saul by taking the heads of "our men"—the Philistines' own troops (cf. 17:51, 54, 57).
- David was renowned in Israel, and his fame was connected with Saul.

The last point is particularly interesting. The little couplet was intended to praise both Saul and David, but it was taken by Saul to be an insult (18:7–8). It turned him against David. Here the Philistines used the same bit of verse to link David to Saul. No matter how it was intended to be perceived, the song snippet consistently worked against David every time (18:7–8; 21:12 [ET 21:11]; 29:5).

Achish summoned David in order to dismiss him and send him back to Ziklag. His words were prefaced by an oath in Yahweh's name (29:6). Achish was probably accommodating himself to David by referring to David's God, thinking that David might not adhere to an oath taken in the name of pagan gods. On the other hand, since Achish was a polytheist, he could readily adapt to using the name of David's God. Achish would have acknowledged many gods, with Yahweh simply one among them.

The words of Achish began on a positive note and expressed the Gittite king's trust and confidence in David before delivering the news of the hostility of his fellow Philistine rulers. Achish characterized David as a "straight" or "honorable" man (יָשָׁר; see the second textual note on 29:6). This word implies justice and honesty, and readers ought to find its use ironic and hopelessly naive on Achish's lips. David had been deceiving the Gittite ruler all along (27:8–12). Achish also stated his approval for David to go out and come back, i.e., to wage war,[8] with the rest of the Philistines. Moreover, Achish had found no fault (29:3) or wrong (רָעָה, "evil," 29:6) in David. It appears as if Achish was trying to soften the blow of rejection for David with these words, and they also emphasized how effective David had been in deceiving Gath's ruler.

After this long preface, the bad news was delivered in one quick sentence— the rest of the Philistine rulers considered David to be "no good" (29:6). Achish then delivered his orders: return, go peaceably, and do not aggravate the situation by doing something offensive to the other Philistines (29:7). Achish not only wanted David to go back to Ziklag but also appeared to have been concerned that David might do something to upset the camp.

David's reply sought information as to why he was being sent home (29:8). What had he done during his time in Achish's service that was causing his dismissal? Perhaps David was concerned that his real activities while at Ziklag had been discovered (27:8–12). However, there is no indication that Achish or the other Philistine governors knew the true nature of David's actions. Most ominously, David's desire was to fight "the enemies of my lord, the king" (29:8). Achish apparently accepted this as a reference to himself. However, David once again had been shrewdly ambiguous and had taken advantage of Achish's own characterization of David as "the servant of Saul" (29:3). Was David expressing his desire to fight on the Philistine side, or, since Achish's own words had acknowledged that Saul was David's master (29:3; cf. "his lord" in 29:4), was the crafty David intending all along to turn on the Philistines, the enemies of Saul? The reader is left to wonder about David's true desires even if Achish appeared to have had no doubts about how David's ambiguous words ought to have been interpreted.

Achish's reassurance to David told him that he considered him "as an angel of God" (29:9). The alert reader will catch the stark difference between the other Philistine commanders and Achish. They were worried that David would become an "adversary" or "Satan" (שָׂטָן; see the fourth textual note on 29:4), while to Achish David was a heavenly angel. Despite this, Achish told David that the other Philistine commanders had overruled him. He ordered David to leave first thing in the morning for Ziklag (29:10). David complied as the Philistines moved on to Jezreel (29:11).

For a chronology of events in 1 Samuel 28–2 Samuel 1, see figure 27.

---

[8] See the first textual note on 18:6.

Figure 27

Chronology of Events in 1 Samuel 28–2 Samuel 1

Day	David	The Philistines and Saul
1	David must accompany Achish (1 Sam 28:1).	The Philistines gather for war (1 Sam 28:1).
	David arrives at Aphek (1 Sam 29:2).	The Philistines arrive at Aphek (1 Sam 29:1).
2	[The Amalekites raid Ziklag (1 Sam 30:13–14).]	Saul camps at the spring in Jezreel (1 Sam 29:1).
	David leaves for Ziklag (1 Sam 29:11).	The Philistines leave for Jezreel (1 Sam 29:11).
3	David travels to Ziklag.	The Philistines march to Jezreel.
4	David arrives at Ziklag (1 Sam 30:1).	The Philistines arrive at Shunem (1 Sam 28:4).
		Saul gathers forces on Gilboa for war (1 Sam 28:4).
	David raids the Amalekites at twilight (1 Sam 30:17).	Saul goes to Endor at night (1 Sam 28:7–8).
		Saul returns to Gilboa at night (1 Sam 28:25).
5	David strikes the Amalekites until evening (1 Sam 30:17).	The Philistines defeat Israel on Gilboa (1 Sam 31:1).
		Saul and his sons die (1 Sam 31:2–6).
6	David returns to Ziklag (1 Sam 30:26).	The Philistines capture Saul's corpse (1 Sam 31:8–10).
7	David is at Ziklag (1 Sam 30:26; 2 Sam 1:1).	
8	David is at Ziklag (2 Sam 1:1).	
9	An Amalekite informs David of Saul's death (2 Sam 1:2–16).	

1 Samuel 30:1–31

David Rescues His Wives
from the Amalekites

Translation

30 ¹When David and his men came to Ziklag on the third day, Amalek had raided the Negev and Ziklag. They struck Ziklag and set it on fire. ²They took the women and all who were in it captive—from the youngest to the oldest. They did not kill anyone, but they carried [them] off and went on their way.

³David and his men came to the city and discovered that it had been set on fire and that their wives, sons, and daughters had been taken captive. ⁴David and the troops with him wept loudly until they could weep no more. ⁵David's two wives had been taken captive: Ahinoam the Jezreelitess and Abigail, the wife of Nabal, the Carmelitess.

⁶David was in a very tight spot because the troops talked about stoning him, since all the troops—each one of them—were bitter and dispirited over [the loss of] their sons and daughters. However, David strengthened himself in Yahweh, his God.

⁷David said to the high priest Abiathar the son of Ahimelech, "Bring the ephod to me." So Abiathar brought the ephod to David. ⁸Then David inquired of Yahweh, "Should I pursue this raiding party? Will I overtake it?"

He said, "Pursue [it], because you will certainly overtake [it], and you will certainly rescue."

⁹So David—he and six hundred men with him—went and came to the Wadi Besor, where some stayed behind. ¹⁰David and four hundred men continued the pursuit, and two hundred men who were too exhausted to cross the Wadi Besor stayed. ¹¹They found an Egyptian man in the field. They took him to David. They gave him food, and he ate. They gave him water to drink. ¹²They gave him a slice of pressed figs and two bunches of raisins. He ate and was revived, because he had not eaten food nor drunk water for three days and three nights.

¹³David said to him, "To whom do you belong, and from where are you?"

He said, "I am a young Egyptian man, a slave belonging to an Amalekite man. My master abandoned me because I fell sick three days ago. ¹⁴We had raided the Negev of the Cherethites and the territory of Judah and the Negev of Caleb, and we had set Ziklag on fire."

¹⁵David said, "Will you lead me down to this raiding party?"

He said, "Take an oath for me by God that you will not kill me and that you will not hand me over to my master, and I will lead you down to this raiding party."

¹⁶So he led them down, and they found them spreading out over the face of the land, eating and drinking and celebrating with all the large amount of spoil that

they took from Philistine territory and from Judah's territory. [17]David attacked them from dusk until the evening of the next day. Not a man of them escaped except four hundred young men who mounted camels and fled.

[18]David rescued all that the Amalekites had taken, and David rescued his two wives. [19]No one of theirs was missing from the youngest to the oldest, including sons and daughters, or anything from the spoil, including anything they had taken for themselves. David returned everything. [20]David took all the sheep and the cattle, and they drove them before that property. They said, "This is David's spoil."

[21]David came to the two hundred men who had been too exhausted to follow David, so he had stationed them at the Wadi Besor. They came out to meet David and to meet the troops with him. David approached the troops and greeted them. [22]But every corrupt and worthless man among the men who had gone with David said in response, "Since they did not go with me, we will not give them anything from the spoil that we rescued except each man's wife and sons. Let them lead [them] away and go!"

[23]But David said, "You must not do this, my brothers, with what Yahweh has given to us. He protected us and handed to us the raiding party that came against us. [24]Who should listen to you regarding this matter? The portion of the one who went down to battle will be equal to the portion of the one who stayed with the equipment. Together they will share." [25]So it was from that day on. He [David] made it a statute and custom for Israel to this day.

[26]When David came to Ziklag, he sent some of the spoil to Judah's elders [and] to his neighbors, saying, "Here is a blessing for you from the spoil of Yahweh's enemies."

[27][He sent them] to those in Beth-zur, to those in Ramoth of the Negev, to those in Jattir, [28]to those in Adadah, to those in Siphmoth, to those in Eshtemoa, [29]to those in Carmel, to those in the cities of the Jerahmeelites, to those in the cities of the Kenites, [30]to those in Hormah, to those in Beersheba, to those in Ether, [31]to those in Hebron, and to all the places where David—he and his men—traveled from time to time.

Textual Notes

30:1 וַעֲמָלֵקִי פָּשְׁטוּ—In almost all Masoretic manuscripts the subject is the singular gentilic noun עֲמָלֵקִי, "Amalekite," which in this context would have to be a collective, referring to Amalekite troops. One Masoretic manuscript has the name of the people, עֲמָלֵק, "Amalek," as does the LXX. "Amalek" fits somewhat better as the subject of the plural verb, פָּשְׁטוּ. Here and in 30:14 פָּשַׁט has the military meaning "make a raid." See the first textual note on 18:4. Chronologically, Amalek had raided Ziklag three days before David arrived there, even though the raid is not narrated until later, in 30:13–14 (see the events on day 1 in figure 27 at the end of the commentary on 29:1–11). Therefore the Qal (G) perfect verb פָּשְׁטוּ is translated with an English pluperfect: "had raided." For the same reason two verbs in 30:3 and one in 30:5 are translated with pluperfects ("had been set on fire" and "had been taken captive" in 30:3 and "had been taken captive" in 30:5).

וַיִּשְׂרְפוּ אֹתָהּ בָּאֵשׁ—Literally "and they burned it with the fire." The Qal (G) of שָׂרַף, "to burn," is used with the prepositional phrase בָּאֵשׁ, "with the fire." Other forms of שָׂרַף are used with the same prepositional phrase in 30:3, 14. The pronominal suffix on the direct object marker אֹתָהּ is feminine (singular) because towns are grammatically feminine. That also explains the use of the feminine Qal passive (Gp) participle שְׂרוּפָה, meaning the city had been "burned," in 30:3.

30:2 וַיִּשְׁבּוּ אֶת־הַנָּשִׁים אֲשֶׁר־בָּהּ—The Qal (G) of שָׁבָה means to "take captive" (BDB). In the MT, the direct object is אֶת־הַנָּשִׁים, "the women," modified by the relative clause אֲשֶׁר־בָּהּ, "who (were) in it [Ziklag]." In the LXX the direct object is longer, τὰς γυναῖκας καὶ πάντα τὰ ἐν αὐτῇ, "the women *and all the things* [neuter plural] that (were) in it." The next clause states that no person was killed (see the next textual note), and in 30:3 we are told that in addition to the women also "their sons and their daughters" (וּבְנֵיהֶם וּבְנֹתֵיהֶם) were captured. It is possible that preceding אֲשֶׁר־בָּהּ the two words וְאֶת־כָּל־, "and all," were in the Hebrew text translated by the LXX but were omitted in the MT. Alternatively, the LXX may have expanded the text here to conform to the next clause and to 30:3. The longer LXX reading is followed in the translation above.[1]

לֹא הֵמִיתוּ אִישׁ—Literally "they did not kill a man/person." In context אִישׁ probably does not refer to men, since at least some of the men defending the city likely were killed in the conquest. Instead, it probably has the generic meaning "person," meaning a member of the groups mentioned: they killed none of the "women" (30:2), none of the "wives, sons, and daughters" (30:3).

וַיִּנְהֲגוּ—The Qal (G) of נָהַג can mean to "drive" animals ahead, as in 30:20, or to "lead away" people, as in 30:22. The appropriate meaning here is "carry off."

30:3 וְהִנֵּה—Literally "and behold," this is rendered as "and discovered that." The particle הִנֵּה is often used to introduce something new and unexpected (*HALOT*, 6).

נִשְׁבּוּ—"They had been taken captive." This is the Niphal (N) perfect of שָׁבָה, whose meaning is the passive of the Qal (G; see the first textual note on 30:2). The same Niphal perfect, נִשְׁבּוּ, recurs in 30:5. These three are the only instances of שָׁבָה in the book of Samuel.

30:4 וְהָעָם—In military contexts "the people" often means "the troops." See the first textual note on 4:3.

וַיִּשָּׂא ... אֶת־קוֹלָם וַיִּבְכּוּ—Literally "and they lifted up their voice, and they wept." The same idiom was in 11:4; 24:17 (ET 24:16). See also 2 Sam 3:32; 13:36.

עַד אֲשֶׁר אֵין־בָּהֶם כֹּחַ לִבְכּוֹת—Literally this means "until (the time) when there was not in them strength to weep."

30:5 וַאֲבִיגַיִל אֵשֶׁת נָבָל הַכַּרְמְלִי—In Codex Leningradensis and most Masoretic manuscripts, the gentilic noun is masculine singular, הַכַּרְמְלִי, "the Carmelite," which must then refer to Nabal. A number of Masoretic manuscripts have the feminine form הַכַּרְמְלִית, "the Carmelitess," which refers to Abigail. The translation follows the feminine reading because Nabal was from "Maon" (25:2) and by ancestry he was a "Calebite" (see the last textual note on 25:3), although his business was in "Carmel"

---

[1] This reading is followed also by McCarter, *I Samuel*, 431; Klein, *1 Samuel*, 280; HCSB; ESV; NIV.

(25:2; see also 25:5). David's servants came to Abigail in "Carmel" (25:40). The same textual issue arises in 2 Sam 2:2; 3:3, where this commentary again follows the feminine reading. See the textual note on the final words in 2 Sam 2:2.

30:6 וַתֵּצֶר לְדָוִד מְאֹד—Literally "and it was very cramped for David," this is rendered as "David was in a very tight spot." For the same idiom, see the second textual note on 28:15. Here, however, the Qal (G) form of the verb צָרַר, "be narrow, cramped," is a third feminine singular preterite (imperfect with *waw* consecutive). Usually an impersonal construction has a masculine verb, but a feminine verb can be used (GKC, § 144 c).

לְסָקְלוֹ—This is the Qal (G) infinitive construct of סָקַל, "to stone," with a third masculine singular suffix. Cf. Ex 17:4, where the people were ready to stone Moses. This Qal verb is used in some prescriptions for the death penalty, e.g., Deut 13:11 (ET 13:10); 17:5; 22:24; cf. Josh 7:25. The only other instances of this verb in the book of Samuel are the Piel (D) forms in 2 Sam 16:6, 13.

מָרָה נֶפֶשׁ כָּל־הָעָם—The feminine noun נֶפֶשׁ in the construct chain "the soul [נֶפֶשׁ] of all the troops" is the subject of the feminine verb מָרָה, the Qal (G) perfect of מָרַר, "to be bitter." The word מָרָה has the postpositive accent *pashṭah* (-ָ֙מָר), which is repeated after the second syllable when the stress is on the first of two syllables (thus מָ֙רָ֙ה). The stress on the first syllable (מָ֙רָה) marks this word as the verb. If it were the feminine form of the adjective מַר, "bitter," the stress would be on the second syllable (מָרָ֙ה), as in 2 Sam 2:26.

אִישׁ—This means "each (one of them)." The noun is used distributively here (*HALOT*, s.v. אִישׁ I, 10).

וַיִּתְחַזַּק—The Hithpael (HtD) of חָזַק, "be strong," has a reflexive meaning: "strengthen oneself" or "take courage in" (see BDB, 1).

30:7 הַכֹּהֵן—In context "the priest" means "the high priest." See the third textual note on 1:9.

הַגִּישָׁה־נָּא לִי הָאֵפֹד—David had used the same imperative (the Hiphil [H] of נָגַשׁ, "bring near," with paragogic *he*) and object noun (הָאֵפֹד, "the ephod") in 23:9.

30:8 וַיִּשְׁאַל דָּוִד בַּיהוָה—"Then David inquired of Yahweh." See the first textual note and the commentary on 22:10.

אֶרְדֹּף אַחֲרֵי הַגְּדוּד־הַזֶּה—The Qal (G) of רָדַף, "pursue," often takes the preposition אַחֲרֵי, "after," as here in 30:8a. It can also take a direct object; see the third textual note on 23:25. Neither a preposition nor a direct object is used with it in 30:8b, 10. The noun גְּדוּד often refers to a "marauding band" (BDB, s.v. גְּדוּד I, 1) of raiding troops. It recurs in 30:15, 23.

הַאַשִּׂגֶנּוּ—"Will I overtake it?" This verb has the interrogative *he* prefix. It is the Hiphil (H) first common singular imperfect of נָשַׂג with a third masculine singular pronominal suffix with paragogic (energic) *nun*.

וְהַצֵּל תַּצִּיל:—"And you will certainly rescue." Yahweh's pledge employs the Hiphil (H) infinitive absolute of נָצַל, "to save, rescue," before its second masculine singular imperfect to emphasize the certainty of the promise. The Hiphil of this verb will recur in 30:18 (twice) and in 30:22 to signify the fulfillment of the divine promise here. No direct object is supplied here to limit the promise. This prepares for the comprehensive fulfillment later in the chapter. David was particularly concerned about rescuing his wives, and the author will record that "David rescued his two wives" (30:18). The narrative also states that David "rescued all that the Amalekites had taken" (30:18), and this all-inclusive rescue specifically included the other men's wives and children (30:22).

30:9 וְהַנּוֹתָרִים עָמָדוּ—Literally "and those left stood/stayed." The next verse (30:10) will reveal that four hundred moved on while two hundred stood/stayed (the Qal [G] of עָמַד again), so the Niphal (N) participle of יָתַר, "be left over," here refers to two hundred men.

30:10 פִּגְּרוּ מֵעֲבֹר—The verb פָּגַר appears only twice in the OT, here and in 30:21, both times in the Piel (D). Aramaic cognates support the meaning "be exhausted." That verb combines with the Qal (G) infinitive construct of עָבַר, "to cross over," with the prefixed preposition מִן, to form an elliptical comparison (Joüon, § 141 i): "too exhausted to cross." In 30:21, the same Piel form, פִּגְּרוּ, is combined with מִלֶּכֶת, the Qal infinitive construct of הָלַךְ with the prefixed preposition מִן, to form the elliptical comparison "too exhausted to follow."

30:11 אִישׁ־מִצְרִי—This means "an Egyptian man." "When two or more nouns or nominal phrases are used in sequence and have the same referents and syntactic function, the trailing noun(s) are said to be *in apposition* to the first noun. ... The second noun may restrict the meaning of the first noun by further defining it as a group contained within the first noun."[2] Thus "a man, Egyptian" is equivalent to "an Egyptian man" in English. See also נַעַר מִצְרִי, "a young Egyptian man," in 30:13; לְאִישׁ עֲמָלֵקִי, "belonging to an Amalekite man," 30:13; and אִישׁ־נַעַר, "a young man" (used collectively), 30:17. Other examples with אִישׁ, "man," or אִשָּׁה, "woman," are אִישׁ כֹּהֵן, "a priest" (Lev 21:9), and אִשָּׁה־אַלְמָנָה, "a widow" (2 Sam 14:5; 1 Ki 7:14; 11:26; 17:9, 10).

וַיַּשְׁקֻהוּ מַיִם:—Biblical Hebrew uses the Qal (G) of שָׁתָה for "to drink" (see שָׁתָה מַיִם in 30:12), but שָׁתָה is not used in the Hiphil (H). Instead, to express the causative meaning "to make [someone] drink," i.e., "to give [someone something] to drink," the Hiphil of שָׁקָה is used, as here (and שָׁקָה is not used in the Qal). The Hiphil of שָׁקָה often takes a double accusative construction (Joüon, § 125 u). Here the first accusative is the third masculine singular pronominal suffix on the verb וַיַּשְׁקֻהוּ, literally "and they made him drink." The second accusative, מָיִם (the pausal form of מַיִם), "water," designates what is given as drink.

30:12 פֶּלַח דְּבֵלָה—In this construct phrase, the first noun, פֶּלַח, denotes a "slice." (The two other OT instances of this word in this sense refer to a "slice" of pomegranate [Song 4:3; 6:7].) The second noun, דְּבֵלָה, "a cake of pressed figs," previously denoted one of Abigail's gifts to David (1 Sam 25:18), as did the second noun in the next construct phrase in 30:12, צִמֻּקִים (25:18; see the next textual note).

וּשְׁנֵי צִמֻּקִים—"And two bunches of raisins" is omitted in the LXX. Some would therefore argue that it is secondary and ought to be omitted as a later expansion.[3] However, it could just as easily have been accidentally omitted from the LXX or its exemplar.

---

[2] *IBH*, § 21 and 21 A. See also Waltke-O'Connor, § 12.3b; Joüon, § 131 b.
[3] McCarter, *I Samuel*, 432; Klein, *1 Samuel*, 280.

וַתָּשָׁב רוּחוֹ אֵלָיו—Literally "and his spirit returned to him."

שְׁלֹשָׁה יָמִים וּשְׁלֹשָׁה לֵילוֹת:—This is an accusative for extent of time (Joüon, § 126 i): "*for* three days and three nights." The noun לַיְלָה, "night," is masculine (its ending, הָ-, is unaccented, and therefore is not the common feminine ending). Therefore the feminine form of the numeral, שְׁלֹשָׁה, "three," is used for both of the masculine nouns here (Joüon, § 89 a, note 2).

30:13 חָלִיתִי הַיּוֹם שְׁלֹשָׁה:—Literally "I am sick today, three," this means "today I have been sick for three days." שְׁלֹשָׁה is another accusative for extent of time (GKC, § 134 o, note 1).

30:15 וְאוֹרִדֵךָ ... הֲתוֹרִדֵנִי—Both forms are Hiphil (H) imperfects of יָרַד, meaning "to bring [someone] down," with pronominal suffixes as direct objects. The first has the interrogative *he* prefix.

הִשָּׁבְעָה ... וְאִם־תַּסְגִּרֵנִי בְּיַד־אֲדֹנִי—In a sworn oath (the Niphal [N] of שָׁבַע, here, its imperative with paragogic *he*), the particle אִם serves as a negative: "swear that you will not …" (as also in 3:14; 19:6; 24:22 [ET 24:21]; 28:10). The Hiphil (H) of סָגַר is used with בְּיַד־ (literally "close me up in the hand of my lord"), as also in 23:11, 12, 20; 30:15.

30:16 וְהִנֵּה—This is translated as "and they found them." See the first textual note on 4:13 (cf. the first textual note on 30:3).

נְטֻשִׁים—The Qal (G) of נָטַשׁ usually means to "leave alone," "abandon," or "permit" (see BDB). This masculine plural Qal passive (Gp) participle here is usually interpreted to mean that they were "spreading out." It might also suggest that they had given themselves over to celebrating with reckless abandon and permissiveness.

30:17 מֵהַנֶּשֶׁף וְעַד־הָעֶרֶב לְמָחֳרָתָם—Literally this means "from twilight until the evening (belonging) to their next day." David plundered them for about twenty-four hours. The noun נֶשֶׁף, "twilight," can refer to that of the dawn (2 Ki 7:5, 7; Is 5:11; 21:4; Ps 119:147; Job 3:9; 7:4; cf. the LXX here: ἑωσφόρου) or of the evening, "dusk" (Is 59:10; Jer 13:16; Job 24:15; Prov 7:9). Since the preceding events narrated in 30:7–16 seem to have taken place during daylight, the translation interprets נֶשֶׁף to refer to "dusk" of the same day.

The noun מָחֳרָת, "the morrow, the next day," is usually used with the prefixed preposition noun מִן (twenty-eight times in the OT), but לְ is prefixed to it here and in Jonah 4:7; 1 Chr 29:21. לְמָחֳרָתָם here may have a suffixed enclitic *mem*.[4] Alternatively, if the final *mem* is the third masculine plural pronominal suffix, it may refer to the Amalekites ("*their* next day"), as did the same pronominal suffix on the first verb of the verse, וַיַּכֵּם. Alternatively, it could refer to David and his men since they were the protagonists who were actively attacking during this time. Most English translations ignore the suffixed *mem*.[5] The LXX reads καὶ τῇ ἐπαύριον, "and to the next day." The Lucianic recension of the LXX reads καὶ τῇ ἐπαύριον καὶ ἐθανατωσεν,[6] "and to the next day and killed them," which might represent an underlying Hebrew text of למחרת להחרמם, to be

---

4   For the classic treatment of the enclitic *mem* in Hebrew, see Hummel, "Enclitic *Mem* in Early Northwest Semitic, Especially Hebrew."

5   HCSB, ESV, GW, NET, NIV.

6   McCarter, *I Samuel*, 432.

vocalized לְמֶחֳרָת לְהַחֲרִמָם, literally "to the next day to devote them to destruction."[7] If so, לְהַחֲרִמָם would be the Hiphil (H) infinitive construct of חָרַם with a third masculine plural object suffix (see לְהַחֲרִימָם in 1 Ki 9:21; 2 Ki 19:11; Is 37:11). If this was the case, the second word probably was a corruption of the first one under the influence of the use of the Hiphil (H) of חָרַם, "devote to destruction, completely destroy," in the narrative of Saul's slaying of the Amalekites (1 Sam 15:3, 8, 9 [twice], 15, 18, 20; those are the only verses in the book of Samuel with חָרַם). Apparently, then, the Lucianic recension combined both readings.

30:18 וְאֶת־שְׁתֵּי נָשָׁיו הִצִּיל דָּוִד:—Since the previous clause stated that David rescued "all" (כָּל־) that the Amalekites had taken, this additional sentence might seem superfluous. However, this detail emphasizes the importance of his rescue of his two wives, since the family line of David was vital for the future of Israel and, indeed, of the world (2 Samuel 7). The value of his wives is highlighted by the word order here; the phrase "his two wives" is the direct object but is placed first: literally "and his two wives David rescued."

30:19 וְלֹא נֶעְדַּר־לָהֶם—Literally "and was not missing (anyone/anything) belonging to them." In the OT the verb עָדַר III appears six times in the Niphal (N), as here, meaning "to be missing, lacking," and once in the Piel (D), meaning "to leave missing." The preposition לְ is used in the sense of possession, hence לָהֶם means "(anyone/anything) belonging to them." It is translated using the English possessive pronoun "theirs."

וּמִשָּׁלָל—The sense of the prefixed preposition מִן is partitive, "some of the spoil" or "(anything) from the spoil." See also the partitive מִן on מֵהַשָּׁלָל, "anything from/some of the spoil," in 30:22, 26.

30:20 נָהֲגוּ—See the third textual note on 30:2.

30:21 פִּגְּרוּ ׀ מֵלֶכֶת—See the textual note on 30:10.

וַיֹּשִׁיבֵם—This is the reading in the majority of Masoretic manuscripts, "and they stationed them" (a third masculine plural Hiphil [H] preterite [imperfect with *waw* consecutive] of יָשַׁב with a third masculine plural object suffix). A few Masoretic manuscripts read וַיֹּשִׁיבֵם, "and he stationed them," which is supported by the LXX (καὶ ἐκάθισεν αὐτούς) and reflected in the translation above.

לִקְרַאת ... וְלִקְרַאת—See the second textual note on 4:1.

וַיִּשְׁאַל לָהֶם לְשָׁלוֹם:—"And he greeted them." See the first textual note on 10:4.

30:22 וּבְלִיַּעַל—See the first textual note on 1:16.

עִמִּי—The MT reads "with me," as if a single man is speaking. A few Masoretic manuscripts read the plural עִמָּנוּ, "with us," in agreement with the LXX (μεθ' ἡμῶν). The plural reading may be a harmonization to the following first common plural verbs נִתֵּן, "we will give," and הִצַּלְנוּ, "we rescued."

30:23 לֹא־תַעֲשׂוּ כֵן אֶחָי אֵת אֲשֶׁר־נָתַן יְהוָה לָנוּ וַיִּשְׁמֹר אֹתָנוּ—The first clause of the MT is the prohibition "you must not do thus, my brothers!" In place of אֶחָי, "my brothers,"

---

[7] However, to translate the Hiphil (H) of חָרַם, the LXX usually uses a different verb, ἐξολεθρεύω (e.g., LXX 15:3, 9 [twice], 15, 18, 20) rather than the verb θανατόω, as used here in the Lucianic recension. The LXX of 1 Samuel usually employs θανατόω to translate the Hiphil (H) of מוּת (e.g., 2:6; 5:10, 11; 11:12).

the LXX reads μετά, "after," which would reflect a Hebrew text with the preposition אַחַר or אַחֲרֵי. The LXX rendition[8] means "you must not do thus after the Lord gave to us and guarded us." It is difficult to decide between these readings, but אֹחִי in the MT seems to be the harder reading, making it more likely the original.

If the prohibition were to end with אֹחִי, as indicated by the Masoretic *athnach* (᠎) on it, then the syntax of the next clause, beginning with אֵת אֲשֶׁר, would be difficult. BDB, s.v. אֵת I, 3 (α), proposes that a verb such as "remember" needs to be supplied, with אֵת marking its direct object; the next sentence would be "[remember] *that which* Yahweh gave to us, and he protected us …" However, most English versions ignore the *athnach* on אֹחִי, take אֵת as the preposition "with" (rather than the direct object marker), and interpret the relative clause with אֲשֶׁר to refer to the spoil: "you must not do thus, my brothers, *with what* Yahweh gave us." The next words (וַיִּשְׁמֹר אֹתָנוּ), then, begin a new sentence: "he guarded/protected us." That is the most expedient construal of the syntax since it does not require any emendations or supplied words.

30:24 כְּחֵלֶק … וּכְחֵלֶק—Literally this means "like the portion … like the portion." Hebrew idiom repeats the preposition כְּ on each of the two items in the comparison to signify that they are comparable or equal (Joüon, § 174 i). The noun חֵלֶק, "a portion, share," is derived from the verb discussed in the next textual note.

יַחְדָּו יַחֲלֹקוּ—This is translated as "together they will share." The Qal (G) of חָלַק I can mean to "divide" the spoil of war (BDB, 5), but here it probably means to "share" (BDB, 4) the spoil, that is, to receive a share or portion after the spoil is divided and apportioned.

30:26 בְּרָכָה—Here "a blessing" refers to a gift; see the first textual note on 25:27.

וַיְשַׁלַּח—In the Piel (D), שָׁלַח, "to send," means "to send away." See the first textual note on 5:10.

לְרֵעֵהוּ—The noun רֵעַ II, "friend, neighbor," is singular. It might be a collective here, but is rarely so elsewhere. The form here with a third masculine singular suffix, רֵעֵהוּ, appears three times in the OT either in a collective sense or as a defective, or *haser*, spelling of the suffixed plural, רֵעֵיהוּ (GKC, § 91 k).

30:27–31 For more information about the places mentioned in these verses, see figure 28 at the end of this pericope.

30:27 בְּבֵית־אֵל—The MT reads "in Bethel," which must be a corruption, since Bethel was in the territory of Benjamin. The LXX reads ἐν Βαιθσουρ, "in Beth-zur," which suggests the Hebrew reading בבת צור. Beth-zur is mentioned in Josh 15:58; Neh 3:16; 1 Chr 2:45; 2 Chr 11:7. Klein suggests that the reading should be "in Bethuel," as in 1 Chr 4:30.[9]

30:28 בַּעֲרֹעֵר—The MT reads "in Aroer." However, Aroer was in the territory of Gad.[10] It is preferable to read בַּעֲדְעָדָה, "in Adadah," based on Josh 15:22. It appears

---

[8] οὐ ποιήσετε οὕτως μετὰ τὸ παραδοῦναι τὸν κύριον ἡμῖν καὶ φυλάξαι ἡμᾶς.

[9] Klein, *1 Samuel*, 280.

[10] Num 32:34; Deut 2:36; 3:12; 4:48; Josh 12:2; 13:9, 16, 25; Judg 11:26, 33; 2 Sam 24:5; 2 Ki 10:33; Is 17:2; Jer 48:19; 1 Chr 5:8.

as if a careless scribe misread the *daleth*s in בַּעֲדְעָדָה as *resh*es, resulting in בַּעֲרְעֶר, adjusting the name to the better-known Transjordanian town. Alternately, since this place in Judah is identified with modern Khirbet ʿArʿarah, it may be that the city name originally was ערער but suffered from the *daleth-resh* confusion to produce עֲדְעָדָה in Josh 15:22.[11] If this occurred at a very early stage in the transmission of the text of Josh 15:22, before *he* was commonly used to indicate final long vowels, the text of Joshua may have read ערער, to which a *he* was added for a terminal long "a." Then with the graphic confusion it could have become עדעדה. In 1 Sam 30:28 then, the Masoretes could easily have used the vowels of the more familiar Gadite city, mispointing the text that ought to read in the MT as בַּעֲרְעָרָה, "in Ararah."

30:29 בְּרָכָל—The MT reads "in Racal," an otherwise unknown town. The LXX reads ἐν Καρμήλῳ, "in Carmel," reflecting a Hebrew text of בְּכַרְמֶל. It appears as if the MT is a corruption resulting from a dropped letter *mem* and a metathesis of the remaining letters. "Carmel" makes good sense since it is mentioned several times in 1 Samuel and also because it was the home of David's in-laws through his wife Abigail (1 Sam 15:12; 25:2, 5, 7, 40; 27:3; 2 Sam 2:2; 3:3).

הַקֵּינִי—This means "the Kenites." The LXX reads τοῦ Κενεζι, "the Kenizites/Kenizzites." See the third textual note on 27:10.

30:30 בְּחָרְמָה—"In Hormah" is the reading in the MT. The LXX reads ἐν Ιεριμουθ, "in Jarmuth," a different town in Judah (Josh 10:3, 5, 23; 12:11; 15:35; 21:29; Neh 11:29). However, "Jarmuth" is in northern Judah and cannot be among the cities where David traveled as he was hiding from Saul.

בְּבוֹר־עָשָׁן—The MT reads "in Bor-ashan," an otherwise unattested city. The LXX reads ἐν Βηρσαβεε, "in Beersheba," reflecting a Hebrew reading בבאר שבע. "Beersheba" is a frequently mentioned city in southernmost Judah. The MT reading appears to be a garbled transmission of it.

בַּעֲתָךְ—The MT reads "in Athach," an otherwise unknown town. The translation "in Ether" is based on the name עֶתֶר in Josh 15:42; 19:7. Apparently the MT reading resulted from confusion of the final *resh* in בַּעֲתֶר with a final *kaph*.

30:31 הִתְהַלֵּךְ—"(He) traveled from time to time" renders the Hithpael (HtD) perfect of הָלַךְ. See the second textual note on 23:13.

Commentary

Nisan (March/April) 1009 BC

This account provides one last comparison between David and Saul.[12] Both fought the Amalekites (Saul: 1 Sam 15:1–35; cf. 1 Sam 28:18; David: 1 Sam 27:8; cf. 2 Sam 1:1), but Saul had not fulfilled God's command concerning

---

[11] *Daleth* and *resh* are similarly shaped in all scripts of all periods, so this type of graphic confusion could have occurred at any time.

[12] For the place of 1 Samuel 30 within the larger structure of 27:1–31:13, see the beginning of the commentary on 27:1–12. See also figure 27, "Chronology of Events in 1 Samuel 28–2 Samuel 1," at the end of the commentary on 29:1–11.

them.[13] At the same point in time,[14] both men would find themselves in a "very tight spot" (28:15; 30:6), but only David would rely on God. Both men would inquire of Yahweh (28:6; 30:7), but only David would receive an answer (30:8). On the same day David defeated the Amalekites, Saul committed suicide as the Philistines were closing in on him.[15]

David Discovers That Ziklag Has Been Sacked (30:1–6)

We are told that David arrived back in Ziklag on the third day of his trip from Aphek (30:1). Apparently, the Amalekite raid on Ziklag and other places in the south of Judah and Philistia (see 30:14) was opportunistic, since both Saul and the Philistines were engaged in battle in the north. While Ziklag had been burnt, the Amalekites did not kill all the inhabitants, as David had when raiding against them (30:2–3; cf. 27:8–9). The author emphasizes the capture of the women in 30:2 (and adds the children only in 30:3). Perhaps this was because David had no children at this time, only his two wives. David's first children were born in Hebron (2 Sam 3:2). Note that the author, who had already stated that all the women had been captured (1 Sam 30:2, 3), made a point of including David's two wives by name, "Ahinoam" and "Abigail" (30:5). His marriages to both of them were narrated in 25:42–43 (see also 27:3).[16]

The reaction of David's men to the loss of their wives and children was as mournful as one would expect. These men had been on the run from Saul, and their families had endured much hardship yet had survived. The irony that they had been captured while David and his men had been with the Philistines at Aphek (29:1) could only have heightened their distress. Out of their bitterness and tragic sense of loss, they turned on David and talked of stoning him (30:6). This afforded the author an opportunity to highlight the difference between David and Saul as David "strengthened himself in Yahweh his God" (30:6). While Saul was turning to demons at Endor,[17] David was turning to the merciful God who had saved Israel and established his covenant of grace with his

---

[13] See the beginning of the commentary on 15:1–35.

[14] Both of these events take place on day 4 in figure 27, "Chronology of Events in 1 Samuel 28–2 Samuel 1," at the end of the commentary on 29:1–11.

[15] Both of these events take place on day 5 in figure 27, "Chronology of Events in 1 Samuel 28–2 Samuel 1," located at the end of the commentary on 29:1–11.

[16] David's first marriage was to Saul's daughter Michal (18:20–27), but Saul later gave Michal to another man (25:44). Whenever Abigail is introduced into a narrative in the book of Samuel (30:5; also 1 Sam 25:3, 14; 27:3; 2 Sam 2:2; 3:3), she is further identified by the name of her former husband, Nabal. Abigail *had* been Nabal's wife (25:3), but he had died (25:38–39). Therefore instead of the literal translation "the *wife* of Nabal" some versions render the phrase אֵשֶׁת נָבָל (30:5) as "the *widow* of Nabal" (e.g., ESV). After Nabal's death she consented to marry David (25:39–42). David had also married Ahinoam (25:43). Consequently, at this time David had only the two wives "Ahinoam" and "Abigail" (27:3; 30:5). See also the textual note on 27:3.

[17] See "Reasons for Saying No" in "Did Samuel Actually Appear to Saul at Endor?" in the commentary on 28:3–25.

people—a prominent theme in the book.[18] David trusted in this gracious God personally; Yahweh was "*his* God."

David Inquires of God (30:7–8)

David's leadership was evident in that he found strength in Yahweh and also because he turned to his God for advice. His command to Abiathar to bring the ephod (30:7) was clearly for the purpose of consulting the Urim and Thummim.[19] Neither Abiathar nor the ephod have been mentioned since the last time David consulted Yahweh (23:6–12). However, the inability of Saul to receive an answer from God by means of the Urim (28:6) stands in sharp contrast to David's receiving advice by this means now (30:7–8). The author uses his *explicit* note that Yahweh did not answer Saul by the Urim to sharpen the contrast with David, since the use of the Urim and Thummim is only *implicit* in David's act of summoning Abiathar to bring the ephod. The author expects his readers to draw the conclusion that David was consulting Yahweh by means of the Urim and Thummim, and in this way the author makes the contrast between Saul and David more vivid for readers.

God assured David that he would be able to overtake the Amalekites and rescue the captives. It is important to observe that Yahweh did more than answer David's two questions (30:8a). After directing David to pursue the Amalekite raiding party and promising that he would overtake it (thus responding affirmatively to the two queries), Yahweh also offered David the comforting assurance that he would "certainly rescue" (30:8b). This act of divine salvation would restore David's wives and the other families together with everything that had been seized by "Yahweh's enemies" (30:26; see further the fourth textual note on 30:8). This creates yet another potent contrast. When Saul asked, God did not reply, but when David inquired, Yahweh gave him more than he asked (cf. Eph 3:20–21).

The Interrogation of an Egyptian (30:9–15)

David's pursuit took him south to the Wadi Besor (30:9). Some commentators identify this as the Wadi Ghazzeh, southwest of Gaza.[20] It is the largest and deepest wadi in southern Judah, and it would make sense that two hundred of David's men who had already marched three days from Aphek to Ziklag would have been too exhausted to traverse it (30:10).

Somewhere in the vicinity of the wadi David's men found an Egyptian upon whom they had compassion and mercifully fed (30:11–12). Since he had not eaten for three full days, the sugar in the figs and raisins provided quick energy

---

[18] The book of Samuel recounts or refers to Yahweh saving his people from Egypt through the exodus redemption in, e.g., 1 Sam 2:27–28; 4:8; 6:6; 8:8; 10:18–19; 12:6–8; 15:2, 6.

[19] See the excursus "The Urim and Thummim" following the commentary on 14:24–46.

[20] E.g., McCarter, *I Samuel*, 435. Tsumura, *The First Book of Samuel*, 639, and Bergen, *1, 2 Samuel*, 276, suggest that as a possibility.

to revive him. The Law of Moses enjoined Israelites to treat Egyptians kindly (Deut 23:8 [ET 23:7]; see also Ex 22:20 [ET 22:21]; 23:9; Lev 19:34). David's questions revealed this man's identity and tactical information—the duration of time since the enemy troops had moved through and abandoned him in this location—and also strategic intelligence about the Amalekite raids (30:13–14). The areas raided appear to be in the southern part of Judah and Philistia. The Cherethites were probably Cretans who served as mercenaries for the Philistines and came to be associated with them (Ezek 25:16; Zeph 2:5). Amos implies that the Philistines were also from Crete (Amos 9:7). Later Cherethites would serve as mercenaries for David (2 Sam 8:18; 15:18; 20:7; 20:23 [Qere]; 1 Ki 1:38, 44). The "Negev of the Cherethites" (1 Sam 30:14) was probably on the Mediterranean coast. The "Negev of Caleb" was probably the land south of Hebron (Josh 14:14; 15:13). Interestingly, the Egyptian mentioned only Ziklag as being burned by the Amalekites. Perhaps they singled out this town to be scorched in retaliation for David's raids on them (27:8).

David appealed to the abandoned slave to betray his Amalekite master by guiding David to the enemy's location (30:15). The Egyptian agreed as long as he was not returned to slavery at the hands of a man who had left him in the wilderness to die. Since the Egyptian complied, David apparently had accepted this condition and sworn the oath, although the writer does not make this explicit. The Egyptian referred to the deity David would invoke when taking the oath by the generic term "God" (אֱלֹהִים, 30:15), which could, on the tongue of a polytheist, mean "gods" (as in 4:8; 28:13; see also 7:2; 8:8; 17:43; 26:19). We are not able to determine the kind or extent of the man's theology, whether he retained the Egyptian pantheon, incorporated or adopted the Canaanite mythology of his captors, or perhaps had come or was being led to trust in the God of Israel. As for David, there is no doubt that he would have sworn this oath in the name of "Yahweh, his God" (30:6; see also 30:8).

David Defeats the Amalekite Raiding Party (30:16–20)

In short order we are told that the Egyptian led David to the Amalekites, who were celebrating their victories prematurely (30:16). We are not told the location, but since it was about twilight when David came upon them, they could not have been far from the Wadi Besor (30:17). While the time signification in the text is ambiguous (see the textual note on 30:17), it is most likely that David caught up with them on the evening of the same day he began the pursuit and immediately started the attack. If the conflict began in the waning light, this would explain how four hundred men escaped on camels. That four hundred escaped while David killed the rest implies that David defeated a much larger Amalekite force with his four hundred men (30:10). The text also says that he continued the attack "until the evening of the next day" (see the textual note on 30:17). This implies that the next day began at the next sunset, which was the normal way to reckon a day in ancient Israel (cf. Ex 12:18; Lev 23:32; Neh 13:19).

The author emphasizes that David succeeded in rescuing everything the Amalekites had taken, especially the wives and children (1 Sam 30:18–19). This stresses the fulfillment of God's earlier promise (see the fourth textual note on 30:8). In addition, the men called the spoil "David's spoil" (30:20), which serves to highlight David's successful leadership in contrast to Saul's failure at Gilboa (31:1).[21]

David Makes His First Statute (30:21–25)

When David returned to the Wadi Besor with the four hundred men who had fought the Amalekites, he faced another potential crisis as some wanted to deny any share in the spoil to the two hundred who had stayed behind (30:21–22). However, David once again showed his skill as a leader in anticipation of his taking the throne. He first of all declared that Yahweh, not the four hundred, deserved credit for the victory (30:23). This implied that the four hundred had no stronger claim to the spoil than the two hundred, since the spoil came from God's "blessing" (30:26). His question to the troublemakers, "who should listen to you regarding this matter?" also demonstrated the foolishness of their position—it would undermine the morale of support troops if they did not share in the spoil of war (30:24). No reasonable person would pay attention to such a demand, since it would divide an army against itself, a self-defeating maneuver (cf. Mt 12:25–26; Mk 3:24; Lk 11:17–18). So we are told that David made his first statute by decree and that this statute was still honored in the author's own day (1 Sam 30:25).

David Sends Gifts to Judah's Elders (30:26–31)

Upon David's return to Ziklag, he made his first move toward returning to Israel by sending gifts to the elders in the southern part of Judah. The gifts were specifically said to be from "Yahweh's enemies" (30:26), a reference to God's judgment on the Amalekites for their hostility to Israel from the time of the exodus (1 Sam 15:2–3; see Ex 17:8–15; Num 24:20; Deut 25:17–19). The spellings of the city names in the list of the cities to which David sent gifts appear to have suffered a number of corruptions in transmission, both in the MT and in the LXX (see the textual notes on 30:27–30). If the MT is followed, six of the thirteen places are mentioned nowhere else in the OT as being in the territory of Judah. While it is possible that some of these are places are mentioned as being in Judah only here in the OT, it is highly unlikely that nearly half of the places in this list would be unmentioned elsewhere. The LXX, on the other hand, appears to contain a corrupted text that holds a different scribal pedigree. At times the MT preserves the better reading, and at times the LXX is better. In some instances both the MT and the LXX appear to be corrupt. See figure 28.

---

[21] See "Prosperity and Success Come Only from God" in "Other Theological Themes in Samuel" in the introduction.

David's generosity in sharing the spoil with cities in southern Judah that likely had been targets of the Amalekite raids not only helped restore some of their lost property, but it was also a shrewd political act. From the massing of Philistine forces against Saul (28:1–5; 29:1, 11), David may well have suspected that his time to take the throne was near. Like all kings, David would need the support of prominent men—in this case the elders of Judah—if he was to rule successfully. Part of what made David more successful than Saul was his sense of how to combine the morally correct actions with socially appropriate and politically astute judgments. While politically motivated acts are often perceived in our day as inherently corrupt, it is neither wrong nor inappropriate for Christians to hold civic offices and take politically advantageous positions unless doing so would violate God's Law or compromise the Gospel. In the civil realm, it is fitting for believers not only to be prudent but also to do what is right and correct in order to carry out God's Law (the natural law built into creation as well as the moral law revealed in Scripture). Even more are Christians called to stand firm when divine Law is assaulted and they, like saints before, are persecuted "on account of the Word of God and the testimony of Jesus" (Rev 1:9; see also Rev 12:17; 20:4).

The author's artistry once again helps readers to see David's acts of redemption and restoration as the beginning of his reign over Judah (see the commentary above on 30:21–25). Key to this is the literary placement of "Hebron" (30:31) last in the list of cities to which David sent gifts. Hebron was the city to which David, upon inquiring of Yahweh, would be directed after the death of Saul (2 Sam 2:1). There he would be anointed as the king of Judah (2 Sam 2:4) and eventually as the king of all Israel (2 Sam 5:1–3). Hebron would serve as David's capital city for seven and a half years (2 Sam 5:5).

Figure 28

Places That Received Gifts from David (1 Sam 30:27–31)

Place	Other References	Probable Modern Location	MT 1 Samuel 30	LXX 1 Samuel 30
Beth-zur	Josh 15:58; Neh 3:16; 1 Chr 2:45; 2 Chr 11:7	Khirbet eṭ-Ṭubeiqah	**Bethel**	Beth-zur
Ramoth of the Negev	Cf. Josh 19:8	Bir Rakhmeh	Ramoth of the Negev	Ramah of the Negev
Jattir	Josh 15:48; 21:14; 1 Chr 6:42 (ET 6:57)	Khirbet ʿAttir	Jattir	Jattir
Adadah	Josh 15:22	Khirbet ʿArʿarah	**Aroer**	**Aroer**, *Ammadi*
Siphmoth	None	Unknown	*Siphmoth*	*Saphi*
Eshtemoa	Josh 21:14; 1 Chr 4:17, 19; 6:42 (ET 6:57)	Es-Semuʿa	Eshtemoa	*Esthie, Gath, Kinan, Saphek, Thimath*
Carmel	Josh 15:55; 1 Sam 15:12; 25:2, 5, 7, 40; cf. 1 Sam 27:3; 1 Chr 3:1	Khirbet al-Karmil	*Racal*	Carmel
Jerahmeelite cities	Cf. 1 Sam 27:10	South of Beersheba	Jerahmeelite cities	Jerahmeelite cities
Kenite cities	Cf. 1 Sam 15:6; 1 Chr 2:55	Near Arad, east of Beersheba	Kenite cites	Kenizite/Kenizzite cities
Hormah	Num 14:45; 21:3; Deut 1:44; Josh 12:14; 15:30; 19:4; Judg 1:17; 1 Chr 4:30	Khirbet el-Meshash	Hormah	Jarmuth
Beersheba	33 times (e.g., 1 Sam 3:20)	Beʾer Shevaʿ	*Bor-ashan*	Beersheba
Ether	Josh 15:42; 19:7	Khirbet el-ʿAter	*Athach*	*Noo*
Hebron	61 times (e.g., 2 Sam 2:1)	Hebron/Al-Khalil	Hebron	Hebron

Cities not in Judah but well-known elsewhere in Israel are in bold. Judahite cities mentioned nowhere else in the OT are in italics.
In some places, the LXX has more than one place-name where the MT has only one.

1 Samuel 31:1–13

Saul Dies in Battle

Translation

31 ¹As the Philistines were fighting with Israel, the men of Israel fled from the Philistines and fell slain on Mount Gilboa. ²The Philistines closely pursued Saul and his sons. The Philistines struck down Jonathan, Abinadab, and Malchi-shua, sons of Saul. ³The battle was intense against Saul, and the archers—men with bows—found him, and he was severely wounded by the archers. ⁴Saul said to his armor bearer, "Draw your sword and stab me with it. Otherwise these uncircumcised men will come and stab me and torture me." But his armor bearer was not willing [to do it], because he was very afraid. So Saul took his sword and fell on it. ⁵When his armor bearer saw that Saul was dead, he also fell upon his sword and died with him. ⁶So Saul and three of his sons and his armor bearer, as well as all his men, died together that day. ⁷When the men who were across the valley and who were across the Jordan saw that the men of Israel had fled and that Saul and his sons were dead, they abandoned their cities and fled. The Philistines came and occupied them.

⁸The next day when the Philistines came to strip the corpses, they found Saul and his three sons fallen on Mount Gilboa. ⁹They cut off his head and stripped his armor and sent messengers around the land of the Philistines to tell the good news in the temples of their idols and to their people. ¹⁰They placed his armor in the temple of the Astartes, but they attached his body to the wall of Beth-shan.

¹¹When the inhabitants of Jabesh-gilead heard what the Philistines had done to Saul, ¹²every skilled soldier arose and traveled all that night and took the body of Saul and the bodies of his sons from the wall of Beth-shan. They brought them to Jabesh and cremated them there. ¹³They took their bones and buried them under the tamarisk tree in Jabesh. And they fasted for seven days.

Textual Notes

31:1 נִלְחָמִים—"Were fighting" is the Niphal (N) masculine plural participle of לָחַם. The parallel in 1 Chr 10:1 reads נִלְחֲמוּ, "(they) fought," the Niphal third common plural perfect.

וַיָּנֻסוּ—"And they fled." The same Qal (G) third masculine plural preterite (imperfect with *waw* consecutive) of נוּס, "flee," recurs in 31:7b, and the Qal perfect נָסוּ is in 31:7a. The Qal of נוּס refers to Israelites fleeing from Philistines also in 1 Sam 4:10, 16, 17; 17:24; 2 Sam 1:4.

וַיִּפְּלוּ חֲלָלִים—Literally "and slain (men) fell." Cf. וַיִּפְּלוּ חַלְלֵי פְלִשְׁתִּים in 17:52. The adjective חָלָל literally means "pierced" (BDB, 1) since it is derived from the verb חָלַל I, "to bore, pierce," but it is commonly used with the meanings "fatally wounded" or "slain" (BDB, 1, 2). Its masculine plural recurs in 31:8. It also appears in 2 Sam 1:19, 22, 25; 23:8, 18.

31:2 וַיַּדְבְּקוּ פְלִשְׁתִּים אֶת־שָׁאוּל וְאֶת־בָּנָיו—The expected form of the third masculine plural Hiphil (H) preterite (imperfect with *waw* consecutive) is וַיַּדְבִּיקוּ (as in, e.g., Judg 18:22), but this is a rare instance of a Hiphil in which the long *hireq* in the accented syllable (-בִּי-) has been reduced to *shewa* (-בְּ-); see GKC, § 53 n. In the Qal (G), דָּבַק usually means "to cling" to someone in love, as in marriage (e.g., Gen 2:24). However, in the Hiphil, as here, the verb often has military meanings, "closely pursue" retreating enemies (see BDB, Hiphil, 2) or "overtake" them (BDB, Hiphil, 3). Here the Hiphil (H) takes two definite direct objects (each introduced with אֶת־), "Saul and his sons." The parallel in 1 Chr 10:2 has prepositional phrases instead of direct objects:

וַיַּדְבְּקוּ פְלִשְׁתִּים אַחֲרֵי שָׁאוּל וְאַחֲרֵי בָנָיו

And the Philistines closely pursued after Saul and after his sons.

בְּנֵי שָׁאוּל:—This construct phrase is translated indefinitely, "sons of Saul," rather than definitely, "*the* sons of Saul." These are three of Saul's sons (see the second textual note on 31:6), but not all of them. Ish-bosheth/Eshbaal would survive to be assassinated later (2 Sam 2:8–10; 4:1–12). Armoni and Mephibosheth, the two sons of Saul's concubine Rizpah, would be executed during David's reign (2 Sam 21:8–9). See further the discussion of the first inaccurate prediction of the "Samuel" apparition in "Reasons for Saying No" in "Did Samuel Actually Appear to Saul at Endor?" in the commentary on 28:3–25.

31:3 וַתִּכְבַּד הַמִּלְחָמָה—Literally "and the battle was heavy." The definite feminine noun הַמִּלְחָמָה is the subject of the third feminine singular Qal (G) preterite (imperfect with *waw* consecutive) of כָּבֵד. The identical clause is in the parallel 1 Chr 10:3. A similar clause is in Judg 20:34 (see also Is 21:15).

הַמּוֹרִים אֲנָשִׁים בַּקֶּשֶׁת—Literally this means "the archers, men with the bow." הַמּוֹרִים is the Hiphil (H) masculine plural participle (with the definite article) of יָרָה, "to shoot [arrows]" (see BDB, Hiphil, 2).

וַיָּחֶל—"And he was wounded." This is the Qal (G) third masculine singular preterite (imperfect with *waw* consecutive) of חִיל I, "be in pain, be in labor; writhe" (so *HALOT* and *DCH*; in BDB this verb is listed as חוּל [חִיל] I).

31:4 לְנֹשֵׂא כֵלָיו—For this participial phrase, "to his armor bearer," see the second textual note on 14:1.

שְׁלֹף חַרְבְּךָ—The Qal (G) of שָׁלַף refers to "drawing" a sword (חֶרֶב) also in 1 Sam 17:51; 2 Sam 24:9. The form here is the masculine singular imperative. The suffixed noun חַרְבְּךָ, "your sword," might refer to the armor bearer's personal weapon, but more likely it refers to Saul's own sword, which the armor bearer carried for him.

וְדָקְרֵנִי ... וּדְקָרֻנִי—"And stab me. ... And (they will) stab me." Both verbs are Qal (G) forms of דָּקַר, "pierce through," with a first common singular object suffix. The first is the masculine singular imperative, and the second is the third common plural perfect with *waw* consecutive. The second verb is omitted in 1 Chr 10:4. When דָּקַר is used in Zech 12:10, it may refer to impaling or a form of execution akin to crucifixion: "and they shall gaze on me, whom they have pierced" (cf. Ps 22:17 [ET 22:16]). See also the discussion of Deut 21:22–23 in the commentary on 1 Sam 31:11–13.

וְהִתְעַלְּלוּ־בִי—"And they will torture me." The verb is a Hithpael (HtD) third common plural perfect with *waw* consecutive of עָלַל I. In this stem the verb always takes the preposition בְּ and can be rendered as "deal wantonly/ruthlessly with [someone]; abuse."[1]

הַחֶרֶב—Literally "the sword," this is translated as "his sword," since it likely refers to Saul's own sword, carried by his armor bearer. See the second textual note on 31:4.

31:5 עִמּוֹ:—"With him" is omitted in 1 Chr 10:5.

31:6 וַיָּמָת שָׁאוּל—Literally "and Saul died." In the context here, the verb, the Qal (G) preterite (imperfect with *waw* consecutive) of מוּת, sums up the preceding action (Joüon, § 118 i). It is common Hebrew style for a verb to agree with the nearest part of its compound subject. Here the verb is singular even though the rest of the verse will include four other individuals and then "all his men" (כָל־אֲנָשָׁיו) among those who died "together" (יַחְדָּו) on the same day. The singular verb focuses attention on Saul as the most important person in this part of the narrative. He is the sole focus in 31:9–11. In comparison to the singular verb here, the plural verb in 31:7, מֵתוּ שָׁאוּל וּבָנָיו, "Saul and his sons died," may attach greater significance to the sons' deaths. Cf. Joüon, § 150 q.

וּשְׁלֹשֶׁת בָּנָיו—This construct phrase (with the conjunction וְ) could be translated as "and his three sons" but is rendered as "and three of his sons" since other sons of Saul survived; see the second textual note on 31:2.

31:7 הֶעָרִים—The MT reads "the cities." 1 Chr 10:7 reads עָרֵיהֶם, "their cities," in agreement with the LXX in both verses (τὰς πόλεις αὐτῶν). In some contexts the definite article can be translated by a possessive (see הַחֶרֶב in the last textual note on 31:4), but some attribute הֶעָרִים here to a corruption caused by a misplaced *he*.

וַיֵּשְׁבוּ בָּהֶן:—Literally "and they dwelt in them." The pronominal suffix on בְּ is feminine plural (בָּהֶן), in agreement with the feminine plural הֶעָרִים, "the cities." This form of the suffix is rare; see GKC, § 103 g.

31:8 וַיְהִי מִמָּחֳרָת—The noun מָחֳרָת, "the morrow, the next day," is almost always used with the prefixed preposition noun מִן (twenty-eight times in the OT). The identical clause was in 11:11; 18:10; 20:27.

לְפַשֵּׁט אֶת־הַחֲלָלִים—This means "to strip the corpses." The verb פָּשַׁט can refer to taking off one's own garment (the Qal [G] in 19:24; the Hithpael [HtD] in 18:4) or to military raiding (the Qal in 23:27; 27:8, 10; 30:1, 14). However, the Piel (D) here and in 2 Sam 23:10 (an infinitive construct with לְ in both verses) and the Hiphil (H) in the next verse (וַיַּפְשִׁטֻוּ, 31:9) refer to despoiling dead enemy soldiers, i.e., taking their weapons, clothing, and anything else of value. See the first textual note on 18:4. For הַחֲלָלִים, see the third textual note on 31:1.

וַיִּמְצְאוּ ... נֹפְלִים—"They found ... fallen." A Hebrew participle itself is atemporal and can be used for the past, present, or future. The preterite (imperfect with *waw* consecutive) וַיִּמְצְאוּ establishes the time frame of past action, and so the Qal (G) masculine

---

[1] See BDB; *HALOT*; *DCH*.

plural participle of נָפַל is translated accordingly. They had died on the previous day and now lay dead, thus "fallen." See Joüon, § 121 f. The LXX, appropriately, translates נֹפְלִים with a perfect participle, πεπτωκότας.

31:9 וַיְשַׁלְּחוּ ... לְבַשֵּׂר—"And they sent ... to tell the good news." The Piel (D) of שָׁלַח here and in the parallel verse 1 Chr 10:9 (וַיְשַׁלְּחוּ) means "send (messengers)" or "**send** ... [a] herald" (*DCH*, Piel, 4 b). It is unlikely that the verb here refers to "sending" spoils of war, as the Piel meant in 30:26, and as the LXX interprets it here (ἀποστέλλουσιν αὐτά). The Piel of בָּשַׂר (here the infinitive construct with לְ: לְבַשֵּׂר) usually refers to proclaiming good news (BDB, Piel, 1, 3), even preaching the Gospel, as does the Suffering Servant (Is 61:1, quoted in Lk 4:18; cf. Acts 10:36). See the Piel of בָּשַׂר in a Gospel sense also in, e.g., Is 40:9; 41:27; 52:7; Nah 2:1 (ET 1:15); Ps 96:2. Of course, a message that is "good news" (Gospel) for one people is "bad news" (Law) for their enemies, and here the Philistines triumph—for now. The Piel of בָּשַׂר involves this dual significance of "good news"/"bad news" here and in 1 Sam 4:17; 2 Sam 1:20; 4:10; 18:19, 20, 26 (see also 2 Sam 18:31).

בֵּית עֲצַבֵּיהֶם—This means "the temples of their idols." The noun עָצָב denotes a statue meant to represent a god. The identical suffixed plural recurs in 2 Sam 5:21, where again עֲצַבֵּיהֶם, "their idols," refers to those of the Philistines. In a construct phrase, a singular *nomen regens* (בֵּית) can be used with a plural *nomen rectum* (עֲצַבֵּיהֶם) to express the plural of the phrase, thus "temples of ..." (see GKC, § 124 r). Contrast the singular בֵּית דָּגוֹן, "the temple of Dagon," in 1 Sam 5:2, 5, where only one temple is meant (the ark of Yahweh could be put in only one).

31:10 עַשְׁתָּרוֹת—This feminine plural noun is translated as "the Astartes." See the second textual note on 7:3.

וְאֶת־גְּוִיָּתוֹ תָּקְעוּ בְּחוֹמַת בֵּית שָׁן:—"And they attached his body to the wall of Beth-shan." The feminine noun גְּוִיָּה (also twice in 31:12) refers to a body of a human or an animal, whether alive (e.g., Gen 47:18) or dead (e.g., Judg 14:8). 1 Chr 10:10 states וְאֶת־גֻּלְגָּלְתּוֹ תָקְעוּ בֵּית דָּגוֹן, "and they attached his skull to the temple of Dagon" (for "the temple of Dagon," see 1 Sam 5:2, 5). This is not a contradiction, since Saul head's had been removed from his body (1 Sam 31:9). The verb תָּקַע can mean "to thrust, drive" a weapon into someone, e.g., into Absalom in 2 Sam 18:14, but here and in 1 Chr 10:10 it refers to "fastening" a body/head to a wall (see BDB, Qal, 1). It can also refer to "blowing" the shofar (1 Sam 13:3; 2 Sam 2:28; 18:16; 20:1, 22).

31:11 וַיִּשְׁמְעוּ אֵלָיו יֹשְׁבֵי יָבֵישׁ גִּלְעָד אֵת אֲשֶׁר־עָשׂוּ פְלִשְׁתִּים לְשָׁאוּל:—The MT must mean "when the inhabitants of Jabesh-gilead heard *about him*, what the Philistines had done to Saul." The preposition אֶל can mean "regarding, concerning" (see BDB, 6). However, the LXX, the Syriac, and the Vulgate omit any translation of the suffixed preposition אֵלָיו, leaving only the direct object (... אֵת). This simplifies the syntax: "when the inhabitants of Jabesh-gilead heard what the Philistines had done to Saul." 1 Chr 10:11 is similar to those versions, but includes two instances of the noun כֹּל, "all" (which is also in the next verse, 1 Sam 31:12 ‖ 1 Chr 10:12a):

וַיִּשְׁמְעוּ כֹּל יָבֵישׁ גִּלְעָד אֵת כָּל־אֲשֶׁר־עָשׂוּ פְלִשְׁתִּים לְשָׁאוּל:

When all Jabesh-gilead heard all that the Philistines did to Saul ...

31:12 אִישׁ חַיִל—This means "a skilled soldier." This construct phrase is similar to בֶּן־חַיִל, for which, see the third textual note on 14:52.

וַיִּשְׂרְפוּ אֹתָם—Literally "and they burned them." The pronominal suffix on אֹתָם is masculine plural, whereas the noun גְּוִיָּה, referring to their bodies in 31:10, 12, is feminine. The verb שָׂרַף often denotes the burning of portions of sacrifices. It also frequently denotes burning in order to destroy objects that are contaminated or unclean, including the cities and possessions of enemies (e.g., Deut 13:17 [ET 13:16]; Josh 6:24), the bodies and possessions of Israelite apostates (Josh 7:15, 25), and false gods (Deut 7:5, 25; 9:21; 12:3, 31). This method was also used for human sacrifice (e.g., Jer 7:31; 19:5). In reference to human bones it can be rendered as "cremate" (*DCH*, s.v. שׂרף I, Qal [G], 4, citing 1 Ki 13:2; 2 Ki 23:16, 20; Amos 2:1; 2 Chr 34:5). In many contexts the verb has a decidedly negative connotation. As for why the men of Jabesh deemed it necessary to burn the bodies and bury only the remaining bones (1 Sam 31:13), they may have considered the bodies to have been defiled by the Philistines' capture, possession, and abuse of them.

31:13 הָאֶשֶׁל—This means "the tamarisk tree." See the second textual note on 22:6. 1 Chr 10:12 states that the bodies were burned under "the terebinth in Jabesh" (הָאֵלָה בְּיָבֵשׁ), but does not say where the bones were buried. (For אֵלָה, "terebinth," see the second textual note on 10:3, which has אֵלוֹן, which also means "terebinth.")

בְּיָבֵשָׁה—This means "in Jabesh." Occasionally the locative *he* is appended to a noun with a preposition. In such cases the locative *he* has lost its original directional force (GKC, § 90 e) and need not be reflected in translation.

וַיָּצֻמוּ—"And they fasted." The verb צוּם can refer to participating in a national or communal fast in mourning or penitence.[2]

Commentary

Nisan (March/April) 1009 BC

Parallel: 1 Sam 31:1–13 ‖ 1 Chr 10:1–12

With no notice the author quickly shifts the scene[3] to the battle on Mount Gilboa with an immediate report of the rout of Israel's army (31:1). Next the narrative focuses directly on Saul and his sons, and the author reports the death of the three sons fighting for Israel (31:2). "Abinadab" is mentioned here for the first time. While it is tempting to equate him with "Ishvi" (14:49), there is no warrant for doing so. It is possible that "Abinadab" was born after Saul began to reign and so has not been mentioned earlier. Alternately, he may have been

---

[2] Judg 20:26; 1 Sam 7:6; 2 Sam 1:12; Zech 7:5; Esth 4:16; Ezra 8:23; hypocritically, Is 58:3, 4; Jer 14:12.

[3] For the place of 1 Samuel 31 within the larger structure of 27:1–31:13, see the beginning of the commentary on 27:1–12. See also figure 27, "Chronology of Events in 1 Samuel 28–2 Samuel 1," at the end of the commentary on 29:1–11.

a son of Saul's concubine, Rizpah.[4] With these three sons of Saul slain,[5] the Philistines concentrated their fight on Saul's position, and we are told that the Philistine "archers … found him" (31:3).

Saul, though "severely wounded," was still alive. The Israelite king might have been evacuated—he expected another blow of a sword would be necessary to finish him off (31:4). However, he apparently had accepted the prediction that he would fall into the hands of the Philistines (28:19). His fear was that the Philistines would make sport of him and torture him. His characterization of them as "uncircumcised" mirrors the contempt shown for them previously by Jonathan and David when fighting the Philistines in God's name (14:6; 17:26, 36). This creates an irony, since Saul was not fighting Yahweh's battle here. Yahweh had turned against him because of his persistent infidelity to the divine Word (28:16–19; see also, previously, 15:22–16:1). In fact, his disobedience had begun as soon as he had been anointed king.[6] Considering the Philistines' abuse of Samson some years earlier (Judg 16:20–21), Saul's fear of Philistine torture was not unfounded. Saul, therefore, asked his armor bearer to slay him (1 Sam 31:4). The request shares similar wording with Abimelech's request to his armor bearer (Judg 9:54). By recording Saul's words in this way the author is leading his readers to compare the two men—the first one illegitimately claimed Israel's throne without Yahweh's blessing, and the second clung to the throne after Yahweh had removed his blessing.[7] One would die from an armor bearer's blow, the other from a self-inflicted wound (1 Sam 31:4).

We are told that the armor bearer was not willing to grant the king's demand because he was "very afraid" (31:4). We are not told what made him afraid, but this allows the author to set up a contrast between Saul's armor bearer and the Amalekite who falsely claimed to have killed Saul (2 Sam 1:2–16) and was "not afraid" to do so (2 Sam 1:14). Thus, the author *implies* that the armor bearer, like David before him,[8] would not kill Yahweh's anointed king out of fear and reverence for God.

The next two verses summarize the defeat: Saul, his sons, his armor bearer, and "all his men" died together (31:5–6). The reference to all of Saul's men ought not to be read too broadly and probably denotes only Saul's immediate squadron of elite troops and bodyguards, since the army's commander, Abner, did not die in the battle (2 Sam 2:8). In addition, the men across the valley— that is, on the north of the Jezreel Valley—fled their settlements, as did the

---

[4] For Rizpah, see 2 Sam 3:7; 21:8–10. See further the discussion of all of Saul's sons in the commentary on 1 Sam 14:47–52.

[5] See the second textual notes on 31:2 and 31:6.

[6] See the discussion of 10:7 in "Samuel Anoints Saul (9:26–10:8)" in the commentary on 9:26–10:16, including figure 16, "Saul's Faltering Accession." See also the beginning of the commentary on 10:17–27a.

[7] E.g., 15:22–16:1. Saul also acknowledged David's ascendancy in 24:18, 21 (ET 24:17, 20); 26:21, 25.

[8] See 1 Samuel 24 and 1 Samuel 26.

men across the Jordan Valley east of the Jezreel Valley (31:7). The Philistines' occupation of these sites may have been intended to enable a deeper penetration into Israelite Galilee.

It was not until the next day that the Philistines found the bodies of Saul and his three sons (31:8). We are not told how they treated the sons, but we are given the details of their treatment of Saul's body (31:9). The cutting off of the dead monarch's head parallels David's treatment of Goliath's corpse (17:51). The stripping off of armor also was part of collecting trophies of their victory (cf. 17:54). More importantly, there is no mention of any Philistine capture of the symbols of Saul's royal authority—his crown and armlet—since these had already been confiscated by the Amalekite, who would later report Saul's death to David (2 Sam 1:10). The "gospel" or "good news"[9] of the triumph was sent throughout Philistia, with the Philistines using their pagan temples as the pulpits from which to proclaim their dominance over Israel and their gods' victory over Israel's God.[10] That Saul's armor was placed in the temple of the Astartes implies this, though we are not told where that temple was located (31:10). Astarte was the goddess of fertility, sexuality, and war (see the second textual note on 7:3).

The Philistines affixed Saul's body to the walls of Beth-shan, a city in the eastern end of the Jezreel Valley, near the Jordan Valley. The site is now called Tell el-Husn. This indicates the impressive nature of the Philistine conquest. It also suggests why the men of Jabesh in Transjordan Gilead heard about it the same day and could travel all night to retrieve Saul's remains (31:11–12). These verses also supplement the earlier notice when readers were told only of Saul's body being affixed to the wall of Beth-shan (31:10). Now we know that the bodies of his sons were also placed there.

The retrieval of the bodies of Saul and his sons by the soldiers of Jabesh accorded them the honor and respect that was proper to show to the royal family (31:12–13). This was an especially appropriate act for the men of Jabesh-gilead, since Saul had rescued Jabesh at the beginning of his reign (10:27b–11:15). The bones were buried in a prominent spot, and later David would have the bones of Saul and Jonathan moved to the tomb of Saul's father, Kish (2 Sam 21:12–14).

Saul's death was not an honorable one. He had consulted a medium and encountered a demonic specter representing itself as Samuel (28:3–25). He

---

[9] The tidings were a kind of "gospel" from the Philistine perspective; see the first textual note on 31:9.

[10] Contrast 5:2–7, where Yahweh, enthroned on his ark, engaged in personal combat with the grain god Dagon and decapitated him. Both Israel and its foes recognized that battles between the armies of Yahweh and the forces of pagan peoples were direct confrontations of God with pagan gods. See the fourth textual note and the commentary on 1:3; also, e.g., 4:3a. From the Philistine vantage point, see 4:6–8. Their placement of the ark of Yahweh in the temple of Dagon (5:2) was their way of showing that, in their mind, their defeat of the Israelites meant that the God of Israel was now subservient to their own god (even though their assumption was short-lived [5:3–7]).

believed the demon's prediction, and his misplaced faith led to his suicide.[11] His last recorded meal was of the occultist's food in her house (28:23–25; cf. Prov 9:13–18). Apparently unrepentant to the end, he despaired of God's help when he was wounded and broke the Fifth Commandment (Ex 20:13; Deut 5:17) by committing suicide. The cremation of his body also suggests defilement.[12]

However, in the burial of his bones, his remains were treated honorably as befitting the high office to which God had called him. The men of Jabesh showed respect to God and the authority he had established over them. Their reverence for the body of the fallen king and his sons was in keeping with the Fourth Commandment (Ex 20:12; Deut 5:16), as well as Deut 21:22–23, which likely influenced the way the body of Jesus was retrieved from the cross and buried instead of being left exposed.[13] The sanctity of human life requires the body (even of an unbeliever who has perished in sin) to be treated reverently. This also reminds Christians that they, too, ought to honor all authority that God has established even though the actions and character of the person holding the office may not be in keeping with the demands of God's holy Law (Rom 13:7). Indeed, despite all of Saul's sins, God used him to bring some blessings to Israel (1 Sam 14:47–48; 2 Sam 1:24).

The portion of the book of Samuel we know as 1 Samuel concludes on this somber note of the defeat of Israel by "Yahweh's enemies" (30:26) and the shameful death and unusual burial of Israel's first king. However, that is only half the story. "Yahweh kills and makes alive; he brings down to Sheol and brings up [again]" (2:6). David had been anointed (16:1–13) and was alive, and the narrative would continue. The nation would undergo a "resurrection"

---

[11] See "Reasons for Saying No" in "Did Samuel Actually Appear to Saul at Endor?" in the commentary on 28:3–25.

[12] See the second textual note on 31:12. In the NT, eternal damnation is often described as burning in the fires of hell (e.g., Mt 5:22; 18:9; Lk 16:23–24; James 3:6; Rev 19:20; 20:10–15). However, given the depiction of Jonathan throughout the book of Samuel as a devout believer in Yahweh, the cremation of his remains here in 1 Sam 31:12 should not be interpreted as a sign of his eternal condemnation.

[13] The removal of Jesus' body from the cross before the Sabbath (Jn 19:31–42) is consistent with Deut 21:22–23. For the reverent care of Jesus' body, see Jn 19:38–42; see also Lk 23:50–24:1. A body left on a cross or otherwise exposed would become carrion for birds of prey (2 Sam 21:10; see also 1 Sam 17:44, 46). The OT refers to "hanging" or "impaling" as methods of execution; they were precursors to the Roman practice of crucifixion. The bodies of Saul and his sons may well have been affixed (תָּקַע; see the second textual note on 31:10) to the city wall by some form of impalement. 2 Sam 21:12 uses the verb תָּלָא (Qere) or its by-form תָּלָה (Kethib), "hang," for the way in which the Philistines attached the bodies of Saul and his sons to the wall. (For תָּלָה, "hang," see 2 Sam 4:12; see also, e.g., Gen 40:19, 22; 41:13; Josh 8:29; 10:26; Esth 2:23; 7:10; 9:13–14.) This (תָּלָה) is the verb in Deut 21:22–23 for "hanging" a body on a tree, which precipitates a divine curse, literally "a hanged man is a curse of God" (Deut 21:23). The apostle Paul largely follows LXX Deut 21:23 in translating that clause as "cursed is everyone who is hung on a tree" (ἐπικατάρατος πᾶς ὁ κρεμάμενος ἐπὶ ξύλου) to support the declaration "Christ redeemed us from the curse of the law by becoming a curse for us" (Gal 3:13; cf. 2 Cor 5:21). Cf. the public display in the city of the bodies of the "two witnesses" prior to their resurrection and ascension to heaven (Rev 11:3–12). Cf. also the third textual note on 1 Sam 31:4.

as the people were delivered from their enemies (cf. 2:1) under the faithful reign of their new anointed king. Moreover, the promises of Yahweh concerning a greater Anointed One would be fulfilled: "He [Yahweh] will give strength to his King and lift up the horn of his Anointed One" (2:10). "I [Yahweh] will raise for myself a faithful priest. ... I will build a secure house for him, and my Anointed One will serve in my presence forever" (2:35). And to the new king of Israel and to the whole people of God would be given still more promises of that Anointed One, the Son of David, who would build Yahweh's house and reign on David's throne forever.[14]

---

[14] See 2 Samuel 7 and "Christ in Samuel" in the introduction. See also, e.g., Is 9:5–6 (ET 9:6–7); Mt 1:1; 22:42–45; Lk 1:32; Rom 1:3.

Index of Subjects

Aaron, 24–25, 88, 103–6, 116–17, 224, 297, 349, 383

Abdon, 14, 219, 280

Abel-meholah, 358

Abiathar, 104, 256, 429, 432–33, 435–36, 441–42, 534, 559

Abiel, 176, 279–80

Abigail, 25, 360, 472, 481, 506–7, 551, 558

Abihu, 152

Abijah, 2–3, 64, 116, 223, 482

Abimelech, 253, 417, 436, 569

Abinadab (of Kiriath-jearim), 124, 148, 152

Abinadab (son of Jesse), 310, 312

Abinadab (son of Saul), 15, 278, 280, 530, 568

Abiram, 88

Abishai, 313, 456, 460, 463, 465, 493, 500–501

Abner, 9, 15, 18, 194, 199, 277, 279–80, 343, 399, 461, 463, 495, 501–2, 531, 535, 569

Abraham, 23, 64, 73, 240, 270, 299, 308, 340, 402, 425, 481, 501

Absalom, 3, 20–22, 26, 66, 131, 240, 313, 344, 349, 366, 402, 404, 487, 508

Absolution, 56, 95, 179. See also Forgiveness

Abstinence, 410–12

Achan, 203, 267

Achish, 17, 416–19, 508–9, 511–17, 544, 546–47

Adadah, 556, 563

Adam, 66, 242, 297, 496, 501

Adonijah, 66, 313, 319, 429

Adoption, 54

Adriel, 278, 358, 361

Adullam, 372–73, 421–22, 440–41

Adultery, 10, 20, 22, 25–26, 65, 106, 298, 311, 383

Adversaries. See Enemies

Aeneas, 416

Agag, 289–90, 294, 300, 384

Age, 16–17, 19, 55, 91, 101–2, 104, 223, 231, 238–39, 329

Aggravation, 45

Agreement, 369, 390, 397–400, 404, 449. See also Covenant

Ahab, 64, 528–29

Ahaziah, 11–12

Ahijah, 251, 253, 256

Ahimelech, 256, 401, 409–13, 431, 492–93, 499–500

Ahinoam, 21, 278, 488, 506–7, 558

Ahitub, 132, 256

Aijalon, 42, 245, 262, 267

'Ain Jalud, 542

Al-Khalil, 563

"All Israel," 9, 85

Alliteration, 233

Allusion, 121, 159, 527, 529, 538

Alphabet, 273

Altar, 30, 73, 187, 268. See also Offering; Sacrifice

Amalekites, 16, 29, 245, 278, 293–94, 512, 532–33, 550, 558

Amarna Letters, 356

Amasa, 535

Ambiguity, 160, 214, 269, 319. See also Deception

Aminadab, 148–49

Ammonites, 19–20, 22, 160, 198, 206–7, 211, 245, 277–78

Amnon, 20–22, 26, 66, 344, 488, 508

Amputation, 138

Anagram, 106

Ancestors, 220. See also Genealogy

Ancients, 456, 508

Angels, 44, 317–18, 544, 547. See also Demons

Animals, 293–94, 296, 340–41, 412, 436, 497, 512

Anna, 381

Anointed One, 24–25, 74, 77–78, 80–81, 102, 104–7, 223, 254, 303, 308, 380, 458–59, 495, 572. See also Christ

Anointing, 77, 306, 311, 500. *See also* Baptism; David, anointing of; Saul, anointing of

Anonymity, 183–84

Anthropomorphism, 295

Antiquity, 508

Aphek, 119, 124–25, 245, 372–73, 525–27, 545, 548, 558–59

Aphorism, 378

Apostasy, 67, 83, 204, 262, 299, 477, 501–2, 534, 568
of Saul, 286, 295, 308, 318, 378, 398, 418, 425, 429, 529, 538

Appearance, 303, 311, 319, 347, 383

Appointment, 106, 163, 224

Approval, 59

Arad, 512, 563

Araunah, 21, 30

Archaeology, 11–13, 132, 158, 334, 542

Arimathea, 42

Ark of the covenant, 4–5, 13, 19–20, 27–28, 96, 105, 110, 120, 122–24, 126, 134–35, 138–40, 142–43, 147–53, 250–51

Armoni, 530, 565

Armor, 17, 327–28, 336, 338, 340–42, 345, 570
of God, 256, 342

Armor bearer, 247, 253, 320, 337, 565, 569

Army, 16–17, 44, 122, 164, 171, 202, 244, 277, 284, 326, 348, 411, 421, 436, 439, 515, 526. *See also* Soldier; War; Yahweh, of armies

Aroer, 556, 563

Arrogance, 70, 78–79, 136, 288, 331, 473

Ashdod, 124, 138, 245, 514, 526

Asherah, 155

Ashhur, 64

Ashkelon, 124, 137, 514, 526

Astarte, 155, 226, 570

Astuteness, 345, 472, 483

Atonement, 79, 111, 144, 156. *See also* Offering; Sacrifice

Atonement, Day of, 89, 275

Author of Samuel, 1–3

Authority, 26, 56, 80, 114, 186, 270–71, 273, 459, 466, 501

Azariah, 417

Azekah, 245, 325

Baal, 15, 17, 130, 152, 155, 171, 226, 278, 402, 476

Baal (of Saul's genealogy), 280

Baalah, 123

Baal-shalishah, 183

Bag, 332

Baking, 165

Balaam, 299

Ban, 283–84, 287, 293, 296, 555

Baptism, 150, 153, 159, 194, 196, 227, 253–54, 256, 311, 381, 500. *See also* Grace, means of; John the Baptist; Sacraments

Barak, 226, 535

Barrenness, 27–28, 52–54, 72, 77, 79

Barzillai, 404

Bathsheba, 20, 26–27, 29, 56, 313

Battle, 119, 125, 127, 159–60, 172, 197, 214, 226, 245, 266, 293–94, 325–26, 328, 330, 350, 525, 534, 570. *See also* War

Battle, spiritual, 256, 355

Beam, 328, 338

Bear, 341

Beauty, 304–5, 472, 483, 487. *See also* Appearance; Eyes

Bedan, 219

Beer, 50

Beersheba, 169, 425, 512, 557, 563

Belief. *See* Faith; Trust

Believers. *See* Christians

Beliya'al, 50

Beloved, 12

Belshazzar, 64

Benediction, 55, 90. *See also* Blessing

Benedictus, 77–78, 307

Benjamin, 42, 131–32, 176, 182, 213, 341, 347, 430

Bereavement, 290

Beth-aven, 233

Beth-car, 157

Bethel, 133, 161, 169, 195, 197, 233, 245, 556, 563

Bethlehem, 43, 158, 195, 245, 307, 338–39, 343, 383, 409

Beth-shemesh, 124, 147–48, 151–52

Beth-zur, 556, 563

Bezek, 214

Bias, 4, 78, 168–69

Bilhah, 56, 66

Binding, 344, 347

Biography, 8–9

Bir Rakhmeh, 563

Birth, 349, 395, 403

Bishops, 356. *See also* Pastors

Bitterness, 48, 289, 420

Blame, 242, 297

Blessing, 55, 90, 105, 179, 185, 234, 368, 445, 450, 478–80, 498, 504

Blindness, 129, 131

Blood, 171, 262, 268, 369, 477. *See also* Lord's Supper; Meat

Boaz, 310, 312, 319

Body, 73, 110, 533, 567–68, 570–71. *See also* Lord's Supper

Body of Christ, 67, 481. *See also* Church

Bodyguard, 427, 432, 516–17

Boiling, 84

Bottle, 191, 483, 487

Bow, 71, 565

Bowdlerization, 15, 17, 278, 476

Bowing, 403. *See also* Worship

Boy, 62, 88, 109, 177, 331–32, 335, 397. *See also* Servant

Bozez, 248

Bread, 44, 60, 191–92, 195, 316, 319, 431

Bread, unleavened, 525, 540

Bread of the Presence, 408, 410–12, 426, 430

Bribes, 169–70, 217, 223

Bride of Christ, 67, 481

Bridegroom, 358, 481

Bride-price, 65, 359–62

Bronze, 328, 338

Bronze Age, 132

Brother, 257, 324, 330, 335–36, 339, 349, 433, 473, 493, 555–56

Bull (bovine), 60, 62

Bull (deity), 132

Bundle, 478, 487

Burial, 425, 468, 471, 568, 570–71

Caleb, 43, 152, 360, 450, 472, 483, 560

Calf, 171, 330, 524

Call, 114, 381, 495, 503

Calvin, John, 404

Camel, 433, 512

Camp, 338, 491, 515–17

Canaan, 6–7, 170, 471, 493, 535. *See also* Gods; Philistines

Capture, 129, 201, 263, 276, 439, 442, 451, 551, 558. *See also* Ark of the covenant; Spoils

Carmel, 482, 506, 551, 563, 557

Cattle, 60, 62, 145, 150–51, 171, 302, 307, 330, 441, 524. *See also* Bull; Calf; Cows

Census, 21–22, 25–26, 30, 290

Chair, 54

Change, 91, 193, 285, 289, 291, 295, 299, 308, 378, 415. *See also* Regret; Repentance

Chapter divisions, 404

Chariot, 233

Cheese, 339

Cherethites, 560

Chiasm, 483, 540

Chieftain, claim that David was, 13, 418

Children, 48, 52, 56, 90

Chileab, 488

Choosing, 25, 98, 203–4, 243, 304, 308, 328, 466. *See also* Election; Foreknowledge; Predestination

Christ, 23–25, 28–29, 56, 66, 81, 96, 103, 106, 254, 256, 295, 299, 311, 318, 337, 355–56, 363, 381, 412, 418, 422, 448, 458, 467, 481, 488, 572. *See also* Anointed One; Son of David
death and resurrection of, 79, 378, 389, 440, 501, 571

Christians, 26, 56, 67, 73, 151, 214, 309, 342, 382–83, 402, 433, 503, 562, 571

Chronicle, 116

Chronicles (book), 9–10, 31

Chronology, 13–23, 226, 525, 548. *See also* Time; Year

Church, 56, 114. *See also* Body of Christ

Church, early, 187

Circle, 447

Circumcision, 253, 340, 412, 569

Cistern, 376

Cities, 556–57, 561, 563

Clan, 181, 201, 394

Cleverness, 446

Clothing, 512. *See also* Ephod; Garments; Robe; Spoils

Cognates, 375

Commander, 427

Commandment, Eighth, 402

Commandment, Fifth, 369, 398, 402, 440, 571

Commandment, First, 158, 499

Commandment, Fourth, 369, 459, 571

Commandment, Second, 126, 270

Commandments, Ten, 125, 346

Communion. *See* Lord's Supper

Company, 375

Compassion, 295

Composition of Samuel, 1–8, 166–69

Conception, 380

Concubines, 20, 64–65, 279

Confession
   of sin, 292, 298

Confirmation (of Saul as king), 198

Conscience, 256, 383, 440, 454, 458–59, 479, 487

Consecration, 152–53. *See also* Sanctification

Conspiring, 425–26

Cook, 164, 181

Coregency, 14

Counsel, 481

Counting, 250, 291. *See also* Census

Courtroom, 217

Covenant, 5, 24, 166, 209, 253, 268, 308, 339–40, 345–46, 348, 392, 404, 426, 468, 558. *See also* Agreement

Cowardice, 204, 232, 327, 338–39, 451, 534

Cows, 145, 150–51, 302, 307

Crag, 248

Craziness. *See* Insanity

Creation, 79, 225, 228, 562

Creditor, 420

Cremation, 568, 571

Crete, 416, 560

Criticism, biblical, 3–8, 31, 33–34, 77–78, 122, 166–68, 324, 368, 379, 459–60, 525

Cross, 254, 378, 415

Crucifixion, 378, 389, 565, 571. *See also* Impaling

Cubit, 326–27. *See also* Height

Curse, 105, 111, 259–60, 266–68, 270, 272, 299, 496, 502, 571. *See also* Oath

Custom, 509

Cutting, 209, 457. *See also* Covenant; Robe

Dagon, 27–28, 135, 138–40, 150, 567, 570

Damnation, 73, 378, 534, 571. *See also* Judgment; Predestination

Dan, 11–12, 42

Dance, 30, 351

Daniel, 488

Date of Samuel, 2–4

Dathan, 88

Daughter, 50, 64–65, 171, 337, 346, 360, 362, 551

David, 1–5, 8–10, 64, 76, 78–79, 82, 105–6, 160. *See also* Son of David
   anointing of, 25, 77, 80–81, 307, 355, 418, 422, 441, 458–59, 562, 571–72
   as compared to Saul, 239, 243, 292, 305–6, 308, 311, 317, 341, 362, 418, 432, 439, 466, 476, 498, 513, 538, 559, 561
   heart or character of, 25–26, 29, 236, 292, 308–9, 343, 433, 465, 467, 481, 500, 558–59

Day, 44–45, 58, 86, 121, 185, 262, 287, 329, 352, 378, 389, 394, 507, 560. *See also* Atonement, Day of; Day, Last; Sabbath; "To this day"

Day, Last, 73, 433. *See also* Eschatology

Deacon, 67

Dead Sea, 450

Death, 72–73. *See also* Christ, death and resurrection of; Samuel (prophet), apparition of; Saul, death of

Deborah, 486, 535

Debt, 420

Deception, 126–27, 307, 371, 401–3, 409–10, 513, 517, 546–47. *See also* Ambiguity; Fraud; Prophecy, false

Dedication, 90–91

Deliverance. *See* Salvation

Demeanor, 415

Demons, 317–18, 342, 481, 521, 529–30, 533, 536, 539, 558, 570–71. *See also* Devil; Possession, spiritual; Samuel (prophet), apparition of

Depression, 46

Derision. *See* Insult

Derogation. *See* Insult

Descendants, 90, 101, 104, 400, 404, 467–68. *See also* Dynasty

Desert, 221, 445, 450. *See also* Wilderness

Deserting, 241, 474, 542

Designation. *See* Ruler, designated

Despising, 100, 285

Destruction, 236, 244, 283, 293

Devil, 127, 342, 355, 440, 448. *See also* Demons; Divination; Idolatry; Necromancy; Possession, spiritual; Satan

Dhahret el-Kolah, 444

Dibon, 12

Dinah, 362, 477

Directions, 445

Disciples, 194, 501

Discipline, 95

Discretion, 480, 487–88

Disguise, 535

Disrespect, 88. *See also* Insult

Divination, 142, 149–297, 521, 535–36

Division, 448. *See also* Army; Chapter divisions; Spoils
of Israel, 9, 14, 67, 214, 355–56
of Samuel, 1, 33

Divorce, 66–67

Dod, 12

Dodo, 336

Doeg, 409, 411–13, 430–32

Dog, 341, 456, 466, 472

Drawing, 158

Dream, 534

Drinking, 47, 553

Drunkenness, 49, 55, 487–88

Dummy, 367, 371

Duty, 93

Dwelling, 99

Dynasty, 12, 23, 242, 478, 486, 539

Ears, 110, 388

Earth, 73, 249

East, 445

Eating, 47, 262. *See also* Lord's Supper; Nourishment

Ebenezer, 123, 125, 157, 160

Ecstaticism. *See* Prophecy, ecstatic

Edom, 245, 278, 304

Egypt, 28, 50, 121–22, 138, 150, 186, 218, 284, 294, 336, 338

Egyptian, 553, 559–60

Ekron, 124, 139, 160, 334, 508, 514, 526

Elah Valley, 12, 325

Elders, 170, 375

Eleazar, 152

Election, 73, 244, 292. *See also* Choosing; Foreknowledge; Predestination

Elhanan, 4, 335–36

Eli, 13–14, 26–27, 29, 53–56, 63, 75–76, 95–96, 103–7, 113–15, 122–23, 131, 170, 253, 256, 381, 429

Eliab, 43, 339

Eliel, 43

Elihu, 43, 310

Elijah, 117, 377

Elisha, 117, 195, 349, 358

Elizabeth, 381

Elkanah, 43, 52–59, 62–63, 91, 113

Encouragement, 449

Endor, 527, 535, 558

Enemies, 74–75, 78, 245, 277–78, 360, 467, 523, 543, 547, 561

En-gedi, 372–73, 450–51, 458–59, 463–64, 482–83

Ephes-dammim, 325

Ephod, 89, 91, 98, 103, 250–51, 253, 413, 437, 441, 559

Ephraim, 42–43, 183

Ephrath, 43, 152, 195

Equipment, 408, 411

Esau, 64, 304, 349

Eschatology, 80, 85, 101, 249–50. *See also* Day, Last; Judgment

Eshbaal, 14–15, 18, 278. *See also* Ish-bosheth

Eshtemoa, 563

Es-Semuʿa, 563

Establishing, 59–60

Ether, 557, 563

Eunuchs, 171–72

Euphemism, 453, 475

Euphony, 51

Eve, 56, 66, 297, 340, 496, 501

Evening, 185, 211, 329, 389, 554

Excavation, 11–12

Exile, 2–6, 10, 225
of ark, 129–32

Exodus, 121, 127, 145, 150, 171, 191, 200, 218, 224–25, 283, 310, 559

Exploitation, 223, 346, 361

Eyes, 112, 206, 209, 212, 303–5, 311

Face, 45

Faith, 83, 221, 297, 337, 340, 371, 378, 384, 403, 440, 486. *See also* Trust

Faithfulness, 228–29, 262, 498, 503

Fall, 378

Family, 372, 422, 426, 466, 485, 502, 555. *See also* Brother; Daughter; Father; Husband; Marriage; Mother; Parent; Son; Wife

Fasting, 158, 267, 539, 568

Fat, 85, 87

Father, 194, 369, 466–67, 502. *See also* Patriarchs; Patristics
God as, 23, 79–81, 311, 337, 381, 472

Favor, 56, 81, 96, 150, 179, 234, 292, 320, 359, 368–69. *See also* Grace

Fear, 314, 409
of God, 29, 213–14, 227, 307

Feasts, 52, 487

Feet, 463, 488

Fellowship, 187–88, 195, 503

Fertility, 72, 79, 155

Festus, 418

Figs, 474, 485, 553

Firstborn, 43, 66, 329, 357

Fish, 138, 327

Flask, 191, 195

Flea, 456, 466–67, 497

Flour, 60, 62

Flow, 260

Following, 220, 227

Food, 71, 330

Foolishness, 235, 243, 259, 266, 472, 477, 483, 486, 539

Foot, 445

Forbearance, 295

Force. *See* Strength

Foreigners, 33, 172, 437

Foreknowledge, 448. *See also* Choosing; Election; Predestination

Foreskin, 359

Forest, 260, 422–23

Forever, 59, 102

Forgiveness, 150, 291, 381, 412. *See also* Absolution; Grace; Justification

Fork, 84, 87

Fornication, 65

Fragrance. *See* Odor

Fraud, 529. *See also* Deception; Divination; Necromancy

Friend, 397–98

Fur, 332

Gad (prophet), 1, 30, 116, 292, 423

Gad (tribe), 206

Garments, 376–77. *See also* Clothing

Gath, 124, 138, 160, 245, 326, 334, 338, 372–73, 414, 508, 510–11, 514, 526

Gather, 155

Gaza, 124, 245, 508, 512, 526, 559

Geba, 232, 245, 247

Genealogy, 182, 279–80, 310, 312–13

Generations, 310

Geshurites, 507–8

Gezer, 7, 508

Giantism, 341. *See also* Goliath

Gibeah, 182, 192, 212–13, 232, 247

Gibeonites, 21, 133, 361

Gideon, 64, 169, 226, 240

Gift, 178, 184, 319, 561, 563

Gilboa, Mount, 245, 520, 524, 526–27, 531, 540, 542, 568

Gilead, 42

Gilgal, 161, 196–97, 215, 245

Giving, 98–99

Gizrites, 508

Glory, 129–30, 132, 145, 150, 289

Glow, 274

Goad, 237

Goats, 275, 319

Gob, 334

Goddess, 50, 155, 570

Gods, 120–21, 170, 221, 522, 536–37, 560, 568. *See also* Idolatry; Polytheism

Going out, 214, 268, 350, 421

Goliath, 4, 12–13, 17, 25, 28, 33, 160, 197, 245, 309, 326, 335, 369, 479, 517

"Good-for-nothing," 50, 86, 102, 202, 204, 221, 485

Gospel, 23–24, 37, 114, 156, 172, 196, 223, 256, 311, 449. *See also* Law and Gospel; News

Gospels, 23, 81, 114

Governors, 417, 545–46

Grace, 29, 56, 73, 91, 179, 191, 221–22, 243, 292, 299, 337, 365, 384, 486. *See also* Favor
    means of, 150, 153, 186, 256, 381, 503 (*See also* Baptism; Lord's Supper)

Grain, 138, 140, 441

Grave, 79

Greatness, 94, 397, 498

Greave, 328

Greek, Old, 33–34

Grief, 384

Growth, 94, 96, 112

Guarding, 152, 429, 516, 555–56

Guilt, 429, 466, 495. *See also* Conscience; Offering, guilt; Repentance; Sins

Guy, 203, 475, 543

Hachilah, 444, 450, 459–60, 491, 499

Hagar, 52, 66

Haggai (prophet), 117

Hair, 217, 269, 304, 311

Hand, 120–21, 145, 163, 193, 228, 261, 286, 302, 326, 333, 407, 415, 428, 437, 444–45, 449, 457, 461–62, 494, 498

Hand, left, 341

Hanging, 571

Hannah, 24, 27, 52–56, 62–63, 66, 86, 89–90, 106, 380. *See also* Songs

Hanun, 19–20

Hapax legomena, 102, 178, 237–38, 249, 261, 328, 332, 351–52, 389, 393, 395, 409, 446–47, 479

Harassment, 473

Hardening, 94

Harem, 172, 511

Harm, 455. *See also* Wickedness

Haughtiness, 70, 78–79

Hazael, 11–12

Head, 210, 328, 342–43, 367, 463, 493, 499, 516–17, 570

Hearing, 51, 56, 93, 368. *See also* Obedience

Heart, 46, 78–79, 158, 193–94, 202, 228, 248, 331, 378, 383, 488, 505
    of David, 25, 236, 308–9, 481
    of God, 236, 242–43

Heaviness, 145, 565. *See also* Honor

Hebrews, 120, 232, 254, 545

Hebron, 10, 14–16, 18, 21, 116, 274, 277, 296, 325, 425, 441, 444, 450–51, 489, 558, 560, 562–63

Height, 42, 177, 202, 310, 326–27, 338, 340, 524

Heirs, 53–54. *See also* Inheritance

Hell, 73, 534, 571. *See also* Sheol

Helmet, 327

Hem, 462–63

Heman, 116, 169

Hemorrhoids. *See* Swellings

Hendiadys, 51, 177–78, 211, 263, 272, 283, 288, 333, 359, 393, 445, 474, 509

Hereth, 372–73, 422–23, 436

Herod, 65

Heth, 493

Hezron, 509

Hiding, 202–3, 365, 444, 446, 475

High place, 185, 194, 425

Hill, 136, 192, 194, 376. *See also* Ephraim; Hachilah

Hiring, 71. *See also* Mercenaries

History, 4–7, 10–13, 117, 166–67, 224, 239, 462–64

Hittites, 326–27, 409, 492–93, 520

Holiness, 75, 78, 149, 152–53, 224, 303, 407, 410–12

Holy Place, 114

Holy Spirit, 77, 125, 159, 193, 229, 254, 309, 311, 315–19, 355, 375, 377–78, 381, 418, 481, 500. *See also* Spirit

Hometown, 471

Homosexuality, 341, 347–49

Honey, 260–61, 266

Honor, 79, 100, 178, 544, 546

Hope, 1, 23–24, 27, 81

Hophni, 26–27, 53, 83–84, 86–88, 95–96, 103–4, 106–7, 122–23, 126, 131, 152, 256–57

Hoplite, 336

Horesh, 372–73

Hormah, 512, 557, 563

Horn, 75, 78, 81, 195, 306–7

Hosea (prophet), 117

Hospitality, 398, 411, 488, 515

Host, 44, 178

House. *See* Descendants; Dynasty; Temple

Humiliation, 46, 473

Humility, 27, 74, 80, 110, 158

Hunger, 69. *See also* Nourishment

Hurrian culture, 7

Husband, 62, 67, 506, 535. *See also* Elkanah; Polygamy

Hyenas, 236

Ibex, 453

Ichabod, 122, 129–30, 132

Idolatry, 125, 140, 150, 221, 288, 370, 384, 477, 497, 499, 502, 567

Immutability, 95, 285, 295, 299, 354, 379

Impaling, 494, 500, 565, 571. *See also* Crucifixion

Incarnation, 109, 114, 220. *See also* Christ

Incense, 103

Incest, 93

Inclusio, 306

Income, dishonest, 169–70

Incomparability, 78

Infantry, 122. *See also* Army

Infants, 381

Inheritance, 64, 66, 74, 191, 497, 502–3. *See also* Dynasty; Heirs

Inquiring (of Yahweh), 203, 268, 273–74, 309, 430–31, 435, 437, 439, 441–42, 520, 559

Insanity, 415–16, 418–19

Inscription, 11–13, 416, 475

Inspiration, 38, 318, 342

Insult, 19, 69, 120, 203, 254, 338–39, 341–42, 354, 396, 401, 403, 430, 473, 484, 486, 543, 546

Intent, 331

Intercession, 94–96, 116, 156, 380

Invitation, 142, 179, 182, 200

Iron, 244, 328

Iron Age, 336, 341

Irony, 152, 320, 340–41, 343, 355, 379, 412, 418, 432, 500, 536–37, 545, 558, 569

Isaac, 52, 91, 270, 349. *See also* Patriarchs

Isaiah (prophet), 117

Ish-bosheth, 15, 245, 278, 530, 539, 565. *See also* Eshbaal

Ishmael, 52

Ishtar, 155

Ishvi, 15, 278, 568

Israel, 9–10, 27, 67, 120, 123, 125, 156, 166, 186, 222, 224, 228–29, 355–56. *See also* "All Israel" as Northern Kingdom, 14–15, 18, 214

Issachar, 520, 535

Izates, 65

ʿIzbet Sartah, 125

Jabesh-gilead, 212–15, 226, 245, 570

Jabin, 218, 535

Jacob, 64–66, 161, 195, 224, 267, 347, 349, 362. *See also* Patriarchs

Jael, 479

Jair, 335

Jarmuth, 557, 563

Jattir, 563

Jealousy, 66, 320, 346, 355, 370, 409, 481, 502

Jebel Fuquʿah, 520

Jebusites, 334, 342–43

Jehoiachin, 64

Jehoram, 64

Jehoshaphat, 195, 213

Jehu, 12, 195, 402

Jephthah, 219, 226, 267, 353

Jerahmeel, 64, 509, 512, 563

Jeremiah, 116

Jerusalem, 2–3, 11, 14–15, 67, 124, 133, 197, 245, 342–43, 409, 501, 521
    David's reign in, 18–22

Jeshanah, 157

Jeshimon, 445, 450, 460, 491, 499

Jesse, 303, 307–8, 310, 312, 315, 319, 338–39, 343, 496

Jesus. *See* Christ

Jethro, 349, 403

Jezreel (north), 245, 278, 464, 488, 499, 515–16, 526

Jezreel (south), 542, 547–48

Joab, 9, 11, 18, 20–22, 25, 253, 290, 292, 313, 320, 337, 493, 500

Joash, 64, 239

Joel (son of Samuel), 116, 169, 223

John the Baptist, 77, 81, 96, 381. *See also* Baptism

Jonah, 275

Jonathan, 15, 28, 131, 160, 240, 245, 252, 255–56, 268–71, 377, 449, 530, 571

Joram, 11–12, 195

Joseph (guardian of Jesus), 381

Joseph (son of Jacob), 66, 319, 349, 422

Joshua (son of Nun), 7, 14, 76, 152, 228, 251, 268, 273, 283, 355, 450, 512

Joshua the Beth-shemeshite, 151

Josiah, 6–7, 116, 519

Judah
    kingdom of, 2, 10, 14, 18, 214
    as son of Jacob, 402, 509
    territory of, 151, 160, 284, 294, 325, 373, 399, 409, 421–22, 436, 441, 449–50, 464, 471, 482, 488, 499, 511–13, 557–63
    tribe of, 43, 152, 214, 291, 355–56, 430, 448

Judas, 203, 295

Judges, 8, 14, 105, 117, 156, 159–61, 169–70, 222–24, 226, 229

Judgment, 73, 80, 112, 114, 157, 163, 249–50, 273, 368, 384, 429, 456, 466

Jug, 462–63, 495, 501

Justice, 105, 112, 163, 169–70, 220, 223, 270, 401, 440, 456, 509, 546

Justification, 114, 153, 340, 403, 457, 481, 486, 513. *See also* Righteousness

Kaige, 33–34

Keilah, 274, 372–73, 440–42

Kenites, 294, 509, 512, 514, 557, 563

Kenizzites, 509, 557, 563

Khirbet al-Karmil, 296, 563

Khirbet ʿArʿarah, 557, 563

Khirbet ʿAttir, 563

Khirbet el-ʿAter, 563

Khirbet el-Meshash, 563

Khirbet es-Shuweikeh, 325

Khirbet eṭ-Ṭubeiqah, 563

Khirbet Khoreisa, 422, 449

Khirbet Qeiyafa, 12–13, 334

Khirbet Safsafeh, 521

Khirbet Shuweikeh, 325

Kimchi, 138

King, 1, 4, 27, 30, 53, 57, 64–65, 74, 77, 80–81, 106, 126, 156, 164, 170–72, 299, 343, 346, 356, 410, 417, 546, 572. *See also* Ruler, designated

Kingdom, 13, 23–24, 242–43, 245, 346, 355, 368, 458. *See also* Monarchy

Kiriath-jearim, 123–24, 152–53, 251

Kish, 176–77, 182–83, 279–80, 570

Kiss, 348–49, 397, 403–4

Knowing, 51, 83, 221, 348, 407, 520

Kohath, 43, 52, 116

Korah, 88

Laban, 349, 362, 371

Lachmi, 336

Lamb, 81, 84–85, 156, 159, 284

Lament, 155, 158. *See also* Mourning; Weeping

Lamp, 113–14, 277

Land, 171–72, 260, 451

Land, promised, 152, 161, 191, 224–25, 293, 411, 450, 513

Langton, Stephen, 404

Law. *See also* Law and Gospel; Torah
as opposed to Gospel, 26, 80, 95, 220, 467
uses of, 26, 214

Law, civic, 186

Law, natural, 440, 562

Law and Gospel, 26–29, 38, 79, 103, 156, 186, 220, 229–30, 285, 467, 562, 567

Lawsuit, 456, 480

Laymen, 410, 412

Leadership, 14, 26, 82, 105, 115, 123, 156, 170, 224

Leah, 52, 56, 66, 362

Levites, 14, 42–43, 52, 54–55, 82, 88, 91, 151, 179, 191, 433

Lex talionis, 290

Life, 79, 478, 498–99, 501, 536, 571. *See also* Soul

Life, book of, 73

Life, eternal, 73, 256, 412, 478–79, 499, 501

Light, 28, 272

Linen, 89

Lion, 340–41

Listening. *See* Hearing; Obedience

Little, 267

Livestock, 171

Lord, 543. *See also* Yahweh

Lord's Supper, 44, 150, 153, 381, 411–12. *See also* Grace, means of; Sacraments

Lots, 203, 264–65, 269, 275

Love, 52–53, 320, 344–47, 349, 356, 361, 382, 481

Lowliness. *See* Humility

Loyalty, 320, 349, 369, 515

Luther, Martin, 380–85

Lying. *See* Deception

Lying down, 92

Lymph nodes, 136

Maacah, 56, 417, 508

Magnificat, 77–81

Malachi (prophet), 117

Malchi-shua, 15, 530

Malcontents, 420, 422, 442

Man, ascending, 24

"Man of God," 103–4, 106, 110, 183–85, 380

Man, old, 104, 375, 522

Man, young, 165, 304, 331–32

Manasseh, 417, 535

Mankind, 24, 496

Maoch, 417

Maon, 372–73, 450, 506

Marriage, 358, 410. *See also* Polygamy

Mary, 77–80, 381, 422, 479

Masada, 422

Masorah Magna, 111

Masoretic Text, 31–35

Matri, 203

Meadow, 147

Means of grace. *See* Grace, means of

Meat, 45, 53, 84–87, 147

Medium, 25, 29, 385, 519–21, 527–33

Meeting, tent of, 92–93, 95. *See also* Tabernacle; Tent

Melanchthon, Philip, 381

Melchizedek, 106

Mephibosheth, 10, 17, 28, 279–80, 346, 348, 456, 476, 530, 565

Merab, 357, 360–61, 467, 489

Mercenaries, 17, 255, 336, 417, 419, 560

Mercy, 156, 169, 292, 298, 368, 404, 411, 467

Merib-baal, 17, 476. *See also* Mephibosheth

Merism, 147

Messiah. *See* Anointed One; Christ

Metaphor, 67, 69, 78, 128, 217, 232, 290, 295, 344, 358, 426, 451, 454, 479, 488, 497, 503

Metonymy, 288

Micaiah, 528

Michal, 28, 105, 278, 357, 362, 370–72, 401, 466–67, 489, 506–7, 558

Michmash, 197, 240, 242, 244–45, 267, 271

Midianites, 240

Midwives, 402

Migron, 247

Military. *See* Army

Millo, 2

Ministry, 76, 81–82, 88, 156. *See also* Bishops; Pastors

Ministry, public, 114, 308, 381, 383, 410, 432–33. *See also* Pastors

Miracle, 381

Miriam, 353

Mistake, 497

Mizpah, 13, 124, 158, 161, 422

Mizpeh, 372, 421–22

Moab, 12, 226, 245, 277–78, 372, 422

Monarchy, 4, 8–10, 166–69, 173, 202, 215, 242. *See also* Kingdom

Monarchy, united, 14–16

Monergism, 101. *See also* Salvation

Monobazus, 65

Monogamy, 65–67

Monotheism, 78, 121, 158, 537

Month, 2, 157, 208, 389, 394, 507. *See also* Nisan; Sivan; Tishri; Ziv

Moon, 389, 394, 399

Moses, 14, 23, 76, 78, 103, 106, 116–17, 183, 223–24, 228, 273, 293, 339, 349, 380, 383, 403, 410. *See also* Torah

Mother, 56, 66, 300, 348–49. *See also* Parent

Mound, 393

Mountain, 447, 475. *See also* Gilboa, Mount; Sinai; Temple

Mourning, 131, 290, 384, 471, 482, 568. *See also* Lament; Weeping

Mouth, 69, 288

Murder, 25, 309, 369, 398, 402, 498. *See also* Abner; Amnon
as aim of Saul, 378, 401, 404, 440, 484
as committed by David, 25, 106, 292, 298

Music, 30, 116, 195, 315, 318–19, 351. *See also* Songs

Myriad, 351, 354

Mystery, 244, 292, 458

Nabal, 401, 472, 477, 483, 486–88, 505, 551, 558

Nadab, 152

Nahash, 32, 206–8, 212, 214, 254

Nahath, 43

Nakedness, 348–49, 377–78, 395

Name, 51, 56, 171, 227, 401, 430, 472, 474, 476–77, 486–87. *See also* Title of God, 75, 126, 390

Naomi, 349, 403

Naphtali (tribe), 42

Narrative, 8

Narrowness, 316, 523, 552

Nathan, 1, 23–25, 28, 30, 116, 380

Nations, 1, 166, 170, 182–83, 226, 278, 299

Nazirite, 55

Near East, ancient, 275, 397

Neck, 129

Necromancy, 385, 519, 521, 527–33, 535

Negev, 42, 512

Negev (Kenites, Judah, Jerahmeel), 509, 512, 514

News, 567, 570

Night, 287

Ninevites, 295

Nisan, 2, 14

Nob, 124, 133, 372–73, 409, 430–32

Nose, 45

Nourishment, 79, 267, 485, 559–60. *See also* Bread; Honey

Numbers, 16, 32, 43, 148, 231, 327, 353–54, 428. *See also* Counting

Oath, 61, 100, 259, 261, 265, 270–71, 334, 391, 399–400, 404, 468, 475, 487, 536, 546. *See also* Agreement; Covenant; Curse; Promise; Vow

Obedience, 8, 163, 217, 242, 294, 297–98, 384, 445. *See also* Hearing

Occult. *See* Demons; Devil; Divination; Idolatry; Necromancy; Satan

Odor, 232, 240, 496, 510

Offering, 98, 111, 195, 502. *See also* Sacrifice

Offering, burnt, 89, 147, 234, 242

Offering, fire, 99

Offering, guilt, 94, 143, 150

Offering, peace, 53, 58, 60, 62, 193, 212, 242

Office, 54–55, 103, 115, 186, 228, 433, 458, 533, 562, 571

Offspring, 81, 348. *See also* Children; Seed

Oil, 87, 195, 306. *See also* Anointing

Omniscience, 79, 295

Oppression, 186, 200, 217, 223–24, 259

Oracle, 23–24, 30, 251, 275. *See also* Divination; Medium

Orality, 1, 275

Orientation. *See* Directions

Orpah, 349

Overhearing, 368

Overseeing, 300, 356

Oxen, 213, 255

Paganism. *See* Polytheism

Palace, 20–22

Palti, 489

Panic, 137, 139, 149, 157, 159–60, 241, 249–52, 255, 339

Parallelism, 9–11, 290–92, 295, 305–6, 354, 362, 460–62, 510, 528, 565, 570 as literary device, 354, 480, 519

Paran, 471

Parent, 95, 349, 369, 372, 397, 422, 483. *See also* Father; Mother

Partridge, 497, 503

Passover, 52, 84–85, 116

Pastors, 67, 114, 186, 223–24, 228, 356, 383, 419. *See also* Bishops; Ministry

Pasture, 374

Patriarchs, 64, 172, 225. *See also* Abraham; Father; Isaac; Jacob

Patristics, 527

Paul, 67, 223, 371, 418

Peace, 55, 192, 302, 317, 330, 449, 468, 473. *See also* Offering, peace

Peninnah, 52–53, 66, 78

Pentapolis, 137. *See also* Ashdod; Ashkelon; Ekron; Gath; Gaza

Pentateuch, 3, 65–66, 348. *See also* Torah

Pentecost, 52, 159, 311

Peresh, 56

Perez, 509

Perfection, 272

Perfume, 164

Pharaoh, 83, 94, 145, 172

Pharisees, 23, 28

Philistines, 13–14, 16, 19, 21, 27–28, 33, 96, 120–23, 125, 137–40, 149–51, 159–60, 196–98, 224, 232, 240, 253, 279, 416–18, 441, 513, 531–37, 545–48, 564–65. *See also* Achish; Dagon; Goliath; Pentapolis; Polytheism; War

Phinehas, 26–27, 53, 83–84, 86–88, 95–96, 103–4, 106–7, 122–23, 126, 131, 152, 256–57

Pidgin text, 37

Pilgrimage, 52

Pim, 45, 237

Plague, 121–22, 138–39

Plague, bubonic, 136, 139

Plow, 164, 237

Plunder, 276, 296, 342, 554. *See also* Spoils

Poetry, 8, 72–80, 297, 354. *See also* Songs

Politics, 64–66, 156, 348–49, 404, 458, 562

Polygamy, 54, 64–67

Polytheism, 121, 333, 342, 535–37, 543, 546, 560. *See also* Gods; Worship

Poor, 27, 64, 74, 359, 361

Portion, 45, 53, 84, 86–87, 182, 187, 556

Possession, spiritual, 317–18, 418, 520, 529. *See also* Demons; Devil

Pot, 84

Pouncing, 296

Pouring, 55, 158–59

Power, 77, 79, 186, 270, 448, 486. *See also* Authority

Prayer, 48–50, 80, 94, 159, 228–29, 286, 383, 450. *See also* Blessing; Inquiring (of Yahweh); Intercession

Predestination, 94, 243–44. *See also* Choosing; Election; Foreknowledge

Prefiguring, 25–26, 380. *See also* Typology

Presence, divine, 88, 100, 104, 106, 149, 151–53, 273, 308, 341, 355, 572

Pretending, 415

Priest, 14, 24–25, 48, 85–89, 91, 94, 102–6, 151, 410, 412, 432–33

Priest, faithful, 104–6

Priest, high, 48, 95, 98, 253, 272–75, 406, 410, 412, 432–33

Priest, pagan, 149–51

Prominence, 176, 319

Promise, 6, 91, 105–6, 214, 222, 227, 255–56, 268, 299, 340, 439–40, 465, 487, 552. *See also* Gospel; Land, promised; Vow
  as made by Saul, 343, 358, 360–62, 489, 503
  as made to Hannah, 59–60, 62
  of Messiah, 23–25, 27, 74, 90, 156, 159, 191, 448, 478, 486, 572

Prophecy, 30, 77–78, 101–2, 104, 111, 114–15, 123, 193, 195, 199, 298–99, 346, 368, 378, 422–23, 441
  of Messiah, 23, 25, 78, 81, 105–7, 303, 380

Prophecy, ecstatic, 30, 318, 352, 377

Prophecy, false, 318, 530, 532–33, 539

Prophets, 57, 103, 105–6, 109, 114, 116–17, 183–84, 194, 418, 433, 441, 529, 534

Prosperity, 29, 79. *See also* Success

Prostitute, 341, 410

Protection, 80, 371, 401–3, 448. *See also* Guarding

Proverb, 194, 199

Psalms, 77

Pun. *See* Wordplay

Question, rhetorical, 95, 148, 195, 331, 431, 467

Quilt, 367

Qumran, 34–36

Rabbah, 11, 20–22

Rachel, 28, 52, 56, 66, 132, 195, 349, 362, 371

Rahab, 371, 403

Raiding, 236, 244, 345, 441, 451, 508, 512–14, 558–60

Rain, 221, 228

Raisin, 474, 485

Ramah, 42, 124, 161, 183, 197, 372–74

Ramathaim, 42, 52

Ramoth of the Negev, 42, 563

Ramoth-gilead, 42, 528

Ransom, 265, 269

Rape, 66, 477

Rashi, 138

Rats, 138–40, 144, 150

Rawness, 85–87

Razor, 55

Rebekah, 28

Rebellion, 99, 220, 288, 297, 395, 533, 536
  of Absalom, 20–22, 26, 290
  of Sheba, 26, 290

Recognizing, 437

Red, 304, 311

Redactions, 6–8, 167, 463, 525

Redemption, 79, 91, 191, 229, 265, 300, 562, 571. *See also* Salvation

Regret, 285, 291–92, 295, 298, 300. *See also* Change; Repentance

Rehoboam, 2, 19–20, 64

Rejoicing, 69, 212, 353

Relenting. *See* Regret

Remains, 468

Remembering, 51

Rempthis, 42

Renewal, 211–12, 215, 309

Rentis, 42

Repentance, 25–26, 29, 140, 158–59, 292, 309, 464, 497. *See also* Change; Regret

Report, 93, 131

Reputation, 362, 418, 431
of Yahweh, 222, 228–29

Request, 51, 56, 61, 90–91, 171, 227, 273–74, 335, 537. *See also* Inquiring (of Yahweh); Wordplay

Rescue, 200, 552–53, 561. *See also* Salvation

Restoration, 72, 90, 238

Resurrection
of body, 73, 79
of Christ, 72, 74, 79, 227, 440

Retribution, 498

Return, 157

Reuben (tribe), 206

Revelation, 109, 114, 185, 381

Revenge, 66, 260, 361, 456, 467, 478, 487

Reverence, 458–59

Reversal, 28–29, 79–80

Righteousness, 73, 170, 229, 340, 371, 403, 457, 467, 498, 503, 544. *See also* Justification; Works-righteousness

Ritual, 536

Rivalry, 45, 66, 78

Rizpah, 530, 569

Roasting, 84–85

Robe, 89, 298, 346, 377, 454, 462–63, 465–66, 535, 537. *See also* Ephod

Rock, 78, 151, 447–48, 450, 488

Ruler, designated, 168, 180, 186–87, 195, 198, 213, 242, 319, 349, 404, 513

Runners, 431–32

Ruth, 422

Ruthlessness, 396

Sabbath, 408, 410, 412, 571

Sacraments, 356, 503. *See also* Baptism; Grace, means of; Lord's Supper

Sacrifice, 53, 58, 62, 83–88, 103, 105, 185, 212, 215, 241, 296–97, 307–8, 380, 394, 399–400, 412, 496, 502, 568. *See also* Atonement; Offering; Offering, burnt; Offering, fire; Offering, guilt; Offering, peace

Salvation, 78, 83, 200–201, 221, 254, 337, 368–69, 378, 380, 384, 448–49, 477, 479, 513. *See also* Monergism; Redemption
God's acts of, 78, 80–81, 126, 221, 229, 342, 435, 486, 559

Samaria, 67. *See also* Israel

Samson, 55, 138, 195, 219

Samuel (book)
author of, 1–3
chronology of, 13–23, 226, 525, 548
composition of, 1–8, 166–69, 525
dating of, 2–4
text of, 31–35, 69–70, 177–78, 182, 190–91, 201, 206–7, 232–33, 236, 250–51, 259, 263, 265, 286, 289, 323–25, 391–92, 394, 428, 436, 446, 473–74, 509, 523, 544–45, 555–56, 561, 567

Samuel (prophet), 1–2, 13–14, 17, 26–27, 51, 62–63, 77, 81–82, 86, 88, 96, 105, 113–17, 123, 156, 159–61, 226, 311, 380–85, 482
apparition of, 385, 522, 528–34, 536
sons of, 116, 169–70, 223

Sanctification, 26, 153, 303, 307–8. *See also* Holiness; Works, good

Sarah, 28, 52, 66, 91, 402

Satan, 317, 528, 533, 543, 547. *See also* Devil

Saul, 3, 8–10, 13, 25, 28, 30, 61, 63, 77, 82, 106, 160, 171, 215, 227, 286, 292. *See also* Apostasy, of Saul; Murder, as aim of Saul; Promise, as made by Saul
anointing of, 14, 306, 381, 458–59, 466
death of, 16, 131, 519, 530–31, 539
heart of, 25, 187, 308–9, 355, 378
inaction or failure of, 26, 29, 196, 198–99, 203, 215, 239, 242, 256, 290, 340–41, 343, 362, 432, 451, 467, 513, 534
piety of, 268–69, 292, 296, 445, 536
reign of, 13, 16–17, 231, 238, 277
sons of, 278, 280, 530–31, 539, 566, 569

Savior, 156, 201. *See also* Christ; Salvation

Scales, 327 Schism, 188

Scimitar, 328, 336

Scream, 474

Scribbling, 415

Scribes (NT), 23

Scripture. *See* Word, of God

Seah, 474

Second, 449

Secu, 376

Security, 219, 485. *See also* Bodyguard

Seed, 23, 48, 90, 340, 348, 457

Seeking, 177, 388, 506

Seer, 30, 109, 184–85, 187. *See also* Prophets

Seizure, 488

Selling, 437

Seneh, 248

Sensibility, 472. *See also* Astuteness

Serpent, 208, 446

Servant, 48, 51, 87–88, 93, 110, 165, 171, 177, 318, 320, 337–38, 456, 476, 478, 484–85, 535, 547. *See also* Armor bearer; Bodyguard; Levites; Ministry; Slave

Servant, Suffering, 94, 488

Serving, 100, 102, 227

Seth, 56

Seven, 79

Sexual relations, 51, 92–93, 348, 410

Shaalim, 183

Shaaraim, 334

Shaharaim, 64

Shalishah, 183

Shame, 212, 348–49, 378, 403. *See also* Bowdlerization

Shammah, 304

Share, 556. *See also* Portion; Spoils

Sheba, 21–22, 401

Shechem, 42, 158, 267, 362

Sheep, 330, 464

Shekel, 45, 184, 237, 328

Shemaᶜ, 158

Sheol, 72–73, 521, 527, 530. *See also* Hell

Shepherd, 304, 343, 409, 484. *See also* Bishops; Ministry; Pastors

Shield, 206, 328, 336, 338, 342

Shiloh, 13, 52–54, 91, 124, 131–33

Shimei, 203, 456, 465, 500

Shining, 261, 266–67. *See also* Glow; Light

Shua, 56

Shual, 183

Shunem, 245, 517, 520, 527, 534–35, 548

Shur, 285, 294

Sickle, 237

Sidon, 245

Simeon, 381, 512

Sinai, 5, 285, 339, 410, 471

Sins, 26, 96, 265, 267–68, 287, 291, 296, 369, 381, 467, 486, 497

Siphmoth, 563

Sisera, 224, 535

Sivan, 228

Skin, 304, 400, 412. *See also* Wine

Slave, 51, 65, 165, 171–72, 232, 338, 476, 560. *See also* Servant

Sleep, 188, 493, 495, 501

Sling, 332, 341, 479

Smell. *See* Odor

Snake. *See* Serpent

Socoh, 245, 325, 334, 343

Sodom, 182

Soldier, 326, 411. *See also* Army; Warrior

Solem, 520

Solomon, 2, 13–14, 19–20, 56, 64–66, 344, 429

Son, 53–54, 66, 165, 171, 202, 551

Son of David, 23, 81, 299, 355, 368, 412, 440, 481, 486, 572

Songs, 76–78, 94, 353–54, 488, 501, 546

Soul, 101, 105, 334, 344, 347, 389, 478

South, 445

Spaciousness, 316

Span, 326

Spear, 328, 338, 462–63, 501

Spies, 492

Spirit. *See also* Holy Spirit of God/Yahweh, 30, 192–93, 195–96, 306, 315–19, 340–41, 378

Spirit, evil, 30, 315–18, 355, 378, 520–21, 528

Spittle, 415–16

Spoils, 276, 296, 413, 442, 451, 512, 561

Spring, 451, 542

Staff, 341

Stars, 44

Starvation, 87

Stele, 11–12

Stone, 147, 332, 552

Strength, 71, 86, 101, 234–35, 276, 288, 524, 540, 552. *See also* Army; Power; Prominence

Stripping, 378, 451, 566

Stroke, 488

Stronghold, 19, 372–73, 421–22, 443, 464, 468, 482

Stupidity. *See* Foolishness

Submission, 481

Success, 29, 345–47, 355, 362, 464, 483, 562

Succoth, 52

Suicide, 533–34, 571

Summons, 200. *See also* Invitation

Superlative, 165

Swellings, 136, 139, 146, 150

"Swept away," 222, 505, 510–11

Sword, 328, 413

Syncretism, 370, 535

Synecdoche, 272

Tabernacle, 54, 93, 113–14, 116, 132. *See also* Tent

Tabor, 195, 197

Talisman, 120, 125

Talmai, 508

Tamar (daughter of David), 20–22, 26, 66, 344, 508

Tamar (daughter-in-law of Judah), 402, 509

Tamarisk, 425, 430

Tasting, 267

Taunt. *See* Insult

Taxation, 171, 331

Teaching, 222, 229, 383–84

Tearing, 454

Tel Aviv, 42, 119, 125

Tel Dan, 11–12

Tel en-Nasbeh, 158

Tell Abû Sûs, 358

Tell el-Husn, 570

Tell el-Maqlub, 358

Tell esh-Shariah, 512

Tell esh-Sheikh Madhkur, 421

Tell Jezer, 508

Tell Ma'in, 450

Tell Qila, 440

Tell Ras el-'Ain, 125

Tell Zaqareyeh, 325

Tell Ziph, 444

Temple, 14, 23, 30, 54, 113, 136. *See also* Dagon; Idolatry

Tent, 95, 122, 343, 413. *See also* Meeting, tent of; Tabernacle

Terebinth, 191, 325–26, 338–39

Test, 151, 399

Theology, 7–8, 29–30, 150, 156, 168–69, 368

Thigh, 187

Thousands, 353–54

Three, 351

Threshing floor, 21, 30

Thunder, 46, 75, 160, 221, 228

Time, 51, 59, 185, 206, 208, 507, 532–33, 542, 554, 560. *See also* Chronology; Day; Year

Timothy, 103

Tishri, 2, 14

Tithe, 165, 191

Title, 80–81, 183, 257, 417, 431, 546
for ark of the covenant, 120, 126, 132, 134, 142
for God, 52, 72, 77, 93, 289, 293, 303, 339

"To this day," 2–3, 138, 151

Toah, 43

Tohu, 43

Tomb, 195

Tooth, 84, 157, 248

Torah, 11, 23, 54, 84, 87, 89, 94, 99, 110, 121, 149–50, 158–59, 170, 172, 186–87, 227, 267–68, 273, 297, 308, 346, 399, 411, 440, 519, 528–29, 536, 560. *See also* Pentateuch

Traits, 305

Transformation, 193

Translation, 37–38

Transliteration, 33, 129, 155, 236

Trap, 521

Trembling, 289, 302

Trinity, 337. *See also* Christ; Father, God as; Holy Spirit

Troops. *See* Army

Trouble, 420

Trust, 25–26, 29, 219, 227, 255, 309, 339–40, 439–40, 509. *See also* Faith

Tumors. *See* Swellings

Typology, 25–26, 380. *See also* Prefiguring

Unbelief, 73, 83, 86, 140, 378, 418, 477, 486, 534

Uncle, 194, 199, 279

Uncleanness, 400–401, 407, 410–11

Uriah, 28–29, 361, 411, 493, 498

Urim and Thummim, 203, 251, 255, 264, 268–69, 272–75, 437, 439, 441, 534, 559

Urination, 475. *See also* Vulgarity

Uselessness, 228. *See also* "Good-for-nothing"

Valley, 12, 236, 253, 325, 334, 338, 450, 542, 569–70

Ventriloquist, 521

Versification, 32–33, 404–5

Vestments. *See* Ephod

Victory, 214–15, 255–56

Virgin, 335, 362, 410

Vision, 109, 113, 221, 341

Visit, 91

Vocation, 54, 381–82

Voice, 163, 221, 521

Vow, 58–59, 62, 267, 269–70

Vulgarity, 476, 485

Wadi, 248

Wadi Besor, 559–61

Wadi es-Sant, 325

Wadi es-Surar, 325

Wadi Ghazzeh, 559

Wages, 102

Wall, 371, 485

War, 19–21, 93, 119, 123–24, 197–98, 240, 268, 279, 360, 370, 478, 515, 548. *See also* Amalekites; Ammonites; Battle; Philistines; Warrior

War, Yahweh's, 360, 411, 477–78, 512–13

Warrior, 71, 176, 277, 305, 319, 336–37, 339

Watching, 128–29, 131, 211, 429

Water, 158–59, 185, 412, 464. *See also* Baptism; Drinking; Spring

Weaning, 62

Weeping, 48, 54, 210, 212, 397, 467, 551

Wickedness, 222, 233, 288, 466, 472

Widow, 67, 410, 488

Wife, 481, 488–89, 551, 555
of Phinehas, 150

Wilderness, 121–22, 221, 225, 471. *See also* Desert

Will of God, 24, 79, 94–96, 187, 268–69, 271, 285, 292, 297, 299, 318, 368, 450, 458, 511

Wine, 50, 60, 62, 319, 483, 487. *See also* Lord's Supper

Wisdom, 345, 446, 480–81, 487

Witch. *See* Medium

Witness, 391, 399–400

Woman from Tekoa, 28

Women, 93, 95, 353–54, 481, 486, 551

Woods, 444. *See also* Hereth

Word. *See also* Grace, means of
of God, 25–26, 29–30, 38, 56, 83, 114, 125–26, 150, 184, 186–87, 215, 221, 227, 242, 288, 299, 317, 356, 378, 380–81, 384, 440–41, 503
of Yahweh, 59, 109, 113, 115, 123, 220, 283, 291–92, 298, 418, 475

Wordplay, 61, 102, 109, 180, 184, 266, 320, 352, 359, 361, 412, 478, 483, 487, 503, 545
on names, 56, 75, 106–7, 171, 201, 227, 263, 335, 390, 427, 474, 486, 520, 538

Works, good, 62, 73, 101, 221–22, 229, 256, 381–82, 403. *See also* Sanctification

Works-righteousness, 150, 384, 486

Worship, 44, 54, 63, 78, 91, 105, 116, 150, 404, 454–55, 503. *See also* Idolatry; Offering; Polytheism; Sacrifice

Worthless. *See* "Good-for-nothing"

Xerxes, 64

Yahweh, 9, 28, 54, 62, 74–80, 87, 91, 109, 125, 127, 149, 151, 166, 168–69, 171, 191, 204, 224, 228, 286, 339–40, 348, 399, 455, 543–44, 558, 561. *See also* Word, of Yahweh
of armies, 44, 52, 54, 120, 293

Year, 2, 44, 46, 58, 157, 231, 238–39, 329, 507. *See also* Chronology; Time

Zadok, 20, 30, 104, 116, 133, 306, 429, 432

Zechariah (of NT), 77–78, 81

Zechariah (of Saul's genealogy), 280

Zechariah (prophet), 117

Zedekiah, 64

Zelzah, 195, 197

Zephaniah, 535

Zeruiah, 312, 493, 500

Ziklag, 2–3, 7, 372–73, 489, 511–12, 514, 517, 526–27, 546–48, 550–51, 558–61

Zilpah, 56, 66

Ziph, 174, 372–73, 444, 449–50, 463, 488, 499, 502

Ziv, 14

Zobah, 245, 277–78

Zuph, 42–43, 52, 183

Zwickau, 381

Index of Passages

Old Testament

Genesis

1:1–2:3, 79
1:2, 221, 228
1:3, 273
1:14, 44
1:26–27, 348
1:27–28, 66
1:31, 317
2:1, 44
2:11, 446
2:18, 65
2:21, 495, 501
2:21–23, 67
2:22, 65
2:24, 65–66, 489, 565
2:25, 378
3:1, 208, 446
3:1–5, 499
3:7–12, 378
3:8–12, 242
3:12, 297
3:13, 297
3:14, 208, 260
3:15, 23, 340, 486
3:17, 260
3:24, 496
4:1, 51
4:2, 129
4:19–24, 64
4:25, 56
5:24, 479
6:3, 383
6:4, 235
6:5, 194
6:6, 295
6:7, 295
8:12, 234
8:21, 194, 496, 502
9:1, 348
9:3–4, 268
9:6, 498
9:11, 209
9:16, 508
9:20–27, 378
9:25, 260, 266
10:14, 416
10:15, 493
10:19, 334

10:30, 334
11:5, 496
11:10, 231
11:30, 28
12:1, 220
12:1–3, 299, 340, 486
12:3, 103
12:11, 305
12:16, 51
13:3, 446
13:4, 446
13:10, 285, 334
13:14, 446
14:4, 231
14:6, 471
14:7, 451
15:1, 109
15:6, 308, 340, 509
15:9–18, 209
15:11, 262
15:12, 495, 501
15:18, 209, 294
15:18–19, 509
15:20, 493
16, 52
16:1, 51
16:6, 59
16:7, 285
17:1, 100
17:6, 23
17:7–14, 340
17:8, 508
17:10–13, 412
17:10–14, 253
17:14, 209, 340
18:4, 488
18:11, 329
18:12, 402
18:13, 402
18:14, 51
18:17–18, 299, 340
19–20, 56
19:1–11, 182
19:2, 488
19:3, 525
19:21, 480
19:27, 446
19:33, 525
19:33–34, 93

19:35, 525
19:36–37, 278
19:38, 278
20:1, 285
20:6, 222
20:18, 46
21, 52
21:1, 91
21:8, 58
21:8–21, 66
21:16, 210
21:21, 471
21:22, 112
21:33, 425
22:17, 240
22:17–18, 299, 340
23:3, 493
23:5, 493
23:7, 493
23:10, 493
23:13, 210
23:16, 210, 493
23:18, 493
23:20, 493
24:1, 329
24:2–4, 270
24:11, 185
24:15–20, 185
24:26, 455
24:32, 488
24:40, 100
24:43, 335
24:48, 455
24:67, 347
25:9, 493
25:10, 493
25:18, 285, 334
25:21, 28
25:24, 129
25:25, 304, 311
25:30, 278
25:30–34, 304
25:31, 86
25:33, 86
26:3, 112
26:3–4, 299, 340
26:24, 525
26:28, 112
26:34, 493

27:5, 251
27:24, 211
27:26, 349
27:27, 349
27:29, 103, 260
27:33, 302
27:38, 210
28, 161
28:2, 177
28:9, 64
28:11, 493
28:13–14, 299, 340
28:15, 112
28:18, 493
29, 362
29:1–10, 185
29:11, 210, 349
29:12, 349
29:13, 349
29:15–30, 362
29:17, 305, 319, 472
29:18, 52, 347, 362
29:23, 362
29:23–31, 28
29:27, 362, 447
29:30, 347
29:31, 52
29:31–30:24, 66
29:32, 56, 347
29:33, 56
29:34, 56
29:35, 28, 56
30:1, 28
30:4–6, 56
30:7–8, 56
30:10–11, 56
30:12–13, 56
30:16, 525
30:17–18, 56
30:21, 56
30:22, 52
30:22–24, 56
31:13, 446
31:19, 285, 288, 371
31:27, 351
31:28, 349
31:30, 285
31:34, 288, 371
31:34–35, 371
31:35, 288, 371
31:41, 362
32:1 (ET 31:55), 349
32:13 (ET 32:12), 240
32:14 (ET 32:13), 525

32:14–19 (ET 32:13–18), 204
32:21 (ET 32:20), 480
32:22 (ET 32:21), 525
32:23 (ET 32:22), 525
33:4, 349
33:11, 478
33:19, 446
34:2, 93
34:3, 347
34:7, 93, 477
34:12, 359, 362
34:30, 267
35:15, 446
35:16–18, 56
35:16–20, 195
35:17–18, 132
35:22, 93
35:27, 446
36:1, 278
36:2, 64, 493
36:6, 64
36:13, 43
36:17, 43
37:2, 65–66, 304
37:14, 55
37:23, 377
37:31–32, 401
37:35, 72
38, 509
38:1, 421
38:4, 56
38:5, 56
38:7, 72
38:12, 421
38:20, 421
38:24, 208
38:26, 402
38:27–30, 402
39:2, 42, 112
39:6, 305, 319, 472
39:10, 251
39:14–15, 401
39:17–18, 401
39:21, 112
39:23, 300
40, 165
40:3, 446
40:19, 571
40:22, 571
41:2, 305
41:4, 305
41:13, 571
41:14, 329

41:18, 305, 472
41:49, 240
42:15, 265
42:35, 478
42:38, 72
43:9, 102
43:24, 488
43:27, 192
44, 347
44:20, 347
44:29, 72
44:30, 347
44:31, 72
44:32, 102
45:15, 349
45:18, 87
45:20, 455
46:34, 220
47:3, 220
47:11–12, 422
47:18, 567
48:10, 349
48:15, 100
48:20, 90
49:7, 266
49:8–10, 448
49:29–30, 493
49:32, 493
50:1, 349
50:10, 446
50:13, 493
50:15–21, 467
50:17, 251
50:24–25, 91

Exodus
1:15–21, 402
2:8, 335
2:11, 516
2:15–19, 185
2:17, 200
2:21, 259
2:23, 172, 186, 218, 516
2:23–25, 186
2:25, 186
3:2–4, 248
3:7, 180, 186, 218
3:8, 200, 493
3:9, 200, 218
3:17, 200, 493
3:20–22, 150
4:18, 55
4:23, 145
4:25, 209

4:27, 349
4:31, 455
5:1, 145
5:2, 83
5:7, 360
6:6, 200
6:11, 145
6:18, 52
6:32, 152
7:2, 145
7:14, 145
7:16, 145
7:18, 232
7:21, 232
8:10 (ET 8:14), 232
8:28 (ET 8:32), 145
9:7, 145
9:9–11, 136
9:17, 145
9:23, 221
9:29, 221
9:33, 221
9:35, 145
10:2, 145
10:24, 135
11:1, 145
11:2, 210
12:6, 211
12:8–9, 85
12:8–20, 525
12:9, 84–85
12:15, 209
12:17, 525
12:18, 560
12:23, 236
12:27, 455
12:33, 145
12:36, 61
12:38, 283
12:39, 525
12:48, 253
13:2, 153
13:5, 493
13:6–7, 525
13:10, 44
13:11, 220
13:17, 145
13:18, 122, 283
13:20, 122
14:3, 122
14:4, 202
14:11–12, 122
14:24, 211
14:24–25, 255

14:28, 28
14:30, 200
15:3, 120
15:15, 250
15:20, 351
15:20–21, 353
15:22, 285
16:7, 130, 361
16:10, 251
16:12, 211
16:31, 480
17:4, 552
17:8–13, 293
17:8–15, 561
17:14–16, 293, 513
18:4, 200
18:7, 192, 349, 403
18:8–10, 200
18:21, 164, 170
18:25, 164
19:5–6, 166
19:6, 410
19:9, 251
19:10, 153, 308, 410
19:11, 411
19:14, 153, 308
19:15, 410
19:16, 221, 302
19:18, 302
19:23, 153
20, 95
20:1–11, 125
20:2–6, 499
20:3, 158, 502
20:5–6, 499
20:7, 126, 270
20:12, 369, 422, 459, 571
20:13, 369, 398, 402, 440, 502, 571
20:16, 401–2
21:7–11, 64–65
21:10, 65
21:13, 456
22:15 (ET 22:16), 359
22:15–16 (ET 22:16–17), 362
22:16 (ET 22:17), 359, 362
22:20 (ET 22:21), 200, 560
22:24 (ET 22:25), 420
22:29 (ET 22:30), 159
22:30 (ET 22:31), 341

23:2–8, 170
23:9, 200, 560
23:14–17, 52
23:15, 525
23:23, 493
23:27, 255
23:28, 493, 496
24:7, 210
24:8, 209
24:13, 76
25–40, 503
25:7, 89
25:22, 114, 132
25:30, 408
26:34, 114
27:3, 87
27:4, 367
27:20–21, 113
28, 103
28:2–12, 103
28:3, 149, 153
28:4, 89
28:4–30, 89
28:28, 441
28:30, 250–51, 255, 268–69, 272–73
28:31, 89
28:34, 89
28:41, 105, 149, 153, 308
28:42–43, 89
29:1, 149, 153
29:4, 201
29:5, 89
29:7, 105
29:9, 103
29:13, 85
29:18, 496
29:25, 496
29:27, 153
29:28, 508
29:31, 84
29:33, 153
29:41, 99, 496
29:44, 153
30:6, 114
30:7–8, 98
30:21, 508
30:30, 105, 153
31:14, 209
32, 171
32:2–6, 297
32:14, 295
32:21–24, 297

32:25–29, 52
33:2, 493, 496
34:6, 228
34:11, 493
34:13, 155
34:18, 525
34:20, 59
34:22, 51
34:23, 59
34:24, 59
35:9, 89
35:13, 408
35:16, 367
35:27, 89
36:6, 93
38:3, 87
38:4, 367
38:5, 367
38:8, 93, 95
38:30, 367
39:1–7, 103
39:2–21, 89
39:22–26, 89
39:36, 408
39:39, 367
40:9–11, 149
40:13, 105, 149, 153
40:15, 103, 105, 508
40:27, 98
40:32, 201
40:34, 130

Leviticus
1:2, 201
1:3, 179, 201
1:3–17, 147
1:4, 111
1:5, 201
1:9, 85, 99, 179, 496
1:10, 201
1:13, 85, 99, 179
1:15, 85
1:17, 85, 99, 179, 454
2:2, 179, 496
2:2–3, 99
2:9, 179
2:10, 99
2:12, 98, 179
3:1–17, 193
3:3–16, 99
3:5, 85, 496
3:16, 85
4:3, 105
4:5, 105
4:13, 143, 497

4:16, 105
4:19, 85
4:20, 150
4:22, 143
4:26, 85, 150
4:27, 143
4:31, 85, 150, 496
4:35, 85, 150
5:2–3, 400
5:2–5, 143
5:4–6, 267
5:6, 111
5:10, 150
5:13, 84, 150
5:14–26 (ET 5:14–6:7), 143
5:16, 150
5:18, 150
5:24 (ET 6:5), 475
5:26 (ET 6:7), 150
6:3 (ET 6:10), 89
6:4 (ET 6:11), 377
6:5 (ET 6:12), 85
6:9 (ET 6:16), 84
6:11 (ET 6:18), 99
6:13 (ET 6:20), 105
6:15 (ET 6:22), 105
6:19 (ET 6:26), 84
6:22 (ET 6:29), 84
7:1–7, 143
7:6–9, 84
7:11–36, 53, 193
7:14, 84
7:16, 58
7:20–21, 400
7:21, 400
7:23–25, 87
7:31, 85, 87
7:31–34, 84
7:35, 99
7:36, 105
8:7, 89
8:7–8, 441
8:8, 251, 255, 268, 272–73
8:12, 105, 153
8:30, 153
8:31, 84
9:22, 90
9:22–23, 179
9:23, 90
10:1–2, 94
10:1–3, 152
10:10, 407

10:13–14, 84
11:9, 327
11:10, 327
11:12, 327
11:24–38, 400
12:1–5, 400
13:1–46, 401
13:2–5, 412
13:23, 248
13:24–28, 412
13:28, 248
13:29–32, 412
13:38, 412
13:39, 412
13:59, 401
14:33–47, 401
14:43, 47
15:2–17, 400
15:15, 412
15:18, 410
15:18–26, 400
16:2, 114
16:4, 89
16:6, 111
16:8, 269
16:10–11, 111
16:16–18, 111
16:23, 89, 377
16:32, 89, 105
17:6, 87, 179
17:10–14, 268
18:22, 348
19:2, 294
19:5, 179
19:11–12, 401
19:12, 475
19:14, 479
19:15, 480
19:18, 346
19:22, 150
19:26, 262, 268, 528
19:31, 519–20, 528
19:34, 560
20:6, 519–20
20:7–8, 308
20:8, 149, 153
20:11–12, 93
20:13, 93, 348
20:20, 93
20:26, 294, 308
20:27, 519–20, 528
21:6, 410
21:6–8, 308
21:7–15, 410

21:8, 149, 153, 410
21:15, 149, 153
21:22, 410
21:23, 149, 153
22:4–7, 410
22:9, 149, 153
22:16, 149, 153
22:19–21, 179
22:21, 58
22:24, 172, 493
22:27, 159
22:31–33, 308
22:32, 149, 153
23:6, 525
23:11, 179
23:17, 192
23:32, 560
24:2–3, 113
24:5, 410
24:5–6, 408
24:5–9, 410
24:8, 408
24:9, 410
25:18–19, 219, 226
25:48, 47
26:5, 219, 226
26:6, 317
26:21, 121
26:37, 208
26:40, 220
26:41, 391

Numbers
1, 17
1:3, 16
1:9, 43
1:32–33, 43
1:47–54, 52
2:7, 43
3:3, 105
3:10, 103
4:2–3, 55
4:14, 87
4:15, 251
4:19, 180
4:22–23, 55
4:23, 93
4:29–30, 55
4:34–35, 55
5:6–7, 143
6:11, 153
6:19, 84
6:23–27, 90, 179
6:24–26, 55, 90
6:26, 90

6:27, 55
7:24, 43
7:29, 43
7:89, 114, 132
8:19, 98
8:24, 93
8:24–25, 55, 91
9:6, 42
10:4, 201
10:12, 471
10:16, 43
11:1, 221
11:3, 221
11:8, 480
11:33, 121
12:7, 106
12:11, 266
12:16, 471
13:3, 471
13:26, 471
13:29, 493
13:30, 152, 450
14:1, 210, 525
14:6–9, 450
14:15, 210
14:24, 152
14:24–38, 450
14:28, 210
14:45, 563
15:3, 58
15:8, 58
15:8–10, 62
15:9, 60
15:10, 60
15:22, 497
15:25–26, 150
15:28, 150
15:30–31, 209
15:39–40, 294
16:1, 43
16:11, 361
16:12, 43
16:14, 209
16:15, 383
16:30, 72, 88
16:33, 72
16:35, 148
17:5 (ET 16:40), 98
18:7, 103
18:12, 87
18:19, 508
18:20, 191
18:21–26, 191
18:29, 87

19:2, 150
20:26, 377
20:28, 377
21, 122
21:3, 563
21:6, 208
21:20, 450
21:28, 194
22:3, 353
22:6, 103
22:7, 142
22:11, 163
22:12, 260
22:38, 163
23:3, 376
23:19, 295
23:19–20, 299
23:23, 142
23:28, 450
24:9, 103, 260
24:18, 276
24:20, 561
24:20–21, 294, 512
25, 171
25:7–8, 494
25:13, 508
26:2, 17
26:4, 17
26:8–9, 43
26:10, 148
26:65, 450
27:1–11, 64
27:16–18, 355
27:18–23, 437
27:21, 250–51, 255,
    264, 268–69,
    272–73
28:9–10, 412
28:11–15, 399
30:3 (ET 30:2), 270
*30:11–16 (ET 30:10–
    15)*, 62
32:2–38, 207
32:11–12, 450
32:12, 227, 509
32:16, 453
32:24, 453
32:33, 122
32:34, 556
32:36, 453
34:5, 294

Deuteronomy
1:1, 471
1:15, 164

1:17, 353
1:35–36, 152, 450
1:36, 227
1:44, 563
2:14–16, 273
2:18–3:11, 122
2:27, 70
2:36, 556
3:12, 556
3:18, 277
4:10, 102
4:20, 191
4:30, 163
4:34–40, 243
4:35, 112
4:37, 98
4:39, 112
4:40, 102
4:43, 42
4:48, 556
5, 95
5:1, 210
5:1–15, 125
5:2–3, 209
5:6–10, 499
5:7, 158, 502
5:11, 126, 270
5:16, 369, 422, 459, 571
5:17, 369, 398, 402, 440, 571
5:20, 401–2
5:26, 339–40, 501, 536
5:29, 102
5:33, 220
6:4, 112, 158
6:5, 158, 372, 499
6:12, 224
6:13–15, 536
6:14, 502
6:24, 102
7:1, 493
7:3–4, 502
7:5, 155, 568
7:6–7, 98
7:6–16, 243
7:16, 455
7:22–23, 255
7:25, 568
8:3, 220
8:11, 224
8:14, 224
8:19, 224
8:20, 170

9:5, 59
9:21, 568
9:26, 191
9:29, 191
10:8, 90, 179
10:11, 177
10:11–15, 243
10:12, 353
10:16, 253
10:17, 480
10:17–19, 403
11:1, 102
11:4, 202
11:6, 43
11:16, 502
11:22, 353
11:28, 502
12:1, 102
12:3, 155, 568
12:4–26, 98
12:6, 58
12:10, 219, 226
12:11, 58
12:15–16, 268
12:20, 389
12:30, 521
12:31, 568
13:2–12 (ET 13:1–11), 502
13:5 (ET 13:4), 227
13:11 (ET 13:10), 552
13:14 (ET 13:13), 50, 204
13:17 (ET 13:16), 568
13:19 (ET 13:18), 163
14:2, 98
14:9, 327
14:10, 327
14:22, 165
14:23, 102
14:23–25, 98
14:26, 389
15:10, 46
15:17, 508
16:5–16, 98
16:7, 84
16:9, 237
16:16, 52, 59, 525
16:19, 170
16:20, 70
17:5, 552
17:9, 516
17:14–20, 23, 65, 166, 170

17:17, 65
17:20, 242
18:1–8, 98
18:3, 84
18:5, 98, 102
18:9–11, 385
18:9–12, 385
18:9–14, 299, 528
18:10, 142, 533
18:11, 519–20
18:13, 294
18:14, 142, 533
18:15, 106, 117
18:15–18, 106
18:16, 221
18:18, 106
18:20, 502
18:21–22, 183
18:22, 353
19:9, 102
19:10, 191, 369
19:13, 455
19:14, 191
19:17, 516
19:18–19, 401
19:21, 455
20:1, 200
20:4, 200, 268, 486
20:10–18, 293
20:16, 191
20:17, 493
20:19, 244
21:3, 150, 302
21:5, 90, 179
21:8, 144, 369
21:11, 305, 472
21:15, 347
21:15–17, 66
21:16, 347
21:22–23, 566, 571
21:23, 571
22:21, 477
22:24, 552
23:2 (ET 23:1), 172
23:4–7 (ET 23:3–6), 422
23:8 (ET 23:7), 560
23:10–15 (ET 23:9–14), 411, 413
23:15 (ET 23:14), 200, 412
23:19 (ET 23:18), 341
23:26 (ET 23:25), 237
24:1–4, 66

24:17, 170, 403
25:3, 121
25:17–19, 293, 561
26:3, 516
26:7, 200, 224
26:12, 165
27:15–26, 260
27:19, 403
27:25, 369
28:1–12, 299
28:15, 294
28:20, 226
28:27, 136
28:29, 102
28:33, 102, 223
28:34, 416
28:50, 480
28:53, 420
28:55, 420
28:57, 420
28:59, 121
28:61, 121
29:22, 121
30:1, 299
30:2, 163
30:6, 253
30:8, 163
30:10, 163
30:16, 299
30:19, 299
30:20, 163
31:11, 59
31:13, 102
31:16, 226
31:17–18, 111
31:25, 251
31:30, 210, 273
32, 78
32:4, 78, 498
32:6, 477
32:7, 59, 235
32:10, 221, 450
32:12, 78
32:13, 194
32:14, 87
32:15, 78, 99
32:18, 78
32:21, 45, 477
32:27, 437
32:30, 78, 224, 354
32:31, 78
32:35, 467
32:37, 78
32:39, 72, 78–79, 94

32:44, 210
33:1, 103, 183, 299
33:2, 471
33:8, 268, 272–73
33:16, 248
33:17, 354
33:19, 521

Joshua
1:1, 76
1:4, 493
2:1–6, 403
2:1–24, 371, 513
2:9, 250
2:15, 370–71
2:18, 371
2:24, 250
3:5, 308, 411
3:10, 493, 501
4:3, 238
4:9, 238
4:14, 228
4:19–20, 161
4:24, 102, 477
6, 251
6:3–15, 428
6:15, 190
6:17–25, 371, 403
6:21, 284
6:24, 568
6:26, 266
7:2, 233
7:9, 228
7:13, 153, 308
7:14–18, 201
7:15, 477, 568
7:16–18, 203
7:25, 267, 552, 568
8:3, 277
8:9, 525
8:13, 525
8:29, 571
9:1, 493
9:14, 273
9:17, 152
10:3, 7, 557
10:5, 557
10:10, 255
10:10–11, 326
10:23, 557
10:26, 571
11:3, 493
11:4, 240
11:23, 191
12:1, 417

12:2, 556
12:7, 417
12:8, 493
12:11, 557
12:15, 421
13:1, 329
13:2–3, 507, 512
13:3, 136–37, 417
13:6–8, 191
13:9, 556
13:16, 556
13:22, 299
13:25, 556
13:26, 42
14:6, 103, 152, 183, 509
14:8–9, 227
14:13, 152
14:13–14, 450
14:14, 227, 509, 560
15:3, 471
15:4, 294
15:9, 123, 152
15:13, 152, 560
15:14, 7
15:16, 360
15:21–30, 512
15:22, 556–57, 563
15:24, 284
15:30, 563
15:31, 512
15:35, 325–26, 421, 557
15:35–36, 334
15:41, 135
15:42, 557, 563
15:44, 441
15:47, 294
15:48, 325
15:55, 296, 563
15:55–56, 488
15:58, 556, 563
15:60, 152
15:63, 334
16:10, 7, 508
17:11, 521
17:11–13, 535
17:12, 259
18:1, 132
18:6, 269
18:8, 269
18:10, 269
18:14–15, 152
18:25, 42

19:4, 563
19:5, 512
19:7, 557, 563
19:8, 42, 563
19:27, 135
19:29, 42
19:36, 42
20:5, 438
20:6, 516
20:8, 42
21:8–16, 151
21:12, 450
21:14, 563
21:20–22, 42, 52
21:23–24, 42
21:29, 557
21:38, 42
21:45, 112
22:5, 353
23:1, 329
23:2, 329
23:14, 112
24:11, 493
24:12, 496
24:14, 264
24:16, 226
24:17, 220
24:20, 226

Judges
1:1, 273
1:12, 360
1:16, 294, 512
1:17, 563
1:22, 112
1:26, 493
1:27, 259
1:27–36, 535
1:29, 508
1:35, 259
2:4, 210, 251
2:10, 83
2:11, 226
2:13, 155, 226
2:14, 226, 437
2:16, 156, 169
2:18, 156
3:3, 136, 417
3:5, 493
3:7, 155, 224
3:8, 224, 437
3:9, 156, 172
3:10, 169
3:12–30, 226
3:13, 293

3:15, 156, 172, 204
3:24, 453
3:31, 156, 224
4, 224
4–5, 219, 226
4:2, 224, 437
4:3, 86, 207
4:5, 42
4:7, 218
4:9, 437
4:10, 200, 478
4:11–21, 294, 512
4:13, 200
4:21, 359
5:2–31, 486
5:24, 479
5:24–27, 294, 512
6–9, 226
6:2, 240
6:3, 293
6:4, 244, 285, 334
6:6–14, 172
6:9, 99
6:12, 112
6:14, 156
6:15, 156, 201, 360
6:16, 210
6:18, 204
6:25, 525
6:33, 293
6:34–35, 240
6:36, 156
6:37, 156
6:40, 525
7:1, 542
7:2, 486
7:2–8, 240
7:2–14, 240
7:6, 240
7:7, 156
7:8, 122
7:9, 525
7:12, 240, 293
7:19, 211
7:19–21, 255
7:21, 248
7:22, 358
8:1, 86
8:5, 478
8:22, 156
8:22–23, 169
8:22–9:29, 4
8:26, 512
8:27, 89

8:34, 226
9:4, 396
9:16, 264
9:17, 156
9:19, 264
9:23–24, 318
9:24, 444
9:54, 249, 253, 569
10:1, 156
10:3, 231
10:7, 123, 224, 437
10:7–9, 160
10:10, 226
10:12, 156, 293
10:15, 59
11–12, 226
11:1, 176, 219
11:26, 556
11:30–35, 267
11:33, 285, 334, 556
11:34, 353
11:35, 267
11:40, 44
12:3, 369
12:5, 43
12:13–15, 219
13:1, 123
13:1–16:31, 224–26
13:2, 42, 219
13:4–5, 55
13:5, 49, 55, 156
14:3, 253
14:6, 193, 454
14:8, 567
14:10, 177
14:16, 211, 347
14:19, 193
15:14, 193, 330
15:16, 316
15:18, 254
16:4, 347
16:5, 136, 417
16:8, 136, 417
16:10, 163
16:15, 347
16:17, 49, 55
16:18, 136, 417
16:20–21, 569
16:21, 138, 209
16:22, 218
16:23, 135–36, 417
16:23–25, 138
16:27, 136, 417
16:30, 136, 417

17–21, 186
17:1, 42
17:5, 89, 288
17:6, 186
17:11, 259
18:1, 186
18:2, 277
18:6, 55
18:14, 288
18:14–20, 89
18:15, 192
18:17, 288
18:18, 288
18:20, 288
18:22, 252, 565
19–21, 182, 213
19:1, 42, 186, 516
19:6, 454
19:11, 343
19:13, 42
19:16–26, 182
19:21, 488
19:22, 50, 204
19:23–24, 477
19:24, 59
19:29, 213
20–21, 158
20:1, 210
20:2, 263
20:6, 477
20:8, 122, 210
20:11, 210
20:15–16, 341
20:16, 333
20:18, 132, 273
20:23, 273
20:26, 568
20:26–28, 132
20:27, 273
20:34, 565
20:35, 148
20:45, 252
21:1–3, 213
21:2, 210
21:5, 213
21:6–7, 213
21:8–9, 213
21:8–11, 213
21:12–14, 213
21:18, 266
21:19, 44
21:25, 186

Ruth
1:2, 43
1:9, 210, 349, 403
1:14, 210, 349
1:17, 265, 400
2:1, 176, 277, 319
2:4, 234
2:20, 501
3:7, 359
3:8, 302
3:10, 177
4:1, 407
4:11, 43
4:13, 312, 422
4:18–22, 310, 422
4:21, 312
4:22, 312

1 Samuel, 1, 18–19, 21, 33–34
1, 27
1–3, 4, 113, 123, 132
1–4, 115–16, 257, 380
1–7, 53, 105
1–8, 8
1–28, 116
1:1, 42–43, 49, 52, 82, 103, 105, 179, 182–83, 329, 383, 433
1:1–3, 52, 82, 179, 182
1:1–8, 42
1:1–20, 41, 58, 63, 82, 110, 179, 212
1:2, 28, 43, 52
1:3, 44, 51–52, 62, 90, 93, 102, 105, 120, 132, 142, 283, 288–89, 293, 333, 397, 454, 476, 515, 570
1:3–5, 46
1:4, 44, 49, 53
1:4–8, 53, 58, 212
1:5, 45–46, 52–53, 344, 347
1:6, 45–46, 48, 58, 75, 84, 93, 366, 438
1:6–7, 46, 78
1:7, 44–47, 157
1:8, 46–47, 53, 64, 144
1:9, 13, 36, 46–47, 54, 76, 110, 113, 142, 406, 426, 552
1:9–10, 47

1:9–18, 54, 63, 110
1:10, 48–49, 61, 69, 94, 229
1:10–11, 63
1:11, 48, 51–52, 55, 58–59, 62, 84, 90, 93, 110, 120, 221, 264, 331, 366, 380, 390, 427, 438, 456, 477–78
1:11–13, 36
1:12, 48–49, 61, 94, 229
1:13, 49
1:14, 49
1:15, 49, 55, 351
1:16, 50, 83, 86, 102, 202, 221, 474, 555
1:17, 48–49, 51, 55–56, 58–59, 61, 84, 90, 93, 120, 351, 366
1:17–18, 36
1:18, 48, 51, 56
1:19, 44, 51, 183, 190, 348
1:19–20, 56, 63
1:20, 49, 51, 56, 61, 90
1:21, 53, 58, 62, 84, 90, 93, 120, 147, 156, 366, 390
1:21–23, 62
1:21–28, 53, 58
1:22, 58, 86, 88
1:22–23, 62
1:22–27, 109, 304
1:22–28, 36
1:23, 27, 59, 62, 221
1:24, 53, 58, 60, 62, 88, 483
1:24–25, 61
1:24–28, 53, 62
1:25, 60–62, 88
1:26, 48, 61, 94, 130, 229, 238, 365, 388, 477, 495, 522, 536, 543
1:27, 48, 51, 56, 61, 88, 90, 94, 229
1:28, 44, 56, 61, 63, 90, 102, 171, 201, 220, 222, 227, 263, 335, 390, 427, 454, 476, 520
2, 27, 103

2:1, 48, 69, 78, 81, 94, 229, 465, 572
2:1–3, 78
2:1–10, 8, 36, 77
2:1–11, 68, 105
2:2, 69, 72, 78
2:2–3, 78
2:3, 70, 78
2:4, 71–72, 79
2:4–7, 79
2:5, 69, 71–72, 77, 79
2:6, 27, 72, 79, 94, 156, 249, 501, 521, 555, 571
2:6–8, 72
2:7, 28, 73, 79–80
2:7–8, 488
2:8, 74, 80, 130, 248
2:8–9, 74
2:8–10, 80, 105
2:9, 74, 80
2:10, 1, 24, 27, 46, 69, 74–75, 77–78, 80–81, 105–6, 160, 164, 180, 282, 303, 307, 329, 343, 380, 454, 481, 495, 572
2:11, 48, 63, 76, 81, 88–89, 107, 109, 183, 304
2:11–17, 89
2:11–35, 142
2:12, 50, 83–84, 86, 105, 113, 126
2:12–17, 29, 53, 63, 83, 95, 103, 107, 109, 170, 177, 304
2:12–36, 26
2:13, 83–84, 87–88, 93, 109, 120, 147, 304, 366
2:13–14, 84, 86–87
2:14, 10, 84–85, 156
2:15, 84–88, 98, 109, 304
2:15–16, 84–85
2:15–17, 94
2:16, 86, 389
2:16–36, 36
2:17, 86–88, 93, 103, 105, 109, 304
2:18, 52, 55, 76, 81, 88–89, 91, 98, 103, 107, 109, 304

2:18–21, 89, 179
2:19, 44, 58, 89, 91, 147, 346, 454, 522, 537
2:20, 48, 56, 90, 112, 179, 479, 498
2:21, 79, 88, 91, 96, 109, 112, 291, 304
2:22, 10, 92, 95, 104–5, 348
2:22–23, 92
2:22–24, 94, 96
2:22–25, 29
2:22–26, 92
2:22–29, 170
2:23, 92–93, 95, 144
2:23–25, 95
2:24, 93, 95, 120, 366
2:25, 48, 93–96, 249
2:26, 88, 91, 94, 96, 109, 112, 304
2:27, 97–99, 103–4, 106, 110, 178, 183, 380
2:27–28, 559
2:27–30, 103, 178
2:27–33, 24
2:27–36, 29, 53, 96–97, 110, 114, 178, 429, 539
2:28, 89, 98, 103, 248, 250, 428
2:29, 99–100, 103, 144
2:30, 100, 102–3, 105, 217, 222, 265, 388, 399, 427, 454, 495
2:31, 100–101, 104
2:31–32, 100
2:31–36, 104, 539
2:32, 99–102, 104
2:33, 98, 101, 104, 209
2:34, 104, 106, 131, 190
2:35, 24, 100–106, 112, 180, 282, 303, 343, 380, 454, 481, 495, 572
2:36, 44, 102, 106
3, 27, 35, 114, 381
3:1, 30, 76, 81, 88, 109, 113–14, 177, 184, 190, 291–92, 304
3:1–4, 36
3:1–21, 96, 108

3:2, 109, 111, 113, 129, 131
3:3, 54, 110, 113, 120, 142
3:4, 110, 114, 426
3:4–10, 109
3:5, 110, 426
3:6, 110, 179, 290, 359, 365, 426, 435, 446, 507
3:7, 83, 109, 113, 291–92
3:8, 88, 109–10, 304, 359, 426, 446, 507
3:9, 48, 109–10, 381, 477
3:10, 109–10, 114, 201, 394, 456
3:11, 110, 114
3:11–14, 26–27
3:11–17, 156
3:12, 109, 111, 114
3:13, 95, 111, 114, 156
3:14, 111, 114, 554
3:14–18, 35–36
3:15, 30, 109, 111, 113–14
3:16, 110–11, 426
3:17, 111, 113, 115, 392, 400, 475
3:17–18, 110
3:18, 59, 112, 115
3:18–21, 36
3:19, 112, 115, 178, 183, 368
3:19–21, 156
3:19–4:1, 91, 123
3:20, 10, 30, 105, 112, 115, 184, 192, 478, 563
3:21, 109–10, 112, 114–15, 119, 184, 291–92, 507
4, 27, 113, 137, 145, 159
4–6, 110
4–7, 226
4:1, 10, 96, 113, 118–19, 123–24, 157, 159, 194, 234, 286, 302, 333, 407, 541, 555
4:1–4, 124
4:1–5, 123, 127

4:1–10, 123
4:1–11, 118, 250–51
4:1–7:1, 4, 122
4:2, 119, 125, 128–29, 157
4:3, 110, 119–21, 125–27, 129, 132, 135, 142–44, 156, 210, 233, 260, 339, 345, 437, 465, 492, 495, 551, 570
4:3–4, 36
4:3–5, 110
4:4, 110, 114, 120, 123, 126, 132, 135, 142–43, 251
4:4–5, 120
4:5, 10, 120, 126, 143, 366
4:6, 119–20, 232, 254, 542
4:6–7, 159
4:6–8, 544, 570
4:6–11, 127
4:7, 120–21, 127, 156, 159, 191, 194, 213, 252, 365, 393, 408, 411
4:7–8, 544
4:8, 120–21, 127, 145, 537, 559–60
4:9, 101, 120, 122–23, 127, 232, 254
4:9–10, 36
4:10, 121–22, 125, 129, 157, 232, 564
4:10–11, 127
4:11, 27, 104, 120, 122–24, 126, 429, 539
4:11–22, 123
4:12, 36, 119, 128, 131, 138
4:12–18, 131
4:12–22, 122, 128
4:13, 54, 120, 128, 131–32, 302, 554
4:14, 129
4:14–15, 131
4:15, 13, 95, 129, 131, 184
4:15–18, 104
4:16, 119, 128, 564
4:16–17, 131

4:17, 49, 96, 104, 129, 131–32, 135, 144, 146, 564, 567
4:17–19, 120
4:18, 13, 22, 27, 54, 129–32, 145, 156, 429, 539
4:19, 129, 132
4:19–21, 257
4:19–22, 132
4:20, 130, 181, 425
4:21, 129–32
4:21–22, 120, 129–30, 150
4:22, 129–30, 132
5, 28, 139
5–6, 136
5:1, 110, 124, 134, 142, 157, 251
5:1–5, 137–38
5:1–12, 134
5:2, 134–35, 567, 570
5:2–7, 570
5:3, 134–36, 138, 190
5:3–7, 570
5:4, 134–35, 138, 190
5:5, 2–3, 136, 138, 142, 567
5:6, 135–36, 138–39, 144–46, 477
5:6–7, 138
5:6–12, 138
5:7, 121, 135
5:7–8, 544
5:8, 124, 135–37, 417, 542, 546
5:8–9, 138
5:8–12, 36
5:9, 47, 136–37, 139, 477
5:10, 124, 134–37, 143, 521, 555–56
5:10–11, 249
5:10–12, 139
5:11, 135–37, 139, 143, 145, 417, 546, 555
5:12, 137, 139–40
6, 140, 145, 297, 333
6:1, 13, 138, 142, 149, 507
6:1–12, 149
6:1–13, 36
6:1–7:1, 141

6:2, 142–43, 149, 297, 299, 521, 535, 544
6:3, 142–43, 149–50
6:3–5, 142
6:4, 136, 138–40, 143–44, 150, 417, 545–46
6:5, 130, 136, 138–39, 144–45, 149–50
6:6, 127, 143–45, 150, 559
6:7, 145, 150
6:7–8, 150
6:8, 142–43, 146
6:9, 146, 148, 156
6:10, 145–46
6:11, 138–39, 142, 146
6:11–12, 22
6:11–16, 124
6:12, 95, 136, 146, 151, 376, 417, 546
6:13, 13, 121, 146–47, 149
6:13–18, 151
6:14, 146–47, 151, 193, 234
6:15, 142, 146–47, 151, 193, 234, 251
6:16, 136, 151, 417, 546
6:16–18, 36, 545
6:17, 137, 143, 146, 240, 338, 414, 507, 517
6:17–18, 151
6:17–25, 513
6:18, 2–3, 136, 138–39, 142, 147, 202, 417, 546
6:19, 121, 142, 147–48, 152, 290, 351, 366
6:19–7:1, 151–52
6:20, 148, 151–52, 156
6:20–21, 36
6:21, 142
6:21–7:2, 123
7, 28, 226
7–12, 116
7–13, 380
7:1, 36, 124, 142, 148, 151–52, 158, 251
7:1–2, 251
7:2, 27, 155, 158, 227, 560

7:2–3, 123
7:2–6, 13, 158
7:2–17, 154
7:3, 123, 155, 158, 170,
    219, 221, 228, 255,
    339, 380, 498, 567,
    570
7:3–4, 159, 226
7:3–17, 27, 123
7:4, 155
7:5, 10, 48, 94, 155–56,
    158, 229, 515
7:5–11, 203
7:5–12, 116
7:6, 14, 93, 117,
    155–60, 163, 170,
    471, 520, 568
7:7, 136, 155–56,
    158–59, 163, 417,
    546
7:7–14, 159
7:8, 156, 159, 186, 190,
    339, 380, 435
7:8–9, 156, 159
7:8–10, 380
7:9, 116, 156, 159, 186,
    193, 234
7:10, 46, 75, 157,
    159–60, 193, 234,
    255
7:10–11, 161
7:11, 157–58, 160, 447
7:12, 123, 157–58, 160
7:13, 110, 157, 160,
    196, 228, 477, 507
7:14, 160, 380, 498
7:15, 14, 117, 156–57,
    170
7:15–17, 160, 307
7:16, 14, 46, 156–58,
    196
7:16–17, 59
7:17, 14, 156–57, 161,
    183, 382
8, 1, 166
8–10, 36, 293
8–12, 166–68
8:1, 163, 169, 537
8:1–3, 169, 223
8:1–6, 105
8:1–22, 61, 162, 201,
    220, 227, 263, 335,
    390, 427, 520
8:2, 169

8:3, 163, 169–70, 223
8:4, 156, 163, 170, 183
8:4–5, 182, 187
8:4–9, 170
8:4–22, 167
8:5, 1, 163–64, 166–67,
    170, 178, 182–83,
    203, 217, 226–27,
    243, 299
8:5–6, 156, 163, 229
8:6, 48, 94, 163–64,
    166, 229
8:6–7, 223
8:7, 27, 36, 53, 126,
    163, 171, 203, 217,
    227, 295
8:7–8, 166
8:7–9, 172
8:8, 2, 164, 170–71,
    559–60
8:9, 163–64, 166,
    170–71
8:9–11, 202
8:9–14, 36
8:10, 57, 164, 171, 283,
    291–92, 520
8:10–22, 61, 171, 201,
    220, 227, 263, 335,
    390, 427, 520
8:11, 164, 170–71
8:11–12, 171
8:11–17, 299
8:11–18, 166
8:12, 164, 330, 355,
    425, 430, 542
8:13, 164, 171, 181
8:14, 165, 171, 177,
    181, 285, 358, 430
8:15, 165, 171–72
8:16, 165, 171, 177,
    453
8:16–17, 165
8:16–20, 36
8:17, 165, 171–72
8:18, 164–65, 172, 186
8:19, 163–64, 203, 219
8:19–20, 172, 187, 297
8:20, 126, 164–67, 170,
    182–83, 196, 208,
    226, 229, 243, 299,
    327, 343, 355, 370,
    439, 478, 486, 513
8:21, 165
8:21–22, 172

8:22, 163–66, 172, 212,
    217, 223, 286
9, 8, 166, 171
9–11, 28
9–12, 17
9:1, 42, 176, 178, 182,
    279–80, 305, 316,
    319
9:1–3, 52, 182
9:1–25, 175, 195, 303
9:1–10:13, 198, 215
9:1–10:16, 166–67, 305
9:2, 171, 176, 181–82,
    187, 202, 280, 296,
    305–6, 308, 327,
    340, 453, 524
9:3, 177–79, 183, 211
9:4, 176–77, 183
9:4–13, 183, 303
9:5, 43, 177–79, 183,
    191, 195, 247
9:6, 112, 115, 145, 163,
    178, 183–84
9:6–8, 36
9:6–10, 103
9:7, 177–78, 184
9:8, 110, 177–79, 184,
    507
9:9, 30, 178–79, 184,
    187, 192, 211, 247,
    303
9:10, 177–79, 184
9:10–12, 36
9:11, 30, 158, 178, 185,
    303
9:12, 163, 179
9:12–13, 185
9:13, 52, 90, 156, 179,
    185, 479, 498
9:14, 180, 184–85
9:14–18, 185
9:14–25, 185, 195
9:15, 180, 389, 426
9:15–16, 4, 166, 185,
    307
9:15–17, 166
9:15–10:13, 440
9:16, 185–87, 190–91,
    196, 208, 213, 236,
    242, 255, 271, 282,
    302, 339, 380, 435,
    454, 479, 495
9:16–24, 36

9:17, 180, 186, 306,
    412
9:18, 30, 180, 185, 187
9:18–19, 303
9:19, 30, 181, 184–85,
    187
9:19–20, 187
9:19–10:1, 306
9:20, 130, 181, 187,
    195
9:20–21, 184
9:21, 49, 144, 176–77,
    181, 187, 296,
    305–6, 360, 425
9:22, 177, 179, 181,
    187
9:22–24, 187
9:23, 164, 181
9:23–24, 187
9:24, 164, 181, 184,
    187
9:25, 182, 188
9:26, 190, 195, 286,
    544
9:26–10:8, 168, 195,
    203–4, 212, 226,
    240, 252, 277, 305,
    317, 341, 362, 382,
    419, 433, 439, 451,
    465, 513, 534, 569
9:26–10:16, 168, 189,
    203–4, 212, 215,
    226, 240, 252, 277,
    305, 317, 341, 362,
    382, 419, 433, 439,
    451, 465, 513, 534,
    569
9:27, 177–78, 190
9:27–10:1, 195, 306
9:27–10:8, 529
10, 166, 439
10–12, 16
10–31, 16
10:1, 77, 180, 186, 190,
    195, 198, 213, 223,
    242, 282, 293, 295,
    297, 302, 305, 349,
    397, 454, 495
10:1–8, 187, 197
10:1–10, 500
10:2, 191, 195
10:3, 191, 352, 393,
    474, 568
10:3–4, 195, 319

10:3–12, 36
10:4, 192, 555
10:5, 192, 194, 196,
    199, 215, 226, 232,
    238–39, 351–52,
    376–77
10:5–6, 195
10:5–7, 277, 341
10:5–8, 239
10:5–13, 30
10:6, 30, 192, 195–96,
    295, 305, 308, 311,
    377, 418
10:6–7, 381
10:6–13, 311
10:7, 193, 196, 198–99,
    212, 214–15, 226,
    240, 252, 277, 317,
    341, 362, 382, 419,
    433, 439–40, 451,
    465, 513, 534, 569
10:7–8, 168, 196, 203,
    240, 242
10:8, 52–53, 58, 147,
    193, 196–98, 212,
    215, 234, 239–42,
    296, 380, 382
10:9, 187, 193, 199,
    305, 308, 378
10:9–12, 196, 199
10:9–13, 418
10:9–16, 382
10:10, 30, 182, 192,
    194, 196, 213, 295,
    305–6, 311, 317,
    341, 377, 418
10:10–11, 305, 318
10:10–12, 192, 199
10:10–13, 30
10:11, 121, 183, 192,
    194, 308, 377
10:11–12, 30, 378
10:12, 194, 199, 379
10:13, 192, 194, 199,
    344, 377
10:13–16, 199
10:14, 36, 194, 199
10:14–16, 187, 194–95,
    198
10:15–16, 199
10:16, 36, 168, 195
10:17, 158, 196, 200,
    203, 232

10:17–27, 166–68, 198,
    200, 207, 212, 226,
    240, 252, 277, 305,
    311, 317, 341, 362,
    382, 419, 433, 439,
    451, 465, 513, 534,
    569
10:18, 36, 221, 339,
    399, 498
10:18–19, 200, 203,
    209, 218, 276, 283,
    435, 559
10:19, 201, 203, 218,
    295, 435
10:20, 201, 263, 305
10:20–21, 203, 263
10:21, 183, 201, 203,
    305
10:21–22, 187
10:22, 61, 171, 201,
    203, 220, 227, 233,
    263, 274, 335, 390,
    427, 446, 520
10:23, 30, 201–2, 296,
    305, 327, 340, 524
10:23–24, 182, 203,
    308
10:24, 202, 213–14,
    295, 440
10:24–27, 36
10:25, 5, 202, 204
10:26, 182, 201–2, 305,
    373, 398
10:26–27, 204
10:27, 32, 50, 156,
    202, 204, 206, 208,
    211–12, 214, 219,
    226–27, 242, 414,
    543
10:27–11:1, 207
10:27–11:15, 205, 208,
    219, 227, 305, 570
11, 206, 224, 226
11:1, 32, 156, 206, 208,
    212, 226, 345, 392,
    426, 444, 520
11:1–2, 36, 209
11:1–11, 19, 245, 305
11:1–13, 167–68, 198,
    215, 242
11:1–15, 166, 223
11:2, 10, 206–7, 209,
    212, 426

11:3, 209, 212, 287, 291

11:4, 210, 212, 305, 457, 551

11:5, 210, 213, 305, 474

11:6, 29–30, 192–93, 196, 213, 295, 305, 311, 317, 395, 418

11:7, 210, 213–14, 400

11:7–8, 222

11:7–12, 36

11:8, 210, 214, 236, 291, 355

11:9, 210, 214, 380

11:10, 59, 214

11:11, 210–11, 214, 425, 566

11:12, 210–11, 214, 249, 265, 555

11:13, 210–11, 214, 305, 380

11:14, 210–11, 215, 296, 382

11:14–15, 198, 215, 222, 242

11:14–12:25, 167

11:15, 147, 166, 193, 210, 212, 215, 242, 296

12, 1, 166, 222

12:1, 10, 166, 217–18, 221–23

12:1–2, 217

12:1–5, 217, 222–23

12:1–25, 198, 216

12:2, 2, 100, 169, 217, 223

12:2–3, 383

12:3, 36, 77, 80, 217, 223

12:4, 223

12:5, 80, 217–18, 222–23, 391

12:5–6, 36

12:6, 218, 224

12:6–8, 559

12:6–19, 222, 224

12:7, 218, 224, 498

12:7–8, 36

12:8, 218, 220, 224–25, 251

12:8–13, 224

12:9, 44, 218, 224, 437

12:9–11, 225

12:10, 93, 155, 218, 221, 226, 251, 498

12:10–11, 380

12:10–19, 36

12:11, 218–21, 226, 339, 465, 498

12:12, 206–8, 219, 226–27

12:12–13, 224–26

12:13, 57, 61, 171, 201, 207–8, 219–20, 227, 263, 308, 335, 390, 427

12:13–19, 520

12:14, 213, 217, 220–21, 227, 229, 233, 286, 288, 428, 453

12:14–15, 208, 298

12:15, 217, 220–21, 228, 288

12:16–17, 228

12:16–19, 4

12:17, 57, 166, 220–21, 474

12:17–18, 160

12:18, 213, 221, 228, 415, 444, 520

12:19, 48, 57, 94, 220–22, 228–29

12:19–20, 229

12:20, 228–29, 233

12:20–25, 222, 228

12:21, 218, 220–21, 228, 233

12:22, 221, 228

12:23, 48, 93–94, 222, 229, 383

12:24, 213, 222, 229

12:24–25, 229

12:25, 222, 229, 495, 505, 511

13, 116, 196

13–14, 16–17, 271

13–15, 8

13–26, 231

13–31, 231

13:1, 15–16, 32–33, 213, 231–32, 238–39, 476

13:1–3, 168, 198

13:1–7, 245

13:1–15, 26

13:1–23, 230, 247, 253

13:1–14:48, 160

13:2, 122, 232–33, 240, 244, 464

13:2–3, 239

13:2–23, 239

13:2–14:46, 277

13:3, 192, 196–97, 232, 238, 240, 247, 254, 567

13:3–4, 239–40

13:4, 10, 196–97, 232–33, 238–40, 252, 296, 510

13:4–15, 168, 198

13:5, 196, 233, 240, 252, 325

13:6, 233, 240–41, 252, 259, 446

13:6–7, 255

13:7, 206, 232–33, 239–41, 249, 296, 302, 513, 534

13:7–8, 239

13:7–14, 317

13:8, 233, 239, 241, 296

13:8–9, 241

13:8–10, 382

13:8–15, 240, 311

13:9, 156, 193, 234

13:9–10, 239

13:10, 234, 239, 241, 479

13:11, 233–34, 241, 325

13:11–12, 241

13:12, 234, 239, 296, 513, 534

13:13, 235, 242–43, 266, 497

13:13–14, 16, 242

13:14, 105, 180, 186, 235–36, 242–43, 248, 308

13:15, 233, 236, 239, 244, 253, 291, 296

13:16, 233, 236, 244, 247

13:17, 183, 236, 244, 249

13:17–18, 244

13:18, 236

13:19, 120, 232, 237, 254, 352
13:19–22, 244
13:20, 10, 237
13:20–21, 237
13:21, 45, 237–38
13:22, 233, 238
13:23, 238, 244, 247, 249
13:23–14:23, 197
14, 28, 276
14–23, 36
14:1, 45, 238, 247, 252–53, 316, 320, 331, 565
14:1–16, 419, 433, 451, 513
14:1–23, 246, 439, 534
14:1–46, 245
14:2, 192, 247, 249, 253, 430
14:2–3, 253, 257
14:3, 98, 132, 248, 251–53, 409
14:4, 238, 248, 253
14:4–5, 232, 253
14:5, 247–48
14:6, 145, 238, 247–48, 253, 256, 268, 339–40, 380, 435, 569
14:7, 247–48, 254
14:8, 248
14:8–10, 254
14:9, 248
14:10, 268, 444
14:11, 120, 232, 238, 248–49, 252, 254, 446
14:12, 247, 249, 254, 268, 340, 444
14:13, 247, 249, 334
14:13–14, 255
14:14, 121, 247, 249
14:15, 236, 238, 249–50, 255, 302
14:16, 128, 247, 249, 252, 255
14:17, 247, 250, 255, 283, 291
14:18, 250–51, 255, 257, 274
14:18–19, 274, 409
14:19, 95, 251–52, 255

14:20, 251, 254–55, 513
14:21, 121, 232, 252, 255, 546
14:22, 252, 255, 446
14:23, 252, 255, 266, 268, 339, 380, 435
14:24, 256, 259, 266, 268–70, 272, 286, 317, 496
14:24–25, 36
14:24–30, 266
14:24–46, 203, 258, 441, 534, 539, 559
14:25, 260, 335
14:25–26, 266
14:26, 260–61
14:27, 259–61, 266–67, 270
14:27–28, 392
14:28, 259, 261, 266, 272, 286, 496
14:28–34, 36
14:29, 260–61, 267, 269–70
14:30, 121, 262, 267
14:31, 262, 267, 351
14:31–35, 267
14:32, 262, 268, 270, 287, 296, 474
14:32–35, 296
14:33, 93, 262
14:33–34, 268
14:34, 93, 262
14:35, 109, 262, 268
14:36, 59, 201, 263, 268
14:36–37, 253
14:36–38, 439
14:36–41, 251
14:36–46, 268
14:37, 61, 171, 201, 220, 227, 251, 263, 268, 275, 335, 390, 427, 444, 520
14:37–41, 253
14:38, 263, 268, 474
14:38–42, 203
14:39, 61, 263, 268–70, 339, 380, 435, 536
14:40, 10, 59, 263
14:40–41, 269

14:41, 31–32, 263–64, 272, 274–75, 327, 399
14:41–42, 36, 272, 275
14:42, 264, 269, 275
14:43, 265
14:43–44, 269
14:43–45, 430
14:44, 112, 265, 269–70, 392, 400, 475
14:45, 61, 265, 269–70, 365, 369, 388, 477, 495, 522, 536, 543
14:46, 265
14:47, 190, 197, 276, 422, 465
14:47–48, 215, 245, 277, 571
14:47–51, 36
14:47–52, 276, 569
14:48, 276, 334, 380, 435
14:49, 15, 239, 278, 280, 357, 568
14:49–50, 280
14:50, 18, 44, 194, 199, 277–79, 535
14:50–51, 176, 279–80
14:51, 183, 280
14:52, 277, 279, 284, 358, 568
15, 16–17, 28, 116, 278, 284, 287, 291, 295, 317, 432–33, 440, 458, 524
15–16, 380
15:1, 109, 180, 282, 291–93, 454, 495, 538
15:1–3, 533
15:1–9, 245, 284, 293, 428
15:1–31, 29
15:1–33, 512
15:1–35, 26, 281, 311, 384, 428, 432, 538, 557–58
15:2, 283, 291, 293, 559
15:2–3, 292, 465, 504, 533, 538, 561

15:3, 283, 287, 290, 293, 296, 428, 432, 555

15:4, 283–84, 291, 294, 437

15:5, 284, 294

15:6, 283–84, 294, 509, 512, 559, 563

15:7, 284–85, 294, 334, 508

15:7–23, 106

15:8, 283, 294, 428, 555

15:9, 283–86, 289, 294, 555

15:10, 109, 291–92, 298

15:10–11, 295

15:10–35, 295, 298

15:11, 166, 285, 289, 291–92, 295–96, 298, 300, 390

15:12, 190, 238, 286, 296, 482, 557, 563

15:13, 234, 283, 286, 291–92, 296, 445, 479, 498, 504, 536

15:14, 292, 296–97

15:15, 283, 285–86, 292, 296–97, 555

15:16, 287, 291, 296

15:17, 180, 282, 295–96, 454, 495

15:17–18, 36

15:17–19, 292, 533

15:17–28, 242

15:18, 283, 287, 296, 432, 465, 555

15:19, 144, 262, 287, 296, 474, 533, 538

15:20, 283–84, 287, 296, 298, 555

15:20–21, 36, 292, 384

15:21, 284, 286–87, 297–98

15:22, 287, 289, 297

15:22–23, 77, 292, 297–98, 502, 533

15:22–29, 296

15:22–16:1, 569

15:23, 142, 215, 287–88, 290–92, 295, 297–99, 303, 307–8, 366, 370,

378, 384, 398, 418, 425, 429, 432, 465, 521, 536

15:23–29, 546

15:24, 93, 287–88, 290–91, 298, 441, 497

15:24–25, 292

15:24–28, 188

15:24–32, 36

15:25, 44, 287–88, 291, 298

15:26, 215, 283, 288, 290–91, 295, 298, 303, 307–8, 418, 425, 429, 533

15:26–28, 16

15:26–29, 279, 292, 295, 298, 307, 343, 354, 356, 362, 377–79, 403, 432, 465

15:27, 288, 298, 346, 454, 537

15:27–28, 346, 466

15:28, 26, 289, 299, 368, 432, 524, 533, 538–39

15:28–29, 287, 533

15:29, 285, 289, 291, 295, 298, 300

15:30, 44, 93, 286–88, 291–92, 299, 497

15:31, 44, 62, 286, 288–89, 300

15:32, 289, 300, 411

15:33, 290, 300, 307, 384

15:34, 300, 370

15:35, 110, 166, 285, 290–92, 295, 300–301, 306, 378, 507

15:35–16:1, 384

16, 16–17, 25, 28, 116, 195, 306, 324, 337, 347–48

16–17, 17

16:1, 195, 215, 279, 288, 290, 301–3, 305–7, 319, 384, 398, 418, 432

16:1–11, 36

16:1–12, 52, 182

16:1–13, 25–27, 300–301, 305–6, 310, 315, 418, 422, 439, 449, 458, 465, 467, 481–82, 486–88, 513, 546, 571

16:2, 52, 302, 307

16:2–3, 307

16:3, 180, 282, 302, 307, 454, 495

16:4, 211, 302, 305, 307, 406, 409

16:5, 147, 149, 153, 302–3, 307

16:6, 43, 303, 308, 310, 411

16:6–12, 324

16:6–13, 339

16:7, 25, 79, 105, 183, 187, 243, 288, 299, 303, 308, 383–84, 481, 524

16:8, 303

16:8–10, 98, 304, 310, 313

16:9, 303–4

16:10, 303–4

16:10–11, 339

16:11, 304, 306, 310, 319, 329

16:11–13, 279

16:12, 180, 282, 303–6, 310–11, 316, 333, 454, 472, 495, 524

16:12–13, 25, 116, 355–56, 432–33, 441

16:13, 29–30, 77, 180, 192–96, 282, 300, 305–6, 309, 311, 317, 320, 359, 418, 446, 454, 495, 500, 523

16:13–14, 340

16:14, 4, 29–30, 193, 300, 306, 314–19, 366, 398, 418, 523, 538

16:14–15, 317

16:14–16, 317, 375, 528

16:14–23, 3, 26, 305, 314, 352, 355, 366, 370, 375, 378, 418

16:15, 30, 314–16, 352, 366, 375

16:15–16, 316, 318

16:16, 10, 30, 315–16, 352, 366

16:17, 315, 318

16:18, 29, 112, 305–6, 315, 318, 324–25, 337, 351, 483, 522–23

16:19, 305, 319, 337

16:20, 60, 316, 319

16:21, 247, 253, 316, 319–20, 324, 329, 339, 344

16:21–23, 337

16:22, 316, 320, 329, 337

16:23, 30, 306, 314–18, 320, 366, 375, 528

17, 12, 25, 28, 324, 336–37, 347, 354, 369, 419, 479

17–18, 33–34, 323, 327

17:1, 284, 325, 337–38

17:1–11, 337

17:1–58, 33, 160, 305, 320–21, 344, 350, 357

17:1–18:30, 33, 323, 335, 344, 350, 357

17:2, 119, 325–26, 328, 330, 338, 409

17:3, 338

17:3–8, 36

17:4, 325–27, 338, 340–41, 369

17:5, 327, 332

17:5–7, 327, 336, 338

17:6, 328, 333, 336

17:7, 327–28, 352

17:8, 119, 144, 326, 328, 338, 435

17:8–10, 330

17:9, 328, 338

17:10, 119, 328–29, 333, 338, 342

17:10–11, 418

17:11, 10, 329, 338, 534

17:12, 43, 152, 305, 310, 329

17:12–14, 324

17:12–15, 338

17:12–19, 338

17:12–31, 33, 324

17:13, 43, 304, 310, 329

17:13–14, 329

17:14, 329

17:15, 305, 316, 319, 329

17:16, 190, 329, 339

17:17, 325, 329

17:17–19, 339

17:18, 164, 291, 330

17:19, 326, 328

17:20, 190, 328–30, 350, 492

17:20–21, 339

17:20–22, 119

17:20–30, 339

17:21, 326, 328, 330

17:22, 192, 328, 330

17:22–24, 339

17:23, 326, 328, 330–31, 369

17:24, 330, 564

17:24–25, 330

17:25, 325, 329–31, 333, 337, 339, 342–43, 360–62, 467, 489

17:26, 253, 309, 328–29, 331, 333, 339–40, 342, 361, 501, 536, 569

17:27, 331, 400

17:28, 43, 144, 310, 329–31, 339, 395

17:29, 331, 340

17:29–30, 339

17:30, 331

17:31, 331, 340

17:31–39, 431

17:31–40, 340

17:32, 17, 328, 331, 340

17:32–37, 254

17:32–39, 4

17:33, 17, 319, 325, 328, 331, 337, 339–40

17:34, 304, 331–32

17:34–36, 319, 325

17:34–37, 305, 319, 337, 340, 513

17:35, 332, 498

17:36, 253, 328–29, 331–33, 339–40, 342, 501, 536, 569

17:37, 197, 221, 305, 309, 319, 332, 340–42, 362, 380, 498, 523

17:38, 327, 332, 345

17:38–39, 17, 340

17:39, 332, 345

17:40, 319, 332, 337, 341, 479

17:40–41, 36

17:40–53, 534

17:40–54, 439

17:41, 95, 324–25, 333, 341

17:41–51, 355

17:42, 17, 304–5, 333, 341, 472

17:42–44, 341

17:43, 111, 332–33, 341–42, 472, 537, 560

17:43–44, 341

17:43–47, 418

17:44, 333, 571

17:45, 44, 309, 328–29, 333, 337

17:45–46, 305

17:45–47, 305, 309, 342, 513

17:46, 138, 309, 325, 333, 337, 342, 445, 457, 494, 517, 571

17:47, 309–10, 333, 337, 342, 352, 380, 435, 444

17:48, 326, 328, 333, 359

17:48–51, 305, 342

17:48–54, 513

17:49, 325, 332–33, 479

17:49–50, 319

17:50, 4, 324–25, 479

17:51, 138, 249, 325, 328, 334, 413, 517, 546, 565, 570

17:52, 214, 285, 334, 342, 355, 447, 564
17:52–58, 342
17:53, 325, 334, 338
17:53–54, 342
17:54, 334, 342–43, 413, 517, 546, 570
17:55, 44, 61, 326, 334–35, 337, 445, 515
17:55–56, 343
17:55–58, 324–25, 337
17:55–18:6, 324
17:56, 334, 393
17:57, 343, 546
17:58, 305, 331, 335, 343–44
18, 17, 361
18:1, 344–47, 361, 368, 425
18:1–4, 325, 449
18:1–5, 33, 252, 254, 325, 344, 347, 392
18:1–6, 324
18:2, 346
18:3, 209, 344–48, 361, 368, 390, 392, 398–99, 404, 426, 444, 449, 457, 466
18:3–4, 346, 369
18:4, 89, 345–47, 377, 400, 447, 451, 454, 550, 566
18:4–5, 36
18:5, 325, 345–46, 350, 353–54, 360–61, 448, 483
18:5–30, 197
18:6, 325, 350, 353, 408, 414, 421, 439, 456, 515, 543–44, 547
18:6–7, 325
18:6–8, 353
18:6–9, 353
18:6–11, 346
18:6–16, 252, 350
18:7, 77, 351, 353, 361, 414, 418, 431, 543
18:7–8, 546
18:8, 320, 324–25, 350–51, 354, 390
18:9, 320, 352, 355, 393

18:10, 10, 30, 192–93, 318, 352, 355, 366, 375, 377, 418, 430, 528, 566
18:10–11, 26, 33, 324–25, 350, 352, 370, 403, 500
18:10–13, 355
18:11, 320, 351–52, 355, 366, 396, 398, 411, 494
18:11–12, 318
18:12, 29, 112, 319, 347, 352, 355, 362, 444, 523, 538
18:12–13, 346
18:13, 164, 345, 350, 352, 354–55, 421, 425, 431
18:14, 29, 112, 319, 345–46, 353, 361, 483, 523
18:14–15, 347, 355, 360
18:14–16, 325, 355
18:15, 320, 345–46, 353, 483
18:16, 10, 214, 344–45, 350, 353, 355–56, 361, 421
18:17, 277, 357–58, 360–62, 411, 467, 478, 486, 489, 512–13
18:17–18, 36
18:17–19, 33, 278, 324–25, 357
18:17–29, 337
18:17–30, 357
18:18, 358, 360–61
18:19, 358, 361, 467, 489
18:20, 344, 347, 358, 361, 401
18:20–21, 361
18:20–27, 346, 489, 506, 558
18:21, 324–25, 357–58, 361, 411
18:21–27, 466–67, 502
18:22, 344, 358, 361, 365, 368–69, 454
18:23, 358–61
18:24, 358

18:24–25, 361
18:25, 254, 359–60, 362
18:26, 324–25, 357–59, 362
18:27, 17, 278, 313, 358–59, 362, 401, 431, 446, 488
18:28, 29, 112, 344, 347, 359, 361, 523
18:28–29, 319, 346, 362
18:29, 110, 360, 362
18:29–30, 324–25, 357
18:30, 339, 345–46, 350, 360, 362–63, 431, 439, 483, 546
19, 116, 297, 311, 371, 380
19–21, 17
19–24, 17
19–26, 362
19:1, 347, 365–69, 400
19:1–6, 346
19:1–7, 252, 367–68, 388, 398, 429–30, 438, 444, 453, 491, 506
19:1–17, 364, 388, 401, 409, 429, 438, 453, 482, 491, 506
19:2, 365, 368–70, 388, 429, 446, 453, 475, 491, 506
19:2–3, 400
19:3, 365, 368–69
19:3–5, 369
19:4, 93, 365, 369, 455
19:5, 10, 93, 144, 365, 369, 380, 435
19:6, 61, 265, 365, 370, 536, 554
19:7, 121, 365, 368, 370
19:8, 110, 121, 365, 370, 436, 507
19:8–10, 368, 370
19:9, 10, 30, 366, 375, 418, 430, 528
19:9–10, 318, 325, 352, 370, 398, 403, 500
19:10, 366, 369–70, 374, 395, 398, 420,

428–29, 453, 491, 494, 506, 525
19:10–13, 36
19:11, 365–66, 370–71
19:11–12, 370
19:11–16, 402
19:11–17, 288, 362, 368, 370, 398, 401, 409, 513
19:12, 366, 370–71, 374, 388, 414, 428
19:13, 288, 366–67, 370–71, 493
19:13–17, 517
19:14, 367, 371, 375, 409
19:15, 365, 367, 372
19:15–17, 36
19:16, 288, 367, 371–72, 493
19:17, 144, 366–67, 370–72, 402, 522
19:18, 366, 370, 374, 377, 388, 401
19:18–24, 300, 318, 373–74, 398, 401, 530
19:19, 374–75, 377
19:19–24, 30, 199
19:20, 30, 192, 194, 196, 238, 375–76, 378, 425
19:20–21, 377
19:21, 110, 192, 376
19:22, 374–77
19:23, 30, 95, 192, 196, 374–78
19:23–24, 318, 418
19:24, 30, 192, 345, 376–79, 566
20, 348, 398
20:1, 320, 347, 366, 369, 388, 398, 429, 506
20:1–10, 398
20:1–21:1 (ET 20:1–42), 373, 386, 409, 449
20:2, 180, 388–89, 391, 398, 426, 444
20:3, 61, 388, 396, 399, 403–4, 536
20:4, 33, 389, 399

20:5, 365, 389, 391, 398, 444, 507
20:5–7, 399
20:6, 58, 61, 171, 201, 227, 263, 291, 389–90, 392, 394, 427, 520
20:7, 390, 396
20:8, 144, 345–46, 348–49, 390, 398–99, 404, 449, 496
20:9, 388, 390–91, 399
20:10, 391, 399
20:11, 389, 391, 399
20:11–24, 399
20:12, 180, 389, 391, 399
20:13, 112, 180, 319, 389, 391–92, 399–400, 475, 523
20:14, 392
20:14–15, 468
20:14–17, 400, 404
20:15, 209, 392, 457
20:15–16, 465
20:16, 392, 426, 444, 457, 466
20:17, 110, 222, 344–45, 347, 368, 392, 404, 507
20:18, 389, 392, 473
20:18–23, 400
20:19, 393, 397, 400, 444
20:20, 222, 393
20:21, 61, 388, 393, 396, 404, 536
20:22, 335, 352, 393
20:23, 391, 393, 400
20:24, 389, 394, 400, 444
20:24–25, 400
20:24–34, 400, 409
20:25, 389, 392–94, 447, 473
20:26, 394, 400, 411
20:26–42, 36
20:27, 389, 394, 401, 430, 473, 484, 566
20:28, 61, 171, 201, 220, 227, 263, 390, 394, 520

20:28–29, 371, 401–2, 409, 513, 517
20:29, 366, 370, 394
20:30, 347–49, 395, 401, 403, 484
20:30–31, 242, 430
20:30–33, 430
20:31, 102, 395, 401, 403, 484, 496
20:32, 144, 396, 403
20:33, 352, 365, 390, 396, 398, 403
20:34, 388–89, 394, 396, 403, 473
20:35, 389, 396
20:35–40, 403
20:35–21:1 (ET 20:35–42), 397, 403
20:36, 222, 396–97
20:37, 352, 393, 396–97
20:37–40, 36
20:38, 397, 543
20:40, 397
20:41, 44–45, 62, 347–48, 393, 397, 403
20:41–42, 325
20:42, 55, 90, 345–46, 348–49, 398–400, 404, 449, 457, 468
21, 417
21–22, 257
21:1 (ET 20:42b), 33, 389, 397, 404, 446
21:1–3 (ET 20:42b–2), 36
21:2 (ET 21:1), 48, 406, 409, 411
21:2–7 (ET 21:1–6), 499
21:2–10 (ET 21:1–9), 132, 373, 406, 430–31, 435, 439
21:2–16 (ET 21:1–15), 33
21:3 (ET 21:2), 48, 401, 406–7, 409
21:3–4 (ET 21:2–3), 371, 401, 513, 517
21:4 (ET 21:3), 192, 407, 410
21:5 (ET 21:4), 406–7, 410–11

21:5–6 (ET 21:4–5), 407

21:5–7 (ET 21:4–6), 426, 430

21:5–10 (ET 21:4–9), 36

21:6 (ET 21:5), 149, 406–8, 411–12

21:7 (ET 21:6), 406, 408, 410–11

21:8 (ET 21:7), 408, 411–12

21:9 (ET 21:8), 407, 409, 413

21:10 (ET 21:9), 326, 328, 342, 406, 409, 413, 430

21:11 (ET 21:10), 366, 414–17, 511

21:11–16 (ET 21:10–15), 373, 414, 417, 510–11, 513

21:12 (ET 21:11), 77, 351, 414, 417–18, 511, 543, 546

21:13 (ET 21:12), 414, 418–19, 444

21:13–14 (ET 21:12–13), 371, 401, 409–10, 513, 517

21:14 (ET 21:13), 415, 418, 436, 480

21:14–16 (ET 21:13–15), 419

21:15 (ET 21:14), 144, 416, 418

21:15–16 (ET 21:14–15), 418

21:16 (ET 21:15), 203, 416, 418, 475

22–23, 257

22:1, 366, 370, 420–22, 426

22:1–2, 373, 441

22:1–5, 420

22:1–23:6, 436

22:2, 156, 420, 422, 436, 442, 466, 511

22:3, 420–22

22:3–4, 373

22:4, 421–22

22:4–5, 443

22:5, 30, 116, 373, 421–23, 433, 436, 439, 441, 444

22:6, 192, 425–26, 430, 568

22:6–10, 430

22:6–23, 424

22:7, 164, 401, 425, 430, 484

22:8, 180, 209, 389, 392, 401, 425, 427–28, 430–31, 444, 449, 466, 468, 484

22:8–9, 36

22:9, 257, 406, 425–26, 430, 484

22:9–10, 412, 466

22:10, 274, 309, 326, 328, 426, 430–31, 435, 552

22:10–11, 36

22:11, 48, 426, 429, 431

22:11–19, 431

22:11–23, 104

22:12, 426, 431

22:13, 144, 274, 309, 401, 425–26, 431, 435, 484

22:14, 427, 431

22:14–15, 409, 413

22:15, 109, 309, 426–27, 429, 431, 435, 445, 480

22:16, 426, 431

22:16–20, 499

22:16–23, 435

22:17, 180, 366, 388, 425–27, 429, 431, 494

22:17–18, 429

22:17–19, 412

22:18, 89, 98, 427–28, 432

22:18–19, 409

22:19, 132, 284, 428, 432

22:20, 366, 428

22:20–21, 432

22:20–22, 257

22:20–23, 432, 436, 441–42, 534

22:22, 104, 426, 428–29, 432, 466

22:23, 369, 429, 432–33, 506

23, 448, 482

23:1, 334, 434, 440, 447

23:1–4, 439

23:1–5, 440

23:1–6, 423

23:1–13, 373, 434, 439

23:2, 274, 309, 380, 430, 435, 441, 525

23:2–4, 437, 439, 442, 465

23:3, 435, 441

23:4, 110, 274, 309, 430, 435, 444, 525

23:4–5, 441

23:5, 121, 380, 435, 437, 439, 441

23:6, 257, 366, 413, 436, 441–42, 534

23:6–12, 559

23:6–13, 25, 442

23:6–14, 432

23:7, 434, 437, 439–42

23:7–8, 442

23:7–18, 423

23:8, 284, 437, 442

23:8–23, 36

23:9, 48, 251, 257, 437–38, 441, 552

23:9–10, 442

23:9–12, 274, 439, 441–42

23:9–13, 268

23:10, 369, 399, 438, 506

23:10–12, 309

23:11, 399, 437–38, 442, 445, 457, 494, 554

23:12, 33, 438, 442, 445, 457, 462, 494, 554

23:13, 366, 370, 422, 435–36, 438–39, 442, 451, 466, 511, 557

23:14, 369, 443, 449, 460, 506

23:14–18, 373

23:14–24:1 (ET 23:14–29), 443, 499

23:15, 369, 422–23, 444, 460, 506

23:15–16, 449

23:15–18, 449

23:16, 423, 444, 446, 449

23:17, 444, 449

23:18, 209, 345–46, 348–49, 390, 392, 398–99, 404, 423, 426, 444, 449, 457, 466

23:19, 192, 423, 443–44, 447, 450, 460, 466, 491, 499

23:19–20, 483, 497, 499, 502

23:19–24, 450, 499

23:19–28, 373

23:20, 438, 445, 450, 457, 462, 494, 554

23:21, 445, 450, 479, 496, 498, 504, 536

23:22, 445–46, 474

23:22–23, 450

23:23, 446, 474, 492, 521

23:24, 445–46, 450, 482, 491

23:24–24:1 (ET 23:24–29), 450

23:25, 369, 444, 447, 450, 456, 496, 506, 552

23:26, 447, 451

23:27, 345, 444, 447, 451, 566

23:27–28, 511

23:28, 447, 451

24, 25, 459, 461–64, 482, 498, 505, 569

24:1 (ET 23:29), 33, 443, 451, 464

24:1–22 (ET 23:29–24:21), 373

24:2 (ET 24:1), 453, 460, 464, 497, 499, 502

24:2–8 (ET 24:1–7), 464

24:2–23 (ET 24:1–22), 33, 320, 343, 452, 482, 498

24:3 (ET 24:2), 10, 369, 453, 455, 460, 464, 491, 499, 506

24:3–5 (ET 24:2–4), 36

24:4 (ET 24:3), 453, 459–60, 463, 465

24:5 (ET 24:4), 89, 346, 359, 444, 453, 455, 457, 460–61, 465, 500, 522

24:6 (ET 24:5), 454, 458–59, 465

24:6–7 (ET 24:5–6), 25, 458

24:7 (ET 24:6), 25, 80, 454, 458, 460–61, 465, 494–95, 498, 500

24:8 (ET 24:7), 454, 459–60, 465

24:8–9 (ET 24:7–8), 466

24:8–16 (ET 24:7–15), 465

24:9 (ET 24:8), 44–45, 62, 454, 461, 522

24:10 (ET 24:9), 144, 453, 455, 461, 466, 506

24:10–16 (ET 24:9–15), 463, 466

24:11 (ET 24:10), 25, 80, 444, 454–55, 461, 466, 494–95, 498, 500

24:12 (ET 24:11), 93, 346, 454–55, 461–62, 466, 474, 502

24:13 (ET 24:12), 456, 466

24:13–16 (ET 24:12–15), 466

24:14 (ET 24:13), 455–56, 466, 472

24:15 (ET 24:14), 341, 447, 456, 461, 466, 472, 497, 503

24:16 (ET 24:15), 456–57, 461, 466

24:17 (ET 24:16), 210, 344, 457, 461, 467, 502, 551

24:17–19 (ET 24:16–18), 464

24:17–22 (ET 24:16–21), 463, 467

24:17–23 (ET 24:16–22), 467

24:18 (ET 24:17), 457, 462, 467, 485, 503, 569

24:18–20 (ET 24:17–19), 467

24:19 (ET 24:18), 333, 445, 457, 461–62, 467, 494

24:20 (ET 24:19), 457, 461–62, 467

24:21 (ET 24:20), 243, 346, 449, 457, 462, 467, 482, 504, 569

24:21–22 (ET 24:20–21), 464, 467

24:22 (ET 24:21), 90, 457, 467, 554

24:22–23 (ET 24:21–22), 320

24:23 (ET 24:22), 373, 421, 443, 462, 464, 468, 482

25, 25, 519

25:1, 2, 10, 17, 22, 116, 155, 160, 380, 464, 471, 482, 516, 519, 534

25:1–43, 373

25:1–44, 469, 499

25:2, 472, 482, 499, 506, 551, 557, 563

25:2–3, 472, 477, 482

25:2–42, 296

25:2–43, 464

25:3, 305, 319, 345, 450, 472, 477, 481, 483, 486–87, 506, 522, 551, 558

25:3–12, 36

25:4, 472, 483

25:4–8, 483

25:5, 192, 219, 473, 484, 551, 557, 563

25:6, 473, 484

25:7, 473, 485, 557, 563
25:7–8, 484–85
25:8, 473, 484
25:9, 473, 484
25:9–22, 484
25:10, 401, 474, 484, 543
25:11, 181, 474, 483–84, 487
25:12, 51, 484
25:13, 422, 442, 484
25:14, 234, 262, 472, 474, 479, 484, 543, 558
25:15, 291, 473–74, 485
25:15–16, 485
25:16, 143, 485
25:17, 50, 474, 484–85, 543
25:18, 472, 474, 483, 485, 488, 553
25:19, 475, 485
25:20, 475, 485
25:20–21, 36
25:21, 473, 475, 485
25:22, 112, 400, 465, 475, 485, 487
25:23, 44–45, 472, 476, 481, 485
25:23–31, 485
25:24, 476, 478, 486
25:25, 50, 130, 204, 472, 474, 476–77, 483, 486
25:25–27, 36
25:26, 61, 96, 369, 465–66, 477, 479–80, 486, 536
25:26–33, 498
25:27, 477–78, 481, 486, 556
25:28, 105, 360, 476–78, 486, 512–13
25:29, 333, 369, 447, 478, 487–88, 498, 501, 506
25:30, 180, 186, 479
25:30–31, 487
25:30–32, 36
25:31, 365, 466, 476–79

25:31–34, 96
25:32, 399, 472, 487
25:32–33, 478–80, 486–87
25:32–35, 487
25:33, 477–78, 480, 487–88, 498
25:34, 61, 399, 476–77, 480, 487, 536
25:35, 480, 487
25:36, 427, 472, 480, 487
25:36–42, 487
25:37, 480, 483, 487–88
25:37–39, 499
25:38, 488, 495
25:38–39, 500, 506, 558
25:38–40, 36
25:39, 472, 477, 480, 498
25:39–40, 488
25:39–42, 506, 558
25:40, 472, 480, 552, 557, 563
25:41, 44–45, 476–78, 481, 488
25:42, 313, 472, 478, 481, 488, 534
25:42–43, 17, 499, 558
25:43, 21, 278, 313, 499, 506, 542, 558
25:43–44, 488, 499, 507
25:44, 489, 502, 507, 558
26, 25, 459, 461–64, 482, 498, 504–5, 569
26:1, 192, 444–45, 450, 460, 491, 497, 499, 502
26:1–3, 499
26:1–25, 320, 343, 373, 490
26:2, 369, 453, 460, 491, 499, 506
26:3, 445, 450, 460, 491, 499
26:4, 492, 499
26:4–6, 499
26:5, 330, 491–92, 499, 515, 542

26:6, 49, 492, 499–500
26:6–11, 465
26:7, 330, 463, 492–93, 500
26:7–12, 500
26:8, 333, 352, 445, 457, 460–62, 465, 494, 500
26:9, 25, 80, 454, 461, 465, 494, 498, 500–501
26:9–12, 36
26:10, 25, 61, 222, 495, 500, 505, 511, 536
26:10–11, 458
26:11, 25, 80, 454, 460–61, 463, 465, 494–95, 498, 500–501
26:12, 460, 463, 493–95, 501
26:13, 501, 503
26:13–16, 501
26:14, 49, 461, 463, 492, 495, 501, 503
26:15, 144, 461, 494–95, 502, 543
26:15–16, 463
26:16, 25, 61, 80, 395, 454, 461, 463, 465, 494–96, 502, 536, 543
26:17, 461, 463, 496, 502
26:17–20, 463
26:17–25, 502
26:18, 144, 447, 461, 496, 502
26:18–20, 514
26:19, 191, 461, 496, 499, 502, 511, 560
26:19–20, 464, 498, 503
26:20, 369, 447, 461, 491, 496–97, 503, 506
26:21, 93, 235, 266, 291, 461–63, 497–98, 503, 569
26:21–24, 36
26:21–25, 464
26:22, 49, 497, 503
26:22–24, 320, 463

26:23, 25, 80, 444, 454, 461–62, 465, 494–95, 497–98, 503

26:24, 461, 497–98, 504

26:25, 449, 461–64, 496, 498, 504, 536, 569

27, 17, 417, 503

27:1, 222, 366, 369–70, 464, 495, 505, 510–11

27:1–2, 36

27:1–4, 373, 510

27:1–12, 417, 505, 510, 516–17, 525, 545, 557, 568

27:1–28:2, 517

27:1–31:13, 516, 545, 557, 568

27:2, 417, 422, 442, 506, 511

27:2–3, 506

27:3, 21, 278, 296, 482, 489, 499, 506–7, 511, 542, 557–58, 563

27:4, 110, 366, 369, 506–7, 511

27:4–5, 422

27:5, 144, 395, 507, 511

27:5–6, 511

27:5–12, 373

27:6, 2–3, 7, 507, 512, 546

27:7, 17, 142, 231, 417, 507, 512, 542

27:7–12, 512

27:8, 235, 285, 334, 345, 451, 507–8, 512, 557, 560, 566

27:8–9, 558

27:8–12, 36, 419, 546–47

27:9, 508, 512–13

27:9–11, 508

27:9–12, 517

27:10, 345, 451, 507–9, 512, 557, 563, 566

27:10–11, 371, 401, 409, 508, 517

27:11, 102, 142, 509, 513

27:12, 232, 240, 508–9, 513, 544

27:12–28:2, 512

28, 25, 29, 116, 160, 385, 547, 557–58, 568

28–31, 526

28:1, 155, 214, 439, 515–17, 520, 541, 548

28:1–2, 510, 515–17, 519, 525

28:1–3, 36

28:1–5, 562

28:1–25, 482

28:2, 515–17, 545

28:3, 10, 116, 380, 471, 482, 516, 519–22, 534–35

28:3–25, 385, 510, 518, 520, 525, 530, 534, 545, 558, 565, 570–71

28:4, 10, 155, 515, 517, 520, 527, 534, 548

28:5, 197, 252, 444, 520, 524, 534

28:6, 251, 264, 268, 272, 274–75, 520–21, 525, 534, 538, 558–59

28:7, 519–21, 530, 535, 540

28:7–8, 548

28:7–19, 378

28:8, 142, 297, 299, 446, 519, 521–22, 528, 533, 535

28:8–25, 527

28:9, 144, 520–21, 536

28:10, 61, 522, 536, 538, 554

28:11, 380, 521–22, 528, 530, 536

28:12, 144, 380, 522, 527–28, 530, 533, 536

28:12–19, 528

28:13, 520, 522–23, 529, 536–37, 544, 560

28:14, 44–45, 62, 346, 380, 454–55, 522, 528–30, 537

28:15, 144, 380, 522, 528, 530, 533–34, 537–38, 552, 558

28:15–19, 295

28:16, 144, 380, 523, 530, 538–39

28:16–18, 538

28:16–19, 528, 530, 539, 569

28:17, 523, 533, 538–39

28:17–19, 539

28:18, 295, 524, 538, 557

28:19, 444, 530–32, 539, 569

28:20, 380, 444, 520, 524, 530, 539

28:20–22, 540

28:21, 369, 524

28:21–22, 540

28:22, 524

28:22–25, 36

28:23, 524, 540

28:23–25, 571

28:24, 165, 524, 540

28:25, 446, 525, 540, 548

29–30, 17

29:1, 36, 155, 515–16, 527, 541, 545, 548, 558, 562

29:1–11, 255, 373, 417, 510, 514, 525, 538, 541, 545, 550, 557–58, 568

29:2, 136, 417, 517, 542, 545–46, 548

29:3, 2, 120, 232, 254, 512, 542–47

29:3–5, 512

29:4, 517, 521, 542, 546–47

29:4–5, 517, 546

29:5, 77, 203, 351, 414, 543, 546

29:6, 2, 61, 136, 350, 417, 421, 536, 542–44, 546–47

29:7, 55, 136, 417, 546–47

29:8, 2, 542, 544, 547
29:9, 49, 544, 546–47
29:10, 190, 543–44, 547
29:11, 190, 516, 544, 547–48, 562
29:11–30:1, 527
30, 557, 563
30:1, 345, 451, 548, 550, 558, 566
30:1–6, 558
30:1–31, 373, 510, 549
30:2, 551, 555, 558
30:2–3, 558
30:3, 550–51, 554, 558
30:4, 210, 551
30:5, 278, 296, 489, 550–51, 558
30:6, 538, 552, 558, 560
30:7, 48, 251, 257, 552, 558–59
30:7–8, 309, 432, 441, 534, 559
30:7–16, 554
30:8, 274, 380, 430, 435, 447, 525, 552, 558–61
30:9, 442, 553, 559
30:9–10, 422
30:9–15, 559
30:10, 447, 552–53, 555, 559–60
30:11, 553
30:11–12, 485, 559
30:12, 553
30:13, 553–54
30:13–14, 548, 550, 560
30:14, 345, 550–51, 558, 560, 566
30:15, 438, 445, 457, 494, 552, 554, 560
30:16, 554, 560
30:16–20, 560
30:17, 366, 548, 553–54, 560
30:18, 552–53, 555
30:18–19, 561
30:19, 555
30:20, 436, 551, 555, 561
30:21, 180, 192, 553, 555

30:21–22, 561
30:21–25, 561–62
30:22, 50, 552–53, 555
30:22–31, 36
30:23, 444, 552, 555, 561
30:24, 556, 561
30:25, 2–3, 561
30:26, 465, 548, 555–56, 559, 561, 567, 571
30:26–31, 561
30:27, 42, 556
30:27–30, 561
30:27–31, 556
30:28, 556–57
30:29, 557
30:30, 557
30:31, 557, 562
31, 25, 28, 160, 245, 270, 295, 531, 568
31:1, 531–32, 548, 561, 564, 566, 568
31:1–4, 36
31:1–6, 341, 525, 527
31:1–13, 11, 26, 510, 564, 568
31:2, 15, 252, 278, 280, 530, 532, 565–66, 568–69
31:2–6, 548
31:3, 222, 532, 565, 569
31:4, 254, 532, 565–66, 569, 571
31:4–6, 247, 253
31:5, 566
31:5–6, 569
31:6, 531–32, 565–66, 569
31:7, 531–32, 564, 566, 570
31:8, 345, 531–32, 565–66, 570
31:8–10, 548
31:9, 28, 138, 345, 532–33, 566–67, 570
31:9–11, 566
31:10, 155, 567–68, 570
31:11, 567
31:11–12, 570
31:11–13, 532, 566

31:12, 446, 531, 567–68, 571
31:12–13, 570
31:13, 425, 471, 568

2 Samuel, 1, 33–34, 257
1, 5, 8, 547, 557–58, 568
1–4, 10
1:1, 548, 557
1:1–16, 131
1:1–11:1, 33
1:2, 44, 62, 131
1:2–16, 548, 569
1:3–4, 131
1:4, 287, 532, 564
1:4–5, 36
1:6, 252
1:9, 249
1:10, 249, 533, 570
1:10–13, 36
1:12, 471, 568
1:14, 77, 80, 454, 458, 465, 494–95, 569
1:14–16, 343, 495
1:15, 428
1:16, 77, 80, 249, 454, 458, 465, 477, 495
1:17–27, 10, 76
1:18, 5
1:19, 565
1:19–27, 8, 320
1:20, 253, 567
1:21, 77, 180, 282
1:22, 565
1:22–24, 215
1:23, 344
1:23–24, 320
1:24, 571
1:25, 565
1:26, 345, 347
2, 1
2–4, 18
2–24, 8, 18
2:1, 274, 430, 435, 441, 525, 562–63
2:1–7, 18
2:1–11, 355
2:2, 278, 296, 552, 557–58
2:2–4, 489
2:4, 180, 282, 454, 495, 512, 562
2:4–5, 471
2:5, 445

2:5–16, 36
2:6, 112, 222
2:7, 180, 282, 454, 495
2:8, 278, 280, 476, 531, 569
2:8–9, 18
2:8–10, 15, 18, 530, 565
2:8–11, 539
2:8–4:12, 18
2:9, 166
2:10, 14–15, 214, 231, 278, 280, 355, 476
2:10–11, 15, 213
2:11, 14, 277
2:11–32, 18
2:12, 204, 278, 476
2:13, 500
2:14, 351
2:15, 278, 476
2:17, 119, 157
2:18, 500
2:22, 110, 144
2:25, 156
2:25–32, 36
2:26, 552
2:27, 61
2:28, 110, 567
2:29, 525
2:30, 155, 515
2:32, 471
3, 18
3:1, 95
3:1–15, 36
3:2, 278, 488, 558
3:2–5, 21, 313, 348
3:3, 296, 488, 508, 552, 557–58
3:7, 348, 569
3:8, 278, 291, 341, 390, 476
3:9, 112, 475
3:10, 214, 243, 355, 400
3:12, 10, 209
3:12–13, 345
3:13, 209
3:14, 278, 476
3:14–16, 489
3:15, 278, 476, 489
3:16, 95
3:17, 18, 36
3:18, 380, 435, 465
3:19, 530

3:21, 10, 36, 155, 209, 389, 515
3:23–39, 36
3:24, 95, 144
3:28, 477
3:31, 471
3:32, 210, 471, 551
3:33, 477
3:33–34, 77
3:34, 110
3:35, 112, 400, 475
3:36, 496
3:37, 10
3:39, 180, 282, 454, 495, 500
4, 15, 18
4:1, 10
4:1–4, 36
4:1–12, 530, 565
4:3, 2–3, 366
4:4, 17, 476
4:5, 278, 476
4:8, 90, 278, 465, 476
4:9, 61, 536
4:9–12, 36
4:10, 567
4:12, 278, 471, 476, 571
5, 18
5–24, 18–19
5:1–3, 11, 36, 277, 562
5:1–8, 15, 18
5:2, 121, 180, 186, 350, 421
5:3, 180, 209, 282, 454, 495
5:4, 14, 16, 239
5:4–5, 417, 426
5:4–16, 213, 277
5:5, 10, 14, 214, 355, 512, 562
5:6–8, 343
5:6–10, 11
5:6–16, 36
5:6–25, 22
5:7, 19, 276, 292, 421
5:8, 343
5:9, 2, 19, 292, 421
5:9–16, 18
5:10, 4, 29, 95, 292, 319
5:11, 19–20, 22
5:11–12, 19
5:11–16, 11

5:12, 243, 292
5:13–16, 19, 313
5:14, 313
5:14–16, 11
5:16, 292
5:17, 19, 180, 421, 282, 454, 495
5:17–25, 11, 19, 513
5:18–19, 36
5:19, 274, 430, 435, 441, 444, 525
5:21, 567
5:22, 110
5:23, 274, 430, 435
5:23–24, 274–75, 441, 525
6, 4, 19, 22, 28, 105, 122–23
6:1, 453
6:1–3, 251
6:1–11, 11
6:1–23, 124
6:2, 114, 120, 123, 125–26, 446
6:2–3, 152
6:2–18, 36
6:3, 251
6:5, 351
6:6–8, 251
6:8, 2–3, 344, 390
6:9, 444
6:11–12, 479
6:12, 156
6:12–16, 11
6:13, 105, 251
6:14, 89, 105
6:16, 105
6:17, 95, 105, 135, 156, 193
6:17–19, 11
6:18, 105, 193, 344
6:18–20, 179
6:19, 284
6:21, 180, 186, 351
6:22, 103, 105
6:23, 105, 278
7, 1, 22–24, 27, 29, 307, 380, 440–41, 448, 486, 555, 572
7–24, 105
7:1, 21
7:1–17, 11, 30
7:2, 30, 116
7:3, 112, 319, 445

615

7:4, 109, 291–92, 525
7:6, 2, 54, 95
7:6–7, 36
7:7, 144
7:8, 180, 186
7:8–9, 368
7:9, 21
7:10, 110
7:10–11, 243, 368
7:11, 21, 23, 106, 465
7:11–17, 478
7:12, 23, 90, 92, 243
7:12–13, 14, 106
7:13, 23, 254
7:14, 23, 106, 532
7:15–16, 23
7:16, 23, 243, 254, 368,
    478, 486
7:17, 30
7:18, 360
7:18–20, 543
7:18–29, 11
7:19, 24, 486
7:20, 110
7:21, 236, 243
7:22, 78, 543
7:22–29, 36
7:23–24, 228
7:25, 59
7:26, 228
7:27, 48, 94, 180, 388
7:28, 543
7:29, 478, 543
8:1, 513
8:1–8, 36
8:1–14, 11
8:2, 204
8:4, 276
8:6, 204, 238, 351, 380,
    435
8:10, 192, 473
8:11, 149
8:11–12, 277
8:14, 238, 380, 435
8:15, 10, 498
8:15–18, 1, 11
8:16, 500
8:17, 104, 257
8:18, 560
9, 10, 28, 346, 348
9–20, 4
9:1–13, 400, 468
9:3, 17

9:6, 17, 44, 62, 180,
    476, 530
9:8, 44, 62, 180, 341,
    361, 456, 466
9:8–10, 36
9:10–13, 476
9:16, 180
9:18, 180
9:19, 180
10:1–5, 19
10:1–11:1, 11, 19, 22
10:2, 19, 214
10:2–3, 285
10:3, 492
10:4–5, 378
10:4–7, 36
10:6, 193, 232, 240
10:9, 119, 193, 453
10:12, 59
10:17, 10
10:18–19, 36
11, 28, 106, 486
11–12, 22, 311
11:1, 10, 20, 214, 439
11:1–12:12, 309
11:1–12:23, 20, 26
11:2–12, 36
11:2–12:28, 10
11:2–24:25, 34
11:3, 493
11:4, 93, 149, 348
11:6, 493
11:8–11, 411
11:11, 61, 92, 214, 348,
    355
11:15, 498
11:15–20, 36
11:17, 493
11:20, 222
11:21, 144, 493
11:24, 222, 493
11:26, 471
11:27, 351
12, 28, 361, 433, 441
12:1, 36, 361
12:1–13, 95
12:3, 361
12:3–5, 36
12:4, 260, 361
12:5, 61, 395, 536
12:7, 180, 282, 399,
    454, 495, 498
12:7–9, 459
12:8, 98, 214, 355

12:8–9, 36
12:9, 291–92, 493
12:9–12, 27
12:10, 493
12:11, 93, 348
12:12, 10
12:13, 25, 29, 93,
    291–92, 298, 309
12:13–20, 36
12:14, 96, 475
12:16, 298
12:20, 44, 62
12:22–23, 298
12:23, 144
12:24, 20, 56, 92, 285,
    344, 348
12:24–25, 22
12:25, 30, 116
12:26–29, 276
12:26–31, 11
12:29–31, 19, 22, 36
12:30, 109
12:30–31, 11
12:31, 330
13–19, 20
13–20, 10
13:1, 344, 347
13:1–6, 36
13:1–22, 20, 22, 66
13:3, 304
13:4, 344, 347
13:5, 300
13:8, 193
13:11, 93, 348
13:12, 93, 348
13:12–13, 477
13:13–34, 36
13:14, 93, 348
13:15, 177, 344–45,
    347
13:17, 76, 203
13:18, 76, 346, 454
13:19, 95, 376
13:20, 20, 130
13:21, 390
13:22, 348
13:23, 20
13:23–28, 487
13:23–33, 20, 66
13:23–39, 22
13:25, 221, 524
13:26, 144
13:27, 524
13:28, 191, 480

13:32, 304, 348
13:33, 130
13:34, 128, 366, 447
13:34–39, 20
13:36, 210, 344. 551
13:36–39, 36
13:37, 366
13:37–38, 508
13:38, 20, 366
13:39, 344
14, 28
14:1, 500
14:1–3, 36
14:1–27, 20, 22
14:4, 44–45
14:5, 553
14:7–33, 36
14:10, 110
14:11, 61, 269, 536
14:13, 144
14:14, 36
14:15, 145
14:16, 191
14:17, 544
14:18–19, 36
14:19, 61
14:22, 44, 62
14:23, 446
14:25, 10
14:27, 305
14:28–33, 20, 22
14:31, 144
14:32, 144
14:33, 36, 44–45, 62, 349
15–18, 290
15:1, 171
15:1–7, 36
15:1–11, 20
15:1–15, 36
15:2, 190
15:5, 44
15:5–6, 404
15:6, 10
15:7, 20
15:9, 55, 446
15:10, 492
15:12, 95, 147, 251, 426
15:13–19:43, 20, 22
15:14, 366
15:16, 478
15:17, 478
15:18, 478, 560

15:19, 144
15:20–21, 36
15:21, 61, 536
15:22, 411
15:23, 36
15:24, 120, 143, 251, 257
15:24–29, 20
15:26–31, 36
15:27, 30, 48, 116, 257
15:29, 257
15:31, 235
15:32, 44
15:35–36, 257
15:37, 36
16:1, 192, 476
16:1–2, 36
16:4, 44, 476
16:5, 203
16:5–13, 111
16:6, 552
16:6–8, 36
16:7, 50, 204, 477
16:8, 444, 477
16:9, 144, 341, 456, 466, 500
16:10, 500
16:10–13, 36
16:11, 163
16:12, 145
16:13, 95, 376, 552
16:17, 144
16:17–18, 36
16:20–22, 27, 36
16:21, 10, 232, 240
16:22, 10, 20
17:2–3, 36
17:9, 446
17:10, 10, 236, 277
17:11, 10, 241
17:13, 10
17:14, 402
17:15, 257
17:18–20, 402
17:23, 446, 471
17:23–25, 36
17:25, 500
17:29, 36
18:1, 164, 291
18:1–11, 36
18:2, 500
18:3, 130
18:6, 119
18:7, 157

18:11, 178
18:12, 494
18:14, 567
18:15, 247, 320, 337
18:16, 567
18:17, 10, 122, 238
18:18, 2–3, 238, 286
18:19, 567
18:19–32, 131
18:20, 567
18:21, 44, 62
18:22, 144
18:24–27, 128
18:25, 95
18:26, 567
18:28, 44–45, 62, 333
18:28–29, 36
18:29, 211
18:31, 567
19:1 (ET 18:33), 33
19:2–44 (ET 19:1–43), 33
19:6–12 (ET 19:5–11), 36
19:7 (ET 19:6), 344, 347
19:9 (ET 19:8), 122
19:10 (ET 19:9), 366
19:10–44 (ET 19:9–43), 355
19:11 (ET 19:10), 144, 180, 214, 282
19:12 (ET 19:11), 10, 144, 257, 355
19:13 (ET 19:12), 144
19:14 (ET 19:13), 112, 265, 400, 475
19:14–16 (ET 19:13–15), 36
19:15 (ET 19:14), 210
19:18 (ET 19:17), 177
19:19 (ET 19:18), 59
19:20 (ET 19:19), 130
19:21 (ET 19:20), 93, 465
19:22 (ET 19:21), 80, 111, 458, 500
19:23 (ET 19:22), 500, 543
19:25 (ET 19:24), 36, 476
19:26 (ET 19:25), 144, 476

19:27 (ET 19:26), 522
19:27–29 (ET 19:26–28), 36
19:28 (ET 19:27), 59, 492, 544
19:30 (ET 19:29), 144
19:31 (ET 19:30), 476
19:36 (ET 19:35), 144
19:37 (ET 19:36), 144
19:38 (ET 19:37), 36
19:39 (ET 19:38), 59
19:40 (ET 19:39), 404
19:40–43 (ET 19:39–42), 214
19:41–44 (ET 19:40–43), 355
19:43 (ET 19:42), 144, 390
19:44 (ET 19:43), 119
20, 22, 290
20:1, 50, 77, 122, 176, 191, 401, 567
20:1–2, 36
20:2, 214, 355
20:3, 348
20:4, 36, 200
20:5, 200
20:6–10, 36
20:7, 560
20:8, 345
20:9–14, 36
20:19, 36, 144, 191, 503
20:20, 49
20:21–25, 36
20:22, 122, 567
20:23, 560
20:25, 257, 429
21, 21
21–24, 4, 6
21:1, 21, 477
21:1–9, 468
21:1–14, 10, 21
21:2, 214, 355
21:3, 111, 191, 503
21:3–6, 36
21:5–9, 361
21:7, 468, 476
21:8, 278, 476
21:8–9, 36, 530, 565
21:8–10, 569
21:8–14, 279
21:9, 444, 326
21:10, 143, 571

21:12, 36, 571
21:12–14, 468, 570
21:13, 156
21:14, 183, 471
21:15–17, 10, 36
21:15–22, 5, 21, 513
21:16–18, 36
21:17, 214, 439, 500
21:18–19, 334
21:18–22, 11
21:19, 4, 326, 328, 335
21:20, 42
21:21, 304, 329
22, 10, 77
22:1, 195
22:1–51, 11
22:2, 421
22:2–51, 8
22:3, 339
22:3–4, 435
22:5, 50
22:6, 72
22:7, 54, 113
22:8, 249, 390
22:12, 492
22:14, 46, 75, 80–81, 157, 160
22:16, 80
22:17, 36
22:19, 36
22:21, 36, 498
22:24, 36
22:25, 498
22:26–28, 36
22:29, 28
22:30–51, 36
22:32, 78
22:36, 435
22:40, 71, 79
22:47, 61, 78, 435, 536
22:51, 77, 80–81, 90, 254, 435, 459
23:1, 2, 77, 80, 459
23:1–2, 30
23:1–6, 1, 36
23:1–7, 8, 10, 29, 77
23:2, 30, 196
23:3, 29, 78, 213
23:3–5, 486
23:5, 23–24, 27, 29, 435
23:6, 50
23:8, 565
23:8–39, 1, 5, 11

23:9, 329
23:9–12, 36
23:10, 345, 435, 566
23:12, 435
23:13, 421
23:14, 238, 421
23:14–16, 36
23:16, 158
23:18, 500, 565
23:21–22, 36
23:22–23, 431
23:23, 427
23:24, 336
23:37, 247, 253, 500
23:38–39, 36
23:39, 493
24, 21–22, 25, 27, 106, 290–91, 441
24:1, 110, 214, 355, 390
24:1–25, 10–11, 26
24:2, 290–91
24:3, 25, 144
24:3–4, 292
24:4, 291
24:5, 206, 556
24:7, 512
24:9, 214, 291, 355, 565
24:10, 25, 93, 235, 243, 291–92, 454
24:10–14, 298
24:11, 30, 109, 116, 291–92
24:11–13, 30, 292
24:11–19, 423
24:12, 352
24:13, 474
24:14, 292, 411
24:16, 32, 236, 285, 291–92, 295, 494
24:16–22, 36
24:16–24, 435
24:16–25, 21
24:17, 93, 291, 298
24:18, 30
24:20, 44–45, 62
24:22, 59
24:24, 365
24:25, 156, 193

1 Kings, 33
1, 22
1–2, 4
1–4, 257

1:1, 329
1:5, 171
1:5–27, 66
1:5–2:12, 14
1:6, 319
1:7, 257
1:16, 455
1:19, 257
1:24, 211
1:25, 257
1:31, 455
1:37, 112
1:38, 560
1:39, 195, 306
1:42, 257
1:44, 560
1:49, 302
1:51, 86
1:52, 269
2, 5
2:1–11, 417
2:6, 72
2:9, 72
2:10–12, 22
2:11, 14, 239
2:13, 211, 302
2:22, 257
2:23, 265, 400
2:26–27, 101, 104, 257, 429
2:35, 104, 257
2:39, 417
2:39–46, 417
3:5, 187
3:7, 19
4:4, 257
4:12, 358
4:13, 42
5:15 (ET 5:1), 347
6:1, 14
7:9–11, 109
7:14, 553
7:48, 408
8:4, 133, 251
8:9, 209, 426
8:11, 130
8:23, 78
8:26, 264
8:39, 496
8:40, 102
8:42, 228
8:56, 112
8:58, 353
8:65, 294

9:7, 209
9:15, 2
9:16–17, 7
9:20, 493
9:21, 555
9:24, 2
10:29, 493
11, 3
11:1, 347, 493
11:1–8, 65
11:1–10, 106
11:5, 155
11:6, 227
11:17–18, 422
11:18, 471
11:26, 43, 553
11:26–40, 368
11:27, 2
11:28, 176
11:29–31, 253, 298
11:33, 155
11:37, 389
11:40, 422
11:42, 239
12:1–24, 356
12:2, 422
12:26–29, 233
12:31, 187
13:2, 568
13:32, 187
14:3, 184, 483
14:4, 129
14:10, 476, 485
14:11, 341
14:13, 482
14:18, 482
14:20, 231
14:21, 19, 22
14:21–24, 213
14:23, 155
14:27, 432
14:28, 432
15:1–3, 213
15:5, 493
15:9–10, 417
15:9–11, 213
15:17, 42
15:22, 158
15:25, 231
15:25–26, 213
15:33–34, 213
16:4, 341
16:8, 231
16:11, 476, 485
16:23, 231

16:29, 231
17:9, 553
17:10, 553
17:12, 495
17:14, 495
17:16, 495
18:19, 155
18:29, 98
18:38, 221
18:46, 285, 334
19:2, 400
19:6, 493, 495
19:13, 409
19:16, 358
19:18, 207, 404
19:20, 349
20:2–7, 64
20:10, 400, 478
20:12, 283
20:35, 194
20:38, 521
21:7, 454
21:10, 50, 204
21:13, 50, 204, 401
21:19, 341
21:21, 476, 485
21:23, 341
21:24, 341
22, 127, 528
22:1–40, 368
22:3–4, 42
22:5, 86
22:6, 529
22:9, 171
22:10–12, 529
22:19, 283
22:19–23, 317–18, 352, 528
22:27, 203, 475
22:30, 521, 528
22:34, 327
22:38, 341
22:49 (ET 22:48), 165
22:52 (ET 22:51), 231

2 Kings, 33
1:2–17, 377
1:9, 164
1:11, 164
1:12, 221
1:13, 164
2, 114
2:3, 194
2:5, 194
2:7, 194

2:12, 194
2:15, 194
2:24, 232
3:1, 231
3:9, 478
3:15–19, 195
3:25, 341
4:1, 194
4:7–27, 103, 183
4:8, 45
4:11, 45
4:18, 45
4:23, 399
4:27, 209
4:29, 234
4:38, 194
4:42, 184
5:1, 176
5:5, 184
5:8–20, 103, 183
5:15–16, 184
5:19, 55
5:22, 194
5:22–27, 401
5:23, 524
5:24, 136
6:1, 194
6:8, 407
6:15, 103, 183
6:17, 44
6:21, 194
6:31, 265, 400
7:1, 283
7:2, 178
7:5, 554
7:6, 493
7:7, 554
7:8, 512
7:15, 447
7:18, 251
8:1–6, 64
8:6, 171
8:8, 204
8:12, 177
8:13, 341
8:15, 367
8:17, 231
8:19, 102
8:26, 231
8:28, 42
8:29, 12, 42, 300
9:1, 191, 194
9:1–3, 195
9:3, 191

9:8, 476, 485
9:10, 341
9:11, 211, 416, 418
9:14–28, 12
9:16, 300
9:32, 171–72
9:36, 341
10:5, 59
10:10, 112
10:15, 234
10:18–28, 402
10:25, 432
10:33, 556
11:4, 432
11:6, 432
11:11, 432
11:13, 432
11:19, 432
12:2 (ET 12:1), 239
13:14, 194
13:17, 47
14:12, 122
15:1–2, 417
15:2, 231
15:23, 231
17:10, 155
17:13, 109
17:15, 170
17:16, 155
17:17, 142, 299
17:23, 130
17:29, 187
17:32, 187
18:4, 155
18:26, 210
19:4, 339
19:7, 318
19:11, 555
19:15, 114, 132
19:16, 339
19:18, 342
19:27, 421
19:35, 525
20:3, 100
20:16, 283
20:17, 101
21:1, 231, 417
21:3, 155
21:6, 519–20
21:12, 110, 114
21:16, 369
21:19, 231
22:1–23:25, 7
22:19, 222

23:3, 227
23:11, 171
23:13, 155
23:14, 155
23:16, 568
23:19, 187
23:20, 568
23:24, 288, 371, 519–20
24:4, 369
24:7, 294
24:12, 171
24:15, 64, 171
24:15–16, 130
25:19, 171
25:21, 130
25:24, 454
25:26, 422
25:27–30, 7

1 Chronicles
1:13, 493
1:37, 43
2, 310
2:3–5, 509
2:7, 267
2:9, 509
2:13, 43, 304, 310, 312
2:13–15, 310
2:14, 312
2:15, 312
2:16, 312, 493
2:16–17, 312
2:17, 312, 535
2:19, 43, 152
2:26, 64
2:42, 450
2:45, 556, 563
2:50, 43, 152
2:50–51, 152
2:52, 152
2:55, 563
3:1, 278, 488, 563
3:1–4, 21
3:1–9, 313
3:5, 313
3:5–8, 11
4, 310
4:4, 43
4:5, 64
4:17, 563
4:19, 563
4:30, 512, 556, 563
5:8, 556
5:11, 257

5:18, 277
5:24, 277, 358
5:27–29 (ET 6:1–3), 52
5:29–34 (ET 6:3–8),
  104
6:1–15 (ET 6:16–30),
  383
6:3 (ET 6:18), 52
6:7–12 (ET 6:22–27),
  43, 52
6:10–12 (ET 6:25–27),
  43
6:11 (ET 6:26), 43
6:12 (ET 6:27), 43
6:13 (ET 6:28), 116,
  169, 380
6:16–33 (ET 6:31–48),
  10
6:17 (ET 6:32), 82
6:18 (ET 6:33), 116,
  169, 380
6:19 (ET 6:34), 43
6:20 (ET 6:35), 43, 183
6:39–45 (ET 6:54–60),
  151
6:42 (ET 6:57), 563
6:51–54 (ET 6:66–69),
  42
6:54 (ET 6:69), 42
6:65 (ET 6:80), 42
7:16, 56
7:17, 219
8:8, 64
8:33, 15, 278–79, 476
8:34, 476
8:40, 277
9:1, 9
9:22, 116, 184, 380
9:35, 280
9:35–36, 279
9:35–39, 279
9:36, 279–80
9:37, 280
9:37–38, 280
9:38, 280
9:39, 15, 278–80, 476
9:40, 476
10:1, 564
10:1–12, 11, 568
10:2, 252, 278, 565
10:3, 565
10:4, 145, 254, 565
10:5, 566
10:7, 566

10:9, 567
10:10, 135, 567
10:11, 567
10:12, 567–68
10:13, 519–20
11–21, 18
11–29, 18
11:1, 9
11:1–3, 11
11:3, 116, 380
11:4, 9
11:4–9, 11, 22
11:10, 9
11:10–41, 11
11:13, 326
11:15, 421
11:16, 238
11:18, 158
11:23, 328
11:24–25, 431
11:25, 427
11:26, 336
11:41, 493
12:2, 341
12:10 (ET 12:9), 43
12:20 (ET 12:19), 136,
  417
12:21 (ET 12:20), 43
12:29 (ET 12:28), 176
12:39 (ET 12:38), 9
12:41 (ET 12:40), 432,
  512
13, 19, 22
13:1–14, 11
13:3, 251
13:5, 9
13:5–6, 123
13:6, 9, 114, 132, 152
13:8, 9–10
14, 22
14:1, 20, 22
14:1–2, 19
14:1–7, 11
14:3–7, 19, 313
14:4, 313
14:8, 9
14:8–16, 11
14:8–17, 19
14:10, 274
14:14, 274
15–16, 19
15:1, 19
15:2, 251
15:3, 9

15:12, 251
15:14–15, 251
15:16–19, 169
15:16–24, 10
15:17, 116
15:18, 43
15:19, 116
15:20, 43, 335
15:25–29, 11
15:26–27, 251
15:27, 89
15:28, 9
16, 22
16:1, 105
16:1–2, 105
16:1–3, 11
16:4, 82, 251
16:5, 43
16:39, 133
16:41–42, 10
17, 22
17:1–15, 11
17:2, 319
17:3, 525
17:6, 9
17:8, 21
17:10, 21
17:11–12, 14
17:16–27, 11
17:17, 24
17:19, 236, 243
17:23, 105
17:24, 228
18:1–13, 11
18:10, 192, 473
18:13, 238
18:14, 9
18:14–17, 11
18:16, 257
19:1–5, 19
19:1–20:1, 11
19:1–20:3, 19, 22
19:2, 19
19:10, 453
19:13, 59
19:17, 9
20:1, 11, 20
20:2–3, 11
20:3, 330
20:4, 21
20:4–8, 11, 21
20:5, 326, 328, 335–36
20:6, 42
20:7, 304

21, 21–22
21:1, 543
21:1–22:1, 10–11
21:4, 9
21:5, 9, 148
21:9–19, 423
21:13, 221
21:15, 295
21:15–22:1, 21
21:16, 32
21:23, 59
22:2–29:25, 21–22
22:5, 19
23–26, 433
23–29, 14
23:1, 22
23:13, 90, 179
23:14, 103, 183
24:6, 257
24:31, 264, 269
25:1–31, 10
25:5, 75, 78
25:8, 264, 269
26:13–14, 264, 269
26:28, 116, 184, 380
27:18, 310
27:19, 358
27:30, 432, 512
28:1, 171, 176
28:3, 14
28:4, 9
28:8, 9
28:17, 87
29:10, 59
29:21, 9, 554
29:23, 9
29:25, 9
29:26, 9
29:26–30, 22
29:27, 239
29:29, 1, 116, 184, 380, 423

2 Chronicles
1:2, 9
1:3, 133
1:4, 123
1:7, 525
1:13, 133
1:14, 421
1:17, 493
3:1, 10, 30
4:16, 87
4:19, 408
5:4, 251

5:5, 133
5:10, 209, 426
5:12, 116
6:25, 220
6:30, 496
6:31, 102
6:32, 228
7:6, 9–10
7:8, 9, 294
8:7, 493
8:11, 129
9:25, 421
9:30, 9, 239
10:1, 9
10:3, 9
10:16, 9, 122
11:3, 10
11:7, 325, 421, 556, 563
11:9, 326
11:13, 10
11:18, 43, 310
11:21, 64, 347
11:23, 64
12:1, 10
12:10, 432
12:11, 432
12:13, 22
13:3, 176
13:4, 10
13:5, 10
13:7, 50, 204
13:8, 10
13:10, 82
13:11, 98
13:15, 10
13:19, 157
13:21, 64
14:2 (ET 14:3), 155
14:13 (ET 14:14), 213
16:5, 42
16:6, 158
16:13, 417
17:2, 238
17:6, 155
17:10, 213
17:16–17, 176
18:4, 86
18:8, 171
18:16, 10
18:18, 283
18:26, 475
18:29, 521
18:33, 327

19:3, 155
19:7, 213–14
20:2, 451
21:5, 231
21:7, 10, 102
21:14, 64
21:17, 64
22:5, 42
22:6, 42, 300
23:3, 10
23:6, 82
23:8, 366
23:12, 432
23:18, 10
24:1, 239
24:3, 64
24:5, 10, 157
24:7, 422
24:23, 51
25:6, 176
25:13, 451
25:15, 221
25:19, 163
25:22, 122
26:3, 231, 417
26:14, 327, 341
27:3, 136
28:7, 449
28:18, 325
28:23, 10
29:5, 153
29:11, 82
29:24, 10
29:25, 423
29:25–27, 10
29:30, 10
30:1, 10
30:5, 10, 93
30:6, 10, 431
30:10, 431
30:27, 90
31:1, 10, 155
31:13, 43
32:21, 176
33:1, 231, 417
33:3, 155
33:6, 519–20
33:14, 136
33:19, 155
33:21, 231
34:3, 155
34:4, 155
34:5, 568
34:7, 155

34:31, 227
35:3, 10, 251
35:13, 84, 329
35:15, 10, 116
35:18, 116, 184, 380
35:22, 521
36:17, 177
36:22, 93

Ezra

1:1, 93
1:6, 444
2:26, 42
2:51, 483
2:63, 250–51, 272, 274
3:1, 210
3:4–5, 399
3:11, 330
4:15, 59, 235
4:19, 59, 235
6:22, 444
7:4, 483
7:11, 48
8:23, 568
9:1, 493
9:4, 129
10:7, 93
10:10, 48
10:16, 48

Nehemiah

2:2, 331
2:6, 99
2:9, 99
2:18, 444
3:16, 556, 563
3:26–27, 136
4:10 (ET 4:16), 177, 327
4:17 (ET 4:23), 377
5:7–11, 420
5:14, 231
6:5, 177
6:9, 444
7:30, 42
7:53, 483
7:65, 250–51, 272, 274
8:1, 210
8:2, 48
8:6, 455
8:9, 48
8:10, 285
8:15, 93
9:6, 225
9:7, 225

9:8, 493
9:9–12, 225
9:13–21, 225
9:22–25, 225
9:26–28, 225
9:29–30, 225
9:30–32, 225
9:34–35, 225
9:36–37, 225
10:33–34 (ET 10:32–33), 399
10:35 (ET 10:34), 264, 269
11:1, 264, 269
11:21, 136
11:29, 557
11:30, 326, 421
11:32, 409
12:26, 48
13:6, 390
13:13, 48
13:19, 560

Esther

2:2, 177
2:3, 172
2:5, 176
2:6, 131
2:7, 305, 319, 472
2:17, 347
2:23, 571
3:7, 208, 264, 269
3:13, 431
3:15, 431
4:16, 568
5:9, 480
6:1, 525
7:10, 571
8:10, 431
8:14, 431
9:13–14, 571
9:24, 264, 269
9:26, 269
10:2–3, 449
10:10–11, 269

Job

1–2, 317
1:1, 42
1:5, 153, 308
1:6, 45
1:6–9, 543
1:10, 46
1:13, 45
1:15, 177

1:16, 221, 447
1:17, 451
2:1, 45
2:10, 477
2:12, 210
3:6, 525
3:7, 525
3:9, 554
3:23, 46
3:24, 102
4:2, 180
4:3, 444
4:13, 495
4:19, 102
5:12, 446
5:19, 353
6:5, 147
6:6, 416
6:18, 221
6:27, 264, 269
7:4, 554
7:14, 314
9:8, 194
9:34, 314
12:15, 180
12:17, 415
12:20, 480
12:22, 73
12:23, 73
12:24, 221
13:11, 314
13:14, 369
13:21, 314
14:20, 73
15:5, 446
15:10, 217
15:24, 314
18:11, 314
19:29, 353
20:17, 521
21:29, 437
22:6, 377
22:15, 235
22:30, 130
24:15, 554
26:7, 221
27:19, 360
28:7, 262
29:9, 180
30:1, 341
30:18, 521
31:35, 415
31:40, 273
32:2, 43

32:5–6, 43
32:20, 316
32:21, 221, 480
33:7, 314
33:14, 358
33:15, 495
34:1, 43
34:19, 437, 480
36:1, 43
36:4, 71
38:12, 407
38:31, 289
40:28 (ET 41:4), 508
42:7, 47
42:15, 64

Psalms
2:2, 164
2:6, 164
2:7, 106
2:8, 99
2:12, 404
5:3 (ET 5:2), 410
5:7 (ET 5:6), 401
5:13 (ET 5:12), 447
6:6 (ET 6:5), 72
7:15–16 (ET 7:14–15), 401
8:5 (ET 8:4), 361
8:6 (ET 8:5), 447
9:17 (ET 9:16), 521
10:14, 403
10:16, 59
10:17–18, 403
14:1, 477
15:1–5, 514
16:9–10, 440
16:10, 74, 79
18, 10–11, 77
18:3 (ET 18:2), 78
18:6 (ET 18:5), 72
18:8 (ET 18:7), 249
18:12 (ET 18:11), 492
18:14 (ET 18:13), 75, 80
18:16 (ET 18:15), 80
18:32 (ET 18:31), 78
18:33 (ET 18:32), 73
18:47 (ET 18:46), 78
18:48 (ET 18:47), 73
18:51 (ET 18:50), 23
19:7 (ET 19:6), 51
21:5 (ET 21:4), 59
22, 79

22:17 (ET 22:16), 341, 566
22:17–32 (ET 22:16–31), 440
22:19 (ET 22:18), 264, 269
22:21 (ET 22:20), 341
22:23 (ET 22:22), 503
22:24 (ET 22:23), 353
22:26 (ET 22:25), 503
23:2, 375
23:3, 222
23:6, 411, 440
24, 77
24:1–2, 80
24:7–10, 410
25:6, 411
25:11, 222
25:20, 221
27:13, 501
28:6, 411
28:9, 191
29:3, 132
29:3–9, 221
29:5, 73
29:10, 410
30, 77
30:4 (ET 30:3), 79
31:4 (ET 31:3), 222
31:9 (ET 31:8), 438
31:19 (ET 31:18), 70
33:12, 191
33:13, 496
34:1, 417–18, 480
35:18, 503
35:21, 69
36:6 (ET 36:5), 498
37:22, 103
38:7 (ET 38:6), 395
38:13 (ET 38:12), 521
40:10–11 (ET 40:9–10), 503
41:7 (ET 41:6), 300
42:3 (ET 42:2), 59, 501
45:7 (ET 45:6), 59
46:1 (ET superscription), 335
46:7 (ET 46:6), 250
48:6 (ET 48:5), 447
48:15 (ET 48:14), 59
49:15 (ET 49:14), 72
50:9, 297
51, 309

51:2 (ET superscription), 348
51:3 (ET 51:1), 411
51:8 (ET 51:6), 194
51:11–13 (ET 51:9–11), 309
51:12 (ET 51:10), 194, 211
51:18 (ET 51:16), 297
51:19 (ET 51:17), 194
51:21 (ET 51:19), 98
52:3 (ET 52:1), 102
52:10 (ET 52:8), 59
53:2 (ET 53:1), 477
54:2 (ET superscription), 450
54:9 (ET 54:7), 45
55:2 (ET 55:1), 411
55:16 (ET 55:15), 72
55:24 (ET 55:23), 72
56:14 (ET 56:13), 100
59:7 (ET 59:6), 341
59:15 (ET 59:14), 341
60:14 (ET 60:12), 276
63:7 (ET 63:6), 211
63:12 (ET 63:11), 437
65:12 (ET 65:11), 447
68:6 (ET 68:5), 403, 456
68:8 (ET 68:7), 450
68:24 (ET 68:23), 341
68:25 (ET 68:24), 410
68:26 (ET 68:25), 335
68:27 (ET 68:26), 503
69:7 (ET 69:6), 264
69:10 (ET 69:9), 432
69:12 (ET 69:11), 99
71:20, 72, 79
73:24, 479
74:2, 191
74:22, 477
75:5 (ET 75:4), 78
75:5–6 (ET 75:4–5), 78
75:6 (ET 75:5), 70, 78
75:8 (ET 75:7), 447
75:11 (ET 75:10), 78
76:2 (ET 76:1), 228
77:19 (ET 77:18), 249
78:12–14, 225
78:15–43, 225
78:31, 177
78:40, 450
78:44–51, 225
78:52–53, 225

78:54–55, 225
78:56–66, 225
78:57, 262
78:60, 14
78:60–66, 132
78:67–72, 225
79:9, 222
81:11 (ET 81:10), 69
81:17 (ET 81:16), 87
82:3, 403
82:8, 157
83:4 (ET 83:3), 446
83:8 (ET 83:7), 211
83:10–11 (ET 83:9–10), 535
83:11 (ET 83:10), 521
84:3 (ET 84:2), 501
84:5 (ET 84:4), 59
89:2–3 (ET 89:1–2), 498
89:4–5 (ET 89:3–4), 23
89:18 (ET 89:17), 75, 78
89:21 (ET 89:20), 23
89:25 (ET 89:24), 75, 78
89:36–37 (ET 89:35–36), 23
89:38 (ET 89:37), 59
89:49 (ET 89:48), 72
89:50 (ET 89:49), 23
90:1, 183
90:4, 211
91:7, 354
91:11, 353
92:11 (ET 92:10), 75, 78
94:4, 70
94:21, 369
96:2, 567
99:1, 249
99:3, 228
99:6, 116, 380
100:5, 498
102:27–28 (ET 102:26–27), 295
103:4, 447
103:5, 212
103:17, 59
104:5, 59
104:7, 447
104:30, 211
104:32, 73, 202
105:1–45, 227

105:8–25, 225
105:26–39, 225
105:40–41, 225
105:42–45, 225
106:7–12, 225
106:8, 222
106:13–33, 225
106:14, 450
106:34–35, 225
106:36–45, 225
106:38, 369
106:45, 295
106:46–47, 225
107:4, 450
107:32, 503
107:40, 73, 221
108:14 (ET 108:13), 276
109:7, 218
109:11, 521
109:21, 222
109:28, 103
110, 25, 106
110:1, 23, 486
110:1–7, 440
110:4, 295
111:1, 503
111:8, 59
112:6, 508
112:9, 75, 78
113, 77, 80
113:7–8, 80
113:9, 79
116:9, 100, 501
118:8–9, 224
118:15–16, 276
119:9, 227
119:21, 497
119:66, 480
119:118, 497
119:143, 420
119:147, 554
119:148, 211
121:8, 421
132, 307
132:6, 43, 152
132:10–18, 23
132:11, 254
132:17, 307
135:6–7, 225
135:8–9, 225
135:10–12, 225
135:17, 409
136:5–9, 225

136:10–15, 225
136:16, 225
136:17–22, 225
136:23–24, 225
136:25, 225
138:2, 228
138:7, 45
139:20, 523
142:6 (ET 142:5), 501
143:11, 45, 222
144:5, 202
144:7–8, 401
144:11, 401
144:13, 354
145:1, 410
145:14, 522
145:17, 353
146, 224
146:8, 522
146:9, 403
148:4, 78
148:6, 59
148:14, 75
149:3, 351
150:4, 351

Proverbs
1:14, 264
1:19, 170
2:8, 80
3:6, 353
3:30, 467
3:31, 353
5:5, 72
6:12, 50, 204
6:16, 353
6:16–19, 401
6:17, 369
6:35, 480
7:9, 554
7:13, 349
7:14, 58
7:27, 72
9:13–18, 571
11:22, 480, 487
11:29, 267
12:8, 395
12:15, 481
12:16, 262
12:23, 446
13:10, 481
13:24, 95
14:5, 401
14:8, 446
14:15, 446

14:25, 401
15:5, 446
15:15, 480
15:27, 170
16:27, 50, 204
16:33, 203
17:13, 485
17:14, 366
17:18, 330
17:23, 170
18:5, 480
18:16, 421
19:5, 401
19:9, 401
19:11, 472
19:20, 481
19:21, 450
19:25, 446
19:28, 50, 204
20:18, 481
20:26, 73
21:20, 87
21:31, 268
22:6, 95
22:28, 59, 235
23:10, 59, 235
23:24, 472
24:13–14, 267
25:21, 411
25:21–22, 467
26:1, 228
26:2, 270
26:11, 341
26:16, 480
28:16, 170
30:4, 24
30:15–16, 53
30:17, 209
30:19, 335
31:4–5, 487
31:8–9, 401
31:12, 467
31:26–27, 481

Ecclesiastes
1:6, 492
1:9, 389
1:17, 99
2:8, 496
3:2, 130
3:14, 352
3:18–19, 496
3:21, 496
7:7, 170, 415
7:24, 70

8:11, 496
8:12, 352
8:13, 352
9:3, 496
9:4, 341
9:7, 480
9:9, 347
9:12, 496
12:11, 238

Song of Songs
1:2, 349
1:3, 335
1:13, 451, 478
1:13–14, 451
1:14, 451
1:15, 305
3:11, 447
4:1, 305
4:3, 553
4:9, 305
5:1, 260
5:3, 377
5:12, 305
6:5, 305
6:7, 553
6:8, 335
7:5 (ET 7:4), 305
8:1, 349
8:6, 72

Isaiah
1:1, 109
1:3, 83
1:10, 283
1:10–11, 297
1:12, 59
1:13, 297
1:13–14, 399
1:16–17, 403
1:23, 170
2:1, 109
2:10, 213
2:11, 111
2:17, 111
2:19, 213
2:21, 213
3:2, 533
3:16, 305
4:2, 111
4:5, 328
5:11, 554
5:13, 130
5:14, 69
5:23, 170

6, 114
6:3, 447
6:7, 111
6:8, 110, 426
7:14, 335
7:21, 302
8:19, 520
9:5–6 (ET 9:6–7), 572
9:6 (ET 9:7), 23, 254, 363
9:16 (ET 9:17), 177
10:17, 328
10:28, 247
10:29, 42, 302
10:30, 489
10:32, 409
11:1–5, 481
11:1–16, 23, 368
11:2, 303
11:3, 303, 496
11:5, 498
11:14, 427
11:17, 483
12:9, 483
13:8, 130
13:13, 249
14:30, 72
14:31, 250
17:2, 556
17:9, 422
18:6, 262
19:2, 255
19:3, 519–20
19:4, 437
19:13, 263, 266
19:13–14, 318
19:18–24, 111
19:21, 83
20:3–4, 378
21:3, 130, 395
21:4, 314, 554
21:6, 128
21:15, 565
22:14, 111
22:17, 352
23:8, 447
23:12, 521
24:6, 143
24:11, 329
25, 483
25:1, 498
25:7, 409
26:17, 129
27:1, 208
27:4, 389

27:12, 294
28:14, 283
28:15, 72
28:18, 72
29:10, 495, 501
30:16, 100
31:8, 177
31:9, 272
32:5–6, 477
32:5–8, 486
32:11, 302, 377–78
32:14, 136
33:14, 213
33:15, 170
34:17, 264
35:10, 508
36:11, 210
37:4, 339, 501
37:11, 555
37:16, 132
37:17, 339, 501
37:19, 342
37:22, 521
37:28, 421
38:3, 100
38:18, 72
39:2, 87
39:5, 283
39:6, 101
40:5, 130
40:9, 567
40:11, 159
40:15, 352
40:26, 44
40:28, 83
40:30, 177
41:5, 302
41:18, 376
41:27, 567
41:29, 221
43:18, 456
43:19, 450
43:20, 450
44:3, 159
44:9, 221
44:9–17, 342
44:11, 213
44:16, 85, 272
44:19, 85
44:25, 415, 533
45:5, 83
45:12, 44
45:15, 264
45:18, 221

45:21–22, 228
46:11, 262
47:12, 221
47:14, 272
49:9, 376
50:11, 272
51:9, 235
52:1, 253
52:7, 567
52:8, 128
53:1, 477
53:10, 94
53:12, 96
54:8, 508
54:17, 191
55:3, 23, 209, 299
56:3–4, 172
56:5, 508
56:10, 501
57:4, 69
57:15, 194
57:17, 170
58:3, 568
58:4, 568
58:12, 235
58:14, 194
59:3–4, 401
59:4, 218
59:7, 369
59:10, 554
59:16, 96
59:17, 327
60:1, 130
60:7, 98
61:1, 567
61:1–3, 481
61:4, 235
61:8, 209
61:10, 67
62:3, 500
62:5, 67
63:7, 467
63:9, 235, 352
63:11, 235
64:3 (ET 64:4), 235
64:6 (ET 64:7), 250
65:15, 72
65:25, 159
66:2, 129
66:5, 283
66:14, 477
66:23, 157

Jeremiah
1, 114
1:3, 130, 273

1:11–13, 184
2:2, 67
2:3, 143
2:4, 283
2:7, 191
2:8, 83, 221
2:11, 221, 342
3:2, 376
3:8, 262
3:11, 262
3:15, 236
3:20, 262
3:21, 376
3:23, 475
3:25, 220
4:4, 253
4:11, 376
4:23, 221
4:28, 295
5:2, 475
5:4, 266
5:11, 262
6:16, 235
7:2, 283
7:6, 369
7:6–7, 403
7:7, 59
7:11, 222
7:12–14, 14, 132
7:16, 96, 116
7:21–26, 297
7:29, 376
7:31, 568
8:10, 170
9:2 (ET 9:3), 83
9:4 (ET 9:5), 401
9:20 (ET 9:21), 177
9:22–23 (ET 9:23–24),
    75
10:6, 228
10:10, 339, 501, 536
10:18, 333
11:14, 116
11:22, 177
12:9, 262
12:12, 376
13:16, 554
14:6, 376
14:11, 116
14:12, 568
14:14, 109, 142, 299,
    533
15:1, 116, 380
15:1–9, 116

15:6, 295
15:9, 72
16:14, 101
16:20, 342
17:5–8, 224
17:11, 497
17:20, 283
18:8, 295
18:10, 295
18:15, 235
18:21, 177
19:3, 110, 114, 283
19:4, 220, 437
19:5, 568
19:9, 420
20:14, 260
20:17, 508
21:11, 283
22:2, 283
22:3, 369, 403
22:14, 316
22:17, 170
22:29, 283
23:5, 101
23:5–6, 23
23:14, 401, 444
23:17, 317
23:32, 221
23:36, 339, 501, 536
23:39, 220
24:7, 194
24:10, 220
25:5, 59, 220
25:16, 415
25:37, 74
26:3, 295
26:6, 14, 132
26:9, 14, 132
26:13, 295
26:15, 210, 369
26:19, 295
27:9, 142, 299, 533
27:15, 475
28:1, 231
28:3, 231
28:7, 210
28:8, 59, 235
29:2, 171
29:8, 299, 533
29:20, 283
29:22, 90
29:23, 477
29:26, 416, 418
30:9, 23

31:10, 283
31:15, 42
31:31, 101
31:32, 67
31:34, 83
32:2, 202
32:39, 102, 194
33:11, 67
33:15–18, 23
34:4, 283
34:7, 326
34:19, 171
35:2, 181
35:4, 181
35:15, 220
36:26, 358
38:7, 171–72
38:23, 64
41:16, 47, 171
42:10, 295
42:15, 283
44:17, 220
44:21, 220
44:24, 283
44:26, 228, 283
46:4, 327
46:9, 415
46:21, 524
48:19, 556
49:23, 250
49:26, 74, 177
50:30, 74, 177
50:32, 492
50:36, 266
50:38, 415
51:3, 177
51:6, 74
51:7, 415
51:39, 501
51:47, 101
51:52, 101
51:57, 501
52:25, 171

Lamentations
1:15, 177
2:7, 438
2:17, 78
2:19, 211
3:7, 46
3:28, 352
4:2, 60
5:14, 177

Ezekiel
1–2, 114
1:1, 130, 184
1:28, 130
2:3, 220
3:17, 128
5:2, 272
7:3, 157
7:19, 479
7:26, 109
9:4, 415
9:5, 455
10, 455
10:19, 456
11:1, 456
12:3, 130
12:14, 492
12:27, 109
13:2, 283
13:3, 477
13:6, 142, 533
13:9, 142, 299, 533
13:22, 444
13:23, 299, 533
14:3–4, 479
16, 67, 425
16:7, 378
16:11, 99
16:22, 378
16:24, 425
16:25, 425
16:31, 425
16:35, 283
16:39, 377–78, 425
16:47, 353
18:31, 194
20:1–26, 228
20:5–10, 225
20:9, 222, 228
20:11–26, 225
20:12, 153
20:14, 222, 228
20:22, 222, 228
20:27–29, 225
20:44, 222
21:3 (ET 20:47), 283
21:20 (ET 21:15), 250
21:26 (ET 21:21), 142, 288
21:26–28, 533
21:34, 533
22:13, 170
22:26, 407
22:27, 170

22:28, 533
23, 67
23:24, 327
23:29, 378
25:16, 560
26:18, 302
27:10, 327
27:35, 46
28:8, 72
28:10, 254
28:13, 109
29:4, 327
29:21, 111
30:12, 437
30:17, 177
31:3, 422
31:15, 72
31:16, 72
31:17, 72
31:18, 254
32:18, 155
32:19–32, 254
32:22, 492
32:25, 492
32:26, 492
32:27, 72
33:7, 128
33:25, 262
34:4, 86
34:9, 283
34:23–24, 23
34:25, 317
35:11, 157
36:1, 283
36:2, 235
36:22, 222
36:23, 228
36:25–26, 194
36:25–27, 159
37:4, 283
37:24–25, 23
38:5, 327
38:17, 456
39:4, 262
39:29, 159
40, 181
42, 181
42:20, 407
44:9, 253
44:12, 479
44:19, 377
44:23, 407
45:17, 399
45:20, 497

46:6–7, 399
46:20–24, 84
47:18, 456
48:15, 407

Daniel
1:10, 429
2:1, 99
2:7, 50
2:15, 50
2:20, 50
2:21, 356, 368, 501
3:9, 50
3:14, 50
3:19, 50
3:24, 50
3:25, 50
3:26, 50
3:28, 50
4:16 (ET 4:19), 50
4:29 (ET 4:32), 356,
    368
5:2, 64
5:3, 64
5:17, 50
5:23, 64
6:14 (ET 6:13), 50
6:21 (ET 6:20), 501
6:27 (ET 6:26), 501
7:2, 50
9:3, 99
12:2–3, 73, 501

Hosea
1–3, 67
2:1 (ET 1:10), 501
2:4–5 (ET 2:2–3), 378
2:5 (ET 2:3), 377
2:10 (ET 2:8), 87
2:12 (ET 2:10), 477
2:15 (ET 2:13), 224
2:18–23 (ET 2:16–21),
    111
2:22 (ET 2:20), 83
2:24 (ET 2:22), 87
3:1, 347
3:4, 288
3:5, 23
4:1, 283
4:15, 233
5:4, 83
5:8, 233
5:11, 223
6:2, 72, 79
6:3, 83

6:6, 297
6:7, 262
8:14, 224
9:7, 416, 418
9:8, 128, 418
9:16, 72
10:5, 131, 233
11:10, 227
12:11 (ET 12:10), 109
13:4, 70
13:6, 224
13:14, 72

Joel
1:2, 220
1:20, 333
2:10, 249
2:13, 295
2:14, 295
2:16, 153
2:17, 191
2:20, 456
3:1–2 (ET 2:28–29),
    159
3:5 (ET 2:32), 140
4:3 (ET 3:3), 269
4:8 (ET 3:8), 437

Amos
1:1, 231
2:1, 568
2:11, 177
3:6, 302, 317
4:1, 223
4:7, 222
4:10, 177
5:7–12, 170
5:21–24, 297
6:4, 524
7:3, 295
7:6, 295
7:8, 184
7:12, 184
7:14–15, 114
7:16, 283
8:2, 184
8:4–5, 399
8:8, 249
9:5, 202, 250
9:7, 560
9:9, 367
9:11, 111
9:11–15, 23
9:13, 101

Obadiah

11, 269

Jonah

1, 114, 275
1:2, 177
1:7, 264, 269, 275
3, 140
3:1–3, 114
3:2, 177
3:5, 509
3:7, 200
3:8, 86
3:9, 295
3:9–10, 285
3:10, 295
4:2, 285, 295
4:7, 554

Micah

1:11, 378
1:15, 421
2:4, 111, 155
2:8, 377
3:5, 184
3:6–7, 533
3:11, 533
3:12, 194
4:8, 136
5:1 (ET 5:2), 23, 43
5:13 (ET 5:14), 155
6:6–8, 297
6:7, 354
6:9, 261
7:4, 128
7:14, 235
7:18, 191

Nahum

1:5, 250
2:1 (ET 1:15), 567
2:5 (ET 2:4), 415
3:4, 521
3:10, 269

Habakkuk

2:4, 136, 214, 229
2:5, 72, 136
2:9, 170
2:18, 221
3:3, 471
3:13, 380

Zephaniah

1:9–10, 111
2:5, 560
2:6, 375, 453
3:4, 396

Zechariah

3:1–2, 543
7:5, 568
7:10, 403
9:9, 254
10:2, 288, 371, 533
12:10, 159, 565
14:8, 456
14:16, 157
14:21, 84

Malachi

1:8, 480
1:9, 480
1:11, 228
2:2, 103
2:9, 480
2:14–16, 489
3:4, 235, 456
3:6, 295
3:20 (ET 4:2), 524

New Testament

Matthew

1, 381
1:1, 23, 81, 368, 440,
    486, 572
1:1–17, 310
1:1–18, 299
1:5, 371, 403
1:21, 254
1:23, 363
2:13, 440
2:16, 363
3:13–17, 481
3:15, 50
3:16, 500
4:1–11, 355, 440
4:4, 50
4:21, 114
5:19, 294
5:22, 571
5:31–32, 66
5:33–37, 270
5:43–48, 467
5:48, 294
6:10, 112
6:12, 383
7:6, 341
8:12, 487
9:27, 23, 81
9:32–34, 318
10:1, 114
10:8, 318
10:32–33, 103

10:33, 288
10:37, 372
11:4, 50
11:25, 50
11:27, 23
12:1, 412
12:1–8, 411
12:3–4, 132, 410, 412
12:5, 412
12:8, 412
12:11, 412
12:14, 440
12:22–28, 318
12:23, 23, 81
12:25–26, 561
12:26, 533
12:43–45, 317–18
13:41, 479
15:4–6, 459
15:22, 23, 81
15:26–27, 341
16:21, 389
17:14–18, 318
17:23, 389
18:7, 479
18:9, 571
18:20, 503
19:3–12, 66
19:4–6, 489
19:19, 346, 459
20:19, 389
20:30–31, 23, 81
21:9, 23, 81
21:15, 23, 81
22:13, 487
22:37, 372
22:37–38, 499
22:39, 346
22:41–42, 23
22:42–45, 9, 23, 363,
    572
23:37, 125
24:4–5, 127
24:11, 127
24:24, 127
25, 73
25:1–13, 481
25:30, 487
25:31, 130
25:31–46, 73
25:40, 433
26:20–30, 412
26:21–25, 295
26:28, 153

26:40–46, 501
26:59–61, 401
26:63, 23
26:63–64, 270
27:24–26, 215
27:35, 269
27:45, 185
27:46, 79
27:57, 42
27:57–66, 79
28, 355
28:10, 433
28:19, 23
28:19–20, 114, 355,
    433

Mark
1:24, 539
1:34, 318
1:39, 318
2:25–26, 410–12
3:6, 440
3:15, 318
3:21–35, 418
3:22, 318
3:24, 561
3:26, 533
7:26–30, 318
7:27–28, 341
9:14–27, 318
10:2–12, 66
10:47–48, 23, 81
11:18, 440
12:28–34, 297
12:30, 372
12:35, 23
12:35–37, 486
14:37–42, 501
15:24, 269
15:33, 185
15:34, 79
15:43, 42
16:9, 318

Luke
1–2, 381
1:26–38, 81
1:32, 254, 363, 572
1:35, 23
1:38, 112
1:42, 479
1:45, 479
1:46, 78, 81
1:46–55, 77
1:51–52, 80

1:53, 79–80
1:67–79, 77
1:68–70, 81
1:69, 81, 307
1:71, 78
1:74, 78
1:80, 96
2:40, 96
3:21–22, 311
4:18, 500, 567
4:18–19, 481
4:33–36, 318
4:34, 539
4:41, 318
6:3–4, 410–12
6:27–28, 467
7:21, 318
8:1–3, 318
8:27–39, 318
9:1, 318
9:22, 389
9:32, 501
9:37–42, 318
9:38–42, 318
10:16, 288
11:4, 383
11:14–20, 318
11:17–18, 561
11:18, 533
11:24–26, 318
12:8–9, 103
12:9, 288
12:42–48, 115
12:51–53, 372
13:15, 411–12
13:32, 318, 389
14:5, 411–12
14:26–27, 372
16:21, 341
16:22, 73
16:23–24, 73, 571
18:31, 440
18:33, 389
18:38–39, 23, 81
20:37–38, 479
20:41–44, 440
21:18, 269
22:2, 440
22:44–47, 501
23, 363
23:34, 269
23:43, 73
23:44, 185
23:50–51, 42

23:50–24:1, 571
24:7, 389
24:19–27, 440
24:46, 72, 79, 389, 440

John
1:14, 23, 109, 114, 130,
    220
1:32–33, 254
1:41, 77, 81, 254
1:42, 114
1:49, 23
2:11, 130
2:19–21, 23
3:13, 24
3:29, 67
4, 158, 185
4:6, 185
4:25, 77, 81
5:18, 440
5:19–23, 23
5:39, 227
6:64, 295
6:71, 295
7:1, 440
7:22–23, 411–12
9:37, 114
10:35, 299
10:36, 308
11:49–52, 215
13:5–17, 488
14:6, 227
17, 96, 412
17:3, 224
17:17–19, 153, 308
17:24, 130
19:10–11, 186
19:14, 185
19:23–24, 203, 378
19:24, 269
19:26–27, 422
19:31–42, 571
19:38, 42
19:38–42, 571
20:9, 440
20:21–23, 114
20:23, 56
20:29, 221

Acts
1:5, 311
1:23–26, 203
1:26, 269
2, 196, 311
2:17–18, 159

2:27, 74
2:27–31, 79
2:34–35, 486
2:38, 382
2:38–39, 311
2:38–41, 500
2:38–46, 187
2:41–44, 503
3:6, 363
3:18, 116
3:18–26, 116
3:22, 117
3:24, 117, 380
3:26, 117
4:12, 127, 363
5:29, 402
6:11–14, 401
7:2, 132
8:12–16, 311
8:27–39, 172
8:38, 311
9, 371
9:4, 114
9:16, 222
9:18, 311
9:23–25, 370–71
9:24, 371
10:36, 567
10:38, 500
10:40, 389
10:44–46, 196
10:48, 311
11:16, 311
13:20, 117, 184, 380
13:21, 15, 238
13:22, 243
13:34–37, 79
13:35, 74
14:15, 501
15:9, 153
15:29, 502
16, 378
16:6–7, 378
16:15, 311
16:33, 311
17:6, 29
18:8, 311
19:3–5, 311
19:6, 196
19:13–16, 318
19:15, 539
22:7, 114
22:16, 311, 500
26:14, 114

26:18, 153, 529
26:24–25, 419
27:34, 269

Romans
1:1, 114
1:3, 572
1:4, 355
1:5, 222, 502
1:16–17, 229
1:17, 214
1:23–31, 94
1:24, 94
1:26, 94
1:27, 348
1:28, 94
2:4, 229, 295
2:22, 502
2:25–29, 253
3:4, 100
3:6, 100
4, 308, 340, 481, 486
4:11, 253
4:11–16, 340
4:16, 481
4:16–6:13, 227
5:2, 229
6:1–4, 382, 500
6:1–6, 311
6:2, 100
6:15, 100
7:2–3, 506
7:22–25, 355
8:9–11, 319
8:29–30, 244
8:34, 96
9:17–18, 94
9:26, 501
10:9–13, 140
10:17, 37
12:1–2, 309, 382
12:4–5, 67
12:14, 467
12:19–20, 467
13:1, 186, 270, 356, 368
13:1–2, 501
13:1–7, 186, 215
13:1–10, 459
13:5, 459
13:7, 571
13:8, 223
13:9, 346
14:9, 501
14:13, 479

14:20, 479
15:3, 432
16:20, 355
16:26, 502

1 Corinthians
1:1, 114
1:2, 153
1:21, 28
1:23, 28
1:27–28, 28
1:30, 308
2:8, 130, 132
3:16, 319
4:12, 223
6:9, 127, 348
6:11, 153
7:8, 67
7:18–19, 253
7:39, 67, 481, 506
8:7, 502
9:1–27, 223
10:4, 220
10:16–17, 67
10:18–20, 342
10:19–20, 529
11:17–34, 411–12, 503
11:27–34, 411
12:10, 196
12:12–13, 67
12:13, 311, 500
14:5–6, 196
14:22, 196
14:26, 503
15:4, 72, 79, 389
15:26, 73
15:33, 127
15:54–57, 355
15:57, 254

2 Corinthians
1:21, 500
3:3, 501
3:18, 244
4:4, 130
5:21, 571
6:15, 50
6:16, 501–2
11:2, 67
11:7–9, 223
11:14, 529
11:32–33, 370–71

Galatians
1–2, 114
1:5, 59

1:15, 114
2:17, 100
2:20, 227
3, 340, 486
3:7–14, 340
3:13, 571
3:21, 100
3:26–29, 253, 311
4:4, 254
4:8, 342
5:2–6, 253
5:3, 294
5:14, 346
6:7, 127
6:15, 253

Ephesians
1:3–14, 244
1:4, 73
2:8–9, 486
2:10, 381
3:20–21, 559
4:4–6, 67, 311
4:10, 24
4:11–13, 356
4:22–24, 309
5:21–33, 481
5:22–33, 67
5:25–27, 67
5:26, 153, 159, 308
6:2, 459
6:4, 466
6:10–17, 342, 355
6:10–20, 256
6:12, 256, 317

Philippians
2:5–11, 467
2:9–10, 363
3:2, 341
4:3, 73
4:20, 59

Colossians
2:11–13, 253
3:4, 227
3:10, 244
3:11, 253

1 Thessalonians
1:10, 481
2:5–9, 223
5:12–13, 433

2 Thessalonians
2:9, 529
3:7–10, 223

1 Timothy
1:9–10, 348
1:17, 59
2:4, 317
2:5, 103
3:2, 65, 67, 383
3:12, 65, 67
3:15, 501
4:1, 529
4:10, 501
5:15, 529
5:17, 433
5:17–18, 356, 433
6:1, 459
6:11, 103

2 Timothy
1:14, 319
2:11–12, 27
2:12, 500
3:13, 126
3:16–17, 103
4:18, 59

Titus
1:6, 65, 67
2:13, 130
3:3–7, 309

Philemon
18–19, 223

Hebrews
1:1–2, 114, 227
1:3, 130
1:5, 23
1:8, 23, 254
2:11, 308
2:17, 24, 106, 412
3–9, 107
3:1, 412
3:2, 106
3:5, 106
3:12, 501
4:14–15, 412
5:5–6, 106, 412
6:16, 270
7:11–16, 24
7:17, 412
7:21, 295
7:25, 96
8:11, 83
9:5, 132
9:11, 412
9:14, 501
9:25–26, 412
10:10, 153

10:23–25, 503
10:24–25, 503
10:29, 153
10:31, 501
11:4, 384
11:6, 214
11:31, 371, 403, 513
11:32, 117, 380
12:2, 378
12:22, 501
13:9–10, 503
13:12, 153, 308
13:17, 433
13:20, 24, 356
13:21, 59

James
1:16, 127
1:17, 295, 481
1:18, 381
2:1, 132
2:8, 346
2:10, 294
2:24–25, 403
2:25, 371, 513
3:1, 115
3:6, 571
3:14–15, 481
3:17, 481
4:5, 319

1 Peter
1:2, 308
1:3, 501
1:8, 221
1:10–12, 117, 227
2:4–7, 363
2:5, 311, 412
2:9, 311, 412, 500
2:13–14, 186
2:17, 459
2:25, 356
3:1–6, 481
3:21, 311
4:11, 59
5:1–5, 356

2 Peter
1:10, 229
2:22, 341
3:2, 117
3:9, 229, 295
3:15, 229

1 John
1:6–10, 103
1:8, 126

2:10, 479
2:20, 500
2:26, 127
2:27, 500
3:7, 127
5:4, 355
5:21, 502

Revelation
1:6, 59
1:9, 562
1:18, 59, 73, 501
2:7, 73
2:14, 502
2:20, 127, 502
3:5, 73
3:7, 23
3:18, 378
4:9–10, 59
5:5, 23
5:6, 81
5:10, 500
5:13, 59
6:6, 87
6:8, 73
6:9, 73
7:2, 501
7:12, 59
9:20, 502
9:20–21, 140, 317
10:6, 59
11:3–12, 571
11:15, 59
12:3–4, 317
12:9, 127
12:17, 562
13:8, 73
13:13–14, 127
15:7, 59
16:9–11, 140, 317
16:15, 378
17:8, 73
19:3, 59
19:7, 67
19:13, 220
19:20, 127, 571
20:1–10, 317
20:2–3, 127
20:4, 562
20:6, 27, 73
20:7–8, 127
20:10, 59, 127
20:10–15, 571
20:12, 73
20:12–13, 73

20:13, 73
20:13–14, 73
20:14, 73
20:15, 73
21:1–4, 501
21:2, 67
21:9, 67
21:23, 130
21:27, 73
22:2, 73
22:5, 59, 500
22:14, 73
22:15, 341
22:16, 23
22:17, 67, 481
22:19, 73

**Apocrypha,
Old Testament
Pseudepigrapha, and
Other Jewish Literature**

Judith
12:5, 211

Sirach
9:9, 304
11:18, 429
35:1, 304
37:5, 523
37:11, 45
37:19, 266
39:18, 248
46:19, 217
46:20, 527
47:7, 523
50:26, 483

1 Maccabees
3:18–19, 254

2 Maccabees
7:27, 62

4 Maccabees
18:24, 59

Jubilees
49:10–12, 211

Qumran
*1QMysteries (1Q27),
   fragment 1, column
   1, lines 3–4*, 389
1QSam, 35–36
4Q160, 35–36
*4Q481ᵇ, fragment 1,
   line 3*, 389

*4QMysteriesᵇ (4Q300),
   fragment 3, lines
   3–4*, 389
4QSamᵃ, 32, 34, 36,
   47, 55, 59–61,
   69–71, 74–75, 86,
   90–92, 98–99, 101,
   110, 137, 142–44,
   148, 164–65, 182,
   191–92, 195, 202,
   206–11, 218,
   276, 288–89, 323,
   326, 426, 456–57,
   472–75, 497, 515,
   525
4QSamᵇ, 35–36, 302–3,
   394–97, 407–9, 438,
   444–46
4QSamᶜ, 35–36, 479
4QTohBᵃ (4Q275) 1.2,
   429

Josephus
Antiquities, 2.102, 65
Antiquities, 5.318, 253
Antiquities, 5.338, 253
Antiquities, 5.345, 55,
   253
Antiquities, 5.347, 55
Antiquities, 5.358, 253
Antiquities, 5.360, 130
Antiquities, 5.361–62,
   253
Antiquities, 6.3, 139
Antiquities, 6.7.79, 148
Antiquities, 6.16, 148
Antiquities, 6.18, 148
Antiquities, 6.32, 169
Antiquities, 6.52,
   181–82
Antiquities, 6.66–72, 32
Antiquities, 6.67–68,
   207
Antiquities, 6.68, 206,
   208
Antiquities, 6.68–70,
   206, 212
Antiquities, 6.78, 210
Antiquities, 6.79, 214
Antiquities, 6.90, 219
Antiquities, 6.107, 253
Antiquities, 6.122, 132
Antiquities, 6.122–23,
   253
Antiquities, 6.130, 279

Antiquities, 6.166, 314

Antiquities, 6.171, 326

Antiquities, 6.230, 391

Antiquities, 6.242, 253

Antiquities, 6.254, 253

Antiquities, 6.260, 428

Antiquities, 6.260–61, 253

Antiquities, 6.261, 253

Antiquities, 6.271, 441

Antiquities, 6.274, 442

Antiquities, 6.294, 14, 160, 253

Antiquities, 6.297, 473

Antiquities, 6.303, 479

Antiquities, 6.323, 508

Antiquities, 6.325, 516

Antiquities, 6.330, 535

Antiquities, 6.332–36, 527

Antiquities, 6.378, 15, 238

Antiquities, 7.200, 253

Antiquities, 7.260, 253

Antiquities, 7.293, 253

Antiquities, 7.346, 253

Antiquities, 7.359, 253

Antiquities, 7.366, 253

Antiquities, 8.206, 253

Antiquities, 9.7, 451

Antiquities, 10.143, 238

Antiquities, 17.19, 65

Antiquities, 20.17–20, 65

Antiquities, 20.85, 65

Antiquities, 20.89, 65

Jewish War, 1.477, 65

Jewish War, 1.480, 65

Jewish War, 1.562–63, 65

Talmud

Baba Meẓiʿa, 87a, 402

Rosh Hashanah, 25a, 219

Yebamoth, 65b, 402

Midrash Rabbah Shmuel, 535

Pirqe de Rabbi Eliezer

33, 535

Early Christian Literature

Ambrose of Milan

On the Duties of the Clergy, 2.7, 398

On the Duties of the Clergy, 3.21, 398

Augustine

The City of God, 17.5, 104

The City of God, 17.6, 458

The City of God, 17.6.2, 242

Letter 158.6, 527

On Care for the Dead, 18, 527

On Christian Doctrine, 2.23, 527

On the Soul and Its Origin, 4.29, 527

Eusebius

Onomasticon, 11/1.32.21–23, 42

Onomasticon, 144.27–29, 42

Preparation for the Gospel, 1.10.16, 138

Gregory of Nyssa

Answer to Eumonius' Second Book, 12.3, 295

Gregory the Great

The Book of Pastoral Rule, 3.4, 459

Hippolytus

On the Sorceress, 530

Jerome

De situ et nominibus, 42

John Chrysostom

Homilies on the Gospel of Matthew, 6.4, 527

Justin Martyr

Dialogue with Trypho, 105, 527

Lactantius

The Divine Institutes, 4.14, 104

Methodius

Discourse on the Resurrection, 3.2.19, 527

Tertullian

Treatise on the Soul, 57, 530

Lutheran Confessions

Augsburg Confession

IV 122–39, 62

V, 114

XIV, 114, 381

XXIII, 412

XXVII 40, 270

XXVIII 11, 186

Apology of the Augsburg Confession

IV 142–44, 317

IV 219, 317

IV 275–76, 256

IV 370–74, 73

XX 13, 229, 317

Smalcald Articles

III III 43–45, 317

III IV, 503

III XIII 1, 153

Large Catechism

I 31, 499

I 45–47, 440

I 51, 126

I 54, 126

I 66, 271

I 95, 126

I 161, 433

II 14–15, 186

II 36, 318

Small Catechism

The Office of the Keys, 56

Formula of Concord Epitome

IV 19, 317

VI, 214

Formula of Concord Solid Declaration

II, 292

II 36–39, 62

II 57, 125

II 58, 125

IV 33–34, 229

VI 12, 79

XI, 25, 244, 292

XI 6, 448

Works of Martin Luther

American Edition

2:19, 383

2:50, 384

2:91, 384

3:283, 384

3:285, 384

5:152–53, 384

7:356, 382

7:367, 382

11:277, 380

15:291, 24

17:195, 382

19:234, 380

22:397, 384

25:323, 381

26:172–79, 29

26:276–91, 29

27:203, 382

28:284, 382–83

29:232, 384

30:136, 382–83

30:225, 29

31:297–99, 29

31:327–77, 29

31:351–52, 29

34:77, 384

36:196, 385, 530

40:269, 382

43:113–38, 139

44:26, 382

45:96, 384

47:269, 384

48:12–13, 29

48:366, 381

51:273, 382–83

51:316, 29

52:180, 385, 530

Weimarer Ausgabe

7.25, 29

Weimarer Ausgabe Deutsche Bibel

9/1.258–59, 404

Lutheran Hymnals

Lutheran Service Book

326, 56

Lutheran Service Book: Agenda

166, 224

Ancient Near Eastern Literature

Amarna Letters, 356

Ashurbanipal, cylinder of, 416

Coptos Decree, 475

Egyptian text with list of Cretan names, 416

Ekron, inscription from, 416

Esarhaddon, prism of, 416

Khirbet Qeiyafa Inscription, 12–13

Mesha Stele, 12

Sanchuniathon, writing of, 138

Tell Dan Inscription, 11–12

Classical Literature

Homer

Iliad, 2.819, 416

Iliad, 20.160, 416

Philo of Byblos, 138